1

Who Sang What
on Broadway, 1866–1996

ALSO BY RUTH BENJAMIN AND ARTHUR ROSENBLATT

Movie Song Catalog: Performers and Supporting Crew for the Songs Sung in 1460 Musical and Nonmusical Films, 1928–1988 (McFarland, 1993)

Who Sang What on Broadway, 1866–1996

RUTH BENJAMIN and
ARTHUR ROSENBLATT

Volume 1 : The Singers A–L

McFarland & Company, Inc., Publishers

Jefferson, North Carolina, and London

1

LIBRARY OF CONGRESS CATALOGUING-IN-PUBLICATION DATA

Benjamin, Ruth, 1934–
Who sang what on Broadway, 1866–1996 / Ruth Benjamin
and Arthur Rosenblatt.
p.   cm.
Includes bibliographical references and indexes.

ISBN 0-7864-1506-1 (2 volume set : softcover : 50# alkaline paper) ∞
ISBN 0-7864-2189-4 (v. 1 : softcover : 50# alkaline paper)
ISBN 0-7864-2190-8 (v. 2 : softcover : 50# alkaline paper)

1. Singers — New York (State) — New York — Dictionaries.
2. Musicals — New York (State) — New York — Dictionaries.
I. Rosenblatt, Arthur, 1931–2005.   II. Title.
ML107.N44B46   2006   782.1'4'0922 — dc22   2005011055

British Library cataloguing data are available

On the cover: *foreground* ©2005 Photofest; *background* ©2005 PhotoSpin

Manufactured in the United States of America

*McFarland & Company, Inc., Publishers
Box 611, Jefferson, North Carolina 28640
www.mcfarlandpub.com*

VOLUME 1 : 0-7864-2189-4
TWO VOLUME SET : 0-7864-1506-1

To Petra, Paul, Judy and Becky

CONTENTS

PREFACE

This is a book about musical theater between 1866 and 1996. And about the people who sang their hearts out on Broadway.

Broadway is perhaps the most famous street in the most famous city in the world. Its name has been synonymous with show business for more than a century.

Before that, Broadway — laid out by the Dutch in the seventeenth century as their *Heere Straas,* or High Street — had been another kind of thoroughfare. Beginning at Bowling Green, and moving steadily north with the rest of the city, by the middle and end of the nineteenth century it had become an elegant boulevard of expensive hotels, restaurants and shops such as Lord & Taylor, B. Altman and A.T. Stewart.

In 1866, *The Black Crook*, an extravaganza generally considered to be the first Broadway musical, settled in for a long stay at a Broadway theater in lower Manhattan called Niblo's Garden.

The census of 1870 showed New York City's population to be 942,347. There were 16 theaters. A lively playgoing public, many of them tourists, brought in revenues of up to $8,000,000 a year.

In 1904, Longacre Square on 42nd Street was renamed Times Square with the completion of the New York Times Building, headquarters for that newspaper. Simultaneously, many theaters and music publishers were moving uptown, locating on Broadway and its adjacent streets.

Broadway had begun to be Broadway.

Musical theater has always been extremely important to its audiences. Especially in the early years of the musical, an evening at the theater was an event; women theatergoers would jot down in their programs impressions of the shows they had seen, complete with fashion comments. One program noted: "I wore my blue silk. It perfectly matched Vivienne Segal's."

This book is for anyone who has ever stood in line to buy a ticket to a musical. Or browsed through a program. Or felt the thrill of excitement as the house lights dimmed, the curtain rose and the orchestra began to play. In other words, for anyone who loves musical theater and wants to find out more about the performers who, over the years, have entertained so many audiences with so many songs.

But where to begin work on this rather daunting project?

To start, we decided to make an alphabetical listing of show titles, each of which would become a small file of basic information about a show. For example:

Name of Musical: *The Black Crook*
Theater: Niblo's Garden
Opening date: 9/12/1866
Number of performances: 475

Next, armed with our files of show titles, we began the search for cast members and the songs they sang. We looked mostly at programs, but also at clippings, sheet music and scrapbook collections of memorabilia. In those interesting early days, we often found ourselves heading toward the New York Pub-

lic Library at Lincoln Center and to the Theatre Collection of the Museum of the City of
New York. We also visited the Library of the
Players, the New-York Historical Society and
the New York Society Library. We developed
an infinite admiration for keepers of archives.

Heaven forbid, a collection should close for
renovations! It once did happen to us; we lost
several months of precious time while materi-
als we needed were being packed, shipped to
another location, and unpacked.

While all this was going on, our daughter,
intrigued by our findings, offered to begin
searching the Internet for performer's dates
and birthplaces and spouses and divorces and
offspring — the bits and pieces that, fitted together, would make a more interesting book.
We didn't turn down her offer. Thank you,
Judy!

Our bookshelves at home were accumulat-
ing all sorts of wonderful second-hand vol-
umes to browse among, from church sales and
thrift shops. And our collection of *Playbills*
was growing. And growing some more. Everybody seemed to possess a treasured stack of
these little beauties, for us to borrow. Or, in
a few cases, to keep.

Our list of performers, what they sang, and
who they were on and off the stage was growing into the book you now hold.

We decided to include cast replacements,
and casts of revivals. Not included are Off
Broadway productions and road company or
out of town shows, too many to count. We
had to leave out Gilbert and Sullivan; they're
a volume unto themselves. And there were
shows whose Broadway programs we couldn't
locate; either they were being used when we
needed them, or not in their file folders for
some other reason.

Little by little, the facts emerged to become
parts of each numbered entry, in the following order (though not all facts were available
for every entry):

The name of the performer begins the entry,
in boldface; alternate name or names, if any,
follow in parentheses and are also in boldface
type.

Life dates are next, in parentheses, followed

by birthplace (indicated with "B") and information about marriage and divorce ("M").
The name of a performer's spouse, partner, or
relative given in CAPITAL LETTERS indicates that the person has his or her own listing in this book.

Highlights of the performer's career outside
of the theater are then listed, if significant.

Next comes the listing of songs performed
in musicals on Broadway, laid out in the following format:

In italics, the name of the musical.

In parentheses, the theatre where it played;
a right-pointing device [>] followed by another theater name if the show moved to another location; a notation of "revival" or "return" as appropriate; in quotation marks, the
name of the character played; "CR" if the performer was a cast replacement; a date, if available, indicating when the performer began in
or re-entered the role.

Title of each song sung by that performer
in that musical.

Following a slash mark, "W" preceding the
name of the show's lyricist and "M" preceding the name of the show's composer.

In brackets, the title and date of any song
(sung by that performer) interpolated into the
show during its run.

A period indicates the end of the information on that show. Information on other shows
follows in the same format.

In keeping with this arrangement, a typical
entry looks like this:

Luther Adler (May 4, 1903–Dec. 8, 1984)
B: New York, NY. M: film star Sylvia Sidney,
1938–1946. A cousin of FRANCINE LARRI-
MORE. Member of a distinguished acting
family; he debuted on stage at the Thalia Theater on the Bowery in 1908 in a Yiddish play
titled *Schmendrick*. Well known for work with
the Group Theater, and on screen as a character actor and villain. *Fiddler of the Roof* (Imperial, CR, "Tevye." Jan. 18, 1965/Aug. 15,
1965): Anatevka; Do You Love Me?; If I Were
a Rich Man; Sabbath Prayer; Sunrise, Sunset;
The Tailor, Motel Kamzoil; To Life; Tradi-
tion/W: Sheldon Harnick, M: Jerry Bock.

We did encounter some difficulty, mostly having to do with songs in early shows — those from the late nineteenth and early twentieth century. These songs were sometimes added or interpolated during the run of the show. Stars had a tendency, whenever they pleased, to burst into the songs most popular with their audiences — even between scenes of an entirely different show. In the days before ASCAP and strict copyright laws, shows were more fluid and changeable than they were later on. As Cole Porter might have noted, pretty much anything went.

So it came as no great surprise to find that those early programs were less reliable than later ones when it came to connecting songs with their singers. Who sang what? Who knows! We had to leave a great many of these tempting titles behind us.

And who did write those lyrics? Who composed that music? Why does this song seem to have two different titles? There were times, though we tried to avoid them, when we had to resort to the dreaded question mark. We preferred to err on the side of inclusiveness and rescue an unknown title from the program where we'd found it and hope someone else would recognize in our book a song that we didn't know about.

If only we could have found more biographical material. We know there are too many blank spaces. It's true that a number of actors prefer not to give out information about their ages or birthplaces. And there's never time enough to fill in every space. Maybe that's part of the challenge.

The past and the present live together on Broadway as they always have. We're still singing tunes that were popular more than 100 years ago. Revivals of musicals by generations new to them are on the boards somewhere all the time.

Young actors come to New York, as they always have, to be on Broadway. All of us, actors and audiences, are part of the same theatrical tradition. It's part of us. We want to celebrate that tradition, and learn more about it, for the future.

We hope you'll join us in a toast. Here's to Broadway!

THE SINGERS (A–L)

1. Eric Aaron (Oct. 27, 1954–) B: Eugene, OR. *The Best Little Whorehouse in Texas* (Eugene O'Neill, CR, "Shy Kid" and "Aggie #21, May 1982): The Aggie Song; 20 Fans/WM: Carol Hall.

2. Lina Abarbanell (Feb. 3, 1879–Jan. 6, 1963) B: Berlin, Germany. Her father, Paul Abarbanell, was a conductor; her son-in-law was composer Marc Blitzstein. After singing opera in Berlin, she came to the U.S. in 1905 to perform in Humperdinck's *Hansel and Gretel* at the Metropolitan Opera. *The Student King* (Garden, "Ilsa," Dec. 25, 1906): Nudel, Nudel, Nup, Nup; Off to Paris; The Pretty Tyrolees/W: Frederick Ranken, Stanislas Stange, M: Reginald De Koven. *The Merry Widow* (New Amsterdam, CR, "Sonia, the Widow," Apr. 13, 1908): I Love You So (The Merry Widow Waltz); In Marsovia; The Silly Cavalier; Vilia/W: Adrian Ross, M: Franz Lehar. *The Love Cure* (New Amsterdam, CR, "Nellie Vaughn," Oct. 11, 1909): Forget Me Not; I Wonder What the Audience Would Say; I'm an Indian; A Pretty Part for Me to Play; A Toast; When Skies Are Bright/W: Oliver Herford, M: Edmund Eysler. *Madame Sherry* (New Amsterdam, "Yvonne Sherry, ex–Jane," Aug. 30, 1910): The Birth of Passion; The Butterfly; Dunnerwetter; I Want to Play House with You; I'm All Right; The Other Fellow; The Smile She Means for You; Uncle Says I Mustn't, So I Won't/W: Otto Harbach, M: Karl Hoschna. *Miss Princess* (Park, "Princess Polonia," Dec. 23, 1912): Come My Sweetheart; Give Me Love, Love, Love; It Might Have Been; Queen Thou Art; The Wireless Way/W: Will B. Johnstone, M: Alexander Johnstone. *The Geisha* (44th Street, revival, "Molly Seamore," Mar. 27, 1913): Chon Kina; The Interfering Parrot; The Toy Duet/W: Harry Greenbank, M: Sidney Jones. *Flora Bella* (Casino > 44th Street, "Princess Manja Demidoff" and "Flora Bella,"

Sept. 11, 1916): Blossom of My Own; It Is Very Hard to Bring Up Father/W: Percy Waxman, M: Milton Schwarzwald — Give Me All of You/W: Earl Carroll, M: Milton Schwarzwald — The Hypnotizing Duet; Love Is a Dance; On to Petrograd/W: Percy Waxman, M: Charles Cuvillier. *Happy Go Lucky* (Liberty, "Elsie Dayly," Sept. 30, 1926): Free, Free, Free; Zip/W: Helena Evans, M: Lucien Denni — Love Thoughts/W: Gwynne Denni, M: Lucien Denni. *The Well of Romance* (Craig, "Frau Schlitzl," Nov. 7, 1930): Be Oh So Careful, Ann; One Night/W: Preston Sturges, M: H. Maurice Jacquet.

3. Harold Abbey *Bitter Sweet* (44th Street, revival, "Mr. Bethel," May 7, 1934): The Last Dance; Tarara Boom-de-Ay/WM: Noel Coward.

4. Bessie Abbott (1878–Feb. 9, 1919) B: New York, NY. *Rob Roy* (Liberty, revival, "Janet," Sept. 15, 1913): Love Land; The Merry Miller; My Hame Is Where the Heather Blooms; Rustic Song/W: Harry B. Smith, M: Reginald De Koven.

5. Bud Abbott (Oct. 2, 1895–Apr. 24, 1974) B: Asbury Park, NJ. Straight man with comic LOU COSTELLO of classic comedy team Abbott and Costello, in movies and on TV, until their breakup in 1957 and Abbott's subsequent retirement. *The Streets of Paris* (Broadhurst, revue, June 19, 1939): The French Have a Word for It/WM: Harold Rome.

6. Joan Abbott (c 1910–Sept. 25, 1968) *George White's Scandals of 1931* (Apollo, revue, Sept. 14, 1931): Here It Is/W: Lew Brown, M: Ray Henderson. *Keep Moving* (Forrest, revue, Aug. 23, 1934): Hot-Cha Chiquita (Rumba Lumbago); Mother Eve; Wake Up, Sleepy Moon/W: Jack Scholl, M: Max Rich.

7. Marion Abbott (Jan. 27, 1867–Jan. 15, 1937) B: Danville KY. *The Girl from Montmartre* (Criterion, "Gabrielle," Aug. 5, 1912): Ghost Quintette/W: Harry B. Smith, Robert B. Smith, M: Henry Bereny.

5

8. Marion Abel *Katja* (44th Street, CR, "Maud Sumerdal," c 1926): In Jail; Night Birds; When Love's in the Air/W: Harry Graham, M: Jean Gilbert.

9. Edward Abeles (Nov. 4, 1869–July 10, 1919) B: St. Louis, MO. *Oh, Lady! Lady!!* (Princess > Casino, "Spike Hudgins," Feb. 1, 1918): Do It Now; Greenwich Village; Our Little Nest/W: P.G. Wodehouse, M: Jerome Kern.

10. Robert Abelson B: Brooklyn, NY. *Those Were the Days* (Edison, revue, Nov. 7, 1990): A Cantor for the Sabbath; I Wish I Were Single Again; Nochum, My Son/WM: trad.— Motele/WM: M. Gebirtig—Those Were the Days/WM: Gene Raskin.

11. Arline Aber With CHARLINE ABER, they were known as the Aber Twins. *Smiles* (Ziegfeld, "Arline," Nov. 18, 1930): Blue Bowery/W: Harold Adamson, M: Vincent Youmans.

12. Charline Aber *Smiles* (Ziegfeld. "Charline," Nov. 18, 1930): same as ARLINE ABER.

13. Betty Aberlin (Dec. 30, 1942–) B: New York, NY. On TV's *Smothers Brothers Comedy Hour (1975). Cafe Crown* (Martin Beck, "Sarah," Apr. 17, 1964): A Mother's Heart/W: Marty Brill, M: Albert Hague.

14. Caroljane Abney *The Girls Against the Boys* (Alvin, revue, Nov. 2, 1959): I Gotta Have You/W: Arnold B. Horwitt, M: Richard Lewine — Light Travelin' Man/W: Arnold B. Horwitt, M: Albert Hague.

15. David Abraham *Mr. Wix of Wickham* (Bijou, "Frolicsome Kangaroo," Sept. 19, 1904): The Dancing Kangaroo/WM: Jerome Kern. *The Lady of the Slipper* (Globe, "Mouser," Oct. 28, 1912): Meow! Meow! Meow!/W: James O'Dea, M: Victor Herbert.

16. Rae Abruzzo *Alive and Kicking* (Winter Garden, revue, Jan. 17, 1950): Cry, Baby, Cry/WM: Harold Rome — One! Two! Three!/W: Ray Golden, Paul Francis Webster, M: Sonny Burke.

17. Mabel Acker *Bye, Bye, Bonnie* (Ritz > Cosmopolitan, "Mrs. Noah Z. Shrivell," Jan. 13, 1927): Just Across the River from Queens/W: Neville Fleeson, M: Albert Von Tilzer.

18. Bernice Ackerman *Ziegfeld Follies of 1924-1925* (New Amsterdam, revue, June 24, 1924): Toyland/W: Glen MacDonough, M: Victor Herbert. *Just Fancy* (Casino, "Jane Stafford," Oct. 11, 1927): Coo-Coo; Humpty-Dumpty/W: Leo Robin, M: Joseph Meyer, Phil Charig. *Animal Crackers* (44th Street, "Mary Stewart," Oct. 23, 1928): Watching the Clouds Roll By; Who's Been List'ning to My Heart?/WM: Bert Kalmar, Harry Ruby.

19. Loni (Zoe) Ackerman (Apr. 10, 1949–) B: New York, NY. *George M!* (Palace, "Rose," Apr. 10, 1968): Forty-Five Minutes from Broadway; So Long, Mary/WM: George M. Cohan. *No, No, Nanette* (46th Street, revival, "Betty Brown," Jan. 19, 1971): Telephone Girlie/W: Otto Harbach, M: Vincent Youmans. *The Magic Show* (Cort, CR, "Charmin," Aug. 1975): Charmin's Lament; The Goldfarb Variations; Sweet, Sweet, Sweet/WM: Stephen Schwartz. *So Long, 174th Street* (Harkness, "Wanda," Apr. 27, 1976): Being with You; It's Like; Men/WM: Stan Daniels. *Evita* (Broadway, CR, "Eva," Apr. 5, 1982): The Actress Hasn't Learned (The Lines You'd Like to Hear); The Art of the Possible; Buenos Aires; Dice Are Rolling; Don't Cry for Me Argentina; Eva Beware of the City; Eva's Final Broadcast; Goodnight and Thank You; High Flying Adored; I'd Be Surprisingly Good for You; Lament; A New Argentina; Peron's Latest Flame; Rainbow High; Rainbow Tour; Waltz for Eva and Che/W: Tim Rice, M: Andrew Lloyd Webber. *Cats* (Winter Garden, CR, "Grizabella," Sept. 5, 1988): Grizabella, the Glamour Cat/W: T.S. Eliot, M: Andrew Lloyd Webber.— Memory/W: Trevor Nunn, based on T.S. Eliot, M: Andrew Lloyd Webber.

20. Elizabeth Acosta *Cyrano: The Musical* (Neil Simon, "Mother Superior," Nov. 21, 1993): He Loves to Make Us Laugh; A Visit from De Guiche/W: Peter Reeves, Koen Van Dijk, M: Ad Van Dijk.

21. Alma Adair *The Passing Show of 1922* (Winter Garden, revue, Sept. 20, 1922): Eleanor; Love of Long Ago; The Passing Show/W: Harold Atteridge, M: Alfred Goodman.

22. Ann Adair *The Alaskan* (Knickerbocker, "Mrs. Good-Better-Best," Aug. 12, 1907): Alimony; Glittering Gold/W: Joseph Blethen, M: Harry Girard.

23. Frank Adair *The Marriage Market* (Knickerbocker, "Captain on the Mariposa," Sept. 22, 1913): All the Little Ladies Love a Sailor Man/W: Percy Greenbank, M: Victor Jacobi.

24. Janet Adair (c 1903–?) *The Passing Show of 1921* (Winter Garden, revue, Dec. 29, 1920): In Little Old New York; Ta-Voo (Ta-Hoo)/W: Harold Atteridge, M: Jean Schwartz. *Bombo* (Al Jolson > Winter Garden, "Soothsayer" and "Mona Tessa," Oct. 6, 1921): I'm Glad I'm Spanish; In the Way Off There/ W: Harold Atteridge, M: Sigmund Romberg. *The Passing Show of 1922* (Winter Garden, revue, Sept. 20, 1922): Poor J'en-Ai-Marre/W: Harold Atteridge, M: Alfred Goodman. *The Grab Bag* (Globe, revue, Oct. 6, 1924): The Grab Bag/WM: Ed Wynn.

25. John Adair (1885–Jan. 22, 1952) B: New

York, NY. *Caroline* (Ambassador, "Roderick Gray," Jan. 31, 1923): Who Cares for a Name/W: Harry B. Smith, Edward Delaney Dunn, M: Edward Kunneke. *Sadie Thompson* (Alvin, CR, "Quartermaster Bates," Dec. 10, 1944): Siren of the Tropics/W: Howard Dietz, M: Vernon Duke.

26. Josephine Adair *Lady Billy* (Liberty, "Eloise," Dec. 14, 1920): Greenwich Village; Love Comes Like a Butterfly; The Tune They Play/W: Zelda Sears, M: Harold A. Levey. *The Clinging Vine* (Knickerbocker, "Mildred Mayo," Dec. 25, 1922): Lady Luck; Roumania/W: Zelda Sears, M: Harold A. Levey. *Greenwich Village Follies of 1923* (Winter Garden, revue, Sept. 20, 1923): The Birthday of the Infantata/W: Josephine Adair, M: Louis A. Hirsch — Kama's Garden/W: John Murray Anderson, Irving Caesar, M: Louis A. Hirsch. *Say When* (Morosco, "Miss Stuart," June 26, 1928): In My Love Boat/W: Max Lief, Nathaniel Lief, M: Ray Perkins.

27. Yvonne Adair (1925–) *Lend an Ear* (National > Broadhurst, revue, Dec. 16, 1948): Doin' the Old Yahoo Step; The Gladiola Girl; I'm Not in Love; Who Hit Me?/WM: Charles Gaynor. *Gentlemen Prefer Blondes* (Ziegfeld, "Dorothy Shaw," Dec. 8, 1949): Homesick Blues; House on Rittenhouse Square [Sept. 11, 1950]; I Love What I'm Doing; It's High Time; Just a Kiss Apart; Keeping Cool with Coolidge; Sunshine/W: Leo Robin, M: Jule Styne.

28. Noelle Adam (Dec. 24, 1933–) *No Strings* (54th Street, "Jeanette Valmy," Mar. 15, 1962): La, La, La/WM: Richard Rodgers.

29. Bil Adams *Oh! Oh! Oh! Nurse* (Cosmopolitan, "Will Plant," Dec. 7, 1925): Under My Umbrella; Who Bites the Holes in Schweitzer Cheese?; You May Have Planted Many a Lily/W: Monte Carlo, M: Alma Schwartz.

30. Edie (Edith) Adams (Apr. 16, 1927–) B: Kingston, PA. M: comedian Ernie Kovacs. A singer on live TV variety shows, *Ernie in Kovacsland* (1951) and *The Ernie Kovacs Show* (1952). *Wonderful Town* (Winter Garden, "Eileen," Feb. 25, 1953): Conquering New York; A Little Bit in Love; My Darlin' Eileen; Ohio; Wrong Note Rag/W: Betty Comden, Adolph Green; M: Leonard Bernstein. *L'il Abner* (St. James, "Daisy Mae," Nov. 15, 1956): If I Had My Druthers; I'm Past My Prime; Love in a Home; Namely You; Unnecessary Town/W: Johnny Mercer, M: Gene de Paul.

31. Gail Adams *My Romance* (Shubert, "Veronica De Witt," Oct. 19, 1948): Debutante/W: Rowland Leigh, M: Sigmund Romberg.

32. Ida M. Adams (c 1888–Nov. 4, 1960) *The Pink Lady* (New Amsterdam, "Desiree," Mar. 13, 1911/Sept. 4, 1911): By the Saskatchewan/W: C.M.S. McLellan, M: Ivan Caryll. *A Winsome Widow* (Moulin Rouge, "Tony," Apr. 11, 1912): I Never Knew What Eyes Could Do (Till Yours Looked into Mine) [May 6, 1912]/ W: Stanley Murphy, M: Henry I. Marshall — Songs of Yesterday/W: ?, M: Raymond Hubbell *Ziegfeld Follies of 1912* (Moulin Rouge, revue, Oct. 21, 1912): Beautiful, Beautiful Girl/W: John E. Hazzard, M: Raymond Hubbell — Mother Doesn't Know; You Might as Well Stay on Broadway/W: Harry B. Smith, M: Raymond Hubbell.

33. J.K. Adams *Mr. Pickwick* (Herald Square, "Mr. Wardle," Jan. 19, 1903): Boys Will Be Boys/W: Grant Stewart, M: Manuel Klein.

34. Kenny Adams (c 1916–) *The Most Happy Fella* (New York City Center, revival, "Jake," Feb. 10, 1959): Standing on the Corner/WM: Frank Loesser. *South Pacific* (New York City Center, revival, "Yeoman Herbert Quale," Apr. 13, 1961): There Is Nothin' Like a Dame/W: Oscar Hammerstein II, M: Richard Rodgers. *Brigadoon* (New York City Center, revival, "Sandy Dean," May 30, 1962): Down on MacConnachy Square/ W: Alan Jay Lerner, M: Frederick Loewe.

35. Laurette Adams *Boom-Boom* (Casino, CR, "Gussie," Feb. 25, 1929): Messin' Round; Shake High, Shake Low/W: Mann Holiner, J. Keirn Brennan, M: Werner Janssen.

36. Leslie Adams (1887–Mar. 26, 1936) B: Stark, FL. *As Thousands Cheer* (Music Box, revue, Sept. 30, 1933): Majestic Sails at Midnight/WM: Irving Berlin.

37. Margaret Adams *The Student Prince* (Majestic, revival, "Princess Margaret," Jan. 29, 1931): Just We Two/W: Dorothy Donnelly, M: Sigmund Romberg. *Melody* (Casino, CR, "Paula de Laurier" and "Andrea de Namours," 1933): Give Me a Roll on the Drum; Good Friends Surround Me; I Am the Singer, You Are the Song; In My Garden; Melody; Tonight May Never Come Again/W: Irving Caesar, M: Sigmund Romberg. *Jubilee* (Imperial, "Princess Diana," Oct. 12, 1935): Mr. and Mrs. Smith; We're Off to Feathermore; When Love Comes Your Way; Why Shouldn't I?/WM: Cole Porter.

38. Mary Adams (1910–Nov. 30, 1973) In the mid 1950s, she played Mother Barbour on radio and TV versions of the long-running soap, *One Man's Family. Artists and Models of 1930* (Majestic, revue, June 10, 1930): My Real Ideal/ W: Sammy Lerner, M: Burton Lane — Two Perfect Lovers/WM: Haydn Wood, Joseph Tunbridge, Jack Waller, Burton Lane — Without a Shadow of a Doubt/WM: Ord Hamilton. *Hello, Paris* (Shubert, "Gracie Jones," Nov. 15, 1930): Dance Your Troubles Away; Give It; Pack Your Suitcase with Love; You Made a Hit with Me [Nov. 24, 1930]/WM: ?. *Hello, Paris* (Shubert, CR, "Opal Peters," Dec. 1930): Deep Sea Roll; Give It; Pack Your Suitcase with Love; Paris; Unaccustomed as I Am; You Made a Hit with Me/WM: ?— Every Bit of You/WM: Kenneth Friede, Adrian Samish — I Stumbled Over You and Fell in Love/W: Henry Dagand, M: Maurie Rubens.

39. Neile Adams (July 10, 1936–) M: actor Steve McQueen, 1956–1971. *The Pajama Game* (St. James, CR, "Gladys," c 1955): Her Is; Hernando's Hideaway; Steam Heat/WM: Richard Adler, Jerry Ross.

40. Ruth Adams *Bitter Sweet* (44th Street, revival, "Honor," May 7, 1934): Alas, the Time Is Past; The Last Dance; Tarara Boom-de-Ay/WM: Noel Coward.

41. Trude Adams (June 19, 1931–) B: Brooklyn, NY. *Catch a Star!* (Plymouth, revue, Sept. 6, 1955): To Be or Not to Be in Love/W: Ray Golden, Dan Shapiro, Milton Pascal, M: Phil Charig. *She Loves Me* (Eugene O'Neill, CR, "Amalia Balash," Nov. 12, 1963): Dear Friend; I Don't Know His Name; Ice Cream; No More Candy; Three Letters; Where's My Shoe?; Will He Like Me?/W: Sheldon Harnick, M: Jerry Bock.

42. Janet Williams Adderley *Starlight Express* (Gershwin, "Belle," Mar. 15, 1987): Belle/W: Richard Stilgoe, M: Andrew Lloyd Webber.

43. Patrick Adiarte (Aug. 2, 1943–) He played Ho-Jon on TV's long-running *M*A*S*H* (1972). *The King and I* (New York City Center, revival, "Prince Chulalongkorn," Apr. 18, 1956): A Puzzlement/W: Oscar Hammerstein II, M: Richard Rodgers. *Flower Drum Song* (St. James, "Wang San," Dec. 1, 1958): Chop Suey; The Other Generation/W: Oscar Hammerstein II, M: Richard Rodgers.

44. Bruce Adler (Nov. 27, 1944–) B: New York, NY. *Oklahoma!* (Palace, revival, "Ali Hakim," Dec. 13, 1979): It's a Scandal! It's a Outrage!/W: Oscar Hammerstein II, M: Richard Rodgers. *Those Were the Days* (Edison, revue, Nov. 7, 1990): At the Fireplace/WM: M. Warshavsky — Bei Mir Bist Du Schoen/W: Sammy Cahn, Saul Chaplin, Jacob Jacobs, M: Sholom Secunda — Hudl with the Shtrudl/WM: A. Lebedeff — Litvak/Galitsyaner/WM: Hymie Jacobson — Nochum, My Son/WM: trad.— The Palace of the Czar/WM: Mel Tolkin — Rumania, Rumania/WM: A. Lebedeff, Sholom Secunda — Yosi Ber/W: Itsik Manger, M: trad. *Crazy for You* (Sam S. Shubert, "Bela Zangler," Feb. 19, 1992/c 1995): What Causes That?/W: Ira Gershwin, M: George Gershwin.

45. Felix Adler (Jan. 22, 1884–Mar. 25, 1963) B: Chicago, IL. *The Queen of the Movies* (Globe, "Billy Hilton," Jan. 12, 1914): Girls, Run Along; Pardon Me If I Stutter; When the Moon Slyly Winks in the Night/W: Edward A. Paulton, M: Jean Gilbert. *See America First* (Maxine Elliott, "Chief Blood-in-His-Eye," Mar. 28, 1916): Something's Got to Be Done; When I Used to Lead the Ballet; Will You Love Me When My Flivver Is a Wreck?/WM: T. Lawrason Riggs, Cole Porter.

46. Hyman Adler (c 1883–June 27, 1945) *Tales of Rigo* (Lyric, "Rigo," May 30, 1927): I'll Tell You All Someday; In Romany; Zita/WM: Ben Schwartz — Rigo's Last Lullaby/WM: Evelyn Adler. *There You Are* (George M. Cohan, "Senor Cambro," May 16, 1932): Legend of the Mission Bells; Love Lives On/WM: William Heagney, Tom Connell.

47. Larry Adler (Feb. 10, 1914–Aug. 6, 2001) B: Baltimore, MD. Harmonica player extraordinaire. *Keep Off the Grass* (Broadhurst, revue, May 23, 1940): On the Old Park Bench/W: Howard Dietz, M: Jimmy McHugh.

48. Luther Adler (May 4, 1903–Dec. 8, 1984) B: New York, NY. M: film star Sylvia Sidney, 1938–1946. A cousin of FRANCINE LARRIMORE. Member of a distinguished acting family; he debuted on stage at the Thalia Theater on the Bowery in 1908 in a Yiddish play titled *Schmendrick*. Well known for work with the Group Theater, and on screen as a character actor and villain. *Fiddler on the Roof* (Imperial, CR, "Tevye," Jan. 18, 1965/Aug. 15, 1965): Anatevka; Do You Love Me?; If I Were a Rich Man; Sabbath Prayer; Sunrise, Sunset; The Tailor, Motel Kamzoil; To Life; Tradition/W: Sheldon Harnick, M: Jerry Bock.

49. Jere Admire (Apr. 29–) B: Fort Worth, TX. *Cabaret* (Broadhurst, "Bobby," Nov. 20, 1966): If You Could See Her/W: Fred Ebb, M: John Kander.

50. Max Adrian (Nov. 1, 1903–Jan. 19, 1973) B: Enniskillen, Ireland. He starred in the film version of *The Boy Friend* (1972). *Candide* (Martin Beck, "Dr. Pangloss," Dec. 1, 1956): The Best of All Possible Worlds/W: Richard Wilbur, M: Leonard Bernstein — Gavotte/W: Dorothy Parker, M: Leonard Bernstein.

51. Adrienne She sang torch songs in English, Spanish and French, and appeared as a hostess wearing glamorous gowns on TV's musical show *Champagne and Orchids* (1948). *If the Shoe Fits* (Century, "Widow Willow," Dec. 5, 1946): My Business Man/W: June Carroll, M: David Raksin.

52. Effie Afton (Dec. 28, 1904–Aug. 7, 1987) B: Steubenville, OH. *Courtin' Time* (National, "Harriet Hearn," June 13, 1951): Masculinity/W: Jack Lawrence, M: Don Walker.

53. Mark Agnes *Cyrano: The Musical* (Neil Simon, "Montfleury," Nov. 21, 1993): Aria/W: Peter Reeves, Koen Van Dijk, M: Ad Van Dijk)

54. Ted Agress (Apr. 20, 1945–) B: Brooklyn, NY. *Shenandoah* (Alvin, "Jacob," Jan. 7, 1975): Next to Lovin' (I Like Fightin')/W: Peter Udell, M: Gary Geld.

55. William Ahearn (Oct. 9, 1896–May 16, 1983) B: Waterbury, CT. *Sidewalks of New York* (Knickerbocker, "Willie," Oct. 3, 1927): Oh, for the Life of a Cowboy; Way Down Town/W: Eddie Dowling, M: James F. Hanley. *Simple Simon* (Ziegfeld, "Jack Horner," Feb. 18, 1930): Don't Tell Your Folks; Roping; Sweetenheart/W: Lorenz Hart, M: Richard Rodgers.

56. Townsend Ahern *The Love Letter* (Globe, "Michael," Oct. 4, 1921): To the Girl You Dance With/W: William Le Baron, M: Victor Jacobi.

57. Ahi *East Wind* (Manhattan, "Tsoi Tsing," Oct. 27, 1931): Congai/W: Oscar Hammerstein II, M: Sigmund Romberg.

58. Helen Ahola *My Fair Lady* (Mark Hellinger, CR, "Eliza Doolittle,"): I Could Have Danced All Night; Just You Wait; The Rain in Spain; Show Me; Without You; Wouldn't It Be Loverly?/W: Alan Jay Lerner, M: Frederick Loewe.

59. Norman Ainsley see NORMAN A. BLUME.

60. Paul Ainsley (Apr. 11, 1945–) B: Boston, MA. *Jesus Christ Superstar* (Mark Hellinger, "King Herod," Oct. 12, 1971): King Herod's Song/W: Tim Rice, M: Andrew Lloyd Webber.

61. Karen Akers (Oct. 13, 1945–) B: New York, NY. Tall, swell cabaret singer in chic clubs in the U.S. and Europe. *Nine* (46th Street, "Luisa," May 9, 1982): Be on Your Own; My Husband Makes Movies/WM: Maury Yeston. *Grand Hotel* (Martin Beck, "Raffaela," Nov. 12, 1989): How Can I Tell Her?; What She Needs/WM: Robert Wright, George Forrest, Maury Yeston — Twenty-Two Years/WM: Maury Yeston — Villa on a Hill/WM: Robert Wright, George Forrest.

62. Frances Alain *The Wife Hunters* (Herald Square, "Mlle. Follette Folarie," Nov. 2, 1911): Follette/W: David Kempner, M: Anatole Friedland, Malvin F. Franklin.

63. Lloyd Alann (Aug. 15, 1952–) B: Bronx, NY. *Grease* (Broadhurst, CR, "Eugene Florczyk," c 1974): Alma Mater/WM: Jim Jacobs, Warren Casey. *Grease* (Broadhurst, CR, "Danny Zuko," June 14, 1976): All Choked Up; Alone At a Drive-In Movie; Summer Nights/WM: Jim Jacobs, Warren Casey.

64. Olga Albani *The New Moon* (Imperial > Casino, "Flower Girl," Sept. 19, 1928): Tavern Song (Red Wine)/W: Oscar Hammerstein II, M: Sigmund Romberg.

65. E. Albano *Blossom Time* (Ambassador, CR, "Von Schwind," Aug. 7, 1922): Keep It Dark; My Springtime Thou Art; Serenade/W: Dorothy Donnelly, M: Sigmund Romberg.

66. Mary Elizabeth Albano *A Christmas Carol* (Paramount Madison Square Garden, "Fan at 6," Dec. 1, 1994): God Bless Us, Every One/ W: Lynn Ahrens, M: Alan Menken.

67. Anna Maria Alberghetti (May 15, 1936–) B: Pesaro, Italy. Sister of CARLA ALBERGHETTI. Classically trained as a coloratura soprano, she made her American debut at Carnegie Hall in 1949. *Carnival!* (Imperial, "Lili," Apr. 13, 1961): Beautiful Candy; I Hate Him; Magic, Magic; Mira (Can You Imagine That?); The Rich (Puppet Song); A Very Nice Man; Yes, My Heart; Yum Ticky-Ticky Tum Tum (Puppet Song)/WM: Bob Merrill.

68. Carla Alberghetti (1939–) *Carnival!* (Imperial, CR, "Lili," Nov. 19, 1962): same as ANNA MARIA ALBERGHETTI.

69. Donnie Ray Albert (Jan. 10, 1950–) B: New Orleans, LA. *Porgy and Bess* (Uris, revival, "Porgy," Sept. 25, 1976): Bess, You Is My Woman Now; I Got Plenty o' Nuttin'; I Loves You, Porgy/W: Ira Gershwin, DuBose Heyward, M: George Gershwin — Oh, Bess, Oh Where's My Bess?/W: Ira Gershwin, M: George Gershwin — They Pass By Singing/W: DuBose Heyward, M: George Gershwin.

70. Eddie Albert (Apr. 22, 1908–) B: Rock Island, IL. M: movie star Margo. The likeable and versatile star played Oliver Douglas on the popular TV series, *Green Acres* (1965). *The Boys from Syracuse* (Alvin, "Antipholus of Syracuse," Nov. 23, 1938): Dear Old Syracuse; This Can't Be Love; You Have Cast Your Shadow on the Sea/W: Lorenz Hart, M: Richard Rodgers. *Miss Liberty* (Imperial, "Horace Miller," July 15, 1949): Just One Way to Say I Love You; Let's Take an Old-Fashioned Walk; A Little Fish in a Big Pond; Me an' My Bundle; Only for Americans/WM: Irving Berlin. *Say, Darling* (ANTA,

CR, "Jack Jordan," c 1959): The Husking Bee; Something's Always Happening on the River/W: Betty Comden, Adolph Green, M: Jule Styne. *The Music Man* (Majestic, CR, "Harold Hill," Jan. 1960): Goodnight, My Someone; Marian, the Librarian; The Sadder-but-Wiser Girl; Seventy-Six Trombones; Shipoopi; Till There Was You; Trouble (in River City)/WM: Meredith Willson.

71. Frank Albertson (Feb. 2, 1909–Feb. 29, 1964) B: Fergus Falls, MN. In films, he began as a prop boy in 1922, later becoming a leading man, then a character actor. *Seventeen* (Broadhurst, "Mr. Baxter," June 21, 1951): Headache and a Heartache/W: Kim Gannon, M: Walter Kent.

72. Jack Albertson (June 16, 1907–Nov. 24, 1981) B: Malden, MA. This character actor of film, television and theater arrived in New York penniless during the Depression, sleeping in subways and on park benches before finding work in vaudeville and later in burlesque with PHIL SILVERS. *Meet the People* (Mansfield, revue, Dec. 25, 1940): It's the Same Old South/W: Edward Eliscu, M: Jay Gorney. *The Cradle Will Rock* (Mansfield > Broadway, revival, "Yasha," Dec. 26, 1947): Art for Art's Sake; The Rich/WM: Marc Blitzstein. *High Button Shoes* (New Century, CR, "Mr. Pontdue," May 1949): He Tried to Make a Dollar; Nobody Ever Died for Dear Old Rutgers; You're My Girl/W: Sammy Cahn, M: Jule Styne. *Tickets, Please!* (Coronet, revue, Apr. 27, 1950): Back at the Palace/W: Mel Tolkin, Lucille Kallen, Jack Fox, M: Clay Warnick — Spring Has Come/WM: Mel Tolkin, Max Liebman — You Can't Take It with You/WM: Lyn Duddy, Joan Edwards. *Top Banana* (Winter Garden, "Vic Davis," Nov. 1, 1951): O.K. for TV; Slogan Song (You Gotta Have a Slogan); Top Banana/WM: Johnny Mercer. *Show Boat* (New York City Center, revival, "Frank Schultz," Apr. 8, 1954): Goodbye, My Lady Love/WM: Joe Howard — I Might Fall Back on You/W: Oscar Hammerstein II, M: Jerome Kern.

73. Jessica Albright *Bye Bye Birdie* (Martin Beck, "Deborah Sue," Apr. 14, 1960): One Boy (One Girl)/W: Lee Adams, M: Charles Strouse.

74. Arthur Albro *Gypsy Love* (Globe, "Jozsi," Oct. 17, 1911): Gypsy Love; There Is a Land of Fancy/W: Harry B. Smith, Robert B. Smith, M: Franz Lehar. *Lady Luxury* (Casino > Comedy, "Count Piniaselli," Dec. 25, 1914): Kiss Me Once More; When I Sing in Grand Opera/W: Rida Johnson Young, M: William Schroeder. *Maytime* (Shubert > 44th Street > Broadhurst, "Rudolfo" and "Signor Vivalla," Aug. 16, 1917): Gypsy Song; Will You Remember? (Sweetheart)/W: Rida Johnson Young, M: Sigmund Romberg.

75. Mlle Alcorn *The Passing Show of 1922* (Winter Garden, revue, Sept. 20, 1922): My Diamond Girls/W: Jack Stanley, M: Alfred Goodman.

76. Alan Alda (Jan. 28, 1936–) B: New York, NY. Son of ROBERT ALDA. Director, writer and actor in motion pictures and television, notably the long-running TV series *M*A*S*H*, in which he played Hawkeye (1972). *Cafe Crown* (Martin Beck, "Dr. Irving Gilbert," Apr. 17, 1964): That's the Life for Me; What's the Matter with Buffalo?; You're a Stranger in This Neighborhood/W: Marty Brill, M: Albert Hague. *The Apple Tree* (Shubert, "Adam" and "Captain Sanjar" and "Flip, the Prince Charming," Oct. 18, 1966/July 3, 1967): Beautiful, Beautiful World; Eve; Forbidden Love (in Gaul); It's a Fish; Which Door?; You Are Not Real/W: Sheldon Harnick, M: Jerry Bock.

77. Delyle Alda (Aug. 1894–Aug. 27, 1927) B: Chicago, IL. In vaudeville with LOUIS JOHN BARTELS. *Ziegfeld Nine O'Clock Revue and Midnight Frolic* (New Amsterdam roof, revue, Dec. 9, 1918): After the First of July; I Love to Linger with You/W: Gene Buck, M: Dave Stamper. *Ziegfeld Follies of 1919* (New Amsterdam, revue, June 16, 1919): My Baby's Arms/W: Joseph McCarthy, M: Harry Tierney — Tulip Time/W: Gene Buck, M: Dave Stamper. *Ziegfeld Follies of 1920* (New Amsterdam, revue, June 22, 1920): Tell Me, Little Gypsy/WM: Irving Berlin. *Blue Eyes* (Casino, "Kitty Higgins," Feb. 21, 1921): Just Suppose; Without a Girl Like You/W: Zeke Meyers, M: I.B. Kornblum — Wanting You/W: Irving Caesar, M: George Gershwin. *Snapshots of 1921* (Selwyn, revue, June 2, 1921): The Bamboula/W: E. Ray Goetz, M: Jose Padilla — On the Brim of Her Old-Fashioned Bonnet/W: E. Ray Goetz, M: George Gershwin — Sky High Bungalow/W: E. Ray Goetz, M: George W. Meyer — Yokohama Lullaby/W: Grant Clarke, M: James V. Monaco. *George White's Scandals of 1923* (Globe, revue, June 18, 1923): Let's Be Lonesome Together/W: B.G. DeSylva, E. Ray Goetz, M: George Gershwin.

78. Robert Alda (Feb. 26, 1914–May 3, 1986) B: New York, NY. Father of ALAN ALDA. He'd planned to be an architect; instead, he made his stage debut in vaudeville at the RKO New York, singing in an act called Charlie Ahearn and His Millionaires. His first film role was as George Gershwin in *Rhapsody in Blue.* (1945). *Guys and Dolls* (46th Street, "Sky Masterson," Nov. 24,

1950): I'll Know; I've Never Been in Love Before; Luck Be a Lady; My Time of Day/WM: Frank Loesser. *What Makes Sammy Run?* (54th Street, "Al Manheim," Feb. 27, 1964): Lites — Camera — Platitude; Maybe Some Other Time; A New Pair of Shoes; Something to Live For; You Help Me/WM: Ervin Drake.

79. Clare Alden *Show Boat* (New York City Center, revival, "Ellie May Chipley," Sept. 7, 1948): Goodbye, My Lady Love/WM: Joe Howard — Life Upon the Wicked Stage/W: Oscar Hammerstein II, M: Jerome Kern.

80. Jane Alden *Say When* (Morosco, "Sydney Farnham," June 26, 1928): Little White Lies/W: Helen Wallace, M: Arthur Sheekman. *The Street Singer* (Shubert, "Mabel Brown," Sept. 17, 1929): You Never Can Tell/W: Graham John, M: ?.

81. Else Alder *Around the Map* (New Amsterdam, revue, "Tootsi," Nov. 1, 1915): Dolly Dear; Here Comes Tootsi; It's a Very Fine World; Let Us Stay Where the Crowd Is; Little Maud Isn't Meant for You; Some Girl Has Got to Darn His Socks/W: C.M.S. McLellan, M: Herman Finck. *Miss Springtime* (New Amsterdam, CR, "Rosika Wenzel," Dec. 4, 1916): In the Garden of Romance; A Little Bid for Sympathy; A Little Country Mouse/W: Herbert Reynolds, M: Emmerich Kalman — My Castle in the Air/W: P.G. Wodehouse, M: Jerome Kern — Once Upon a Time/WM: ? — Some One/W: Herbert Reynolds, M: Jerome Kern.

82. James Alderman *Vogues of 1924* (Shubert, revue, Mar. 27, 1924): Medicos/W: Clifford Grey, M: Herbert Stothart.

83. Tom Aldredge (Feb. 28, 1928–) B: Dayton, OH. *Rex* (Lunt-Fontanne, "Will Somers," Apr. 25, 1976): The Chase; In Time; The Masque; The Wee Golden Warrior/W: Sheldon Harnick, M: Richard Rodgers. *Where's Charley?* (Circle in the Square, revival, "Mr. Spettigue," Dec. 20, 1974): The New Ashmoleon Marching Society and Students Conservatory Band; Serenade with Asides/WM: Frank Loesser. *Into the Woods* (Martin Beck, "Narrator" and "Mysterious Man," Nov. 5, 1987/Sept. 13, 1988): Ever After; No More/WM: Stephen Sondheim.

84. Sean Aldrich *The Me Nobody Knows* (Longacre, CR, "Clorox," Nov. 1971): Black; Jail-Life Walk; Rejoice/W: Will Holt, M: Gary William Friedman.

85. Billy Alessi (1954–) B: Long Island, NY. Billy and identical twin BOBBY ALESSI were singer-songwriters in the 1970s. *Dude* (Broadway, "Extra," Oct. 9, 1972): The Days of This Life/W: Gerome Ragni, M: Galt MacDermot.

86. Bobby Alessi (1954–) B: Long Island,

NY. *Dude* (Broadway, "Esso," Oct. 9, 1972): same as BILLY ALESSI.

87. Jimmy Alex *The Boy Friend* (Royale, "Phillipe," Sept. 30, 1954): Riviera; Sur La Plage/WM: Sandy Wilson.

88. Adrienne Alexander *The Utter Glory of Morrissey Hall* (Mark Hellinger, "Boody," May 13, 1979): Lost; You Will Know When the Time Has Arrived/WM: Clark Gesner.

89. Alex Alexander *The Merry Widow* (Majestic, revival, "Cascada," Aug. 4, 1943): Women/W: Adrian Ross, M: Franz Lehar. *The Merry Widow* (New York City Center, revival, "Cascada," Apr. 10, 1957): In Marsovia/W: Adrian Ross, M: Franz Lehar.

90. Amy Alexander *The Fortune Teller* (Al Jolson, revival, "Rafael," Nov. 4, 1929): Romany Life (Czardas)/W: Harry B. Smith, M: Victor Herbert.

91. Barbara Alexander *Anya* (Ziegfeld, "Tinka," Nov. 29, 1965): Snowflakes and Sweethearts (The Snowbird Song)/WM: Robert Wright, George Forrest.

92. Cheryl Alexander B: Philadelphia, PA. Jazz singer and recording artist. *The News* (Helen Hayes, "Reporter," Nov. 7, 1985): Beautiful People; Classifieds; The Contest; Editorial; Front Page Expose; Horoscope; Hot Flashes I; Hot Flashes II; Hot Flashes III; Personals; Pyramid Lead; Super Singo; Violent Crime; What in the World; What's the Angle/WM: Paul Schierhorn.

93. Chris Alexander (1920–) B: Tulsa, OK. *On the Town* (Adelphi, "Chip," Dec. 28, 1944): Come Up to My Place; New York, New York; Some Other Time; Ya Got Me/W: Betty Comden, Adolph Green, M: Leonard Bernstein. *Wonderful Town* (Winter Garden, "Frank Lippencott," Feb. 25, 1953): Conversation Piece (Nice Talk, Nice People)/W: Betty Comden, Adolph Green, M: Leonard Bernstein.

94. C.K. Alexander (May 4, 1919–Sept. 2, 1980) B: Cairo, Egypt. Actor, producer and director. *Ari* (Mark Hellinger, "Mandria, the Greek," Jan. 15, 1971): Aphrodite; The Lord Helps Those Who Help Themselves; The Saga of the Haganah/W: Leon Uris; M: Walt Smith. *Threepenny Opera* (Vivian Beaumont, revival, "Jonathan Peachum," May 1, 1976): Concerning the Insecurity of the Human State; No They Can't; Song of the Insufficiency of Human Endeavor/W: Bertolt Brecht; M: Kurt Weill.

95. Geraldine Alexander *The Night Boat* (Liberty, "Alice," Feb. 2, 1920): I Love the Lassies (I Love Them All)/W: Anne Caldwell, M: Jerome Kern.

96. Jason Alexander (Sept. 23, 1959–) B:

Newark, NJ. Character actor and singer. Memorable as George Costanza on the TV series *Seinfeld* (1990). *Merrily We Roll Along* (Alvin, "Joe Josephson," Nov. 16, 1981): It's a Hit!; Opening Doors/WM: Stephen Sondheim. *The Rink* (Martin Beck, "Lenny," Feb. 9, 1984): Marry Me; Mrs. A.; Not Enough Magic/W: Fred Ebb, M: John Kander. *Jerome Robbins' Broadway* (Imperial, revue, Feb. 26, 1989): Comedy Tonight/WM: Stephen Sondheim — I Still Get Jealous/W: Sammy Cahn, M: Jule Styne — Sunrise, Sunset; Tradition/W: Sheldon Harnick, M: Jerry Bock.

97. Louise Alexander *Peggy* (Casino, "Polly Polino," Dec. 7, 1911): Go Away, Little Girl, Go Back to School/W: C.H. Bovill, M: Leslie Stuart.

98. Mara Alexander (Feb. 7, 1914–May 23, 1965) B: New York, NY. *Who's Who* (Hudson, revue, Mar. 1, 1938): Croupier/W: June Sillman, M: Baldwin Bergersen.

99. Newton Alexander *George White's Scandals of 1922* (Globe, revue, Aug. 28, 1922): I'll Build a Stairway to Paradise/W: B.G. DeSylva, Arthur Francis, M: George Gershwin. *Gay Paree* (Winter Garden, revue, CR, Jan. 10, 1927): There Never Was a Town Like Paris/W: Mann Holiner, M: Alberta Nichols.

100. Rod Alexander (Jan. 23, 1922–) B: Colorado. A dancer, with BAMBI LINN, on Max Liebman's TV variety shows of the 1950s; he also worked in nightclubs with Jack Coles's dancers. *Great to Be Alive* (Winter Garden, "Albert," Mar. 23, 1950): Headin' for a Weddin'; When the Sheets Come Back from the Laundry/W: Walter Bullock, M: Abraham Ellstein.

101. Roy Alexander *Up in the Clouds* (Lyric, "Willie Tuttle," Jan. 2, 1922): Rum Tum Tiddle/W: Will B. Johnstone, M: Tom Johnstone.

102. Vada Alexander *George White's Scandals of 1929* (Apollo, revue, Sept. 23, 1929): 18 Days Ago/W: B.G. DeSylva, Lew Brown, M: Ray Henderson.

103. Virginia Alexander *Ned Wayburn's Gambols* (Knickerbocker, revue, Jan. 15, 1929): Gypsy Days/W: Morrie Ryskind, M: Arthur Schwartz — 'Tis the Last Rose of Summer/W: Thomas Moore, M: based on song by Richard Alfred Milliken.

104. Sarina Alexe *The Geisha* (Daly's, "Nami," Sept. 9, 1896): The Dear Little Jappy-jap-jappy/W: Harry Greenbank, M: Sidney Jones.

105. Rhonda Alfaro *The Me Nobody Knows* (Longacre, CR, "Lillie Mae," Nov. 1971): Black; Fugue for Four Girls; Robert, Alvin, Wendell

and Jo Jo/W: Will Holt, M: Gary William Friedman.

106. George Ali (1866–Apr. 26, 1947) B: Freeport, NY. An animal impersonator. *Buster Brown* (Majestic, "Tige," Jan. 24, 1905): Bo-Peep/W: Paul West, M: John W. Bratton.

107. Edgar Allan *Parade* (Guild, revue, May 20, 1935): Join Our Ranks; On Parade/W: Paul Peters, George Sklar, M: Jerome Moross.

108. Edward Allan *Three Cheers* (Globe, "Spike," Oct. 15, 1928): Gee It's Great to Be Alive; Look Pleasant; Putting on the Ritz/W: B.G. DeSylva, M: Ray Henderson.

109. Martine Allard (Aug. 24, 1970–) B: Brooklyn, NY. *The Tap Dance Kid* (Broadhurst, "Emma," Dec. 21, 1983): Another Day; Four Strikes Against Me; Like Him; Someday; They Never Hear What I Say/W: Robert Lorick, M: Henry Krieger.

110. Beatrice Allen *Kosher Kitty Kelly* (Times Square > Daly's 63rd St., "Rosie Feinbaum," June 15, 1925): What's in Store for You/WM: Leon DeCosta.

111. Betty Allen (?– Aug. 17, 1979) *George White's Scandals of 1931* (Apollo, revue, Sept. 14, 1931): Back from Hollywood/W: Lew Brown, M: Ray Henderson. *Of Thee I Sing* (Imperial, return engagement, CR, "Diana Devereaux," May 15, 1933): Because, Because; I Was the Most Beautiful Blossom; Jilted! Jilted!; Some Girls Can Bake a Pie; Who Is the Lucky Girl to Be?/W: Ira Gershwin, M: George Gershwin. *Red, Hot and Blue!* (Alvin, "Reporter," Oct. 29, 1936): Five Hundred Million/WM: Cole Porter. *George White's Scandals of 1939-40* (Alvin, revue, Aug. 28, 1939): Smart Little Girls/W: Jack Yellen, M: Sammy Fain. *Du Barry Was a Lady* (46th Street, CR, "May Daley" and Du Barry," Aug. 1940): But in the Morning, No!; Come On In; Do I Love You?; Du Barry Was a Lady; Friendship; Give Him the Oo-La-La; Katie Went to Haiti; When Love Beckoned/WM: Cole Porter. *Dream with Music* (Majestic, "Ella" and "Mrs. Sinbad," May 18, 1944): I'll Take the Solo; Mr. and Mrs. Wrong; Relax and Enjoy It/W: Edward Eager, M: Clay Warnick.

112. Betty Allen (1930–) *Treemonisha* (Palace, "Monisha," Oct. 21, 1975): The Bag of Luck; Confusion; I Want to See My Child; The Sacred Tree; Treemonisha's Bringing Up; Treemonisha's Return; We Will Trust You As Our Leader; We're Goin' Around; The Wreath/WM: Scott Joplin.

113. Clarice Allen *Rain or Shine* (George M. Cohan, CR, "Frankie Schultz," Oct. 29, 1928): Add a Little Wiggle/W: Jack Yellen, M: Milton

Ager—Feelin' Good/W: Jack Yellen, M: Owen Murphy.

114. Cliff Allen *New Faces of 1936* (Vanderbilt, revue, May 19, 1936): I Was a Gyp in Egypt; Sixty Second Romance [May 25, 1936]/W: Lawrence Harris, M: Bud Harris—It Must Be Religion/WM: Forman Brown.

115. Clint Allen (c 1961–) B: Petersburg, IN. *Big River: The Adventures of Huckleberry Finn* (Eugene O'Neill, CR, "Tom Sawyer," Aug. 22, 1985): The Boys; Hand for the Hog/WM: Roger Miller.

116. Debbie (Deborah) Allen (Jan. 16, 1950–) B: Houston, TX. Sister of PHYLICIA RASHAD. Actress, choreographer, director. She appeared on the TV drama series *Fame* (1982). *Raisin* (46th Street, "Beneatha Younger," Oct. 18, 1973): Alaiyo; Measure the Valleys; Not Anymore/W: Robert Brittan, M: Judd Woldin. *Ain't Misbehavin'* (Longacre, revue, CR, Mar. 5, 1979): How Ya Baby/W: James C. Johnson, M: Fats Waller—I Can't Give You Anything but Love/W: Dorothy Fields, M: Jimmy McHugh—I've Got My Fingers Crossed/W: Ted Koehler, M: Jimmy McHugh—Keepin' Out of Mischief Now/W: Andy Razaf, M: Fats Waller—Lounging at the Waldorf/W: Richard Maltby, Jr., M: Fats Waller—When the Nylons Bloom Again/W: George Marion, Jr., M: Fats Waller—Yacht Club Swing/W: James C. Johnson, M: Fats Waller, Herman Autry. *West Side Story* (Minskoff, revival, "Anita," Feb. 14, 1980): America; A Boy Like That; I Have a Love/W: Stephen Sondheim, M: Leonard Bernstein. *Sweet Charity* (Minskoff, revival, "Charity Hope Valentine," Apr. 27, 1986): Charity's Soliloquy; If My Friends Could See Me Now; I'm a Brass Band; I'm the Bravest Individual; There's Gotta Be Something Better Than This; Where Am I Going?; You Should See Yourself/W: Dorothy Fields, M: Cy Coleman.

117. Domenick Allen (Oct. 5, 1958–) B: Glasgow, Scotland. *Blood Brothers* (Music Box, CR, "Narrator," Feb. 7, 1995): Light Romance; Madman; Shoes Upon the Table/WM: Willy Russell.

118. Edward Allen *Judy* (Royale, "Dick Wetherbee," Feb. 7, 1927): The Curfew Shall Not Ring Tonight; Hard to Get Along With; Hobohemia; Judy, Who D'Ya Love?; Looking for a Thrill; Start Stompin'; When Gentlemen Grew Whiskers and Ladies Grew Old/W: Leo Robin, M: Charles Rosoff. *Ripples* (New Amsterdam, "Malcolm Fairman," Feb. 11, 1930): Gentlemen of the Press/W: Irving Caesar, Graham John, M: Oscar Levant, Albert Sirmay.

119. Effie Allen *Miss 1917* (Century, revue, Nov. 5, 1917): The Picture I Want to See/W: P.G. Wodehouse, M: Jerome Kern.

120. Elizabeth Allen (Jan. 25, 1934–) B: Jersey City, NJ. On TV sit-coms she was Martha Simms on the *Paul Lynde Show* (1972) and Capt. Quinlan on *C.P.O. Sharkey* (1976). *The Gay Life* (Shubert, "Magda," Nov. 18, 1961): Come A-Wandering with Me/W: Howard Dietz, M: Arthur Schwartz. *Do I Hear a Waltz?* (46th Street, "Leona Samish," Mar. 18, 1965): Do I Hear a Waltz?; Here We Are Again; Moon in My Window; Perfectly Lovely Couple; Someone Woke Up; Thank You So Much; Thinking; What Do We Do? We Fly!/W: Stephen Sondeim, M: Richard Rodgers. *Sherry!* (Alvin, "Maggie Cutler," Mar. 27, 1967): How Can You Kiss Those Times Goodbye?; Imagine That; Maybe It's Time for Me; Turn On Your Radio; With This Ring/W: James Lipton, M: Laurence Rosenthal. *42nd Street* (Winter Garden, CR, "Dorothy Brock," Apr. 26, 1983/Jan. 20, 1987): About a Quarter to Nine; I Know Now; Shadow Waltz; You're Getting to Be a Habit with Me/W: Al Dubin, M: Harry Warren—Getting Out of Town/W: Mort Dixon, M: Harry Warren.

121. Ernest Allen *Rhapsody in Black* (Sam H. Harris, revue, CR, May 18, 1931): Exhortation/W: Henry Creamer, M: Con Conrad—St. Louis Blues/WM: W.C. Handy.

122. Fred Allen (May 31, 1894–Mar. 17, 1956) B: Cambridge, MA. Fondly remembered for his radio program, *The Fred Allen Show* (1932), and the characters who lived in "Allen's Alley." James Thurber said of him: "You can count on the thumb of one hand the American who is at once a comedian, a humorist, a wit and a satirist, and his name is Fred Allen." *Three's a Crowd* (Selwyn, revue, Oct. 15, 1930): Right at the Start of It/W: Howard Dietz, M: Arthur Schwartz.

123. Harry Allen (July 10, 1883–Dec. 4, 1951) B: Sydney, New South Wales, Australia. *Happy as Larry* (Coronet, "4th Tailor," Jan. 6, 1950): And So He Died; The Dirty Dog; Give the Doctor the Best in the House; He's a Bold Rogue; Oh, Mrs. Larry; Without a Stitch/W: Donagh MacDonagh, M: Mischa Portnoff, Wesley Portnoff.

124. Hazel Allen *The Never Homes* (Broadway, "Daisy Copp," Oct. 5, 1911): Just a Little Bit of Lingerie/W: E. Ray Goetz, M: A. Baldwin Sloane.

125. Jay Edward Allen *Snow White and the Seven Dwarfs* (Radio City Music Hall, "Bashful," Oct. 18, 1979): Bluddle-Uddle-Um-Dum

(The Washing Song); The Dwarf's Yodel Song (The Silly Song); Heigh Ho/W: Larry Morey, M: Frank Churchill.

126. Jennifer Allen *Guys and Dolls* (Martin Beck, revival, CR, "Miss Adelaide," June 1993): Adelaide's Lament; A Bushel and a Peck; Marry the Man Today; Sue Me; Take Back Your Mink/WM: Frank Loesser.

127. Jonelle Allen (July 18, 1944–) B: New York, NY. On TV she played Doreen Jackson, a recovering drug addict, on the soap *Generations* (1990) and Grace, wife of the town's blacksmith, on *Dr. Quinn, Medicine Woman* (1997). *George M!* (Palace, "Secretary," Apr. 10, 1968): Down by the Erie Canal/WM: George M. Cohan. *Two Gentlemen of Verona* (St. James, "Silvia," Dec. 1, 1971): Eglamour; Love Me; Night Letter; To Whom It May Concern Me; Where's North?/W: John Guare, M: Galt MacDermot.

128. Joseph Allen, Sr. (Feb. 23,1873–Sept. 9, 1952) B: Worcester, MA. *The Red Widow* (Astor, "Baron Maximillian Scareovich, " Nov. 6, 1911): When Woman Is the Question/W: Rennold Wolf, Channing Pollock, M: Charles J. Gebest. *Oh, My Dear!* (Princess > 39th Street, "Bagshott," Nov. 27, 1918): Childhood Days/W: P.G. Wodehouse, M: Louis A. Hirsch — What's the Use?/W: Howard Dietz, M: Jerome Kern.

129. Josephine Allen *Hurly-Burly* (Weber and Fields Music Hall, "Sissy Oxford," Sept. 8, 1898): Clink, Clink/W: Harry B. Smith, M: John Stromberg.

130. Keith Allen (Feb. 18, 1964–) B: Daytona Beach, FL. *Starlight Express* (Gershwin, CR, "Dustin," c 1987): Belle; Final Selection; Race Two/W: Richard Stilgoe, M: Andrew Lloyd Webber.

131. Lee Allen *Funny Girl* (Winter Garden, CR, "Eddie Ryan," during run): Find Yourself a Man; If a Girl Isn't Pretty; Who Taught Her Everything?/W: Bob Merrill, M: Jule Styne.

132. Lester Allen (Nov. 17, 1891–Nov. 6, 1949) B: Liverpool, England. He began as a circus acrobat. *George White's Scandals of 1922* (Globe, revue, Aug. 28, 1922): Oh, What She Hangs Out/W: B.G. DeSylva, M: George Gershwin. *George White's Scandals of 1923* (Globe, revue, June 18, 1923): Katinka/W: B.G. DeSylva, E. Ray Goetz, Ballard Macdonald, M: George Gershwin. *Florida Girl* (Lyric, "Sandy," Nov. 2, 1925): Oranges; Smile On/W: Paul Porter, Benjamin Hapgood Burt, M: Milton Suskind. *The Three Musketeers* (Lyric, "Planchet," Mar. 13, 1928): The Colonel and the Major/W: Clifford Grey, P.G. Wodehouse, M: Rudolf Friml — Ev'ry Little While/W: Clifford

Grey, M: Rudolf Friml. *Top Speed* (46th Street, "Elmer Peters," Dec. 25, 1929): Keep Your Undershirt On; You Couldn't Blame Me for That/WM: Bert Kalmar, Harry Ruby. *Shady Lady* (Shubert, "Al Darcy," July 5, 1933): I'll Betcha That I'll Getcha/W: Stanley Adams, M: Jesse Greer — Swingy Little Thingy; Your Type Is Coming Back/W: Bud Green, M: Sam H. Stept.

133. Louise Allen (1873–Nov. 9, 1909) B: New York, NY. M: WILLIAM COLLIER. *Twirly-Whirly* (Weber and Fields Music Hall, "Mary MacPain," Sept. 11, 1902): In Stage Land/W: Edgar Smith, M: William T. Francis.

134. Louise Allen *The Amber Express* (Globe, "Trixie Scott," Sept. 19, 1916): Don't Lose Your Way; It's the Only One for Me; Melody Will Keep You Young/W: Marc Connelly, M: Zoel Parenteau. *Eileen* (Shubert, "Rosie Flynn," Mar. 19, 1917): I'd Love to Be a Lady Someday; My Little Irish Rose/W: Henry Blossom, M: Victor Herbert. *Toot-Toot!* (George M. Cohan, "Marjorie Newton," Mar. 11, 1918): Every Girl in All America; Girlie; If; Let's Go/W: Berton Braley, M: Jerome Kern. *Somebody's Sweetheart* (Central > Casino, "Bessie Williams," Dec. 23, 1918): Girl of My Heart; Somebody's Sweetheart; Then I'll Marry You/W: Alonzo Price, M: Antonio Bafunno. *Tickle Me* (Selwyn, "Mary Fairbanks," Aug. 17, 1920): Broadway Swell and Bowery Bum; Little Hindoo Man; Then Love Again; Tickle Me/W: Otto Harbach, Oscar Hammerstein II, M: Herbert Stothart. *The Gingham Girl* (Earl Carroll, "Libby O'Day," Aug. 28, 1922): The Down East Flapper; The 42nd Street and Broadway Strut; Gingham Girl; Libby [Sept. 18, 1922]; Newlyweds; The Twinkle in Your Eye/W: Neville Fleeson, M: Albert Von Tilzer. *Little Jessie James* (Longacre, CR, "Jessie Jamieson," Nov. 12, 1923): From Broadway to Main Street; Little Jack Horner; Little Jessie James; My Home Town in Kansas/W: Harlan Thompson, M: Harry Archer.

135. Mae Allen *The Girl Behind the Counter* (Herald Square, "Hattie Tryon," Oct. 1, 1907): Shopping/W: Arthur Anderson, M: Howard Talbot.

136. Marianna Allen *Merrily We Roll Along* (Alvin, "Girl Auditioning," Nov. 16, 1981): Opening Doors/WM: Stephen Sondheim.

137. Michael Allen *The King and I* (St. James, CR, "Louis Leonowens," c 1952): I Whistle a Happy Tune/W: Oscar Hammerstein II, M: Richard Rodgers.

138. Michael K. Allen (Jan. 23, 1940–) B: New York, NY. He was discovered by LAUREN

BACALL on the TV variety show *Celebrity Talent Scouts* (1960). *New Faces of 1968* (Booth, revue, May 2, 1968): Evil/WM: Sydney Shaw — Right About Here/WM: Arthur Siegel — Where Is the Waltz?/W: Paul Nassau, M: Alonzo Levister.

139. Norman Allen (Dec. 24, 1939–) B: London, England. *Half a Sixpence* (Broadhurst, "Buggins," Apr. 25, 1965): All in the Cause of Economy; Flash! Bang! Wallop!; If the Rain's Got to Fall; The Party's on the House; A Proper Gentleman/WM: David Heneker.

140. Peter Allen (Feb. 10, 1944–June 18, 1992) B: Tenterfield, Australia. M: LIZA MINNELLI. Discovered by Liza's mother JUDY GARLAND in Hong Kong in 1964, singer-songwriter Allen became a popular cabaret and concert entertainer. *Legs Diamond* (Mark Hellinger, "Jack Diamond," Dec. 26, 1988): All I Wanted Was the Dream; Cut of the Cards; Gangland Chase; Knockers; Now You See Me, Now You Don't; Only an Older Woman; Only Steal from Thieves; Say It Isn't So; Sure Thing Baby; Taxi Dancer's Tango; Tropicabana Rhumba; When I Get My Name in Lights/WM: Peter Allen.

141. Rae Allen (July 23, 1926–) B: Brooklyn, NY. *Damn Yankees* (46th Street, "Gloria," May 5, 1955): Shoeless Joe from Hannibal, Mo./WM: Richard Adler, Jerry Ross. *Fiddler on the Roof* (Imperial, CR, "Golde," July 15, 1968): Anatevka; Do You Love Me?; Sabbath Prayer; Sunrise, Sunset; The Tailor, Motel Kamzoil/W: Sheldon Harnick, M: Jerry Bock. *Dude* (Broadway, "Reba," Oct. 9, 1972): The Earth; Goodbyes/W: Gerome Ragni, M: Galt MacDermot.

142. Raymond Allen (?–Jan. 29, 1994) For 21 years, until its demise in 1990, he was an artistic director of the Light Opera of Manhattan, playing leading roles in most of their Gilbert and Sullivan productions. *My Fair Lady* (New York City Center, revival, "Jamie," May 20, 1964): Get Me to the Church on Time; With a Little Bit of Luck/W: Alan Jay Lerner, M: Frederick Loewe.

143. Robert Lee Allen *Music Hath Charms* (Majestic, "Sen. Ballanqua," Dec. 29, 1934): Scandal Number/W: Rowland Leigh, John Shubert, M: Rudolf Friml.

144. Seth Allen (July 13, 1941–Aug. 14, 1986) B: Brooklyn, NY. *Jesus Christ Superstar* (Mark Hellinger, CR, "Pontius Pilate," Jan. 24, 1972): Pilate and Christ; Pilate's Dream; Trial Before Pilate/W: Tim Rice, M: Andrew Lloyd Webber.

145. Vivienne Allen (?–Sept. 24, 1963) *Pal Joey* (Ethel Barrymore > Shubert > St. James, CR, "Gladys Bumps," July 1941): Do It the Hard Way; The Flower Garden of My Heart; Plant You Now, Dig You Later; That Terrific Rainbow; You Mustn't Kick It Around/W: Lorenz Hart, M: Richard Rodgers. *Stars on Ice* (Center, revue, July 2, 1942): Big Broad Smile; Gin Rummy, I Love You; Juke Box Saturday Night; Little Jack Frost; You're Awfully Smart/W: Al Stillman, M: Paul McGrane — Put Your Cares on Ice [June 24, 1943]/WM: James Littlefield — You Must Be Part of a Dream [June 24, 1943]/W: James Littlefield, M: Marten Lowell. *Oklahoma!* (St. James, CR, "Ado Annie Carnes," Apr. 1947/Jan. 1948): All er Nothin'; The Farmer and the Cowman; I Cain't Say No/W: Oscar Hammerstein II, M: Richard Rodgers.

146. Michael Allinson (Dec. 30, 1920–) B: London, England. President of The Players. *My Fair Lady* (Mark Hellinger, CR, "Henry Higgins," Feb. 10, 1960): A Hymn to Him; I'm an Ordinary Man; I've Grown Accustomed to Her Face; The Rain in Spain; Why Can't the English?; You Did It/W: Alan Jay Lerner, M: Frederick Loewe.

147. Bernie Allison *Runaways* (Plymouth, "Sundar," May 13, 1978): Every Now and Then; Lonesome of the Road/WM: Elizabeth Swados.

148. May Allison (June 14, 1890–Mar. 27, 1989) B: Rising Fawn, GA. Leading lady in silent pictures from 1915 until her retirement in the 1920s. *Iole* (Longacre, "Dione," Dec. 29, 1913): Back to Nature; Comes an Exquisite Situation; If Dreams Come True; Nude Descending a Staircase; Think of That/WM: ? — None but the Brave Deserve the Fair/W: Will M. Hough, Frank R. Adams, M: Joseph E. Howard — Oh Precious Thoughts/W: Robert W. Chambers, M: William F. Peters.

149. Patti Allison (June 26, 1942–) B: St. Louis, MO. *Angel* (Minskoff, "Mrs. Fatty Pert," May 10, 1978): Astoria Gloria; A Dime Ain't Worth a Nickel/W: Peter Udell, M: Gary Geld.

150. Clint (Clinton) Allmon (June 13, 1941–) B: Monahans, TX. *The Best Little Whorehouse in Texas* (46th Street, "Farmer" and "Melvin P. Thorpe," June 19, 1978): The Sidestep; Texas Has a Whorehouse in It; 20 Fans; Watch Dog Theme/WM: Carol Hall.

151. Jacqueline Alloway B: San Diego, CA. *George M!* (Palace, "Fay Templeton," Apr. 10, 1968): Mary's a Grand Old Name/WM: George M. Cohan.

152. June Allyson (Oct. 7, 1917–) B: Bronx, NY. M: Actor Dick Powell, 1945-1963. The girl with the husky voice and homespun charm was

15, pretending to be 17, when she landed a job on a Broadway chorus line. Many movies were to follow her stage career. *Best Foot Forward* (Ethel Barrymore, "Minerva," Oct. 1, 1941): Don't Sell the Night Short; The Three B's; What Do You Think I Am?/WM: Hugh Martin, Ralph Blane.

153. Joan Almedia (Sept. 19, 1973–) B: Cebu City, Philippines. *Miss Saigon* (Broadway, CR, "Kim," c 1995): Back in Town; The Ceremony; The Guilt Inside Your Head; I Still Believe; I'd Give My Life for You; The Last Night of the World; Little God of My Heart; The Movie in My Mind; Please; Room 317; Sun and Moon; You Will Not Touch Him/W: Richard Maltby, Jr., Alain Boublil, M: Claude-Michel Schonberg.

154. Brooks Almy (July 15, 1950–) B: Fort Belvoir, VA. *A Change in the Heir* (Edison, "Aunt Julia," Apr. 29, 1990): Exactly the Same as It Was; Hold That Crown; The Weekend; When/W: George H. Gorham, M: Dan Sticco.

155. Maria Conchita Alonso (June 26, 1957–) B: Cienfuegos, Cuba. When she was 5, her parents moved to Venezuela; in 1975 the actress-singer became Miss Venezuela. *Kiss of the Spider Woman* (Broadhurst, CR, "Spider Woman" and "Aurora," Mar. 20, 1995): Anything for Him; Come; Gimme Love; Good Times; Her Name Is Aurora; I Do Miracles; Kiss of the Spider Woman; Russian Movie; A Visit; Where You Are/W: Fred Ebb, M: John Kander.

156. Larry Alpert (?– Mar. 9, 1975) *Let It Ride!* (Eugene O'Neill, "Frankie," Oct. 12, 1961): Broads Ain't People; He Needs You; If Flutterby Wins/WM: Jay Livingston, Ray Evans.

157. Greta Alpeter *Blossom Time* (Ambassador, revival, "Mitzi," Mar. 23, 1931): Love Is a Riddle; Only One Love Ever Fills the Heart; Peace to My Lonely Heart; Song of Love; Tell Me, Daisy; Three Little Maids/W: Dorothy Donnelly, M: Sigmund Romberg.

158. Barbara Alston *Ain't Supposed to Die a Natural Death* (Ethel Barrymore > Ambassador, Oct. 20, 1971): Lily Done the Zampoughi Every Time I Pulled Her Coattail/WM: Melvin Van Peebles.

159. Natalie Alt B: New York, NY. *The Fascinating Widow* (Liberty, "Ivy Tracy, " Sept. 11, 1911): Love Is the Theme of My Dreams [Sept. 25, 1911]/WM: Kerry Mills — Put Your Arms Around Me Honey/W: Sam M. Lewis, M: Kerry Mills. *The Quaker Girl* (Park, CR, "Princess Mathilde," Dec. 11, 1911): A Runaway Match; Wonderful/W: Adrian Ross, M: Lionel Monckton. *Adele* (Longacre > Harris, "Adele," Aug. 28,

1913): Adele; The Clock Is Striking Ten; Close Your Eyes; Is It Worth While?; It's Love!; Strawberries and Cream; A Waste of Time to Plan; When the Little Birds Are Sleeping; Yesterday; Yours for Me and Mine for You/W: Edward A. Paulton, M: Adolf Philipp, Jean Briquet. *The Girl Who Smiles* (Lyric > Longacre, "Marie," Aug. 9, 1915): Baby Mine; A Girl from Paree; Join the Families; Life Has Just Begun; Teach Me to Smile/W: Edward A. Paulton, M: Adolf Philipp, Jean Briquet. *The Grass Widow* (Liberty > Princess, "Denise," Dec. 3, 1917): Farewell (Letter Song); The Grass Widow; Just You and Me; The Song of Love/W: Channing Pollock, Rennold Wolf, M: Louis A. Hirsch.

160. Derin Altay (Nov. 10, 1954–) B: Chicago, IL. *Evita* (Broadway, CR, "Eva," Jan. 12, 1981): The Actress Hasn't Learned (The Lines You'd Like to Hear); The Art of the Possible; Buenos Aires; Dice Are Rolling; Don't Cry for Me Argentina; Eva Beware of the City; Eva's Final Broadcast; Goodnight and Thank You; High Flying Adored; I'd Be Surprisingly Good for You; Lament; A New Argentina; Peron's Latest Flame; Rainbow High; Rainbow Tour; Waltz for Eva and Che/W: Tim Rice, M: Andrew Lloyd Webber.

161. Bella Alten *Robin Hood* (New Amsterdam, revival, "Maid Marian," May 6, 1912): All Nature Is at Peace and Rest (Forest Song)/W: Harry B. Smith, M: Reginald De Koven.

162. Ruth Altman *Say When* (Morosco, "Miss Randall," June 26, 1928): In My Love Boat/W: Max Lief, Nathaniel Lief, M: Ray Perkins. *Luana* (Hammerstein's, "Luana," Sept. 17, 1930): Aloha; By Welawela; Magic Spell of Love; My Bird of Paradise/W: J. Keirn Brennan, M: Rudolf Friml. *The Merry Widow* (Erlanger's, revival, "Natalie, Baroness Popoff," Sept. 14, 1931): A Dutiful Wife; Love in My Heart/W: Adrian Ross, M: Franz Lehar. *The Boy Friend* (Royale, "Madame Dubonnet," Sept. 30, 1954): Fancy Forgetting; Poor Little Pierrette; The You-Don't-Want-to-Play-with-Me Blues/WM: Sandy Wilson.

163. Marjorie Alton *The Greenwich Village Follies of 1924* (Shubert > Winter Garden, revue, CR, Oct. 27, 1924): I'm in Love Again/WM: Cole Porter.

164. Trini Alvarado (Jan. 10, 1967–) B: New York, NY. She was 12 when she appeared in her first movie, *Rich Kids* (1979). *Runaways* (Plymouth, "Melinda," May 13, 1978): Lullaby from Baby to Baby/WM: Elizabeth Swados.

165. Anita Alvarez (Oct. 13, 1920–) B: Tyrone, PA. *Gentlemen Prefer Blondes* (Ziegfeld,

"Gloria Stark," Dec. 8, 1949): Mamie Is Mimi/W: Leo Robin, M: Jule Styne.

166. Carmen Alvarez (July 2–) B: Los Angeles, CA. M: CHAD BLOCK. *The Yearling* (Alvin, "Twink," Dec. 10, 1965): Everything in the World I Love; I'm All Smiles/W: Herbert Martin; M: Michael Leonard. *The Apple Tree* (Shubert, CR, "Eve" and "Princess Barbara" and "Ella" and "Passionella," Aug. 9, 1967, mats.): Feelings; Forbidden Love (in Gaul); Friends; Gorgeous; Here in Eden; I've Got What You Want; Lullaby (Go to Sleep, Whatever You Are); Oh to Be a Movie Star; Tiger, Tiger; Wealth; What Makes Me Love Him?; Which Door?/W: Sheldon Harnick, M: Jerry Bock. *Zorba* (Imperial, "Widow," Nov. 17, 1968): The Butterfly; Why Can't I Speak?/W: Fred Ebb, M: John Kander. *Look to the Lilies* (Lunt-Fontanne, "Rosita," Mar. 29, 1970): I'd Sure Like to Give It a Shot; Meet My Seester/W: Sammy Cahn, M: Jule Styne. *Irene* (Minskoff, revival, "Helen Mc-Fudd," Mar. 13, 1973): The Great Lover Tango/W: Otis Clements, M: Charles Gaynor — We're Getting Away with It/W: Joseph McCarthy, M: Harry Tierney.

167. Farah Alvin *Grease* (New York City Center, return engagement, "Jan," Nov. 29, 1996): Mooning/WM: Jim Jacobs, Warren Casey.

168. Dolly Alwyn *The Velvet Lady* (New Amsterdam, "Dolly," Feb. 3, 1919): I've Danced to Beat the Band/W: Henry Blossom, M: Victor Herbert.

169. John Aman (Sept. 28–) B: Hollywood, FL. *South Pacific* (New York City Center, revival, "R.O. Bob McCaffrey," Apr. 13, 1961): There Is Nothin' Like a Dame/W: Oscar Hammerstein II, M: Richard Rodgers.

170. Martin Ambrose *How Now, Dow Jones* (Lunt-Fontanne, "Jones," Dec. 7, 1967): A Little Investigation/W: Carolyn Leigh, M: Elmer Bernstein.

171. Don Ameche (May 31, 1908–Dec. 6, 1993) B: Kenosha, WI. Popular star of radio and TV, he also appeared in more than 40 films. *Silk Stockings* (Imperial, "Steve Canfield," Feb. 24, 1955): All of You; As On Through the Seasons We Sail; Paris Loves Lovers; Silk Stockings/WM: Cole Porter. *Goldilocks* (Lunt-Fontanne, "Max Grady," Oct. 11, 1958): I Can't Be in Love; No One'll Ever Love You (Like You Do); There Never Was a Woman (Who Couldn't Be Had)/W: Joan Ford, Walter Kerr, Jean Kerr, M: Leroy Anderson. *13 Daughters* (54th Street, "Chun," Mar. 2, 1961): House on the Hill; 13 Daughters; You Set My Heart to Music/WM: Eaton

Magoon, Jr.— Oriental Plan/WM: Sid Wayne, Sherman Edwards. *Henry, Sweet Henry* (Palace, "Henry Orient," Oct. 23, 1967): Forever; Pillar to Post; To Be Artistic/WM: Bob Merrill.

172. Don Amendolia (Feb. 1, 1945–) B: Woodbury, NJ. *My One and Only* (St. James, CR, "Prince Nicolai Erraclyovitch Tchatch-avadze," Nov. 1, 1984): Funny Face; I Can't Be Bothered Now; In the Swim; What Are We Here For?/W: Ira Gershwin, M: George Gershwin.

173. April Ames *Louisiana Purchase* (Imperial, "Emmy-Lou," May 28, 1940): Louisiana Purchase; You Can't Brush Me Off/WM: Irving Berlin.

174. Ed Ames (July 9, 1927–) B: Boston, MA. One of the 4 Ames Brothers, hit recording artists of the late 1940s and 50s. *Carnival!* (Imperial, CR, "Paul Berthalet," c 1963): Ev'rybody Likes You; Her Face; I've Got to Find a Reason; She's My Love/WM: Bob Merrill.

175. Florenz Ames (1884–?) B: Rochester, NY. He played Inspector Richard Queen, Ellery's dad, on TV's *Adventures of Ellery Queen* (1950); he was also Dagwood's boss, J.C. Dithers, on the sitcom *Blondie* (1957). *Lady Butterfly* (Globe, "Alfred Hopper," Dec. 22, 1923): Beautiful Love; The Booze of Auld Lang Syne/W: Clifford Grey, M: Werner Janssen. *Madame Pompadour* (Martin Beck, "Joseph Calicot," Nov. 11, 1924): Inspiration [Jan. 5, 1925]; Oh! Joseph; Oh Pom-Pom-Pom-Pompadour!; One, Two and One, Two, Three/W: Clare Kummer, M: Leo Fall — When the Cherry Blossoms Fall (Love Is Love)/W: William Cary Duncan, M: Anselm Goetzl. *Sky High* (Shubert > Winter Garden > Casino, "Alfred Horridge, Esq.," Mar. 2, 1925): Find a Good Time/W: Clifford Grey, M: Carleton Kelsey, Maurie Rubens — Sky High; There's Life in the Old Dog Yet [Mar. 23, 1925]/W: P.G. Wodehouse, M: Ivan Caryll. *The Great Tempta-tions* (Winter Garden, revue, May 18, 1926): Dancing Town/W: Clifford Grey, M: Maurie Rubens. *Angela* (Ambassador, "Grand Duke Herbert," Dec. 3, 1928): The Regal Romp; The Weaker Sex/W: Mann Holiner, M: Alberta Nichols. *The Silver Swan* (Martin Beck, "Gen. Van Auen," Nov. 27, 1929): None But the Brave Deserve the Fair/W: Will M. Hough, Frank R. Adams, M: Joseph E. Howard. *The Count of Luxembourg* (Jolson's, revival, "Grand Duke Rutzinoff," Feb. 17, 1930): Cousins of the Czar; I Am in Love/W: Basil Hood, M: Franz Lehar — Rootsie-Pootsie/W: Adrian Ross, Basil Hood, M: Franz Lehar. *Of Thee I Sing* (Music Box, "French Ambassador," Dec. 26, 1931): Entrance of the French Ambassador; The Illegitimate

Daughter; Jilted! Jilted!/W: Ira Gershwin, M: George Gershwin. *Let 'Em Eat Cake* (Imperial, "Gen. Adam Snookfield, U.S.A.," Oct. 21, 1933): I've Brushed My Teeth; My Fellow Soldiers/W: Ira Gershwin, M: George Gershwin. *I'd Rather Be Right* (Alvin > Music Box, "James B. Maxwell," Nov. 2, 1937): Labor Is the Thing/W: Lorenz Hart, M: Richard Rodgers. *Oklahoma!* (St. James, CR, "Andrew Carnes," Jan. 14, 1945): The Farmer and the Cowman/W: Oscar Hammerstein II, M: Richard Rodgers. *Arms and the Girl* (46th Street, "Capt. Aaron Kirkland," Feb. 2, 1950): That's What I Told Him Last Night/ W: Dorothy Fields, M: Morton Gould. *Of Thee I Sing* (Ziegfeld, revival, "French Ambassador," May 5, 1952): The Illegitimate Daughter/W: Ira Gershwin, M: George Gershwin.

176. Genevieve Ames *The New Yorkers* (Edyth Totten, revue, Mar. 10, 1927): Romany/ W: Henry Myers, M: Arthur Schwartz — A Side Street Off Broadway/W: Henry Myers, M: Edgar Fairchild — Words and Music/W: Henry Myers, M: Charles M. Schwab.

177. Kenston Ames *Harrigan 'n Hart* (Longacre, "Chester Fox," Jan. 31, 1985): The Old Barn Floor/W: Edward Harrigan, M: Dave Braham.

178. Nancy Ames (1937–) B: Washington, DC. She appeared in the TV political satire *That Was the Week That Was* (1964) *Kiss Me, Kate* (New York City Center, revival, "Lois Lane" and "Bianca," May 12, 1965): Always True to You in My Fashion; Tom, Dick or Harry; We Open in Venice; Why Can't You Behave?/WM: Cole Porter.

179. Percy Ames (1874–Mar. 28, 1936) B: Brighton, England. *The Prince of Pilsen* (New York, revival, "Arthur St. John Wilberforce, Lord Somerset," Apr. 3, 1905): Artie; Walk, Mister, Walk; The Widow/W: Frank Pixley, M: Gustav Luders. *Funabashi* (Casino, "Monty Beauchamp," Jan. 6, 1908): Her Baggage Was Checked for Troy/WM: Safford Waters. *The Balkan Princess* (Herald Square > Casino, "Max Hein," Feb. 9, 1911): The Opera Ball/WM: Arthur Wimperis, Paul Rubens. *He Didn't Want to Do It* (Broadhurst, "O. Vivian Smith," Aug. 20, 1918): It's the Scotch; What Would You Do in a Case Like That?/W: George Broadhurst, M: Silvio Hein. *Be Yourself!* (Sam H. Harris, CR, "Joseph Peabody Prescott," Sept. 29, 1924): Life in Town/WM: ?.

180. Alan Amick *The King and I* (Uris, revival, "Louis Leonowens, May 2, 1977): I Whistle a Happy Tune/W: Oscar Hammerstein II, M: Richard Rodgers.

181. Robert Amirante *Cats* (Winter Garden, CR, "Munkustrap," c 1988): The Awefull Battle of the Pekes and Pollicles; The Marching Songs of the Pollicle Dogs; Old Deuteronomy/ W: T.S. Eliot, M: Andrew Lloyd Webber.

182. Keith Lorenzo Amos (Oct. 26, 1962– Nov. 22, 1998) B: Annapolis, MD. He worked extensively on TV and became well known for the "Got Milk?" commercial. *Amen Corner* (Nederlander, "David," Nov. 10, 1983): I'm Already Gone; That Woman Can't Play No Piano; We Got a Good Thing Goin'/W: Peter Udell, M: Garry Sherman.

183. Monte Amundsen (1930–) M: GIORGIO TOZZI. *Juno* (Winter Garden, "Mary Boyle," Mar. 9, 1959): Bird Upon the Tree; For Love; I Wish It So; My True Heart/WM: Marc Blitzstein. *Cafe Crown* (Martin Beck, "Norma Roberts," Apr. 17, 1964): All Those Years; A Lifetime Love/W: Marty Brill, M: Albert Hague.

184. John Anania (July 12, 1923–) B: Sicily, Italy. *Sweethearts* (Shubert, revival, "Adolphus," Jan. 21, 1947): Pilgrims of Love/W: Robert B. Smith, M: Victor Herbert. *Hello, Dolly!* (Lunt-Fontanne, revival, "Rudolph," Mar. 5, 1978): Hello, Dolly!/WM: Jerry Herman.

185. Jean Andalman (May 5, 1951–) B: Chicago, IL. *Oh! Calcutta!* (Edison, revue, revival, Sept. 24, 1976): Clarence; Spread Your Love Around/WM: Robert Dennis, Peter Schickele, Stanley Walden.

186. Darlene Anders *The Three Musketeers* (Broadway, revival, "Queen Anne of France," Nov. 11, 1984): L'Amour, Toujours, L'Amour/W: Catherine Chisholm Cushing, M: Rudolf Friml.

187. Glenn Anders (Sept. 1, 1889–Oct. 26, 1981) B: Los Angeles, CA. *Three Waltzes* (Majestic, "Karl Brenner," Dec. 25, 1937): The Olden Days/W: Clare Kummer, M: Oscar Straus.

188. Karen Anders (July 30, 1928–Jan. 18, 1994) B: Massachusetts. *Almost Crazy* (Longacre, revue, June 20, 1955): I Can Live Without It/WM: Ray Taylor — Mother's Day/W: Joyce Geary, M: Portia Nelson.

189. Anne Renee Anderson (July 9, 1920–) B: New York, NY. *Lend an Ear* (National > Broadhurst, revue, Dec. 16, 1948): Ballade; Neurotic You and Psychopathic Me; Three Little Queens of the Silver Screen/WM: Charles Gaynor.

190. Carl Anderson (Feb. 27, 1945–Feb. 23, 2004) B: Lynchburg, VA. He recreated the role in the movie in 1973. *Jesus Christ Superstar* (Mark Hellinger, CR, "Judas Iscariot," May 1972): Damned for All Time; Everything's Alright; Heaven on Their Minds; Judas' Death; The Last

Supper; Strange Thing Mystifying; Superstar/ W: Tim Rice, M: Andrew Lloyd Webber. *Jesus Christ Superstar* (Paramount Madison Square Garden, revival, "Judas Iscariot," Jan. 17, 1995): same as above.

191. Delbert Anderson *Brigadoon* (Ziegfeld, "Stuart Dalrymple," Mar. 13, 1947): Down on MacConnachy Square/W: Alan Jay Lerner, M: Frederick Loewe. *A Tree Grows in Brooklyn* (Alvin, Apr. 19, 1951): If You Haven't Got a Sweetheart/W: Dorothy Fields, M: Arthur Schwartz. *Paint Your Wagon* (Shubert, "Jack," Nov. 12, 1951): Movin'/W: Alan Jay Lerner, M: Frederick Loewe. *Wonderful Town* (Winter Garden, "Drunk" and "Policeman," Feb. 25, 1953): My Darlin' Eileen/W: Betty Comden, Adolph Green, M: Leonard Bernstein. *New Girl in Town* (46th Street, "Oscar," May 14, 1957): Sunshine Girl/WM: Bob Merrill.

192. Dolores Anderson *The Boys from Syracuse* (Alvin, "Assistant Courtesan," Nov. 23, 1938): The Shortest Day of the Year/W: Lorenz Hart, M: Richard Rodgers.

193. Dorian Anderson *Maytime* (Shubert > 44th Street > Broadhurst, CR, "Little Dick Wayne," Dec. 24, 1917): Reminiscence/W: Rida Johnson Young, M: Sigmund Romberg.

194. George Anderson (Mar. 6, 1886–Aug. 26, 1948) B: New York, NY. M: FRITZI SCHEFF. *Up and Down Broadway* (Casino, revue, July 18, 1910): Come Down to Earth, My Dearie; Go on Your Mission; I Want a Lot of Girlies, Girlies (I Want a Whole Lot of Girls)/W: William Jerome, M: Jean Schwartz. *He Came from Milwaukee* (Casino, "Egbert Keskiesko, Duke of Zurach," Sept. 21, 1910): Love Is Like a Red, Red Rose; Merry Wedding Bells/W: Edward Madden, M: Ben M. Jerome, Louis A. Hirsch. *The Duchess* (Lyric, "Philippe, Marquis de Montreville," Oct. 16, 1911): The Land of Sultans' Dreams/W: Joseph W. Herbert, Harry B. Smith, M: Victor Herbert. *Tantalizing Tommy* (Criterion, "Paul Normand," Oct. 1, 1912): I Am a Tomboy; Irish Stew; Just Like You/W: Adrian Ross, M: Hugo Felix. *Nobody Home* (Princess > Maxine Elliott, "Vernon Popple," Apr. 20, 1915): Another Little Girl/W: Herbert Reynolds, M: Jerome Kern — Cupid at the Plaza/WM: ? — You Know and I Know/W: Schuyler Greene, M: Jerome Kern. *A Night in Spain* (44th Street, revue, May 3, 1927): International Vamp/W: Alfred Bryan, M: Jean Schwartz.

195. Greta Anderson *Keep Shufflin'* (Eltinge, revue, CR, Apr. 23, 1928): Teasing Mama (Teasing Baby)/W: Henry Creamer, M: James P. Johnson.

196. Ida Anderson *Pansy* (Belmont, "Miss Wright," May 14, 1929): A Stranger Interlude/ WM: Maceo Pinkard.

197. Ivar Anderson *The Prince of Pilsen* (New York, revival, "Lieut. Tom Wagner," Apr. 3, 1905): The Message of the Violet/W: Frank Pixley, M: Gustav Luders. *The Rich Mr. Hoggenheimer* (Wallack's, "Ned Brandon," Oct. 22, 1906): Au Revoir My Little Hyacinth [Oct. 29, 1906]/W: A.E. Sidney Davis, M: Herman Darewski — The Homesick Yankee (You're Thinking of Home Sweet Home) [Oct. 29, 1906]/WM: Kenneth S. Clark — Little Old America for Me/W: Harry B. Smith, M: Ludwig Englander.

198. Joel Anderson (Nov. 19, 1955–) B: San Diego, CA. *The Best Little Whorehouse in Texas* (Eugene O'Neill, CR, "Governor's Aide," May 1982): The Sidestep/WM: Carol Hall.

199. John Anderson (Oct. 20, 1922–Aug. 7, 1992) B: Clayton, IL. He appeared in the long-running TV western, *The Life and Legend of Wyatt Earp* (1959). *Paint Your Wagon* (Shubert, "Johansen," Nov. 12, 1951): Movin'/W: Alan Jay Lerner, M: Frederick Loewe.

200. Katherine Anderson She played Margaret Allen, the Professor's wife, in the daily radio soap, *Against the Storm* (1949). *Courtin' Time* (National, "Louisa Windeatt, June 13, 1951): Masculinity/W: Jack Lawrence, M: Don Walker.

201. Lawrence Anderson (May 18, 1964–) B: Poughkeepsie, NY. *Les Miserables* (Broadway, CR, "Enjolras," c 1992): Do You Hear the People Sing?; Red and Black/W: Herbert Kretzmer, M: Claude-Michel Schonberg.

202. Leona Anderson (Nov. 23, c 1897–Mar. 29, 1985) B: Philadelphia, PA. *The Sultan of Sulu* (Wallack's, CR, "Miss Newton," May 18, 1903): The Peachy Teacher; Ten Little Gentlemen of Spooney Town/W: George Ade, M: Alfred G. Wathall. *Moonshine* (Liberty, "Countess of Broadlawns," Oct. 30, 1905): A Hundred Years from Now/W: George V. Hobart, Edwin Milton Royle, M: Silvio Hein. *The Honeymooners* (New Amsterdam roof, "Susie Sprightling," June 3, 1907): I'll Be There in the Public Square; In a One-Night Stand; Mysterious Maid/WM: George M. Cohan. *Marcelle* (Casino, "Mrs. Darlington," Oct. 1, 1908): It's Not the Proper Thing/W: Frank Pixley, M: Gustav Luders.

203. Lillian Anderson *Helen Goes to Troy* (Alvin, "Helen," Apr. 24, 1944 mats.): Advice to Husbands; Come with Me; Is It a Dream?; Love at Last; Sweet Helen; Take My Advice; Where Is Love?/W: Herbert Baker, M: Jacques Offenbach, adapted by Eric Wolfgang Korngold.

204. Thomas Charles Anderson (Nov. 28, 1906–Jan. 12, 1996) B: Pasadena, CA. *70, Girls, 70* (Broadhurst, Apr. 15, 1971): Broadway, My Street; See the Light; You and I, Love/W: Fred Ebb, M: John Kander. *Don't Play Us Cheap!* (Ethel Barrymore, "Mr. Percy," May 16, 1972): 8 Day Week/WM: Melvin Van Peebles.

205. Warner Anderson (Mar. 10, 1911–Aug. 26, 1976) B: Brooklyn, NY. A supporting actor in many movies, his career began in silents at the age of 4. On TV he starred in the long-running police drama, *The Lineup* (1954). *Maytime* (Shubert, "Little Dick Wayne," Aug. 16, 1917): Reminiscence/W: Rida Johnson Young, M: Sigmund Romberg.

206. Jeffrey Anderson-Gunter B: Jamaica, West Indies. *But Never Jam Today* (Longacre, "Cheshire Cat" and "Mock Turtle," July 31, 1979): Jumping from Rock to Rock; The More I See People/WM: Bob Larimer, Bert Keyes.

207. Keith Andes (July 12, 1920–) B: Ocean City, NJ. *The Chocolate Soldier* (Century, revival, "Lieut. Bumerli," Mar. 12, 1947): The Chocolate Soldier; Falling in Love; The Letter Song; Seek the Spy; Sympathy; The Tale of a Coat/W: Stanislaus Stange, M: Oscar Straus — Forgive/W: Bernard Hanighen, M: Oscar Straus. *Kiss Me, Kate* (New Century, CR, "Fred Graham" and "Petruchio," June 1950): I've Come to Wive It Wealthily in Padua; Kiss Me, Kate; So in Love; We Open in Venice; Were Thine That Special Face; Where Is the Life That Late I Led?; Wunderbar/WM: Cole Porter. *Maggie* (National, "John Shand," Feb. 18, 1953): He's the Man; I Never Laughed in My Life; Long and Weary Wait; People in Love; Thimbleful; You Become Me/WM: William Roy. *Wildcat* (Alvin, "Joe Dynamite," Dec. 16, 1960): Corduroy Road; Give a Little Whistle (and I'll Be There); You're a Liar!; You've Come Home/W: Carolyn Leigh, M: Cy Coleman.

208. David Andrada (Dec. 27, 1865–Jan. 3, 1941) B: Brooklyn, NY. *A Broken Idol* (Herald Square, "Lord Dunby," Aug. 16, 1909): The Sign of a Honeymoon/W: Harry Williams, M: Egbert Van Alstyne. *The Madcap Duchess* (Globe, "Watteau," Nov. 11, 1913): Far Up the Hill/W: David Stevens, M: Victor Herbert.

209. Ann Andre *The Red Mill* (Ziegfeld, revival, "Gretchen," Oct. 16, 1945): I Want You to Marry Me; In the Isle of Our Dreams; Moonbeams; Wedding Bells (Wedding Chorus)/W: Henry Blossom, Forman Brown, M: Victor Herbert.

210. Christine Andreas (Oct. 1, 1951–) B: Camden, NJ. Popular cabaret singer. *My Fair Lady* (St. James, revival, "Eliza Doolittle," Mar. 25, 1976): I Could Have Danced All Night; Just You Wait; The Rain in Spain; Show Me; Without You; Wouldn't It Be Loverly?/W: Alan Jay Lerner, M: Frederick Loewe. *Oklahoma!* (Palace, revival, "Laurey Williams," Dec. 13, 1979): Many a New Day; Oh, What a Beautiful Mornin'; Oklahoma!; Out of My Dreams; People Will Say We're in Love; The Surrey with the Fringe on Top/W: Oscar Hammerstein II, M: Richard Rodgers. *On Your Toes* (Virginia, revival, "Frankie Frayne," Mar. 6, 1983): Glad to Be Unhappy; It's Got to Be Love; On Your Toes; There's a Small Hotel/W: Lorenz Hart, M: Richard Rodgers.

211. Barbara Andres (Feb. 11, 1939–) B: New York, NY. *The Boy Friend* (Ambassador, revival, "Hortense," Apr. 14, 1970): It's Nicer in Nice; Perfect Young Ladies/WM: Sandy Wilson. *Rex* (Lunt-Fontanne, "Queen Catherine," Apr. 25, 1976): As Once I Loved You/W: Sheldon Harnick, M: Richard Rodgers. *Doonesbury* (Biltmore, "Joanie," Nov. 21, 1983): Another Memorable Meal; Mother/W: Garry Trudeau; M: Elizabeth Swados.

212. Stella Andreva B: England. *Yours Is My Heart* (Shubert, "Claudette Vernay," Sept. 5, 1946): Chinese Ceremony; A Cup of China Tea; Free As the Air; Love, What Has Given You This Magic Power?; Upon a Moonlight Night in May/W: Karl Farkas, Ira Cobb, Harry Graham, M: Franz Lehar — Paris Sings Again/W: ?, M: Paul Durant.

213. Albert G. Andrews (c 1857–Nov. 26, 1950) B: Buffalo, NY. His first stage performance was in 1862; his last was in 1944. He played 255 roles. *Marjolaine* (Broadhurst, "Admiral Sir Peter Antrobus," Jan. 24, 1922): Punch and Judy/W: Brian Hooker, M: Hugo Felix.

214. Avis Andrews (?–July 14, 1972) B: Houston, TX. *Rhapsody in Black* (Sam H. Harris, revue, May 4, 1931): Eli Eli/WM: trad. *Smile at Me* (Fulton, revue, Aug. 23, 1935): Calcutta; Goona, Goona; Tired of the South/WM: Edward J. Lambert, Gerald Dolin — Doin' the Truck/WM: Edward J. Lambert. *Virginia* (Center, "Miranda," Sept. 2, 1937): Good and Lucky; I'll Be Sitting in de Lap o' de Lord/W: Al Stillman, M: Arthur Schwartz — Send One Angel Down/W: Al Stillman, Laurence Stallings, M: Arthur Schwartz.

215. Billy Andrews *Pansy* (Belmont, "Bob," May 14, 1929): Pansy/WM: Maceo Pinkard.

216. Brian Andrews *Cats* (Winter Garden, CR, "Rumpus Cat" and "Macavity"): The Awefull Battle of the Pekes and Pollicles; Macavity;

The Marching Songs of the Pollicle Dogs/W: T.S. Eliot, M: Andrew Lloyd Webber.

217. George Lee Andrews (Oct. 13, 1942–) B: Milwaukee, WI. Father of JENNIFER LEE ANDREWS. *Sondheim: A Musical Tribute* (Shubert, revue, Mar. 11, 1973): Silly People/WM: Stephen Sondheim. *On the Twentieth Century* (St. James, "Max Jacobs," Feb. 19, 1978): Max Jacobs/W: Betty Comden, Adolph Green, M: Cy Coleman. *Merlin* (Mark Hellinger, "Old Merlin," Feb. 13, 1983): It's About Magic; Put a Little Magic in Your Life/W: Don Black, M: Elmer Bernstein. *The Phantom of the Opera* (Majestic, CR, "Monsieur Firmin," during run): Notes; Prima Donna; Twisted Every Way/W: Charles Hart, Richard Stilgoe, M: Andrew Lloyd Webber.

218. Jennifer Lee Andrews Daughter of GEORGE LEE ANDREWS. *Les Miserables* (Broadway, CR, "Cosette," Nov. 19, 1996): A Heart Full of Love; In My Life/W: Herbert Kretzmer, M: Claude-Michel Schonberg.

219. Jerome Andrews *The Straw Hat Revue* (Ambassador, revue, Sept. 29, 1939): Four Young People/WM: James Shelton.

220. Julie Andrews (Oct. 1, 1935–) B: Walton-on-Thames, England. This bright star began appearing on the English stage as a child in variety and pantomime. Famous for her film role as Mary Poppins (1964); and as Maria von Trapp in *The Sound of Music,* originated on Broadway by MARY MARTIN. *The Boy Friend* (Royale, "Polly Browne," Sept. 30, 1954): The Boy Friend; I Could Be Happy with You; Poor Little Pierrette; A Room in Bloomsbury/WM: Sandy Wilson. *My Fair Lady* (Mark Hellinger, "Eliza Doolittle," Mar. 15, 1956): I Could Have Danced All Night; Just You Wait; The Rain in Spain; Show Me; Without You; Wouldn't It Be Loverly?/W: Alan Jay Lerner, M: Frederick Loewe. *Camelot* (Majestic, "Queen Guenevere," Dec. 3, 1960): Before I Gaze at You Again; Camelot; I Loved You Once in Silence; The Lusty Month of May; The Simple Joys of Maidenhood; Then You May Take Me to the Fair; What Do the Simple Folk Do?/W: Alan Jay Lerner, M: Frederick Loewe. *Victor/Victoria* (Marquis, "Victoria Grant," Oct. 25, 1995/ Feb.2, 1997): Almost a Love Song; Crazy World; If I Were a Man; Le Jazz Hot; The Tango; Victor/Victoria; You and Me/W: Leslie Bricusse, M: Henry Mancini — Living in the Shadows; Trust Me/W: Leslie Bricusse, M: Frank Wildhorn.

221. Linda Andrews *Look to the Lilies* (Lunt-Fontanne, "Sister Agnes," Mar. 29, 1970): Casamagordo, New Mexico; Follow the Lamb;

Gott Is Gut; Himmlisher Vater; Look to the Lilies; One Little Brick at a Time; Them and They/W: Sammy Cahn, M: Jule Styne.

222. Lois Andrews (Mar. 24, 1924–Apr. 5, 1968) B: Huntington Park, CA. M: GEORGE JESSEL. *George White's Scandals of 1939-40* (Alvin, revue, Aug. 28, 1939): Our First Kiss; Smart Little Girls/W: Jack Yellen, M: Sammy Fain.

223. Maidie Andrews (c 1893–Oct. 13, 1986) B: London, England. *Conversation Piece* (44th Street, "Rose," Oct. 23, 1934): Charming, Charming; Dear Little Soldiers/WM: Noel Coward.

224. Maxene Andrews (Jan. 3, 1916–Oct. 21, 1995) B: Minneapolis, MN. One of the 3 Andrews Sisters, the others being PATTY and Laverne (1913-1967), best remembered for singing roles in movies and for their hit recordings of the 1940s. *Over Here!* (Shubert, "Pauline de Paul," Mar. 6, 1974): The Big Beat; Charlie's Place; No Goodbyes; Over Here; Wartime Wedding; We Got It/WM: Richard M. Sherman, Robert B. Sherman.

225. Nancy Andrews (Dec. 16, 1920–July 29, 1989) B: Minneapolis, MN. She began as a cabaret singer and pianist, and toured with the USO during WWII. *Touch and Go* (Broadhurst > Broadway, revue, Oct. 13, 1949): Be a Mess; Miss Platt Selects Mate; This Had Better Be Love; Wish Me Luck/W: Walter Kerr, Jean Kerr, M: Jay Gorney. *Hazel Flagg* (Mark Hellinger, CR, "Laura Carew," May 1953): Everybody Loves to Take a Bow; Hello, Hazel; A Little More Heart; My Wild Imagination/W: Bob Hilliard, M: Jule Styne. *Plain and Fancy* (Mark Hellinger, "Emma Miller," Jan. 27, 1955): City Mouse, Country Mouse; How Do You Raise a Barn?; Plenty of Pennsylvania/W: Arnold B. Horwitt, M: Albert Hague. *Pipe Dream* (Shubert, CR, "Fauna," June 1956): All at Once You Love Her; Bums' Opera; The Happiest House on the Block; How Long?; Suzy Is a Good Thing; Sweet Thursday; We Are a Gang of Witches; Will You Marry Me?/W: Oscar Hammerstein II, M: Richard Rodgers. *Juno* (Winter Garden, "Mrs. Brady," Mar. 9, 1959): You Poor Thing/WM: Marc Blitzstein. *Christine* (46th Street, "Auntie," Apr. 28, 1960): Freedom Can Be a Most Uncomfortable Thing; How to Pick a Man a Wife; I'm Just a Little Sparrow; Welcome Song/W: Paul Francis Webster, M: Sammy Fain. *Little Me* (Lunt-Fontanne, "Belle Poitrine," Nov. 17, 1962): Here's to Us; Little Me; The Truth/W: Carolyn Leigh, M: Cy Coleman.

226. Patty Andrews (Feb. 16, 1918–1992) B:

Minneapolis, MN. Sister of MAXENE AN-
DREWS. *Over Here!* (Shubert, "Paulette de
Paul," Mar. 6, 1974): The Big Beat; The Good-
Time Girl; No Goodbyes; Over Here; Wartime
Wedding; We Got It; Where Did the Good
Times Go?/WM: Richard M. Sherman, Robert
B. Sherman.

227. Talleur Andrews *The School Girl* (Daly's
> Herald Square, "Edgar Verney," Sept. 1, 1904):
Jolly Little Japs/WM: Paul Rubens — She's an
English Girl/WM: Adrian Ross, Leslie Stuart —
Sweet Sanaoo [Oct. 31, 1904]/W: Vernon Roy,
M: William T. Francis.

228. Ada Androva *Robinson Crusoe, Jr.*
(Winter Garden, Feb. 17, 1916): My Voodoo
Maiden/W: Harold Atteridge, M: Sigmund
Romberg.

229. Lou Angel (Aug. 18, 1940–) B:
Chicago, IL. *Hallelujah, Baby!* (Martin Beck,
"Calhoun," Apr. 26, 1967): Farewell, Farewell/
W: Betty Comden, Adolph Green, M: Jule
Styne.

230. June Angela (Aug. 18, 1959–) B: New
York, NY. *The King and I* (Uris, revival, "Tup-
tim," May 2, 1977): I Have Dreamed; My Lord
and Master; We Kiss in a Shadow/W: Oscar
Hammerstein II, M: Richard Rodgers. *Shogun:
The Musical* (Marquis, "Lady Mariko," Nov. 20,
1990): Absolution; Born to Be Together; Cha-
No-Yu; Fireflies; He Let Me Live; How Nice to
See You; Impossible Eyes; No Word for Love;
One Candle; Poetry Competition; Trio/W: John
Driver, M: Paul Chihara.

231. Aimee Angeles (Feb. 6, 1880–?) *A Chi-
nese Honeymoon* (Casino, "Mi Mi," Sept. 1,
1902): Tid Bits from the Plays/W: George
Dance; M: Howard Talbot. *Mother Goose* (New
Amsterdam, "Caroline Evelyn Gwendolyn
Scraggs," Dec. 2, 1903): I Don't Want to Be a
Lady/W: J.M. Glover, Matthew Woodward, M:
Ben M. Jerome — Under the Mistletoe Bough/
W: Will Heelan, M: J. Fred Helf. *Higgledy-Pig-
gledy* (Weber Music Hall, "Gertie Keith," Oct.
20, 1904): Big Indian and His Little Maid; For
You, Honey, for You/W: Edgar Smith, M: Mau-
rice Levi. *Wonderland* (Majestic, "Gladys," Oct.
24, 1905): The Crew of the Peek-a-Boo; Jogra-
fee; The Voice for It/W: Glen MacDonough, M:
Victor Herbert.

232. Ebba Angeles *The Broadway Whirl*
(Selwyn, revue, CR, Aug. 15, 1921): Baby Dolls/
W: B.G. DeSylva, John Henry Mears, M:
George Gershwin — Button Me Up the Back/W:
Joseph McCarthy, M: Harry Tierney.

233. Charles Angelo *Kitty Grey* (New Amsterdam, "Ernest III, King of Illyria," Jan. 25,

1909): Incognito/W: J. Smyth Piggot, M: Lionel
Monckton — King Hal's Gals/WM: St. John
Hamund, Richard Kenneth. *Madame Trouba-
dour* (Lyric > 39th Street, "Marquis de Kerga-
zon," Oct. 10, 1910): Don't Be Rash; Trou-Trou-
Ba-Ba-Troubadour/W: Joseph W. Herbert, M:
Felix Albini. *The Wedding Trip* (Broadway,
"Szigetti," Dec. 25, 1911): The Family Council;
The Interrupted Love Song/W: Harry B. Smith,
M: Reginald De Koven. *The Merry Widow*
(Knickerbocker, revival, "Camille De Jolidon,"
Sept. 5, 1921): A Dutiful Wife; I Love You So
(The Merry Widow Waltz); Love in My Heart;
Oh, Say No More/W: Adrian Ross, M: Franz
Lehar. *The DuBarry* (George M. Cohan, "Baron
Charmard," Nov. 22, 1932): Pantalettes/W:
Rowland Leigh, M: Carl Millocker.

234. Muriel Angelus (Mar. 10, 1909–) B:
London, England. *The Boys from Syracuse* (Alvin,
"Adriana," Nov. 23, 1938): Falling in Love with
Love; Sing for Your Supper/W: Lorenz Hart, M:
Richard Rodgers. *Sunny River* (St. James, "Marie
Sauvinet," Dec. 4, 1941): Along the Winding
Road; Call It a Dream; Can You Sing?; It Can
Happen to Anyone; Let Me Live Today; Mak-
ing Conversation; Time Is Standing Still/W:
Oscar Hammerstein II, M: Sigmund Romberg.
Early to Bed (Broadhurst, "Madame Rowena,"
June 17, 1943): The Ladies Who Sing with a
Band; Long Time No Song; There's a Man in
My Life; This Is So Nice/W: George Marion,
Jr., M: Fats Waller.

235. Charles Angle *The Student Prince*
(Majestic, revival, "Von Asterberg," Jan. 29,
1931): Come Boys, Let's All Be Gay, Boys (Students' March Song); Serenade; Student Life; To
the Inn We're Marching/W: Dorothy Donnelly,
M: Sigmund Romberg.

236. D. Angulliar *The Passing Show of 1919*
(Winter Garden, revue, Mar. 15, 1920): The
King's Favorite/W: Harold Atteridge, M: Sig-
mund Romberg, Jean Schwartz.

237. Paul Anka (July 30, 1941–) B: Ottawa,
Ontario, Canada. The singer-songwriter wrote
over 200 songs, many of which became hits, by
the time he was 21. *What Makes Sammy Run?*
(54th Street, CR, "Sammy Glick," July 13,
1964): I Feel Humble; I See Something; Kiss Me
No Kisses; Lites — Camera — Platitude; My
Hometown; A New Pair of Shoes; A Room
Without Windows; Some Days Everything Goes
Wrong; You Can Trust Me; You Help Me; You're
No Good/WM: Ervin Drake.

238. Annabelle (July 6, c 1878–Nov. 30,
1961) B: Chicago, IL. Her full name was ANNA-
BELLE WHITFORD. Flo Ziegfeld proclaimed

her one of the great beauties of her era; she was chosen by artist Charles Dana Gibson as the original Gibson Girl. In 1894, Thomas Edison photographed her dancing in a butterfly costume; the image was shown in peepshows and projected on screen. *Ziegfeld Follies of 1908* (Jardin de Paris, New York roof > New York, revue, June 15, 1908): The Nell Brinkley Girl/W: Harry B. Smith, M: Maurice Levi. *Ziegfeld Follies of 1909* (Jardin de Paris, New York roof, revue, June 14, 1909): The Bathing Girls; Madame Venus (Take a Tip from Venus)/W: Harry B. Smith, M: Maurice Levi. *The Happiest Night of His Life* (Criterion, "Minnie Randolph," Feb. 20, 1911): The Fiddler Must Be Paid; Oh, You Chicago, and Oh, You New York; We Are Laughing Widows/W: Junie McCree, M: Albert Von Tilzer.

239. Marie Annis *Fluffy Ruffles* (Criterion, "Celeste," Sept. 7, 1908): Echo of My Heart/W: Wallace Irwin, M: William T. Francis.

240. Emmett Anthony *Liza* (Daly's, "Bodiddily," Nov. 27, 1922): My Old Man/WM: Nat Vincent, Maceo Pinkard.

241. Eugene J. Anthony *On Your Toes* (Virginia, revival, "Phil Dolan II," Mar. 6, 1983): Two-a-Day for Keith/W: Lorenz Hart, M: Richard Rodgers.

242. John D. Anthony *Porgy and Bess* (Uris, revival, "Crown," Sept. 25, 1976): A Red Headed Woman/W: Ira Gershwin, M: George Gershwin — What You Want wid Bess?/W: DuBose Heyward, M: George Gershwin.

243. Susan Anton (Oct. 12, 1950–) B: Oak Glen, CA. Concert and nightclub singer. She succeeded EDIE ADAMS advertising Muriel Cigars on TV. *The Will Rogers Follies* (Palace, CR, "Ziegfeld's Favorite," Dec. 9, 1991): Will-a-Mania/W: Betty Comden, Adolph Green, M: Cy Coleman.

244. Harry Antrim (Aug. 27, 1884–Jan. 18, 1967) B: Chicago, IL. *Frivolities of 1920* (44th Street, revue, Jan. 8, 1920): Araby/WM: William B. Friedlander.

245. Johnny Anzalone *Cats* (Winter Garden, CR, "Mungojerrie"): Mungojerrie and Rumpleteazer/W: T.S. Eliot, M: Andrew Lloyd Webber.

246. Hy Anzell (c 1924–Aug. 25, 2003) B: New York, NY. *Oklahoma!* (St. James, CR, "Ali Hakim," Feb. 1948): It's a Scandal! It's a Outrage!/W: Oscar Hammerstein II, M: Richard Rodgers.

247. Boris Aplon (July 14, 1910–Nov. 27, 1995) B: Chicago, IL. He played the villain, Ivan Shark, on radio's *Captain Midnight* (1939). *Anya*

(Ziegfeld, "Josef," Nov. 29, 1965): Here Tonight, Tomorrow Where?; On That Day; So Proud; That Prelude!; Vodka, Vodka!/WM: Robert Wright, George Forrest. *Fiddler on the Roof* (Imperial, CR, "Lazar Wolf," Aug. 1967): Anatevka; To Life/W: Sheldon Harnick, M: Jerry Bock.

248. Arthur Appel *Innocent Eyes* (Winter Garden, CR, "Harry," July 7, 1924): Let's Have a Rattling Good Time/W: Alfred Bryan, M: Jean Schwartz — Organdie Days/W: Tot Seymour, M: Jean Schwartz — Surrounded by the Girls/WM: ?.

249. Dorothy Appleby (Jan. 6, 1906–Aug. 9, 1990) B: Portland, ME. While still at school, she was chosen by film star Rudolph Valentino to be Miss Maine in a beauty contest. *Princess April* (Ambassador, "Marjorie Hale," Dec. 1, 1924): Dumb-Bells May Be Foolish; String 'Em Along/WM: Monte Carlo, Alma Sanders. *Puzzles of 1925* (Fulton, revue, Feb. 2, 1925): The Doo-Dab/W: Bert Kalmar, M: Harry Ruby — When the Cat's Away/WM: Blanche Merrill.

250. Walter Appler *Polonaise* (Alvin, "Count Gronski," Oct. 6, 1945): An Imperial Conference/W: John Latouche, M: Bronislau Kaper, based on Frederic Chopin.

251. Lewis Appleton *Stars on Ice* (Center, revue, CR, June 24, 1943): Big Broad Smile [Sept. 26, 1943]/W: Al Stillman, M: Paul McGrane — Put Your Cares on Ice/WM: James Littlefield.

252. April *Right This Way* (46th Street, "The Girl," Jan. 4, 1938): Doughnuts and Coffee/W: Irving Kahal, M: Sammy Fain.

253. Raul Aranas (Oct. 1, 1947–) B: Manila, Philippines. *Miss Saigon* (Broadway, CR, "The Engineer," c 1994): The American Dream; Back in Town; The Heat Is On in Saigon; If You Want to Die in Bed; The Morning of the Dragon; The Telephone; What a Waste/W: Richard Maltby, Jr., Alain Boublil, M: Claude-Michel Schonberg.

254. Flavia Arcaro (June 22, 1876–Apr. 8, 1937) B: Mejico, TX. *The Newlyweds and Their Baby* (Majestic, "Gwendolin," Mar. 22, 1909): Girls Who Want to Go Upon the Stage/W: A. Seymour Brown, M: Nat D. Ayer — My Black Dove/W: Paul West, M: John W. Bratton. *The Chocolate Soldier* (Lyric > Herald Square > Lyric > Casino, "Aurelia Popoff," Sept. 13, 1909): Seek the Spy; The Tale of a Coat; Thank the Lord the War Is Over; We Too, Are Lonely/W: Stanislas Stange, M: Oscar Straus. *The Red Rose* (Globe, "Mme. Joyant," June 22, 1911): A Brass Band's Good Enough for Me/W: James Harvey, M:

Robert Hood Bowers — I'd Like to Go on a Honeymoon with You/W: Harry B. Smith, M: Robert Hood Bowers — The Old Ballet Days/W: Harry B. Smith, Robert B. Smith, M: Robert Hood Bowers. *Hop o' My Thumb* (Manhattan Opera House, "Amber Witch," Nov. 26, 1913): Love Me, Love Me, Won't You?/W: Sydney Rosenfeld, M: Manuel Klein. *Dearest Enemy* (Knickerbocker, "Mrs. Robert Murray," Sept. 18, 1925): Full Blown Roses; Heigh-Ho, Lackaday; The Hermits (What Do All the Hermits Do in Springtime); War Is War; Where the Hudson River Flows/W: Lorenz Hart, M: Richard Rodgers. *Oh, Ernest!* (Royale, "Lady Bracknell," May 9, 1927): Ancestry/W: Francis De Witt, M: Robert Hood Bowers. *Mlle. Modiste* (Jolson, revival, "Mme. Cecelie," Oct. 7, 1929): When the Cat's Away the Mice Will Play/W: Henry Blossom, M: Victor Herbert.

255. Adele Archer *The Show Girl or The Cap of Fortune* (Wallack's, CR, "Diana," May 1902): Katrina/WM: Edward W. Corliss. *The American Maid* (Broadway, "Mrs. Vandeveer," Mar. 3, 1913): The Matrimonial Mart; This Is My Busy Day/W: Leonard Liebling, M: John Philip Sousa. *Wars of the World* (Hippodrome, revue, Sept. 5, 1914): Baby Eyes; In Siam; You're Just the One I've Waited For/WM: Manuel Klein.

256. Jane Archer *The Two Bouquets* (Windsor, "Flora Grantley," May 31, 1938): Dearest Miss Flo/W: Elcanor Farjeon, Herb Farjeon, M: trad., based on All Around the Ring.

257. John Archer (May 8, 1915–Dec. 3, 1999) B: Osceola, NB. Father of actress Anne Archer. Leading man in B movies. As a winner of the Jesse L. Lasky Gateway to Hollywood talent search in 1939, Ralph Bowman was given the new name of John Archer. *The Day Before Spring* (National, "Peter Townsend," Nov. 22, 1945): Where's My Wife?/W: Alan Jay Lerner, M: Frederick Loewe.

258. William Archibald (Mar. 7, 1915–Dec. 27, 1970) B: Trinidad. He came to the U.S. in 1937, joining Charles Weidman's dance company. *All in Fun* (Majestic, revue, Dec. 27, 1940): That Man and Woman Thing/WM: John Rox.

259. Will Archie *The Babes and the Baron* (Lyric, "Charlie," Dec. 25, 1905): I Didn't Mean No Harm/W: ?, M: J. Fred Helf — It's a Jolly Good Thing to Be Alive/W: Charles M. Taylor, Robert B. Smith, M: Herbert E. Haines. *The Never Homes* (Broadway, "Jimmy Louder," Oct. 5, 1911): There's a Girl in Havana/WM: E. Ray Goetz, Irving Berlin, Ted Snyder. *Go To It* (Princess, "The Bandmaster," Oct. 24, 1916):

Girls, If You Ever Get Married/WM: John L. Golden, Anne Caldwell, John E. Hazzard.

260. Kenneth Ard *Cats* (Winter Garden, "Rumpus Cat" and "Macavity," Oct. 7, 1982): The Awefull Battle of the Pekes and Pollicles; Macavity; The Marching Songs of the Pollicle Dogs/W: T.S. Eliot, M: Andrew Lloyd Webber. *Starlight Express* (Gershwin, "Electra," Mar. 15, 1987): AC/DC; Final Selection; First Final; One Rock & Roll Too Many; Race One; Wide Smile, High Style, That's Me/W: Richard Stilgoe, M: Andrew Lloyd Webber. *Jelly's Last Jam* (Virginia, CR, "Chimney Man," Feb. 9, 1993): The Chicago Stomp; Good Ole New York; Somethin' More/W: Susan Birkenhead, M: Jelly Roll Morton — The Last Rites/W: Susan Birkenhead, M: Luther Henderson, Jelly Roll Morton. *Smokey Joe's Cafe* (Virginia, revue, Mar. 2, 1995): Dance with Me; Keep on Rollin'; Little Egypt; Love Potion #9; Loving You; On Broadway; Poison Ivy; Ruby Baby; Searchin'; Shoppin' for Clothes; Young Blood/WM: Jerry Lieber, Mike Stoller — Spanish Harlem/WM: Phil Spector, Jerry Lieber.

261. David Ardao (July 24, 1951–) B: Brooklyn, NY. *Joseph and the Amazing Technicolor Dreamcoat* (Royale, revival, "Potiphar," Jan. 27, 1982): Potiphar/W: Tim Rice, M: Andrew Lloyd Webber.

262. Franklyn Ardell (May 1, 1885–Apr. 17, 1960) B: New Jersey. *Katinka* (44th Street > Lyric, "Thaddeus Hopper," Dec. 23, 1915): In a Hurry; Skidiskischatch/W: Otto Harbach, M: Rudolf Friml. *The Lady in Red* (Lyric, "Darius Dirks," May 12, 1919): Family Faces; I Want Somebody/W: Anne Caldwell, M: Richard Winterberg. *Sweet Little Devil* (Astor > Central, "Sam Wilson," Jan. 21, 1924): Hooray for the U.S.A.!/W: B.G. DeSylva, M: George Gershwin. *Cross My Heart* (Knickerbocker, "Tommy Fitzgerald," Sept. 17, 1928): Good Days and Bad Days; Such Is Fame/W: Joseph McCarthy, M: Harry Tierney.

263. Doris Arden *Fifty-Fifty, Ltd.* (Comedy, "Claire Crosby," Oct. 27, 1919): Honey Bunch; Silence of Love/WM: Leon De Costa — Without a Beautiful Girl/WM: Arthur Swanstrom, Carey Morgan.

264. Eve Arden (Apr. 30, 1908–Nov. 12, 1990) B: Mill Valley, CA. Her tongue was biting, but her heart was warm. The comic actress appeared in at least 60 movies and is widely remembered for her popular radio and TV series, *Our Miss Brooks.* (1948/1952). *Parade* (Guild, revue, May 20, 1935): Send for the Militia/WM: Marc Blitzstein. *Ziegfeld Follies of 1936* (Winter

Garden, revue, Jan. 30, 1936): Dancing to Our Score/WM: Ira Gershwin, Billy Rose, Vernon Duke — The Economic Situation; I Can't Get Started/W: Ira Gershwin, M: Vernon Duke. *Very Warm for May* (Alvin, "Winnie Spofford," Nov. 17, 1939): In Other Words, Seventeen/W: Oscar Hammerstein II, M: Jerome Kern. *Let's Face It!* (Imperial, "Maggie Watson," Oct. 29, 1941): Baby Games; A Lady Needs a Rest; Let's Not Talk About Love/WM: Cole Porter.

265. Helen Arden *Street Scene* (Adelphi, "Greta Fiorentino," Jan. 9, 1947): Ain't It Awful, the Heat?; Get a Load of That; When a Woman Has a Baby/W: Langston Hughes, Elmer Rice, M: Kurt Weill.

266. Helene Arden *Gypsy Blonde* (Lyric, "Baba," June 25, 1934): Bliss Forever Past/W: Frank Gabrielson, M: Michael Balfe.

267. Jane Arden B: Beaumont, TX. *Follow the Girls* (44th Street > Broadhurst, CR, "Betty Deleaninnion," Apr. 1, 1945): Where You Are/W: Dan Shapiro, Milton Pascal, M: Phil Charig.

268. Ottie Ardine M: GEORGE MCKAY. *Honey Girl* (Cohan and Harris, "Esther Blake," May 3, 1920): You're Just the Boy for Me/W: Neville Fleeson, M: Albert Von Tilzer.

269. Adele Ardsley *High Jinks* (Lyric > Casino, CR, "Florence," June 8, 1914): High Jinks; Something Seems Tingle-ingleing; When Sammy Sang the Marseillaise/W: Otto Harbach, M: Rudolf Friml. *The Show of Wonders* (Winter Garden, revue, CR, Apr. 4, 1917): Get a Girlie/ W: Harold Atteridge, M: Herman Timberg — Girls Prepare/W: Harold Atteridge, M: Sigmund Romberg — Wedding by the Sea/W: Harold Atteridge, M: ?.

270. Yancey Arias (June 27, 1971–) B: New York, NY. *Miss Saigon* (Broadway, CR, "Thuy," c 1993): Back in Town; The Guilt Inside Your Head; The Morning of the Dragon; You Will Not Touch Him/W: Richard Maltby, Jr., Alain Boublil, M: Claude-Michel Schonberg.

271. Juki Arkin B: Israel. Known in Israel and Europe as a pantomimist. *Milk and Honey* (Martin Beck, "Adi," Oct. 10, 1961): Milk and Honey; That Was Yesterday/WM: Jerry Herman.

272. Dee Arlen B: Montana. *Tickets, Please!* (Coronet, revue, Apr. 27, 1950): Darn It, Baby, That's Love/WM: Lyn Duddy, Joan Edwards.

273. Steve Arlen *Cry for Us All* (Broadhurst, "Matt Stanton," Apr. 8, 1970): Call in to Her; The Confessional; The End of My Race; Home Free All; How Are Ya Since?; This Cornucopian Land; The Verandah Waltz/W: Alfred Robinson, Phyllis Robinson, M: Mitch Leigh. *La Cage*

aux Folles (Palace, CR, "Georges," Nov. 12, 1985/July 29, 1986): Cocktail Counterpoint; Look Over There; Masculinity; Song on the Sand; With You on My Arm/WM: Jerry Herman.

274. Charles Arling (Aug. 22, 1880–?) B: Toronto, Canada. *The Tourists* (Majestic, "Noorian," Aug. 25, 1906): Love Is a Wonderful Thing/W: R.H. Burnside, M: Gustave Kerker.

275. George Armand *South Pacific* (Majestic > Broadway, CR, "Jerome"): Dites-Moi/W: Oscar Hammerstein II, M: Richard Rodgers.

276. Richard Armbruster *Goldilocks* (Lunt-Fontanne, "Andy," Oct. 11, 1958): Bad Companions/W: Joan Ford, Walter Kerr, Jean Kerr, M: Leroy Anderson. *South Pacific* (New York City Center, revival, "Lieut. Joseph Cable, U.S.M.C.," June 2, 1965): Bali Ha'i; Younger Than Springtime; You've Got to Be Carefully Taught/W: Oscar Hammerstein II, M: Richard Rodgers.

277. Armida (Mar. 29, 1911–Oct. 23, 1989) B: Sonora, Mexico. Her full name was Armida Vendrell. She played opposite John Barrymore in his first talking picture, a 1930 swashbuckler titled *General Crack*. *Nina Rosa* (Majestic, "Corinna," Sept. 20, 1930): A Kiss I Must Refuse You; Pay Day; Serenade of Love/W: Irving Caesar, M: Sigmund Romberg. *Broadway Sho-Window* (Broadway, revue, CR, Apr. 19, 1936): Spring Is in the Air/W: Eugene Conrad, M: Gus Edwards.

278. Walter Armin *The Blue Paradise* (Casino > 44th Street, "Josef Stransky," Aug. 5, 1915): Here's to You, My Sparkling Wine/W: Blanche Merrill, M: Leo Edwards. *Caviar* (Forrest, "Count Chipolita," June 7, 1934): Here's to You/W: Edward Heyman, M: Harden Church.

279. Frances Arms (Dec. 25, 1892–Sept. 1, 1976) *Sharlee* (Daly's, "Dolly Dare," Nov. 22, 1923): Leaping Leopards; Love Is the Bunk; Loving Is a Habit/W: Alex Rogers, M: C. Luckeyth Roberts.

280. Joshie Jo Armstead (Oct. 8, 1944–) B: Yazoo City, MS. Singer and songwriter. Member of the Ikettes, 1961. *Don't Play Us Cheap!* (Ethel Barrymore, "Mrs. Washington," May 16, 1972): You Cut Up the Clothes in the Closet of My Dreams/WM: Melvin Van Peebles.

281. Louis (Satchmo) Armstrong (July 4, 1900–July 6, 1971) B: New Orleans, LA. One of the great jazz musicians of all time, he played trumpet, and was a singer, actor and composer on Broadway, in films, radio and TV. His house in Queens, NY is now a museum and archive. *Swingin' the Dream* (Center, "Bottom," Nov. 29, 1939): Darn That Dream; Peace, Brother;

There's Gotta Be a Weddin'/W: Eddie DeLange, M: James Van Heusen.

282. Vanessa Bell Armstrong B: Detroit, MI. *Don't Get God Started* (Longacre, revue, "Female Lead Vocalist," Oct. 29, 1987): After Looking for Love; Bring Back the Days of Yea and Nay; Can I Build My Home in You; Cry Loud (Lift Your Voice Like a Trumpet); Denied Stone; Don't Turn Your Back; I Made It; Let the Healing Begin; Slipping Away from You; Turn Us Again; What's Wrong with Our Love/WM: Marvin Winans — Always/WM: ?.

283. William M. Armstrong *The Girl from Paris* (Herald Square, CR, "Tom Everleigh," June 28, 1897): The Festive Continong; Somebody/W: George Dance, M: Ivan Caryll. *The French Maid* (Herald Square, "Lieut. Harry Fife, R.N.," Sept. 27, 1897): Charity's Useful Disguise; Love That Is True/W: Basil Hood, M: Walter Slaughter — You Can Read It in My Eyes/W: Henry Norman, M: Herman Perlet.

284. Sidney Armus (Dec. 19, 1924–) B: Bronx, NY. *Wish You Were Here* (Imperial, "Itchy Flexner," June 25, 1952): Ballad of a Social Director; Don Jose from Far Rockaway; Flattery/WM: Harold Rome.

285. Desi Arnaz (Mar. 2, 1915–Dec. 2, 1986) B: Santiago, Cuba. At 17 he was singing with a band in Miami Beach, FL.; later he formed his own Latino band. Best remembered for his role opposite his wife, LUCILLE BALL, in the long-running TV series *I Love Lucy* (1951). *Too Many Girls* (Imperial, "Manuelito," Oct. 18, 1939): She Could Shake the Maracas; Tempt Me Not; Too Many Girls/W: Lorenz Hart, M: Richard Rodgers.

286. France Arnell *La Grosse Valise* (54th Street, "La Nana," Dec. 14, 1965): C'est Defendu; Delilah Done Me Wrong; Hawaii; La Java; Xanadu/W: Harold Rome, M: Gerard Calvi.

287. Patricia Arnell (Oct. 13, 1950–) B: New Orleans, LA. *Ambassador* (Lunt-Fontanne, "Flower Girl," Nov. 19, 1972): Lilas; Lilas, What Happened to Paris/W: Hal Hackady, M: Don Gohman.

288. Sig Arno (Dec. 27, 1895–Aug. 17, 1975) B: Hamburg, Germany. One of Germany's top comedy actors. He went to Hollywood in 1939 where he was usually cast in waiter or butler roles. On TV he played Professor Kropotkin in the popular sitcom *My Friend Irma* (1952). *Song of Norway* (Imperial, "Count Peppi Le Loup," Aug. 21, 1944): Bon Vivant/WM: Robert Wright, George Forrest, based on Edvard Grieg. *The Merry Widow* (New York State Theater,

revival, "Nish," Aug. 17, 1964): Women/W: Forman Brown, M: Franz Lehar.

289. Florine Arnold (?–July 3, 1925) *You're in Love* (Casino, "Mrs. Payton," Feb. 6, 1917): Keep Off the Grass; The Musical Snore; Things That They Must Not Do/W: Otto Harbach, Edward Clark, M: Rudolf Friml.

290. Hattie Arnold *The Duke of Duluth* (Majestic, "Princess Flirtino," Sept. 11, 1905): The Sweetest Part of Loving Is to Dream/W: George Broadhurst, M: Max S. Witt. *The Man from Now* (New Amsterdam, "Matricula," Sept. 3, 1906): Come Along My Boys; What Says Your Heart?/W: Vincent Bryan, M: Manuel Klein — Mary Ann/W: ?, M: Harry Von Tilzer. *The Enchantress* (New York, "Mamoute," Oct. 19, 1911): Come to Sunny Spain/W: Harry B. Smith, M: Victor Herbert.

291. Helen Arnold *George White's Music Hall Varieties* (Casino, revue, Nov. 22, 1932): Hold Me Closer/WM: Jack Scholl, Max Rich, Frank Littau — The Waltz That Brought You Back to Me/W: Irving Caesar, M: Carmen Lombardo.

292. Jack Arnold (c 1903–June 15, 1962) *The Greenwich Village Follies of 1925* (Shubert, revue, CR, Mar. 15, 1926): White Cargo/WM: ? — Wouldn't You?/WM: Owen Murphy.

293. Jeanne Arnold (July 30–) B: Berkeley, CA. *Coco* (Mark Hellinger, "Pignol, " Dec. 18, 1969): The World Belongs to the Young/W: Alan Jay Lerner; M: Andre Previn.

294. Laura Arnold (c 1888–Aug. 17, 1962) B: Indianapolis, IN. *Maytime* (Shubert > 44th Street > Broadhurst, "Alice Tremaine," Aug. 16, 1917): It's a Windy Day at the Battery/W: Rida Johnson Young, M: Sigmund Romberg. *Maytime* (Lyric, CR, "Ottilie Van Zandt," Aug. 1918): In Our Little Home Sweet Home; The Road to Paradise; Will You Remember? (Sweetheart)/W: Rida Johnson Young, M: Sigmund Romberg — Selling Gowns/W: Cyrus D. Wood, M: Sigmund Romberg. *Adrienne* (George M. Cohan, "Nora Malone" or "Nadja," May 28, 1923): As Long as the Wife Don't Know; Sing Sing/W: A. Seymour Brown, M: Albert Von Tilzer.

295. Lois Arnold (1877–Jan. 26, 1947) B: St. Augustine, FL. *Sally, Irene and Mary* (44th Street, revival, "First Dresser to Girls," Mar. 23, 1925): Do You Remember?/W: Raymond Klages, M: J. Fred Coots.

296. Lucille Arnold *Princess Flavia* (Century, "Charlotte," Nov. 2, 1925): Yes or No/W: Harry B. Smith, M: Sigmund Romberg.

297. Michael Arnold *Cats* (Winter Garden,

CR, "Mistoffolees"): The Invitation to the Jellicle Ball; Mr. Mistoffolees; Mungojerrie and Rumpleteazer/W: T.S. Eliot, M: Andrew Lloyd Webber.

298. Bobbe Arnst (Oct. 11, 1903–Nov. 25, 1980) B: New York, NY. M: Johnny (Tarzan) Weissmuller; she was one of his 6 wives. *The Greenwich Village Follies of 1924* (Shubert > Winter Garden, revue, Sept. 16, 1924): Bring Me a Radio; Broadcast a Jazz; I'm in Love Again [Oct. 27, 1924]/WM: Cole Porter. *Rufus Le Maire's Affairs* (Majestic, revue, Mar. 28, 1927): I Can't Get Over a Girl Like You (Loving a Boy Like Me)/W: Harry Ruskin, M: Martin Broones — Mexico/W: Ballard Macdonald, M: Martin Broones. *A la Carte* (Martin Beck, revue, Aug. 17, 1927): Baby's Blue; The Calinda; Sort o' Lonesome/WM: Herman Hupfeld — I'm Stepping Out with Lulu/W: Henry Creamer, M: James P. Johnson. *Rosalie* (New Amsterdam, "Mary O'Brien," Jan. 10, 1928): Ev'rybody Knows I Love Somebody [Jan. 16, 1928]; How Long Has This Been Going On?; New York Serenade; Show Me the Town/W: Ira Gershwin, M: George Gershwin. *Simple Simon* (Ziegfeld, "Gilly Flower" or "Jill," Feb. 18, 1930): Don't Tell Your Folks; I Want That Man (Apr. 1930); Magic Music; Sweetenheart/W: Lorenz Hart, M: Richard Rodgers.

299. Joel Aroeste (Apr. 10, 1949–) B: New York, NY. *Raggedy Ann* (Nederlander, "Camel with Wrinkled Knees," Oct. 16, 1986): Blue; A Little Music/WM: Joe Raposo.

300. Ellyn Arons (Oct. 29, 1956–) B: Philadelphia, PA. *Jerry's Girls* (St. James, revue, Dec. 18, 1985): Have a Nice Day; It Takes a Woman; It's Today; Just Go to the Movies; Mame; Milk and Honey; We Need a Little Christmas/WM: Jerry Herman.

301. Luann Aronson *The Phantom of the Opera* (Majestic, CR, "Christine Daae," June 1992): All I Ask of You; Angel of Music; Bravo, Bravo; I Remember; Little Lotte; The Mirror; Notes; The Point of No Return; Raoul, I've Been There; Stranger Than You Dreamt It; Think of Me; Twisted Every Way; Wandering Child; Why Have You Brought Me Here; Wishing You Were Somehow Here Again/W: Charles Hart, Richard Stilgoe, M: Andrew Lloyd Webber — The Phantom of the Opera/W: Mike Batt, Richard Stilgoe, M: Andrew Lloyd Webber.

302. Nicole Arrington *A Christmas Carol* (Paramount Madison Square Garden, return engagement, "Blind Hag," Nov. 20, 1995): Nothing to Do with Me/W: Lynn Ahrens, M: Alan Menken.

303. Beatrice Arthur (May 13, 1923–) B: New York, NY. The versatile comic actress starred in the popular TV series *Maude* (1972) and *The Golden Girls* (1985). *Seventh Heaven* (ANTA, "Mme. Suze," May 26, 1955): C'est la Vie/W: Stella Unger, M: Victor Young. *Fiddler on the Roof* (Imperial, "Yente," Sept. 22, 1964): Anatevka; I Just Heard/W: Sheldon Harnick, M: Jerry Bock. *Mame* (Winter Garden, "Vera Charles," May 24, 1966/Apr. 10, 1967): Bosom Buddies; The Man in the Moon/WM: Jerry Herman.

304. Carol Arthur (Aug. 4, 1935–) B: Hackensack, NJ. M: DOM DELUISE, and appeared with him on his summer TV variety show (1968). *The Music Man* (City Center 55th Street, revival, "Mrs. Paroo," June 5, 1980): Piano Lesson/WM: Meredith Willson. *Woman of the Year* (Palace, CR, "Jan Donovan," Oct. 13, 1981): The Grass Is Always Greener/W: Fred Ebb, M: John Kander.

305. Charles Arthur *The Ballet Girl* (Manhattan, "Lord Comarthy," Dec. 21, 1897): The Elopement; Wedding Bells/W: Adrian Ross, M: Carl Kiefert.

306. Dorothy Arthur *90 in the Shade* (Knickerbocker, "Dot," Jan. 25, 1915): Courtship de Dance; Peter Pan/WM: ?.

307. Florence Arthur *Bunk of 1926* (Heckscher, revue, Feb. 16, 1926): Chatter/WM: Gene Lockhart.

308. Helene Arthur *The Student Prince* (Broadway, revival, "Princess Margaret," June 8, 1943): Just We Two/W: Dorothy Donnelly, M: Sigmund Romberg. *Blossom Time* (Ambassador, revival, "Bellabruna," Sept. 4, 1943): Keep It Dark; Let Me Awake; Melody Triste/W: Dorothy Donnelly, M: Sigmund Romberg. *Marinka* (Ethel Barrymore, CR, "Countess Von Diefendorfer," Nov. 4, 1945): Cab Song/W: George Marion, Jr., M: Emmerich Kalman.

309. Henry Arthur *Right This Way* (46th Street, "Phil Doane," Jan. 4, 1938): He Can Dance/W: Irving Kahal, M: Sammy Fain — You Click with Me/W: Marianne Brown Waters, M: Bradford Greene.

310. John (Johnny) Arthur (May 20, 1883–Dec. 31, 1951) B: Scottsdale, PA. Character actor usually in meek or whiny movie roles. *Elsie* (Vanderbilt, "Alfie Westford," Apr. 2, 1923): Jazzing Thunder Storming Dance/WM: Noble Sissle, Eubie Blake.

311. Maureen Arthur (Apr. 15, 1934–) B: San Jose, CA. *How to Succeed in Business Without Really Trying* (46th Street, CR, "Hedy La Rue," Aug. 31, 1964): Been a Long Day; Love from a Heart of Gold/WM: Frank Loesser.

312. Tom Arthur *New Faces of 1962* (Alvin, revue, Feb. 1, 1962): Johnny Mishuga/WM: David Rogers, Mark Bucci — Moral Rearmament/WM: Jack Holmes.

313. Michelle Artigas *Cats* (Winter Garden, CR, "Tantomile," c 1991): The Moments of Happiness/W: T.S. Eliot, M: Andrew Lloyd Webber.

314. Edyth Artley *Mlle. Modiste* (Jolson, revival, "Fanchette," Oct. 7, 1929): When the Cat's Away the Mice Will Play/W: Henry Blossom, M: Victor Herbert.

315. Cleve Asbury (Dec. 29, 1958–) B: Houston, TX. *West Side Story* (Minskoff, revival, "Snowboy," Feb. 14, 1980): Gee, Officer Krupke!/W: Stephen Sondheim, M: Leonard Bernstein. *Harrigan 'n Hart* (Longacre, "Billy Gross," Jan. 31, 1985): Ada with the Golden Hair; The Silly Boy; The Skidmore Fancy Ball/W: Edward Harrigan, M: Dave Braham.

316. Sam Ash (Aug. 28, 1884–Oct. 21, 1951) B: Kentucky. The popular tenor recorded 13 hit songs from 1915 to 1923. *Katinka* (44th Street > Lyric, "Ivan Dimitri," Dec. 23, 1915): I Want All the World to Know; In Vienna; Katinka; My Paradise; Skidiskischatch; 'Tis the End, So Farewell/W: Otto Harbach, M: Rudolf Friml. *The Highwayman* (44th Street, revival, "Lieut. Rodney," May 2, 1917): Gretna Green; While the Four Winds Blow/W: Harry B. Smith, M: Reginald De Koven. *Doing Our Bit* (Winter Garden, revue, "Mr. Smile" and "Mr. Army Man," Oct. 18, 1917): For the Sake of Humanity/W: Harold Atteridge, M: Sigmund Romberg — Perfect Jewels; The Phantom of Your Smile/W: Harold Atteridge, M: Sigmund Romberg, Herman Timberg. *Monte Cristo, Jr.* (Winter Garden, "Julian," Feb. 12, 1919): Indoor Sports; My Lady's Dress; Sentimental Knights/W: Harold Atteridge, M: Sigmund Romberg, Jean Schwartz. *Oh, What a Girl!* (Shubert, "Jack Rushton," July 28, 1919): The Breeze Through the Trees; Oh, What a Girl!/W: Edgar Smith, M: Charles Jules, Jacques Presburg. *Some Party* (Al Jolson, revue, Apr. 15, 1922): In Rose Time/W: R.H. Burnside, M: Mary Earl. *The Passing Show of 1922* (Winter Garden, revue, Sept. 20, 1922): I Came, I Saw, I Fell; Love of Long Ago/W: Harold Atteridge, M: Alfred Goodman — My Diamond Girls; Radiance/W: Jack Stanley, M: Alfred Goodman. *Rose-Marie* (Imperial, CR, "Jim Kenyon," June 1925): I Love Him; Indian Love Call; Rose-Marie/W: Otto Harbach, Oscar Hammerstein II, M: Rudolf Friml. *White Lights* (Ritz, "Danny Miles," Oct. 11, 1927): I'll Keep on Dreaming of You/WM: J. Fred Coots, Al

Dubin, Walter S. Rode — Some Other Day/W: Dolph Singer, M: Jimmie Steiger. *The Houseboat on the Styx* (Liberty, "Ponce De Leon," Dec. 25, 1928): The Fountain of Youth; Men of Hades; My Heaven; Soul Mates/W: Monte Carlo, M: Alma Sanders. *The Singing Rabbi* (Selwyn, "Nuchem Sheindel," Sept. 10, 1931): Hear O Israel/W: L. Wolfe Gilbert, M: J. Rumshinsky.

317. Camila Ashland *Follies* (Winter Garden, CR, "Emily Whitman," May 1972): Rain on the Roof/WM: Stephen Sondheim.

318. Barbara Ashley (Mar. 3, c 1928–Mar. 1, 1978) B: Brooklyn, NY. *The Liar* (Broadhurst, "Cleonice Anselmi," May 18, 1950): Out of Sight, Out of Mind; 'Twill Never Be the Same/W: Edward Eager, M: John Mundy. *Out of This World* (New Century, "Chloe," Dec. 21, 1950): Cherry Pies Ought to Be You; What Do You Think About Men?; Where Oh Where?/WM: Cole Porter.

319. Minnie Ashley (1875–June 19, 1946) B: Fall River, MA. *San Toy* (Daly's, "Dudley," Oct. 1, 1900): The Lady's Maid/W: Harry Greenbank, Adrian Ross, M: Lionel Monckton — Pletty Little Chinee; Samee Gamee; We'll Keep the Feast in Pynka Pong/W: Harry Greenbank, Adrian Ross, M: Sidney Jones — Rhoda and Her Pagoda/W: Adrian Ross, M: Lionel Monckton. *San Toy* (Daly's, revival, "Dudley," Apr. 7, 1902): same as above. *A Country Girl* (Daly's, "Madame Sophie," Sept. 22, 1902): Quarrelling; Two Little Chicks/W: Percy Greenbank, M: Paul Rubens — The Real Smart Set/W: Adrian Ross, M: Lionel Monckton.

320. Brooks Ashmanskas *How to Succeed in Business Without Really Trying* (Richard Rodgers, revival, CR, "Bud Frump," Feb. 19, 1996): Been a Long Day; Coffee Break; The Company Way/WM: Frank Loesser.

321. Marie Ashton *Marriage a la Carte* (Casino, "Euryanthe Bowers," Jan. 2, 1911): Toddle Go the Girls/W: C.M.S. McLellan, M: Ivan Caryll.

322. Asia B: Shanghai, China. *Whoop-Up* (Shubert, "Billie Mae Littlehorse," Dec. 22, 1958): 'Til the Big Fat Moon Falls Down/W: Norman Gimbel, M: Moose Charlap.

323. Perry Askam (Aug. 31, 1898 — Oct. 22, 1961) B: Seattle, WA. *The Passing Show of 1921* (Winter Garden, revue, CR, Apr. 25, 1921): Broadway Is Sahara/WM: ?. *Blossom Time* (Ambassador, "Erkmann," Sept. 29, 1921): Love Is a Riddle/W: Dorothy Donnelly, M: Sigmund Romberg.

324. Darrell J. Askey *Donnybrook!* (46th Street, "Tim O'Connell," May 18, 1961): The

Day the Snow Is Meltin'; Sez I/WM: Johnny Burke.

325. Brad Aspel *A Funny Thing Happened on the Way to the Forum* (St. James, revival, "A Protean," Apr. 18, 1996): Bring Me My Bride; Comedy Tonight/WM: Stephen Sondheim.

326. Algernon Aspland *When Johnny Comes Marching Home* (New York, "Maj. George Buckle," Dec. 16, 1902): I Could Waltz On Forever; Marry the Man and Be Merry/W: Stanislaus Stange, M: Julian Edwards.

327. Armand Assante (Oct. 4, 1949–) B: New York, NY. *Boccaccio* (Edison, "Masetto," Nov. 24, 1975): God Is Good; Masetto's Song/W: Kenneth Cavander, M: Richard Peaslee.

328. Adele Astaire (Sept. 10, 1897–Jan. 25, 1981) B: Omaha, NE. FRED ASTAIRE's famous sister and dancing partner in vaudeville, stage revues and musicals. She retired to marry the younger son of the Duke of Devonshire, Charles Cavendish, in 1932, and take up residence in Lismore Castle, Co. Waterford, Ireland. *Over the Top* (44th Street roof, revue, Nov. 28, 1917): The Justine Johnstone Rag/W: Charles Manning, M: Frank Carter, Sigmund Romberg — Where Is the Language to Tell?/W: Philip Bartholomae, M: Sigmund Romberg, Herman Timberg. *The Love Letter* (Globe, "Aline Moray," Oct. 4, 1921): Dreaming; I'll Say I Love You; Upside Down/W: William Le Baron, M: Victor Jacobi. *For Goodness Sake* (Lyric, "Suzanne Hayden," Feb. 20, 1922): All to Myself; The Whichness of the Whatness/W: Arthur Jackson, M: Paul Lannin, William Daly — Oh Gee, Oh Gosh, I Love You/W: Arthur Jackson, M: William Daly. *The Bunch and Judy* (Globe, "Paulina" and "Judy Jordan," Nov. 28, 1922): Every Day in Every Way; How Do You Do, Katinka; Morning Glory; Pale Venetian Moon; Peach Girl; Times Square/W: Anne Caldwell, M: Jerome Kern. *Lady, Be Good!* (Liberty, "Susie Trevor," Dec. 1, 1924): Fascinating Rhythm; Hang On to Me; Juanita; So Am I/W: Ira Gershwin, M: George Gershwin — Swiss Miss/W: Ira Gershwin, Arthur Jackson, M: George Gershwin. *Funny Face* (Alvin, "Frankie Wynne," Nov. 22, 1927): The Babbitt and the Bromide; Funny Face; He Loves and She Loves; Let's Kiss and Make Up; 'S Wonderful/W: Ira Gershwin, M: George Gershwin. *Smiles* (Ziegfeld, "Dot Hastings," Nov. 18, 1930): Anyway, We've Had Fun; Be Good to Me; If I Were You, Love (I'd Jump Right in the Lake)/W: Ring Lardner, M: Vincent Youmans — Hotcha Ma Chotch/W: Harold Adamson, Clifford Grey, M: Vincent Youmans — You're Driving Me Crazy [Dec. 1930]/WM: Walter Donaldson. *The Band*

Wagon (New Amsterdam, revue, June 3, 1931): Hoops; I Love Louisa; Miserable with You; Sweet Music; White Heat/W: Howard Dietz, M: Arthur Schwartz.

329. Fred Astaire (May 10, 1899–June 22, 1987) B: Omaha, NE. Incomparable dancer, singer, charmer, who performed on stage with sister ADELE ASTAIRE before going on to an illustrious film career and GINGER ROGERS. *Over the Top* (44th Street roof, revue, Nov. 28, 1917): The Justine Johnstone Rag/W: Charles Manning, M: Frank Carter, Sigmund Romberg — Where Is the Language to Tell?/W: Philip Bartholomae, M: Sigmund Romberg, Herman Timberg. *The Love Letter* (Globe, "Richard Kolnar," Oct. 4, 1921): Dreaming; I'll Say I Love You; Upside Down/W: William Le Baron, M: Victor Jacobi. *For Goodness Sake* (Lyric, "Teddy Lawrence," Feb. 20, 1922): All to Myself; When You're in Rome; The Whichness of the Whatness/W: Arthur Jackson, M: Paul Lannin, William Daly — The French Pastry Walk/W: Arthur Jackson, Ira Gershwin, M: Paul Lannin, William Daly — Oh Gee, Oh Gosh, I Love You/W: Arthur Jackson, M: William Daly. *The Bunch and Judy* (Globe, "Antonio" and "Gerald Lane," Nov. 28, 1922): Every Day in Every Way; How Do You Do, Katinka; Pale Venetian Moon; Peach Girl/W: Anne Caldwell, M: Jerome Kern. *Lady, Be Good!* (Liberty, "Dick Trevor," Dec. 1, 1924): Fascinating Rhythm; The Half of It, Dearie, Blues; Hang On to Me/W: Ira Gershwin, M: George Gershwin — Swiss Miss/W: Ira Gershwin, Arthur Jackson, M: George Gershwin. *Funny Face* (Alvin, "Jimmie Reeve," Nov. 22, 1927): The Babbitt and the Bromide; Funny Face; High Hat; Let's Kiss and Make Up; My One and Only/W: Ira Gershwin, M: George Gershwin. *Smiles* (Ziegfeld, "Bob Hastings," Nov. 18, 1930): Anyway, We've Had Fun; Be Good to Me; If I Were You, Love (I'd Jump Right in the Lake)/W: Ring Lardner, M: Vincent Youmans — I'm Glad I Waited/W: Harold Adamson, Clifford Grey, M: Vincent Youmans — Say, Young Man of Manhattan/W: Clifford Grey, M: Vincent Youmans. *The Band Wagon* (New Amsterdam, revue, June 3, 1931): Hoops; I Love Louisa; New Sun in the Sky; Sweet Music; White Heat/W: Howard Dietz, M: Arthur Schwartz. *Gay Divorce* (Ethel Barrymore > Shubert, "Guy Holden," Nov. 29, 1932): After You, Who?; I've Got You on My Mind; Night and Day; You're in Love/WM: Cole Porter.

330. Lilyan Astaire *Belmont Varieties* (Belmont, revue, Sept. 26, 1932): Etiquette/W: Sam Bernard, Jr., Bobby Burk, M: Henry Lloyd.

331. Ben Astar (June 15, 1909–Oct. 20, 1988) B: Jaffa, Israel. *On Your Toes* (46th Street, revival, "Sergei Alexandrovitch," Oct. 11, 1954): Too Good for the Average Man/W: Lorenz Hart, M: Richard Rodgers.

332. Suzanne Astor *New Faces of 1968* (Booth, revue, May 2, 1968): Hungry/WM: Murray Grand — Luncheon Ballad/W: Michael McWhinney, M: Jerry Powell.

333. Marie Astrova *Suzette* (Princess, "Suzette," Nov. 24, 1921): Dreams of Tomorow; A Forest Legend; Gypsy Rose; Honey Love Moon; No! No!; Sweetheart Mine/W: Roy Dixon, M: Arthur Gutman.

334. Yona Atari *To Live Another Summer, To Pass Another Winter* (Helen Hayes, revue, Oct. 21, 1971): Better Days; To Live Another Summer, To Pass Another Winter/W: David Paulsen, M: Dov Seltzer — Can You Hear My Voice?/W: George Sherman, M: Samuel Kraus — Sorry We Won/W: David Paulsen, M: David Krivoshei.

335. Edgar Atchison-Ely *The Mocking Bird* (Bijou, "Bob Finchley," Nov. 10, 1902): From a Different Point of View; The Rigadoon; What's the Matter with the Moon Tonight?/W: Sydney Rosenfeld, M: A. Baldwin Sloane. *Mrs. Black Is Back* (Bijou, "Jack Dangerfield," Nov. 7, 1904): Guess, Guess, Guess (Can't You Guess)/W: Paul West, M: John W. Bratton — I'm Worried to Death About That/WM: May Irwin. *The White Cat* (New Amsterdam, "Prince Paragon," Nov. 2, 1905): Down the Line with Arabella/W: William Jerome, M: Jean Schwartz — Where Broadway Meets Fifth Avenue/W: John Kemble, M: Lester Keith. *The Boys and Betty* (Wallack's, "Paul Gerard," Nov. 2, 1908): Gee! But You Look Awfully Good to Me/W: Will D. Cobb, M: Silvio Hein — I Love to Go Shopping/W: George V. Hobart, M: Silvio Hein.

336. Rosco Ates (Jan. 20, 1892–Mar. 1, 1962) B: Hattiesburg, MS. In movies from 1929, often as a comic sidekick to cowboys. He appeared briefly in a TV western called *The Marshall of Gunsight Pass* (1950), that was produced live from a Los Angeles studio. *Sea Legs* (Mansfield, "James McCracken," May 18, 1937): Looks Like Love Is Here to Stay/W: Arthur Swanstrom, M: Michael H. Cleary.

337. Alice Atherton (1860–Feb. 4, 1899) B: Cincinnati, OH. M: WILLIE EDOUIN. Successful as a singing comedienne in vaudeville and burlesque in Britain and the U.S. *Hiawatha* (Standard, "Hiawatha," Feb. 21, 1880): Ah! Never More Sadly! Now, Away; Behold in Me; God of Love; Goodbye for a Little While; He's Won! He's Won! Good Night; Indians Never Lie; Tea and Toast and Kisses; That's What Puzzles the Quaker/ W: Nathaniel Childs, M: Edward E. Rice.

338. Norman Atkins *The Most Happy Fella* (New York City Center, revival, "Tony," Feb. 10, 1959): Happy to Make Your Acquaintance; How Beautiful the Days; Mama Mama; The Most Happy Fella; My Heart Is So Full of You; Rosabella; Young People/WM: Frank Loesser. *Street Scene* (New York City Center, revival, "Frank Maurrant," Feb. 13, 1960): I Loved Her, Too; Let Things Be Like They Always Was; There'll Be Trouble/W: Langston Hughes, Elmer Rice, M: Kurt Weill. *The Most Happy Fella* (New York City Center, revival, "Tony," May 11, 1966): same as above.

339. Roy Atkins *Blackbirds of 1930* (Royale, revue, Oct. 22, 1930): Blackbirds on Parade/W: Andy Razaf, M: Eubie Blake.

340. Win Atkins *Canterbury Tales* (Rialto, revival, "Miller," Feb. 12, 1980): Beer Is Best (Beer, Beer, Beer)/W: Nevill Coghill, M: Richard Hill, John Hawkins.

341. David Atkinson (Oct. 20, 1921–) B: Montreal, Canada. *Inside U.S.A.* (New Century, revue, CR, Oct. 4, 1948): Haunted Heart; My Gal Is Mine Once More/W: Howard Dietz, M: Arthur Schwartz. *The Girl in Pink Tights* (Mark Hellinger, "Clyde Hallam," Mar. 5, 1954): In Paris and in Love; Lost in Loveliness; My Heart Won't Say Goodbye; Up in the Elevated Railway/W: Leo Robin, M: Sigmund Romberg. *The Vamp* (Winter Garden, "Oliver J. Oxheart," Nov. 10, 1955): Have You Met Delilah?; The Impossible She; Why Does It Have to Be You?/W: John Latouche, M: James Mundy. *Kiss Me, Kate* (New York City Center, revival, "Fred Graham" and "Petruchio," May 9, 1956): I've Come to Wive It Wealthily in Padua; Kiss Me, Kate; So in Love; We Open in Venice; Were Thine That Special Face; Where Is the Life That Late I Led?; Wunderbar/WM: Cole Porter. *Brigadoon* (New York City Center, revival, "Tommy Albright," Mar. 27, 1957): Almost Like Being in Love; From This Day On; The Heather on the Hill; There but for You Go I/W: Alan Jay Lerner, M: Frederick Loewe. *Annie Get Your Gun* (New York City Center, revival, "Frank Butler," Feb. 19, 1958): Anything You Can Do; The Girl That I Marry; I'm a Bad, Bad Man; My Defenses Are Down; There's No Business Like Show Business; They Say It's Wonderful/WM: Irving Berlin. *The Cradle Will Rock* (New York City Center, revival, "Larry Foreman," Feb. 11, 1960): The Cradle Will Rock; Ex-Foreman; Leaflets; Polyphonic; Stuck Like a Sandwich/

WM: Marc Blitzstein. *Man of La Mancha* (ANTA Washington Square > Martin Beck, CR, "Don Quixote," July 14, 1967/Sept. 8, 1969/Apr. 7, 1971): The Combat; Dulcinea; Golden Helmet; The Impossible Dream (The Quest); Man of La Mancha (I, Don Quixote)/W: Joe Darion, M: Mitch Leigh. *Man of La Mancha* (Vivian Beaumont, revival, "Don Quixote," June 22, 1972 mats.): same as above.

342. Sarah Atkinson (Dec. 21, 1944–) B: Bishop's Stortford, England. *Wait a Minim!* (John Golden, revue, Mar. 7, 1966): Hoshoryu/WM: Japanese folk song — I Know Where I'm Going/WM: Irish folk song — Kapurapura Kupika/WM: Pounding Song, Nyasaland — Sir Oswald Sodde/WM: Jeffrey Smith — This Is Worth Fighting For/WM: ?.

343. Joseph Attles (Apr. 7, 1903–Oct. 29, 1990) B: James Island, SC. *John Henry* (44th Street, "Bad Stacker Lee" and "Man Named Sam," Jan. 10, 1940): Bad, Bad Stacker Lee; Now You Talks Mighty Big in the Country; Take Me a Drink of Whiskey/W: Roark Bradford, M: Jacques Wolfe. *Kwamina* (54th Street, "Akufo," Oct. 23, 1961): Seven Sheep, Four Red Shirts and a Bottle of Gin/WM: Richard Adler. *Bubbling Brown Sugar* (ANTA, "Checkers" and "Dusty," Mar. 2, 1976/July 4, 1977): In Honeysuckle Time; Pray for the Lights to Go Out/WM: Renton Tunnan, Will Skidmore.

344. Rick Atwell Dancer and choreographer. *The Selling of the President* (Shubert, "Van Denisovich," Mar. 22, 1972): If You Like People; Sunset/W: Jack O'Brien, M: Bob James.

345. Roy Atwell (May 2, 1878–Feb, 6, 1962) B: Syracuse, NY. M: BLANCHE WEST. The composer and comedian was a double talk artist specializing in spoonerisms on FRED ALLEN's radio show (1932). *Moonshine* (Liberty, "Lord Dumgarven," Oct. 30, 1905): Foolish; How Happy Would This Chappie Be/W: George V. Hobart, M: Silvio Hein — A Hundred Years from Now/W: George V. Hobart, Edwin Milton Royle, M: Silvio Hein. *Marrying Mary* (Daly's, "Willie Drinkwater, No. 3," Aug. 27, 1906): Noah Knew a Thing or Two; Old Reliable Jokes; Three Men in a Boat/W: Benjamin Hapgood Burt, M: Silvio Hein. *The Orchid* (Herald Square > Casino, CR, "Hon. Guy Scrymageour," June 17, 1907): I Must Propose to You/WM: Paul Rubens — Oh, Mr. Registrar!/W: Percy Greenbank, M: Lionel Monckton. *Mlle. Mischief* (Lyric, "Freddy Meline," Sept. 28, 1908): Ev'ry Hour Brings Its Flower; Ladies Beware; My Own Vienna; A Single Day/W: Sydney Rosenfeld, M: Carl M. Ziehrer. *The*

Firefly (Lyric > Casino, "Jenkins," Dec. 2, 1912): De Trop; Something/W: Otto Harbach, M: Rudolf Friml. *Alone at Last* (Shubert, "Count Willigard," Oct. 14, 1915): Not Now but By the Moon/W: Matthew Woodward, M: Franz Lehar — Oh My Darling Tilly/W: Joseph W. Herbert, M: Franz Lehar — Some Little Bug Is Going to Find You Some Day/W: Benjamin Hapgood Burt, Roy Atwell, M: Silvio Hein. *Oh, My Dear!* (Princess > 39th Street, "Broadway Willy Burbank," Nov. 27, 1918): I Shall Be All Right Now/W: P.G. Wodehouse, M: Louis A. Hirsch. *Apple Blossoms* (Globe, "Harvey," Oct. 7, 1919): The Marriage Knot/W: William Le Baron, M: Fritz Kreisler. *Helen of Troy, New York* (Selwyn > Times Square, "C. Warren Jennings," June 19, 1923): We Must Be Up on Our Toes; What Makes a Business Man Tired?/W: Bert Kalmar, M: Harry Ruby.

346. Lionel Atwill (Mar. 1, 1885–Apr. 22, 1946) B: Croydon, England. The actor, producer and manager had intended to be an architect and surveyor. In Hollywood from 1932 he played villains and mad scientists in countless B pictures. *Fioretta* (Earl Carroll, "Count Matteo Di Brozzo," Feb. 5, 1929): Alone with You/W: Grace Henry, Jo Trent, M: George Bagby.

347. Rene Auberjonois (June 1, 1940–) B: New York, NY. A Tony winner for his role in *Coco*. On TV he appeared as Clayton Endicott III on the popular sitcom, *Benson* (1980). *Coco* (Mark Hellinger, "Sebastian Baye," Dec. 19, 1969): Fiasco; The World Belongs to the Young/W: Alan Jay Lerner, M: Andre Previn. *Tricks* (Alvin, "Scapin," Jan. 8, 1973): Anything Is Possible; Somebody's Doin' Somebody All the Time; A Sporting Man; Tricks; Trouble's a Ruler/W: Lonnie Burstein, M: Jerry Blatt. *Big River: The Adventures of Huckleberry Finn* (Eugene O'Neill, "The Duke," Apr. 25, 1985): The Royal Nonesuch; When the Sun Goes Down in the South/WM: Roger Miller. *City of Angels* (Virginia, "Buddy Fidler," Dec. 11, 1989): The Buddy System; Double Talk/W: David Zippel, M: Cy Coleman.

348. Jeanne (Jane) Aubert (Feb. 21, 1906–Mar. 6, 1988) B: Paris, France. *Gay Paree* (Winter Garden, revue, Nov. 9, 1926): Je T'Aime Means I Love You/WM: Powers Gouraud. *Princess Charming* (Imperial, "Countess Wanda Navarro," Oct. 13, 1930): I Love Love/W: Walter O'Keefe, M: Robert Emmett Dolan — I'll Be There/W: Arthur Swanstrom, M: Arthur Schwartz, Albert Sirmay. *America's Sweetheart* (Broadhurst, "Denise Torel," Feb. 10, 1931): How About It?; I Want a Man; A Lady Must Live;

There's So Much More/W: Lorenz Hart, M: Richard Rodgers. *The Laugh Parade* (Imperial, revue, Nov. 2, 1931): Ooh! That Kiss; You're My Everything/W: Mort Dixon, Joe Young, M: Harry Warren. *Ballyhoo of 1932* (44th Street, revue, Sept. 6, 1932): Thrill Me; What Have You Got to Have? [added]/W: E.Y. Harburg, M: Lewis E. Gensler. *Melody* (Casino, "Eugenie Revelle," Feb. 14, 1933): Pompadour; Rendezvous/W: Irving Caesar, M: Sigmund Romberg.

349. Mischa Auer (Nov. 17, 1905–Mar. 5, 1967) B: St. Petersburg, Russia. Comic character actor with a lanky frame and prominent eyes. He went to Hollywood in 1928 where he played dozens of roles in broken English. *The Merry Widow* (New York State, revival, "Baron Popoff," Aug. 17, 1964): When in France; Women/W: Forman Brown, M: Franz Lehar.

350. Edna Aug (1878–Nov. 30, 1938) B: Cincinnati, OH. *The Girl from Up There* (Herald Square, "Lais" and "Bebe," Jan. 7, 1901): Seraphina and Her Concertina/W: Hugh Morton, M: Gustave Kerker. *Hello, Paris and A La Broadway* (Folies Bergere, revue, CR?, "Mrs. Mazie Kummer," Sept. 25, 1911): A Very Ambitious Girl/WM: ?.

351. Adrienne Augarde (May 12, 1882–Mar. 17, 1913) B: England. *The Dollar Princess* (Knickerbocker, "Daisy," Sept. 6, 1909): The Dollar Princess; Paragraphs; Reminiscence; The Riding Lesson/W: George Grossmith, M: Leo Fall. *The Rose Maid* (Globe, "Daphne," Apr. 22, 1912): I Live for You Alone; Now His Choice We See; Roses Bloom for Lovers; When Two Little Hearts Beat Together/W: Robert B. Smith, M: Bruno Granichstaedten—A Yankee Millionairess/W: Raymond W. Peck, M: Robert Hood Bowers.

352. Stephanie Augustine *Peter Pan* (Imperial, "Mermaid," Apr. 24, 1950): Never Land/WM: Leonard Bernstein. *The King and I* (St. James, CR, "Tuptim," Apr. 1952): I Have Dreamed; My Lord and Master; We Kiss in a Shadow/W: Oscar Hammerstein II, M: Richard Rodgers.

353. Helen Ault *Sweet Adeline* (Hammerstein's, "Maizie O'Rourke," Sept. 3, 1929): Mollie O'Donahue/W: Oscar Hammerstein II, M: Jerome Kern.

354. Jean Pierre Aumont (Jan. 5, 1909–Jan. 30, 2001) B: Paris, France. Star of stage and screen in France, he went to Hollywood for several years in the 1940s. *Tovarich* (Broadway, "Prince Mikail," Mar. 18, 1963): All for You; I Go to Bed; Make a Friend; Managed; Nitchevo;

No! No! No!; You Love Me/W: Anne Crosswell, M: Lee Pockriss.

355. Jerry Austen *Barefoot Boy with Cheek* (Martin Beck, "Kermit McDermott," Apr. 3, 1947): It's Too Nice a Day to Go to School; Who Do You Think You Are?/W: Sylvia Dee, M: Sidney Lippman.

356. Beth (Elizabeth) Austin (May 22, 1952–) B: Philadelphia, PA. *Whoopee!* (ANTA, revival, "Sally Morgan," Feb. 14, 1979): I'm Bringing a Red, Red Rose; Out of the Dawn; Until You Get Somebody Else/W: Gus Kahn, M: Walter Donaldson. *Onward Victoria* (Martin Beck, "Tennie Claflin," Dec. 14, 1980): The Age of Brass; I Depend on You; Magnetic Healing; Read It in the Weekly; Respectable; Unescorted Women; Victoria's Banner; You Cannot Drown the Dreamer/W: Charlotte Anker, Irene Rosenberg, M: Keith Herrmann. *Raggedy Ann* (Nederlander, "Mommy," Oct. 16, 1986): The Shooting Star; What Did I Lose; Why Not/WM: Joe Raposo.

357. Carrie Ellen Austin *Grease* (Eugene O'Neill, revival, CR, "Patty Simcox," c 1994): Rydell Fight Song/WM: Jim Jacobs, Warren Casey.

358. Ivy Austin (Jan. 19, 1958–) B: Brooklyn, NY. *Raggedy Ann* (Nederlander, "Raggedy Ann," Oct. 16, 1986): Blue; A Little Music; Make Believe; Rag Dolly; So Beautiful; Somewhere; You'll Love It/WM: Joe Raposo.

359. Patti Austin (Aug. 1, 1948–) B: New York, NY. Her hit single with James Ingram became the love theme for the soap *General Hospital* (1982). *Ain't Misbehavin'* (Ambassador, revue, revival, CR, Dec. 20, 1988): Find Out What They Like/W: Andy Razaf, M: Fats Waller—I've Got My Fingers Crossed/W: Ted Koehler, M: Jimmy McHugh—Lounging at the Waldorf/W: Richard Maltby, Jr., M: Fats Waller—Squeeze Me/W: Clarence Williams, M: Fats Waller—That Ain't Right/WM: Nat King Cole, add. W: Richard Maltby, Jr., Murray Horwitz—Two Sleepy People/W: Frank Loesser, M: Hoagy Carmichael—When the Nylons Bloom Again/W: George Marion, Jr., M: Fats Waller.

360. Phyllis Austin *Oh, Ernest!* (Royale, "Jessica Esmond," May 9, 1927): Didoes; On the Beach/W: Francis De Witt, M: Robert Hood Bowers.

361. Ralph Austin *The Top o' th' World* (Majestic > Casino, "Candy Kid," Oct. 19, 1907): Hand Me Out a Laugh; Riddle Ma Ree; Yankee Doodle Yarns/W: James O'Dea, M: Anne Caldwell. *Hop o' My Thumb* (Manhattan Opera House, "Tango," Nov. 26, 1913): Bird Talk; The

Date Tree; Run Along Mr. Ogre Man/WM: Manuel Klein. *Let's Go* (Fulton, revue, Mar. 9, 1918): Why Can't a Girl Be a Soldier?/WM: ?.

362. Paul Avedisian (Mar. 1, 1962–) B: Detroit, MI. *Les Miserables* (Broadway, CR, "Enjolras," Oct. 29, 1996): Do You Hear the People Sing?; Red and Black/W: Herbert Kretzmer, M: Claude-Michel Schonberg.

363. Tom Avera (Feb. 21, 1923–) B: Rocky Mount, NC. *Oklahoma!* (St. James, CR, "Will Parker," July 1945): All er Nothin'; The Farmer and the Cowman; Kansas City/W: Oscar Hammerstein II, M: Richard Rodgers. *On the Town* (Imperial, revival, "Pitkin," Oct. 31, 1971): I Understand/W: Betty Comden, Adolph Green, M: Leonard Bernstein. *The Best Little Whorehouse in Texas* (46th Street, CR, "Governor" and "Traveling Salesman" and "Scruggs," Aug. 6, 1979): The Sidestep; Texas Has a Whorehouse in It; 20 Fans/WM: Carol Hall.

364. Brian Avery (July 13, 1940–) B: Los Angeles, CA. *A Time for Singing* (Broadway, "Ivor Morgan," May 21, 1966): Three Ships/ WM: Gerald Freedman, John Morris.

365. Kathleen Ayers *Hello, Daddy* (Erlanger's, CR, "Dot," June 10, 1929): Three Little Maids from School/W: Dorothy Fields, M: Jimmy McHugh.

366. Ken Ayers *South Pacific* (New York City Center, revival, "Seebee Richard West," June 2, 1965): There Is Nothin' Like a Dame/W: Oscar Hammerstein II, M: Richard Rodgers.

367. Ethel Ayler (1934–) B: Whistler, AL. *Kwamina* (54th Street, "Naii," Oct. 23, 1961): Nothing More to Look Forward To/WM: Richard Adler.

368. Arthur Aylesworth (Aug. 12, 1883– June 26, 1946) B: Apponaugh, RI. M: SADIE HARRIS. *Roly Poly* (Weber and Fields, CR, "Percy Fitzsimmons," Dec. 23, 1912): Dear Old Heidelberg/W: E. Ray Goetz, M: A. Baldwin Sloane — Float Away/WM: ?. *Go Easy, Mabel* (Longacre, "George MacDonald," May 8, 1922): I Want a Regular Man/WM: Charles George.

369. Percival Aylmer *The Girl of My Dreams* (Criterion, "Socrates Primmer," Aug. 7, 1911): Dear Little Game of Guessing/W: Otto Harbach, M: Karl Hoschna.

370. Jean Aylwin (Oct. 10, 1885–Jan. 2, 1964) B: Hawick, Scotland. *Our Miss Gibbs* (Knickerbocker, "Mme. Jeanne," Aug. 29, 1910): Dougal/WM: ? — Hats/W: Percy Greenbank, Adrian Ross, M: Ivan Caryll — I Love MacIntosh/W: George Arthurs, M: Harold Lonsdale. *La Belle Paree* (Winter Garden, "Mme. Clarice," Mar. 20, 1911): The Edinboro Wriggle/W: M.E.

Rourke, M: Jerome Kern — Widows/W: Edward Madden, M: Frank Tours.

371. Neva Aymar (Apr. 19, 1889–Feb. 2, 1932) B: Pike, NY. *Rogers Brothers in London* (Knickerbocker, "Evelyn Birmingham," Sept. 7, 1903): Mr. Breezy/W: Ed Gardenier, M: Melville Ellis — Queen of the Bungalow/W: Ed Gardenier, M: Gus Rogers, Max Rogers. *Fritz in Tammany Hall* (Herald Square, "Susette Sorbonne," Oct. 16, 1905): East Side Walk/W: William Jerome, M: Jean Schwartz. *Nearly a Hero* (Casino, "Edith," Feb. 24, 1908): I Don't Want to Marry You/WM: Edward B. Claypoole — The Walking Tour/W: ?, M: Seymour Furth.

372. Charlotte Ayres *Mayflowers* (Forrest, "Miss Watkins," Nov. 24, 1925): Put Your Troubles in a Candy Box/W: Clifford Grey, M: J. Fred Coots.

373. Christine Ayres B: Detroit, MI. She appeared in burlesque as Charmaine. *A Lady Says Yes* (Broadhurst, "Christine," Jan. 10, 1945): A Lesson in Terpsichore/W: Stanley Adams, M: Fred Spielman, Arthur Gershwin.

374. Arminae Azarian *A Chorus Line* (Shubert, CR, "Diana," Feb. 13, 1989): Nothing; What I Did for Love/W: Edward Kleban, M: Marvin Hamlisch.

375. Tony Azito (July 18, 1948–May 26, 1995) B: New York, NY. *Happy End* (Martin Beck, revival, "Governor Nakamura," May 7, 1977): The Bilbao Song; The Liquor Dealer's Dream; Song of the Big Shot/W: Bertolt Brecht, M: Kurt Weill. *Gotta Getaway!* (Radio City Music Hall, revue, June 16, 1984): Gotta Getaway/WM: Glen Roven — Hello Beautiful/WM: Walter Donaldson — Here in Minipoora; Manhattan; Take Good Care of That Lady/WM: Marc Shaiman, Marc Elliot — I'll Build a Stairway to Paradise/W: B.G. DeSylva, Ira Gershwin, M: George Gershwin — I'm Throwing a Ball Tonight/WM: Cole Porter.

376. Charles Aznavour (May 22, 1924–) B: Paris, France. One of the most famous singer songwriters, he began as a cabaret singer in Paris where his Armenian actor parents had opened a family restaurant. Encouraged by Edith Piaf, he went on to become a top performer in France and then an international star. *The World of Charles Aznavour* (Ambassador, solo revue, Oct. 14, 1965): Avec; The Boss Is Dead; C'est Fini; For Me Formidable; I Dig You That Way; I'm Wrong; Isabelle; J'ai Perdu la Tete; Je Te Rechaufferais; L'amour C'est Comme un Jour; Love at Last You Have Found Me; Never Again; Parceque; Paris Is at Her Best in May; Quand

Tu Viens Chez Moi; Reste; The Time Is Now; Two Guitars; Who; You've Got to Learn; You've Let Yourself Go/WM: Charles Aznavour — Et Pourtant/W: Georges Garvarentz, M: Charles Aznavour — La Boheme; Les Comediens/W: J. Plante, M: Charles Aznavour — La Mamma/W: Gail, M: Charles Aznavour — Le Temps/W: Charles Aznavour, M: J. Davis — Que C'est Triste Venice/W: Charles Aznavour, M: F. Dorin. *Charles Aznavour* (Music Box, solo revue, Feb. 4, 1970): All Those Pretty Girls/WM: Charles Aznavour, trans. B. Kaye — And I in My Chair/WM: Charles Aznavour, trans. D. Newburg — Apaga La Luz/WM: Charles Aznavour, trans. R. Deleon — August Days in Paree/W: Georges Garvarentz, M: Charles Aznavour, trans. D. Newburg — De t'Avoir Aimee; Emmenez-Moi; Isabelle; Le Toreador; Les Bons Moments; Reste/WM: Charles Aznavour — Desormais; Et Pourtant/W: Georges Garvarentz, M: Charles Aznavour — Happy Anniversary; Who; Yesterday When I Was Young/WM: Charles Aznavour, trans. Herbert Kretzmer — I Will Give to You; It Will Be My Day; To My Daughter; The Wine of Youth/WM: Charles Aznavour, trans. B. Morrisson — I Will Warm Your Heart/WM: Charles Aznavour, trans. G. Lees — La Boheme; Les Comediens/W: Charles Aznavour, M: J. Plante — Le Tamos/W: J. Davis, M: Charles Aznavour — My Hand Needs Your Hand/W: P. Roche, M: Charles Aznavour, trans. B. Kaye — Sunday's Not My Day/W: T. Veran, M: Charles Aznavour, trans: B. Morrisson — Venice Dressed in Blue/W: Charles Aznavour, M: F. Dorin, trans. B. Kaye — We'll Drift Away/W: Georges Garvarentz, M: Charles Aznavour, trans. B. Kaye — You've Got to Learn/WM: Charles Aznavour, trans. M. Stellman. *Aznavour* (Lunt-Fontanne, solo revue, Mar. 14, 1983): And I in My Chair/WM: Charles Aznavour, trans. D. Newburg — De t'Avoir Aimee; The First Dance; The Happy Days; I Didn't See the Time Go By; Ils Sont Tombes; In Your Room; Isabelle; L'Amour, Bon Dieu, L'Amour; Mon Ami, Mon Judas; Mon Emouvant Amour; Mourir d'Aimer; Qui; Take Me Along; To Be a Soldier; What Makes a Man/WM: Charles Aznavour — Etre; I'll Be There; Non Je N'ai Rien Oublie; Nous n'Avons Pas d'Enfant; The Old Fashioned Way/W: Charles Aznavour, M: Georges Garvarentz — Happy Anniversary/WM: Charles Aznavour, trans. Herbert Kretzmer — I Act as If; In Times to Be; La Boheme; Les Comediens/W: J. Plante, M: Charles Aznavour — La Mama/W: Gail, M: Charles Aznavour — Le Temps/W: Charles Aznavour, M: J.

Davis — Que C'est Triste Venice/W: Charles Aznavour, M: F. Dorin — She/W: Herbert Kretzmer, M: Charles Aznavour.

377. Obba Babatunde B: Jamaica, NY. Actor, singer, dancer and choreographer. He became a professional performer at age 14. *Reggae* (Biltmore, "Rockets," Mar. 27, 1980): Gotta Take a Chance/WM: Max Romeo, Michael Kamen — Mash 'Em Up/WM: Kendrew Lascelles, Ras Karbi, Jackie Mittoo, Michael Kamen — Mash Ethiopia/WM: Kendrew Lascelles, Ras Karbi, Jackie Mittoo, Michael Kamen, Stafford Harrison. *It's So Nice to Be Civilized* (Martin Beck, "Sharky," June 3, 1980): Keep Your Eye on the Red; Step Into My World; Wake Up, Sun/WM: Micki Grant. *Dreamgirls* (Imperial, "C.C. White," Dec. 20, 1981): Cadillac Car; Family; I Miss You Old Friend; Quintette; The Rap; Steppin' to the Bad Side/W: Tom Eyen, M: Henry Krieger.

378. Kevin Babb *Comin' Uptown* (Winter Garden, "Tiny Tim," Dec. 20, 1979): What Better Time to Love/W: Peter Udell, M: Garry Sherman.

379. Dorothy Babbs (1926–May 13, 1998) B: Amarillo, TX. The dancer appeared in movies from 1939, and retired in the 1950s. *Lend an Ear* (National > Broadhurst, revue, Dec. 16, 1948): Give Your Heart a Chance to Sing/WM: Charles Gaynor.

380. Donald Babcock *The Student Gypsy or The Prince of Liederkranz* (54th Street, "Osgood the Good," Sept. 30, 1963): There's Life in the Old Folks Yet/WM: Rick Besoyan.

381. John Babcock *The Secret Garden* (St. James, "Colin," Apr. 25, 1991): Come to My Garden; Round-Shouldered Man/W: Marsha Norman, M: Lucy Simon.

382. Theodore Babcock (Feb. 14, 1868–Sept. 7, 1930) B: Brooklyn, NY. *Pretty Mrs. Smith* (Casino, "Ferdinand Smith," Sept. 21, 1914): The Plain Ol' Name of Smith/W: Earl Carroll, M: Alfred G. Robyn.

383. Sue Babel *Fiddler on the Roof* (Imperial, "Grandma Tzeitel," Sept. 22, 1964): The Tailor, Motel Kamzoil/W: Sheldon Harnick, M: Jerry Bock.

384. Vivienne Baber *Shuffle Along of 1933* (Mansfield, revue, "Alice Walker," Dec. 26, 1932): Sugar Babe/W: Noble Sissle, M: Eubie Blake.

385. Lauren Bacall (Sept. 16, 1924–) B: Bronx, NY. M: actors Humphrey Bogart and Jason Robards. Major motion picture star from the mid 1940s on. *Applause* (Palace, "Margo Channing," Mar. 30, 1970): But Alive; Good Friends; Hurry Back; Inner Thoughts; One of a

Kind; Something Greater; Welcome to the Theater; Who's That Girl?/W: Lee Adams, M: Charles Strouse. *Woman of the Year* (Palace, "Tess Harding," Mar. 29, 1981/Dec. 15, 1981): The Grass Is Always Greener; Happy in the Morning; I Wrote the Book; One of the Boys; Shut Up, Gerald; Table Talk; The Two of Us; We're Gonna Work It Out; When You're Right, You're Right; Who Would Have Dreamed? [Dec. 1, 1981]; Woman of the Year [Dec. 1, 1981]/W: Fred Ebb, M: John Kander.

386. Charles Bachman (?–Mar. 1919) *Running for Office* (14th Street, "Quick Hall," Apr. 27, 1903): Johnny, Get Off the Corner/WM: George M. Cohan.

387. Agostino (Gus) Baci *Hello, Paris and A La Broadway* (Folies Bergere, revue, "Tom Jackson," Sept. 22, 1911): In Loving Time/W: William Le Baron, Mabel H. Hollins, M: Harold Orlob. *Rock-a-Bye Baby* (Astor, "Finnegan," May 22, 1918): Bella Mia/W: Herbert Reynolds, M: Jerome Kern.

388. Robert Bacigalupi see ROBERT FOX.

389. Richard Backus (Mar. 28, 1945–) B: Goffstown, NH. *Camelot* (Winter Garden, revival, "Mordred," Nov. 15, 1981): Fie on Goodness; The Seven Deadly Virtues/W: Alan Jay Lerner, M: Frederick Loewe.

390. Olga Baclanova (Aug. 19, 1899–Sept. 6, 1974) B: Moscow, Russia. She came to the U.S. in 1923, and appeared in several films, including the horror classic *Freaks* (1932). *Murder at the Vanities* (New Amsterdam > Majestic, "Sonya Sonya," Sept. 12, 1933): You Love Me/WM: Herman Hupfeld.

391. Hermione Baddeley (Nov. 13, 1906–Aug. 19, 1986) B: Broseley, England. A star of the British stage by the age of 15, she went on to play comedic roles in theater and movies on both sides of the Atlantic. Memorable as Mrs. Nell Naugatuck on TV's popular sitcom, *Maude* (1974). *Canterbury Tales* (Eugene O'Neill, "Wife of Bath," Feb. 3, 1969): Come on and Marry Me Honey; It Depends on What You're At/W: Nevill Coghill, M: Richard Hill, John Hawkins.

392. Annette Bade *Morris Gest Midnight Whirl* (Century Grove, revue, Dec. 27, 1919): Doughnuts; Let Cutie Cut Your Cuticle/W: B. G. DeSylva, John Henry Mears, M: George Gershwin. *Ziegfeld Midnight Frolic (11th Edition) aka Ziegfeld New Midnight Frolic* (New Amsterdam roof, revue, Feb. 9, 1921): Love Is Like a Mushroom; The Ziegfeld Dollies/W: Gene Buck, M: Dave Stamper. *Vogues of 1924* (Shubert, revue, Mar. 27, 1924): Hush, Look Away; Rain/W: Clifford Grey, M: Herbert Stothart.

393. Enjio Badii *A Night in Venice* (Shubert, CR, "Beppo," July 8, 1929): One Night of Love/W: J. Keirn Brennan, M: Maurie Rubens.

394. Dean Badolato (June 6, 1952–) B: Chicago, IL. *The Most Happy Fella* (Majestic, revival, "Clem," Oct. 11, 1979): Standing on the Corner/WM: Frank Loesser.

395. Marian Baer (Aug. 18, 1926–) B: Sedalia, MO. *My Fair Lady* (Uris, revival, "Mrs. Pearce," Aug. 18, 1981): I Could Have Danced All Night; You Did It/W: Alan Jay Lerner, M: Frederick Loewe.

396. Jeanette Bageard *Rogers Brothers in Wall Street* (Victoria, "Carrie Rafferty," Sept. 18, 1899): Beware of an Innocent Maid/WM: Richard Carle, Maurice Levi. *Rogers Brothers in Washington* (Knickerbocker, "Clara Braley," Sept. 2, 1901): In the Swim; The Wedding of the Reuben and the Maid/W: Harry B. Smith, M: Maurice Levi. *The Prince of Pilsen* (Broadway, "Sidonie," Mar. 17, 1903): Keep It Dark/W: Frank Pixley, M: Gustav Luders.

397. Eleanore Bagley (Apr. 20, 1924–) B: Philadelphia, PA. *Of V We Sing* (Concert, revue, Feb. 11, 1942): Brooklyn Cantata/W: Mike Stratton, M: George Kleinsinger — Gertie the Stool Pigeon's Daughter/W: Joe Darion, M: Ned Lehac. *Make Mine Manhattan* (Broadhurst, revue, Jan. 15, 1948): Saturday Night in Central Park/W: Arnold B. Horwitt, M: Richard Lewine.

398. Frank Baier *The News* (Helen Hayes, "Circulation Editor," Nov. 7, 1985): Dear Felicia/WM: Paul Schierhorn.

399. Adrian Bailey (Sept. 23–) B: Detroit, MI. *Smokey Joe's Cafe* (Virginia, revue, Mar. 2, 1995): Dance with Me; Don't; Keep on Rollin'; Little Egypt; Love Me; Love Potion #9; On Broadway; Poison Ivy; Ruby Baby; Searchin'; Shoppin' for Clothes; Stand By Me; Teach Me How to Shimmy; There Goes My Baby; Young Blood/WM: Jerry Leiber, Mike Stoller.

400. Bill Bailey (Dec. 8, 1912–Dec. 12, 1978) B: Newport News, VA. Brother of PEARL BAILEY. *Blackbirds of 1930* (Royale, revue, Oct. 22, 1930): Blackbirds on Parade/W: Andy Razaf, M: Eubie Blake. *Swingin' the Dream* (Center, "Cupid," Nov. 29, 1939): Darn That Dream/W: Eddie DeLange, M: James Van Heusen.

401. Larry G. Bailey *A Chorus Line* (Shubert, CR, "Richie," Jan. 1979): And.../W: Edward Kleban, M: Marvin Hamlisch.

402. Maureen Bailey *The Girls Against the Boys* (Alvin, revue, Nov. 2, 1959): Where Do We Go? Out/W: Arnold B. Horwitt, M: Richard Lewine.

403. Melissa Bailey *Marilyn* (Minskoff, "Elda," Nov. 20, 1983): Swing Shift (Miss Parachute)/WM: Beth Lawrence, Norman Thalheimer.

404. Pearl Bailey (Mar. 29, 1918–Aug. 17, 1990) B: Newport News, VA. Sister of BILL BAILEY. Known as Pearlie Mae, the versatile entertainer with her chatty, effervescent charm worked in vaudeville, nightclubs, as a band singer with NOBLE SISSLE, CAB CALLOWAY and others, and in movies and TV. *St. Louis Woman* (Martin Beck, "Butterfly," Mar. 30, 1946): Cakewalk Your Lady; Legalize My Name; A Woman's Prerogative/W: Johnny Mercer, M: Harold Arlen. *Arms and the Girl* (46th Street, "Connecticut," Feb. 2, 1950): Nothin' for Nothin'; Plantation in Philadelphia; There Must Be Somethin' Better Than Love/W: Dorothy Fields, M: Morton Gould. *Bless You All* (Mark Hellinger, revue, Dec. 14, 1950): Bless You All; When; You Never Know What Hit You When It's Love/WM: Harold Rome. *House of Flowers* (Alvin, "Madame Fleur," Dec. 30, 1954): Don't Like Goodbyes; Has I Let You Down?; One Man Ain't Quite Enough; What Is a Friend For?/WM: Truman Capote, Harold Arlen. *Hello, Dolly!* (St. James, CR, "Mrs. Dolly Gallagher Levi," Nov. 12, 1967/Jan. 23, 1969/July 28, 1969/Oct. 9, 1969): Before the Parade Passes By/WM: Lee Adams, Charles Strouse, Jerry Herman — Dancing; Hello, Dolly!; I Put My Hand In; Put on Your Sunday Clothes; So Long, Dearie/WM: Jerry Herman — Motherhood/WM: Bob Merrill, Jerry Herman. *Hello, Dolly!* (Minskoff, revival, "Mrs. Dolly Gallagher Levi," Nov. 6, 1975): same as above.

405. Robin Bailey (Oct. 5, 1919–Jan. 14, 1999) B: Nottingham, England. Comedy character actor in film and TV. *Jennie* (Majestic, "Christopher Lawrence Cromwell," Oct. 17, 1963): Over Here; Where You Are/W: Howard Dietz, M: Arthur Schwartz.

406. Shirley Baines *Porgy and Bess* (Uris, revival, "Serena," Sept. 25, 1976): My Man's Gone Now; Time and Time Again/W: DuBose Heyward, M: George Gershwin. *Porgy and Bess* (Radio City Music Hall, revival, "Serena," Apr. 7, 1983): My Man's Gone Now/W: DuBose Heyward, M: George Gershwin — Oh, Bess, Oh Where's My Bess?/W: Ira Gershwin, M: George Gershwin — Oh, Doctor Jesus/W: DuBose Heyward, Ira Gershwin, M: George Gershwin.

407. Fay Bainter (Dec. 7, 1891–Apr. 16, 1968) B: Los Angeles, CA. Aunt of DOROTHY BURGESS. Supporting character actress in a long career on stage and screen. She received an

Academy Award for the movie *Jezebel* (1938), starring BETTE DAVIS. *The Kiss Burglar* (Cohan, "Aline, Grand Duchess of Orly," May 9, 1918): Because You Do Not Know; I Want to Learn to Dance; The Mantelpiece Tragedy/W: Glen MacDonough, M: Raymond Hubbell. *The Dream Girl* (Ambassador, "Elspeth," Aug. 20, 1924): Dancing 'Round; My Dream Girl; My Hero; Stop, Look and Listen/W: Rida Johnson Young, M: Victor Herbert — I Want to Go Home/W: Harold Atteridge, M: Sigmund Romberg.

408. Joey Baio (July 24, 1953–) B: Brooklyn, NY. Cousin of Scott Baio, brother of Jimmy Baio, popular TV actors. *Oliver!* (Martin Beck, "The Artful Dodger," Aug. 2, 1965): Be Back Soon; Consider Yourself; I'd Do Anything/WM: Lionel Bart.

409. Eugenie Baird *Angel in the Wings* (Coronet, CR, revue, Feb. 9, 1948): Breezy; Holler Blue Murder; If It Were Easy to Do; Tambourine/WM: Bob Hilliard, Carl Sigman.

410. Stewart Baird (c 1881–Oct. 28, 1947) B: Boston, MA. For a while he was associate drama critic at The Boston Transcript. *Little Boy Blue* (Lyric, CR, "Gaston, the Marquis de la Tour," Feb. 19, 1912): In the Heart of the Golden Wine/W: Grant Stewart, M: Henry Bereny — Kiss Me, Dearest, Kiss Me Do; Love Never Dies; You're Very Like Your Sister, Dear/W: Edward A. Paulton, M: Henry Bereny. *All for the Ladies* (Lyric, "Hector Renaud," Dec. 30, 1912): I'd Like to Have a Little Girl Like You Like Me; The Sunday Dress Parade; Women, Women!/W: Henry Blossom, M: Alfred G. Robyn. *The Man with Three Wives* (Weber and Fields, "Capt. Adhemar," Jan. 23, 1913): Kisses That I Have Missed; There's Always a Girl Who Is Waiting; We Are Free/W: Paul M. Potter, Harold Atteridge, M: Franz Lehar. *Iole* (Longacre, "Lionel Frawley," Dec. 29, 1913): And That Is All; Take It from Me/WM: ?. *The Debutante* (Knickerbocker, "Armand," Dec. 7, 1914): All for the Sake of a Girl; The Gay Life; Never Mention Love When We're Alone; The Will-o'-the-Wisp/W: Robert B. Smith, M: Victor Herbert. *Sybil* (Liberty, "Capt. Paul Petrow," Jan. 10, 1916): Letter Duet (My Dearest Paul)/W: Harry Graham, Harry B. Smith, M: Victor Jacobi. *Rambler Rose* (Empire, "Marcel Petipas," Sept. 10, 1917): I Might Say Yes to You; Just a Little Bit in Love/W: Harry B. Smith, M: Victor Jacobi. *The Kiss Burglar* (Cohan, CR, "Bert Duvivier," June 3, 1918): Because You Do Not Know; The Girl I Can't Forget; Since I Met Wonderful You; Your Kiss Is Champagne/W: Glen MacDonough, M:

Raymond Hubbell. *Little Simplicity* (Astor > 44th Street, "Jack Sylvester," Nov. 4, 1918): Days of Youth; First Love; Hush! Hush!; My Lulu; National Air's Medley; Same Old Way/W: Rida Johnson Young, M: Augustus Barratt — My Caravan/WM: Augustus Barratt. *Shubert Gaieties of 1919* (44th Street, revue, July 14, 1919): Beautiful American Girl/WM: ? — Cherry Blossom Lane; I've Made Up My Mind to Mind a Maid Made Up Like You/W: Alfred Bryan, M: Jean Schwartz — Coat o' Mine; This Is the Day/W: Blanche Merrill, M: M.K. Jerome. *Cinderella on Broadway* (Winter Garden, revue, "Prince Charming," June 24, 1920): Just Like the House That Jack Built; Phantom Loves; Primrose Ways/W: Harold Atteridge, M: Bert Grant. *The Rose Girl* (Ambassador, "Count Henri de Guise," Feb. 11, 1921): Beauty's Candy Shop; Flirtation Quartette; May and September/W: William Cary Duncan, M: Anselm Goetzel. *The Hotel Mouse* (Shubert, "Don Esteban," Mar. 13, 1922): Nearly True to You/W: Clifford Grey, M: Ivan Caryll — Where Lanterns Gleam/W: Clifford Grey, M: Armand Vecsey.

411. Bob Bakanic *Seventeen* (Broadhurst, "Don," June 21, 1951): Reciprocity; Weatherbee's Drug Store/W: Kim Gannon, M: Walter Kent.

412. Belle Baker (Dec. 25, 1893–Apr. 28, 1957) B: New York, NY. M: producer Lew Leslie; composer Maurice Abrahams. On stage as a child in Yiddish productions, at 20 she was a vaudeville headliner at NY's Palace. During her career in England and the US, she introduced more than 150 songs, many by Irving Berlin. *Betsy* (New Amsterdam, "Ruth," Dec. 28, 1926): Blue Skies/WM: Irving Berlin — Push Around; Sing; This Funny World/W: Lorenz Hart, M: Richard Rodgers.

413. Benny Baker (May 5, 1907–Sept. 20, 1994) B: St. Joseph MO. *Du Barry Was a Lady* (46th Street > Royale, "Charley," Dec. 6, 1939): Dream Song/WM: Cole Porter. *Let's Face It* (Imperial, "Frankie Burns," Oct. 29, 1941): Baby Games; Farming/WM: Cole Porter. *Jackpot* (Alvin, "Winkie Cotter," Jan. 13, 1944): A Piece of a Girl; Sugarfoot; What's Mine Is Yours/W: Howard Dietz, M: Vernon Duke. *No, No, Nanette* (46th Street, revival, CR, "Jimmy Smith," Jan. 10, 1972): I Want to Be Happy/W: Irving Caesar, M: Vincent Youmans.

414. David Aaron Baker (Aug. 14, 1963–) B: Durham, NC. *110 in the Shade* (New York State, revival, "Jimmie Curry," July 18, 1992): Little Red Hat; Lizzie's Comin' Home; Poker Polka/W: Tom Jones, M: Harvey Schmidt. *Once*

Upon a Mattress (Broadhurst, revival, "Prince Dauntless," Dec. 19, 1996): Goodnight, Sweet Princess; Man to Man Talk; An Opening for a Princess; Song of Love; Swamps of Home/W: Marshall Barer, M: Mary Rodgers.

415. D.L. Baker *The Pied Piper* (Majestic, "Official Reminder," Dec. 3, 1908): It All Depends; We Tell Him Just What to Do/W: R.H. Burnside, M: Manuel Klein.

416. Doris Baker (Aug. 8, 1908–) *Rain or Shine* (George M. Cohan, CR, "Katie," June 25, 1928): Oh, Baby!/WM: Owen Murphy — Who's Goin' to Get You?/W: Jack Yellen, M: Milton Ager.

417. Earl Baker *Trumpets of the Lord* (Brooks Atkinson, revival, "Singer," Apr. 29, 1969): There's a Man/WM: based on gospel hymn.

418. Edythe Baker *The Blushing Bride* (Astor, "Rose," Feb. 6, 1922): Love's Highway; Rosy Posy/W: Cyrus D. Wood, M: Sigmund Romberg. *Innocent Eyes* (Winter Garden, revue, "Rose Longuebois," May 20, 1924): Garden of Love/W: Tot Seymour, M: Jean Schwartz — Last Night on the Back Porch (I Loved Her Best of All)/W: Lew Brown, M: Carl Schraubstader — Let's Have a Rattling Good Time/W: Alfred Bryan, M: Jean Schwartz. *Big Boy* (Winter Garden, "Phyllis Carter," Jan. 7, 1925): Come On and Play; The Dance from Down Yonder; Lead 'Em On/W: B.G. DeSylva, M: Joseph Meyer, James F. Hanley. *Big Boy* (44th Street, CR, "Annabelle Bedford," Aug. 24, 1925): Born and Bred in Old Kentucky; The Dance from Down Yonder; Tap the Toe; True Love/W: B.G. DeSylva, M: Joseph Meyer, James F. Hanley. *Hello, Lola* (Eltinge, "Lola Pratt," Jan. 12, 1926): Don't Stop; Hello, Cousin Lola; My Baby Talk Lady; Swinging on the Gate/W: Dorothy Donnelly, M: William B. Kernell.

419. Elden Baker *Blossom Time* (Century, CR, "Binder," Nov. 20, 1922): Love Is a Riddle/W: Dorothy Donnelly, M: Sigmund Romberg.

420. Florence L. Baker (?–Jan 17, 1900) B: Boston, MA. *Hiawatha* (Standard, "Sally Bohee," Feb. 21, 1880): Pretty Little Boys/W: Nathaniel Childs, M: Edward E. Rice.

421. Grafton Baker *A Million Dollars* (New York, "Harold Spotwood," Sept. 27, 1900): Phoebe, Dear, I Love You/W: Louis Harrison, George V. Hobart, M: A. Baldwin Sloane.

422. Gregg Baker *Porgy and Bess* (Radio City Music Hall, revival, "Crown," Apr. 7, 1983): A Red Headed Woman/W: Ira Gershwin, M: George Gershwin — What You Want Wid Bess?/W: DuBose Heyward, M: George Gershwin. *The Wiz* (Lunt-Fontanne, revival, "Lion," May 24, 1984): Be a Lion; Mean Ole Lion/WM: Charlie Smalls.

423. Guelma L. Baker (Oct. 1–Feb. 5, 1923) B: Los Angeles, CA. *Florodora* (Casino > New York, "Valleda," Nov. 10, 1900): We Get Up at 8 A.M./WM: Leslie Stuart. *Peggy from Paris* (Wallack's, "Lutie Plummer," Sept. 10, 1903): The Girl Who Comes in from the West; Highfalutin' Music/W: George Ade, M: William Lorraine.

424. Ivena Baker *Animal Crackers* (44th Street, CR, "Arabella Rittenhouse," Mar. 11, 1929): When Things Are Bright and Rosy/WM: Bert Kalmar, Harry Ruby.

425. Jennifer Baker (Feb. 9, 1946–) B: London, England. *Stop the World—I Want to Get Off* (Shubert, "Jane Littlechap," Oct. 3, 1962): Family Fugue; Nag! Nag! Nag!/WM: Leslie Bricusse, Anthony Newley.

426. Josephine Baker (June 3, 1906–Apr. 12, 1975) B: St. Louis, MO. Major star of Paris in the 1920s and 30s. The legendary dancer, singer and actress led a tempestuous life. At one time she was the most fashionable and highly paid entertainer in Europe. After WWII she sheltered and cared for many adopted orphans. *Ziegfeld Follies of 1936* (Winter Garden, revue, Jan. 30, 1936): Five A.M.; Maharanee/W: Ira Gershwin, M: Vernon Duke.

427. Karin Baker *Different Times* (ANTA, "Columbia" and "Mae Verne," May 1, 1972): I Miss Him; Marianne/WM: Michael Brown.

428. Kenny Baker (Sept. 20, 1912–Aug. 10, 1985) B: Monrovia, CA. Tenor star of stage, screen and radio. He started out to be a violinist, but won a talent competition at the Cocoanut Grove in Los Angeles, and a contract to sing with Eddie Duchin's Orchestra. In the 1930s he was a vocalist on Jack Benny's radio program. In 1939 he starred in the legendary film version of Gilbert and Sullivan's *The Mikado. One Touch of Venus* (Imperial, "Rodney Hatch," Oct. 7, 1943): How Much I Love You; Speak Low; The Trouble with Women; Way Out West in Jersey; Wooden Wedding/W: Ogden Nash, M: Kurt Weill.

429. LaVern Baker (Nov. 11, 1928–Mar. 10, 1997) B: Chicago, IL. Jazz and blues singer and recording artist. *Black and Blue* (Minskoff, CR, revue): Black and Blue/W: Andy Razaf, M: Fats Waller, Harry Brooks— Body and Soul/W: Edward Heyman, Robert Sour, Frank Eyton, M: Johnny Green— If I Can't Sell It, I'll Keep Sittin' on It/WM: Alexander Hill, Andy Razaf— I'm a Woman/WM: Elias McDaniel, Cora

Taylor— St. Louis Blues/WM: W.C. Handy— 'Taint Nobody's Biz-ness If I Do/WM: Clarence Williams, Porter Grainger, Graham Prince.

430. Lenny Baker (Jan. 17, 1945–Apr. 12, 1982) B: Boston, MA. *I Love My Wife* (Ethel Barrymore, "Alvin," Apr. 17, 1977): By Three's; Everybody Today Is Turning On; I Love My Wife; Married Couple Seeks Married Couple; Monica; A Mover's Life; Sexually Free/W: Michael Stewart, M: Cy Coleman.

431. Mark Baker (Oct. 2, 1946–) B: Cumberland, MD. *Candide* (Broadway, revival, "Candide," Mar. 10, 1974): The Best of All Possible Worlds; Life Is Happiness Indeed; Sheep's Song; This World (Candide's Lament)/W: Stephen Sondheim, M: Leonard Bernstein — I Am Easily Assimilated/WM: Leonard Bernstein — It Must Be So; Oh Happy We/W: Richard Wilbur, M: Leonard Bernstein — You Were Dead, You Know/W: Richard Wilbur, John Latouche, M: Leonard Bernstein.

432. May Baker (c 1869–May 17, 1902) *A Runaway Girl* (Daly's, revival, "Dorothy Stanley," Apr. 23, 1900): The Soldiers in the Park/W: Aubrey Hopwood, M: Lionel Monckton.

433. Mildred Baker *The School Girl* (Daly's > Herald Square, "Mother Superior," Sept. 1, 1904): When I Was a Girl Like You/W: Charles H. Taylor, M: Leslie Stuart.

434. Phil Baker (Aug. 24, 1896–Nov. 30, 1963) B: Philadelphia, PA. M: PEGGY CARTWRIGHT. In vaudeville he was a partner of BEN BERNIE, playing the accordian. In the 1940s he hosted a popular radio quiz show called *Take It or Leave It*, which featured the $64 question. *Artists and Models of 1925* (Winter Garden, revue, June 24, 1925): Lucita/W: Clifford Grey, M: Alfred Goodman, Maurie Rubens, J. Fred Coots. *Artists and Models of 1930 (Paris-Riviera Edition)* (Majestic, revue, June 10, 1930): In Old Havana Town/WM: Harold Stern, Ernie Golden. *Crazy Quilt* (44th Street, revue, May 19, 1931): I Found a Million Dollar Baby (in a Five and Ten Cent Store)/W: Mort Dixon, Billy Rose, M: Harry Warren — Kept in Suspense/W: Billy Rose, James Dyrenforth, M: Carroll Gibbons — Under the Clock at the Astor/W: Ned Wever, M: Manning Sherwin.

435. Raymond Baker (July 9, 1948–) B: Omaha, NE. *Is There Life After High School?* (Ethel Barrymore, revue, May 7, 1982): Beer; Second Thoughts/WM: Craig Carnelia.

436. Sam Baker (?–May 6, 1982) *Sporting Days* (Hippodrome, "Jim Brice," Sept. 5, 1908): Rowing/WM: Manuel Klein.

437. Susan Baker (Feb. 9, 1946–) B: London, England. *Stop the World—I Want to Get Off* (Shubert, "Susan Littlechap," Oct. 3, 1962): Family Fugue; Nag! Nag! Nag!/WM: Leslie Bricusse, Anthony Newley.

438. Suzie Baker *Nellie Bly* (Adelphi, "Singer," Jan. 21, 1946): How About a Date?/W: Johnny Burke, M: James Van Heusen.

439. Ed Bakey (Nov. 13, 1917–May 4, 1988) B: Havre de Grace, MD. *Walking Happy* (Lunt-Fontanne, "George Beenstock," Nov. 26, 1966): Think of Something Else/W: Sammy Cahn, M: James Van Heusen.

440. Scott Bakula (Oct. 9, 1954–) B: St. Louis, MO. M: KRISTA NEUMANN, 1981-1995. He appeared intermittantly on the TV sitcom *Murphy Brown* (1993), as Murphy's sometime boyfriend Peter Hunt. *Marilyn* (Minskoff, "Joe DiMaggio," Nov. 20, 1983): Don't Hang Up the Telephone/WM: Jeanne Napoli, Gary Portnoy — I'll Send You Roses; My Heart's an Open Door/WM: Beth Lawrence, Norman Thalheimer. *Romance Romance* (Helen Hayes, "Alfred Von Wilmers" and "Sam," May 1, 1988): Great News; Happy, Happy, Happy; I'll Always Remember the Song; It's Not Too Late; Let's Not Talk About It; The Little Comedy; Moonlight Passing Through a Window; Oh, What a Performance!; A Rustic Country Inn; Women of Vienna; Words He Doesn't Say/W: Barry Harman, M: Keith Herrmann.

441. Jeanne Bal (May 3, 1928–) B: Santa Monica, CA. *The Gay Life* (Shubert, "Helene," Nov. 18, 1961): Why Go Anywhere at All?/W: Howard Dietz, M: Arthur Schwartz.

442. Brian R. Baldomero (c 1987–) *Miss Saigon* (Broadway, "Tam," Apr. 11, 1991): Little God of My Heart/W: Richard Maltby, Jr., Alain Boublil, M: Claude-Michel Schonberg.

443. George Baldwin *He Came from Milwaukee* (Casino, CR, "Egbert Keskiesko, Duke of Zurach," Aug. 28, 1911): Love Is Like a Red, Red Rose; Merry Wedding Bells/W: Edward Madden, M: Ben M. Jerome, Louis A. Hirsch. *The Girl Who Smiles* (Lyric > Longacre, "Francois Dechanelle," Aug. 9, 1915): Baby Mine; A Breath from Bohemia; Teach Me to Smile; Your Picture/WM: Edward A. Paulton, Adolf Philipp, Jean Briquet. *The Passing Show of 1916* (Winter Garden, revue, June 22, 1916): Romeo and Juliet; Wine, Women and Song/W: Harold Atteridge, M: Sigmund Romberg, Otto Motzan — What's the Matter with You?/WM: Clifton Crawford. *The Show of Wonders* (Winter Garden, revue, Oct. 26, 1916): Pajama Girlie; Wedding Bells/W: Harold Atteridge, M: Otto Motzan. *Love o' Mike* (Shubert, "Jack Vaughn," Jan. 15, 1917): Don't

Tempt Me; Lulu/W: Harry B. Smith, M: Jerome Kern.

444. Robert Baldwin *Three Cheers* (Globe, CR, "Prince Josef," Mar. 4, 1929): Two Boys/W: B.G. DeSylva, M: Ray Henderson.

445. Winnie Baldwin *So Long Letty* (Shubert, "Chita Alvarez," Oct. 23, 1916): Letter Trio; Maryland; On a Beautiful Beach; Pass Around the Apples Once Again; Play Me a Ukulele; When You Hear Jackson Moan on His Saxophone/WM: Earl Carroll.

446. Sandra Balesti *Oklahoma!* (Music Theater of Lincoln Center, revival, "Girl Who Falls Down," June 23, 1969): Many a New Day/W: Oscar Hammerstein II, M: Richard Rodgers.

447. Arthur Ball (c 1895–Aug. 27, 1951) B: Massachusetts. One of 36 founders of the Academy of Motion Picture Arts and Sciences. He died of carbon monoxide poisoning. *The Broadway Whirl* (Selwyn, revue, CR, Aug. 15, 1921): All Girls Are Like the Rainbow/W: Joseph McCarthy, M: Harry Tierney. *George White's Scandals of 1925* (Apollo, revue, June 22, 1925): The Girl of Tomorrow; Room Enough for Me; Rose Time/W: B.G. DeSylva, Lew Brown, M: Ray Henderson.

448. George Ball B: Pittsburgh, PA. *Jacques Brel Is Alive and Well and Living in Paris* (Royale, revue, revival, Sept. 15, 1972): Alone; Bachelor's Dance/W: Eric Blau, M: Jacques Brel — The Bulls/W: Eric Blau, Mort Shuman, M: Jacques Brel, Gerard Jouannest, Jean Corti — Fannette; Girls and Dogs; The Middle Class; The Statue/W: Eric Blau, Mort Shuman, M: Jacques Brel.

449. Lucille Ball (Aug. 6, 1910–Apr. 26, 1989) B: Jamestown, NY. Actress and comedienne loved by generations of kids and grownups for her TV series with Cuban bandleader husband DESI ARNAZ, *I Love Lucy* (1951). She was president of Desilu Productions, Inc. and executive producer of *The Lucy Show* (1962). *Wildcat* (Alvin, "Wildcat Jackson," Dec. 16, 1960): Dancing on My Tippy Tippy Toes; El Sombrero; Give a Little Whistle (and I'll Be There); Hey, Look Me Over!; That's What I Want for Janie; What Takes My Fancy; Wildcat; You're a Liar!/W: Carolyn Leigh, M: Cy Coleman.

450. Michael Ball (June 27, 1963–) B: Stratford-on-Avon, England. *Aspects of Love* (Broadhurst, "Alex Dillingham," Apr. 8, 1990): Falling; Hand Me the Wine and the Dice; Love Changes Everything; Mermaid Song; Other Pleasures; Parlez Vous Francais?; Seeing Is Believing; She'd Be Far Better Off with You/W: Don Black, Charles Hart, M: Andrew Lloyd Webber.

451. Patsy Ball *The Merry Malones* (Erlanger's, "Annie," Sept. 26, 1927): Our Own Way of Going Along (If You Like Coffee and I Like Tea)/WM: George M. Cohan.

452. Carl Ballantine (Sept. 27, 1922–) B: Chicago, IL. He played Lester Gruber in the TV sitcom *McHale's Navy* (1962), and for the subsequent 1964 movie. *A Funny Thing Happened on the Way to the Forum* (Lunt-Fontanne, revival, "Lycus," Mar. 30, 1972): Everybody Ought to Have a Maid; The House of Marcus Lycus/WM: Stephen Sondheim.

453. Dave Ballard *Dream with Music* (Majestic, "Genie," May 18, 1944): Battle of the Genie/W: Edward Eager, M: Clay Warnick.

454. Kaye Ballard (Nov. 20, 1926–) B: Cleveland, OH. She began as an impressionist, singer and actress at the Stage Door Canteen in Cleveland, then played in vaudeville with Spike Jones all over the country. TV credits include: *The Perry Como Show* (1961); *The Mothers-in-Law* (1967); *The Doris Day Show* (1970); *The Steve Allen Comedy Hour* (1980). *The Golden Apple* (Alvin, "Helen," Apr. 20, 1954): Lazy Afternoon; My Picture in the Papers; Nothing Ever Happens in Angel's Roost/W: John Latouche, M: Jerome Moross. *Carnival!* (Imperial, "The Incomparable Rosalie," Apr. 13, 1961/Aug. 13, 1962): Direct from Vienna; Humming; It Was Always You; Magic, Magic/WM: Bob Merrill. *Wonderful Town* (New York City Center, revival, "Ruth Sherwood," Feb. 13, 1963): Conga!; Conversation Piece (Nice Talk, Nice People); Ohio; One Hundred Easy Ways; Swing!; Wrong Note Rag/W: Betty Comden, Adolph Green, M: Leonard Bernstein. *The Beast in Me* (Plymouth, revue, May 16, 1963): Eat Your Breakfast; Hallelujah; So Beautiful; When I'm Alone; Why?/W: James Costigan, M: Don Elliott. *Molly* (Alvin, "Molly Goldberg," Nov. 1, 1973) Cahoots; If Everyone Got What They Wanted; So I'll Tell Him; There's Gold on the Trees/W: Mack David, M: Jerry Livingston — Go in the Best of Health; Oak Leaf Memorial Park/W: Leonard Adelson, M: Jerry Livingston — I See a Man; A Piece of the Rainbow/WM: Norman L. Martin.

455. Lucille Ballentine *The Broadway Whirl* (Times Square > Selwyn, revue, June 8, 1921): Button Me Up the Back/W: Joseph McCarthy, M: Harry Tierney — Let Cutie Cut Your Cuticle/W: B.G. DeSylva, John Henry Mears, M: George Gershwin — Three Little Maids/W: Joseph McCarthy, B.G. DeSylva, M: Harry Tierney.

456. Julia Ballew *Shubert Gaieties of 1919*

(44th Street, revue, July 14, 1919): Baby Vampire Land; Cosy Corner/W: Alfred Bryan, M: Jean Schwartz.

457. Matthew Ballinger (Apr. 22, 1985–) B: New York, NY. *A Christmas Carol* (Madison Square Garden, return engagement, "Tiny Tim," Nov. 22, 1996): Christmas Together/W: Lynn Ahrens, M: Alan Menken.

458. Marion Ballou (Oct. 17, 1870–Mar. 25, 1939) B: Boston, MA. *My Maryland* (Al Jolson, "Mrs. Hunter," Sept. 12, 1927): Something Old, Something New; Strawberry Jam/W: Dorothy Donnelly, M: Sigmund Romberg.

459. Buddy Balou (1953–) B: Seattle, WA. *A Chorus Line* (Shubert, CR, "Mike," June 1980): I Can Do That/W: Edward Kleban, M: Marvin Hamlisch. *A Chorus Line* (Shubert, CR, "Al," Mar. 1983): Sing!/W: Edward Kleban, M: Marvin Hamlisch.

460. Martin Balsam (Nov. 4, 1919–Feb. 12, 1996) B: New York, NY. Distinguished character actor of stage, screen and TV. He won an Oscar for *A Thousand Clowns* (1964). *Nowhere to Go but Up* (Winter Garden, "Moe Smith," Nov. 10, 1962): Ain't You Ashamed?; Baby, Baby; Dear Mom; Follow the Leader Septet; I Love You for That; Live a Little; Nowhere to Go but Up; When a Fella Needs a Friend/W: James Lipton, M: Sol Berkowitz.

461. Carmen Balthrop (c 1950–) The soprano has performed on stage and in concert halls all over the world. *Treemonisha* (Palace, "Treemonisha," Oct. 21, 1975): Abuse; The Bag of Luck; Conjurer's Forgiven; The Corn Huskers; Going Home; The Rescue; Surprise; Treemonisha's Bringing Up; Treemonisha's Return; We Will Trust You As Our Leader; We're Goin' Around; The Wreath/WM: Scott Joplin.

462. George Bancroft (Sept. 30, 1882–Oct. 2, 1956) B: Philadelphia, PA. M: OCTAVIA BROSKE. He started out in blackface, in minstrel shows. From the 1920s he played tough guys and villains in Hollywood. In 1942 he retired to a ranch. *The Rise of Rosie O'Reilly* (Liberty, "Johnson," Dec. 25, 1923): Born and Bred in Brooklyn (Over the Bridge); The Plot Again/WM: George M. Cohan.

463. Millicent Bancroft *The Houseboat on the Styx* (Liberty, "Lucretia Borgia," Feb. 4, 1929): Someone Like You/W: Monte Carlo, M: Alma Sanders.

464. Paula Bane B: Seattle, WA. *Call Me Mister* (National > Plymouth, revue, Apr. 18, 1946): Along with Me; His Old Man; When We Meet Again/WM: Harold Rome.

465. Xenia Bank *The Merry Widow* (New York City Center, revival, "Natalie, Baroness Popoff," Oct. 8, 1944): A Dutiful Wife/W: Adrian Ross, M: Franz Lehar.

466. Herbert Banke *Oklahoma!* (New York City Center, revival, "Curly McLain," Mar. 19, 1958): The Farmer and the Cowman; Oh, What a Beautiful Mornin'; Oklahoma!; People Will Say We're in Love; Pore Jud; The Surrey with the Fringe on Top/W: Oscar Hammerstein II, M: Richard Rodgers.

467. Richard Banke *Kismet* (New York State, revival, "The Caliph," June 22, 1965): And This Is My Beloved; He's in Love!; Night of My Nights; Stranger in Paradise/WM: Robert Wright, George Forrest.

468. Ada Banks *Mr. Lode of Koal* (Majestic, "A. Saylor," Nov. 1, 1909): In Far Off Mandalay/W: Alex Rogers, M: Al Johns.

469. Baby Banks *Americana of 1928* (Lew Fields, revue, Oct. 30, 1928): Hot Pants; Young Black Joe/W: Irving Caesar, M: Roger Wolfe Kahn — Life as a Twosome/W: Irving Caesar, M: Roger Wolfe Kahn, Joseph Meyer.

470. Diana Banks *Kismet* (New York State, revival, "Princess of Ababu," June 22, 1965): He's in Love!; Not Since Ninevah; Rahadlakum/WM: Robert Wright, George Forrest.

471. Ernie Banks (Jan. 30, 1931–) B: Dallas, TX. *Don't Get God Started* (Longacre, revue, "Wise Old Man," Oct. 29, 1987): Millions/WM: Marvin Winans.

472. Hugh Banks *Big Boy* (Winter Garden > 44th Street, "Joe Warren," Jan. 7, 1925): The Dance from Down Yonder; Lead 'Em On; Tap the Toe/W: B.G. DeSylva, M: Joseph Meyer, James F. Hanley.

473. Gary Bankston *Jesus Christ Superstar* (Paramount Madison Square Garden, revival, "3rd Priest," Jan. 17, 1995): This Jesus Must Die/W: Tim Rice, M: Andrew Lloyd Webber.

474. Billy Bann *Parisiana* (Edyth Totten, revue, Feb. 9, 1928): Gettin' Gertie's Gumdrop; Her First Affair/WM: Vincent Valentini.

475. John Banner (Jan. 28, 1910–Jan. 28, 1973) B: Vienna, Austria. He went to New York in 1939. On TV's *Hogan's Heroes* (1965) he played Sgt. Hans Schultz. *From Vienna* (Music Box, revue, June 20, 1939): Salzburg Puppet Show/W: Lothar Metzl, Werner Michel, Eva Franklin, M: Otto Andreas.

476. Leslie Bannister *Bitter Sweet* (Ziegfeld, "Mr. Vale," Nov. 5, 1929): The Last Dance; Tarara Boom-de-Ay/WM: Noel Coward.

477. Christine Baranski (May 2, 1952–) B: Cheektowaga, NY. Sophisticated actress-singer with a generous dash of humor stirred in. *Cybill's* best TV sitcom friend, Maryann (1995). *Nick & Nora* (Marquis, "Tracy Gardner," Dec. 8, 1991): Everybody Wants to Do a Musical; Is There Anything Better Than Dancing?; May the Best Man Win; Men/W: Richard Maltby, Jr., M: Charles Strouse.

478. Joseph Barbara (Dec. 5, 1967–) B: New Smyrna Beach, FL. *Grease* (Eugene O'Neill, revival, CR, "Danny Zuko"): Alone at a Drive-In Movie; Summer Nights/WM: Jim Jacobs, Warren Casey.

479. Burrell Barbaretto (c 1877–Oct. 27, 1918) B: Ft. Wayne, IN. *Nearly a Hero* (Casino, "Fred Doolittle," Feb. 24, 1908): After Office Hours/W: Edward B. Claypoole, Will Heelan, M: Seymour Furth — I Don't Want to Marry You/WM: Edward B. Claypoole. *Tillie's Nightmare* (Herald Square, "Smiley Bragg," May 5, 1910): I Want to Bring You a Ring/WM: John L. Golden. *The Pearl Maiden* (New York, "Bob Norris," Jan. 22, 1912): If One Little Girl Loves Me; My Old Brass Band; You Can Never Tell Till You Try/W: Arthur F. Kales, Earle C. Anthony, M: Harry Auracher. *High Jinks* (Lyric > Casino, "Dick Wayne," Dec. 10, 1913): The Bubble; Chi-Chi; High Jinks; Is This Love at Last? [Jan. 26, 1914]; Love's Own Kiss; Something Seems Tingle-ingleing/W: Otto Harbach, M: Rudolf Friml. *Good Night, Paul* (Hudson, "Robert Hayward," Sept. 3, 1917): I've Given My Heart to You, Dear; Nothing Seems Right, Oh! the World Is All Wrong; Serenade/W: Roland Oliver, M: Harry B. Olsen.

480. Eileen Barbaris *West Side Story* (New York State, revival, "Francisca," June 24, 1968): I Feel Pretty/W: Stephen Sondheim, M: Leonard Bernstein.

481. Adrienne Barbeau (June 11, 1945–) B: Sacramento, CA. She played Carol on the TV sitcom *Maude* (1972). *Fiddler on the Roof* (Imperial, CR, "Hodel," Oct. 1968): Far from the Home I Love; Matchmaker, Matchmaker; Now I Have Everything/W: Sheldon Harnick, M: Jerry Bock. *Grease* (Broadhurst, "Betty Rizzo," June 7, 1972): Freddy, My Love; Look at Me, I'm Sandra Dee; There Are Worse Things I Could Do/WM: Jim Jacobs, Warren Casey.

482. Victor Barbee (1954–) B: Raleigh, NC. *Woman of the Year* (Palace, CR, "Alexi Petrikov," Feb. 1983): Happy in the Morning/W: Fred Ebb, M: John Kander.

483. Dorothy Barber *Betty Lee* (44th Street, "Maridetta," Dec. 25, 1924): Along the Rio Grande; Sweet Cactus Rose/ W: Otto Harbach, Irving Caesar, M: Louis A. Hirsch, Con Conrad. *Luckee Girl* (Casino, "Celina," Sept. 15, 1928): Hold Your Man/W: Max Lief, Nathaniel Lief, M: ?

484. Joan Barber *A Christmas Carol* (Madison Square Garden, return engagement, "Blind Hag" and "Scrooge's Mother," Nov. 22, 1996): God Bless Us, Every One; Nothing to Do with Me/W: Lynn Ahrens, M: Alan Menken.

485. James Barbour (Apr. 25, 1966–) B: Cherry Hill, NJ. *Carousel* (Lincoln Center, revival, CR, "Billy Bigelow," Dec. 1994): If I Loved You; Soliloquy/W: Oscar Hammerstein II, M: Richard Rodgers.

486. Joyce Barbour (Mar. 27, 1901–Mar. 14, 1977) B: Birmingham, England. *Sky High* (Shubert > Winter Garden > Casino, "Florence Horridge," Mar. 2, 1925): Give Your Heart in June Time/W: Clifford Grey, Harold Atteridge, M: Victor Herbert — Hello the Little Birds Have Flown; Intermezzo; The Letter Song; Sky High; Somewhere in Lovers' Land/W: Harold Atteridge, M: Robert Stolz. *Present Arms* (Mansfield, "Edna Stevens," Apr. 26, 1928): I'm a Fool, Little One; You Took Advantage of Me/W: Lorenz Hart, M: Richard Rodgers. *Spring Is Here* (Alvin, "Rita Conway," Mar. 11, 1929): You Never Say Yes/W: Lorenz Hart, M: Richard Rodgers. *Jonica* (Craig, "Fanny," Apr. 7, 1930): My Story Ends That Way; One Step Nearer the Moon; Tie Your Cares to a Melody/W: Billy Moll, M: Joseph Meyer — Tonight or Never/WM: William B. Friedlander.

487. Virginia Barbour *Naughty-Naught ('00)* (Old Knickerbocker Music Hall, revival, "Cathleen," Oct. 19, 1946): Zim-Zam-Zee/W: Ted Fetter, M: Richard Lewine.

488. Don Barclay (Dec. 26, 1892–Oct. 16, 1975) B: Ashland, OR. *Ziegfeld Follies of 1916* (New Amsterdam, revue, June 12, 1916): There's Ragtime in the Air/W: Gene Buck, M: Dave Stamper. *Go-Go* (Daly's, "Oswald Piper," Mar. 12, 1923): Uno/W: Alex Rogers, M: C. Luckeyth Roberts. *China Rose* (Martin Beck, CR, "Lo," Mar. 16, 1925): I'm Hi, I'm Lo; I'm No Butterfly/W: Harry L. Cort, George E. Stoddard, M: A. Baldwin Sloane. *Oh! Oh! Oh! Nurse* (Cosmopolitan, "I. Dye," Dec. 7, 1925): No, I Won't!; Who Bites the Holes in Schweitzer Cheese?/W: Monte Carlo, M: Alma Sanders. *Merry-Go-Round* (Klaw, revue, CR, May 31, 1927): In the Bathroom Tra La (Bathroom Tenor) [July 18, 1927]/W: Howard Dietz, M: Jay Gorney.

489. Paul Barclay *Carnival!* (New York City Center, revival, "Paul Berthalet," Dec. 12, 1968): Ev'rybody Likes You; Her Face; I've Got to Find a Reason; She's My Love/WM: Bob Merrill.

490. Edgar Nelson Barclift (Sept. 14, 1917–1993) B: Hopewell, VA. Actor, dancer, songwriter. At the time of the Berlin show, he was a Corporal in the U.S. Army. *This Is the Army* (Broadway, revue, July 4, 1942): I'm Getting Tired So I Can Sleep/WM: Irving Berlin.

491. Robert Bard *New Faces of 1936* (Vanderbilt, revue, May 19, 1936): Too Too Too!/W: Everett Marcy, M: Irvin Graham — You Better Go Now [June 15, 1936]/W: Bickley Reichner, M: Irvin Graham.

492. James Bardin *Blossom Time* (Jolson, revival, "Vogl," Mar. 8, 1926): Keep It Dark; My Springtime Thou Art; Serenade/W: Dorothy Donnelly, M: Sigmund Romberg.

493. Lenny Bari (Mar. 1, 1955–) B: Bronx, NY. *The Me Nobody Knows* (Longacre, CR, "Donald," Nov. 1971): I Love What the Girls Have; Jail-Life Walk/W: Will Holt, M: Gary William Friedman.

494. Christine Barker (Nov. 26–) B: Jacksonville, FL. She played Kristine in the original London production. *A Chorus Line* (Shubert, CR, "Kristine," Mar. 1979/Oct. 1981): Sing!/W: Edward Kleban, M: Marvin Hamlisch.

495. Irene Barker *Ziegfeld Midnight Frolic of 1919* (New Amsterdam roof, revue, Jan. 26, 1920): Under Cover/W: Gene Buck, M: Dave Stamper.

496. Jack (John) Barker (c 1895–July 18, 1950) *Sally* (New Amsterdam, "Harry Burton," Dec. 21, 1920): On with the Dance/W: Clifford Grey, M: Jerome Kern. *No, No, Nanette* (Globe, "Tom Trainor," Sept. 16, 1925): I'm Waiting for You/W: Otto Harbach, M: Vincent Youmans — Tea for Two/W: Irving Caesar, M: Vincent Youmans. *The Cocoanuts* (Lyric > Century, "Robert Adams," Dec. 8, 1925): A Little Bungalow; Lucky Boy; We Should Care; Why Do You Want to Know Why? [May 16, 1927]/WM: Irving Berlin. *The Love Call* (Majestic, "Lieut. Denton," Oct. 24, 1927): Eyes That Love; Good Pals; Hear the Trumpet Call; I Am Captured; The Ranger's Song/W: Harry B. Smith, M: Sigmund Romberg. *Follow Thru* (46th Street, "Jerry Downs," Jan. 9, 1929): He's a Man's Man; My Lucky Star; (If There Were) No More You; You Wouldn't Fool Me, Would You?/W: B.G. DeSylva, Lew Brown, M: Ray Henderson. *The Gang's All Here* (Imperial, "Andy Lennox," Feb. 18, 1931): How Can I Get Rid of Those Blues?; The Moon, the Wind and the Sea; Speaking of You; What Have You Done to Me?/W: Owen Murphy, Robert A. Simon, M: Lewis E. Gensler. *The Band Wagon* (New Amsterdam, revue, June 3, 1931): Dancing in the Dark; Nanette [Jan. 4,

1932]/W: Howard Dietz, M: Arthur Schwartz — High and Low/W: Howard Dietz, Desmond Carter, M: Arthur Schwartz. *Face the Music* (44th Street, return engagement, "Pat Mason, Jr.," Jan. 31, 1933): I Say It's Spinach; Let's Have Another Cup of Coffee; Manhattan Madness; On a Roof in Manhattan; Soft Lights and Sweet Music/WM: Irving Berlin.

497. Charles Barlow *New Faces of 1962* (Alvin, revue, Feb. 1, 1962): I Want You to Be the First to Know/W: June Carroll, M: Arthur Siegel.

498. Henry Clay Barnabee (Nov. 14, 1833–Dec. 16, 1917) B: Portsmouth, NH. The comedic member of the famed Boston Ideal Comic Opera Company, known as the Bostonians. His greatest role was as the Sheriff of Nottingham which he played about 2,000 times. *Robin Hood* (Standard, "Sheriff of Nottingham," Sept. 28, 1891): Churning, Churning; I Am the Sheriff of Nottingham; O, See the Lambkins Play!; Tinkers' Song; When a Peer Makes Love to a Damsel Fair/W: Harry B. Smith, M: Reginald De Koven. *The Serenade* (Knickerbocker, "Duke of Santa Cruz," Mar. 16, 1897): Dreaming, Dreaming; The Funny Side of That; Woman, Lovely Woman/W: Harry B. Smith, M: Victor Herbert. *The Viceroy* (Knickerbocker, "Viceroy of Sicily," Apr. 9, 1900): By This Sweet Token; I'm the Leader of Society; A Sailor's Life; So They Say/W: Harry B. Smith, M: Victor Herbert.

499. Ida Barnard *Marriage a la Carte* (Casino, "Primrose Farmilow," Jan. 2, 1911): Toddle Go the Girls/W: C.M.S. McLellan, M: Ivan Caryll.

500. Sophye Barnard (Feb. 23, 1888–?) B: Philadelphia, PA. *The Red Widow* (Astor, "Anna Varvara, the Red Widow," Nov. 6, 1911): The Avenue of Palms; I Love Love; In Society It's Always Dress Parade; Just for You; Soldiers of the Czar; When Woman Is the Question/W: Rennold Wolf, Channing Pollock, M: Charles J. Gebest. *The Man with Three Wives* (Weber and Fields, CR, "Colette," Jan. 27, 1913): Kisses That I Have Missed; Love's Flower Is Always Blooming; Lullaby; Rose of Yesterday; We Are Free; Woman of Temperament/W: Paul M. Potter, Harold Atteridge, M: Franz Lehar.

501. Charles Barnes *Murray Anderson's Almanac* (Erlanger's, revue, Aug. 14, 1929): Builders of Dreams/W: John Murray Anderson, M: Henry Sullivan — Same Old Moon/W: Clifford Orr, John Murray Anderson, M: Henry Sullivan — Wait for the Happy Ending/W: Jack Yellen, M: Milton Ager. *The Vanderbilt Revue* (Vanderbilt, revue, Nov. 5, 1930): Button Up

Your Heart/W: Dorothy Fields, M: Jimmy McHugh — Half Way to Heaven/W: David Sidney, M: Mario Braggiotti — I Give Myself Away/W: Edward Eliscu, M: Jacques Fray. *Babes in Toyland* (Imperial, revival, "Alan," Dec. 22, 1930): Before and After; Fioretta; Go to Sleep, Slumber Deep; I Can't Do the Sum; Song of the Poet (Rock-a-Bye Baby)/W: Glen MacDonough, M: Victor Herbert.

502. Cheryl Barnes *The Magic Show* (Cort, "Dina," May 28, 1974): Before Your Very Eyes; A Bit of Villainy; The Goldfarb Variations; Solid Silver Platform Shoes; Two's Company/WM: Stephen Schwartz.

503. Fred J. Barnes (May 1, 1884–Oct. 23, 1938) B: Birmingham, England. The baritone comedian toured variety theaters in Britain, Australia, South Africa and the U.S. Ill from alcoholism and TB, he committed suicide after publicity revealed that he was homosexual. *The District Leader* (Wallack's, "Mr. Partridge," Apr. 30, 1906): Old Broadway/WM: Joseph E. Howard.

504. Helen Barnes *Oh, My Dear!* (Princess, "Georgie Van Alstyne," Nov. 27, 1918): Ask Dad; Childhood Days/W: P.G. Wodehouse, M: Louis A. Hirsch.

505. Irving Barnes *Porgy and Bess* (Ziegfeld, revival, "Porgy," Mar. 10, 1953): Bess, You Is My Woman Now; I Got Plenty o' Nuttin'; I Loves You, Porgy/W: Ira Gershwin, DuBose Heyward, M: George Gershwin — Oh, Bess, Oh Where's My Bess?/W: Ira Gershwin, M: George Gershwin — They Pass By Singing/W: DuBose Heyward, M: George Gershwin. *Porgy and Bess* (New York City Center, revival, alt, "Porgy," May 17, 1961): same as above. *Porgy and Bess* (New York City Center, revival, alt, "Jake," May 17, 1961): It Takes a Long Pull to Get There; A Woman Is a Sometime Thing/W: DuBose Heyward, M: George Gershwin. *Porgy and Bess* (New York City Center, revival, alt, "Porgy," May 6, 1964): same as above. *Porgy and Bess* (New York City Center, revival, alt, "Jake," May 6, 1964): same as above. *Raisin* (46th Street, CR, "Bobo Jones," Oct. 1, 1974): Booze/W: Robert Brittan, M: Judd Woldin. *Wind in the Willows* (Nederlander, "Badger," Dec. 19, 1985): That's What Friends Are For/WM: Roger McGough, William Perry.

506. Mae Barnes (Jan. 23, 1907–Dec. 13, 1996) B: New York, NY. Known as "the bronze ANN PENNINGTON" because of her dancing, she, along with ELISABETH WELCH and others, introduced the Charleston to Broadway and became an international favorite of high society. After a car accident in 1938, she could no longer dance and turned to singing instead. *Runnin' Wild* (Colonial, revue, CR, "Miss Little Bit," Apr. 7, 1924): Charleston; Pay Day on the Levee/W: Cecil Mack, M: James P. Johnson. *Lucky Sambo* (Colonial, June 6, 1925): Charley from That Charleston Dancin' School/WM: Porter Grainger, Freddie Johnson. *Rang-Tang* (Royale, revue, July 12, 1927): Sammy and Topsy/W: Jo Trent, M: Ford Dabney. *Hot Rhythm* (Times Square > Waldorf, revue, Aug. 21, 1930): Say the Word That Will Make You Mine/W: Donald Heywood, M: Porter Grainger. *By the Beautiful Sea* (Majestic, "Ruby Monk," Apr. 8, 1954): Hang Up!; Happy Habit/W: Dorothy Fields, M: Arthur Schwartz.

507. Marcel Barnes *Broadway Brevities of 1920* (Winter Garden, revue, Sept. 29, 1920): We've Got the Stage Door Blues/W: Bert Kalmer, M: Harry Ruby.

508. Rob Barnes *Rock 'n Roll! The First 5,000 Years* (St. James, revue, Oct. 24, 1982): I'll Be There/WM: Hal Davis, Berry Gordy, Jr., Willie Hutch, Bob West — Say It Loud — I'm Black and I'm Proud/WM: James Brown, Alfred Ellis — Why Do Fools Fall in Love?/WM: Frank Lymon, Morris Levy.

509. Roy Barnes *The Student Prince* (Broadway, revival, "Detlef," June 8, 1943): Come Boys, Let's All Be Gay, Boys (Students' March Song); Drinking Song (Drink! Drink! Drink!); Serenade; Student Life; To the Inn We're Marching/W: Dorothy Donnelly, M: Sigmund Romberg. *Blossom Time* (Ambassador, revival, "Vogl," Sept. 4, 1943): Keep It Dark; My Springtime Thou Art; Serenade/W: Dorothy Donnelly, M: Sigmund Romberg.

510. Thomas Roy Barnes (Aug. 11, 1880– Mar. 30, 1937) B: Lincolnshire, England. He came to the U.S. as a child. M: BESSIE CRAWFORD, his vaudeville partner. *The Passing Show of 1914* (Winter Garden > Lyric, revue, June 10, 1914): The Crinoline Girl/W: Harold Atteridge, M: Sigmund Romberg.

511. Art Barnett *Annie Get Your Gun* (Imperial, "Foster Wilson," May 16, 1946): Doin' What Comes Natur'lly/WM: Irving Berlin. *How to Succeed in Business Without Really Trying* (New York City Center, revival, "Bratt," Apr. 20, 1966): Brotherhood of Man; I Believe in You; A Secretary Is Not a Toy/WM: Frank Loesser.

512. Eileen Barnett (May 8–) B: Chicago, IL. *Nine* (46th Street, CR, "Luisa," Nov. 1983): Be on Your Own; My Husband Makes Movies/WM: Maury Yeston.

513. Ken Barnett *A Christmas Carol* (Paramount Madison Square Garden, return engagement, "Young Marley" and "Undertaker," Nov. 20, 1995): Dancing on Your Grave; The Lights of Long Ago/W: Lynn Ahrens, M: Alan Menken. *A Christmas Carol* (Madison Square Garden, return engagement, "Young Marley" and "Undertaker," Nov. 22, 1996): same as above.

514. Lee Barnett *Bless You All* (Mark Hellinger, revue, Dec. 14, 1950): Just a Little White House/WM: Harold Rome.

515. Mary Barnett *Tattle Tales* (Broadhurst, revue, June 1, 1933): Jig Saw Jamboree/W: William Walsh, M: Eddie Bienbryer — Sing American Tunes/W: Frank Fay, William Walsh, M: Edward Ward — You Gotta Do Better Than That/WM: ?.

516. Nancy Barnett *Bitter Sweet* (Ziegfeld, "Freda," Nov. 5, 1929): Ladies of the Town/WM: Noel Coward.

517. Nate Barnett (c 1940–May 29, 1988) *Don't Play Us Cheap!* (Ethel Barrymore, "Rat," May 16, 1972): Some Days It Seems That It Just Don't Even Pay to Get Out of Bed/WM: Melvin Van Peebles. *Ride the Winds* (Bijou, "Joshu," May 16, 1974): Flower Song; The Gentle Buffoon; Those Who Speak/WM: John Driver. *A Broadway Musical* (Lunt-Fontanne, "Policeman," Dec. 21, 1978): Broadway, Broadway/W: Lee Adams, M: Charles Strouse.

518. Zoe Barnett *All Aboard* (44th Street roof garden, revue, "Marime Sinkavitch," June 5, 1913): Sarafina/WM: Joaquin Valverde. *The Debutante* (Knickerbocker, "Irma," Dec. 7, 1914): When I Played Carmen/W: Robert B. Smith, M: Victor Herbert. *Jim Jam Jems* (Cort, "Rosie Robbins," Oct. 4, 1920): They're Making Them Wonderful; When the Right Little Girl Comes Along/W: Harry L. Cort, George E. Stoddard, M: James F. Hanley. *The Rose Girl* (Ambassador, "Nadine Bankoff," Feb. 11, 1921): Flirtation Quartette; Lingerie; That's Me/W: William Cary Duncan, M: Anselm Goetzel. *Blossom Time* (Ambassador, "Bellabruna," Sept. 29, 1921): Keep It Dark; Let Me Awake; Melody Triste/W: Dorothy Donnelly, M: Sigmund Romberg.

519. Charles Baron *Just Fancy* (Casino, "Bobby Vanderpool," Oct. 11, 1927): Ain't Love Grand; You Came Along/W: Leo Robin, M: Joseph Meyer, Phil Charig. *Treasure Girl* (Alvin, Nov. 8, 1928): Got a Rainbow/W: Ira Gershwin, M: George Gershwin.

520. Christy Baron *Les Miserables* (Broadway, CR, "Fantine"): Come to Me; I Dreamed a Dream/W: Herbert Kretzmer, M: Claude-Michel Schonberg.

521. Evalyn Baron (Apr. 21, 1948–) B: Atlanta, GA. *Fearless Frank* (Princess, "Mrs. Mayhew" and "Mrs. Clapton" and "Mrs. Clayton," June 15, 1980): My Own, or True Love at Last; Oh, Catch Me, Mr. Harris, Cause I'm Falling for You!; Oh, Mr. Harris, You're a Naughty Naughty Man!/W: Andrew Davies, M: Dave Brown. *Les Miserables* (Broadway, CR, "Mme. Thenardier," Jan. 15, 1990): Beggars at the Feast; Master of the House; Thenardier Waltz/W: Herbert Kretzmer, M: Claude-Michel Schonberg.

522. Irina Baronova (Mar. 13, 1919–) B: Petrograd, Russia. At 14, she became prima ballerina of the original Ballet Russe de Monte Carlo. *Follow the Girls* (New Century > 44th Street, "Anna Viskinova," Apr. 8, 1944): Where You Are/W: Dan Shapiro, Milton Pascal, M: Phil Charig.

523. Edith Barr *The Liberty Belles* (Madison Square, "Ethel Love," Sept. 30, 1901): Lesson Book Song/W: ?, M: Aimee Lachaume.

524. Edna Barr *Africana* (Daly's > National, revue, July 11, 1927): Clorinda [Aug. 1927]/WM: Donald Heywood.

525. Sydney Barraclough (Aug. 9, 1869– Mar. 1930) B: York, England. *The Little Duchess* (Casino, "Capt. Ralph Edgerton," Oct. 14, 1901): Violets/W: Julian Fane, M: Ellen Wright. *Florodora* (Winter Garden, CR, "Frank Abercoed," Jan. 27, 1902): The Shade of the Palm/W: Owen Hall, M: Leslie Stuart — Somebody/WM: ?.

526. Augustus Barratt *Lady Teazle* (Casino, "Sir Benjamin Backbite," Dec. 24, 1904): Here's to a Bashful Girl of Fifteen; Macaronis We/W: John Kendrick Bangs, M: A. Baldwin Sloane.

527. Gabriel Barre (Aug. 26, 1957–) B: Brattleboro, VT. *Ain't Broadway Grand* (Lunt-Fontanne, "Marvin Fischbein," Apr. 18, 1993): Ain't Broadway Grand; The Theater, the Theater/W: Lee Adams, M: Mitch Leigh.

528. Stella Barre *All Aboard* (44th Street roof garden, revue, CR, "Alice Brown," 1913): Over the Ocean; Tulip Time/WM: E. Ray Goetz, Malvin F. Franklin.

529. Brent Barrett (Feb. 28, 1957–) B: Quinter KS. *Dance a Little Closer* (Minskoff, "Charles Castleton," May 11, 1983): I Don't Know; Why Can't the World Go and Leave Us Alone?/W: Alan Jay Lerner, M: Charles Strouse. *Grand Hotel* (Martin Beck, CR, "Baron Felix Von Gaigern," May 8, 1990): As It Should Be; Fire and Ice/WM: Robert Wright, George Forrest, Maury Yeston — Love Can't Happen; Roses at the Station/WM: Maury Yeston.

530. Fenton Barrett *My Maryland* (Al Jolson, CR, "Edgar Strong," Mar. 26, 1928): Boys in Gray; The Mocking Bird; Strolling with the One I Love the Best/W: Dorothy Donnelly, M: Sigmund Romberg. *The DuBarry* (George M. Cohan, "Prince de Soubise," Nov. 22, 1932): Pantalettes/W: Rowland Leigh, M: Carl Millocker.

531. Helen Barrett *Hip! Hip! Hooray!* (Music Hall, revue, "Erminie Rellick," Oct. 10, 1907): Let's Wander Off Nowhere/W: Edgar Smith, M: Gus Edwards.

532. James Barrett *Strut Miss Lizzie* (Times Square, revue, June 19, 1922): Crooning; I Love Sweet Angeline; Mandy; Wyoming Lullaby/WM: Henry Creamer, Turner Layton.

533. Louise Barrett *Lovely Lady* (Sam H. Harris, "Desiree," Dec. 29, 1927): At the Barbecue/W: Harry A. Steinberg, Edward Ward, M: Dave Stamper, Harold A. Levey — The Lost Step; Make Believe You're Happy/W: Cyrus D. Wood, M: Dave Stamper, Harold A. Levey.

534. Mace Barrett *The Girls Against the Boys* (Alvin, revue, Nov. 2, 1959): The Girls Against the Boys; Where Did We Go? Out/W: Arnold B. Horwitt, M: Richard Lewine. *La Cage aux Folles* (Palace, CR, "Georges," Nov. 19, 1987): Cocktail Counterpoint; Look Over There; Masculinity; Song on the Sand; With You On My Arm/WM: Jerry Herman.

535. Nancy Barrett (Oct. 5, 1943–) B: Shreveport, LA. *Pickwick* (46th Street, "Mary," Oct. 4, 1965): A Gentleman's Gentleman/W: Leslie Bricusse, M: Cyril Ornadel.

536. Pauline Barrett *Hip! Hip! Hooray!* (Music Hall, revue, "Georgette Marion," Oct. 10, 1907): same as HELEN BARRETT.

537. Sondra Barrett *Pal Joey* (Ethel Barrymore > Shubert > St. James, "The Kid," Dec. 25, 1940): You Mustn't Kick It Around/W: Lorenz Hart, M: Richard Rodgers. *New Faces of 1943* (Ritz, revue, CR, Feb. 28, 1943): Animals Are Nice/W: J.B. Rosenberg, M: Lee Wainer — New Shoes/W: June Carroll, M: Will Irwin — Richard Crudnut's Charm School/W: June Carroll, John Lund, M: Lee Wainer.

538. Ann Barrie *Music in the Air* (Alvin > 44th Street, CR, "Sieglinde Lessing," Mar. 1933): I've Told Ev'ry Little Star; Prayer (Our Journey May Be Long); We Belong Together; When the Spring Is in the Air/W: Oscar Hammerstein II, M: Jerome Kern. *Saluta* (Imperial, "Eleanor Bradley," Aug. 28, 1934): La Vita; Night; You Have My Heart/W: Will Morissey, M: Frank D'Armond — We, Incorporated/W: Maurice Sigler, Milton Berle, M: Frank D'Armond. *White Horse Inn* (Center, CR, "Natalie," Feb. 1937): Blue Eyes/W: Irving Caesar, M: Robert Stolz — We Prize Most the Things We Miss/W: Irving Caesar, M: Ralph Benatzky — White Sails/W: Irving Caesar, M: Vivian Ellis.

539. Barbara Barrie (May 23, 1931–) B: Chicago, IL. She played Elizabeth on the TV sitcom *Barney Miller* (1975). *Company* (Alvin, "Sarah," Apr. 26, 1970): Poor Baby/WM: Stephen Sondheim.

540. Gracie Barrie (c 1917–) M: Dick Stabile, orchestra leader and saxophonist. She was a vocalist with his band, and fronted for him in 1942 when he went into the service. *Strike Me Pink* (Majestic, revue, Mar. 4, 1933): It's Great to Be Alive/W: Lew Brown, M: Ray Henderson. *George White's Scandals of 1936* (New Amsterdam, revue, Dec. 25, 1935): Anything Can Happen/W: Jack Yellen, Ballard Macdonald, M: Ray Henderson — I'm the Fellow Who Loves You; I've Got to Get Hot; Life Begins at Sweet Sixteen/W: Jack Yellen, M: Ray Henderson. *The Show Is On* (Winter Garden, revue, Dec. 25, 1936): By Strauss/W: Ira Gershwin, M: George Gershwin — Casanova; Now/W: Ted Fetter, M: Vernon Duke — Long as You've Got Your Health/W: E.Y. Harburg, Norman Zeno, M: Will Irwin — The Show Is On/W: Ted Fetter, M: Hoagy Carmichael. *Crazy with the Heat* (44th Street, revue, Jan. 14, 1941): Crazy with the Heat/W: Irvin Graham, M: Rudi Revil — It Should Happen to Me/W: Richard Kollmar, M: Elsie Thompson — Time of Your Life/W: Peter K. Smith, M: William Provost — Yes, My Darling Daughter/WM: Jack Lawrence.

541. Lee Barrie *Of V We Sing* (Concert, revue, Feb. 11, 1942): Sisters Under the Skin/W: Sylvia Marks, M: Baldwin Bergersen — You've Got to Appease with a Strip Tease/W: Lewis Allan, M: Toby Sacher.

542. Nigel Barrie (Feb. 5, 1889–Oct. 8, 1971) B: Calcutta, India. *The Laughing Husband* (Knickerbocker, "Hans Zimt," Feb. 2, 1914): Bought and Paid For; You're Here and I'm Here/W: Harry B. Smith, M: Jerome Kern. *The Queen of the Movies* (Globe, CR, "Baron Victor de Gardennes," Mar. 23, 1914): Forgive and Forget; Who Is to Know?/W: Edward A. Paulton, M: Jean Gilbert.

543. Anthony Barrile *The Who's Tommy* (St. James, "Cousin Kevin," Apr. 22, 1993): Cousin Kevin/WM: John Entwistle — Pinball Wizard; Sally Simpson/WM: Pete Townshend.

544. Michael Barriskill *Cats* (Winter Garden, CR, "Mistoffolees," c 1988): The Invitation to the Jellicle Ball; Mr. Mistoffolees;

Mungojerrie and Rumpleteazer/W: T.S. Eliot, M: Andrew Lloyd Webber.

545. Mabel Barrison (1882–Oct. 31, 1912) B: Toronto, Canada. M: JOSEPH E. HOWARD. *Babes in Toyland* (Majestic, "Jane," Oct. 13, 1903): Go to Sleep, Slumber Deep!; I Can't Do the Sum/W: Glen MacDonough, M: Victor Herbert. *The Land of Nod* (New York, "Bonnie," Apr. 1, 1907): Cross Your Heart; Love Is Contagious; The Same Old Moon; You Look Awful Good to Father/W: Will M. Hough, Frank R. Adams, M: Joseph E. Howard.

546. David Barron (May 11, 1938–) B: Pilot Point, TX. *Sweeney Todd* (Circle in the Square, revival, "Judge Turpin," Sept. 14, 1989): Ladies in Their Sensitivities; Pretty Women/WM: Stephen Sondheim.

547. Judith Barron *Ziegfeld Follies of 1934* (Winter Garden, revue, Jan. 4, 1934): I Like the Likes of You/W: E.Y. Harburg, M: Vernon Duke — A Sidewalk in Paris; That's Where We Come In/W: E.Y. Harburg, M: Samuel Pokrass.

548. Julia Barron *Nikki* (Longacre, "Entertainer," Sept. 29, 1931): My Heart Is Calling/W: James Dyrenforth, M: Phil Charig.

549. William Barrows *The Lady from Lane's* (Lyric > Casino, "Front," Aug. 19, 1907): I Never Do It Now/W: George Broadhurst, M: Gustave Kerker.

550. Bobby Barry (Oct. 1886–Mar. 23, 1964) B: Brooklyn, NY. Brother of CHARLES BARRY and LYDIA BARRY. *Foxy Grandpa* (14th Street, "Bunt," Feb. 17, 1902): The Bathing Lesson/WM: Joseph Hart — The Story of Two Bad Boys; The Submarine Boat/WM: Joseph Hart, R. Melville Baker. *A Stubborn Cinderella* (Broadway, CR, "Skeeter," Mar. 22, 1909): If They'd Only Left Poor Adam's Rib Alone; I'm in Love with All the Girls I Know/W: Will M. Hough, Frank R. Adams, M: Joseph E. Howard.

551. Charles Barry (June 9, 1876–Jan. 22, 1914) B: New York, NY. *Wonderland* (Majestic, "Capt. Montague Blue," Oct. 24, 1905): The Crew of the Peek-a-Boo; The Ossified Man/W: Glen MacDonough, M: Victor Herbert.

552. Fred Barry (?–Aug. 17, 1964) B: England. Known as The Barrys, he and wife Elaine danced together in New York nightclubs before he entered the theater. She was killed in a car crash in 1948. *Up in Central Park* (Century, "Joe Stewart," Jan. 27, 1945): Currier and Ives; The Fireman's Bride; Rip Van Winkle/W: Dorothy Fields, M: Sigmund Romberg.

553. Gene Barry (June 14, 1919–) B: New York, NY. Leading man in forgettable films. On TV, however, he starred on *Bat Masterson* (1959) and *Burke's Law* (1963). *The Merry Widow* (Majestic, revival, "Novakovich," Aug. 4, 1943): Women/W: Adrian Ross, M: Franz Lehar. *Happy as Larry* (Coronet, "The Doctor," Jan. 6, 1950): A Cup of Tea; It's Pleasant and Delightful; Mrs. Larry, Tell Me This; Oh, Mrs. Larry/ W: Donagh MacDonagh, M: Mischa Portnoff, Wesley Portnoff. *La Cage aux Folles* (Palace, "Georges," Aug. 21, 1983/Feb. 27, 1984): Cocktail Counterpoint; Look Over There; Masculinity; Song on the Sand; With You on My Arm/ WM: Jerry Herman.

554. Jimmie Barry M: MRS. JIMMIE BARRY *Our Nell* (Nora Bayes, "Peleg Doolittle," Dec. 4, 1922): Gol Durn!; Names I Love to Hear/W: Brian Hooker, M: George Gershwin, William Daly.

555. Joan Barry (Nov. 5, 1901–Apr.10, 1989) B: England. *You'll See Stars* (Maxine Elliott, revue, "Martha," Dec 29, 1942): Time and Time Again/W: Herman Timberg, M: Leo Edwards.

556. John Barry (June 13, 1915–) B: Amsterdam, NY. *Follow the Girls* (44th Street > Broadhurst, CR, "Bob Monroe," Apr. 1, 1945): John Paul Jones; Today Will Be Yesterday Tomorrow; Where You Are/W: Dan Shapiro, Milton Pascal, M: Phil Charig.

557. Katie Barry *A Chinese Honeymoon* (Casino, "Fi Fi," June 2, 1902): I Want to Be a Laidy/W: George Dance, M: George Dee — Martha Spanks the Grand Pianner/W: George Dance, M: Howard Talbot — The Twiddley Bits/W: George Dance, H. Adams, M: Ernie Woodville. *Fantana* (Lyric, "Jessie," Jan. 14, 1905): Darby and Joan; Drop In on Me at Luncheon; My Word/W: Robert B. Smith, M: Raymond Hubbell.

558. Lee Barry *The Conquering Hero* (ANTA, "Doorman," Jan. 16, 1961): Girls! Girls!/W: Norman Gimbel, M: Moose Charlap.

559. Lydia Barry (c 1876–July 3, 1932) B: New York, NY. Sister of BOBBY BARRY and CHARLES BARRY *The Revue of Revues* (Winter Garden, revue, Sept. 27, 1911): (I Met You in) Pittsburgh, PA/W: Harold Atteridge, M: Louis A. Hirsch.

560. Mrs. Jimmie Barry M: JIMMIE BARRY. *Our Nell* (Nora Bayes, "Malvina Holcombe," Dec. 4, 1922): Little Villages; Names I Love to Hear/W: Brian Hooker, M: George Gershwin, William Daly.

561. Raymond J. Barry (Mar. 14, 1939–) B: Hempstead, NY. *Happy End* (Martin Beck, revival, "Baby Face Flint," May 7, 1977): The Bilbao Song/W: Bertolt Brecht, M: Kurt Weill.

562. Tom Barry *Earl Carroll's Sketch Book of* *1935* (Winter Garden > Majestic, revue, CR, June 24, 1935/Sept. 16, 1935): Anna Louise of Louisiana/W: Norman Zeno, M: Will Irwin — At Last/W: Charles Tobias, Sam M. Lewis, M: Henry Tobias — The Day You Were Born [Oct. 14, 1935]/WM: Edward Heyman, Dana Suesse — Silhouettes Under the Stars; Through These Portals Pass the Most Beautiful Girls in the World/W: Charles Newman, Charles Tobias, M: Murray Mencher — There's Music in a Kiss/ WM: Abner Silver, Al Lewis, Al Sherman.

563. Chick Barrymore *Hello, Alexander* (44th Street, "Gloria Carter," Oct. 7, 1919): Baseball/W: Alfred Bryan, M: Jean Schwartz.

564. John Barrymore (Feb. 15, 1882–May 29, 1942) B: Philadelphia, PA. The great Shakespearian actor wasted much of his life and talent on alcohol and womanizing. He starred in a silent film version of *Dr. Jekyll and Mr. Hyde* (1921). *A Stubborn Cinderella* (Broadway, "Mac," Jan. 25, 1909): If They'd Only Left Poor Adam's Rib Alone/W: Will M. Hough, Frank R. Adams, M: Joseph E. Howard.

565. Delight Barsch *Love's Lottery* (Broadway, "Sally Lunn," Oct. 3, 1904): Hoax and Coax/W: Stanislaus Stange, M: Julian Edwards.

566. Barbara Barsky (July 7, 1955–) B: Winnipeg, Canada. *Anne of Green Gables* (City Center 55th Street, "Josie Pye," Dec. 21, 1971): Did You Hear?/WM: Donald Harron, Norman Campbell.

567. Roger Bart (Sept. 29, 1962–) B: Norwalk, CT. *Big River: The Adventures of Huckleberry Finn* (Eugene O'Neill, "Tom Sawyer," Apr. 7, 1987): The Boys; Hand for the Hog/WM: Roger Miller.

568. Jean Bartel She was Miss America of 1943. *The Desert Song* (New York City Center, revival, "Clementina," Jan. 8, 1946): My Little Castagnette; One Good Man Gone Wrong; Song of the Brass Key/W: Otto Harbach, Oscar Hammerstein II, M: Sigmund Romberg.

569. Louis John Bartels (Oct. 19, 1895– Mar. 4, 1932) B: Bunker Hill, IL. He played in vaudeville with DELYLE ALDA. *The 5 O'Clock Girl* (44th Street, "Hudgins," Oct. 10, 1927): Any Little Thing/W: Bert Kalmar, M: Harry Ruby.

570. Fred Barth *Manhattan Mary* (Apollo, Sept. 26, 1927): Memories/W: B.G. DeSylva, Lew Brown, M: Ray Henderson.

571. Perle Barti *The Baron Trenck* (Casino, "Mariza," Mar. 11, 1912): Cupid Is a Cruel Master/W: Henry Blossom, M: Alfred G. Robyn — I'd Like to Be a Soldier Gay; I'm from the Court of the Empress Queen; This Handsome Soldier

Is Too Bold/W: Frederick F. Schrader, M: Felix Albini. *The Rose Maid* (Globe, CR, "Daphne," July 1, 1912): I Live for You Alone; Now His Choice We See; Roses Bloom for Lovers; When Two Little Hearts Beat Together/W: Robert B. Smith, M: Bruno Granichstaedten — A Yankee Millionairess/W: Raymond W. Peck, M: Robert Hood Bowers.

572. Josephine Bartlett (c 1862–Oct. 13, 1910) B: Morris, IL. *The Viceroy* (Knickerbocker, "Ortensia," Apr. 9, 1900): By This Sweet Token; On My Nuptial Day; One Fellow's Joy Is Another Fellow's Woe/W: Harry B. Smith, M: Victor Herbert. *Babette* (Broadway, "Eva," Nov. 16, 1903): My Lady of the Manor; There Once Was an Owl; To the Sound of the Pipe and the Roll of the Drum/W: Harry B. Smith, M: Victor Herbert. *Mlle. Modiste* (Knickerbocker, "Mme. Cecelie," Dec. 25, 1905): When the Cat's Away the Mice Will Play/W: Henry Blossom, M: Victor Herbert.

573. Michael Bartlett (Aug. 25, 1901–?) B: North Oxford, MA. He sang in theater, concerts, film and opera. A Princeton graduate, he started the racoon coat craze of the 1920s. *Through the Years* (Manhattan, "Kenneth Wayne" and "Jeremiah Wayne," Jan. 28, 1932): I'll Come Back to You; Kathleen, Mine/W: Edward Heyman, M: Vincent Youmans. *The Cat and the Fiddle* (Globe, CR, "Victor Florescu," Aug. 1932): The Breeze Kissed Your Hair; A New Love Is Old; One Moment Alone/W: Otto Harbach, M: Jerome Kern. *Three Waltzes* (Majestic, "Count Rudolph Von Hohenbrunn" and "Count Max Von Hohenbrunn," Dec. 25, 1937): Do You Recall?; Maytime in the Air/W: Clare Kummer, M: based on Johann Strauss, Sr. — The Only One; To Love Is to Live/W: Clare Kummer, M: based on Johann Strauss, Jr. — Our Last Valse/W: Clare Kummer, M: Oscar Straus. *Follies* (Winter Garden, "Roscoe," Apr. 4, 1971): Beautiful Girls/WM: Stephen Sondheim.

574. Peter Bartlett (Aug. 28, 1942–) B: Chicago, IL. *Beauty and the Beast* (Palace, CR, "Cogsworth," c 1995): Be Our Guest; Something There/W: Howard Ashman, M: Alan Menken.

575. Richard Bartlett *The Only Girl* (39th Street > Lyric, "Sylvester Martin [Corksey]," Nov. 2, 1914): Be Happy, Boys, Tonight; Connubial Bliss; When You're Wearing the Ball and the Chain/W: Henry Blossom, M: Victor Herbert.

576. Betty Lou Barto Sister of NANCY WALKER. *As the Girls Go* (Winter Garden > Broadway, "Mickey Wellington," Nov. 13, 1948):

It's More Fun Than a Picnic/W: Harold Adamson, M: Jimmy McHugh.

577. Dianne Barton *Man of La Mancha* (Vivian Beaumont, revival, "Antonia," June 22, 1972): I'm Only Thinking of Him/W: Joe Darion, M: Mitch Leigh.

578. Eileen Barton (Nov. 24, 1929–) B: New York, NY. *Angel in the Wings* (Coronet, revue, Dec. 11, 1947): Holler Blue Murder; If It Were Easy to Do; Tambourine/WM: Bob Hilliard, Carl Sigman.

579. James Barton (Nov. 1, 1890–Feb. 19, 1962) B: Gloucester, NJ. A star of his era, the singer, actor and clog dancer was on stage from the age of 2. He became known in burlesque and vaudeville for his imitations of drunks. *The Passing Show of 1919* (Winter Garden, revue, Oct. 23, 1919): A la Hockey; Shimmy a la Egyptian/W: Harold Atteridge, M: Sigmund Romberg, Jean Schwartz. *The Last Waltz* (Century, "Matt Maltby," May 10, 1921): The Charming Ladies/W: Harold Atteridge, M: Alfred Goodman — Ladies' Choice/WM: ?. *The Mimic World* (Century roof, revue, Aug. 17, 1921): Ma Femme; Mighty Like a Rosenbloom/WM: ? — Rose of the Rotisserie/W: Joe Goodwin, James Hussey, M: James F. Hanley. *The Rose of Stamboul* (Century, "Bob," Mar. 7, 1922): Little Blue Book of Girls/W: Harold Atteridge, M: Leo Fall — Mazuma/W: Harold Atteridge, M: Sigmund Romberg — Ting-a-ling/W: Harold Atteridge, M: Sigmund Romberg, Leo Fall — Why Do They Die at the End of a Classical Dance?/W: William Jerome, Alex Gerber, M: Jean Schwartz. *Dew Drop Inn* (Astor, "Ananias Washington," May 17, 1923): Porter! Porter!; The Struttingest Strutter; Travesty; You Can't Experiment on Me/W: Cyrus D. Wood, M: Alfred Goodman. *Sweet and Low* (46th Street > 44th Street, revue, Nov. 17, 1930): Dancing with Tears in Their Eyes/W: Mort Dixon, Billy Rose, M: Will Irwin. *Bright Lights of 1944* (Forrest, revue, Sept. 16, 1943): Damned Ole Jeeter/W: George Blake, M: Dick Liebert — I Can't Give You Anything but Love/W: Dorothy Fields, M: Jimmy McHugh. *Paint Your Wagon* (Shubert, "Ben Rumson," Nov. 12, 1951): I Still See Elisa; Wand'rin Star; Whoop-ti-ay!/W: Alan Jay Lerner, M: Frederick Loewe.

580. Marion Barton *Blossom Time* (Ambassador, CR, "Kitzi," Aug. 7, 1922): Love Is a Riddle; Peace to My Lonely Heart; Three Little Maids/W: Dorothy Donnelly, M: Sigmund Romberg.

581. Ottilia Barton *The Rose of Stamboul* (Century, "Saada," Mar. 7, 1922): Ting-a-ling/

W: Harold Atteridge, M: Sigmund Romberg, Leo Fall.

582. Steve Barton (June 26, 1954–July 21, 2001) B: Hot Springs, AR. He grew up in Nederland, TX. He originated the role of Raoul and was the first understudy for the Phantom. *The Phantom of the Opera* (Majestic, "Raoul, Vicomte de Chagny," Jan. 26, 1988): All I Ask of You; Bravo, Bravo; Little Lotte; The Mirror; Notes; Prima Donna; Raoul, I've Been There; Think of Me; Twisted Every Way; Wandering Child; Why Have You Brought Me Here/W: Charles Hart, Richard Stilgoe, M: Andrew Lloyd Webber. *The Phantom of the Opera* (Majestic, CR, "The Phantom of the Opera," Mar. 19, 1990): All I Ask of You; Bravo, Bravo; I Remember; Little Lotte; The Mirror; The Music of the Night; Notes; Prima Donna; The Point of No Return; Stranger Than You Dreamt It; Twisted Every Way; Wandering Child/W: Charles Hart, Richard Stilgoe, M: Andrew Lloyd Webber — The Phantom of the Opera/W: Mike Batt, Richard Stilgoe, M: Andrew Lloyd Webber. *The Red Shoes* (Gershwin, "Boris Lermontov," Dec. 16, 1993): Am I to Wish Her Love; Come Home; Impresario; It's a Fairy Tale; Miss Page; Top of the Sky; When You Dance for a King/W: Bob Merrill, M: Jule Styne.

583. Annabelle Bascom *Cohan and Harris Minstrels* (New York, revue, Aug. 16, 1909): The Gibson Coon; Oh! You Coon/WM: George M. Cohan.

584. George Basely *Chu Chin Chow* (Manhattan Opera House > Century, "Nur Al-Huda," Oct. 22, 1917): Corraline/W: Oscar Asche, M: Frederic Norton — I Love You So/W: Hartley Carrick, M: Frederic Norton.

585. Phyllis Bash *Porgy and Bess* (Uris, revival, "Bess," Sept. 25, 1976): Bess, You Is My Woman Now; I Loves You, Porgy/W: Ira Gershwin, DuBose Heyward, M: George Gershwin — Leavin' fo' de Promis' Lan'; What You Want wid Bess?/W: DuBose Heyward, M: George Gershwin — There's a Boat Dat's Leavin' Soon for New York/W: Ira Gershwin, M: George Gershwin.

586. Charles Basile *Pal Joey* (New York City Center, revival, "Victor," May 29, 1963): That Terrific Rainbow/W: Lorenz Hart, M: Richard Rodgers.

587. Philip Michael Baskerville *Cats* (Winter Garden, CR, "Plato" and "Macavity," c 1994): The Awefull Battle of the Pekes and Pollicles; Macavity; The Marching Songs of the Pollicle Dogs/W: T.S. Eliot, M: Andrew Lloyd Webber.

588. Priscilla Baskerville B: Brooklyn, NY.

Sophisticated Ladies (Lunt-Fontanne, revue, Mar. 1, 1981): Drop Me Off in Harlem/W: Nick Kenny, M: Duke Ellington — My Love/WM: Duke Ellington — Solitude/W: Eddie DeLange, Irving Mills, M: Duke Ellington. *Porgy and Bess* (Radio City Music Hall, revival, alt, "Clara," Apr. 7, 1983): Summertime/W: DuBose Heyward, M: George Gershwin. *Porgy and Bess* (Radio City Music Hall, revival, alt, "Bess," Apr. 7, 1983): Bess, You Is My Woman Now; I Loves You, Porgy/W: Ira Gershwin, DuBose Heyward, M: George Gershwin — Leavin' fo' de Pomis' Lan'; What You Want Wid Bess?/W: DuBose Heyward, M: George Gershwin — There's a Boat Dat's Leavin' Soon for New York/W: Ira Gershwin, M: George Gershwin.

589. Jimmy Baskette (James Baskett) (Feb. 16, 1904–July 9, 1948) B: Indianapolis, IN. Immortalized as Uncle Remus in Disney's animated and live action film *Song of the South* (1946). *Hot Chocolates* (Hudson, revue, June 20, 1929): Goddess of Rain; That Rhythm Man/W: Andy Razaf, M: Fats Waller, Harry Brooks — Redskinland/W: Andy Razaf, M: Fats Waller — The Unloaded Gun/WM: ?. *Blackbirds of 1930* (Royale, revue, Oct. 22, 1930): Blackbirds on Parade; You're Lucky to Me [Nov. 17, 1930]/W: Andy Razaf, M: Eubie Blake.

590. Johnsie Bason *Nellie Bly* (Adelphi, "Singer," Jan. 21, 1946): How About a Date?/W: Johnny Burke, M: James Van Heusen.

591. Paul Bass *My Magnolia* (Mansfield, revue, "Harvey," July 8, 1926): My Magnolia/W: Alex Rogers, M: C. Luckeyth Roberts. *Africana* (Daly's > National, revue, July 11, 1927): Clorinda [Aug. 1927]/WM: Donald Heywood. *Hot Chocolates* (Hudson, revue, June 20, 1929): Ain't Misbehavin'; Sweet Savannah Sue/W: Andy Razaf, M: Fats Waller, Harry Brooks.

592. Edward Basse *When Johnny Comes Marching Home* (New Amsterdam > Manhattan Opera House, revival, "Col. John Graham aka John Johnson [Johnny]," May 7, 1917): Flag of My Country; Katie, My Southern Rose; Love's Night; My Own United States; The Suwanee River; Who Knows?/W: Stanislaus Stange, M: Julian Edwards. *Girl o' Mine* (Bijou, CR, "Teddy," Mar. 4, 1918): Girl o' Mine/W: Philip Bartholomae, M: Frank Tours — Omar Khayyam/W: Harold Atteridge, M: Sigmund Romberg.

593. Stephanie Bast (Oct. 4, 1972–) B: Seoul, Korea. *A Christmas Carol* (Paramount Madison Square Garden, return engagement, "Sally," Nov. 20, 1995): Christmas Together/W: Lynn Ahrens, M: Alan Menken.

594. Dorothy Bate *Criss Cross* (Globe, "Goldie Digger," Oct. 12, 1926): The Ali Baba Babies/W: Anne Caldwell, Otto Harbach, M: Jerome Kern.

595. Tom Bate (c 1900–1985) *Where's Charley?* (New York City Center, revival, "Brassett," May 25, 1966): The New Ashmoleon Marching Society and Students Conservatory Band; Where's Charley?/WM: Frank Loesser.

596. Charles H. Bates *Foxy Grandpa* (14th Street, "Pietro," Feb. 17, 1902): Napoli/WM: Joseph Hart.

597. Edna Bates *The Lady of the Slipper* (Globe, "Irma," Oct. 28, 1912): Fond of the Ladies/W: James O'Dea, M: Victor Herbert. *Jack O'Lantern* (Globe, "Janet," Oct. 16, 1917): Come and Have a Swing with Me/W: Anne Caldwell, M: Ivan Caryll — Knit, Knit/W: Anne Caldwell, R.H. Burnside, M: Ivan Caryll. *The Canary* (Globe, "Mrs. Beasley," Nov. 4, 1918): That's What Men Are For/W: P.G. Wodehouse, M: Ivan Caryll. *Honey Girl* (Cohan and Harris, "Honora Parker [Honey]," May 3, 1920): Anything You Liked; Close to Your Heart; Mytyl and Tyltyl (The Bluebird Song)/W: Neville Fleeson, M: Albert Von Tilzer.

598. Kenneth Bates *New Faces of 1934* (Fulton, revue, Mar. 15, 1934): Something You Lack/W: June Sillman, Nancy Hamilton, M: Warburton Guilbert.

599. Lulu Bates *Great to Be Alive* (Winter Garden, "Blodgett," Mar. 23, 1950): There's Nothing Like It; What a Day!; Who Done It?/W: Walter Bullock, M: Abraham Ellstein. *Flahooley* (Broadhurst, "Elsa Bullinger," May 14, 1951): Happy Hunting/W: E.Y. Harburg, M: Sammy Fain. *New Girl in Town* (46th Street, "Lily," May 14, 1957): Flings/WM: Bob Merrill. *A Family Affair* (Billy Rose, "Mother Lederer," Jan. 27, 1962): My Son, the Lawyer/W: James Goldman, William Goldman, M: John Kander.

600. Sally Bates *The Manhatters* (Selwyn, revue, Aug. 3, 1927): Down on the Delta/W: George S. Oppenheimer, M: Alfred Nathan.

601. Thorpe Bates (Feb. 11, 1883–May 23, 1958) B: London, England. Performing mainly in England, this baritone sang heroic roles in operettas as well as musical comedy. *The Yankee Princess* (Knickerbocker, "Prince Radjami of Lahore," Oct. 2, 1922): Eyes So Dark and Luring; I Still Can Dream; My Bajadere; Roses, Lovely Roses/W: B.G. DeSylva, M: Emmerich Kalman.

602. Franklyn A. Batie (1880–Dec. 31, 1949) B: Norwich, NY. Before working as straight man to Al Jolson, Batie was with Dock-stader, Primrose and West Minstrels. *A World of Pleasure* (Winter Garden, revue, Oct. 14, 1915): Fascination; The Girl of the Fan; Miss Innovation; The Ragtime Pipes of Pan/W: Harold Atteridge, M: Sigmund Romberg. *The Passing Show of 1917* (Winter Garden, revue, Apr. 26, 1917): America's Fighting Back/WM: ?— My Bedouin Girl; Ring Out Liberty Bell/W: Harold Atteridge, M: Sigmund Romberg. *Sinbad* (Winter Garden > Century > Casino, "Jack Randall," Feb. 14, 1918): Bagdad/W: Harold Atteridge, M: Al Jolson — A Thousand and One Arabian Nights/W: Harold Atteridge, M: Sigmund Romberg. *Bombo* (Al Jolson > Winter Garden, Paul Marcus," Oct. 6, 1921): In Old Granada; Wait Until My Ship Comes In/W: Harold Atteridge, M: Sigmund Romberg.

603. Elena Jeanne Batman *The Phantom of the Opera* (Majestic, CR, "Carlotta Guidicelli," c 1992): Notes; Poor Fool, He Makes Me Laugh; Prima Donna; Think of Me; Twisted Every Way/W: Charles Hart, Richard Stilgoe, M: Andrew Lloyd Webber.

604. Susan Batson (1944–) B: Roxbury, MA. *George M!* (Palace, "Little Girl," Apr. 10, 1968): Down by the Erie Canal/WM: George M. Cohan.

605. Bryan Batt (Mar. 1, 1963–) B: New Orleans, LA. *Starlight Express* (Gershwin, CR, "Rocky I," c 1987): Belle; Poppa's Blues; Right Place, Right Time/W: Richard Stilgoe, M: Andrew Lloyd Webber. *Cats* (Winter Garden, CR, "Munkustrap"): The Awefull Battle of the Pekes and Pollicles; The Marching Songs of the Pollicle Dogs; Old Deuteronomy/W: T.S. Eliot, M: Andrew Lloyd Webber.

606. Tom Batten B: Oklahoma City, OK. *Gantry* (George Abbott, "Bill Morgan," Feb.14, 1970): He's Never Too Busy; Wave a Hand/W: Fred Tobias, M: Stanley Lebowsky. *On the Twentieth Century* (St. James, "Conductor Flanagan," Feb. 19, 1978): I Have Written a Play; On the Twentieth Century/W: Betty Comden, Adolph Green, M: Cy Coleman. *Into the Light* (Neil Simon, "Archbishop Parisi," Oct. 22, 1986): Fede, Fede; Let There Be Light/W: John Forster, M: Lee Holdridge.

607. Lloyd Battista (May 14, 1937–) B: Cleveland, OH. *King of Schnorrers* (Playhouse, "Da Costa," Nov. 28, 1979): Chutzpah/WM: Judd Woldin, Amy Seidman — The Fine Art of Schnorring; Hail to the King/WM: Judd Woldin.

608. Hinton Battle (Nov. 29, 1956–) B: Neubraecke, Germany. A member of the Dance Theater of Harlem. *The Wiz* (Majestic, "Scarecrow," Jan. 5, 1975): Ease on Down the Road; I Was Born on the Day Before Yesterday; Slide Some Oil to Me/WM: Charlie Smalls. *Sophisticated Ladies* (Lunt-Fontanne, revue, Mar. 1, 1981): Drop Me Off in Harlem/W: Nick Kenny, M: Duke Ellington — I Love You Madly; I've Got to Be a Rug Cutter/WM: Duke Ellington — Old Man Blues/W: Irving Mills, M: Duke Ellington — Perdido/W: Hans Lengsfelder, Ervin Drake, M: Juan Tizol. *Dreamgirls* (Imperial, CR, "James Thunder Early," July 25, 1983): Ain't No Party; Cadillac Car; Fake Your Way to the Top; Family; I Meant You No Harm; I Want You Baby; Quintette; The Rap; Steppin' to the Bad Side/W: Tom Eyen, M: Henry Krieger. *The Tap Dance Kid* (Broadhurst, "Dipsey Bates," Dec. 21, 1983): Class Act; Dance If It Makes You Happy; Fabulous Feet; Man in the Moon; My Luck Is Changing; Tap Tap/W: Robert Lorick, M: Henry Krieger. *Miss Saigon* (Broadway, "John," Apr. 11, 1991): Bui-doi; The Confrontation; The Guilt Inside Your Head; Please; The Telephone/W: Richard Maltby, Jr., Alain Boublil, M: Claude-Michel Schonberg.

609. Kathleen Battle (Aug. 13, 1948–) B: Portsmouth, OH. The internationally acclaimed soprano has performed with the great orchestras and in the great opera houses of the world. *Treemonisha* (Palace, "Treemonisha," Oct. 21, 1975): Abuse; The Bag of Luck; Conjurer's Forgiven; The Corn Huskers; Going Home; The Rescue; Surprise; Treemonisha's Bringing Up; Treemonisha's Return; We Will Trust You As Our Leader; We're Goin' Around; The Wreath/WM: Scott Joplin.

610. George Battles *Keep Shufflin'* (Daly's > Eltinge, revue, "Henry," Feb. 27, 1928): Exhortation/W: Henry Creamer, M: Con Conrad.

611. John Battles (1921–) B: New York, NY. *On the Town* (Adelphi, "Gabey," Dec. 28, 1944): Lonely Town; Lucky to Be Me; New York, New York/W: Betty Comden, Adolph Green, M: Leonard Bernstein. *Allegro* (Majestic, "Joseph Taylor, Jr.," Oct. 10, 1947): Allegro; A Darn Nice Campus; You Are Never Away/W: Oscar Hammerstein II, M: Richard Rodgers.

612. Richard Bauer (Mar. 14, 1939–Mar. 1, 1999) B: Missouri. *Boccaccio* (Edison, "Anichino" and "Nuto" and "Abbot," Nov. 24, 1975): Apples in the Garden; Egano D'Galluzzi; Masetto's Song; My Holy Prayer; Only in My Song/W: Kenneth Cavander, M: Richard Peaslee.

613. Renee Baughman *A Chorus Line* (Shubert, "Kristine," July 25, 1975): Sing!/W: Edward Kleban, M: Marvin Hamlisch.

614. Mordecai Bauman *Let Freedom Sing* (Longacre, revue, Oct. 5, 1942): The House I Live In/W: Lewis Allan, M: Earl Robinson.

615. K.T. (Kathryn) Baumann (Aug. 13, 1946–) B: Bronx, NY. *Hello, Dolly!* (Lunt-Fontanne, revival,"Ermengarde," Mar. 5, 1978): Put on Your Sunday Clothes/WM: Jerry Herman.

616. Franklyn Baur (c 1904–Feb. 24, 1950) B: New York, NY. He was one of the two original soloists on radio's concert music program, *The Voice of Firestone*. (1929). *Ziegfeld Follies of 1927* (New Amsterdam, revue, Aug. 16, 1927): Learn to Sing a Love Song; Ooh, Maybe It's You; Rainbow of Girls/WM: Irving Berlin.

617. Michele Bautier *Stardust* (Biltmore, revue, Feb. 19, 1987): Carolina Rolling Stone/W: Mitchell Parish, M: Eleanor Young, Harry D. Squires — Deep Purple/W: Mitchell Parish, M: Peter DeRose — Don't Be That Way/W: Mitchell Parish, M: Edgar Sampson, Benny Goodman — Evenin'/W: Mitchell Parish, M: Harry White — Forgotten Dreams/W: Mitchell Parish, M: Leroy Anderson — Hands Across the Table/W: Mitchell Parish, M: Jean Delettre — Moonlight Serenade/W: Mitchell Parish, M: Glenn Miller — Riverboat Shuffle/W: Mitchell Parish, M: Hoagy Carmichael, Dick Voynow, Irving Mills — Sentimental Gentleman from Georgia/W: Mitchell Parish, M: Frank Perkins — Star Dust/W: Mitchell Parish, M: Hoagy Carmichael — Volare/W: Mitchell Parish, M: Domenico Modugno.

618. Tony Bavaar (June 22, 1921–) B: Brooklyn, NY. *Paint Your Wagon* (Shubert, "Julio Valveras," Nov. 12, 1951): Another Autumn; Carino Mio; I Talk to the Trees/W: Alan Jay Lerner, M: Frederick Loewe.

619. Yolande Bavan (June 1, 1942–) B: Ceylon. *Heathen!* (Billy Rose, "Kalialani" and "Kali," May 21, 1972): Battle Cry; Kalialani; No Way in Hell; This Is Someone I Could Love/WM: Eaton Magoon, Jr.

620. Frances Baviello *The Count of Luxembourg* (Jolson's, revival, "Franchot," Feb. 17, 1930): Rootsie-Pootsie/W: Adrian Ross, Basil Hood, M: Franz Lehar.

621. Barbara Baxley (Jan. 1, 1925–June 7, 1990) B: Porterville, CA. *She Loves Me* (Eugene O'Neill, "Ilona Ritter," Apr. 23, 1963/Dec. 2, 1963): Good Morning, Good Day; Goodbye, Georg; I Don't Know His Name; I Resolve; Thank You, Madam; A Trip to the Library/W: Sheldon Harnick, M: Jerry Bock.

622. Anne Baxter (May 7, 1923–Dec. 12, 1985) B: Michigan City, IN. Her grandfather was the famous architect Frank Lloyd Wright. Best remembered for her role as Eve opposite rival BETTE DAVIS in the film *All About Eve* (1950). In a twist of irony, she replaced that rival, being played by LAUREN BACALL, on stage. Then, in 1983, she took over for an ailing Davis, in the TV drama *Hotel*. *Applause* (Palace, CR, "Margo Channing," July 19, 1971): But Alive; Good Friends; Hurry Back; Inner Thoughts; One of a Kind; Something Greater; Welcome to the Theater; Who's That Girl?/W: Lee Adams, M: Charles Strouse.

623. Connie Baxter *Carousel* (Majestic, CR, "Carrie Pipperidge," Apr. 1947): June Is Bustin' Out All Over; Mister Snow; A Real Nice Clambake; When the Children Are Asleep; You're a Queer One, Julie Jordan/W: Oscar Hammerstein II, M: Richard Rodgers.

624. Gladys Baxter *Peg o' My Dreams* (Al Jolson, "Blossom," May 5, 1924): Right-O; Shy Little Irish Smile/W: Anne Caldwell, M: Hugo Felix. *Piggy* (Royale, "Lady Mildred Vane," Jan. 11, 1927): I Need a Little Bit, You Need a Little Bit (A Little Bit of Love)/W: Lew Brown, M: Cliff Friend. *Cherry Blossoms* (44th Street > Cosmopolitan, "Mary Temple," Mar. 28, 1927): I Want to Be There/W: Harry B. Smith, M: Sigmund Romberg. *Music in May* (Casino, "Comtesse Olga," Apr. 1, 1929): Lips That Laugh at Love; No Other Love Was Meant for Me; There's Love in the Heart I Hold/W: J. Keirn Brennan, M: Maurie Rubens. *Sweethearts* (Jolson's, revival, "Princess Sylvia," Sept. 21, 1929): The Angelus; The Cricket on the Hearth; Garden of Roses; In the Convent They Never Taught Me That; Mother Goose/W: Robert B. Smith, M: Victor Herbert. *Blossom Time* (Ambassador, revival, "Bellabruna," Mar. 23, 1931): Keep It Dark; Let Me Awake; Melody Triste/W: Dorothy Donnelly, M: Sigmund Romberg.

625. Robin Baxter B: Maryland. *A Christmas Carol* (Paramount Madison Square Garden, return engagement, "Mrs. Cratchit," Nov. 20, 1995): Christmas Together/W: Lynn Ahrens, M: Alan Menken.

626. Sue Baxter *The New Yorkers* (Edyth Totten, revue, Mar. 10, 1927): Burn 'Em Up/W: Henry Myers, M: Edgar Fairchild — Slow River; Words and Music/W: Henry Myers, M: Charles M. Schwab.

627. Robert Bay *What's Up* (National, "2nd Lieut. Murray Bacchus," Nov. 11, 1943): You Wash and I'll Dry/W: Alan Jay Lerner, M: Frederick Loewe.

628. Gary Bayer *A History of the American Film* (ANTA, revue, "Jimmy," Mar. 30, 1978): Search for Wisdom; Shanty Town Romance/W: Christopher Durang, M: Mel Marvin.

629. Nora Bayes (Jan. 1, 1880–Mar. 19, 1928) B: Milwaukee, WI. M: JACK NORWORTH; HARRY CLARKE. Popular performers and songwriters, Bayes and Norworth billed themselves as The Happiest Married Couple on Stage, until their divorce. He was the second of her five husbands; the movie *Shine On Harvest Moon* (1944) purported to be about their lives together. *Rogers Brothers in Washington* (Knickerbocker, "Esther Pace," Sept. 2, 1901): Watermelon Party/W: Harry B. Smith, M: Maurice Levi. *Nearly a Hero* (Casino, CR, "Angeline De Vere," 1908): I'm So Particular; The Queen of Belle Paree/W: Edward B. Claypoole, Will Heelan, M: Seymour Furth — My Sahara Belle/W: Harry B. Smith, M: Edward B. Claypoole. *Ziegfeld Follies of 1908* (Jardin de Paris > New York, revue, June 15, 1908): Nothing Ever Troubles Me [June 29, 1908]; Since Mother Was a Girl; You Will Have to Sing an Irish Song/W: Jack Norworth, M: Albert Von Tilzer — Rosa Rosetta/W: Earle C. Jones, Jack Norworth, M: Albert Von Tilzer — Shine On, Harvest Moon [added]/WM: Jack Norworth, Nora Bayes, Gus Edwards, Edward Madden. *Ziegfeld Follies of 1909* (Jardin de Paris, revue, June 14, 1909): I Wish I was a Boy and I Wish I Was a Girl (I'm Glad I'm a Boy and I'm Glad I'm a Girl)/WM: Jack Norworth, Nora Bayes. *The Jolly Bachelors* (Broadway, "Astarita Vandergould," Jan. 6, 1910): Come Along My Mandy/WM: Tom Mellor, Alfred J. Lawrence, Harry Gifford, Jack Norworth, Nora Bayes — Has Anybody Here Seen Kelly?/WM: William J. McKenna, C.W. Murphy, Will Letters — Rosa Rosetta/W: Earle C. Jones, Jack Norworth, M: Albert Von Tilzer — What Am I Going to Do to Make You Love Me?/W: Glen MacDonough, M: Raymond Hubbell — Young America/WM: Jack Norworth, Nora Bayes. *Little Miss Fix-It* (Globe, "Delia Wendell," Apr. 3, 1911): I've a Garden in Sweden; Mister Moon Man, Turn Off Your Light; The Only Bit of Ireland in New York; Please Go Find My Billy Boy/WM: R. Weston, Fred Barnes — Strawberries/W: Herbert Rule, M: James McGhee. *Roly Poly* (Broadway > Weber and Fields, "La Frolique," Nov. 21, 1912): In My Birch Bark Canoe (With Emmy Lou)/WM: Jack Norworth, Nora Bayes — Way Down in C-U-B-A/WM: Jack Norworth, Nora Bayes, Antonio Torroella Chijo — When It's Apple Blossom Time in Normandy/WM: Harry Gifford, Tom Mellor, Huntley Trevor. *Maid in America* (Winter Garden, revue "Nettie, Belle of the Broadway Knitting Club," Feb. 18, 1915): The Stolen Melody/WM: Phil Schwartz, Nora

Bayes, Harold Atteridge — There's a Little Bit of Everything on Broadway/WM: Leo Edwards — When Grandma Was a Girl/W: Harold Atteridge, M: Sigmund Romberg. *The Cohan Revue of 1918* (New Amsterdam, revue, Dec. 31, 1917): Polly, Pretty Polly (Polly with a Past)/W: George M. Cohan, M: Irving Berlin — Regretful Blues/W: Grant Clarke, M: Cliff Hess — Who Do You Love?/W: Gene Buck, M: James F. Hanley. *Her Family Tree* (Lyric > Shubert > Nora Bayes, Dec. 27, 1920): As We Sow, So Shall We Reap; No Other Gal; Ouija Board; Where Tomorrows Begin; Why Worry?/WM: Seymour Simons — The Broadway Blues [Mar. 7, 1921]/W: Arthur Swanstrom, M: Carey Morgan. *Snapshots of 1921* (Selwyn, revue, June 2, 1921): Ambition; Chinish/W: Morrie Ryskind, M: Lewis E. Gensler — Rendezvous/W: Sidney D. Mitchell, M: Leopold Godowsky — Saturday/W: Sidney D. Mitchell, M: Harry Brooks — Sentence Me for Life/WM: Al Bloomberg, Lewis E. Gensler. *Queen o' Hearts* (George M. Cohan, "Elizabeth Bennett," Oct. 10, 1922): Dear Little Girlie/W: Nora Bayes, M: Dudley Wilkinson — My Busy Day; System/W: Oscar Hammerstein II, M: Lewis E. Gensler, Dudley Wilkinson — That's That/W: Nora Bayes, Harry Richman, M: Dudley Wilkinson — You Need Someone/W: Oscar Hammerstein II, M: Lewis E. Gensler.

630. St. Clair Bayfield B: England. *The King of Cadonia* (Daly's, "Laborde," Jan.10, 1910): It's a Bomb/W: Adrian Ross, M: Sidney Jones.

631. Emy Baysic (c 1971–) B: San Carlos, CA. *Miss Saigon* (Broadway, CR, alt, "Kim," c 1993): Back in Town; The Ceremony; The Guilt Inside Your Head; I Still Believe; I'd Give My Life for You; The Last Night of the World; Little God of My Heart; The Movie in My Mind; Please; Room 317; Sun and Moon; You Will Not Touch Him/W: Richard Maltby, Jr., Alain Boublil, M: Claude-Michel Schonberg.

632. Raymond Bazemore (c 1946–2001) B: He grew up in Norfolk, VA. *Treemonisha* (Palace, "Simon," Oct. 21, 1975): Superstition; Treemonisha in Peril; The Wasp Nest/WM: Scott Joplin. *1600 Pennsylvania Avenue* (Mark Hellinger, "Henry," May 4, 1976): Welcome Home Miz Adams/W: Alan Jay Lerner, M: Leonard Bernstein.

633. Gary Beach (Oct. 10, 1947–) B: Alexandria, VA. *Annie* (Alvin, CR, "Rooster Hannigan," Jan. 29, 1980): Easy Street/W: Martin Charnin, M: Charles Strouse. *The Mooney Shapiro Songbook* (Morosco, revue, May 3, 1981): Bring Back Tomorrow; Climbin'; East River Rhapsody; Happy Hickory; I Found Love; I'm Gonna Take Her Home to Momma; Lovely Sunday Mornin'; Messages II; Pretty Face; A Storm in My Heart; Talking Picture Show/W: Julian More, M: Monty Norman. *Doonesbury* (Biltmore, "Duke," Nov. 21, 1983): Guilty; Real Estate/W: Garry Trudeau, M: Elizabeth Swados. *Beauty and the Beast* (Palace, "Lumiere," Apr. 18, 1994/c 1996): Be Our Guest; Human Again; Something There/W: Howard Ashman, M: Alan Menken.

634. George Beach *Blossom Time* (Ambassador, revival, "Erkmann," Sept. 4, 1943): Love Is a Riddle/W: Dorothy Donnelly, M: Sigmund Romberg.

635. Louis Beachner (June 9, 1923–Sept. 19, 1986) B: Jersey City, NJ. *Georgy* (Winter Garden, "Ted," Feb. 26, 1970): Sweet Memory/W: Carole Bayer Sager, M: George Fischoff. *Where's Charley?* (Circle in the Square, revival, "Brassett," Dec. 20, 1974): The New Ashmoleon Marching Society and Students Conservatory Band/WM: Frank Loesser.

636. Harrison Beal *Beauty and the Beast* (Palace, CR, "Lefou," c 1995): Belle; Gaston; The Mob Song/W: Howard Ashman, M: Alan Menken — Maison des Lunes/W: Tim Rice, M: Alan Menken.

637. John Beal (Aug. 13, 1909–Apr. 26, 1997) B: Joplin, MO. M: HELEN CRAIG. The clean-cut actor played opposite KATHARINE HEPBURN in the 1935 film *The Little Minister*. In later years he appeared in horror movies. *Billy* (Billy Rose, "Dansker," Mar. 22, 1969): In the Arms of a Stranger/WM: Ron Dante, Gene Allen.

638. Robert Beam B: Baltimore, MD. *One Touch of Venus* (Imperial, CR, "Rodney Hatch," Dec. 1944): How Much I Love You; Speak Low; The Trouble with Women; Way Out West in Jersey; Wooden Wedding/W: Ogden Nash, M: Kurt Weill.

639. Hazel Beamer *Mayflowers* (Forrest, "Miss Kaye," Nov. 24, 1925): Put Your Troubles in a Candy Box/W: Clifford Grey, M: J. Fred Coots.

640. Orson Bean (July 22, 1928–) B: Burlington, VT. He was a panelist on TV quiz shows *I've Got a Secret* (1952) and *To Tell the Truth* (1964). He played Loren Bray on the TV western drama, *Dr. Quinn, Medicine Woman* (1993). *John Murray Anderson's Almanac* (Imperial, revue, Dec. 10, 1953): Merry Little Minuet/WM: Sheldon Harnick. *Subways Are for Sleeping* (St. James, "Charlie Smith," Dec. 27, 1961): I Just Can't Wait; Strange Duet (When You Help a Friend Out); What Is This Feeling in the Air?/W: Betty Comden, Adolph Green, M: Jule Styne. *The Roar of the Greasepaint—The Smell of the Crowd* (Shubert, CR, "Cocky," Nov. 22, 1965): It Isn't Enough; The Joker; My First Love Song; My Way; Nothing Can Stop Me Now; Sweet Beginning; This Dream; What a Man; Where Would You Be Without Me?; Who Can I Turn To (When Nobody Needs Me); A Wonderful Day Like Today/WM: Leslie Bricusse, Anthony Newley. *Illya Darling* (Mark Hellinger, "Homer Thrace," Apr. 11, 1967): Golden Land; I Think She Needs Me; The Lesson; Po, Po, Po/W: Joe Darion, M: Manos Hadjidakis.

641. Reathel Bean (Aug. 24, 1942–) B: Missouri. *Doonesbury* (Biltmore, "Roland," Nov. 21, 1983): Baby Boom Boogie Boy; Graduation; It's the Right Time to Be Rich/W: Garry Trudeau, M: Elizabeth Swados.

642. George A. Beane *The Maid and the Mummy* (New York, "Dr. Elisha Dobbins," July 25, 1904): My Gasoline Automobile/W: Richard Carle, M: Robert Hood Bowers. *Oh! Oh! Delphine* (Knickerbocker > New Amsterdam, "Uncle Noel Jolibeau," Sept. 30, 1912): Hush! Hush! Hush!; Oh, P-P-P-Poor Bouchette/W: C.M.S. McLellan, M: Ivan Caryll.

643. James Beard (Feb 27–) B: New York, NY. *My Fair Lady* (New York City Center, revival, "Jamie," June 13, 1968): Get Me to the Church on Time; With a Little Bit of Luck/W: Alan Jay Lerner, M: Frederick Loewe.

644. Stella Beardsley *The Belle of Mayfair* (Daly's, "Lady Peter Robinson," Dec. 3, 1906): Eight Little Debutantes Are We/W: William Caine, M: Leslie Stuart.

645. Madeline Beasley *The Prince of Pilsen* (Daly's, revival, "Nellie Wagner," Apr. 4, 1904): Back to the Boulevards; Pictures in the Smoke; The Tale of the Sea Shell/W: Frank Pixley, M: Gustav Luders.

646. Frank Beaston *Big Boy* (Winter Garden, "Jack Bedford," Jan. 7, 1925): The Dance from Down Yonder; Tap the Toe/W: B.G. DeSylva, M: Joseph Meyer, James F. Hanley. *Judy* (Royale, "Harry Danforth," Feb. 7, 1927): The Curfew Shall Not Ring Tonight; Hard to Get Along With; Hobohemia; Judy, Who D'Ya Love?; Looking for a Thrill; One Baby; When Gentlemen Grew Whiskers and Ladies Grew Old/W: Leo Robin, M: Charles Rosoff.

647. Betzi Beaton *The Only Girl* (44th Street, revival, "Birdie Martin," May 21, 1934): Connubial Bliss/W: Henry Blossom, M: Victor Herbert — I Always Go to Parties Alone/WM: James Shelton. *Fools Rush In* (The Playhouse,

revue, Dec. 25, 1934): Love All; Sitting Over There/W: Norman Zeno, M: Will Irwin.

648. Ethel Beatty *Bubbling Brown Sugar* (ANTA, "Ella," Mar. 2, 1976): I Got It Bad (and That Ain't Good)/W: Paul Francis Webster, M: Duke Ellington — Love Will Find a Way/W: Noble Sissle, M: Eubie Blake. *Eubie!* (Ambassador, revue, Sept. 20, 1978): Gee, I Wish I Had Someone to Rock Me in the Cradle of Love; I'm Just Wild About Harry; Oriental Blues; There's a Million Little Cupids in the Sky/W: Noble Sissle, M: Eubie Blake — Goodnight Angeline/W: Noble Sissle, James Reese Europe, M: Eubie Blake — Memories of You/W: Andy Razaf, M: Eubie Blake. *Dreamgirls* (Imperial, CR, "Michelle Morris," Mar. 1984): Quintette/W: Tom Eyen, M: Henry Krieger.

649. Roberta Beatty (Dec. 29, 1891–1978) B: Rochester, NY. *The Bunch and Judy* (Globe, "Lady Janet," Nov. 28, 1922): Lovely Lassie/W: Anne Caldwell, M: Jerome Kern. *Peg o' My Dreams* (Al Jolson, "Ethel," May 5, 1924): A Dainty Nosegay; Her Bright Shawl; Rose in the Snow/W: Anne Caldwell, M: Hugo Felix. *The Student Prince [in Heidelberg]* (Al Jolson, "Princess Margaret," Dec. 2, 1924): Just We Two/W: Dorothy Donnelly, M: Sigmund Romberg. *The Love Call* (Majestic, "Estrella," Oct. 24, 1927): Hear the Trumpet Call; I Am Captured; The Lark; 'Tis Love/W: Harry B. Smith, M: Sigmund Romberg.

650. Susan Beaubian *Honky Tonk Nights* (Biltmore, "Countess Aida," Aug. 7, 1986): Roll with the Punches/W: Ralph Allen, David Campbell, M: Michael Valenti. *Dreamgirls* (Ambassador, revival, "Michelle Morris," June 28, 1987): Quintette/W: Tom Eyen, M: Henry Krieger.

651. Louise Beaudet (c 1860–Dec. 31, 1947) B: St. Emilie, Quebec, Canada. *Jacinta* (Fifth Avenue, "Jacinta," Nov. 26, 1894): A Soldier Need Not Fear/W: William H. Lepere, M: Alfred G. Robyn.

652. Rose Beaudet *The Girl from Paris* (Wallack's, revival, "Mrs. Honeycomb," Jan. 17, 1898): Cock-a-doodle/W: George Dance, M: Ivan Caryll.

653. Marie Beaugarde *The Merry Whirl* (New York, "Cherie" and "Mlle. De Baron," May 30, 1910): I'll Be There With You; La Belle Francaise; Ring the Wedding Bells/W: Ed Ray, M: Leo Edwards.

654. Nellie (Nelly) Beaumont (Oct. 11, 1870–Oct. 26, 1938) B: Ramsgate, England. Sister of ROSE BEAUMONT. They were billed as The Clever, Fascinating Beaumont Sisters.

Hurly-Burly (Weber and Fields Music Hall, "Tottie Cambridge," Sept. 8, 1898): Clink, Clink/W: Harry B. Smith, Edgar Smith, M: John Stromberg. *The Knickerbocker Girl* (Herald Square, "La Rosa Estrobana," June 15, 1903): My Linda Love/W: George Totten Smith, M: Alfred E. Aarons.

655. Rose Beaumont (?–May 11, 1938) *Hurly-Burly* (Weber and Fields Music Hall, "Suzzannah," Sept. 8, 1898): Clink, Clink; A Loidy Wot Is Studyin' for the Stoige/W: Harry B. Smith, Edgar Smith, M: John Stromberg. *The Wild Rose* (Knickerbocker, CR, "Vera Von Lahn," 1902): Nancy Brown (A Bucolic Wail)/WM: Clifton Crawford. *The Jersey Lily* (Victoria, "Senorita Marquita," Sept. 14, 1903): Rosie Lee/W: George V. Hobart, M: Reginald De Koven.

656. Sascha Beaumont *Merry, Merry* (Vanderbilt, "Sadi La Salle," Sept. 24, 1925): My Own; What a Life/W: Harlan Thompson, M: Harry Archer. *Oh, Kay!* (Imperial, "Constance Appleton," Nov. 8, 1926): Bride and Groom/W: Ira Gershwin, M: George Gershwin.

657. Bertee Beaumonte (c 1889–June 27, 1934) *The Lady in Red* (Lyric, "Peppina Cattaneo," May 12, 1919): Garibaldi Band; I Want to Be Like Cleo/W: Anne Caldwell, M: Richard Winterberg. *The Magic Melody* (Shubert, "Eifine," Nov. 11, 1919): Down by the Nile/W: Frederic Arnold Kummer, M: Sigmund Romberg. *The Gingham Girl* (Earl Carroll, "Sonya Maison," Aug. 28, 1922): Down Greenwich Village Way; The Wonderful Thing We Call Love/W: Neville Fleeson, M: Albert Von Tilzer.

658. Jeanne Beauvais *The Beggar's Opera* (New York City Center, revival, "Lucy Lockit," Mar. 13, 1957): Come Sweet Lass; I'm Like a Skiff on the Ocean Toss'd; Is Then His Fate Decreed, Sir?; Why How Now Madam Flirt; Would I Might Be Hanged/WM: John Gay. *The Boy Friend* (Ambassador, revival, "Madame Dubonnet," Apr. 14, 1970): Fancy Forgetting; Poor Little Pierrette; The You-Don't-Want-to-Play-with-Me Blues/WM: Sandy Wilson.

659. George Beban (Nov. 5, 1873–Oct. 5, 1928) B: San Francisco, CA. Although of Scottish and Irish ancestry, he played Italians and Frenchmen in silent films and on stage. *Moonshine* (Liberty, "Marcel Barbier," Oct. 30, 1905): I Want to Go Back to the Boulevard/W: George V. Hobart, M: Silvio Hein — Mister Bonaparte/W: Benjamin Hapgood Burt, M: Silvio Hein. *The Girl Behind the Counter* (Herald Square, "Henri Duval," Oct. 1, 1907): The Enterprising Frenchman/W: Arthur Anderson, M:

Howard Talbot. *The American Idea* (New York, "Souchet," Oct. 5, 1908): Cohan's Pet Names (That's the Pet Name for Me); F-A-M-E/WM: George M. Cohan.

660. Don Becker *South Pacific* (New York City Center, revival, "Seebee Richard West," Apr. 13, 1961): There Is Nothin' Like a Dame/W: Oscar Hammerstein II, M: Richard Rodgers.

661. Edward Becker B: Astoria, NY. *Guys and Dolls* (New York City Center, revival, "Rusty Charlie," Apr. 28, 1965): Fugue for Tinhorns/WM: Frank Loesser. *The Most Happy Fella* (New York City Center, revival, "Ciccio," May 11, 1966): Abbondanza; Benvenuta/WM: Frank Loesser. *Guys and Dolls* (New York City Center, revival, "Rusty Charlie," June 8, 1966): same as above. *Jimmy* (Winter Garden, "Francis Xavier Aloysius O'Toole," Oct. 23, 1969): It's a Nice Place to Visit; They Never Proved a Thing/WM: Bill Jacob, Patti Jacob. *Goodtime Charley* (Palace, "Pope," Mar. 3, 1975): History/W: Hal Hackady, M: Larry Grossman.

662. Lee Becker *Tenderloin* (46th Street, "Gertie," Oct. 17, 1960): How the Money Changes Hands; Little Old New York; Reform/W: Sheldon Harnick, M: Jerry Bock.

663. Willard Beckham *The Utter Glory of Morrissey Hall* (Mark Hellinger, "Richard Tidewell," May 13, 1979): Duet/WM: Clark Gesner.

664. Linden Beckwith (May 21, 1885–Feb. 23, 1913) B: Oakland, CA. *The Midnight Sons* (Broadway, "Claire Voyant," May 22, 1909): True Blue/W: Glen MacDonough, M: Raymond Hubbell.

665. Don Beddoe (July 1, 1891–Jan. 19, 1991) B: Pittsburgh, PA. He began in silent films, often playing a sheriff, cop or reporter. *Kismet* (New York State, revival, "Omar Khayyam," June 22, 1965): He's in Love!/WM: Robert Wright, George Forrest.

666. Bonnie Bedelia (Mar. 25, 1946–) B: New York, NY. In movies and TV from 1969. *Street Scene* (New York City Center, revival, "Mary Hildebrand," Feb. 13, 1960): Catch Me If You Can/W: Langston Hughes, Elmer Rice, M: Kurt Weill.

667. David Bedella *Jesus Christ Superstar* (Paramount Madison Square Garden, revival, "Caiaphas," Jan. 17, 1995): The Arrest; Damned for All Time; Hosanna; Judas' Death; This Jesus Must Die; Trial Before Pilate/W: Tim Rice, M: Andrew Lloyd Webber.

668. Irving Beebe *Head Over Heels* (George M. Cohan, "Edward Sterling," Aug. 29, 1918): I Was Lonely; Ladies, Have a Care!; The Moments of the Dance/W: Edgar Allan Woolf, M: Jerome

Kern. *Afgar* (Central, "Don Juan, Jr.," Nov. 8, 1920): Give the Devil His Due; Neath Thy Casement; We're the Gentlemen of the Harem/ W: Douglas Furber, M: Charles Cuvillier. *Marjolaine* (Broadhurst, "Lieut. the Hon. Jack Sayle," Jan. 24, 1922): Marjolaine; Song of a Sailor/W: Brian Hooker, M: Hugo Felix. *Sweet Little Devil* (Astor > Central, "Tom Nesbitt," Jan. 21, 1924): Just Supposing; The Matrimonial Handicap; Someone Believes in You/W: B.G. DeSylva, M: George Gershwin. *Florida Girl* (Lyric, "Henry Elkins," Nov. 2, 1925): Lady of My Heart/W: Paul Porter, Benjamin Hapgood Burt, M: Milton Suskind.

669. Rachel Beech *Messin' Around* (Hudson, revue, Apr. 22, 1929): I Don't Love Nobody but You; Roustabouts/W: Perry Bradford, M: James P. Johnson.

670. Sylvia Beecher *Paris by Night* (Madison Square roof garden, "Margueritta Hottomoleo," July 2, 1904): Follow the Crowd on a Sunday/W: James Morrison, Richard Gerard, M: Harry Armstrong — I Loves You Lady Deed I Do/WM: Joseph Nathan — Twinkle, Twinkle, Little Star/WM: Henry I. Marshall, Alfred Solman, Robert W. Edwards.

671. Laurie Beechman (Apr. 4, 1954–Mar. 8, 1998) B: Philadelphia, PA. Broadway, cabaret and concert singer. For over 5 years, she played Grizabella in *Cats,* on tour and, when BETTY BUCKLEY stepped down, on Broadway. *Annie* (Alvin, "Cecille" and "Star to Be" and "Bonnie Boylan," Apr. 21, 1977): I Think I'm Gonna Like It Here; N.Y.C.; You Won't Be an Orphan for Long; You're Never Fully Dressed Without a Smile/W: Martin Charnin, M: Charles Strouse. *Joseph and the Amazing Technicolor Dreamcoat* (Royale, revival, "Narrator," Jan. 27, 1982): The Brothers Came to Egypt; A Coat of Many Colors; Go, Go, Go, Joseph; Grovel, Grovel; Jacob and Sons; Jacob in Egypt; Joseph All the Time; Joseph's Dreams; One More Angel in Heaven; Pharaoh's Story; Poor, Poor Joseph; Poor, Poor Pharaoh; Potiphar; Song of the King; Stone the Crows/W: Tim Rice, M: Andrew Lloyd Webber. *Cats* (Winter Garden, CR, "Grizabella," Apr. 9, 1984/ c 1996): Grizabella, the Glamour Cat/W: T.S. Eliot, M: Andrew Lloyd Webber — Memory/W: Trevor Nunn, based on T.S. Eliot/ M: Andrew Lloyd Webber. *Les Miserables* (Broadway, CR, "Fantine," Jan. 15, 1990): Come to Me; I Dreamed a Dream/W: Herbert Kretzmer, M: Claude-Michel Schonberg.

672. Elaine Beener *Raisin* (46th Street, "Bar Girl," Oct. 18, 1973): Booze/W: Robert Brittan, M: Judd Woldin.

673. Leo Beers *The Century Revue* (Century, revue, July 12, 1920): Marcelle/W: Alfred Bryan, M: Jean Schwartz. *Honeymoon Lane* (Knickerbocker, "Leo Scamp," Sept. 20, 1926): Little Old New Hampshire/W: Eddie Dowling, M: James F. Hanley.

674. Leigh (Lee) Beery (Mar. 20–) B: Minneapolis, MN. *Oklahoma!* (Music Theater of Lincoln Center, revival, "Laurey Williams," June 23, 1969): Many a New Day; Oh, What a Beautiful Mornin'; Oklahoma!; Out of My Dreams; People Will Say We're in Love; The Surrey with the Fringe on Top/W: Oscar Hammerstein II, M: Richard Rodgers. *Cyrano* (Palace, "Roxana," May 13, 1973): Autumn Carol; Bergerac; Love Is Not Love; You Have Made Me Love/W: Anthony Burgess, M: Michael J. Lewis.

675. Noah Beery, Sr. (Jan. 17, 1882–Apr. 1, 1946) B: Kansas City, MO. The movieland bad guy was half-brother of WALLACE BEERY. *Up in Central Park* (Century, "William Marcey Tweed, Grand Sachem of Tammany Hall," Jan. 27, 1945): Boss Tweed; Rip Van Winkle/W: Dorothy Fields, M: Sigmund Romberg.

676. Wallace Beery (Apr. 1, 1885–Apr. 15, 1949) B: Kansas City, MO. M: movie star Gloria Swanson, 1916-1918. Like his half-brother, NOAH BEERY, SR, he also achieved stardom playing movie villains. *The Yankee Tourist* (Astor, CR, "Copeland Schuyler," Nov. 4, 1907): Come and Have a Smile with Me; The Yankee Millionaire/W: Wallace Irwin, M: Alfred G. Robyn — So What's the Use?/WM: Edward Montagu.

677. Malcolm Lee Beggs (1907–Dec. 10, 1956) *Up in Central Park* (New York City Center, revival, "William Marcey Tweed, Grand Sachem of Tammany Hall," May 19, 1947): Boss Tweed; Rip Van Winkle/W: Dorothy Fields, M: Sigmund Romberg. *The Vamp* (Winter Garden, "Stark Clayton," Nov. 10, 1955): I'm Everybody's Baby/W: John Latouche, M: James Mundy.

678. Edward Begley *The Red Mill* (Knickerbocker, "Jan Van Borkem," Sept. 24, 1906): You Can Never Tell About a Woman/W: Henry Blossom, M: Victor Herbert. *The Passing Show of 1913* (Winter Garden, revue, July 24, 1913): Ragging the Nursery Rhymes/W: Harold Atteridge, M: Al W. Brown. *Going Up* (Liberty, "Sam Robinson," Dec. 25, 1917): Down! Up! Left! Right!/W: Otto Harbach, M: Louis A. Hirsch.

679. Carrie Behr *The Babes and the Baron* (Lyric, "Lena Pickles," Dec. 25, 1905): It's a Jolly Good Thing to Be Alive/W: Charles M. Taylor, Robert B. Smith, M: Herbert E. Haines.

680. Richard Bekins *Happy New Year*

(Morosco, "Edward Seton, Jr.," Apr. 27, 1980): At Long Last Love; Once Upon a Time; When Your Troubles Have Started/WM: Cole Porter.

681. Harry Belafonte (Mar. 1, 1924–) B: New York, NY. Popular singer since the 1950s of West Indian ballads, calypso style. He acted memorably, but did not sing, in the 1954 film, *Carmen Jones. John Murray Anderson's Almanac* (Imperial, revue, Dec. 10, 1953): Acorn in the Meadow/WM: Richard Adler, Jerry Ross— Hold 'Em Joe/WM: Harry Thomas — Mark Twain/WM: Harry Belafonte. *3 for Tonight* (Plymouth, revue, Apr. 6, 1955): In That Great Gettin' Up Mornin'/WM: Jester Herston — Jerry; Noah; Sylvie; Take My Mother Home/WM: ?— Mark Twain/WM: Harry Belafonte — Matilda/ WM: Harry Belafonte, Millard Thomas — Scarlet Ribbons/W: Jack Segal, M: Evelyn Danzig — When the Saints Go Marching In/W: Katherine E. Purvis, M: James M. Black.

682. Leon Belasco (Oct. 11, 1902–June 1, 1988) B: Odessa, Russia. In movies he played headwaiters, ballet masters and landlords, to perfection. *Silk Stockings* (Imperial, "Brankov," Feb. 24, 1955): Hail, Bibinski; Siberia; Too Bad/ WM: Cole Porter. *Happy Hunting* (Majestic, "Arturo," Dec. 6, 1956): A New Fangled Tango/ W: Matt Dubey, M: Harold Karr.

683. Frank H. Belcher (1869–Feb. 27, 1947) B: San Francisco, CA. *Mary's Lamb* (New York, "Bill Blackwell," May 25, 1908): I Idolize Ida; Never Borrow Trouble/WM: Richard Carle. *When Sweet Sixteen* (Daly's, "John Hammond," Sept. 14, 1911): A Man's a Man for A' That; My Toast to You; There's Money in Graft (There's a Raft of Money in Graft! Graft! Graft!)/W: George V. Hobart, M: Victor Herbert. *My Best Girl* (Park, "Gus Bludge," Sept. 12, 1912): A Regular Army Man/W: Rennold Wolf, M: Augustus Barratt. *Sweethearts* (New Amsterdam > Liberty, "Petrus Von Tromp," Sept. 8, 1913): Jeannette and Her Little Wooden Shoes; The Monks' Quartette; Pilgrims of Love; Pretty As a Picture/W: Robert B. Smith, M: Victor Herbert.

684. Tavie Belge *Fiddlers Three* (Cort, "Anina Andreani," Sept. 3, 1918): Can It Be Love at Last?; The Love That Is Gone/W: William Cary Duncan, M: Alexander Johnstone.

685. Katherine Belknap *The Red Petticoat* (Daly's > Broadway, "Parrot," Nov. 13, 1912): Where Did the Bird Hear That?/W: Paul West, M: Jerome Kern.

686. Digby Bell (Nov. 8, 1849–June 20, 1917) B: Milwaukee, WI. M: LAURA JOYCE, 1883. He went to Italy in 1872 to study music and debuted as a concert singer 4 years later in New York's Chickering Hall. During a career of over 30 years, he became one of the best loved singing comedians of the American musical theater. *Cinderella at School* (Daly's, CR, "Jack Polo," Aug. 9, 1881): Columbia Won the Race Today; I Kiss My Hand to Thee; No Regular Wife; Swing with Me; 'Tis Not Becoming in a Maiden; What a Shocking Sight/WM: Woolson Morse. *The Black Hussar* (Wallack's, "Piffkow," May 4, 1885): Read the Answer in the Stars/W: Sydney Rosenfeld, M: Carl Millocker. *Mr. Pickwick* (Herald Square, "Sam Weller," Jan. 19, 1903): The Forest Air; Gratitude; On the Side/W: Grant Stewart, M: Manuel Klein.

687. George Bell *Timbuktu!* (Mark Hellinger, "Wazir," Mar. 1, 1978): And This Is My Beloved/WM: Robert Wright, George Forrest, M: based on Alexander Borodin.

688. Glynis Bell (July 30, 1947–) B: London, England. *My Fair Lady* (Virginia, revival, "Mrs. Pearce," Dec. 9, 1993): I Could Have Danced All Night; You Did It/W: Alan Jay Lerner, M: Frederick Loewe.

689. Ida Bell *Adonis* (Bijoux, "Lady Mattie," Sept. 4, 1884): We Are the Duchess' Daughters/W: William F. Gill, Henry E. Dixey, M: Edward E. Rice. *Adonis* (Star, revival, "Talamea," Nov. 22, 1888): Golden Chains/W: William F. Gill, Henry E. Dixey, M: Edward E. Rice — The Wall Street Broker/W: H.S. Hewitt, M: Edward E. Rice.

690. Leslie Bell *State Fair* (Music Box, "Jeanne," Mar. 27, 1996): The Man I Used to Be/W: Oscar Hammerstein II, M: Richard Rodgers.

691. Marion Bell (Nov. 16, 1919–Dec. 14, 1997) B: St. Louis, MO. M: lyricist and author Alan Jay Lerner, 1947–1949. Under contract to MGM, she sang a duet with Metropolitan Opera tenor James Melton in the film, *Ziegfeld Follies* (1946). *Brigadoon* (Ziegfeld, "Fiona MacLaren," Mar. 13, 1947): Almost Like Being in Love; Come to Me, Bend to Me; From This Day On; The Heather on the Hill; Waitin' for My Dearie/W: Alan Jay Lerner, M: Frederick Loewe.

692. Michel Bell *Show Boat* (Gershwin, revival, "Joe," Oct. 2, 1994): Can't Help Lovin' Dat Man; Ol' Man River/W: Oscar Hammerstein II, M: Jerome Kern.

693. Blanche Bellaire *Listen Lester* (Knickerbocker, CR, "Miss Down," Apr. 7, 1919): When the Shadows Fall/W: Harry L. Cort, George E. Stoddard, M: Harold Orlob.

694. Kathryn Belle *The Rich Mr. Hoggenheimer* (Wallack's, CR, "Violet Moss," Dec. 24,

1906): Poker Love (Card Duet)/WM: Paul West, Jerome Kern.

695. Cal Bellini (1936–) B: San Francisco, CA. *Her First Roman* (Lunt-Fontanne, "Apollodorus," Oct. 20, 1968): In Vino Veritas; The Things We Think We Are/WM: Ervin Drake.

696. Grace Belmont *Miss Simplicity* (Casino, "Patty Yarrell," Feb. 10, 1902): You'd Better Take It Back/W: R.A. Barnet, M: H.L. Heartz. *The Knickerbocker Girl* (Herald Square, "Eleanor De Reuyter," June 15, 1903): Today/W: George Totten Smith, M: Alfred E. Aarons. *Sergeant Kitty* (Daly's, "Ninon," Jan. 18, 1904): An Accident; Cupid's Cure/W: R.H. Burnside, M: A. Baldwin Sloane.

697. Bertha Belmore (Dec. 20, 1882–Dec. 14, 1953) B: Manchester, England. Top character actor in British musicals of the 1930s and 40s. *Show Boat* (Casino, return engagement, CR, "Parthy Ann Hawks," June 1932): Why Do I Love You?/W: Oscar Hammerstein II, M: Jerome Kern. *By Jupiter* (Shubert, "Pomposia," June 3, 1942): Life with Father/W: Lorenz Hart, M: Richard Rodgers.

698. Daisy Belmore (June 30, 1874–Dec. 12, 1954) B: London, England. *Marjolaine* (Broadhurst, "Mrs. Pamela Poskett," Jan. 24, 1922): Punch and Judy/W: Brian Hooker, M: Hugo Felix.

699. Madeline Belt *Hot Chocolates* (Hudson, revue, June 20, 1929): Can't We Get Together/W: Andy Razaf, M: Fats Waller, Harry Brooks — Pickaninny Land [July 11, 1929]/WM: ?. *Hot Rhythm* (Times Square > Waldorf, revue, Aug. 21, 1930): Alabamy; Rector Rhythm; Steppin' on It/W: Donald Heywood, M: Porter Grainger — Loving You the Way I Do/W: Jack Scholl, Will Morrissey, M: Eubie Blake.

700. Neal Ben-Ari (Mar. 20, 1952–) B: Brooklyn, NY. *Roza* (Royale, "Yussef Kadir," Oct. 1, 1987): Yussef's Visit/W: Julian More, M: Gilbert Becaud. *Chess* (Imperial, "Gregor Vassey," Apr. 28, 1988): Lullaby (Apukad Eros Kezen); The Story of Chess/W: Tim Rice, M: Benny Anderson, Bjorn Ulvaeus. *Joseph and the Amazing Technicolor Dreamcoat* (Minskoff, revival, "Simeon," Nov. 10, 1993): Those Canaan Days/W: Tim Rice, M: Andrew Lloyd Webber.

701. Daniel Ben-Zali *Music Is* (St. James, "William Shakespeare" and "Feste," Dec. 20, 1976): Big Bottom Betty; The Duel; Music Is; Sing Hi; What You Will/W: Will Holt, M: Richard Adler.

702. Sidney Ben-Zali (Dec. 20, 1945–) B: Rio de Janeiro. *The Rothschilds* (Lunt-Fontanne, CR, "Amshel Rothschild," Apr. 20, 1971):

Bonds; Everything; Rothschild & Sons/W: Sheldon Harnick, M: Jerry Bock.

703. Charles Bender *The New Yorkers* (Edyth Totten, revue, Mar. 10, 1927): He Who Gets Slapped; Romany/W: Henry Myers, M: Arthur Schwartz — Nothing Left but Dreams/W: Henry Myers, M: Edgar Fairchild — Words and Music/W: Henry Myers, M: Charles M. Schwab.

704. Victor Bender *Bloomer Girl* (Shubert, "Herman Brasher," Oct. 5, 1944): The Farmer's Daughter; Welcome Hinges/W: E.Y. Harburg, M: Harold Arlen. *Bloomer Girl* (New York City Center, revival, "Herman Brasher," Jan. 6, 1947): same as above.

705. Frances Bendsten *Linger Longer Letty* (Fulton, "Lazelle," Nov. 20, 1919): Parisienne Mechanical Marvels/W: Bernard Grossman, M: Alfred Goodman.

706. Marc Benecke He worked as a doorman at Studio 54 in New York. *Got Tu Go Disco* (Minskoff, "Marc," June 25, 1979): In and Out/WM: Kenny Lehman, John Davis, Ray Chew, Nat Adderley, Jr., Thomas Jones, Wayne Morrison, Steve Boston, Eugene Narmore, Betty Rowland, Jerry Powell.

707. Gail K. Benedict (May 7–) B: Storm Lake, IA. *Dancin'* (Broadhurst, revue, Mar. 27, 1978): Gary Owen/WM: trad. — Pack Up Your Troubles in Your Old Kit Bag (and Smile, Smile, Smile)/W: George Asaf, M: Felix Powell. *Raggedy Ann* (Nederlander, "Bat," Oct. 16, 1986): You'll Love It/WM: Joe Raposo.

708. Dorothy Benham (Dec. 11, 1955–) B: Minneapolis, MN. *Jerome Robbins' Broadway* (Imperial, revue, Feb. 26, 1989): Somewhere/W: Stephen Sondheim, M: Leonard Bernstein.

709. Earl Benham (c 1887–Mar. 21, 1976) *Fritz in Tammany Hall* (Herald Square, "Slim Jim," Oct. 16, 1905): My Sweet/W: William Jerome, M: Jean Schwartz. *Cohan and Harris Minstrels* (New York, revue, Aug. 3, 1908): Meet Me in Rose Time Rosie/W: William Jerome, M: Jean Schwartz. *Cohan and Harris Minstrels* (New York, revue, Aug. 16, 1909): The Hat My Father Wore on St. Patrick's Day/W: William Jerome, M: Jean Schwartz. *The Little Millionaire* (George M. Cohan, "Danny Wheeler," Sept. 25, 1911): Come with Me to My Bungalow (Cohan's Bungalow Song); Musical Moon/WM: George M. Cohan. *Very Good Eddie* (39th Street > Princess, CR, "Dick Rivers," Sept. 1916): If I Find the Girl/W: John E. Hazzard, Herbert Reynolds, M: Jerome Kern — Nodding Roses/W: Schuyler Greene, Herbert Reynolds, M: Jerome Kern — Old Boy Neutral; The Same Old Game/W:

Schuyler Greene, M: Jerome Kern — On the Shore at Le Lei Wi/W: Herbert Reynolds, M: Henry Kailimai, Jerome Kern — Some Sort of Somebody (All of the Time)/W: Elsie Janis, M: Jerome Kern. *Toot-Toot!* (George M. Cohan, "Mr. Colt," Mar. 11, 1918): Runaway Colts/W: Berton Braley, M: Jerome Kern. *Hitchy-Koo of 1918* (Globe, revue, June 6, 1918): Hitchy-Koo Girl/W: ?, M: Percy Wenrich — Resurrection Rag/W: ?, M: Raymond Hubbell. *The Magic Melody* (Shubert, "Richard Palmer Adams," Nov. 11, 1919): The Little Church Around the Corner/W: Alex Gerber, M: Sigmund Romberg — Two's Company, Three's a Crowd; We Are the Fixers/W: Frederic Arnold Kummer, M: Sigmund Romberg. *Ed Wynn Carnival* (New Amsterdam, revue, Apr. 5, 1920): Goodbye Sunshine, Hello Moon/W: Gene Buck, M: William Eckstein — My Sahara Rose; Rather Than See You Once in a While/W: Grant Clarke, M: Walter Donaldson. *The Right Girl* (Times Square, "Anthony Stanton," Mar. 15, 1921): Girls All Around Me; Harmony; Old Flames; The Right Girl/W: Raymond W. Peck, M: Percy Wenrich.

710. Harry Benham (Feb. 26, 1886–July 17, 1969) B: Valparaiso, IN. *The Rainbow Girl* (New Amsterdam, "Robert Vernon Dudley," Apr. 1, 1918): In a Month or Two; Just You Alone; My Rainbow Girl/W: Rennold Wolf, M: Louis A. Hirsch.

711. Ted Beniades (Nov. 17–) B: New York, NY. *Golden Boy* (Majestic, "Roxy Gottlieb," Oct. 20, 1964): The Road Tour/W: Lee Adams, M: Charles Strouse. *Oklahoma!* (Music Theater of Lincoln Center, revival, "Ali Hakim," June 23, 1969): It's a Scandal! It's a Outrage!/W: Oscar Hammerstein II, M: Richard Rodgers.

712. P.J. Benjamin (Sept. 2, 1951–) B: Chicago, IL. *Sarava* (Mark Hellinger, "Vadinho," Feb. 23, 1979): Makulele; Play the Queen; Remember; Sarava; A Single Life/W: N. Richard Nash, M: Mitch Leigh. *Charlie and Algernon* (Helen Hayes, "Charlie," Sept. 14, 1980): Charlie and Algernon; Hey Look at Me; I Can't Tell You; I Got a Friend; I Really Loved You; The Maze; Now; Reading; Some Bright Morning; Somebody New; Whatever Time There Is/W: David Rogers, M: Charles Strouse. *Sophisticated Ladies* (Lunt-Fontanne, revue, Mar. 1, 1981): Bliblip/WM: Duke Ellington, Sid Kuller — Drop Me Off in Harlem/W: Nick Kenny, M: Duke Ellington — Fat and Forty/WM: Duke Ellington, Al Hibbler — Hey Baby/WM: Duke Ellington — Satin Doll/W: Johnny Mercer, M: Billy Strayhorn, Duke Ellington. *Wind in the Willows* (Nederlander, "Chief Weasel," Dec. 19, 1985):

Evil Weasel; Moving Up in the World; You'll Love It in Jail/WM: Roger McGough, William Perry.

713. Sue Benjamin Using the name Sue Bennett, she was a regular on TV Quiz *Kay Kyser's Kollege of Musical Knowledge* (1949), and a vocalist on *Your Hit Parade* (1951). *Small Wonder* (Coronet, revue, Nov. 29, 1948): Nobody Told Me/W: Phyllis McGinley, M: Baldwin Bergersen.

714. Andy Bennett *Head Over Heels* (George M. Cohan, "Buxaume," Aug. 29, 1918): Me/W: Edgar Allan Woolf, M: Jerome Kern.

715. David Bennett *The Office Boy* (Victoria, "Reggy Wiggins," Nov. 2, 1903): Bohemia; An Embassy Burglarious (The Burglars); Plain Mamie O'Hooley/W: Harry B. Smith, M: Ludwig Englander.

716. Eloise Bennett *Lovely Lady* (Sam H. Harris, "Parthenia," Dec. 29, 1927): At the Barbecue/W: Harry A. Steinberg, Eddie Ward, M: Dave Stamper, Harold A. Levey. *Yeah Man* (Park Lane, revue, May 26, 1932): At the Barbecue/W: Harry A. Steinberg, Edward Ward, M: Dave Stamper, Harold A. Levey — I've Got What It Takes/WM: Al Wilson, Charles Weinberg, Ken Macomber.

717. Evelyn Bennett *Americana of 1926* (Belmont, revue, July 26, 1926): Blowin' the Blues Away/W: Ira Gershwin, M: Phil Charig — Tabloid Papers/W: J.P. McEvoy, M: Con Conrad — Why Do Ya Roll Those Eyes?/W: Morrie Ryskind, M: Phil Charig. *Merry-Go-Round* (Klaw, revue, May 31, 1927): Cider Ella/W: ?, M: Gene Salzer — Let's Be Happy Now/W: Howard Dietz, Morrie Ryskind, M: Henry Souvaine, Jay Gorney. *Allez-Oop* (Earl Carroll, revue, Aug. 2, 1927/Oct. 3, 1927): Hoof, Hoof; A Kiss with a Kick; What Does It Mean?/W: Leo Robin, M: Phil Charig, Richard Myers. *Good Boy* (Hammerstein's, "Elvira Hobbs," Sept. 5, 1928): I Have My Moments; I Wanna Be Loved by You; What Makes You So Wonderful?/W: Bert Kalmar, M: Harry Ruby, Herbert Stothart.

718. Joe Bennett *West Side Story* (New York City Center, revival, "Action," Apr. 8, 1964): Gee, Officer Krupke!/W: Stephen Sondheim, M: Leonard Bernstein.

719. Johnstone Bennett (Nov. 3, 1870–Apr. 15, 1906) B: at sea. He was a famous female impersonator. *A Female Drummer* (Star > Manhattan, "Haza Bargain" and "Baby" and "Saleslady," Dec. 26, 1898): A Female Drummer; My Own Best Love; Pinkey, My Darling; A Terpsichorean Trifle/W: Charles E. Blaney, M: Frank David. *The Silver Slipper* (Broadway, CR, "Belle

Jimper," Nov. 24, 1902): Class/W: Charles H. Taylor, M: Leslie Stuart.

720. Jordan Bennett *Cyrano: The Musical* (Neil Simon, "Cyrano," Nov. 21, 1993): Aria; Balcony Scene; Cyrano's Story; The Duel; The Evening; Every Day, Every Night; Hate Me; The Letter; A Letter for Roxane; Loving Her; A Message from Roxane; Moonsong; An Old Wound; Poetry; Roxane's Confession; Tell Her Now; Two Musketeers; When I Write; Where's All This Anger Coming From; A White Sash/W: Peter Reeves, Koen Van Dijk, Add. W: Sheldon Harnick, M: Ad Van Dijk.

721. Keith Robert Bennett *The High Rollers Social and Pleasure Club* (Helen Hayes, revue, "Wonder Boy #1," Apr. 21, 1992): Challenge Dance; Feet Don't Fail Me Now; Fun Time; Injuns Here We Come; Jelly Roll/WM: ?.

722. Linda Bennett (June 19, 1942–) B: Salt Lake City, UT. *Brigadoon* (New York City Center, revival, "Fiona MacLaren," Dec. 23, 1964): Almost Like Being in Love; From This Day On; The Heather on the Hill; Waitin' for My Dearie/W: Alan Jay Lerner, M: Frederick Loewe. *Wonderful Town* (New York City Center, revival, "Eileen Sherwood," May 17, 1967): Conversation Piece (Nice Talk, Nice People); A Little Bit in Love; My Darlin' Eileen; Ohio; Wrong Note Rag/W: Betty Comden, Adolph Green, M: Leonard Bernstein.

723. Lois Bennett *Ziegfeld Follies of 1924-1925* (New Amsterdam, revue, Aug. 3, 1925): In the Shade of the Alamo/W: Gene Buck, M: Raymond Hubbell — Toddle Along/W: Gene Buck, M: Werner Janssen.

724. Meg Bennett (Oct. 4, 1948–) B: Los Angeles, CA. *Grease* (Broadhurst, CR, "Marty"): Freddy, My Love/WM: Jim Jacobs, Warren Casey.

725. Wilda Bennett (Dec. 19, 1894–Dec. 20, 1967) B: Asbury Park, NJ. *The Only Girl* (39th Street > Lyric, "Ruth Wilson," Nov. 2, 1914): The Compact; When You're Away; You're the Only One for Me/W: Henry Blossom, M: Victor Herbert. *The Riviera Girl* (New Amsterdam, "Sylva Vareska," Sept. 24, 1917): The Fall of Man; Gypsy Bring Your Fiddle; Just a Voice to Call Me, Dear; Life's a Tale; Man, Man, Man; Will You Forget?/W: P.G. Wodehouse, M: Emmerich Kalman. *The Girl Behind the Gun* (New Amsterdam, "Lucienne Lambrissac," Sept. 16, 1918): The Girl Behind the Man Behind the Gun; Some Day Waiting Will End; There's a Light in Your Eyes; There's Life in the Old Dog Yet/W: P.G. Wodehouse, M: Ivan Caryll. *Apple Blossoms* (Globe, "Nancy," Oct. 7, 1919): I'll Be

True to You; When the Wedding Bells Are Ringing; You Are Free/W: William Le Baron, M: Victor Jacobi — Star of Love; Who Can Tell?/W: William Le Baron, M: Fritz Kreisler. *Music Box Revue of 1921* (Music Box, revue, Sept. 22, 1921): Behind the Fan; The Legend of the Pearls; Say It with Music/WM: Irving Berlin. *The Lady in Ermine* (Ambassador, "Mariana," Oct. 2, 1922): Childhood Days/WM: ?— Farewell to Adrian; When Hearts Are Young (in Springtime)/W: Cyrus D. Wood, M: Sigmund Romberg, Alfred Goodman — Mariana/W: Harry Graham, M: Jean Gilbert. *Madame Pompadour* (Martin Beck, "Mme. la Marquise de Pompadour," Nov. 11, 1924): By the Light of the Moon; I'll Be Your Soldier; Magic Moments; Oh! Joseph; Reminiscence; Tell Me What Your Eyes Were Made For/W: Clare Kummer, M: Leo Fall. *Lovely Lady* (Sam H. Harris, CR, "Folly Watteau," Apr. 9, 1928): Boy Friends; Breakfast in Bed; Lovely Lady/W: Cyrus D. Wood, M: Dave Stamper, Harold A. Levey.

726. Bruce Bennetts *Jesus Christ Superstar* (Mark Hellinger, CR, "Old Man," May 1972): Peter's Denial/W: Tim Rice, M: Andrew Lloyd Webber.

727. Ben Benny *Paradise Alley* (Casino, "Dusty," Mar. 31, 1924): In the Musical Comedy Shows; We're Looking for the Bobbed Hair Bandit/WM: Howard Johnson — Put on the Ritz/W: Howard Johnson, M: Irving Bibo.

728. Victor Benoit (1876–Jan. 16, 1943) B: Ottawa, Canada. *Girl o' Mine* (Bijou, CR, "Duc de Bouvais," Mar. 4, 1918): The Winning Race/W: Philip Bartholomae, M: Frank Tours.

729. Albertine Benson *Little Nemo* (New Amsterdam, "Valentine Fairy" and "Barometer Girl," Oct. 20, 1908): Different Kinds of Weather; Give Us a Fleet; When Cupid Is the Postman; Won't You Be My Valentine?/W: Harry B. Smith, M: Victor Herbert.

730. Betty Benson M: Film producer Sam Spiegel. *3 for Tonight* (Plymouth, revue, Apr. 6, 1955): Fly Bird/W: Robert Wells, M: Walter Schumann.

731. Cindy Benson (Oct. 2, 1951–) B: Attleboro, MA. *Cats* (Winter Garden, CR, "Jennyanydots"): Bustopher Jones; The Old Gumbie Cat/W: T.S. Eliot, M: Andrew Lloyd Webber.

732. Harry Benson (May 25, 1870–Feb. 17, 1937) B: Halifax, Nova Scotia, Canada. *The New Yorkers* (Edyth Totten, revue, Mar. 10, 1927): He Who Gets Slapped/W: Henry Myers, M: Arthur Schwartz — Slow River/W: Henry Myers, M: Charles M. Schwab.

733. Jodi Benson (Oct. 10, 1961–) B: Rockford, IL. *Smile* (Lunt-Fontanne, "Doria Hudson," Nov. 24, 1986): Disneyland; Dressing Room Scene; Postcard #3/W: Howard Ashman, M: Marvin Hamlisch. *Welcome to the Club* (Music Box, "Betty Bursteter," Apr. 13, 1989): At My Side/WM: A.E. Hotchner, Cy Coleman. *Crazy for You* (Sam S. Shubert, "Polly Baker," Feb. 19, 1992): But Not for Me; Could You Use Me?; Embraceable You; I Got Rhythm; Shall We Dance?; Someone to Watch Over Me; Stiff Upper Lip/W: Ira Gershwin, M: George Gershwin.

734. Lucille Benson (July 17, 1914–Feb. 17, 1984) B: Scottsboro, AL. *Walking Happy* (Lunt-Fontanne, "Mrs. Figgins," Nov. 26, 1966): A Joyful Thing/W: Sammy Cahn, M: James Van Heusen.

735. Robby Benson (Jan. 21, 1956–) B: Dallas, TX. He was the voice of the Beast in the Disney cartoon version of *Beauty and the Beast* (1991). *The Rothschilds* (Lunt-Fontanne, "Young Solomon Rothschild," Oct. 19, 1970): Sons/W: Sheldon Harnick, M: Jerry Bock.

736. Marion Bent (Dec. 23, 1879–July 28, 1940) B: New York, NY. M: PAT ROONEY, JR., her childhood sweetheart, and performed with him for many years in vaudeville. *Love Birds* (Apollo, "Mamie O'Grady," Mar. 15, 1921): Can Macy Do Without Me?; Girl Like Grandma/W: Ballard Macdonald, M: Sigmund Romberg.

737. Irene Bentley (c 1870–June 3, 1940) B: Baltimore, MD. M: songwriter Harry B. Smith, her second husband. *The Casino Girl* (Casino, "Lotta Rocks," Mar. 19, 1900): The Casino Girl/W: Harry B. Smith, M: Harry T. MacConnell. *The Belle of Bohemia* (Casino, "Geraldine McDuffy," Sept. 24, 1900): Always Make Allowances for Love; Fairies' Lullaby; The Girl Who Is Up to Date; The Lady in the Moon/W: Harry B. Smith, M: Ludwig Englander. *The Strollers* (Knickerbocker, June 24, 1901): A Lesson in Flirtation/W: Harry B. Smith, M: Ludwig Englander. *The Wild Rose* (Knickerbocker, "Rose Romany," May 5, 1902): The Little Gipsy Maid/W: Harry B. Smith, Cecil Mack, M: Will Marion Cook. *The Girl from Dixie* (Madison Square, "Kitty Calvert," Dec. 14, 1903): The Dissipated Kitten/W: Harry B. Smith, M: A. Baldwin Sloane — When the Moon Comes Peeping O'er the Hill/W: Bob Cole, M: J. Rosamond Johnson. *The Belle of Mayfair* (Daly's, H.S.H. Princess Carl of Ehbreneitstein," Dec. 3, 1906): And the Weeping Willow Wept/W: George Arthurs, M: Leslie Stuart — Come to St. George's; Said I to Myself; We've Come from Court/WM: Leslie Stuart. *The Mimic World* (Casino, revue, "Sonia," July 9, 1908): Your Lips Say No but Your Eyes Say Yes/W: Edward Madden, M: Ben M. Jerome.

738. John Bentley (Jan. 31, 1940–) B: Jackson Heights, NY. *A Funny Thing Happened on the Way to the Forum* (Lunt-Fontanne, revival, CR, "Prologus" and "Pseudolus," July 24, 1972): Bring Me My Bride; Comedy Tonight; Everybody Ought to Have a Maid; Free; The House of Marcus Lycus; Lovely/WM: Stephen Sondheim.

739. Jordan Bentley *Wonderful Town* (Winter Garden, "Wreck," Feb. 25, 1953): Pass the Football/W: Betty Comden, Adolph Green, M: Leonard Bernstein. *Wonderful Town* (New York City Center, revival, "Wreck," Mar. 5, 1958): same as above.

740. Marjorie Bentley *Oh, My Dear!* (Princess > 39th Street, "Grace Spelvin," Nov. 27, 1918): Childhood Days; Come Where Nature Calls; I Wonder Whether (I've Loved You All My Life); Try Again; You Never Know/W: P.G. Wodehouse, M: Louis A. Hirsch.

741. Robert Bentley (1895–Apr. 19, 1958) *Strike Up the Band* (Times Square, "Richard K. Sloane," Jan. 14, 1930): Fletcher's American Chocolate Choral Society; He Knows Milk/W: Ira Gershwin, M: George Gershwin.

742. Fremont Benton *The Midnight Girl* (44th Street, "Clarisse," Feb. 23, 1914): Burglars/WM: Adolf Philipp, Edward A. Paulton, Jean Briquet.

743. Marguerite Benton *Let's Face It!* (Imperial, "Madge Hall," Oct. 29, 1941): A Little Rumba Numba/WM: Cole Porter.

744. Mimi Benzell (Apr. 6, 1922–Dec. 23, 1970) B: Bridgeport, CT. She sang leads with the Metropolitan Opera from 1944-1950, and often appeared as a guest artist on TV variety shows. *Milk and Honey* (Martin Beck, "Ruth," Oct. 10, 1961): As Simple as That; Shalom; That Was Yesterday; There's No Reason in the World; The Wedding/WM: Jerry Herman.

745. Roger Berdahl *Shenandoah* (Alvin, CR, "Jacob," July 29, 1976): Next to Lovin' (I Like Fightin')/W: Peter Udell, M: Gary Geld.

746. Beatrice Berenson *Bitter Sweet* (44th Street, revival, "Gloria" and "Freda," May 7, 1934): Alas, the Time Is Past; Ladies of the Town; The Last Dance; Tarara Boom-de-Ay/WM: Noel Coward.

747. Florence Beresford *Little Simplicity* (Astor > 44th Street, "Maude McCall," Nov. 4, 1918): A Military Fox Trot Tune/W: Rida Johnson Young, M: Augustus Barratt.

748. Kitty Berg *Broadway Brevities of 1920* (Winter Garden, revue, Sept. 29, 1920): We've Got the Stage Door Blues/W: Bert Kalmar, M: Harry Ruby.

749. Sallie Berge *The Vanderbilt Cup* (Broadway, "Mrs. Dillenberg," Jan. 16, 1906): The Fatal Curse of Beauty/W: Raymond W. Peck, M: Robert Hood Bowers.

750. Nella Bergen (Dec. 2, 1873–Apr. 24, 1919) B: New York, NY. M: DE WOLF HOPPER. *Wang* (Lyric, revival, "Marie," Apr. 18, 1904): Dear Golden Days; Where Are You Going, My Pretty Maid?/W: J. Cheever Goodwin, M: Woolson Morse. *The Free Lance* (New Amsterdam, "Princess Yolande," Apr. 16, 1906): The Carrier Pigeon; Come, My Dear; Three Love Stories/W: Harry B. Smith, M: John Philip Sousa. *The Talk of New York* (Knickerbocker, "Grace Palmer," Dec. 3, 1907): Burning Up the Boulevard; I Want You/WM: George M. Cohan. *He Came from Milwaukee* (Casino, "Leska," Sept. 21, 1910): Come Back to Bohemia; In Gypsy Land/W: Edward Madden, M: Ben M. Jerome, Louis A. Hirsch.

751. Polly Bergen (July 14, 1930–) B: Knoxville, TN. M: JEROME COURTLAND. The singer and actress often appeared on TV dramas, but may be best remembered for the popular quiz *To Tell the Truth* (1956). *John Murray Anderson's Almanac* (Imperial, revue, Dec. 10, 1953): The Earth and the Sky/WM: John Rox — Fini/WM: Richard Adler, Jerry Ross — I Dare to Dream/ W: Sammy Gallup, M: Michael Grace, Carl Tucker — La Loge/WM: Herb Farjeon — My Love Is a Wanderer/WM: Bart Howard. *First Impressions* (Alvin, "Elizabeth Bennet," Mar. 19, 1959): Fragrant Flower; The Heart Has Won the Game; I Suddenly Find You Agreeable; I'm Me; Let's Fetch the Carriage; Love Will Find Out the Way; A Perfect Evening; This Really Isn't Me; Wasn't It a Simply Lovely Wedding?/ WM: Robert Goldman, Glenn Paxton, George David Weiss.

752. Lauree Berger *A Chorus Line* (Shubert, CR, "Maggie," Apr. 26, 1976): At the Ballet/W: Edward Kleban, M: Marvin Hamlisch.

753. Stephen Berger (May 16, 1954–) B: Philadelphia, PA. *Little Me* (Eugene O'Neill, revival, "Doctor," Jan. 21, 1982): Goodbye/W: Carolyn Leigh, M: Cy Coleman. *Wonderful Town* (New York State, revival, "Chick Clark," Nov. 8, 1994): Conversation Piece (Nice Talk, Nice People)/W: Betty Comden, Adolph Green, M: Leonard Bernstein.

754. Lee Bergere (Apr. 10, 1924–) B: Brooklyn, NY. On TV he played Joseph Anders on *Dynasty* (1981) and Justin Nash on *Falcon Crest*

(1989). *Man of La Mancha* (Vivian Beaumont, revival, "Dr. Carrasco," June 22, 1972): I'm Only Thinking of Him/W: Joe Darion, M: Mitch Leigh.

755. Gertrude Berggrem *Revenge with Music* (New Amsterdam, CR, "Consuela," Feb. 11, 1935): In the Noonday Sun/W: Howard Dietz, M: Arthur Schwartz.

756. Herbert Berghof (Sept. 13, 1909–Nov. 5, 1990) B: Vienna, Austria. Distinguished actor for many years in Vienna and Berlin, and founder, with his wife Uta Hagen, of the Herbert Berghof Studio in NYC. *Reunion in New York* (Little, revue, Feb. 21, 1940): Dachau/W: Jura Soyfer, Milton Hindus, M: Andre Singer. *Oklahoma!* (St. James, CR, "Ali Hakim," July 1944): It's a Scandal! It's a Outrage!/W: Oscar Hammerstein II, M: Richard Rodgers.

757. Michael Berglund *Starlight Express* (Gershwin, "Weltschaft," Mar. 15, 1987): Race One/W: Richard Stilgoe, M: Andrew Lloyd Webber.

758. Brenda Bergman *Man on the Moon* (Little, "Miss America," Jan. 29, 1975): Mission Control/WM: John Phillips.

759. Caryl Bergman *Sweet Adeline* (Hammerstein's, "Nellie Schmidt," Sept. 3, 1929): Out of the Blue/W: Oscar Hammerstein II, M: Jerome Kern. *The Gang's All Here* (Imperial, CR, "Julie Winterbottom," Mar. 1931): Adorable Julie; The Moon, the Wind and the Sea; Speaking of You; What Have You Done to Me?/W: Owen Murphy, Robert A. Simon, M: Lewis E. Gensler.

760. Henry Bergman (c 1887–Nov. 6, 1962) M: GLADYS CLARK, who performed with him. *Step This Way* (Shubert > Astor, May 29, 1916): By the Sad Luana Shore/WM: E. Ray Goetz — When the Sun Goes Down in Romany (My Heart Goes Roaming Back to You)/W: Sam M. Lewis, Joe Young, M: Bert Grant. *The Passing Show of 1917* (Winter Garden, revue, Apr. 26, 1917): Meet Me at the Station, Dear/W: Sam M. Lewis, Joe Young, M: Ted Snyder — My Yokohama Girl/W: Alfred Bryan, M: Harry Tierney — A Table for Two/W: Harold Atteridge, M: Ray Perkins.

761. Sandahl Bergman (Nov. 14, 1951–) B: Kansas City, MO. *A Chorus Line* (Shubert, CR, "Judy," Apr. 26, 1976): And.../W: Edward Kleban, M: Marvin Hamlisch. *Dancin'* (Broadhurst, revue, Mar. 27, 1978): Here You Come Again/WM: Barry Mann, Cynthia Weil — Stouthearted Men/W: Oscar Hammerstein II, M: Sigmund Romberg — Was Dog a Doughnut/WM: Cat Stevens.

762. Beth Beri *Jack and Jill* (Globe, "Phyllis Sisson," Mar. 22, 1923): Dancing in the Dark/W: Oliver Deerin, M: Muriel Pollock. *Kid Boots* (Earl Carroll > Selwyn, "Beth," Dec. 31, 1923): I'm in My Glory; In the Swim at Miami; When the Cocoanuts Call/W: Joseph McCarthy, M: Harry Tierney.

763. Marguerite Beriza *Maid in America* (Winter Garden, revue, "Diana," Feb. 18, 1915): Diana; Garden of Paradise/W: Harold Atteridge, M: Sigmund Romberg.

764. Busby Berkeley (Nov. 29, 1895–Mar. 14, 1976) B: Los Angeles, CA. Dance director, famous for his unique choreography in Hollywood musicals of the 1930s. *Present Arms* (Mansfield, "Douglas Atwell," Apr. 26, 1928): I'm a Fool, Little One; A Kiss for Cinderella; Tell It to the Marines (A Bunch o' Nuts); You Took Advantage of Me/W: Lorenz Hart, M: Richard Rodgers.

765. John (Johnnie; Johnny) Berkes (June 13, 1895–July 5, 1951) B: Trenton, NJ. With partner FRANK GRACE they were known as Grace and Berkes. *Robinson Crusoe, Jr.* (Winter Garden, Feb. 17, 1916): (Go Ahead and) Dance a Little More/W: Harold Atteridge, M: James F. Hanley — Don't Be a Sailor; Happy Hottentots/W: Harold Atteridge, M: Sigmund Romberg. *Sinbad* (Winter Garden > Century, Feb. 14, 1918): The Bedalumbo/W: Harold Atteridge, M: Al Jolson — Love Ahoy; The Rag Lad of Bagdad; Raz-Ma-Taz/W: Harold Atteridge, M: Sigmund Romberg. *The Passing Show of 1921* (Winter Garden, revue, Dec. 29, 1920): The Dancing Blues; I'm Oriental [May 2, 1921]/W: Harold Atteridge, M: Lew Pollack — The Sweetest Melody/WM: Abner Silver.

766. Milton Berle (July 12, 1908–Mar. 27, 2002) B: New York, NY. More than one generation of TV viewers remembers the popular comic as Uncle Miltie. Before that, he was a child actor in silent movies. *Saluta* (Imperial, "Windy Walker," Aug. 28, 1934): The Great Dictator and Me/W: Will Morrissey, Milton Berle, M: Frank D'Armond — I'll Produce for You; La Vita/W: Will Morrissey, M: Frank D'Armond. *Ziegfeld Follies of 1943* (Winter Garden, revue, Apr. 1, 1943): The Micromaniac/WM: Harold Rome.

767. Irving Berlin (May 11, 1888–Sept. 21, 1989) B: Temun, Russia. One of the great songwriters of all time. *Up and Down Broadway* (Casino, revue, July 18, 1910): Oh, That Beautiful Rag/W: Irving Berlin, M: Ted Snyder. *Yip, Yip, Yaphank* (Century > Lexington Avenue Opera House, revue, Aug. 19, 1918): Oh! How I Hate to Get Up in the Morning/WM: Irving Berlin. *This Is the Army* (Broadway, revue, July 4, 1942): Oh! How I Hate to Get Up in the Morning/WM: Irving Berlin.

768. Warren Berlinger (Aug. 31, 1937–) B: Brooklyn, NY. He played Chief Engineer Dobritch on the TV sitcom *Operation Petticoat* (1978). *A Broadway Musical* (Lunt-Fontanne, "Eddie Bell," Dec. 21, 1978): A Broadway Musical; Don't Tell Me; Lawyers; Together; What You Go Through/W: Lee Adams, M: Charles Strouse.

769. Shelley Berman (Feb. 3, 1926–) B: Chicago, IL. A humorist known for cabaret monologues. *The Girls Against the Boys* (Alvin, revue, Nov. 2, 1959): Light Travelin' Man/W: Arnold B. Horwitt, M: Albert Hague — Overspend; Rich Butterfly/W: Arnold B. Horwitt, M: Richard Lewine. *A Family Affair* (Billy Rose, "Alfie Nathan," Jan. 27, 1962): Beautiful; Harmony; I'm Worse Than Anybody; Revenge; Right Girls/W: James Goldman, William Goldman, M: John Kander.

770. Mina Bern (May 5, 1920–) B: Poland. *Those Were the Days* (Edison, revue, Nov. 7, 1990): Dear Mama/W: Mani Leib, M: trad. — I Wish I Were Single Again; In a Poor Little House/WM: trad. — Welcoming the Sabbath/W: Ben Bonus, M: Ben Yomen.

771. Barry K. Bernal (?–Oct. 31, 1994) B: San Diego, CA. *Starlight Express* (Gershwin, "Red Caboose," Mar. 15, 1987): Final Selection; First Final; One Rock & Roll Too Many; Race One; There's Me; Wide Smile, High Style, That's Me/W: Richard Stilgoe, M: Andrew Lloyd Webber. *Miss Saigon* (Broadway, "Thuy," Apr. 11, 1991): Back in Town; The Guilt Inside Your Head; The Morning of the Dragon; You Will Not Touch Him/W: Richard Maltby, Jr., Alain Boublil, M: Claude-Michel Schonberg. *Cats* (Winter Garden, CR, "Mistoffolees"): The Invitation to the Jellicle Ball; Mr. Mistoffolees; Mungojerrie and Rumpleteazer/W: T.S. Eliot, M: Andrew Lloyd Webber.

772. Barney Bernard (Aug. 17, 1877–Mar. 21, 1924) B: Rochester, NY. *The Soul Kiss* (New York, "Sol Skevinsky," Jan. 28, 1908): The Dollar Sign/W: Jessie Villars, M: Fleta Jan Brown — My Affinity; Under the Bargain Tree [Mar. 2, 1908]/W: Harry B. Smith, M: Maurice Levi. *The Silver Star* (New Amsterdam, "Mr. Wiseheimer," Nov. 1, 1909): If Only I Were Santa Claus/W: Harry B. Smith, M: Robert Hood Bowers. *The Whirl of Society* (Winter Garden, revue, Mar. 5, 1912): Lead Me to That Beautiful Band [Apr. 29, 1912]/WM: E. Ray Goetz, Irving Berlin.

773. Dick Bernard (Dec. 21, 1866–Dec. 25, 1925) B: Birmingham, England. Brother of SAM BERNARD. *The Belle of Bohemia* (Casino, "Rudolph Dinkelhauser," Sept. 24, 1900): Beer, Beautiful Beer/W: Harry B. Smith, M: Ludwig Englander.

774. Frank Bernard *Bombo* (Al Jolson > Winter Garden, "Alfred" and "Alfredo," Oct. 6, 1921): In a Curio Shop; No One Loves a Clown/ W: Harold Atteridge, M: Sigmund Romberg.

775. Sam Bernard (June 3, 1863–May 18, 1927) B: Birmingham, England. Brother of DICK BERNARD. He came to the U.S. as a child and worked in vaudeville, becoming a dialect comedian before joining Weber and Fields. *The Man in the Moon* (New York, "Conan Doyle," Apr. 24, 1899): In Spite of Puck and Judge/W: Louis Harrison, Stanislaus Stange, M: Ludwig Englander. *The Casino Girl* (Casino, "The Khedive of Egypt," Mar. 19, 1900): I'll Put a Tax On That/W: Harry B. Smith, M: Harry T. MacConnell. *The Belle of Bohemia* (Casino, "Adolph Klotz," Sept. 24, 1900): Always Make Allowances for Love; He Was a Married Man; Never Again/W: Harry B. Smith, M: Ludwig Englander. *The Silver Slipper* (Broadway, "Henny Bismark Henschs," Oct. 27, 1902): I'd Be Satisfied with Life/WM: George M. Cohan. *The Girl from Kay's* (Herald Square, "Max Hoggenheimer [Piggy]," Nov. 2, 1903): Mr. Hoggenheimer of Park Lane/W: Adrian Ross, M: Ivan Caryll — Sufficiency/WM: Clare Kummer. *Nearly a Hero* (Casino, "Ludwig Knoedler," Feb. 24, 1908): I Was a Hero Too/W: Harry Williams, M: Egbert Van Alstyne — A Singer Sang a Song/W: Will Heelan, M: Seymour Furth. *The Girl and the Wizard* (Casino, "Herman Scholz," Sept. 27, 1909): How Can You Toot a Toot-Toot?/W: Will Heelan, M: Seymour Furth — Opera Comique [Nov. 1, 1909]/WM: Melville Gideon. *He Came from Milwaukee* (Casino, "Herman von Schnellenvein," Sept. 21, 1910): Bring Back My Lena to Me/WM: Irving Berlin, Ted Snyder — Consequences/W: Edward Madden, M: Ben M. Jerome, Louis A. Hirsch. *All for the Ladies* (Lyric, "Leo von Laubenheim," Dec. 30, 1912): It's Permissible/W: Henry Blossom, M: Alfred G. Robyn. *The Belle of Bond Street* (Shubert, "Max Hoggenheimer," Mar. 30, 1914): Mr. Hoggenheimer of Park Lane/W: Adrian Ross, M: Ivan Caryll — Who Paid the Rent for Mrs. Rip Van Winkle When Rip Van Winkle Went Away?/W: Alfred Bryan, M: Fred Fisher. *As You Were* (Central, revue, "Wolfie Wafflestein," Jan. 27, 1920): Who Ate Napoleons with Josephine When Bonaparte Was Away?/W: Alfred Bryan, M: E. Ray Goetz. *Music Box Revue of 1921* (Music Box, revue, Sept. 22, 1921): They Call It Dancing/WM: Irving Berlin. *Piggy* (Royale, "Piggy Hoggenheimer," Jan. 11, 1927): Didn't It?; It's Easy to Say Hello (But So Hard to Say Goodbye)/W: Lew Brown, M: Cliff Friend.

776. Herschel Bernardi (Oct. 30, 1923–May 9, 1986) B: New York, NY. He grew up in an acting family, appearing on stage from the age of 6 months. He played Tevye over 700 times, and was Lt. Jacoby on the TV police drama *Peter Gunn* (1958). In commercials, his was the voice of the Jolly Green Giant and Charlie the Tuna. *Bajour* (Shubert, "Cockeye Johnny," Nov. 23, 1964): Bajour; Honest Man; Move Over, New York; Words, Words, Words/WM: Walter Marks. *Fiddler on the Roof* (Imperial, CR, "Tevye," Nov. 8, 1965/Sept. 18, 1967): Anatevka; Do You Love Me?; If I Were a Rich Man; Sabbath Prayer; Sunrise, Sunset; The Tailor, Motel Kamzoil; To Life; Tradition/W: Sheldon Harnick, M: Jerry Bock. *Zorba* (Imperial, "Zorba," Nov. 17, 1968): The First Time; Goodbye, Canavaro; Grandpapa; I Am Free; No Boom Boom; Y'Assou/W: Fred Ebb, M: John Kander. *Fiddler on the Roof* (New York State, revival, "Tevye," July 9, 1981): same as above.

777. Keith Bernardo *Cats* (Winter Garden, CR, "Munkustrap," Sept. 20, 1993): The Awefull Battle of the Pekes and Pollicles; The Marching Songs of the Pollicle Dogs; Old Deuteronomy/W: T.S. Eliot, M: Andrew Lloyd Webber.

778. Ben Bernie (May 31, 1891–Oct. 20, 1943) B: Bayonne, NJ. Vaudeville partner for a time of PHIL BAKER. The comedian, violinist and bandleader formed his first band in 1922, calling himself The Old Maestro. *Here's Howe!* (Broadhurst, "Dan Dabney," May 1, 1928): Crazy Rhythm/W: Irving Caesar, M: Joseph Meyer, Roger Wolfe Kahn.

779. Peggy Bernier (Mar. 19, 1907–Mar. 5, 2001) B: Rhinebeck, NY. M: MILTON WATSON. *Sons o' Guns* (Imperial, CR, "Bernice Pearce," Mar. 31, 1930): Let's Merge; Red Hot and Blue Rhythm; There's a Rainbow on the Way/W: Arthur Swanstrom, Benny Davis, M: J. Fred Coots. *You Said It* (46th Street, "Hattie Hudson," Jan. 19, 1931): Sweet and Hot; They Learn About Women from Me; You'll Do/W: Jack Yellen, M: Harold Arlen.

780. Mabel Berra *Little Nemo* (New Amsterdam, CR, "Valentine Fairy" and "Barometer Girl," Dec. 28, 1908): Different Kinds of Weather; Give Us a Fleet; When Cupid Is the

Postman; Won't You Be My Valentine?/W: Harry B. Smith, M: Victor Herbert.

781. Maud Lillian Berri M: FRANK MOULAN. *The Sultan of Sulu* (Wallack's, "Henrietta Budd," Dec. 29, 1902): Carmena; Engaged in a Sort of Way; Foolish Wedding Bells; Oh, What a Bump; Palm Branches Waving; Since I First Met You/W: George Ade, M: Alfred G. Wathall. *Humpty Dumpty* (New Amsterdam, "Prince Rudolph," Nov. 14, 1904): Cupid Reigns King/W: Bob Cole, James Weldon Johnson, M: Frederic Solomon — Mexico/W: James Weldon Johnson, M: Bob Cole — On Lalawana's Shore/W: James Weldon Johnson, M: J. Rosamond Johnson. *The Grand Mogul* (New Amsterdam, "Ruth Walker," Mar. 25, 1907): Love Is Not for a Day; Nestle by My Side/W: Frank Pixley, M: Gustav Luders.

782. Audrey Berry (Oct. 23, 1906–) *Take the Air* (Waldorf, "Marguerite," Nov. 22, 1927): All Aboard for Times Square/W: Gene Buck, M: Dave Stamper.

783. Eric Berry (Jan. 9, 1913–Sept. 2, 1993) B: London, England. He appeared in *Pippin* for its entire Broadway run. *The Boy Friend* (Royale, "Percival Browne," Sept. 30, 1954): Fancy Forgetting; The You-Don't-Want-to-Play-with-Me Blues/WM: Sandy Wilson. *Pippin* (Imperial, "Charles," Oct. 23, 1972): War Is a Science; Welcome Home, Son/WM: Stephen Schwartz.

784. Ken Berry (Nov. 3, 1933–) B: Moline, IL. He appeared as Capt. Wilton Parmenter on the TV sitcom *F-Troop* (1965), and as Sam Jones in *Mayberry R.F.D.* (1968). *The Billy Barnes People* (Royale, revue, June 13, 1961): Don't Bother; The End?; Let's Get Drunk; Where Is the Clown?/WM: Billy Barnes.

785. Marilyn Berry *Simply Heavenly* (Playhouse, "Joyce Lane," Aug. 20, 1957): Love Is Simply Heavenly/W: Langston Hughes, M: David Martin.

786. Mary Sue Berry *Camelot* (Majestic, "Nimue," Dec. 3, 1960): Follow Me/W: Alan Jay Lerner, M: Frederick Loewe.

787. Sarah Uriarte Berry see SARAH URIARTE.

788. Beulah Berson *George White's Scandals of 1923* (Globe, revue, June 18, 1923): Let's Be Lonesome Together [June 25, 1923]/W: B.G. DeSylva, E. Ray Goetz, M: George Gershwin — You and I (in Old Versailles)/W: B.G. DeSylva, M: George Gershwin, Jack Green. *Blossom Time* (Jolson, revival, "Mitzi," Mar. 8, 1926): Love Is a Riddle; Moment Musicale; Only One Love Ever Fills the Heart; Peace to My Lonely Heart; Song of Love; Tell Me, Daisy; Three Little

Maids/W: Dorothy Donnelly, M: Sigmund Romberg.

789. Barron Berthald *Rob Roy* (Herald Square, "Prince Charles Edward Stuart," Oct. 29, 1894): The Lay of the Cavalier; My True Love Is a Shepherdess/W: Harry B. Smith, M: Reginald De Koven.

790. Helen Bertram (1869–) B: Tuscola, IL. *The Viceroy* (Knickerbocker, "Tivolini," Apr. 9, 1900): Hear Me; 'Neath the Blue Neapolitan Skies; That's My Idea of Love/W: Harry B. Smith, M: Victor Herbert. *Foxy Quiller* (Broadway, "La Colomba," Nov. 5, 1900): The Legend of the Tarantella; Poor Shepherds We; Song to Fishermen; The Vendetta/W: Harry B. Smith, M: Reginald De Koven. *The Prince of Pilsen* (Broadway, "Mrs. Madison Crocker," Mar. 17, 1903): The American Girl (Song of the Cities); Floral Fete (Our Floral Queen); A Season at the Shore; The Widow/W: Frank Pixley, M: Gustav Luders. *The Gingerbread Man* (Liberty > New York, "Jack Horner," Dec. 25, 1905): Beautiful Land of Bon Bon; Mazie/W: Frederic Ranken, M: A. Baldwin Sloane. *The Land of Nod* (New York, "Jack of Hearts," Apr. 1, 1907): Love Is Contagious; My Cinderella/W: Will M. Hough, Frank R. Adams; M: Joseph E. Howard.

791. Joe Besser (Aug. 12, 1907–Mar. 1, 1988) B: St. Louis, MO. One of the Three Stooges in the 1950s. *If the Shoe Fits* (Century, "Herman," Dec. 5, 1946): Am I a Man or a Mouse?; In the Morning/W: June Carroll, M: David Raksin.

792. Mimi Bessette (Jan. 15, 1956–) B: Midland, MI. *The Best Little Whorehouse in Texas* (Eugene O'Neill, CR, "Angelette Imogene Charlene" and "Dawn," May 1982): Angelette March; Hard Candy Christmas/WM: Carol Hall.

793. Alvah Bessie (June 4, 1904–July 21, 1985) B: New York, NY. Screenwriter and novelist, he was blacklisted in 1949 as one of the so called Hollywood Ten. *The Garrick Gaieties of 1925* (Garrick, revue, May 17, 1925): The Guild Gilded/W: Lorenz Hart, M: Richard Rodgers.

794. Paul Best (Aug. 30, 1908–) B: Berlin, Germany. *The Firebrand of Florence* (Alvin, "Marquis," Mar. 22, 1945): Come to Paris/W: Ira Gershwin, M: Kurt Weill. *Sweethearts* (Shubert, revival, "Baron Petrus Von Tromp," Jan. 21, 1947): Jeannette and Her Little Wooden Shoes; Pilgrims of Love/W: Robert B. Smith, M: Victor Herbert.

795. David Bethea *Early to Bed* (Broadhurst, "Gardener," June 17, 1943): Hi De Hi Ho in Harlem; Slightly Less Than Wonderful/W: George Marion, Jr., M: Fats Waller.

796. Valerie Bettis (Dec. 2, 1919–Sept. 26,

1982) B: Houston, TX. Dancer, choreographer, actress and director, she was a member of the 1939 World's Fair's "Railroads on Parade" ballet. *Great to Be Alive* (Winter Garden, "Kitty," Mar. 23, 1950): Headin' for a Weddin'; The Riddle; When the Sheets Come Back from the Laundry/W: Walter Bullock, M: Abraham Ellstein. *Bless You All* (Mark Hellinger, revue, Dec. 14, 1950): Bless You All; Voting Blues/WM: Harold Rome.

797. Isla Bevan (1911–) B: Isle of Wight, England. *Bitter Sweet* (Ziegfeld, "Honor," Nov. 5, 1929): Alas, the Time Is Past; The Last Dance; Tarara Boom-de-Ay/WM: Noel Coward.

798. Philippa Bevans (Feb. 10, 1913–May 10, 1968) B: London, England. Her mother was actress VIOLA ROACHE. *My Fair Lady* (Mark Hellinger, "Mrs. Pearce," Mar. 15, 1956): I Could Have Danced All Night; You Did It/W: Alan Jay Lerner, M: Frederick Loewe.

799. Gaile Beverley *Innocent Eyes* (Winter Garden, revue, May 20, 1924): Africa/W: Henry Creamer, M: James F. Hanley. *Mayflowers* (Forrest, "Ursula," Nov. 24, 1925): The Grecian Bend; The Lancers/W: Clifford Grey, M: Edward Kunneke — Play Me a New Tune; Take a Little Stroll with Me/W: Clifford Grey, M: J. Fred Coots, Maurie Rubens. *Queen High!* (Ambassador, "Coddles," Sept. 7, 1926): Sez You? Sez I!; Springtime/W: B.G. DeSylva, M: Lewis E. Gensler. *Present Arms* (Mansfield, "Hortense Mossback," Apr. 26, 1928): I'm a Fool, Little One/W: Lorenz Hart, M: Richard Rodgers.

800. Salome Bey (1944–) B: Newark, NJ. *Dude* (Broadway, "Mother Earth," Oct. 9, 1972): Baby Breath; I Love My Boo Boo; I Never Knew; The Mountains; No One/W: Gerome Ragni, M: Galt MacDermot. *Your Arms Too Short to Box with God* (Lyceum, revue, Dec. 22, 1976): Be Careful When You Kiss; See How They Done My Lord; Something Is Wrong in Jerusalem/WM: Alex Bradford.

801. Bhaskar (Feb. 11, 1930–) B: Madras, India. *Christine* (46th Street, "Rainath," Apr. 28, 1960): The Divali Festival; I'm Just a Little Sparrow; Welcome Song/W: Paul Francis Webster, M: Sammy Fain.

802. Leon Bibb (Feb. 2, 1926–) B: Louisville, KY. *A Hand Is on the Gate* (Longacre, program of poetry and song, Sept. 21, 1966): 'Buked and Scorned; Eas' Man; Glory, Glory; Little Boy, Little Boy; Oh Shenandoah/WM: ? — Harlem Sweeties/WM: Langston Hughes — Rocks and Gravel/WM: Arr. Leon Bibb. *Carnival!* (New York City Center, revival, "Paul Berthalet," Dec. 12, 1968): Ev'rybody Likes You; Her Face; I've

Got to Find a Reason; She's My Love/WM: Bob Merrill.

803. Teri Bibb *The Phantom of the Opera* (Majestic, CR, alt., "Christine Daae," c 1995): All I Ask of You; Angel of Music; Bravo, Bravo; I Remember; Little Lotte; The Mirror; Notes; The Point of No Return; Raoul, I've Been There; Stranger Than You Dreamt It; Think of Me; Twisted Every Way; Wandering Child; Why Have You Brought Me Here; Wishing You Were Somehow Here Again/W: Charles Hart, Richard Stilgoe, M: Andrew Lloyd Webber — The Phantom of the Opera/W: Mike Batt, Richard Stilgoe, M: Andrew Lloyd Webber.

804. Ken Bichel *I Love My Wife* (Ethel Barrymore, "Norman," Apr. 17, 1977): Hey There, Good Times; Lovers on Christmas Eve; Scream/W: Michael Stewart, M: Cy Coleman.

805. George Bickel (Feb. 17, 1863–June 5, 1941) B: Saginaw, MI. *The Silver Star* (New Amsterdam, "Prof. Alonzo Dingelblatz," Nov. 1, 1909): If Only I Were Santa Claus/W: Harry B. Smith, M: Robert Hood Bowers — (You Can Have Your "Oh, You Kids" but) It's a Loving Wife for Mine/WM: Herbert Ingraham — To Bring Up a Girl/W: Harry B. Smith, M: Karl Hoschna. *Paradise Alley* (Casino, "Rudolf Zatz," Mar. 31, 1924): If We Could Live on Promises/W: Howard Johnson, M: Harry Archer — In the Musical Comedy Shows/WM: Howard Johnson — Success/W: Howard Johnson, M: Harry Archer, Carle Carlton.

806. Cyril Biddulph *The Dollar Princess* (Knickerbocker, "Lord Herbert Fitz-Jones," Sept. 6, 1909): A Boat Sails on Wednesday/W: Adrian Ross, George Grossmith, M: Jerome Kern — I Can Say Truly Rural/WM: Worton David, George Arthurs.

807. Charles A. Bigelow (Dec. 12, 1862–Mar. 12, 1912) B: Cleveland OH. *Excelsior, Jr.* (Olympia > Broadway, "Courier Gyde," Nov. 29, 1895): I'm a Very Fly Conductor/W: R.A. Barnet, M: A. Baldwin Sloane. *The Girl from Paris* (Herald Square, "Ebenezer Honeycomb," Dec. 8, 1896): Cock-a-doodle; It's a Good Thing to Have; So Take You a Warning; Tweedledum and Tweedledee/W: George Dance, M: Ivan Caryll. *The French Maid* (Herald Square, "Charles Brown," Sept. 27, 1897): Do Not Jump at Your Conclusions; It Is Their Nature To/W: Basil Hood, M: Walter Slaughter — Rhapsodie Table d'Hote/W: William Barton, M: Edward E. Rice. *The Little Duchess* (Casino, "Gustave," Oct. 14, 1901): Make Allowances for Love; Menagerie Song; The Swimming Master/W: Harry B. Smith, M: Reginald De Koven. *Twirly-*

Whirly (Weber and Fields Music Hall, "Ebenezer Doolittle," Sept. 11, 1902): Romeo/W: Edgar Smith, M: William T. Francis. *An English Daisy* (Casino, "Daniel Crab," Jan. 18, 1904): At the Music Hall/W: Edgar Smith, M: Jean Schwartz. *Higgledy-Piggledy* (Weber's Music Hall, "Sandy Walker," Oct. 20, 1904): Big Indian and His Little Maid; A Game of Love; I'm So Lonesome; Socrates Jackson (An Educated Coon)/W: Edgar Smith, M: Maurice Levi. *Twiddle-Twaddle* (Weber's Music Hall, "Ebenezer Dodge," Jan. 1, 1906): Days of My Boyhood; My Syncopated Gypsy Maid; 'Tis Dreadful! 'Tis Astounding/W: Edgar Smith, M: Maurice Levi. *A Parisian Model* (Broadway, "Silas Goldfinch," Nov. 27, 1906): I'm the Man in Washington/W: Vincent Bryan, M: Gertrude Hoffmann — Kiss, Kiss, Kiss (If You Want to Learn to Kiss)/W: Harry B. Smith, M: Gertrude Hoffmann. *A Waltz Dream* (Broadway, "Joachim XIII," Jan. 27, 1908): The Family's Ancient Tree; Two Is Plenty/W: Joseph W. Herbert, M: Oscar Straus — When the Song of Love Is Heard/W: Joseph W. Herbert, M: Arthur Weld. *Miss Innocence* (New York, "Ezra Pettingill," Nov. 30, 1908): I Used to Be Afraid to Go Home in the Dark/W: Harry Williams, M: Egbert Van Alstyne — My Cousin Carus/W: Edward Madden, M: Gus Edwards — Please Tell Me What They Mean/W: Harry B. Smith, M: Ludwig Englander. *Alma, Where Do You Live?* (Weber's, "Theobald," Sept. 26, 1910): Boogie Boo; Never More/W: George V. Hobart, M: Jean Briquet.

808. Dorothie Bigelow *See America First* (Maxine Elliott, "Polly Huggins," Mar. 28, 1916): Buy Her a Box at the Opera; Damsel, Damsel (Prithee, Come Crusading with Me); Ever and Ever Yours; I've a Shooting Box in Scotland; I've Got an Awful Lot to Learn/WM: T. Lawrason Riggs, Cole Porter.

809. Susan Bigelow (Apr. 11, 1952–) B: Abington, PA. *Working* (46th Street, "Kate Rushton," May 14, 1978): Just a Housewife/WM: Craig Carnelia. *Oklahoma!* (Palace, revival, CR, "Ado Annie Carnes," June 10, 1980): All er Nothin'; The Farmer and the Cowman; I Cain't Say No/W: Oscar Hammerstein II, M: Richard Rodgers. *Into the Light* (Neil Simon, "Kate Prescott," Oct. 22, 1986): Neat, Not Neat; The Rose and I; A Talk About Time; The Three of Us; To Measure the Darkness/W: John Forster, M: Lee Holdridge.

810. Isabel Bigley B: New York, NY. *Guys and Dolls* (46th Street, "Sarah Brown," Nov. 24, 1950): Follow the Fold; If I Were a Bell; I'll Know; I've Never Been in Love Before; Marry

the Man Today/WM: Frank Loesser. *Me and Juliet* (Majestic, "Jeanie," May 28, 1953): I'm Your Girl; It's Me; No Other Love; That's the Way It Happens; A Very Special Day/W: Oscar Hammerstein II, M: Richard Rodgers.

811. Theodore Bikel (May 2, 1924–) B: Vienna, Austria. Actor, guitarist, singer, on stage, TV, film and cabaret. President of Actors' Equity, 1973-1982. *The Sound of Music* (Lunt-Fontanne, "Capt. Georg Von Trapp," Nov. 16, 1959): Do-Re-Mi; Edelweiss; How Can Love Survive?; No Way to Stop It; An Ordinary Couple; So Long, Farewell; The Sound of Music/W: Oscar Hammerstein II, M: Richard Rodgers. *Cafe Crown* (Martin Beck, "Samuel Cole," Apr. 17, 1964): A Lifetime Love; Magical Things in Life; A Man Must Have Something to Live For; So Long as It Isn't Shakespeare; That's the Life for Me/W: Marty Brill, M: Albert Hague. *Pousse-Cafe* (46th Street, "Prof. George Ritter," Mar. 18, 1966): C'est Comme Ca; Old World Charm; Rules and Regulations; Someone to Care For; Thank You, Ma'am/W: Marshall Barer, M: Duke Ellington.

812. James Billings B: Springfield, MO. *Johnny Johnson* (Edison, revival, "Grandpa Joe" and "Dr. Mahodan," Apr. 11, 1971): The Psychiatry Song; Up Chuckamauga Hill/W: Paul Green, M: Kurt Weill.

813. Emily Bindiger (May 10, 1955–) B: Brooklyn, NY. *Shenandoah* (Alvin, CR, "Jenny Anderson," May 31, 1977): Next to Lovin' (I Like Fightin'); Over the Hill; Papa's Gonna Make It Alright; Violets and Silverbells; We Make a Beautiful Pair/W: Peter Udell, M: Gary Geld.

814. Bob Bingham (Oct. 29, 1946–) B: Seattle, WA. *Jesus Christ Superstar* (Mark Hellinger, "Caiaphas," Oct. 12, 1971): The Arrest; Damned for All Time; Hosanna; Judas' Death; This Jesus Must Die; Trial Before Pilate/W: Tim Rice, M: Andrew Lloyd Webber.

815. Constance Binney (June 28, 1896– Nov. 15, 1989) B: New York, NY. *Sweet Little Devil* (Astor > Central, "Virginia Araminta Culpepper," Jan. 21, 1924): Just Supposing; The Same Old Story; Someone Believes in You; Virginia (Don't Go Too Far)/W: B.G. DeSylva, M: George Gershwin — System/W: Oscar Hammerstein II, M: Lewis E. Gensler, Dudley Wilkinson.

816. Paul Binotto *Dreamgirls* (Imperial, "Dave," Dec. 20, 1981): Cadillac Car/W: Tom Eyen, M: Henry Krieger.

817. Dorothy Bird (?–Nov. 12, 1996) *The Straw Hat Revue* (Ambassador, revue, Sept. 29, 1939): Four Young People/WM: James Shelton.

818. Muriel Birkhead *The Most Happy Fella* (New York City Center, revival, "Marie," Feb. 10, 1959): How Beautiful the Days; Young People/WM: Frank Loesser.

819. Virginia Birmingham *The Broadway Whirl* (Times Square > Selwyn, revue, June 8, 1921): Button Me Up the Back/W: Joseph McCarthy, M: Harry Tierney — Three Little Maids/W: Joseph McCarthy, B.G. DeSylva, M: Harry Tierney.

820. Estelle Birney *The Magic Ring* (Liberty, "Stella," Oct. 1, 1923): The Love Song (of Today)/W: Zelda Sears, M: Harold A. Levey.

821. Adelaide Bishop *Blossom Time* (Ambassador, revival, "Fritzi," Sept. 4, 1943): Love Is a Riddle; Three Little Maids/W: Dorothy Donnelly, M: Sigmund Romberg. *The Girl from Nantucket* (Adelphi, "Betty Ellis," Nov. 8, 1945): From Morning Till Night; Hammock in the Blue; I Want to See More of You; Isn't It a Lovely View?; What's He Like?; Your Fatal Fascination/W: Kay Twomey, M: Jacques Belasco.

822. George Bishop *The Girl from Utah* (Knickerbocker, CR, "Lord Amersham," Sept. 30, 1914): Mother Will Be Pleased/WM: ?— The Music of Love; Where Has Una Gone?/W: Percy Greenbank, M: Paul Rubens.

823. Joey Bishop (Feb. 3, 1918–) B: Bronx, NY. Popular comic and member of Frank Sinatra's "rat pack" in the 1950s. A frequent visitor to Jack Paar's late night TV show, he was host of his own show in 1961. *Sugar Babies* (Mark Hellinger, revue, CR, Feb. 2, 1981): Down at the Gaiety Burlesque; Every Day Another Tune; Mr. Banjo Man/WM: Arthur Malvin — A Good Old Burlesque Show/W: Arthur Malvin, M: Jimmy McHugh — I Can't Give You Anything but Love; On the Sunny Side of the Street/W: Dorothy Fields, M: Jimmy McHugh — I Want a Girl (Just Like the Girl That Married Dear Old Dad)/W: William Dillon, M: Harry Von Tilzer — I'm Shooting High/W: Ted Koehler, M: Jimmy McHugh — Immigration Rose/W: Eugene West, Irwin Dash, M: Jimmy McHugh — When You and I Were Young, Maggie Blues/W: Jack Frost, M: Jimmy McHugh.

824. Kelly (Carole) Bishop (Feb. 28, 1944–) B: Colorado Springs, CO. She changed her first name from Carole to Kelly in March 1976. *A Chorus Line* (Shubert, "Sheila," Oct. 19, 1975/ Oct. 19, 1983/Mar. 1984): At the Ballet/W: Edward Kleban, M: Marvin Hamlisch.

825. Philip Bishop *Nothing but Love* (Lyric, "Brooks," Oct. 14, 1919): It's Not What You Say/W: Frank Stammers, M: Harold Orlob.

826. Esther Bissett *Marriage a la Carte* (Casino, "Sheila Wragge," Jan. 2, 1911): Take Him Away to the Mountains; Toddle Go the Girls/W: C.M.S. McLellan, M: Ivan Caryll. *Peggy* (Casino, "Diamond," Dec. 7, 1911): Go Away, Little Girl, Go Back to School/W: C.H. Bovill, M: Leslie Stuart.

827. Jack Bittner (c 1917–June 22, 1993) B: Omaha, NE. Best known for Shakespearian roles. *Little Johnny Jones* (Alvin, revival, "Starter," Mar. 21, 1982): The Cecil in London Town/WM: George M. Cohan.

828. Valerie Leigh Bixler (Feb. 17, 1956–) B: Des Moines, IA. *The Best Little Whorehouse in Texas* (46th Street > Eugene O'Neill, CR, "Linda Lou," c 1980): Hard Candy Christmas/WM: Carol Hall.

829. W.W. Black *Little Nemo* (New Amsterdam, "Morpheus," Oct. 20, 1908): There's Nothing the Matter with Me/W: Harry B. Smith, M: Victor Herbert. *Little Nemo* (New Amsterdam, CR, "An Officer of the Continentals," Dec. 28, 1908): Remember the Old Continentals/W: Harry B. Smith, M: Victor Herbert.

830. George Blackwell *Happy Town* (54th Street, "Lint Richards," Oct. 7, 1959): It Isn't Easy/WM: Paul Nassau, Gordon Duffy, Harry M. Haldane.

831. Harolyn Blackwell *West Side Story* (Minskoff, revival, "Francisca," Feb. 14, 1980): I Feel Pretty/W: Stephen Sondheim, M: Leonard Bernstein.

832. Jennifer Blain *A Christmas Carol* (Madison Square Garden, return engagement, "Grace Smythe," Nov. 22, 1996): Nothing to Do with Me/W: Lynn Ahrens, M: Alan Menken.

833. Howard Blaine *The Cradle Will Rock* (Mansfield > Broadway, revival, "Pres. Prexy," Dec. 26, 1947): Lovely Morning/WM: Marc Blitzstein.

834. Vivian Blaine (Nov. 21, 1921–Dec. 1995): B: Newark NJ. She sang professionally from age 14 with bands such as Al Kavelin and Art Kessel. Later, she starred in movie musicals with Perry Como, Dick Haymes, Frank Sinatra and others. *Guys and Dolls* (46th Street, "Miss Adelaide," Nov. 24, 1950): Adelaide's Lament; A Bushel and a Peck; Marry the Man Today; Sue Me; Take Back Your Mink/WM: Frank Loesser. *Say, Darling* (ANTA, "Irene Lovelle," Apr. 3, 1958): The Carnival Song; Chief of Love; Dance Only with Me; Something's Always Happening on the River; Try to Love Me/W: Betty Comden, Adolph Green, M: Jule Styne. *Guys and Dolls* (New York City Center, revival, "Miss Adelaide," June 8, 1966): same as above. *Com-

pany (Alvin, CR, "Joanne," Nov. 1, 1971): The Ladies Who Lunch; The Little Things You Do Together; Poor Baby/WM: Stephen Sondheim. *Zorba* (Broadway, revival, CR, "Madame Hortense," Jan. 10, 1984): Goodbye Canavaro; Happy Birthday; No Boom Boom; Only Love/W: Fred Ebb, M: John Kander.

835. Barbara Blair *George White's Scandals of 1931* (Apollo, revue, Sept. 14, 1931): Back from Hollywood/W: Lew Brown, M: Ray Henderson.

836. Edith Blair *My Lady's Maid or Lady Madcap* (Casino, "Mrs. Layton," Sept. 20, 1906): Flirtation/WM: Percy Greenbank, Paul Rubens.

837. Jack Blair *New Faces of 1936* (Vanderbilt, revue, CR, June 8, 1936): Off to the Deacon/W: June Sillman, M: Robert Sour. *Who's Who* (Hudson, revue, Mar. 1, 1938): Sunday Morning in June/W: Neville Fleeson, M: Paul McGrane. *Night of Love* (Hudson, "Andor," Jan. 7, 1941): Loosen Up/W: Rowland Leigh, M: Robert Stolz.

838. June Blair *New Faces of 1936* (Vanderbilt, revue, CR, June 8, 1936): Off to the Deacon/W: June Sillman, M: Robert Sour. *Who's Who* (Hudson, revue, Mar. 1, 1938): Sunday Morning in June/W: Neville Fleeson, M: Paul McGrane.

839. Pamela Blair (Dec. 5, 1949–) B: Arlington, VT. *A Chorus Line* (Shubert, "Val," July 25, 1975): And...; Dance: Ten, Looks: Three/W: Edward Kleban, M: Marvin Hamlisch. *The Best Little Whorehouse in Texas* (46th Street, "Amber," June 19, 1978): Hard Candy Christmas/WM: Carol Hall. *King of Hearts* (Minskoff, "Jeunefille," Oct. 22, 1978): King of Hearts; Nothing, Only Love/W: Jacob Brackman, M: Peter Link.

840. Laine Blaire *The Merry World* (Imperial, revue, June 8, 1926): Dangerous Devil; Military Charleston/WM: ? — Deauville/WM: Herman Hupfeld. *Bye, Bye, Bonnie* (Ritz > Cosmopolitan, "Flossie," Jan. 13, 1927): Promise Not to Stand Me Up Again/W: Neville Fleeson, M: Albert Von Tilzer. *The Silver Swan* (Martin Beck, "Denise," Nov. 27, 1929): I Like the Military Man; Shoe Clap Platter/W: William Brady, M: H. Maurice Jacquet. *Top Speed* (46th Street, "Molly," Dec. 25, 1929): Fireworks/W: Bert Kalmar, M: Harry Ruby. *The Well of Romance* (Craig, "Ann," Nov. 7, 1930): At Lovetime; For You and for Me; How Can You Tell?; The Well of Romance/W: Preston Sturges, M: H. Maurice Jacquet.

841. Brad Blaisdell (Mar. 15, 1949–) B: Baltimore, MD. *Going Up* (John Golden, revival,

"Robert Street," Sept. 19, 1976): Down! Up! Left! Right!; Going Up; If You Look in Her Eyes/W: Otto Harbach, M: Louis A. Hirsch — I'll Think of You/W: Rennold Wolf, M: Louis A. Hirsch.

842. Geoffrey Blaisdell (Apr. 16, 1958–) B: Danville, KY. *Cyrano: The Musical* (Neil Simon, "Man" and "Capt. De Castel Jaloux," Nov. 21, 1993): Courage Makes a Man/W: Peter Reeves, Koen Van Dijk, M: Ad Van Dijk.

843. William Blaisdell (c 1865–Jan. 31, 1931) *The Girl from Paris* (Herald Square, CR, "Auguste Pompier," June 28, 1897): Cock-a-doodle; I'm All the Way from Gay Paree; Tootle, Tootle/W: George Dance, M: Ivan Caryll. *The Toreador* (Knickerbocker, "Pettifer," Jan. 6, 1902): My Zoo/W: Percy Greenbank, M: Ivan Caryll.

844. Beulah Blake *Bitter Sweet* (44th Street, revival, "Effie," May 7, 1934): Alas, the Time Is Past; The Last Dance; Tarara Boom-de-Ay/WM: Noel Coward.

845. Doris Blake *Helen Goes to Troy* (Alvin, "Minerva" and "Parthenis," Apr. 24, 1944): The Judgment of Paris; Tsing-la-la/W: Herbert Baker, M: Jacques Offenbach, adapted by Eric Wolfgang Korngold.

846. Eubie Blake (Feb. 7, 1883–Feb. 12, 1983) B: Baltimore, MD. One of the great names in music of his time. The jazz pianist, dancer and composer grew up with ragtime and vaudeville. In his teens he played piano and organ in sporting houses and cafes. He met lyricist NOBLE SISSLE in 1915. In 1981, he was awarded the Presidential Medal of Honor; his last public appearance was at Lincoln Center in New York City at the age of 99. *Shuffle Along of 1933* (Mansfield, revue, Dec. 26, 1932): Reminiscing/W: Noble Sissle, M: Eubie Blake. *Shuffle Along of 1952* (Broadway, revue, May 8, 1952): same as above.

847. Josh Blake (Jan. 7, 1975–) *The Human Comedy* (Royale, "Ulysses Macauley," Apr. 5, 1984): Hi Ya, Kid; We're a Little Family/W: William Dumaresq, M: Galt MacDermot. *Rags* (Mark Hellinger, "David Hershkowitz," Aug. 21, 1986): Brand New World; Children of the Wind; Easy for You; The Sound of Love/W: Stephen Schwartz, M: Charles Strouse.

848. Kimberly Blake *Starlight Express* (Gershwin, CR, "Joule," c 1987): AC/ DC; Pumping Iron; Race One; Wide Smile, High Style, That's Me/W: Richard Stilgoe, M: Andrew Lloyd Webber.

849. Nena (Nina) Blake *Comin' Thro' the Rye* (Herald Square, "Bossie Claude," Jan. 9, 1906): My Broncho Boy/W: George V. Hobart, M: A.

Baldwin Sloane — The Sand Man/W: ?, M: MacArthur, Varley. *A Certain Party* (Wallack's, "Grace Fairweather," Apr. 24, 1911): I Want a Boy/W: Edgar Smith, M: Tom Kelly — Love's Wireless Telephone/W: Raymond W. Peck, M: Robert Hood Bowers.

850. Pamela Blake (Aug. 6, 1918–) B: Oakland, CA. *Evita* (Broadway, CR, "Eva," May 25, 1983, mats.): The Actress Hasn't Learned (The Lines You'd Like to Hear); The Art of the Possible; Buenos Aires; Dice Are Rolling; Don't Cry for Me Argentina; Eva Beware of the City; Eva's Final Broadcast; Goodnight and Thank You; High Flying Adored; I'd Be Surprisingly Good for You; Lament; A New Argentina; Peron's Latest Flame; Rainbow High; Rainbow Tour; Waltz for Eva and Che/W: Tim Rice, M: Andrew Lloyd Webber.

851. Richard H. Blake (May 17, 1975–) B: Providence, RI. *Teddy & Alice* (Minskoff, "Archie Roosevelt," Nov. 12, 1987): Charge; Private Thoughts/W: Hal Hackady, M: John Philip Sousa, Richard Kapp. *Prince of Central Park* (Belasco, "Jay Jay," Nov. 9, 1989): All I've Got Is Me; Follow the Leader; Here's Where I Belong; I Fly by Night; One of a Kind; The Prince of Central Park; Zap!/W: Gloria Nissenson, M: Don Sebesky.

852. Robin Blake *Shenandoah* (Virginia, revival, "Henry," Aug. 8, 1989): Next to Lovin' (I Like Fightin')/W: Peter Udell, M: Gary Geld.

853. Sydney Blake (Feb. 4, 1951–) B: Rome, Italy. *So Long, 174th Street* (Harkness, "Miss B," Apr. 27, 1976): Bolero on Rye/WM: Stan Daniels.

854. Bidda Blakeley *Sing for Your Supper* (Adelphi, revue, Apr. 24, 1939): At Long Last/W: Robert Sour, M: Lee Wainer.

855. James Blakeley (1873–Oct. 19, 1915) B: Hull, Yorkshire, England. *The School Girl* (Daly's > Herald Square, "Tubby Bedford," Sept. 1, 1904): In Black and White [Oct. 31, 1904]/W: Paul West, M: John W. Bratton — Looking for a Needle in a Haystack/WM: Adrian Ross, Leslie Stuart — We Want to Be Simpler/WM: Leslie Stuart. *The Little Cherub* (Criterion, "Algernon Southdown," Aug. 6, 1906): The Doggie in Our Yard/WM: Marie Doro — Little Willie Brown/W: Edward Montague, George V. Hobart, M: Silvio Hein — Tom the Piper's Son/WM: ?. *The Girls of Gottenburg* (Knickerbocker, "Max," Sept. 2, 1908): Berlin on the Spree; The Itsy Bitsy Girl/W: Basil Hood, M: Lionel Monckton — Sprechen Sie Deutsch, Mein Herr?/W: Adrian Ross, M: Lionel Monckton — Two Little Sausages/WM: Lionel Monckton. *Tonight's the*

Night (Shubert, "Montagu Lovitt Lovitt," Dec. 24, 1914): Tonight's the Night; Too Particular/WM: Paul Rubens, Percy Greenbank.

856. Michelle Blakely (July 27, 1969–) B: Harrisonburg, VA. *Grease* (Eugene O'Neill, revival, "Patty Simcox," May 11, 1994): Rydell Fight Song/WM: Jim Jacobs, Warren Casey.

857. Ronee Blakley (1946–) B: Stanley or Caldwell, ID. The country and western singer appeared in the film *Nashville* (1975). *Pump Boys and Dinettes* (Princess, CR, "Rhetta Cupp," Sept. 29, 1982): Be Good or Be Gone/WM: Jim Wann.

858. Nan Blakstone (1905–Dec. 24, 1951) In the 1930s and 40s she sang in clubs and cafes all over the country. Her face was disfigured in a car accident in 1937, but she continued to perform. *Nine-Fifteen Revue* (George M. Cohan, revue, Feb. 11, 1930): Breakfast Dance/W: Edward Eliscu, M: Ralph Rainger — Toddlin' Along/W: Ira Gershwin, M: George Gershwin. *The Garrick Gaieties of 1930* (Guild, revue, June 4, 1930): I Am Only Human After All/W: E.Y. Harburg, Ira Gershwin, M: Vernon Duke — I've Got It Again/W: Allen Boretz, M: Ned Lehac — Lazy Levee Loungers/WM: Willard Robison.

859. Scott Blanchard *South Pacific* (New York City Center, revival, "Seabee Morton Wise," June 2, 1965): There Is Nothin' Like a Dame/W: Oscar Hammerstein II, M: Richard Rodgers.

860. Steve Blanchard (Dec. 4, 1958–) B: York, PA. *Camelot* (Gershwin, revival, "Lancelot Du Lac," June 21, 1993): C'est Moi; If Ever I Would Leave You/W: Alan Jay Lerner, M: Frederick Loewe. *A Christmas Carol* (Paramount Madison Square Garden, return engagement, "Fred," Nov. 20, 1995): Christmas Together; Nothing to Do with Me/W: Lynn Ahrens, M: Alan Menken.

861. Belle Blanche (June 2, 1891–Mar. 27, 1963) B: New York, NY. *Hello, Broadway!* (Astor, revue, "Ruth Chatterbox," Dec. 25, 1914): My Miracle Man/WM: George M. Cohan.

862. Ralph Blane (July 26, 1914–Nov. 13, 1995) B: Broken Arrow, OK. The singer, arranger and composer met partner HUGH MARTIN at Northwestern University in 1937. Together, they formed The Martins, a vocal quartet that sang on Fred Allen's radio program. They went on to write words and music for many Hollywood musicals. *New Faces of 1936* (Vanderbilt, revue, May 19, 1936): Give Me a Song I Can Whistle; Tonight's the Night [July 6, 1936]/W: June Sillman, M: Alex Fogarty — Your Face Is So Familiar/W: Edwin Gilbert, M: Alex

Fogarty. *Hooray for What!* (Winter Garden, revue, Dec. 1, 1937): A Fashion Girl; In the Shade of the New Apple Tree/W: E.Y. Harburg, M: Harold Arlen.

863. Lillian Blauvelt (Mar. 16, 1874–Aug. 29, 1947) B: New York, NY. *Dream City* (Weber's, "Elsa," Dec. 25, 1906): I'm Such a Modest Maiden [Mar. 18, 1907]; Oh, Look Who's Here [Mar. 18, 1907]/W: Edgar Smith, M: Victor Herbert.

864. Enid Blaymore *Musical Chairs* (Rialto, "Millie," May 14, 1980): Better Than Broadway/WM: Tom Savage.

865. Judith (Judy) Blazer (Oct. 22, 1956–) B: Dover, NJ. *Me and My Girl* (Marquis, revival, CR, "Sally Smith," July 4, 1989): Hold My Hand/W: Harry Graham, M: Maurice Elwin, Noel Gay — The Lambeth Walk; Me and My Girl; Take It on the Chin/W: Douglas Furber, M: Noel Gay — Once You Lose Your Heart/ WM: Noel Gay. *A Change in the Heir* (Edison, "Prince Conrad," Apr. 29, 1990): By Myself; Can't I?; Duet; A Fairy Tale; Here I Am; I Tried and I Tried and I Tried; Look at Me/W: George H. Gorham; M: Dan Sticco.

866. Jules Bledsoe (Dec. 29, 1898–July 14, 1943) B: Waco, TX. He introduced the song "Ol' Man River" in its original Broadway production, then went on to perform it more than 3500 times throughout his lifetime. *Show Boat* (Ziegfeld, "Joe," Dec. 27, 1927): Can't Help Lovin' Dat Man; Ol' Man River/W: Oscar Hammerstein II, M: Jerome Kern.

867. Gloria Bleezarde (Oct. 12, 1940–) B: Albany, NY. *New Faces of 1968* (Booth, revue, May 2, 1968): #X9RL220/W: Michael McWhinney, M: Jerry Powell.

868. James Blendick *Cyrano* (Palace, "Le Bret," May 13, 1973): Paris Cuisine; Pocapdedious; Tell Her/W: Anthony Burgess, M: Michael J. Lewis.

869. Christine Blessing *The Ballet Girl* (Manhattan, "Vrouw Schomberg," Dec. 21, 1897): Janken and Mieken/W: Adrian Ross, M: Carl Kiefert.

870. Timothy Robert Blevins *Miss Saigon* (Broadway, CR, "John," c 1992): Bui-doi; The Confrontation; The Guilt Inside Your Head; Please; The Telephone/W: Richard Maltby, Jr., Alain Boublil, M: Claude-Michel Schonberg.

871. Helena Bliss (Dec. 31, 1917–) B: St. Louis, MO. *Song of Norway* (Imperial, "Nina Hagerup," Aug. 21, 1944): At Christmastime; Hill of Dreams; I Love You; Midsummer's Eve; Strange Music; Three Loves/WM: Robert Wright, George Forrest, based on Edvard Grieg.

Gypsy Lady (Century, "Musetta," Sept. 17, 1946): My First Waltz; Springtide; Young Lady a la Mode/W: Robert Wright, George Forrest, M: Victor Herbert — Romany Life (Czardas)/W: Harry B. Smith, M: Victor Herbert. *Show Boat* (New York City Center, revival, "Julie La Verne," Apr. 8, 1954): Bill/W: Oscar Hammerstein II, P.G. Wodehouse, M: Jerome Kern — Can't Help Lovin' Dat Man/W: Oscar Hammerstein II, M: Jerome Kern.

872. Lela Bliss (May 11, 1896– May 15, 1980) B: Los Angeles, CA. *Rose-Marie* (Imperial, "Ethel Brander," Sept. 2, 1924): I Love Him; Pretty Things/W: Otto Harbach, Oscar Hammerstein II, M: Rudolf Friml.

873. Louise Bliss *The Enchantress* (New York, "Princess Stellina," Oct. 19, 1911): Art Is Calling to Me (I Want to Be a Prima Donna)/W: Harry B. Smith, M: Victor Herbert.

874. Chad Block (May 1, 1938–June 18, 2002) B: Twin Falls, ID. M: CARMEN ALVAREZ. Actor, singer, dancer, choreographer on stage, screen and TV. *A Funny Thing Happened on the Way to the Forum* (Lunt-Fontanne, revival, "A Protean," Mar. 30, 1972): Bring Me My Bride; Comedy Tonight/WM: Stephen Sondheim.

875. Eric Blore (Dec. 23, 1887–Mar. 1, 1959) B: London, England. The perfect waiter, butler and gentleman's gentleman in more than 70 films. *Here Goes the Bride* (46th Street, "Roddy Trotwood," Nov. 3, 1931): Remarkable People We/W: Edward Heyman, M: Richard Myers. *Gay Divorce* (Ethel Barrymore > Shubert, "Waiter," Nov. 29, 1932): What Will Become of Our England?/WM: Cole Porter.

876. Helon Blount (Jan. 15, 1929–) B: Big Spring, TX. *How to Succeed in Business Without Really Trying* (46th Street, CR, "Miss Jones," 1963): Brotherhood of Man; Paris Original/ WM: Frank Loesser. *Musical Chairs* (Rialto, CR, "Roberta," May 20, 1980): Better Than Broadway/WM: Tom Savage. *Woman of the Year* (Palace, "Cleaning Woman," Mar. 29, 1981): I Wrote the Book/W: Fred Ebb, M: John Kander.

877. Peggie Blue *The Wiz* (Lunt-Fontanne, revival, "Aunt Em," May 24, 1984): The Feeling We Once Had/WM: Charlie Smalls.

878. Joel Blum (May 19, 1952–) B: San Francisco, CA. *Show Boat* (Gershwin, revival, "Frank," Oct. 2, 1994): Goodbye, My Lady Love/WM: Joseph E. Howard — Till Good Luck Comes My Way/W: Oscar Hammerstein II, M: Jerome Kern.

879. Norman A. Blume or NORMAN AINSLEY (May 4, 1881–Jan. 23, 1948) B: Edinburgh, Scotland. *Marriage a la Carte* (Casino, "Jimmy Wragge," Jan. 2, 1911): Toddle Go the Girls/W: C.M.S. McLellan, M: Ivan Caryll.

880. Jeff Blumenkrantz (June 3, 1965–) B: Long Branch, NJ. *How to Succeed in Business Without Really Trying* (Richard Rodgers, revival, "Bud Frump," Mar. 23, 1995): Been a Long Day; Coffee Break; The Company Way/WM: Frank Loesser.

881. Larry Blyden (June 23, 1925–June 6, 1975) B: Houston, TX. M: CAROL HANEY. *Flower Drum Song* (St. James, "Sammy Fong," Dec. 1, 1958): Don't Marry Me; Sunday/W: Oscar Hammerstein II, M: Richard Rodgers. *Foxy* (Ziegfeld, "Doc," Feb. 16, 1964): I'm Way Ahead of the Game; It's Easy When You Know How; Larceny and Love; Many Ways to Skin a Cat; Money Isn't Everything/W: Johnny Mercer, M: Robert Emmett Dolan. *The Apple Tree* (Shubert, "Snake" and "Balladeer," Oct. 18, 1966): The Apple Tree (Forbidden Fruit); I'll Tell You a Truth/W: Sheldon Harnick, M: Jerry Bock. *A Funny Thing Happened on the Way to the Forum* (Lunt-Fontanne, revival, "Hysterium," Mar. 30, 1972): Everybody Ought to Have a Maid; I'm Calm; Lovely/WM: Stephen Sondheim. *Sondheim: A Musical Tribute* (Shubert, revue, Mar. 11, 1973): Buddy's Blues (The God-Why-Don't-You-Love-Me Blues); Love Is in the Air/WM: Stephen Sondheim.

882. Frank Blyler *Earl Carroll's Vanities of 1923* (Earl Carroll, revue, CR, Dec. 17, 1923): Girls Were Made for Dancing/WM: Earl Carroll.

883. Jimmie Blyler *The Century Revue* (Century, revue, July 12, 1920): Millions of Tunes/W: Alfred Bryan, M: Jean Schwartz.

884. Coralie Blythe (1880–July 24, 1928) B: England. M: LAWRENCE GROSSMITH. Her brother was VERNON CASTLE. She appeared in flirtatious supporting roles in musical comedy, mostly in London. *About Town* (Herald Square, "Millie Bounden," Oct. 29, 1906): There's a Baby in the House/W: Addison Burkhardt, M: Melville Ellis. *The Blue Moon* (Casino, CR, "Evelyn Ormsby," Dec. 31, 1906): Don't You Think It's Time to Marry?/W: Addison Burkhardt, M: Gus Edwards — The Loveland Volunteers/WM: Percy Greenbank, Paul Rubens, Howard Talbot.

885. Walter Bobbie (Nov. 18, 1945–) B: Scranton, PA. Former artistic director of City Center's Encore series, bringing back to the stage concert versions of forgotten Broadway musicals. *Grease* (Broadhurst, "Roger," June 7, 1972): Mooning; Rock 'n' Roll Party Queen/WM: Jim

Jacobs, Warren Casey. *Tricks* (Alvin, "Octave," Jan. 8, 1973): Believe Me; Enter Hyacinthe; Trouble's a Ruler; Who Was I?/W: Lonnie Burstein, M: Jerry Blatt. *Going Up* (John Golden, revival, "Hopkinson Brown," Sept. 19, 1976): Do It for Me; Down! Up! Left! Right!; I Want a Boy Who's Determined to Do as I Say/W: Otto Harbach, M: Louis A. Hirsch. *Anything Goes* (Vivian Beaumont, revival, CR, "Lord Evelyn Oakleigh," Apr. 14, 1989): The Gypsy in Me/WM: Cole Porter. *Guys and Dolls* (Martin Beck, revival, "Nicely Nicely Johnson," Apr. 14, 1992): Fugue for Tinhorns; Guys and Dolls; The Oldest Established; Sit Down, You're Rockin' the Boat/WM: Frank Loesser.

886. Anne Marie Bobby (Dec. 12, 1967–) B: Paterson, NJ. *The Human Comedy* (Royale, "Helen," Apr. 5, 1984): The Assyrians/W: William Dumaresq, M: Galt MacDermot. *Smile* (Lunt-Fontanne, "Robin Gibson," Nov. 24, 1986): Dressing Room Scene; Orientation; Postcard #1; Postcard #2; Postcard #3; Pretty as a Picture/W: Howard Ashman, M: Marvin Hamlisch.

887. Chris Bocchino *A Chorus Line* (Shubert, CR, "Diana," Oct. 1978/Dec. 1979/Aug. 1980): Nothing; What I Did for Love/W: Edward Kleban, M: Marvin Hamlisch.

888. Duane Bodin (Dec. 31, 1932–) B: Duluth, MN. *Fiddler on the Roof* (Winter Garden, revival, "Grandma Tzeitel," Dec. 28, 1976): The Tailor, Motel Kamzoil/W: Sheldon Harnick, M: Jerry Bock.

889. Jane Bodle (Nov. 12–) B: Lawrence, KS. *Cats* (Winter Garden, CR, "Demeter," Mar. 1984): Grizabella, the Glamour Cat; Macavity/W: T.S. Eliot, M: Andrew Lloyd Webber. *Miss Saigon* (Broadway, CR, "Ellen," c 1991): The Confrontation; I Still Believe; Now That I've Seen Her; Room 317/W: Richard Maltby, Jr., Alain Boublil, M: Claude-Michel Schonberg.

890. Penelope Bodry (1948–) *Threepenny Opera* (Vivian Beaumont, revival, CR, "Lucy Brown"): Jealousy Duet/W: Bertolt Brecht, M: Kurt Weill.

891. Jessica Boevers (Aug. 24, 1972–) B: Chicago, IL. *A Funny Thing Happened on the Way to the Forum* (St. James, revival, "Philia," Apr. 18, 1996): Lovely; That'll Show Him/WM: Stephen Sondheim.

892. Stephen Bogardus (Mar. 11, 1954–) B: Norfolk, VA. *Falsettos* (John Golden, revival, "Whizzer," Apr. 29, 1992): The Chess Game; Everyone Tells Jason to See a Psychiatrist; Four Jews in a Room Bitching; The Games I Play; I

Never Wanted to Love You; Jason's Therapy; Love Is Blind; Making a Home; March of the Falsettos; Marvin at the Psychiatrist; Marvin Hits Trina; This Had Better Come to a Stop; Thrill of First Love; Unlikely Lovers; What More Can I Say?; What Would I Do?; You Gotta Die Sometime/WM: William Finn.

893. Matt Bogart *Miss Saigon* (Broadway, CR, "Chris," Dec. 20, 1997): The Ceremony; The Confrontation; The Guilt Inside Your Head; The Last Night of the World; Sun and Moon; The Telephone; Why God Why?/W: Richard Maltby, Jr., Alain Boublil, M: Claude-Michel Schonberg.

894. Gail Boggs (Aug. 10, 1951–) B: Glen Ridge, NJ. *Mother Earth* (Belasco, revue, Oct. 19, 1972): Corn on the Macabre/WM: Ron Thronson, Roger Ailes, Ray Golden — Pills/WM: Ray Golden — Save the World for Children/W: Ron Thronson, M: Toni Shearer. *Candide* (Broadway, revival, "Penitente" and "Whore" and "Houri," Mar. 10, 1974): O Miserere/W: Richard Wilbur, M: Leonard Bernstein.

895. Ron Bohmer (Aug. 15, 1961–) B: Cincinnati, OH. *Les Miserables* (Broadway, CR, "Enjolras," c 1993): Do You Hear the People Sing?; Red and Black/W: Herbert Kretzmer, M: Claude-Michel Schonberg.

896. John Bohn *Love o' Mike* (Shubert > Maxine Elliott, "Ted Watson," Jan. 15, 1917): Don't Tempt Me; Lulu/W: Harry B. Smith, M: Jerome Kern.

897. Peanuts Bohn *Keep Off the Grass* (Broadhurst, revue, May 23, 1940): The Cabby's Serenade/W: Al Dubin, M: Jimmy McHugh — On the Old Park Bench/W: Howard Dietz, M: Jimmy McHugh.

898. Roman Bohnen (Nov. 24, 1899–Feb. 24, 1949) B: St. Paul, MN. *Johnny Johnson* (44th Street, "Grandpa Joe," Nov. 19, 1936): The Battle of San Juan Hill/W: Paul Green, M: Kurt Weill.

899. Curt Bois (Apr. 5, 1901–Dec. 25, 1991) B: Berlin, Germany. In movies he played comic head waiters and clerks. *Polonaise* (Alvin, "Sgt. Wacek Zapolski," Oct. 6, 1945): Hay, Hay, Hay; Laughing Bells; Motherhood/W: John Latouche, M: Bronislau Kaper.

900. Mary Boland (Jan. 28, 1880–June 23, 1965) B: Philadelphia, PA. In a stage and screen career that lasted nearly 50 years, she appeared in more than 40 movies, most memorably as a flighty grande dame. *Jubilee* (Imperial, "The Queen," Oct. 12, 1935): Me and Marie; Mr. and Mrs. Smith; We're Off to Feathermore/WM: Cole Porter.

901. Richard Bold *Frivolities of 1920* (44th Street, revue, Jan. 8, 1920): Music/WM: William B. Friedlander. *Love Birds* (Apollo, "Arthur Harwood Hines," Mar. 15, 1921): Is It Hard to Guess?; Love Will Always Find a Way; Two Little Love Birds/W: Ballard Macdonald, M: Sigmund Romberg. *The Greenwich Village Follies of 1921* (Shubert, revue, Aug. 31, 1921): The Haunted Violin; I'm Up in the Air Over You; When Dreams Come True/W: John Murray Anderson, Arthur Swanstrom, M: Carey Morgan — Three O'Clock in the Morning/W: Dorothy Terris, M: Julian Robledo. *George White's Scandals of 1922* (Globe, revue, Aug. 28, 1922): Argentina [Oct. 16, 1922]; Cinderelatives [Oct. 16, 1922]; I Found a Four Leaf Clover; Just a Tiny Cup of Tea/W: B.G. DeSylva, M: George Gershwin — I'll Build a Stairway to Paradise/W: B.G. DeSylva, Arthur Francis, M: George Gershwin — My Heart Will Sail Across the Sea [Sept. 18, 1922]/W: B.G. DeSylva, E. Ray Goetz, M: George Gershwin. *George White's Scandals of 1923* (Globe, revue, June 18, 1923): The Life of a Rose; Lo-La-Lo/W: B.G. DeSylva, M: George Gershwin — Let's Be Lonesome Together; There Is Nothing Too Good for You/W: B.G. DeSylva, E. Ray Goetz, M: George Gershwin. *George White's Scandals of 1924* (Apollo, revue, June 30, 1924): Night Time in Araby; Rose of Madrid; Year After Year (We're Together)/W: B.G. DeSylva, M: George Gershwin. *Gay Paree* (Shubert, revue, Aug.18, 1925): The Glory of the Morning Sunshine; Wedgewood Maid/WM: ?— (My) Sugar Plum/W: B.G. DeSylva, M: Joseph Meyer, J. Fred Coots — Venetian Nights [Nov. 23, 1925]/WM: Clarence Gaskill — A Vision of Hassan/W: Clifford Grey, M: Alfred Goodman, J. Fred Coots. *Gay Paree* (Winter Garden, revue, Nov. 9, 1926): Kandahar Isle/W: Mann Holiner, M: Alberta Nichols — Oriental Nights/WM: ?. *The Optimists* (Casino de Paris, revue, Jan. 30, 1928): If I Gave You a Rose/W: Granville English, M: Melville Gideon — London Town; Rolling Stones/WM: ?. *Earl Carroll's Vanities of 1928* (Earl Carroll, revue, Aug. 6, 1928): Once in a Lifetime/W: Raymond W. Klages, M: Jesse Greer — Painting a Vanities Girl/WM: Ernie Golden — Raquel/W: George Whiting, M: Joe Burke.

902. Virginia Bolen *Sing for Your Supper* (Adelphi, revue, Apr. 24, 1939): At Long Last/W: Robert Sour, M: Lee Wainer — Legitimate/W: John Latouche, M: Lee Wainer.

903. John Boles (Oct. 28, 1895–Feb. 27, 1969) B: Greenville, TX. The popular baritone was discovered by Hollywood star Gloria Swanson while he was performing on Broadway. Between 1929 and 1943 he starred in screen musicals, mainly for Fox. *Little Jessie James* (Longacre, CR, "Paul Revere," Dec. 24, 1923): I Love You (Je T'aime!); Little Jack Horner; Suppose I Had Never Met You/W: Harlan Thompson, M: Harry Archer. *Mercenary Mary* (Longacre, "Lyman Webster," Apr. 13, 1925): Everything's Going to Be All Right/WM: William B. Friedlander, Con Conrad — Tomorrow/WM: William B. Friedlander, Con Conrad, M: based on Frederic Chopin. *Kitty's Kisses* (Playhouse, "Robert Mason," May 6, 1926): I'm in Love/W: Gus Kahn, Otto Harbach, M: Con Conrad — Kitty's Kisses; Whenever I Dream/W: Gus Kahn, M: Con Conrad. *One Touch of Venus* (Imperial, Whitelaw Savory," Oct. 7, 1943): Catch Hatch; Dr. Crippen; New Art Is True Art; The Trouble with Women; West Wind/W: Ogden Nash, M: Kurt Weill.

904. Arline Boley *Ziegfeld Follies of 1912* (Moulin Rouge, revue, CR, Dec. 2, 1912): Mother Doesn't Know/W: Harry B. Smith, M: Raymond Hubbell.

905. May Boley (May 29, 1881–Jan. 7, 1963) B: Washington, DC. She combined a theater career with vaudeville and movies. *The Chaperons* (New York > New York Theatre roof, "Hortense," June 5, 1902): Bois D'Boulogne; In My Official Capacity/W: Frederick Ranken, M: Isidore Witmark. *The Maid and the Mummy* (New York, "Trixie Evergreen," July 25, 1904): Letters; The Sales Lady/W: Richard Carle, M: Robert Hood Bowers — Peculiar Julia/WM: Richard Carle. *The Hurdy Gurdy Girl* (Wallack's, "Miss Cuticle," Sept. 23, 1907): The Modest Manicure; Style/W: Richard Carle, M: H.L. Heartz. *The Balkan Princess* (Herald Square > Casino, "Magda," Feb. 9, 1911): I Char; Lady and Gentleman; The Opera Ball/W: Arthur Wimperis, M: Paul Rubens. *The Duchess* (Lyric, "Angelique," Oct. 16, 1911): It's the Bump/W: Joseph W. Herbert, M: Victor Herbert. *The Whirl of the World* (Winter Garden, revue, "Viola," Jan. 10, 1914): A Broadway in Paree/WM: Henry Lehman. *So Long Letty* (Shubert, "Grace Miller," Oct. 23, 1916): All the Comforts of Home/WM: Earl Carroll. *Toot Sweet* (Princess > Nora Bayes, revue, May 7, 1919): Baby Vampire; One of the Ruins of France/WM: Roy K. Moulton — Toot Sweet/W: Raymond B. Egan, M: Richard A. Whiting. *Roly-Boly Eyes* (Knickerbocker, "Kitty Rice," Sept. 25, 1919): All Washed Up; Spring/W: Edgar Allen Woolf, M: Eddy Brown, Louis Gruenberg. *The Rose Girl* (Ambassador, "Mme. Donay," Feb. 11, 1921):

Flirtation Quartette; The Proteges/W: William Cary Duncan, M: Anselm Goetzl. *Go-Go* (Daly's, "Mrs. Phyllis Full," Mar. 12, 1923): Honey; Lolly Papa/W: Alex Rogers, M: C. Luckeyth Roberts. *Oh! Oh! Oh! Nurse* (Cosmopolitan, "Mrs. Rose d'Brac," Dec. 7, 1925): Cleopatra; No, I Won't/W: Monte Carlo, M: Alma Sanders. *Jubilee* (Imperial, "Eve Standing," Oct. 12, 1935): Mr. and Mrs. Smith; My Most Intimate Friend/WM: Cole Porter.

906. Ray Bolger (Jan. 10, 1903–Jan. 15, 1987) B: Dorchester, MA. The versatile and endearing dancer and singer began his career as a bank clerk, a vacuum cleaner salesman and an accountant. His stage debut was with Bob Ott's Musical Comedy repertory as they toured New England. He is, of course, best remembered for his role as the Scarecrow in the classic film *The Wizard of Oz* (1939), and for his rendition of Frank Loesser's song "Once in Love with Amy" from *Where's Charley? Heads Up!* (Alvin, "Georgie," Nov. 11, 1929): Knees; Me for You; Play Boy/W: Lorenz Hart, M: Richard Rodgers. *Life Begins at 8:40* (Winter Garden, revue, Aug. 27, 1934): All the Elks and Masons; C'est la Vie; Life Begins at City Hall (Beautifying the City); Quartet Erotica; You're a Builder-Upper/W: Ira Gershwin, E.Y. Harburg, M: Harold Arlen. *On Your Toes* (Imperial > Majestic, "Phil Dolan III," Apr. 11, 1936): The Heart Is Quicker Than the Eye; It's Got to Be Love; On Your Toes; There's a Small Hotel; The Three B's/W: Lorenz Hart, M: Richard Rodgers. *Keep Off the Grass* (Broadhurst, revue, May 23, 1940): Crazy as a Loon; A Latin Tune, a Manhattan Moon and You; Old Jitterbug; Rhett, Scarlet, Ashley/W: Al Dubin, M: Jimmy McHugh. *By Jupiter* (Shubert, "Sapiens," June 3, 1942): Ev'rything I've Got; Life with Father; No, Mother, No; Nobody's Heart (Belongs to Me); Now That I've Got My Strength/W: Lorenz Hart, M: Richard Rodgers. *Three to Make Ready* (Adelphi, revue, Mar. 7, 1946): The Old Soft Shoe/W: Nancy Hamilton, M: Morgan Lewis. *Where's Charley?* (St. James > Broadway, "Charley Wykeham," Oct. 11, 1948): Better Get Out of Here; Make a Miracle; The New Ashmoleon Marching Society and Students Conservatory Band; Once in Love with Amy; Pernambuco/WM: Frank Loesser. *All American* (Winter Garden, "Professor Fodorski," Mar. 19, 1962): The Fight Song; Have a Dream; If I Were You; I'm Fascinating; It's Fun to Think; Melt Us! (The Old Immigration and Naturalization Rag); Once Upon a Time; Our Children; We Speak the Same Language; What a Country/W: Lee Adams, M: Charles Strouse.

Come Summer (Lunt-Fontanne, "Phineas Sharp," Mar. 18, 1969): Come Summer; Faucett Falls Fancy; Feather in My Shoe; Good Time Charlie; Goodbye, My Bachelor; The Loggers' Song; Moonglade; No; Skin and Bones; Think Spring/ W: Will Holt, M: David Baker.

907. Shannon Bolin (Jan. 1, 1917–) B: South Dakota. *Damn Yankees* (46th Street, "Meg," May 5, 1955): A Man Doesn't Know; Near to You; Six Months Out of Every Year/WM: Richard Adler, Jerry Ross. *The Student Gypsy or The Prince of Liederkranz* (54th Street, "Zampa Allescu," Sept. 30, 1963): A Gypsy Dance; The Gypsy Life; There's Life in the Old Folks Yet; Walk-on/WM: Rick Besoyan.

908. Helen Bolton B: St. Louis, MO. *See-Saw* (Cohan, "Cleo Ray," Sept. 23, 1919): Senorita, Senorita; When You Come Near I Feel All of a Ooh!/W: Earl Derr Biggers, M: Louis A. Hirsch. *My Golden Girl* (Nora Bayes, "Helen Randolph," Feb. 2, 1920): If We Had Met Before; A Song Without (Many) Words/W: Frederic Arnold Kummer, M: Victor Herbert. *Pitter Patter* (Longacre, "Mrs. George Meriden," Sept. 28, 1920): Any Afternoon; Love Me Tonight/W: ?, M: William B. Friedlander — Send for Me/W: Will M. Hough, M: William B. Friedlander — The Wedding Blues/WM: William B. Friedlander. *Up She Goes* (Playhouse, "Ella Mayer," Nov. 6, 1922): Let's Kiss; Settle Down, Travel 'Round; Takes a Heap of Love; The Visitors; We'll Do the Riviera/W: Joseph McCarthy, M: Harry Tierney. *My Girl* (Vanderbilt, "Cynthia Redding," Nov. 24, 1924): Desert Isle; A Solo on the Drum; They Say/W: Harlan Thompson, M: Harry Archer.

909. Lewis Bolyard *Pal Joey* (Broadhurst, revival, "Louis," Jan. 3, 1952): The Flower Garden of My Heart/W: Lorenz Hart, M: Richard Rodgers.

910. Elaine Bonazzi *The Most Happy Fella* (New York State, revival, "Marie," Sept. 4, 1991): How Beautiful the Days; Young People/WM: Frank Loesser.

911. Brenda Bond B: Hudson or Winchester, MA. *Yes, Yes, Yvette* (Harris, "Ethel Clark," Oct. 3, 1927): What Kind of Boy?/W: Irving Caesar, M: Phil Charig, Ben M. Jerome. *Just a Minute* (Ambassador > Century, "Kay Bolton," Oct. 8, 1928): We'll Just Be Two Commuters/W: Walter O'Keefe, M: Harry Archer.

912. Francine Bond *Dance Me a Song* (Royale, revue, Jan. 20, 1950): It's the Weather/WM: James Shelton.

913. Frederic Bond (Sept. 12, 1861–Feb. 9, 1914) B: New York, NY. *The Social Whirl*

(Casino > Majestic, "James Ellingham," Apr. 7, 1906): Just Kids/WM: Charles J. Ross.

914. Helen Bond *Go to It* (Princess, "Grape Juice," Oct. 24, 1916): Extra!/WM: John L. Golden, Anne Caldwell, John E. Hazzard — There's Something About You Dear That Appeals to Me/W: Frank Craven, M: John L. Golden, Silvio Hein. *Hitchy-Koo of 1917* (Cohan and Harris > Liberty > 44th Street, revue, June 7, 1917): The Ragtime Alphabet/WM: ?.

915. Julie Bond B: Houston, TX. *Joseph and the Amazing Technicolor Dreamcoat* (Minskoff, revival, "Mrs. Potiphar," Nov. 10, 1993): Potiphar/W: Tim Rice, M: Andrew Lloyd Webber.

916. Lillian Bond (Jan. 18, 1910–Jan. 25, 1991) B: London, England. She began her career as a costume designer. In the 1930s she appeared in Hollywood movies. *Luana* (Hammerstein's, "Neikia," Sept. 17, 1930): Hawaii's Shore; Wanapoo Bay; Yankyula/W: J. Keirn Brennan, M: Rudolf Friml.

917. Ridge Bond (July 12, 1923–) B: McAlester, OK. *Oklahoma!* (New York City Center, revival, "Curly McLain," Aug. 31, 1953): The Farmer and the Cowman; Oh, What a Beautiful Mornin'; Oklahoma!; People Will Say We're in Love; Pore Jud; The Surrey with the Fringe on Top/W: Oscar Hammerstein II, M: Richard Rodgers.

918. Rudy Bond (Oct. 1, 1913–Mar. 29, 1982) B: Philadelphia, PA. *Illya Darling* (Mark Hellinger, "Captain," Apr. 11, 1967): Birthday Song/W: Joe Darion, M: Manos Hadjidakis.

919. Ruth Bond *Du Barry Was a Lady* (46th Street > Royale, CR, "Alice Barton" and "Alisande," June 1940): Ev'ry Day a Holiday; Katie Went to Haiti; Well, Did You Evah!/WM: Cole Porter. *One Touch of Venus* (Imperial, "Gloria Kramer," Oct. 7, 1943): Way Out West in Jersey/W: Ogden Nash, M: Kurt Weill.

920. Sheila Bond (Mar. 16, 1928–) B: New York, NY. *Street Scene* (Adelphi, "Mae Jones," Jan. 9, 1947): Moon-Faced, Starry-Eyed/W: Langston Hughes, M: Kurt Weill. *Make Mine Manhattan* (Broadhurst, revue, Jan. 15, 1948): My Brudder and Me/W: Arnold B. Horwitt, M: Richard Lewine. *Wish You Were Here* (Imperial, "Fay Fromkin," June 25, 1952): Certain Individuals; Everybody Loves Everybody; Flattery; Goodbye Love; Shopping Around/WM: Harold Rome. *Damn Yankees* (46th Street, CR, "Lola," June 1956): A Little Brains, a Little Talent; Two Lost Souls; Whatever Lola Wants (Lola Gets); Who's Got the Pain?/WM: Richard Adler, Jerry Ross. *Pal Joey* (New York City Center, revival, "Gladys Bumps," May 31, 1961): Do It the Hard

Way; The Flower Garden of My Heart; Plant You Now, Dig You Later; That Terrific Rainbow; You Mustn't Kick It Around/W: Lorenz Hart, M: Richard Rodgers.

921. Sudie Bond (July 13, 1928–Nov. 10, 1984) B: Louisville, KY. Wisecracking character actress in films from 1965. She was Flo on the TV sitcom *Alice* (1980). *Grease* (Broadhurst, CR, "Miss Lynch," June 1972): Alma Mater/WM: Jim Jacobs, Warren Casey.

922. John A. Boni *The Most Happy Fella* (New York City Center, revival, "Al," May 11, 1966): Standing on the Corner/WM: Frank Loesser.

923. Marion Bonnell *Crazy Quilt* (44th Street, revue, May 19, 1931): Crazy Quilt/W: Bud Green, M: Harry Warren.

924. Letitia Bonta *The Greenwich Village Follies of 1925* (46th Street, revue, CR, Jan. 18, 1926): The Curse of Cinderella/W: Owen Murphy, M: Harold A. Levey.

925. Nace Bonville *Florodora* (Casino > New York, "Leandro," Nov. 10, 1900): We Got Up at 8/WM: Leslie Stuart. *The Tattooed Man* (Criterion, "Hashish," Feb. 18, 1907): Take Things Easy; Things We Are Not Supposed to Know/W: Harry B. Smith, M: Victor Herbert.

926. Elise Bonwit *Poor Little Ritz Girl* (Central, "Helen Bond," July 28, 1920): The Bombay Bombashay/W: Alex Gerber, M: Sigmund Romberg, Ray Perkins — The Daisy and the Lark/W: Lorenz Hart, M: Richard Rodgers — In the Land of Yesterday/W: Alex Gerber, M: Sigmund Romberg.

927. Leta Bonynge (May 11, 1917–) B: Los Angeles, CA. *How to Succeed in Business Without Really Trying* (46th Street, CR, "Miss Jones," Mar. 1964): Brotherhood of Man; Paris Original/WM: Frank Loesser. *My Fair Lady* (New York City Center, revival, "Mrs. Pearce," June 13, 1968): I Could Have Danced All Night; You Did It/W: Alan Jay Lerner, M: Frederick Loewe.

928. Sorrell Booke (Jan. 4, 1926–Feb. 11, 1994) B: Buffalo, NY. The chubby character actor is best remembered for his role as Boss Hogg in the TV series *The Dukes of Hazzard* (1979). *Fiorello!* (New York City Center, revival, "Fiorello LaGuardia," June 13, 1962): The Name's LaGuardia; Unfair/W: Sheldon Harnick, M: Jerry Bock.

929. George Booker (1911–Feb. 17, 2001) *Swing It* (Adelphi, "Gabby," July 22, 1937): Blah-Blah-Blah/W: Ira Gershwin, M: George Gershwin — Captain, Mate and Crew; The Susan Belle and the Liza Jane/W: Cecil Mack, Milton Reddie, M: Eubie Blake.

930. Michael C. Booker B: Wichita, KS. *Hello, Dolly!* (Lunt-Fontanne, revival, "Ambrose Kemper," Mar. 5, 1978): Put on Your Sunday Clothes/WM: Jerry Herman.

931. Debby Boone (Sept. 22, 1956–) B: Hackensack, NJ. Singing daughter of Pat Boone. Her major hit song was "You Light Up My Life" (WM: Joe Brooks). *Seven Brides for Seven Brothers* (Alvin, "Milly," July 8, 1982): Glad That You Were Born; Love Never Goes Away; One Man; You Gotta Make It Through the Winter/WM: Al Kasha, Joel Hirschhorn — Goin' Courting; Wonderful, Wonderful Day/W: Johnny Mercer, M: Gene de Paul. *The Sound of Music* (New York State, revival, "Maria Rainer," Mar. 8, 1990): Do-Re-Mi; Edelweiss; The Lonely Goatherd; My Favorite Things; An Ordinary Couple; Sixteen, Going on Seventeen; So Long, Farewell; The Sound of Music/W: Oscar Hammerstein II, M: Richard Rodgers. *Grease* (Eugene O'Neill, revival, CR, "Betty Rizzo," c 1994): Greased Lightnin'; Look at Me, I'm Sandra Dee; There Are Worse Things I Could Do/WM: Jim Jacobs, Warren Casey.

932. Kailip Boonrai *Miss Saigon* (Broadway, CR, "Tam," c 1993): Little God of My Heart/W: Richard Maltby, Jr., Alain Boublil; M: Claude-Michel Schonberg.

933. Anne Booth B: Liverpool, England. *Virginia* (Center, "Sylvia Laurence," Sept. 2, 1937): My Bridal Gown; An Old Flame Never Dies; You and I Know/W: Al Stillman, Laurence Stallings, M: Arthur Schwartz — My Heart Is Dancing/W: Al Stillman, M: Arthur Schwartz.

934. Joyce Booth *Merry-Go-Round* (Klaw, revue, May 31, 1927): Sentimental Silly/W: Howard Dietz, Morrie Ryskind, M: Henry Souvaine, Jay Gorney.

935. Marjorie Booth *Suzette* (Princess, "Dora Dolores," Nov. 24, 1921): A Forest Legend; Oh, Waiter/W: Roy Dixon, M: Arthur Gutman.

936. Rachel Booth M: JAMES T. POWERS. *A Runaway Girl* (Daly's, revival, "Alice," Apr. 23, 1900): The Pickaninnies/W: Aubrey Hopwood, M: Ivan Caryll. *The Messenger Boy* (Daly's, "Rosa," Sept. 16, 1901): Aspirations/W: Adrian Ross, M: Lionel Monckton — The Mummies/W: Adrian Ross, M: Ivan Caryll. *The Jewel of Asia* (Criterion > Daly's, "Mimi," Feb. 16, 1903): My Honey Bunch/W: George V. Hobart, M: Max Hirschfeld — Pierre; Wanted: A Fly/W: Frederic Ranken, M: Ludwig Englander.

937. Shirley Booth (Aug. 30, 1898–Oct. 16, 1992) B: New York, NY. A versatile actress capable of both humor and pathos. Best remembered on TV in the sitcom *Hazel* (1961). *A Tree Grows in Brooklyn* (Alvin, "Cissy," Apr. 19, 1951): He Had Refinement; Is That My Prince?; Look Who's Dancing; Love Is the Reason/W: Dorothy Fields, M: Arthur Schwartz. *By the Beautiful Sea* (Majestic, "Lottie Gibson," Apr. 8, 1954): Alone Too Long; Coney Island Boat; I'd Rather Wake Up by Myself; Lottie Gibson Specialty (Please Send Me Down a Baby Brother); The Sea Song (By the Beautiful Sea)/W: Dorothy Fields, M: Arthur Schwartz. *Juno* (Winter Garden, "Juno Boyle," Mar. 9, 1959): Bird Upon the Tree; Old Sayin's; On a Day Like This; Song of the Ma; Where?/WM: Marc Blitzstein. *Look to the Lilies* (Lunt-Fontanne, "Mother Maria," Mar. 29, 1970): Follow the Lamb; Gott Is Gut; Himmlisher Vater; I, Yes, Me, That's Who; Look to the Lilies; One Little Brick at a Time; Them and They; When I Was Young; Why Can't He See/W: Sammy Cahn, M: Jule Styne.

938. Johnny Borden *Bye Bye Birdie* (Martin Beck, "Randolph MacAfee," Apr. 14, 1960): Hymn for a Sunday Evening; Kids/W: Lee Adams, M: Charles Strouse. *Milk and Honey* (Martin Beck, "Shepherd Boy," Oct. 10, 1961): Shepherd's Song/WM: Jerry Herman.

939. Edwin (Ed) Bordo (Mar. 3, 1931–) B: Cleveland, OH. *Annie* (Alvin, "Drake," Apr. 21, 1977): Annie; I Think I'm Gonna Like It Here; You Won't Be an Orphan for Long/W: Martin Charnin, M: Charles Strouse.

940. Irene Bordoni (Jan. 16, 1895–Mar. 19, 1953) B: Corsica. M: Broadway producer, playwright, songwriter E. Ray Goetz. Her stage career began in Paris in 1907. Singer, dancer, comedienne, she usually played flirtatious French coquettes. *Miss Information* (George M. Cohan, "Elaine Foazane," Oct. 5, 1915): A Little Love (But Not for Me)/W: Elsie Janis, M: Jerome Kern — Two Big Eyes/W: John L. Golden, M: Cole Porter. *Hitchy-Koo of 1917* (Cohan and Harris > Liberty > 44th Street, revue, June 7, 1917): Lady of the Sea/WM: E. Ray Goetz. *Hitchy-Koo of 1918* (Globe, revue, June 6, 1918): Clara/W: E. Ray Goetz, Glen MacDonough, M: ?. *As You Were* (Central, "Gervaise" and "Ninon de L'Esclos" and "Cleopatra," Jan. 27, 1920): I Am Cleopatra/WM: E. Ray Goetz — If You Could Care for Me; Ninon Was a Naughty Girl/W: Arthur Wimperis, M: Herman Darewski. *Little Miss Bluebeard* (Lyceum, "Colette," Aug. 28, 1923): The Gondola and the Girl/W: Percy Graham Paul, E. Ray Goetz, M: Paul Rubens — I Won't Say I Will, But I Won't Say I Won't/W: B.G. DeSylva, Arthur Francis, M: George Gershwin — So This Is Love/WM: E. Ray Goetz — Who'll Buy My Violets? (La Violetera)/W: E. Ray Goetz, M: Jose Padilla. *Naughty Cinderella* (Lyceum, "Germaine Leverrier," Nov. 9, 1925): Do I Love You?/WM: E. Ray Goetz, Henri Christine — J'ai Deux Amants/W: Sacha Guitry, M: Andre Messager — Nothing but Yes in My Eyes/WM: E. Ray Goetz — That Means Nothing to Me/WM: Lee Sterling, A.L. Keith. *Paris* (Music Box, "Vivienne Rolland," Oct. 8, 1928): Don't Look at Me That Way; Let's Do It (Let's Fall in Love); Two Little Babes in the Wood/WM: Cole Porter — The Land of Going to Be/WM: E. Ray Goetz, Walter Kollo — Paris/W: E. Ray Goetz, M: Louis Alter. *Great Lady* (Majestic, "Mme. Colette," Dec. 1, 1938): And So Will You; May I Suggest Romance?/W: Earle Crooker, M: Frederick Loewe. *Louisiana Purchase* (Imperial, "Madame Bordelaise," May 28, 1940): It's a Lovely Day Tomorrow; Latins Know How/WM: Irving Berlin.

941. Emil Boreo (1885–July 27, 1951) B: Poland. He played Boris the hotel manager in Hitchcock's classic film *The Lady Vanishes* (1938). *The Merry World* (Imperial, revue, June 8, 1926): Don't Fall in Love with Me/WM: Herman Hupfeld.

942. Yamil Borges (June 8, 1958–) B: San Lorenzo, PR. *West Side Story* (Minskoff, revival, "Rosalia," Feb. 14, 1980): I Feel Pretty/W: Stephen Sondheim, M: Leonard Bernstein. *Roza* (Royale, "Jasmine," Oct. 1, 1987): Different; Is Me; Sweet Seventeen/W: Julian More, M: Gilbert Becaud.

943. Alexandra Borrie *Happy End* (Martin Beck, revival, "Sister Jane," May 7, 1977): Brother, Give Yourself a Shove; Don't Be Afraid; In Our Childhood's Bright Endeavor; Lieutenants of the Lord; The Liquor Dealer's Dream; March Ahead/W: Bertolt Brecht, M: Kurt Weill.

944. Alonzo Bosan (Oct. 7, 1886–June 24, 1959) B: Shelbyville, OH. *Seventeen* (Broadhurst, "Mr. Genesis," June 21, 1951): I Could Get Married Today/W: Kim Gannon, M: Walter Kent.

945. Philip Bosco (Sept. 26, 1930–) B: Jersey City, NJ. An important stage actor, he was in films from 1962. *Threepenny Opera* (Vivian Beaumont, revival, CR, "Mack the Knife," c 1976): Ballad in Which Macheath Begs All Men for Forgiveness; Ballad of Gracious Living; Ballad of Immoral Earnings; Call from the Grave; The Cannon Song; Liebeslied; What Keeps Mankind Alive?/W: Bertolt Brecht, M: Kurt Weill.

946. Tom Bosley (Oct. 1, 1927–) B: Chicago, IL. He appeared in all 796 Broadway performances of *Fiorello!*. He was Howard Cunningham on the TV sitcom *Happy Days* (1974), and Sheriff Amos Tupper on the popular mystery series *Murder, She Wrote* (1984). *Fiorello!* (Broadhurst, "Fiorello LaGuardia," Nov. 23, 1959): The Name's LaGuardia; Unfair/W: Sheldon Harnick, M: Jerry Bock. *Nowhere to Go but Up* (Winter Garden, "Izzy Einstein," Nov. 10, 1962): Ain't You Ashamed; Dear Mom; Follow the Leader Septet; Live a Little; Natural Allies; Nowhere to Go but Up; When a Fella Needs a Friend/W: James Lipton, M: Sol Berkowitz. *The Education of H*Y*M*A*N K*A*P*L*A*N* (Alvin, "Hyman Kaplan," Apr. 4, 1968): Anything Is Possible; I Never Felt Better in My Life; Julius Caesar; Lieben Dich; OOOO-EEEE/WM: Paul Nassau, Oscar Brand. *Beauty and the Beast* (Palace, "Maurice," Apr. 18, 1994): No Matter What/W: Tim Rice, M: Alan Menken.

947. Gretha Boston (Apr. 18, 1959–) B: Crossett, AR. *Show Boat* (Gershwin, revival, "Queenie," Oct. 2, 1994): Can't Help Lovin' Dat Man; Mis'ry's Comin' Aroun'; Queenie's Ballyhoo/W: Oscar Hammerstein II, M: Jerome Kern.

948. Barry Bostwick (Feb. 24, 1945–) B: San Mateo, CA. *Grease* (Broadhurst, "Danny Zuko," June 7, 1972): All Choked Up; Alone at a Drive-In Movie; Summer Nights/WM: Jim Jacobs, Warren Casey. *The Robber Bridegroom* (Biltmore, return engagement, "Jamie Lockhart," Oct. 9, 1976): Love Stolen; Riches; Steal with Style; Where Oh Where?/W: Alfred Uhry, M: Robert Waldman. *Nick & Nora* (Marquis, "Nick Charles," Dec. 8, 1991): As Long as You're Happy; A Busy Night at Lorraine's; Is There Anything Better Than Dancing?; Let's Go Home; Look Who's Alone Now; May the Best Man Win; Swell/W: Richard Maltby, Jr., M: Charles Strouse.

949. Jill Bosworth *The Sound of Music* (New York State, revival, "Sister Berthe," Mar. 8, 1990): Maria/W: Oscar Hammerstein II, M: Richard Rodgers.

950. Rose Botti *The Yankee Consul* (Broadway > Wallack's, "Papinta," Feb. 22, 1904): The Hammers Will Go Rap, Rap, Rap; I'd Like to Be a Soldier; The Mosquito and the Midge; We Were Taught to Walk Demurely/W: Henry Blossom, M: Alfred G. Robyn.

951. Roland Bottomley (Oct. 19, 1879–Jan. 5, 1947) B: Liverpool, England. On stage as a child in England, he gained fame in the U.S. as an actor in silent pictures. *The Laughing Husband* (Knickerbocker, "Lutz Nachitgall," Feb. 2, 1914): Forbidden Fruit/W: Arthur Wimperis, M:

Edmund Eysler—Since Grandpa Learned to Tango/W: L. Williams, M: Pedro Dezulueta. *High Jinks* (Casino, CR, "Dick Wayne," June 8, 1914): High Jinks; Is This Love at Last?; Love's Own Kiss; Something Seems Tingle-ingleing/W: Otto Harbach, M: Rudolf Friml. *Lassie* (Nora Bayes, CR, "Lieut. The Hon. David Graham," Apr. 6, 1920): Lassie; Lovely Corals; Skeletons; A Teacup and a Spoon/W: Catherine Chisholm Cushing, M: Hugo Felix. *The Yankee Princess* (Knickerbocker, "Phillipe La Tourette," Oct. 2, 1922): Forbidden Fruit; Friendship; Love the Wife of Your Neighbor/W: B.G. DeSylva, M: Emmerich Kalman.

952. John Bottoms (1939–) B: Dayton, OH. *Two Gentlemen of Verona* (St. James, "Launce," Dec. 1, 1971): Don't Have the Baby; Follow the Rainbow; Hot Lover; Love's Revenge; Milkmaid; Pearls/W: John Guare, M: Galt MacDermot.

953. Aubrey Boucicault (June 23, 1868–July 10, 1913) B: London, England. *Higgledy-Piggledy* (Weber Music Hall, "Charley Stringham," Oct. 20, 1904): For You, Honey, for You/W: Edgar Smith, M: Maurice Levi. *The Vanderbilt Cup* (Broadway, "Dexter Joyce," Jan. 16, 1906): So I've Been Told; Somewhere in the World (There's a Little Girl for Me)/W: Raymond Peck, M: Robert Hood Bowers.

954. John Bouie *Finian's Rainbow* (New York City Center, revival, "First Passion Pilgrim Gospeleer," May 18, 1955): The Begat/W: E.Y. Harburg, M: Burton Lane. *Carmen Jones* (New York City Center, revival, "Dink," May 31, 1956): Whizzin' Away Along de Track/W: Oscar Hammerstein II, M: Georges Bizet. *Simply Heavenly* (Playhouse, "Melon," Aug. 20, 1957): Did You Ever Hear the Blues?; When I'm in a Quiet Mood/W: Langston Hughes, M: David Martin.

955. Alice Boulden B: Boston, MA. M: JOE COOK. *Gay Paree* (Shubert, revue, Aug. 18, 1925): Baby's Baby Grand/W: Clifford Grey, M: J. Fred Coots—Bamboo Babies/W: Ballard Macdonald, M: Joseph Meyer, James F. Hanley—Every Girl Must Have a Little Bull/W: Clifford Grey, M: Alfred Goodman, J. Fred Coots. *Gay Paree* (Winter Garden, revue, Nov. 9, 1926): Broken Rhythm/WM: ?—Shaking the Blues Away/WM: Irving Berlin. *Hold Everything!* (Broadhurst, "Betty Dunn," Oct. 10, 1928): Don't Hold Everything/W: B.G. DeSylva, Lew Brown, M: Ray Henderson. *Heads Up!* (Alvin, "Peggy Pratt," Nov. 11, 1929): Knees; My Man Is on the Make/W: Lorenz Hart, M: Richard Rodgers. *Fine and Dandy* (Erlanger's, "Nancy

Ellis," Sept. 23, 1930): Can This Be Love?; Fine and Dandy; Let's Go Eat Worms in the Garden; Nobody Breaks My Heart [Jan. 26, 1931]/W: Paul James, M: Kay Swift.

956. Kathryn Boule (Dec. 27–) B: Washington, D.C. *Annie* (Alvin, CR, "Grace Farrell," July 29, 1980): Annie; I Think I'm Gonna Like It Here; A New Deal for Christmas; N.Y.C.; You Won't Be an Orphan for Long/W: Martin Charnin, M: Charles Strouse.

957. Frank Bouley (May 6, 1928–) B: Spokane, WA. M: JOAN BOWMAN. *Carmelina* (St. James, "Father Tommaso," Apr. 8, 1979): Signora Campbell/W: Alan Jay Lerner, M: Burton Lane.

958. Fan Bourke (July 12, 1886–Mar. 9, 1959) B: Brooklyn, NY. *Kitty's Kisses* (Playhouse, "Mrs. Dennison," May 6, 1926): I Don't Want Him/W: Gus Kahn, M: Con Conrad.

959. Philip Bourneuf (Jan. 7, 1908–Mar. 23, 1979) B: Somerville, MA. *Miss Liberty* (Imperial, "Joseph Pulitzer," July 15, 1949): The Most Expensive Statue in the World/WM: Irving Berlin.

960. Stephen Bourneuf (Nov. 24, 1957–) B: St. Louis, MO. *A Chorus Line* (Shubert, CR, "Al," Mar. 27, 1989): Sing!/W: Edward Kleban, M: Marvin Hamlisch.

961. Yvonne Bouvier *The Streets of Paris* (Broadhurst, revue, June 19, 1939): History Is Made at Night/WM: Harold Rome — Rendezvous Time in Paree; We Can Live on Love (We Haven't Got a Pot to Cook In)/W: Al Dubin, M: Jimmy McHugh.

962. Joseph (Joe) Bova (May 25, 1924–) B: Cleveland, OH. *Once Upon a Mattress* (Alvin, "Prince Dauntless," Nov. 25, 1959): Man to Man Talk; An Opening for a Princess; Song of Love; Swamps of Home/W: Marshall Barer, M: Mary Rodgers. *Irma La Douce* (Plymouth, CR, "Bob Le Hontu," Aug. 1961): Le Grisbi Is le Root of le Evil in Man; That's a Crime; Valse Milieu/ Eng. W: Julian More, David Heneker, Monty Norman, M: Marguerite Monnot. *Hot Spot* (Majestic, "Shim," Apr. 19, 1963): I Had Two Dregs; I Think the World of You; A Little Trouble Goes a Long, Long Way; Rich, Rich, Rich/ W: Martin Charnin, M: Mary Rodgers. *42nd Street* (Winter Garden, "Bert Barry," Aug. 25, 1980): Getting Out of Town/W: Mort Dixon, M: Harry Warren — Shuffle Off to Buffalo/W: Al Dubin, M: Harry Warren.

963. Mark Bove (Jan. 9, 1960–) B: Pittsburgh, PA. *West Side Story* (Minskoff, revival, "Action," Feb. 14, 1980): Gee, Officer Krupke!/ W: Stephen Sondheim, M: Leonard Bernstein.

A Chorus Line (Shubert, CR, "Mike," c 1986): I Can Do That/W: Edward Kleban, M: Marvin Hamlisch.

964. Sibyl Bowan (Jan. 31–) B: New York, NY. *Donnybrook!* (46th Street, "Sadie McInty," May 18, 1961): Mr. Flynn/WM: Johnny Burke. *The Music Man* (New York City Center, revival, "Mrs. Paroo," June 16, 1965): Piano Lesson/ WM: Meredith Willson. *Maggie Flynn* (ANTA, "Mrs. Vanderhoff," Oct. 23, 1968): How About a Ball?/WM: Hugo Peretti, Luigi Creatore, George David Weiss.

965. Joyce Leigh Bowden *Rock 'n Roll! The First 5,000 Years* (St. James, revue, Oct. 24, 1982): Boogie Woogie Bugle Boy (of Company B)/WM: Don Raye, Hughie Prince — I Feel the Earth Move/WM: Carole King — When Will I Be Loved?/WM: Phil Everly.

966. Rae Bowdin *Sweet Little Devil* (Astor > Central, "Rena," Jan. 21, 1924): Hooray for the U.S.A.; Strike, Strike, Strike/W: B.G. DeSylva, M: George Gershwin.

967. Elgie Bowen *The Love Cure* (New Amsterdam, "Nellie Vaughn," Sept. 1, 1909): Forget Me Not; I Wonder What the Audience Would Say; I'm an Indian; A Pretty Part for Me to Play; A Toast; When Skies Are Bright/W: Oliver Herford, M: Edmund Eysler. *The Spring Maid* (Liberty, "Annamirl," Dec. 26, 1910): Dance with Me; Interrupted Allegory/W: Robert B. Smith, M: Heinrich Reinhardt — The Loving Cup; Take Me Dear/W: Robert B. Smith, M: Robert Hood Bowers.

968. Charles H. Bowers *Cyrano de Bergerac* (Knickerbocker, "Christian de Neuvillette," Sept. 18, 1899): The King's Musketeers; Let the Sun of Thine Eyes; Since I Am Not for Thee/W: Harry B. Smith, M: Victor Herbert.

969. Clent Bowers *The First* (Martin Beck, "Cool Minnie Edwards," Nov. 17, 1981): The National Pastime (This Year's Nigger); You Do-Do-Do-It Good/W: Martin Charnin, M: Bob Brush. *Harrigan 'n Hart* (Longacre, "Sam Nichols," Jan. 31, 1985): Maggie Murphy's Home; The Skidmore Fancy Ball/W: Edward Harrigan, M: Dave Braham — Sam Johnson's Colored Cakewalk/WM: ?. *Cats* (Winter Garden, CR, "Old Deuteronomy," c 1986): The Addressing of Cats; The Moments of Happiness; Old Deuteronomy/W: T.S. Eliot, M: Andrew Lloyd Webber. *Big* (Sam S. Shubert, "Barrett," Apr. 28, 1996): Coffee, Black/W: Richard Maltby, Jr., M: David Shire.

970. Edward Bowers *Robinson Crusoe, Jr.* (Winter Garden, Feb. 17, 1916): Sailor's Fling/ WM: ?.

971. Frederick V. Bowers *The Ham Tree* (New York, CR, Nov. 6, 1905): Goodbye Sweet Old Manhattan Isle; Sweethearts in Every Town/W: William Jerome, M: Jean Schwartz. *The Young Turk* (New York, "Otis Knott," Jan. 31, 1910): I'll Be Happy Too; The Parisian Glide; Under the Oriental Moon/W: Harry Williams, M: Max Hoffmann.

972. George Vining Bowers (Apr. 23, 1835–Aug. 18, 1878) B: Philadelphia, PA. *The White Fawn* (Niblo's Garden, "Lord Twaddledum," Jan. 17, 1868): I'll Never Ride Again/W: James Mortimer, M: Edward Mollenhauer.

973. Kenneth (Kenny) Bowers (Mar. 10, 1923–) B: Jersey City, NJ. *Best Foot Forward* (Ethel Barrymore, "Hunk Hoyt," Oct. 1, 1941): The Guy Who Brought Me/WM: Richard Rodgers, Hugh Martin — Just a Little Joint with a Juke Box; Three Men on a Date; What Do You Think I Am?/WM: Hugh Martin, Ralph Blane. *Annie Get Your Gun* (Imperial, "Tommy Keeler," May 16, 1946): I'll Share It All with You; Who Do You Love, I Hope/WM: Irving Berlin.

974. Teresa Bowers *Ain't Misbehavin'* (Longacre, revue, CR, Sept. 1979): Find Out What They Like/W: Andy Razaf, M: Fats Waller — I've Got My Fingers Crossed/W: Ted Koehler, M: Jimmy McHugh — Lounging at the Waldorf/W: Richard Maltby, Jr., M: Fats Waller — Squeeze Me/W: Clarence Williams, M: Fats Waller — That Ain't Right/WM: Nat King Cole, Add. W: Richard Maltby, Jr., Murray Horwitz — Two Sleepy People/W: Frank Loesser, M: Hoagy Carmichael — When the Nylons Bloom Again/W: George Marion, Jr., M: Fats Waller.

975. Martha Bowes *Head Over Heels* (George M. Cohan, "Miss Wentworth," Aug. 29, 1918): With Type a-Ticking/W: Edgar Allan Woolf, M: Jerome Kern.

976. Sibylla Bowhan *Mary* (Knickerbocker, "Golden Girl," Oct. 18, 1920): Don't Fall Until You've Seen Them All/W: Otto Harbach, M: Louis A. Hirsch. *Ginger* (Daly's, "Majorie Frayne," Oct. 16, 1923): Before You Take a Man; Don't Judge a Girl by Her Name; He Failed to Underwrite a Happy Home/W: H.I. Phillips, M: Harold Orlob — Beware/W: Frank Stammers, M: Harold Orlob. *Who Cares?* (46th Street, revue, July 8, 1930): The Hunt/W: Harry Clark, M: Percy Wenrich.

977. Betty Bowman *Pleasure Bound* (Majestic, "Marcella Standish," Feb. 18, 1929): We'll Get Along/W: Max Lief, Nathaniel Lief, M: Muriel Pollock.

978. Carrie Bowman *The Rich Mr. Hoggenheimer* (Wallacks, "Violet Moss," Oct. 22, 1906): Poker Love (Card Duet)/WM: Paul West, Jerome Kern. *The American Idea* (New York, "Catherine Budmeyer," Oct. 5, 1908): Brothers and Sisters; That's Some Love/WM: George M. Cohan. *The Girl of My Dreams* (Criterion, "Carolyn Swifton [Cuddle]," Aug. 7, 1911): Belles of the Tally-Ho Boarding School; Dear Little Game of Guessing; Dearest Little Marionette/W: Otto Harbach, M: Karl Hoschna.

979. Grace Bowman *Innocent Eyes* (Winter Garden, revue, "Prima Donna" and "Singer," May 20, 1924): Day Dreams [June 16, 1924]/W: Harold Atteridge, Tot Seymour, M: Sigmund Romberg — Inspiration/W: Clare Kummer, M: Leo Fall — Organdie Days/W: Tot Seymour, M: Jean Schwartz. *A Night in Spain* (44th Street, revue, May 3, 1927): Argentina; Columbus at the Court of Queen Isabel [May 23, 1927]; My Rose of Spain [May 23, 1927]; The Nocturne; The Sky Girl/W: Alfred Bryan, M: Jean Schwartz. *Ned Wayburn's Gambols* (Knickerbocker, revue, Jan. 15, 1929): Crescent Moon/W: Morrie Ryskind, M: Walter G. Samuels — The Sun Will Shine/W: Morrie Ryskind, M: Arthur Schwartz — What Is the Good?/W: Clifford Grey, M: Lew Kessler.

980. Joan Bowman (Nov. 15, 1930–) B: Westminster, MD. M: FRANK BOULEY. *Seventeen* (Broadhurst, "Nan," June 21, 1951): Ode to Lola; Things Are Gonna Hum This Summer/W: Kim Gannon, M: Walter Kent.

981. Polly Bowman *Papa's Darling* (New Amsterdam, "Mignon," Nov. 2, 1914): The Land of the Midnight Sun; The Popular Pop/W: Harry B. Smith, M: Ivan Caryll.

982. Paul Bown (c 1854–July 29, 1889) *Cinderella at School* (Daly's, "Professor Kindergarten," Mar. 5, 1881): Corn Beef Hashed; A Cotton Cloth Ghost; Origin of Love/WM: Woolson Morse.

983. Richard Bowne (Nov. 12, 1949–May 19, 1990) B: Bronxville, NY. *Snow White and the Seven Dwarfs* (Radio City Music Hall, "Prince Charming," Oct. 18, 1979): One Song/W: Larry Morey, M: Frank Churchill — Will I Ever See Her Again/W: Joe Cook, M: Jay Blackton.

984. James (Thomas) Boxwill *Blackbirds of 1933-34* (Apollo, revue, Dec. 2, 1933): Great Gettin' Up Mornin'/W: Mann Holiner, M: Alberta Nichols — Let Me Be Born Again/W: Joe Young, Ned Washington, M: Victor Young. *Swing It* (Adelphi, "Jasper," July 22, 1937): By the Sweat of Your Brow; Jungle Swing/W: Cecil Mack, Milton Reddie, M: Eubie Blake.

985. Monica Boyar (Dec. 20–) B: Dominican Republic. *13 Daughters* (54th Street,

"Emmaloa," Mar. 2, 1961): Hiaka; Ka Wahine Akamai; You Set My Heart to Music/WM: Eaton Magoon, Jr.

986. Bonnie Boyce *When Johnny Comes Marching Home* (New Amsterdam > Manhattan Opera House, revival, "Mrs. Constance Pemberton," May 7, 1917): Marry the Man and Be Merry; The Suwanee River; When Our Lips in Kisses Met; Years Touch Not the Heart/W: Stanislaus Stange, M: Julian Edwards.

987. Anna Boyd (?–June 4, 1916) M: JOSEPH P. COYNE. *Aladdin, Jr.* (Broadway, "Aladdin, Jr.," Apr. 8, 1895): I Didn't Think She'd Do It; Message of the Rose; The Rackety Boys; Women, Wine and Song/W: J. Cheever Goodwin, M: W.H. Batchelor. *The Tourists* (Majestic, "Letitia Hemmingway," Aug. 25, 1906): Ruth, She Always Told the Truth/W: R.H. Burnside, M: Gustave Kerker. *A Skylark* (New York, "Amelia Parling," Apr. 4, 1910): The Broadway Lament; I Just Can't Wait/W: William B. Harris, Jr., M: Frank Dossert.

988. Ethel Boyd *Rambler Rose* (Empire, "Claire," Sept. 10, 1917): Just a Little Bit in Love/W: Harry B. Smith, M: Victor Jacobi.

989. Sydney Boyd (Feb. 25, 1901–) B: Glasgow, Scotland. *Are You With It?* (New Century, "Mr. Bixby," Nov. 10, 1945): Nutmeg Insurance/W: Arnold B. Horwitt, M: Harry Revel.

990. Carol Boyer *Bitter Sweet* (44th Street, revival, "Lotte," May 7, 1934): Ladies of the Town/WM: Noel Coward.

991. Lucienne Boyer (c 1903–Dec. 6, 1983) *Continental Varieties* (Little, revue, Oct. 3, 1934): Buy My Roses/W: Chamfleury, M: Fugaro — Come Dance Anyway/W: Jamblan, M: Jean Delettre — From Love to Love/W: Leo Delievre, M: Jean Delettre — Hands Across the Table/W: Mitchell Parish, M: Jean Delettre — I Did Not Know/W: Maurice Aubert, M: Jean Delettre — I Spit in the Water/WM: Jean Tranchant — Is It the Singer or Is It the Song?/WM: Annette Mills — So Small/W: Pierre Bayle, M: Gaston Claret — Speak to Me of Love (Parlez-Moi d'Amour)/WM: Bruce Sievier, Jean Lenoir — Speak to Me of Something Else/WM: Jean Lelettre — The Street Walkers/W: French song, M: Vincent Scotto — Wait!/W: Jacques-Charles, M: Jean Lenoir.

992. Martha Boyer *Bitter Sweet* (44th Street, revival, "Victoria," May 7, 1934): Alas, the Time Is Past; The Last Dance; Tarara Boom-de-Ay/WM: Noel Coward.

993. Francis J. Boyle *Yankee Circus on Mars* (Hippodrome, CR, "Signor Thunderairo," Sept. 4, 1905): The Bogie Man; Get a Horse; Hold Your Horses/W: Harry Williams, M: Jean Schwartz. *A Society Circus* (Hippodrome, "Bolesla, King of the Gypsies," Dec. 13, 1905): The Good, Kind, Jolly Man/WM: Manuel Klein. *The Peasant Girl* (44th Street, "Pan Jan Zaremba," Mar. 2, 1915): Advice to the Young/W: Herbert Reynolds, Harold Atteridge, M: Oscar Nedbal — Love's Awakening/W: ?, M: Oscar Nedbal, Rudolf Friml.

994. Jack Boyle *The Passing Show of 1916* (Winter Garden, revue, CR, Sept. 4, 1916): Broadway School Days/W: Harold Atteridge, M: Sigmund Romberg, Otto Motzan — The Making of a Girl/W: Harold Atteridge, M: George Gershwin, Sigmund Romberg. *Meet the People* (Mansfield, revue, Dec. 25, 1940): Let's Steal a Tune (from Offenbach); Senate in Session/W: Henry Myers, M: Jay Gorney.

995. John Boyle (Sept. 1, 1891–Sept. 28, 1959) B: Memphis, TN. *Miss Daisy* (Shubert > Lyric, "Billy," Sept. 9, 1914): Cheer Up; I Adore the American Girl; Kissing; Pierrot's Ball; The Race of Life; Won't You Dance?; Youth/W: Philip Bartholomae, M: Silvio Hein. *The Cohan Revue of 1916* (Astor, revue, "Col. Smith," Feb. 9, 1916): The Dancing Pirates/WM: George M. Cohan. *Hello, Alexander* (44th Street, "Simons," Oct. 7, 1919): Ghost of Old Black Joe; Tampa Bay; Those Dixie Melodies; When Those Mason Dixon Minstrels Hit Town/W: Alfred Bryan, M: Jean Schwartz — Yazoo Rag/WM: ?.

995a. Victor Bozardt *The Hurdy Gurdy Girl* (Wallack's, "Porter No. 1," Sept. 23, 1907): Bluff/W: Richard Carle, M: H.L. Heartz.

996. Beverley (Beverlee) Bozeman (July 20, 1927–) B: Fresno, CA. *Where's Charley?* (Broadway, CR, "Amy Spettigue"): Better Get Out of Here; Make a Miracle; The New Ashmoleon Marching Society and Students Conservatory Band; Where's Charley?; The Woman in His Room/WM: Frank Loesser. *Pal Joey* (Broadhurst, revival, CR, "Gladys Bumps," Mar. 1953): The Flower Garden of My Heart; Plant You Now, Dig You Later; That Terrific Rainbow; You Mustn't Kick It Around/W: Lorenz Hart, M: Richard Rodgers.

997. Sidney (Sydney) Bracey (Dec. 18, 1877–Aug. 5, 1942) B: Melbourne, Australia. *Robin Hood* (New Amsterdam, revival, "Guy of Gisborne," May 6, 1912): Roundelay; Tinkers' Song/W: Harry B. Smith, M: Reginald De Koven. *Rob Roy* (Liberty, revival, "Sandy MacSherry," Sept. 15, 1913): Town Crier's Song/W: Harry B. Smith, M: Reginald De Koven.

998. Eddie Bracken (Feb. 7, 1920–Nov. 14, 2002) B: Astoria, Queens, NY. The comic actor's best films were made for director Preston Sturges. *Too Many Girls* (Imperial, "Jojo Jordan," Oct. 18, 1939): I Like to Recognize the Tune/W: Lorenz Hart, M: Richard Rodgers. *Beg, Borrow or Steal* (Martin Beck, "Pistol," Feb. 10, 1960): Little People; You've Got Something to Say; Zen Is When/W: Bud Freeman, M: Leon Prober. *Hello, Dolly!* (Lunt-Fontanne, revival, "Horace Vandergelder," Mar. 5, 1978): Before the Parade Passes By/WM: Lee Adams, Charles Strouse, Jerry Herman — Hello, Dolly!; It Takes a Woman; So Long, Dearie/WM: Jerry Herman — Motherhood/WM: Bob Merrill, Jerry Herman. *Sugar Babies* (Mark Hellinger, revue, CR, May 31, 1982): Down at the Gaiety Burlesque; Every Day Another Tune; Mr. Banjo Man/WM: Arthur Malvin — A Good Old Burlesque Show/W: Arthur Malvin, M: Jimmy McHugh — I Can't Give You Anything but Love; On the Sunny Side of the Street/W: Dorothy Fields, M: Jimmy McHugh — I Want a Girl (Just Like the Girl That Married Dear Old Dad)/W: William Dillon, M: Harry Von Tilzer — I'm Shooting High/W: Ted Koehler, M: Jimmy McHugh — Immigration Rose/W: Eugene West, Irwin Dash, M: Jimmy McHugh — When You and I Were Young, Maggie Blues/W: Jack Frost, M: Jimmy McHugh.

999. Jessie Bradbury *The Spring Maid* (Liberty, "Ursula," Dec. 26, 1910): On the Track [Jan. 16, 1911]/W: Robert B. Smith, M: Heinrich Reinhardt.

1000. Lane Bradbury *Gypsy* (Broadway, "June," May 21, 1959): If Momma Was Married/W: Stephen Sondheim, M: Jule Styne.

1001. Alberta Bradford *Don't Bother Me, I Can't Cope* (Playhouse, revue, Apr. 19, 1972): All I Need; Fighting for Pharaoh; I Gotta Keep Movin'/WM: Micki Grant.

1002. Alex Bradford same as ALBERTA BRADFORD.

1003. Billy Bradford *A la Carte* (Martin Beck, revue, Aug. 17, 1927): Baby's Blue/WM: Herman Hupfeld.

1004. Edith Bradford (June 24, 1884–?) B: Bangor, ME. M: CHARLES MEAKINS. *The Pearl and the Pumpkin* (Broadway, CR, "Mother Carey," Oct. 2, 1905): The Submarine Fire Brigade (Fighters of Flame Are We)/W: Paul West, M: John W. Bratton. *The Chocolate Soldier* (Lyric > Herald Square > Lyric > Casino, "Mascha," Sept. 13, 1909): After Today; Falling in Love; Seek the Spy; The Tale of a Coat; Thank the Lord the War Is Over; We, Too, Are Lonely/W: Stanislaus Stange, M: Oscar Straus. *Adele* (Longacre > Harris, "Babiole," Aug. 28,

1913): The Clock Is Striking Ten; Gay Soldier Boy; It's Love!; Wedding Bells; Yours for Me and Mine for You/WM: Edward A. Paulton, Adolf Philipp, Jean Briquet. *The Fortune Teller* (Century roof, revival, "Borisa," Sept. 29, 1923): Serenade/W: Harry B. Smith, M: Victor Herbert.

1005. Ted Bradford *Earl Carroll's Vanities of 1928* (Earl Carroll, revue, Aug. 6, 1928): Painting a Vanities Girl/WM: Ernie Golden.

1006. Frank Bradley *Kitty Darlin'* (Casino, "Mallow," Nov. 7, 1917): You're Plenty of a Lady as You Are/WM: ?.

1007. Harry C. Bradley (Apr. 15, 1869–Oct. 18, 1947) B: San Francisco, CA. *Adele* (Longacre > Harris, "Jacques," Aug. 28, 1913): The Clock Is Striking Ten; Gay Soldier Boy; It's Love!; Wedding Bells; Yours for Me and Mine for You/WM: Edward A. Paulton, Adolf Philipp, Jean Briquet.

1008. Charles Bradshaw *Miss Dolly Dollars* (Knickerbocker > New Amsterdam, "Samuel Gay," Sept. 4, 1905): Life's a Masquerade; The Self-Made Family; She's a Lady with Money/W: Harry B. Smith, M: Victor Herbert.

1009. Alice Brady (Nov. 2, 1892–Oct. 28, 1939) B: New York, NY. The versatile actress alternated between stage and screen, comedy and drama. 52 of her 78 films were silents. Her creation of Lavinia in Eugene O'Neill's 1931 play *Mourning Becomes Electra* was a great theatrical event. *The Balkan Princess* (Herald Square > Casino, "Olga," Feb. 9, 1911): Dreaming; Holidays/WM: Arthur Wimperis, Paul Rubens.

1010. Bee Brady *Blossom Time* (Jolson, revival, "Kitzi," May 19, 1924): Love Is a Riddle; Peace to My Lonely Heart; Three Little Maids/W: Dorothy Donnelly, M: Sigmund Romberg.

1011. June Brady *Alive and Kicking* (Winter Garden, revue, Jan. 17, 1950): I Didn't Want Him/W: Leonard Gershe, M: Irma Jurist.

1012. Olne Brady *Girl Crazy* (Alvin, Oct. 14, 1930): Barbary Coast/W: Ira Gershwin, M: George Gershwin.

1013. Bonnie Brae *Seventeen* (Broadhurst, "Madge," June 21, 1951): Ode to Lola/W: Kim Gannon, M: Walter Kent.

1014. Ruby Braff (1927–) B: Boston, MA. *Pipe Dream* (Shubert, "Pancho," Nov. 30, 1955): Bums' Opera/W: Oscar Hammerstein II, M: Richard Rodgers.

1015. Nellie Braggins *The Highwayman* (Broadway, "Doll Primrose," Dec. 13, 1897): Bread, Cheese and Kisses/W: Harry B. Smith, M: Reginald De Koven.

1016. David (Dave) Braham, Jr. (c 1877–June 30, 1915) *Marty Malone* (Bijou, Aug. 31,

1896): Savannah Sue/W: Edward Harrigan, M: Dave Braham.

1017. Harry Braham (c 1850– Sept. 21, 1923) B: London, England. M: LILLIAN RUSSELL for a short time. He came to the U.S. in 1874. *Sergeant Kitty* (Daly's, "Pierre Picorin," Jan. 18, 1904): I Have Thought of a Scheme; I'm the King of Bakers/W: R.H. Burnside, M: A. Baldwin Sloane.

1018. Lionel Braham (Apr. 1, 1879–Oct. 6, 1947) B: Yorkshire, England. *Mecca* (Century, "Ali Shar," Oct. 4, 1920): From Bagdad We Come/W: Oscar Asche, M: Percy E. Fletcher.

1019. Ralph Brainard *The Fortune Teller* (Century roof, revival, "Capt. Ladislas," Sept. 29, 1923): Hungaria's Hussars/W: Harry B. Smith, M: Victor Herbert.

1020. Wilfrid Brambell (Mar. 22, 1912–Jan. 18, 1985) B: Dublin, Ireland. Star of British TV show *Steptoe and Son*, on which the U.S. TV sitcom *Sanford and Son* (1972) was based. *Kelly* (Broadhurst, "Dan Kelly," Feb. 6, 1965): Life Can Be Beautiful; Me and the Elements/W: Eddie Lawrence, M: Moose Charlap.

1021. Gretchen Branche *Blackbirds of 1933-34* (Apollo, revue, Dec. 2, 1933): I Just Couldn't Take It, Baby/W: Mann Holiner, M: Alberta Nichols — Three Little Maids from School/W: Mann Holiner, M: Alberta Nichols, based on Gilbert and Sullivan.

1022. Gibby Brand (May 20, 1946–) B: New York, NY. *Little Me* (Eugene O'Neill, revival, "Yulnick," Jan. 21, 1982): Goodbye (The Prince's Farewell)/W: Carolyn Leigh, M: Cy Coleman. *Beauty and the Beast* (Palace, CR, "Cogsworth," c 1996): Be Our Guest; Something There/W: Howard Ashman, M: Alan Menken.

1023. John E. Brand (1846–June 24, 1907) B: Boston, MA. *Cinderella at School* (Daly's, "Jack Polo," Mar. 5, 1881): Columbia Won the Race Today; I Kiss My Hand to Thee; No Regular Wife; Swing with Me; 'Tis Not Becoming in a Maiden; What a Shocking Sight/WM: Woolson Morse.

1024. Phoebe Brand *Johnny Johnson* (44th Street, "Minny Belle Tompkins," Nov. 19, 1936): Democracy's Call; Oh, Heart of Love/W: Paul Green, M: Kurt Weill.

1025. Sophie Brandt (July 4, 1896–Feb. 4, 1946) B: St. Louis, MO. *A Waltz Dream* (Broadway, "Franzi Steingruber," Jan. 27, 1908): A Country Lass and a Courtly Dame; A Lesson in Love; Life Is Love and Laughter; Sweetest Maid of All/W: Joseph W. Herbert, M: Oscar Straus — Piccolo, Tsin, Tsin, Tsin/W: Grace Colbron, M: Oscar Straus. *The Gay Musician* (Wallack's,

"Marie Dubois," May 18, 1908): At Last I Hold You; Not as Simple as I Look; The Saucy Sparrow; Take That; That Melody/W: Charles J. Campbell, M: Julian Edwards.

1026. Phil Branson *The Man from Now* (New Amsterdam, "John P. Pennypacker," Sept. 3, 1906): I Want to Go Home Now/W: John Kendrick Bangs, M: Manuel Klein.

1027. Marion Brantley *Swing It* (Adelphi, "Ethel," July 22, 1937): Old Time Swing/W: Cecil Mack, Milton Reddie, M: Eubie Blake.

1028. John Brascia *Hazel Flagg* (Mark Hellinger,"Willie," Feb. 11, 1953): You're Gonna Dance with Me, Willie/W: Bob Hilliard, M: Jule Styne.

1029. Marion Brash She played Eunice on the TV soap *Search for Tomorrow* (1951). *She Loves Me* (Eugene O'Neill, CR, "Ilona Ritter," Nov. 2, 1963): Good Morning, Good Day; Goodbye, Georg; I Don't Know His Name; I Resolve; Thank You, Madam; A Trip to the Library/W: Sheldon Harnick, M: Jerry Bock.

1030. George Brasno (Dec. 23, 1911–Aug. 15, 1982) One of a family of midgets who played in vaudeville, he appeared in a few movies in the 1930s and 40s. *Are You With It?* (New Century, "George," Nov. 10, 1945): Slightly Slightly/W: Arnold B. Horwitt, M: Harry Revel.

1031. Olive Brasno (Oct. 7, 1917–Jan. 25, 1998) B: Oak Bridge, NJ. same as GEORGE BRASNO.

1032. Richard Brasno same as GEORGE BRASNO.

1033. Charles Braswell (Sept. 7, 1925–May 17, 1974) B: McKinney, TX. *Wildcat* (Alvin, "Matt," Dec. 16, 1960): Tall Hope/W: Carolyn Leigh, M: Cy Coleman. *Sail Away* (Broadhurst, "Joe" and "Ali," Oct. 3, 1961): The Customer's Always Right; The Passenger's Always Right/WM: Noel Coward. *Mame* (Winter Garden, "Beauregard Jackson Pickett Burnside," May 24, 1966): Mame; We Need a Little Christmas/WM: Jerry Herman. *Company* (Alvin, "Larry," Apr. 26, 1970): Have I Got a Girl for You; Sorry-Grateful/WM: Stephen Sondheim. *Company* (Alvin, CR, "Harry," Mar. 29, 1971): Have I Got a Girl for You; Sorry-Grateful/WM: Stephen Sondheim.

1034. George Bratt *The Grand Street Follies of 1928* (Booth, revue, May 28, 1928): Husky Dusky Annabel/W: Agnes Morgan, M: Max Ewing.

1035. Ralph Braun (Aug. 20, 1946–) B: Milwaukee, WI. *The Music Man* (City Center 55th Street, revival, "Olin Britt," June 5, 1980): It's You; Lida Rose; Sincere/WM: Meredith

Willson. *Copperfield* (ANTA, "Mr. Quinion," Apr. 13, 1981): Copperfield/WM: Al Kasha, Joel Hirschhorn.

1036. Alan Braunstein (Apr. 30, 1947–) B: Brooklyn, NY. *Dude* (Broadway, "Hero," Oct. 9, 1972): A Dawn; Hum Drum Life; I'm Small/W: Gerome Ragni, M: Galt MacDermot.

1037. Brenda Braxton *Cats* (Winter Garden, CR, "Demeter"): Grizabella, the Glamour Cat; Macavity/W: T.S. Eliot, M: Andrew Lloyd Webber. *Legs Diamond* (Mark Hellinger, "Madge," Dec. 26, 1988): The Man Nobody Could Love/WM: Peter Allen. *Smokey Joe's Cafe* (Virginia, revue, Mar. 2, 1995): Don Juan; I'm a Woman; Neighborhood; Trouble; You're the Boss/WM: Jerry Leiber, Mike Stoller — Spanish Harlem/WM: Phil Spector, Jerry Leiber.

1038. Stephen Bray (June 22, 1956–June 10, 1990) *Going Up* (John Golden, revival, "John Gordon," Sept. 19, 1976): Paging Mr. Street/W: Otto Harbach, M: Louis A. Hirsch.

1039. Will Bray *When Johnny Comes Marching Home* (New York, "Uncle Tom," Dec. 16, 1902): My Honeysuckle Girl (Ma Honeysuckle Gal)/W: Stanislaus Stange, M: Julian Edwards.

1040. Walter Brazil Partner of JOHN BOYLE. *The Cohan Revue of 1916* (Astor, revue, "Capt. Jones," Feb. 9, 1916): The Dancing Pirates/WM: George M. Cohan. *Hello, Alexander* (44th Street, "Slocum," Oct. 7, 1919): Ghost of Old Black Joe; Tampa Bay; Those Dixie Melodies; When Those Mason Dixon Minstrels Hit Town/W: Alfred Bryan, M: Jean Schwartz — Yazoo Rag/WM: ?.

1041. Toney Brealond *Ain't Supposed to Die a Natural Death* (Ethel Barrymore, Oct. 20, 1971): Funky Girl on Motherless Broadway/WM: Melvin Van Peebles.

1042. Marc Breaux *Catch a Star!* (Plymouth, revue, Sept. 6, 1955): To Be or Not to Be in Love/W: Ray Golden, Dan Shapiro, Milton Pascal, M: Phil Charig — Twist My Arm/W: Paul Francis Webster, M: Sammy Fain. *Li'l Abner* (St. James, "Dr. Schleifitz," Nov. 15, 1956): Oh Happy Day/W: Johnny Mercer, M: Gene de Paul. *Destry Rides Again* (Imperial, "Gyp Watson," Apr. 23, 1959): Every Once in a While/WM: Harold Rome.

1043. Patricia Bredin B: England. *Camelot* (Majestic, CR, "Queen Guenevere," Apr. 16, 1962): Before I Gaze at You Again; Camelot; I Loved You Once in Silence; The Jousts; The Lusty Month of May; The Simple Joys of Maidenhood; Then You May Take Me to the Fair; What Do the Simple Folk Do?/W: Alan Jay Lerner, M: Frederick Loewe.

1044. David Breen *The Cocoanuts* (Lyric > Century, CR, "Eddie," between May 17, 1926 and Aug. 7, 1926): The Bellhops; They're Blaming the Charleston; We Should Care/WM: Irving Berlin.

1045. Grace Breen *Eileen* (Shubert, "Eileen Mulvaney," Mar. 19, 1917): Thine Alone; Too-re-loo-re; When Love Awakes (Love's Awakening)/W: Henry Blossom, M: Victor Herbert.

1046. J. Patrick Breen (Oct. 26, 1960–) B: Brooklyn, NY. *Big River: The Adventures of Huckleberry Finn* (Eugene O'Neill, CR, "Young Fool"): Arkansas/WM: Roger Miller.

1047. Margaret Breen (Feb. 3, 1907–Dec. 5, 1960) B: Missouri. *Princess Flavia* (Century, "Helga," Nov. 2, 1925): Marionettes; Only One/W: Harry B. Smith, M: Sigmund Romberg. *The Merry World* (Imperial, revue, June 8, 1926): Dancing Jim/W: Donovan Parsons, Marc Anthony — Deauville/WM: Herman Hupfeld — Jabberwalky; Military Charleston; Tallahassee/WM: ?. *Peggy-Ann* (Vanderbilt, "Patricia Seymour," Dec. 27, 1926): Havana (Havana Opening); Hello!/W: Lorenz Hart, M: Richard Rodgers.

1048. Nellie Breen (c 1898–Apr. 26, 1986) Dancer and comedienne. In 1922 she tapdanced on radio, a first. *The Passing Show of 1922* (Winter Garden, revue, Sept. 20, 1922): A Study in Black and White/W: Harold Atteridge, M: Alfred Goodman. *Ginger* (Daly's, "Ruth Warewell," Oct. 16, 1923): Beware/W: Frank Stammers, M: Harold Orlob — Mating Time; Pretty Girl; Take a Chance; That Ought to Count for Something/W: H.I. Phillips, M: Harold Orlob. *Mercenary Mary* (Longacre, "Norah," Apr. 13, 1925): Cherchez la Femme (Get Your Woman); Just You and I and the Baby/WM: William B. Friedlander, Con Conrad. *Florida Girl* (Lyric, "Betty," Nov. 2, 1925): Beautiful Sea; Smile On/W: Paul Porter, Benjamin Hapgood Burt, M: Milton Suskind. *The Desert Song* (Casino, "Susan," Nov. 30, 1926): I'll Be a Buoyant Girl; It; Let's Have a Love Affair/W: Otto Harbach, Oscar Hammerstein II, M: Sigmund Romberg.

1049. Beverly Ann Bremers (Mar. 10, 1950–) B: Chicago, IL. *The Me Nobody Knows* (Orpheum > Helen Hayes, "Catherine," May 18, 1970/Dec. 18, 1970): Fugue for Four Girls; How I Feel; Sounds/W: Will Holt, M: Gary William Friedman. *Hair* (Biltmore, CR, "Sheila"): Easy to Be Hard; Good Morning, Starshine; I Believe in Love; Let the Sunshine In (The Flesh Failures)/W: Gerome Ragni, James Rado, M: Galt MacDermot.

1050. El Brendel (Mar. 25, 1891–Apr. 9,

1964) B: Philadelphia, PA. M: FLO BURT. In vaudeville at age 13, he played comic Germans; during WWI he switched to comic Swedes. He appeared in silent films and more than 40 sound movies. On TV he played Joan Davis' father in the sitcom *I Married Joan* (1952). *Cinderella on Broadway* (Winter Garden, revue, June 24, 1920): Cindy/W: Harold Atteridge, M: Bert Grant.

1051. Dan Brennan *Red Pepper* (Shubert, "Jimmy Swift," May 29, 1922): Bugaboo; Ginger/WM: Howard E. Rogers, Albert Gumble, Owen Murphy — Strut Your Stuff/W: Howard E. Rogers, M: Albert Gumble. *Topsy and Eva* (Harris, CR, "Gee Gee," Mar. 23, 1925): Kiss Me/WM: Vivian Duncan, Rosetta Duncan.

1052. Eileen Brennan (Sept. 3, 1935–) B: Los Angeles, CA. She recreated her movie role as Capt. Doreen Lewis in *Private Benjamin* (1980) for the 1981 TV remake, but was unable to continue in it beyond Oct. 1982 due to a serious car injury. *The King and I* (New York City Center, revival, "Anna Leonowens," June 12, 1963): Getting to Know You; Hello, Young Lovers; I Whistle a Happy Tune; The Royal Bangkok Academy; Shall I Tell You What I Think of You?; Shall We Dance?/W: Oscar Hammerstein II, M: Richard Rodgers. *The Student Gypsy or The Prince of Liederkranz* (54th Street, "Merry May Glockenspiel," Sept. 30, 1963): The Drinking Song; The Gypsy Life; Merry May; My Love Is Yours; Our Love Has Flown Away; Romance; Seventh Heaven Waltz/WM: Rick Besoyan. *Hello, Dolly!* (St. James, "Irene Molloy," Jan. 16, 1964): Dancing; Elegance; It Only Takes a Moment; Motherhood; Ribbons Down My Back/WM: Jerry Herman.

1053. James Brennan (Oct. 31, 1950–) B: Newark, NJ. *So Long, 174th Street* (Harkness, "Soda Jerk," Apr. 27, 1976): Men/WM: Stan Daniels. *42nd Street* (Winter Garden, CR, "Billy Lawlor," Dec. 13, 1983): Dames; 42nd Street; I Know Now; We're in the Money; Young and Healthy; You're Getting to Be a Habit with Me/W: Al Dubin, M: Harry Warren. *Me and My Girl* (Marquis, revival, CR, "Bill Snibson," Mar. 1, 1988/Jan. 31, 1989): Hold My Hand/W: Harry Graham, M: Maurice Elwin, Noel Gay — The Lambeth Walk; Me and My Girl; You Would If You Could/W: Douglas Furber, M: Noel Gay — Leaning on a Lamppost; Love Makes the World Go Round; Song of Hareford/WM: Noel Gay. *Crazy for You* (Sam S. Shubert, CR, "Bobby Child," Jan. 2, 1995): Could You Use Me?; Embraceable You; I Can't Be Bothered Now; I Got Rhythm; K-ra-zy for You;

Nice Work If You Can Get It; Shall We Dance?; Slap That Bass; Stiff Upper Lip; They Can't Take That Away from Me; Things Are Looking Up; What Causes That?/W: Ira Gershwin, M: George Gershwin.

1054. Jay Brennan (Dec. 6, 1882–Jan. 14, 1961) B: Baltimore, MD. Vaudeville partner of BERT SAVOY. *The Greenwich Village Follies of 1922* (Shubert, revue, Sept. 12, 1922): Greenwich Village Nights/W: Irving Caesar, John Murray Anderson, M: Louis A. Hirsch. *Fioretta* (Earl Carroll, "Caponetti," Feb. 5, 1929): Wicked Old Willage of Wenice/WM: G. Romilli.

1055. Maureen Brennan (Oct. 11, 1952–) B: Washington, DC. *Candide* (Broadway, revival, "Cunegonde," Mar. 10, 1974): The Best of All Possible Worlds; Life Is Happiness Indeed/W: Stephen Sondheim, M: Leonard Bernstein — Glitter and Be Gay; Oh Happy We/W: Richard Wilbur, M: Leonard Bernstein — I Am Easily Assimilated/WM: Leonard Bernstein — You Were Dead, You Know/W: Richard Wilbur, John Latouche, M: Leonard Bernstein. *Going Up* (John Golden, revival, "Madeline Manners," Sept. 19, 1976): Do It for Me; I Want a Boy Who's Determined to Do as I Say; If You Look in Her Eyes/W: Otto Harbach, M: Louis A. Hirsch. *Little Johnny Jones* (Alvin, revival, "Goldie Gates," Mar. 21, 1982): Let's You and I Just Say Goodbye; Oh, You Wonderful Boy/WM: George M. Cohan. *Stardust* (Biltmore, revue, Feb. 19, 1987): Belle of the Ball; Forgotten Dreams; Sleigh Ride; The Syncopated Clock/W: Mitchell Parish, M: Leroy Anderson — Carolina Rolling Stone/W: Mitchell Parish, M: Eleanor Young, Harry D. Squires — Deep Purple/W: Mitchell Parish, M: Peter DeRose — Midnight at the Onyx; Sophisticated Swing/W: Mitchell Parish, M: Will Hudson — Moonlight Serenade/W: Mitchell Parish, M: Glenn Miller — One Morning in May; Star Dust/W: Mitchell Parish, M: Hoagy Carmichael — Riverboat Shuffle/W: Mitchell Parish, M: Hoagy Carmichael, Dick Voynow, Irving Mills — The Scat Song/W: Mitchell Parish, M: Frank Perkins, Cab Calloway — Sentimental Gentleman from Georgia; Stars Fell on Alabama/W: Mitchell Parish, M: Frank Perkins — Take Me in Your Arms/W: Mitchell Parish, M: Fred Markush — Volare/W: Mitchell Parish, M: Domenico Modugno.

1055a. Nan Brennan (?–July 21, 1965) *The Girl Behind the Counter* (Herald Square, "Kitty Ermine," Oct. 1, 1907): Shopping/W: Arthur Anderson, M: Howard Talbot. *The Never Homes*

(Broadway, "Lotta Lipp," Oct. 5, 1911): Just a Little Bit of Lingerie/W: E. Ray Goetz, M: Raymond Hubbell. *The Sun Dodgers* (Broadway, "Vera Light," Nov. 30, 1912): The Night Brigade; Rag Me Around/W: E. Ray Goetz, M: A. Baldwin Sloane.

1056. Nora Brennan (Dec. 1, 1953–) B: East Chicago, IN. *Cats* (Winter Garden, CR, "Cassandra"): The Old Gumbie Cat/W: T.S. Eliot, M: Andrew Lloyd Webber.

1057. Dorothy Brenner *A Stubborn Cinderella* (Broadway, "Sallie," Jan. 25, 1909): Don't Teach Me to Swim Alone; The Land of the Sky (Adios, Senorita) [Mar. 22, 1909]/W: Will M. Hough, Frank R. Adams, M: Joseph E. Howard. *The Wife Hunters* (Herald Square, "Henrietta Lampton," Nov. 2, 1911): Honeyland; Little Dancing Jumping Jigger/W: David Kempner, M: Anatole Friedland, Malvin F. Franklin. *The Three Romeos* (Globe, CR, "Nancy Mallory," Dec. 11, 1911): Humpty and Dumpty; In the Spring It's Nice to Have Someone to Love You; The Lily and the Rose/W: R.H. Burnside, M: Raymond Hubbell.

1058. Romney Brent (Jan. 26, 1902–Sept. 24, 1976) B: Saltillo, Mexico, where his father was ambassador to France and Spain. M: GINA MALO. *The Garrick Gaieties of 1925* (Garrick, revue, May 17, 1925): April Fool; Soliciting Subscriptions/W: Lorenz Hart, M: Richard Rodgers — Stage Managers' Chorus (Walk Upon Your Toes)/W: Dudley Digges, Lorenz Hart, M: Richard Rodgers. *The Garrick Gaieties of 1926* (Garrick, revue, "King Arthur" and "Helen Wills," May 10, 1926): Idles of the King; Tennis Champs (Helen! Susanna! and Bill!)/W: Lorenz Hart, M: Richard Rodgers. *The Little Show* (Music Box, revue, Apr. 30, 1929): The Theme Song/W: Howard Dietz, M: Arthur Schwartz — What Every Little Girl Should Know/W: Henry Myers, M: Arthur Schwartz.

1059. Tommy (Tom) Breslin (Mar. 24, 1946–) B: Norwich, CT. *70, Girls, 70* (Broadhurst, Apr. 15, 1971): Go Visit Your Grandmother/W: Fred Ebb, M: John Kander. *Good News* (St. James, revival, "Sylvester," Dec. 23, 1974): Happy Days/W: B.G. DeSylva, Lew Brown, M: Ray Henderson. *Musical Chairs* (Rialto, "Blue Suit," May 14, 1980): Musical Chairs/WM: Tom Savage.

1060. Sherri (Peaches) Brewer (May 29–) B: Chicago, IL. *Hello, Dolly!* (St. James, CR, "Ermengarde," Nov. 12, 1967): Put on Your Sunday Clothes/WM: Jerry Herman. *Hello, Dolly!* (St. James, CR, "Minnie Fay," Mar. 1968): Dancing/WM: Jerry Herman — Elegance;

Motherhood/WM: Bob Merrill, Jerry Herman.

1061. Betty Brewster *See America First* (Maxine Elliott, "Gwendolyn," Mar. 28, 1916): Beautiful, Primitive Indian Girls; Indian Girls' Chant/WM: T. Lawrason Riggs, Cole Porter.

1062. Henrietta Brewster *The Velvet Lady* (New Amsterdam, "Guest," Feb. 3, 1919): Way Down in Yucatan/W: Henry Blossom, M: Victor Herbert. *Peg o' My Dreams* (Al Jolson, "Rita," May 5, 1924): Right-O; Shy Little Irish Smile/W: Anne Caldwell, M: Hugo Felix.

1063. Pat Brewster *Laffing Room Only* (Winter Garden, revue, Dec. 23, 1944): Feudin' and Fightin'/WM: Al Dubin, Burton Lane — Hooray for Anywhere; The Steps of the Capitol; Stop That Dancing [May 27, 1945]; Sunny California [May 27, 1945]; This Is as Far as I Go [May 27, 1945]/WM: Burton Lane.

1064. Antony Brian *Conversation Piece* (44th Street, "Lord Doyning," Oct. 23, 1934): Regency Rakes/WM: Noel Coward.

1065. Donald Brian (Feb. 17, 1871–Dec. 22, 1948) B: St. John's, Newfoundland. M: VIRGINIA O'BRIEN. After his appearance as Prince Danilo in *The Merry Widow*, Brian became one of the first matinee idols of the musical stage. *Florodora* (Winter Garden, CR, "Capt. Arthur Donegal," Jan. 27, 1902): Galloping/W: Ernest Boyd-Jones, M: Leslie Stuart — I Want to Be a Military Man/W: Frank Clement, M: Leslie Stuart. *Little Johnny Jones* (Liberty > New York, "Henry Hapgood," Nov. 7, 1904): Good Old California/WM: George M. Cohan. *Forty-Five Minutes from Broadway* (New Amsterdam > New York, "Tom Bennett," Jan. 1, 1906/Nov. 5, 1906): I Want to Be a Popular Millionaire/WM: George M. Cohan. *The Merry Widow* (New Amsterdam, "Prince Danilo," Oct. 21, 1907): I Love You So (The Merry Widow Waltz); Maxim's; The Silly Cavalier/W: Adrian Ross, M: Franz Lehar. *The Dollar Princess* (Knickerbocker, "Freddy Smythe," Sept. 6, 1909): The Dollar Princess; Inspection; Love's a Race; My Dream of Love; Then You Go?; Typewriting/W: George Grossmith, M: Leo Fall. *The Siren* (Knickerbocker, "Armand Marquis de Ravaillac," Aug. 28, 1911): The Donkey and the Hay; Hail, She Is the One Girl; Little Girls Beware; Wallflower Sweet/W: Harry B. Smith, M: Leo Fall — The Siren's Honeymoon (Sirens So Fair)/WM: Donald Brian. *The Marriage Market* (Knickerbocker, CR, "Edward Fleetwood [Teddy Tulare]," Sept. 22, 1913): Compliments/WM: ?— The Futurist Whirl/W: M.E. Rourke, M: Edwin Burch — Hand in Hand; June Is in the Air/W: Arthur

Anderson, M: Victor Jacobi — I'm Looking for an Irish Husband/W: M.E. Rourke, M: Jerome Kern — The Mendocino Stroll/WM: Donald Brian — Naval Manoeuvres; Oh, How Near and Yet How Far/W: Adrian Ross, M: Victor Jacobi. *The Girl from Utah* (Knickerbocker, "Sandy Blair," Aug. 24, 1914): The Donald Brian Polka; I Want to Be the Captain; In the Movies; Step This Way; When We Meet the Mormon [Sept. 30, 1914]/WM: ? — Gilbert the Filbert/W: Arthur Wimperis, M: Herman Finck — The Girl in Clogs and Shawl/WM: Harry Castling, C.W. Murphy, Donald Brian — The Land of Let's Pretend; Same Sort of Girl/W: Harry B. Smith, M: Jerome Kern — They Didn't Believe Me/W: M.E. Rourke, M: Jerome Kern — Where Has Una Gone?/WM: Paul Rubens, Percy Greenbank. *Sybil* (Liberty, "The Grand Duke Constantine," Jan. 10, 1916): Girls, You Are Wonderful Things; When Cupid Calls (The Rat-Tat-Tat Song)/W: Harry B. Smith, M: Victor Jacobi — Lift Your Eyes to Mine; Love May Be a Mystery/W: Harry Graham, M: Victor Jacobi. *Her Regiment* (Broadhurst, "Andre De Courcy," Nov. 12, 1917): A Little Farm in Normandy; Oh, My!; Some Day; Superlative Love; 'Twixt Love and Duty/W: William Le Baron, M: Victor Herbert. *The Girl Behind the Gun* (New Amsterdam, "Robert Lambrissac," Sept. 16, 1918): Back to the Dear Old Trenches; Happy Family; I Like It; Oh, How Warm It Is Today; There's a Light in Your Eyes; There's Life in the Old Dog Yet/W: P.G. Wodehouse, M: Ivan Caryll. *Buddies* (Selwyn, "Sonny," Oct. 27, 1919): Darling I; My Indispensable Girl; The Wail of the Tale of the Long Long Trail/WM: B.C. Hilliam. *The Chocolate Soldier* (Century, revival, "Lieut. Bumerli," Dec. 12, 1921): The Chocolate Soldier; Seek the Spy; Sympathy; The Tale of a Coat; That Would Be Lovely/W: Stanislaus Stange, M: Oscar Straus. *Up She Goes* (Playhouse, "Albert Bennett," Nov. 6, 1922): Journey's End; Lady Luck Smile on Me; Let's Kiss; Nearing the Day; The Strike; Tyup (Hitch Your Wagon to a Star)/W: Joseph McCarthy, M: Harry Tierney. *Yes, Yes, Yvette* (Harris, CR, "Robert Bennett"): How'd You Like To?/W: Irving Caesar, M: Stephen Jones — My Lady/WM: Frank Crumit, Ben M. Jerome. *The Merry Widow* (Erlanger's, revival, "Prince Danilo," Sept. 14, 1931): Maxim's; Silly Cavalier; Women/W: Adrian Ross, M: Franz Lehar. *Music in the Air* (44th Street, CR, "Bruno Mahler," July 1933): I Am So Eager; I'm Coming Home; One More Dance; The Song Is You/W: Oscar Hammerstein II, M: Jerome Kern. *The Chocolate Sol-dier* (St. James, revival, alt, "Lieut. Bumerli," May 2, 1934): The Chocolate Soldier; The Letter Song; That Would Be Lovely/W: Stanislas Stange, M: Oscar Straus. *Very Warm for May* (Alvin, William Graham," Nov. 17, 1939): In Other Words, Seventeen/W: Oscar Hammerstein II, M: Jerome Kern.

1066. Suzanne Briar (Feb. 8, 1946–) B: Washington, DC. *Aspects of Love* (Broadhurst, "Elizabeth," Apr. 8, 1990): She'd Be Far Better Off with You/W: Don Black, Charles Hart, M: Andrew Lloyd Webber.

1067. Denise Briault *Icetime* (Center, revue, June 20, 1946): Cossack Love; The Dream Waltz; Ole King Cole; Song of the Silver Blades/WM: James Littlefield, John Fortis.

1068. Carol Brice (1918–1985) *Saratoga* (Winter Garden, "Kakou," Dec. 7, 1959): Gettin' a Man; Goose Never Be a Peacock/W: Johnny Mercer, M: Harold Arlen. *Show Boat* (New York City Center, revival, "Queenie," Apr. 12, 1961): C'mon Folks (Ballyhoo); Can't Help Lovin' Dat Man/W: Oscar Hammerstein II, M: Jerome Kern. *Finian's Rainbow* (New York City Center, revival, "Maude," Apr. 5, 1967): Necessity/W: E.Y. Harburg, M: Burton Lane. *The Grass Harp* (Martin Beck, "Catherine Creek," Nov. 2, 1971): Dropsy Cure Weather; If There's Love Enough; Indian Blues; Marry with Me; Take a Little Sip; Whooshin' Through My Flesh; Yellow Drum/W: Kenward Elmslie, M: Claibe Richardson.

1069. Elizabeth Brice (c 1885–Jan. 25, 1965) B: Findlay, OH. The beautiful singer, dancer, actress began in vaudeville. *Nearly a Hero* (Casino, "Francine," Feb. 24, 1908): Don't You Ever Tell I Told You; I Want a Steam Yacht; The Walking Tour/W: Edward B. Claypoole, Will Heelan, M: Seymour Furth. *The Motor Girl* (Lyric, "Louise," June 15, 1909): All the World Loves a Lover/W: Charles J. Campbell, Ralph Skinner, M: Julian Edwards — I'm Old Enough to Do a Little Thinking; In Philadelphia; Just Like This/W: Charles J. Campbell, M: Julian Edwards. *The Jolly Bachelors* (Broadway, "Carola Gayley," Jan. 6, 1910): The Luncheon Line; Walk This Way; What Am I Going to Do to Make You Love Me?/W: Glen MacDonough, M: Raymond Hubbell. *The Hen-Pecks* (Broadway, CR, "Henolia Peck," Aug. 14, 1911): It's the Skirt; Just Tell Me with Your Eyes; Try This on Your Pianna, Anna/W: E. Ray Goetz, M: A. Baldwin Sloane. *A Winsome Widow* (Moulin Rouge, "Isabel," Apr. 11, 1912): Be My Little Baby Bumble Bee [May 6, 1912]/W: Stanley Murphy, M: Henry I. Marshall — String a Ring of Roses

'Round Your Rosie/W: William Jerome, M: Jean Schwartz — You're a Regular Girl/W: A. Seymour Brown, M: Nat D. Ayer. *Tantalizing Tommy* (Criterion, "Tommy," Oct. 1, 1912): Fairy Bells; I Am a Tomboy; Irish Stew; Just Like You/W: Adrian Ross, M: Hugo Felix. *Ziegfeld Follies of 1912* (Moulin Rouge, revue, CR, Dec. 2, 1912): Good Old Circus Band/W: Harry B. Smith, M: Raymond Hubbell — Row, Row, Row/W: William Jerome, M: James V. Monaco — There's One in a Million Like You/W: Grant Clarke, M: Jean Schwartz. *Ziegfeld Follies of 1913* (New Amsterdam, revue, June 16, 1913): Going There; Hello, Honey/W: George V. Hobart, M: Raymond Hubbell — Without You/W: Gene Buck, M: Dave Stamper. *Watch Your Step* (New Amsterdam, "Stella Spark," Dec. 8, 1914): I Love to Have the Boys Around Me; Move Over; Settle Down in a One-Horse Town/WM: Irving Berlin — When I Discovered You/WM: E. Ray Goetz, Irving Berlin. *Miss 1917* (Century, revue, Nov. 5, 1917): Be My Little Baby Bumble Bee/W: Stanley Murphy, M: Henry I. Marshall — The Land Where the Good Songs Go; The Picture I Want to See/W: P.G. Wodehouse, M: Jerome Kern. *Toot Sweet* (Princess > Nora Bayes, revue, May 7, 1919): America's Answer; Carolina; Give Him Back His Job; Just Around the Corner from Easy Street; Salvation Sal/W: Raymond B. Egan, M: Richard A. Whiting. *Buzzin' Around* (Casino, "Betty Barrett," July 6, 1920): Buzzin' Around; Ching-A-Ling Fling; I'll Be Just the Same; Voulez-Vous/WM: Will Morrissey, Edward Madden.

1070. Fanny Brice (Oct. 29, 1891–May 29, 1951) B: New York, NY. M: showman, producer, songwriter Billy Rose. One of the most beloved names in comedy of any era. She took her stage character Baby Snooks into radio in 1938 where she remained for 11 years. Barbra Streisand played her in the movie *Funny Girl* (1968). *Ziegfeld Follies of 1910* (Jardin de Paris — New York roof, revue, June 20, 1910): Good-bye Becky Cohen/WM: ? — Lovie Joe/W: Will Marion Cook, M: Joe Jordan. *Ziegfeld Follies of 1911* (Jardin de Paris, revue, June 26, 1911): Doggone That Chilly Man/WM: Irving Berlin — Ephraham Played Upon the Piano/WM: Vincent Bryan, Irving Berlin. *The Honeymoon Express* (Winter Garden, "Marcelle," Feb. 6, 1913): My Coca-Cola Belle; My Raggyadore; Syncopatia Land/W: Harold Atteridge, M: Jean Schwartz. *Ziegfeld Follies of 1916* (New Amsterdam, revue, June 12, 1916): The Dying Swan; The Hat/W: Blanche Merrill, M: Leo Edwards — Nijinski/W: Gene Buck, M: Dave Stamper. *Ziegfeld Follies*

of 1917 (New Amsterdam, revue, June 12, 1917): Egyptian/W: Blanche Merrill, M: Leo Edwards — Just You and Me; Ziegfeld Follies Rag/W: Gene Buck, M: Dave Stamper. *Ziegfeld Midnight Frolic [7th Edition]* (New Amsterdam roof, revue, May 20, 1918): Becky Is Back at the Ballet; Egyptian/W: Blanche Merrill, M: Leo Edwards. *Ziegfeld Midnight Frolic of 1919 [9th Edition]* (New Amsterdam roof, revue, Oct. 3, 1919): Rose of Washington Square/W: Ballard Macdonald, M: James F. Hanley. *Ziegfeld Follies of 1920* (New Amsterdam, revue, June 22, 1920): I Was a Florodora Baby/W: Ballard Macdonald, M: Harry Carroll — I'm a Vamp from East Broadway/WM: Irving Berlin, Bert Kalmar, Harry Ruby. *Ziegfeld Follies of 1921* (Globe, revue, June 21, 1921): Allay Up!/W: Ballard Macdonald, M: James F. Hanley — I'm a Hieland Lassie/W: Blanche Merrill, M: Leo Edwards — My Man/W: Channing Pollock, M: Maurice Yvain — Second Hand Rose/W: Grant Clarke, M: James F. Hanley. *Ziegfeld Follies of 1923* (New Amsterdam, revue, Oct. 20, 1923): The Fool/W: Benton Levy, M: Lee David — Russian Art/W: Blanche Merrill, M: Leo Edwards — That Society Bud (I'm a Society Bud)/W: Bert Kalmar, M: Harry Ruby. *Music Box Revue of 1924* (Music Box, revue, Dec. 1, 1924): Bandanna Ball; Don't Send Me Back to Petrograd; I Want to Be a Ballet Dancer/WM: Irving Berlin — Polly of Hollywood [Mar. 23, 1925]/W: B.G. DeSylva, M: James F. Hanley — Poor Little Moving Picture Baby/W: Blanche Merrill, M: Leo Edwards. *Fioretta* (Earl Carroll, "Marchesa Vera Di Livio," Feb. 5, 1929): Wicked Old Willage of Wenice/WM: G. Romilli. *Sweet and Low* (46th Street > 44th Street, revue, Nov. 17, 1930): Dancing with Tears in Their Eyes/W: Mort Dixon, Billy Rose, M: Will Irwin — I Knew Him Before He Was Spanish/W: Ballard Macdonald, Billy Rose, M: Dana Suesse — I Wonder Who's Keeping Him Now [Jan. 19, 1931]; Overnight/W: Charlotte Kent, Billy Rose, M: Louis Alter. *Crazy Quilt* (44th Street, revue, May 19, 1931): I Found a Million Dollar Baby (in a Five and Ten Cent Store)/W: Mort Dixon, Billy Rose, M: Harry Warren — I Want to Do a Number with the Boys/W: Ned Wever, M: Rowland Wilson — Peter Pan/W: Billy Rose, James Dyrenforth, M: Carroll Gibbons — Rest Room Rose [June 1931]/W: Lorenz Hart, M: Richard Rodgers. *Ziegfeld Follies of 1934* (Winter Garden, revue, Jan. 4, 1934): Countess Dubinsky; Sarah, the Sunshine Girl; Soul Saving Sadie/W: Ballard Macdonald, Billy Rose, M: Joseph Meyer — Rose of Washington Square/W: Ballard Macdonald,

M: James F. Hanley. *Ziegfeld Follies of 1936* (Winter Garden, revue, Jan. 30, 1936): Fancy, Fancy; He Hasn't a Thing Except Me/W: Ira Gershwin, M: Vernon Duke — The Gazooka/WM: Ira Gershwin, David Freedman — Modernistic Moe/WM: Ira Gershwin, Billy Rose, Vernon Duke.

1071. Lew Brice (Oct. 26, 1893–June 16, 1966) B: New York, NY. M: MAE CLARKE, for awhile. The younger brother of FANNY BRICE was a song and dance man, and a compulsive gambler. *The Passing Show of 1913* (Winter Garden, revue, July 24, 1913): Whistling Cowboy Joe/W: Harold Atteridge, M: Al W. Brown. *The Passing Show of 1914* (Winter Garden, revue, June 10, 1914): Good Old Levee Days/W: Harold Atteridge, M: Harry Carroll — The Grape Dance/W: Harold Atteridge, M: Sigmund Romberg. *Maid in America* (Winter Garden, revue, Feb. 18, 1915): Castles in the Air; The Girlie of the Cabaret; The Times Square Arguments/W: Harold Atteridge, M: Sigmund Romberg. *Americana of 1926* (Belmont, revue, July 26, 1926/Jan. 17, 1927): Blowin' the Blues Away/W: Ira Gershwin, M: Phil Charig — Kosher Kleagle [added]/W: J.P. McEvoy, M: Phil Charig — The Volga Boatman/W: Dailey Paskman, M: Alexei Archangelsky — Why Do Ya Roll Those Eyes?/W: Morrie Ryskind, M: Phil Charig. *Crazy Quilt* (44th Street, revue, May 19, 1931): Crazy Quilt/W: Bud Green, M: Harry Warren — I Found a Million Dollar Baby (in a Five and Ten Cent Store)/W: Mort Dixon, Billy Rose, M: Harry Warren — I Want to Do a Number with the Boys/W: Ned Wever, M: Rowland Wilson.

1072. Kenneth Bridges *The Rothschilds* (Lunt-Fontanne, "2nd Vendor," Oct. 19, 1970): He Tossed a Coin/W: Sheldon Harnick, M: Jerry Bock. *Goodtime Charley* (Palace, CR, "Phillip of Burgundy," during run): History/W: Hal Hackady, M: Larry Grossman.

1073. Dee Dee Bridgewater (May 27, 1950–) B: Memphis, TN. *The Wiz* (Majestic, "Glinda," Jan. 5, 1975): If You Believe (Believe in Yourself); A Rested Body Is a Rested Mind/WM: Charlie Smalls.

1074. Joel Briel *Cats* (Winter Garden, CR, "Bustopher Jones" and "Asparagus" and "Growltiger," c 1994): Bustopher Jones; Growltiger's Last Stand; Gus: The Theater Cat/W: T.S. Eliot, M: Andrew Lloyd Webber.

1075. Jean Briggs *New Faces of 1934* (Fulton, revue, Mar. 15, 1934): So Low/W: June Sillman, Nancy Hamilton, M: Donald Honrath.

1076. Matt Briggs (Nov. 18, 1883–June 10, 1962) B: St. Louis, MO. *Bloomer Girl* (Shubert, "Horatio Applegate," Oct. 5, 1944): Welcome Hinges/W: E.Y. Harburg, M: Harold Arlen. *Bloomer Girl* (New York City Center, revival, "Horatio Applegate," Jan. 6, 1947): same as above.

1077. Constance Brigham *The Beggar's Opera* (New York City Center, revival, "Jenny Diver," Mar. 13, 1957): When Young at the Bar/WM: John Gay.

1078. Lee Bright *Blossom Time* (Jolson, revival, "Binder," May 19, 1924): Love Is a Riddle/W: Dorothy Donnelly, M: Sigmund Romberg.

1079. Patricia Bright A satirical comedienne and singer in clubs. *You'll See Stars* (Maxine Elliott, revue, "Hildegarde," Dec. 29, 1942): What a Pretty Baby You Are/W: Herman Timberg, M: Leo Edwards. *Tickets, Please!* (Coronet, revue, Apr. 27, 1950): The Ballet Isn't Ballet Any More/WM: Jack Weinstock, Willie Gilbert, Herb Hecht — Spring Has Come/WM: Mel Tolkin, Max Liebman — Tough on Love; You Can't Take It with You/WM: Lyn Duddy, Joan Edwards.

1080. Sarah Brightman (Aug. 14, 1960–) B: London, England. M: composer Andrew Lloyd Webber. She appeared in London in the original cast of *Cats*. *The Phantom of the Opera* (Majestic, "Christine Daae," Jan. 26, 1988): All I Ask of You; Angel of Music; Bravo, Bravo; I Remember; Little Lotte; The Mirror; Notes; The Point of No Return; Raoul, I've Been There; Stranger Than You Dreamt It; Think of Me; Twisted Every Way; Wandering Child; Why Have You Brought Me Here; Wishing You Were Somehow Here Again/W: Charles Hart, Richard Stilgoe, M: Andrew Lloyd Webber — The Phantom of the Opera/W: Mike Batt, Richard Stilgoe, M: Andrew Lloyd Webber. *Aspects of Love* (Broadhurst, CR, "Rose Vibert," Dec. 14, 1990): Anything but Lonely; Chanson d'Enfance; Falling; Hand Me the Wine and the Dice; Other Pleasures; Parlez Vous Francais?; Seeing Is Believing; She'd Be Far Better Off with You; There Is More to Love/W: Don Black, Charles Hart, M: Andrew Lloyd Webber.

1081. Lorelle Brina *Grease* (Broadhurst, CR, "Betty Rizzo"): Freddy, My Love; Look at Me, I'm Sandra Dee; There Are Worse Things I Could Do/WM: Jim Jacobs, Warren Casey.

1082. Lillie Brink *The Dress Parade [Mid Summer Night's Fancies]* (Crystal Gardens, revue, June 22, 1903): The Marriage of the Daffodil and Daisy/W: Nicholas Biddle, M: Ben M. Jerome.

1083. Robert Brink *Dream with Music* (Majestic, "Robert" and "Sultan," May 18, 1944): I'm Afraid I'm in Love; Love at Second Sight; Relax and Enjoy It/W: Edward Eager, M: Clay Warnick.

1084. Lynn Brinker *Greenwillow* (Alvin, "Martha Briggs," Mar. 8, 1960): Clang Dang the Bell; Greenwillow Christmas/WM: Frank Loesser.

1085. Grace Brinkley *The Greenwich Village Follies of 1928* (Winter Garden, revue, Apr. 9, 1928): High, High Up in the Clouds; Little Boy's Blue [Apr. 23, 1928]/W: Max Lief, Nathaniel Lief, M: Maurie Rubens — What's the Reason?/W: Harold Atteridge, M: Maurie Rubens. *White Lilacs* (Shubert, "Delphine Potocka," Sept. 10, 1928): Adorable You/W: David Goldberg, M: Maurie Rubens — Be Happy in Your Dreams; White Lilacs/W: J. Keirn Brennan, M: Karl Hajos, based on Frederic Chopin — Our Little Castle of Love/W: J. Keirn Brennan, M: Sam Timberg. *Pleasure Bound* (Majestic, revue, "Betty," Feb. 18, 1929): Just Suppose/W: Sid Silvers, Moe Jaffe, M: Phil Baker, Maurie Rubens — Park Avenue Strut/W: Moe Jaffe, Harold Atteridge, M: Phil Baker, Maurie Rubens. *Flying High* (Apollo, "Eileen Cassidy," Mar. 3, 1930): I'll Know Him; Thank Your Father (Thank Your Mother); Wasn't It Beautiful While It Lasted?; Without Love/W: B.G. DeSylva, Lew Brown, M: Ray Henderson. *Here Goes the Bride* (46th Street, "Betty Fish," Nov. 3, 1931): My Sweetheart 'Tis of Thee/W: Edward Heyman, M: Johnny Green — It Means So Little to You/W: Edward Heyman, M: Richard Myers. *Of Thee I Sing* (Music Box, "Diana Devereaux," Dec. 26, 1931): Because, Because; I Was the Most Beautiful Blossom; Jilted! Jilted!; Some Girls Can Bake a Pie; Who Is the Lucky Girl to Be?/W: Ira Gershwin, M: George Gershwin.

1086. Ruth Brisbane *The Wiz* (Majestic, CR, "Evillene," Sept. 1976): No Bad News/WM: Charlie Smalls.

1087. Lauretta Brislin *The Chocolate Soldier* (St. James, revival, "Mascha," May 2, 1934): Falling in Love/W: Stanislaus Stange, M: Oscar Straus.

1088. Carl Brisson (Dec. 24, 1893–Sept. 26, 1958) B: Copenhagen, Denmark. As Carl Pedersen, he became amateur lightweight boxing champion of Denmark at the age of 15. His son, producer Frederick Brisson, was married to ROSALIND RUSSELL. *Forbidden Melody* (New Amsterdam, "Gregor Fiorescu," Nov. 2, 1936): Blame It on the Night; Just Hello; Lady in the Window; Moonlight and Violins; No Use Pre-tending; When a Girl Forgets to Scream; You Are All I've Wanted/W: Otto Harbach, M: Sigmund Romberg.

1089. George Britton (Oct. 19, 1910–) B: Chicago, IL. An opera singer in Europe and New York. *Gypsy Lady* (Century, "Sandor," Sept. 17, 1946): Gypsy Love Song (Slumber On, My Little Gypsy Sweetheart)/W: Harry B. Smith, M: Victor Herbert — My Treasure/W: Robert Wright, George Forrest, M: Victor Herbert. *South Pacific* (Majestic, CR, "Emile de Becque," Jan. 1952): A Cockeyed Optimist; Dites-Moi; I'm Gonna Wash That Man Right Outa My Hair; Some Enchanted Evening; This Nearly Was Mine; Twin Soliloquies; A Wonderful Guy/W: Oscar Hammerstein II, M: Richard Rodgers.

1090. Pamela Britton (Mar. 19, 1923–June 17, 1974) B: Milwaukee, WI. She starred in the TV sitcom *Blondie* (1957), and played Mrs. Lorelei Brown in *My Favorite Martian* (1963). *Brigadoon* (Ziegfeld, "Meg Brockie," Mar. 13, 1947): Down on MacConnachy Square; The Love of My Life; My Mother's Wedding Day/W: Alan Jay Lerner, M: Frederick Loewe.

1091. Frances Brock *The Hot Mikado* (Broadhurst, "Pitti-Sing," Mar. 23, 1939): The Flowers That Bloom in the Spring; So Pardon Us; Three Little Maids/W: William S. Gilbert, M: Arthur Sullivan.

1092. Harrison Brockbank (Oct. 2, 1867–Nov. 30, 1947) B: Liverpool, England. He came to the U.S. in 1909. *The Enchantress* (New York, "Miloch, Regent of Zergovia," Oct. 19, 1911): If You Can't Be as Happy as You'd Like to Be (Just Be as Happy as You Can)/W: Harry B. Smith, M: Victor Herbert. *The Purple Road* (Liberty > Casino, "Napoleon," Apr. 7, 1913): The Love Spell/WM: ?. *Sometime* (Shubert > Casino, "Henry Vaughn," Oct. 4, 1918): Picking Peaches/W: Rida Johnson Young, M: Rudolf Friml. *The Last Waltz* (Century, "Prince Paul," May 10, 1921): The Whip Hand/W: Harold Atteridge, M: Rudolf Nelson. *Caroline* (Ambassador, "Brig. Gen. Randolph Calhoun," Jan. 31, 1923): When I Say It's So, It's So/W: Harry B. Smith, M: Edward Delaney Dunn, Edward Kunneke — Will o' the Wisp/W: Harry B. Smith, M: Edward Kunneke.

1093. Roy Brocksmith (Sept. 15, 1945–Dec. 16, 2001) B: Quincy, IL. *Threepenny Opera* (Vivian Beaumont, revival in new translation, "Ballad Singer," May 1, 1976): Ballad of Mack the Knife (Moritat)/W: Bertolt Brecht, M: Kurt Weill.

1094. Diana Broderick *The Best Little*

Whorehouse in Texas (Eugene O'Neill, CR, "Ruby Rae," May 1982): Hard Candy Christmas/WM: Carol Hall.

1095. Edna Broderick *Eva* (New Amsterdam, "Yvonne," Dec. 30, 1912): The Starlight Guards/W: Glen MacDonough, M: Franz Lehar.

1096. Helen Broderick (Aug. 11, 1891–Sept. 25, 1959) B: Philadelphia, PA. Daughter of WILLIAM E. BRODERICK. The singer-dancer-comedienne went to Hollywood in 1935, where her caustic wit enhanced films such as *Top Hat* (1935) and *Swing Time* (1936). *Puzzles of 1925* (Fulton, revue, Feb. 2, 1925): We're Jumping Into Something/WM: Blanche Merrill. *Oh, Please!* (Fulton, "Emma Bliss," Dec. 17, 1926): Homely but Clean/W: Anne Caldwell, M: Vincent Youmans. *Fifty Million Frenchmen* (Lyric, "Violet Hildegarde," Nov. 27, 1929): The Tale of an Oyster; Where Would You Get Your Coat?/WM: Cole Porter. *The Band Wagon* (New Amsterdam, revue, June 3, 1931): Where Can He Be?/W: Howard Dietz, M: Arthur Schwartz. *As Thousands Cheer* (Music Box, revue, Sept. 30, 1933): Majestic Sails at Midnight/WM: Irving Berlin.

1097. James Broderick (Mar. 7, 1927–Nov. 1, 1982) B: Charlestown, NH. Father of MATTHEW BRODERICK. *Maggie* (National, "James Wylie," Feb. 18, 1953): The New Me; Thimbleful; The Train with the Cushioned Seats/WM: William Roy.

1098. Matthew Broderick (Mar. 21, 1962–) B: New York, NY. *How to Succeed in Business Without Really Trying* (Richard Rodgers, revival, "J. Pierrepont Finch," Mar. 23, 1995/Mar. 19, 1996): Been a Long Day; Brotherhood of Man; The Company Way; Grand Old Ivy; How To; I Believe in You; Rosemary; A Secretary Is Not a Toy/WM: Frank Loesser.

1099. William E. Broderick (c 1859–Apr. 29, 1904) B: Ohio. Father of HELEN BRODERICK. *Erminie* (Broadway, revival, "Ravennes," Oct. 3, 1893): Downy Jailbirds of a Feather/W: Claxson Bellamy, Harry Paulton, M: Edward Jakobowski. *The Girl from Paris* (Wallack's, revival, "Maj. Fossdyke," Jan. 17, 1898): The Battersea Butterfly Shooters/W: George Dance, M: Ivan Caryll. *Hodge, Podge & Co.* (Madison Square, "Don Antonio d'Careera Cararra," Oct. 23, 1900): Dream Days of Seville; A Soldier of Love/W: Walter Ford, M: John W. Bratton — What a Funny Story/W: Walter Ford, M: Herman Perlet. *The Toreador* (Knickerbocker, "Carajola," Jan. 6, 1902): Toreador's Song (I'm the Glory and Pride of the Land of Spain)/W: Adrian Ross, M: Ivan Caryll. *Erminie*

(Casino, revival, "Ravennes," Oct. 19, 1903): same as above.

1100. Lee Brody *Shoot the Works!* (George M. Cohan, revue, July 21, 1931): The First Lady of the Land/W: Max Lief, Nathaniel Lief, M: Michael H. Cleary.

1101. Patricia Brogan *Double Dublin* (Little, revue, Dec. 26, 1963): Bonnet Trimmed with the Blue/WM: ?.

1102. Ivar Brogger (Jan. 10–) B: St. Paul, MN. *Blood Brothers* (Music Box, "Mr. Lyons," Apr. 25, 1993): Take a Letter, Miss Jones/WM: Willy Russell.

1103. Walter Brogsdale *Messin' Around* (Hudson, revue, Apr. 22, 1929): Mississippi; Shout On!/W: Perry Bradford, M: James P. Johnson.

1104. J. Edward Bromberg (Dec. 25, 1903–Dec. 6, 1951) B: Temesvar, Hungary. A character actor in movies, 1936-1950. After being blacklisted from working in Hollywood, he died while in London for his first appearance on the English stage. *Toplitzky of Notre Dame* (Century, "Toplitzky," Dec. 26, 1946): All-American Man; Common Sense; Let Us Gather at the Goal Line/W: George Marion, Jr., M: Sammy Fain.

1105. Cleveland Bronner *The Passing Show of 1921* (Winter Garden, revue, Dec. 29, 1920): Dream Fantasies/WM: ?.

1106. Edna Bronson *The Fisher Maiden* (Victoria, "Marjory," Oct. 5, 1903): A Daughter of the Moon Am I; He Dandled Me on His Knee; I'm a Fisher Maiden; On a Beautiful Distant Island; When You Go to London Town, Gay Paree or Dixieland/W: Arthur J. Lamb, M: Harry Von Tilzer.

1107. Percy Bronson *The Lady from Lane's* (Lyric > Casino, "Arthur Gilbert," Aug. 19, 1907): Four Little Pigs [Sept. 16, 1907]; I Never Do It Now; Take a Maid/W: George Broadhurst, M: Gustave Kerker. *So Long Letty* (Shubert, "Philip Brown," Oct. 23, 1916): Letter Trio; Maryland; Pass Around the Apples Once Again; Play Me a Ukulele; When You Hear Jackson Moan on His Saxophone/WM: Earl Carroll.

1108. Claudio Brook (Aug. 28, 1927–Oct. 18, 1995) B: Mexico City, Mexico. In movies from 1956. *Man of La Mancha* (ANTA Washington Square, CR, "Don Quixote," Sept. 22, 1969): The Combat; Dulcinea; Golden Helmet; The Impossible Dream (The Quest); Man of La Mancha (I, Don Quixote)/W: Joe Darion, M: Mitch Leigh.

1109. John Brooke *Nikki* (Longacre, "Francis [the Washout]," Sept. 29, 1931): Taking Off/W: James Dyrenforth, M: Phil Charig.

1110. Tyler Brooke (June 6, 1886–Mar. 2, 1943) B: New York, NY. *Very Good Eddie* (Casino, CR, "Dick Rivers," Aug. 1916): If I Find the Girl/W: John E. Hazzard, Herbert Reynolds, M: Jerome Kern — Nodding Roses/W: Schuyler Greene, Herbert Reynolds, M: Jerome Kern — Old Boy Neutral; The Same Old Game/W: Schuyler Greene, M: Jerome Kern — On the Shore at Le Lei Wi/W: Herbert Reynolds, M: Henry Kailimai, Jerome Kern — Some Sort of Somebody (All of the Time)/W: Elsie Janis, M: Jerome Kern. *Go To It* (Princess, "Lieutenant," Oct. 24, 1916): Come Along Little Girls/WM: ? — Girls, If You Ever Get Married; Where's the Little Boy for Me?/W: Schuyler Greene, M: Charles N. Grant — A Little World of Our Own/WM: John L. Golden. *Angel Face* (Knickerbocker, "Arthur Griffin," Dec. 29, 1919): If You Can Love Like You Can Dance; A Man Should Have a Double When He's Single; Sow Your Wild Oats Early; Those Since-I-Met-You Days/W: Robert B. Smith, M: Victor Herbert. *Hitchy-Koo of 1920* (New Amsterdam, revue, Oct. 19, 1920): I Am Daguerre/W: Glen MacDonough, Anne Caldwell, M: Jerome Kern.

1111. Ada Brooks *Gentleman Joe, the Hansom Cabby* (Bijou, "Hon. Mabel Cavanaugh," Jan. 30, 1896): It's Money That Makes the World Go Round/W: Basil Hood, M: Walter Slaughter.

1112. Alan Brooks (July 11, 1950–) B: Bakersfield, CA. *The Midnight Sons* (Broadway, CR, "Souseberry Lushmore," Nov. 8, 1909): Call Me Bill/W: Glen MacDonough, M: Raymond Hubbell.

1113. Catherine Brooks *Hummin' Sam* (New Yorker, "Emmaraldae," Apr. 8, 1933): If I Didn't Have You; I'll Be True, but I'll Be Blue/WM: Alexander Hill.

1114. David Brooks (Sept. 24, 1917–Mar. 31, 1999) B: Portland, OR. *Bloomer Girl* (Shubert, "Jeff Calhoun," Oct. 5, 1944): Evelina; The Rakish Young Man with the Whiskers; Right as the Rain; Welcome Hinges/W: E.Y. Harburg, M: Harold Arlen. *Brigadoon* (Ziegfeld, "Tommy Albright," Mar. 13, 1947): Almost Like Being in Love; From This Day On; The Heather on the Hill; There but for You Go I/WAlan Jay Lerner, M: Frederick Loewe. *Park* (John Golden, "Man," Apr. 22, 1970): Elizabeth; He Talks to Me; I'd Marry You Again; Jamie/W: Paul Cherry, M: Lance Mulcahy.

1115. Eleanor Brooks *Artists and Models of 1927* (Winter Garden, revue, Nov. 15, 1927): Bangaway Isle; Start the Band/WM: ?.

1116. Ellanore Brooks *The Student King* (Garden, "Gretchen," Dec. 25, 1906): The Same Old Game/W: Frederic Ranken, Stanislaus Stange, M: Reginald De Koven.

1117. Evelyn Brooks *Beat the Band* (46th Street, "Band Girl," Oct. 14, 1942): The Steam Is on the Beam/W: George Marion, Jr., M: Johnny Green. *New Faces of 1943* (Ritz, revue, CR, Jan. 10, 1943): Animals Are Nice; Yes, Sir, I've Made a Date/W: J.B. Rosenberg, M: Lee Wainer — Hey, Gal!; New Shoes/W: June Carroll, M: Will Irwin — Love, Are You Raising Your Head Again?/W: June Carroll, M: Lee Wainer — Richard Crudnut's Charm School/W: June Carroll, John Lund, M: Lee Wainer.

1118. Georgie Brooks *The Student King* (Garden, "Frieda," Dec. 25, 1906): The Same Old Game/W: Frederic Ranken, Stanislaus Stange, M: Reginald De Koven.

1119. Irving Brooks *Around the Map* (New Amsterdam, revue "Hoppolyte Boun," Nov. 1, 1915): I'm the Boom Boom Boomer/W: C.M.S. McLellan, M: Herman Finck.

1120. Jeff Brooks (Apr. 7, 1950–) B: Vancouver, Canada. *Nick & Nora* (Marquis, "Spider Malloy," Dec. 8, 1991): A Busy Night at Lorraine's; Swell/W: Richard Maltby, Jr., M: Charles Strouse. *Guys and Dolls* (Martin Beck, revival, CR, "Benny Southstreet," c 1992): Fugue for Tinhorns; Guys and Dolls; The Oldest Established/WM: Frank Loesser. *Guys and Dolls* (Martin Beck, revival, CR, "Nathan Detroit," c 1993): The Oldest Established; Sue Me/WM: Frank Loesser.

1121. Lawrence Brooks (Aug. 7, 1912–) B: Westbrook, ME. *Song of Norway* (Imperial, "Edvard Grieg," Aug. 21, 1944): Bon Vivant; Hill of Dreams; Midsummer's Eve; Strange Music; Three Loves/WM: Robert Wright, George Forrest, based on Edvard Grieg. *My Romance* (Shubert > Adelphi, "Bishop Armstrong," Oct. 19, 1948): Desire; From Now Onward; In Love with Romance; Love and Laughter; Paradise Stolen; Souvenir; Written in Your Hand/W: Rowland Leigh, M: Sigmund Romberg. *Buttrio Square* (New Century, "Capt. Steve Dickson," Oct. 14, 1952): Every Day Is a Holiday; Let's Make It Forever; More and More; One Is a Lonely Number/W: Gen Genovese, M: Fred Stamer — There's No Place Like the Country/W: Gen Genovese, M: Arthur Jones.

1122. Virginia Fox Brooks *Sinbad* (Winter Garden > Century > Casino, "Nan Van Decker," Feb. 14, 1918): A Thousand and One Arabian Nights/W: Harold Atteridge, M: Sigmund Romberg.

1123. Leroy Broomfield *How Come?*

(Apollo, "Brother Wire Nail," Apr. 16, 1923): Gingerena; Pretty Malinda/WM: Ben Harris, Henry Creamer, Will Vodery.

1124. Octavia Broske (June 4, 1886–Mar. 19, 1967) B: Pennsylvania. M: GEORGE BANCROFT. *Tillie's Nightmare* (Herald Square, "Maude Blobbs," May 5, 1910): Life Is Only What You Make It, After All/W: Edgar Smith, M: A. Baldwin Sloane. *Hello, Paris and A La Broadway* (Folies Bergere, revue, "Mrs. Morris," Sept. 22, 1911): In Loving Time/W: William Le Baron, Mabel H. Hollins, M: Harold Orlob. *Oh! Oh! Delphine* (Knickerbocker > New Amsterdam, "Bimboula," Sept. 30, 1912): Allaballa Goo-Goo; The Venus Waltz/W: C.M.S. McLellan, M: Ivan Caryll. *Papa's Darling* (New Amsterdam, "Sophie," Nov. 2, 1914): Oh, This Love/W: Harry B. Smith, M: Ivan Caryll. *A Lonely Romeo* (Shubert > Casino, "Alexina Tripp," June 10, 1919): Don't Do Anything Till You Hear from Me/W: Robert B. Smith, M: Malvin F. Franklin.

1125. Eric Brotherson (May 10, 1911–Oct. 21, 1989) B: Chicago, IL. *Lady in the Dark* (Alvin, CR, "Russell Paxton," Sept. 1941): The Best Years of His Life; The Greatest Show on Earth; One Life to Live; Tschaikowsky/W: Ira Gershwin, M: Kurt Weill. *My Dear Public* (46th Street, revue, "Byron Burns," Sept. 9, 1943): Last Will and Testament/WM: ?— This Is Our Private Love Song/WM: Sammy Lerner, Gerald Marks, Irving Caesar. *Gentlemen Prefer Blondes* (Ziegfeld, "Henry Spofford," Dec. 8, 1949): Homesick Blues; Just a Kiss Apart; Sunshine; You Say You Care/W: Leo Robin, M: Jule Styne. *My Fair Lady* (St. James, revival, CR, "Jamie," Dec. 1976): Get Me to the Church on Time; With a Little Bit of Luck/W: Alan Jay Lerner, M: Frederick Loewe.

1126. Heywood Broun (Dec. 7, 1888–Dec. 18, 1939) B: Brooklyn, NY. M: RUTH HALE. Well-known drama critic for the *New York World* in the 1920s, and drama editor of *Vanity Fair*. *Shoot the Works!* (George M. Cohan, revue, July 21, 1931): I Want to Chisel In on Your Heart/ W: Max Lief, Nathaniel Lief, M: Michael Cleary.

1127. A. Seymour Brown (May 28, 1885– Dec. 22, 1947) B: Philadelphia, PA. Songwriter and actor. *The White Cat* (New Amsterdam, "Migonet," Nov. 2, 1905): Henny Klein; Meet Me on the Fence Tonight/W: William Jerome, M: Jean Schwartz. *The Grand Mogul* (New Amsterdam, "Hannibal," Mar. 25, 1907): Help Yourself/W: Frank Pixley, M: Gustav Luders.

1128. Ada Brown (May 1, 1890–Mar. 31,

1950) B: Junction City, KS. Daughter of a minister. *Brown Buddies* (Liberty, Oct. 7, 1930): Dancin' 'Way Your Sin/WM: James C. Johnson — When a Black Man's Blue/WM: George A. Little, Ed G. Nelson, Art Sizemore. *Memphis Bound!* (Broadway > Belasco, "Mrs. Paradise," May 24, 1945): A-Many Years Ago; I'm Called Little Buttercup/WM: Clay Warnick, Don Walker, based on W.S. Gilbert and Arthur Sullivan.

1129. Agnes Cain Brown *The Isle of Spice* (Majestic, "Teresa," Aug. 23, 1904): Little Maid of Nicobar/W: Allen Lowe, M: Paul Schindler — Star of Fate/WM: ?— You and I/W: Allen Lowe, M: Paul Schindler, Ben M. Jerome. *The Alaskan* (Knickerbocker, "Arlee Easton," Aug. 12, 1907): Glittering Gold; Mother Did; Party of the Second Part; Rainbow and the Thistle/W: Joseph Blethen, M: Harry Girard.

1130. Alice Brown *Strut Miss Lizzie* (Times Square, revue, June 19, 1922): Breakin' the Leg; I'm Nobody's Gal; Lovesick Blues/WM: Henry Creamer, Turner Layton. *How Come?* (Apollo, "Miss Disappear," Apr. 16, 1923): Charleston Cutout; I Didn't Grieve Over Daniel; Keep the Man You've Got; Syncopated Strain/W: Ben Harris, Henry Creamer, M: Will Vodery.

1131. Ann Brown (Dec. 1, 1960–) B: Westwood, NJ. *Once Upon a Mattress* (Broadhurst, revival, "Nightingale of Samarkand," Dec. 19, 1996): Lullaby/W: Marshall Barer, M: Mary Rodgers.

1132. Anne Brown (1912–) B: Baltimore, MD. *Porgy and Bess* (Alvin, "Bess," Oct. 10, 1935): Bess, You Is My Woman Now; I Loves You, Porgy/W: Ira Gershwin, DuBose Heyward, M: George Gershwin — Leavin' fo' de Promis' Lan'; What You Want wid Bess?; Woman to Lady/W: DuBose Heyward, M: George Gershwin — There's a Boat Dat's Leavin' Soon for New York/W: Ira Gershwin, M: George Gershwin. *Porgy and Bess* (Majestic, revival, "Bess," Jan. 22, 1942): same as above.

1133. Bill Brown *Happy* (Earl Carroll > Daly's, "Tommy," Dec. 5, 1927/Feb. 13, 1928): Hitting on High; Mad About You; Plastic Surgery; The Serpentine/W: Earle Crooker, McElbert Moore, M: Frank Grey.

1134. Blair Brown (Apr. 23, 1947–) B: Washington, DC. She was Molly Dodd on TV's *The Days and Nights of Molly Dodd* (1987). *Threepenny Opera* (Vivian Beaumont, revival in new translation, "Lucy Brown," May 1, 1976): Jealousy Duet/W: Bertolt Brecht, M: Kurt Weill. *Threepenny Opera* (Vivian Beaumont, revival in new translation, CR, "Polly

Peachum"): Barbara Song; Concerning the Insecurity of the Human State; For That's My Way; Jealousy Duet; Liebeslied; Polly's Lied/W: Bertolt Brecht, M: Kurt Weill.

1135. Brandy Brown (Jan. 18, 1976–) B: Mobile, AL *Les Miserables* (Broadway, CR, "Eponine"): A Heart Full of Love; In My Life; A Little Fall of Rain; On My Own/W: Herbert Kretzmer, M: Claude-Michel Schonberg.

1136. Candy Brown *Chicago* (46th Street, "June," June 3, 1975): Cell Block Tango/W: Fred Ebb, M: John Kander.

1137. Charles Brown (c 1891–?) *Marriage a la Carte* (Casino, "Cuthbert Coddington," Jan. 2, 1911): Cassie's Not a Bit Like Mother; Toddle Go the Girls/W: C.M.S. McLellan, M: Ivan Caryll. *Peggy* (Casino, "Auberon Blow," Dec. 7, 1911): Any Old Tune at All/W: C.H. Bovill, M: Leslie Stuart — In Sunny Kokomo/WM: ?. *The American Maid* (Broadway, "Duke of Branford," Mar. 3, 1913): The American Girl; Cheer Up; Cleopatra's a Strawb'ry Blonde; Sweetheart; This Is My Busy Day/W: Leonard Liebling, M: John Philip Sousa. *Little Simplicity* (Astor, CR, "Prof. Erasmus Duckworth"): Learning to Love; Maybe You'll Look Good to Me; My Lulu; National Air's Medley/W: Rida Johnson Young, M: Augustus Barratt. *Red Pepper* (Shubert, "Lord Gathe-Coyne," May 29, 1922): Butterfly; Game of Love; Wedding Bells; Wedding Day/WM: Howard E. Rogers, Albert Gumble, Owen Murphy.

1138. Charles D. Brown (July 1, 1887–Nov. 25, 1948) B: Council Bluffs, IA. In movies from 1929, he played detectives, officials and businessmen. *Parade* (Guild, revue, May 20, 1935): Bon Voyage/W: Kyle Crichton, M: Jerome Moross.

1139. Charlie Brown *See-Saw* (Cohan, "Lord Harrowby," Sept. 23, 1919): I'll Take Care of Him; You'll Have to Find Out/W: Earl Derr Biggers, M: Louis A. Hirsch.

1140. Dorothy Brown *Music Box Revue of 1922* (Music Box, revue, CR, July 30, 1923): Porcelain Maid/WM: Irving Berlin. *Hassard Short's Ritz Revue* (Ritz > Winter Garden, revue, CR, Dec. 15, 1924): A Midsummer Night's Dream; Monsieur Beaucaire; Our Crystal Wedding Day/W: Anne Caldwell, M: Frank Tours — Springtime/W: Kenneth Webb, M: Roy Webb.

1141. Eleanor Brown *A World of Pleasure* (Winter Garden, revue, Oct. 14, 1915): At the Toy Shop/W: Harold Atteridge, M: Sigmund Romberg. *The Show of Wonders* (Winter Garden, revue, Oct. 26, 1916): Pajama Girlies/W: Harold Atteridge, M: Otto Motzan.

1142. Flo Brown *Hummin' Sam* (New

Yorker, "Mae Carter," Apr. 8, 1933): Change Your Mind About Me/WM: Alexander Hill.

1143. Fodi Brown *A Night in Spain* (44th Street, revue, CR, Nov. 7, 1927): International Vamp/W: Alfred Bryan, M: Jean Schwartz.

1144. Georgia Brown (Oct. 21, 1933–June 6, 1992) B: London, England. Actress and cabaret singer in Britain and the U.S. In 1955 she played Lucy Lockit in London's Royal Court Theatre production of *The Threepenny Opera*. *Oliver!* (Imperial, "Nancy," Jan. 6, 1963/Aug. 5, 1963): As Long as He Needs Me; I'd Do Anything; It's a Fine Life; Oom-Pah-Pah/WM: Lionel Bart. *Carmelina* (St. James, "Signora Carmelina Campbell," Apr. 8, 1979): I'm a Woman; It's Time for a Love Song; Love Before Breakfast; Signora Campbell; Someone in April; Why Him?/W: Alan Jay Lerner, M: Burton Lane. *Roza* (Royale, "Madame Roza," Oct. 1, 1987): Bravo, Bravo; Different; Don't Make Me Laugh; Get the Lady Dressed; Happiness; House in Algiers; Live a Little; Max's Visit; Yussef's Visit/W: Julian More, M: Gilbert Becaud. *3 Penny Opera* (Lunt-Fontanne, revival, "Mrs. Peachum," Nov. 5, 1989): Ballad of the Prisoner of Sex; Why-Can't-They Song/W: Bertolt Brecht, M: Kurt Weill, translated by Michael Feingold.

1145. Georgie Brown *Queen o' Hearts* (George M. Cohan, "Alabama Smith," Oct. 10, 1922): My Highbrow Fling/W: Oscar Hammerstein II, M: Lewis E. Gensler, Dudley Wilkinson.

1146. Harry Brown *The Serenade* (Knickerbocker, "Colombo," Mar. 16, 1897): The Singing Lesson/W: Harry B. Smith, M: Victor Herbert. *Nancy Brown* (Bijou, "Socrates Finis," Feb. 16, 1903): I'm Glad I'm Not Methusalem/WM: Eugene Ellsworth.

1147. J. Mardo Brown *Hummin' Sam* (New Yorker, "Drum Major," Apr. 8, 1933): Stompin' 'Em Down/WM: Alexander Hill.

1148. Jean Brown *Sally, Irene and Mary* (Casino, "Sally," Sept. 4, 1922): Something In Here; Wedding Time/W: Raymond W. Klages, M: J. Fred Coots.

1149. Jeb Brown (Aug. 11, 1964–) B: New York, NY. *Bring Back Birdie* (Martin Beck, "Gary," Mar. 5, 1981): Movin' Out/W: Lee Adams, M: Charles Strouse.

1150. Jessica Brown (c 1895–) M: Bert Kalmar, writer of stage scores, screenplays and songs. *Cinderella on Broadway* (Winter Garden, revue, June 24, 1920): Any Little Melody/W: Harold Atteridge, M: Bert Grant.

1151. Joe E. Brown (July 28, 1892–July 6,

1973) B: Holgate, OH. At age 9 he joined a circus, later becoming an acrobat. His specialty was slapstick comedy and the widest smile in show business. Best remembered for his part in the movie *Some Like It Hot* (1959). *The Greenwich Village Follies of 1921* (Shubert, revue, CR, Nov. 14, 1921): Miss Dooley and Mr. Brown/W: Eddie Dowling, Raymond W. Klages, M: J. Fred Coots. *Greenwich Village Follies of 1923* (Winter Garden, revue, Sept. 20, 1923): Cock-A-Doodle Doo/W: Cliff Friend, M: Con Conrad. *Betty Lee* (44th Street, "Lawrence Glass," Dec. 25, 1924): Give Him Your Sympathy; They Always Run a Little Faster/W: Otto Harbach, Irving Caesar, M: Louis A. Hirsch, Con Conrad. *Captain Jinks* (Martin Beck, "Hap Jones," Sept. 8, 1925): Ain't Love Wonderful?/W: B.G. DeSylva, M: Stephen Jones — The New Game; Oh! How I Hate Women/W: B.G. DeSylva, M: Lewis E. Gensler. *Twinkle Twinkle* (Liberty, "P.T. Robinson [Peachy]," Nov. 16, 1926): Crime; Reuben; When We're Bride and Groom/W: Harlan Thompson, M: Harry Archer — Day Dreams [Apr. 4, 1927]/W: Bert Kalmar, M: Harry Ruby. *Courtin' Time* (National, "Samuel Rilling," June 13, 1951): Fixin' for a Long, Cold Winter; Golden Moment; Heart in Hand; Today at Your House, Tomorrow at Mine; Too Much Trouble/W: Jack Lawrence, M: Don Walker. *Show Boat* (New York City Center, revival, "Cap'n Andy Hawks," Apr. 12, 1961): Oh! That Show Boat; Why Do I Love You?/W: Oscar Hammerstein II, M: Jerome Kern.

1152. Johnny Brown (June 11, 1937-) B: St. Petersburg, FL. Father of SHARON BROWN. A regular on TV's *Laugh-In* (1970); Nathan Bookman on the sitcom *Good Times* (1977) *Golden Boy* (Majestic, "Ronnie," Oct. 20, 1964): Don't Forget 127th Street/W: Lee Adams, M: Charles Strouse.

1153. Kay Brown B: Peoria, IL. *The Conquering Hero* (ANTA, "Libby Callan," Jan. 16, 1961): I'm Beautiful; Rough Times; Wonderful, Marvelous You; Won't You Marry Me?/W: Norman Gimbel, M: Moose Charlap.

1154. Kelly Brown (Sept. 24, 1928–Mar. 13, 1981) B: Jackson MS. *From A to Z* (Plymouth, revue, Apr. 20, 1960): Time Step/W: Fred Ebb, M: Paul Klein. *I Can Get It for You Wholesale* (Shubert, "Buggo," Mar. 22, 1962): What Are They Doing to Us Now?/WM: Harold Rome. *Kiss Me, Kate* (New York City Center, revival, "Bill Calhoun" and "Lucentio," May 12, 1965): Bianca; I Sing of Love; Tom, Dick or Harry; We Open in Venice/WM: Cole Porter.

1155. Leonard Brown *Runaways* (Plymouth,

"EZ," May 13, 1978): The Basketball Song; We Are Not Strangers/WM: Elizabeth Swados.

1156. Lillyan Brown *Kiss Me, Kate* (Broadway, revival, "Hattie," Jan. 8, 1952): Another Op'nin', Another Show/WM: Cole Porter.

1157. Linda Leilani Brown *Dreamgirls* (Imperial, CR, "Deena Jones," June 5, 1984): Family; Hard to Say Goodbye, My Love; I'm Somebody; One Night Only; Only the Beginning; Quintette; When I First Saw You/W: Tom Eyen, M: Henry Krieger.

1158. Lisa Brown (Aug. 2, 1954-) B: Kansas City, MO. *The Best Little Whorehouse in Texas* (46th Street, "Angelette Imogene Carlene" and "Dawn," June 19, 1978): Angelette March; Hard Candy Christmas/WM: Carol Hall. *42nd Street* (Winter Garden, CR, "Peggy Sawyer," July 26, 1982/Mar. 1985): About a Quarter to Nine; 42nd Street; Go Into Your Dance; We're in the Money; Young and Healthy; You're Getting to Be a Habit with Me/W: Al Dubin, M: Harry Warren.

1159. Louise Brown B: Madison, WI. She began as a dancer in the U.S., billed as The Spinning Top, but spent most of her later career on the British stage. Nothing is known of her after about 1938. *Sally, Irene and Mary* (44th Street, revival, "Sally," Mar. 23, 1925): Something In Here; Wedding Time/W: Raymond Klages, M: J. Fred Coots. *Captain Jinks* (Martin Beck, "Mlle. Suzanne Trentoni," Sept. 8, 1925): Fond of You; I Do; Kiki; Wanna Lotta Love/W: B.G. DeSylva, M: Lewis E. Gensler — You Need a Man, Suzanne/W: B.G. DeSylva, M: ?. *Ziegfeld's American Revue of 1926 aka No Foolin'* (Globe, revue, June 24, 1926): No Foolin'/W: Gene Buck, M: James F. Hanley. *Rainbow* (Gallo, "Virginia Brown," Nov. 21, 1928): Hay! Straw!; I Like You as You Are; Let Me Give All My Love to Thee; Virginia/W: Oscar Hammerstein II, M: Vincent Youmans. *Lady Fingers* (Vanderbilt > Liberty, "Hope Quayle," Jan. 31, 1929): I Love You More Than Yesterday/W: Lorenz Hart, M: Richard Rodgers — I Want You All to Myself [Mar. 4, 1929]; The Life of a Nurse; My Wedding; An Open Book; Shah! Raise the Dust!; There's Something in That; You're Perfect/W: Edward Eliscu, M: Joseph Meyer. *Woof, Woof* (Royale, "Susie Yates," Dec. 25, 1929): A Girl Like You; I Mean What I Say; I'll Take Care of You; Won't I Do?/WM: Eddie Brandt, Edward Pola.

1160. Marjorie Brown *A Hero Is Born* (Adelphi, "Lady Kathleena," Oct. 1, 1937): Prigio Didn't Know; Woe Is Me/W: Agnes Morgan, M: A. Lehman Engel.

1161. Martin Brown (June 22, 1885–Feb. 13, 1936) B: Montreal, Canada. *The Girl Behind the Counter* (Herald Square, CR, "Dudley Cheatham," Jan. 27, 1908): If You'll Walk with Me/W: Edgar Selden, M: Paul Rubens — The Way of Trade/W: Arthur Anderson, M: Howard Talbot. *The Motor Girl* (Lyric, "Dick Willoughby," June 15, 1909): Coffee and Cheese; What Can a Fellow Do?/W: Charles J. Campbell, M: Julian Edwards — Just Suppose You Loved Me/W: Charles J. Campbell, Ralph Skinner, M: Julian Edwards. *The Belle of Brittany* (Daly's, "Baptiste Boubillon," Nov. 8, 1909): The Girl with the Clocking on Her Stocking; In the Oven; A Little Cafe; Two Giddy Goats/W: Percy Greenbank, M: Howard Talbot. *He Came from Milwaukee* (Casino, "Bruce Chetwynde," Sept. 21, 1910): Merry Wedding Bells; There's an Aeroplane Air About You; The Zinga-Zulu Man/W: Edward Madden, M: Ben M. Jerome, Louis A. Hirsch — When We Are Married to You and Me/W: Edward Madden, M: Louis A. Hirsch. *Up and Down Broadway* (Casino, revue, July 18, 1910): The Dope Fiend/W: ?, M: Melville Ellis — The Pretty Little Girl Inside; The Spanish Fandango Rag (Dreamy Fandango Tune)/W: William Jerome, M: Jean Schwartz. *The Kiss Waltz* (Casino, "Paul von Gervais," Sept. 18, 1911): Do As You Please/WM: ? — Love's Charming Art (The Dove Duet); Ta-Ta, Little Girl/W: Matthew Woodward, M: Jerome Kern. *Vera Violetta* (Winter Garden, CR, "Andrew Mason," Feb. 5, 1912): Come and Dance with Me/W: Melville Gideon, M: Louis A. Hirsch — The Gaby Glide/W: Harry Pilcer, M: Louis A. Hirsch. *The Whirl of Society* (Winter Garden, revue, Mar. 5, 1912): The Gaby Glide/W: Harry Pilcer, M: Louis A. Hirsch — How Do You Do, Miss Ragtime/WM: Louis A. Hirsch. *Hello, Broadway!* (Astor, revue, Dec. 25, 1914): That Old Fashioned Cakewalk/WM: George M. Cohan.

1162. Maxine Brown (Apr. 12, 1897–Dec. 28, 1956) B: Denver, CO. *Odds and Ends of 1917* (Bijou, revue, Nov. 19, 1917): Where Did You Get Those Irish Eyes?/W: Bide Dudley, Jack Norworth, M: James Byrnes. *Buddies* (Selwyn, "Louise Maitland," Oct. 27, 1919): My Indispensable Girl/WM: B.C. Hilliam. *The Right Girl* (Times Square, CR, "Dera Darcy," May 2, 1921): A Girl in Your Arms; Harmony/W: Raymond W. Peck, M: Percy Wenrich. *Sue, Dear* (Times Square, "Minerva West," July 10, 1922): Key to My Heart; Lady Lingerie; Love's Corporation/W: Bide Dudley, M: Frank Grey. *Moonlight* (Longacre, "Betty Duncan," Jan. 30, 1924): I

Love Them All; If I Were of the Hoi Polloi; Old Man in the Moon/W: William B. Friedlander, M: Con Conrad.

1163. Nancy Brown (1910–) B: Sydney, New South Wales, Australia. *Bitter Sweet* (Ziegfeld, "Gloria," Nov. 5, 1929): Alas, the Time Is Past; The Last Dance; Tarara Boom-de-Ay/WM: Noel Coward.

1164. Norma Brown *The Midnight Sons* (Broadway, "Rose Raglan," May 22, 1909): The Cynical Owl; Lithograph Land; The Little Mary Gardeners/W: Glen MacDonough, M: Raymond Hubbell.

1165. Peggy Brown *The Mimic World* (Century roof, revue, Aug. 17, 1921): Broadway Pirates; A Posty and a Maid/WM: ?

1166. Rosa Brown B: Savannah, GA. *The Hot Mikado* (Broadhurst, "Katisha," Mar. 23, 1939): I, Living I; I'm the Emperor of Japan/W: William S. Gilbert, M: Arthur Sullivan.

1167. Rose Brown *My Dear Public* (46th Street, revue, "Rose Brown," Sept. 9, 1943): There Ain't No Color Line Around the Rainbow/WM: Sammy Lerner, Gerald Marks, Irving Caesar.

1168. Russ Brown (May 30, 1892–Oct. 19, 1964) B: Philadelphia, PA. The singer and actor appeared in vaudeville with BERT WHEELER. *Ups-A-Daisy!* (Shubert, "Jimmy Ridgeway," Oct. 8, 1928): A Great Little Guy; Tell Me Who You Are; Ups-A-Daisy!/W: Robert A. Simon, M: Lewis E. Gensler. *Flying High* (Apollo, "Sport Wardell," Mar. 3, 1930): Good for You, Bad for Me/W: B.G. DeSylva, Lew Brown, M: Ray Henderson. *Hold On to Your Hats* (Shubert, "Dinky," Sept. 11, 1940): Don't Let It Get You Down/W: E.Y. Harburg, M: Burton Lane. *Viva O'Brien* (Majestic, "Don Jose O'Brien," Oct. 9, 1941): Broken Hearted Romeo; Don Jose O'Brien; To Prove My Love/W: Raymond Leveen, M: Maria Grever. *Up in Central Park* (New York City Center, revival, "Timothy Moore," May 19, 1947): The Birds and the Bees; Boss Tweed; Up from the Gutter; When the Party Gives a Party/W: Dorothy Fields, M: Sigmund Romberg. *Damn Yankees* (46th Street, "Van Buren," May 5, 1955): Heart/WM: Richard Adler, Jerry Ross.

1169. Ruth Brown (Jan. 31, 1928–) B: Portsmouth, VA. The best selling R&B singer and recording artist left home in her teens to sing jazz and blues, against the wishes of her father, a Methodist preacher. *Amen Corner* (Nederlander, "Odessa," Nov. 10, 1983): In His Own Good Time; Leanin' on the Lord; Somewhere Close By/W: Peter Udell, M: Garry Sherman. *Black and Blue* (Minskoff, revue, Jan. 26, 1989): Black and Blue/W: Andy Razaf, M: Fats Waller, Harry Brooks — Body and Soul/W: Edward Heyman, Robert Sour, Frank Eyton, M: Johnny Green — If I Can't Sell It, I'll Keep Sittin' on It/WM: Alexander Hill, Andy Razaf — I'm a Woman/WM: Elias McDaniel, Cora Taylor — St. Louis Blues/WM: W.C. Handy — 'Taint Nobody's Biz-ness If I Do/WM: Clarence Williams, Porter Grainger, Graham Prince.

1170. Sharon Brown (Jan. 11, 1962–) B: New York, NY. Daughter of JOHNNY BROWN. She played the lawyer Chantel Marshall on the TV soap *Generations* (1990). *Joseph and the Amazing Technicolor Dreamcoat* (Royale, revival, CR, "Narrator," Dec. 1, 1982): The Brothers Came to Egypt; A Coat of Many Colors; Go, Go, Go, Joseph; Grovel, Grovel; Jacob and Sons; Joseph All the Time; Joseph's Dreams; Pharaoh's Story; Poor, Poor Joseph; Poor, Poor Pharaoh; Potiphar; Song of the King; Stone the Crows/W: Tim Rice, M: Andrew Lloyd Webber. *Dreamgirls* (Ambassador, revival, CR, "Effie Melody White," Oct. 27, 1987): And I Am Telling You I'm Not Going; Faith in Myself; I Am Changing; I Miss You Old Friend; One Night Only; Only the Beginning/W: Tom Eyen, M: Henry Krieger.

1171. Tener Brown *The Phantom of the Opera* (Majestic, CR, "Meg Giry," c 1992): Angel of Music; Magical Lasso; Notes; Prima Donna/W: Charles Hart, Richard Stilgoe, M: Andrew Lloyd Webber.

1172. Tom Brown *Mr. Lode of Koal* (Majestic, "Gimlet," Nov. 1, 1909): Chink-Chink Chinyman/W: Alex Rogers, M: Bert Williams.

1173. Troy Brown, Jr. (Mar. 17, 1901–Nov. 18, 1944) B: Tennessee. *Swingin' the Dream* (Center, "Snout," Nov. 29, 1939): Peace, Brother; There's Gotta Be a Weddin'/W: Eddie DeLange, M: James Van Heusen.

1174. Walter P. Brown (Apr. 18, 1926–) B: Newark, NJ. *South Pacific* (New York City Center, revival, "Yeoman Herbert Quale," June 2, 1965): There Is Nothin' Like a Dame/W: Oscar Hammerstein II, M: Richard Rodgers. *Raisin* (46th Street, "Willie Harris," Oct. 18, 1973): Booze/W: Robert Brittan, M: Judd Woldin.

1175. Bothwell Browne (Mar. 7, 1877–Dec. 12, 1947) B: Copenhagen, Denmark. The second best known female impersonator in vaudeville, after JULIAN ELTINGE. *Miss Jack* (Herald Square, "Jack Hayward," Sept. 4, 1911): The Fencing Girl; The Serpent of the Nile/W: Mark Swan, M: William F. Peters.

1176. Florence Browne *Head Over Heels*

(George M. Cohan, "Miss Collins," Aug. 29, 1918): With Type a-Ticking/W: Edgar Allan Woolf, M: Jerome Kern.

1177. Harry C. Browne *Her Regiment* (Broadhurst, CR, "Eugene de Merriame," Dec. 10, 1917): Art Song/W: William Le Baron, M: Victor Herbert. *Oh, Lady! Lady!!* (Princess > Casino, "Hale Underwood," Feb. 1, 1918): Do It Now; It's a Hard, Hard World for a Man; The Picture I Want to See; You Found Me and I Found You/W: P.G. Wodehouse, M: Jerome Kern. *The Little Whopper* (Casino, "John Harding," Oct. 13, 1919): I Have a Date; It Can't Be Wrong; It's Great to Be Married; I've Got to Leave You; The Kiss; There's Only One Thing to Do; We May Meet Again/W: Otto Harbach, Bide Dudley, M: Rudolf Friml.

1178. Roscoe Lee Browne (May 2, 1925–) B: Woodbury, NJ. He played Saunders on the TV sitcom *Soap* (1980), and Rosemont on the long-running drama *Falcon Crest* (1988). *A Hand Is on the Gate* (Longacre, program of poetry and song, Sept. 21, 1966): Harlem Sweeties/WM: Langston Hughes — A Negro Love Song/WM: Paul Laurence Dunbar. *My One and Only* (St. James, "Rt. Rev. J.D. Montgomery," May 1, 1983): Just Another Rhumba/W: Ira Gershwin, M: George Gershwin — Kickin' the Clouds Away/W: B.G. DeSylva, Ira Gershwin, M: George Gershwin.

1179. Susan Browning (Feb. 25, 1941–) B: Baldwin, NY. *Company* (Alvin, "April," Apr. 26, 1970): Barcelona; You Could Drive a Person Crazy/WM: Stephen Sondheim. *Shelter* (John Golden, "Wednesday November," Feb. 6, 1973): He's a Fool; I Bring Him Seashells; Welcome to a New World/W: Gretchen Cryer, M: Nancy Ford. *Sondheim: A Musical Tribute* (Shubert, revue, Mar. 11, 1973): Love Is in the Air; So Many People; You Could Drive a Person Crazy/WM: Stephen Sondheim. *Goodtime Charley* (Palace, "Agnes Sorel," Mar. 3, 1975): Merci, Bon Dieu; Why Can't We All Be Nice?/W: Hal Hackady, M: Larry Grossman.

1180. Dell Brownlee B: Paris, France. *Man of La Mancha* (ANTA Washington Square, CR, "Aldonza," Jan. 21, 1971, mats.): The Abduction; Aldonza; The Combat; Dulcinea; It's All the Same; Knight of the Woeful Countenance (The Dubbing); What Do You Want of Me?/W: Joe Darion, M: Mitch Leigh.

1181. John Brownlee *The Vagabond King* (Shubert, revival, "Francois Villon," June 29, 1943): Love Me Tonight; Only a Rose; Song of the Vagabonds; Tomorrow/W: Brian Hooker, M: Rudolf Friml.

1182. Wallace Brownlow *Love's Lottery* (Broadway, "Sgt. Bob Trivet," Oct. 3, 1904): Cupid's a Lad; Follow the Flag; If We Part; The Temptation/W: Stanislas Stange, M: Julian Edwards.

1183. Bobbie (Roberta) Brox (Nov. 28, 1901–May 2, 1999) B: Riveton, IA. One of three performers known as the Brox Sisters. *Music Box Revue of 1921* (Music Box, revue, Sept. 22, 1921): Everybody Step; The Schoolhouse Blues/WM: Irving Berlin. *Music Box Revue of 1923* (Music Box, revue, Sept. 22, 1923): Learn to Do the Strut; When You Walked Out Someone Else Walked Right In/WM: Irving Berlin. *Music Box Revue of 1924* (Music Box, revue, Dec. 1, 1924): Alice in Wonderland (Come Along with Alice); Tokio Blues; Who/WM: Irving Berlin. *Ziegfeld Follies of 1927* (New Amsterdam, revue, Aug. 16, 1927): It's Up to the Band; Jungle Jingle/WM: Irving Berlin.

1184. Lorayne (Lorraine) Brox (Nov. 11, 1900–June 14, 1993) B: Memphis, TN. same as BOBBIE (ROBERTA) BROX.

1185. Robert Brubaker *Brigadoon* (New York State, revival, "Stuart Dalrymple," Feb. 28, 1986): Down on MacConnachy Square/W: Alan Jay Lerner, M: Frederick Loewe.

1186. Betty Bruce (May 2, 1921–July 18, 1974) B: New York, NY. *Keep Off the Grass* (Broadhurst, revue, May 23, 1940): I'll Applaud You with My Feet; A Latin Tune, a Manhattan Moon and You/W: Al Dubin, M: Jimmy McHugh. *High Kickers* (Broadhurst, "Mamie," Oct. 31, 1941): Cigarettes; The Girls; My Sweetheart Mamie; A Panic in Panama/W: Bert Kalmar, M: Harry Ruby. *Something for the Boys* (Alvin, "Betty-Jean," Jan. 7, 1943): Hey, Good Lookin'/WM: Cole Porter. *Something for the Boys* (Alvin, CR, "Chiquita Hart," Sept. 5, 1943): By the Mississinewah; There's a Happy Land in the Sky; When We're Home on the Range/WM: Cole Porter. *Up in Central Park* (Century, "Bessie O'Cahane," Jan. 27, 1945): The Birds and the Bees; Currier and Ives; The Fireman's Bride; It Doesn't Cost You Anything to Dream; Rip Van Winkle; Up from the Gutter/W: Dorothy Fields, M: Sigmund Romberg. *Up in Central Park* (New York City Center, revival, "Bessie O'Cahane," May 19, 1947): same as above.

1187. Carol Bruce (Nov. 15, 1919–) B: Great Neck, NY. The singer of stage, screen and radio began at 17 as a band singer with Lloyd Huntley in Montreal, Canada. *Louisiana Purchase* (Imperial, "Beatrice," May 28, 1940): The Lord Done Fixed Up My Soul; Louisiana Purchase/WM: Irving Berlin. *Show Boat* (Ziegfeld, revival,

"Julie La Verne," Jan. 5, 1946): Bill/W: Oscar Hammerstein II, P.G. Wodehouse, M: Jerome Kern — Can't Help Lovin' Dat Man/W: Oscar Hammerstein II, M: Jerome Kern. *Show Boat* (New York City Center, revival, "Julie La Verne," Sept. 7, 1948): same as above. *Along Fifth Avenue* (Broadhurst, revue, Jan. 13, 1949): The Best Time of Day; Weep No More/W: Tom Adair, M: Gordon Jenkins — Call It Applefritters/W: Milton Pascal, M: Richard Stutz. *Pal Joey* (New York City Center, revival, "Vera Simpson," May 31, 1961): Bewitched, Bothered and Bewildered; Den of Iniquity; Take Him; What Is a Man?/W: Lorenz Hart, M: Richard Rodgers. *A Family Affair* (Billy Rose, CR, "Tilly Siegal," Feb. 1962): Beautiful; Harmony; I'm Worse Than Anybody; Kalua Bay; My Son, the Lawyer; Summer Is Over/W: James Goldman, William Goldman, M: John Kander. *Do I Hear a Waltz?* (46th Street, "Signora Floria," Mar. 18, 1965): Moon in My Window; No Understand; Perfectly Lovely Couple; This Week Americans/W: Stephen Sondheim, M: Richard Rodgers. *Henry, Sweet Henry* (Palace, "Mrs. Boyd," Oct. 23, 1967): To Be Artistic/WM: Bob Merrill.

1188. Eddie Bruce *Smile at Me* (Fulton, revue, Aug. 23, 1935): I Love to Flutter/WM: Edward J. Lambert, Gerald Dolin.

1189. Judy Bruce *Oliver!* (Imperial, CR, "Nancy," July 1964): As Long as He Needs Me; I'd Do Anything; It's a Fine Life; Oom-Pah-Pah/WM: Lionel Bart.

1190. Nigel Bruce (Feb. 4, 1895–Oct. 8, 1953) B: Ensenada, Mexico. Though best remembered as Dr. Watson in the 1940s *Sherlock Holmes* movie series, the English-educated actor appeared in dozens of other films. *Virginia* (Center, "His Excellency, Gov. of the Colony," Sept. 2, 1937): It's Our Duty to the King/W: Al Stillman, M: Arthur Schwartz.

1191. Shelley Bruce (May 5, 1965–) B: Passaic, NJ. *Annie* (Alvin, CR, "Annie," Mar. 6, 1978): I Don't Need Anything but You; I Think I'm Gonna Like It Here; It's the Hard-Knock Life; Maybe; A New Deal for Christmas; N.Y.C.; Tomorrow/W: Martin Charnin, M: Charles Strouse.

1192. Larry Brucker *Funny Girl* (Winter Garden > Majestic, CR, "Ziegfeld Tenor"): His Love Makes Me Beautiful/W: Bob Merrill, M: Jule Styne.

1193. David Brummel (Nov. 1, 1942–) B: Brooklyn, NY. *Oklahoma!* (Palace, revival, CR, "Jud Fry," 1979): Lonely Room; Pore Jud/W: Oscar Hammerstein II, M: Richard Rodgers.

1194. Gabrielle Brune (Feb. 12, 1912–) B: Bournemouth, Dorset, England. Her mother was London musical star Adrienne Brune. *The Two Bouquets* (Windsor, "Patty Moss," May 31, 1938): Git on de Boat, Chillun; She Did the Fandango/W: Eleanor Farjeon, Herb Farjeon, M: Trad.— How Can We Bring the Old Folks Round/W: Eleanor Farjeon, Herb Farjeon, M: Henry Smart — Pretty Patty Moss/W: Eleanor Farjeon, Herb Farjeon, M: Nordendorff, based on Mozzer Bought a Baby — Yes or No/W: Eleanor Farjeon, Herb Farjeon, M: based on Offenbach.

1195. Ralph Bruneau (Sept. 22, 1952–) B: Phoenix, AZ. *King of Schnorrers* (Playhouse, "Harry Tinker," Nov. 28, 1979): Just for Me; Murder/WM: Judd Woldin. *Doonesbury* (Biltmore, "Mike Doonesbury," Nov. 21, 1983): Another Memorable Meal; Get Together; Graduation; Just One Night; Muffy & the Topsiders/W: Garry Trudeau, M: Elizabeth Swados.

1196. Philip Bruns (May 2, 1931–) B: Pipestone, MN. He was a regular on *Jackie Gleason's* TV variety show (1964), and played George Schumway on the soap spoof *Mary Hartman, Mary Hartman* (1977). *The Cradle Will Rock* (New York City Center, revival, "Prof. Trixie," Feb. 11, 1960): Listen, Fellas!/WM: Marc Blitzstein. *Blood Red Roses* (John Golden, "Pvt. John Smalls," Mar. 22, 1970): The Cream of English Youth; The English Rose; How Fucked Up Things Are/W: John Lewin, M: Michael Valenti.

1197. Marcia Brushingham *The Music Man* (City Center 55th Street, revival, "Alma Hix," June 5, 1980): It's You; Pick-a-Little, Talk-a-Little/WM: Meredith Willson.

1198. Buddy Bryan *Kismet* (New York State, revival, "Akbar," June 22, 1965): Bazaar of the Caravans; He's in Love!; Not Since Ninevah/WM: Robert Wright, George Forrest.

1199. Fred Bryan *Two on the Aisle* (Mark Hellinger, revue, July 19, 1951): Everlasting/W: Betty Comden, Adolph Green, M: Jule Styne.

1200. Gertrude Bryan *Little Boy Blue* (Lyric, "Daisy," Nov. 27, 1911): Angus Gordon Donald Douglas Ewart John McKee/WM: Edward A. Paulton — Flirt/W: William Kirk, Edward Madden, M: Henry Bereny — King of the Boulevards/W: Edward A. Paulton, A.E. Thomas, M: Paul Rubens — Kiss Me, Dearest, Kiss Me Do; Love Never Dies; You're Very Like Your Sister, Dear/W: Edward A. Paulton, M: Henry Bereny. *Sitting Pretty* (Fulton, "May Tolliver," Apr. 8, 1924): All You Need Is a Girl; The Enchanted Train; On a Desert Island with You; Shadow of the Moon; There Isn't One Girl; Worries; A Year

from Today/W: P.G. Wodehouse, M: Jerome Kern.

1201. Kenneth Bryan (July 30, 1953–Mar. 3, 1986) B: New Jersey. *Joseph and the Amazing Technicolor Dreamcoat* (Royale, revival, "Butler," Jan. 27, 1982): Go, Go, Go, Joseph/W: Tim Rice, M: Andrew Lloyd Webber.

1202. Tom Bryan *Her Family Tree* (Lyric > Shubert, Dec. 27, 1920): Boom Whee! [Feb. 14, 1921]; I Love You/WM: Seymour Simons.

1203. Wayne Bryan (Aug. 13, 1947–) B: Compton, CA. *Good News* (St. James, revival, "Bobby Randall," Dec. 23, 1974): Button Up Your Overcoat/W: B.G. DeSylva, Lew Brown, M: Ray Henderson.

1204. Ben Bryant *Pousse-Cafe* (46th Street, "Bill," Mar. 18, 1966): Rules and Regulations/W: Marshall Barer, M: Duke Ellington.

1205. David Bryant (May 26, 1936–) B: Nashville, TN. *Bubbling Brown Sugar* (ANTA, CR, "Bill" and "Time Man" and "Emcee" and "Bumpy," June 22, 1976): C'mon Up to Jive Time; Goin' Back in Time; Harlem-Time/W: ?; M: Danny Holgate — Moving Uptown/W: Loften Mitchell, M: Danny Holgate — Sophisticated Lady/W: Mitchell Parish, Irving Mills, M: Duke Ellington. *Les Miserables* (Broadway, "Marius," Mar. 12, 1987): Empty Chairs at Empty Tables; A Heart Full of Love; In My Life; A Little Fall of Rain; Red and Black/W: Herbert Kretzmer, M: Claude-Michel Schonberg. *Show Boat* (Gershwin, revival, "Pete," Oct. 2, 1994): Till Good Luck Comes My Way/W: Oscar Hammerstein II, M: Jerome Kern.

1206. Glenn Bryant B: New York, NY. A member of the police department, he was given leave by Mayor Fiorello La Guardia and Commissioner Lewis J. Valentine to perform in *Carmen Jones*. *Carmen Jones* (Broadway, "Husky Miller," Dec. 2, 1943): Poncho de Panther from Brazil; Stan' Up an' Fight/W: Oscar Hammerstein II, M: Georges Bizet. *Carmen Jones* (New York City Center, revival, "Husky Miller," Apr. 7, 1946): same as above.

1207. Nana Bryant (Nov. 23, 1888–Dec. 24, 1955) B: Cincinnati, OH. Character actress of stage, screen and TV. Her career lasted more than 50 years. *The Wild Rose* (Martin Beck, "Countess Nita," Oct. 20, 1926): L'Heure d'Or (One Golden Hour)/W: Otto Harbach, J.B. Kantor, M: Rudolf Friml — Love Me, Don't You?/W: Otto Harbach, Oscar Hammerstein II, M: Rudolf Friml. *A Connecticut Yankee* (Vanderbilt, "Fay Morgan," Nov. 3, 1927): A Ladies' Home Companion/W: Lorenz Hart, M: Richard Rodgers.

1208. Edward S. Bryce (Sept. 24, 1921–) B: Allentown, PA. *The Cradle Will Rock* (Broadway, revival, CR, "Larry Foreman," Feb. 2, 1948): The Cradle Will Rock; Ex-Foreman; Leaflets; Polyphonic; Stuck Like a Sandwich/ WM: Marc Blitzstein.

1209. Barbara Bryne (Apr. 1, 1929–) B: London, England. *Sunday in the Park with George* (Booth, "Old Lady," May 2, 1984): Beautiful; Gossip/WM: Stephen Sondheim.

1210. Yul Brynner (July 12, 1911–Oct. 10, 1985) B: Sakhalin, an island east of Siberia, north of Japan. Facts about his early life are contradictory, but he came to the U.S. in 1940, a protege of actor Michael Chekov. He played the role of The King in *The King and I* 4,625 times in a period of 30 years, for which he was awarded a special Tony in 1985, when he was dying of lung cancer. *Lute Song* (Plymouth, "Tsai-Yong, the husband," Feb. 6, 1946): The Lute Song; Mountain High, Valley Low; Vision Song; Willow Tree/W: Bernard Hanighen, M: Raymond Scott. *The King and I* (St. James, "The King," Mar. 29, 1951): A Puzzlement; Shall We Dance?; Song of the King/W: Oscar Hammerstein II, M: Richard Rodgers. *Home Sweet Homer* (Palace, "Odysseus," Jan. 4, 1976): The Contest; The Departure; Home Sweet Homer; How Could I Dare to Dream?; I Was Wrong; Love Is the Prize/ W: Charles Burr, Forman Brown, M: Mitch Leigh. *The King and I* (Uris, revival, "The King," May 2, 1977): same as above. *The King and I* (Broadway, revival, "The King," Jan. 7, 1985): same as above, except for A Puzzlement, omitted in June, when Brynner missed performances due to illness.

1211. Arthur Bryson *Hot Rhythm* (Times Square > Waldorf, revue, Aug. 21, 1930): Loving You the Way I Do/W: Jack Scholl, Will Morrissey, M: Eubie Blake.

1212. Claiborne Bryson *Earl Carroll's Vanities of 1930* (New Amsterdam, revue, July 1, 1930): Going Up/W: E.Y. Harburg, M: Jay Gorney — Rumba Rhythm/W: Stella Unger, M: James P. Johnson.

1213. John W. Bubbles (Feb. 19, 1902–May 18, 1986) B: Louisville, KY. His full name was JOHN W. (BUBBLES) SUBLETT. With his vaudeville partner from childhood, FORD LEE (BUCK) WASHINGTON, the song and dance team was known as Buck & Bubbles. *Blackbirds of 1930* (Royale, revue, Oct. 22, 1930): Blackbirds on Parade; You're Lucky to Me [Nov. 17, 1930]/W: Andy Razaf, M: Eubie Blake. *Porgy and Bess* (Alvin, "Sportin' Life," Oct. 10, 1935): It Ain't Necessarily So; There's a Boat Dat's

Leavin' Soon for New York/W: Ira Gershwin, M: George Gershwin. *Virginia* (Center, "Scipio," Sept. 2, 1937): Good and Lucky; Goodbye, Jonah; I'll Be Sitting in de Lap o' de Lord/ W: Al Stillman, M: Arthur Schwartz. *Carmen Jones* (New York City Center, revival, "Rum," Apr. 7, 1946): Poncho de Panther from Brazil; Whizzin' Away Along de Track/W: Oscar Hammerstein II, M: Georges Bizet.

1214. Aleen Buchanan *Great to Be Alive* (Winter Garden, "Maybelle," Mar. 23, 1950): Headin' for a Weddin'; When the Sheets Come Back from the Laundry/W: Walter Bullock, M: Abraham Ellstein.

1215. Donald Buchanan *The Girl and the Wizard* (Casino, "Carl Behrend," Sept. 27, 1909): When I Sang Toreador/WM: Melville Gideon.

1216. Jack Buchanan (Apr. 2, 1890–Oct. 20, 1957) B: Helensburgh, Scotland. Dapper song and dance star of the London stage, he produced and directed several films during the 1930s and appeared in Hollywood's *The Band Wagon* (1953). *Charlot Revue of 1924* (Times Square > Selwyn, revue, Jan. 9, 1924): I Did Feel a Dreadful Ass/W: Jack Hulbert, M: Philip Braham — It's a Far Far Better Thing/W: Douglas Furber, M: Philip Braham — You Were Meant for Me/WM: Eubie Blake, Noble Sissle. *Charlot Revue of 1926* (Selwyn, revue, Nov. 10, 1925): A Cup of Coffee, a Sandwich and You/W: Billy Rose, Al Dubin, M: Joseph Meyer — The Fox Has Left His Lair/W: Douglas Furber, M: Peggy Connor — Gigolette/W: Irving Caesar, M: Franz Lehar — Oxford Bags/W: Arthur Wimperis, M: Philip Braham — Take Them All Away/WM: Jack Strachey. *Wake Up and Dream* (Selwyn, revue, Dec. 30, 1929): Fancy Our Meeting/W: Douglas Furber, M: Joseph Meyer, Phil Charig — She's Such a Comfort to Me [added]/ W: Douglas Furber, Max Lief, Nathaniel Lief, Donovan Parsons, M: Arthur Schwartz. *Between the Devil* (Imperial, "Peter Anthony" and "Pierre Antoine," Dec. 22, 1937): By Myself; Don't Go Away, Monsieur; Experience; The Gendarme; I See Your Face Before Me; I've Made Up My Mind/W: Howard Dietz, M: Arthur Schwartz.

1217. Ford Lee Buck (Oct. 16, 1903–Jan. 31, 1955) B: Louisville, KY. Song and dance man, pianist and trumpet player. His full name was FORD LEE (BUCK) WASHINGTON. With his childhood friend and partner JOHN W. BUBBLES, they were known as Buck & Bubbles. *Virginia* (Center, "Hannibal," Sept. 2, 1937): Good and Lucky; Goodbye, Jonah; I'll Be Sitting in de Lap o' de Lord/W: Al Stillman,

M: Arthur Schwartz. *Carmen Jones* (New York City Center, revival, "Dink," Apr. 7, 1946): Whizzin' Away Along de Track/W: Oscar Hammerstein II, M: Georges Bizet.

1218. Anna Buckley *The Girl from Paris* (Wallack's, revival, "Ruth," Jan. 17, 1898): Sister Mary Jane's Top Note/W: F. Bowyer, M: Ivan Caryll. *Nancy Brown* (Bijou, CR, "Muriel," Apr. 27, 1903): A Little Birdie Told Me/W: Frederick Ranken, M: Henry Hadley.

1219. Annie Buckley (1872–Nov. 26, 1916) B: New York, NY. *Marrying Mary* (Daly's, "Flourette," Aug. 27, 1906): Gwendolyn/W: Benjamin Hapgood Burt, M: Silvio Hein.

1220. Betty Buckley (July 3, 1947–) B: Big Spring, TX. Her career has included film and cabaret as well as musical theater. On TV she played Abby Bradford on *Eight Is Enough* (1977). *1776* (46th Street, "Martha Jefferson," Mar. 16, 1969/Oct. 5, 1970): He Plays the Violin/WM: Sherman Edwards. *Pippin* (Imperial, CR, "Catherine," June 11, 1973): Kind of Woman; Love Song/WM: Stephen Schwartz. *Cats* (Winter Garden, "Grizabella," Oct. 7, 1982): Grizabella, the Glamour Cat/W: T.S. Eliot, M: Andrew Lloyd Webber — Memory/W: Trevor Nunn, based on T.S. Eliot, M: Andrew Lloyd Webber. *The Mystery of Edwin Drood* (Imperial, "Edwin Drood," Dec. 2, 1985): Ceylon; No Good Can Come from Bad; Perfect Strangers; Two Kinsmen/WM: Rupert Holmes. *Song & Dance* (Royale, CR, "Emma," Oct. 6, 1986): Capped Teeth and Caesar Salad; Come Back with the Same Look in Your Eyes; Married Men; Tell Me on a Sunday; Unexpected Song; You Made Me Think You Were in Love/W: Don Black, M: Andrew Lloyd Webber — English Girls; First Letter Home; I Love New York; Let Me Finish; Second Letter Home; So Much to Do in New York; So Much to Do in New York II; So Much to Do in New York III; Take That Look Off Your Face; Third Letter Home; What Have I Done?/W: Don Black, Richard Maltby, M: Andrew Lloyd Webber. *Carrie* (Virginia, "Margaret White," May 12, 1988): And Eve Was Weak; Carrie; Evening Prayers; Heaven; I Remember How Those Boys Could Dance; Open Your Heart; When There's No One/W: Dean Pitchford, M: Michael Gore. *Sunset Boulevard* (Minskoff, CR, "Norma Desmond," July 4, 1995): As If We Never Said Goodbye; The Greatest Star of All; The Lady's Paying; New Ways to Dream; The Perfect Year; Salome; Surrender; With One Look/W: Don Black, Christopher Hampton, M: Andrew Lloyd Webber.

1221. Dennis Buckley *Jesus Christ Superstar* (Mark Hellinger, "Simon Zealotes," Oct. 12, 1971): Simon Zealotes/W: Tim Rice, M: Andrew Lloyd Webber.

1222. Kay Buckley (Dec. 23, 1921–Nov. 2, 1982) B: Philadelphia, PA. *Sally* (Martin Beck, revival, "Rosie," May 6, 1948): Bungalow in Quogue/W: P.G. Wodehouse, M: Jerome Kern — The Church 'Round the Corner/W: Clifford Grey, P.G. Wodehouse, M: Jerome Kern.

1223. Melinda Buckley (Apr. 17, 1954–) B: Attleboro, MA. *Crazy for You* (Sam S. Shubert, CR, "Tess"): Slap That Bass/W: Ira Gershwin, M: George Gershwin.

1224. Belle Bucklin *The Idol's Eye* (Broadway, "Bidalia," Oct. 25, 1897): Minding the Baby/W: Harry B. Smith, M: Victor Herbert.

1225. Gladys Buckridge *Monte Cristo, Jr.* (Winter Garden, "Gladys," Feb. 12, 1919): Festive Nights; The Military Glide/W: Harold Atteridge, M: Sigmund Romberg, Jean Schwartz.

1226. Norman Budd (Jan. 27, 1914–) B: Liverpool, England. *The Merry Widow* (Majestic, revival, CR, "Nish," Dec. 19, 1943): Women/W: Adrian Ross, M: Franz Lehar. *The Merry Widow* (New York City Center, revival, "Nish," Oct. 8, 1944): same as above.

1227. Bill Buell (Sept. 21, 1952–) B: Paipai, Taiwan. *The First* (Martin Beck, "Frog," Nov. 17, 1981): Is This Year Next Year?/W: Martin Charnin, M: Bob Brush. *Welcome to the Club* (Music Box, "Gus Bottomly," Apr. 13, 1989): It's Love! It's Love!; Miami Beach; Rio/WM: Cy Coleman, A.E. Hotchner. *The Who's Tommy* (St. James, "Minister" and "Mr. Simpson," Apr. 22, 1993): Christmas; Sally Simpson/WM: Pete Townshend.

1228. Katherine Buffaloe (Nov. 7, 1953–) B: Greenville, SC. *The Phantom of the Opera* (Majestic, CR, "Christine Daae," June 5, 1989, Mon. and Wed. eves.): All I Ask of You; Angel of Music; Bravo, Bravo; I Remember; Little Lotte; The Mirror; Notes; The Point of No Return; Raoul, I've Been There; Stranger Than You Dreamt It; Think of Me; Twisted Every Way; Wandering Child; Why Have You Brought Me Here; Wishing You Were Somehow Here Again/W: Charles Hart, Richard Stilgoe, M: Andrew Lloyd Webber — The Phantom of the Opera/W: Mike Batt, Richard Stilgoe, M: Andrew Lloyd Webber.

1229. Kenny Buffett (Oct. 2, 1926–) B: Philadelphia, PA. *Hold It!* (National, "Judge Rogers," May 5, 1948): About Face; Hold It!;

You Took Possession of Me/W: Sammy Lerner, M: Gerald Marks.

1230. Donald Buka (Aug. 17, 1921–) B: Cleveland, OH. While studying drama at Carnegie Institute of Technology, he was discovered by the Lunts, who took him on tour with them. *Helen Goes to Troy* (Alvin, "Orestes," Apr. 24, 1944): A Little Chat; Take My Advice; Tsing-la-la/W: Herbert Baker, M: Jacques Offenbach, adapted by Eric Wolfgang Korngold.

1231. Harry Bulger (1872–Apr. 15, 1926) *By the Sad Sea Waves* (Herald Square, "Boston Budge," Feb. 21, 1899): Buttercups and Daisies; Yankee Banners/W: J. Sherrie Mathews, Harry Bulger, M: Gustav Luders. *By the Sad Sea Waves* (Grand Opera House, revival, "Hi Ball," Mar. 5, 1900): The Under-Takers' Frolic; You Told Me Yo' Had Money in the Bank/W: J. Sherrie Mathews, Harry Bulger, M: Gustav Luders. *The Sleeping Beauty and the Beast* (Broadway, "King Bardout," Nov. 4, 1901): B'Gosh!; Hygiene/W: J. Cheever Goodwin, M: Frederic Solomon, J.M. Glover — Flora I Am Your Adorer/W: Vincent Bryan, M: Charles Robinson — My Princess Zulu Lulu [Mar. 3, 1902]/WM: Dave Reed, Jr. — Rip Van Winkle Was a Lucky Man/W: William Jerome, M: Jean Schwartz — Tell Me, Dusky Maiden (A Travesty)/W: Bob Cole, James Weldon Johnson, M: J. Rosamond Johnson. *Mother Goose* (New Amsterdam, "Jack," Dec. 2, 1903): Always Leave Them Laughing When You Say Good-bye; Rube Song/WM: George M. Cohan — Laughing Water/W: George Totten Smith, M: Frederick W. Hager — Still in the Old Front Line/WM: Matthew Woodward — Under the Mistletoe Bough/W: Will Heelan, M: J. Fred Helf — We Marched Away/W: George V. Hobart, M: Frederic Solomon. *Woodland* (New York > Herald Square, "Blue Jay," Nov. 21, 1904): Bye-Bye Baby; They'll Have to Go; The Valley of Hokus-Pocus/W: Frank Pixley, M: Gustav Luders — No Bird Ever Flew So High He Didn't Have to Light/W: Will D. Cobb, M: Harry Bulger. *The Man from Now* (New Amsterdam, "Steve Waffles," Sept. 3, 1906): College Chums/ W: Vincent Bryan, M: Gertrude Hoffmann — The Irresistible Tune/WM: Manuel Klein — There Isn't Anything That Can't Be Cured/W: Vincent Bryan, M: Harry Bulger — What Says Your Heart?/W: Vincent Bryan, M: Manuel Klein.

1232. Donna Bullock (Dec. 11, 1955–) B: Dallas, TX. *City of Angels* (Virginia, CR, "Bobbi" and "Gabby"): It Needs Work; What You Don't Know About Women; With Every Breath I Take; You're Nothing Without Me/W: David Zippel, M: Cy Coleman.

1233. Wynne Bullock *Music Box Revue of 1922* (Music Box, revue, CR, July 30, 1923): Diamond Horseshoe; Lady of the Evening; Will She Come from the East? (East-North-West or South)/WM: Irving Berlin.

1234. Joseph Buloff (Dec. 6, 1899–Feb. 27, 1985) B: Vilna, Lithuania. He came to the U.S. in the 1920s and worked in New York with the Yiddish Art Theater. In movies from 1940. *Oklahoma!* (St. James, "Ali Hakim," Mar. 31, 1943): It's a Scandal! It's a Outrage!/W: Oscar Hammerstein II, M: Richard Rodgers.

1235. George Bumson *The Desert Song* (New York City Center, revival, "Ali Ben Ali," Jan. 8, 1946): Let Love Go/W: Otto Harbach, Oscar Hammerstein II, M: Sigmund Romberg.

1236. Alan Bunce (June 28, 1902–Apr. 27, 1965) B: Westfield, NJ. He played Albert Arbuckle first on radio in the 1940s, then on TV in the popular sitcom *Ethel and Albert* (1953). *Copper and Brass* (Martin Beck, "Captain," Oct. 17, 1957): Argentine Tango/W: David Craig, M: David Baker.

1237. Eleanor Bunker *New Faces of 1936* (Vanderbilt, revue, May 19, 1936): Too Too Too!/W: Everett Marcy, M: Irvin Graham.

1238. Ralph Bunker (c 1889–Apr. 28, 1966) B: Boston, MA. *The Girl Who Smiles* (Lyric > Longacre, "Theodore," Aug. 9, 1915): Join the Families/WM: Edward A. Paulton, Adolf Philipp, Jean Briquet.

1239. John Bunny (Sept. 21, 1863–Apr. 26, 1915) B: New York, NY. Audiences loved the rotund comedy star of more than 150 silent short motion pictures, made from 1910 until his death. *Tom Jones* (Astor, "Gregory," Nov. 11, 1907): The Barley Mow; Let's Be Merry; Uncle John Tappit/W: Charles M. Taylor, M: Edward German.

1240. Mabel Bunyea *See-Saw* (Cohan, CR, "Cleo Ray," Nov. 17, 1919): Senorita-Senorita; When You Come Near I Feel All of a Ooh!/W: Earl Derr Biggers, M: Louis A. Hirsch.

1241. Stephen R. Buntrock *Les Miserables* (Broadway, CR, "Enjolras," Mar. 12, 1997): Do You Hear the People Sing?; Red and Black/W: Herbert Kretzmer, M: Claude-Michel Schonberg.

1242. Shelly Burch (Mar. 19, 1960–) B: Tucson, AZ. *Stop the World — I Want to Get Off* (New York State, revival, "Jane Littlechap," Aug. 3, 1978): Family Fugue; Nag! Nag! Nag!/WM: Leslie Bricusse, Anthony Newley. *Nine* (46th Street, "Claudia," May 9, 1982): A Man Like You; Unusual Way/WM: Maury Yeston.

1243. Harry B. Burcher *The Belle of Mayfair* (Daly's, "The Earl of Mount Highgate,"

Dec. 3, 1906): I Am a Military Man/W: William Caine, M: Leslie Stuart — I Know a Girl/WM: Leslie Stuart.

1244. Frederick Burchinal *The Most Happy Fella* (Majestic, revival, "Tony," Oct. 11, 1979, mats.): Happy to Make Your Acquaintance; How Beautiful the Days; Mamma, Mamma, The Most Happy Fella; My Heart Is So Full of You; Rosabella; Young People/WM: Frank Loesser.

1245. Arthur Burckley *The Riviera Girl* (New Amsterdam, "Charles Lorenz," Sept. 24, 1917): The Fall of Man/W: P.G. Wodehouse, M: Emmerich Kalman — Man, Man, Man/W: James Weldon Johnson, M: Bob Cole. *Irene* (Vanderbilt, "J.P. Bowden," Nov. 18, 1919): To Love You/W: Joseph McCarthy, M: Harry Tierney. *Bye, Bye Barbara* (National, "Stanley Howard," Aug. 25, 1924): Bo Peep Waltz; Harmony; Quaint Little House for Two/WM: Monte Carlo, Alma Sanders. *Mlle. Modiste* (Jolson, revival, "Gaston," Oct. 7, 1929): Love Me, Love My Dog; Ze English Language/W: Henry Blossom, M: Victor Herbert.

1246. Florence Burdett *Tom Jones* (Astor, "Hostess of the Inn," Nov. 11, 1907): My Lady's Coach Has Been Attacked/W: Charles M. Taylor, M: Edward German. *A Country Girl* (Herald Square, revival, "Nan," May 29, 1911): Molly the Marchioness; Try Again Johnnie/W: Adrian Ross, M: Lionel Monckton.

1247. David Burdick *Peter Pan* (Minskoff, return engagement of revival, "John Darling," Nov. 27, 1991): I'm Flying; Tender Shepherd/W: Carolyn Leigh, M: Moose Charlap.

1248. Gregg Burge (Nov. 15, 1957–July 4, 1998) B: New York, NY. *The Wiz* (Majestic, CR, "Scarecrow," Dec. 1976): Ease on Down the Road; I Was Born on the Day Before Yesterday; Slide Some Oil to Me/WM: Charlie Smalls. *Sophisticated Ladies* (Lunt-Fontanne, revue, Mar. 1, 1981): Caravan/W: Irving Mills, M: Juan Tizol, Duke Ellington — Drop Me Off in Harlem/W: Nick Kenny, M: Duke Ellington — I Love You Madly; I've Got to Be a Rug Cutter/WM: Duke Ellington — Imagine My Frustration/WM: Duke Ellington, Billy Strayhorn, Gerald Wilson — It Don't Mean a Thing/ W: Irving Mills, M: Duke Ellington. *Oh, Kay!* (Richard Rodgers, revival, "Billy Lyles," Nov. 1, 1990): Heaven on Earth; Oh, Kay!/W: Ira Gershwin, Howard Dietz, M: George Gershwin — Show Me the Town; Slap That Bass; Sleepless Nights; You've Got What Gets Me/W: Ira Gershwin, M: George Gershwin.

1249. Dorothy Burgess (Mar. 4, 1905–Aug.

20, 1961) B: Los Angeles, CA. Leading lady in B pictures of the 1930s and 40s. FAY BAINTER was her aunt. *Bye, Bye, Bonnie* (Ritz > Cosmopolitan, "Bonnie Quinlan," Jan. 13, 1927): Bye, Bye, Bonnie; Look in Your Engagement Book; You and I Love You and Me/W: Neville Fleeson, M: Albert Von Tilzer.

1250. Marjorie Burgess B: Little Cosby, England. As a child she played roles in *Peter Pan* and *The Blue Bird*. *Monsieur Beaucaire* (New Amsterdam, "Lucy," Dec. 11, 1919): That's a Woman's Way; We Are Not Speaking Now/W: Adrian Ross, M: Andre Messager.

1251. Billie Burke (Aug. 7, 1884–May 14, 1970) B: Washington, D.C. M: producer Florenz Ziegfeld, 1914. Her father was a singing clown who traveled through Europe with The Barnum and Bailey Circus; her mother worked for the Dept. of the Treasury in Washington. Best remembered as Glinda, the Good Witch of the East in the classic movie *The Wizard of Oz* (1939). *Annie Dear* (Times Square, "Annie Leigh," Nov. 4, 1924): Annie; Come to My Party; I Want to Be Loved; Slither, Slither/WM: Clare Kummer.

1252. Harriett Burke *Americana of 1926* (Belmont, revue, July 26, 1926): Dreaming/W: J.P. McEvoy, M: Henry Souvaine, Con Conrad.

1253. Ione Burke *Evangeline, or The Belle of Arcadia* (Niblo's Garden, "Evangeline," July 27, 1874): Come Back to the Heart That Is Thine; Fie Upon You, Fie; Go Not Happy Day; My Best Beloved; Thinking, Love, of Thee; Where Art Thou Now, My Beloved?/W: J. Cheever Goodwin, M: Edward E. Rice.

1254. John J. Burke (c 1853–July 6, 1898) B: New York, NY. *Aladdin, Jr.* (Broadway, "Crambo," Apr. 8, 1895): I Don't Suppose You Have; The Stars Alone Can Tell/W: J. Cheever Goodwin, M: W.H. Batchelor, Jesse Williams.

1255. Karen G. Burke *Dancin'* (Broadhurst, revue, Mar. 27, 1978): Dixie/WM: Daniel Decatur Emmett — Here You Come Again/ WM: Barry Mann, Cynthia Weil.

1256. Katherine Burke *Rio Rita* (Ziegfeld, "Montezuma's Daughter," Feb. 2, 1927): Montezuma's Daughter/W: Joseph McCarthy, M: Harry Tierney.

1257. Marie Burke (Oct. 18, 1894–Mar. 21, 1988) B: London, England. M: briefly, to TOM BURKE. Trained in Italy for an operatic career, she returned to the British musical stage in 1917. *Make It Snappy* (Winter Garden, revue, Apr. 13, 1922): Blossom Time; Gay Butterfly on the Wheel/W: Alfred Bryan, M: Jean Schwartz — Good-Bye Main Street; My Castillian Girl/W:

Harold Atteridge, M: Jean Schwartz. *The Lady in Ermine* (Ambassador, "Sophia Lavalle," Oct. 2, 1922): Gay Butterfly on the Wheel/W: Alfred Bryan, M: Jean Schwartz — How Fiercely You Dance; Men Grow Older/WM: ?— I'll Follow You to Zanzibar (Follow You All Over the World)/W: Cyrus D. Wood, M: Alfred Goodman. *The Great Waltz* (Center, "Countess Olga Baranskaja," Sept. 22, 1934): For We Love You Still; Like a Star in the Sky; Love's Never Lost/W: Desmond Carter, M: Johann Strauss.

1258. Michele Burke B: Pittsburgh, PA. M: dancer PETER CONLOW. *The President's Daughter* (Billy Rose, "Frances," Nov. 3, 1970): Welcome, Mr. Golden!/W: Jacob Jacobs, M: Murray Rumshinsky.

1259. Tom Burke (1890–Sept. 13, 1969) B: Leigh, England. M: MARIE BURKE. In 1919 he sang with opera star Melba at Covent Garden in London, the high point in a career of musical comedy, variety and concerts. *The Dancing Girl* (Winter Garden, "Rudolpho" and "Old Man," Jan. 24, 1923): That Romance of Mine/WM: ?— Venetian Carnival/W: Harold Atteridge, M: Sigmund Romberg — Why Am I So Sad?/W: ?, M: George Gershwin. *The Greenwich Village Follies of 1923* (Winter Garden, revue, CR, Oct. 29, 1923): Golden Trail/W: John Murray Anderson, Irving Caesar, M: Louis A. Hirsch. *Hassard Short's Ritz Revue* (Ritz, revue, Sept. 17, 1924): Monsieur Beaucaire; Our Crystal Wedding Day; Sun Girl/W: Anne Caldwell, M: Frank Tours — The Wanderer/W: Owen Murphy, M: Jay Gorney, Tom Burke.

1260. Thomas Burke, Jr. *Holka-Polka* (Lyric, "Rudi Munz," Oct. 14, 1925): Fairy Tale/W: Gus Kahn, Raymond B. Egan, M: Will Ortman.

1261. Virginia Burke *'Tis of Thee* (Maxine Elliott, revue, Oct. 26, 1940): The Lady/W: Alfred Hayes, M: Elsie Peters — What's Mine Is Thine/W: Alfred Hayes, M: Al Moss.

1262. Walter Burke (Aug. 25, 1908–Aug. 4, 1984) B: Brooklyn, NY. *Sadie Thompson* (Alvin, "Quartermaster Bates," Nov. 16, 1944): Siren of the Tropics/W: Howard Dietz, M: Vernon Duke. *Up in Central Park* (Century, "Danny O'Cahane," Jan. 27, 1945): The Birds and the Bees; Up from the Gutter; When the Party Gives a Party/W: Dorothy Fields, M: Sigmund Romberg. *Up in Central Park* (New York City Center, revival, "Danny O'Cahane," May 19, 1947): same as above.

1263. Willi Burke *On the Twentieth Century* (St. James, "Imelda," Feb. 19, 1978): Indian Maiden's Lament/W: Betty Comden, Adolph Green, M: Cy Coleman.

1264. Gerry Burkhardt (June 14, 1946–) B: Houston, TX. *The Best Little Whorehouse in Texas* (46th Street, "Shy Kid" and "Aggie #7," June 19, 1978): 20 Fans/WM: Carol Hall.

1265. Arthur Burkley *Mlle. Modiste* (Jolson, revival, "Gaston," Oct. 7, 1929): Love Me, Love My Dog; Ze English Language/W: Henry Blossom, M: Victor Herbert.

1266. Hattie Burks *His Little Widows* (Astor, "Murilla Lloyd," Apr. 30, 1917): I Need Someone's Love/W: William Cary Duncan, M: William Schroeder — That Creepy Weepy Feeling/W: Rida Johnson Young, M: William Schroeder. *Oh, My Dear!* (39th Street, CR, "Hilda Rockett," Apr. 21, 1919): City of Dreams; Come Where Nature Calls; I Wonder Whether (I've Loved You All My Life); Isn't It Wonderful?; Try Again; You Never Know/W: P.G. Wodehouse, M: Louis A. Hirsch — Go Little Boat/W: P.G. Wodehouse, M: Jerome Kern. *Jimmie* (Apollo, "Beatrice," Nov. 17, 1920): Don' Yo' Want to See de Moon?; She Alone Could Understand/W: Oscar Hammerstein II, Otto Harbach, M: Herbert Stothart.

1267. Leo Burmester (Feb. 1, 1944–) B: Louisville, KY. *Big River: The Adventures of Huckleberry Finn* (Eugene O'Neill, CR, "Pap Finn," Sept. 3, 1985): Guv'ment/WM: Roger Miller. *Raggedy Ann* (Nederlander, "General D," Oct. 16, 1986): I Come Riding; Make Believe/WM: Joe Raposo. *Les Miserables* (Broadway, "Thenardier," Mar. 12, 1987): Beggars at the Feast; Dog Eats Dog; Master of the House; Thenardier Waltz/W: Herbert Kretzmer, M: Claude-Michel Schonberg.

1268. G. Davy Burnaby (Apr. 7, 1881–Apr. 18, 1949) B: Buckland, England. A favorite light comedian of the London musical stage. He also appeared in numerous British comedy films, and wrote song lyrics and a libretto. *Tonight's the Night* (Shubert, "Robin Carraway," Dec. 24, 1914): Dancing Mad; Round the Corner; When the Boys Come Home to Tea/WM: Paul Rubens, Percy Greenbank.

1269. Brevard Burnett *Strut Miss Lizzie* (Times Square, revue, June 19, 1922): Four Fo' Me; Jazz Blues/W: Henry Creamer, M: Turner Layton.

1270. Carol Burnett (Apr. 26, 1933–) B: San Antonio, TX. The popular comic actress starred in her own TV show (1967). *Once Upon a Mattress* (Alvin, "Princess Winnifred," Nov. 25, 1959): Happily Ever After; Shy; Song of Love; Swamps of Home/W: Marshall Barer, M: Mary Rodgers. *Fade Out— Fade In* (Mark Hellinger, "Hope Springfield," May 26, 1964/Feb.

15, 1965): Call Me Savage; Fade Out — Fade In; Go Home Train; I'm With You; It's Good to Be Back Home; Lila Tremaine; The Usher from the Mezzanine; You Mustn't Be Discouraged/W: Betty Comden, Adolph Green, M: Jule Styne.

1271. Connie Burnett *West Side Story* (New York State, revival, "Teresita," June 24, 1968): I Feel Pretty/W: Stephen Sondheim, M: Leonard Bernstein.

1272. Martha Burnett *George White's Scandals of 1939-40* (Alvin, revue, Aug. 28, 1939): Goodnight, My Beautiful/W: Jack Yellen, M: Sammy Fain. *By Jupiter* (Shubert, "1st Sentry," June 3, 1942): Jupiter Forbid/W: Lorenz Hart, M: Richard Rodgers.

1273. Robert Burnett (Feb. 28, 1960–) B: Goshen, NY. *Cats* (Winter Garden, CR, "Skimbleshanks," c 1986): Skimbleshanks/W: T.S. Eliot, M: Andrew Lloyd Webber.

1274. Steve Burney *Fearless Frank* (Princess, "Tobin" and "Whitehouse" and "Smith" and "Chapman" and "Oscar Wilde," June 15, 1980): The Examination Song, or Get Me on That Boat/W: Andrew Davies, M: Dave Brown.

1275. Harry Burnham *Take It from Me* (44th Street, "Wilkins," Mar. 31, 1919): It's Different Now [Apr. 7, 1919]/W: Will B. Johnstone, M: Will R. Anderson.

1276. Martine Burnley *The Broadway Whirl* (Selwyn, revue, CR, Aug. 15, 1921): Let Cutie Cut Your Cuticle/W: B.G. DeSylva, John Henry Mears, M: George Gershwin.

1277. Barry Burns B: New York, NY. *West Side Story* (New York City Center, revival, "Snowboy," Apr. 8, 1964): Gee, Officer Krupke!/W: Stephen Sondheim, M: Leonard Bernstein.

1278. David Burns (June 22, 1902–Mar. 12, 1971) B: New York, NY. M: MILDRED TODD. Character actor who often played comic gangster roles. His early career was spent on the London musical stage. While in Philadelphia rehearsing a song from *70, Girls, 70* just a month before its Broadway opening date, he suffered a fatal heart attack. *Pal Joey* (Ethel Barrymore > Shubert > St. James, CR, "Ludlow Lowell," Aug. 1941): Do It the Hard Way; Plant You Now, Dig You Later/W: Lorenz Hart, M: Richard Rodgers. *My Dear Public* (46th Street, revue, "Walters," Sept. 9, 1943): My Spies Tell Me (You Love Nobody but Me)/WM: Irving Caesar, Sammy Lerner, Gerald Marks. *Billion Dollar Baby* (Alvin, "Dapper Welch," Dec. 21, 1945): Speaking of Paris/W: Betty Comden, Adolph Green, M: Morton Gould. *Oklahoma!* (St. James, CR, "Ali Hakim," Aug. 1946): It's a Scandal! It's a Outrage!/W: Oscar Hammerstein II, M: Richard

Rodgers. *Make Mine Manhattan* (Broadhurst, revue, Jan. 15, 1948): The Good Old Days/W: Arnold B. Horwitt, Ted Fetter, M: Richard Lewine. *Heaven on Earth* (New Century, "H.M. Hutton," Sept. 16, 1948): Push a Button in a Hutton/W: Barry Trivers, M: Jay Gorney. *Out of This World* (New Century, "Niki Skolianos," Dec. 21, 1950): Cherry Pies Ought to Be You; Climb Up the Mountain/WM: Cole Porter. *Do Re Mi* (St. James, "Brains Berman," Dec. 26, 1960): It's Legitimate/W: Betty Comden, Adolph Green, M: Jule Styne. *A Funny Thing Happened on the Way to the Forum* (Alvin, "Senex," May 8, 1962): Everybody Ought to Have a Maid; Impossible/WM: Stephen Sondheim. *Hello, Dolly!* (St. James, "Horace Vandergelder," Jan. 16, 1964): Before the Parade Passes By/WM: Lee Adams, Charles Strouse, Jerry Herman — Hello, Dolly!; It Takes a Woman; So Long, Dearie/WM: Jerry Herman Motherhood/WM: Bob Merrill, Jerry Herman. *Lovely Ladies, Kind Gentlemen* (Majestic, "Col. Wainwright Purdy III," Dec. 28, 1970): Right Hand Man; You've Broken a Fine Woman's Heart/WM: Franklin Underwood, Stan Freeman.

1279. George Burns *When Johnny Comes Marching Home* (New Amsterdam > Manhattan Opera House, revival, "Maj. George Buckle," May 7, 1917): I Could Waltz On Forever/W: Stanislaus Stange, M: Julian Edwards.

1280. Karla Burns *Show Boat* (Uris, revival, "Queenie," Apr. 24, 1983): Can't Help Lovin' Dat Man; Queenie's Ballyhoo/W: Oscar Hammerstein II, M: Jerome Kern.

1281. Paul Burns (Jan. 26, 1881–May 17, 1967) B: Philadelphia, PA. *Go-Go* (Daly's, "Otis Hubbard," Mar. 12, 1923): Go-Go Bug; New York Town; Pat Your Feet/W: Alex Rogers, M: C. Luckeyth Roberts. *Music Hath Charms* (Majestic, "Sen. Burranto," Dec. 29, 1934): Scandal Number/W: Rowland Leigh, John Shubert, M: Rudolf Friml.

1282. Donald Burr (July 31, 1907–Feb. 27, 1979) B: Cincinnati, OH. M: BILLIE WORTH. *The Garrick Gaieties of 1930* (Guild, revue, return engagement, Oct. 16, 1930): The Butcher, the Baker, the Candle-Stick Maker/W: Benjamin M. Kaye, M: Mana-Zucca — I Am Only Human After All/W: E.Y. Harburg, Ira Gershwin, M: Vernon Duke — Johnny Wanamaker/W: Paul James, M: Kay Swift — Rose of Arizona/W: Lorenz Hart, M: Richard Rodgers. *Marching By* (46th Street, "Sasha Sachaloff," Mar. 3, 1932): Forward March into My Arms/W: Harry B. Smith, M: Jean Gilbert — It Might Have Been

You/W: George Waggoner, M: Gus Arnheim, Neil Moret—I've Gotta Keep My Eye on You/W: Mack Gordon, M: Harry Revel. *Walk a Little Faster* (St. James, revue, Dec. 7, 1932): A Penny for Your Thoughts [Feb. 20, 1933]; Speaking of Love; Unaccustomed as I Am; Where Have We Met Before?/W: E.Y. Harburg, M: Vernon Duke. *Sherry!* (Alvin, "Ernest W. Stanley," Mar. 27, 1967): Harriet Sedley/W: James Lipton, M: Laurence Rosenthal.

1283. Fritzi Burr *Funny Girl* (Winter Garden > Majestic, CR, "Mrs. Strakosh" and "Mrs. Brice," c 1965): Find Yourself a Man; If a Girl Isn't Pretty; Who Taught Her Everything?/W: Bob Merrill, M: Jule Styne.

1284. Robert Burr (Mar. 5, 1922–May 13, 2000) B: Jersey City, NJ. *The Beggar's Opera* (New York City Center, revival, "Matt of the Mint," Mar. 13, 1957): Fill Every Glass/WM: John Gay. *Bajour* (Shubert, "Lou MacNiall," Nov. 23, 1964): Living Simply/WM: Walter Marks. *Wild and Wonderful* (Lyceum, "Lionel Masters," Dec. 7, 1971): Little Bits and Pieces; She Should Have Me/WM: Bob Goodman.

1285. Deborah Burrell Sister of TERRY (TERESA) BURRELL. *The Wiz* (Majestic, CR, "Glinda," Apr. 12, 1976): If You Believe (Believe in Yourself); A Rested Body Is a Rested Mind/WM: Charlie Smalls. *Eubie!* (Ambassador, CR, revue, Mar. 1979): Gee, I Wish I Had Someone to Rock Me in the Cradle of Love; I'm Just Wild About Harry; Oriental Blues; There's a Million Little Cupids in the Sky/W: Noble Sissle, M: Eubie Blake—Goodnight Angeline/W: Noble Sissle, James Reese Europe, M: Eubie Blake—Memories of You/W: Andy Razaf, M: Eubie Blake. *Dreamgirls* (Imperial, "Michelle Morris," Dec. 20, 1981): Quintette/W: Tom Eyen, M: Henry Krieger. *Dreamgirls* (Imperial, CR, "Deena Jones," c 1985): Family; Hard to Say Goodbye, My Love; I'm Somebody; One Night Only; Only the Beginning; Quintette; When I First Saw You/W: Tom Eyen, M: Henry Krieger. *The High Rollers Social and Pleasure Club* (Helen Hayes, revue, "Queen," Apr. 21, 1992): Dance the Night; Don't You Feel My Leg; Heebie Jeebie Dance; Such a Night; You're the One/WM: ?—Sea Cruise/WM: Huey P. Smith—Tell It Like It Is/WM: George Davis, Jr., Lee Diamond.

1286. Pamela Burrell (Aug. 4, 1945–) B: Tacoma, WA. *Where's Charley?* (Circle in the Square, revival, "Young Lady," Dec. 20, 1974): The Gossips; Lovelier Than Ever/WM: Frank Loesser.

1287. Terry (Teresa) Burrell (Feb. 8, 1952–)

B: Trinidad, West Indies. Sister of DEBORAH BURRELL. *Eubie!* (Ambassador, revue, Sept. 20, 1978): Roll Jordan; Weary/W: Andy Razaf, M: Eubie Blake. *Dreamgirls* (Imperial, CR, "Michelle Morris," Mar. 1983/Apr. 1984/Oct. 1984): Quintette/W: Tom Eyen, M: Henry Krieger. *Dreamgirls* (Imperial, CR, "Lorell Robinson," June 5, 1984): Ain't No Party; Family; Quintette; The Rap/W: Tom Eyen, M: Henry Krieger. *Honky Tonk Nights* (Biltmore, "Lily Meadows," Aug. 7, 1986): Eggs; Hot and Bothered; I Took My Time; I've Had It; Lily of the Alley; Little Dark Bird; Withered Irish Rose/W: Ralph Allen, David Campbell, M: Michael Valenti. *Swinging on a Star* (Music Box, revue, Oct. 22, 1995): Ain't It a Shame About Mame/W: Johnny Burke, M: James V. Monaco—Annie Doesn't Live Here Anymore/W: Johnny Burke, Joe Young, M: Harold Spina—But Beautiful; Imagination; Personality; When Stanislaus Got Married; You Don't Have to Know the Language/W: Johnny Burke, M: James Van Heusen—Whoopsie Daisy Day/WM: Johnny Burke.

1288. William Burress (Aug. 19, 1867–Oct. 30, 1948) B: Newcomerstown, OH. *The Spring Maid* (Liberty, Prince Nepomuk," Dec. 26, 1910): Interrupted Allegory; The Next May Be the Right/W: Robert B. Smith, M: Heinrich Reinhardt. *The Dancing Duchess* (Casino, "Adolphus Spiggott," Aug. 20, 1914): Fol-De-Rol-Lol/W: C.H. Kerr, R.H. Burnside, M: Milton Lusk. *Miss Millions* (Punch and Judy, "Ephraim Tutt," Dec. 9, 1919): Since Hiram Came Back/W: R.H. Burnside, M: Raymond Hubbell. *The Girl from Home* (Globe, "Gen. Santos Campos," May 3, 1920): El Presidente/W: Frank Craven, M: Silvio Hein.

1289. Bennett Burrill *Street Scene* (Adelphi, "Charlie Hildebrand," Jan. 9, 1947): Catch Me If You Can/W: Langston Hughes, Elmer Rice, M: Kurt Weill.

1290. Glenn Burris *The Liar* (Broadhurst, "Florindo Pallido," May 18, 1950): Lack-a-Day; You've Stolen My Heart/W: Edward Eager, M: John Mundy.

1291. Don Burroughs *Jimmie* (Apollo, "Tom O'Brien," Nov. 17, 1920): Cute Little Two by Four; Jimmie; Just a Smile/W: Oscar Hammerstein II, Otto Harbach, M: Herbert Stothart.

1292. James Burroughs *Blossom Time* (Century, CR, "Erkmann," Nov. 20, 1922): Love Is a Riddle/W: Dorothy Donnelly, M: Sigmund Romberg.

1293. Judyth Burroughs (June 6, 1940–) B: Miami, FL. *Along Fifth Avenue* (Broadhurst, revue, Jan. 13, 1949): A Trip Doesn't Care at All/W: Thomas Howell, M: Philip Kadison.

1294. Jay Bursky (Mar. 27, 1954–) B: Cleveland, OH. *The Best Little Whorehouse in Texas* (46th Street, "Governor's Aide," June 19, 1978): The Sidestep/WM: Carol Hall.

1295. Mike Burstyn (July 1, 1945–) B: Bronx, NY. His parents, Pesach'ke Burstyn and Lillian Lux, were stars of the Yiddish theater. *Barnum* (St. James, CR, "Phineas Taylor Barnum," Oct. 13, 1981): Black and White; The Colors of My Life; I Like Your Style; Join the Circus; Museum Song; One Brick at a Time; Out There; The Prince of Humbug; There's a Sucker Born Ev'ry Minute/W: Michael Stewart, M: Cy Coleman. *Those Were the Days* (Edison, revue, CR): At the Fireplace/WM: M. Warshavsky — Bei Mir Bist Du Schoen/W: Sammy Cahn, Saul Chaplin, Jacob Jacobs, M: Sholom Secunda — Hudl with the Shtrudl/WM: A. Lebedeff — Litvak/Galitsyaner/WM: Hymie Jacobson — Nochum, My Son/WM: trad.— The Palace of the Czar/WM: Mel Tolkin — Rumania, Rumania/WM: A. Lebedeff, Sholom Secunda — Yosl Ber/W: Itsik Manger, M: trad. *Ain't Broadway Grand* (Lunt-Fontanne, "Mike Todd," Apr. 18, 1993): Ain't Broadway Grand; Class; On the Street; They'll Never Take Us Alive; You're My Star/W: Lee Adams, M: Mitch Leigh.

1296. Flo Burt M: EL BRENDEL. *Cinderella on Broadway* (Winter Garden, revue, "Miss Moffet," June 24, 1920): Any Little Melody; Whistle and I'll Come to Meet You/W: Harold Atteridge, M: Bert Grant. *The Mimic World* (Century roof, revue, Aug. 17, 1921): Weep No More, My Mammy/W: Sidney Clare, M: Lew Pollack.

1297. Harriet Burt (Oct. 5, 1885–May 22, 1935) B: Troy, NY. *The Time, the Place and the Girl* (Wallack's, "Mrs. Talbot," Aug. 5, 1907): Waning Honeymoon/W: Frank R. Adams, Will M. Hough, M: Joseph E. Howard. *Algeria* (Broadway, "Millicent Madison, MD," Aug. 31, 1908): Ask Her While the Band Is Playing; Bohemia, Good-Bye; You'll Feel Better Then/ W: Glen MacDonough, M: Victor Herbert. *The Boys and Betty* (Wallack's, CR, "Nanon Duval," Feb. 1, 1909): At the Folies Bergere; I Want to Go to Paris/W: George V. Hobart, M: Silvio Hein. *Modest Suzanne* (Liberty, "Rose," Jan. 1, 1912): Father and Son/W: Robert B. Smith, M: Jean Gilbert — Tangolango Tap [Jan. 8, 1912]/W: Grant Clarke, M: Jean Schwartz. *The Purple Road* (Liberty > Casino, "The Duchess of Dantzic," Apr. 7, 1913): To Make a Hit in Par-ee/W: ?, M: William F. Peters.

1298. Herschell Burton B: Georgia. *Buck White* (George Abbott, "Hunter," Dec. 2, 1969): Beautiful Allelujah Days; Nobody Does My Thing/WM: Oscar Brown, Jr.

1299. Irving Burton (Aug. 5, 1923–) *Chu Chem* (Ritz, "Yakob," Mar. 17, 1989): What Happened, What?/W: Jim Haines, Jack Wohl, M: Mitch Leigh.

1300. Kate Burton (Sept. 10, 1957–) B: Geneva, Switzerland. Daughter of RICHARD BURTON. *Doonesbury* (Biltmore, "J.J.," Nov. 21, 1983): Another Memorable Meal; Get Together; Just One Night; Mother/W: Garry Trudeau, M: Elizabeth Swados.

1301. Miriam Burton *House of Flowers* (Alvin, "Mother," Dec. 30, 1954): Mardi Gras/ WM: Truman Capote, Harold Arlen.

1302. Richard Burton (Nov. 10, 1925–Aug. 5, 1984) B: Pontrhydyfen, S. Wales. M: actress Elizabeth Taylor. Father of KATE BURTON. Talented actor who drank too much. *Camelot* (Majestic, "King Arthur," Dec. 3, 1960): Camelot; How to Handle a Woman; I Wonder What the King Is Doing Tonight; The Jousts; What Do the Simple Folk Do?/W: Alan Jay Lerner, M: Frederick Loewe. *Camelot* (New York State, revival, "King Arthur," July 8, 1980): same as above.

1303. Robert Burton (c 1909–June 17, 1955) M: IMOGENE COCA. *Fools Rush In* (The Playhouse, revue, Dec. 25, 1934): Building Up to a Let-Down/W: Lee Brody, Norman Zeno, M: Will Irwin — Love All; Willie's Little Whistle/W: Norman Zeno, M: Will Irwin — Wicked, Unwholesome, Expensive/WM: John Rox. *New Faces of 1936* (Vanderbilt, revue, May 19, 1936): Too Too Too!/W: Everett Marcy, M: Irvin Graham — You Better Go Now [Oct. 19, 1936]/W: Bickley Reichner, M: Irvin Graham. *The Straw Hat Revue* (Ambassador, revue, Sept. 29, 1939): The Swingaroo Trio/WM: Sylvia Fine.

1304. Sarah Burton (Mar. 20, 1912–) B: London, England. *Tonight at 8:30* (National, revival, "Lavinia Featherways," Feb. 20, 1948): Music Box/WM: Noel Coward.

1305. Albert Busby *The Wedding Trip* (Broadway, "Major Vathek," Dec. 25, 1911): The Miraculous Cure/W: Harry B. Smith, M: Reginald De Koven.

1306. Betty Ann Busch *Sweethearts* (Shubert, revival, "Pauline," Jan. 21, 1947): Every Lover Must Meet His Fate; Game of Love; Sweethearts/W: Robert B. Smith, M: Victor Herbert.

1307. Mae Busch (Jan. 20, 1891–Apr. 19, 1946) B: Melbourne, Australia. A leading lady in 1920s silent films; a foil for Laurel and Hardy in the 1930s. *Over the River* (Globe, CR, "Phyllis Melba" and "Myrtle Mirabeau," Feb. 19, 1912): Chop Stick Rag/W: Grant Clarke, M: Jean Schwartz — Coontown Quartet [Mar. 25, 1912]; When There's No Light at All/WM: John L. Golden — For de Lawd's Sake, Play a Waltz/WM: Elsie Janis — The Raggety Man/W: Harry Williams, M: Egbert Van Alstyne — Ring-Ting-a-Ling/W: William Jerome, M: Jean Schwartz.

1308. Joseph Bush At this time, he was a Private in the U.S. Army. *This Is the Army* (Broadway, revue, July 4, 1942): This Is the Army, Mr. Jones/WM: Irving Berlin.

1309. Jessie Busley (Mar. 10, 1869–Apr. 20, 1950) B: Albany, NY. *The Hen-Pecks* (Broadway, CR, "Honoria Peck," Aug. 14, 1911): The Manicure Girl/W: Frederick Day, M: Jerome Kern.

1310. Anna Bussert *The Gay Hussars* (Knickerbocker, "Baroness Risa Von Marbach," July 29, 1909): The Army Directory; Dreaming of Love; Heart to Heart; O, Silver Moon! (Forgive! Forgive!)/W: Grant Stewart, M: Emmerich Kalman.

1311. Meg Bussert (Oct. 21, 1949–) B: Chicago, IL. *The Music Man* (City Center 55th Street, revival, "Marian Paroo," June 5, 1980): Goodnight, My Someone; My White Knight; Piano Lesson; Seventy-Six Trombones; Shipoopi; Till There Was You; Will I Ever Tell You?/WM: Meredith Willson. *Brigadoon* (Majestic, revival, "Fiona MacLaren," Oct. 16, 1980): Almost Like Being in Love; Come to Me, Bend to Me; From This Day On; The Heather on the Hill; There But for You Go I; Waitin' for My Dearie/W: Alan Jay Lerner, M: Frederick Loewe. *Camelot* (Winter Garden, revival, "Queen Guenevere," Nov. 15, 1981): Before I Gaze at You Again; Camelot; I Loved You Once in Silence; The Jousts; The Lusty Month of May; The Simple Joys of Maidenhood; What Do the Simple Folk Do?/W: Alan Jay Lerner, M: Frederick Loewe.

1312. Keith Buterbaugh *The Phantom of the Opera* (Majestic, CR, "Raoul, Vicomte de Chagny," c 1992): All I Ask of You; Bravo, Bravo; Little Lotte; The Mirror; Notes; Prima Donna; Raoul, I've Been There; Think of Me; Twisted Every Way; Wandering Child; Why Have You Brought Me Here/W: Charles Hart, Richard Stilgoe, M: Andrew Lloyd Webber.

1313. Ann Butler She worked with HAL PARKER in vaudeville. *Keep Kool* (Morosco > Globe > Earl Carroll, revue, May 22, 1924): Painted Rose/W: Paul Gerard Smith, M: Jack Frost.

1314. Charles Butler (c 1826–Sept. 17, 1920)

Funabashi (Casino, "Wilkinson," Jan. 6, 1908): I Walked Around/W: Vincent Rose, Ted Snyder, M: Safford Waters.

1315. Dean Butler (May 20, 1956–) B: Prince George, Canada. He played Almanzo Wilder in the popular TV series *Little House on the Prairie* (1979). *Into the Woods* (Martin Beck, CR, "Rapunzel's Prince," Mar. 7, 1989): Agony/WM: Stephen Sondheim.

1316. Etta Butler (c 1879–Jan. 7, 1903) B: San Francisco, CA. *The Liberty Belles* (Madison Square, "Margery Lee," Sept. 30, 1901): Jack O'Lantern/W: Harry B. Smith, M: Mae A. Sloane — A Little Child Like Me/W: Harry B. Smith, M: A. Baldwin Sloane.

1317. Joseph Campbell Butler *Hair* (Biltmore, CR, "Claude," Jan. 1969): Hair; I Got Life; Let the Sunshine In (The Flesh Failures); Manchester; Where Do I Go/W: Gerome Ragni, James Rado, M: Galt MacDermot.

1318. Kerry Butler B: Brooklyn, NY. *Blood Brothers* (Music Box, CR, "Miss Jones," c 1993): Take a Letter, Miss Jones/WM: Willy Russell. *Beauty and the Beast* (Palace, CR, "Belle," c 1995): Belle; Something There/W: Howard Ashman, M: Alan Menken — Home; Me; No Matter What; Transformation/W: Tim Rice, M: Alan Menken.

1319. Rhoda Butler (July 25, 1949–) B: Sanford, ME. *Goodtime Charley* (Palace, "Queen Kate," Mar. 3, 1975): History/W: Hal Hackady, M: Larry Grossman.

1320. Sam Butler, Jr. *The Gospel at Colonus* (Lunt-Fontanne, "Singer," Mar. 24, 1988): Evil; Oh Sunlight of No Light; Stop, Do Not Go On; A Voice Foretold/W: Lee Breuer, M: Bob Telson.

1321. Jennifer Butt (May 17, 1958–) B: Valparaiso, IN. *Les Miserables* (Broadway, "Mme. Thenardier," Mar. 12, 1987): Beggars at the Feast; Master of the House/W: Herbert Kretzmer, M: Claude-Michel Schonberg.

1322. Charles Butterworth (July 26, 1896–June 13, 1946) B: South Bend, IN. The comic actor who never got the girl in several dozen 1930s and 40s movies started his career as a newspaper reporter. He was known for humorous monologues. His death was due to a car accident. *Good Boy* (Hammerstein's, "Cicero Meakin," Sept. 5, 1928): I Have My Moments; I Wanna Be Loved by You; What Makes You So Wonderful?/W: Bert Kalmar, M: Harry Ruby, Herbert Stothart. *Sweet Adeline* (Hammerstein's, "Ruppert Day," Sept. 3, 1929): First Mate Martin; Naughty Boy; Spring Is Here; Take Me for a Honeymoon Ride/W: Oscar Hammerstein II,

M: Jerome Kern. *Flying Colors* (Imperial, revue, Sept. 15, 1932): All's Well; Fatal Fascination [added]; Lost in a Crowd/W: Howard Dietz, M: Arthur Schwartz. *Count Me In* (Ethel Barrymore, "Papa," Oct. 8, 1942): The Way My Ancestors Went/WM: Ann Ronell.

1323. Red Buttons (Feb. 5, 1919–) B: New York, NY. The vaudeville and TV slapstick comic won an Oscar for his role as Sgt. Kelly in the film *Sayonara* (1957). *Barefoot Boy with Cheek* (Martin Beck, "Shyster Fiscal," Apr. 3, 1947): Alice in Boogieland; There's Lots of Things You Can Do with Two (But Not with Three); We Feel Our Man Is Definitely You/W: Sylvia Dee, M: Sidney Lippman. *Hold It!* (National, "Dinky Bennett," May 5, 1948): About Face; Friendly Enemy; Fundamental Character; Hold It!/W: Sammy Lerner, M: Gerald Marks.

1324. Eddie Buzzell (Nov. 13, 1895–Jan. 11, 1985) B: Brooklyn, NY. M: ONA MUNSON, 1926-1930. A child actor with Gus Edwards' troupe, later a director. *Broadway Brevities of 1920* (Winter Garden, revue, Sept. 29, 1920): Love, Honor and Oh Baby!/W: Blair Treynor, M: Archie Gottler. *The Gingham Girl* (Earl Carroll, "John Cousins," Aug. 28, 1922): As Long as I Have You; Gingham Girl; The Wonderful Thing We Call Love; You Must Learn the Latest Dances/W: Neville Fleeson, M: Albert Von Tilzer. *No Other Girl* (Morosco, "Ananias Jones," Aug. 13, 1924): After the Curfew Rings; In the Corner of My Mind; No Other Girl; You Flew Away from the Nest/W: Bert Kalmar, M: Harry Ruby. *Sweetheart Time* (Imperial, "Dion Woodbury," Jan. 19, 1926): A Girl in Your Arms/W: Irving Caesar, M: Jay Gorney — Rue de la Paix/W: Ballard Macdonald, M: Walter Donaldson. *The Desert Song* (Casino, "Bennie Kidd," Nov. 30, 1926): It; Let's Have a Love Affair; One Good Man Gone Wrong/W: Otto Harbach, Oscar Hammerstein II, M: Sigmund Romberg. *Good Boy* (Hammerstein's, "Walter Meakin," Sept. 5, 1928): Good Boy; Some Sweet Someone/W: Bert Kalmar, M: Harry Ruby, Herbert Stothart. *Lady Fingers* (Vanderbilt > Liberty, "Jim Bailey," Jan. 31, 1929): Ga-Ga!/W: Edward Eliscu, M: Joseph Meyer.

1325. John Byam *The Midnight Rounders of 1920* (Century roof, revue, July 12, 1920): Heartbreakers; My Lady of the Cameo [Oct. 4, 1920]; O You Heavenly Body/W: Alfred Bryan, M: Jean Schwartz. *Make It Snappy* (Winter Garden, revue, Apr. 13, 1922): Blossom Time; Bouquet of Girls; Good-Bye Main Street/W: Harold Atteridge, M: Jean Schwartz. *Earl Carroll's Vanities of 1923* (Earl Carroll, revue, CR, Dec. 17,

1923): Chasing Little Rainbows; Cretonne Girl; Mr. Wagner's Wedding March; When the Snowflakes Fall/WM: Earl Carroll. *My Girl* (Vanderbilt, CR, "Harold Gray," Mar. 16, 1925): Before the Dawn; Desert Isle; They Say/W: Harlan Thompson, M: Harry Archer. *Bye, Bye, Bonnie* (Ritz > Cosmopolitan, "Richard Van Buren," Jan. 13, 1927): In My Arms Again; Love Is Like a Blushing Rose; When You Get to Congress/W: Neville Fleeson, M: Albert Von Tilzer. *Ned Wayburn's Gambols* (Knickerbocker, revue, Jan. 15, 1929): Indian Prayer; March Gypsies; The Palm Beach Walk; Savannah Stomp; Sweet Old Fashioned Waltz/W: Morrie Ryskind, M: Walter G. Samuels. *A Night in Venice* (Shubert, "Harry De Costa," May 21, 1929): The Stork Don't Come Around Anymore/WM: Betty Morse Laidlaw — Strolling on the Lido (Lido Shores)/W: J. Keirn Brennan, Moe Jaffe, M: Lee David, Maurie Rubens.

1326. Irene Byatt *South Pacific* (Music Theater of Lincoln Center, revival, "Bloody Mary," June 12, 1967): Bali Ha'i; Happy Talk/W: Oscar Hammerstein II, M: Richard Rodgers.

1327. Patricia Bybell *Allegro* (Majestic, "Addie," Oct. 10, 1947): Money Isn't Everything/W: Oscar Hammerstein II, M: Richard Rodgers. *Alive and Kicking* (Winter Garden, revue, Jan. 17, 1950): One! Two! Three!/W: Ray Golden, Paul Francis Webster, M: Sonny Burke — A World of Strangers/W: Ray Golden, Paul Francis Webster, M: Sammy Fain.

1328. Lehman Byck *The Manhatters* (Selwyn, revue, Aug. 3, 1927): Close Your Eyes; Sailor Boy; Too Bad/W: George S. Oppenheimer, M: Alfred Nathan.

1329. Lyman Byck *Americana of 1926* (Belmont, revue, July 26, 1926): Thanks Awful/W: Sam M. Lewis, Joe Young, M: Con Conrad — Why Do Ya Roll Those Eyes?/W: Morrie Ryskind, M: Phil Charig.

1330. Karen Byers *Jesus Christ Superstar* (Paramount Madison Square Garden, revival, "Maid by the Fire," Jan. 17, 1995): Peter's Denial/W: Tim Rice, M: Andrew Lloyd Webber.

1331. Carolyn Byrd B: Paterson, NJ. *Bubbling Brown Sugar* (ANTA, "Carolyn" and "Gospel Lady" and "Female Nightclub Singer," Mar. 2, 1976): His Eye Is on the Sparrow; Swing Low, Sweet Chariot/WM: trad. — Stormy Monday Blues/WM: Earl Hines, Billy Eckstine, Bob Crowder.

1332. Debra Byrd B: Cleveland, OH. *The Human Comedy* (Royale, "Beautiful Music," Apr. 5, 1984): Beautiful Music; When I Am Lost/W: William Dumaresq, M: Galt MacDermot.

1333. Joe Byrd *Lucky Sambo* (Colonial, "Rufus Johnson," June 6, 1925): If You Can't Bring It, You've Got to Send It; Runnin'/WM: Porter Grainger, Freddie Johnson.

1334. Gaylea Byrne B: Baltimore, MD. *The Music Man* (New York City Center, revival, "Marian Paroo," June 16, 1965): Goodnight, My Someone; My White Knight; Piano Lesson; Seventy-Six Trombones; Shipoopi; Till There Was You; Will I Ever Tell You?/WM: Meredith Willson. *Man of La Mancha* (ANTA Washington Square, revival, CR, "Aldonza," May 5, 1969): The Abduction; Aldonza; The Combat; Dulcinea; It's All the Same; Knight of the Woeful Countenance (The Dubbing); What Do You Want of Me?/W: Joe Darion, M: Mitch Leigh.

1335. Gypsy Byrne *Just a Minute* (Ambassador > Century, "Helen," Oct. 8, 1928): Heigh-Ho Cheerio; You'll Kill 'Em/W: Walter O'Keefe, M: Harry Archer.

1336. Richard Byrne *The Most Happy Fella* (New York State, revival, "Pasquale," Sept. 4, 1991): Abbondanza; Benvenuta/WM: Frank Loesser.

1337. Betty Byron *Babes in Toyland* (Jolson, revival, "Jane," Dec. 23, 1929): Go to Sleep, Slumber Deep; I Can't Do the Sum/W: Glen MacDonough, M: Victor Herbert. *Babes in Toyland* (Imperial, revival, "Jane," Dec. 22, 1930): same as above.

1338. George Byron *New Faces of 1936* (Vanderbilt, revue, May 19, 1936): Love Is a Dancer/W: Jean Sothern, M: Muriel Pollock — Off to the Deacon/W: June Sillman, M: Robert Sour — Tonight's the Night/W: June Sillman, M: Alex Fogarty — You Better Go Now [May 25, 1935]/W: Bickley Reichner, M: Irvin Graham.

1339. Helen Byron *The Wizard of Oz* (Majestic, "Cynthia Cynch," Jan. 20, 1903): Niccolo's Piccolo/W: Glen MacDonough, M: A. Baldwin Sloane — The Witch Behind the Moon/W: Louis Weslyn, M: Charles Albert. *Madame Troubadour* (39th Street, CR, "Juliette," Dec. 12, 1910): Don't Be Rash; Tra-la-la, Etcetera/W: Joseph W. Herbert, M: Felix Albini.

1340. Henrietta Byron (?–June 1, 1924) *Sally, Irene and Mary* (Casino, "1st Lady Dresser," Sept. 4, 1922): Do You Remember?/W: Raymond Klages, M: J. Fred Coots.

1341. Lorna Byron *The Red Mill* (Ziegfeld, revival, "Juliana," Oct. 16, 1945): Because You're You; The Legend of the Mill; Wedding Bells (Wedding Chorus)/W: Henry Blossom, Forman Brown, M: Victor Herbert.

1342. Christophe Caballero *Jerome Robbins' Broadway* (Imperial, revue, Feb. 26, 1989): Somewhere/W: Stephen Sondheim, M: Leonard Bernstein.

1343. Roxann Cabellero *A Chorus Line* (Shubert, CR, "Diana," Oct. 1982/Jan. 1983/c 1985): Nothing; What I Did for Love/W: Edward Kleban, M: Marvin Hamlisch.

1344. Christopher Cable *Jesus Christ Superstar* (Longacre, revival, "Caiaphas," Nov. 23, 1977): The Arrest; Damned for All Time; Hosanna; Judas' Death; This Jesus Must Die; Trial Before Pilate/W: Tim Rice, M: Andrew Lloyd Webber.

1345. Ethel Cadman (Jan. 5, 1886–?) B: Hill Top, Staffordshire, England. *The Arcadians* (Liberty > Knickerbocker, "Sombra," Jan. 17, 1910): Arcady Is Ever Young; The Pipes of Pan Are Calling/W: Arthur Wimperis, M: Lionel Monckton — The Joy of Life; Light Is My Heart/W: Arthur Wimperis, M: Howard Talbot. *The Three Romeos* (Globe, "Nancy Mallory," Nov. 13, 1911): Humpty and Dumpty; In the Spring It's Nice to Have Someone to Love You; The Lily and the Rose/W: R.H. Burnside, M: Raymond Hubbell.

1346. Sid Caesar (Sept. 8, 1922–) B: Yonkers, NY. An all-time comedy great, star of TV's *Your Show of Shows* (1950) and *Caesar's Hour* (1954). *Make Mine Manhattan* (Broadhurst, revue, Jan. 15, 1948): The Good Old Days/W: Arnold B. Horwitt, Ted Fetter, M: Richard Lewine. *Little Me* (Lunt-Fontanne, "Noble Eggleston" and "Mr. Pinchley" and "Val du Val" and "Fred Poitrine" and "Prince Cherney," Nov. 17, 1962/June 13, 1963): Boom-Boom (Le Grand Boom-Boom); Deep Down Inside; I Love You (As Much as I Am Able); The Prince's Farewell (Goodbye); Real Live Girl/W: Carolyn Leigh, M: Cy Coleman.

1347. James Cagney (July 17, 1899–Mar. 30, 1986) B: New York, NY. A long career from vaudeville to the screen, as hoofer and singer and tough guy. His portrayal of GEORGE M. COHAN in *Yankee Doodle Dandy* (1942) was one of his best. *The Grand Street Follies of 1929* (Booth, revue, "Harlequin," May 1, 1929): I Need You So/W: David Goldberg, Howard Dietz, M: Arthur Schwartz.

1348. Jack Cagwin *The Melting of Molly* (Broadhurst, CR, "John Moore" and "Dr. Moore," Jan. 27, 1919): Darling; Lodger; Oh Doctor, Doctor; Reminiscence/W: Cyrus D. Wood, M: Sigmund Romberg. *Hello, Alexander* (44th Street, "Lieut. Jack Winslow," Oct. 7, 1919): Give Me the South All the Time; Old Fashioned Rag; Two Lips from Georgia; Up in the Air/W: Alfred Bryan, M: Jean Schwartz —

Tell Me (Why Nights Are Lonely)/W: J. Will Callahan, M: Max Kortlander.

1349. Alfred Cahill *The Tourists* (Majestic, CR, "Loofah," Sept. 10, 1906): Keep on Doing Something/W: R.H. Burnside, M: Gustave Kerker.

1350. Marie Cahill (Feb. 7, 1870–Aug. 23, 1933) B: Brooklyn, NY. Popular musical comedienne known as a "coon shouter" due to the way she belted out a tune. To the anger of some, most notably composer Victor Herbert, she liked to interpolate songs of others into any role she played. *Excelsior, Jr.* (Olympia > Broadway, "Blanche Calve Santootsie," Nov. 29, 1895): I Love You, Evaline/W: R.A. Barnet, M: George Lowell Tracy. *The Gold Bug* (Casino, "Lady Patty Larceny," Sept. 21, 1896): When I First Began to Marry, Years Ago/W: Glen MacDonough, M: Victor Herbert. *Monte Carlo* (Herald Square, "Bertie Galatine," Mar. 21, 1898): If I Only Knew the Way; The Sisters Galatine/W: Harry Greenbank, M: Howard Talbot. *The Wild Rose* (Knickerbocker, "Vera Von Lahn," May 5, 1902): Nancy Brown (A Bucolic Wail)/WM: Clifton Crawford. *Sally in Our Alley* (Broadway, "Sally," Aug. 29, 1902): Under the Bamboo Tree (If You Lak-a Me Lak I Lak-a You)/W: Bob Cole, M: J. Rosamond Johnson. *Nancy Brown* (Bijou, "Nancy Brown," Feb. 16, 1903): Congo Love Song; Cupid's Ramble/W: Bob Cole, James Weldon Johnson, M: J. Rosamond Johnson — The Glow Worm and the Moth/W: Frederick Ranken, M: Max S. Witt — The Katy-did, the Cricket and the Frog; Under the Bamboo Tree (If You Lak-a Me Lak I Lak-a You)/WM: Bob Cole, J. Rosamond Johnson — Navajo Jo/W: Harry Williams, M: Egbert Van Alstyne — Sweet Nellie Wood [Apr. 27, 1903]/W: Vincent Bryan, M: James Mullen — You Can't Fool All the People All the Time/W: Frederick Ranken, M: Henry Hadley. *It Happened in Nordland* (Lew Fields, "Katherine Peepfogle," Dec. 5, 1904): Any Old Tree/WM: Dick Temple — Bandanna Land; Beatrice Barefacts; Commanderess-in-Chief; The Coon Banshee/W: Glen MacDonough, M: Victor Herbert — My Hindoo Man/W: Harry Williams, M: Egbert Van Alstyne. *Moonshine* (Liberty, "Molly Moonshine," Oct. 30, 1905): The Conjure Man/WM: James Weldon Johnson, Bob Cole — Don't Be What You Ain't; Friendship/W: George V. Hobart, Edwin Milton Royle, M: Silvio Hein — Foolish; How Happy Would This Chappie Be; (They Never Do That) In Our Set/W: George V. Hobart, M: Silvio Hein — Robinson Crusoe's Isle/WM: Benjamin Hapgood Burt. *Marrying Mary* (Daly's, "Mary Montgomery," Aug. 27, 1906): He's a Cousin of Mine/W: Cecil Mack, M: Chris Smith, Silvio Hein — The Hottentot Love Song; Mr. Cupid/W: Benjamin Hapgood Burt, M: Silvio Hein. *The Boys and Betty* (Wallack's, "Betty Barbeau," Nov. 2, 1908): Auf Wiedersehn; I Love to Go Shopping; A Little Further; Marie Cahill's Arab Love Song/W: George V. Hobart, M: Silvio Hein — She Was a Dear Little Girl/W: Irving Berlin, M: Ted Snyder — Take Plenty of Shoes/W: Will D. Cobb, M: Melville Gideon. *Judy Forgot* (Broadway, "Judy Evans," Oct. 6, 1910): Good Morning Judge/WM: John L. Golden, Silvio Hein, Avery Hopwood — The Quarrel; Students' Serenade; Thinky Thanky Thunk; Turkish Love Song/W: Avery Hopwood, M: Silvio Hein — Whoop 'er Up (with a Whoop-La-La)/W: Andrew B. Sterling, M: Will Marion Cook. *90 in the Shade* (Knickerbocker, "Polly Bainbridge," Jan. 25, 1915): Human Nature/WM: ? — Lonely in Town/WM: Clare Kummer — My Lady's Dress; Whistling Dan/W: Harry B. Smith, M: Jerome Kern — My Mindanao Chocolate Soldier/W: Clare Kummer, M: Henri Christine — The Triangle/W: Guy Bolton, M: Jerome Kern. *Merry-Go-Round* (Klaw, revue, May 31, 1927): Gabriel Is Blowing His Horn/W: Howard Dietz, Morrie Ryskind, M: Henry Souvaine, Jay Gorney.

1351. Larry Cahn (Dec. 19, 1955–) B: Nassau, NY. *The Music Man* (City Center 55th Street, revival, "Ewart Dunlop," June 5, 1980): It's You; Lida Rose; Sincere/WM: Meredith Willson. *Guys and Dolls* (Martin Beck, revival, CR, "Rusty Charlie," June 1993): Fugue for Tinhorns/WM: Frank Loesser. *Guys and Dolls* (Martin Beck, revival, CR, "Nicely-Nicely Johnson," c 1993): Fugue for Tinhorns; Guys and Dolls; The Oldest Established; Sit Down, You're Rockin' the Boat/WM: Frank Loesser.

1352. Billie Cain *Dixie to Broadway* (Broadhurst, revue, Oct. 29, 1924): Jazz Time Came from the South; Trottin' to the Land of Cotton Melodies/W: Grant Clarke, Roy Turk, M: George W. Meyer, Arthur Johnston.

1353. John E. Cain *Aladdin, Jr.* (Broadway, "Chow Chow," Apr. 8, 1895): Beauteous Widow Bohea; The Stars Alone Can Tell; Women, Wine and Song/W: J. Cheever Goodwin, M: W.H. Batchelor, Jesse Williams.

1354. Michael-Demby Cain B: Mississippi. *Honky Tonk Nights* (Biltmore, "Montgomery Boyd," Aug. 7, 1986): Lily of the Alley; Tapaholics; Withered Irish Rose/W: Ralph Allen, David Campbell, M: Michael Valenti.

1355. Sibol Cain *Fast and Furious* (New

Yorker, revue, Sept. 15, 1931): East Coast Blues/ WM: ?.

1356. Viola Cain *The Riviera Girl* (New Amsterdam, "Claire Ferrier," Sept. 24, 1917): Man, Man, Man; There'll Never Be Another Girl Like Daisy/W: P.G. Wodehouse, M: Emmerich Kalman.

1357. Georgia Caine (Oct. 30, 1876–Apr. 4, 1964) B: San Francisco, CA. *The Girl from Paris* (Herald Square, CR, "Mlle. Julie Bon-Bon," Sept. 20, 1897): Cock-a-doodle; I'm All the Way from Gay Paree; It's a Good Thing to Have; The Proper Air; Reste La; Tweedledum and Tweedledee/W: George Dance, M: Ivan Caryll. *The Girl from Paris* (Wallack's, revival, "Mlle. Julie Bon-Bon," Jan. 17, 1898): I'm All the Way from Gay Paree/W: George Dance, M: Ivan Caryll. *A Reign of Error* (Victoria, "Mlle. Georgie Gelee," Mar. 2, 1899): Bonnie Little Johnnie; Mlle. Gelee/W: ?, M: Maurice Levi. *Rogers Brothers in Wall Street* (Victoria, "Georgette Jollier," Sept. 18, 1899): Gay Georgette; The Summer Man/W: ?, M: Maurice Levi. *Foxy Quiller* (Broadway, "Polly Prime," Nov. 5, 1900): Poor Shepherds We/W: Harry B. Smith, M: Reginald De Koven. *The Messenger Boy* (Daly's, "Nora," Sept. 16, 1901): Ask Papa/W: Percy Greenbank, M: Ivan Caryll. *Peggy from Paris* (Wallack's, "Peggy Plummer," Sept. 10, 1903): Gay Fleurette; When He's Not Near/W: George Ade, M: William Lorraine. *The Medal and the Maid* (Broadway, CR, "Miss Ventnor," Feb. 8, 1904): Frills Upon Their Petticoats; In My Curriculum; Publicity/W: Charles H. Taylor, M: Sidney Jones. *The Sho-Gun* (Wallack's, "Omee-Omi," Oct. 10, 1904): Love You Must Be Blind; The Man She'll Never Meet/W: George Ade, M: Gustav Luders. *The Earl and the Girl* (Casino, "Elphin Haye," Nov. 4, 1905): How'd You Like to Spoon with Me?/W: Edward Laska, M: Jerome Kern — I Would Like to Marry You [Jan. 15, 1906]/W: Edward Laska, M: Tom Kelly — One Night Only/W: Percy Greenbank, M: Ivan Caryll. *The Rich Mr. Hoggenheimer* (Wallack's, "Flora Fair," Oct. 22, 1906): The Bagpipe Serenade/WM: Jerome Kern — Be Demure/W: Harry B. Smith, M: Ludwig Englander — Don't You Want a Paper, Dearie? (Newspaper Song)/ WM: Paul West, Jerome Kern — The World Is a Toy Shop/W: A. Baldwin Sloane, M: Ludwig Englander. *Miss Hook of Holland* (Criterion, "Mina," Dec. 31, 1907): The Flying Dutchman; A Pink Petty from Peter/WM: Paul Rubens. *The Merry Widow* (New Amsterdam, CR, "Sonia," Aug. 31, 1908/Oct. 5, 1908): I Love You So (The Merry Widow Waltz); In Marsovia; The Silly Cavalier; Vilia/W: Adrian Ross, M: Franz Lehar. *The Motor Girl* (Lyric, "Dorothy Dare," June 15, 1909): All the World Loves a Lover; The Belle of the Dairy Lunch; Finesse; Just Suppose You Loved Me; The Motor Girl/W: Charles J. Campbell, Ralph Skinner, M: Julian Edwards — Coffee and Cheese/W: Charles J. Campbell, M: Julian Edwards. *Madame Troubadour* (Lyric > 39th Street, "Juliette," Oct. 10, 1910): Don't Be Rash; Tra-la-la, Etcetera/W: Joseph W. Herbert, M: Felix Albini. *The Three Romeos* (Globe, "Gussie Gibson," Nov. 13, 1911): Divorce; I've Been Looking for a Girl Like You; Mary Carey; A Matter of Experience/W: R.H. Burnside, M: Raymond Hubbell. *Adele* (Longacre > Harris, "Mme. Myrianne de Neuville," Aug. 28, 1913): The Clock Is Striking Ten; A Honeymoon with You; Like Swallow Flying; Matter of Opinion; A Waste of Time to Plan; Yours for Me and Mine for You/WM: Edward A. Paulton, Adolf Philipp, Jean Briquet. *Oh, My Dear!* (Princess > 39th Street, "Mrs. Rockett," Nov. 27, 1918): Come Where Nature Calls/W: P.G. Wodehouse, M: Louis A. Hirsch. *Mary* (Knickerbocker, "Mrs. Keene," Oct. 18, 1920): The Love Nest/W: Otto Harbach, M: Louis A. Hirsch. *The O'Brien Girl* (Liberty, "Mrs. Drexel," Oct. 3, 1921): Give, Give/W: Otto Harbach, M: Louis A. Hirsch. *Be Yourself!* (Sam H. Harris, "Grandma Brennan," Sept. 3, 1924): Grandma's a Flapper Too; Life in Town/W: Addison Burkhardt, M: Max Hoffmann.

1358. Gladys Caire *The Mimic World* (Casino, revue, "Polly," July 9, 1908): Miss Hook of Holland/WM: Paul Rubens.

1359. Angus Cairns (Mar. 29, 1910–Oct. 14, 1975) B: Fitchburg, MA. *Paint Your Wagon* (Shubert, "Edgar Crocker," Nov. 12, 1951): I'm on My Way/W: Alan Jay Lerner, M: Frederick Loewe.

1360. Mae Cairns *Innocent Eyes* (Winter Garden, revue, CR, July 7, 1924): Love Is Like a Pinwheel/W: Harold Atteridge, Tot Seymour, M: Sigmund Romberg.

1361. Jack Caito *Artists and Models of 1925* (Winter Garden, revue, June 24, 1925): Take a Little Baby Home with You/W: Clifford Grey, M: J. Fred Coots.

1362. Eleanor Calbes (Feb. 20, 1940–) B: Aparri, Philippines. *South Pacific* (Music Theater of Lincoln Center, revival, "Liat," June 12, 1967): Bali Ha'i; Happy Talk/W: Oscar Hammerstein II, M: Richard Rodgers. *The King and I* (New York City Center, revival, "Tuptim," May 23, 1968): I Have Dreamed; My Lord and Master; We Kiss in a Shadow/W: Oscar Hammerstein II, M: Richard Rodgers. *Lovely Ladies, Kind Gentlemen* (Majestic, "Lotus Blossom," Dec. 28, 1970): Geisha; Simple Word/WM: Franklin Underwood, Stan Freeman.

1363. E.J. Caldwell *The Yankee Girl* (Herald Square, "Pedro," Feb. 10, 1910): Whoop Daddy Ooden Dooden Day/W: George V. Hobart, M: Silvio Hein.

1364. Gladys Caldwell *The Girl from Home* (Globe, "Lucy Sheridan," May 3, 1920): By the Palmest Tree; Manana; Nine Little Missionaries/W: Frank Craven, M: Silvio Hein. *Tip Top* (Globe, revue, Oct. 5, 1920): Wonderful Girl, Wonderful Boy/W: Anne Caldwell, M: Ivan Caryll. *Bombo* (Al Jolson > Winter Garden, "Patricia Downing" and "Princess Isabella," Oct. 6, 1921): In a Curio Shop; In the Way Off There/W: Harold Atteridge, M: Sigmund Romberg.

1365. Neal Caldwell *The Garrick Gaieties of 1930* (Guild, revue, return engagement, Oct. 16, 1930): Johnny Wanamaker/W: Paul James, M: Kay Swift — Rose of Arizona; The Three Musketeers/W: Lorenz Hart, M: Richard Rodgers.

1366. Mickey Calin (Nov. 22, 1935–) B: Philadelphia, PA. *West Side Story* (Winter Garden, "Riff," Sept. 26, 1957): Cool/W: Stephen Sondheim, M: Leonard Bernstein.

1367. Michael Calkins (Apr. 27, 1948–) B: Chicago, IL. *Annie* (Alvin, "Rooster Hannigan," Sept. 19, 1982): Easy Street/W: Martin Charnin, M: Charles Strouse.

1368. Catherine Call *The Duke of Duluth* (Majestic, "Jhansi," Sept. 11, 1905): My Dainty Dresden Shepherdess; Nicodemus/W: George Broadhurst, M: Max S. Witt.

1369. John Call (Nov. 3, 1915–Apr. 3, 1973) B: Philadelphia, PA. *Pickwick* (46th Street, "Tracy Tupman," Oct. 4, 1965): A Bit of a Character; I Like the Company of Men; The Pickwickians/W: Leslie Bricusse, M: Cyril Ornadel. *A Time for Singing* (Broadway, "Dai Bando," May 21, 1966): What a Party/WM: Gerald Freedman, John Morris.

1370. Charles (Chuck) Callahan (Aug. 7, 1891–Nov. 12, 1964) *The Royal Vagabond* (Cohan and Harris, "The Queen's Guard," Feb. 17, 1919): Here Come the Soldiers/WM: George M. Cohan — Messenger Number and Dance/WM: George M. Cohan, Anselm Goetzl.

1371. Ethel Callahan *Broadway Brevities of 1920* (Winter Garden, revue, Sept. 29, 1920): We've Got the Stage Door Blues/W: Bert Kalmar, M: Harry Ruby.

1372. George W. Callahan *The Motor Girl* (Lyric, "Mynheer Alehoff, Burgomaster of Saar-

daam," June 15, 1909): Prosit/W: Charles J. Campbell, M: Julian Edwards. *Betsy* (Herald Square, "Augustus Tutwiler," Dec. 11, 1911): Snoop, Snoop/W: Will B. Johnstone, M: Alexander Johnstone. *Kitty Darlin'* (Casino, "Col. Kimby McFinton," Nov. 7, 1917): Dear Old Dublin/W: P.G. Wodehouse, M: Rudolf Friml.

1373. Marie Callahan *Ziegfeld Follies of 1923* (New Amsterdam, revue, Oct. 20, 1923): I'm Bugs Over You/W: Gene Buck, M: Dave Stamper. *Kid Boots* (Earl Carroll, "Jane Martin," Dec. 31, 1923): The Cake-Eaters' Ball; Let's Do and Say We Didn't/W: Joseph McCarthy, M: Harry Tierney. *The New Moon* (Imperial > Casino, "Julie," Sept. 19, 1928): Gorgeous Alexander; Love Is Quite a Simple Thing; The Trial; Try Her Out at Dances/W: Oscar Hammerstein II, M: Sigmund Romberg.

1374. William (Bill) Callahan (Aug. 23, 1925–Mar. 18, 1981) B: New York, NY. The dancer, actor, business executive, was found, apparently murdered, in a Wisconsin nature preserve. *Something for the Boys* (Alvin, "Corp. Burns," Jan. 7, 1943): Hey, Good Lookin'/WM: Cole Porter. *Call Me Mister* (National > Plymouth, revue, Apr. 18, 1946): Call Me Mister; A Home of Our Own/WM: Harold Rome. *As the Girls Go* (Winter Garden > Broadway, "Kenny Wellington," Nov. 13, 1948): I Got Lucky in the Rain; Nobody's Heart but Mine; Rock, Rock, Rock!; You Say the Nicest Things, Baby/W: Harold Adamson, M: Jimmy McHugh. *Two's Company* (Alvin, revue, Dec. 15, 1952): Theater Is a Lady/W: Ogden Nash, M: Vernon Duke.

1375. Alexander Callam *Boom-Boom* (Casino, CR, "Tony Smith," Feb. 25, 1929): What Could I Do?/W: Mann Holiner, J. Keirn Brennan, M: Werner Janssen. *The Student Prince* (Majestic, revival, "Capt. Tamitz," Jan. 29, 1931): Just We Two/W: Dorothy Donnelly, M: Sigmund Romberg.

1376. Christopher (Chris) Callan (July 14, 1944–) B: Fresno, CA. *1776* (46th Street, CR, "Martha Jefferson," July 4, 1971): He Plays the Violin/WM: Sherman Edwards. *The Desert Song* (Uris, revival, "Margo Bonvalet," Sept. 5, 1973): The Desert Song; French Military Marching Song; I Want a Kiss; One Alone; Romance/W: Otto Harbach, Oscar Hammerstein II, M: Sigmund Romberg — The Sabre Song; Then You Will Know/W: Otto Harbach, Oscar Hammerstein II, Frank Mandel, M: Sigmund Romberg. *Fiddler on the Roof* (Winter Garden, revival, "Hodel," Dec. 28, 1976): Far from the Home I Love; Matchmaker, Matchmaker; Now I Have

Everything/W: Sheldon Harnick, M: Jerry Bock.

1377. Liz Callaway (Apr. 13, 1961–) B: Chicago, IL. *Baby* (Ethel Barrymore, "Lizzie Fields," Dec. 4, 1983): Baby, Baby; I Want It All; The Ladies Singin' Their Song; The Story Goes On; Two People in Love; We Start Today; What Could Be Better?/W: Richard Maltby, Jr., M: David Shire. *The Three Musketeers* (Broadway, revival, "Lady Constance Bonacieux," Nov. 11, 1984): Ma Belle/W: Clifford Grey, M: Rudolf Friml — Only a Rose/W: Brian Hooker, M: Rudolf Friml. *Miss Saigon* (Broadway, "Ellen," Apr. 11, 1991): The Confrontation; I Still Believe; Now That I've Seen Her; Room 317/W: Richard Maltby, Jr., Alain Boublil, M: Claude-Michel Schonberg. *Cats* (Winter Garden, CR, "Grizabella," May 3, 1993): Grizabella, the Glamour Cat/W: T.S. Eliot, M: Andrew Lloyd Webber — Memory/W: Trevor Nunn, based on T.S. Eliot, M: Andrew Lloyd Webber.

1378. Betty Callish *The Laughing Husband* (Knickerbocker, "Hella Bruckner," Feb. 2, 1914): Away from Thee; Go to Paris or Vienna; Little Miss Understood; Silken Screen; Telephone Duet/W: Arthur Wimperis, M: Edmund Eysler — Love Is Like a Violin/W: Harry B. Smith, M: Jerome Kern.

1379. Cab Calloway (Dec. 24, 1907–Nov. 18, 1994) B: Rochester, NY. Father of CHRIS CALLOWAY. Famous band leader, singer and composer, known as the King of Hi-De-Ho. Appearing on radio and TV, in nightclubs and films, he made scat singing a major feature of his work. His theme song was "Minnie the Moocher," which he wrote with Clarence Gaskill and Irving Mills in 1931, and introduced at the Cotton Club in New York. *Hot Chocolates* (Hudson, revue, CR): Ain't Misbehavin'/W: Andy Razaf, M: Fats Waller, Harry Brooks. *Porgy and Bess* (Ziegfeld, revival, "Sportin' Life," Mar. 10, 1953): I Ain't Got No Shame; It Ain't Necessarily So; There's a Boat Dat's Leavin' Soon for New York/W: Ira Gershwin, M: George Gershwin — A Woman Is a Sometime Thing/W: DuBose Heyward, M: George Gershwin. *Hello, Dolly!* (St. James, CR, "Horace Vandergelder," Nov. 12, 1967): Before the Parade Passes By/WM: Lee Adams, Charles Strouse, Jerry Herman — Hello, Dolly!; It Takes a Woman; So Long, Dearie/WM: Jerry Herman — Motherhood/WM: Bob Merrill, Jerry Herman. *The Pajama Game* (Lunt-Fontanne, revival, "Hines," Dec. 9, 1973): I'll Never Be Jealous Again; The Pajama Game; Think of the Time I Save/WM: Richard Adler, Jerry Ross.

1380. Chris Calloway Singer and actress, daughter of CAB CALLOWAY, with whom she performed all over the world. *Hello, Dolly!* (St. James, CR, "Minnie Fay," Nov. 12, 1967): Dancing/WM: Jerry Herman — Elegance; Motherhood/WM: Bob Merrill, Jerry Herman.

1381. Harriett Calloway *Blackbirds of 1928* (Eltinge, revue, CR, May 27, 1929): Bandanna Babies; Diga Diga Doo; Here Comes My Blackbird; I Must Have That Man!/W: Dorothy Fields, M: Jimmy McHugh.

1382. Northern J. Calloway (c 1949–Jan. 9, 1990) B: New York, NY. *The Me Nobody Knows* (Helen Hayes, "Lloyd," Dec. 18, 1970): Black; The Horse; Jail-Life Walk; War Babies; What Happens to Life/W: Will Holt, M: Gary William Friedman. *Pippin* (Imperial, CR, "Leading Player," Feb. 18, 1974/May 24, 1976): Glory; On the Right Track; Simple Joys/WM: Stephen Schwartz.

1383. Alex Calm *Sidewalks of New York* (Knickerbocker, "Izzy," Oct. 3, 1927): Way Down Town/W: Eddie Dowling, M: James F. Hanley.

1384. Annette Calud (Nov. 1963–) B: Milwaukee, WI. *Miss Saigon* (Broadway, CR, "Kim"): Back in Town; The Ceremony; The Guilt Inside Your Head; I Still Believe; I'd Give My Life for You; The Last Night of the World; Little God of My Heart; The Movie in My Mind; Please; Room 317; Sun and Moon; You Will Not Touch Him/W: Richard Maltby, Jr., Alain Boublil, M: Claude-Michel Schonberg.

1385. Joe Calvan *A Tree Grows in Brooklyn* (Alvin, "Allie," Apr. 19, 1951): Look Who's Dancing/W: Dorothy Fields, M: Arthur Schwartz.

1386. Margaret Calvert *Funabashi* (Casino, "Kitty," Jan. 6, 1908): Boo-Ra-Boo; A Little Japan Lady/WM: Safford Waters.

1387. Henry Calvin (May 25, 1918–Oct. 6, 1975) B: Dallas, TX. He was Sgt. Garcia in the TV Western series *Zorro* (1957). *The Chocolate Soldier* (Century, revival, "Massakroff," Mar. 12, 1947): Seek the Spy/W: Stanislaus Stange, M: Oscar Straus. *Happy as Larry* (Coronet, "5th Tailor," Jan. 6, 1950): And So He Died; The Dirty Dog; Double Murder, Double Death; Give the Doctor the Best in the House; He's a Bold Rogue; Oh, Mrs. Larry; Without a Stitch/W: Donagh MacDonagh, M: Mischa Portnoff, Wesley Portnoff. *Kismet* (Ziegfeld, "The Wazir of Police," Dec. 3, 1953): And This Is My Beloved; Not Since Ninevah; Was I Wazir?/WM: Robert Wright, George Forrest. *Kismet* (New York State, revival, "The Wazir of Police," June 22, 1965): same as above.

1388. Dorothy Cameron *Ned Wayburn's Town Topics* (Century, revue, "Rosie Century," Sept. 23, 1915): It's the Gown That Makes the Girl/WM: ?.

1389. Frances Cameron (Oct. 23, 1886–?) B: New York, NY. *Two Little Brides* (Casino, "Honoka," Apr. 23, 1912): Are We Widows, Wives or What?; I Like All Girls; Meet Me at Eight in the Hall (The Letter Song)/W: Arthur Anderson, M: Gustave Kerker. *The Count of Luxembourg* (New Amsterdam, "Juliette," Sept. 16, 1912): A Carnival for Life; In Society/W: Adrian Ross, M: Franz Lehar — Land of Make Believe; Love Spats/W: ?, M: Franz Lehar. *His Little Widows* (Astor, "Blanche Hale," Apr. 30, 1917): I'm Keeping My Love a Secret/W: Rida Johnson Young, M: William Schroeder — In Cabaret-Land; Johnnie Come Follow Me/W: William Cary Duncan, M: William Schroeder. *Sometime* (Shubert > Casino, "Sylvia De Forrest," Oct. 4, 1918): Beautiful Night; Keep on Smiling; The Tune You Can't Forget/W: Rida Johnson Young, M: Rudolf Friml. *A Lonely Romeo* (Shubert > Casino, "Mazie Gay," June 10, 1919): Don't Do Anything Till You Hear from Me/W: Robert B. Smith, M: Malvin F. Franklin — Save a Little Daylight for Me; Wait for Me/W: Robert B. Smith, M: Robert Hood Bowers — Will o' Wisp/W: Robert B. Smith, M: Malvin F. Franklin, Otis Spencer. *Afgar* (Central, "Isilda," Nov. 8, 1920): Ceremony of Veils; Rose of Seville; Sunshine Valley/W: Douglas Furber, M: Charles Cuvillier.

1390. Grace Cameron (Aug. 1, 1879–?) B: Storm Lake, IA. *The Viceroy* (Knickerbocker, "Beatrice," Apr. 9, 1900): By This Sweet Token; On My Nuptial Day; The Robin and the Rose/W: Harry B. Smith, M: Victor Herbert. *Foxy Quiller* (Broadway, "Daphne," Nov. 5, 1900): Winding, Winding; Youth Is the Golden Age/W: Harry B. Smith, M: Reginald De Koven. *Piff! Paff!! Pouf!!!* (Casino, "Cora Melon," Apr. 2, 1904): Since Dolly Dimples Made a Hit (Dolly Dimples); We Really Ought to Be Married/W: William Jerome, M: Jean Schwartz.

1391. Hugh Cameron (May 15, 1879–Nov. 9, 1941) B: Duluth, MN. *Hanky-Panky* (Broadway, "Sir J. Rufus Wallingford," Aug. 5, 1912): The Dollar Bill's the Flag That Rules the World/W: E. Ray Goetz, M: A. Baldwin Sloane — Opera Burlesque on the Sextette (from Lucia Di Lammermoor)/WM: Irving Berlin. *Princess Virtue* (Central, "Bourbon," May 4, 1921): Clothes/WM: Gitz Rice, B.C. Hilliam. *Song of the Flame* (44th Street, "Nicholas," Dec. 30, 1925): Great Big Bear; I Want Two Husbands/

W: Otto Harbach, Oscar Hammerstein II, M: Herbert Stothart. *Cavier* (Forrest, "Wallace," June 7, 1934): Here's to You/W: Edward Heyman, M: Harden Church. *Ziegfeld Follies of 1936-1937* (Winter Garden, revue, Sept. 14, 1936): The Gazooka/WM: Ira Gershwin, David Freedman.

1392. Jean Cameron *Half a Sixpence* (Broadhurst, CR, "Mrs. Walsingham"): A Proper Gentleman/WM: David Heneker.

1393. Lawrence Cameron *The Highwayman* (44th Street, revival, "Lieut. Lovelace," May 2, 1917): Marching Away/W: Harry B. Smith, M: Reginald De Koven.

1394. Madeleine Cameron (?–May 23, 1990) M: WILLIAM GAXTON. *Betty Lee* (44th Street, "Jeanne Chapin," Dec. 25, 1924): Athletic Boy; Baby Be Good; Just Lean on Me; Little Pony of Mine/W: Otto Harbach, Irving Caesar, M: Louis A. Hirsch, Con Conrad. *Happy Go Lucky* (Liberty, "Laura La Guerre," Sept. 30, 1926): Happy Melody/W: Gwynne Denni, M: Lucien Denni — In Vaudeville; It's Wonderful/W: Helena Evans, M: Lucien Denni. *Betsy* (New Amsterdam, "Winnie Hill," Dec. 28, 1926): Bugle Blow; The Kitzel Engagement; One of Us Should Be Two; Shuffle/W: Lorenz Hart, M: Richard Rodgers. *Hit the Deck* (Belasco, "Charlotte Payne," Apr. 25, 1927): What's a Kiss Among Friends?; Why, Oh Why?/W: Clifford Grey, Leo Robin, M: Vincent Youmans. *Follow Thru* (46th Street, "Ruth Van Horn," Jan. 9, 1929/ Sept. 30, 1929): Follow Thru; He's a Man's Man; It's a Great Sport/W: B.G. DeSylva, Lew Brown, M: Ray Henderson.

1395. Rudolph Cameron (Oct. 12, 1894–Feb. 17, 1958) B: Washington DC. *Sitting Pretty* (Fulton, "Bill Pennington," Apr. 8, 1924): All You Need Is a Girl; The Enchanted Train; Is This Not a Lovely Spot?; There Isn't One Girl; Worries; A Year from Today/W: P.G. Wodehouse, M: Jerome Kern. *Bye, Bye, Bonnie* (Ritz, "Ted Williams," Jan. 13, 1927): Just Across the River from Queens; Out of Town Buyers; Toodle-oo; You and I Love You and Me/W: Neville Fleeson, M: Albert Von Tilzer.

1396. William Cameron *The Belle of New York* (Casino, "Blinky Bill," Sept. 28, 1897): She Is the Belle of New York/W: Hugh Morton, M: Gustave Kerker. *The Jewel of Asia* (Criterion > Daly's, "Mufti," Feb. 16, 1903): Oh, What's the Use?/W: Frederick Ranken, M: Ludwig Englander — A Woman's No Means Yes/W: Harry B. Smith, M: Ludwig Englander. *The Darling of the Gallery Gods [Mid Summer Night's Fancies]* (Crystal Gardens, "Doggon," June 22, 1903): Ida

Bell/W: Matthew Woodward, M: Ben M. Jerome. *The Dress Parade [Mid Summer Night's Fancies]* (Crystal Gardens, revue, June 22, 1903): The Marriage of the Daffodil and Daisy/W: Nicholas Biddle, M: Ben M. Jerome. *The Jersey Lily* (Victoria, "Max Bennett," Sept. 14, 1903): Rosie Lee/W: George V. Hobart, M: Reginald De Koven. *My Lady's Maid or Lady Madcap* (Casino, CR, "Posh Jenkins," Oct. 8, 1906): Don't You Care?/W: Joseph E. Miller, M: Harold Orlob — We Get There Just the Same/WM: Percy Greenbank, Paul Rubens. *The Pied Piper* (Majestic, "Official Adviser," Dec. 3, 1908): It All Depends; We Tell Him Just What to Do/W: R.H. Burnside, M: Manuel Klein.

1397. William Cameron *Elsie* (Vanderbilt, "Parker," Apr. 2, 1923): A Regular Guy/WM: Noble Sissle, Eubie Blake. *Bringing Up Father* (Lyric, "Sandy MacPherson," Apr. 6, 1925): Play Me a Bagpipe Tune/W: R.F. Carroll, M: Seymour Furth, Leo Edwards.

1398. Yukona Cameron *The Second Little Show* (Shubert, revue, CR, Oct. 20, 1930): My Intuition/W: Howard Dietz, M: Arthur Schwartz.

1399. Grace Camp *Wars of the World* (Hippodrome, revue, Sept. 5, 1914): In Siam; When You Come Home Again Johnny/WM: Manuel Klein.

1400. Shep Camp (July 16, 1876–Nov. 20, 1929) B: West Point, GA. *Good Morning, Judge* (Shubert, "Mr. Burridge," Feb. 6, 1919): Young Folks and Old Folks/WM: ?. *Flossie* (Lyric, "Uncle Ezra," June 3, 1924): The Battle Cry of Freedom; Walla Walla/W: Ralph Murphy, M: Armand Robi. *The Love Call* (Majestic, "Slim Carter," Oct. 24, 1927): When I Take You All to London/W: Harry B. Smith, M: Sigmund Romberg.

1401. Frank Campanella Brother of JOSEPH CAMPANELLA. *Nowhere to Go but Up* (Winter Garden, "Lupo," Nov. 10, 1962): Dear Mom/W: James Lipton, M: Sol Berkowitz.

1402. Joseph Campanella (Nov. 21, 1925–) B: New York, NY. On TV he was Lou Wickersham in the detective series *Mannix* (1967). *Hot Spot* (Majestic, "Gabriel Snapper," Apr. 19, 1963): Don't Laugh/WM: Martin Charnin, Stephen Sondheim, Mary Rodgers — Gabie; A Matter of Time; This Little Yankee/W: Martin Charnin, M: Mary Rodgers.

1403. Alan Campbell (Apr. 22, 1957–) B: Homestead, FL. He played Derek Mitchell on the TV legal drama *Jake and the Fatman* (1987). *Sunset Boulevard* (Minskoff, "Joe Gillis," Nov. 17, 1994): Every Movie's a Circus; Girl Meets Boy; The Lady's Paying; Let's Have Lunch; The Perfect Year; Salome; Sunset Boulevard; This Time Next Year; Too Much in Love to Care/W: Don Black, Christopher Hampton, M: Andrew Lloyd Webber.

1404. Allan Campbell *Show Boat* (Ziegfeld, "Windy McLain," Dec. 27, 1927): Can't Help Lovin' Dat Man/W: Oscar Hammerstein II, M: Jerome Kern. *Show Boat* (Casino, return engagement, "Windy McLain," May 19, 1932): same as above.

1405. Arthur Campbell *Mystery Moon* (Royale, "Don Bradley," June 23, 1930): It's All OK; Mystery Moon/W: Monte Carlo, M: Alma Sanders. *Ziegfeld Follies of 1931* (Ziegfeld, revue, July 1, 1931): Mailu/W: E.Y. Harburg, M: Jay Gorney, Hugo Riesenfeld.

1406. Charles Campbell *The Gay Musician* (Wallack's, "A. Corker," May 18, 1908): It's a Long, Long Time/W: Charles J. Campbell, M: Julian Edwards.

1407. Charles Campbell *Don't Bother Me, I Can't Cope* (Playhouse, revue, Apr. 19, 1972): Fighting for Pharaoh; I Gotta Keep Movin'/WM: Micki Grant.

1408. Claudia Campbell *A Tree Grows in Brooklyn* (Alvin, "Annie," Apr. 19, 1951): Love Is the Reason/W: Dorothy Fields, M: Arthur Schwartz.

1409. Colin Campbell (Mar. 20, 1883–Mar. 25, 1966) B: Falkirk, Scotland. He appeared in Hollywood movies from 1915. *The Better 'Ole* (Greenwich Village > Cort > Booth, "Alf," Oct. 19, 1918): I Wish I Was in Blighty/W: W.R. Titterton, M: Herman Darewski — My Word! Ain't We Carrying On/WM: James Heard, Melville Gideon, Percival Knight, Herman Darewski. *Marjolaine* (Broadhurst, "Rev. Jacob Sternroyd, D.D.," Jan. 24, 1922): Oh Dr. Sternroyd/W: Brian Hooker, M: Hugo Felix. *Hammerstein's Nine O'Clock Revue* (Century roof, revue, Oct. 4, 1923): I Wonder Why the Glow-worm Winks His Eye at Me/W: Oscar Hammerstein II, M: Herbert Stothart. *Big Boy* (Winter Garden > 44th Street, "Steve Leslie," Jan. 7, 1925): The Day I Rode Half Fare/W: B.G. DeSylva, M: Joseph Meyer, James F. Hanley.

1410. Craig Campbell (Oct. 18, 1884–Jan. 12, 1965) B: London, Ontario, Canada. *The Love Cure* (New Amsterdam, CR, "Alfred Blake," Sept. 20, 1909): How Fair the World; Oh Be Jolly; A Pretty Part for Me to Play; When Skies Are Bright/W: Oliver Herford, M: Edmund Eysler. *The Red Rose* (Globe, "Andre," June 22, 1911): Sleigh Bells May Be Wedding Bells/W: Harry B. Smith, M: Robert Hood Bowers. *The Firefly* (Lyric > Casino, "Jack Travers," Dec. 2,

1912): He Says Yes, She Says No!; We're Going to Make a Man of You; When a Maid Comes Knocking at Your Heart; A Woman's Smile/W: Otto Harbach, M: Rudolf Friml. *Over the Top* (44th Street roof, revue, Nov. 28, 1917): The Golden Pheasant/W: Matthew Woodward, M: Sigmund Romberg, Herman Timberg — My Rainbow Girl/W: Philip Bartholomae, M: Sigmund Romberg, Herman Timberg — Oh, Galatea/W: Philip Bartholomae, M: Sigmund Romberg.

1411. Dean Campbell *Look Ma, I'm Dancin'* (Adelphi, "Bell Boy," Jan. 29, 1948): If You'll Be Mine/WM: Hugh Martin.

1412. Flo Campbell *Artists and Models of 1924* (Astor > Casino, revue, Oct. 15, 1924): Call It What You Like [added]/WM: ?— Pull Your Strings/W: Sam Coslow, Clifford Grey, M: Sigmund Romberg.

1413. Graeme Campbell (Nov. 30, 1940–1993) B: Australia. *Oliver!* (Mark Hellinger, revival, "Bill Sikes," Apr. 29, 1984): It's a Fine Life; My Name/WM: Lionel Bart.

1414. John Campbell *Sing for Your Supper* (Adelphi, revue, Apr. 24, 1939): Bonnie Banks/W: Robert Sour, M: Lee Wainer.

1415. Maude Campbell *The Only Girl* (Lyric, CR, "Patrice La Montrose [Patsy]," Mar. 22, 1915): Here's How; Here's to the Land We Love, Boys!; The More I See of Others, Dear, the Better I Love You; Personality; You Have to Have a Part to Make a Hit/W: Henry Blossom, M: Victor Herbert.

1416. Peggy Campbell (Aug. 11, 1912–) B: Vancouver, British Columbia, Canada. *Bloomer Girl* (New York City Center, revival, "Daisy," Jan. 6, 1947): I Never Was Born; T'morra, T'morra/W: E.Y. Harburg, M: Harold Arlen.

1417. Charles Cannefax (Apr. 18, 1899–Nov. 30, 1973) B: Missouri. *Artists and Models of 1924* (Astor > Casino, revue, Oct. 15, 1924): Artists and Models/W: Sam Coslow, Clifford Grey, M: Sigmund Romberg — Who's the Lucky Fellow?/W: ?, M: J. Fred Coots.

1418. James J. Canning (July 2, 1946–) B: Chicago, IL. *Grease* (Broadhurst, "Doody," June 7, 1972): Rock 'n' Roll Party Queen; Those Magic Changes/WM: Jim Jacobs, Warren Casey.

1419. Alice Cannon (June 25–) B: Rochester, NY. *Company* (Alvin, CR, "Susan," Oct. 5, 1970): Poor Baby/WM: Stephen Sondheim. *Johnny Johnson* (Edison, revival, "Minny Belle Tompkins," Apr. 11, 1971): Democracy's Call; Farewell, Goodbye; Oh, Heart of Love/W: Paul Green, M: Kurt Weill.

1420. Maureen Cannon (Dec. 3, 1926–) B:

Chicago, IL. She began her career dancing with her brother, then went on to study classical singing. She was still in high school when she was chosen for her first Broadway ingenue role. On TV she was a regular on *Paul Whiteman's Goodyear Revue* (1951). *Best Foot Forward* (Ethel Barrymore, "Helen Schlessinger," Oct. 1, 1941): Ev'ry Time; Shady Lady Bird; Where Do You Travel?/WM: Hugh Martin, Ralph Blane. *Up in Central Park* (Century, "Rosie Moore," Jan. 27, 1945): April Snow; The Birds and the Bees; Carousel in the Park; Close As Pages in a Book; The Fireman's Bride; It Doesn't Cost You Anything to Dream; Rip Van Winkle; Up from the Gutter/W: Dorothy Fields, M: Sigmund Romberg. *Up in Central Park* (New York City Center, revival, "Rosie Moore," May 19, 1947): same as above.

1421. Judy Canova (Nov. 20, 1916–Aug. 5, 1983) B: Jacksonville, FL. The singer, actress, comedienne and yodeller started out to be an opera singer. She sang on the radio with Paul Whiteman's band in the 1930s and had her own radio show from 1943-1953. *Calling All Stars* (Hollywood, revue, Dec. 13, 1934): If It's Love/W: Lew Brown, M: Harry Akst. *Yokel Boy* (Majestic, "Judy," July 6, 1939): A Boy Named Lem (and a Girl Named Sue); Catherine the Great; Comes Love/W: Lew Brown, Charles Tobias, M: Sam H. Stept — Time for Jookin/W: Lew Brown, Charles Tobias, M: Walter Kent.

1422. Eddie Cantor (Jan. 31, 1892–Oct. 10, 1964) B: New York, NY. The nickname of this well loved comedian-singer was Banjo Eyes. He started in vaudeville at age 15, and starred in movies, radio and TV. *Ziegfeld Midnight Frolic [4th Edition]* (New Amsterdam roof, revue, Oct. 3, 1916): Oh! How She Could Yacki, Hacki, Wicki, Wacki, Woo (Love in Honolulu)/W: Stanley Murphy, Charles McCarron, M: Albert Von Tilzer. *Ziegfeld Follies of 1917* (New Amsterdam, revue, June 12, 1917): Just You and Me/W: Gene Buck, M: Dave Stamper — The Modern Maiden's Prayer/W: Ballard Macdonald, M: James F. Hanley — That's the Kind of a Baby for Me/W: Alfred C. Harriman, M: John C. Egan. *Ziegfeld Follies of 1918* (New Amsterdam > Globe, revue, June 18, 1918): But After the Ball Was Over! (Then He Made Up for Lost Time)/WM: B.G. DeSylva, Arthur Jackson — Would You Rather Be a Colonel with an Eagle on Your Shoulder, or a Private with a Chicken on Your Knee?/W: Sidney D. Mitchell, M: Archie Gottler. *Ziegfeld Follies of 1919* (New Amsterdam, revue, June 16, 1919): I'd Rather See a Minstrel Show; I've Got My Captain Working for Me

Now; You'd Be Surprised [added]/WM: Irving Berlin. *Broadway Brevities of 1920* (Winter Garden, revue, Sept. 29, 1920): Beautiful Faces (Need Beautiful Clothes)/WM: Irving Berlin. *Make It Snappy* (Winter Garden, revue, Apr. 13, 1922): I Love Her, She Loves Me (I'm Her He, She's My She)/WM: Irving Caesar, Eddie Cantor — The Sheik of Araby/W: Harry B. Smith, Francis Wheeler, M: Ted Snyder — Yes! We Have No Bananas/WM: Frank Silver, Irving Cohn. *Kid Boots* (Earl Carroll > Selwyn, "Kid Boots," Dec. 31, 1923): Alabamy Bound [added]/W: B.G. DeSylva, Bud Green, M: Ray Henderson — Dinah/W: Sam M. Lewis, Joe Young, M: Harry Akst — Down 'Round the 19th Hole; In the Rough; Keep Your Eye on the Ball; Let's Do and Say We Didn't; Some One Loves You After All; Win for Me/W: Joseph McCarthy, M: Harry Tierney — If You Knew Susie (Like I Know Susie)/W: B.G. DeSylva, M: Joseph Meyer — I'm Goin' South/WM: Abner Silver, Harry Woods. *Ziegfeld Follies of 1927* (New Amsterdam, revue, Aug. 16, 1927): My Blue Heaven/W: George Whiting, M: Walter Donaldson — You Got to Have "It" in Hollywood/WM: Irving Berlin. *Whoopee* (New Amsterdam, "Henry Williams," Dec. 4, 1928): I Faw Down and Go Boom/WM: James Brockman, Leonard Stevens, B.B.B. Donaldson — Makin' Whoopee; My Baby Just Cares for Me; Until You Get Somebody Else/W: Gus Kahn, M: Walter Donaldson. *Earl Carroll's Sketch Book* (Earl Carroll > 44th Street > 46th Street, revue, July 1, 1929): Legs, Legs, Legs/W: E.Y. Harburg, M: Jay Gorney. *Banjo Eyes* (Hollywood, "Erwin Trowbridge," Dec. 25, 1941): I'll Take the City; Who Started the Rumba?/W: John Latouche, M: Vernon Duke — It Could Only Happen in the Movies; We're Having a Baby/W: Harold Adamson, M: Vernon Duke.

1423. Vandy Cape *Fools Rush In* (Playhouse, revue, Dec. 25, 1934): Willie's Little Whistle/W: Norman Zeno, M: Will Irwin.

1424. Ruby Capen *The Good Mister Best* (Garrick, "Lottie," Aug. 30, 1897): Puff, Puff/W: John J. McNally, M: ?.

1425. Virginia Capers (Sept. 22, 1925–May 6, 2004) B: Sumter, SC. *Saratoga* (Winter Garden, "Charwoman," Dec. 7, 1959): Petticoat High/W: Johnny Mercer, M: Harold Arlen. *Raisin* (46th Street, "Mama Lena Younger," Oct. 18, 1973): He Come Down This Morning; It's a Deal; Measure the Valleys; Not Anymore; A Whole Lotta Sunlight; You Done Right/W: Robert Brittan, M: Judd Woldin.

1426. Kendall Capps *Boom-Boom* (Casino,

"Skippy Carr," Jan. 28, 1929): Blow the Blues Away; On Top; Pick 'Em Up and Lay 'Em Down; Shake High, Shake Low; We're Going to Make Boom-Boom; What a Girl/W: Mann Holiner, J. Keirn Brennan, M: Werner Janssen.

1427. Robert Capron *Naughty Marietta* (Jolson, revival, "Silas Slick," Nov. 16, 1931): If I Were Anybody Else but Me; It's Pretty Soft for Silas/W: Rida Johnson Young, M: Victor Herbert. *The Firefly* (Erlanger's, revival, "Jenkins," Nov. 30, 1931): De Trop; Something/W: Otto Harbach, M: Rudolf Friml. *There You Are* (George M. Cohan, "Dick Longwood [Klondike]," May 16, 1932): Just a Little Penthouse and You; There You Are/WM: William Heagney, Tom Connell.

1428. Christopher Cara *Happy End* (Martin Beck, revival, "Brother Ben Owens," May 7, 1977): Brother, Give Yourself a Shove; Don't Be Afraid; In Our Childhood's Bright Endeavor; Lieutenants of the Lord; The Liquor Dealer's Dream; March Ahead/W: Bertolt Brecht, M: Kurt Weill.

1429. Irene Cara (Mar. 18, 1957–) B: Bronx, NY. She starred in the musical movie *Fame* (1980). *The Me Nobody Knows* (Orpheum > Helen Hayes, "Lillie Mae," May 18, 1970/Dec. 18, 1970): Black; Fugue for Four Girls; Robert, Alvin, Wendell and Jo Jo/W: Will Holt, M: Gary William Friedman. *Via Galactica* (Uris, "Storyteller," Nov. 28, 1972): Dance the Dark Away!; Via Galactica/W: Christopher Gore, M: Galt MacDermot. *Got Tu Go Disco* (Minskoff, "Cassette," June 25, 1979): All I Need; Bad Glad, Good and Had; Disco Shuffle/WM: Kenny Lehman, John Davis, Ray Chew, Nat Adderley, Jr., Thomas Jones, Wayne Morrison, Steve Boston, Eugene Narmore, Betty Rowland, Jerry Powell.

1430. Melanie Carabuena *Miss Saigon* (Broadway, CR, "Tam," c 1993): Little God of My Heart/W: Richard Maltby, Jr., Alain Boublil, M: Claude-Michel Schonberg.

1431. Philip Lee Carabuena (Oct. 18, 1986–) B: New York, NY. *Miss Saigon* (Broadway, CR, "Tam," c 1991): Little God of My Heart/W: Richard Maltby, Jr., Alain Boublil, M: Claude-Michel Schonberg.

1432. Richard Carafa *The Sound of Music* (Lunt-Fontanne, CR, "Friedrich," Aug. 1962): Do-Re-Mi; Edelweiss; The Lonely Goatherd; So Long, Farewell; The Sound of Music/W: Oscar Hammerstein II, M: Richard Rodgers.

1433. Fanny Carby (Feb. 2, 1925–Sept. 20, 2002) B: Sutton, Surrey, England. *Oh What a Lovely War* (Broadhurst, revue, Sept. 30, 1964):

Hitchy-Koo/W: L. Wolfe Gilbert, M: Lewis F. Muir, Maurice Abrahams.

1434. Tony Cardell *Billion Dollar Baby* (Alvin, "Violin Player," Dec. 21, 1945): Speaking of Pals/W: Betty Comden, Adolph Green, M: Morton Gould.

1435. Tom Carder *Joseph and the Amazing Technicolor Dreamcoat* (Royale, revival, "Pharaoh," Jan. 27, 1982): Poor, Poor Pharaoh; Song of the King; Stone the Crows/WM: Tim Rice, Andrew Lloyd Webber.

1436. Beryl Carew *Meet the People* (Mansfield, revue, Dec. 25, 1940): The Stars Remain/ W: Henry Myers, M: Jay Gorney.

1437. Ann Carey *The Geisha* (Erlanger's, revival, "Lady Constance Wynne," Oct. 5, 1931): We Are Going to Call on the Marquis/W: Henry Greenbank, M: Sidney Jones. *Naughty Marietta* (Erlanger's, revival, "Adah," Nov. 16, 1931): Live for Today; 'Neath the Southern Moon/W: Rida Johnson Young, M: Victor Herbert.

1438. Darrell Carey *La Cage aux Folles* (Palace, CR, "Jacob," Jan. 1987): Cocktail Counterpoint/WM: Jerry Herman.

1439. Frank Carey (Oct. 12, 1934–) B: Tarrytown, NY. *Don't Play Us Cheap!* (Ethel Barrymore, "Cockroach," Dec. 21, 1978): Some Days It Seems That It Just Don't Even Pay to Get Out of Bed/WM: Melvin Van Peebles.

1440. Joseph Carey *A Waltz Dream* (Broadway, "Sigismund," Jan. 27, 1908): A Soldier Stole Her Heart/W: Joseph W. Herbert, M: Oscar Straus.

1441. Joyce Carey (Mar. 30, 1898–Feb. 28, 1993) B: London, England. Stage, film and TV actress with a long distinguished career in Britain and the U.S. She also wrote plays using the name Jay Mallory. *Tonight at 8:30* (National, "Lavinia Featherways," Nov. 24, 1936): Music Box/WM: Noel Coward.

1442. Macdonald Carey (Mar. 15, 1913– Mar. 21, 1994) B: Sioux City, IA. Nice guy in more than 35 movies and numerous TV dramas. He played Dr. Tom Horton on the long-running soap *Days of Our Lives* (1965). *Lady in the Dark* (Alvin, "Charley Johnson," Jan. 23, 1941): The Best Years of His Life/W: Ira Gershwin, M: Kurt Weill.

1443. Carmine Caridi (1933–) His TV credits include *Phyllis* (1976), *Fame* (1982), and *NYPD Blue* (1994). *Carnival!* (New York City Center, revival, "Mr. Schlegel," Dec. 12, 1968): Direct from Vienna; Humming/WM: Bob Merrill.

1444. Martha Carine *The Cingalee* (Daly's, "Lady Patricia Vane," Oct. 24, 1904): My Heart's At Your Feet/W: Percy Greenbank, M: Lionel Monckton.

1445. Len Cariou (Sept. 30, 1939–) B: Winnipeg, Canada. *Applause* (Palace, "Bill Sampson," Mar. 30, 1970): Fasten Your Seat Belts; One of a Kind; Think How It's Gonna Be/W: Lee Adams, M: Charles Strouse. *A Little Night Music* (Shubert, "Fredrik Egerman," Feb. 25, 1973): It Would Have Been Wonderful; Now; Soon; You Must Meet My Wife/WM: Stephen Sondheim. *Sweeney Todd, the Demon Barber of Fleet Street* (Uris, "Sweeney Todd," Mar. 1, 1979): The Barber and His Wife; Epiphany; God, That's Good!; A Little Priest; My Friends; No Place Like London; Pirelli's Miracle Elixir; Pretty Women/WM: Stephen Sondheim. *Dance a Little Closer* (Minskoff, "Harry Aikens," May 11, 1983): Dance a Little Closer; Happy, Happy New Year; He Always Comes Home to Me; I Don't Know; I Got a New Girl; I Never Want to See You Again; It Never Would Have Worked; Mad; There's Always One You Can't Forget; There's Never Been Anything Like Us/W: Alan Jay Lerner, M: Charles Strouse. *Teddy & Alice* (Minskoff, "Theodore Roosevelt," Nov. 12, 1987): Can I Let Her Go?; Charge; The Coming-Out Party; The Fourth of July; Her Father's Daughter; This House; Wave the Flag/W: Hal Hackady, M: John Philip Sousa, Richard Kapp.

1446. Cynthia Carle (Mar. 4, 1951–) B: Hollywood, CA. *Is There Life After High School?* (Ethel Barrymore, revue, May 7, 1982): I'm Glad You Didn't Know Me/WM: Craig Carnelia.

1447. Richard Carle (July 7, 1871–June 28, 1941) B: Somerville, MA. Comedy star of the British and U.S. stage, he also produced plays, wrote lyrics and librettos, and from 1928 on, appeared in over 60 films. *The Tenderfoot* (New York, "Prof. Zachary Pettibone, LL.D, B.A.," Feb. 22, 1904): Dancing; I'm a Peaceable Party; My Alamo Love; The Tortured Thomas Cat/W: Richard Carle, M: H.L. Heartz. *The Mayor of Tokio* (New York, "Marcus Orlando Kidder," Dec. 4, 1905): Cheer Up Everybody; A Comic Opera Capsule; Cruising Home/W: Richard Carle, M: William F. Peters—Foolishness/W: Arthur Gillespie, M: William F. Peters—I Like You/W: Charles J. Campbell, Ralph Skinner, M: William F. Peters. *The Spring Chicken* (Daly's > New Amsterdam > Daly's, "Ambrose Girdle," Oct. 8, 1906): All the Girls Love Me; Marching/WM: Richard Carle—In Seville; A Lemon in the Garden of Love/W: M.E. Rourke, M: Richard Carle—No Doubt You'd Like to Cuddle Up to Baby (Baby and Nursie)/W: Richard

Carle, M: Robert Hood Bowers. *The Girl from Montmartre* (Criterion, "Dr. Petypon," Aug. 5, 1912): Ghost Quintette; In Spirit Land/W: Harry B. Smith, Robert B. Smith, M: Henry Bereny — I've Taken Such a Fancy to You/W: Clifford Harris, M: Jerome Kern. *The Doll Girl* (Globe, "Marquis de la Tourelle," Aug. 25, 1913): Come On Over Here/W: Harry B. Smith, Jerome Kern, M: Walter Kollo — Foolishness/W: Arthur Gillespie, M: William F. Peters — A Little Thing Like a Kiss/W: Harry B. Smith, M: Jerome Kern — Papa; Rosalilla of Sevilla; When You're on the Stage/W: Harry B. Smith, M: Leo Fall. *90 in the Shade* (Knickerbocker, "Willoughby Parker," Jan. 25, 1915): Foolishness/W: Arthur Gillespie, M: William F. Peters — Human Nature/WM: ? — Jolly Good Fellow/WM: Clare Kummer — A Package of Seeds/W: Herbert Reynolds, P.G. Wodehouse, M: Jerome Kern — The Triangle/W: Guy Bolton, M: Jerome Kern. *The Cohan Revue of 1916* (Astor, revue, "Dr. Booberang," Feb. 9, 1916): He Can Cure You of Love; Julia and Donald and Joe; My Musical Comedy Maiden/WM: George M. Cohan. *The Broadway Whirl* (Times Square > Selwyn, revue, June 8, 1921): Wood Alcohol Blues/W: J. Hershkowitz, M: E.S. Hutchinson. *Adrienne* (George M. Cohan, "John Grey," May 28, 1923): As Long as the Wife Don't Know; King Solomon/W: A. Seymour Brown, M: Albert Von Tilzer.

1448. William P. (W.P.) Carleton (Oct. 3, 1872–Apr. 6, 1947) B: London, England. He started in silent movies in the 1910s. He died after a car accident. *Florodora* (New York, CR, "Frank Abercoed," Dec. 9, 1901): The Shade of the Palm/W: Owen Hall, M: Leslie Stuart — Somebody/WM: ?. *Winsome Winnie* (Casino, "Desmond Poverish," Dec. 1, 1903): I Don't Remember That; My Winsome Winnie/W: Frederick Ranken, M: Gustave Kerker. *The Tattooed Man* (Criterion, "Abdallah," Feb. 18, 1907): Hear My Song of Love; The Legend of the Djin; Watch the Professor/W: Harry B. Smith, M: Victor Herbert. *A Knight for a Day* (Wallack's, "Marco," Dec. 16, 1907): Life Is a See-Saw/W: Robert B. Smith, M: Raymond Hubbell. *The Yankee Girl* (Herald Square, "Capt. John Lawrence," Feb. 10, 1910): I'll Make a Ring Around Rosie; The Yankee Girl/W: George V. Hobart, M: Silvio Hein. *The Wall Street Girl* (Grand Opera House, revival, "Dexter Brown," Nov. 18, 1912): Every Day/WM: Earle C. Jones, Charles Daniels — I Never Knew What Eyes Could Do (Till Yours Looked into Mine)/W: Stanley Murphy, M: Henry I. Marshall. *Follow*

Me (Casino, "Hector," Nov. 29, 1916): A Tete-a-Tete with You/W: Robert B. Smith, M: Sigmund Romberg — When a Man Is Single/W: Robert B. Smith, M: Frank Tours.

1449. W.T. Carleton (1859–Sept. 28, 1930) B: England. *The Medal and the Maid* (Broadway, "Admiral Lord Belton," Jan. 11, 1904): Go to Sea/W: Charles H. Taylor, M: Sidney Jones. *Lady Teazle* (Casino, "Sir Peter Teazle," Dec. 24, 1904): The Pretty Little Milliner; Were I Happily Married/W: John Kendrick Bangs, M: A. Baldwin Sloane. *Mlle. Mischief* (Lyric, "Lieut. Berner," Sept. 28, 1908): The Joy Duet/W: Sydney Rosenfeld, M: Carl M. Ziehrer.

1450. Gertie Carlisle *The Pearl and the Pumpkin* (Broadway, "Pearl Pringle," Aug. 21, 1905): My Baby Elephant; My Party; A String of Pearls/W: Paul West, M: John W. Bratton. *The Tattooed Man* (Criterion, "Alma," Feb. 18, 1907): There's Just One Girl I'd Like to Marry/W: Harry B. Smith, M: Victor Herbert.

1451. Kitty Carlisle (Sept. 3, 1914–) B: New Orleans, LA. Singer and actress, in movies, on radio and TV. Her appearance with the Marx Brothers in the classic film *A Night at the Opera* (1935) remains a delight. In 1976 she began as Chairman of the New York State Council on the Arts. *White Horse Inn* (Center, "Katarina," Oct. 1, 1936): High Up in the Hills; I Cannot Live Without Your Love; Market Day in the Village; We Prize Most the Things We Miss; The White Horse Inn/W: Irving Caesar, M: Ralph Benatzky — Leave It to Katarina/W: Irving Caesar, M: Jara Benes. *Three Waltzes* (Majestic, "Marie Hiller" and "Charlotte Hiller" and "Franzi Corot Hiller," Dec. 25, 1937): Do You Recall?; My Heart Controls My Head; Springtime in the Air/W: Clare Kummer, M: based on Johann Strauss, Sr.— Our Last Valse/W: Clare Kummer, M: Oscar Straus — Paree; To Love Is to Live/W: Clare Kummer, M: based on Johann Strauss, Jr. *Walk with Music* (Ethel Barrymore, "Pamela Gibson," June 4, 1940): Friend of the Family; How Nice for Me; I Walk with Music; Smile for the Press; Today I Am a Glamour Girl; Wait Till You See Me in the Morning/W: Johnny Mercer, M: Hoagy Carmichael. *Kiss Me, Kate* (New York City Center, revival, "Lilli Vanessi" and "Katherine," May 9, 1956): I Am Ashamed That Women Are So Simple; I Hate Men; Kiss Me, Kate; So In Love; We Open in Venice; Wunderbar/WM: Cole Porter. *On Your Toes* (Virginia, revival, CR, "Peggy Porterfield," June 14, 1983/Dec. 20, 1983): The Heart Is Quicker Than the Eye; Too Good for the Average Man/W: Lorenz Hart, M: Richard Rodgers.

1452. Margaret Carlisle (July 14, 1905–)
B: Elgin, IL. M: LEONARD CEELEY. *The New Moon* (Casino, CR, "Marianne Beaunoir," Aug. 1929): The Girl on the Prow; An Interrupted Love Song; Lover, Come Back to Me; Never for You; One Kiss; Wanting You/W: Oscar Hammerstein II, M: Sigmund Romberg.

1453. Marion Carlisle *Bitter Sweet* (44th Street, revival, "Harriet" and "Hansi," May 7, 1934): Alas, the Time Is Past; Ladies of the Town; The Last Dance; Tarara Boom-de-Ay/WM: Noel Coward.

1454. P. Carlos *Music Box Revue of 1921* (Music Box, revue, CR, Sept. 18, 1922): Dancing the Seasons Away/WM: Irving Berlin.

1455. Richard Carlson (Apr. 29, 1912–Nov. 25, 1977) B: Albert Lea, MN. He wrote novels and short stories and directed films as well as appearing in them. On TV he played the lead role of Herbert Philbrick in the McCarthy era drama series *I Led Three Lives* (1952). *Stars in Your Eyes* (Majestic, "John Blake," Feb. 9, 1939): All the Time/W: Dorothy Fields, M: Arthur Schwartz.

1456. Stanley Carlson *The Liar* (Broadhurst, "Ottavio Ossimorsi," May 18, 1950): Stop Holding Me Back; Supper Trio/W: Edward Eager, M: John Mundy. *Show Boat* (New York City Center, revival, "Cap'n Andy Hawks," Apr. 8, 1954): Why Do I Love You?/W: Oscar Hammerstein II, M: Jerome Kern.

1457. Violet Carlson (c 1900–Dec. 3, 1997) B: Oak Park, IL. The tiny, energetic soubrette began in vaudeville, winning a singing contest and touring with NINA OLIVETTE in a kid novelty act. She played in *The Student Prince* on Broadway for 2 years, before taking it to London in 1926. *The Student Prince [in Heidelberg]* (Al Jolson, "Gretchen," Dec. 2, 1924): Student Life/W: Dorothy Donnelly, M: Sigmund Romberg. *The Nightingale* (Jolson, "Josephine," Jan. 3, 1927): Breakfast in Bed/W: P.G. Wodehouse, M: Armand Vecsey — Josephine/W: Clifford Grey, M: Armand Vecsey. *The Love Call* (Majestic, "Miss McCullagh," Oct. 24, 1927): If That's What You Want; Spanish Love; You Appeal to Me/W: Harry B. Smith, M: Sigmund Romberg. *The Red Robe* (Shubert, "Marie," Dec. 25, 1928): I've Got It/W: Mann Holiner, M: Alberta Nichols — The Thrill of a Kiss/W: Harry B. Smith, M: Jean Gilbert. *Sweet Adeline* (Hammerstein's, "Dot," Sept. 3, 1929): Here Am I; Out of the Blue; Play Us a Polka Dot; Spring Is Here; Take Me for a Honeymoon Ride/W: Oscar Hammerstein II, M: Jerome Kern. *Caviar* (Forrest, "Jeannine," June 7, 1934): I Feel Sorta... ; Tarts and Flowers/W: Edward Heyman, M: Harden Church.

1458. Claudia Carlstedt *The Idol's Eye* (Broadway, "Chief Priestess of the Temple of the Ruby," Oct. 25, 1897): Song of the Priestess/W: Harry B. Smith, M: Victor Herbert.

1459. Evelyn Carlton *Ziegfeld Follies of 1912* (Moulin Rouge, revue, Oct. 21, 1912): I'm Such a Romantic Girl; Mother Doesn't Know/W: Harry B. Smith, M: Raymond Hubbell. *Ziegfeld Follies of 1913* (New Amsterdam, revue, June 16, 1913): You Must Have Experience/W: George V. Hobart, M: Raymond Hubbell.

1460. Thelma Carlton *Her Family Tree* (Lyric > Shubert, Dec. 27, 1920): Boom Whee!; The Gold-Diggers; A Romantic Knight/WM: Seymour Simons.

1461. Carolee Carmello B: Albany, NY. M: GREGG EDELMAN. *City of Angels* (Virginia, CR, "Oolie" and "Donna," Oct. 10, 1991): The Buddy System; What You Don't Know About Women; You Can Always Count on Me/W: David Zippel, M: Cy Coleman. *Falsettos* (John Golden, revival, "Cordelia," Apr. 29, 1992): Something Bad Is Happening; Unlikely Lovers/WM: William Finn.

1462. Lillian Carmen *Earl Carroll's Sketch Book of 1935* (Winter Garden > Majestic, revue, June 4, 1935): Gringola; Let's Swing It/W: Charles Newman, Charles Tobias, M: Murray Mencher — Let the Man Who Makes the Gun/W: Raymond B. Egan, M: Gerald Marks — The Rustle of Your Bustle [June 24, 1935]/W: Norman Zeno, M: Will Irwin.

1463. Sybil Carmen *Ziegfeld Midnight Frolic [1st Edition]* (New Amsterdam roof, revue, Jan. 5, 1915): I Want Someone to Make a Fuss Over Me/W: Gene Buck, M: Dave Stamper. *Ziegfeld Midnight Frolic [4th Edition]* (New Amsterdam roof, revue, Oct. 3, 1916): The Balloonatica; Don't You Wish You Were a Kid Again?/W: Gene Buck, M: Dave Stamper. *Ziegfeld Midnight Frolic [5th Edition]* (New Amsterdam roof, revue, Apr. 24, 1917): The Midnight Zeppo/W: Gene Buck, M: Dave Stamper.

1464. Bill Carmichael (June 18, 1954–) B: Oceanside, CA. *Cats* (Winter Garden, CR, "Bustopher Jones" and "Asparagus" and "Growltiger," c 1986): Bustopher Jones; Growltiger's Last Stand; Gus: The Theater Cat/W: T.S. Eliot, M: Andrew Lloyd Webber.

1465. Tullio Carminati (Sept. 21, 1894–Feb. 26, 1971) B: Zara, Dalmatia, Italy. Formerly an Italian aristocrat (or so the story goes), he appeared on the European stage before going to Hollywood in 1926. *Music in the Air* (Alvin >

44th Street, "Bruno Mahler," Nov. 8, 1932): I Am So Eager; I'm Coming Home; One More Dance; The Song Is You/W: Oscar Hammerstein II, M: Jerome Kern. *Great Lady* (Majestic, "Stephen Jumel," Dec. 1, 1938): In the Carefree Realm of Fancy; Keep Your Hand on My Heart; Though Tongues May Wag/W: Earle Crooker, M: Frederick Loewe.

1466. Eileen Carmody *The Nightingale* (Jolson, "Dolly," Jan. 3, 1927): Fairyland/W: P.G. Wodehouse, M: Armand Vecsey.

1467. Kirsti Carnahan (June 29–) B: Evanston, IL. *Kiss of the Spider Woman* (Broadhurst, "Marta," May 3, 1993): Dear One; I Do Miracles/W: Fred Ebb, M: John Kander.

1468. Judy Carne (Apr. 27, 1939–) B: Northampton, England. M: actor Burt Reynolds. The "sock-it-to-me" girl of TV's *Laugh-In* comedy variety series (1967). *The Boy Friend* (Ambassador, revival "Polly," Apr. 14, 1970): The Boy Friend; I Could Be Happy with You; Poor Little Pierrette; A Room in Bloomsbury/WM: Sandy Wilson.

1469. Grace Carney (Sept. 15, 1911–) B: Hartford, CT. *Donnybrook!* (46th Street, "Birdy Monyhan," May 18, 1961): Mr. Flynn/WM: Johnny Burke.

1470. Morris Carnovsky (Sept. 5, 1897–Sept. 1, 1992) B: St. Louis, MO. The distinguished stage and screen actor was an original member of the Group Theater in the 1930s and was blacklisted during the McCarthy era of the 1950s. *Johnny Johnson* (44th Street, "Dr. Mahodan," Nov. 19, 1936): The Psychiatry Song/W: Paul Green, M: Kurt Weill. *A Family Affair* (Billy Rose, "Morris Siegal," Jan. 27, 1962): I'm Worse Than Anybody; Kalua Bay; Now, Morris/W: James Goldman, William Goldman, M: John Kander.

1471. Carleton Carpenter (July 10, 1926–) B: Bennington, VT. The songwriter and actor sang "Aba Daba Honeymoon" with DEBBIE REYNOLDS in the movie *Two Weeks with Love* (1950). *John Murray Anderson's Almanac* (Imperial, revue, Dec. 10, 1953): When Am I Going to Meet Your Mother?; You're So Much a Part of Me/WM: Richard Adler, Jerry Ross. *Hello, Dolly!* (St. James, CR, "Cornelius Hackl," 1966): Dancing; It Only Takes a Moment; Put On Your Sunday Clothes/WM: Jerry Herman — Elegance; Motherhood/WM: Bob Merrill, Jerry Herman.

1472. Constance Carpenter (Apr. 19, 1905–Dec. 26, 1992) B: Bath, England. As a child, she studied ballet with the great Russian dancer, Anna Pavlova. *Oh, Kay!* (Imperial, "Mae," Nov.

8, 1926): Clap Yo' Hands; The Woman's Touch/W: Ira Gershwin, M: George Gershwin — Heaven on Earth/W: Ira Gershwin, Howard Dietz, M: George Gershwin. *A Connecticut Yankee* (Vanderbilt, "Alice Carter," Nov. 3, 1927): My Heart Stood Still; Nothing's Wrong; Thou Swell/W: Lorenz Hart, M: Richard Rodgers. *Hello, Daddy* (Mansfield > Erlangers, CR, "Connie Block," Mar. 1929): As Long as We're in Love; Let's Sit and Talk About You; Your Disposition Is Mine/W: Dorothy Fields, M: Jimmy McHugh. *The Third Little Show* (Music Box, revue, June 1, 1931): Falling in Love/W: Earle Crooker, M: Henry Sullivan — You Forgot Your Gloves/W: Edward Eliscu, M: Ned Lehac — You Might as Well Pretend/W: Ted Fetter, Edward Eliscu, M: Morgan Lewis. *Music Hath Charms* (Majestic, "Gioconda" and "Marella," Dec. 29, 1934): It's Three O'Clock; A Smile, a Kiss; Sweet Fool/W: Rowland Leigh, John Shubert, M: Rudolf Friml. *The King and I* (St. James, CR, "Anna Leonowens," Sept. 1952): Getting to Know You; Hello, Young Lovers; I Whistle a Happy Tune; The Royal Bangkok Academy; Shall I Tell You What I Think of You?; Shall We Dance?/W: Oscar Hammerstein II, M: Richard Rodgers.

1473. Imogen Carpenter (Feb. 2, 1919–) B: Hot Springs, AK. Composer, singer in nightclubs and on radio, she was also a concert pianist. *Ziegfeld Follies of 1943* (Winter Garden, revue, Apr. 1, 1943): Come Up and Have a Cup of Coffee; Hold That Smile; This Is It/W: Jack Yellen, M: Ray Henderson.

1474. Jean Carpenter *The Vanderbilt Revue* (Vanderbilt, revue, Nov. 5, 1930): Half Way to Heaven/W: David Sidney, M: Mario Braggiotti — You're the Better Half of Me/W: Dorothy Fields, M: Jimmy McHugh.

1475. John Carpenter (Jan. 16, 1948–) B: Carthage, NY. *Guys and Dolls* (Martin Beck, revival, "Arvide Abernathy," Apr. 14, 1992): Follow the Fold; More I Cannot Wish You/WM: Frank Loesser.

1476. Thelma Carpenter (June 15, 1922–May 15, 1997) B: Brooklyn, NY. *Memphis Bound!* (Broadway > Belasco, "Henny Paradise," May 24, 1945): Love or Reason/WM: Clay Warnick, Don Walker, based on William S. Gilbert and Arthur Sullivan. *Inside U.S.A.* (New Century, revue, Apr. 30, 1948): Blue Grass/W: Howard Dietz, M: Arthur Schwartz. *Shuffle Along* (Broadway, "Cpl. Betty Lee," May 8, 1952): Bitten by Love; Give It Love/W: Floyd Huddleston, M: Joseph Meyer — Swanee Moon/W: Noble Sissle, M: Eubie Blake. *Ankles Aweigh*

(Mark Hellinger, "Chipolata," Apr. 18, 1955): Headin' for the Bottom/W: Dan Shapiro, M: Sammy Fain. *Hello, Dolly!* (St. James, CR, "Mrs. Dolly Gallagher Levi," Jan.10, 1969/Jan. 29, 1969 Wed. mats./July 19, 1969/Sept. 6, 1969/ Nov. 11, 1969 all mats.): Before the Parade Passes By/WM: Lee Adams, Charles Strouse, Jerry Herman — Dancing; Hello, Dolly!; I Put My Hand In; Put on Your Sunday Clothes; So Long, Dearie/WM: Jerry Herman — Motherhood/ WM: Bob Merrill, Jerry Herman.

1477. Alexander Carr (Mar. 7, 1878–Sept. 19, 1946) B: Rumni, Russia. Comedian of films as well as the stage. *The Gay White Way* (Casino, revue, "Montgomery Bernstein Brewster," Oct. 7, 1907): Brewster the Millionaire; Climbing the Ladder of Love/W: Sydney Rosenfeld, M: Ludwig Englander.

1478. Jamie Carr *The Selling of the President* (Shubert, "Casey Steele," Mar. 22, 1972): If You Like People; Little Moon; Take My Hand/W: Jack O'Brien, M: Bob James.

1479. Patti Carr *Look to the Lilies* (Lunt-Fontanne, "Juanita," Mar. 29, 1970): I'd Sure Like to Give It a Shot; Meet My Seester/W: Sammy Cahn, M: Jule Styne.

1480. Percy Carr (1865–Nov. 22, 1926) B: England. *The Three Musketeers* (Manhattan Opera House, "Athos," May 17, 1921): Now Drink a Glass with Me My Friends; Oh Friendship!; Oh! Who Will Be a Queen!; Yes, I Am Here/WM: Richard W. Temple.

1481. Lucy Carr-Shaw *Shamus O'Brien* (Broadway, "Kitty O'Toole," Jan. 5, 1897): Where Is the Man?/W: George H. Jessop, M: Charles Villiers Stanford.

1482. John Carradine (Feb. 5, 1906–Nov. 27, 1988) B: New York, NY. M: DORIS RICH. The tall, sinister-looking character actor was well known for Shakespearian roles and for appearances in hundreds of movies, plays, and TV dramas. Early in his career he went to Hollywood as a scenic designer for Cecil B. de Mille. *A Funny Thing Happened on the Way to the Forum* (Alvin, "Lycus," May 8, 1962/Sept. 2, 1963): Everybody Ought to Have a Maid/WM: Stephen Sondheim.

1483. Keith Carradine (Aug. 8, 1949–) B: San Mateo, CA. Son of JOHN CARRADINE. The singer-songwriter-guitarist with the cynical smile appeared in movies from 1970. *Hair* (Biltmore, CR, "Claude," Oct. 1969): Hair; I Got Life; Let the Sunshine In (The Flesh Failures); Manchester; Where Do I Go/W: Gerome Ragni, James Rado, M: Galt MacDermot. *The Will Rogers Follies* (Palace, "Will Rogers," May 1,

1991): The Big Time; Favorite Son; Give a Man Enough Rope; Marry Me Now; Never Met a Man I Didn't Like; Presents for Mrs. Rogers; So Long Pa; Will-a-Mania/W: Betty Comden, Adolph Green, M: Cy Coleman.

1484. Mabel Carrier *The Runaways* (Casino, CR, "Dorothy Hardtack," July 27, 1903): Love Is an Ailment; Strolling/W: Addison Burkhardt, M: Raymond Hubbell.

1485. Cely Carrillo Mother of CYNTHIA ONRUBIA. *Flower Drum Song* (St. James, CR, "Mei Li," Jan. 1960): Don't Marry Me; A Hundred Million Miracles; I Am Going to Like It Here/W: Oscar Hammerstein II, M: Richard Rodgers.

1486. Evelyn Carter (Sept. 22, 1876–Nov. 21, 1942) *Miss Daisy* (Shubert > Lyric, "Mrs. Swigget," Sept. 9, 1914): Interruptions/W: Philip Bartholomae, M: Silvio Hein.

1487. Helen Carrington (1895–Oct. 22, 1963) *Plain Jane* (New Amsterdam, "Countess Suzanne D'Arcy," May 12, 1924): Don't Take Your Troubles to Bed; Winning the Prize/W: Phil Cook, M: Tom Johnstone. *Dear Sir* (Times Square, "Gladys Barclay," Sept. 23, 1924): If You Think It's Love You're Right/W: Howard Dietz, M: Jerome Kern.

1488. Katherine (Kay) Carrington (c 1910– May 2, 1953) B: East Orange, NJ. M: composer Arthur Schwartz. *The Garrick Gaieties of 1930* (Guild, revue, return engagement, Oct. 16, 1930): I Am Only Human After All/W: E.Y. Harburg, Ira Gershwin, M: Vernon Duke — Rose of Arizona/W: Lorenz Hart, M: Richard Rodgers — There Ain't No Love/W: E.Y. Harburg, M: Vernon Duke. *Face the Music* (New Amsterdam, "Kit Baker," Feb. 17, 1932): Crinoline Days; I Say It's Spinach; Let's Have Another Cup of Coffee; On a Roof in Manhattan; Soft Lights and Sweet Music/WM: Irving Berlin. *Music in the Air* (Alvin > 44th Street, "Sieglinde Lessing," Nov. 8, 1932): I've Told Ev'ry Little Star; Prayer (Our Journey May Be Long); We Belong Together; When the Spring Is in the Air/W: Oscar Hammerstein II, M: Jerome Kern.

1489. Nell Carrington *The Passing Show of 1917* (Winter Garden, revue, CR, Sept. 24, 1917): The Golden West/W: Harold Atteridge, M: Sigmund Romberg, Otto Motzan — The Language of the Fan/W: Harold Atteridge, M: Sigmund Romberg.

1490. Paul Carrington *Raisin* (46th Street, CR, "Travis Younger," Sept. 3, 1974): He Come Down This Morning; Sidewalk Tree/W: Robert Brittan, M: Judd Woldin.

1491. Reginald Carrington (Aug. 4, 1890–

July 9, 1959) *Mam'selle Napoleon* (Knickerbocker, "Choquille," Dec. 8, 1903): Flowers, Feathers, Ribbons and Laces/W: Joseph W. Herbert, M: Gustav Luders.

1492. Adam Carroll (Mar. 19, 1897–) B: Philadelphia, PA. He played piano in Paul Whiteman's orchestra. *The Little Show* (Music Box, revue, Apr. 30, 1929): The Theme Song/ W: Howard Dietz, M: Arthur Schwartz.

1493. Albert Carroll (c 1895–Dec. 2, 1956) B: Oak Park, IL. *The Grand Street Follies of 1928* (Booth, revue, May 28, 1928): Command to Love/W: Agnes Morgan, M: Serge Walter. *The Grand Street Follies of 1929* (Booth, revue, May 1, 1929): I Love You but I Like You Even More (I Love You and I Like You)/W: Max Lief, Nathaniel Lief, M: Arthur Schwartz — I'll Never Forget/W: Albert Carroll, M: Max Ewing. *The Garrick Gaieties of 1930* (Guild, revue, June 4, 1930): George and Mary [July 21, 1930]/W: Thomas McKnight, M: Charles M. Schwab — Shavian Shivers/W: E.Y. Harburg, M: Vernon Duke. *The Garrick Gaieties of 1930* (Guild, return engagement, Oct. 16, 1930): George and Mary/W: Thomas McKnight, M: Charles M. Schwab — Rose of Arizona/W: Lorenz Hart, M: Richard Rodgers. *Americana of 1932* (Shubert, revue, Oct. 5, 1932): Five Minutes of Spring/W: E.Y. Harburg, M: Jay Gorney — Let Me Match My Private Life with Yours/W: E.Y. Harburg, M: Vernon Duke.

1494. Art Carroll *Touch and Go* (Broadhurst > Broadway, revue, Oct. 13, 1949): It Will Be All Right (in a Hundred Years)/W: Walter Kerr, Jean Kerr, M: Jay Gorney. *Michael Todd's Peep Show* (Winter Garden, revue, June 28, 1950): Blue Night/WM: King Bhumibol of Thailand, B. Chakraband, N. Tong Yai — Violins from Nowhere/W: Herb Magidson, M: Sammy Fain.

1495. Claire Carroll *Innocent Eyes* (Winter Garden, revue, CR, July 7, 1924): Love Is Like a Pinwheel/W: Harold Atteridge, Tot Seymour, M: Sigmund Romberg.

1496. Danny Carroll (May 30, 1940–) B: Maspeth, NY. *The Music Man* (Majestic, "Tommy Djilas," Dec. 19, 1957): Shipoopi/WM: Meredith Willson. *Flora, the Red Menace* (Alvin, "Joe," May 11, 1965): You Are You/W: Fred Ebb, M: John Kander. *Billy* (Billy Rose, "Rawley," Mar. 22, 1969): The Fiddlers' Green/WM: Ron Dante, Gene Allen. *42nd Street* (Winter Garden, "Andy Lee," Aug. 25, 1980): Audition; Go Into Your Dance/W: Al Dubin, M: Harry Warren.

1497. David (David James) Carroll (July 30, 1950–Mar. 11, 1992) B: Rockville Centre, NY. *Oh, Brother!* (ANTA, "Eastern Mousada,"

Nov. 10, 1981): A Man; Tell Sweet Saroyana/W: Donald Driver, M: Michael Valenti. *Seven Brides for Seven Brothers* (Alvin, "Adam," July 8, 1982): Bless Your Beautiful Hide; Sobbin' Women/W: Johnny Mercer, M: Gene de Paul — Love Never Goes Away; A Woman Ought to Know Her Place/WM: Al Kasha, Joel Hirschhorn. *Wind in the Willows* (Nederlander, "Rat," Dec. 19, 1985): I'd Be Attracted; Messing About in Boats; That's What Friends Are For; When Springtime Comes to My River/WM: Roger McGough, William Perry. *Chess* (Imperial, "Anatoly," Apr. 28, 1988): Anthem; Endgame; A Model of Decorum & Tranquility; Terrace Duet; Where I Want to Be; You and I/W: Tim Rice, M: Benny Anderson, Bjorn Ulvaeus. *Grand Hotel* (Martin Beck, "Baron Felix Von Gaigern," Nov. 12, 1989/Dec. 2, 1990): As It Should Be; Fire and Ice/WM: Robert Wright, George Forrest, Maury Yeston — Love Can't Happen; Roses at the Station/WM: Maury Yeston.

1498. Diahann Carroll (July 17, 1935–) B: Bronx, NY. M: singer Vic Damone. As a teenager in the 1950s, her singing career was launched on the TV talent show *Chance of a Lifetime*, which she won 3 weeks in a row. Star of the popular sitcom *Julia* (1958), she played singer Dominique Deveraux on the soap *Dynasty* (1981). *House of Flowers* (Alvin, "Ottilie" alias "Violet," Dec. 30, 1954): House of Flowers; I Never Has Seen Snow; A Sleepin' Bee; Turtle Song/WM: Truman Capote, Harold Arlen. *No Strings* (54th Street, "Barbara Woodruff," Mar. 15, 1962): Loads of Love; Look No Further; Maine; No Strings; Nobody Told Me; An Orthodox Fool; The Sweetest Sounds; You Don't Tell Me/WM: Richard Rodgers.

1499. Dorothy Carroll *Earl Carroll's Sketch Book of 1929* (Earl Carroll > 44th Street > 46th Street, revue, July 1, 1929): Crashing the Golden Gate/W: E.Y. Harburg, M: Jay Gorney, Phil Cohan — Rhythm of the Waves/W: Charles Tobias, Harry Tobias, M: Vincent Rose.

1500. George Carroll *My Lady's Maid or Lady Madcap* (Casino, "Cpl. Ham," Sept. 20, 1906): I've No Patience with a Soldier/WM: Percy Greenbank, Paul Rubens.

1501. Harry Carroll (Nov. 28, 1892–Dec. 26, 1962) B: Atlantic City, NJ. Composer and musical director of many Broadway shows, and performer in vaudeville and nightclubs, he was one of the original members of ASCAP. *Maid in America* (Winter Garden, revue, "The Made in America Song Writer," Feb. 18, 1915): Dancing Around the U.S.A./W: Jack Yellen, M: Harry Carroll, George L. Cobb — Made in the U.S.A./

W: Harold Atteridge, M: Harry Carroll — The Times Square Arguments/W: Harold Atteridge, M: Sigmund Romberg.

1502. Helena Carroll (c 1941–) B: Edinburgh, Scotland. *Oliver!* (Imperial, "Mrs. Sowerberry," Jan. 6, 1963): That's Your Funeral/WM: Lionel Bart. *Oliver!* (Imperial, CR, "Mrs. Corney," c 1963): I Shall Scream; Oliver!/WM: Lionel Bart. *Pickwick* (46th Street, "Rachel," Oct. 4, 1965): There's Something About You/W: Leslie Bricusse, M: Cyril Ornadel.

1503. Jane Carroll *Leave It to Jane* (Longacre, "Sally," Aug. 28, 1917): There It Is Again/ W: P.G. Wodehouse, M: Jerome Kern. *The Greenwich Village Follies of 1919* (Nora Bayes, revue, c Sept. 15, 1919): My Little Javanese/W: Philip Bartholomae, John Murray Anderson, M: A. Baldwin Sloane. *The Love Letter* (Globe, "Betty Parker," Oct. 4, 1921): Rainbow; You're Mine/W: William Le Baron, M: Victor Jacobi. *The Blushing Bride* (Astor, "Doris Mayne," Feb. 6, 1922): Springtime Is the Time for Loving/W: Cyrus D. Wood, M: Sigmund Romberg. *The Yankee Princess* (Knickerbocker, "Princess Odys," Oct. 2, 1922): A Husband's Only a Husband/W: B.G. DeSylva, M: Emmerich Kalman. *Lady Butterfly* (Astor, CR, "Enid Crawford," Mar. 26, 1923): Don't Tell the Old Home Town; Kiss Time; Lady Butterfly; My Cottage in Sunshine Lane/W: Clifford Grey, M: Werner Janssen. *The Vagabond King* (Casino, "Huguette Du Hamel," Sept. 21, 1925): Huguette Waltz; Love for Sale/W: Brian Hooker, M: Rudolf Friml.

1504. Jean Carroll (1909–July 29, 1972) M: Buddy Howe, an acrobatic dancer with whom she teamed as a comedienne in vaudeville. After his death in 1945, she worked on her own. *Earl Carroll's Vanities of 1940* (St. James, revue, Jan. 13, 1940): The Starlit Hour/W: Mitchell Parish, M: Peter De Rose.

1505. Joan Carroll (Jan. 18, 1932–) B: Elizabeth, NJ. Since Miss Carroll was only 8 and forbidden to sing on stage due to child labor laws, Porter wrote her song as a recitation. *Panama Hattie* (46th Street, "Geraldine Bullett," Oct. 30, 1940): Let's Be Buddies/WM: Cole Porter.

1506. June Carroll (June 22–) B: Detroit, MI. Singer and lyric writer. Sister of LEONARD SILLMAN. She used the name JUNE SILLMAN early in her career as a performer. *Who's Who* (Hudson, revue, Mar. 1, 1938): The Girl with the Paint on Her Face/WM: Irvin Graham — I Dance Alone/WM: James Shelton — Let Your Hair Down with a Bang; Train Time/W: June Sillman, M: Baldwin Bergersen.

New Faces of 1952 (Royale, revue, May 16, 1952): Guess Who I Saw Today/W: Elisse Boyd, M: Murray Grand — Love Is a Simple Thing; Penny Candy/W: June Carroll, M: Arthur Siegel — Waltzing in Venice with You/WM: Ronny Graham.

1507. Leo G. Carroll (Oct. 25, 1886–Oct. 16, 1972) B: Weedon, England. From 1934 until 1966, this distinguished character actor of the stage made more than 40 films. Perhaps best remembered for his TV role of Cosmo Topper in the *Topper* series (1953), and as the spymaster in *The Man from U.N.C.L.E* (1964). *May Wine* (St. James, "Uncle Pishka," Dec. 5, 1935): Just Once Around the Clock/W: Oscar Hammerstein II, M: Sigmund Romberg. *The Two Bouquets* (Windsor, "Mr. Gill," May 31, 1938): The Course of Nature/W: Eleanor Farjeon, Herb Farjeon, M: A. Scott Gatly, based on Voices of the Past — A Health to Dear Mama/W: Eleanor Farjeon, Herb Farjeon, M: trad., based on Schneider, How Was You — Her Lily-white Hand/W: Eleanor Farjeon, Herb Farjeon, M: Herold — I Wish I Was in Texas/W: Eleanor Farjeon, Herb Farjeon, M: Paladine, based on Mandolinata — When I Was but a Bounding Boy/W: Eleanor Farjeon, Herb Farjeon, M: trad. — Yes or No/W: Eleanor Farjeon, Herb Farjeon, M: based on Offenbach.

1508. Marcelle Carroll (1897–Nov. 18, 1936) B: Biarritz, France. *Come Along* (Nora Bayes > 39th Street, "Madelon," Apr. 8, 1919): Big Offensive; Cuckoo/WM: John L. Nelson.

1509. Marie Carroll *Oh, Boy!* (Princess > Casino, "Lou Ellen Carter," Feb. 20, 1917): Oh, Daddy, Please; Words Are Not Needed/W: P.G. Wodehouse, M: Jerome Kern — An Old-Fashioned Wife; You Never Knew About Me/W: P.G. Wodehouse, Guy Bolton, M: Jerome Kern. *The Kiss Burglar* (Broadhurst > Nora Bayes, revival, "Aline, Grand Duchess of Orly," Mar. 17, 1919): Because You Do Not Know; I Want to Learn to Dance; The Rose/W: Glen MacDonough, M: Raymond Hubbell. *My Golden Girl* (Nora Bayes, "Peggy Mitchell," Feb. 2, 1920): Change Partners; Darby and Joan; I'd Like a Honeymoon with You; Shooting Star/W: Frederic Arnold Kummer, M: Victor Herbert. *Love Dreams* (Times Square > Apollo, "Cherry O'Moore," Oct. 10, 1921): Lonesome Boy; Pity Me/W: Oliver Morosco, M: Werner Janssen.

1510. Nancy Carroll (Nov. 19, 1904–Aug. 6, 1965) B: New York, NY. One of the first major stars of talking pictures. *Mayflowers* (Forrest, "Jane," Nov. 24, 1925): Oh! Sam/W: Clifford Grey, M: J. Fred Coots, Maurie Rubens — Put

Your Troubles in a Candy Box/W: Clifford Grey, M: J. Fred Coots — Whoa, Emma!/W: Clifford Grey, M: Edward Kunneke.

1511. Philip Carroll *3 Penny Opera* (Lunt-Fontanne, revival, "Ed," Nov. 5, 1989): Wedding Song/W: Bertolt Brecht, M: Kurt Weill, translated by Michael Feingold.

1512. Richard F. Carroll (Oct. 27, 1864–June 26, 1925) B: Boston, MA. *Rob Roy* (Herald Square, "Dugaid MacWheeble, Mayor of Perth," Oct. 29, 1894): My Hairt Is in the Highlands; My True Love Is a Shepherdess; Song of the Balladmongers/W: Harry B. Smith, M: Reginald De Koven. *The Burgomaster* (Manhattan, "E. Booth Talkington," Dec. 31, 1900): We've Never Discovered Him Yet/W: Frank Pixley, M: Gustav Luders. *The Maid and the Mummy* (New York, "Washington Stubbs," July 25, 1904): I Fell in Love with Polly/WM: Richard Carle — Letters; Sad Experiences/W: Richard Carle, M: Robert Hood Bowers. *The Belle of Mayfair* (Daly's, "Sir John Chaldicott," Dec. 3, 1906): I Know a Girl/WM: Leslie Stuart.

1513. Ronn Carroll *Annie Get Your Gun* (Music Theater of Lincoln Center > Broadway, revival, return engagement, "Foster Wilson" and "Mr. Schuyler Adams," May 31, 1966): Doin' What Comes Natur'lly; There's No Business Like Show Business/WM: Irving Berlin. *The Rink* (Martin Beck, "Dino's Father" and "Mrs. Silverman," Feb. 9, 1984): Not Enough Magic; What Happened to the Old Days?/W: Fred Ebb, M: John Kander. *The Best Little Whorehouse Goes Public* (Lunt-Fontanne, "Sen. A. Harry Hardast," May 10, 1994): Down and Dirty (The Smut Song)/WM: Carol Hall. *How to Succeed in Business Without Really Trying* (Richard Rodgers, revival, "J.B. Biggley," Mar. 23, 1995): Been a Long Day; Grand Old Ivy; Love from a Heart of Gold/WM: Frank Loesser.

1514. Elisabeth Carron *Street Scene* (New York City Center, revival, "Anna Maurrant," Feb. 13, 1960): A Boy Like You; Somehow I Never Could Believe/W: Langston Hughes, M: Kurt Weill — There'll Be Trouble; When a Woman Has a Baby/W: Langston Hughes, Elmer Rice, M: Kurt Weill.

1515. Louis Carry *Snow White and the Seven Dwarfs* (Radio City Music Hall, "Sneezy," Oct. 18, 1979/Jan. 11, 1980): Bluddle-uddle-um-dum (The Washing Song); The Dwarf's Yodel Song (The Silly Song); Heigh-Ho/W: Larry Morey, M: Frank Churchill.

1516. Doris Carson (Dec, 25, 1910–Feb. 20, 1995) B: New York, NY. Daughter of JAMES B.

CARSON. *Americana of 1928* (Lew Fields, revue, Oct. 30, 1928): The Ameri-can-can; Hot Pants/W: Irving Caesar, M: Roger Wolfe Kahn — Life as a Twosome/W: Irving Caesar, M: Roger Wolfe Kahn, Joseph Meyer. *Strike Up the Band* (Times Square, "Anne Draper," Jan. 14, 1930): Hangin' Around with You; I Mean to Say; I've Got a Crush on You/W: Ira Gershwin, M: George Gershwin. *Luana* (Hammerstein's, "Polly Hatch," Sept. 17, 1930): Wanapoo Bay; Yankyula/W: J. Keirn Brennan, M: Rudolf Friml. *The Cat and the Fiddle* (Globe, "Angie Sheridan," Oct. 15, 1931): Try to Forget/W: Otto Harbach, M: Jerome Kern. *On Your Toes* (Imperial > Majestic, "Frankie Frayne," Apr. 11, 1936): Glad to Be Unhappy; It's Got to Be Love; On Your Toes; There's a Small Hotel/W: Lorenz Hart, M: Richard Rodgers.

1517. Emma Carson *Adonis* (Bijoux, CR, "Artea," Mar. 19, 1885): Golden Chains/W: William F. Gill, Henry E. Dixey, M: Edward E. Rice.

1518. Jack Carson (Oct. 27, 1910–Jan. 2, 1963) B: Carman, Manitoba, Canada. The comedy actor with the sheepish grin started out in vaudeville and went on to the stage, TV and more than 70 movies. *Of Thee I Sing* (Ziegfeld, revival, "John P. Wintergreen," May 5, 1952): Love Is Sweeping the Country; Mine; Of Thee I Sing; Some Girls Can Bake a Pie; Who Cares?; Who Is the Lucky Girl to Be?/W: Ira Gershwin, M: George Gershwin.

1519. James B. Carson (Dec. 22, 1884–Nov. 18, 1958) B: Missouri. Father of DORIS CARSON. *The Motor Girl* (Lyric, "Ludwig Liebling," June 15, 1909): All the World Loves a Lover/W: Robert B. Smith, M: Jean Gilbert. *Judy Forgot* (Broadway, "Dr. Kuno Lauberscheimer," Oct. 6, 1910): My Soldier Boy/W: Avery Hopwood, M: Silvio Hein. *Miss Jack* (Herald Square, "Otto-Von-Hertz," Sept. 4, 1911): The English Language; There Really Isn't Any More to Tell/W: Mark Swan, M: William F. Peters. *The Red Petticoat* (Daly's > Broadway, "Otto Schmaltz," Nov. 13, 1912): Oo-Oo-Oo; Where Did the Bird Hear That?/W: Paul West, M: Jerome Kern. *Flo Flo* (Cort, "Isidor Moser," Dec. 20, 1917): Business Is Business; Don't Trust Them; If It Wasn't for My Wife and Family; A Wonderful Creature/W: Edward A. Paulton, M: Silvio Hein — Sarah from Sahara/W: George Edwards, M: Hugo Frey. *The Girl in the Spotlight* (Knickerbocker, "Max Preiss," July 12, 1920): Catch 'Em Young, Treat 'Em Rough, Tell 'Em Nothing; I'll Be There/W: Robert B. Smith, M: Victor Herbert. *The Magic Ring* (Liberty,

"Moe Bernheimer," Oct. 1, 1923): Malaiya/W: Zelda Sears, M: Harold A. Levey.

1520. Jeannie Carson (May 28, 1928–) B: Yorkshire, England. M: BIFF MCGUIRE. Best remembered for her TV series, *Hey Jeannie!* (1956). *Finian's Rainbow* (New York City Center, revival, "Sharon McLonergan," Apr. 27, 1960): How Are Things in Glocca Morra?; If This Isn't Love; Look to the Rainbow; Old Devil Moon; Something Sort of Grandish; That Great Come-and-Get-It Day; When the Idle Poor Become the Idle Rich/W: E.Y. Harburg, M: Burton Lane. *The Sound of Music* (Lunt-Fontanne, CR, "Maria Rainer," July 1962): Do-Re-Mi; Edelweiss; The Lonely Goatherd; My Favorite Things; An Ordinary Couple; Sixteen, Going on Seventeen; So Long, Farewell; The Sound of Music/W: Oscar Hammerstein II, M: Richard Rodgers. *Blood Red Roses* (John Golden, "Queen Victoria" and "Bessie Bellwood" and "Alice Crabbe" and "Florence Nightingale," Mar. 22, 1970): A Garden in the Sun; (O Rock Eternal) Soldier's Prayer; Song of Greater Britain; Song of the Fair Dissenter Lass/W: John Lewin, M: Michael Valenti.

1521. Maxine Carson *Sunny Days* (Imperial, "Lulu," Feb. 8, 1928): A Belle, a Beau and a Boutonniere; One Sunny Day/W: Clifford Grey, William Cary Duncan, M: Jean Schwartz.

1522. Mindy Carson (July 16, 1926–) B: New York, NY. Radio singer in the late 1940s; host of her own TV show in the 1950s. *The Body Beautiful* (Broadway, "Ann," Jan. 23, 1958): All of These and More; The Body Beautiful; Just My Luck; Leave Well Enough Alone; A Relatively Simple Affair/W: Sheldon Harnick, M: Jerry Bock.

1523. Susan Dawn Carson *Les Miserables* (Broadway, CR, "Fantine," Jan. 17, 1989/Nov. 19, 1992): Come to Me; I Dreamed a Dream/W: Herbert Kretzmer, M: Claude-Michel Schonberg.

1524. Kenneth Carten (Aug. 29, 1915–) B: London, England. He appeared as Sub Lieutenant R.N.V.R. in the British film, written and directed by Noel Coward, *In Which We Serve* (1942). *Set to Music* (Music Box, revue, Jan. 18, 1939): The Stately Homes of England/WM: Noel Coward.

1525. Brent Carter *Shenandoah* (Alvin, CR, "Gabriel," Oct. 20, 1975): Freedom; Why Am I Me?/W: Peter Udell, M: Gary Geld.

1526. Dixie Carter (May 25, 1939–) B: McLemoresville, TN. M: HAL HOLBROOK, 1984. She was Julia Sugarbaker on the TV sitcom *Designing Women* (1986). *Sextet* (Bijou, "Ann," Mar. 3, 1974): I Wonder; Visiting Rights/W: Lee Goldsmith, M: Lawrence Hurwit. *Pal Joey* (Circle in the Square, revival, "Melba Snyder," June 27, 1976): Zip/W: Lorenz Hart, M: Richard Rodgers.

1527. Frank Carter (c 1888–May 9, 1920) M: MARILYN MILLER. The handsome young song and dance man was married in May 1919, only a year before he was killed in a car accident. *Dancing Around* (Winter Garden, "Lieut. Harry Graham," Oct. 10, 1914): The Dancing Maniacs; Oh, You John/WM: ?—There's Something About You/W: Harold Atteridge, M: Sigmund Romberg, Harry Carroll. *Dancing Around* (Winter Garden, CR, "Lieut. Hartley," Jan. 23, 1915): The Broadway Triangle; Oh, You John/WM: ?—The Call to the Colors/W: Harold Atteridge, M: Sigmund Romberg, Harry Carroll—It's a Long Way to Tipperary/WM: Jack Judge, Harry Williams—My Lady of the Telephone/W: Harold Atteridge, M: Jean Gilbert—My Rainbow Beau/W: Harold Atteridge, M: Sigmund Romberg. *Robinson Crusoe, Jr.* (Winter Garden, "Dick Hunter," Feb. 17, 1916): (Go Ahead and) Dance a Little More; Pretty Little Mayflower Girl/W: Harold Atteridge, M: James F. Hanley—Hunter's Fox Trot Ball; My Pirate Lady/W: Harold Atteridge, M: Sigmund Romberg. *Doing Our Bit* (Winter Garden, "Bud Travers," Oct. 18, 1917): Hello, Miss Tango!; Let Her Go; Sally Down Our Alley/W: Harold Atteridge, M: Sigmund Romberg, Herman Timberg. *Ziegfeld Midnight Frolic [6th Edition]* (New Amsterdam roof, revue, Dec. 29, 1917): Beautiful Girl; I'm Looking for the Gay White Way (I'm Looking for Old Broadway); Uncle Sam Is Santa Claus to the World/W: Gene Buck, M: Dave Stamper—My Tiger Rose/WM: Gene Buck. *Ziegfeld Midnight Frolic [7th Edition]* (New Amsterdam roof, revue, Apr. 24, 1918): The Motor Girl/W: Gene Buck, M: Dave Stamper. *Ziegfeld Follies of 1918* (New Amsterdam > Globe, revue, June 18, 1918): Garden of My Dreams/W: Gene Buck, M: Louis A. Hirsch, Dave Stamper—I'm Gonna Pin My Medal on the Girl I Left Behind/WM: Irving Berlin. *See-Saw* (Cohan, "Richard Minot," Sept. 23, 1919): The Happiest Moment I've Ever Known; I'll Take Care of Him; When Two Hearts Discover/W: Earl Derr Biggers, M: Louis A. Hirsch.

1528. Jack Carter (June 24, 1923–Nov. 9, 1967) B: New York, NY. Comic performer in nightclubs and movies. *Mr. Wonderful* (Broadway, "Fred Campbell," Mar. 22, 1956): Charlie Welch; I've Been Too Busy; Without You I'm Nothing/W: Larry Holofcener, George Weiss, M: Jerry Bock.

1529. Lavada Carter *Shuffle Along of 1933* (Mansfield, revue, "Edith Wilkes," Dec. 26, 1932): Chickens Come Home to Roost; Here 'Tis; Sing and Dance Your Troubles Away; Sugar Babe/W: Noble Sissle, M: Eubie Blake.

1530. Nell Carter (Sept. 13, 1948–Jan. 23, 2003) B: Birmingham, AL. She starred as Nell Harper in the TV sitcom *Gimme a Break* (1981). *Dude* (Broadway, "Suzie Moon," Oct. 9, 1972): I Love My Boo Boo; Suzie Moon; Wah Wah Wah/W: Gerome Ragni, M: Galt MacDermot. *Ain't Misbehavin'* (Longacre, revue, May 9, 1978): Cash for Your Trash/W: Ed Kirkeby, M: Fats Waller — Find Out What They Like; Honeysuckle Rose/W: Andy Razaf, M: Fats Waller — It's a Sin to Tell a Lie/WM: Billy Mayhew — I've Got a Feeling I'm Falling/W: Billy Rose, M: Fats Waller, Harry Link — Lounging at the Waldorf/W: Richard Maltby, Jr., M: Fats Waller — Mean to Me/WM: Roy Turk, Fred E. Ahlert — This Is So Nice; When the Nylons Bloom Again/W: George Marion, Jr., M: Fats Waller. *Ain't Misbehavin'* (Ambassador, revue, revival, Aug. 15, 1988): same as above.

1531. Ralph Carter (May 30, 1961–) B: New York, NY. He played Michael Evans in the TV sitcom *Good Times* (1974). *The Me Nobody Knows* (Longacre, CR, "Benjamin," Nov. 1971): Black; Flying Milk and Runaway Plates/W: Will Holt, M: Gary William Friedman. *Raisin* (46th Street, "Travis Younger," Oct. 18, 1973): He Come Down This Morning; Sidewalk Tree/W: Robert Brittan, M: Judd Woldin.

1532. Rex Carter *The Last Waltz* (Century, "Ensign Orsinski," May 10, 1921): Ladies' Choice/W: Harold Atteridge, Edward Delaney Dunn, M: Oscar Strauss.

1533. Robert Peyton Carter (?–June 1918) *Fad and Folly [orig. Tommy Rot]* (Mrs. Osborn's Playhouse, "Lord Dope," Nov. 27, 1902): Sally/WM: Safford Waters. *The Lady from Lane's* (Lyric > Casino, "Wayland Clingstone," Aug. 19, 1907): I Never Do It Now/W: George Broadhurst, M: Gustave Kerker.

1534. Roland Carter *The Mocking Bird* (Bijou, "Gen. Aubrey," Nov. 10, 1902): The King of France/W: Sydney Rosenfeld, M: A. Baldwin Sloane.

1535. Terry Carter He played Sgt. Joe Broadhurst on the TV police drama *McCloud* (1970). *Kwamina* (54th Street, "Kwamina," Oct. 23, 1961): Did You Hear That?; Ordinary People; Something Big/WM: Richard Adler.

1536. Joan Carter-Waddell *Ups-A-Daisy!* (Shubert, "Madge Mallory," Oct. 8, 1928): Ups-A-Daisy!/W: Robert A. Simon, M: Lewis E. Gensler. *The Little Show* (Music Box, revue, Apr. 30, 1929): Caught in the Rain/W: Howard Dietz, M: Henry Sullivan. *Hey Nonny Nonny!* (Shubert, revue, June 6, 1932): The Season Ended/W: Max Lief, Nathaniel Lief, M: Michael H. Cleary.

1537. Dan Carthay *Keep Moving* (Forrest, revue, Aug. 23, 1934): Now Is the Time for All Good Men to Come to the Aid of the Party/W: Jack Scholl, M: Max Rich.

1538. Jeanne Cartier *See America First* (Maxine Elliott, "Notonah," Mar. 28, 1916): The Language of Flowers/WM: T. Lawrason Riggs, Cole Porter.

1539. Peggy Cartwright (Nov. 14, 1912–June 13, 2001) B: Vancouver, British Columbia, Canada. M: PHIL BAKER. *Americana of 1932* (Shubert, revue, Oct. 5, 1932): Would'ja for a Big Red Apple?/W: Johnny Mercer, Everett Miller, M: Henry Souvaine — You're Not Pretty but You're Mine/W: E.Y. Harburg, M: Burton Lane.

1540. Emma Carus (Mar. 18, 1879–Nov. 18, 1927) B: Berlin, Germany. The popular heavyset singing comedienne preferred vaudeville to the legitimate stage. Billed as The Human Dialect Cocktail, she was also able to leap from contralto to baritone. *The King's Carnival* (New York, revue, May 13, 1901): My Sailor Boy/W: Sidney Rosenfeld, George V. Hobart, M: A. Baldwin Sloane. *The Defender* (Herald Square, "Mrs. Jack Orchard," July 3, 1902): I'll Be Your Rainbeau/W: Ed Gardenier, M: J. Fred Helf— Jack O'Lantern Man; Queens of Society/W: Allen Lowe, M: Charles Denee. *The Dress Parade [Mid Summer Night's Fancies]* (Crystal Gardens, revue, June 22, 1903): Keep On A-Shining, Sil'vry Moon/W: Arthur J. Lamb, M: Ben M. Jerome. *The Darling of the Gallery Gods [Mid Summer Night's Fancies]* (Crystal Gardens, "Foxy Woman," June 22, 1903): Ida Bell/W: Matthew Woodward, M: Ben M. Jerome — Mozart Lincoln/W: John Gilroy, M: Ben M. Jerome — Watch Me Tonight in the Torchlight Parade/W: Arthur J. Lamb, M: Ben M. Jerome. *The Medal and the Maid* (Broadway, "Mrs. Habbicombe," Jan. 11, 1904): I'm Going to Be a Marquis; In Society/W: Charles H. Taylor, M: Sidney Jones — In Zanzibar (My Little Chimpanzee)/W: Will D. Cobb, M: Gus Edwards. *Woodland* (New York > Herald Square, "Lady Peacock," Nov. 21, 1904): Society; Will You Be My Little Bride?/W: Frank Pixley, M: Gustav Luders. *Up and Down Broadway* (Casino, revue, July 18, 1910): Go on Your Mission; I Am Melpomene; Samson and Delilah (My Operatic Samson)/W:

William Jerome, M: Jean Schwartz — In 1861/W: Junie McCree, M: Albert Von Tilzer — Mary Ann/W: Andrew B. Sterling, A. Costello, M: Albert Von Tilzer. *The Wife Hunters* (Herald Square, "Mrs. Homer Van Pelt," Nov. 2, 1911): Down at Mammy Jinny's; Leonara/WM: David Kempner, Anatole Friedland, Malvin Franklin — Girls, Girls, Keep Your Figures/W: David Kempner, M: Anatole Friedland.

1541. Brent Carver (Nov. 17, 1951–) B: Cranbrook, BC, Canada. *Kiss of the Spider Woman* (Broadhurst, "Molina," May 3, 1993): Anything for Him; Bluebloods; Dear One; Dressing Them Up; Gimme Love; Good Times; Her Name Is Aurora; I Draw the Line; Mama, It's Me; Only in the Movies; Over the Wall II; Russian Movie; She's a Woman; A Visit/W: Fred Ebb, M: John Kander.

1542. Ronny Carver *You'll See Stars* (Maxine Elliott, revue, "Joseph Kelly," Dec. 29, 1942): It Could Happen, It's Possible/W: Herman Timberg, M: Leo Edwards.

1543. Marjorie Carville *The Mimic World* (Century roof, revue, Aug. 17, 1921): Fine Feathers/W: Harold Atteridge, M: Sigmund Romberg.

1544. Claiborne Cary B: Iowa. Sister of CLORIS LEACHMAN. Cabaret singer and actress. *Beg, Borrow or Steal* (Martin Beck, "Frieda," Feb. 10, 1960): Poetry and All That Jazz/W: Bud Freeman, M: Leon Prober.

1545. Jeanne Caryl (July 11–) B: Thatcher, AZ. Formerly CAROL JEANNE TENNEY; CAROLINE TENNEY; CARYL TENNEY. *Two by Two* (Imperial, CR, "Goldie," Aug. 16, 1971): The Golden Ram/W: Martin Charnin, M: Richard Rodgers. *The Desert Song* (Uris, revival, "Margo Bonvalet," Sept. 5, 1973 mats.): The Desert Song; French Military Marching Song; I Want a Kiss; One Alone; Romance; The Sabre Song; Then You Will Know/W: Otto Harbach, Oscar Hammerstein II, M: Sigmund Romberg. *Carmelina* (St. James, "Katherine Smith," Apr. 8, 1979): The Image of Me; One More Walk Around the Garden/W: Alan Jay Lerner, M: Burton Lane. *Camelot* (New York State, revival, "Nimue," July 8, 1980): Follow Me/W: Alan Jay Lerner, M: Frederick Loewe. *Camelot* (Winter Garden, revival, "Nimue," Nov. 15, 1981): same as above.

1546. Primrose Caryll *Kissing Time* (Lyric, "Tashi," Oct. 11, 1920): Bill and Coo/W: George V. Hobart, M: Ivan Caryll — Keep a Fox Trot for Me/W: ?, M: Ivan Caryll. *Stepping Stones* (Globe, "Radiola," Nov. 6, 1923): Little Angel Cake/W: Anne Caldwell, M: Jerome Kern. *Step-* *ping Stones* (Globe, revival, "Radiola," Sept. 1, 1924): same as above. *Criss Cross* (Globe, "Renee," Oct. 12, 1926): Leaders of the Modern Regime/W: Anne Caldwell, Otto Harbach, M: Jerome Kern.

1547. Louis Casavant *The Red Feather* (Lyric, "Col. MacPatrick," Nov. 9, 1903): The Humorous Ghost; Our Cabinet/W: Charles Emerson Cook, M: Reginald De Koven. *The Golden Butterfly* (Broadway, "Prince Sergius Orloffsky," Oct. 12, 1908): The Man About Town/W: J. Hayden-Clarendon, M: Reginald De Koven. *The Princess Pat* (Cort, "Gen. John Holbrook," Sept. 29, 1915): When a Girl's About to Marry/W: Henry Blossom, M: Victor Herbert. *The Riviera Girl* (New Amsterdam, "Count Michael Lorenz," Sept. 24, 1917): There'll Never Be Another Girl Like Daisy/W: P.G. Wodehouse, M: Emmerich Kalman. *Louie the 14th* (Cosmopolitan, "The Major Domo," Mar. 3, 1925): The Major Domo/W: Arthur Wimperis, M: Sigmund Romberg.

1548. Clare Cascelles *The Belle of Mayfair* (Daly's, "Lady Hayward," Dec. 3, 1906): Eight Little Debutantes Are We/W: William Caine, M: Leslie Stuart.

1549. Allen Case (c 1935–Aug. 25, 1986) B: Dallas, TX. *Damn Yankees* (46th Street, CR, "Joe Hardy," Aug. 1957): Goodbye, Old Girl; A Man Doesn't Know; Near to You; Two Lost Souls/WM: Richard Adler, Jerry Ross. *Once Upon a Mattress* (Alvin, "Sir Harry," Nov. 1959): In a Little While; Yesterday I Loved You/W: Marshall Barer, M: Mary Rodgers. *Hallelujah, Baby!* (Martin Beck, "Harvey," Apr. 26, 1967): Another Day; Farewell, Farewell; I Don't Know Where She Got It; Not Mine; Talking to Yourself/W: Betty Comden, Adolph Green, M: Jule Styne.

1550. Anita Case *A Night in Venice* (Shubert, "Maria Livia," May 21, 1929): The One Girl/W: Oscar Hammerstein II, M: Vincent Youmans — One Night of Love/W: J. Keirn Brennan, M: Maurie Rubens.

1551. Helen Case (May 8, 1885–Mar. 1977) B: Petersburgh, IN. *Topsy and Eva* (Harris, "Mrs. Shelby," Dec. 23, 1924): Rememb'ring/WM: Vivian Duncan, Rosetta Duncan.

1552. Florence Caselle *Mlle. Modiste* (Jolson, revival, "Nanette," Oct. 7, 1929): When the Cat's Away the Mice Will Play/W: Henry Blossom, M: Victor Herbert.

1553. Dorothy Casey *The Great Temptations* (Winter Garden, revue, CR, July 19, 1926): The Spider's Web/W: ?, M: Milton Schwarzwald.

1554. Eileen Casey *Dancin'* (Broadhurst,

revue, CR, May 8, 1979): Pack Up Your Troubles in Your Old Kit Bag (and Smile, Smile, Smile)/W: George Asaf, M: Felix Powell.

1555. Marilyn Caskey *The Utter Glory of Morrissey Hall* (Mark Hellinger, "Elizabeth Wilkins," May 13, 1979): Duet; Elizabeth's Song; Give Me That Key; Proud, Erstwhile, Upright, Fair/WM: Clark Gesner. *The Phantom of the Opera* (Majestic, CR, "Carlotta Guidicelli," Jan. 2, 1989): Notes; Poor Fool, He Makes Me Laugh; Prima Donna; Think of Me; Twisted Every Way/W: Charles Hart, Richard Stilgoe, M: Andrew Lloyd Webber.

1556. Vic Casmore *Tickle Me* (Selwyn, "Marcel Poisson," Aug. 17, 1920): Safe in the Arms of Bill Hart; You're the Type/W: Otto Harbach, Oscar Hammerstein II, M: Herbert Stothart.

1557. Philip Casnoff (Aug. 3, 1953–) B: Philadelphia, PA. *Grease* (Broadhurst, CR, "Teen Ager," c 1974): Beauty School Dropout; Born to Hand-Jive/WM: Jim Jacobs, Warren Casey. *Chess* (Imperial, "Freddie," Apr. 28, 1988): Endgame; How Many Women; No Contest; One Night in Bangkok; Pity the Child; Press Conference; So You Got What You Want; A Whole New Board Game; You Want to Lose Your Only Friend?/W: Tim Rice, M: Benny Anderson, Bjorn Ulvaeus. *Shogun: The Musical* (Marquis, "John Blackthorne," Nov. 20, 1990): Born to Be Together; Death Walk; Escape; Fireflies; Honto; Impossible Eyes; Mad Rum Below; Night of Screams; No Man; One Candle; Rum Below; Sail Home; Trio/W: John Driver, M: Paul Chihara.

1558. Bradley Cass *Americana of 1928* (Lew Fields, revue, Oct. 30, 1928): No Place Like Home/W: Irving Caesar, M: Roger Wolfe Kahn.

1559. Lee Cass *Greenwillow* (Alvin, "Thomas Clegg," Mar. 8, 1960): Could've Been a Ring/WM: Frank Loesser.

1560. Maurice Cass (Oct. 12, 1884–June 8, 1954) B: Vilna, Lithuania. *La, La, Lucille* (Henry Miller, "Nicholas Grimsby," May 26, 1919): It's Hard to Tell [Sept. 8, 1919]/W: Arthur Jackson, B.G. DeSylva, M: George Gershwin.

1561. Peggy Cass (May 21, 1924–Mar. 8, 1999) B: Boston, MA. She was a regular on TV's late night *Jack Paar Show* (1958), and a panelist on the quiz *To Tell the Truth* (1964). *Touch and Go* (Broadhurst > Broadway, revue, Oct. 13, 1949): Be a Mess/W: Walter Kerr, Jean Kerr, M: Jay Gorney. *42nd Street* (Winter Garden, CR, "Maggie Jones," Sept. 1981/c 1985): Getting Out of Town/W: Mort Dixon, M: Harry Warren —

Go Into Your Dance; Shadow Waltz; Shuffle Off to Buffalo/W: Al Dubin, M: Harry Warren.

1562. Frances Cassard *On the Town* (Adelphi, "Singer," Dec. 28, 1944): I'm Blue/W: Betty Comden, Adolph Green, M: Leonard Bernstein.

1563. Claire Casscles *The Girl Behind the Counter* (Herald Square, "Dottie Styles," Oct. 1, 1907): Shopping/W: Arthur Anderson, M: Howard Talbot.

1564. Walter Cassel *Stars in Your Eyes* (Majestic, "Leading Man," Feb. 9, 1939): One Brief Moment; This Is It/W: Dorothy Fields, M: Arthur Schwartz. *All in Fun* (Majestic, revue, Dec. 27, 1940): It's a Big, Wide Wonderful World/WM: John Rox — Love and I/W: June Sillman, Irvin Graham, M: Baldwin Bergersen. *The Desert Song* (New York City Center, revival, "Pierre Birabeau" and "Red Shadow," Jan. 8, 1946): The Desert Song; Farewell; I Want a Kiss; One Alone; The Riff Song; Then You Will Know/W: Otto Harbach, Oscar Hammerstein II, M: Sigmund Romberg.

1565. Kerry Casserly (Oct. 26, 1953–) B: Minneapolis, MN. *A Chorus Line* (Shubert, CR, "Kristine," Aug. 1981): Sing!/W: Edward Kleban, M: Marvin Hamlisch.

1566. David Cassidy (Apr. 12, 1950–) B: New York, NY. Son of JACK CASSIDY; stepson of SHIRLEY JONES. Half-brother of SHAUN CASSIDY and PATRICK CASSIDY. He played Keith Partridge on the TV series *The Partridge Family* (1970). *The Fig Leaves Are Falling* (Broadhurst, "Billy," Jan. 2, 1969): For Our Sake; Lillian, Lillian, Lillian/W: Allan Sherman, M: Albert Hague. *Joseph and the Amazing Technicolor Dreamcoat* (Royale, revival, CR, "Joseph," Mar. 6, 1983): Any Dream Will Do; The Brothers Came to Egypt; Close Ev'ry Door to Me; A Coat of Many Colors; Go, Go, Go, Joseph; Grovel, Grovel; Jacob and Sons; Jacob in Egypt; Joseph All the Time; Joseph's Dreams; Pharaoh's Dream Explained; Potiphar; Stone the Crows; Who's the Thief?/WM: Tim Rice, Andrew Lloyd Webber. *Blood Brothers* (Music Box, CR, "Mickey," Aug. 16, 1993): Kids Game; Long Sunday Afternoon; My Friend; That Guy/WM: Willy Russell.

1567. Jack Cassidy (Mar. 5, 1925–Dec. 12, 1976) B: Richmond Hills, NY. M: SHIRLEY JONES. Father of DAVID, SHAUN and PATRICK CASSIDY. The actor-singer-dancer burned to death in his Los Angeles apartment. *Small Wonder* (Coronet, revue, Sept. 15, 1948): Nobody Told Me/W: Phyllis McGinley, M: Baldwin Bergersen — William McKinley High/W: Burt Shevelove, M: Albert Selden. *South*

Pacific (Majestic, CR, "Seabee Richard West," Jan. 1952): There Is Nothin' Like a Dame/W: Oscar Hammerstein II, M: Richard Rodgers. *Wish You Were Here* (Imperial, "Chick Miller," June 25, 1952): Mix and Mingle; They Won't Know Me; Where Did the Night Go?; Wish You Were Here/WM: Harold Rome. *Shangri-La* (Winter Garden, "Charles Mallinson," June 13, 1956): Somewhere; The World Outside/W: Jerome Lawrence, Robert E. Lee, M: Harry Warren. *The Beggar's Opera* (New York City Center, revival, "Macheath," Mar. 13, 1957): At the Tree I Shall Suffer with Pleasure; The Charge Was Prepar'd; Let Us Take the Road; My Heart Was So Free; O, What Pain It Is to Part; The Ways of the World; Were I Laid on Greenland Coast; Why How Now Madam Flirt/WM: John Gay. *She Loves Me* (Eugene O'Neill, "Steven Kodaly," Apr. 23, 1963): Good Morning, Good Day; Goodbye, Georg; Grand Knowing You; Ilona; Sounds While Selling; Thank You, Madam/W: Sheldon Harnick, M: Jerry Bock. *Fade Out—Fade In* (Mark Hellinger, "Byron Prong," May 26, 1964): Close Harmony; Fear; The Fiddler and the Fighter; I'm With You; My Fortune Is My Face; Oh Those Thirties/W: Betty Comden, Adolph Green, M: Jule Styne. *It's a Bird It's a Plane It's Superman* (Alvin, "Max Mencken," Mar. 29, 1966): So Long, Big Guy; We Need Him; The Woman for the Man; You've Got What I Need/W: Lee Adams, M: Charles Strouse. *Maggie Flynn* (ANTA, "Phineas," Oct. 23, 1968): Don't You Think It's Very Nice?; How About a Ball?; Learn How to Laugh; Look Around Your Little World; Maggie Flynn; Mr. Clown; Pitter Patter; Why Can't I Walk Away?/WM: Hugo Peretti, Luigi Creatore, George David Weiss. *Sondheim: A Musical Tribute* (Shubert, revue, Mar. 11, 1973): So Many People/WM: Stephen Sondheim.

1568. Margie Cassidy *Ziegfeld Midnight Frolic [6th Edition]* (New Amsterdam roof, revue, Dec. 29, 1917): My Tiger Rose/WM: Gene Buck.

1569. Patrick Cassidy (Jan. 4, 1961–) B: Los Angeles, CA. See JACK CASSIDY. *Leader of the Pack* (Ambassador, "Jeff Barry," Apr. 8, 1985): Do Wah Diddy Diddy; Hanky Panky/ WM: Jeff Barry, Ellie Greenwich — I Can Hear Music/ WM: Jeff Barry, Ellie Greenwich, Phil Spector.

1570. Shaun Cassidy (Sept. 27, 1958–) B: Los Angeles, CA. See JACK CASSIDY. Shaun was a teen idol of the late 1970s. *Blood Brothers* (Music Box, CR, "Eddie," c 1993): I'm Not Saying a Word; Long Sunday Afternoon; My Friend; That Guy/WM: Willy Russell.

1571. Tim Cassidy (Mar. 22, 1952–) B: Alliance, OH. *A Chorus Line* (Shubert, CR, "Bobby," Nov. 1978): And.../W: Edward Kleban, M: Marvin Hamlisch. *Dreamgirls* (Ambassador, revival, "Frank," June 28, 1987): The Rap/W: Tom Eyen, M: Henry Krieger.

1572. Irene Cassini *The Geisha* (44th Street, revival, "Nami," Mar. 27, 1913): The Dear Little Jappy-jap-jappy/W: Harry Greenbank, M: Sidney Jones.

1573. Judy Cassmore (Mar. 27, 1942–) B: San Francisco, CA. *Fade Out— Fade In* (Mark Hellinger, CR, "Gloria Currie," June 22, 1964/ Feb. 15, 1965): Close Harmony; L.Z. in Quest of His Youth/W: Betty Comden, Adolph Green, M: Jule Styne.

1574. Gene Castle B: New York, NY. He made his NY debut in *Gypsy* at age 11. *George M!* (Palace, "Willie," Apr. 10, 1968): Popularity/ WM: George M. Cohan.

1575. Irene Castle (Apr. 7, 1893–Jan. 25, 1969) B: New Rochelle, NY. M: VERNON CASTLE. Dancing partners until his death, they innovated many dance steps, such as the turkey-trot and the one-step. She went on to become the most famous ballroom dancer of her time. *Watch Your Step* (New Amsterdam, revue, "Mrs. Vernon Castle," Dec. 8, 1914): Show Us How to Do the Fox Trot/WM: Irving Berlin.

1576. John Castle (Jan. 14, 1940–) *Georgy* (Winter Garden, "Jos," Feb. 26, 1970): A Baby; Howdjadoo; Life's a Holiday; Ol' Pease Puddin'; Something Special; There's a Comin' Together/ W: Carole Bayer Sager, M: George Fischoff.

1577. Joyce Castle *Brigadoon* (New York State, revival, "Meg Brockie," Nov. 7, 1991): Down on MacConnachy Square; The Love of My Life/W: Alan Jay Lerner, M: Frederick Loewe.

1578. Roy Castle (Aug. 31, 1932–Sept. 2, 1994) B: Huddersfield, W. Yorkshire, England. *Pickwick* (46th Street, "Sam Weller," Oct. 4, 1965): A Gentleman's Gentleman; Talk; You Never Met a Feller Like Me/W: Leslie Bricusse, M: Cyril Ornadel.

1579. Vernon Castle (May 2, 1887–Feb. 15, 1918) B: Norwich, England. M: IRENE CASTLE, his dance partner, in 1911. His sister was CORALIE BLYTHE; his brother-in-law was LAWRENCE GROSSMITH. Castle was killed in an airplane crash in Houston, TX. *The Story of Vernon and Irene Castle* (1939), starring Fred Astaire and Ginger Rogers, is the film version of their lives together. *The Midnight Sons* (Broadway, "Souseberry Lushmore," May 22, 1909): Call Me Bill/W: Glen MacDonough, M: Raymond Hubbell. *Old Dutch* (Herald Square, "Hon. Algernon Clymber," Nov. 22, 1909): Algy/W: George V. Hobart, M: Victor Herbert. *The Summer Widowers* (Broadway, "Oxford Tighe," June 4, 1910): I Never Know How to Behave When I'm with Girls, Girls, Girls/W: Glen MacDonough, M: A. Baldwin Sloane. *The Hen-Pecks* (Broadway, "Zowie," Feb. 4, 1911): It's Not the Trick Itself, but It's the Tricky Way It's Done/W: E. Ray Goetz, Vincent Bryan, M: A. Baldwin Sloane. *The Sunshine Girl* (Knickerbocker,"Lord Bicester," Feb. 3, 1913): The Butler; Josephine; Ladies; Little Girl, Mind How You Go!; Who's the Boss?/WM: Paul Rubens, Arthur Wimperis. *Watch Your Step* (New Amsterdam, "Joseph Lilyburn," Dec. 8, 1914): I'm a Dancing Teacher Now/WM: Irving Berlin.

1580. Dolly Castles *The Woman Haters* (Astor, "Tilly Von Eberhart," Oct. 7, 1912): Come On Over Here/W: Jerome Kern, George V. Hobart, M: Walter Kollo — The Jag of Joy; Little Girl Come Back to Me/W: M.E. Rourke, M: Edmund Eysler — Love Is the Joy of Living; Love's Alphabet/W: George V. Hobart, M: Edmund Eysler. *The Man with Three Wives* (Weber and Fields, "Olivia," Jan. 23, 1913): All in a Little Dance; Love's Flower Is Always Blooming; We Are Free/W: Paul M. Potter, Harold Atteridge, M: Franz Lehar.

1581. Jean Casto B: Boston, MA. *Pal Joey* (Ethel Barrymore > Shubert > St. James, "Melba Snyder," Dec. 25, 1940): Zip/W: Lorenz Hart, M: Richard Rodgers.

1582. Paul Castree B: Rockford, IL. *Grease* (Eugene O'Neill, revival, "Eugene Florczyk," May 11, 1994): Born to Hand-Jive/WM: Jim Jacobs, Warren Casey.

1583. Claudia Catania *The Most Happy Fella* (Booth, revival, "Marie," Feb. 13, 1992): How Beautiful the Days; Young People/WM: Frank Loesser.

1584. Mary Jo Catlett (Sept. 2, 1938–) B: Denver, CO. She played Pearl Gallagher on the TV sitcom *Diff'rent Strokes* (1982). *Canterbury Tales* (Eugene O'Neill, CR, "Nun" and "Miller's Wife"): Beer Is Best (Beer, Beer, Beer); It Depends on What You're At/W: Nevill Coghill, M: Richard Hill, John Hawkins. *Different Times* (ANTA, "Mrs. Daniel Webster Hepplewhite" and "The Kaiser" and "Hazel Hughes," May 1, 1972): Forward Into Tomorrow; I Feel Grand; Marianne/WM: Michael Brown. *The Pajama Game* (Lunt-Fontanne, revival, "Mabel," Dec. 9, 1973): I'll Never Be Jealous Again/WM: Richard Adler, Jerry Ross.

1585. Walter Catlett (Feb. 4, 1889–Nov. 14,

1960) B: San Francisco, CA. In movies from the 1920s he was a comical performer in hundreds of cameo roles. *Little Simplicity* (Astor > 44th Street, "Prof. Erasmus Duckworth," Nov. 4, 1918): Learning to Love; Maybe You'll Look Good to Me; My Lulu; National Air's Medley/ W: Rida Johnson Young, M: Augustus Barratt. *Sally* (New Amsterdam, "Otis Hooper," Dec. 21, 1920): The Church 'Round the Corner/W: Clifford Grey, P.G.Wodehouse, M: Jerome Kern — The Lorelei/W: Anne Caldwell, M: Jerome Kern — On with the Dance/W: Clifford Grey, M: Jerome Kern. *Dear Sir* (Times Square, "Andrew Bloxom," Sept. 23, 1924): If You Think It's Love You're Right; A Mormon Life; My Houseboat on the Harlem/W: Howard Dietz, M: Jerome Kern. *Lady, Be Good!* (Liberty, "J. Watterson Watkins," Dec. 1, 1924): Oh, Lady Be Good!/W: Ira Gershwin, M: George Gershwin. *Lucky* (New Amsterdam, "Charlie," Mar. 22, 1927): By the Light of the Silvery Moon/W: Edward Madden, M: Gus Edwards — Spring Is Here; Without Thinking of You/WM: ?. *Rio Rita* (Lyric, CR, "Ed Lovett," Jan. 30, 1928): The Best Little Lover in Town; I Can Speak Espagnol/W: Joseph McCarthy, M: Harry Tierney. *Treasure Girl* (Alvin, "Larry Hopkins," Nov. 8, 1928): Got a Rainbow/W: Ira Gershwin, M: George Gershwin.

1586. Minto Cato (Aug. 23, 1900–Oct. 26, 1979) B: Little Rock, AK. *Blackbirds of 1930* (Royale, revue, Oct. 22, 1930): Memories of You/W: Andy Razaf, M: Eubie Blake. *John Henry* (44th Street, "Old Aunt Dinah," Jan. 10, 1940): Jaybird/W: Roark Bradford, M: Jacques Wolfe.

1587. Irene Cattell *The Fortune Teller* (Century roof, revival, "Vaninka," Sept. 29, 1923): Serenade/W: Harry B. Smith, M: Victor Herbert.

1588. Rebekah Cauble *Sinbad* (Casino, CR, "Harriet," Feb. 14, 1918): Beauty and the Beast/ W: Harold Atteridge, M: Sigmund Romberg. *Tangerine* (Casino, "Elsie Loring," Aug. 9, 1921): (You and I) Atta Baby [Apr. 10, 1922]/W: Howard Johnson, M: Carle Carlton — Man Is the Lord of It All/W: Carle Carlton, M: Jean Schwartz — There's a Sunbeam for Every Drop of Rain; We'll Never Grow Old/W: Howard Johnson, M: Monte Carlo, Alma Sanders. *Oh! Oh! Oh! Nurse* (Cosmopolitan, "Marion Gay," Dec. 7, 1925): Good Night, My Lady Love; Is It Any Wonder?; The Newlywed Express; Way Out in Rainbow Land/W: Monte Carlo, M: Alma Sanders.

1589. Zachary Caully *Nina Rosa* (Majestic,

"Harry," Sept. 20, 1930): Nina Rosa/W: Irving Caesar, M: Sigmund Romberg.

1590. Chief Caupolican B: poss. Chile. A baritone, he sang with the Metropolitan Opera, 1920-1922. *Whoopee* (New Amsterdam, "Black Eagle," Dec. 4, 1928): The Song of the Setting Sun (Love Is the Mountain)/W: Gus Kahn, M: Walter Donaldson.

1591. Joseph Cauto *San Toy* (Daly's, CR, "Sing-Hi," Mar. 18, 1901): We're the Cream of Courtly Creatures/W: Harry Greenbank, Adrian Ross, M: Sidney Jones.

1592. Thomas Cavanagh (Oct. 26, 1968–) B: Ottawa, Ontario, Canada. *Shenandoah* (Virginia, revival, "Sam," Aug. 8, 1989): Violets and Silverbells/W: Peter Udell, M: Gary Geld.

1593. Alice Cavanaugh *Sue, Dear* (Times Square, "Zoe," July 10, 1922): Dance Me Darling Dance Me; Pidgie Widgie/W: Bide Dudley, M: Frank Grey. *Lady Butterfly* (Astor, CR, "Mabel Stockbridge," Apr. 2, 1923): Doll's House; Good Evening — Good Night; Sailors Sail Away; When the Wedding Bells Ring Out/W: Clifford Grey, M: Werner Janssen. *Flossie* (Lyric, "Bessie," June 3, 1924): Blind Man's Bluff; Flossie; I'm in Wonderland; Poogie-Woo/W: Ralph Murphy, M: Armand Robi.

1594. Evelyn Cavanaugh *The Kiss Burglar* (Cohan, "Miss Tinkle," May 9, 1918): He Loves Me, He Loves Me Not/W: Glen MacDonough, M: Raymond Hubbell. *My Golden Girl* (Nora Bayes > Casino, "Kitty Mason," Feb. 2, 1920): A Little Nest for Two; Name the Day/W: Frederic Arnold Kummer, M: Victor Herbert. *Love Birds* (Apollo, "Violet Morley," Mar. 15, 1921): Carnival Night; Is It Hard to Guess?; Let's Pretend/W: Ballard Macdonald, M: Sigmund Romberg. *Wildflower* (Casino, "Bianca Benedetto," Feb. 7, 1923): The Best Dance I've Had Tonight/W: Otto Harbach, Oscar Hammerstein II, M: Vincent Youmans, Herbert Stothart. *Dew Drop Inn* (Astor, "Edith Toober," May 17, 1923): A Girl May as Well Marry Well; Moonlight Waltz; The Primrose Path/W: Cyrus D. Wood, M: Alfred Goodman — I'm a Flapper/W: McElbert Moore, M: Jean Schwartz, J. Fred Coots. *The Girl Friend* (Vanderbilt, "Wynn Spencer," Mar. 17, 1926): Good Fellow Mine; What Is It?/W: Lorenz Hart, M: Richard Rodgers.

1595. Hobart Cavanaugh (Sept. 22, 1886– Apr. 25, 1950) B: Virginia City, NV. Meek, bald character actor, in movies from 1927. *Irene* (Vanderbilt, "Robert Harrison," Nov. 18, 1919): We're Getting Away with It/W: Joseph McCarthy, M: Harry Tierney. *Tangerine* (Casino, CR, "Fred Allen," Apr. 10, 1922): It's Great to Be Married

(and Lead a Single Life)/W: Howard Johnson, M: Monte Carlo, Alma Sanders, Carle Carlton — Love Is a Business; South Sea Island Blues/ W: Howard Johnson, M: Monte Carlo, Alma Sanders — Man Is the Lord of It All/W: Carle Carlton, M: Jean Schwartz. *Tell Her the Truth* (Cort, "Maclean," Oct. 28, 1932): Horrortorio!/W: R.P. Weston, Bert Lee, M: Joseph Tunbridge, Jack Waller.

1596. Lucille Cavanaugh *Ziegfeld Follies of 1915* (New Amsterdam, revue, June 21, 1915): Oriental Love/WM: ?.

1597. Robert D. Cavanaugh *Teddy & Alice* (Minskoff, "Ted Roosevelt, Jr.," Nov. 12, 1987): Charge; Private Thoughts/W: Hal Hackady, M: John Philip Sousa, Richard Kapp.

1598. Lisa Dawn Cave *Cats* (Winter Garden, CR, "Tantomile"): The Moments of Happiness/W: T.S. Eliot, M: Andrew Lloyd Webber.

1599. Millie Cavendish (?–Jan. 23, 1867) B: England. *The Black Crook* (Niblo's Garden, "Carline," Sept. 12, 1866): You Naughty, Naughty Men/WM: T. Kennick, G. Bicknell.

1600. Pamela Caveness *Show Boat* (New York City Center, revival, "Magnolia Hawks Ravenal," Sept. 7, 1948): After the Ball/WM: Charles K. Harris — Can't Help Lovin' Dat Man; Make Believe; Why Do I Love You?; You Are Love/W: Oscar Hammerstein II, M: Jerome Kern.

1601. Dick Cavett (Nov. 19, 1936–) B: Kearny, NE. M: CARRIE NYE. Actor, comedy writer, TV talk show host. *Into the Woods* (Martin Beck, CR, "Narrator," July 19, 1988): Ever After/WM: Stephen Sondheim.

1602. Joe Antony Cavise (Jan. 7, 1958–) B: Syracuse, NY. *Cats* (Winter Garden, CR, "Mungojerrie," Mar. 1984): Mungojerrie and Rumpleteazer/W: T.S. Eliot, M: Andrew Lloyd Webber.

1603. Joseph Cawthorn (Mar. 29, 1867– Jan. 21, 1949) B: New York, NY. M: QUEENIE VASSAR. The popular Dutch dialect comedian first appeared on the stage in 1871, at Robinson's Music Hall in New York. He was brought to England at age 9, where he performed in music halls until he was 13. He went to Hollywood in 1926. *The Fortune Teller* (Wallack's, "Boris," Sept. 26, 1898): The Power of the Human Eye; Romany Life (Czardas)/W: Harry B. Smith, M: Victor Herbert. *The Sleeping Beauty and the Beast* (Broadway, "Lena," Nov. 4, 1901): B'Gosh!; Let Them Go/W: J. Cheever Goodwin, M: Frederic Solomon, J.M. Glover — Nursery Rhymes/W: William Jerome, M: Jean Schwartz. *Mother Goose* (New Amsterdam, "Mother Goose," Dec.

2, 1903): On the Go; Our Goose Has a Mint in Her Little Insides; We Marched Away/W: George V. Hobart, M: Frederic Solomon — Social Eclat/WM: Clifton Crawford — Still in the Old Front Line/WM: Matthew Woodward — The Stories Adam Told to Eve/W: William Jerome, M: Jean Schwartz. *Fritz in Tammany Hall* (Herald Square, "Fritz von Swobenfritz," Oct. 16, 1905): The Dear Little Wise Old Bowery; The Dear Old Farm; In Bad Man's Land; Yankee Doodle Boodle/W: William Jerome, M: Jean Schwartz. *The Free Lance* (New Amsterdam, "Siegmund Lump," Apr. 16, 1906): Come, My Dear; It Depends on the Hair; The Mystery of History; Song of the Free Lance (I Am a Salaried Warrior)/W: Harry B. Smith, M: John Philip Sousa. *Little Nemo* (New Amsterdam, "Dr. Pill," Oct. 20, 1908): I Wouldn't Take a Case Like That; Is My Face On Straight?; Newspaper Song (Read the Papers Every Day); There's Nothing the Matter with Me/W: Harry B. Smith, M: Victor Herbert. *Girlies* (New Amsterdam, "Oscar Spiel," June 13, 1910): Concertina [June 20, 1910]; You Can Find It in the Papers Every Day/W: Harry Williams, M: Egbert Van Alstyne — Life Is a Merry-Go-Round/W: John L. Golden, M: Benjamin Hapgood Burt. *The Sunshine Girl* (Knickerbocker, "Schlump," Feb. 3, 1913): The Butler; Two Nuts; Who's the Boss?/WM: Paul Rubens, Arthur Wimperis — You Can't Play Every Instrument in the Band/W: Joseph Cawthorn, M: John L. Golden. *The Girl from Utah* (Knickerbocker, "Trimpel," Aug. 24, 1914): Follow Me; I Want to Be the Captain; In the Movies; We're Getting On Very Well; Where Has Una Gone?/W: Percy Greenbank, Adrian Ross, M: Paul Rubens, Sidney Jones — Gilbert the Filbert/W: Arthur Wimperis, M: Herman Finck — The Girl in Clogs and Shawl/WM: Harry Castling, C.W. Murphy — They Didn't Believe Me/W: M.E. Rourke, M: Jerome Kern. *Sybil* (Liberty, "Otto Spreckles," Jan. 10, 1916): At a Grand Hotel/W: Harry Graham, Harry B. Smith, M: Victor Jacobi — Good Advice; When Cupid Calls (The Rat-Tat-Tat Song)/W: Harry B. Smith, M: Victor Jacobi — I Can Dance with Everybody but My Wife/WM: Joseph Cawthorn, John L. Golden. *Rambler Rose* (Empire, "Joseph Guppy," Sept. 10, 1917): Bundle of Nerves; But Not for You; Smile a Little Smile for Me/W: Harry B. Smith, M: Victor Jacobi — Poor Little Rich Girl's Dog/WM: Irving Berlin. *The Canary* (Globe, "Timothy," Nov. 4, 1918): Love Me in the Spring/W: Richard Fecheimer, M: William B. Kernell — That Little German Band/W: Benjamin Hapgood Burt, M: Ivan Caryll — You're So Beautiful/WM: Irving Berlin. *The Half Moon* (Liberty, "Henry Hudson Hobson," Nov. 1, 1920): What Is the Matter with Women?; When You Smile/W: William Le Baron, M: Victor Jacobi. *The Blue Kitten* (Selwyn, "Theodore Vanderpop," Jan. 13, 1922): The Best I Ever Get Is the Worst of It/W: William Cary Duncan, M: Rudolf Friml — Cutie/W: Otto Harbach, M: Rudolf Friml — Tact/W: Otto Harbach, William Cary Duncan, M: Rudolf Friml.

1604. Susie Forrester Cawthorn *The Yankee Tourist* (Astor, "Mrs. Sybil Schwartz," Aug. 12, 1907): Irish Memories/W: Wallace Irwin, M: Alfred G. Robyn.

1605. Herbert Cawthorne *Mr. Bluebeard* (Knickerbocker, "Irish Patshaw," Jan. 21, 1903): Julie/W: William Jerome, M: Jean Schwartz. *The Isle of Spice* (Majestic, "Mickey O'Grady," Aug. 23, 1904): Silly Sailors/W: George E. Stoddard, M: Paul Schindler. *Marcelle* (Casino, "Herr Schwindle," Oct. 1, 1908): The Schwindle Corps/W: Frank Pixley, M: Gustav Luders.

1606. Hilarion (Larry) Ceballos (Oct. 21, 1887–Sept. 12, 1978) B: Iquique, Chile. He was a dance director and choreographer of 1940 and early 50s movies. *The Hen-Pecks* (Broadway, CR, "Hiram," Aug. 14, 1911): Don't Forget the Beau You Left Behind/W: E. Ray Goetz, M: A. Baldwin Sloane.

1607. Rene Ceballos (Apr. 7, 1953–) B: Boston, MA. *A Chorus Line* (Shubert, CR, "Bebe," Sept. 1977/Mar. 1981): At the Ballet/W: Edward Kleban, M: Marvin Hamlisch. *Dancin'* (Broadhurst, revue, Mar. 27, 1978): Here You Come Again/WM: Barry Mann, Cynthia Weil — Pack Up Your Troubles in Your Old Kit Bag (and Smile, Smile, Smile)/W: George Asaf, M: Felix Powell — Rally Round the Flag [May 1978]/WM: trad. *Cats* (Winter Garden, "Cassandra," Oct. 7, 1982): The Old Gumbie Cat/W: T.S. Eliot, M: Andrew Lloyd Webber. *Grand Hotel* (Martin Beck, CR, "Elizaveta Grushinskaya," Nov. 12, 1990): Bonjour Amour; Love Can't Happen/WM: Maury Yeston — Fire and Ice/WM: Robert Wright, George Forrest, Maury Yeston — No Encore/WM: Robert Wright, George Forrest.

1608. Joey Cee *Peter Pan* (Minskoff, return engagement of revival, "Michael Darling," Nov. 27, 1991): I'm Flying; Tender Shepherd/W: Carolyn Leigh, M: Moose Charlap.

1609. Leonard Ceeley (Aug. 14, 1892–May 7, 1977) B: England. M: MARGARET CARLISLE. *Lollipop* (Knickerbocker, "Don Carlos," Jan. 21, 1924): Deep in My Heart; Love in a Cottage; When We Are Married/W: Zelda Sears, M: Vincent Youmans. *My Princess* (Shubert, "Guiseppe Ciccolini [Chick]," Oct. 6, 1927): Dear Girls, Goodbye; Follow the Sun to the South; Our Bridal Night/W: Dorothy Donnelly, M: Sigmund Romberg. *The Desert Song* (Imperial, CR, "Red Shadow" and "Pierre Birabeau," Nov. 1927): The Desert Song; Farewell; I Want a Kiss; One Alone; The Riff Song; Then You Will Know/W: Otto Harbach, Oscar Hammerstein II, M: Sigmund Romberg. *Nina Rosa* (Majestic, "Pablo," Sept. 20, 1930): A Gaucho Love Song; Pablo; Serenade of Love/W: Irving Caesar, M: Sigmund Romberg. *Marching By* (46th Street, "Col. Petroff," Mar. 3, 1932): All's Fair in Love and War/W: Harry B. Smith, M: Jean Gilbert — Finery; Light Up/WM: ? — Let Fate Decide/W: Harry B. Smith, M: Maurie Rubens.

1610. Baby Cele (Mar. 22, 1972–) B: Durban, South Africa. *Sarafina!* (Cort, "Mistress It's a Pity," Jan. 28, 1988): Give Us Power; Mama/WM: Mbongeni Ngema — The Lord's Prayer/W: The Bible, M: Albert Hay Malotte — Talking About Love; Yes! Mistress It's a Pity/WM: Hugh Masekela, Mbongeni Ngema.

1611. Marie Celeste (c 1876–Dec. 17, 1954) B: New York, NY. *A Runaway Girl* (Daly's, revival, "Winifred Grey," Apr. 23, 1900): The Boy Guessed Right/WM: Lionel Monckton — No One in the World Like You/W: Aubrey Hopwood, Harry Greenbank, M: Alfred D. Cammeyer — The Singing Girl/W: Aubrey Hopwood, Harry Greenbank, M: Ivan Caryll — The Cigarette Song/W: Aubrey Hopwood, M: Lionel Monckton. *San Toy* (Daly's, "San Toy," Oct. 1, 1900): The Little China Maid; When You Are Wed to Me/W: Harry Greenbank, Adrian Ross, M: Sidney Jones. *San Toy* (Daly's, revival, "San Toy," Apr. 7, 1902): same as above.

1612. Mona Celete *Just a Minute* (Cort, "Margaret Gibson," Oct. 27, 1919): Because You're Different; The Girl I Want to Call My Wife; I'll Say I Will; Some Other Girl/WM: Harry L. Cort, George E. Stoddard, Harold Orlob. *The Greenwich Village Follies of 1920* (Shubert, revue, Aug. 31, 1921): Just Sweet Sixteen/W: Arthur Swanstrom, John Murray Anderson, M: A. Baldwin Sloane.

1613. Frank H. Celli (1842–Dec. 27, 1904) B: London, England. *A Runaway Girl* (Fifth Avenue, CR, "Prof. Tamarind," Dec. 26, 1898): Barcelona/W: Aubrey Hopwood, Harry Greenbank, M: Ivan Caryll.

1614. Michael Cerveris (Nov. 6, 1960–) B: Bethesda, MD. *The Who's Tommy* (St. James, "Tommy," Apr. 22, 1993): Amazing Journey; I'm Free; Listening to You; Pinball Wizard; See Me, Feel Me; Sensation; Welcome; We're Not Going to Take It/WM: Pete Townshend.

1615. Carlos Cestero (May 4, 1949–) B: San Juan, Puerto Rico. *Two Gentlemen of Verona* (St. James, CR, "Proteus," Oct. 23, 1972): Calla Lily Lady; Dragon Fight; Follow the Rainbow; I Love My Father; I'd Like to Be a Rose; Love's Revenge; Symphony; That's a Very Interesting Question; Thou, Julia, Thou Hast Metamorphosed; What Does a Lover Pack?; What's a Nice Girl Like Her/W: John Guare, M: Galt MacDermot — Who Is Silvia?/W: William Shakespeare, M: Galt MacDermot.

1616. Christopher Chadman (?–Apr. 30, 1995) *Rockabye Hamlet* (Minskoff, "Rosencrantz," Feb. 17, 1976): Have I Got a Girl for You; Hey…!/WM: Cliff Jones. *Pal Joey* (Circle in the Square, revival, "Joey Evans," June 27, 1976): Den of Iniquity; Happy Hunting Horn; I Could Write a Book; Pal Joey (What Do I Care for a Dame?); Take Him; You Mustn't Kick It Around/W: Lorenz Hart, M: Richard Rodgers. *A Chorus Line* (Shubert, CR, "Bobby," June 1977): And…/W: Edward Kleban, M: Marvin Hamlisch. *Dancin'* (Broadhurst, revue, Mar. 27, 1978/Apr. 17, 1979): Easy; If It Feels Good, Let It Ride/WM: Carol Bayer Sager, Melissa Manchester — Was Dog a Doughnut/WM: Cat Stevens.

1617. Cyril Chadwick (June 11–?) B: London, England. On Mar. 24, 1913, he appeared in a one-act musical comedy, part of the opening program of the brand new Palace Theater in New York. *Yvette* (39th Street, "Lord Silverhampton," Aug. 10, 1916): Galloping Major; Silly Ass; Tick-Tick/WM: Frederick Herendeen. *The Kiss Burglar* (Cohan, "E. Chatterton-Pym," May 9, 1918): I Want to Learn to Dance/W: Glen MacDonough, M: Raymond Hubbell.

1618. Ida May Chadwick *Paradise Alley* (Casino, "Quinnie La Salle," Mar. 31, 1924): As Long as They Keep on Making 'Em; In the Musical Comedy Shows; Rolland from Holland/WM: Howard Johnson — If We Could Live on Promises/W: Howard Johnson, M: Harry Archer — Put on the Ritz/W: Howard Johnson, M: Irving Bibo — Success/W: Howard Johnson, M: Harry Archer, Carle Carlton.

1619. Thomas Chadwick *Sweet Adeline* (Hammerstein's, "The Sultan," Sept. 3, 1929): Oriental Moon/W: Oscar Hammerstein II, M: Jerome Kern.

1620. Dell Chain *Sunkist* (Globe, revue, "A Nut Applicant," May 23, 1921): Use Your Own Judgment/WM: Fanchon Wolff, Marco Wolff.

1621. Lucille Chalfant *The Greenwich Village Follies of 1922* (Shubert, revue, Sept. 12, 1922): Nightingale, Bring Me a Rose/W: Irving Caesar, John Murray Anderson, M: Louis A. Hirsch — Vienna Nights/WM: ?.

1622. Bessie Challenger *By the Sad Sea Waves* (Grand Opera House, revival, "Sis Hopkins," Mar. 5, 1900): I'se Found Yo', Honey, Found Yo', Now Be Mine/W: Harry Bulger, J. Sherrie Mathews, M: Gustav Luders.

1623. Peggy Chamberlain *Here's Howe!* (Broadhurst, "Cora Bibby," May 1, 1928): Crazy Rhythm; Dismissal Whistle; I'd Rather Dance Here Than Hereafter/W: Irving Caesar, M: Joseph Meyer, Roger Wolfe Kahn.

1624. Richard Chamberlain (Mar. 31, 1935–) B: Beverly Hills, CA. *My Fair Lady* (Virginia, revival, "Henry Higgins," Dec. 9, 1993): A Hymn to Him; I'm an Ordinary Man; I've Grown Accustomed to Her Face; The Rain in Spain; Why Can't the English?; You Did It/W: Alan Jay Lerner, M: Frederick Loewe.

1625. Howard Chambers (1873–Mar. 15, 1911) B: England. M: BLANCHE MORRISON. *Mlle. Modiste* (Knickerbocker, "Lieut. Rene La Motte," Dec. 25, 1905): The Dear Little Girl Who Is Good/W: Henry Blossom, M: Victor Herbert. *The Tourists* (Majestic, "Capt. of the Guard," Aug. 25, 1906): A Game of Hearts/W: R.H. Burnside, M: Gustave Kerker.

1626. Lindsay Chambers *Cats* (Winter Garden, CR, "Mistoffelees," c 1992): The Invitation to the Jellicle Ball; Mr. Mistoffelees; Mungojerrie and Rumpleteazer/W: T.S. Eliot, M: Andrew Lloyd Webber.

1627. Madelaine Chambers *Alive and Kicking* (Winter Garden, revue, Jan. 17, 1950): What a Delightful Day/W: Ray Golden, Paul Francis Webster, M: Sammy Fain.

1628. Peter Chambers *The Band Wagon* (New Amsterdam, revue, June 3, 1931): Nanette/W: Howard Dietz, M: Arthur Schwartz. *The Cat and the Fiddle* (Globe, "Jean Colbert," Oct. 15, 1931): Poor Pierrot/W: Otto Harbach, M: Jerome Kern.

1629. Ralph Chambers (Mar. 1, 1892–Mar. 16, 1968) B: Uniontown, PA. *Call Me Madam* (Imperial, "Sen. Gallagher," Oct. 12, 1950): They Like Ike/WM: Irving Berlin.

1630. Gower Champion (June 22, 1919–Aug. 25, 1980) B: Geneva, IL. M: MARGE CHAMPION, 1947-1973. At 15 he won a dance contest and went to New York. Dancer, choreographer and director of several Broadway hits, he died on the day that the last of them, *42nd Street*, opened. *3 For Tonight* (Plymouth, revue,

Apr. 6, 1955): The Auction; By-Play for Drums; The Clock; Dance, Dance, Dance; Here I Stand; It Couldn't Be a Better Day; Summer in Fairview Falls/W: Robert Wells, M: Walter Schumann — By the Light of the Silvery Moon/W: Edward Madden, M: Gus Edwards — Shine On, Harvest Moon/WM: Jack Norworth, Nora Bayes.

1631. Marge Champion (Sept. 2, 1921–) B: Los Angeles, CA. M: GOWER CHAMPION. They appeared together in several 1950s MGM musicals. Her father was a ballet coach to movie stars. She was the model for Disney's animated *Snow White*. *3 for Tonight* (Plymouth, revue, Apr. 6, 1955): same as above. *Five-Six-Seven-Eight … Dance!* (Radio City Music Hall, revue, June 15, 1983): I Love to Dance/W: Marilyn Bergman, Alan Bergman, M: Billy Goldenberg.

1632. David Shoiche Chan *Roza* (Royale, "Michel," Oct. 1, 1987): Get the Lady Dressed; Is Me/W: Julian More, M: Gilbert Becaud.

1633. Nicholas Chan *Miss Saigon* (Broadway, CR, "Tam," c 1993): Little God of My Heart/W: Richard Maltby, Jr., Alain Boublil, M: Claude-Michel Schonberg.

1634. Jamie Beth Chandler *Starlight Express* (Gershwin, "Buffy," Mar. 15, 1987): Engine of Love/W: Peter Reeves, Richard Stilgoe, M: Andrew Lloyd Webber — Lotta Locomotion; Pumping Iron; Race Two; Rolling Stock; U.N.C.O.U.P.L.E.D./W: Richard Stilgoe, M: Andrew Lloyd Webber.

1635. David Chaney *That's Entertainment* (Edison, revue, "Greg," Apr. 14, 1972): Come, O, Come to Pittsburgh; Experience; Hammacher Schlemmer, I Love You; If There Is Someone Lovelier Than You; Keep Off the Grass; Triplets; We Won't Take It Back/W: Howard Dietz, M: Arthur Schwartz.

1636. Jan Chaney *Portofino* (Adelphi, "Angela," Feb. 21, 1958): A Dream for Angela/W: Richard Ney, M: Louis Bellson.

1637. Betsy Chang (Aug. 24, 1963–) B: Oakland, CA. *Cats* (Winter Garden, CR, "Demeter," c 1993): Grizabella, the Glamour Cat; Macavity/W: T.S. Eliot, M: Andrew Lloyd Webber.

1638. Jeffrey Chang *Miss Saigon* (Broadway, CR, "Tam," c 1992): Little God of My Heart/W: Richard Maltby, Jr., Alain Boublil, M: Claude-Michel Schonberg.

1639. Carol Channing (Jan. 31, 1921–) B: Seattle, WA. Superb comic actress who will always be "Dolly" to us all. *Let's Face It!* (Imperial, CR, "Maggie Watson," Oct. 1941): Baby Games; A Lady Needs a Rest; Let's Not Talk About Love/WM: Cole Porter. *Lend an Ear* (National > Broadhurst, revue, Dec. 16, 1948):

The Gladiola Girl; Three Little Queens of the Silver Screen/WM: Charles Gaynor — Power of the Press/WM: Joseph Stein, Will Glickman. *Gentlemen Prefer Blondes* (Ziegfeld, "Lorelei Lee," Dec. 8, 1949): Button Up with Esmond; Bye Bye Baby; Diamonds Are a Girl's Best Friend; Gentlemen Prefer Blondes; Homesick Blues; It's Delightful Down in Chile; A Little Girl from Little Rock/W: Leo Robin, M: Jule Styne. *Wonderful Town* (Winter Garden, CR, "Ruth Sherwood," 1953): Conga; Conversation Piece (Nice Talk, Nice People); Ohio; One Hundred Easy Ways; Swing!; Wrong Note Rag/W: Betty Comden, Adolph Green, M: Leonard Bernstein. *The Vamp* (Winter Garden, "Flora Weems," Nov. 10, 1955): Delilah's Dilemma; I'm Everybody's Baby; I've Always Loved You; Keep Your Nose to the Grindstone; Samson and Delilah; That's Where a Man Fits In; Yeemy Yeemy/W: John Latouche, M: James Mundy. *Show Girl* (Eugene O'Neill, revue, Jan. 12, 1961): Calypso Pete; The Girl in the Show; In Our Teeny Little Weeny Nest; Love Is a Sickness; My Kind of Love; The Story of Marie/WM: Charles Gaynor. *Hello, Dolly!* (St. James, "Mrs. Dolly Gallagher Levi," Jan. 16, 1964): Before the Parade Passes By/WM: Lee Adams, Charles Strouse, Jerry Herman — Dancing; Hello, Dolly!; I Put My Hand In; Put on Your Sunday Clothes; So Long, Dearie/WM: Jerry Herman — Motherhood/WM: Bob Merrill, Jerry Herman. *Lorelei or Gentlemen Still Prefer Blondes* (Palace, "Lorelei Lee," Jan. 27, 1974): Button Up with Esmond; Bye Bye Baby; Diamonds Are a Girl's Best Friend; Homesick Blues; It's Delightful Down in Chile; A Little Girl from Little Rock; Mamie Is Mimi/W: Leo Robin, M: Jule Styne — Looking Back; Men!/W: Betty Comden, Adolph Green, M: Jule Styne. *Hello, Dolly!* (Lunt-Fontanne, revival, "Mrs. Dolly Gallagher Levi," Mar. 5, 1978): same as above. *Hello, Dolly!* (Lunt-Fontanne, revival, "Mrs. Dolly Gallagher Levi," Oct. 19, 1995): same as above.

1640. Stockard Channing (Feb. 13, 1944–) B: New York, NY. Serious actress, in movies and TV dramas as well as on the stage. *The Rink* (Martin Beck, CR, "Angel," July 14, 1984): All the Children in a Row; Angel's Rink and Social Center; The Apple Doesn't Fall; Colored Lights; Don't Ah Ma Me; Mrs. A.; Not Enough Magic; Under the Roller Coaster; Wallflower/W: Fred Ebb, M: John Kander.

1641. Marina Chapa *Miss Saigon* (Broadway, "Gigi," Apr. 11, 1991): The Movie in My Mind/W: Richard Maltby, Jr., Alain Boublil, M: Claude-Michel Schonberg.

1642. Alyce Chapelle *You Said It* (46th Street, CR, "Grace Carroll," May 18, 1931): Wha'd' We Come to College For?/W: Jack Yellen, M: Harold Arlen.

1643. Brian Chapin *Jennie* (Majestic, "Kevin O'Conner," Oct. 17, 1963): When You're Far Away from New York Town/W: Howard Dietz, M: Arthur Schwartz.

1644. Harry Chapin (Dec. 7, 1942–July 16, 1981) B: New York, NY. Brother of TOM CHAPIN. The folk-rock composer and performer was killed in a car accident. *The Night That Made America Famous* (Ethel Barrymore, revue, Feb. 26, 1975): Better Place to Be; Cat's in the Cradle; Great Divide; Mr. Tanner; The Night That Made America Famous; Six String Orchestra; Sniper; Sunday Morning Sunshine; Taxi; Too Much World/WM: Harry Chapin.

1645. Tom Chapin (Mar. 13, 1945–) B: Charlotte, NC. *Pump Boys and Dinettes* (Princess, CR, "Jim," Jan. 5, 1983): Mamaw/WM: Jim Wann.

1646. Chapine *Yvette* (39th Street, "Yvette," Aug. 10, 1916): I Love You So; Just One More Kiss; Love Holds Sway; Love Letters; Since I Met You; Some Girls; Tick-Tick/WM: Frederick Herendeen.

1647. Sydney Chaplin (Mar. 31, 1926–) B: Los Angeles, CA. His father was actor Charles Chaplin, with whom he appeared in the film, *Limelight* (1952). *Bells Are Ringing* (Shubert, "Jeff Moss," Nov. 29, 1956): Better Than a Dream [Apr. 14, 1958]; Hello, Hello There!; I Met a Girl; Independent (On My Own); Just in Time; Long Before I Knew You; You've Got to Do It/W: Betty Comden, Adolph Green, M: Jule Styne. *Subways Are for Sleeping* (St. James, "Tom Bailey," Dec. 27, 1961): Be a Santa; Comes Once in a Lifetime; How Can You Describe a Face?; I'm Just Taking My Time; Ride Through the Night; Subway Directions; Swing Your Projects; What Is This Feeling in the Air?; Who Knows What Might Have Been?/W: Betty Comden, Adolph Green, M: Jule Styne. *Funny Girl* (Winter Garden, "Nick Arnstein," Mar. 26, 1964): I Want to Be Seen with You Tonight; You Are Woman/W: Bob Merrill, M: Jule Styne.

1648. Blanche Chapman (1851–June 7, 1941) B: Covington, KY. *An Arabian Girl and Forty Thieves* (Herald Square, "Nicotina Zaza," Apr. 29, 1899): Operatic Mountebanks; Pictures/W: J. Cheever Goodwin, M: ?.

1649. Frank Chapman (c 1900–July 26, 1966) *Nikki* (Longacre, "Frank Chapman," Sept. 29, 1931): My Heart Is Calling; Now I Know/W: James Dyrenforth, M: Phil Charig.

1650. Gary Chapman (Apr. 20, 1953–) B: Brooklyn, NY. *Sophisticated Ladies* (Lunt-Fontanne, revue, CR, Jan. 5, 1982): Drop Me Off in Harlem/W: Nick Kenny, M: Duke Ellington — I Love You Madly; I've Got to Be a Rug Cutter/WM: Duke Ellington — Old Man Blues/W: Irving Mills, M: Duke Ellington — Perdido/W: Hans Lengsfelder, Ervin Drake, M: Juan Tizol. *Big Deal* (Broadway, "Kokomo" and "Dancin' Dan," Apr. 10, 1986): I've Got a Feelin' You're Foolin'/W: Arthur Freed, M: Nacio Herb Brown — Me and My Shadow/W: Billy Rose, M: Al Jolson, Dave Dreyer.

1651. George Chapman (c 1871–Jan. 23, 1914) *Mr. Pickwick* (Herald Square, "Snodgrass," Jan. 19, 1903): The Lay of the Merry Ha! Ha!/W: Grant Stewart, M: Manuel Klein.

1652. William Chapman (Apr. 30, 1923–) B: Los Angeles, CA. *Candide* (Martin Beck, "Ferone," Dec. 1, 1956): What's the Use?/W: Richard Wilbur, M: Leonard Bernstein. *Greenwillow* (Alvin, "Reverend Lapp," Mar. 8, 1960): The Sermon/WM: Frank Loesser. *South Pacific* (New York City Center, revival, "Emile de Becque," Apr. 13, 1961): A Cockeyed Optimist; Dites-Moi; I'm Gonna Wash That Man Right Outa My Hair; Some Enchanted Evening; This Nearly Was Mine; Twin Soliloquies; A Wonderful Guy/W: Oscar Hammerstein II, M: Richard Rodgers. *Shenandoah* (Alvin, CR, "Charlie Anderson," Nov. 2, 1976): It's a Boy; I've Heard It All Before; Meditation; Papa's Gonna Make It Alright; The Pickers Are Comin'/W: Peter Udell, M: Gary Geld.

1653. Vickie D. Chappell (Oct. 1957–) B: Wedowee, AL. *It's So Nice to Be Civilized* (Martin Beck, "Sissy," June 3, 1980): It's So Nice to Be Civilized; Why Can't Me and You?/WM: Micki Grant.

1654. Chappy Chappelle Partner of JUANITA STINNETTE. They were a black team who, unusual for their day, played the white vaudeville circuit. *Plantation Revue* (48th Street, revue, July 17, 1922): Gypsy Blues/W: Noble Sissle, M: Eubie Blake — I Want to Be Vamped in Georgia; Minstrels on Parade/W: Roy Turk, M: J. Russel Robinson — Mandy/W: Henry Creamer, M: Turner Layton *How Come?* (Apollo, "A Smart Lawyer," Apr. 16, 1923): E-Gypsy-Ann; Pickaninny Vamp; Sweetheart, Farewell/WM: Ben Harris, Henry Creamer, Will Vodery — Love Will Bring You Happiness/WM: Ben Harris.

1655. Cyd Charisse (Mar. 8, 1921–) B: Amarillo, TX. M: singer and actor Tony Martin. Aunt of ZAN CHARISSE and IAN

TUCKER. Best dancing in movie musicals such as *Singin' in the Rain* (1952), *Band Wagon* (1953) and *Silk Stockings* (1957). *Grand Hotel* (Martin Beck, CR, "Elizaveta Grushinskaya," Jan. 1992): Bonjour Amour; Love Can't Happen/WM: Maury Yeston — Fire and Ice/WM: Robert Wright, George Forrest, Maury Yeston — No Encore/WM: Robert Wright, George Forrest.

1656. Zan Charisse (Nov. 14, 1951–) B: New York, NY. Niece of CYD CHARISSE. Sister of IAN TUCKER. Model and actress. *Gypsy* (Winter Garden, revival, "Louise," Sept. 23, 1974): All I Need Is the Girl; If Momma Was Married; Let Me Entertain You; Little Lamb; Madame Rose's Toreadorables; Together Wherever We Go/W: Stephen Sondheim, M: Jule Styne.

1657. Ernest Charles (Nov. 21, 1895–) B: Minneapolis, MN. *Earl Carroll's Vanities of 1928* (Earl Carroll, revue, Aug. 6, 1928): Pretty Girl/W: Grace Henry, M: Morris Hamilton — Tell Me Truly/WM: George Bagby, G. Romilli. *George White's Scandals of 1929* (Apollo, revue, Sept. 23, 1929): You Are My Day Dream/W: Irving Caesar, M: Cliff Friend.

1658. Keith Charles (Mar. 4, 1934–) B: San Francisco, CA. *Celebration* (Ambassador, "Potemkin," Jan. 22, 1969): Celebration; Love Song; My Garden; Not My Problem; Survive; Winter and Summer/W: Tom Jones, M: Harvey Schmidt. *Applause* (Palace, CR, "Bill Sampson," May 3, 1971): Fasten Your Seat Belts; One of a Kind; Think How It's Gonna Be/W: Lee Adams, M: Charles Strouse.

1659. Pamela Charles (June 10, 1932–) B: Croydon, Surrey, England. *My Fair Lady* (Mark Hellinger, CR, "Eliza Doolittle," Feb. 2, 1959): I Could Have Danced All Night; Just You Wait; The Rain in Spain; Show Me; Without You; Wouldn't It Be Loverly?/W: Alan Jay Lerner, M: Frederick Loewe.

1660. Richard Charles *The Desert Song* (New York City Center, revival, "Sid El Kar," Jan. 8, 1946): High on a Hill; One Flower Grows Alone in Your Garden; The Riff Song/W: Otto Harbach, M: Oscar Hammerstein II, M: Sigmund Romberg.

1661. Walter Charles (Apr. 4, 1945–) B: East Stroudsburg, PA. *La Cage aux Folles* (Palace, CR, "Albin," July 22, 1986): The Best of Times; I Am What I Am; La Cage aux Folles; A Little More Mascara; Masculinity; Song on the Sand; With You on My Arm/WM: Jerry Herman. *Aspects of Love* (Broadhurst, "Marcel Richard," Apr. 8, 1990): Hand Me the Wine and the Dice; Leading Lady/W: Don Black, Charles Hart, M:

Andrew Lloyd Webber. *Aspects of Love* (Broadhurst, CR, "George Dillingham"): Falling; The First Man You Remember; A Memory of a Happy Moment; Other Pleasures; She'd Be Far Better Off with You; Stop. Wait. Please./W: Don Black, Charles Hart, M: Andrew Lloyd Webber. *110 in the Shade* (New York State, revival, "Noah Curry," July 18, 1992): Lizzie's Comin' Home; Poker Polka/W: Tom Jones, M: Harvey Schmidt. *A Christmas Carol* (Paramount Madison Square Garden, "Scrooge," Dec. 1, 1994): Abundance and Charity; Christmas Together; Link by Link; Nothing to Do with Me; A Place Called Home; Yesterday, Tomorrow and Today/W: Lynn Ahrens, M: Alan Menken.

1662. Zachary A. Charles B: New York, NY. *Top Banana* (Winter Garden, "Russ Wiswell," Nov. 1, 1951): O.K. for TV; Slogan Song (You Gotta Have a Slogan)/WM: Johnny Mercer.

1663. Tom Charlesworth *Kismet* (Ziegfeld, "Chief Policeman," Dec. 3, 1953): He's in Love; Was I Wazir?/WM: Robert Wright, George Forrest, M: based on Alexander Borodin.

1664. Spencer Charters (Mar. 25, 1875–Jan. 25, 1943) B: Duncannon, PA. In 36 years on stage the character actor appeared in 475 plays and was in movies from the 1920s. *Annie Dear* (Times Square, "James Ludgate," Nov. 4, 1924): Help, Help, Help/WM: Clare Kummer.

1665. Arline Chase (1900–Apr. 19, 1926) *Leave It to Jane* (Longacre, "Louella," Aug. 28, 1917): I'm Going to Find the Girl; Just You Watch My Step/W: P.G. Wodehouse, M: Jerome Kern. *The Night Boat* (Liberty, "Betty," Feb. 2, 1920): Girls Are Like a Rainbow; I Love the Lassies (I Love Them All)/W: Anne Caldwell, M: Jerome Kern.

1666. Diana Chase *Luana* (Hammerstein's, "Diana Larned," Sept. 17, 1930): Where You Lead/W: J. Keirn Brennan, M: Rudolf Friml.

1667. Ilka Chase (Apr. 8, 1900–Feb. 15, 1978) B: New York, NY. M: actor Louis Calhern. Primarily known as a novelist and commentator, her career included acting in movies and plays. *Keep Off the Grass* (Broadhurst, revue, May 23, 1940): Rhett, Scarlett, Ashley/W: Al Dubin, M: Jimmy McHugh.

1668. Norman Chase *Johnny Johnson* (Edison, revival, "Capt. Valentine," Apr. 11, 1971): Captain Valentine's Tango/W: Paul Green, M: Kurt Weill.

1669. Pauline Chase (May 20, 1885–Mar. 3, 1962) B: Washington, D.C. *The Liberty Belles* (Madison Square, "Kathleen Gay," Sept. 30, 1901): Lesson Book Song/W: ?, M: Aimee Lachaume. *Our Miss Gibbs* (Knickerbocker, "Mary Gibbs," Aug. 29, 1910): I Don't Want You to Be a Sister to Me/W: Frederick Day, M: Jerome Kern — In Yorkshire/W: Ralph Roberts, Leslie Mayne, M: Lionel Monckton — Mary; Not That Sort of Person/W: Adrian Ross, M: Lionel Monckton — Moonstruck; Our Farm/WM: Lionel Monckton.

1670. Don Chastain (Sept. 2, 1935–Aug. 9, 2002) B: Oklahoma City, OK. *No Strings* (54th Street, "Mike Robinson," Mar. 15, 1962): Be My Host; Eager Beaver/WM: Richard Rodgers. *It's a Bird It's a Plane It's Superman* (Alvin, "Jim Morgan," Mar. 29, 1966): We Don't Matter at All/W: Lee Adams, M: Charles Strouse. *42nd Street* (Winter Garden, CR, "Julian Marsh," Apr. 1985): 42nd Street; Lullaby of Broadway/W: Al Dubin, M: Harry Warren.

1671. Ruth Chatterton (Dec. 24, 1893–Nov. 24, 1961) B: New York, NY. M: RALPH FORBES; movie actor George Brent, 1932-34. A good actress who appeared mostly in not so good movies. She was also a novelist. *The Magnolia Lady* (Shubert, "Lily-Lou Ravenel," Nov. 25, 1924): The French Lesson; Liza Jane; Moon Man; My Heart's in the Sunny South; The Old Red Gate; Tiger Lily-Lou/W: Anne Caldwell, M: Harold A. Levey.

1672. Richard Chawner *The Little Cherub* (Criterion, CR, "Alderman Briggs," Oct. 22, 1906): My Wife Will Be My Lady/W: Owen Hall, M: Ivan Caryll.

1673. Mireille Chazal *La Grosse Valise* (54th Street, "Mireille," Dec. 14, 1965): Spanish Dance/W: Harold Rome, M: Gerard Calvi.

1674. Chubby Checker (Oct. 3, 1941–) B: Philadelphia, PA. Early 60s rock 'n' roller, most connected with the Twist dance craze. *Grease* (Eugene O'Neill, revival, CR, "Teen Angel"): Beauty School Dropout/WM: Jim Jacobs, Warren Casey.

1675. Jean Cheek *Amen Corner* (Nederlander, "Sister Moore," Nov. 10, 1983): In His Own Good Time; Leanin' on the Lord/W: Peter Udell, M: Garry Sherman.

1676. Larry Chelsi *The Golden Apple* (Alvin, "Patroclus," Apr. 20, 1954): Come Along, Boys; Helen Is Always Willing; It Was a Glad Adventure/W: John Latouche, M: Jerome Moross.

1677. Ed Cheney *The Laugh Parade* (Imperial, revue, Nov. 2, 1931): Excuse for Song and Dance; Gotta Go to Town/W: Mort Dixon, Joe Young, M: Harry Warren.

1678. Chun-Tao Cheng *Paint Your Wagon* (Shubert, "Lee Zen," Nov. 12, 1951): I'm on My Way; Movin'/W: Alan Jay Lerner, M: Frederick Loewe.

1679. Kam Cheng (Mar. 28, 1969–) B: Hong Kong. *Miss Saigon* (Broadway, "Kim," Apr. 11, 1991): Back in Town; The Ceremony; The Guilt Inside Your Head; I Still Believe; I'd Give My Life for You; The Last Night of the World; Little God of My Heart; The Movie in My Mind; Please; Room 317; Sun and Moon; You Will Not Touch Him/W: Richard Maltby, Jr., Alain Boublil, M: Claude-Michel Schonberg.

1680. Frances H. Cherry *Holka-Polka* (Lyric, "Marie Karin," Oct. 14, 1925): Spring in Autumn/W: Gus Kahn, Raymond B. Egan, M: Will Ortman.

1681. John Cherry (c 1888–Jan. 11, 1968) *Suzette* (Princess, "Armand," Nov. 24, 1921): No! No!/W: Roy Dixon, M: Arthur Gutman. *Glory* (Vanderbilt, "Sumner Holbrook," Dec. 25, 1922): Saw Mill River Road; We've Got to Build/W: Joseph McCarthy, M: Harry Tierney — When the Curfew Rings at Nine/WM: Al W. Brown. *Robin Hood* (Jolson, revival, "Sir Guy of Gisborne," Nov. 18, 1929): Churning, Churning; I Am the Sheriff of Nottingham; Oh, See the Lambkins Play!; Tinkers' Song/W: Harry B. Smith, M: Reginald De Koven. *The Serenade* (Jolson's, revival, "Colombo," Mar. 4, 1930): The Singing Lesson/W: Harry B. Smith, M: Victor Herbert. *Robin Hood* (Erlanger's, revival, "Sir Guy of Gisborne," Feb. 8, 1932): same as above. *Viva O'Brien* (Majestic, "Prof. Sherwood," Oct. 9, 1941): Mozambamba/W: Raymond Leveen, M: Maria Grever.

1682. Rex Cherryman (Oct. 30, 1896–Aug. 10, 1928) B: Grand Rapids, MI. *Topsy and Eva* (Harris, "George Shelby," Dec. 23, 1924): Give Me Your Heart and Give Me Your Hand; Kiss Me; Rememb'ring/WM: Vivian Duncan, Rosetta Duncan.

1683. Charles Chesney *Music in May* (Casino, CR, "Hans," June 3, 1929): High, High, High!; Open Your Window/W: J. Keirn Brennan, M: Maurie Rubens. *The Student Prince* (Majestic, revival, "Detlef," Jan. 29, 1931): Come Boys, Let's All Be Gay, Boys (Students' March Song); Drinking Song (Drink! Drink! Drink!); Serenade; Student Life; To the Inn We're Marching/W: Dorothy Donnelly, M: Sigmund Romberg. *The Student Prince* (Broadway, revival, "Capt. Tarnitz," June 8, 1943): Just We Two/W: Dorothy Donnelly, M: Sigmund Romberg.

1684. Alfred Chester *Pansy* (Belmont, "Bill," May 14, 1929): I'd Be Happy/WM: Maceo Pinkard.

1685. Eddie Chester *Artists and Models of 1927* (Winter Garden, revue, Nov. 15, 1927): Bangaway Isle/WM: ?.

1686. Nona Chester *How Come?* (Apollo, "Sister Jones," Apr. 16, 1923): Charleston Cutout; Pretty Malinda; Syncopated Strain/WM: Ben Harris, Henry Creamer, Will Vodery.

1687. Maurice Chevalier (Sept. 12, 1888–Jan. 1, 1972) B: Paris, France. Debonair singer, actor, songwriter; international superstar of stage, screen, night clubs and TV. *Maurice Chevalier in Songs and Impressions* (Lyceum, one-person revue, Sept. 28, 1955): A Barcelone/W: Maurice Chevalier, M: Henri Betti — A Boy and a Girl; She and He/Eng. W: Ben Smith, M: Henri Betti — A Las Vegas/Eng. W: Maurice Chevalier, M: Louis Guiglielmi Louiguy — Ca Va, Ca Va; C'est Fort la Musique/W: Maurice Chevalier, M: Fred Freed — Folies-Bergere/W: Maurice Chevalier, M: Francis Lopez — I Wonder Who's Kissing Her Now/W: Will M. Hough, Frank R. Adams, M: Joseph E. Howard, Harold Orlob — Les Pas Perdus/W: Robert Lamoureux, Maurice Chevalier, M: Henri Bourtsyre — L'Illusioniste/W: Vittonet, M: Jean Constantin — L'Orientale; Paris Oui Oui/W: Andre Hornez, M: Henri Betti — Louise/W: Leo Robin, M: Richard A. Whiting — Seems Like Old Times/WM: Carmen Lombardo, John Jacob Loeb — Un Gentleman/WM: Maurice Chevalier. *Maurice Chevalier* (Ziegfeld, one-person revue, Jan. 28, 1963): A Las Vegas/W: Albert Willemetz, M: Louis Guiglielmi Louiguy — Ah Donnez M'en de la Chanson/WM: Rene Rouzaud, Marguerite Monnot — Contre L'Amour y'a Rien a Faire/WM: Michel Rivgauche, Eva Wallis — How to Handle a Woman; I Still See Elisa; I'm Glad I'm Not Young Anymore; Thank Heaven for Little Girls/W: Alan Jay Lerner, M: Frederick Loewe — La Tete de Roi/WM: Jean-Pierre Moulin — Le Twist Canotier/WM: Noel Roux, Georges Garvarentz — Les Chapeaux/WM: Jacques Mareuil, Fred Freed — Louise/W: Leo Robin, M: Richard A. Whiting — Mimi/W: Lorenz Hart, M: Richard Rodgers — Place Pigalle; Quai de Bercy/WM: Maurice Chevalier, Louis P. Alstone — There's a Rainbow 'Round My Shoulder/WM: Dave Dreyer, Billy Rose, Al Jolson — Valentine/W: Albert Willemetz, M: Henri Christine — Yankee Doodle Parisien/WM: George M. Cohan — You Made Me Love You (I Didn't Want to Do It)/W: Joseph McCarthy, M: James V. Monaco — You Must Have Been a Beautiful Baby/W: Johnny Mercer, M: Harry Warren. *Maurice Chevalier at 77* (Alvin, one-person revue, Apr. 1, 1965): A Las Vegas/W: Albert Willemetz, M: Louis Guiglielmi Louiguy — Ah Donnez M'en de la Chanson/WM: Rene Rouzaud, Marguerite Monnot—Au Revoir/WM: Jean Drejac, Fred Freed—Hello! Beautiful!/WM: Walter Donaldson—Hello, Dolly!/WM: Jerry Herman—I Remember It Well; I'm Glad I'm Not Young Anymore; Thank Heaven for Little Girls/W: Alan Jay Lerner, M: Frederick Loewe—La Lecon de Piano/WM: Maurice Vandair, Henri Betti—La Miss/WM: Henri Salvador—La Tendresse/WM: Noel Roux, Hubert Giraud—Louise/W: Leo Robin, M: Richard A. Whiting—Mimi/W: Lorenz Hart, M: Richard Rodgers—Mimi la Blonde/WM: Jean Drejac, Heino Gaze—Paris Je T'aime/WM: Battaille-Henri, Victor Schertzinger—Paris Tu Rajeunis/WM: Noel Roux, Andre Popp—Place Pigalle/WM: Maurice Chevalier, Louis P. Alstone—Some People/W: Stephen Sondheim, M: Jule Styne—Un Clochard M'a Dit/WM: Noel Roux, Georges Garvarentz—Un P'tit Air/W: Albert Willemetz, M: Mireille—Valentine/W: Albert Willemetz, M: Henri Christine—When You're Smiling (The Whole World Smiles with You)/WM: Mark Fisher, Joe Goodwin, Larry Shay—You Brought a New Kind of Love to Me/WM: Sammy Fain, Irving Kahal, Pierre Norman Connor—You Must Have Been a Beautiful Baby/W: Johnny Mercer, M: Harry Warren.

1688. Walter Chiari (Mar. 2, 1924–Dec. 20, 1991) B: Verona, Italy. *The Gay Life* (Shubert, "Anatol," Nov. 18, 1961): For the First Time; I Never Had a Chance; Now I'm Ready for a Frau; This Kind of a Girl; Who Can? You Can!; You're Not the Type/W: Howard Dietz, M: Arthur Schwartz.

1689. Roy Chicas *Grease* (New York City Center, return engagement, "Doody," Nov. 29, 1996): Rock 'n' Roll Party Queen; Those Magic Changes/WM: Jim Jacobs, Warren Casey.

1690. Harry Child *Pom-Pom* (Cohan, "Bidage," Feb. 28, 1916): Zim-Zim/W: Anne Caldwell, M: Hugo Felix.

1691. Marilyn Child B: Santa Monica, CA. *New Faces of 1968* (Booth, revue, May 2, 1968): Luncheon Ballad/W: Michael McWhinney, M: Jerry Powell—A New Waltz/W: Fran Minkoff, M: Fred Hellerman—Prisms/W: Hal Hackady, M: Carl Friberg—Where Is Me?/W: June Carroll, M: Arthur Siegel. *Man of La Mancha* (ANTA Washington Square, CR, "Aldonza," May 28, 1969 mats.): The Abduction; Aldonza; The Combat; Dulcinea; It's All the Same; Knight of the Woeful Countenance (The Dubbing); What Do You Want of Me?/W: Joe Darion, M: Mitch Leigh. *Promises, Promises* (Shubert, CR, "Marge MacDougall," May 1971): A Fact Can Be a Beautiful Thing/W: Hal David, M: Burt Bacharach.

1692. Eddie Childs *By the Way* (Central, revue, CR, Apr. 19, 1926): My Castle in Spain/WM: Isham Jones.

1693. Jeanette Childs *Dr. Deluxe* (Knickerbocker, "Kittie Melville," Apr. 17, 1911): Harem Scarem; That's the Way to Treat a Little Doggie/W: Otto Harbach, M: Karl Hoschna.

1694. Kirsten Childs *Jerry's Girls* (St. James, revue, Dec. 18, 1985): Have a Nice Day; It Takes a Woman; Just Go to the Movies; Kiss Her Now; La Cage aux Folles; Milk and Honey; Song on the Sand; We Need a Little Christmas/WM: Jerry Herman.

1695. William Ching (Oct. 2, 1913–July 1, 1989) B: St. Louis, Mo. *Allegro* (Majestic, "Dr. Joseph Taylor," Oct. 10, 1947): A Fellow Needs a Girl/W: Oscar Hammerstein II, M: Richard Rodgers.

1696. Kevin Chinn *A Chorus Line* (Shubert, CR, "Richie," Jan. 1981): And.../W: Edward Kleban, M: Marvin Hamlisch.

1697. Lori (Tan) Chinn (July 7–) B: Seattle, WA. *Lovely Ladies, Kind Gentlemen* (Majestic, "Miss Higa Jiga," Dec. 28, 1970): Find Your Own Cricket/WM: Franklin Underwood, Stan Freeman.

1698. Sam Chip (c 1881–Apr. 11, 1917) *Wonderland* (Majestic, "Dr. Fax," Oct. 24, 1905): I and Myself and Me/W: Vincent Bryan, M: Victor Herbert—The Ossified Man; The Voice for It/W: Glen MacDonough, M: Victor Herbert.

1699. Robert Chisholm (Apr. 18, 1898–Nov. 4, 1960) B: Melbourne, Australia. *Golden Dawn* (Hammerstein's, "Shep Keyes," Nov. 30, 1927): Here in the Dark; When I Crack My Whip/W: Oscar Hammerstein II, Otto Harbach, M: Emmerich Kalman, Herbert Stothart. *Sweet Adeline* (Hammerstein's, "James Day," Sept. 3, 1929): Don't Ever Leave Me; Out of the Blue; Some Girl Is on Your Mind; The Sun About to Rise/W: Oscar Hammerstein II, M: Jerome Kern. *Luana* (Hammerstein's, "Robert Dean," Sept. 17, 1930): In the Clouds; A Son of the Sun; Where You Lead/W: J. Keirn Brennan, M: Rudolf Friml. *The Threepenny Opera* (Empire, "Capt. Macheath," Apr. 13, 1933): Ballad of the Easy Life; Love Duet; Soldier Song; Tango Ballad/W: Bertolt Brecht, M: Kurt Weill. *The Two Bouquets* (Windsor, "George," May 31, 1938): Git on de Boat, Chillun; She Did the Fandango; Toddy's the Drink for Me/W: Eleanor Farjeon, Herb Farjeon, M: trad.—Yes or No/W: Eleanor Farjeon, Herb Farjeon, M: based on Jacques Offenbach. *Higher and Higher* (Shubert, "Byng," Apr. 4, 1940): Blue Monday; Disgustingly Rich; From Another World/W: Lorenz

Hart, M: Richard Rodgers. *A Connecticut Yan-kee* (Martin Beck, revival, "King Arthur," Nov. 17, 1943): You Always Love the Same Girl/W: Lorenz Hart, M: Richard Rodgers. *On the Town* (Adelphi, "Pitkin," Dec. 28, 1944): I Under-stand/W: Betty Comden, Adolph Green, M: Leonard Bernstein. *Billion Dollar Baby* (Alvin, "M.M. Montague," Dec. 21, 1945): Faithless; There I'd Be/W: Betty Comden, Adolph Green, M: Morton Gould. *Park Avenue* (Shubert, "Charles Crowell," Nov. 4, 1946): The Dew Was on the Rose; The Land of Opportunitee; There's Nothing Like Marriage for People/W: Ira Gersh-win, M: Arthur Schwartz.

1700. Joyce Chittick *Big* (Sam S. Shubert, "Deathstarette," Apr. 28, 1996): Dr. Death-star/W: Richard Maltby, Jr., M: David Shire.

1701. Hye-Young Choi *The King and I* (Uris, revival, "Lady Thiang," May 2, 1977): Something Wonderful; Western People Funny/W: Oscar Hammerstein II, M: Richard Rodgers.

1702. Joohee Choi *The King and I* (Neil Simon, revival, "Tuptim," Apr. 11, 1996/Mar. 24, 1997): I Have Dreamed; My Lord and Master; We Kiss in a Shadow/W: Oscar Hammerstein II, M: Richard Rodgers.

1703. Ruth Chorpenning (Feb. 11, 1905–) B: Springfield, OH. *The Garrick Gaieties of 1930* (Guild, revue, June 4, 1930): Do Tell/W: Henry Myers, M: Charles M. Schwab — Four Infant Prodigies/W: Allen Boretz, M: Ned Lehac. *The Garrick Gaieties of 1930* (Guild, return engage-ment, Oct. 16, 1930): Four Infant Prodigies/W: Allen Boretz, M: Ned Lehac — Rose of Ari-zona/W: Lorenz Hart, M: Richard Rodgers.

1704. Jerry Christakos (Sept. 9, 1960–) B: Chicago, IL. *Kiss of the Spider Woman* (Broad-hurst, "Gabriel," May 3, 1993): Gabriel's Letter; My First Woman/W: Fred Ebb, M: John Kan-der.

1705. Audrey Christie (June 27, 1911–Dec. 19, 1989) B: Chicago, IL. M: GUY ROBERT-SON. *Sweet and Low* (44th Street, revue, CR, Mar. 1931): Cheerful Little Earful/W: Ira Gersh-win, Billy Rose, M: Harry Warren — Revival Day/W: Malcolm McComb, M: Will Irwin — Sweet So and So/W: Ira Gershwin, M: Phil Charig, Joseph Meyer — Would You Like to Take a Walk? (Sump'n Good'll Come from That)/W: Mort Dixon, Billy Rose, M: Harry Warren. *Shady Lady* (Shubert, "Francine," July 5, 1933): Any Way the Wind Blows; Get Hot Foot; Live, Laugh and Love; Swingy Little Thingy/W: Bud Green, M: Sam H. Stept. *I Married an Angel* (Shubert, "Anna Murphy," May 11, 1938): At the Roxy Music Hall; How to Win Friends and

Influence People/W: Lorenz Hart, M: Richard Rodgers. *Banjo Eyes* (Hollywood, "Mabel," Dec. 25, 1941): It Could Only Happen in the Movies; Make with the Feet/W: Harold Adamson, M: Vernon Duke. *The Duchess Misbehaves* (Adelphi, "Duchess of Alba" and "Crystal," Feb. 13, 1946): I Hate Myself in the Morning; Katie Did in Madrid; Nuts/W: Gladys Shelley, M: Frank Black. *Mame* (Winter Garden, CR, "Vera Charles," Apr. 1, 1968): Bosom Buddies; The Man in the Moon/WM: Jerry Herman.

1706. George Stuart Christie (Feb. 27, 1873–May 20, 1949) B: Philadelphia, PA. *Oh! Oh! Delphine* (Knickerbocker > New Amster-dam, "Louis Gigoux," Sept. 30, 1912): Oh, P-P-P-Poor Bouchette/W: C.M.S. McLellan, M: Ivan Caryll.

1707. Marice Christie *Blossom Time* (Am-bassador, revival, "Greta," Mar. 23, 1931): Peace to My Lonely Heart/W: Dorothy Donnelly, M: Sigmund Romberg.

1708. Bobette Christine *Roberta* (New Ams-terdam, "Angele," Nov. 18, 1933): Hot Spot/W: Otto Harbach, M: Jerome Kern.

1709. David Christmas (May 2, 1942–) B: Pasadena, CA. *Very Good Eddie* (Booth, revival, "Mr. Dick Rivers," Dec. 21, 1975): Nodding Roses/W: Schuyler Greene, Herbert Reynolds, M: Jerome Kern — Old Boy Neutral/W: Schuy-ler Greene, M: Jerome Kern — Some Sort of Somebody (All of the Time)/W: Elsie Janis, M: Jerome Kern.

1710. Eileen Christy (Feb. 6, 1927–) B: California. *Carousel* (New York State, revival, "Julie Jordan," Aug. 10, 1965): If I Loved You; A Real Nice Clambake; What's the Use of Wond'rin'; You're a Queer One, Julie Jordan/W: Oscar Hammerstein II, M: Richard Rodgers.

1711. Lew Christy *Half a Widow* (Waldorf, "Gyp," Sept. 12, 1927): I'm Thru with War/W: Frank Dupree, Harry B. Smith, M: Shep Camp.

1712. Molly Chrysty *Miss Daisy* (Shubert > Lyric, "Edna Barber," Sept. 9, 1914): Kissing; My Little Queen Bee; Pierrot's Ball; Tea Leaves; Won't You Dance?; Youth/W: Philip Bartholo-mae, M: Silvio Hein.

1713. George Church (Oct. 8, 1912–) B: Springfield, MA. *Hold On to Your Hats* (Shu-bert, "Lon," Sept. 11, 1940): Life Was Pie for the Pioneer; Then You Were Never in Love/W: E.Y. Harburg, M: Burton Lane. *110 in the Shade* (Broadhurst, "Toby," Oct. 24, 1963): Everything Beautiful Happens at Night/W: Tom Jones, M: Harvey Schmidt.

1714. Sandra Church (Jan. 13, 1943–) B: San Francisco, CA. *Gypsy* (Broadway, "Louise,"

May 21, 1959): All I Need Is the Girl; If Momma Was Married; Let Me Entertain You; Little Lamb; Madame Rose's Toreadorables; Together Wherever We Go/W: Stephen Sondheim, M: Jule Styne.

1715. Stewart Churchill He was a Private in the U.S. Army when he appeared in the show. *This Is the Army* (Broadway, revue, July 4, 1942): A Soldier's Dream/WM: Irving Berlin.

1716. Chester Chute *The New Yorkers* (Edyth Totten, revue, Mar. 10, 1927): Pretty Little So-and-So/W: Henry Myers, M: Edgar Fairchild.

1717. Eduardo Cianelli (Aug. 30, 1887–Oct. 8, 1969) B: The Island of Ischia, off Italy. In Italy he was a doctor and an opera singer. On Broadway he appeared in operettas and plays. In Hollywood he was a villain in movies such as *Gunga Din* (1939). *Always You* (Central, "East Indian Peddler," Jan. 5, 1920): The Voice of Bagdad/W: Oscar Hammerstein II, M: Herbert Stothart. *Rose-Marie* (Imperial, "Emile La Flamme," Sept. 2, 1924): I Love Him; Rose-Marie/W: Otto Harbach, Oscar Hammerstein II, M: Rudolf Friml. *Sari* (Liberty, revival, "Count Estragon," Jan. 29, 1930): Follow Me; Long Live the King (Vive le Roi); My Faithful Stradivari/W: Catherine Chisholm Cushing, E.P. Heath, M: Emmerich Kalman.

1718. Alfred Cibelli, Jr. *Oklahoma!* (New York City Center, revival, "Jud Fry," Aug. 31, 1953): Lonely Room; Pore Jud/W: Oscar Hammerstein II, M: Richard Rodgers.

1719. Wayne Cilento (Aug. 25, 1949–) B: Bronx, NY. *A Chorus Line* (Shubert, "Mike," July 25, 1975): I Can Do That [added]/W: Edward Kleban, M: Marvin Hamlisch. *Dancin'* (Broadhurst, revue, Mar. 27, 1978): Crunchy Granola Suite; Hot August Night/WM: Neil Diamond — Easy; If It Feels Good, Let It Ride/WM: Carol Bayer Sager, Melissa Manchester — Mr. Bojangles/WM: Jerry Jeff Walker — Under the Double Eagle/WM: trad. — Was Dog a Doughnut/WM: Cat Stevens. *Big Deal* (Broadway, "1st Narrator," Apr. 10, 1986): Ain't She Sweet?/W: Jack Yellen, M: Milton Ager — Chicago/WM: Fred Fisher — Everybody Loves My Baby (But My Baby Don't Love Nobody But Me)/WM: Jack Palmer, Spencer Williams — For No Good Reason at All/W: Sam M. Lewis, Joe Young, M: Abel Baer — I've Got a Feelin' You're Foolin'/W: Arthur Freed, M: Nacio Herb Brown — Love Is Just Around the Corner/W: Leo Robin, M: Lewis E. Gensler — Now's the Time to Fall in Love (Potatoes Are Cheaper — Tomatoes Are Cheaper)/WM: Al Sherman, Al Lewis.

1720. Paula Cinko (Dec. 14, 1950–) *Good News* (St. James, revival, "Millie," Dec. 23, 1974): Happy Days; He's a Ladies' Man; Just Imagine/W: B.G. DeSylva, Lew Brown, M: Ray Henderson. *Candide* (Broadway, CR, "Paquette," Sept. 1975): The Best of All Possible Worlds; Life Is Happiness Indeed; Sheep's Song/W: Stephen Sondheim, M: Leonard Bernstein.

1721. Monique Cintron *Roza* (Royale, "Salima," Oct. 1, 1987): Get the Lady Dressed; Is Me/W: Julian More, M: Gilbert Becaud.

1722. Danny Cistone (Apr. 10, 1974–) B: Philadelphia, PA. *She Loves Me* (Criterion Center, revival, CR, "Arpad Laszlo," Mar. 1, 1994): Good Morning, Good Day; Ilona; Try Me/W: Sheldon Harnick, M: Jerry Bock.

1723. A.C. Ciulla *Starlight Express* (Gershwin, "Bobo," Mar. 15, 1987): Race Two/W: Richard Stilgoe, M: Andrew Lloyd Webber.

1724. Bernice Claire (Mar. 22, 1907–Jan. 17, 2003) B: Oakland, CA. *The Chocolate Soldier* (St. James, revival, "Nadina Popoff," May 2, 1934): The Chocolate Soldier; The Letter Song; My Hero; Never Was There Such a Lover; That Would Be Lovely/W: Stanislaus Stange, M: Oscar Straus.

1725. Dorothy Claire Vocalist in the 1930s and 1940s with bands such as Bobby Byrne, Sonny Dunham and Glenn Miller. *Finian's Rainbow* (46th Street, CR, "Sharon McLonergan," during original run): How Are Things in Glocca Morra?; If This Isn't Love; Look to the Rainbow; Old Devil Moon; Something Sort of Grandish; That Great Come-and-Get-It Day; When the Idle Poor Become the Idle Rich/W: E.Y. Harburg, M: Burton Lane. *Jimmy* (Winter Garden, "Texas Guinan," Oct. 23, 1969): Our Jimmy; The Walker Walk/WM: Bill Jacob, Patti Jacob.

1726. Ina Claire (Oct. 15, 1892–Feb. 21, 1985) B: Washington, DC. M: silent film star John Gilbert, 1929-1931. In Mar. 1909, the blonde, hazel-eyed vaudeville comedienne appeared at the American Music Hall in New York with an impersonation of Harry Lauder. She made occasional movies, before and after sound. *A Quaker Girl* (Park, "Prudence Pym," Oct. 23, 1911): A Bad Boy and a Good Girl/W: Percy Greenbank, M: Lionel Monckton — A Quaker Girl; Take a Step/W: Adrian Ross, M: Lionel Monckton — Tony from America/WM: Lionel Monckton. *The Honeymoon Express* (Winter Garden, CR, "Marcelle," Apr. 28, 1913): My Coca-Cola Belle; My Raggyadore; Syncopatia Land/W: Harold Atteridge, M: Jean Schwartz. *Lady Luxury* (Casino > Comedy, "Eloise Van Cuyler," Dec. 25, 1914): Birthday Ensemble; It's

Written in the Book of Destiny; Lady Luxury; Longing Just for You; Moon, Moon [Jan. 4, 1915]; Pick, Pick, Pickaninny; Those Awful Tattle-Tales/W: Rida Johnson Young, M: William Schroeder. *Ziegfeld Follies of 1915* (New Amsterdam, revue, June 21, 1915): Hello, Frisco! (I Called You Up to Say Hello!)/W: Gene Buck, M: Louis A. Hirsch — Marie Odile/W: Rennold Wolf, Channing Pollock, M: Louis A. Hirsch. *Ziegfeld Follies of 1916* (New Amsterdam, revue, June 12, 1916): Ain't It Funny What a Difference Just a Few Drinks Make?; Have a Heart; When the Lights Are Low/W: Gene Buck, M: Jerome Kern.

1727. Marion Claire *The Great Waltz* (Center, "Therese [Resi]," Sept. 22, 1934): Danube So Blue; Love Will Find You; Morning; While You Love Me; With All My Heart; You Are My Song/W: Desmond Carter, M: Johann Strauss.

1728. Rosalie Claire *The Greenwich Village Follies of 1924* (Shubert > Winter Garden, revue, CR, Oct. 27, 1924): Toy of Destiny/WM: Cole Porter. *White Lights* (Ritz, "Flossie Finch," Oct. 11, 1927): Don't Throw Me Down/W: Al Dubin, M: J. Fred Coots. *Sunny Days* (Imperial, "Angele Larue," Feb. 8, 1928): Hang Your Hat on the Moon; One Sunny Day/W: Clifford Grey, William Cary Duncan, M: Jean Schwartz.

1729. Stella Claire *The Boy Friend* (Royale, "Fay," Sept. 30, 1954): The Boy Friend; Perfect Young Ladies; Sur La Plage; The You-Don't-Want-to-Play-with-Me Blues/WM: Sandy Wilson.

1730. Teddy Claire *Artists and Models of 1925* (Winter Garden, revue, June 24, 1925): The Rotisserie/W: Clifford Grey, M: ?.

1731. Phyllis Clare (c 1905–Nov. 1, 1947) B: London, England. *The Band Wagon* (New Amsterdam, revue, CR, Jan. 4, 1932): High and Low/W: Howard Dietz, Desmond Carter, M: Arthur Schwartz.

1732. Wyn Clare *This Year of Grace* (Selwyn, revue, Nov. 7, 1928): Mother's Complaint/WM: Noel Coward.

1733. Alexander Clark (c 1866–Nov. 10, 1932) B: Bordentown, NJ. *The Girl from Paris* (Herald Square, CR, "Ebenezer Honeycomb," June 28, 1897): Cock-a-doodle; It's a Good Thing to Have; The Proper Air; So Take You a Warning; Tweedledum and Tweedledee/W: George Dance, M: Ivan Caryll. *Monte Carlo* (Herald Square, "James," Mar. 21, 1898): The Use of French/W: Harry Greenbank, M: Howard Talbot. *The Defender* (Herald Square, "Sam Keno," July 3, 1902): Heart-to-Heart Talks; The Man Who Hypnotized McCarthy/

W: Allen Lowe, M: Charles Denee. *The Runaways* (Casino, "Gen. Hardtack, U.S.A.," May 11, 1903): In a General Sort of Way; Our Cause Is the Cause/W: Addison Burkhardt, M: Raymond Hubbell. *The Student King* (Garden, "Rudolph," Dec. 25, 1906): I Took Them All; In Bohemia; My Old Bassoon; The Same Old Game/W: Frederick Ranken, Stanislaus Stange, M: Reginald De Koven. *Mlle. Mischief* (Lyric, "Meline," Sept. 28, 1908): Verily, Merrily/W: Sydney Rosenfeld, M: Carl M. Ziehrer. *The Red Rose* (Globe, "Alonzo Lorimer," June 22, 1911): You Can Go as Far as You Like with Me/W: Harry B. Smith, M: Robert Hood Bowers. *The Princess Pat* (Cort, "Si Perkins," Sept. 29, 1915): The Shoes of Husband Number One As Seen by Number Two/W: Henry Blossom, M: Victor Herbert. *Glorianna* (Liberty, "Alexander Galloway," Oct. 26, 1918): The Best Man Never Gets the Worst of It; Everyday Will Be Sunday When the Town Goes Dry/W: Catherine Chisholm Cushing, M: Rudolf Friml. *Natja* (Knickerbocker, "Count Panin," Feb. 16, 1925): Ups and Downs; You'll Have to Guess/W: Harry B. Smith, M: Karl Hajos, based on Peter I. Tchaikovsky.

1734. Bert Clark (c 1884–Jan. 26, 1920) B: San Francisco, Calif. *The Maid of the Mountains* (Casino, "Tonio," Sept. 11, 1918): Dirty Work; Dividing the Spoils/W: Clifford Harris, M: Harold Fraser-Simpson — Husbands and Wives; Over There and Over Here/W: Harry Graham, M: Harold Fraser-Simpson.

1735. Billy Clark *Come Along* (Nora Bayes > 39th Street, "Pvt. Jeff Scroggins," Apr. 8, 1919): Rollin' de Bones at Coblenz on de Rhine/W: Bide Dudley, M: John L. Nelson.

1736. Bobby Clark (June 16, 1888–Feb. 12, 1960) B: Springfield, OH. Comedy partner and friend from childhood of PAUL MCCULLOUGH. In their teens, they toured together in minstrel shows and circuses, beginning in vaudeville in 1912. Between 1928 and 1936 when McCullough died, they appeared in 36 RKO comedies. *Music Box Revue of 1922* (Music Box, revue, Oct. 23, 1922): Three Cheers for the Red, White and Blue/WM: Irving Berlin. *The Ramblers* (Lyric, "Prof. Cunningham," Sept. 20, 1926): Oh! How We Love Our Alma Mater/W: Bert Kalmar, M: Harry Ruby. *Strike Up the Band* (Times Square, "Col. Holmes," Jan. 14, 1930): He Knows Milk; How About a Boy Like Me?; If I Became the President; Mademoiselle in New Rochelle; A Man of High Degree; The Unofficial Spokesman/W: Ira Gershwin, M: George Gershwin. *Here Goes the Bride* (46th Street,

"Hives," Nov. 3, 1931): Well, You See, I-Oh, You Know/W: Edward Heyman, M: Johnny Green. *Walk a Little Faster* (St. James, revue, Dec. 7, 1932): Can-Can; End of a Perfect Night; That's Life/W: E.Y. Harburg, M: Vernon Duke — Frisco Fanny/W: Earle Crooker, M: Henry Sullivan. *Ziegfeld Follies of 1936-1937* (Winter Garden, revue, Sept. 14, 1936): The Gazooka/WM: Ira Gershwin, David Freedman — I Can't Get Started/W: Ira Gershwin, M: Vernon Duke. *The Streets of Paris* (Broadhurst, revue, June 19, 1939): The French Have a Word for It/WM: Harold Rome — Is It Possible?; Robert the Roue from Reading, PA/W: Al Dubin, M: Jimmy McHugh. *Star and Garter* (Music Box, revue, June 24, 1942): For a Quarter/W: Jerry Seelen, M: Lester Lee — Robert the Roue from Reading, PA/W: Al Dubin, M: Jimmy McHugh. *Mexican Hayride* (Winter Garden, "Joe Bascom, alias Humphrey Fish," Jan. 28, 1944): Count Your Blessings; Girls/WM: Cole Porter. *Sweethearts* (Shubert, revival, "Mikel Mikeloviz," Jan. 21, 1947): Jeannette and Her Little Wooden Shoes; Pilgrims of Love; Pretty as a Picture/W: Robert B. Smith, M: Victor Herbert. *As the Girls Go* (Winter Garden > Broadway, "Waldo Wellington," Nov. 13, 1948): American Cannes; As the Girls Go; Brighten Up and Be a Little Sunbeam; It Takes a Woman to Take a Man; I've Got the President's Ear; You Say the Nicest Things, Baby/W: Harold Adamson, M: Jimmy McHugh.

1737. Buddy Clark (July 26, 1912–Oct. 1, 1949) Popular singer in the 1930s and 1940s with bands such as Ben Bernie, Wayne King and Freddy Martin. He was killed in a plane crash over Los Angeles, returning from a football game. *Bright Lights of 1944* (Forrest, revue, Sept. 16, 1943): Thoughtless; Your Face Is Your Fortune/W: Mack David, M: Jerry Livingston.

1738. Cheryl Clark (Dec. 7, 1950–) B: Boston, MA. *Chicago* (46th Street, "Liz," June 3, 1975): Cell Block Tango/W: Fred Ebb, M: John Kander. *A Chorus Line* (Shubert, CR, "Cassie," Dec. 1978/Oct. 1983): The Music and the Mirror/W: Edward Kleban, M: Marvin Hamlisch.

1739. Dort Clark (Oct. 1, 1917–Mar. 30, 1989) B: Wellington, KS. *Wonderful Town* (Winter Garden, "Chick Clark," Feb. 25, 1953): Conversation Piece (Nice Talk, Nice People)/W: Betty Comden, Adolph Green, M: Leonard Bernstein. *South Pacific* (New York City Center, revival, "Luther Billis," Apr. 13, 1961): Bloody Mary; Honey Bun; There Is Nothin' Like a Dame/W: Oscar Hammerstein II, M: Richard

Rodgers. *Fiorello!* (New York City Center, revival, "Floyd Macduff," June 13, 1962): I Love a Cop/W: Sheldon Harnick, M: Jerry Bock.

1740. Eliza Atkins Clark *A Christmas Carol* (Paramount Madison Square Garden, return engagement, "Fan at 10," Nov. 20, 1995): A Place Called Home/W: Lynn Ahrens, M: Alan Menken.

1741. Erminie Clark *Girlies* (New Amsterdam, "Susie Smith," June 13, 1910): Going Up (in My Aeroplane)/W: Harry Williams, M: Egbert Van Alstyne.

1742. Eva Clark *Sunkist* (Globe, revue, "Anabelle Foster," May 23, 1921): Lo! Hear the Gentle Lark; The Love a Gypsy Knows/WM: Fanchon Wolff, Marco Wolff. *Our Nell* (Nora Bayes, "Helen Ford," Dec. 4, 1922): By and By/W: Brian Hooker, M: George Gershwin — Old New England Home/W: Brian Hooker, M: William Daly. *Mary Jane McKane* (Imperial, "Louise Dryer," Dec. 25, 1923): My Boy and I/W: William Cary Duncan, Oscar Hammerstein II, M: Vincent Youmans — Not in Business Hours; You're Never Too Old [Feb. 1924]/W: William Cary Duncan, Oscar Hammerstein II, M: Vincent Youmans, Herbert Stothart — Thistledown/W: William Cary Duncan, Oscar Hammerstein II, M: Herbert Stothart. *Madame Pompadour* (Martin Beck, "Madeleine," Nov. 11, 1924): Tell Me What Your Eyes Were Made For/W: Clare Kummer, M: Leo Fall.

1743. Gladys Clark (c 1883–Mar. 31, 1965) M: HENRY BERGMAN, who was also her partner on stage. *Step This Way* (Shubert > Astor, May 29, 1916): By the Sad Luana Shore/WM: E. Ray Goetz — When the Sun Goes Down in Romany (My Heart Goes Roaming Back to You)/W: Sam M. Lewis, Joe Young, M: Bert Grant. *The Passing Show of 1917* (Winter Garden, revue, Apr. 26, 1917): Meet Me at the Station, Dear/W: Sam M. Lewis, Joe Young, M: Ted Snyder — My Yokohama Girl/W: Alfred Bryan, M: Harry Tierney — A Table for Two/W: Harold Atteridge, M: Ray Perkins.

1744. Harry Clark (c 1911–Feb. 28, 1956) *One Touch of Venus* (Imperial, "Stanley," Oct. 7, 1943): The Trouble with Women/W: Ogden Nash, M: Kurt Weill. *Call Me Mister* (National > Plymouth, revue, Apr. 18, 1946): Military Life (The Jerk Song); The Senators' Song/WM: Harold Rome. *Kiss Me, Kate* (New Century, "First Man," Dec. 30, 1948): Brush Up Your Shakespeare/WM: Cole Porter.

1745. Helen Clark *La, La, Lucille* (Henry Miller, "Mrs. Britton Hughes [Peggy]," May 26, 1919): It's Great to Be in Love; Nobody but You

[Sept. 8, 1919]/W: Arthur Jackson, B.G. De-Sylva, M: George Gershwin — Ooo, How I Love to Be Loved By You/W: Lou Paley, M: George Gershwin — There's More to the Kiss Than the Sound/W: Irving Caesar, M: George Gershwin.

1746. Hilda Clark (c 1873–May 4, 1932) B: Leavenworth, KS. *The Highwayman* (Broadway, "Lady Constance Sinclair," Dec. 13, 1897): Do You Remember, Love?; Vive la Bagatelle/W: Harry B. Smith, M: Reginald De Koven.

1747. Jacqueline Clark (June 21, 1949–) B: Portland, OR. *Where's Charley?* (Circle in the Square, revival, "Young Lady," Dec. 20, 1974): The Gossips; Lovelier Than Ever/WM: Frank Loesser.

1748. Les Clark *Tattle Tales* (Broadhurst, revue, June 1, 1933): Jig Saw Jamboree/W: William Walsh, M: Eddie Bienbryer — Sing American Tunes/W: Frank Fay, William Walsh, M: Edward Ward — You Gotta Do Better Than That/WM: ?.

1749. Lillion Clark *Forbidden Melody* (New Amsterdam, "Katcha," Nov. 2, 1936): Bucharest; Just Hello; Lady in the Window; No Use Pretending; Shadows That Walk in the Night/W: Otto Harbach, M: Sigmund Romberg.

1750. Marguerite Clark (Feb. 22, 1883–Sept. 25, 1940) B: Avondale, OH. Star of silent pictures from 1914, playing innocent young things. *Mr. Pickwick* (Herald Square, "Polly," Jan. 19, 1903): Acting; The Forest Air; Gratitude; The Lay of the Merry Ha! Ha!; Love/W: Grant Stewart, M: Manuel Klein. *Happyland or The King of Elysia* (Lyric > Casino > Majestic, "Sylvia," Oct. 2, 1905): Cupid's Grammar; Girls, Girls, Girls; Robin Redbreast; 'Twas the Rose; What Is the Difference?/W: Frederick Ranken, M: Reginald De Koven. *The Pied Piper* (Majestic, "Elvira," Dec. 3, 1908): The Dresden China Plate; I Should Like to Know the Reason; I'm Looking for a Sweetheart and I Think You'll Do; It Really Was a Very Pretty Story; Whose Little Girl Are You?/W: R.H. Burnside, M: Manuel Klein. *The Beauty Spot* (Herald Square, "Nadine," Apr. 10, 1909): The Boulevard Glide/W: E. Ray Goetz, M: Melville Gideon — Goo-Goo; In a Hammock (Hammock Love Song); Ode to Aphrodite; Pas Seul; Pretty Punchinello; A Song of the Sea; Toujours la Politesse/W: Joseph W. Herbert, M: Reginald De Koven. *The King of Cadonia* (Daly's, "Princess Marie," Jan. 10, 1910): Coo-oo Coo-oo/W: Maurice Stonehill, M: Jerome Kern — Mother and Father/W: M.E. Rourke, M: Jerome Kern — The Portrait; When a Fellow Loves a Girl/W: Adrian Ross, M: Sidney Jones — Spar-

row and Hippopotamus/W: Adrian Ross, M: Jerome Kern.

1751. Patrice Clark *The Bunch and Judy* (Globe, "Hazel," Nov. 28, 1922): Times Square/W: Anne Caldwell, M: Jerome Kern.

1752. Petula Clark (Nov. 15, 1932–) B: Epsom, Surrey, England. International singing star and movie actress. She started as a band singer at 8 and became a radio star in England during WWII. *Blood Brothers* (Music Box, CR, "Mrs. Johnstone," Aug. 16, 1993): Bright New Day; Easy Terms; Light Romance; Marilyn Monroe; My Child; Tell Me It's Not True/WM: Willy Russell.

1753. Sylvia Clark (?–Mar. 31, 1970) *Hitchy-Koo of 1919* (Liberty, revue, Oct. 6, 1919): I'm an Anaesthetic Dancer/WM: Cole Porter. *The Greenwich Village Follies of 1920* (Shubert, revue, Aug. 31, 1921): Murder in My Heart/W: Arthur Swanstrom, John Murray Anderson, M: A. Baldwin Sloane.

1754. Victoria Clark (Oct. 10–) B: Dallas, TX. *A Grand Night for Singing* (Criterion Center, revue, Nov. 17, 1993): Don't Marry Me; The Gentleman Is a Dope; Hello, Young Lovers; Honey Bun; I Cain't Say No; I Have Dreamed; I Know It Can Happen Again; I'm Gonna Wash That Man Right Outa My Hair; Impossible; It's a Grand Night for Singing; Kansas City; A Lovely Night; The Man I Used to Be; My Little Girl (from Soliloquy); So Far; Some Enchanted Evening; Stepsisters' Lament; When the Children Are Asleep; When You're Driving Through the Moonlight; Wish Them Well/W: Oscar Hammerstein II, M: Richard Rodgers. *How to Succeed in Business Without Really Trying* (Richard Rodgers, revival, "Smitty," Mar. 23, 1995): Been a Long Day; Coffee Break; How To; Paris Original/WM: Frank Loesser.

1755. William H. Clark *The Auto Race* (Hippodrome, "William Worthington," Nov. 25, 1907): Those Days Gone By/WM: Manuel Klein.

1756. Alexander Clarke *The Isle of Spice* (Majestic, "Bompopka," Aug. 23, 1904): The Goo-Goo Man/W: Toby Lyons, M: Paul Schindler, Ben M. Jerome — Mercenary Mary Ann/W: George E. Stoddard, M: Ben M. Jerome — The Sporting King of Nicobar/W: George E. Stoddard, M: Paul Schindler.

1757. Edwin A. Clarke (Nov. 14, 1871–?) B: Worcester, MA. *A Society Circus* (Hippodrome, "Paul Pasky," Dec. 13, 1905): Moon Dear/WM: Manuel Klein. *Pioneer Days* (Hippodrome, "Pierre," Nov. 28, 1906): Lucia My Italian Maid/WM: Manuel Klein. *The Auto Race* (Hippodrome, "Dick Spanker," Nov. 25, 1907): Starlight Maid/WM: Manuel Klein. *Sporting Days* and *Battle in the Skies* (Hippodrome, "Jack Vanderveer" and "Geoffrey Gedison," Sept. 5, 1908): Dear Motherland; The Whole Year Round/WM: Manuel Klein — I'm Looking for a Sweetheart and I Think You'll Do [Feb. 22, 1909]/W: R.H. Burnside, M: Manuel Klein. *A Trip to Japan* (Hippodrome, "Dick Gordon, U.S.N.," Sept. 4, 1909): Meet Me Where the Lanterns Glow; Our Navy's the Best in the World/WM: Manuel Klein. *The International Cup* (Hippodrome, "John Gordon," Sept. 3, 1910): There Is No North or South Today; Yachting/WM: Manuel Klein.

1758. Gordon B. Clarke (May 2, 1906–Jan. 11, 1972) B: St. Paul, MN. *Sing for Your Supper* (Adelphi, revue, Apr. 24, 1939): Ballad for Americans (Ballad of Uncle Sam)/W: John Latouche, M: Earl Robinson. *The Yearling* (Alvin, "Doc Wilson," Dec. 10, 1965): What a Happy Day/W: Herbert Martin, M: Michael Leonard.

1759. Harry Clarke (Oct. 4, 1885–July 19, 1938) B: Chelsea, MA. M: NORA BAYES. *The Tattooed Man* (Criterion, "Algy Cuffs," Feb. 18, 1907): There's Just One Girl I'd Like to Marry/W: Harry B. Smith, M: Victor Herbert. *The Red Widow* (Astor, "Oswald Butts," Nov. 6, 1911): The Avenue of Palms; In Society It's Always Dress Parade; We Will Go Go to Go-Go; You Can't Pay the Landlord with Love/W: Rennold Wolf, Channing Pollock, M: Charles J. Gebest. *Tantalizing Tommy* (Criterion, "Biff," Oct. 1, 1912): Cupid's Car; I Am a Tomboy; A Tandem/W: Adrian Ross, M: Hugo Felix. *The Sun Dodgers* (Broadway, "A. Goode Lamb," Nov. 30, 1912): At the Picture Show/WM: E. Ray Goetz, Irving Berlin — Dixie Love; Rag Me Around; When You Said How Do You Do/W: E. Ray Goetz, M: A. Baldwin Sloane. *Dancing Around* (Winter Garden, CR, "Lieut. Harry Graham," Jan. 23, 1915): The Dancing Maniacs; Oh, You John/WM: ?— There's Something About You/W: Harold Atteridge, M: Sigmund Romberg, Harry Carroll. *You're in Love* (Casino, "Hobby Douglas," Feb. 6, 1917): Buck Up; Things That They Must Not Do; A Year Is a Long, Long Time/W: Otto Harbach, Edward Clark, M: Rudolf Friml. *The Kiss Burglar* (Cohan, "Tommy Dodd," May 9, 1918): A Little Class of One; On the Shimmering, Glimmering Nile/W: Glen MacDonough, M: Raymond Hubbell. *The Kiss Burglar* (Broadhurst > Nora Bayes, revival, "Tommy Dodd," Mar. 17, 1919): A Little Class of One; On the Shimmer-

ing, Glimmering Nile; The Rose; Temperament/W: Glen MacDonough, M: Raymond Hubbell. *A Lonely Romeo* (Shubert > Casino," Larry Tripp," June 10, 1919): Don't Do Anything Till You Hear from Me/W: Robert B. Smith, M: Malvin F. Franklin — Jolly Me/W: Robert B. Smith, M: Robert Hood Bowers. *Dew Drop Inn* (Astor, "Jack Newton," May 17, 1923): I'm a Flapper/W: McElbert Moore, M: Jean Schwartz, J. Fred Coots — The Primrose Path/W: Cyrus D. Wood, M: Alfred Goodman. *Princess April* (Ambassador, "A. Sharpe Quill," Dec. 1, 1924): Dumb-Bells May Be Foolish; Scandal; String 'Em Along/WM: Monte Carlo, Alma Sanders. *China Rose* (Martin Beck, "Lo," Jan. 19, 1925): I'm Hi, I'm Lo; I'm No Butterfly/W: Harry L. Cort, George E. Stoddard, M: A. Baldwin Sloane.

1760. Harry (Henry) Corson Clarke (Jan. 13, 1863–Mar. 3, 1923) B: New York, NY. *Mr. Wix of Wickham* (Bijou, "Mr. Wix," Sept. 19, 1904): One Thing Different/WM: Jerome Kern, Herbert Darnley — Sergeant Wix/WM: Herbert Darnley — Waiting for You/WM: John Wagner, Jerome Kern. *The Mimic World* (Casino, revue, "Lemuel Sawwood," July 8, 1908): Woman, Lovely Woman/W: George Broadhurst, M: Gustave Kerker. *The Mimic World* (Casino, revue, "George M. Cohan," Aug. 24, 1908): All the Stars and Stripes Belong to Me/WM: ? *The Blushing Bride* (Astor, "Judge Redwood," Feb. 6, 1922): Different Days/W: Cyrus D. Wood, M: Sigmund Romberg.

1761. Helen Clarke *Love o' Mike* (Shubert > Maxine Elliott, "Helen," Jan. 15, 1917): Don't Tempt Me; Drift with Me/W: Harry B. Smith, M: Jerome Kern. *Oh, My Dear!* (Princess, "Babe," Nov. 27, 1918): Ask Dad; Childhood Days/W: P.G. Wodehouse, M: Louis A. Hirsch.

1762. Hope Clarke (1943–) B: Washington DC. *West Side Story* (Winter Garden, revival, "Teresita," Apr. 27, 1960): I Feel Pretty/W: Stephen Sondheim, M: Leonard Bernstein. *Don't Bother Me, I Can't Cope* (Playhouse, revue, Apr. 19, 1972): Help; Love Power; So Long Sammy; When I Feel Like Moving/WM: Micki Grant.

1763. Hughie Clarke A Private in the U.S. Army during World War I. *Yip, Yip, Yaphank* (Century, revue, Aug. 19, 1918): Ever Since I Put on a Uniform (What a Difference a Uniform Will Make); Ragtime Razor Brigade/WM: Irving Berlin. *You Said It* (46th Street, "Kewpie Andrews," Jan. 19, 1931): Sweet and Hot; Wha'd' We Come to College For?; What Do We Care?/W: Jack Yellen, M: Harold Arlen.

1764. John Clarke B: Nottingham, England. In opera, he sang leading tenor roles. *Monsieur Beaucaire* (New Amsterdam, "Philip Molyneux," Dec. 11, 1919): Honor and Love; We Are Not Speaking Now/W: Adrian Ross, M: Andre Messager. *Ziegfeld Follies of 1921* (Globe, revue, June 21, 1921): Bring Back My Blushing Rose/W: Gene Buck, Brian Hooker, M: Rudolf Friml — Princess of My Dreams/W: Gene Buck, M: Victor Herbert. *The Dream Girl* (Ambassador, "Will Levison," Aug. 20, 1924): Maiden, Let Me In/W: Rida Johnson Young, M: Victor Herbert. *Princess Flavia* (Century, "Rupert of Hentzau," Nov. 2, 1925): I Love Them All; Yes or No/W: Harry B. Smith, M: Sigmund Romberg. *The Three Musketeers* (Lyric, "Duke of Buckingham," Mar. 13, 1928): Love Is the Sun; Queen of My Heart/W: Clifford Grey, M: Rudolf Friml. *Music Hath Charms* (Majestic, "Rudolfo," Dec. 29, 1934): It's Three O'Clock/W: Rowland Leigh, John Shubert, M: Rudolf Friml. *The Boys from Syracuse* (Alvin, "Angelo," Nov. 23, 1938): Come with Me/W: Lorenz Hart, M: Richard Rodgers.

1765. Mae Clarke (Aug. 16, 1907–Apr. 29, 1992) B: Philadelphia, PA. M: LEW BRICE when she was 17. The union did not last. Between 1929 and 1967, she made many Hollywood films, but is probably remembered best for the grapefruit scene with JAMES CAGNEY in *Public Enemy* (1931). *Manhattan Mary* (Apollo, "Viola Fay," Sept. 26, 1927): It Won't Be Long Now; My Blue Bird's Home Again/W: B.G. DeSylva, Lew Brown, M: Ray Henderson.

1766. Patricia Clarke *Two Little Girls in Blue* (George M. Cohan, "Ophelia," May 3, 1921): Here, Steward/W: Ira Gershwin, M: Vincent Youmans.

1767. Robert Clarke *The Gay Hussars* (Knickerbocker, "Corp. Ludwig," July 29, 1909): A Soldier's Life; Vagrant Fancies/W: Grant Stewart, M: Emmerich Kalman.

1768. Wilfred Clarke (June 12, 1866–Apr. 27, 1945) B: Philadelphia, PA. Actor, author, producer and a leading comedian on the Keith-Orpheum Circuits in vaudeville. *The Little Blue Devil* (Central, "Mr. Lewellyn," Nov. 3, 1919): Shimmy-Shaking Love/W: Harold Atteridge, M: Harry Carroll.

1769. John Clarkson (Jan. 19, 1932–) B: London, England. *My Fair Lady* (St. James, revival, "Harry," Mar. 25, 1976): Get Me to the Church on Time; With a Little Bit of Luck/W: Alan Jay Lerner, M: Frederick Loewe.

1770. Robert Clary (Mar. 1, 1926–) B: Paris, France. He played La Beau on TV's *Hogan's Heroes* (1965). *New Faces of 1952* (Royale,

revue, May 16, 1952): I'm in Love with Miss Logan; Lucky Pierre; Raining Memories/WM: Ronny Graham — Love Is a Simple Thing/W: June Carroll, M: Arthur Siegel. *Seventh Heaven* (ANTA, "Fleegle, the Rat," May 26, 1955): C'est la Vie; Happy Little Crook; Love Sneaks Up on You/W: Stella Unger, M: Victor Young.

1771. Wilton Clary *The Desert Song* (New York City Center, revival, "Capt. Paul Fontaine," Jan. 8, 1946): All Hail to the General; I Want a Kiss; Margot/W: Otto Harbach, Oscar Hammerstein II, M: Sigmund Romberg. *Oklahoma!* (St. James, CR, "Curly McLain," July 1947): The Farmer and the Cowman; Oh, What a Beautiful Mornin'; Oklahoma; People Will Say We're in Love; Pore Jud; The Surrey with the Fringe on Top/W: Oscar Hammerstein II, M: Richard Rodgers.

1772. Toby Claude (Jan. 29, 1877–Oct. 27, 1962) B: Dublin, Ireland. *Florodora* (Winter Garden, CR, "Angela Gilfain," Jan. 27, 1902): Galloping/W: Ernest Boyd-Jones, M: Leslie Stuart — Willie Was a Gay Boy/W: Alfred Murray, M: ?.

1773. Dane Claudius *Ziegfeld Midnight Frolic [6th Edition]* (New Amsterdam roof, revue, Dec. 29, 1917): Long, Long Ago/W: Gene Buck, Dave Stamper.

1774. Joy Claussen B: Chicago, IL. *How to Succeed in Business Without Really Trying* (46th Street, CR, "Hedy LaRue," Aug. 27, 1962): Been a Long Day; Love from a Heart of Gold/WM: Frank Loesser.

1775. Cassius Clay (Jan. 17, 1942–) B: Louisville, KY. The prizefighter, later known as Muhammed Ali. *Buck White* (George Abbott, "Buck White," Dec. 2, 1969): Better Far; Big Time Buck; Black Balloons; Get Down; Mighty Whitey; We Came in Chains/WM: Oscar Brown, Jr.

1776. Edwin Clay *Oklahoma!* (St. James, "Fred," Mar. 31, 1943): The Farmer and the Cowman; Oklahoma/W: Oscar Hammerstein II, M: Richard Rodgers. *Kiss Me, Kate* (New Century, CR, "First Suitor," Jan. 24, 1949): Tom, Dick or Harry/WM: Cole Porter.

1777. Hilda Clay *The Serenade* (Knickerbocker, CR, "Yvonne," Apr. 22, 1897): Cupid and I; Dreaming, Dreaming; In Fair Andalusia; The Singing Lesson/W: Harry B. Smith, M: Victor Herbert.

1778. Jill Clayburgh (Apr. 30, 1944–) B: New York, NY. In movies from 1969; best remembered for *An Unmarried Woman* (1978). *The Rothschilds* (Lunt-Fontanne, "Hannah Cohen," Oct. 19, 1970): I'm in Love! I'm in

149 CLEALE

Love!/W: Sheldon Harnick, M: Jerry Bock. *Pippin* (Imperial, "Catherine," Oct. 23, 1972): Kind of Woman; Love Song/WM: Stephen Schwartz.

1779. Bessie Clayton (c 1878–July 16, 1948) B: Philadelphia, PA. *It Happened in Nordland* (Lew Fields, "Parthenia Schmitt," Dec. 5, 1904): The Jack O'Lantern Girl; The Man Meant Well/W: Glen MacDonough, M: Victor Herbert. *The Belle of Mayfair* (Daly's, "Pincott," Dec. 3, 1906): Bells in the Morning/W: William Caine, M: Leslie Stuart — My Little Girl Is a Shy Little Girl/W: Basil Hood, M: Leslie Stuart. *Hip! Hip! Hooray!* (Music Hall, revue, "Tootsie Tripper," Oct. 10, 1907): The College Boy's Dream; Let's Wander Off Nowhere; Tootsie Tripper/W: Edgar Smith, M: Gus Edwards. *Roly Poly* (Broadway > Weber and Fields, "Cerita," Nov. 21, 1912): The Regimental Roly Poly Girl/W: E. Ray Goetz, M: A. Baldwin Sloane. *The Passing Show of 1913* (Winter Garden, revue, July 24, 1913): Dance of the Perfume; The White House Glide/W: Harold Atteridge, M: Jean Schwartz.

1780. Gilbert Clayton (June 18, 1859–Mar. 1, 1950) B: Polo, IL. *A Million Dollars* (New York, "Chasem," Sept. 27, 1900): We Are the Men of Law/W: Louis Harrison, George V. Hobart, M: A. Baldwin Sloane. *The Wizard of Oz* (Majestic, "Pastoria II," Jan. 20, 1903): In Michigan/W: Glen MacDonough, M: A. Baldwin Sloane — When the Circus Comes to Town/W: James O'Dea, M: Bob Adams. *The Office Boy* (Victoria, "Damon Ketcham," Nov. 2, 1903): After Business Hours; An Embassy Burglarious (The Burglars)/W: Harry B. Smith, M: Ludwig Englander. *The Tattooed Man* (Criterion, "Ali," Feb. 18, 1907): Take Things Easy; Things We Are Not Supposed to Know/W: Harry B. Smith, M: Victor Herbert. *The Enchantress* (New York, "Poff," Oct. 19, 1911): They All Look Good When They're Far Away/W: Harry B. Smith, M: Victor Herbert. *The Madcap Duchess* (Globe, "M. de Secherat," Nov. 11, 1913): Tweedledum and Tweedledee/W: David Stevens, M: Victor Herbert.

1781. Jan Clayton (Aug. 26, 1917–Aug. 28, 1983) B: Alamogardo, NM. She played the mother in the TV adventure series *Lassie* (1954). *Carousel* (Majestic, "Julie Jordan," Apr. 19, 1945): If I Loved You; A Real Nice Clambake; What's the Use of Wond'rin'; You're a Queer One, Julie Jordan/W: Oscar Hammerstein II, M: Richard Rodgers. *Show Boat* (Ziegfeld, revival, "Magnolia Hawks Ravenal" and "Kim," Jan. 5, 1946): After the Ball/WM: Charles K. Harris — Can't Help Lovin' Dat Man; Make Believe; Nobody Else but Me; Why Do I Love You?; You Are Love/W: Oscar Hammerstein II, M: Jerome Kern. *The King and I* (New York City Center, revival, "Anna Leonowens," Apr. 18, 1956): Getting to Know You; Hello, Young Lovers; I Whistle a Happy Tune; The Royal Bangkok Academy; Shall I Tell You What I Think of You?; Shall We Dance?/W: Oscar Hammerstein II, M: Richard Rodgers.

1782. Lawrence Clayton (Oct. 10, 1956–) B: Mocksville, NC. *Dreamgirls* (Imperial, CR, "C.C. White," Sept. 1984): Cadillac Car; Family; I Miss You Old Friend; Quintette; The Rap; Steppin' to the Bad Side/W: Tom Eyen, M: Henry Krieger. *The High Rollers Social and Pleasure Club* (Helen Hayes, revue, "King," Apr. 21, 1992): Black Widow Spider; Dance the Night; Don't You Feel My Leg; You're the One/WM: ? — Such a Night/WM: Lincoln Chase — Tell It Like It Is/W: Lee Diamond, M: George Davis, Jr. *Jesus Christ Superstar* (Paramount Madison Square Garden, revival, "Simon Zealotes," Jan. 17, 1995): Simon Zealotes/W: Tim Rice, M: Andrew Lloyd Webber. *Once Upon a Mattress* (Broadhurst, revival, "Minstrel," Dec. 19, 1996): Many Moons Ago; The Minstrel, the Jester and I; Normandy/W: Marshall Barer, M: Mary Rodgers.

1783. Lou Clayton (Mar. 12, 1887–Sept. 12, 1950) B: Brooklyn, NY. With EDDIE JACKSON and JIMMY DURANTE, whose manager he later became, he was part of the team known as CLAYTON, JACKSON and DURANTE. *Show Girl* (Ziegfeld, "Gypsy," July 2, 1929): Can Broadway Do Without Me?/WM: Jimmy Durante — Spain/W: Gus Kahn, M: Isham Jones. *The New Yorkers* (Broadway, "Oscar Gregory," Dec. 8, 1930): Data; The Hot Patata; Money; Sheikin' Fool; Wood/WM: Jimmy Durante — Venice/WM: Cole Porter.

1784. Philip Clayton (June 4, 1954–) B: Billings, MT. *Starlight Express* (Gershwin, "Espresso," Mar. 15, 1987): Race Two/W: Richard Stilgoe, M: Andrew Lloyd Webber.

1785. Ruth Clayton *Viva O'Brien* (Majestic, "Betty Dayton," Oct. 9, 1941): Mozambamba/W: Raymond Leveen, M: Maria Grever.

1786. Lewis Cleale *Swinging on a Star* (Music Box, revue, Oct. 22, 1995): Ain't Got a Dime to My Name; Apalachicola; Going My Way; Moonlight Becomes You; Pakistan; Polka Dots and Moonbeams; Road to Morocco; You Don't Have to Know the Language/W: Johnny Burke, M: James Van Heusen — Annie Doesn't Live Here Anymore; Shadows on the Swanee/W: Johnny Burke, Joe Young, M: Harold Spina — Irresistible/W: Johnny Burke, M: Harold

Spina — Pennies from Heaven/W: Johnny Burke, M: Arthur Johnston — Whoopsie Daisy Day/ WM: Johnny Burke. *Once Upon a Mattress* (Broadhurst, revival, "Sir Harry," Dec. 19, 1996): In a Little While; Yesterday I Loved You/W: Marshall Barer, M: Mary Rodgers.

1787. Ardelle Cleaves *Poor Little Ritz Girl* (Central, "Dorothy Arden," July 28, 1920): All You Need to Be a Star; Love's Intense in Tents/ W: Lorenz Hart, M: Richard Rodgers — In the Land of Yesterday; My Violin/W: Alex Gerber, M: Sigmund Romberg.

1788. John Cleese (Oct. 27, 1939–) B: Weston-Super-Mare, Somerset, England. Popular comedy actor and screenwriter, best known in the U.S. for the British TV series *Monty Python's Flying Circus* and *Fawlty Towers*. *Half a Sixpence* (Broadhurst, "Young Walsingham," Apr. 25, 1965): A Proper Gentleman/WM: David Heneker.

1789. Richard Clemence *Street Scene* (New York City Center, revival, "Charlie Hildebrand," Feb. 13, 1960): Catch Me If You Can/W: Langston Hughes, Elmer Rice, M: Kurt Weill.

1790. Gertrude Clemens *Oh, Please!* (Fulton, "Miss Topeka," Dec. 17, 1926): Homely but Clean/W: Anne Caldwell, M: Vincent Youmans.

1791. Joan Clement *She's My Baby* (Globe, "Joan," Jan. 3, 1928): Wasn't It Great (It's All Over Now); Where Can the Baby Be?/W: Lorenz Hart, M: Richard Rodgers.

1792. Rene Clemente (July 2, 1950–) B: El Paso, TX. *Cats* (Winter Garden, "Mungojerrie," Oct. 7, 1982): Mungojerrie and Rumpleteazer/W: T.S. Eliot, M: Andrew Lloyd Webber.

1793. Dudley Clements (Mar. 31, 1889– Nov. 4, 1947) B: New York, NY. *A Night in Venice* (Shubert, "Ambrose Trainer," May 21, 1929): The Stork Don't Come Around Anymore/WM: Betty Morse Laidlaw. *Strike Up the Band* (Times Square, "Horace J. Fletcher," Jan. 14, 1930): Fletcher's American Chocolate Choral Society; He Knows Milk; How About a Boy Like Me?; A Man of High Degree; A Typical Self-Made American/W: Ira Gershwin, M: George Gershwin. *Caviar* (Forrest, "Pavel," June 7, 1934): I Feel Sorta.../W: Edward Heyman, M: Harden Church.

1794. Hazel Clements *The O'Brien Girl* (Liberty, "Dickey," Oct. 3, 1921): Partners/W: Otto Harbach, M: Louis A. Hirsch.

1795. Joy Clements *Street Scene* (New York City Center, revival, "Rose Maurrant," Feb. 13, 1960): Don't Forget the Lilac Bush; I Loved Her, Too; There'll Be Trouble/W: Langston Hughes, Elmer Rice, M: Kurt Weill — Remember That I

Care; We'll Go Away Together; What Good Would the Moon Be?/W: Langston Hughes, M: Kurt Weill. *The King and I* (New York City Center, revival, "Tuptim," May 11, 1960): I Have Dreamed; My Lord and Master; We Kiss in a Shadow/W: Oscar Hammerstein II, M: Richard Rodgers. *The King and I* (New York City Center, revival, "Tuptim," June 12, 1963): same as above.

1796. L.D. Clements *The King and I* (New York City Center, revival, "Lun Tha," June 12, 1963): I Have Dreamed; We Kiss in a Shadow/ W: Oscar Hammerstein II, M: Richard Rodgers.

1797. James Clemons *Maid in America* (Winter Garden, revue, "The Made in America Dancer," Feb. 18, 1915): Castles in the Air; The Girlie of the Cabaret/W: Harold Atteridge, M: Sigmund Romberg. *The Passing Show of 1916* (Winter Garden, revue, June 22, 1916): Any Night on Old Broadway/W: Harold Atteridge, M: Sigmund Romberg, Otto Motzan — Ragging the Apache/W: Harold Atteridge, M: Otto Motzan. *Doing Our Bit* (Winter Garden, "Mr. Resorter," Oct. 18, 1917): Egyptian Rag; Mister Rag and I/W: Harold Atteridge, M: Sigmund Romberg, Herman Timberg.

1798. Camille Cleveland *The Good Mister Best* (Garrick, "Mrs. Isabella Best," Aug. 30, 1897): Puff, Puff; Waltz of the Mazy/W: John J. McNally, M: ?.

1799. Phyllis Cleveland *Annie Dear* (Times Square, "Ethel Deane," Nov. 4, 1924): Help, Help, Help/WM: Clare Kummer — Louwanna/ W: Clifford Grey, M: Sigmund Romberg, Jean Schwartz. *Tell Me More!* (Gaiety, "Peggy Van de Leur," Apr. 13, 1925): Kickin' the Clouds Away; My Fair Lady (Lady Fair); Tell Me More!; Three Times a Day/W: Ira Gershwin, B.G. DeSylva, M: George Gershwin. *The City Chap* (Liberty, "Betty Graham," Oct. 26, 1925): He Is the Type; No One Knows (How Much I'm in Love); Sympathetic Someone; Walking Home with Josie; When I Fell in Love with You/W: Anne Caldwell, M: Jerome Kern — Journey's End/W: P.G. Wodehouse, M: Jerome Kern. *The Cocoanuts* (Lyric > Century, CR, "Polly Potter," May 17, 1926): A Little Bungalow; We Should Care; Why Do You Want to Know Why? [May 16, 1927]; With a Family Reputation/WM: Irving Berlin.

1800. Bessie Clifford *Fluffy Ruffles* (Criterion, "Mattie Swizzle," Sept. 7, 1908): Won't You Let Me Carry Your Parcel?/W: C.H. Bovill, M: Jerome Kern. *The Never Homes* (Broadway, "Wisteria Bunn," Oct. 5, 1911): The Kiss Burglar; That Spooky Tune/W: E. Ray Goetz, M: A. Baldwin Sloane.

1801. Billy Clifford (1869–1930) *Go-Go* (Daly's, "Sen. Locksmith," Mar. 12, 1923): I'm Scared of You/W: Alex Rogers, M: C. Luckeyth Roberts.

1802. George Clifford *Piggy* (Royale, "Totsie," Jan. 11, 1927): I Wanna Go Voom Voom/W: Lew Brown, M: Cliff Friend.

1803. Kathleen Clifford (Feb. 16, 1887–Jan. 11, 1963) B: Charlottesville, VA. Billed as The Smartest Chap in Town, she was a male impersonator in vaudeville from about 1910. *Fascinating Flora* (Casino, "Rose Gayboy," June 3, 1907): What Will Happen Then?/W: R.H. Burnside, M: Gustave Kerker. *The Top o' th' World* (Majestic > Casino, "Maida," Oct. 19, 1907): Cupid and You and I/WM: Manuel Klein — My Shaggy Old Polar Bear; Riddle-Ma-Ree/W: James O'Dea, M: Anne Caldwell. *Vera Violetta* (Winter Garden, "Mlle. Angelique," Nov. 20, 1911): Angelique of the Opera Comique/W: Melville Gideon, M: Louis A. Hirsch. *A Winsome Widow* (Moulin Rouge, "Willie Grow," Apr. 11, 1912): I Take After Dad/W: Robert B. Smith, M: Raymond Hubbell — Toodle-oodle-oodle on Your Piccolo [July 1, 1912]/WM: S. T. Griffin, Henry Murtagh.

1804. Larry Clifford (May 4, 1877–Feb. 9, 1955) B: Ohio. *Hello, Alexander* (44th Street, "Jim Delily," Oct. 7, 1919): I'm Glad I'm from Dixie/W: Alfred Bryan, M: Jean Schwartz.

1805. William Clifton (c 1855–Sept. 18, 1951) *The Newlyweds and Their Baby* (Majestic, "Mr. Newlywed," Mar. 22, 1909): The Boogie-Boo; Napoleon/W: A. Seymour Brown, M: Nat D. Ayer — Mr. Jiggers/W: Paul West, M: John W. Bratton.

1806. Lynne Clifton-Allen *But Never Jam Today* (Longacre, "Black Queen," July 31, 1979): Long Live the Queen/WM: Bob Larimer, Bert Keyes.

1807. Jeffrey Clonts *Cats* (Winter Garden, CR, "Bustopher Jones" and "Asparagus" and "Growltiger," c 1991): Bustopher Jones; Growltiger's Last Stand; Gus: The Theater Cat/W: T.S. Eliot, M: Andrew Lloyd Webber.

1808. Glenn Close (Mar. 19, 1947–) B: Greenwich, CT. *Rex* (Lunt-Fontanne, "Princess Mary," Apr. 25, 1976): Christmas at Hampton Court; The Masque; The Wee Golden Warrior/W: Sheldon Harnick, M: Richard Rodgers. *Barnum* (St. James, "Chairy Barnum," Apr. 30, 1980): Black and White; The Colors of My Life; I Like Your Style; One Brick at a Time/W: Michael Stewart, M: Cy Coleman. *Sunset Boulevard* (Minskoff, "Norma Desmond," Nov. 17, 1994/Mar. 19, 1995): As If We Never Said Good-bye; The Greatest Star of All; The Lady's Paying; New Ways to Dream; The Perfect Year; Salome; Surrender; With One Look/W: Don Black, Christopher Hampton, M: Andrew Lloyd Webber.

1809. Arthur Clough *Two Little Brides* (Casino > Lyric, "King of Wurtenburg," Apr. 23, 1912): I Like All Girls; So Away with Sorrow/W: Arthur Anderson, M: Gustave Kerker.

1810. James Clow (Apr. 15, 1965–) B: White Plains, NY. *Blood Brothers* (Music Box, "Sammy," Apr. 25, 1993): Kids Game/WM: Willy Russell.

1811. Robert C. Cloy *Half a Widow* (Waldorf, "Capt. Wagner," Sept. 12, 1927): France Will Not Forgive/W: Gordon Johnstone, M: Geoffrey O'Hara — Let's Laugh and Be Merry; You're a Wonderful Girl/W: ?, M: Shep Camp — Under the Midsummer Moon/W: Harry B. Smith, M: Shep Camp.

1812. Harry E. Cluett *Sporting Days* and *Battle in the Skies* (Hippodrome, "Joe Van Dyck," Sept. 5, 1908): Rowing/WM: Manuel Klein. *The International Cup* (Hippodrome, "Sgt. Lefevre," Sept. 3, 1910): The Fighting Regiment/WM: Manuel Klein.

1813. Ivy Clyde *Love's Lottery* (Broadway, "Bess Myrtle," Oct. 3, 1904): Behold Our Lady Great; Holiday Joys; Song of the Tub; The Village Recruits/W: Stanislas Stange, M: Julian Edwards.

1814. June Clyde (Dec. 2, 1909–Oct. 1, 1987) B: St. Joseph, MO. In vaudeville at age 7, she was called Baby Tetrazini (her real name). She spent much of her life in Britain with director husband Thornton Freeland, when she appeared in movie musicals and comedies. *Hooray for What!* (Winter Garden, "Annabel Lewis," Dec. 1, 1937): Down with Love; In the Shade of the New Apple Tree; I've Gone Romantic on You; Napoleon's a Pastry/W: E.Y. Harburg, M: Harold Arlen. *Banjo Eyes* (Hollywood, "Sally Trowbridge," Dec. 25, 1941): We're Having a Baby/W: Harold Adamson, M: Vernon Duke.

1815. John Coast *The Student Prince [in Heidelberg]* (Al Jolson, "Capt. Tarnitz," Dec. 2, 1924): Just We Two/W: Dorothy Donnelly, M: Sigmund Romberg.

1816. Daniel Cobb *Sadie Thompson* (Alvin, "Cpl. Hodgson," Nov. 16, 1944): Siren of the Tropics/W: Howard Dietz, M: Vernon Duke.

1817. Charles Coburn (June 19, 1877–Aug. 30, 1961) B: Macon, GA. Versatile character actor, known for his monocle and cigar. In 1905 he organized his own company, The Shakespearan Players, where he acted for many years with his wife. After her death he appeared in almost 100 films. *The Better 'Ole* (Greenwich Village > Cort > Booth, "Old Bill," Oct. 19, 1918): I Wish I Was in Blighty/W: W.R. Titterton, M: Herman Darewski — My Word! Ain't We Carrying On/WM: James Heard, Melville Gideon, Herman Darewski — She's Venus De Milo to Me/WM: Oliver DeGerde, Peter Bernard.

1818. Imogene Coca (Nov. 18, 1908–June 2, 2001) B: Philadelphia, PA. M: ROBERT BURTON. Actress and comedienne. At 11, she made her debut as a tap dancer in vaudeville. Best remembered on TV for her inspired partnership with SID CAESAR on *Your Show of Shows* (1950). *The Garrick Gaieties of 1930* (Guild, revue, June 4, 1930): I Am Only Human After All/W: E.Y. Harburg, Ira Gershwin, M: Vernon Duke — Put It Away Till Spring/W: Joshua Titzell, M: Peter Nolan — Shavian Shivers/W: E.Y. Harburg, M: Vernon Duke — You Lost Your Opportunity/W: Henry Myers, M: Charles M. Schwab. *The Garrick Gaieties of 1930* (Guild, revue, return engagement, Oct. 16, 1930): I Am Only Human After All/W: E.Y. Harburg, Ira Gershwin, M: Vernon Duke — There Ain't No Love/W: E.Y. Harburg, M: Vernon Duke. *Shoot the Works!* (George M. Cohan, revue, July 21, 1931): Let's Go Out in the Open Air/WM: Ann Ronell — My Heart's a Banjo/W: E.Y. Harburg, M: Jay Gorney. *Flying Colors* (Imperial, revue, Sept. 15, 1932): It Was Never Like This/W: Howard Dietz, M: Arthur Schwartz. *New Faces of 1934* (Fulton, revue, Mar. 15, 1934): 'Cause You Won't Play House/W: E.Y. Harburg, Nancy Hamilton, M: Morgan Lewis — The Gangster Influence/W: June Sillman, Viola Brothers Shore, M: Warburton Guilbert — Something You Lack/W: June Sillman, Nancy Hamilton, M: Warburton Guilbert. *Fools Rush In* (The Playhouse, revue, Dec. 25, 1934): Willie's Little Whistle/W: Norman Zeno, M: Will Irwin. *New Faces of 1936* (Vanderbilt, revue, May 25, 1936): Miss Mimsey/WM: Irvin Graham — You Better Go Now [Oct. 19, 1936]/W: Bickley Reichner, M: Irvin Graham. *Who's Who* (Hudson, revue, Mar. 1, 1938): I Must Waltz/W: Irvin Graham, M: Baldwin Bergersen — Skiing at Saks/WM: Irvin Graham. *The Straw Hat Revue* (Ambassador, revue, Sept. 29, 1939): The Swingaroo Trio/WM: Sylvia Fine. *On the Twentieth Century* (St. James, "Letitia Primrose," Feb. 19, 1978/Jan. 22, 1979): Five Zeros; On the Twentieth Century; Repent; Sign, Lily, Sign (Sextet)/W: Betty Comden, Adolph Green, M: Cy Coleman.

1819. June Cochrane (c 1903–Dec. 30,

1967) *The Garrick Gaieties of 1925* (Garrick, revue, May 17, 1925): Ladies of the Boxoffice; Manhattan; On with the Dance [June 1925]; Sentimental Me [June 1925]; Soliciting Subscriptions/W: Lorenz Hart, M: Richard Rodgers. *The Girl Friend* (Vanderbilt, "Irene Covel," Mar. 17, 1926): I'd Like to Take You Home; Town Hall Tonight; Why Do I?/W: Lorenz Hart, M: Richard Rodgers. *A Connecticut Yankee* (Vanderbilt, "Mistress Evelyn La Belle-Ans," Nov. 3, 1927): Evelyn, What Do You Say?; I Feel at Home with You; On a Desert Island with Thee/W: Lorenz Hart, M: Richard Rodgers.

1820. James Coco (Mar. 21, 1928–Feb. 25, 1987) B: New York, NY. Serious comic actor who appeared in films from 1964. *Here's Where I Belong* (Billy Rose, "Lee," Mar. 3, 1968): We Are What We Are; We're Home; Where Have I Been?/W: Alfred Uhry, M: Robert Waldman. *Little Me* (Eugene O'Neill, revival, "Amos Pinchley" and "Prince Chernet" and "Mr. Worst," Jan. 21, 1982): Deep Down Inside; Goodbye (The Prince's Farewell); I Wanna Be Yours/W: Carolyn Leigh, M: Cy Coleman.

1821. Jennifer Cody (Nov. 10, 1969–) B: Rochester, NY. M: HUNTER FOSTER. *Cats* (Winter Garden, CR, "Rumpleteazer," c 1994): Mungojerrie and Rumpleteazer/W: T.S. Eliot, M: Andrew Lloyd Webber.

1822. Kathy Cody *Here's Love* (Shubert, "Hendrika," Oct. 3, 1963): The Bugle/WM: Meredith Willson.

1823. George Coe *Company* (Alvin, "David," Apr. 26, 1970): Have I Got a Girl for You; Sorry-Grateful/WM: Stephen Sondheim. *On the Twentieth Century* (St. James, "Owen O'Malley," Feb. 19, 1978): Five Zeros; I Rise Again; Never; Sign, Lily, Sign (Sextet)/W: Betty Comden, Adolph Green, M: Cy Coleman.

1824. Heidi Coe *Snow White and the Seven Dwarfs* (Radio City Music Hall, "Greta," Oct. 18, 1979): I'm Wishing/W: Larry Morey, M: Frank Churchill.

1825. George M. Cohan (July 3, 1878–Nov. 5, 1942) B: Providence, RI. M: ETHEL LEVEY 1901-1907. Versatile actor, songwriter, director, producer. In vaudeville with his parents and sister JOSEPHINE COHAN, they were known as the Four Cohans. *The Governor's Son* (Savoy, "Algy Wheelock," Feb. 25, 1901): And the Manager Said...; The Governor's Son; Never Breathe a Word of This to Mother; The Story of the Wedding March; Too Many Miles from Broadway/WM: George M. Cohan. *Running for Office* (14th Street, "Augustus Wright," Apr. 27, 1903): Flirtation on the Beach; If I Were Only Mr.

Morgan/WM: George M. Cohan. *Little Johnny Jones* (Liberty > New York, "Johnny Jones," Nov. 7, 1904): Always Leave Them Laughing When You Say Good-bye [Aug. 14, 1905]; A Girl I Know; Give My Regards to Broadway; I'm Mighty Glad I'm Living and That's All; Life's a Funny Proposition After All; The Yankee Doodle Boy/WM: George M. Cohan. *George Washington, Jr.* (Herald Square > New York, "George Belgrave," Feb. 12, 1906): If Washington Should Come to Life; Wedding of the Blue and the Gray; You're a Grand Old Flag/WM: George M. Cohan. *The Honeymooners* (New Amsterdam roof, "Augustus Wright," June 3, 1907): If I'm Going to Die I'm Going to Have Some Fun; Kid Days; Nothing New Beneath the Sun/WM: George M. Cohan. *The Yankee Prince* (Knickerbocker, "Percy Springer," Apr. 20, 1908): The ABC's of the U.S.A.; Cohan's Rag Babe; M-O-N-E-Y; Think It Over Carefully; Yankee Doodle's Come to Town/WM: George M. Cohan. *The Little Millionaire* (George M. Cohan, "Robert Spooner," Sept. 25, 1911): Any Place the Old Flag Flies; Barnum Had the Right Idea; The Dancing Wedding; Echoes of the Past [Nov. 27, 1911]; The Little Millionaire/WM: George M. Cohan. *Hello, Broadway!* (Astor, revue, "George Babbit," Dec. 25, 1914): Alexander's Ragtime Band; Everybody's Doing It Now; That International Rag/WM: Irving Berlin — Hello, Broadway; It Pays to Advertise; Those Irving Berlin Melodies; Two Dandy Darkies; The Two Playhouses/WM: George M. Cohan — That Old Fashioned Cakewalk/WM: George M. Cohan, Jean Schwartz. *The Merry Malones* (Erlanger's, "John Malone," Sept. 26, 1927): A Feeling in Your Heart (You'll See a Great Big Beautiful Smile); God Is Good to the Irish; Molly Malone/WM: George M. Cohan. *I'd Rather Be Right* (Alvin > Music Box, "The President of the United States," Nov. 2, 1937): I'd Rather Be Right; Off the Record; We're Going to Balance the Budget/W: Lorenz Hart, M: Richard Rodgers.

1826. Josephine (Josie) Cohan (Dec. 25, 1876–July 12, 1916) B: Providence, RI. Sister of GEORGE M. COHAN. *The Governor's Son* (Savoy, "Mrs. Dickey Dickson," Feb. 25, 1901): And the Manager Said...; The Governor's Son; The Story of the Wedding March/WM: George M. Cohan. *Running for Office* (14th Street, "Madeleine Tiger," Apr. 27, 1903): Flirtation on the Beach; I Want to Go to Paree, Papa/WM: George M. Cohan. *Rogers Brothers in Paris* (New Amsterdam, "Marjorie Kelliher," Sept. 5, 1904): The Belle of the Silvery Nile; Society/W: Ed

Gardenier, M: Max Hoffmann — The Village Maid/W: George V. Hobart, M: Max Hoffmann. *The Yankee Prince* (Knickerbocker, "Evelyn Fielding," Apr. 20, 1908): The ABC's of the U.S.A.; Cohan's Rag Babe; I'm Going to Marry a Nobleman/WM: George M. Cohan.

1827. Mary Anne Cohan *Can-Can* (Shubert, "Gabrielle," May 7, 1953): If You Loved Me Truly/WM: Cole Porter.

1828. Al Cohen (Oct. 25, 1939–) B: New York, NY. *Billy* (Billy Rose, "Gilbert," Mar. 22, 1969): The Fiddlers' Green/WM: Ron Dante, Gene Allen.

1829. Patti Cohenour (Oct. 17, 1952–) B: Albuquerque, NM. *Big River: The Adventures of Huckleberry Finn* (Eugene O'Neill, "Mary Jane Wilkes," Apr. 25, 1985/Sept. 3, 1985): Leavin's Not the Only Way to Go; You Oughta Be Here with Me/WM: Roger Miller. *The Mystery of Edwin Drood* (Imperial, "Rosa Bud," Dec. 2, 1985): Ceylon; Moonfall; The Name of Love; No Good Can Come from Bad; Perfect Strangers/WM: Rupert Holmes. *The Phantom of the Opera* (Majestic, "Christine Daae," Jan. 26, 1988, Thurs. eves. and Sat. mats./June 7, 1988): All I Ask of You; Angel of Music; Bravo, Bravo; I Remember; Little Lotte; The Mirror; Notes; The Point of No Return; Raoul, I've Been There; Stranger Than You Dreamt It; Think of Me; Twisted Every Way; Wandering Child; Why Have You Brought Me Here; Wishing You Were Somehow Here Again/W: Charles Hart, Richard Stilgoe, M: Andrew Lloyd Webber — The Phantom of the Opera/W: Mike Batt, Richard Stilgoe, M: Andrew Lloyd Webber.

1830. Helen Colbert *Porgy and Bess* (Ziegfeld, revival, "Clara," Mar. 10, 1953): Summertime/W: DuBose Heyward, M: George Gershwin.

1831. Miss Colburn *The Firefly* (Erlanger's, revival, "Geraldine Vandare," Nov. 30, 1931): He Says Yes, She Says No!; Sympathy/W: Otto Harbach, M: Rudolf Friml.

1832. Betty Colby *Almost Crazy* (Longacre, revue, June 20, 1955): Down to Eartha/WM: Ray Taylor — Where Is the Girl?/WM: James Shelton.

1833. Christine Colby (Feb. 27–) B: Cincinnati, OH. *Dancin'* (Broadhurst, revue, CR, July 4, 1978): Stouthearted Men/W: Oscar Hammerstein II, M: Sigmund Romberg — Was Dog a Doughnut/WM: Cat Stevens.

1834. Marion Colby (Aug. 27, 1923–) B: Los Angeles, CA. *Meet the People* (Mansfield, revue, Dec. 25, 1940): Elmer's Wedding Day/WM: Sid Kuller, Ray Golden — The Stars

Remain/W: Henry Myers, M: Jay Gorney. *Toplitzky of Notre Dame* (Century, "Betty," Dec. 26, 1946): All-American Man; I Wanna Go to City College; Wolf Time/W: George Marion, Jr., M: Sammy Fain.

1835. Violet Colby *The Whirl of Society* (Winter Garden, revue, CR, June 24, 1912): Oriental Rose/WM: Louis A. Hirsch.

1836. Bob Cole (July 1, 1868–Aug. 2, 1911) B: Athens, GA. The son of former slaves, he became one of the top songwriters of his era and a performer in vaudeville and on the legitimate stage. *The Shoo Fly Regiment* (Bijou, "Hunter Wilson," Aug. 6, 1907): If Adam Hadn't Seen the Apple Tree; There's Always Something Wrong/W: Bob Cole, M: J. Rosamond Johnson — Won't You Be My Little Brown Bear?/W: James Weldon Johnson, M: J. Rosamond Johnson. *The Red Moon* (Majestic, "Slim Brown," May 3, 1909): Ada, My Sweet Potater/W: Charles A. Hunter, M: Bob Cole, James Reese Europe — Don't Tell Tales Out of School/WM: ?— Run, Brudder Possum, Run (A Negro Warning)/W: James Weldon Johnson, M: J. Rosamond Johnson.

1837. Carol Cole Adopted daughter of singer Nat King Cole. *Seventeen* (Broadhurst, "Ida," June 21, 1951): The Hoosier Way; Ode to Lola/W: Kim Gannon, M: Walter Kent.

1838. Kay Cole (Jan. 13, 1948–) B: Miami, FL. *A Chorus Line* (Shubert, "Maggie," July 25, 1975): At the Ballet/W: Edward Kleban, M: Marvin Hamlisch. *A Chorus Line* (Shubert, CR, "Diana," Aug. 1982): Nothing; What I Did for Love/W: Edward Kleban, M: Marvin Hamlisch.

1839. Lester Cole (June 19, 1904–1985) B: New York, NY. A screenwriter who was blacklisted during the McCarthy era. *Peggy-Ann* (Vanderbilt, "Guy Pendleton," Dec. 27, 1926): I'm So Humble; Maybe It's Me; A Tree in the Park/W: Lorenz Hart, M: Richard Rodgers.

1840. T. Kelley Cole *The Serenade* (Knickerbocker, CR, "Lopez," Mar. 30, 1897): I Envy the Bird/W: Harry B. Smith, M: Victor Herbert.

1841. Vera Bayles Cole *Bombo* (Al Jolson > Winter Garden, "Annabella Downing," Oct. 6, 1921): Rose of Spain/W: Fred Fisher, M: Tom Brown, Billy Fazioli, Ray Miller — Wetona/W: Harold Atteridge, M: Sigmund Romberg.

1842. Charles Coleman *Blues in the Night* (Rialto, "Saloon Singer," June 2, 1982): Baby Doll/WM: Bessie Smith — Four Walls (and One Dirty Window) Blues/WM: Willard Robison — When a Woman Loves a Man/W: Johnny Mercer, M: Bernard Hanighen, Gordon Jenkins —

Wild Women Don't Have the Blues/WM: Ida Cox.

1843. Desiree Coleman (1968–) B: New York, NY. *Big Deal* (Broadway, "Phoebe," Apr. 10, 1986): Ain't She Sweet?; Happy Days Are Here Again/W: Jack Yellen, M: Milton Ager.

1844. Gladys Coleman *The Golden Butterfly* (Broadway, "Lazlov's Wife," Oct. 12, 1908): The Elf King/W: J. Hayden-Clarendon, M: Reginald De Koven.

1845. Harry Coleman (?–Jan. 30, 1928) *Kissing Time* (Lyric, "Emile Grossard," Oct. 11, 1920): Bill and Coo/W: George V. Hobart, M: Ivan Caryll — Keep a Fox Trot for Me/W: ?, M: Ivan Caryll.

1846. Herbert Coleman (Dec. 12, 1907–Oct. 3, 2001) B: Bluefield, WV. Actor, director and producer of films in the 1950s and 60s. *St. Louis Woman* (Martin Beck, "Piggie," Mar. 30, 1946): We Shall Meet to Part, No Never/W: Johnny Mercer, M: Harold Arlen. *Lost in the Stars* (Music Box, "Alex," Oct. 30, 1949): Big Mole/W: Maxwell Anderson, M: Kurt Weill.

1847. Lillian Coleman *The Burgomaster* (Manhattan, CR, "Ruth," Jan. 14, 1901): I Love You Dear and Only You; The Tale of the Kangaroo/W: Frank Pixley, M: Gustav Luders. *The Prince of Pilsen* (Broadway, "Nellie Wagner," Mar. 17, 1903): Back to the Boulevards; Pictures in the Smoke; The Tale of the Sea Shell/W: Frank Pixley, M: Gustav Luders. *Rogers Brothers in London* (Knickerbocker, "Marie Patricia," Sept. 7, 1903): By the Sycamore Tree/W: George V. Hobart, M: Max Hoffmann. *Humpty Dumpty* (New Amsterdam, "Blossom," Nov. 14, 1904): Sambo and Dinah/W: James Weldon Johnson, M: Bob Cole. *The Babes and the Baron* (Lyric, "Cinderella," Dec. 25, 1905): The Firefly and the Rose/W: Charles M. Taylor, M: Nat D. Mann — How D'Ye Do?/WM: F.R. Babcock — Tailor's Dummy/W: Charles M. Taylor, Robert B. Smith, M: H.E. Haines.

1848. Margret Coleman *Man of La Mancha* (Palace, revival, "The Housekeeper," Sept. 15, 1977): I'm Only Thinking of Him/W: Joe Darion, M: Mitch Leigh.

1849. Marilyn B. Coleman *Ain't Supposed to Die a Natural Death* (Ethel Barrymore, Oct. 20, 1971): Come Raising Your Leg on Me/WM: Melvin Van Peebles. *Don't Get God Started* (Longacre, revue, "Wise Old Woman," Oct. 29, 1987): Millions/WM: Marvin Winans.

1850. Warren Coleman (c 1901–Jan. 13, 1968) B: Boston, MA. *Porgy and Bess* (Alvin, "Crown," Oct. 10, 1935): A Red Headed Woman/W: Ira Gershwin, M: George Gershwin — What You Want wid Bess?/W: DuBose Heyward, M: George Gershwin. *Porgy and Bess* (Majestic, revival, "Crown," Jan. 22, 1942): same as above. *Porgy and Bess* (44th Street > New York City Center, revival, "Crown," Sept. 13, 1943): same as above.

1851. Charles (Honi) Coles (Apr. 2, 1911– Nov. 12, 1992) B: Philadelphia, PA. *Bubbling Brown Sugar* (ANTA, CR, "John Sage" and "Rusty," June 20, 1977): Brown Gal/WM: Avon Long, Lil Armstrong — Honeysuckle Rose/W: Andy Razaf, M: Fats Waller — In Honeysuckle Time/WM: Noble Sissle, Eubie Blake — Nobody/W: Alex Rogers, M: Bert Williams. *My One and Only* (St. James, "Mr. Magix," May 1, 1983): High Hat; My One and Only; Sweet and Low Down/W: Ira Gershwin, M: George Gershwin.

1852. Jerry Colker (Mar. 16, 1955–) B: Los Angeles, CA. *A Chorus Line* (Shubert, CR, "Al," May 1981): Sing!/W: Edward Kleban, M: Marvin Hamlisch.

1853. Owen Coll (Oct. 30, 1887–) B: St. John, New Brunswick, Canada. *Walk a Little Faster* (St. James, revue, Dec. 7, 1932): Mayfair/W: Roland Leigh, M: William Waliter.

1854. Beatrice Collenette *Lady Billy* (Liberty, "Mlle. Viorica," Dec. 14, 1920): Greenwich Village; That's All He Wants/W: Zelda Sears, M: Harold A. Levey.

1855. Mildred Collette With RUTH COLLETTE, they were known as the Collette Sisters. *Earl Carroll's Vanities of 1930* (New Amsterdam, revue, July 1, 1930): Going Up/W: E.Y. Harburg, M: Jay Gorney — Out of a Clear Blue Sky/W: Ted Koehler, M: Harold Arlen — Rumba Rhythm/W: Stella Unger, M: James P. Johnson. *Ziegfeld Follies of 1931* (Ziegfeld, revue, July 1, 1931): Dance/W: Mack Gordon, M: Harry Revel.

1856. Ruth Collette same as MILDRED COLLETTE.

1857. William Collier, Sr. (Nov. 1, 1866– Jan. 13, 1944) B: New York, NY. M: LOUISE ALLEN. The comedian started appearing in movies in 1929. *Twirly-Whirly* (Weber and Fields Music Hall, "Bob Upton," Sept. 11, 1902): In Stage Land/W: Edgar Smith, M: William T. Francis. *Hokey-Pokey* and *Bunty, Bulls and Strings* (Broadway, "Josh Kidder," Feb. 8, 1912): The Minstrel Parade; On the Stage/W: E. Ray Goetz, M: A. Baldwin Sloane, William T. Francis. *Hello, Broadway!* (Astor, "Bill Shaverfam," Dec. 25, 1914): Hello, Broadway; Two Dandy Darkies; The Two Playhouses/WM: George M. Cohan — That Old Fashioned Cakewalk/WM:

George M. Cohan, Jean Schwartz. *The Wild Rose* (Martin Beck, "Gideon Holtz," Oct. 20, 1926): Love Me, Don't You?/W: Otto Harbach, Oscar Hammerstein II, M: Rudolf Friml.

1858. Blanche Collins (May 12, 1918–) B: New York, NY. *The Cradle Will Rock* (Windsor > Mercury, "Ella Hammer," Jan. 3, 1938): Joe Worker/WM: Marc Blitzstein. *On a Clear Day You Can See Forever* (Mark Hellinger, "Mrs. Welles," Oct. 17, 1965): Ring Out the Bells/W: Alan Jay Lerner, M: Burton Lane.

1859. Charles Collins (Jan. 7, 1904–June 26, 1999) B: Frederick, OR. M: DOROTHY STONE. *Ripples* (New Amsterdam, "Richard Willoughby," Feb. 11, 1930): Is It Love?; Talk with Your Heel and Your Toe/W: Irving Caesar, M: Oscar Levant. *Smiling Faces* (Shubert, "Arthur Lawrence," Aug. 30, 1932): I Stumbled Over You and Fell in Love/W: Henry Dagand, M: Maurie Rubens — Sweet Little Stranger; Thank You, You're Welcome, Don't Mention It; There Will Be a Girl (There Will Be a Boy)/W: Mack Gordon, M: Harry Revel. *As Thousands Cheer* (Music Box, revue, CR, Mar. 1934): How's Chances?; Not for All the Rice in China; Our Wedding Day/WM: Irving Berlin. *Say When* (Imperial, "Carter Holmes," Nov. 8, 1934): It Must Have Been the Night; So Long For Ever So Long/W: Ted Koehler, M: Ray Henderson. *Sea Legs* (Mansfield, "Bill Halliday," May 18, 1937): Infatuation; The Opposite Sex; Ten O'Clock Town; Touched in the Head/W: Arthur Swanstrom, M: Michael H. Cleary. *Hooray for What!* (Winter Garden, CR, "Breezy Cunningham," Mar. 28, 1938): Down with Love; God's Country; In the Shade of the New Apple Tree; I've Gone Romantic on You; Napoleon's a Pastry/W: E.Y. Harburg, M: Harold Arlen. *The Red Mill* (Ziegfeld, revival, "Gaston," Oct. 16, 1945): Al Fresco; Moonbeams/W: Henry Blossom, Forman Brown, M: Victor Herbert.

1860. Dorothy Collins (Nov. 18, 1926–July 21, 1994) B: Windsor, Ontario, Canada. M: RONALD HOLGATE. Entertainer in nightclubs, radio and TV. Especially remembered for singing on the TV show *Your Hit Parade* (1950). *Follies* (Winter Garden, "Sally Durant Plummer," Apr. 4, 1971): Don't Look at Me; In Buddy's Eyes; Losing My Mind; Love Will See Us Through; Too Many Mornings; Waiting for the Girls Upstairs/WM: Stephen Sondheim. *Sondheim: A Musical Tribute* (Shubert, revue, Mar. 11, 1973): Do I Hear a Waltz?/W: Stephen Sondheim, M: Richard Rodgers — Losing My Mind; Pleasant Little Kingdom; Too Many Mornings/WM: Stephen Sondheim.

1861. Gene Collins *Happy* (Earl Carroll > Daly's, "Teddy," Dec. 5, 1927/Feb. 13, 1928): Hitting on High; Mad About You; Plastic Surgery; The Serpentine/W: Earle Crooker, McElbert Moore, M: Frank Grey.

1862. Jack Collins *Jimmy* (Winter Garden, "Jim Hines," Oct. 23, 1969): The Darlin' of New York; The Little Woman; Our Jimmy; They Never Proved a Thing; The Walker Walk/WM: Bill Jacob, Patti Jacob.

1863. James Collins *Bringing Up Father* (Lyric, "Dinty Moore," Apr. 6, 1925): We Hope to Make a Hit/W: R.F. Carroll, M: Seymour Furth, Leo Edwards.

1864. Jose Collins (May 23, 1887–Dec. 6, 1958) B: London, England. Dubbed The Maid of the Mountains after playing 1,352 performances in London as Theresa, heroine of the musical production of that name. "Ta-Ra-Ra-Boom-De-Ay" was the trademark song of her mother, Lottie Collins, singer-comedienne of British music hall fame. *Vera Violetta* (Winter Garden, "Mme. Von Gruenberg [Vera Violetta]," Nov. 20, 1911): I Wonder If It's True; Olga from the Volga; Vera Violetta/W: Harold Atteridge, M: Edmund Eysler — Ta-Ra-Ra-Boom-De-Ay/WM: Henry J. Sayers. *The Whirl of Society* (Winter Garden, "Angela," Mar. 5, 1912): Which Shall I Choose?/W: Harold Atteridge, M: Louis A. Hirsch. *Ziegfeld Follies of 1913* (New Amsterdam, revue, June 16, 1913): Everybody Sometime Must Love Someone; He's So Good; Just You and I and the Moon/W: Gene Buck, M: Dave Stamper — Isle d'Amour/W: Earl Carroll, M: Leo Edwards — A Little Love, a Little Kiss/W: Nilson Fysher, Adrian Ross, M: Lao Silesu — Panama; Sleep Time, My Honey/W: George V. Hobart, M: Raymond Hubbell — Peg O' My Heart/W: Alfred Bryan, M: Fred Fisher. *The Passing Show of 1914* (Winter Garden, revue, June 10, 1914): California; Dreams of the Past; The Girl of Today/W: Harold Atteridge, M: Sigmund Romberg — Kitty MacKay; You're Just a Little Better (Than the One I Thought Was Best)/W: Harold Atteridge, M: Harry Carroll — That Bohemian Rag/W: Lou Havez, M: Gus Edwards, Louis Silvers. *Suzi* (Casino > Shubert, "Suzi," Nov. 3, 1914): Angling [Nov. 30, 1914]; The Best Toast of All (Kiss Her and Look in Her Eyes); A Fascinating Night; Heaven Measured You for Me; It Thrills! It Thrills!; Life Is a Garden; Secrets; 'Twas in a Garden/W: Otto Harbach, M: Aladar Renyi — Tick-A-Tick (Suzi I'm Ticking Love Taps)/W: Otto Harbach, M: Max Perschk. *Alone at Last* (Shubert, "Tilly Dachau," Oct. 14, 1915): Not Now but By the Moon/W:

Matthew Woodward, M: Franz Lehar — Oh My Darling Tilly; Waltz Entrancing/W: Joseph W. Herbert, M: Franz Lehar — Return to Warm My Heart Again/W: Matthew Woodward, Joseph W. Herbert, M: Gaetano Merola.

1865. Madeline Collins *Natja* (Knickerbocker, "Natja Narishkin," Feb. 16, 1925): Comrade, You Have a Chance Here; Eyes That Haunt Me; I Hear Love Call Me; The Magic of Moonlight and Love; Reminiscence; Shall I Tell Him?/W: Harry B. Smith, M: Karl Hajos, based on Peter I. Tchaikovsky.

1866. Milt Collins *The New Yorkers* (Edyth Totten, revue, Mar. 10, 1927): I Can't Get Into the Quota/W: Henry Myers, M: Arthur Schwartz.

1867. Miriam Collins *Oh, My Dear!* (Princess > 39th Street, "Pickles," Nov. 27, 1918): Ask Dad; Childhood Days/W: P.G. Wodehouse, M: Louis A. Hirsch — A Moment of Peace [Apr. 21, 1919]/WM: ?. *Lassie* (Nora Bayes, "Lily," Apr. 6, 1920): Piper o' Dundee/W: Catherine Chisholm Cushing, M: Hugo Felix.

1868. Russell Collins (Oct. 8, 1897–Nov. 14, 1965) B: Indianapolis, IN. *Johnny Johnson* (44th Street, "Johnny Johnson," Nov. 19, 1936): Listen to My Song (Johnny's Song)/W: Paul Green, M: Kurt Weill. *The Liar* (Broadhurst, "Brighella," May 18 1950): Spring/W: Edward Eager, M: John Mundy.

1869. Samuel Collins *San Toy* (Daly's, revival, "Li," Apr. 7, 1902): Chinee Soje Man/W: Harry Greenbank, Adrian Ross, M: Lionel Monckton — Pletty Little Chinee; Samee Gamee; We'll Keep the Feast in Pynka Pong/W: Harry Greenbank, Adrian Ross, M: Sidney Jones.

1870. Tom Collins *The Dress Parade [Mid Summer Night's Fancies]* (Crystal Gardens, revue, June 22, 1903): The Marriage of the Daffodil and Daisy/W: Nicholas Biddle, M: Ben M. Jerome. *Miss Hook of Holland* (Criterion, "Old Policeman," Dec. 31, 1907): Miss Hook/WM: Paul Rubens.

1871. Dan Collyer (c 1853–Mar. 30, 1918) *Marty Malone* (Bijou, Aug. 31, 1896): Savannah Sue/W: Edward Harrigan, M: Dave Braham.

1872. C. David Colson (Dec. 23, 1941–) B: Detroit, MI. *Purlie* (Broadway, "Charlie," Mar. 15, 1970): Big Fish, Little Fish; Charlie's Songs; Skinnin' a Cat; The World Is Comin' to a Start/W: Peter Udell, M: Gary Geld.

1873. Kevin Colson (Aug. 28, 1938–) B: Sydney, Australia. After major musical roles in Australia and London during the 1960s, he pursued a business career until his 1990 appearance on Broadway. *Aspects of Love* (Broadhurst, "George Dillingham," Apr. 8, 1990): Falling;

The First Man You Remember; A Memory of a Happy Moment; Other Pleasures; She'd Be Far Better Off with You; Stop. Wait. Please/W: Don Black, Charles Hart, M: Andrew Lloyd Webber.

1874. Percy Colston *My Magnolia* (Mansfield, revue, "Jodey," July 8, 1926): Baby Mine/W: Alex Rogers, M: C. Luckeyth Roberts.

1875. Phyllis Colt *It Happens on Ice* (Center, revue, Oct. 10, 1940): Between You, Me, and the Lamp Post; So What Goes?; What's on the Penny/W: Al Stillman, M: Fred E. Ahlert — Long Ago/W: Al Stillman, M: Vernon Duke — The Moon Fell in the River/W: Mitchell Parish, M: Peter De Rose.

1876. Charles Columbus *Oh, Please!* (Fulton, "Buddy Trescott," Dec. 17, 1926): I'm Waiting for a Wonderful Girl/W: Anne Caldwell, M: Vincent Youmans. *Hello, Paris* (Shubert, "Clark McCurley," Nov. 15, 1930): Every Bit of You/WM: Kenneth Friede, Adrian Samish — I Stumbled Over You and Fell in Love/W: Henry Dagand, M: Maurie Rubens — Pack Your Suitcase with Love [Nov. 24, 1930]; You Made a Hit with Me [Nov. 24, 1930]/WM: ?. *Frederika* (Imperial, "Meyer," Feb. 4, 1937): The Bane of Man; Jealousy Begins at Home; Out in the Sun/W: Edward Eliscu, M: Franz Lehar.

1877. Austin Colyer (Oct. 29, 1935–) B: Brooklyn, NY. *Wonderful Town* (New York City Center, revival, "Guide," May 17, 1967): Christopher Street/W: Betty Comden, Adolph Green, M: Leonard Bernstein. *Maggie Flynn* (ANTA, "Donnelly," Oct. 23, 1968): Never Gonna Make Me Fight/WM: Hugo Peretti, Luigi Creatore, George David Weiss.

1878. Betty Comden (May 3, 1913–) B: Brooklyn, NY. Writer and performer, with partner ADOLPH GREEN, of a string of musicals for the stage and movies. *On the Town* (Adelphi, "Claire," Dec. 28, 1944): Carried Away; Some Other Time; Ya Got Me/W: Betty Comden, Adolph Green, M: Leonard Bernstein. *On the Twentieth Century* (St. James, CR, "Letitia Primrose," Jan. 16, 1979): Five Zeros; On the Twentieth Century; Repent; Sign, Lily, Sign (Sextet)/W: Betty Comden, Adolph Green, M: Cy Coleman.

1879. Vaughn Comfort *Cohan and Harris Minstrels* (New York, revue, Aug. 16, 1909): The Wedding Bells/WM: ?.

1880. Betty Compton (c 1907–July 12, 1944) B: Isle of Wight, England. M: James J. Walker, Mayor of New York, one of 4 husbands. *Vogues of 1924* (Shubert, revue, Mar. 27, 1924): Hush, Look Away; Rain/W: Clifford Grey, M: Herbert

Stothart. *Americana of 1926* (Belmont, revue, July 26, 1926): Blowin' the Blues Away/W: Ira Gershwin, M: Phil Charig — Why Do Ya Roll Those Eyes?/W: Morrie Ryskind, M: Phil Charig. *Oh, Kay!* (Imperial, "Molly Morse," Nov. 8, 1926): Clap Yo' Hands; The Woman's Touch/W: Ira Gershwin, M: George Gershwin — Heaven on Earth/W: Ira Gershwin, Howard Dietz, M: George Gershwin. *Funny Face* (Alvin, "Dora Wynne," Nov. 22, 1927): Birthday Party; My One and Only; Once/W: Ira Gershwin, M: George Gershwin. *Hold Everything!* (Broadhurst, "Norine Lloyd," Oct. 10, 1928): For Sweet Charity's Sake; It's All Over but the Shoutin'; An Outdoor Man (for My Indoor Sports)/W: B.G. DeSylva, Lew Brown, M: Ray Henderson. *Fifty Million Frenchmen* (Lyric, "Joyce Wheeler," Nov. 27, 1929): Paree, What Did You Do to Me?; Why Shouldn't I Have You?; You've Got That Thing/WM: Cole Porter.

1881. Fay Compton (Sept. 18, 1894–Dec. 12, 1978) B: London, England. M: LAURI DE FRECE. Mother of ANTHONY PELISSIER. She began on the stage at 12, the start of a long, distinguished career that included film and TV. Best remembered as Shakespeare's Ophelia in *Hamlet*. *Tonight's the Night* (Shubert, "Victoria," Dec. 24, 1914): I'd Like to Bring My Mother; Land and Water/WM: Paul Rubens, Percy Greenbank.

1882. June Lynn Compton *Sherry!* (Alvin, "Cosette," Mar. 27, 1967): Listen Cosette/W: James Lipton, M: Laurence Rosenthal.

1883. Frances Comstock *Life Begins at 8:40* (Winter Garden, revue, Aug. 27, 1934): C'est la Vie/W: Ira Gershwin, E.Y. Harburg, M: Harold Arlen. *One for the Money* (Booth, revue, Feb. 4, 1939): I Only Know; Once Upon a Time/W: Nancy Hamilton; M: Morgan Lewis. *Two for the Show* (Booth, revue, Feb. 8, 1940): How High the Moon/W: Nancy Hamilton, M: Morgan Lewis.

1884. Jeff Conaway (Oct. 5, 1950–) B: New York, NY. He played Bobby Wheeler on the TV sitcom *Taxi* (1978). *Grease* (Broadhurst, CR, "Danny Zuko," June 1973): All Choked Up; Alone at a Drive-In Movie; Summer Nights/WM: Jim Jacobs, Warren Casey. *The News* (Helen Hayes, "Executive Editor," Nov. 7, 1985): Beautiful People; The Contest; Dear Felicia; Editorial; Front Page Expose; I Am the News; Open Letter; Pyramid Lead; She's on File; Super Singo; They Write the News; Violent Crime; What's the Angle/WM: Paul Schierhorn.

1885. Eva Condon *Higher and Higher* (Shubert, "Hilda O'Brien," Apr. 4, 1940): Disgustingly Rich; From Another World/W: Lorenz Hart, M: Richard Rodgers.

1886. Kate Condon *Florodora* (Casino > New York, CR, "Dolores," Feb. 18, 1901): The Queen of the Philippine Islands/WM: Paul Rubens — Somebody; When We're on the Stage/ WM: ?. *Chu Chin Chow* (Manhattan Opera House > Century, "Alcolom," Oct. 22, 1917): Any Time's Kissing Time/WM: Frederic Norton — I Long for the Sun/W: Oscar Asche, M: Frederic Norton.

1887. Max Condon *Stars on Ice* (Center, revue, CR, June 24, 1943): Big Broad Smile [Sept. 26, 1943]/W: Al Stillman, M: Paul McGrane — Put Your Cares on Ice/WM: James Littlefield.

1888. Steve Condos (Oct. 12, 1918–Sept. 16, 1990) B: Pittsburgh, PA. *Heaven on Earth* (New Century, "Sailor with Trumpet," Sept. 16, 1948): Apple Jack; You're the First Cup of Coffee/W: Barry Trivers, M: Jay Gorney.

1889. Michael Cone (Oct. 7, 1952–) B: Fresno, CA. *Brigadoon* (Majestic, revival, "Sandy Dean," Oct. 16, 1980): Down on MacConnachy Square/W: Alan Jay Lerner, M: Frederick Loewe. *Rags* (Mark Hellinger, "Irish Tenor on Recording" and "Frankie," Aug. 21, 1986): For My Mary; What's Wrong with That?/W: Stephen Schwartz, M: Charles Strouse. *A Christmas Carol* (Paramount Madison Square Garden, return engagement, "Fezziwig," Nov. 20, 1995): Mr. Fezziwig's Annual Christmas Ball/W: Lynn Ahrens, M: Alan Menken.

1890. Gino Conforti (Jan. 30, 1932–) B: Chicago, IL. *A Family Affair* (Billy Rose, "Harry Latz," Jan. 27, 1962): Harmony/W: James Goldman, William Goldman, M: John Kander. *She Loves Me* (Eugene O'Neill, "Violinist" and "Caroler," Apr. 23, 1963): A Romantic Atmosphere; Twelve Days to Christmas/W: Sheldon Harnick, M: Jerry Bock. *Man of La Mancha* (ANTA Washington Square, "The Barber," Nov. 22, 1965): Barber's Song; Golden Helmet/W: Joe Darion, M: Mitch Leigh.

1891. James Congdon B: Detroit, MI. *Promises, Promises* (Shubert, CR, "J.D. Sheldrake," Dec. 7, 1970): It's Our Little Secret; Wanting Things/W: Hal David, M: Burt Bacharach. *42nd Street* (Winter Garden, "Pat Denning," Aug. 25, 1980): Getting Out of Town/W: Mort Dixon, M: Harry Warren. *Baby* (Ethel Barrymore, "Alan MacNally," Dec. 4, 1983): And What If We Had Loved Like That; Baby, Baby, Baby; Easier to Love; Fatherhood Blues; The Plaza Song; We Start Today/W: Richard Maltby, Jr., M: David Shire.

1892. Thomas Conkey *The Spring Maid* (Liberty, CR, "Prince Aladar," May 1, 1911): Day Dreams; How I Love a Pretty Face; Interrupted Allegory; Two Little Love Bees/W: Robert B. Smith, M: Heinrich Reinhardt — Take Me Dear/W: Robert B. Smith, M: Robert Hood Bowers. *Sweethearts* (New Amsterdam > Liberty, "Prince Franz," Sept. 8, 1913): The Angelus; The Cricket on the Hearth; Every Lover Must Meet His Fate/W: Robert B. Smith, M: Victor Herbert. *Molly O'* (Cort, "Count Walter von Walden," May 17, 1916): Little Women; The Right Girl; The Voice of Love/W: Robert B. Smith, M: Carl Woess. *The Amber Express* (Globe, "Sheldon Scott," Sept. 19, 1916): Cannonading Eyes/WM: ? — Love Flies Everywhere; Palace or Cot; There's Always One You Can't Forget/W: Marc Connelly, M: Zoel Parenteau, Robert Planquette. *The Land of Joy* (Park > Knickerbocker, CR, "Somerville Ross," Dec. 26, 1917): New York, U.S.A.; Off to Spain; There's a Chapter/W: Ruth Boyd Ober, M: Joaquin Valverde. *Fiddlers Three* (Cort, "Nicolo Colona," Sept. 3, 1918): As the Flitting Swallows Fly; One Hour, Sweetheart, with You/W: William Cary Duncan, M: Alexander Johnstone. *Our Nell* (Nora Bayes, "Frank Hart," Dec. 4, 1922): By and By/W: Brian Hooker, M: George Gershwin.

1893. Harold W. Conklin *The Garrick Gaieties of 1925* (Garrick, revue, May 17, 1925): The Butcher, The Baker, The Candle-Stick Maker/ W: Benjamin M. Kaye, M: Mana-Zucca.

1894. Harold Conkling *A Wonderful Night* (Majestic, CR, "Prince Koslofsky," Nov. 18, 1929): Chacun a Son Gout/W: Fanny Todd Mitchell, M: Johann Strauss.

1895. Harry Conley (c 1877–June 23, 1975) *Broadway Nights* (44th Street, revue, "Wilbur Scrump," July 15, 1929): The Right Man/W: Moe Jaffe, M: Sam Timberg, Maurie Rubens.

1896. Jay Conley *Bitter Sweet* (44th Street, revival, "Marquis of Steere," May 7, 1934): The Last Dance/WM: Noel Coward.

1897. Peter Conlow (July 2, 1929–) B: Philadelphia, PA. M: MICHELE BURKE. *Courtin' Time* (National, "George Mullins," June 13, 1951): Today at Your House, Tomorrow at Mine; The Wishbone Song/W: Jack Lawrence, M: Don Walker. *Three Wishes for Jamie* (Mark Hellinger, "Dennis O'Ryan," Mar. 21, 1952): I'll Sing You a Song; Trottin' to the Fair/WM: Ralph Blane. *Copper and Brass* (Martin Beck, "Brains," Oct. 17, 1957): Baby's Baby/W: David Craig, M: David Baker. *Take Me Along* (Shubert, "Wint," Oct. 22, 1959): Pleasant Beach House/WM: Bob Merrill.

1898. Gordon Connell (Mar. 19, 1923–) B: Berkeley, CA. *The Human Comedy* (Royale, "Mr. Grogan," Apr. 5, 1984): Cocoanut Cream Pie; The Fourth Telegram; Happy Anniversary; I Think the Kid Will Do/W: William Dumaresq, M: Galt MacDermot.

1899. Jane Connell (Oct. 27, 1925–) B: Berkeley, CA. Julius Monk brought her to New York to appear in revues at his clubs, The Upstairs Room and Plaza 9. *New Faces of 1956* (Ethel Barrymore, revue, June 14, 1956): April in Fairbanks/WM: Murray Grand. *Drat! The Cat!* (Martin Beck, "Matilda Van Guilder," Oct. 10, 1965): Dancing with Alice; Drat! The Cat!; It's Your Fault/W: Ira Levin, M: Milton Schafer. *Mame* (Winter Garden, "Agnes Gooch," May 24, 1966): Gooch's Song; St. Bridget; We Need a Little Christmas/WM: Jerry Herman. *Dear World* (Mark Hellinger, "Gabrielle, the Madwoman of Montmartre," Feb. 6, 1969): Dickie; Garbage; Pearls/WM: Jerry Herman. *Mame* (Gershwin, revival, "Agnes Gooch," July 24, 1983): same as above. *Me and My Girl* (Marquis, revival, "Maria, Duchess of Dene," Aug. 10, 1986): Song of Hareford/WM: Noel Gay.

1900. Edward J. Connelly (Dec. 31, 1859– Nov. 21, 1928) B: New York, NY. *Twiddle-Twaddle* (Weber's Music Hall, "Richard Jones," Jan. 1, 1906): Everybody's Looking for a Sure Thing [Apr. 23, 1906]; 'Tis Dreadful! 'Tis Astounding!/ W: Edgar Smith, M: Maurice Levi. *The Dollar Princess* (Knickerbocker, "John W. Cowder," Sept. 6, 1909): A Boat Sails on Wednesday/W: Adrian Ross, George Grossmith, M: Jerome Kern.

1901. Jim Conner *South Pacific* (New York City Center, revival, "Seabee Morton Wise," Apr. 13, 1961): There Is Nothin' Like a Dame/W: Oscar Hammerstein II, M: Richard Rodgers.

1902. Dolly Connolly M: composer Percy Wenrich. *All Aboard* (44th Street roof garden, revue, "Tillie Whiteway," June 5, 1913): Goodbye Poor Old Manhattan/WM: E. Ray Goetz, Malvin F. Franklin. *The Passing Show of 1917* (Winter Garden, revue, Apr. 26, 1917): The Golden West; Pierrot/W: Harold Atteridge, M: Sigmund Romberg, Otto Motzan — The Language of the Fan/W: Harold Atteridge, M: Sigmund Romberg. *Odds and Ends of 1917* (Norworth, revue, CR, Feb. 4, 1918): Every Girl Is Doing Her Bit Today/W: Clifford Harris, P.H. Valentine, M: James W. Tate — The Navy of Today's All Right/WM: ?. *The Right Girl* (Times Square, "Molly Darcy," Mar. 15, 1921): Aladdin; Harmony; Love's Little Journey; You'll Get Nothing from Me/W: Raymond Peck, M: Percy Wenrich.

1903. Don Connolly *Caviar* (Forrest, "Jack," June 7, 1934): Haywire/WM: Edward Heyman — My Heart's an Open Book; One in a Million/W: Edward Heyman, M: Harden Church.

1904. John P. Connolly (Sept. 1, 1950–) B: Philadelphia, PA. *Big River: The Adventures of Huckleberry Finn* (Eugene O'Neill, CR, "Pap Finn," c 1986): Guv'ment/WM: Roger Miller.

1905. Edgar Connor *The Red Moon* (Majestic, "Sambo Simmons," May 3, 1909): Sambo/ W: Bob Cole, M: James Reese Europe.

1906. Kaye Connor (Dec. 20, 1925–) B: Vancouver, British Columbia, Canada. *Gypsy Lady* (Century, "Yvonne," Sept. 17, 1946): The Facts of Life Backstage; Young Lady a la Mode/ W: Robert Wright, George Forrest, M: Victor Herbert.

1907. Thelma Connor With VELMA CONNOR, they were billed as the Connor Twins. *Ziegfeld Follies of 1922* (New Amsterdam, revue, June 5, 1922): Flappers/W: Gene Buck, M: Dave Stamper —'Neath the South Sea Moon/W: Gene Buck, M: Louis A. Hirsch, Dave Stamper — Sing a Swanee Song/W: Nat Sanders, M: Louis Breau.

1908. Velma Connor same as THELMA CONNOR.

1909. Jack Connors *The Royal Vagabond* (Cohan and Harris, "The Queen's Guard," Feb. 17, 1919): Here Come the Soldiers/WM: George M. Cohan — Messenger Number and Dance/ WM: George M. Cohan, Anselm Goetzl.

1910. Mary Beth Conoly *My Maryland* (Al Jolson, CR, "Sally Negly," Mar. 26, 1928): The Bonnie Blue Flag; Boys in Gray; Ker-choo!; The Mocking Bird; Mr. Cupid; Song of Victory; Strolling with the One I Love the Best/W: Dorothy Donnelly, M: Sigmund Romberg. *Sari* (Liberty, revival, "Juliska Fekete," Jan. 29, 1930): Long Live the King (Vive le Roi); Love Has Wings; Marry Me; Softly Thro' the Summer Night; Triumphant Youth/W: Catherine Chisholm Cushing, E.P. Heath, M: Emmerich Kalman.

1911. Harry Conor (c 1856–Apr. 1931) B: England. *A Trip to Chinatown* (Madison Square, "Welland Strong," Nov. 9, 1891): The Bowery; Reuben and Cynthia/W: Charles H. Hoyt, M: Percy Gaunt. *The Chaperons* (New York > New York Theater roof, "Adam Hogg," June 5, 1902): Bois D'Boulogne; In My Official Capacity; The Man Behind the Scenes/W: Frederick Ranken, M: Isidore Witmark. *Fad and Folly [orig. Tommy Rot]* (Mrs. Osborn's Playhouse, "Hezekiah Goop," Nov. 27, 1902): Microbes/W: Paul West,

M: Safford Waters — The Smoke Goes Up the Chimney Just the Same/WM: F. Chandler. *The Girl and the Kaiser* (Herald Square, "Peter Wenzel," Nov. 22, 1910): A Tailor Man/W: Leonard Liebling, M: Georges Jarno. *Marriage a la Carte* (Casino, "Napoleon Pettingill," Jan. 2, 1911): Oh, Rosalie; Thrifty Little Mabel; What's the Use of Going to Bed?/W: C.M.S. McLellan, M: Ivan Caryll. *A Winsome Widow* (Moulin Rouge, "Welland Strong," Apr. 11, 1912): Songs of Yesterday/W: ?, M: Raymond Hubbell. *Lady Luxury* (Casino > Comedy, "Edward Van Cuyler," Dec. 25, 1914): When I Sing in Grand Opera/W: Rida Johnson Young, M: William Schroeder. *Fancy Free* (Astor, "Benjamin Pestlewaite," Apr. 11, 1918): Give Me the Moonlight; Someone Has Your Number/WM: Augustus Barratt.

1912. Arthur Conrad *Bright Eyes* (New York, "William Hawley," Feb. 28, 1910): If Only You Would Take a Tip from Me; The Man on the Box/W: Otto Harbach, M: Karl Hoschna. *The Wife Hunters* (Herald Square, "Paul De Laperra," Nov. 2, 1911): Follette; Little Dancing Jumping Jigger/W: David Kempner, M: Anatole Friedland — Honeyland/WM: David Kempner, Anatole Friedland, Malvin F. Franklin.

1913. Barbara Smith Conrad *Porgy and Bess* (New York City Center, revival, "Bess," May 6, 1964): Bess, You Is My Woman Now; I Loves You, Porgy/W: Ira Gershwin, DuBose Heyward, M: George Gershwin — Leavin' fo' de Promis' Lan'; What You Want wid Bess?/W: DuBose Heyward, M: George Gershwin — There's a Boat Dat's Leavin' Soon for New York/W: Ira Gershwin, M: George Gershwin.

1914. Eddie (Eddy) Conrad (1891–Apr. 1, 1941) B: New York, NY. *Gay Paree* (Shubert, revue, Aug. 18, 1925): Give Me the Rain/WM: Lester Allen, Henry Creamer, Maurie Rubens — (My) Sugar Plum/W: B.G. DeSylva, M: Joseph Meyer, J. Fred Coots. *Cross My Heart* (Knickerbocker, "The Maharajah of Mah-Ha," Sept. 17, 1928): Such Is Fame/W: Joseph McCarthy, M: Harry Tierney.

1915. Harriett Conrad *Man of La Mancha* (Palace, revival, "Antonia," Sept. 15, 1977): I'm Only Thinking of Him/W: Joe Darion, M: Mitch Leigh.

1916. Hans Conried (Apr. 15, 1915–Jan. 5, 1982) B: Baltimore, MD. He played eccentric mostly comic roles in movies and TV. In the cartoon series *Rocky and Bullwinkle* (1961), his was the voice of Snidley Whiplash. *Can-Can* (Shubert, "Boris Adzinidzinadze," May 7, 1953): Come Along with Me; If You Loved Me Truly; Never, Never Be an Artist/WM: Cole Porter. *70,*

Girls, 70 (Broadhurst, Apr. 15, 1971): Believe; Boom Ditty Boom; The Caper; Hit It, Lorraine; Home/W: Fred Ebb, M: John Kander. *Irene* (Minskoff, revival, CR, "Madame Lucy," June 27, 1974): They Go Wild, Simply Wild Over Me/W: Joseph McCarthy, M: Fred Fisher — We're Getting Away with It/W: Joseph McCarthy, M: Harry Tierney — You Made Me Love You (I Didn't Want to Do It)/W: Joseph McCarthy, M: James V. Monaco.

1917. Allen Conroy *New Faces of 1952* (Royale, revue, May 16, 1952): Waltzing in Venice/WM: Ronny Graham.

1918. John Conroy *Rogers Brothers in Paris* (New Amsterdam, "P. Sarsfield Kelliher," Sept. 5, 1904): McNabb (Who Drives the Cab)/W: Ed Gardenier, M: Max Hoffmann.

1919. Beatrice Constance *Lady Billy* (Liberty, "Anastasia Kosiankowski," Dec. 14, 1920): The Futurist Rag/W: Zelda Sears, M: Harold A. Levey.

1920. Yvonne Constant *No Strings* (Broadhurst, CR, "Jeanette Valmy," Dec. 1962): La, La, La/WM: Richard Rodgers.

1921. Carol Conte *Jimmy* (Winter Garden, "Girl in Fur Coat," Oct. 23, 1969): It's a Nice Place to Visit/WM: Bill Jacob, Patti Jacob.

1922. John Conte (Sept. 15, 1915–) B: Palmer, MA. *Carousel* (Majestic, CR, "Jigger Craigin," Nov. 1946): Blow High, Blow Low; There's Nothin' So Bad for a Woman/W: Oscar Hammerstein II, M: Richard Rodgers. *Allegro* (Majestic, "Charlie Townsend," Oct. 10, 1947): Allegro; It May Be a Good Idea; Yatata, Yatata, Yatata/W: Oscar Hammerstein II, M: Richard Rodgers. *Arms and the Girl* (46th Street, "Col. Mortimer Sherwood," Feb. 2, 1950): Don't Talk; Plantation in Philadelphia/W: Dorothy Fields, M: Morton Gould.

1923. Ray Contreras (Apr. 14, 1960–) B: Jersey City, NJ. *Runaways* (Plymouth, "Luis," May 13, 1978): Lonesome of the Road; Lullaby for Luis; Song of a Child Prostitute/WM: Elizabeth Swados.

1924. Fay Conty *Shuffle Along of 1933* (Mansfield, revue, "Sylvia Williams," Dec. 26, 1932): Chickens Come Home to Roost; In the Land of Sunny Sunflowers/W: Noble Sissle, M: Eubie Blake.

1925. Bert Convy (July 23, 1933–July 15, 1991) B: St. Louis, MO. For 2 seasons after high school he played 1st baseman with the Philadelphia Phillies' midwestern farm circuit. *Nowhere to Go but Up* (Winter Garden, "Tommy Dee," Nov. 10, 1962): Follow the Leader Septet; Out of Sight, Out of Mind; When a Fella Needs a

Friend/W: James Lipton, M: Sol Berkowitz. *The Beast in Me* (Plymouth, revue, May 16, 1963): Go, Go, Go; When I'm Alone; Why?; You're Delicious/W: James Costigan, M: Don Elliott. *Fiddler on the Roof* (Imperial, "Perchik," Sept. 22, 1964): Now I Have Everything/W: Sheldon Harnick, M: Jerry Bock. *Cabaret* (Broadhurst, "Clifford Bradshaw," Nov. 20, 1966): Perfectly Marvelous; Why Should I Wake Up?/W: Fred Ebb, M: John Kander. *Nine* (46th Street, CR, "Guido Contini," Jan. 10, 1983): The Bells of St. Sebastian; The Grand Canal; Guido's Song; I Can't Make This Movie; Long Ago; A Man Like You; Nine; Only with You; Unusual Way/WM: Maury Yeston.

1926. Curt Conway (May 4, 1915–Apr. 10, 1974) B: Boston, MA. *Of V We Sing* (Concert, revue, Feb. 11, 1942): Brooklyn Cantata/W: Mike Stratton, M: George Kleinsinger.

1927. Hart Conway (c 1839–June 1, 1919) B: England. *The Royal Middy* (Daly's, "Don Januario Paraguassa Calobrio," Jan. 28, 1880): All We Seem to Agree; I Am Don Januario; Of All the Fine Fellows That Sail on the Sea; Sword in Hand, Man to Man; Through the Night; To Our Flag/W: F. Zell, M: Richard Genee.

1928. Peggy Conway *The Garrick Gaieties of 1925* (Garrick, revue, May 17, 1925): The Guild/W: Lorenz Hart, M: Richard Rodgers.

1929. Shirl Conway (June 13, 1916–) B: Franklinville, NY. M: BILL (WILLIAM) JOHNSON. *Plain and Fancy* (Mark Hellinger, "Ruth Winters," Jan. 27, 1955): It's a Helluva Way to Run a Love Affair; Take Your Time and Take Your Pick; You Can't Miss It/W: Arnold B. Horwitt, M: Albert Hague.

1930. Jack Coogan, Sr. (1880–May 4, 1935) B: Syracuse, NY. Movie star Jackie Coogan's dad. *Maid in America* (Winter Garden, revue, CR, "The Made in America Dancer," May 17, 1915): Castles in the Air; The Girlie of the Cabaret/W: Harold Atteridge, M: Sigmund Romberg. *The Show of Wonders* (Winter Garden, revue, CR, Apr. 2, 1917): Wedding Bells/W: Harold Atteridge, M: Otto Motzan.

1931. Abbie Mitchell Cook (1884–Mar. 16, 1960) B: Baltimore, MD. or New York, NY. M: songwriter Will Marion Cook. *Bandanna Land* (Majestic, "Mandy Lou," Feb. 3, 1908): Corn Song; Red, Red Rose/W: Alex Rogers, M: Will Marion Cook.

1932. Anna Cook M: THEODORE PANKEY. *The Shoo Fly Regiment* (Bijou, "Martha Jones," Aug. 6, 1907): I'll Always Love Old Dixie/W: James Weldon Johnson, M: J. Rosamond Johnson.

1933. Barbara Cook (Oct. 25, 1927–) B: Atlanta, GA. Musical comedy star and sublime cabaret artist. *Flahooley* (Broadhurst, "Sandy," May 14, 1951): Come Back, Little Genie; Here's to Your Illusions; He's Only Wonderful; Who Says There Ain't No Santa Claus?; The World Is Your Balloon/W: E.Y. Harburg, M: Sammy Fain. *Oklahoma!* (New York City Center, revival, "Ado Annie Carnes," Aug. 31, 1953): All er Nothin'; The Farmer and the Cowman; I Cain't Say No/W: Oscar Hammerstein II, M: Richard Rodgers. *Plain and Fancy* (Mark Hellinger, "Hilda Miller," Jan. 27, 1955): Follow Your Heart; I'll Show Him!; Take Your Time and Take Your Pick; This Is All Very New to Me/W: Arnold B. Horwitt, M: Albert Hague. *Candide* (Martin Beck, "Cunegonde," Dec. 1, 1956): Gavotte/W: Dorothy Parker, M: Leonard Bernstein — Glitter and Be Gay; Oh, Happy We; Quiet/W: Richard Wilbur, M: Leonard Bernstein — I Am Easily Assimilated/WM: Leonard Bernstein — My Love; You Were Dead, You Know/W: Richard Wilbur, John Latouche, M: Leonard Bernstein. *Carousel* (New York City Center, revival, "Julie Jordan," Sept. 11, 1957): If I Loved You; A Real Nice Clambake; What's the Use of Wond'rin'; You're a Queer One, Julie Jordan/W: Oscar Hammerstein II, M: Richard Rodgers. *The Music Man* (Majestic, "Marian Paroo," Dec. 19, 1957): Goodnight, My Someone; My White Knight; Piano Lesson; Seventy-Six Trombones; Shipoopi; Till There Was You; Will I Ever Tell You?/WM: Meredith Willson. *The King and I* (New York City Center, revival, "Anna Leonowens," May 11, 1960): Getting to Know You; Hello, Young Lovers; I Whistle a Happy Tune; The Royal Bangkok Academy; Shall I Tell You What I Think of You?; Shall We Dance?/W: Oscar Hammerstein II, M: Richard Rodgers. *The Gay Life* (Shubert, "Liesl Brandel," Nov. 18, 1961): I Wouldn't Marry You; The Label on the Bottle; Magic Moment; Something You Never Had Before; This Kind of a Girl; Who Can? You Can!; You're Not the Type/W: Howard Dietz, M: Arthur Schwartz. *She Loves Me* (Eugene O'Neill, "Amalia Balash," Apr. 23, 1963/Nov. 18, 1963): Dear Friend; I Don't Know His Name; Ice Cream; No More Candy; Three Letters; Where's My Shoe?; Will He Like Me?/W: Sheldon Harnick, M: Jerry Bock. *Something More!* (Eugene O'Neill, "Carol Deems," Nov. 10, 1964): Better All the Time; Grazie Per Niente; I've Got Nothin' to Do; One Long Last Look; Who Fills the Bill/W: Marilyn Bergman, Alan Bergman, M: Sammy Fain — I Feel Like New Year's Eve; Mineola; No Questions/W: Marilyn

Bergman, Alan Bergman, M: Jule Styne. *Show Boat* (New York State, revival, "Magnolia," July 19, 1966): After the Ball/WM: Charles K. Harris — Can't Help Lovin' Dat Man; Only Make Believe; Why Do I Love You?; You Are Love/W: Oscar Hammerstein II, M: Jerome Kern. *The Grass Harp* (Martin Beck, "Dolly Talbo," Nov. 2, 1971): Dropsy Cure Weather; I'll Always Be in Love; Reach Out; Take a Little Sip; Whooshin' Through My Flesh; Yellow Drum/W: Kenward Elmslie, M: Claibe Richardson.

1934. Candace Cook *Different Times* (ANTA, "Angela Adams" and "Pauline Verne," May 1, 1972): I Miss Him; You're Perfect/WM: Michael Brown.

1935. Carole Cook B: Abilene, TX. *42nd Street* (Winter Garden, "Maggie Jones," Aug. 25, 1980): Getting Out of Town/W: Mort Dixon, M: Harry Warren — Go Into Your Dance; Shadow Waltz; Shuffle Off to Buffalo/W: Al Dubin, M: Harry Warren.

1936. Donn Cook *Les Miserables* (Broadway, CR, "Jean Valjean," c 1992): Bring Him Home; Come to Me; In My Life; Soliloquy; Thenardier Waltz; Who Am I?/W: Herbert Kretzmer, M: Claude-Michel Schonberg.

1937. Elisha Cook, Jr. (Dec. 26, 1902–May 18, 1995) B: San Francisco, CA. Thin, dark-eyed, intense character actor in films such as *The Maltese Falcon* (1941) and *The Big Sleep* (1946). *Hello, Lola* (Eltinge, "Joe Bullitt," Jan. 12, 1926): Hello, Cousin Lola; In the Dark; Keep It Up/W: Dorothy Donnelly, M: William B. Kernell.

1938. Harold Cook *Hooray for What!* (Winter Garden, Dec. 1, 1937): In the Shade of the New Apple Tree/W: E.Y. Harburg, M: Harold Arlen.

1939. James Cook (c 1869–Jan. 21, 1931) *Mr. Hamlet of Broadway* (Casino, "Brakebeam Pete," Dec. 23, 1908): Dancing Is Delightful/W: Edward Madden, M: Ben M. Jerome. *The Motor Girl* (Lyric, "Bill Pusher," June 15, 1909): Out in the Barnyard/W: Charles J. Campbell, Ralph Skinner, M: Julian Edwards. *Hello, Paris* and *A La Broadway* (Folies Bergere, revue, "Jim Jamb," Sept. 22, 1911): Antics of the Comics/W: William Le Baron, Mabel H. Hollins, M: Harold Orlob.

1940. Joe Cook (Mar. 29, 1890–May 16, 1959) B: Evansville, IN. M: ALICE BOULDEN. On stage with a traveling show at age 12; he and his brothers were known in vaudeville as The Juggling Kids. *Hitchy-Koo of 1919* (Liberty, revue, Oct. 6, 1919): When I Had a Uniform On/WM: Cole Porter. *Rain or Shine* (George M. Cohan, "Smiley Johnson," Feb. 9, 1928): So

Would I/W: Jack Yellen, M: Milton Ager. *Fine and Dandy* (Erlanger's, "Joe Squibb," Sept. 23, 1930): Fine and Dandy; Giddyup, Back/W: Paul James, M: Kay Swift. *Hold Your Horses* (Winter Garden, "Broadway Joe," Sept. 25, 1933): Hold Your Horses/W: Arthur Swanstrom, M: Louis Alter.

1941. Louise Cook *Hummin' Sam* (New Yorker, "Miss Jitters," Apr. 8, 1933): Jitters/WM: Alexander Hill.

1942. Olga Cook (?–Dec. 15, 1991) *The Passing Show of 1919* (Winter Garden, revue, Oct. 23, 1919): In a Love Boat with You/W: Harold Atteridge, M: Sigmund Romberg, Jean Schwartz — Molly Malone/W: Hale Byers, M: Chris Schonberg — Orient/W: Alfred Bryan, M: Jean Schwartz. *Cinderella on Broadway* (Winter Garden, revue, CR, "Simple Simon," July 12, 1920): Naughty Eyes/WM: Cliff Friend, Harry Richman — Why Don't You Get a Sweetie?/W: Harold Atteridge, M: Bert Grant. *Blossom Time* (Ambassador, "Mitzi," Sept. 29, 1921): Love Is a Riddle; Moment Musicale; Only One Love Ever Fills the Heart; Peace to My Lonely Heart; Song of Love; Tell Me, Daisy; Three Little Maids/W: Dorothy Donnelly, M: Sigmund Romberg.

1943. Ray Cook *Flahooley* (Broadhurst, "Citizen of Capsulanti," May 14, 1951): Sing the Merry/W: E.Y. Harburg, M: Sammy Fain.

1944. Roderick Cook (1932–Aug. 17, 1990) B: London, England. *The Girl Who Came to Supper* (Broadway, "Peter Northbrook," Dec. 8, 1963): Curt, Clear and Concise; My Family Tree; Sir or Ma'am/WM: Noel Coward. *Woman of the Year* (Palace, "Gerald," Mar. 29, 1981): I Told You So; It Isn't Working; Shut Up, Gerald; When You're Right, You're Right!/W: Fred Ebb, M: John Kander. *Oh Coward!* (Helen Hayes, revue, Nov. 17, 1986): Bright Young People; Dance Little Lady; Has Anybody Seen Our Ship?; If Love Were All; I'll See You Again; Let's Say Goodbye; Mad Dogs and Englishmen; Men About Town; Mrs. Worthington; The Party's Over Now; The Passenger's Always Right; Play Orchestra Play; Poor Little Rich Girl; A Room with a View; Someday I'll Find You; Something to Do with Spring; This Is a Changing World; Three White Feathers; We Were Dancing; World Weary; Zigeuner/WM: Noel Coward — Let's Do It/W: Noel Coward, M: Cole Porter.

1945. Victor Trent Cook (Aug. 19, 1967–) B: New York, NY. *Smokey Joe's Cafe* (Virginia, revue, Mar. 2, 1995): D.W. Washburn; Dance with Me; I (Who Have Nothing); Keep on Rollin'; Little Egypt; Love Portion #9; On

Broadway; Poison Ivy; Ruby Baby; Searchin'; Shoppin' for Clothes; Teach Me How to Shimmy; There Goes My Baby; Treat Me Nice; Young Blood/WM: Jerry Leiber, Mike Stoller.

1946. Will A. Cook *Liza* (Daly's, "Sheriff," Nov. 27, 1922): I'm the Sheriff/WM: Nat Vincent, Maceo Pinkard.

1947. Sally Cooke *No, No, Nanette* (46th Street, revival, CR, "Flora Latham," Aug. 1971): Telephone Girlie/W: Otto Harbach, M: Vincent Youmans. *Gypsy* (Winter Garden, revival, "Electra," Sept. 23, 1974): You Gotta Have a Gimmick/W: Stephen Sondheim, M: Jule Styne. *Jacques Brel Is Alive and Well and Living in Paris* (Town Hall, revue, revival, Feb. 19, 1981): Brussels/Eng. W: Eric Blau, M: Jacques Brel, Gerard Jouannest — I Loved/W: Francois Rauber, M: Gerard Jouannest — Timid Frieda/Eng. W: Eric Blau, Mort Shuman, M: Jacques Brel.

1948. Curtis Cooksey (Dec. 9, 1891–Apr. 19, 1962) B: Kentucky or Indiana. *The Vagabond King* (Shubert, revival, "Oliver Le Dain," June 29, 1943): Serenade/W: Brian Hooker, M: Rudolf Friml.

1949. Peter Cookson (May 8, 1915–Jan. 6, 1990) B: Portland, OR. *Can-Can* (Shubert, "Judge Aristide Forestier," May 7, 1953): C'est Magnifique; I Am in Love; It's All Right/WM: Cole Porter. *Wonderful Town* (New York City Center, revival, "Robert Baker," Mar. 5, 1958): Conversation Piece (Nice Talk, Nice People); It's Love; A Quiet Girl; What a Waste/W: Betty Comden, Adolph Green, M: Leonard Bernstein.

1950. Dennis Cooley (May 11, 1948–) B: Huntington Park, CA. *Jesus Christ Superstar* (Mark Hellinger, CR, "Jesus of Nazareth," Apr. 2, 1973): The Arrest; The Crucifixion; Everything's Alright; Gethsemane; Hosanna; I Don't Know How to Love Him; The Last Supper; Pilate and Christ; Poor Jerusalem; Strange Thing Mystifying; The Temple; Trial Before Pilate; What's the Buzz/W: Tim Rice, M: Andrew Lloyd Webber. *Where's Charley?* (Circle in the Square, revival, "Student," Dec. 20, 1974): Lovelier Than Ever; Once in Love with Amy; Where's Charley?/WM: Frank Loesser.

1951. Philip Coolidge (Aug. 25, 1908–May 23, 1967) B: Concord, MA. *The Liar* (Broadhurst, "Dr. Balanzoni," May 18, 1950): A Jewel of a Duel/W: Edward Eager, M: John Mundy. *Kismet* (Ziegfeld, "Omar Khayyam," Dec. 3, 1953): He's in Love!/WM: Robert Wright, George Forrest, M: based on Alexander Borodin.

1952. Frank T. Coombs *Mother Earth* (Belasco, revue, Oct. 19, 1972): Corn on the Macabre/WM: Ron Thronson, Roger Ailes, Ray

Golden — Taking the Easy Way Out/W: Ron Thronson, M: Toni Shearer.

1953. J. Parker Coombs *A Society Circus* (Hippodrome, CR, "Bolesla, King of the Gypsies," Oct. 1, 1906): The Good, Kind, Jolly Man/WM: Manuel Klein. *Sporting Days* and *Battle in the Skies* (Hippodrome, "John P. Vanderveer," Sept. 5, 1908): The Racing Game/WM: Manuel Klein.

1954. Kristi Coombs *Marilyn* (Minskoff, "Young Norma Jean," Nov. 20, 1983): A Single Dream/WM: Jeanne Napoli, Doug Frank.

1955. Kevin Cooney (Oct. 2, 1945–) B: Houston, TX. *The Best Little Whorehouse Goes Public* (Lunt-Fontanne, "I.R.S. Director," May 10, 1994): Brand New Start/WM: Carol Hall.

1956. Catherine Cooper *Miss Hook of Holland* (Criterion, "Freda Voos," Dec. 31, 1907): Amsterdam/WM: Paul Rubens.

1957. Charlotte Cooper *The President's Daughter* (Billy Rose, "Esther," Nov. 3, 1970): Welcome, Mr. Golden!; Women's Liberation/W: Jacob Jacobs, M: Murray Rumshinsky.

1958. Chuck Cooper (Nov. 8, 1954–) B: Cleveland OH. *Amen Corner* (Nederlander, "Brother Boxer," Nov. 10, 1983): In His Own Good Time; In the Real World; Leanin' on the Lord/W: Peter Udell, M: Garry Sherman.

1959. Donny Cooper *Shenandoah* (Alvin, CR, "Gabriel," June 29, 1976): Freedom; Why Am I Me?/W: Peter Udell, M: Gary Geld.

1960. Harry Cooper *Naughty Marietta* (New York, "Simon O'Hara," Nov. 7, 1910): If I Were Anybody Else but Me; It's Pretty Soft for Silas/W: Rida Johnson Young, M: Victor Herbert. *Hanky-Panky* (Broadway, "Solomon Bumpski," Aug. 5, 1912): The Hanky-Panky Glide/WM: Ballard Macdonald, Joe Cooper, Harry Cooper — My Hero (parody on Chocolate Soldier)/W: E. Ray Goetz, M: A. Baldwin Sloane — On the Mississippi [Oct. 18, 1912]/W: Ballard Macdonald, M: Harry Carroll, Arthur Fields — Opera Burlesque on the Sextette (from Lucia Di Lammermoor)/WM: Irving Berlin. *The Pleasure Seekers* (Winter Garden, revue, "Isidore Eisenstein," Nov. 3, 1913): Faust Up to Date; Levi Is a Grand Old Name/WM: E. Ray Goetz — My Arverne Rose/WM: E. Ray Goetz, Bert Grant.

1961. Helmar Augustus Cooper *Oh, Kay!* (Richard Rodgers, revival, "Shorty," Nov. 1, 1990): Dear Little Girl (I Hope You've Missed Me); When Our Ship Comes Sailing In/W: Ira Gershwin, M: George Gershwin.

1962. Horace Cooper B: Queensland, Australia. *Where's Charley?* (St. James > Broadway, "Mr. Spettigue," Oct. 11, 1948): The New Ashmoleon Marching Society and Students Conservatory Band; Serenade with Asides/WM: Frank Loesser.

1963. Jane Cooper *George White's Scandals of 1936* (New Amsterdam, revue, Dec. 25, 1935): Truckin' in My Tails/W: Jack Yellen, M: Ray Henderson.

1964. Jerry Cooper *Boys and Girls Together* (Broadhurst, revue, Oct. 1, 1940): I Want to Live (As Long as You Love Me); The Sun'll Be Up in the Morning/W: Jack Yellen, M: Sammy Fain — Such Stuff as Dreams Are Made Of/W: Irving Kahal, M: Sammy Fain.

1965. Laura Cooper *Purlie* (Billy Rose, revival, "Missy," Dec. 27, 1972): Down Home; The Harder They Fall; He Can Do It/W: Peter Udell, M: Gary Geld.

1966. Lew Cooper *Oh, What a Girl!* (Shubert, "Washington," July 28, 1919): Gimme This, Gimme That/WM: L. Wolfe Gilbert, Alex Sullivan, Nat Vincent.

1967. Lillian Kemble Cooper (Mar. 21, 1898–May 4, 1977) B: London, England. From a prominent British theatrical family. The singer and actress came to the U.S. in 1918. *Hitchy-Koo of 1919* (Liberty, revue, Oct. 6, 1919): Bring Me Back My Butterfly; In Hitchy's Garden; Old-Fashioned Garden; Pagliacci/WM: Cole Porter.

1968. Marilyn Cooper (Dec. 14, 1936–) B: New York, NY. *West Side Story* (Winter Garden, "Rosalia," Sept. 26, 1957): I Feel Pretty/W: Stephen Sondheim, M: Leonard Bernstein. *I Can Get It for You Wholesale* (Shubert, "Ruthie Rivkin," Mar. 22, 1962): Ballad of the Garment Trade; The Family Way; A Funny Thing Happened (On My Way to Love); A Gift Today (The Bar Mitzvah Song); When Gemini Meets Capricorn; Who Knows?/WM: Harold Rome. *West Side Story* (New York City Center, revival, "Rosalia," Apr. 8, 1964): same as above. *Hallelujah, Baby!* (Martin Beck, "Ethel," Apr. 26, 1967): Witches' Brew/W: Betty Comden, Adolph Green, M: Jule Styne. *Mame* (Winter Garden, CR, "Agnes Gooch," Dec. 15, 1969): Gooch's Song; St. Bridget; We Need a Little Christmas/WM: Jerry Herman. *Two by Two* (Imperial, "Leah," Nov. 10, 1970): As Far as I'm Concerned; Put Him Away/W: Martin Charnin, M: Richard Rodgers. *On the Town* (Imperial, revival, "Lucy Schmeeler," Oct. 31, 1971): I Understand/W: Betty Comden, Adolph Green, M: Leonard Bernstein. *Woman of the Year* (Palace, "Jan Donovan," Mar. 29, 1981/Oct. 20, 1981): The Grass Is Always Greener/W: Fred Ebb, M: John Kander. *Grease* (Eugene O'Neill, revival, CR, "Miss Lynch," c 1996): Alma Mater;

Born to Hand-Jive/WM: Jim Jacobs, Warren Casey.

1969. Melville Cooper (Oct. 15, 1896–Mar. 29, 1973) B: Birmingham, England. His career spanned nearly 50 years of, as he said, "being bossed about as a valet, secretary or handyman." His first movie was *The Private Life of Don Juan* (1934). In 1952 he was a panelist on the popular TV quiz *I've Got a Secret*. *Jubilee* (Imperial, "The King," Oct. 12, 1935): Me and Marie; Mr. and Mrs. Smith; We're Off to Feathermore/WM: Cole Porter. *The Merry Widow* (Majestic, revival, "Baron Popoff," Aug. 4, 1943): Women/W: Adrian Ross, M: Franz Lehar. *The Firebrand of Florence* (Alvin, "Duke," Mar. 22, 1945): Allesandro the Wise; I Know Where There's a Cozy Nook (The Cozy Nook); The Nighttime Is No Time for Thinking; A Rhyme for Angela; When the Duchess Is Away/W: Ira Gershwin, M: Kurt Weill. *Gypsy Lady* (Century, "Boris," Sept. 17, 1946): Reality/W: Robert Wright, George Forrest, M: Victor Herbert. *The Liar* (Broadhurst, "Pantalone Bisognosi," May 18, 1950): A Jewel of a Duel/W: Edward Eager, M: John Mundy. *The Merry Widow* (New York City Center, revival, "Baron Popoff," Apr. 10, 1957): same as above. *My Fair Lady* (Mark Hellinger, CR, "Colonel Pickering," July 1959): The Rain in Spain; You Did It/W: Alan Jay Lerner, M: Frederick Loewe.

1970. Peggy Cooper (Mar. 31, 1931–) B: Huntington, WV. *La Strada* (Lunt-Fontanne, "Mama Lambrini," Dec. 14, 1969): What a Man/WM: Lionel Bart. *Goodtime Charley* (Palace, "Yolande," Mar. 3, 1975): History/W: Hal Hackady, M: Larry Grossman.

1971. Richard Cooper (July 16, 1893–June 18, 1947) B: Harrow, Middlesex, England. Character actor most notable on the stage in *Charley's Aunt*. In movies from 1929. *Three Showers* (Harris > Plymouth, "Lincoln Brown," Apr. 5, 1920): You May Be the World to Your Mother/W: Henry Creamer, M: Turner Layton.

1972. Roy Cooper (Jan. 22, 1930–) B: London, England. *Canterbury Tales* (Eugene O'Neill, "Miller" and "Pluto," Feb. 3, 1969): Beer Is Best (Beer, Beer, Beer); Pear Tree Quintet/W: Nevill Coghill, M: Richard Hill, John Hawkins.

1973. Henry Coote (c 1880–June 13, 1949) B: Springfield, MA. *Lifting the Lid* (New Amsterdam roof, "Silas," June 5, 1905): Dear Old Dixie Land/W: William Jerome, M: Jean Schwartz. *The Student King* (Garden, "Francis," Dec. 25, 1906): Give Me Thy Heart, Love/W: Frederick Ranken, Stanislaus Stange, M: Reginald De Koven.

1974. Robert Coote (Feb. 4, 1909–Nov. 26, 1982) B: London, England. His father was Bert Coote, well known comedian of the British music hall. Robert appeared in Hollywood movies from 1931. *My Fair Lady* (Mark Hellinger, "Colonel Pickering," Mar. 15, 1956): The Rain in Spain; You Did It/W: Alan Jay Lerner, M: Frederick Loewe. *My Fair Lady* (St. James, revival, "Colonel Pickering," Mar. 25, 1976): same as above.

1975. Joan Copeland (June 1, 1922–) B: New York, NY. Sister of playwright Arthur Miller. *Tovarich* (Broadway, CR, "Tatiana," Oct. 7, 1963): All for You; I Know the Feeling; Make a Friend; The Only One; Wilkes-Barre, Pa.; You Love Me/W: Anne Crosswell, M: Lee Pockriss — You'll Make an Elegant Butler (I'll Make an Elegant Maid)/WM: Joan Javits, Philip Springer. *Something More!* (Eugene O'Neill, "Marchesa Valentina Crespi," Nov. 10, 1964): In No Time at All/W: Marilyn Bergman, Alan Bergman — M: Sammy Fain. *Two by Two* (Imperial, "Esther," Nov. 10, 1970): An Old Man; Something Doesn't Happen; Two by Two/W: Martin Charnin, M: Richard Rodgers. *Pal Joey* (Circle in the Square, revival, "Vera Simpson," June 27, 1976): Bewitched, Bothered and Bewildered; Den of Iniquity; Take Him; What Is a Man?/W: Lorenz Hart, M: Richard Rodgers.

1976. Virginia Copeland B: Bridgeport, CT. *The Golden Apple* (Alvin, CR, "Penelope" and "Circe," Aug. 2, 1954): Circe, Circe; It's the Going Home Together; My Love Is on the Way; We've Just Begun; Windflowers (When We Were Young)/W: John Latouche, M: Jerome Moross.

1977. Grace Coppin (?–Apr. 7, 1993) *The Fireman's Flame* (American Music Hall, "Vera Violet," Oct. 9, 1937): Doin' the Waltz/W: Ted Fetter, M: Richard Lewine.

1978. Tito Coral (Mar. 4, 1903–Nov. 1972) B: Caracas, Venezuela. *A Night in Spain* (44th Street, revue, May 3, 1927): Columbus at the Court of Queen Isabel [Nov. 7, 1927]; A Spanish Shawl/W: Alfred Bryan, M: Jean Schwartz. *Pleasure Bound* (Majestic, revue, "Tito," Feb. 18, 1929): Spanish Fado/WM: ?. *Hot-cha!* (Ziegfeld, "Ramon La Grande," Mar. 8, 1932): Fiesta/W: Lew Brown, M: Ray Henderson. *My Romance* (Shubert > Adelphi, "Tosatti, the Organ Grinder," Oct. 19, 1948): Bella Donna/W: Rowland Leigh, M: Sigmund Romberg.

1979. Frank J. Corbett *The Dancing Girl* (Winter Garden, CR, "Mr. Jones," Apr. 23, 1923): Venetian Carnival/W: Harold Atteridge, M: Sigmund Romberg. *I'll Say She Is* (Casino, "Chief," May 19, 1924): I'm Saving You for a Rainy Day; Only You; Pretty Girl/W: Will B. Johnstone, M: Tom Johnstone.

1980. Leonora Corbett (June 28, 1907–July 29, 1960) B: London, England. *Park Avenue* (Shubert, "Mrs. Sybil Bennett," Nov. 4, 1946): The Dew Was on the Rose; My Son-in-Law; Sweet Nevada; There's Nothing Like Marriage for People/W: Ira Gershwin, M: Arthur Schwartz.

1981. Don Corby *South Pacific* (New York City Center, revival, "Lieut. Buzz Adams," Apr. 13, 1961): There Is Nothin' Like a Dame/W: Oscar Hammerstein II, M: Richard Rodgers.

1982. Jack Corcoran *Hello, Broadway!* (Astor, "Daddy Long Beard's Brother," Dec. 25, 1914): Sneaky Steps/WM: George M. Cohan.

1983. Ottilie Corday *Sharlee* (Daly's, "Jane Caldwell," Nov. 22, 1923): Honeymoon Row/W: Alex Rogers, M: C. Luckeyth Roberts.

1984. Peggy Corday *Helen Goes to Troy* (Alvin, "Venus," Apr. 24, 1944): The Judgment of Paris/W: Herbert Baker, M: Jacques Offenbach, adapted by Eric Wolfgang Korngold.

1985. Sandyl Cordell *The Vamp* (Winter Garden, "Aunt Hester," Nov. 10, 1955): Keep Your Nose to the Grindstone/W: John Latouche, M: James Mundy.

1986. Leeta Corder *Ginger* (Daly's, "Virginia Warewell," Oct. 16, 1923): Don't Forget; Ginger; If Ever I Get Up My Irish; Love's Art; Mating Time; Quarrel Duet/W: H.I. Phillips, M: Harold Orlob. *Madame Pompadour* (Martin Beck, CR, "Belotte," Jan. 5, 1925): Magic Moments; One, Two and One, Two, Three; Tell Me What Your Eyes Were Made For/W: Clare Kummer, M: Leo Fall — When the Cherry Blossoms Fall (Love Is Love)/W: William Cary Duncan, M: Anselm Goetzl. *Blossom Time* (Jolson, revival, "Bellabruna," Mar. 8, 1926): Keep It Dark; Let Me Awake; Melody Triste/W: Dorothy Donnelly, M: Sigmund Romberg.

1987. Blaine Cordner (Aug. 21, 1895–Mar. 29, 1971) B: Jacksonville, FL. *The Grand Street Follies of 1929* (Booth, revue, "Pierrot," May 1, 1929): I Need You So/W: David Goldberg, Howard Dietz, M: Arthur Schwartz — I've Got You on My Mind/WM: Max Ewing. *Show Girl* (Ziegfeld, July 2, 1929): How Could I Forget?/W: Ira Gershwin, Gus Kahn, M: George Gershwin.

1988. Juliette Cordon *Rob Roy* (Herald Square, "Janet," Oct. 29, 1894): The Merry Miller; My Hame Is Where the Heather Blooms; Rustic Song/W: Harry B. Smith, M: Reginald De Koven.

1989. Norman Cordon *Street Scene* (Adelphi, "Frank Maurrant," Jan. 9, 1947): I Loved

Her, Too; Let Things Be Like They Always Was; There'll Be Trouble/W: Langston Hughes, Elmer Rice, M: Kurt Weill.

1990. Victoria Cordova B: Mexico City, Mexico. *Viva O'Brien* (Majestic, "Lupita Estrada," Oct. 9, 1941): Carinito; El Matador Terrifico; To Prove My Love/W: Raymond Leveen, M: Maria Grever. *Around the World in Eighty Days* (Adelphi, "Lola," May 31, 1946): If You Smile at Me/WM: Cole Porter.

1991. Virginia Cordova *Louisiana Lady* (New Century, "Golondrina," June 4, 1947): The Cuckoo-Cheena; Louisiana's Holiday/W: Monte Carlo, M: Alma Sanders.

1992. Irwin Corey (Jan. 29, 1912–) B: Brooklyn, NY. The World's Foremost Authority has performed in nightclubs, movies, radio and TV. *New Faces of 1943* (Ritz, revue, Dec. 22, 1942): Land of Rockefellera/W: John Lund, M: Lee Wainer. *Happy as Larry* (Coronet, "Seamus," Jan. 6, 1950): A Cup of Tea; The Flatulent Ballad/W: Donagh MacDonagh, M: Mischa Portnoff, Wesley Portnoff. *Flahooley* (Broadhurst, "Abou Ben Atom," May 14, 1951): The Springtime Cometh/W: E.Y. Harburg, M: Sammy Fain.

1993. Corinne (Kimball) (Dec. 25, 1873–1937) B: New Orleans, LA. *A China Doll* (Majestic, "Hi See," Nov. 19, 1904): How to Be Happy Though Married; One Umbrella Would Be Big Enough for Two/W: Harry B. Smith, M: Alfred E. Aarons. *Lifting the Lid* (New Amsterdam roof, "Mathilde Macartini," June 5, 1905): Reminds Me of Home Sweet Home/WM: Frank Bryan — Sombrero/W: James O'Dea, M: William C. Polla. *Rogers Brothers in Ireland* (Liberty > New York, "Alice O'Grady," Sept. 4, 1905): The Irish Girl I Love; Mike Doolin's Jaunting Car; My Irish Maid; The Shamrock of Erin; So Different/W: George V. Hobart, M: Max Hoffmann.

1994. Irene Corlett *The Lady in Red* (Lyric, "Maude Langoon," May 12, 1919): Garibaldi Band; A Little Bit of Scotch; Pretty Little Girls Like You/W: Anne Caldwell, M: Richard Winterberg. *By Jupiter* (Shubert, "Penelope," June 3, 1942): Now That I've Got My Strength/W: Lorenz Hart, M: Richard Rodgers.

1995. Nick Corley *A Christmas Carol* (Paramount Madison Square Garden, "Cratchit," Dec. 1, 1994): Christmas Together; Dancing on Your Grave; Nothing to Do with Me/W: Lynn Ahrens, M: Alan Menken. *A Christmas Carol* (Paramount Madison Square Garden > Madison Square Garden, return engagements, "Cratchit," Nov. 20, 1995 > Nov. 22, 1996): same as above.

1996. William S. Corliss *Winsome Winnie* (Casino, "Demetrius," Dec. 1, 1903): Way Down South/W: Frederick Ranken, M: Gustave Kerker.

1997. Paul A. Corman (Apr. 22, 1946–) B: Dallas, TX. *Fiddler on the Roof* (Winter Garden, revival, "Mendel," Dec. 28, 1976): Anatevka/W: Sheldon Harnick, M: Jerry Bock.

1998. Nord Cornell *Blossom Time* (Ambassador, revival, "Kuppelweiser," Sept. 4, 1943): Keep It Dark; My Springtime Thou Art; Serenade/W: Dorothy Donnelly, M: Sigmund Romberg.

1999. Peggy Cornell (c 1904–Aug. 30, 1986) B: Kansas City. Dancer and Ziegfeld girl. She retired in 1951. *Sunny Days* (Imperial, "Babette," Feb. 8, 1928): A Belle, a Beau and a Boutonniere; I'll Be Smiling; One Sunny Day/W: Clifford Grey, William Cary Duncan, M: Jean Schwartz. *Angela* (Ambassador, CR, "Bijou," Dec. 10, 1928): Bundle of Love; Don't Forget Your Etiquette; Oui, Oui!; The Regal Romp; Tally-Ho/W: Mann Holiner, M: Alberta Nichols. *The Street Singer* (Shubert, "Muriel," Sept. 17, 1929): Somebody Quite Like You; You Never Can Tell/WM: ?.

2000. Don Correia (Aug. 28, 1951–) B: San Jose, CA. M: SANDY DUNCAN. *A Chorus Line* (Shubert, CR, "Mike," June 1979/July 1984): I Can Do That/W: Edward Kleban, M: Marvin Hamlisch. *Little Me* (Eugene O'Neill, revival, "Frankie Polo," Jan. 21, 1982): I've Got Your Number/W: Carolyn Leigh, M: Cy Coleman. *Sophisticated Ladies* (Lunt-Fontanne, revue, CR, Mar. 29, 1982): Bli-Blip/WM: Duke Ellington, Sid Kuller — Drop Me Off in Harlem/W: Nick Kenny, M: Duke Ellington — Fat and Forty/WM: Duke Ellington, Al Hibbler — Hey Baby/WM: Duke Ellington — Satin Doll/W: Johnny Mercer, M: Billy Strayhorn, Duke Ellington. *Five-Six-Seven-Eight...Dance!* (Radio City Music Hall, revue, June 15, 1983): Cheek to Cheek; It Only Happens When I Dance with You/WM: Irving Berlin — I Go to Rio/WM: Peter Allen, Adrienne Anderson — I Love to Dance/W: Marilyn Bergman, Alan Bergman, M: Billy Goldenberg — I'm Flying/W: Carolyn Leigh, M: Moose Charlap — I've Got Your Number/W: Carolyn Leigh, M: Cy Coleman — You Mustn't Kick It Around/W: Lorenz Hart, M: Richard Rodgers. *My One and Only* (St. James, CR, "Capt. Billy Buck Chandler," Nov. 1, 1984): Blah, Blah, Blah; He Loves and She Loves; High Hat; How Long Has This Been Going On?; I Can't Be Bothered Now; My One and Only; 'S Wonderful; Soon; Strike Up the

Band; Sweet and Low Down/W: Ira Gershwin, M: George Gershwin. *Singin' in the Rain* (Gershwin, "Don Lockwood," July 2, 1985): Beautiful Girl; Good Morning; Singin' in the Rain; You Are My Lucky Star/W: Arthur Freed, M: Nacio Herb Brown — Fit as a Fiddle/WM: Arthur Freed, Al Hoffman, Al Goodhart — Moses/W: Betty Comden, Adolph Green, M: Roger Edens.

2001. Billie Cortez *Blackbirds of 1928* (Liberty > Eltinge, revue, May 9, 1928): Porgy (Blues for Porgy)/W: Dorothy Fields, M: Jimmy McHugh.

2002. John Cortez *Pardon My English* (Majestic, "Karl," Jan. 20, 1933): In Three-Quarter Time/W: Ira Gershwin, M: George Gershwin.

2003. Herbert Corthell (Jan. 20, 1875–Jan. 23, 1947) B: Boston, MA. *The White Cat* (New Amsterdam, "Prince Plump," Nov. 2, 1905): Get the Money/W: William Jerome, M: Jean Schwartz. *The Balkan Princess* (Herald Square > Casino, "Henri," Feb. 9, 1911): A Hard Life; The Opera Ball/WM: Arthur Wimperis, Paul Rubens. *The Road to Mandalay* (Park, "Hiram Montgomery," Mar. 1, 1916): Father's Whiskers; Looking for a Girl My Size; See America First; Till You Try/W: William J. McKenna, M: Oreste Vessella. *Canary Cottage* (Morosco, "Billy Moss," Feb. 5, 1917): But in the Morning/WM: Earl Carroll. *Tumble Inn* (Selwyn, "Jim Wilson," Mar. 24, 1919): The Laugh; The Wedding Blues; You'll Do It All Over Again/W: Otto Harbach, M: Rudolf Friml. *Fifty-Fifty, Ltd.* (Comedy, "Cornwallis Crosby," Oct. 27, 1919): The Argentines, Portuguese and the Greeks; Fifty-Fifty/WM: Arthur Swanstrom, Carey Morgan — Girls/WM: Leon DeCosta. *The Vagabond King* (Casino, "Guy Tabarie," Sept. 21, 1925): Drinking Song; Serenade/W: Brian Hooker, M: Rudolf Friml.

2004. Jim Corti *Candide* (Broadway, revival, "Chinese Coolie" and "Westphalian Soldier" and "Priest" and "Spanish Don" and "Rosary Vendor," Mar. 10, 1974): I Am Easily Assimilated/WM: Leonard Bernstein — Sheep's Song/W: Stephen Sondheim, Leonard Bernstein. *A Chorus Line* (Shubert, CR, "Al," Jan. 1979): Sing!/W: Edward Kleban, M: Marvin Hamlisch.

2005. Diana Corto (July 28, 1942–) B: Buffalo, NY. *13 Daughters* (54th Street, "Malia," Mar. 2, 1961): Let-a-Go Your Heart; Throw a Petal/WM: Eaton Magoon, Jr. *West Side Story* (New York City Center, revival, "Francisca," Apr. 8, 1964): I Feel Pretty/W: Stephen Sondheim, M: Leonard Bernstein. *Her First Roman* (Lunt-Fontanne, "Charmian," Oct. 20, 1968): Magic Carpet/WM: Ervin Drake.

2006. Lucita Corvera *Artists and Models of 1924* (Astor > Casino, revue, Oct. 15, 1924): I Love to Dance When I Hear a March; Who's the Lucky Fellow?/W: ?, M: J. Fred Coots — Mediterranean Nights/WM: ?.

2007. Kenneth Cory (July 21, 1941–Jan. 15, 1993) B: Hanover, PA. *Company* (Alvin, CR, "Peter," Apr. 26, 1971): Have I Got a Girl for You/WM: Stephen Sondheim. *Company* (Alvin, CR, "Robert"): Barcelona; Being Alive; Company; Side by Side by Side; Someone Is Waiting; What Would We Do Without You?/WM: Stephen Sondheim.

2008. Valerie Cossart (June 27, c 1907–Dec. 31, 1994) B: London, England. *Tonight at 8:30* (National, revival, "Emily Valance," Feb. 20, 1948): Music Box/WM: Noel Coward.

2009. Suzanne Costallos *Zorba* (Broadway, revival, "Crow," Oct. 16, 1983): The Crow/W: Fred Ebb, M: John Kander.

2010. Diosa Costello *Too Many Girls* (Imperial, "Pepe," Oct. 18, 1939): She Could Shake the Maracas; Spic and Spanish/W: Lorenz Hart, M: Richard Rodgers. *South Pacific* (Majestic, CR, "Bloody Mary," June 1951): Bali Ha'i; Happy Talk/W: Oscar Hammerstein II, M: Richard Rodgers.

2011. Lou Costello (Mar. 6, 1906–Mar. 3, 1959) B: Paterson, NJ. Chubby comedy partner of thin straight man BUD ABBOTT from their first movie together, *One Night in the Tropics* (1940) until their breakup in 1957. *The Streets of Paris* (Broadhurst, revue, June 19, 1939): The French Have a Word for It/WM: Harold Rome.

2012. Nicholas Coster (Dec. 3, 1934–) B: London, England. Among numerous other TV soaps, he played history professor Paul Britton during the run of *The Secret Storm. Seesaw* (Uris, CR, "Jerry Ryan," June 11, 1973): Chapter 54, Number 1909; In Tune; My City; Spanglish; We've Got It; You're a Lovable Lunatic/W: Dorothy Fields, M: Cy Coleman.

2013. James Costigan *The Beast in Me* (Plymouth, revue, May 16, 1963): Calypso Kitty; Eat Your Breakfast; Eat Your Nice Lily, Unicorn; J'ai/W: James Costigan, M: Don Elliott.

2014. Guy Costley *1600 Pennsylvania Avenue* (Mark Hellinger, "Little Lud," May 4, 1976): If I Was a Dove; President Jefferson Sunday Luncheon Party March; Take Care of This House/W: Alan Jay Lerner, M: Leonard Bernstein.

2015. Sivan Cotel *Falsettos* (John Golden, revival, CR, "Jason," Oct. 15, 1992): Another Miracle of Judaism; Canceling the Bar Mitzvah; Everyone Hates His Parents; Everyone Tells Jason to See a Psychiatrist; Father to Son; The

Fight; Four Jews in a Room Bitching; The Games I Play; I Never Wanted to Love You; Jason's Therapy; Love Is Blind; Making a Home; March of the Falsettos; A Marriage Proposal; Marvin at the Psychiatrist; Marvin Hits Trina; My Father's a Homo; Please Come to My House; This Had Better Come to a Stop/WM: William Finn.

2016. Dorothy Cothran *Bloomer Girl* (New York City Center, revival, "Julia," Jan. 6, 1947): Welcome Hinges; When the Boys Come Home/W: E.Y. Harburg, M: Harold Arlen.

2017. Stephanie Cotsirilos (Feb. 24, 1947–) B: Chicago, IL. *Nine* (46th Street, "Stephanie Necrophorus," May 9, 1982): Folies Bergeres/WM: Maury Yeston.

2018. Mathilde Cottrelly (Feb. 7, 1851–June 15, 1933) B: Hamburg, Germany. In the theater from childhood, she married at 15, was singing light opera at 16, became a widow at 18 and moved to the U.S. at 24, where she began appearing in German language plays and musicals. *The Black Hussar* (Wallack's, "Heidekrug's Housekeeper," May 4, 1885): Read the Answer in the Stars/W: Sydney Rosenfeld, M: Carl Millocker. *Mam'selle Napoleon* (Knickerbocker, "Mme. Phillipard," Dec. 8, 1903): Flowers, Feathers, Ribbons and Laces; My Heart Will Be True to You (Too Whoo)/W: Joseph W. Herbert, M: Gustav Luders.

2019. Kevin Coughlin (Dec. 12, 1945–Jan. 19, 1976) B: New York, NY. He played T.R. Ryan on the popular TV comedy-drama *Mama* (1952). *The King and I* (New York City Center, revival, "Louis Leonowens," Apr. 18, 1956): I Whistle a Happy Tune; A Puzzlement/W: Oscar Hammerstein II, M: Richard Rodgers.

2020. Rhonda Coullet (Sept. 23, 1945–) B: Magnolia, AR. *The Robber Bridegroom* (Biltmore, return engagement, "Rosamund," Oct. 9, 1976): Nothin' Up; Riches; Rosamund's Dream; Sleepy Man; Where Oh Where/W: Alfred Uhry, M: Robert Waldman.

2021. Carol Coult *Sing for Your Supper* (Adelphi, revue, Apr. 24, 1939): Bonnie Banks/W: Robert Sour, M: Lee Wainer.

2022. Kay Coulter *On Your Toes* (46th Street, revival, "Frankie Frayne," Oct. 11, 1954): Glad to Be Unhappy; It's Got to Be Love; On Your Toes; There's a Small Hotel/W: Lorenz Hart, M: Richard Rodgers.

2023. Fay Courtenay (1878–July 18, 1943) B: San Francisco, CA. Sister of FLORENCE COURTENAY. *The Whirl of Society* (Winter Garden, revue, Mar. 5, 1912): I Want to Be in Dixie/W: Ted Snyder, M: Irving Berlin — That

Society Bear [June 24, 1912]/WM: Irving Berlin.

2024. Florence Courtenay *The Whirl of Society* (Winter Garden, revue, Mar. 5, 1912): I Want to Be in Dixie/W: Ted Snyder, M: Irving Berlin.

2025. Foster Courtenay (?–Dec. 20, 1909) *The Girl from Paris* (Herald Square, CR, "Cecil Smyth," Apr. 12, 1897): The Festive Continong/W: George Dance, M: Ivan Caryll.

2026. George Courtenay *The Girl from Paris* (Herald Square, CR, "Percy Tooting," June 28, 1897): The Festive Continong/W: George Dance, M: Ivan Caryll.

2027. William Courtenay (June 19, 1875–Apr. 20, 1933) B: Worcester, MA. *The Maid of the Mountains* (Casino, "Baldasarre," Sept. 11, 1918): Dividing the Spoils/W: Clifford Harris, M: Harold Fraser-Simpson.

2028. Jerome Courtland (Dec. 27, 1926–) B: Knoxville, TN. M: POLLY BERGEN. After acting in Western and musical films in the 1940s and 50s he became an executive at Walt Disney Productions. *Flahooley* (Broadhurst, "Sylvester," May 14, 1951): He's Only Wonderful; Here's to Your Illusions; Who Says There Ain't No Santa Claus?; The World Is Your Balloon/W: E.Y. Harburg, M: Sammy Fain.

2029. William Courtleigh, Sr. (June 28, 1867–Dec. 27, 1930) B: Guelph, Ontario, Canada. *Marrying Mary* (Daly's, "Ormsby Kulpepper," Aug. 27, 1906): Mr. Cupid/W: Benjamin Hapgood Burt, M: Silvio Hein.

2030. Charles Courtneidge (?–1935) Brother of CICELY COURTNEIDGE. *By the Way* (Gaiety > Central, revue, Dec. 28, 1925): In the Same Way I Love You/W: Eric Little, M: H.M. Tennant.

2031. Cicely Courtneidge (Apr. 1, 1893–Apr. 26, 1980) B: Sydney, Australia. M: JACK HULBERT. The very popular entertainers appeared separately and together in stage musicals in London and New York, and in films. *By the Way* (Gaiety > Central, revue, Dec. 28, 1925): All Day Long [Apr. 19, 1926]/W: Bert Lee, M: R.P. Weston — High Street, Africa/WM: Cumberland Clark, Huntley Trevor, Everett Lynton — Looking Around [Apr. 19, 1926]/W: Leo Robin, M: Richard Myers — Three Little Hairs [Apr. 19, 1926]/WM: Trevor Butler. *Under the Counter* (Shubert, "Jo Fox," Oct. 3, 1947): Ai Yi Yi; Let's Get Back to Glamor; The Moment I Saw You/W: Harold Purcell, M: Manning Sherwin.

2032. Alex Courtney (?–Dec. 2, 1985) *Babes in Arms* (Shubert > Majestic, "Alex," Apr. 14,

1937): Imagine; Way Out West (on West End Avenue)/W: Lorenz Hart, M: Richard Rodgers.

2033. Florence Courtney M: GEORGE JESSEL. *Snapshots of 1921* (Selwyn, revue, June 2, 1921): Futuristic Melody/W: E. Ray Goetz, M: George Gershwin.

2034. Inez Courtney (Mar. 12, 1908–Apr. 5, 1975) B: New York, NY. *Snapshots of 1921* (Selwyn, revue, June 2, 1921): Futuristic Melody/W: E. Ray Goetz, M: George Gershwin. *The Wild Rose* (Martin Beck, "Luella Holtz," Oct. 20, 1926): Brown Eyes; Won't You Come Across?/W: Otto Harbach, Oscar Hammerstein II, M: Rudolf Friml. *Good News!* (46th Street, "Babe O'Day," Sept. 6, 1927): Baby! What?; Flaming Youth; In the Meantime/W: B.G. DeSylva, Lew Brown, M: Ray Henderson. *Polly* (Lyric, "Betty," Jan. 8, 1929): Be the Secret of My Life; Heel and Toe; Nobody Wants Me/W: Irving Caesar, M: Phil Charig. *Spring Is Here* (Alvin, "Mary Jane," Mar. 11, 1929): Baby's Awake Now; Rich Man! Poor Man!; Spring Is Here (in Person); Why Can't I?/W: Lorenz Hart, M: Richard Rodgers. *America's Sweetheart* (Broadhurst, "Madge Farrell," Feb. 10, 1931): How About It?; My Sweet; You Ain't Got No Savoir Faire/W: Lorenz Hart, M: Richard Rodgers. *Hold Your Horses* (Winter Garden, "Gwen Fordyce," Sept. 25, 1933): High Shoes; I Guess I Love You/W: Owen Murphy, Robert A. Simon, M: Robert Russell Bennett.

2035. Minerva Courtney In vaudeville, she impersonated Charlie Chaplin. *Rogers Brothers in London* (Knickerbocker, "Claire Harte," Sept. 7, 1903): Mr. Breezy/W: Ed Gardenier, M: Melville Ellis. *The Mayor of Tokio* (New York, "Birdie Talcum," Dec. 4, 1905): Cheer Up Everybody/W: Richard Carle, M: William F. Peters.

2036. Perqueta Courtney (?–Nov. 26, 1974) *Merry, Merry* (Vanderbilt, "Mrs. Penwell," Sept. 24, 1925): Oh, Wasn't It Lovely?/W: Harlan Thompson, M: Harry Archer. *Twinkle Twinkle* (Liberty, "Florence Devereaux," Nov. 16, 1926): Get a Load of This/W: Harlan Thompson, M: Harry Archer. *Happy* (Earl Carroll > Daly's, CR, "Marion Brooker," Jan. 9, 1928): Check Your Troubles; Hitting on High; If You'll Put Up with Me; Sunny Side of You; The Younger Generation/W: Earle Crooker, McElbert Moore, M: Frank Grey.

2037. Willie Covan (Mar. 4, 1897–May 7, 1989) B: Savannah, GA. A major tap dancer of his time. He worked in minstrel shows and vaudeville from the age of 12; in 1936, he opened the Covan School of Dance in Hollywood, and with the help of film star, dancer Eleanor Pow-

ell, was hired by MGM to give dance lessons to a number of its players. *Tell Me More!* (Gaiety, "Waiter," Apr. 13, 1925): The Poetry of Motion/W: Ira Gershwin, B.G. DeSylva, M: George Gershwin.

2038. Franklin Cover (Nov. 20, 1928–) B: Cleveland, OH. He was Tom Willis on the long-running sitcom *The Jeffersons* (1975). *Applause* (Palace, CR, "Howard Benedict," Jan. 17, 1972): Fasten Your Seat Belts/W: Lee Adams, M: Charles Strouse.

2039. Minerva Coverdale *Hello, Paris* and *A La Broadway* (Folies Bergere, revue, "Fifi," Aug. 19, 1911): Fascination Waltz; Look Me Over; Loving Moon; The Siberian Dip; You're the Nicest Little Girl I Ever Knew/W: J. Leubrie Hill, M: J. Rosamond Johnson — The Frisco Frizz/W: Collin Davis, M: Ned Wayburn. *Maid in America* (Winter Garden, revue, "The Made in America Chorus Girl," Feb. 18, 1915): Everyone's Moving Up Town; The Girlie of the Cabaret/W: Harold Atteridge, M: Sigmund Romberg — Here's a Bale of Cotton for You/W: Harold Atteridge, M: Harry Carroll. *Maid in America* (Winter Garden, revue, CR, "Appolonora, Bottled in the U.S.A.," Apr. 12, 1915): Dancing Round the U.S.A./W: Jack Yellen, M: Harry Carroll, George L. Cobb — Oh, Those Days; Sister Susie's Started Syncopation/W: Harold Atteridge, M: Sigmund Romberg. *The Velvet Lady* (New Amsterdam, "Bubbles," Feb. 3, 1919): Bubbles; Dancing at the Wedding; Fair Honeymoon; I've Danced to Beat the Band; Little Boy and Girl; Throwing the Bull/W: Henry Blossom, M: Victor Herbert.

2040. Edie Cowan (Apr. 14–) B: New York, NY. *Annie* (Alvin, "Mrs. Pugh" and "Connie Boylan," Apr. 21, 1977): I Think I'm Gonna Like It Here; You Won't Be an Orphan for Long; You're Never Fully Dressed Without a Smile/W: Martin Charnin, M: Charles Strouse.

2041. Jerome Cowan (Oct. 6, 1897–Jan. 24, 1972) B: New York, NY. Supporting actor in over 100 films starting with *Beloved Enemy* in 1936, he also appeared frequently on TV. *As Thousands Cheer* (Music Box, revue, Sept. 30, 1933): Majestic Sails at Midnight; Not for All the Rice in China [July 16, 1934]/WM: Irving Berlin. *Rumple* (Alvin, "Dr. Wellington Winslow," Nov. 6, 1957): In Times Like These; To Adjust Is a Must/W: Frank Reardon, M: Ernest G. Schweikert.

2042. Tom Cowan *Nic-Nax of 1926* (Cort, revue, Aug. 2, 1926): In Old Rangoon/WM: Gitz Rice — When the Sun Kissed the Rose Goodbye/W: Tom Dodd, M: Gitz Rice.

2043. Noel Coward (Dec. 16, 1899–Mar. 26, 1973) B: Teddington, Middlesex, England. Talented, urbane composer, writer of short stories, lyrics, librettos and plays, as well as stage actor and director, he also appeared in films in Britain and the U.S. He and GERTRUDE LAWRENCE were close friends; some of his plays were written for her. *This Year of Grace* (Selwyn, revue, Nov. 7, 1928): Dance, Little Lady; Lilac Time; A Room with a View/WM: Noel Coward. *Tonight at 8:30* (National, "George Pepper" and "Jasper Featherways" and "Karl Sandys" and "Simon Gayforth," Nov. 24, 1936): Drinking Song; Has Anybody Seen Our Ship?; Hearts and Flowers; Men About Town; Music Box; Play, Orchestra, Play!; Then; We Were Dancing; You Were There/WM: Noel Coward.

2044. Margaret Cowie *Lost in the Stars* (Imperial, revival, "Irina," Apr. 18, 1972): Trouble Man/W: Maxwell Anderson, M: Kurt Weill.

2045. Chandler Cowles (Sept. 29, 1917–Nov. 24, 1981) B: New Haven, CT. He was a Lieutenant in the Navy on board the U.S.S. California when it was sunk at Pearl Harbor on Dec. 7, 1941. *Call Me Mister* (National > Plymouth, revue, Apr. 18, 1946): Military Life (The Jerk Song); Yuletide, Park Avenue/WM: Harold Rome. *The Cradle Will Rock* (Mansfield > Broadway, revival, "Dauber," Dec. 26, 1947): Art for Art's Sake; The Rich/WM: Marc Blitzstein. *Small Wonder* (Coronet, revue, Sept. 15, 1948): Ballad for Billionaires; William McKinley High/W: Burt Shevelove, M: Albert Selden. *The Cradle Will Rock* (New York City Center, revival, "Dauber," Feb. 11, 1960): same as above.

2046. Eugene Cowles (1860–Sept. 22, 1948) B: Standstead, Quebec, Canada. He grew up in Vermont, then studied singing while working as a bank clerk. In 1888 he joined the Boston Ideal Opera Company, known as The Bostonians, as their leading bass singer. *Robin Hood* (Standard, "Will Scarlet," Sept. 28, 1891): The Armorers' Song; Come the Bowmen in Lincoln Green; In Sherwood Forest; O, See the Lambkins Play!; The Tailor and the Crow (Jet Black Crow)/W: Harry B. Smith, M: Reginald De Koven. *The Knickerbockers* (Garden, "Antony van Corlear," May 29, 1893): If You and I Should Meet/W: Harry B. Smith, M: Reginald De Koven. *The Serenade* (Knickerbocker, "Romero," Mar. 16, 1897): The Monk and the Maid; Song of the Carbine/W: Harry B. Smith, M: Victor Herbert. *The Fortune Teller* (Wallack's, "Sandor," Sept. 26, 1898): Gypsy Jan; Gypsy Love Song (Slumber On, My Little Gypsy Sweetheart); Ho!

Ye Townsmen; Romany Life (Czardas)/W: Harry B. Smith, M: Victor Herbert. *Babette* (Broadway, "Mondragon," Nov. 16, 1903): My Honor and My Sword; My Lady of the Manor; On the Other Side of the Wall; There Once Was an Owl; Tony the Peddler/W: Harry B. Smith, M: Victor Herbert. *Marrying Mary* (Daly's, "Col. Henry Clay Kulpepper," Aug. 27, 1906): I Love the Last One Best of All/W: Benjamin Hapgood Burt, M: Silvio Hein. *The Boys and Betty* (Wallack's, "Major Gordon, U.S.A.," Nov. 2, 1908): Girls, Girls, Girls/W: George V. Hobart, M: Silvio Hein. *The Rose of Algeria* (Herald Square, "Gen. Petitpons," Sept. 20, 1909): I've Been Decorated; Only One of Anything; You'll Feel Better Then/W: Glen MacDonough, M: Victor Herbert.

2047. Frances Cowles *The Grand Street Follies of 1928* (Booth, revue, May 28, 1928): Husky Dusky Annabel/W: Agnes Morgan, M: Max Ewing.

2048. Adele Cox *The Babes and the Baron* (Lyric, "Cissie," Dec. 25, 1905): It's a Jolly Good Thing to Be Alive/W: Charles M. Taylor, Robert B. Smith, M: H.E. Haines.

2049. Catherine Cox (Dec. 13, 1950–) B: Toledo, OH. *Music Is* (St. James, "Viola," Dec. 20, 1976): The Duel; Lady's Choice; No Matter Where; Should I Speak of Loving You?; Twenty-one Chateaux/W: Will Holt, M: Richard Adler. *Whoopee!* (ANTA, revival, "Harriet Underwood," Feb. 14, 1979): You/W: Gus Kahn, M: Walter Donaldson. *Oklahoma!* (Palace, revival, CR, "Ado Annie Carnes," July 1980): All er Nothin'; The Farmer and the Cowman; I Cain't Say No/W: Oscar Hammerstein II, M: Richard Rodgers. *Barnum* (St. James, CR, "Chairy Barnum," Mar. 3, 1981/Jan. 26, 1982): Black and White; The Colors of My Life; I Like Your Style; One Brick at a Time/W: Michael Stewart, M: Cy Coleman. *Baby* (Ethel Barrymore, "Pam Sakarian," Dec. 4, 1983): Baby, Baby, Baby; I Want It All; Romance; We Start Today; With You/W: Richard Maltby, Jr., M: David Shire. *Oh Coward!* (Helen Hayes, revue, Nov. 17, 1986): Bright Young People; Chase Me, Charlie; Dance Little Lady; Has Anybody Seen Our Ship?; If Love Were All; I'll Follow My Secret Heart; I'll See You Again; Let's Say Goodbye; Mad About the Boy; Mad Dogs and Englishmen; Mrs. Worthington; The Passenger's Always Right; Play Orchestra Play; Poor Little Rich Girl; A Room with a View; Something to Do with Spring; This Is a Changing World; Three White Feathers; Uncle Harry; We Were Dancing; Why Do the Wrong People Travel?;

World Weary; Zigeuner/WM: Noel Coward — Let's Do It/W: Noel Coward, M: Cole Porter.

2050. Eddie Cox *Maid in America* (Winter Garden, revue, CR, "Another Made in America Dancer," May 17, 1925): Castles in the Air; The Girlie of the Cabaret; The Times Square Arguments/W: Harold Atteridge, M: Sigmund Romberg. *The Little Blue Devil* (Central, "Moss" and "Billy," Nov. 3, 1919): Auction Rag; The Office Blues/W: Harold Atteridge, M: Harry Carroll.

2051. Gertrude (Baby) Cox *Hot Chocolates* (Hudson, revue, June 20, 1929): Can't We Get Together?; Dixie Cinderella; Say It with Your Feet/W: Andy Razaf, M: Fats Waller, Harry Brooks. *Hummin' Sam* (New Yorker, "Hummin' Sam," Apr. 8, 1933): Ain'tcha Glad You Got Music?; Pinchin' Myself; They're Off/WM: Alexander Hill.

2052. Hazel Cox *Miss Jack* (Herald Square, "Olive Brook," Sept. 4, 1911): Goodbye, Little Girl/W: Mark Swan, M: William F. Peters. *Around the Map* (New Amsterdam, revue, "Madame Kapinski," Nov. 1, 1915): Goodness, Ain't You Glad?; I'm Madame Kapinski/W: C.M.S. McLellan, M: Herman Finck — Katie Clancy/W: C.M.S. McLellan, M: Louis A. Hirsch. *Sinbad* (Winter Garden > Century, "Patricia de Trait," Feb. 14, 1918): Isle of Youth; A Little Bit of Every Nationality; A Night in the Orient/W: Harold Atteridge, M: Sigmund Romberg. *The Passing Show of 1919* (Winter Garden, revue, Oct. 23, 1919): Dreamy Florence; Water Lily/W: Harold Atteridge, M: Sigmund Romberg, Jean Schwartz.

2053. India Cox *The Prince of Pilsen* (Jolson, revival, "Mrs. Madison Crocker," Jan. 13, 1930): The American Girl (Song of the Cities); A Season at the Shore; The Widow/W: Frank Pixley, M: Gustav Luders.

2054. Louise Cox *Oh, Look!* (Vanderbilt, "Grace Tyler," Mar. 7, 1918): Changeable Girls; Far Apart, Still You're in My Heart; A Kiss for Cinderella; We Will Live for Love and Love Alone/W: Joseph McCarthy, M: Harry Carroll.

2055. Ray Cox *La Belle Paree* (Winter Garden, "Susan Brown," Mar. 20, 1911/Apr. 10, 1911): Susan Brown from a Country Town/W: Edward Madden, M: Frank Tours. *The Never Homes* (Broadway, "Mrs. Daly Bunn," Oct. 5, 1911): Tonight's the Night/W: E. Ray Goetz, M: A. Baldwin Sloane.

2056. Richard Cox (May 6, 1948–) B: New York, NY. *Platinum* (Mark Hellinger, "Dan Danger," Nov. 12, 1978): I Am the Light; Movie Star Mansion; 1945; Ride Baby Ride/W: Will

Holt, M: Gary William Friedman. *Blood Brothers* (Music Box, CR, "Narrator," c 1993): Light Romance; Madman; Shoes Upon the Table/WM: Willy Russell.

2057. Wilbur Cox *When Johnny Comes Marching Home* (New Amsterdam > Manhattan Opera House, revival, "Uncle Tom," May 7, 1917): My Honeysuckle Girl (Ma Honeysuckle Gal)/W: Stanislaus Stange, M: Julian Edwards. *Three Showers* (Harris > Plymouth, CR, "Rastus Redmond Reynolds [Red]," May 10, 1920): B Is the Note; He Raised Everybody's Rent but Katie's/W: Henry Creamer, M: Turner Layton.

2058. Walter Coy (Jan. 31, 1909–Dec. 11, 1974) B: Great Falls, MT. *Lady in the Dark* (Alvin, CR, "Charley Johnson," Sept. 2, 1941): The Best Years of His Life/W: Ira Gershwin, M: Kurt Weill.

2059. Jack Coyle *Footlights* (Lyric, revue, "Roy Royal," Aug. 19, 1927): College Pals/WM: Harry Denny — Roam On, My Little Gypsy Sweetheart/W: Irving Kahal, Francis Wheeler, M: Ted Snyder.

2060. Wally Coyle *Good News!* (46th Street, "Windy," Sept. 6, 1927): Flaming Youth; On the Campus; The Varsity Drag/W: B.G. DeSylva, Lew Brown, M: Ray Henderson. *Murray Anderson's Almanac* (Erlanger's, revue, Aug. 14, 1929): The Almanac Covers/W: Edward Eliscu, M: Henry Sullivan — Educate Your Feet; The New Yorker/W: Jack Yellen, M: Milton Ager. *Three's a Crowd* (Selwyn, revue, Oct. 15, 1930): Forget All Your Books/W: Howard Dietz, Sammy Lerner, M: Burton Lane — Practising Up on You/W: Howard Dietz, M: Phil Charig. *Walk a Little Faster* (St. James, revue, CR, Jan. 2, 1933): A Penny for Your Thoughts/W: E.Y. Harburg, M: Vernon Duke.

2061. Joseph P. Coyne (Mar. 27, 1867–Feb. 17, 1941) B: New York, NY. M: ANNA BOYD. He spent his early years as half of the vaudeville team of Evans and Coyne. He then appeared on Broadway, but became a huge success in London, where he moved in 1907, playing Count Danilo in *The Merry Widow*. *The Good Mister Best* (Garrick, "Marmaduke Mush," Aug. 30, 1897): Beautiful, Gay Paree; The Swellest Thing in Town/W: John J. McNally, M: ?. *The Toreador* (Knickerbocker, "Sir Archibald Slackitt," Jan. 6, 1902): Archie/W: George Grossmith, M: Lionel Monckton — Away to Espana/W: Adrian Ross, M: Ivan Caryll — Everybody's Awfully Good to Me/WM: Paul A. Rubens. *Rogers Brothers in London* (Knickerbocker, "Harold Harvey," Sept. 7, 1903): It's Awfully Hard to Shop/W: George V. Hobart, M: Melville Ellis. *In Newport* (Liberty, "Percy Van Alstyne," Dec. 26, 1904): Don't Go Too Dangerously Nigh; Nobody but You/W: Bob Cole, James Weldon Johnson, M: J. Rosamond Johnson. *The Social Whirl* (Casino > Majestic, "Artie Endicott," Apr. 7, 1906): Love Among the Freaks; Tally Ho!!! (We'll Blow the Jolly Horn)/W: Joseph W. Herbert, M: Gustave Kerker. *My Lady's Maid* or *Lady Madcap* (Casino, "Trooper Smith," Sept. 20, 1906): Flirtation/WM: Percy Greenbank, Paul Rubens — They Handed Me a Lemon/W: Ed Gardenia, M: J. Fred Help.

2062. Phoebe Coyne *The Girl from Paris* (Herald Square, "Mrs. Honeycomb," Dec. 8, 1896): Cock-a-doodle; Tootle, Tootle/W: George Dance, M: Ivan Caryll. *Monte Carlo* (Herald Square, CR, "Mrs. Carthew," Apr. 4, 1898): The Duties of a Ladies' Maid; Very Careful If You Please/W: Harry Greenbank, M: Howard Talbot. *The Sleeping Beauty and the Beast* (Broadway, "Mrs. Malevolentia," Nov. 4, 1901): That Was Years Ago/W: J. Cheever Goodwin, M: Frederic Solomon.

2063. Don Crabtree (Aug. 21, 1928–) B: Borger, TX. *Pousse-Cafe* (46th Street, "Paul," Mar. 18, 1966): The Good Old Days/W: Marshall Barer, M: Duke Ellington. *The Best Little Whorehouse in Texas* (46th Street, "Edsel Mackey," June 19, 1978): Texas Has a Whorehouse in It/WM: Carol Hall.

2064. Paul Crabtree (Nov. 17, 1918–Mar. 21, 1979): B: Pulaski, VA. *Oklahoma!* (St. James, CR, "Will Parker," Jan. 1945): All er Nothin'; The Farmer and the Cowman; Kansas City/W: Oscar Hammerstein II, M: Richard Rodgers.

2065. Earle Craddock *No Other Girl* (Morosco, "Joshua Franklin," Aug. 13, 1924): Look Out for Us, Broadway/W: Bert Kalmar, M: Harry Ruby.

2066. Louis Craddock *Messin' Around* (Hudson, revue, Apr. 22, 1929): I Need You/W: Perry Bradford, M: James P. Johnson.

2067. Charles Crafts *Round the Town* (Century roof, revue, May 21, 1924): Chiquita/WM: Walter Donaldson.

2068. Mrs. Charles G. Craig (Oct. 10, 1866–July 21, 1925) B: Oregon. *The Melting of Molly* (Broadhurst, "Judy," Dec. 30, 1918): Bills; Rolling Exercise/W: Cyrus D. Wood, M: Sigmund Romberg.

2069. Donald Craig (Aug. 14, 1941–) B: Abilene, TX. *Annie* (Alvin, "Bert Healy," Apr. 21, 1977): You're Never Fully Dressed Without a Smile/W: Martin Charnin, M: Charles Strouse.

2070. Helen Craig (May 13, 1912–July 20,

1986) B: San Antonio, TX. M: JOHN BEAL. *New Faces of 1936* (Vanderbilt, revue, May 19, 1936): We Shriek of Chic/W: June Sillman, M: Irvin Graham.

2071. Joel Craig (Apr. 26–) B: New York, NY. *Very Good Eddie* (Booth, revival, "M. de Rougemont," Dec. 21, 1975): I've Got to Dance/ W: Schuyler Greene, M: Jerome Kern.

2072. Noel Craig (Jan. 4–) B: St. Louis, MO. *Going Up* (John Golden, revival, "James Brooks," Sept. 19, 1976): Down! Up! Left! Right!/W: Otto Harbach, M: Louis A. Hirsch.

2073. Richard (Dick) Craig *Sons o' Fun* (Winter Garden, revue, Dec. 1, 1941): Let's Say Goodnight with a Dance/W: Jack Yellen, M: Sammy Fain. *Icetime* (Center, revue, June 20, 1946): Cossack Love; The Dream Waltz; Mary, Mary; Ole King Cole; Song of the Silver Blades/WM: James Littlefield, John Fortis. *Icetime of 1948* (Center, revue, May 28, 1947): Breaking the Ice/WM: Al Stillman, Paul McGrane — The Dream Waltz; Garden of Versailles; Lillian Russell; Lovable You/WM: James Littlefield, John Fortis. *Howdy, Mr. Ice!* (Center, revue, June 24, 1948): Forty-eight States; In the Pink; Plenty More Fish in the Sea; Rocked in the Cradle of Jazz; Santa Claus; World's Greatest Show/W: Al Stillman, M: Alan Moran. *Howdy, Mr. Ice of 1950* (Center, revue, May 26, 1949): Big City; Forty-eight States; Plenty More Fish in the Sea; Rocked in the Cradle of Jazz; We're the Doormen of New York; World's Greatest Show/W: Al Stillman, M: Alan Moran.

2074. Richy Craig, Jr. (c 1902–Nov. 28, 1933) *Hey Nonny Nonny!* (Shubert, revue, June 6, 1932): Hey Nonny Nonny/W: Ogden Nash, M: Will Irwin.

2075. Tony Craig *Follow the Girls* (44th Street, CR, "Bob Monroe," Nov. 5, 1944): John Paul Jones; Today Will Be Yesterday Tomorrow; Where You Are/W: Dan Shapiro, Milton Pascal, M: Phil Charig.

2076. Virginia Craig *Look to the Lilies* (Lunt-Fontanne, "Sister Elizabeth," Mar. 29, 1970): Casamagordo, New Mexico; Follow the Lamb; Gott Is Gut; Himmlisher Vater; Look to the Lilies; One Little Brick at a Time; Them and They/W: Sammy Cahn, M: Jule Styne.

2077. Walter Craig (Dec. 5, 1900–July 5, 1972) B: St. Louis, MO. He later became a producer and executive in radio and TV. *Greenwich Village Follies of 1923* (Winter Garden, revue, CR, Oct. 29, 1923): Cock-a-Doodle Do/W: Cliff Friend, M: Con Conrad. *Hello, Daddy* (Erlanger's, CR, "Lawrence Tucker," June 10,

1929): As Long as We're in Love; Let's Sit and Talk About You; Your Disposition Is Mine/W: Dorothy Fields, M: Jimmy McHugh.

2078. Robert Craik *The Vagabond King* (Casino, CR, "Francois Villon," Nov. 1926): Love Me Tonight; Only a Rose; Song of the Vagabonds; Tomorrow/W: Brian Hooker, M: Rudolf Friml.

2079. Stephen Crain (Oct. 3, 1952–) B: Tokyo, Japan. *Oklahoma!* (Palace, revival, "Slim," Dec. 13, 1979): The Farmer and the Cowman/W: Oscar Hammerstein II, M: Richard Rodgers.

2080. Augustus Cramer *The Girl from Paris* (Wallack's, revival, "Tom Everleigh," Jan. 17, 1898): Somebody/W: George Dance, M: Ivan Caryll. *Monte Carlo* (Herald Square, "Fred Dorian," Mar. 21, 1898): Along the Way Where Lovers Go; I Only Know I Love Thee/W: Harry Greenbank, M: Howard Talbot.

2081. Elizabeth Crandall *Music Hath Charms* (Majestic, "Isabella," Dec. 29, 1934): It's Three O'Clock/W: Rowland Leigh, John Shubert, M: Rudolf Friml.

2082. Harold Crane (Nov. 21, 1875–?) B: Nottingham, England. *Hodge, Podge & Co.* (Madison Square, "Christopher Chinchilla," Oct. 23, 1900): What a Funny Story/W: Walter Ford, M: Herman Perlet — The White and Gray Cadets/W: Walter Ford, M: John W. Bratton. *The Sun Dodgers* (Broadway, "Wakeleigh Knight," Nov. 30, 1912): Marry a Sunshine Girl; Song of the Cocktail/W: E. Ray Goetz, M: A. Baldwin Sloane. *The Blue Paradise* (Casino > 44th Street, CR, "Hans Walther," Jan. 31, 1916): My Model Girl/W: Harold Atteridge, M: Sigmund Romberg — One Step into Love/W: Herbert Reynolds, M: Sigmund Romberg. *Dearest Enemy* (Knickerbocker, "Gen. Sir William Howe," Sept. 18, 1925): Where the Hudson River Flows/W: Lorenz Hart, M: Richard Rodgers. *The DuBarry* (George M. Cohan, "Comte Bordeneau," Nov. 22, 1932): Pantalettes/W: Rowland Leigh, M: Carl Millocker.

2083. Raymond Crane *The Clinging Vine* (Knickerbocker, "Randolph Mayo," Dec. 25, 1922): Age of Innocence; Cupid; Lady Luck; Song Without Words/W: Zelda Sears, M: Harold A. Levey.

2084. Thurston Crane *Red, Hot and Blue!* (Alvin, "Sonny Hadley," Oct. 29, 1936): Carry On; Ours; What a Great Pair We'll Be/WM: Cole Porter.

2085. Viola Crane *The Jolly Bachelors* (Broadway, CR, "Carola Gayley," May 2, 1910): The Luncheon Line; Walk This Way; What Am

I Going to Do to Make You Love Me?/W: Glen MacDonough, M: Raymond Hubbell.

2086. Allene Crater (c 1880–Aug. 13, 1957) M: FRED STONE. Mother of DOROTHY STONE and PAULA STONE. *Aladdin, Jr.* (Broadway, "Badroubladour," Apr. 8, 1895): Message of the Rose/W: J. Cheever Goodwin, M: W.H. Batchelor, Jesse Williams. *The Ballet Girl* (Manhattan, "Violette," Dec. 21, 1897): The Elopement; I Never Saw a Girl Like That; Infant Marriage; Wedding Bells/W: Adrian Ross, M: Carl Kiefert. *Miss Simplicity* (Casino, "Rosalie," Feb. 10, 1902): An Innocent City Maid; Stand Back/W: R.A. Barnet, M. H.L. Heartz. *The Wizard of Oz* (Majestic, CR, "Cynthia Cynch," Sept. 14, 1903): Things That We Don't Learn at School/W: Ed Gardenier, M: Edwin S. Brill. *The Red Mill* (Knickerbocker, "Bertha," Sept. 24, 1906): Because You're You; Go While the Goin' Is Good; The Legend of the Mill; A Widow Has Ways/W: Henry Blossom, M: Victor Herbert. *Jack O'Lantern* (Globe, "Vilanessa," Oct. 16, 1917): Knit, Knit/W: Anne Caldwell, M: Ivan Caryll. *Stepping Stones* (Globe, "Widow Hood," Nov. 6, 1923): Little Red Riding Hood/W: Anne Caldwell, M: Jerome Kern. *Stepping Stones* (Globe, revival, "Widow Hood," Sept. 1, 1924): same as above. *Criss Cross* (Globe, "Countess de Pavazac," Oct. 12, 1926): The Portrait Parade; You Will — Won't You?/W: Anne Caldwell, Otto Harbach, M: Jerome Kern.

2087. Edward Craven (?–1991) *The Babes and the Baron* (Lyric, "Cowardly Policeman," Dec. 25, 1905): Gee, But This Is a Lonesome Town/WM: Billy Gaston — Think It Over/WM: Alex A. Aarons. *Fascinating Flora* (Casino, "Reuben Brown," May 20, 1907): Oshkosh/WM: John Kemble, Lester Keith.

2088. Frank Craven (Aug. 24, 1875–Sept. 1, 1945) B: Boston, MA. Brother of EDWARD CRAVEN. Actor, writer and director. He played the Stage Manager in Thornton Wilder's classic *Our Town. Going Up* (Liberty, "Robert Street," Dec. 25, 1917): Down! Up! Left! Right!; First Act, Second Act, Third Act [Dec. 31, 1917]; Going Up/W: Otto Harbach, M: Louis A. Hirsch — When the Curtain Falls [Apr. 15, 1918]/WM: Irving Berlin.

2089. Pierce Cravens (Jan. 8, 1986–) B: Dallas, TX. *A Christmas Carol* (Madison Square Garden, return engagement, "Tiny Tim," Nov. 22, 1996): Christmas Together/W: Lynn Ahrens, M: Alan Menken.

2090. Bessie Crawford (1882–Nov. 11, 1943) M: THOMAS ROY BARNES. *The Passing Show*

of 1914 (Winter Garden > Lyric, revue, June 10, 1914): Don't Hesitate with Me/W: Harold Atteridge, M: Sigmund Romberg.

2091. Clifton Crawford (1875–June 3, 1920) B: Edinburgh, Scotland. He began as a golf player and songwriter, moving to Boston at age 21 and producing a hit song, "Nancy Brown," for MARIE CAHILL in 1902. He died in a fall from a hotel window in London. *Foxy Grandpa* (14th Street, "Jack Richman," Feb. 17, 1902): The Country Club; Polly/WM: Joseph Hart. *Mother Goose* (New Amsterdam, "Mayor of Chatham," Dec. 2, 1903): Girls Will Be Girls and Boys Will Be Boys/W: George V. Hobart, M: Frederic Solomon — Rafferty/WM: Clifton Crawford. *Three Twins* (Herald Square > Majestic, "Tom Stanhope," June 15, 1908): At a Reception; The Fifth Avenue Brigade; Good Night, Sweetheart, Good Night; Hypnotic Kiss/W: Otto Harbach, M: Karl Hoschna. *The Quaker Girl* (Park, "Tony Chute," Oct. 23, 1911): A Bad Boy and a Good Girl/W: Percy Greenbank, M: Lionel Monckton — I Want to Tell You Something (Something to Tell); Keep Away from a Married Man (I'm a Married Man)/WM: Clifton Crawford — A Runaway Match; Take a Step/W: Adrian Ross, M: Lionel Monckton. *My Best Girl* (Park, "Richard Vanderfleet," Sept. 12, 1912): Come Take a Dance with Me; If the Morning After Were the Night Before/W: Rennold Wolf, M: Augustus Barratt — I Do Like Your Eyes; My Best Girl/WM: Clifton Crawford. *Roly Poly* (Weber and Fields, CR, "Jack Billington," Dec. 23, 1912): Come Along to the Movies/W: Philip Bartholomae, M: Silvio Hein — Come to My Land of Love Dreams/W: George V. Hobart, M: John L. Golden — Milestones; The Moving Picture Man/WM: ?— The Zingaras/W: E. Ray Goetz, M: A. Baldwin Sloane. *The Peasant Girl* (44th Street, "Bronio Von Popiel," Mar. 2, 1915): Childhood Lessons; On to Conquer; One and Only/W: ?, M: Oscar Nedbal — Love Is Like a Butterfly/W: Herbert Reynolds, M: Rudolf Friml — That Little Lamb Was Me (Mary's Li'l Lamb)/WM: Clifton Crawford. *A World of Pleasure* (Winter Garden, revue, Oct. 14, 1915): Girlies Are Out of My Life; I Could Go Home to a Girlie Like You/W: Harold Atteridge, M: Sigmund Romberg. *Her Soldier Boy* (Astor > Lyric > Shubert, "Teddy McLane," Dec. 6, 1916): All Alone in a City Full of Girls/W: Rida Johnson Young, M: Sigmund Romberg — History; Military Stamp; Slavery/WM: Clifton Crawford. *Fancy Free* (Astor, "Albert Van Wyck," Apr. 11, 1918): Eve; If You're Crazy About the Women; Rat-Tat-A-Tat/WM: Clifton Crawford.

2092. Douglas Crawford *Grease* (Eugene O'Neill, revival, CR, "Kenickie," c 1996): Greased Lightnin'; Rock 'n' Roll Party Queen/WM: Jim Jacobs, Warren Casey.

2093. Ellen Crawford B: Normal, IL. Nurse Lydia Wright on the hit TV medical drama, *ER* (1994). *Do Black Patent Leather Shoes Really Reflect Up?* (Alvin, "Sister Lee," May 27, 1982): Cookie Cutters/WM: James Quinn, Alaric Jans.

2094. Kathryn Crawford (Oct. 5, 1908– Dec. 7, 1980) B: Wellsboro, PA. Actress and singer, in movies from 1929. *The New Yorkers* (Broadway, "May," Dec. 8, 1930): Love for Sale/WM: Cole Porter.

2095. Margaret Crawford *Love's Lottery* (Broadway, "Jane Jones," Oct. 3, 1904): Behold Our Lady Great; Holiday Joys; Song of the Tub; The Village Recruits/W: Stanislas Stange, M: Julian Edwards. *America* (Hippodrome, revue, "Mrs. Beacon-Hill," Aug. 30, 1913): A Gay Excursion; Though Hearts We May Secure/WM: Manuel Klein.

2096. Michael Crawford (Jan. 19, 1942–) B: Salisbury, England. He left school at 15 to be on BBC radio, TV and films. He played Cornelius Hackl in the film version of the musical *Hello, Dolly!* (1969). *The Phantom of the Opera* (Majestic, "The Phantom of the Opera," Jan. 26, 1988): All I Ask of You; Bravo, Bravo; I Remember; Little Lotte; The Mirror; The Music of the Night; Notes; The Point of No Return; Prima Donna; Stranger Than You Dreamt It; Twisted Every Way; Wandering Child/W: Charles Hart, Richard Stilgoe, M: Andrew Lloyd Webber — The Phantom of the Opera/W: Mike Batt, Richard Stilgoe, M: Andrew Lloyd Webber.

2097. Henry Creamer (June 21, 1879–Oct. 14, 1930) B: Richmond, VA. Songwriter, actor, dancer, producer. Most of his songs were written with his partner, pianist Turner Layton. *Spice of 1922* (Winter Garden, revue, July 6, 1922): Way Down Yonder in New Orleans/W: Henry Creamer, M: Turner Layton.

2098. Georgia Creighton *Chicago* (46th Street, CR, "Matron," July 1977): Class; When You're Good to Mama/W: Fred Ebb, M: John Kander.

2099. Susan Cremin B: New York, NY. *Gypsy* (Marquis, return engagement of revival, "Baby June," Apr. 28, 1991): May We Entertain You/W: Stephen Sondheim, M: Jule Styne.

2100. James Cresson (Nov. 25, 1935–) B: Seminole, OK. *Flora, the Red Menace* (Alvin, "Bronco Smallwood," May 11, 1965): Knock Knock; Palomino Pal/W: Fred Ebb, M: John Kander.

2101. Laura Hope Crews (Dec. 12, 1879–Nov. 13, 1942) B: San Francisco, CA. A child actress on the stage, she went to Hollywood in the early days of talking pictures as elocution coach for Norma Talmadge and others. Best remembered among her own film roles as Aunt Pittypat in *Gone with the Wind* (1939). *Jubilee* (Imperial, CR, "The Queen," Feb. 24, 1936): Me and Marie; Mr. and Mrs. Smith; We're Off to Feathermore/WM: Cole Porter.

2102. Lyndon Crews *The Student Prince* (Broadway, revival, "Von Asterberg," June 8, 1943): Come Boys, Let's All Be Gay, Boys (Students' March Song); Serenade; Student Life; To the Inn We're Marching/W: Dorothy Donnelly, M: Sigmund Romberg.

2103. Madge Crichton (Oct. 31, 1881–?) B: Scarborough, Yorkshire, England. *Three Little Maids* (Daly's > Garden, "Ada Branscombe," Sept. 1, 1903): Men; Sal/WM: Paul Rubens. *My Lady's Maid* or *Lady Madcap* (Casino, "Lady Betty Framlingham," Sept. 20, 1906): All I Want Is You/W: Paul West, M: Jerome Kern — Flirtation; Mum's the Word; My Lady's Maid; A Soldier of My Own/WM: Percy Greenbank, Paul Rubens.

2104. Florence Crips *The Velvet Lady* (New Amsterdam, "Florence," Feb. 3, 1919): I've Danced to Beat the Band/W: Henry Blossom, M: Victor Herbert.

2105. Louis Criscuolo (Jan. 23, 1934–) B: New York, NY. *Hurry, Harry* (Ritz, "Nick" and "Witch Doctor" and "Chorus Boy," Oct. 12, 1972): Africa Speaks; Hurry, Harry; When a Man Cries/W: David Finkle, M: Bill Weeden.

2106. Kim Criswell (July 19, 1957–) B: Hampton, VA. *The First* (Martin Beck, "Hilda Chester," Nov. 17, 1981): The Opera Ain't Over/W: Martin Charnin, M: Bob Brush. *Nine* (46th Street, CR, "Claudia," Jan. 31, 1983): A Man Like You; Unusual Way/WM: Maury Yeston. *Stardust* (Biltmore, revue, Feb. 19, 1987): Carolina Rolling Stone/W: Mitchell Parish, M: Eleanor Young, Harry D. Squires — Ciao, Ciao, Bambina; Volare/W: Mitchell Parish, M: Domenico Modugno — Deep Purple/W: Mitchell Parish, M: Peter DeRose — Forgotten Dreams; Sleigh Ride; The Syncopated Clock/W: Mitchell Parish, M: Leroy Anderson — It Happens to the Best of Friends/W: Mitchell Parish, M: Rube Bloom — Moonlight Serenade/W: Mitchell Parish, M: Glenn Miller — Riverboat Shuffle/W: Mitchell Parish, M: Hoagy Carmichael, Dick Voynow, Irving Mills — Sentimental Gentleman from Georgia/W: Mitchell Parish, M: Frank Perkins — Sidewalks of Cuba/WM: Mitchell Parish, Irving Mills, Ben Oakland — Sophisticated Swing/W: Mitchell Parish, M: Will Hudson — Stairway to the Stars/W: Mitchell Parish, M: Matt Malneck, Frank Signorelli — Star Dust/W: Mitchell Parish, M: Hoagy Carmichael. *3 Penny Opera* (Lunt-Fontanne, revival, "Lucy," Nov. 5, 1989): Jealousy Duet; Lucy's Aria/W: Bertolt Brecht, M: Kurt Weill, trans: Michael Feingold.

2107. Sam Critcherson *Adrienne* (George M. Cohan, CR, "Stephen Hayes," Oct. 1923): Cheer Up; Love Is All/W: A. Seymour Brown, M: Albert Von Tilzer.

2108. Anthony Crivello (Aug. 2, 1955–) B: Milwaukee, WI. *Evita* (Broadway, CR, "Che," Apr. 5, 1982): The Actress Hasn't Learned (The Lines You'd Like to Hear); And the Money Kept Rolling In (And Out); Goodnight and Thank You; High Flying Adored; Lament; A New Argentina; Oh What a Circus; On the Balcony of the Casa Rosada; Peron's Latest Flame; Rainbow Tour; Waltz for Eva and Che/W: Tim Rice, M: Andrew Lloyd Webber. *The News* (Helen Hayes, "Killer," Nov. 7, 1985): Beautiful People; Classifieds; Dear Editor; Editorial; Open Letter; Ordinary, Extraordinary Day; Personals; Shooting Stars; Talk to Me/WM: Paul Schierhorn. *Les Misérables* (Broadway, "Grantaire," Mar. 12, 1987): Drink with Me to Days Gone By/W: Herbert Kretzmer, M: Claude-Michel Schonberg. *Les Misérables* (Broadway, CR, "Javert," Nov. 30, 1987/Mar. 14, 1988): Soliloquy; Stars/W: Herbert Kretzmer, M: Claude-Michel Schonberg. *Kiss of the Spider Woman* (Broadhurst, "Valentin," May 3, 1993): Anything for Him; The Day After That; Dear One; Dressing Them Up; Gabriel's Letter; Good Times; I Draw the Line; My First Woman; Over the Wall II; Over the Wall III, Marta; Russian Movie/W: Fred Ebb, M: John Kander.

2109. Alfred Crocker *Robinson Crusoe, Jr.* (Winter Garden, Feb. 17, 1916): Sailor's Fling/WM: ?.

2110. Alan Crofoot (June 2, 1929–) B: Toronto, Canada. *Oliver!* (Martin Beck, limited engagement, "Mr. Bumble," Aug. 2, 1965): Boy for Sale; I Shall Scream; Oliver!; That's Your Funeral/WM: Lionel Bart.

2111. Leonard John Crofoot (Sept. 20, 1948–) B: Utica, NY. *Barnum* (St. James, "Tom Thumb," Apr. 30, 1980): Bigger Isn't Better/W: Michael Stewart, M: Cy Coleman.

2112. Charles (C.H.) Croker-King (Apr. 30, 1873–Oct. 25, 1951) B: Rook Holme, Yorkshire, England. *White Lilacs* (Shubert, "Giacomo Meyerbeer," Sept. 10, 1928): Words, Music,

Cash/W: J. Keirn Brennan, M: Karl Hajos, based on Frederic Chopin.

2113. Harold Cromer *Early to Bed* (Broadhurst, "Caddy," June 17, 1943): Early to Bed; A Girl Should Never Ripple When She Bends; Hi De Hi Ho in Harlem; Slightly Less Than Wonderful/W: George Marion, Jr., M: Fats Waller.

2114. John Crone *The Passing Show of 1917* (Winter Garden, revue, CR, Sept. 24, 1917): Ring Out Liberty Bell/W: Harold Atteridge, M: Sigmund Romberg.

2115. Tandy Cronyn (Nov. 27, 1945–) B: Los Angeles, CA. Daughter of actors Hume Cronyn and Jessica Tandy. *Cabaret* (Broadway, CR, "Sally Bowles," June 30, 1969): Cabaret; Don't Tell Mama; Perfectly Marvelous; Why Should I Wake Up?/W: Fred Ebb, M: John Kander.

2116. Harriette Cropper *The White Cat* (New Amsterdam, "The Fairy Queen," Nov. 2, 1905): Cherries Ripe; Sailing Away/W: Harry B. Smith, M: Ludwig Englander.

2117. Roy Cropper (1898–May 14, 1954) B: Boston, MA. *Blossom Time* (Ambassador, "Vogl," Sept. 29, 1921): Keep It Dark; My Springtime Thou Art; Serenade/W: Dorothy Donnelly, M: Sigmund Romberg. *Blossom Time* (Century, CR, "Baron Franz Schober," Nov. 20, 1922): Let Me Awake; Love Is a Riddle; Only One Love Ever Fills the Heart; Serenade/W: Dorothy Donnelly, M: Sigmund Romberg. *Ziegfeld Follies of 1923* (New Amsterdam, revue, Oct. 20, 1923): I'd Love to Waltz Through Life with You/W: Gene Buck, M: Victor Herbert — Lady Fair/W: Gene Buck, M: Rudolf Friml. *The Student Prince [in Heidelberg]* (Al Jolson, CR, "Prince Karl Franz," May 1926): Deep in My Heart, Dear; Golden Days; Nevermore; Serenade; Student Life/W: Dorothy Donnelly, M: Sigmund Romberg. *Rufus Le Maire's Affairs* (Majestic, revue, Mar. 28, 1927): The Mirror Never Lies; Wandering Through Dreamland/W: Ballard Macdonald, M: Martin Broones. *Naughty Marietta* (Jolson, revival, "Capt. Richard Warrington," Oct. 21, 1929): Ah! Sweet Mystery of Life; I'm Falling in Love with Someone; It Never Never Can Be Love; Live for Today; Tramp! Tramp! Tramp!/W: Rida Johnson Young, M: Victor Herbert. *The Fortune Teller* (Al Jolson, revival, "Capt. Ladislas," Nov. 4, 1929): Only in the Play/W: Harry B. Smith, M: Victor Herbert. *Robin Hood* (Jolson, revival, "Robert of Huntington [Robin Hood]," Nov. 18, 1929): Come Dream So Bright; Oh, See the Lambkins Play!; Serenade; Then Hey for the Merry Greenwood/W: Harry B. Smith, M:

Reginald De Koven. *The Prince of Pilsen* (Jolson, revival, "Carl Otto, the Prince of Pilsen," Jan. 13, 1930): Heidelberg (Stein Song); Pictures in the Smoke; The Tale of the Sea Shell/W: Frank Pixley, M: Gustav Luders. *The Chocolate Soldier* (Jolson, revival, "Maj. Alexius Spiridoff," Jan. 27, 1930): Falling in Love; Never Was There Such a Lover; The Tale of a Coat/W: Stanislaus Stange, M: Oscar Straus. *The Count of Luxembourg* (Jolson's, revival, "Count Rene of Luxembourg," Feb. 17, 1930): Are You Going to Dance?; Love Breaks Every Bond/W: Basil Hood, M: Franz Lehar — The Count of Luxembourg; Her Glove/W: Adrian Ross, M: Franz Lehar. *The Serenade* (Jolson's, revival, "Lopez," Mar. 4, 1930): I Envy the Bird/W: Harry B. Smith, M: Victor Herbert. *The Merry Widow* (Erlanger's, revival, "Camille De Jolidon," Sept. 14, 1931): A Dutiful Wife; I Love You So (The Merry Widow Waltz); Love in My Heart/W: Adrian Ross, M: Franz Lehar. *The Chocolate Soldier* (Erlanger's, revival, "Maj. Alexius Spiridoff," Sept. 21, 1931): Falling in Love; Never Was There Such a Lover/W: Stanislaus Stange, M: Oscar Straus. *The Geisha* (Erlanger's, revival, "Reginald Fairfax," Oct. 5, 1931): Here They Come; The Kissing Duet; The Toy Duet/W: Harry Greenbank, M: Sidney Jones. *Naughty Marietta* (Erlanger's, revival, "Capt. Richard Warrington," Nov. 16, 1931): same as above. *The Firefly* (Erlanger's, revival, "Jack Travers," Nov. 30, 1931): He Says Yes, She Says No!; We're Going to Make a Man of You; When a Maid Comes Knocking at Your Heart; A Woman's Smile/W: Otto Harbach, M: Rudolf Friml. *There You Are* (George M. Cohan, "Lloyd Emerson," May 16, 1932): Aces Up; Safe in Your Arms; Wings of the Morning/WM: William Heagney, Tom Connell. *The Show Is On* (Winter Garden, revue, CR, Sept. 18, 1937): By Strauss/W: Ira Gershwin, M: George Gershwin — Now/W: Ted Fetter, M: Vernon Duke. *Blossom Time* (46th Street, revival, "Baron Von Schober," Dec. 26, 1938): Let Me Awake; Love Is a Riddle; My Springtime Thou Art; Only One Love Ever Fills the Heart; Peace to My Lonely Heart; Serenade/W: Dorothy Donnelly, M: Sigmund Romberg. *Blossom Time* (Ambassador, revival, "Baron Von Schober," Sept. 4, 1943): Let Me Awake; Love Is a Riddle; My Springtime Thou Art; Only One Love Ever Fills the Heart; Serenade/W: Dorothy Donnelly, M: Sigmund Romberg.

2118. B.J. Crosby (Nov. 23, 1952–) B: New Orleans, LA. *Smoky Joe's Cafe* (Virginia, revue, Mar. 2, 1995): Dance with Me; Fools Fall in Love; Hound Dog; I'm a Woman; Kansas City;

Neighborhood; Saved; Some Cats Know/WM: Jerry Leiber, Mike Stoller.

2119. Kathryn Crosby (Nov. 25, 1933–) B: Houston, TX. M: crooner Bing Crosby. *State Fair* (Music Box, "Melissa Frake," Mar. 27, 1996): Boys and Girls Like You and Me; Driving at Night; When I Go Out Walking with My Baby/W: Oscar Hammerstein II, M: Richard Rodgers.

2120. Kim Crosby (July 11, 1960–) B: Fort Smith, AR. *Jerry's Girls* (St. James, revue, Dec. 18, 1985): Have a Nice Day; It Takes a Woman; It's Today; Just Go to the Movies; Mame; Milk and Honey; Take It All Off; We Need a Little Christmas/WM: Jerry Herman. *Into the Woods* (Martin Beck, "Cinderella," Nov. 5, 1987): No One Is Alone; On the Steps of the Palace; A Very Nice Prince; Your Fault/WM: Stephen Sondheim. *Guys and Dolls* (Martin Beck, revival, CR, "Sarah Brown," c 1993): Follow the Fold; If I Were a Bell; I'll Know; I've Never Been in Love Before; Marry the Man Today/WM: Frank Loesser.

2121. Miriam Crosby *Lovely Lady* (Sam H. Harris, "Claudette," Dec. 29, 1927): At the Barbecue/W: Harry A. Steinberg, Edward Ward, M: Dave Stamper, Harold A. Levey — The Lost Step; Make Believe You're Happy/W: Cyrus D. Wood, M: Dave Stamper, Harold A. Levey.

2122. Phoebe Crosby *The Magic Ring* (Liberty, "Mrs. Bellamy," Oct. 1, 1923): Malaiya/W: Zelda Sears, M: Harold A. Levey.

2123. Murphy Cross (June 22, 1950–) B: Baltimore, MD. *A Chorus Line* (Shubert, CR, "Judy," Dec. 1977): And.../W: Edward Kleban, M: Marvin Hamlisch.

2124. Sam Cross *Messin' Around* (Hudson, revue, Apr. 22, 1929): I Don't Love Nobody but You/W: Perry Bradford, M: James P. Johnson. *Change Your Luck* (George M. Cohan, "Profit Jones," June 6, 1930): Walk Together Children/WM: James C. Johnson.

2125. Wellington Cross (Apr. 3, 1887–Oct. 12, 1975) B: Boston, MA. *The Wall Street Girl* (Cohan, "Lawrence O'Connor," Apr. 15, 1912): You're Some Girl/W: A. Seymour Brown, M: Nat D. Ayer. *The Passing Show of 1913* (Winter Garden, revue, July 24, 1913): The Golden Stairs of Love; High Lights; It Won't Be the Same Old Broadway/W: Harold Atteridge, M: Jean Schwartz — Won't You Come into My Playhouse?/WM: ?. *Oh, I Say!* (Casino, "Hugo," Oct. 30, 1913): Katy-Did/W: Harry B. Smith, M: Jerome Kern. *Ned Wayburn's Town Topics* (Century, revue, "Brighton Early," Sept. 23, 1915): The Old Fashioned Groom and the Up-to-Date Bride; Take It from Me/W: Robert B. Smith, M: Harold Orlob. *Go To It* (Princess, "The Captain," Oct. 24, 1916): Girls, If You Ever Get Married/WM: ?— Love Me Just a Little Bit/WM: Schuyler Greene, Worton David, William Hargreaves — When You're in Love You'll Know/WM: John L. Golden, Jerome Kern — You're the Girl (That Sets Me Stuttering)/WM: John L. Golden, Charles N. Grant. *Just a Minute* (Cort, "Robert Fulton," Oct. 27, 1919): Because You're Different; The Girl I Want to Call My Wife; Grandfather's Clock; I'll Say I Will; Over and Over Again/WM: Harry L. Cort, George E. Stoddard, Harold Orlob. *No, No, Nanette* (Globe, "Billy Early," Sept. 16, 1925): The Call of the Sea; I Want to Be Happy; You Can Dance with Any Girl at All/W: Irving Caesar, M: Vincent Youmans — Pay Day Pauline; Telephone Girlie/W: Otto Harbach, M: Vincent Youmans.

2126. Charlotte Crossley *Tricks* (Alvin, "Charlotta," Jan. 8, 1973): Believe Me; Enter Hyacinthe; Gypsy Girl; Love or Money; A Man of Spirit; Somebody's Doin' Somebody All the Time; A Sporting Man; Who Was I?/W: Lonnie Burstein, M: Jerry Blatt.

2127. Jack Crowder (Nov. 15, 1939–Oct. 9, 1991) B: Miami, FL. *Hello, Dolly!* (St. James, CR, "Cornelius Hackl," Nov. 12, 1967): Dancing; It Only Takes a Moment; Put on Your Sunday Clothes/WM: Jerry Herman — Elegance; Motherhood/WM: Bob Merrill, Jerry Herman.

2128. Ann Crowley (Oct. 17, 1929–) B: Scranton, PA. *Oklahoma!* (St. James, CR, "Laurey Williams," Feb. 1946): Many a New Day; Oh, What a Beautiful Mornin'; Oklahoma!; Out of My Dreams; People Will Say We're in Love; The Surrey with the Fringe on Top/W: Oscar Hammerstein II, M: Richard Rodgers. *Seventeen* (Broadhurst, "Lola Pratt," June 21, 1951): If We Only Could Stop the Old Town Clock; Reciprocity; Things Are Gonna Hum This Summer; This Was Just Another Day/W: Kim Gannon, M: Walter Kent. *Paint Your Wagon* (Shubert, "Jennifer Rumson," Nov. 12, 1951): All for Him; Carino Mio; How Can I Wait?; I Talk to the Trees/W: Alan Jay Lerner, M: Frederick Loewe.

2129. Ann Crumb *Aspects of Love* (Broadhurst, "Rose Vibert," Apr. 8, 1990): Anything but Lonely; Chanson d'Enfance; Falling; Hand Me the Wine and the Dice; Other Pleasures; Parlez-Vous Francais?; Seeing Is Believing; She'd Be Far Better Off with You; There Is More to Love/W: Don Black, Charles Hart, M: Andrew Lloyd Webber. *Anna Karenina* (Circle in the Square, "Anna Karenina," Aug. 26, 1992): Everything's Fine; I'm Lost; In a Room; Mazurka;

Nothing Has Changed; On a Train; There's More to Life Than Love; This Can't Go On; Waiting for You/W: Peter Kellogg, M: Daniel Levine.

2130. Camilla Crume (1874–Mar. 20, 1952) *Some Night* (Harris, "Mrs. Hardy," Sept. 23, 1918): Something That Money Can't Buy/WM: Harry Delf.

2131. Frank Crumit (Sept. 26, 1888–Sept. 7, 1943) B: Jackson, OH. M: JULIA SANDERSON. Together they broadcast radio variety and quiz shows, such as *The Battle of the Sexes*, NBC (1938) and *The Crumit and Sanderson Quiz*, CBS (1942). *The Greenwich Village Follies of 1920* (Shubert, revue, Jan. 3, 1921): I'm a Lonesome Little Raindrop (Looking for a Place to Fall)/W: Joe Goodwin, Murray Roth, M: James F. Hanley — Just Snap Your Fingers at Care/W: B.G. DeSylva, M: Louis Silvers — The Naked Truth; Tam, Tam, Tam, Tam, Tam/W: Arthur Swanstrom, John Murray Anderson, M: A. Baldwin Sloane. *Tangerine* (Casino, "Dick Owens," Aug. 9, 1921): Listen to Me; Love Is a Business; South Sea Island Blues/W: Howard Johnson, M: Monte Carlo, Alma Sanders — Man Is the Lord of It All/W: Carle Carlton, M: Jean Schwartz — Sweet Lady/W: Frank Crumit, Howard Johnson, M: Dave Zoob. *Moonlight* (Longacre, CR, "Brooks"): If I Were of the Hoi Polloi; On Such a Night/W: William B. Friedlander, M: Con Conrad.

2132. Master Crumpton *Betty* (Globe, "Alf," Oct. 3, 1916): The Duchess of Dreams; I Feel So Happy/WM: Paul Rubens, Adrian Ross.

2133. Ruth Crumpton *Carmen Jones* (New York City Center, revival, "Myrt," Apr. 7, 1946): Beat Out Dat Rhythm on a Drum; De Cards Don't Lie; Poncho de Panther from Brazil; Whizzin' Away Along de Track/W: Oscar Hammerstein II, M: Richard Rodgers.

2134. Buddy Crutchfield (June 4, 1957–) B: Dallas, TX. *The Most Happy Fella* (Booth, revival, "Ciccio," Feb. 13, 1992): Abbondanza; Benvenuta/WM: Frank Loesser.

2135. David Cryer (Mar. 8, 1936–) B: Evanston, IL. M: BRITT SWANSON. *Come Summer* (Lunt-Fontanne, "Jude Scribner," Mar. 18, 1969): Come Summer; Jude's Holler; Let Me Be; The Loggers' Song; Moonglade; Road to Hampton; Rockin'; So Much World; Think Spring; Wild Birds Calling/W: Will Holt, M: David Baker. *1776* (46th Street, CR, "Edward Rutledge," May 30, 1969): Molasses to Rum/WM: Sherman Edwards. *1776* (46th Street, CR, "Thomas Jefferson"): But, Mr. Adams; The Egg/WM: Sherman Edwards. *Ari* (Mark Hellinger,

"Ari Ben Canaan," Jan. 15, 1971): Ari's Promise; My Brother's Keeper; My Galilee; Yerushaliam/W: Leon Uris, M: Walt Smith. *The Desert Song* (Uris, revival, "Red Shadow" and "Pierre Birabeau," Sept. 5, 1973): The Desert Song; I Want a Kiss; One Alone; The Riff Song; The Sabre Song; Then You Will Know/W: Otto Harbach, Oscar Hammerstein II, M: Sigmund Romberg. *Evita* (Broadway, CR, "Peron," Oct. 20, 1980): The Art of the Possible; Dice Are Rolling; I'd Be Surprisingly Good for You; A New Argentina; On the Balcony of the Casa Rosada; Rainbow Tour; She Is a Diamond/W: Tim Rice, M: Andrew Lloyd Webber.

2136. Robert (Bob) Cuccioli (May 3, 1958–) B: Hempstead, NY. *Les Miserables* (Broadway, CR, "Javert," c 1993): Soliloquy; Stars/W: Herbert Kretzmer, M: Claude-Michel Schonberg.

2137. Hugh Cuenod *Bitter Sweet* (Ziegfeld, "Bertram Sellick," Nov. 5, 1929): Green Carnation/WM: Noel Coward.

2138. Alma Cuervo (Aug. 13, 1951–) B: Tampa, FL. *Is There Life After High School?* (Ethel Barrymore, revue, May 7, 1982): Nothing Really Happened/WM: Craig Carnelia.

2139. Frances Cuka (Aug. 21, 1936–) B: London, England. *Oliver!* (Mark Hellinger, revival, "Mrs. Sowerberry," Apr. 29, 1984): That's Your Funeral/WM: Lionel Bart.

2140. Lloyd Culbreath *Honky Tonk Nights* (Biltmore, "Sparks Roberts," Aug. 7, 1986): Lily of the Alley; Tapaholics/W: Ralph Allen, David Campbell, M: Michael Valenti.

2141. Terry Culkin Uncle of actor Macaulay Culkin. *Street Scene* (New York City Center, revival, "Willie Maurrant," Feb. 13, 1960): Catch Me If You Can/W: Langston Hughes, Elmer Rice, M: Kurt Weill.

2142. Karen Culliver (Dec. 30, 1959–) B: Florida. *The Mystery of Edwin Drood* (Imperial, CR, "Rosa Bud," Aug. 16, 1986): Ceylon; Moonfall; The Name of Love; No Good Can Come from Bad; Perfect Strangers/WM: Rupert Holmes. *The Phantom of the Opera* (Majestic, CR, "Christine Daae," c 1990): All I Ask of You; Angel of Music; Bravo, Bravo; I Remember; Little Lotte; The Mirror; Notes; The Point of No Return; Raoul, I've Been There; Stranger Than You Dreamt It; Think of Me; Twisted Every Way; Wandering Child; Why Have You Brought Me Here; Wishing You Were Somehow Here Again/W: Charles Hart, Richard Stilgoe, M: Andrew Lloyd Webber — The Phantom of the Opera/W: Mike Batt, Richard Stilgoe, M: Andrew Lloyd Webber.

2143. John Cullum (Mar. 2, 1930–) B: Knoxville, TN. He played Holling Vincouer on the TV drama *Northern Exposure* (1990). *Camelot* (Majestic, "Sir Dinadan," Dec. 3, 1960): Then You May Take Me to the Fair/W: Alan Jay Lerner, M: Frederick Loewe. *Camelot* (Majestic, CR, "Mordred," May 1961): The Persuasion; The Seven Deadly Virtues/W: Alan Jay Lerner, M: Frederick Loewe. *On a Clear Day You Can See Forever* (Mark Hellinger, "Dr. Mark Bruckner," Oct. 17, 1965): Come Back to Me; Melinda; On a Clear Day You Can See Forever/W: Alan Jay Lerner, M: Burton Lane. *Man of La Mancha* (ANTA Washington Square, CR, "Don Quixote," Feb. 24, 1967): The Combat; Dulcinea; Golden Helmet; The Impossible Dream (The Quest); Man of La Mancha (I, Don Quixote)/W: Joe Darion, M: Mitch Leigh. *1776* (46th Street, CR, "Edward Rutledge," May 19, 1970): Molasses to Rum/WM: Sherman Edwards. *Shenandoah* (Alvin, "Charlie Anderson," Jan. 7, 1975): It's a Boy; I've Heard It All Before; Meditation; Papa's Gonna Make It Alright; The Pickers Are Comin'/W: Peter Udell, M: Gary Geld. *On the Twentieth Century* (St. James, "Oscar Jaffee," Feb. 19, 1978): Five Zeros; I Rise Again; I've Got It All; The Legacy; Lily, Oscar; Mine; Our Private World; Sign, Lily, Sign (Sextet); Together/W: Betty Comden, Adolph Green, M: Cy Coleman. *Shenandoah* (Virginia, revival, "Charlie Anderson," Aug. 8, 1989): same as above. *Aspects of Love* (Broadhurst, CR, "George Dillingham," Oct. 22, 1990): Falling; The First Man You Remember; A Memory of a Happy Moment; Other Pleasures; She'd Be Far Better Off with You; Stop. Wait. Please./W: Don Black, Charles Hart, M: Andrew Lloyd Webber. *Show Boat* (Gershwin, revival, CR, "Cap'n Andy," Jan. 30, 1996): Cap'n Andy's Ballyhoo/W: Oscar Hammerstein II, M: Jerome Kern.

2144. Carol Culver *The Boy Friend* (Ambassador, revival, "Monica," Apr. 14, 1970): The Riviera; Sur La Plage; The You-Don't-Want-to-Play-with-Me Blues/WM: Sandy Wilson. *Grease* (Broadhurst, CR, "Patty Simcox," c 1974): Alma Mater/WM: Jim Jacobs, Warren Casey.

2145. Claudia Cummings *The Sound of Music* (New York State, revival, "The Mother Abbess," Mar. 8, 1990): Climb Ev'ry Mountain; Maria; My Favorite Things/W: Oscar Hammerstein II, M: Richard Rodgers.

2146. Robert (Bob) Cummings (June 9, 1908–Dec. 2, 1990) B: Joplin, MO. Formerly known as BRICE HUTCHINS. His 1950s TV series *The Bob Cummings Show* was a hit. He also appeared in more than 100 movies. *Kid Boots*

(Selwyn, CR, "Peter Pillsbury," May 19, 1924): Down 'Round the 19th Hole/W: Joseph McCarthy, M: Harry Tierney. *Ziegfeld Follies of 1934* (Winter Garden, revue, Jan. 4, 1934): I Like the Likes of You/W: E.Y. Harburg, M: Vernon Duke — A Sidewalk in Paris/W: E.Y. Harburg, M: Samuel Pokrass.

2147. Roy Cummings *Hitchy-Koo of 1918* (Globe, revue, June 6, 1918): When the Girls Get Wise/WM: E. Ray Goetz, Glen MacDonough.

2148. Vicki Charles Cummings (Feb. 15, 1913–Nov. 30, 1969) B: Northampton, MA. *Here Goes the Bride* (46th Street, "June Doyle," Nov. 3, 1931): One Second of Sex/W: Edward Heyman, M: Johnny Green. *Orchids Preferred* (Imperial, "Marion Brown," May 11, 1937): Boy, Girl, Moon; A Million Dollars; My Lady's Hand/W: Frederick Herendeen, M: Dave Stamper. *Sunny River* (St. James, "Emma," Dec. 4, 1941): The Butterflies and the Bees; She Got Him/W: Oscar Hammerstein II, M: Sigmund Romberg.

2149. Arthur Cunningham (c 1888–Nov. 29, 1955) B: San Francisco, CA. *A Runaway Girl* (Daly's, revival, "Leonello," Apr. 23, 1900): My Kingdom/W: Aubrey Hopwood, Harry Greenbank, M: Ivan Caryll. *A China Doll* (Majestic, "Sing Lo," Nov. 19, 1904): How to Be Happy Though Married/W: Robert B. Smith, M: Alfred E. Aarons. *The Wedding Trip* (Broadway, "Capt. Josef," Dec. 25, 1911): Ah, at Last; The Family Council; Here Is the Tunic of a Soldier/W: Harry B. Smith, M: Reginald De Koven. *Lieber Augustin* (Casino, "Jasomir," Sept. 3, 1913): Anna, What's Wrong?/W: Scott Craven, M: Leo Fall — Do You Love Me Best?/W: Harry Beswick, M: Leo Fall. *When Johnny Comes Marching Home* (New Amsterdam > Manhattan Opera House, revival, "Gen. William Allen," May 7, 1917): The Suwanee River; When Our Lips in Kisses Met/W: Stanislaus Stange, M: Julian Edwards. *Hitchy-Koo of 1920* (New Amsterdam, revue, Oct. 19, 1920): Old New York/W: ?, M: Jerome Kern. *My Maryland* (Al Jolson, "Tim Green," Sept. 12, 1927): Old John Barleycorn/W: Dorothy Donnelly, M: Sigmund Romberg.

2150. Cecil Cunningham (Aug. 2, 1888–Apr. 17, 1959): B: Missouri. In movies from 1929. *Somewhere Else* (Broadway, "Mary VIIth, Queen of Somewhere Else," Jan. 20, 1913): Can You Do This?; Dingle-Dangle; Love at First Sight; Somebody's Eyes/W: Avery Hopwood, M: Gustav Luders. *Oh, I Say!* (Casino, "Sydonie de Mornay," Oct. 30, 1913): Well This Is Jolly; A Woman's Heart/W: Harry B. Smith, M: Jerome Kern. *The Maids of Athens* (New Amsterdam,

"Princess Photini," Mar. 18, 1914): Ah Yes, I Am in Love; Bid Me Forget/W: Carolyn Wells, M: Franz Lehar. *Dancing Around* (Winter Garden, "Beulah Elliot," Oct. 10, 1914): The Broadway Triangle/WM: ?—A Fashion's Slave; I Was Born on the Isle of Man/W: Harold Atteridge, M: Sigmund Romberg, Harry Carroll—He Is Sweet, He Is Good/W: Harold Atteridge, M: Sigmund Romberg. *The Rose of China* (Lyric, "Polly Baldwin," Nov. 25, 1919): Down on the Banks of the Subway; Proposals; Romeo and Juliet/W: P.G. Wodehouse, M: Armand Vecsey.

2151. Davis Cunningham *Stars in Your Eyes* (Majestic, "3rd Assistant Director" and "Photographer," Feb. 9, 1939): This Is It/W: Dorothy Fields, M: Arthur Schwartz.

2152. John Cunningham (June 22, 1932–) B: Auburn, NY. *Cabaret* (Broadhurst, CR, "Clifford Bradshaw," July 30, 1968): Perfectly Marvelous; Why Should I Wake Up?/W: Fred Ebb, M: John Kander. *Zorba* (Imperial, "Nikos," Nov. 17, 1968): The Butterfly; No Boom Boom; Y'assou/W: Fred Ebb, M: John Kander. *Company* (Alvin, "Peter," Apr. 26, 1970): Have I Got a Girl for You/WM: Stephen Sondheim. *1776* (46th Street, CR, "John Adams," May 4, 1971): But, Mr. Adams; The Egg; He Plays the Violin; Is Anybody There?; The Lees of Old Virginia; Piddle, Twiddle and Resolve; Sit Down, John; Till Then; Yours, Yours, Yours/WM: Sherman Edwards. *Anna Karenina* (Circle in the Square, "Nicolai Karenin," Aug. 26, 1992): Karenin's List; Only at Night; This Can't Go On/W: Peter Kellogg, M: Daniel Levine.

2153. M. Cunningham *The O'Brien Girl* (Liberty, "Mickey," Oct. 3, 1921): Partners/W: Otto Harbach, M: Louis A. Hirsch.

2154. Robert Cunningham B: Hobart, Tasmania. *Monsieur Beaucaire* (New Amsterdam, "Beau Nash," Dec. 11, 1919): When I Was King of Bath/W: Adrian Ross, M: Andre Messager.

2155. Ronnie Cunningham (Nov. 3, 1923–) B: Washington, DC. *Marinka* (Winter Garden > Ethel Barrymore, "Tilly," July 18, 1945): Cab Song; Treat a Woman Like a Drum; Young Man Danube/W: George Marion, Jr., M: Emmerich Kalman. *Can-Can* (Shubert, CR, "Claudine," c 1955): Can-Can; If You Loved Me Truly/WM: Cole Porter.

2156. Zamah Cunningham (Nov. 29, 1892– June 2, 1967) B: Portland, OR. *On the Town* (Adelphi, "Maude P. Dilly," Dec. 28, 1944): Do-Do-Re-Do/W: Betty Comden, Adolph Green, M: Leonard Bernstein. *The Beggar's Opera* (New York City Center, revival, "Mrs. Peachum,"

Mar. 13, 1957): Our Polly is a Sad Slut/WM: John Gay.

2157. Shepard Curelop *Naughty-Naught ['00]* (Old Knickerbocker Music Hall, revival, "Stub," Oct. 19, 1946): Coney by the Sea/W: Ted Fetter, M: Richard Lewine.

2158. Wilma Curley *I Can Get It for You Wholesale* (Shubert, "Gail," Mar. 22, 1962): What Are They Doing to Us Now?/WM: Harold Rome.

2159. Steve Curry *I Can Get It for You Wholesale* (Shubert, "Sheldon Bushkin," Mar. 22, 1962): A Gift Today (The Bar Mitzvah Song)/WM: Harold Rome. *Hair* (Biltmore, "Woof," Apr. 29, 1968): Ain't Got No; Don't Put It Down/W: Gerome Ragni, James Rado, M: Galt MacDermot. *Hair* (Biltmore, CR, "Berger," Nov. 22, 1968): Donna; Don't Put It Down; Going Down; Hair/W: Gerome Ragni, James Rado, M: Galt MacDermot.

2160. Tim Curry (Apr. 19, 1946–) B: Cheshire, England. *The Rocky Horror Show* (Belasco, "Frank," Mar. 10, 1975): Charles Atlas Song; Planet Schmanet Janet; Sweet Transvestite/WM: Richard O'Brien. *My Favorite Year* (Vivian Beaumont, "Alan Swann," Dec. 10, 1992): Exits; The Gospel According to King; If the World Were Like the Movies; The Lights Come Up; Manhattan; The Musketeer Sketch Rehearsal; Welcome to Brooklyn/W: Lynn Ahrens, M: Stephen Flaherty.

2161. Christopher Curtis *All in Fun* (Majestic, revue, Dec. 27, 1940): It's All in Fun/W: Bob Russell, M: Baldwin Bergersen.

2162. Keene Curtis (Feb. 15, 1923–) B: Salt Lake City, UT. *The Rothschilds* (Lunt-Fontanne, "Prince William" and "Lord Herries" and "Lord Metternich" and "Joseph Fouche," Oct. 19, 1970): Allons; Bonds; Give England Strength; Have You Ever Seen a Prettier Little Congress?; Pleasure and Privilege; Stability/W: Sheldon Harnick, M: Jerry Bock. *Via Galactica* (Uris, "Dr. Isaacs," Nov. 28, 1972): Cross on Over; Isaacs' Equation/W: Christopher Gore, M: Galt MacDermot. *Annie* (Alvin, CR, "Oliver Warbucks," Feb. 6, 1978): I Don't Need Anything but You; N.Y.C.; A New Deal for Christmas; Something Was Missing; Tomorrow; You Won't Be an Orphan for Long/W: Martin Charnin, M: Charles Strouse. *La Cage aux Folles* (Palace, CR, "Albin," Oct. 8, 1984/Feb. 17, 1987): The Best of Times; I Am What I Am; La Cage aux Folles; A Little More Mascara; Masculinity; Song on the Sand; With You on My Arm/WM: Jerry Herman.

2163. Norman Curtis *Treasure Girl* (Alvin,

"Bunce," Nov. 8, 1928): Place in the Country/ W: Ira Gershwin, M: George Gershwin.

2164. Virginia Curtis *Great to Be Alive* (Winter Garden, "Sandra," Mar. 23, 1950): That's a Man Every Time; What a Day!; Who Done It?/W: Walter Bullock, M: Abraham Ellstein.

2165. Vondie Curtis-Hall (Sept. 30, 1956–) B: Detroit, MI. He played Dr. Dennis Hancock on the TV medical drama *Chicago Hope* (1995). *Dreamgirls* (Imperial, "Marty," Dec. 20, 1981): Cadillac Car; I Miss You Old Friend; The Rap/ W: Tom Eyen, M: Henry Krieger.

2166. Willard Curtiss *The Social Whirl* (Casino > Majestic, "Jack Ellingham," Apr. 7, 1906): You're Just the Girl I'm Looking For/WM: E. Ray Goetz.

2167. Gene Curtsinger *Magdalena* (Ziegfeld, "The Old One," Sept. 20, 1948): Magdalena/W: Robert Wright, George Forrest, M: Heitor Villa-Lobos.

2168. Gene Curty *The Lieutenant* (Lyceum, "Judge" and "OCS Sergeant," Mar. 9, 1975): The Indictment; Kill; The Verdict/WM: Gene Curty, Nitra Scharfman, Chuck Strand.

2169. George Curzon (Oct. 18, 1896–May 10, 1976) B: Amersham, Buckinghamshire, England. The grandson of an Earl. In movies from 1932, he usually played aristocrats or villains. *The Lilac Domino* (44th Street, "Vicomte de Brissac," Oct. 28, 1914): Ladies Day; The Lilac Domino/W: Robert B. Smith, M: Charles Cuvillier.

2170. Joe Cusanelli *Fiddler on the Roof* (Imperial, CR, "Avram"): Anatevka/W: Sheldon Harnick, M: Jerry Bock.

2171. Nancy Cushman (Apr. 26, 1913–Sept. 26, 1979) B: Brooklyn, NY. *Skyscraper* (Lunt-Fontanne, "Mrs. Allerton," Nov. 13, 1965): Wrong!/W: Sammy Cahn, M: James Van Heusen.

2172. Lou Cutell *How to Succeed in Business Without Really Trying* (New York City Center, revival, "Mr. Twimble" and "Womper," Apr. 20, 1966): Brotherhood of Man; The Company Way/WM: Frank Loesser.

2173. Ben Cutler *The Fireman's Flame* (American Music Hall, "Harry Howard," Oct. 9, 1937): Do My Eyes Deceive Me?; It's a Lovely Night on the Hudson River/W: Ted Fetter, M: Richard Lewine. *One Touch of Venus* (Imperial, CR, "Rodney Hatch"): How Much I Love You; Speak Low; The Trouble with Women; Way Out West in Jersey; Wooden Wedding/W: Ogden Nash, M: Kurt Weill.

2174. Rudolf Cutten *Leave It to Jane* (Lon-gacre, "Ollie Mitchell," Aug. 28, 1917): I'm Going to Find the Girl/W: P.G. Wodehouse, M: Jerome Kern.

2175. Royal Cutter *The Baron Trenck* (Casino, "Josef," Mar. 11, 1912): I'm from the Court of the Empress Queen/W: Frederick F. Schrader, M: Felix Albini.

2176. Patricia Cutts (July 20, 1926–Sept. 11, 1974) B: London, England. A child actor who had difficulty with her adult career and ended her life with pills. She came to New York in 1955 to be a panelist on the TV show *Down You Go.* The host of this unusually intelligent quizzer was Dr. Bergen Evans, professor of English at Northwestern University. *Kean* (Broadway, "Lady Amy Goswell," Nov. 2, 1961): Mayfair Affair; The Social Whirl/WM: Robert Wright, George Forrest.

2177. Jon Cypher (Jan. 13, 1932–) B: Brooklyn, NY. Among his TV credits: Chief Fletcher P. Daniels on the police drama *Hill Street Blues* (1981); Jeff Munson on *Knots Landing* (1982); Maj. Gen. Marcus Craig on the sitcom *Major Dad* (1990). *Man of La Mancha* (ANTA Washington Square, "Dr. Carrasco," Nov. 22, 1965): I'm Only Thinking of Him/W: Joe Darion, M: Mitch Leigh. *Sherry!* (Alvin, "Bert Jefferson," Mar. 27, 1967): With This Ring/W: James Lipton, M: Laurence Rosenthal. *1776* (46th Street, CR, "Thomas Jefferson," Sept. 16, 1969): But, Mr. Adams; The Egg/WM: Sherman Edwards. *Coco* (Mark Hellinger, "Papa," Dec. 18, 1969): Gabrielle/W: Alan Jay Lerner, M: Andre Previn. *Big* (Sam S. Shubert, "MacMillan," Apr. 28, 1996): Coffee, Black; Fun/W: Richard Maltby, Jr., M: David Shire.

2178. Jack Dabdoub (Feb. 5–) B: New Orleans, LA. *Anya* (Ziegfeld, "Sergei," Nov. 29, 1965): That Prelude!/WM: Robert Wright, George Forrest. *Annie Get Your Gun* (Music Theater of Lincoln Center > Broadway, return engagement of revival, "Major Gordon Lillie [Pawnee Bill]," May 31, 1966): There's No Business Like Show Business/WM: Irving Berlin. *Man of La Mancha* (ANTA Washington Square, CR, "Don Quixote," Oct. 20, 1969 mats.): The Combat; Dulcinea; Golden Helmet; The Impossible Dream (The Quest); Man of La Mancha (I, Don Quixote)/W: Joe Darion, M: Mitch Leigh. *Coco* (Mark Hellinger, "voice of Grand Duke Alexandrovitch," Dec. 18, 1969): But That's the Way You Are/W: Alan Jay Lerner, M: Andre Previn. *Man of La Mancha* (ANTA Washington Square, CR, "The Innkeeper," Oct. 5, 1970): Knight of the Woeful Countenance (The Dubbing)/W: Joe Darion, M: Mitch Leigh. *Man* *of La Mancha* (Vivian Beaumont, revival, "The Innkeeper," June 22, 1972): same as above.

2179. William S. Daboll (c 1857–Aug. 23, 1892) B: Providence, RI. *Erminie* (Casino, "Ravennes," May 10, 1886): Downy Jailbirds of a Feather/W: Claxson Bellamy, Harry Paulton, M: Edward Jakobowski.

2180. Arlene Dahl (Aug. 11, 1924–) B: Minneapolis, MN. M: FERNANDO LAMAS, 1954–60. She left Hollywood after about 2 dozen movies to become a beauty columnist, then an executive in the beauty and fashion industry. She appeared on the TV soap *One Life to Live* (1982). *Applause* (Palace, CR, "Margo Channing," May 1, 1972): But Alive; Good Friends; Hurry Back; Inner Thoughts; One of a Kind; Something Greater; Welcome to the Theater; Who's That Girl?/W: Lee Adams, M: Charles Strouse.

2181. Magda Dahl *A Waltz Dream* (Broadway, "Princess Helene," Jan. 27, 1908): A Husband's Love/W: Joseph W. Herbert, M: Oscar Straus — A Lesson in Love/W: Frank Pixley, M: Gustav Luders. *Sinbad* (Casino, CR, "Patricia de Trait," Oct. 18, 1918): Isle of Youth; A Little Bit of Every Nationality; A Night in the Orient/W: Harold Atteridge, M: Sigmund Romberg.

2182. Mitzi Dahl *Babes in Arms* (Shubert > Majestic, "Mitzi," Apr. 14, 1937): You Are So Fair/W: Lorenz Hart, M: Richard Rodgers.

2183. Lou Dahlman *You'll See Stars* (Maxine Elliott, revue, "Groucho Marx," Dec. 29, 1942): All You Have to Do Is Stand There/W: Herman Timberg, M: Leo Edwards.

2184. Marie Dahm *Ziegfeld Follies of 1922* (New Amsterdam, revue, CR, Oct. 2, 1922): List'ning on Some Radio/W: Gene Buck, M: Louis A. Hirsch, Dave Stamper.

2185. Cora Daigneau *Happyland* or *The King of Elysia* (Majestic, CR, "Lady Patricia," May 7, 1906): Hail, Gentle Eros; Happy Is the Summer's Day/W: Frederick Ranken, M: Reginald De Koven.

2186. Dan Dailey, Jr. (Dec. 14, 1914–Oct. 16, 1978) B: New York, NY. An affable song and dance man with a background in vaudeville, he appeared in movie musicals of the 1940s and 50s. His personal life was beset with problems — alcoholism, a son's suicide, 4 marriages and transvestism, to name a few. *Stars in Your Eyes* (Majestic, "5th Assistant Director," Feb. 9, 1939): As of Today; Never a Dull Moment/W: Dorothy Fields, M: Arthur Schwartz.

2187. Mammy Mae Dailey *Keep It Clean* (Selwyn, revue, June 24, 1929): Broadway Mammy/WM: Clarence Gaskill, Jimmy Duffy.

2188. Peter F. Dailey (Jan. 5, 1868–May 23, 1908) B: New York, NY. A comedian well known for ad-libs and a quick wit. At age 8 he appeared at the Globe Theater in NY as a child dancer. For years he was part of a vaudeville act calling itself The American Four. *Hurly-Burly* (Weber and Fields Music Hall, "Abel Stringer," Sept. 8, 1898): Kiss Me Honey Do (The Dinah Song); There Was a Time When on Broadway/W: Edgar Smith, M: John Stromberg. *Hodge, Podge & Co.* (Madison Square, "Rudolph Roastemsum," Oct. 23, 1900): Billet Doux/W: Walter Ford, George V. Hobart, M: John W. Bratton — Cindy, I Dreams About You/WM: Dave Reed, Jr.— I Love You, Babe, and You Love Me/WM: McConnell, Smith — My Charcoal Charmer/W: Will D. Cobb, M: Gus Edwards — My Sunflower Sue; A Scion of the House of Highball; You Can Never Tell What a Kiss Will Do; You're Altogether Model Girls/W: Walter Ford, M: John W. Bratton. *Twirly-Whirly* (Weber and Fields Music Hall, "Buck Winger" and "Lord Spillberries," Sept. 11, 1902): Etiquette/W: Robert B. Smith, M: William T. Francis — Susie Woosie/ W: Edgar Smith, M: John Stromberg. *In Newport* (Liberty, "Alert Pincherton," Dec. 26, 1904): Hello, Ma Lulu; Roaming Around the Town; When I Am Chief of Police/W: Bob Cole, James Weldon Johnson, M: J. Rosamond Johnson. *About Town* (Herald Square, CR, "Acton Alday" and "Steve," Nov. 15, 1906): A Girl from Everywhere/W: Joseph W. Herbert, M: A. Baldwin Sloane — A Little Class of One/W: Glen MacDonough, M: Victor Herbert — The Piccadilly Crawl/W: Addison Burkhardt, M: Melville Ellis.

2189. Robert L. Dailey (c 1885–Apr. 19, 1934) B: New York, NY. *The Show Girl* or *The Cap of Fortune* (Wallack's, "Garrick Forrest McCready," May 5, 1902): Adeline/W: D.K. Stevens, M: Edward W. Corliss — Invocation to Pie/W: D.K. Stevens, M: M.W. Daniels. *The Vanderbilt Cup* (New York, CR, "Theodore Banting," Jan. 28, 1907): Wine, Women and Song/W: Raymond W. Peck, M: Robert Hood Bowers. *The American Idea* (New York, "Stephen Hustleford," Oct. 5, 1908): American Ragtime; F-A-M-E; Too Long from Longacre Square/ WM: George M. Cohan. *The Jolly Bachelors* (Broadway, "Harold McCann," Jan. 6, 1910): We'uns from Dixie/W: Glen MacDonough, M: Raymond Hubbell.

2190. Marie Dainton (June 30, 1881–Feb. 1, 1938) B: Russia. *The Belle of Bohemia* (Casino, "Paquita," Sept. 24, 1900): The Amateur Entertainer; Be Clever; The Blue Ribbon Girls; The Champagne Waltz/W: Harry B. Smith, M: Ludwig Englander.

2191. Beatrice Dakin *Doing Our Bit* (Winter Garden, revue, Oct. 18, 1917): Egyptian Rag/W: Harold Atteridge, M: Sigmund Romberg, Herman Timberg.

2192. Audrey Dale *The Little Show* (Music Box, revue, CR, Sept. 16, 1929): A Little Hut in Hoboken/WM: Herman Hupfeld — Little Old New York/W: Howard Dietz, M: Arthur Schwartz — Or What Have You?/W: Grace Henry, M: Morris Hamilton — Six Little Sinners/W: Earle Crooker, M: Frank Grey.

2193. Clamma Churita Dale (July 4, 1948–) B: Chester, PA. *Porgy and Bess* (Uris, revival, "Bess," Sept. 25, 1976): Bess, You Is My Woman Now; I Loves You, Porgy/W: DuBose Heyward, Ira Gershwin, M: George Gershwin — Leavin' fo' de Promis' Land; What You Want wid Bess?/W: DuBose Heyward, M: George Gershwin — There's a Boat Dat's Leavin' Soon for New York/W: Ira Gershwin, M: George Gershwin.

2194. Glen Dale *Moonlight* (Longacre, "George Van Horne," Jan. 30, 1924): On Such a Night; Say It Again/W: William B. Friedlander, M: Con Conrad. *Louie the 14th* (Cosmopolitan, CR, "Capt. William Brent, A.E.F.," Oct. 12, 1925): Edelweiss/W: Clifford Grey, M: Sigmund Romberg — Homeland; True Hearts; Wayside Flower/W: Arthur Wimperis, M: Sigmund Romberg — My First Love Letter/W: Irving Caesar, M: Sigmund Romberg. *The Desert Song* (Casino, "Capt. Paul Fontaine," Nov. 30, 1926): All Hail to the General; I Want a Kiss; Margot/W: Otto Harbach, Oscar Hammerstein II, M: Sigmund Romberg. *The Nightingale* (Jolson, CR, "Capt. Rex Gurnee," Feb. 14, 1927): Homeland/W: Arthur Wimperis, M: Sigmund Romberg — May Moon/W: P.G. Wodehouse, M: Armand Vecsey. *Harry Delmar's Revels* (Shubert, revue, Nov. 28, 1927): Say It with a Solitaire/W: Billy Rose, Ballard MacDonald, M: James V. Monaco.

2195. Grover Dale (July 22, 1935–) B: Harrisburg, PA. *West Side Story* (Winter Garden, "Snowboy," Sept. 26, 1957): Gee, Officer Krupke!/W: Stephen Sondheim, M: Leonard Bernstein. *Sail Away* (Broadhurst, "Barnaby Slade," Oct. 3, 1961): Beatnik Love Affair; When You Want Me; Where Shall I Find Her?/WM: Noel Coward. *Half a Sixpence* (Broadhurst, "Pearce," Apr. 25, 1965): All in the Cause of Economy; Flash! Bang! Wallop!; If the Rain's Got to Fall; The Party's on the House; A Proper Gentleman/WM: David Heneker.

2196. Jim Dale (Aug. 15, 1935–) B: Rothwell, Northamptonshire, England. Actor, singer, comedian, songwriter. He received an Oscar nomination for writing the lyrics to the title tune of the movie *Georgy Girl* (1966). *Barnum* (St. James, "Phineas Taylor Barnum," Apr. 30, 1980/May 26, 1981): Black and White; The Colors of My Life; I Like Your Style; Join the Circus; Museum Song; One Brick at a Time; Out There; The Prince of Humbug; There's a Sucker Born Ev'ry Minute/W: Michael Stewart, M: Cy Coleman. *Me and My Gal* (Marquis, revival, CR, "Bill Snibson," Dec. 16, 1986/June 16, 1987/Mar. 15, 1988): Hold My Hand/W: Harry Graham, M: Maurice Elwin, Noel Gay — The Lambeth Walk; Me and My Girl; You Would If You Could/W: Douglas Furber, M: Noel Gay — Leaning on a Lamppost; Love Makes the World Go Round; Song of Hareford/WM: Noel Gay.

2197. John Dale *The Perfect Fool* (George M. Cohan, revue, Nov. 7, 1921): Old Home Week in Maine/WM: Ed Wynn.

2198. Margaret Dale (Mar. 6, 1876–Mar. 23, 1972) B: Philadelphia, PA. *Good Morning Judge* (Shubert, "Millicent Meebles," Feb. 6, 1919): Oh That We Two Were Maying/W: Percy Greenbank, M: Lionel Monckton — Young Folks and Old Folks/WM: ?.

2199. Maryon Dale *Americana of 1926* (Belmont, revue, CR, Jan. 3, 1927): Blowin' the Blues Away/W: Ira Gershwin, M: Phil Charig. *Merry-Go-Round* (Klaw, revue, May 31, 1927): Sentimental Silly [July 18, 1927]; Something Tells Me/W: Howard Dietz, Morrie Ryskind, M: Henry Souvaine, Jay Gorney. *Belmont Varieties* (Belmont, revue, Sept. 26, 1932): Autograph of You; Something New and It's You/W: Mildred Kaufman, M: Alvin Kaufman — Automotivation; Hitting the New High/W: Sam Bernard, Jr., Bobby Burk, M: Henry Lloyd.

2200. Norma Dale *The Broadway Whirl* (Times Square > Selwyn, revue, June 8, 1921): Three Little Maids/W: Joseph McCarthy, B.G. DeSylva, M: Harry Tierney.

2201. Ruby Dale *The Merry Widow* (New Amsterdam, CR, "Sonia, the Widow," Sept. 28, 1908): I Love You So (The Merry Widow Waltz); In Marsovia; The Silly Cavalier; Vilia/W: Adrian Ross, M: Franz Lehar.

2202. Sunny Dale see SUNNIE O'DEA.

2203. Cass Daley (July 17, 1915–Mar. 22, 1975) B: Philadelphia, PA. A comedian best known for her acrobatics and boisterous singing. *Ziegfeld Follies of 1936-1937* (Winter Garden, revue, Sept. 14, 1936): The Gazooka/WM: Ira Gershwin, David Freedman — Harlem Waltz/W: Richard Jerome, M: Walter Kent — Nice Goin'/W: Bob Rothberg, M: Joseph Meyer —

You Don't Love Right/W: Tot Seymour, M: Vee Lawnhurst.

2204. Lee Daley *The Fortune Teller* (Century roof, revival, "Fresco," Sept. 29, 1923): Serenade/W: Harry B. Smith, M: Victor Herbert.

2205. Evelyn Dall (c 1914–) Nightclub singer. *Parade* (Guild, revue, May 20, 1935): I'm All Washed Up on Love/W: Albert Silverman, M: Kay Swift — I'm an International Orphan/W: Paul Peters, George Sklar, M: Jerome Moross.

2206. Mony Dalmes *The Unsinkable Molly Brown* (Winter Garden, "Princess DeLong," Nov. 3, 1960): Happy Birthday, Mrs. J.J. Brown/WM: Meredith Willson.

2207. Aimee Dalmores (?–Jan. 26, 1920) B: New York, NY. *Dancing Around* (Winter Garden, CR, "Mlle. Mitzi," Dec. 7, 1914): When an Englishman Marries a Parisian/W: Harold Atteridge, M: Sigmund Romberg, Harry Carroll.

2208. Dolle Dalnert *The Whirl of Society* (Winter Garden, revue, Mar. 5, 1912): Oriental Rose/WM: Louis A. Hirsch.

2209. Doris Dalton (Mar. 18, 1910–1984) B: Sharon, MA. She taught school before becoming an actress. *Seventeen* (Broadhurst, "Mrs. Baxter," June 21, 1951): Headache and a Heartache/W: Kim Gannon, M: Walter Kent.

2210. Dan Daly (1858–Mar. 26, 1904) B: Boston, MA. Deadpan comedian who began as a circus acrobat. *The Belle of New York* (Casino, "Ichabod Bronson," Sept. 28, 1897): The Anti-Cigarette Society/W: Hugh Morton; M: Gustave Kerker.

2211. Lee Daly *Sweethearts* (Jolson's, revival, "Aristide Caniche," Sept. 21, 1929): Jeannette and Her Little Wooden Shoes; Pilgrims of Love/W: Robert B. Smith, M: Victor Herbert.

2212. Nellie Daly *Humpty Dumpty* (New Amsterdam, "Princess Marie," Nov. 14, 1904): Down at the Bottom of the Sea; Down in Mulberry Bend/W: Bob Cole, James Weldon Johnson, M: J. Rosamond Johnson — The Pussy and the Bow-Wow/W: James Weldon Johnson, M: J. Rosamond Johnson.

2213. Tyne Daly (Feb. 21, 1946–) B: Madison, WI. She was Det. Mary Beth Lacey on the TV police drama *Cagney and Lacey* (1982) and a social worker and Amy's mom on *Judging Amy*. *Gypsy* (St. James, revival, "Rose," Nov. 16, 1989/Feb. 25, 1990): Everything's Coming Up Roses; Mr. Goldstone, I Love You; Rose's Turn; Small World; Some People; Together Wherever We Go; You'll Never Get Away from Me/W: Stephen Sondheim, M: Jule Styne. *Gypsy* (Marquis, re-

turn engagement of revival, "Rose," Apr. 28, 1991): same as above.

2214. Una Daly *A la Carte* (Martin Beck, revue, Aug. 17, 1927): Give Trouble the Air/W: Leo Robin, M: Louis Alter.

2215. John Daman *Teddy & Alice* (Minskoff, "Quentin Roosevelt," Nov. 12, 1987): Charge; Private Thoughts/W: Hal Hackady, M: John Philip Sousa, Richard Kapp.

2216. Charlotte d'Amboise M: TERRENCE V. MANN. Daughter of dancer, choreographer and teacher Jacques d'Amboise. *Cats* (Winter Garden, CR, "Cassandra," c 1984): The Old Gumbie Cat/W: T.S. Eliot, M: Andrew Lloyd Webber. *Carrie* (Virginia, "Chris," May 12, 1988): Do Me a Favor; Don't Waste the Moon; Out for Blood/W: Dean Pitchford, M: Michael Gore. *Jerome Robbins' Broadway* (Imperial, revue, Feb. 26, 1989): America/W: Stephen Sondheim, M: Leonard Bernstein — I'm Flying/W: Carolyn Leigh, M: Moose Charlap. *Damn Yankees* (Marquis, revival, CR, "Lola," Mar. 12, 1995): A Little Brains, a Little Talent; Two Lost Souls; Whatever Lola Wants (Lola Gets); Who's Got the Pain?/WM: Richard Adler, Jerry Ross.

2217. Michael Damian (Apr. 26, 1962–) B: San Diego, CA. *Joseph and the Amazing Technicolor Dreamcoat* (Minskoff, revival "Joseph," Nov. 10, 1993): Any Dream Will Do; The Brothers Came to Egypt; Close Ev'ry Door to Me; A Coat of Many Colors; Go, Go, Go, Joseph; Grovel, Grovel; Jacob and Sons; Joseph All the Time; Joseph's Dreams; Pharaoh's Dream Explained; Potiphar; Stone the Crows; Who's the Thief?/WM: Tim Rice, Andrew Lloyd Webber.

2218. Lili Damita (July 19, 1901–Mar. 21, 1994) B: Bordeaux, France. M: film star Errol Flynn, 1935–42. Samuel Goldwyn saw her on screen in Berlin and brought her to Hollywood where she starred with Ronald Colman in *The Rescue* (1929). *Sons o' Guns* (Imperial, "Yvonne," Nov. 26, 1929): It's You I Love (C'est Vous Que J'aime); Why?/W: Arthur Swanstrom, Benny Davis, M: J. Fred Coots. *George White's Music Hall Varieties* (Casino, revue, Nov. 22, 1932): Let's Put Out the Lights and Go to Sleep/WM: Herman Hupfeld — Oh, Lady; (And) So I Married the Girl/W: Herb Magidson, M: Sam H. Stept — Sweet Liar/WM: Irving Caesar — Two Feet in Two-Four Time/W: Irving Caesar, M: Harold Arlen.

2219. Cathryn Damon (Sept. 11, 1931–May 4, 1987): B: Seattle, WA. She played Mary Campbell in the 1970s TV sitcom *Soap*. *Foxy* (Ziegfeld, "Brandy," Feb. 16, 1964): I'm Way

Ahead of the Game; Larceny and Love; Rollin' in Gold/W: Johnny Mercer, M: Robert Emmett Dolan. *Flora, the Red Menace* (Alvin, "Comrade Charlotte," May 11, 1965): Express Yourself/W: Fred Ebb, M: John Kander. *Come Summer* (Lunt-Fontanne, "Submit Pratt [Mitty]," Mar. 18, 1969): Come Summer; Let Me Be; Moonglade; Wild Birds Calling; Women/W: Will Holt, M: David Baker.

2220. Stuart Damon (Feb. 5, 1937–) B: Brooklyn, NY. He was Dr. Alan Quartermain on the TV soap *General Hospital* (1963). *Do I Hear a Waltz?* (46th Street, "Eddie Yaeger," Mar. 18, 1965): No Understand; Perfectly Lovely Couple; We're Gonna Be All Right; What Do We Do? We Fly!/W: Stephen Sondheim, M: Richard Rodgers.

2221. Paige Dana *Cats* (Winter Garden, CR, "Rumpleteazer," Mar. 1984): Mungojerrie and Rumpleteazer/W: T.S. Eliot, M: Andrew Lloyd Webber.

2222. Dorothy Dandridge (Nov. 9, 1920–Sept. 8, 1965) B: Cleveland, OH. M: HAROLD NICHOLAS, 1942. Sister of VIVIAN DANDRIDGE. She was a child movie actor; in the 1930s, she and Etta and Vivian sang together as the Dandridge Sisters. Later films included *Carmen Jones* (1954) and *Porgy and Bess* (1959), but her singing was dubbed by Marilyn Horne and Adele Addison. Death occurred from an overdose of pills. *Swingin' the Dream* (Center, "2nd Pixie," Nov. 29, 1949): Darn That Dream; Swingin' a Dream/W: Eddie DeLange, M: James Van Heusen.

2223. Etta Dandridge Her name was actually Etta Jones, and she was not the sister of DOROTHY and VIVIAN DANDRIDGE. But because girl trios were then so popular, Etta was called upon to be the third Dandridge sister. *Swingin' the Dream* (Center, "3rd Pixie," Nov. 29, 1949): same as DOROTHY DANDRIDGE.

2224. Vivian Dandridge *Swingin' the Dream* (Center, "1st Pixie," Nov. 29, 1949): same as DOROTHY DANDRIDGE.

2225. Jess Dandy (Nov. 9, 1871–Apr. 15, 1923) B: Rochester, NY. He played the role of Hans Wagner 5,000 times. *The Prince of Pilsen* (New York, revival, "Hans Wagner," Apr. 3, 1905): Didn't Know Exactly What to Do; The Widow/W: Frank Pixley, M: Gustav Luders. *Marcelle* (Casino, "Baron Von Berghof," Oct. 1, 1908): Something's Always Going Wrong/W: Frank Pixley, M: Gustav Luders.

2226. Faith Dane *Gypsy* (Broadway, "Mazeppa," May 21, 1959): You Gotta Have a Gimmick/W: Stephen Sondheim, M: Jule Styne.

2227. Rita Dane *Pom-Pom* (Cohan, "Therese," Feb. 28, 1916): Mon Desir; Ships in the Night/W: Anne Caldwell, M: Hugo Felix.

2228. William (Will) Danforth (May 13, 1867–Apr. 16, 1941) B: Syracuse, NY. M: NORMA KOPP. A partner of FRANK DANIELS, they appeared together in several productions. Danforth played more than 5,000 performances of Gilbert and Sullivan operas. *The Idol's Eye* (Broadway, "Don Pablo Tabasco," Oct. 25, 1897): Cuban Song/W: Harry B. Smith, M: Victor Herbert. *Miss Simplicity* (Casino, "Dr. Willie Pellet," Feb. 10, 1902): But He Said It So Politely/W: R.A. Barnet, M: H.L. Heartz. *The Yankee Consul* (Broadway > Wallack's, "Don Raphael Deschado," Feb. 22, 1904): The Hammers Will Go Rap, Rap, Rap/W: Henry Blossom, M: Alfred G. Robyn. *Happyland* or *The King of Elysia* (Lyric > Casino > Majestic, "Altimus," Oct. 2, 1905): How I Love Flowers/W: Frederick Ranken, M: Reginald De Koven. *The King of Cadonia* (Daly's, "Bran," Jan. 10, 1910): Lena, Lena/W: M.E. Rourke, M: Jerome Kern — Sparrow and Hippopotamus/W: Adrian Ross, M: Jerome Kern — You're Not the Only Cinder in the Grate/W: Adrian Ross, M: Sidney Jones. *Little Miss Fix-It* (Globe, "Henry Burbank," Apr. 3, 1911): Parlor Games/WM: R.P. Weston, Fred Barnes. *The Three Romeos* (Globe, "Titus Bellamy," Nov. 13, 1911): Along Broadway; Anabelle Jerome; He's Crazy; Mary Ann, Where Are You?; A Matter of Experience/W: R.H. Burnside, M: Raymond Hubbell. *The Girl from Montmartre* (Criterion, "Dr. Brumage," Aug. 5, 1912): Ghost Quintette; In Spirit Land/W: Harry B. Smith, Robert B. Smith, M: Henry Bereny. *Adele* (Longacre > Harris, "Henri Parmaceau," Aug. 28, 1913): The Clock Is Striking Ten; It's Love!; My Long Lost Love Lenore/WM: Edward A. Paulton, Adolf Philipp, Jean Briquet. *The Debutante* (Knickerbocker, "Godfrey Frazer," Dec. 7, 1914): The Dancing Lesson/W: Robert B. Smith, M: Victor Herbert. *The Girl Who Smiles* (Lyric > Longacre, "Paul Fabre," Aug. 9, 1915): Join the Families; A Little Difference at Breakfast; The Story of a Sparrow/WM: Edward A. Paulton, Adolf Philipp, Jean Briquet. *The Maid of the Mountains* (Casino, "Gen. Malona," Sept. 11, 1918): Dirty Work/W: Clifford Harris, M: Harold Fraser-Simpson — For Many a Year; Good People Gather 'Round/W: Harry Graham, M: Harold Fraser-Simpson — When You're in Love/W: Clifford Harris, Arthur Valentine, M: James W. Tate. *The Houseboat on the Styx* (Liberty, "Henry VIII," Dec. 25, 1928): Men of Hades; The Roll

Call in the Morning/W: Monte Carlo, M: Alma Sanders. *Robin Hood* (Jolson, revival, "Sheriff of Nottingham," Nov. 18, 1929): Churning, Churning; I Am the Sheriff of Nottingham; O, See the Lambkins Play!; Tinkers' Song/W: Harry B. Smith, M: Reginald De Koven. *Robin Hood* (Erlanger's, revival, "Sheriff of Nottingham," Feb. 8, 1932): same as above.

2229. Beverly D'Angelo (Nov. 15, 1953–) B: Columbus, OH. A visual arts student, she worked as a cartoonist for Hanna-Barbera Studios in Hollywood before her singing and acting career in movies and TV began. *Rockabye Hamlet* (Minskoff, "Ophelia," Feb. 17, 1976): Denmark Is Still; Gentle Lover; Hello-Hello; If Not to You; Rockabye Hamlet; Twist Her Mind/WM: Cliff Jones.

2230. Billie Lynn Daniel *Porgy and Bess* (New York City Center, revival, "Clara," May 17, 1961): Summertime/W: DuBose Heyward, M: George Gershwin.

2231. Tom Daniel *Dolly Varden* (Herald Square, "John Fairfax," Jan. 27, 1902): An Aural Understanding; I'm Twirling, Whirling; The Song of the Sword; We Met in Lover's Lane/W: Stanislaus Stange, M: Julian Edwards.

2232. Graciela Daniele (Dec. 8, 1939–) B: Buenos Aires, Argentina. *What Makes Sammy Run?* (54th Street, "Rita Rio," Feb. 27, 1964): Paint a Rainbow/WM: Ervin Drake. *Chicago* (46th Street, "Hunyak," June 3, 1975): Cell Block Tango/W: Fred Ebb, M: John Kander.

2233. Marlene Danielle (Aug. 16–) B: New York, NY. She appeared in *Cats* for its entire run. *Cats* (Winter Garden, CR, "Demeter"): Grizabella, the Glamour Cat/W: T.S. Eliot, M: Andrew Lloyd Webber — Macavity/W: Trevor Nunn, based on T.S. Eliot, M: Andrew Lloyd Webber. *Cats* (Winter Garden, CR, "Bombalurina," Jan. 9, 1984): Bustopher Jones; Grizabella, the Glamour Cat; Macavity; The Old Gumbie Cat/W: T.S. Eliot, M: Andrew Lloyd Webber.

2234. Martha Danielle *Rex* (Lunt-Fontanne, "Lady Margaret," Apr. 25, 1976): Elizabeth/W: Sheldon Harnick, M: Richard Rodgers.

2235. Susan Danielle (Jan. 30, 1949–) B: Englewood, NJ. *A Chorus Line* (Shubert, CR, "Sheila," Mar. 1981/Sept. 1984/Mar. 27, 1989): At the Ballet/W: Edward Kleban, M: Marvin Hamlisch.

2236. Billy Daniels (Sept. 12, 1915–Oct. 7, 1988) B: Jacksonville, FL. Singer and actor, he worked in nightclubs, radio and movies and briefly on TV during the 1940s and 50s. His theme song: the Johnny Mercer–Harold Arlen classic, "That Old Black Magic." *Memphis*

Bound! (Broadway > Belasco, "Roy Baggott," May 24, 1945): Farewell My Own; A Maiden Fair to See; The Nightingale, the Moon and I; Old Love and Brand New Love/WM: Clay Warnick, Don Walker, based on William S. Gilbert and Arthur Sullivan. *Golden Boy* (Majestic, "Eddie Satin," Oct. 20, 1964): This Is the Life; While the City Sleeps/W: Lee Adams, M: Charles Strouse. *Hello, Dolly!* (Minskoff, revival, "Horace Vandergelder," Nov. 6, 1975): Before the Parade Passes By/WM: Lee Adams, Charles Strouse, Jerry Herman — Hello, Dolly!; It Takes a Woman; So Long, Dearie/WM: Jerry Herman — Motherhood/WM: Bob Merrill, Jerry Herman.

2237. Danny Daniels (Oct. 25, 1924–) B: Albany, NY. *Billion Dollar Baby* (Alvin, "Champ Watson," Dec. 21, 1945): One Track Mind/W: Betty Comden, Adolph Green, M: Morton Gould. *Street Scene* (Adelphi, "Dick McGann," Jan. 9, 1947): Moon-Faced, Starry-Eyed/W: Langston Hughes, M: Kurt Weill. *Make Mine Manhattan* (Broadhurst, revue, Jan. 15, 1948): My Brudder and Me/W: Arnold B. Horwitt, M: Richard Lewine. *Kiss Me, Kate* (New Century, CR, "Bill Calhoun" and "Lucentio"): Bianca; I Sing of Love; Tom, Dick or Harry; We Open in Venice/WM: Cole Porter.

2238. David Daniels (Apr. 10, 1929–) B: Evanston, IL. *Plain and Fancy* (Mark Hellinger, "Peter Reber," Jan. 27, 1955): Follow Your Heart; Young and Foolish/W: Arnold B. Horwitt, M: Albert Hague.

2239. Eleanor Daniels *Kitty Darlin'* (Casino, "Lydie," Nov. 7, 1917): You're Plenty of a Lady as You Are/WM: ?.

2240. Frank Daniels (Aug. 15, 1856–Jan. 12, 1935) B: Dayton, OH. Comedian and sometime partner of WILLIAM DANFORTH. Known for his expressive eyebrows and his curtain speeches. From 1915 he appeared in Vitagraph films. *The Wizard of the Nile* (Casino, "Kibosh," Nov. 4, 1895): My Angeline; There's One Thing a Wizard Can Do/W: Harry B. Smith, M: Victor Herbert. *The Idol's Eye* (Broadway, "Abel Conn," Oct. 25, 1897): I Just Dropped In; I'm Captain Cholly Chumley of the Guards; Talk About Yo' Luck; The Tattooed Man/W: Harry B. Smith, M: Victor Herbert. *Miss Simplicity* (Casino, "My Man Blossoms," Feb. 10, 1902): The Chestnutty Language of Lovers; The Good Little Sunday School Boy/W: R.A. Barnet, M: H.L. Heartz-Don't Mind Me; The Interrogative Child/W: R.A. Barnet, M: Clifton Crawford. *The Office Boy* (Victoria, "Noah Little," Nov. 2, 1903): I Thought Wrong/WM: Richard Morton, R.G.

Knowles — I'm on the Water Wagon Now/W: Paul West, M: John W. Bratton — Plain Mamie O'Hooley; Signs; Will You Be My Hero, Noble Sir?/W: Harry B. Smith, M: Ludwig Englander. *The Tattooed Man* (Criterion, "Omar Khayyam, Jr.," Feb. 18, 1907): Omar Khayyam; Watch the Professor/W: Harry B. Smith, M: Victor Herbert. *The Belle of Brittany* (Daly's, "Marquis de St. Gautier," Nov. 8, 1909): In the Chest; The Old Chateau; Sing to Your Dear One/W: Percy Greenbank, M: Howard Talbot — Oh! I Must Go Home Tonight/WM: William Hargreaves. *Roly Poly* (Broadway > Weber and Fields, "Hiram Fitzsimmons," Nov. 21, 1912): I Cannot Drink the Old Drinks/W: Harry Williams, Vincent Bryan, M: Nat D. Ayer — I'm a Lonesome Romeo; The Zingaras/W: E. Ray Goetz, M: A. Baldwin Sloane.

2241. Grace Daniels *My Lady's Glove* (Lyric, "Charlotte," June 18, 1917): I'll Hate to Leave the Boys/WM: ?. *Good Morning Judge* (Shubert, "Diana Fairlie," Feb. 6, 1919): Make Hay, Little Girl!/W: Percy Greenbank, M: Lionel Monckton-Young Folks and Old Folks/WM: ?.

2242. Howard Daniels One of the quintette known as the Charioteers. *Hellzapoppin* (46th Street > Winter Garden, revue, Sept. 22, 1938): Abe Lincoln/W: Alfred Hayes, M: Earl Robinson-We Won't Let It Happen Here/WM: Don George, Teddy Hall.

2243. Sharon Daniels *The Most Happy Fella* (Majestic, revival, "Rosabella," Oct. 11, 1979): Don't Cry; Happy to Make Your Acquaintance; How Beautiful the Days; My Heart Is So Full of You; Please Let Me Tell You; Somebody Somewhere; Warm All Over/WM: Frank Loesser.

2244. William Daniels (Mar. 31, 1927–) B: Brooklyn, NY. As a child, he was part of a song and dance act with his family. He played Dr. Mark Craig on the TV medical drama *St. Elsewhere* (1982). *On a Clear Day You Can See Forever* (Mark Hellinger, "Warren Smith," Oct. 17, 1965): Wait 'Til We're Sixty-Five/W: Alan Jay Lerner, M: Burton Lane. *1776* (46th Street, "John Adams," Mar. 16, 1969): But, Mr. Adams; The Egg; He Plays the Violin; Is Anybody There?; The Lees of Old Virginia; Piddle, Twiddle and Resolve; Sit Down, John; Till Then; Yours, Yours, Yours/WM: Sherman Edwards. *A Little Night Music* (Shubert, CR, "Fredrik Egerman," Feb. 25, 1974): It Would Have Been Wonderful; Now; Soon; You Must Meet My Wife/WM: Stephen Sondheim.

2245. Alexandra Danilova (Nov. 20, 1904– July 13, 1997) B: Peterhoff, Russia. M: George Balanchine. A dancer with Balanchine and

Diaghileff. *Oh Captain!* (Alvin, "Lisa," Feb. 4, 1958): Hey Madame!/WM: Jay Livingston, Ray Evans.

2246. Jeanne Danjou *Flossie* (Lyric, "Marie," June 3, 1924): Flossie; I Want to Be a Santa Claus/W: Ralph Murphy, M: Armand Robi.

2247. Braden Danner (July 12, 1975–) B: Indianapolis, IN. *Oliver!* (Mark Hellinger, revival, "Oliver Twist," Apr. 29, 1984): Consider Yourself; Food, Glorious Food; I'd Do Anything; Where Is Love?; Who Will Buy/WM: Lionel Bart. *Les Miserables* (Broadway, "Gavroche," Mar. 12, 1987): Look Down/W: Herbert Kretzmer, M: Claude-Michel Schonberg.

2248. Harry Danner Brother of actress Blythe Danner; uncle of Gwyneth Paltrow. *Bajour* (Shubert, "1st Patrolman," Nov. 23, 1964): Living Simply/WM: Walter Marks.

2249. Edward Dano *Up She Goes* (Playhouse, "Simpson," Nov. 6, 1922): The Visitors/ W: Joseph McCarthy, M: Harry Tierney.

2250. Paul Franklin Dano (June 19, 1984–) B: Connecticut. *A Christmas Carol* (Paramount Madison Square Garden, return engagement, "Scrooge at 12," Nov. 20, 1995): A Place Called Home/W: Lynn Ahrens, M: Alan Menken.

2251. Fleury D'Antonakis (May 11, 1939–) B: Athens, Greece. *Do I Hear a Waltz?* (46th Street, "Giovanna," Mar. 18, 1965): No Understand; Perfectly Lovely Couple/W: Stephen Sondheim, M: Richard Rodgers.

2252. Michael Dantuono (July 30, 1942–) B: Providence, RI. *The Three Musketeers* (Broadway, revival, "Comte de la Rochefort," Nov. 11, 1984): Bless My Soul/WM: ?.

2253. Rex Dantzler *What's in a Name?* (Maxine Elliott, revue, Mar. 19, 1920): The Theatrical Blues; What's in a Name? (Love Is Always Love)/W: John Murray Anderson, Jack Yellen, M: Milton Ager.

2254. Philip Darby *I'll Say She Is* (Casino, "Merchant," May 19, 1924): Pretty Girl; When Shadows Fall/W: Will B. Johnstone, M: Tom Johnstone.

2255. Michael Darbyshire *Pickwick* (46th Street, "Dodson," Oct. 4, 1965): That's the Law/W: Leslie Bricusse, M: Cyril Ornadel.

2256. Denise Darcel (Sept. 8, 1925–) B: Paris, France. The nightclub singer went to Hollywood in 1947. *Pardon Our French* (Broadway, revue, Oct. 5, 1950): Dolly from the Folies Bergere/W: Ole Olsen, Chic Johnson, M: Harry Sukman.

2257. Mary (D'Arcy) Darcy (1956–) B: Yardville, NJ. *Sunday in the Park with George* (Booth, "Celeste #2," May 2, 1984): The Day

Off; Gossip/WM: Stephen Sondheim. *Singin' in the Rain* (Gershwin, "Kathy Selden," July 2, 1985): Good Morning; I've Got a Feelin' You're Foolin'; Would You?; You Are My Lucky Star/W: Arthur Freed, M: Nacio Herb Brown — You Stepped Out of a Dream/W: Gus Kahn, M: Nacio Herb Brown. *The Phantom of the Opera* (Majestic, CR, "Christine Daae," c 1992): All I Ask of You; Angel of Music; Bravo, Bravo; I Remember; Little Lotte; The Mirror; Notes; The Point of No Return; Raoul, I've Been There; Stranger Than You Dreamt It; Think of Me; Twisted Every Way; Wandering Child; Why Have You Brought Me Here; Wishing You Were Somehow Here Again/W: Charles Hart, Richard Stilgoe, M: Andrew Lloyd Webber — The Phantom of the Opera/W: Mike Batt, Richard Stilgoe, M: Andrew Lloyd Webber.

2258. Maurice Darcy *The Idol's Eye* (Broadway, "Ned Winner," Oct. 25, 1897): Pretty Isabella and Her Umbrella/W: Harry B. Smith, M: Victor Herbert. *When Johnny Comes Marching Home* (New York, "Maj. Geoffrey Martin," Dec. 16, 1902): Good Day, Yankees!; I Could Waltz On Forever; 'Twas Down in the Garden of Eden/W: Stanislaus Stange, M: Julian Edwards. *Piff! Paff!! Pouf!!!* (Casino, CR, "Dick Dailey," Apr. 18, 1904): I've Interviewed the Wide, Wide World/W: William Jerome, M: Jean Schwartz. *Rogers Brothers in Ireland* (Liberty > New York, "Gerald Fitzgerald," Sept. 4, 1905): The Blarney Stone; The Irish Girl I Love/W: George V. Hobart, M: Max Hoffmann. *When Johnny Comes Marching Home* (New Amsterdam > Manhattan Opera House, revival, "Jonathan Phoenix," May 7, 1917): I Was Quite Upset/W: Stanislaus Stange, M: Julian Edwards.

2259. Pattie Darcy *Leader of the Pack* (Ambassador, "Lounge Singer," Apr. 8, 1985): I Can Hear Music/WM: Jeff Barry, Ellie Greenwich, Phil Spector — Look of Love/WM: Jeff Barry, Ellie Greenwich.

2260. Richard Darcy *Heaven on Earth* (New Century, "A Lover," Sept. 16, 1948): Heaven on Earth/W: Barry Trivers, M: Jay Gorney.

2261. Danny Dare (Mar. 20, 1905–Nov. 20, 1996) B: New York, NY. He later became a movie producer and dance director. *Dew Drop Inn* (Astor, "Bellboy No. 1," May 17, 1923): The Primrose Path/W: Cyrus D. Wood, M: Alfred Goodman. *The 5 O'Clock Girl* (44th Street, "Ronnie Webb," Oct. 10, 1927): I'm One Little Party/W: Bert Kalmar, M: Harry Ruby.

2262. Dorothy Dare (Apr. 4, 1916–) B: Philadelphia, PA. *Hello, Paris* (Shubert, CR, "Gracie Jones," Dec. 1930): Dance Your Troubles Away; Give It; Pack Your Suitcase with Love; You Made a Hit with Me/WM: ?. *America's Sweetheart* (Broadhurst, "Dorith," Feb. 10, 1931): In Califor-n-i-a; Two Unfortunate Orphans/W: Lorenz Hart, M: Richard Rodgers. *Here Goes the Bride* (46th Street, "Diddles Stuyvesant," Nov. 3, 1931): It's My Nature; Shake Well Before Using; What's the Difference/W: Edward Heyman, M: Johnny Green. *Strike Me Pink* (Majestic, revue, Mar. 4, 1933): I Hate to Think That You'll Grow Old, Baby; Strike Me Pink/W: Lew Brown, M: Ray Henderson. *The Only Girl* (44th Street, revival, "Margaret Ayre," May 21, 1934): Connubial Bliss/W: Henry Blossom, M: Victor Herbert — I Paused, I Looked, I Fell/W: Sam Bernard, Jr., Bobby Burk, M: Henry Lloyd.

2263. Bertha Darel *When Johnny Comes Marching Home* (New York, "Susan Graham," Dec. 16, 1902): Good Day, Yankees!; Marry the Man and Be Merry/W: Stanislas Stange, M: Julian Edwards.

2264. Anita Darian *Flower Drum Song* (St. James, CR, "Helen Chao," Dec. 1959): Love, Look Away/W: Oscar Hammerstein II, M: Richard Rodgers. *The King and I* (New York City Center, revival, "Lady Thiang," May 11, 1960): Something Wonderful; Western People Funny/W: Oscar Hammerstein II, M: Richard Rodgers. *Show Boat* (New York City Center, revival, "Julie La Verne," Apr. 12, 1961): Bill/W: P.G. Wodehouse, Oscar Hammerstein II, M: Jerome Kern—Can't Help Lovin' Dat Man/W: Oscar Hammerstein II, M: Jerome Kern. *The King and I* (New York City Center, revival, "Lady Thiang," June 12, 1963/May 23, 1968): same as above.

2265. Yvonne D'Arle *Fancy Free* (Astor, "Yvette," Apr. 11, 1918): Pretty Baby Doll from Paree; The Road to Anywhere; When I Came to America/WM: Augustus Barratt. *Countess Maritza* (Shubert, "Countess Maritza," Sept. 18, 1926): Love Has Found My Heart/W: Harry B. Smith, M: Alfred Goodman — The Music Thrills Me; The One I'm Looking For; Why Is the World So Changed Today?/W: Harry B. Smith, M: Emmerich Kalman. *The Three Musketeers* (Lyric, "Queen Anne of France," Mar. 13, 1928): Love Is the Sun; My Dreams/W: Clifford Grey, M: Rudolf Friml.

2266. Herbert Darley *The Messenger Boy* (Daly's, "Mr. Trotter" and "Purser," Sept. 16, 1901): Bradshaw's Guide/W: Adrian Ross, M: Ivan Caryll.

2267. Beatrice Darling *The Rose Girl* (Ambassador, "Colette," Feb. 11, 1921): The Proteges/W: William Cary Duncan, M: Anselm Goetzl.

2268. Clifton Darling *Babes in Arms* (Shubert > Majestic, "Cliff," Apr. 14, 1937): Imagine; Way Out West (on West End Avenue)/W: Lorenz Hart, M: Richard Rodgers.

2269. Elizabeth Darling *The Rose Girl* (Ambassador, "Denise," Feb. 11, 1921): The Proteges/W: William Cary Duncan, M: Anselm Goetzl.

2270. Hattie Darling *The Passing Show of 1916* (Winter Garden, revue, June 22, 1916): Broadway School Days; Play My Melody/W: Harold Atteridge, M: Sigmund Romberg, Otto Motzan — Walking the Dog/W: Harold Atteridge, M: Otto Motzan. *Tick-Tack-Toe* (Princess, revue, Feb. 13, 1920): Dance Mad; Hoppy Poppy Queen; I'd Like to Know Why I Fell in Love with You/WM: Herman Timberg.

2271. James Darling *Madame Sherry* (New Amsterdam, CR, "Theophilus Sherry," Feb. 13, 1911): The Smile She Means for You; We Are Only Poor Weak Mortals After All/W: Otto Harbach, M: Karl Hoschna — You Can't Argue/W: ?, M: Ben M. Jerome.

2272. Jean Darling (Aug. 23, 1922–) B: Santa Monica, CA. She was the curlyheaded little blonde girl in *Our Gang* comedies. *Carousel* (Majestic, "Carrie Pipperidge," Apr. 19, 1945): June Is Bustin' Out All Over; Mister Snow; A Real Nice Clambake; When the Children Are Asleep; You're a Queer One, Julie Jordan/W: Oscar Hammerstein II, M: Richard Rodgers.

2273. Jennifer Darling (June 19, 1946–) B: Oklahoma City, OK. She played Donna on the TV sitcom *Eight Is Enough* (1978). *Maggie Flynn* (ANTA, "Mary O'Cleary," Oct. 23, 1968): The Thank You Song/WM: Hugo Peretti, Luigi Creatore, George David Weiss.

2274. Isabel D'Armond (Aug. 28, 1887– Nov. 1, 1940) B: St. Louis, MO. *The Girl Question* (Wallack's, "Elsie Davis," Aug. 3, 1908): Be Sweet to Me, Kid; I'd Like to Have You Call Me Honey; There Is No Place Like Home; When Eyes Like Yours Looked Into Eyes Like Mine/W: Frank R. Adams, Will M. Hough, M: Joseph E. Howard.

2275. Nydia d'Arnell *Topsy and Eva* (Harris, "Mariette," Dec. 23, 1924): Give Me Your Heart and Give Me Your Hand; Kiss Me; The Land of Long Ago; Rememb'ring; Smiling Through My Tears [Apr. 27, 1925]/WM: Vivian Duncan, Rosetta Duncan. *Mayflowers* (Forrest, "Rosamond Gill," Nov. 24, 1925): The Grecian Bend; The Lancers/W: Clifford Grey, M: Edward Kunneke — Take a Little Stroll with Me/W: Clifford Grey, M: J. Fred Coots, Maurie Rubens. *Happy Go Lucky* (Liberty, "Mildred

Chapin," Sept. 30, 1926): Choose Your Flowers; When I Make a Million for You (I Want a Million for You, Dear)/W: Helena Evans, M: Lucien Denni — How Are You, Lady Love?/W: Gwynne Denni, M: Lucien Denni. *Golden Dawn* (Hammerstein's, "Johanna," Nov. 30, 1927): We Two/ W: Oscar Hammerstein II, Otto Harbach, M: Emmerich Kalman, Herbert Stothart. *My Maryland* (Al Jolson, CR, "Barbara Frietchie," Mar. 26, 1928): Mother; Mr. Cupid; Old John Barleycorn; The Same Silver Moon; Something Old, Something New; Won't You Marry Me?; Your Land and My Land/W: Dorothy Donnelly, M: Sigmund Romberg.

2276. Robert Darnell (Sept. 26, 1930–Jan. 27, 1991) B: Los Angeles, CA. *Hurry, Harry* (Ritz, "Stavos" and "Native No. 1" and "Chorus Boy," Oct. 12, 1972): Africa Speaks; Hurry, Harry; When a Man Cries/W: David Finkle, M: Bill Weeden.

2277. James Darrah *Hello, Dolly!* (Lunt-Fontanne, revival, "Ambrose Kemper," Oct. 19, 1995): Put on Your Sunday Clothes/WM: Jerry Herman.

2278. Gertrude Darrell *Mlle. Mischief* (Lyric, "Mimi," Sept. 28, 1908): Ev'ry Hour Brings Its Flower; Le Coeur de Ninon; My Own Vienna/ W: Sydney Rosenfeld, M: Carl M. Ziehrer.

2279. Danielle Darrieux (May 1, 1917–) B: Bordeaux, France. Considered one of the finest actresses of the French stage and screen, she was memorable as Maria Vetsera in the film *Mayerling* (1937). During WWII she was accused of collaborating with the Nazis. *Coco* (Mark Hellinger, CR, "Coco," Aug. 3, 1970): Always Mademoiselle; Coco; Mademoiselle Cliche de Paris; The Money Rings Out Like Freedom; On the Corner of the Rue Cambon; Ohrbach's, Bloomingdale's, Best and Saks; The Preparation; The World Belongs to the Young/W: Alan Jay Lerner, M: Andre Previn. *Ambassador* (Lunt-Fontanne, "Marie de Vionnet," Nov. 19, 1972): I Know the Man; Not Tomorrow; She Passed My Way; Surprise; That's What I Need Tonight; Young with Him/W: Hal Hackady, M: Don Gohman.

2280. Camille D'Arville (June 21, 1863– Sept. 10, 1932) B: Overryssel, Holland. *The Knickerbockers* (Garden, "Katrina," May 29, 1893): If There Is a Lad; If You and I Should Meet; Sing Your Merriest Lays/W: Harry B. Smith, M: Reginald De Koven. *The Highwayman* (Broadway, CR, "Lady Constance Sinclair," Feb. 21, 1898): Do You Remember, Love?; Vive la Bagatelle/W: Harry B. Smith, M: Reginald De Koven.

2281. Evelyn Darville *The Greenwich Village Follies of 1921* (Shubert, CR, revue, Nov. 14, 1921): The House That Jack Built; That Reminiscent Melody/W: John Murray Anderson, Jack Yellen, M: Milton Ager. *Orange Blossoms* (Fulton, "Cecilia Malba," Sept. 19, 1922): I Can't Argue with You/W: B.G. DeSylva, M: Victor Herbert. *My Princess* (Shubert, "Maud Satterlee," Oct. 6, 1927): My Passion Flower/W: Dorothy Donnelly, M: Sigmund Romberg.

2282. Cress Darwin *Oh! Calcutta!* (Edison, revival, Sept. 24, 1976): Much Too Soon/WM: Robert Dennis, Peter Schickele, Stanley Walden.

2283. Jeanne Darys *The Only Girl* (39th Street > Lyric, "Renee," Nov. 2, 1914): Antoinette/W: Henry Blossom, M: Victor Herbert.

2284. Howard Da Silva (May 4, 1909–Feb. 16, 1986) B: Cleveland, OH. Distinguished character actor of radio, stage, film and TV. He was blacklisted during the McCarthy era. *The Cradle Will Rock* (Windsor > Mercury, "Larry Foreman," Jan. 3, 1938): The Cradle Will Rock; Leaflets!/WM: Marc Blitzstein. *Oklahoma!* (St. James, "Jud Fry," Mar. 31, 1943): Lonely Room; Pore Jud/W: Oscar Hammerstein II, M: Richard Rodgers. *Fiorello!* (Broadhurst, "Ben Marino," Nov. 23, 1959): The Bum Won; Little Tin Box; Politics and Poker/W: Sheldon Harnick, M: Jerry Bock. *1776* (46th Street, "Benjamin Franklin," Mar. 16, 1969): But, Mr. Adams; The Egg; He Plays the Violin; The Lees of Old Virginia/WM: Sherman Edwards.

2285. Irene Datcher *Guys and Dolls* (Broadway, revival, "Agatha," July 21, 1976): Follow the Fold/WM: Frank Loesser.

2286. Delphie Daughn *Silks and Satins* (George M. Cohan, revue, July 15, 1920): Around the Town/W: Louis Weslyn, M: Leon Rosebrook.

2287. Hollis Davenny *Blossom Time* (Century, CR, "Franz Schubert," Nov. 20, 1922): Moment Musicale; My Springtime Thou Art; Serenade; Song of Love; Tell Me, Daisy/W: Dorothy Donnelly, M: Sigmund Romberg. *The Student Prince* (Majestic, revival, "Dr. Engel," Jan. 29, 1931): Golden Days; Student Life/W: Dorothy Donnelly, M: Sigmund Romberg.

2288. Eva Davenport (c 1857–Sept. 26, 1932) B: London, England. *The Silver Slipper* (Broadway, CR, "Belle Jimper," Mar. 9, 1903): Class/W: Charles H. Taylor, M: Leslie Stuart. *The Yankee Consul* (Broadway > Wallack, "Donna Teresa Rebera-y-Uruburu," Feb. 22, 1904): We Were Taught to Walk Demurely/W: Henry Blossom, M: Alfred G. Robyn. *The Kiss Waltz* (Casino, "Kathi," Sept. 18, 1911): Eleva-

tion; What I Seen I Done/W: Matthew Woodward, M: Louis A. Hirsch — Laughing Song/W: Matthew Woodward, M: Carl M. Ziehrer. *The Sunshine Girl* (Knickerbocker, "Mrs. Blacker," Feb. 3, 1913): The Butler; I've Been to America; Kitchen Range/WM: Paul Rubens, Arthur Wimperis.

2289. Frank Davenport *Cherry Blossoms* (Cosmopolitan, "Nogo," May 2, 1927): Japanese Serenade/W: Harry B. Smith, M: Sigmund Romberg.

2290. Harry Davenport (Jan. 19, 1866–Aug. 9, 1949) B: New York, NY. M: PHYLLIS RANKIN. The character actor, from a distinguished theatrical family, was related to ANNE SEYMOUR and JOHN D. SEYMOUR. He appeared in more than 100 movies as a benevolent gentleman. *The Belle of New York* (Casino, "Harry Bronson," Sept. 28, 1897): Teach Me How to Kiss, Dear/W: Hugh Morton, M: Gustave Kerker. *The Liberty Belles* (Madison Square, "Jack Everleigh," Sept. 30, 1901): De Trop/WM: Clifton Crawford — Follow the Man That Leads the Band/W: ?, M: Aimee Lachaume. *The Defender* (Herald Square, "Sir Thomas Ceylon Teaton," July 3, 1902): Lift the Cup; Little Fly/W: Allen Lowe, M: Charles Denee. *The Girl from Kay's* (Herald Square, CR, "Harry Gordon," 1903): I Don't Care/WM: Paul Rubens — Make It Up/W: Claude Aveling, M: Ivan Caryll — Matilda and the Builder/W: J. Hickory Wood, M: Ernest Bucalossi — Semi-Detached/W: Adrian Ross, M: Ivan Caryll. *It Happened in Nordland* (Lew Fields, "Prince George of Nebula," Dec. 5, 1904): Absinthe Frappe; My Catamaran/W: Glen MacDonough, M: Victor Herbert. *The Dancing Duchess* (Casino, "Max Tokay," Aug. 20, 1914): Fol-De-Rol-Lol; It's the Girls; Never Worry/W: R.H. Burnside, M: Milton Lusk.

2291. Clifford David (June 30, 1932–) B: Toledo, OH. *Wildcat* (Alvin, "Hank," Dec. 16, 1960): One Day We Dance/W: Carolyn Leigh, M: Cy Coleman. *On a Clear Day You Can See Forever* (Mark Hellinger, "Edward Moncrief," Oct. 17, 1965): Don't Tamper with My Sister; She Wasn't You/W: Alan Jay Lerner, M: Burton Lane. *A Joyful Noise* (Mark Hellinger, "Brother Locke," Dec. 15, 1966): Whither Thou Goest/WM: Oscar Brand, Paul Nassau. *1776* (46th Street, "Edward Rutledge," Mar. 16, 1969): Molasses to Rum/WM: Sherman Edwards. *Joseph and the Amazing Technicolor Dreamcoat* (Minskoff, revival, "Jacob" and "Potiphar" and "Guru," Nov. 10, 1993): Any Dream Will Do; A Coat of Many Colors; Go, Go, Go, Joseph;

Jacob and Sons; Jacob in Egypt; One More Angel in Heaven; Potiphar; Those Canaan Days/W: Tim Rice, M: Andrew Lloyd Webber.

2292. Daniel David (May 7, 1960–) B: Torrance, CA. *Cleavage* (Playhouse, June 23, 1982): Bringing Up Badger; Only Love; The Thrill of the Chase/WM: Buddy Sheffield.

2293. Keith David (May 8, 1954–) B: New York, NY. *Jelly's Last Jam* (Virginia, "Chimney Man," Apr. 26, 1992): The Chicago Stomp; Good Ole New York; Somethin' More/W: Susan Birkenhead, M: Jelly Roll Morton — The Last Rites/W: Susan Birkenhead, M: Luther Henderson, Jelly Roll Morton.

2294. John Davidson (Dec. 13, 1941–) B: Pittsburgh, PA. The singer had his own TV variety show from 1969 to 1976. *Foxy* (Ziegfeld, "Ben," Feb. 16, 1964): Talk to Me, Baby; This Is My Night to Howl/W: Johnny Mercer, M: Robert Emmett Dolan. *Oklahoma!* (New York City Center, revival, "Curly McLain," Dec. 15, 1965): The Farmer and the Cowman; Oh, What a Beautiful Mornin'; Oklahoma; People Will Say We're in Love; Pore Jud; The Surrey with the Fringe on Top/W: Oscar Hammerstein II, M: Richard Rodgers. *State Fair* (Music Box, "Abel Frake," Mar. 27, 1996): All I Owe Ioway; Boys and Girls Like You and Me; Driving at Night; When I Go Out Walking with My Baby/W: Oscar Hammerstein II, M: Richard Rodgers — More Than Just a Friend/WM: Richard Rodgers.

2295. Brian Davies (Nov. 15, 1939–) B: South Wales. He came to the U.S. at age 10 with his parents, and grew up in Indianapolis, IN. *The Sound of Music* (Lunt-Fontanne, "Rolf Gruber," Nov. 16, 1959): Sixteen, Going on Seventeen/W: Oscar Hammerstein II, M: Richard Rodgers. *A Funny Thing Happened on the Way to the Forum* (Alvin, "Hero," May 8, 1962): Free; Impossible; Love, I Hear; Lovely; Pretty Little Picture/WM: Stephen Sondheim.

2296. Lilian Davies *Katja* (44th Street, "Katja Karina," Oct. 18, 1926): Dance with You; Those Eyes So Tender/W: Harry Graham, M: Jean Gilbert — Just for Tonight/W: Clifford Grey, M: Maurie Rubens, Ralph Benatzky.

2297. Maitland Davies *The Rose of Algeria* (Herald Square, "Lieut. Bertrand," Sept. 20, 1909): Little Bird of Paradise/W: Glen MacDonough, M: Victor Herbert.

2298. Margaret Davies *The Greenwich Village Follies of 1920* (Shubert, revue, Jan. 3, 1921): At the Krazy Kat's Ball/W: Arthur Swanstrom, John Murray Anderson, M: A. Baldwin Sloane. *Earl Carroll's Vanities of 1923* (Earl Carroll,

revue, CR, July 16, 1923): Chasing Little Rainbows; Girls Were Made for Dancing [Dec. 17, 1923]; Jazzmania/WM: Earl Carroll.

2299. Marion Davies (Jan. 3, 1897–Sept. 22, 1961) B: Brooklyn, NY. Sister of REINE DAVIES. The showgirl met newspaper mogul William Randolph Heart while she was in the Ziegfeld Follies, and became his mistress. Orson Welles' classic film, *Citizen Kane* (1941) is a fictionalized account of their story. *Betty* (Globe, "Jane," Oct. 3, 1916): I Love the Girls; The Little Harlequin/WM: Paul Rubens, Adrian Ross. *Oh, Boy!* (Princess > Casino, "Jane Packard," Feb. 20, 1917): A Little Bit of Ribbon/W: P.G. Wodehouse, M: Jerome Kern — A Package of Seeds/ W: Herbert Reynolds, P.G. Wodehouse, M: Jerome Kern. *Miss 1917* (Century, revue, Nov. 5, 1917): A Dancing M.D./W: P.G. Wodehouse, M: Jerome Kern — Follow On/W: Hugh Morton, M: Gustave Kerker. *Ed Wynn Carnival* (New Amsterdam, revue, Apr. 5, 1920): Goodbye Sunshine, Hello Moon/W: Gene Buck, M: William Eckstein — I Love the Land of Old Black Joe; Rather Than See You Once in a While/W: Grant Clarke, M: Walter Donaldson.

2300. Paul Hyde Davies *The Girl Who Smiles* (Lyric > Longacre, "Pierre Renauld," Aug. 9, 1915): At Last United; Baby Mine; A Breath from Bohemia/WM: Edward A. Paulton, Adolf Philipp, Jean Briquet.

2301. Reine Davies (June 6, 1892–Apr. 2, 1938) B: Montclair, NJ. *Canary Cottage* (Morosco, "Pauline Hugg," Feb. 5, 1917): It's Always Orange Day in California; Such a Chauffeur; That Syncopated Harp/WM: Earl Carroll.

2302. Diana Davila (Nov. 5, 1947–) B: New York, NY. *Two Gentlemen of Verona* (St. James, "Julia," Dec. 1, 1971): Bring All the Boys Back Home; Don't Have the Baby; Follow the Rainbow; I Am Not Interested in Love; Kidnapped; Thou, Proteus, Thou Hast Metamorphosed Me; Two Gentlemen of Verona; What a Nice Idea; What Does a Lover Pack?/W: John Guare, M: Galt MacDermot. *Home Sweet Homer* (Palace, "Nausikaa," Jan. 4, 1976): The Ball/W: Charles Burr, Forman Brown, M: Mitch Leigh.

2303. Rosalina Davila *South Pacific* (Majestic > Broadway, CR, "Ngana"): Dites-Moi/W: Oscar Hammerstein II, M: Richard Rodgers.

2304. Paul Davin *Americana of 1932* (Shubert, revue, Oct. 5, 1932): Whistling for a Kiss/ W: E.Y. Harburg, Johnny Mercer, M: Richard Myers.

2305. Alvin Davis *Guys and Dolls* (Broadway, revival, "Calvin," July 21, 1976): Follow the Fold/WM: Frank Loesser.

2306. Amon Davis (c 1883–June 1, 1934) *How Come?* (Apollo, "Ebenezer Green," Apr. 16, 1923): I Didn't Grieve Over Daniel/WM: Ben Harris, Henry Creamer, Will Vodery.

2307. Bette Davis (Apr. 5, 1908–Oct. 7, 1989) B: Lowell, MA. A great motion picture star and a fine actress. Davis was one of a kind. *Two's Company* (Alvin, revue, Dec. 15, 1952): Just Like a Man; Roll Along, Sadie; Turn Me Loose on Broadway/W: Ogden Nash, M: Vernon Duke.

2308. Brian Davis *Bitter Sweet* (44th Street, revival, "Cedric Ballantyne" and "Lord Sorrel," May 7, 1934): Green Carnation; The Last Dance; Tarara Boom-de-Ay/WM: Noel Coward.

2309. Bruce Anthony Davis (Mar. 4, 1959–) B: Dayton, OH. *Dancin'* (Broadhurst, revue, CR, Jan. 26, 1979): Dixie/WM: Daniel Decatur Emmett — Easy; If It Feels Good, Let It Ride/WM: Carol Bayer Sager, Melissa Manchester — I've Got Them Feelin' Too Good Today Blues/WM: Jerry Leiber, Mike Stoller. *Big Deal* (Broadway, "2nd Narrator," Apr. 10, 1986): Ain't She Sweet?/W: Jack Yellen, M: Milton Ager — Chicago/WM: Fred Fisher — Everybody Loves My Baby (But My Baby Don't Love Nobody but Me)/WM: Jack Palmer, Spencer Williams — For No Good Reason at All/W: Sam M. Lewis, Joe Young, M: Abel Baer — I've Got a Feelin' You're Foolin'/W: Arthur Freed, M: Nacio Herb Brown — Love Is Just Around the Corner/W: Leo Robin, M: Lewis E. Gensler — Now's the Time to Fall in Love (Potatoes Are Cheaper, Tomatoes Are Cheaper)/WM: Al Sherman, Al Lewis. *A Chorus Line* (Shubert, CR, "Richie," Dec. 1986/c 1988): And.../W: Edward Kleban, M: Marvin Hamlisch.

2310. Charles Davis *Shuffle Along of 1921* (63rd Street Music Hall, "Uncle Tom," May 23, 1921): Old Black Joe and Uncle Tom; Shuffle Along [Nov. 14, 1921]/W: Noble Sissle, M: Eubie Blake. *My Magnolia* (Mansfield, revue, "Lightfoot," July 8, 1926): Gee Chee-Charleston; Jazz Land Ball; Spend It/W: Alex Rogers, M: C. Luckeyth Rogers.

2311. Clifton Davis (Oct. 4, 1945–) B: Chicago, IL. He wrote the gold record song "Never Can Say Goodbye" (1970). *Two Gentlemen of Verona* (St. James, "Valentine," Dec. 1, 1971): Dragon Fight; Follow the Rainbow; I'd Like to Be a Rose; Love's Revenge; Mansion; Night Letter; That's a Very Interesting Question; To Whom It May Concern Me; Where's North?/W: John Guare, M: Galt MacDermot.

2312. Diane Davis B: Saskatchewan, Canada. *New Faces of 1943* (Ritz, revue, Dec. 22, 1942): Animals Are Nice; Yes, Sir, I've Made a Date/W: J.B. Rosenberg, M: Lee Wainer — Richard Crudnut's Charm School/W: June Carroll, John Lund, M: Lee Wainer.

2313. Edith Davis (July 16, 1896–Oct. 26, 1987) B: Washington, DC. *Tell Her the Truth* (Cort, "Helen," Oct. 28, 1932) Hoch, Caroline!; Tell Her the Truth/W: R.P.Weston, Bert Lee, M: Joseph Tunbridge, Jack Waller.

2314. Garry Davis (July 28, 1921–) B: Philadelphia, PA. *Bless You All* (Mark Hellinger, revue, "Dec. 14, 1950): Don't Wanna Write About the South/WM: Harold Rome.

2315. Henrietta Elizabeth Davis *Porgy and Bess* (Radio City Music Hall, revival, "Bess," Apr. 7, 1983): Bess, You Is My Woman Now; I Loves You, Porgy/W: DuBose Heyward, Ira Gershwin, M: George Gershwin — Leavin' fo' de Promis' Lan'; What You Want Wid Bess/W: DuBose Heyward, M: George Gershwin — There's a Boat Dat's Leavin' Soon for New York/W: Ira Gershwin, M: George Gershwin.

2316. James Davis *The Whirl of Society* (Winter Garden, revue, CR, May 13, 1912): Hypnotizing Man/W: Harold Atteridge, M: Louis A. Hirsch. *Wars of the World* (Hippodrome, revue, Sept. 5, 1914): In Siam; When You Come Home Again Johnny; You're Just the One I've Waited For/WM: Manuel Klein.

2317. Jeffrey (Jeff) Bryan Davis (Oct. 6, 1973–) *The King and I* (Broadway, revival, "Louis Leonowens," Jan. 7, 1985): I Whistle a Happy Tune; A Puzzlement/W: Oscar Hammerstein II, M: Richard Rodgers.

2318. Jessie Bartlett Davis (Sept. 1859–May 14, 1905) B: Morris, IL. Born on a farm, the contralto took voice lessons in Chicago and was an early member of the Boston Ideal Opera Company. *Robin Hood* (Standard, "Alan-a-Dale," Sept. 28, 1891): The Bells of St. Swithins; Come the Bowmen in Lincoln Green; In Sherwood Forest; The Legend of the Chimes; Milkmaid's Song/W: Harry B. Smith, M: Reginald De Koven — Oh, Promise Me/W: Clement Scott, M: Reginald De Koven. *Prince Ananias* (Broadway, "Idalia," Nov. 20, 1894): Ah! He's a Prince; Amaryllis; The Hamlet of Fancy; I Am No Queen; Love Is Spring/W: Francis Neilson, M: Victor Herbert. *The Serenade* (Knickerbocker, "Dolores," Mar. 16, 1897): The Angelus; Don Jose of Sevilla; I Love Thee, I Adore Thee/W: Harry B. Smith, M: Victor Herbert.

2319. Lanier Davis *Tenderloin* (46th Street, "Martin," Oct. 17, 1960): The Army of the Just/W: Sheldon Harnick, M: Jerry Bock.

2320. Mac Davis (Jan. 21, 1942–) B: Lubbock, TX. The country music singer-songwriter worked his way into show business via ditch digging and pumping gas. His songs have been performed by 150 artists, including Elvis Presley and Nancy Sinatra. *The Will Rogers Follies* (Palace, CR, "Will Rogers," May 18, 1992): The Big Time; Favorite Son; Give a Man Enough Rope; Marry Me Now; Never Met a Man I Didn't Like; Presents for Mrs. Rogers; So Long Pa; Will-a-Mania/W: Betty Comden, Adolph Green, M: Cy Coleman.

2321. Mary Bond Davis (June 3, 1958–) B: Los Angeles, CA. *Mail* (Music Box, "Radio Singer" and "Mama Utility," Apr. 14, 1988): Gone So Long; Helplessness at Midnight; We're Gonna Turn Off Your Juice/W: Jerry Colker, M: Michael Rupert. *Jelly's Last Jam* (Virginia, "Miss Mamie," Apr. 26, 1992): Michigan Water/WM: trad. *Grease* (Eugene O'Neill, revival, CR, "Teen Angel," c 1994): Beauty School Dropout/WM: Jim Jacobs, Warren Casey.

2322. Melissa Anne Davis (Nov. 14–) B: Nashville, TN. *Les Miserables* (Broadway, CR, "Cosette"): A Heart Full of Love; In My Life/W: Herbert Kretzmer, M: Claude-Michel Schonberg.

2323. Michael Davis *The Most Happy Fella* (New York City Center, revival, "Ciccio," Feb. 10, 1959): Abbondanza; Benvenuta/WM: Frank Loesser. *Sweet Charity* (Palace, "Dark Glasses" and "Mike," Jan. 29, 1966): I Love to Cry at Weddings; You Should See Yourself/W: Dorothy Fields, M: Cy Coleman. *Rags* (Mark Hellinger, "Mike," Aug. 21, 1986): Big Tim; What's Wrong with That?/W: Stephen Schwartz, M: Charles Strouse.

2324. Ossie Davis (Dec. 18, 1917–Feb. 4, 2005) B: Cogdell, GA. Actor, writer, producer, director. He played Ponder Blue on the TV sitcom *Evening Shade* (1990). *Jamaica* (Imperial, "Cicero," Oct. 31, 1957): Little Biscuit; What Good Does It Do?/W: E.Y. Harburg, M: Harold Arlen. *The Zulu and the Zayda* (Cort, "Johannes," Nov. 10, 1965): Crocodile Wife; How Cold, Cold, Cold an Empty Room; The Water Wears Down the Stone; Zulu Hunting Song (Tkambuza)/WM: Harold Rome.

2325. Patti Davis (Oct. 21, 1952–) B: Los Angeles, CA. Daughter of Nancy Reagan. *Promises, Promises* (Shubert, CR, "Fran Kubelik," Aug. 17, 1970): I'll Never Fall in Love Again; Knowing When to Leave; Whoever You Are, I Love You; You'll Think of Someone/W: Hal David, M: Burt Bacharach. *Applause* (Palace, CR, "Eve Harrington," Apr. 16, 1971): The Best

Night of My Life; One Halloween/W: Lee Adams, M: Charles Strouse.

2326. Robert Davis (c 1917–July 19, 1993) *Meet the People* (Mansfield, revue, Dec. 25, 1940): The Stars Remain/W: Henry Myers, M: Jay Gorney.

2327. Sammy Davis, Jr. (Dec. 8, 1925–May 16, 1990) B: New York, NY. Actor, singer, dancer, comedian of stage, screen and TV. Son of SAMMY DAVIS, SR. He made his stage debut in vaudeville at age 2 or 3, with his uncle WILL MASTIN's troupe. *Mr. Wonderful* (Broadway, "Charlie Welch," Mar. 22, 1956): Ethel, Baby; I've Been Too Busy; Jacques d'Iraque; There; Too Close for Comfort; Without You I'm Nothing/W: Larry Holofcener, George David Weiss, M: Jerry Bock. *Golden Boy* (Majestic, "Joe Wellington," Oct. 20, 1964): Can't You See It?; Colorful; Don't Forget 127th Street; Gimme Some (Beer and Whiskey); I Want to Be with You; Night Song; No More; Stick Around; This Is the Life/W: Lee Adams, M: Charles Strouse. *Stop the World—I Want to Get Off* (New York State, revival, "Littlechap," Aug. 3, 1978): Family Fugue; Gonna Build a Mountain; I Wanna Be Rich; Lumbered; Melinki Meilchick; Mumbo Jumbo; Nag! Nag! Nag!; Once in a Lifetime; Someone Nice Like You; Typically English; What Kind of Fool Am I?/WM: Leslie Bricusse, Anthony Newley.

2328. Sammy Davis, Sr. (Dec. 12, 1900–May 21, 1988) B: Wilmington, NC. Father of SAMMY DAVIS, JR. Brother of WILL MASTIN. The three became known as the Will Mastin Trio. *Mr. Wonderful* (Broadway, "Dad," Mar. 22, 1956): Jacques d'Iraque/W: Larry Holofcener, George David Weiss, M: Jerry Bock.

2329. Abbott Davison *Nancy Brown* (Bijou, CR, "Muley Mustapha, Bey of Ballyhoo," Apr. 27, 1903): I'm Glad I'm Not Methusalem/WM: Eugene Ellsworth — It's a Most Disagreeable Thing to Do/W: Frederick Ranken, M: Henry Hadley — The Katy-did, the Cricket and the Frog/W: J. Rosamond Johnson, M: Bob Cole.

2330. Jack Davison *Two by Two* (Imperial, CR, "Shem," Sept. 5, 1971): As Far as I'm Concerned; Put Him Away; You Have Got to Have a Rudder on the Ark/W: Martin Charnin, M: Richard Rodgers. *La Cage aux Folles* (Palace, CR, "Albin," July 15, 1986): The Best of Times; I Am What I Am; La Cage aux Folles; A Little More Mascara; Masculinity; Song on the Sand; With You on My Arm/WM: Jerry Herman.

2331. Mae Daw *Ziegfeld Follies of 1924-1925* (New Amsterdam, revue, June 24, 1924): The

Beauty Contest/W: Joseph McCarthy, M: Harry Tierney, Victor Herbert — March of the Toys/W: Glen MacDonough, M: Victor Herbert.

2332. Patrick Dawe *The White Cat* (New Amsterdam, "Knocko," Nov. 2, 1905): Antonio/W: William Jerome, M: Jean Schwartz.

2333. Dominique Dawes *Grease* (Eugene O'Neill, revival, CR, "Patty Simcox," c 1996): Rydell Fight Song/WM: Jim Jacobs, Warren Casey.

2334. Eleanor Dawn *The Clinging Vine* (Knickerbocker, "Janet Milton," Dec. 25, 1922): Lady Luck; Roumania/W: Zelda Sears, M: Harold A. Levey.

2335. Gloria Dawn (1928–Apr. 2, 1978) *Lollipop* (Knickerbocker, "Virginia," Jan. 21, 1924): Deep in My Heart; Love in a Cottage; When We Are Married/W: Zelda Sears, M: Vincent Youmans. *Paradise Alley* (Casino, "Sylvia Van de Veer," Mar. 31, 1924): Friendship Leads Us to Love/W: Howard Johnson, M: Adorjan Otvos.

2336. Hazel Dawn (Mar. 23, 1890–Aug. 28, 1988) B: Ogden City, UT. Her family were Mormons. They moved to England so that she and her sister, MARGARET ROMAINE, could take voice lessons. There Hazel learned the violin, which she played in *The Pink Lady*. From 1914 to 1917 she made 11 silent pictures for The Famous Players Film Company. *Pink Lady* "Claudine, the Pink Lady," Mar. 13, 1911): The Duel; The Intriguers; The Kiss Waltz; My Beautiful Lady/W: C.M.S. McLellan, M: Ivan Caryll — Oh, So Gently/W: George Grossmith, Jr., M: Ivan Caryll. *The Little Café* (New Amsterdam, "Gaby Gaufrette," Nov. 10, 1913): Just Because It's You; So I Smile; Thy Mouth Is a Rose/W: C.M.S. McLellan, M: Ivan Caryll. *The Debutante* (Knickerbocker, "Elaine," Dec. 7, 1914): Call Around Again; The Golden Age; The Love of the Lorelei; Never Mention Love When We're Alone; Professor Cupid; Take Me Home with You/W: Robert B. Smith, M: Victor Herbert. *The Century Girl* (Century, revue, "The Century Girl" and "Eva Brown," Nov. 6, 1916): Alice in Wonderland/WM: Irving Berlin — The Century Girl/W: Henry Blossom, M: Victor Herbert. *Nifties of 1923* (Fulton, revue, "Sept. 25, 1923): Fabric of Dreams/W: B.G. DeSylva, Arthur Francis, M: Raymond Hubbell. *Keep Kool* (Morosco > Globe > Earl Carroll, revue, May 22, 1924): Out Where the Pavement Ends/WM: Jack Frost. *The Great Temptations* (Winter Garden, revue, May 18, 1926): Valencia/W: Clifford Grey, M: Jose Padilla.

2337. Hazel Dawn, Jr. (Sept. 7, 1929–) B:

New York, NY. Niece of HAZEL DAWN. Daughter of MARGARET ROMAINE. *My Romance* (Shubert > Adelphi, "Susan Van Tuyl," Oct. 19, 1948): Debutante; Written in Your Hand/W: Rowland Leigh, M: Sigmund Romberg.

2338. Thera Dawn *Enchanted Isle* (Lyric, "Angela," Sept. 19, 1927): Cowboy Potentate/WM: Ida Hoyt Chamberlain.

2339. Dan Dawson *Around the World* (Hippodrome, revue, "The Spider," Sept. 2, 1911): 'Arry and 'Arriet/WM: Manuel Klein. *Wars of the World* (Hippodrome, revue, Sept. 5, 1914): Baby Eyes/WM: Manuel Klein. *Come Along* (Nora Bayes > 39th Street, "Sgt. Chauncey Holmes," Apr. 8, 1919): Doughnuts for Doughboys/W: Bide Dudley, M: John L. Nelson — It's a Long Long Time Before Pay Day Comes 'Round/WM: John L. Nelson.

2340. Lillian Dawson *Earl Carroll's Vanities of 1931* (Earl Carroll > 44th Street, revue, CR, Jan. 4, 1932): Have a Heart/W: Harold Adamson, M: Burton Lane — Tonight or Never/WM: Raymond Klages, Jack Meskill, Vincent Rose.

2341. Mark Dawson (Mar. 23, 1920–) B: Philadelphia, PA. *By Jupiter* (Shubert, "A Herald," June 3, 1942): Bottoms Up; For Jupiter and Greece/W: Lorenz Hart, M: Richard Rodgers. *Sweethearts* (Shubert, revival, "Prince Franz," Jan. 21, 1947): Every Lover Must Meet His Fate/W: Robert B. Smith, M: Victor Herbert — To the Land of My Own Romance/W: Harry B. Smith, M: Victor Herbert. *High Button Shoes* (New Century, "Hubert Ogglethorpe," Oct. 9, 1947): Can't You Just See Yourself?; Next to Texas, I Love You; Nobody Ever Died for Dear Old Rutgers; You're My Girl/W: Sammy Cahn, M: Jule Styne. *Great to Be Alive* (Winter Garden, "Vince," Mar. 23, 1950): Call It Love; Dreams Ago; It's a Long Time Till Tomorrow; What a Day!/W: Walter Bullock, M: Abraham Ellstein. *Me and Juliet* (Majestic, "Bob," May 28, 1953): It Feels Good; Keep It Gay/W: Oscar Hammerstein II, M: Richard Rodgers. *Ankles Away* (Mark Hellinger, "Lieut. Bill Kelley," Apr. 18, 1955): His and Hers; Kiss Me and Kill Me with Love; Nothing at All/W: Dan Shapiro, M: Sammy Fain. *New Girl in Town* (46th Street, "Bartender," May 14, 1957): Sunshine Girl/WM: Bob Merrill. *Fiorello!* (Broadhurst, "Floyd Macduff," Nov. 23, 1959): I Love a Cop/W: Sheldon Harnick, M: Jerry Bock.

2342. Connie Day (Dec. 26, 1940–) B: New York, NY. *Molly* (Alvin, "Stella Hazelcorn," Nov. 1, 1973): High Class Ladies and Elegant Gentlemen; I Want to Share It with You/W:

Mack David, M: Jerry Livingston. *A Change in the Heir* (Edison, "Countess," Apr. 29, 1990): Exactly the Same as It Was; I Tried and I Tried and I Tried; The Weekend/W: George H. Gorham, M: Dan Sticco.

2343. Dorothy Day (c 1898–June 24, 1975) *The New Yorkers* (Edyth Totten, revue, Mar. 10, 1927): Burn 'Em Up/W: Henry Myers, M: Edgar Fairchild — Floating Thru the Air; He Who Gets Slapped; Here Comes the Prince of Wales; Self-Expression/W: Henry Myers, M: Arthur Schwartz. *Lady Do* (Liberty, CR, "Marion Hobart," May 23, 1927): In the Long Run (You'll Run After Me); Jiggle Your Feet; Lady Do; Snap Into It/W: Sam M. Lewis, Joe Young, M: Abel Baer.

2344. E. Marie Day *Yvette* (39th Street, "Paullette," Aug. 10, 1916): I Want All the Boys; Wonderful Kiss/WM: Frederick Herendeen.

2345. Edith Day (Apr. 10, 1896–May 2, 1971) B: Minneapolis, MN. M: PAT SOMERSET. The beautiful singing actress ingenue was a favorite on the musical stage in Britain and the U.S. *Pom-Pom* (Cohan, "Evelyn" and "Gina," Feb. 28, 1916): Come and Cuddle Me; Mister Love/W: Anne Caldwell, M: Hugo Felix. *Follow Me* (Casino, "Denise," Nov. 29, 1916): How Would You Like to Bounce a Baby on Your Knee?; Milady's Toilette Set/W: Alfred Bryan, Anna Held, M: Harry Tierney. *His Little Widows* (Astor, CR, "Murilla Lloyd," 1917): I Need Someone's Love/W: William Cary Duncan, M: William Schroeder — That Creepy Weepy Feeling/W: Rida Johnson Young, M: William Schroeder. *Going Up* (Liberty, "Grace Douglas," Dec. 25, 1917): First Act, Second Act, Third Act [Dec. 31, 1917]; Going Up; Here's to the Two of You; If You Look in Her Eyes; Kiss Me; (Everybody Ought to Know How to Do) The Tickle Toe; The Touch of a Woman's Hand/W: Otto Harbach, M: Louis A. Hirsch. *Irene* (Vanderbilt, "Irene O'Dare," Nov. 18, 1919): Alice Blue Gown; Irene; Sky Rocket; To Be Worthy (Worthy of You)/W: Joseph McCarthy, M: Harry Tierney. *Orange Blossoms* (Fulton, "Kitty," Sept. 19, 1922): A Dream of Orange Blossoms; In Hennequeville; I've Missed You; A Kiss in the Dark; Laugh All Your Troubles Away; Legend of the Glowworm; The Lonely Nest/W: B.G. DeSylva, M: Victor Herbert. *Wildflower* (Casino, "Nina Benedetto," Feb. 7, 1923): Apple Blossoms; Bambalina; Course I Will; I Can Always Find Another Partner; If I Told You; You Never Can Blame a Girl for Dreaming [Mar. 1923]/W: Otto Harbach, Oscar Hammerstein II, M: Vincent Youmans.

2346. Julietta Day (c 1894–Sept. 18, 1957) *Chin-Chin* (Globe, "Sen-Sen," Oct. 20, 1914): Shopping in the Orient/W: Anne Caldwell, M: Ivan Caryll. *The Riviera Girl* (New Amsterdam, "Birdie Springer," Sept. 24, 1917): Bungalow in Quoque/W: P.G. Wodehouse, M: Jerome Kern. *Oh, My Dear!* (Princess > 39th Street, "Jenny Wren," Nov. 27, 1918): I'd Ask No More; If They Ever Parted Me from You; Phoebe Snow; Try Again/W: P.G. Wodehouse, M: Louis A. Hirsch — The Train That Leaves for Town [Apr. 21, 1919]/W: P.G. Wodehouse, M: ?. *Sharlee* (Daly's, "Sharlee Saunders," Nov. 22, 1923): Love Today; My Sunshine; Toodle-oo/W: Alex Rogers, M: C. Luckeyth Roberts. *The Matinee Girl* (Forrest, "Bess Gordon," Feb. 1, 1926): Do I, Dear? I Do/WM: McElbert Moore — Holding Hands; Like-a-Me, Like-a-You/W: McElbert Moore, M: Frank Grey — What Difference Does It Make?/W: ?, M: Constance Shepard.

2347. Marilyn Day *If the Shoe Fits* (Century, "Delilah," Dec. 5, 1946): I Wish/W: June Carroll, M: David Raksin. *Small Wonder* (Coronet, revue, Sept. 15, 1948): The Commuters' Song; Nobody Told Me/W: Phyllis McGinley, M: Baldwin Bergersen — Show Off; When I Fall in Love/WM: Albert Selden — William McKinley High/W: Burt Shevelove, M: Albert Selden. *Kiss Me, Kate* (Broadway, revival, "Lois Lane" and "Bianca," Jan. 8, 1952): Always True to You in My Fashion; Tom, Dick or Harry; We Open in Venice; Why Can't You Behave?/WM: Cole Porter.

2348. Nola Day *The Golden Apple* (Alvin, "Mother Hare," Apr. 20, 1954): Circe, Circe/W: John Latouche, M: Jerome Moross.

2349. Richard Day *Snow White and the Seven Dwarfs* (Radio City Music Hall, "Happy," Oct. 18, 1979/Jan. 11, 1980): Bluddle-uddle-um-dum (The Washing Song); The Dwarf's Yodel Song (The Silly Song); Heigh-Ho/W: Larry Morey, M: Frank Churchill.

2350. Marie Dayne *The Madcap* (Royale, "Petunia," Jan. 31, 1928): Why Can't It Happen to Me?/W: Clifford Grey, M: Maurie Rubens. *The Red Robe* (Shubert, CR, "Marie," Apr. 22, 1929): I've Got It/W: Mann Holiner, M: Alberta Nichols — The Thrill of a Kiss/W: Harry B. Smith, M: Jean Gilbert.

2351. Danny Dayton (Nov. 20, 1923–Feb. 6, 1999) B: Jersey City, NJ. He played Hank Pivnik on the TV sitcom *All in the Family* (1977). *A Funny Thing Happened on the Way to the Forum* (Alvin, CR, "Lycus," Aug. 19, 1963): Everybody Ought to Have a Maid/WM: Stephen Sondheim. *A Funny Thing Happened on* *the Way to the Forum* (Alvin, CR, "Prologus" and "Pseudolus," Aug. 1964): Bring Me My Bride; Comedy Tonight; Everybody Ought to Have a Maid; Free; Lovely; Pretty Little Picture/WM: Stephen Sondheim.

2352. Richard Deacon (May 14, 1922–Aug. 8, 1984) B: Philadelphia, PA. He was Lumpy's father on the TV sitcom *Leave It to Beaver* (1957), and Melvin Cooley on the classic *Dick Van Dyke Show* (1961). *Hello, Dolly!* (St. James, CR, "Horace Vandergelder," Dec. 26, 1969): Before the Parade Passes By/WM: Lee Adams, Charles Strouse, Jerry Herman — Hello, Dolly!; It Takes a Woman; So Long, Dearie/WM: Jerry Herman — Motherhood/WM: Bob Merrill, Jerry Herman.

2353. Arthur Deagon (Jan. 1, 1873–Sept. 4, 1927) B: Seaforth, Ontario, Canada. *King Dodo* (Daly's, "Pedro," May 12, 1902): The Cat's Quartet (The Miller's Cats); I'll Shut My Eyes and Think It's You; In Lands Unknown; When You Are Mine/W: Frank Pixley, M: Gustav Luders. *Ziegfeld Follies of 1908* (Jardin de Paris > New York, revue, June 15, 1908): The Big Hats; The International Merry Widow; The Rajah of Broadway/W: Harry B. Smith, M: Maurice Levi. *Ziegfeld Follies of 1909* (Jardin de Paris, revue, June 14, 1909): My Cousin Caruso/W: Edward Madden, M: Gus Edwards. *Ziegfeld Follies of 1914* (New Amsterdam, revue, June 1, 1914): I'm a Statesman; Night Life in Old Manhattan/W: Gene Buck, M: Raymond Hubbell — My Little Pet Chicken/W: George V. Hobart, M: Dave Stamper, Raymond Hubbell. *Hip-Hip Hooray* (Hippodrome, revue, "The Chubby Comedian," Sept. 30, 1915): The Wedding of Jack and Jill/W: John L. Golden, M: Raymond Hubbell. *Little Nellie Kelly* (Liberty, "Capt. John Kelly," Nov. 13, 1922): The Great New York Police; The Name of Kelly/WM: George M. Cohan. *Rose-Marie* (Imperial, "Sgt. Malone," Sept. 2, 1924): The Mounties/W: Otto Harbach, Oscar Hammerstein II, M: Rudolf Friml, Herbert Stothart — Only a Kiss; Vive la Canadienne/W: Otto Harbach, Oscar Hammerstein II, M: Herbert Stothart — Rose-Marie/W: Otto Harbach, Oscar Hammerstein II, M: Rudolf Friml.

2354. Grace Deagon *Cinderella on Broadway* (Winter Garden, revue, June 24, 1920): Cinderella on Broadway; Cindy/W: Harold Atteridge, M: Bert Grant.

2355. Augusta Dean *The Passing Show of 1916* (Winter Garden, revue, CR, Sept. 4, 1916): Let Cupid In/W: Harold Atteridge, M: Otto Motzan — So This Is Paris!/W: Harold Atteridge, M: Harry Tierney.

2356. Gerri Dean *The Me Nobody Knows* (Helen Hayes > Longacre, "Melba," Dec. 18, 1970): Black; Dream Babies/W: Will Holt, M: Gary William Friedman.

2357. Laura Dean (May 27, 1963–) B: Smithtown, NY. *Doonesbury* (Biltmore, "Boopsie," Nov. 21, 1983): Another Memorable Meal; Complicated Man; Graduation; I Can Have It All; Muffy & the Topsiders/W: Garry Trudeau, M: Elizabeth Swados. *The Who's Tommy* (St. James, CR, "Mrs. Walker," c 1994): Christmas; Do You Think It's Alright; Go to the Mirror; I Believe My Own Eyes; It's a Boy; Smash the Mirror; There's a Doctor; Twenty-One/WM: Pete Townshend.

2358. Virginia Dean *The Liberty Belles* (Madison Square, "Augusta Glose," Sept. 30, 1901): To Marry a Millionaire/W: Harry B. Smith, M: John W. Bratton.

2359. Peter DeAnda (Mar. 10, 1940–) B: Pittsburgh, PA. *The Zulu and the Zayda* (Cort, "Peter," Nov. 10, 1965): Like the Breeze Blows/WM: Harold Rome.

2360. Berna Deane *The Love Call* (Majestic, "Bonita Canby," Oct. 24, 1927): Bonita; Eyes That Love; Hear the Trumpet Call; I Am Captured; The Lark/W: Harry B. Smith, M: Sigmund Romberg.

2361. Douglas Deane *Guys and Dolls* (46th Street, "Rusty Charlie," Nov. 24, 1950): Fugue for Tinhorns/WM: Frank Loesser.

2362. Sydney (Dean) Deane Part of the dance team known as Reed and Dean. *Florodora* (Casino > New York, "Frank Abercoed," Nov. 10, 1900): The Shade of the Palm/W: Owen Hall, M: Leslie Stuart — Somebody/WM: ?. *The Mocking Bird* (Bijou, "Eugene de Lorme," Nov. 10, 1902): France Glorious France; In Silence/W: Sydney Rosenfeld, M: A. Baldwin Sloane. *The Knickerbocker Girl* (Herald Square, "Sanford Merton," June 15, 1903): Hear the Band; I Only Know I Love You; Just a Smile/W: George Totten Smith, M: Alfred E. Aarons.

2363. Toby Deane *Hit the Trail* (Mark Hellinger, "Aggie July," Dec. 2, 1954): Blue Sierras; It Was Destiny; Men Are a Pain in the Neck; Nevada Hoe Down; The Wide Open Spaces/W: Elizabeth Miele, M: Frederico Valerio.

2364. Jefferson De Angelis (Nov. 30, 1859– Mar. 20, 1933) B: San Francisco, CA. Inspired clown of comic opera and musicals. *Fantana* (Lyric, "Hawkins," Jan. 14, 1905): Darby and Joan; Drop In on Me at Luncheon; That's Art; What Would Mrs. Grundy Say?/W: Robert B. Smith, M: Raymond Hubbell — Tammany [added]/W: Vincent Bryan, M: Gus Edwards.

The Gay White Way (Casino, revue, "George Dane," Oct. 7, 1907): The Great White Way; The School of Acting; Theodore/W: Sydney Rosenfeld, M: Ludwig Englander. *The Beauty Spot* (Herald Square, "Gen. Samovar," Apr. 10, 1909): The Boulevard Glide/W: E. Ray Goetz, M: Melville Gideon — Choose Her in the Morning/WM: Will R. Barnes, R.P. Weston — The Cinematograph; He Loved Her Tender/W: Joseph W. Herbert, M: Reginald De Koven — She Sells Sea Shells/W: Terry Sullivan, M: Harry Gifford. *The Pearl Maiden* (New York, "Pinkerton Kerr," Jan. 22, 1912): Davy Jones; Look at the Package They Handed to Me; You Can Never Tell Until You Try/W: Arthur F. Kales, Earle C. Anthony, M: Harry Auracher. *Rob Roy* (Liberty, revival, "Dugald MacWheeble, Mayor of Perth," Sept. 15, 1913): My Hairt Is in the Highlands; My True Love Is a Shepherdess/W: Harry B. Smith, M: Reginald De Koven. *The Highwayman* (44th Street, revival, "Foxy Quiller," May 2, 1917): The Farmer and the Scarecrow; Gypsy Song; On the Track/W: Harry B. Smith, M: Reginald De Koven. *Some Party* (Al Jolson, revue, Apr. 15, 1922): In Yama Yama Land/W: Henry Creamer, M: Turner Layton.

2365. Delfino De Arco *South Pacific* (New York City Center, revival, "Jerome," Apr. 26, 1961): Dites-Moi/W: Oscar Hammerstein II, M: Richard Rodgers.

2366. Isabel De Armand *The Beauty Spot* (Herald Square, "Pomare," Apr. 10, 1909): Coo-Ee; The Jungle Man/W: Joseph W. Herbert, M: Reginald De Koven.

2367. Ada Deaves (c 1866–Sept. 16, 1920) *Aladdin, Jr.* (Broadway, "Widow Bohea," Apr. 8, 1895): Beauteous Widow Bohea; Laundry Trio; The Stars Alone Can Tell; Women, Wine and Song/W: J. Cheever Goodwin, M: W.H. Batchelor.

2368. Alf De Ball *The Beauty Spot* (Herald Square, "Nikolas Kromeski," Apr. 10, 1909): Toujours la Politesse/W: Joseph W. Herbert, M: Reginald De Koven.

2369. Clara De Beers *The Soul Kiss* (New York, "Cleopatra," Jan. 28, 1908): The Soul Kiss (Just for You from Above)/W: Lewis Gates, M: Maurice Levi.

2370. Cicely Debenham (Apr. 17, 1891–Nov. 7, 1955) B: Aylesbury, Bucks., England. *Hammerstein's Nine O'Clock Revue* (Century roof, revue, Oct. 4, 1923): Girls of the Old Brigade/WM: ?— Susannah's Squeaking Shoes/W: Arthur Weigall, M: Muriel Lillie — That's the Tune/W: Nelson Keys, Graham John, M: Max Darewski.

2371. Dorothy Debenham *Bitter Sweet* (Ziegfeld, "Hansi," Nov. 5, 1929): Ladies of the Town/WM: Noel Coward.

2372. Jeff De Benning *How to Succeed in Business Without Really Trying* (46th Street, CR, "J.B. Biggley," Oct. 19, 1964): Been a Long Day; Brotherhood of Man; Grand Old Ivy; Love from a Heart of Gold/WM: Frank Loesser.

2373. Yvonne De Carlo (Sept. 1, 1922–) B: Vancouver, British Columbia. Screen actress from the 1940s on. Among many TV credits, she was Lily Munster in *The Munsters* (1964). *Follies* (Winter Garden, "Carlotta Campion," Apr. 4, 1971): I'm Still Here/WM: Stephen Sondheim.

2374. Edith Decker *The Duke of Duluth* (Majestic, "Ameera," Sept. 11, 1905): My Sweet Wild Rose; Through All Eternity; Zenedee/W: George Broadhurst, M: Max S. Witt. *The Vanderbilt Cup* (Broadway > New York, "Clarinda Larkspur," Jan. 16, 1906): If You Were Lost to Me [Jan. 29, 1906]; The Little Chauffeur/W: Raymond W. Peck, M: Robert Hood Bowers. *A Parisian Model* (Broadway, CR, "Violette," Jan. 20, 1908): On San Francisco Bay/W: Vincent Bryan, M: Gertrude Hoffmann — The Whistling Yankee Girl/W: Edward P. Moran, M: Seymour Furth. *Miss Innocence* (New York, "Helen Legarde," Nov. 30, 1908): I'm Crazy When the Band Begins to Play/W: William Jerome, M: Jean Schwartz. *Havana* (Casino, "Consuelo," Feb. 11, 1909): I'm a Cuban Girl/W: Adrian Ross, M: Leslie Stuart — What Shall I Do with the Rest?/W: Adrian Ross, George Arthurs, M: Leslie Stuart. *The Girl and the Kaiser* (Herald Square, "Minka," Nov. 22, 1910): Cradled in Thy Arms; Hungarian Rhythmic Air; Only a Gypsy Maid/W: Leonard Liebling, M: Georges Jarno. *The Wife Hunters* (Herald Square, "Juanita De Laperra," Nov. 2, 1911): In Your Arms; On the Avenue/WM: David Kempner, Anatole Friedland, Malvin F. Franklin — Love Waves/W: David Kempner, M: Anatole Friedland. *The Rose Maid* (Globe, "Princess Hilda Von Lahn," Apr. 22, 1912): The Course of True Love; The Happy Family; Liberty Hall; One Waltz, Only One Waltz/W: Robert B. Smith, M: Bruno Granichstaedten. *Katinka* (44th Street > Lyric, "Olga Nashan," Dec. 23, 1915): Allah's Holiday; Charms Are Fairest When They're Hidden; Skidiskischatch; Stamboul/W: Otto Harbach, M: Rudolf Friml. *Two Little Girls in Blue* (George M. Cohan, "Mary Bird," May 3, 1921): Just Like You/W: Ira Gershwin, M: Paul Lannin.

2375. Elsie Decker *The Yankee Princess* (Knickerbocker, "Yvette," Oct. 2, 1922): Lotus

Flower/W: B.G. DeSylva, M: Emmerich Kalman.

2376. Marceline Decker *Man of La Mancha* (Marquis, revival, "The Housekeeper," Apr. 24, 1992): I'm Only Thinking of Him/W: Joe Darion, M: Mitch Leigh.

2377. Paul Decker *The Girl Who Smiles* (Lyric > Longacre, "Anatole," Aug. 9, 1915): Join the Families; A Little Difference at Breakfast/WM: Edward A. Paulton, Adolf Philipp, Jean Briquet.

2378. Al DeCristo (Aug. 14, 1953–) B: Providence, RI. *Roza* (Royale, "Max," Oct. 1, 1987): Max's Visit/W: Julian More, M: Gilbert Becaud.

2379. Pauline Dee *The Houseboat on the Styx* (Liberty, "Queen of Sheba," Dec. 25, 1928): Red River/W: Monte Carlo, M: Alma Sanders. *Mystery Moon* (Royale, "Goldie Del Monte," June 23, 1930): Mystery Moon; One Night in the Rain/W: Monte Carlo, M: Alma Sanders.

2380. Deborah Deeble (Oct. 27, 1945–) B: Plainfield, NJ. *George M!* (Palace, CR, "Agnes Nolan"): Billie/WM: George M. Cohan.

2381. Deedee *Sea Legs* (Mansfield, "Deedee," May 18, 1937): Catalina; The Opposite Sex/W: Arthur Swanstrom, M: Michael H. Cleary.

2382. Sandra Deel *Look Ma, I'm Dancin'* (Adelphi, "Suzy," Jan. 29, 1948): If You'll Be Mine/WM: Hugh Martin.

2383. Mickey Deems (Apr. 22, 1925–) B: Englewood, NJ. *Little Me* (Lunt-Fontanne, "Pinchley, Jr." and "Yulnick," Nov. 17, 1962): Deep Down Inside; Goodbye (The Prince's Farewell)/W: Carolyn Leigh, M: Cy Coleman. *Little Me* (Lunt-Fontanne, CR, "Noble Eggleston" and "Mr. Pinchley," and "Val du Val" and "Fred Poitrine" and "Prince Cherney," June 12, 1963): Boom-Boom (Le Grand Boom-Boom); Deep Down Inside; Goodbye (The Prince's Farewell); I Love You (As Much as I Am Able); Real Live Girl/W: Carolyn Leigh, M: Cy Coleman.

2384. Gladyce Deering *Woof, Woof* (Royale, "Virginia Lee Penny," Dec. 25, 1929): That Certain Thing; You're All the World to Me/WM: Eddie Brandt, Edward Pola.

2385. Jane Deering *Early to Bed* (Broadhurst, "Lois," June 17, 1943): Early to Bed; The Ladies Who Sing with a Band; Slightly Less Than Wonderful; There's Yes in the Air (Martinique)/W: George Marion, Jr., M: Fats Waller.

2386. Alfred Deery *Betsy* (Herald Square, "Earl of Dexminster," Dec. 11, 1911): Aristocracy; The Day Before the Morning After/W: Will B. Johnstone, M: Alexander Johnstone.

2387. Jacy De Filippo *A Christmas Carol* (Paramount Madison Square Garden, "Fan at 10," Dec. 1, 1994): A Place Called Home/W: Lynn Ahrens, M: Alan Menken.

2388. Dora de Fillippe *A Princess of Kensington* (Broadway, "Kenna," Aug. 31, 1903): If You Will Spare the Time; A Mountain Stood Like a Grim Outpost; Twin Butterflies That Fitfully Fall; Who That Knows How I Love You, Love/W: Basil Hood, M: Edward German.

2389. Patsy (Patsie) De Forest *Maytime* (Lyric > Broadhurst, CR, "Ermintrude D'Albert," Aug. 1918): Dancing Will Keep You Young/W: Cyrus D. Wood, M: Sigmund Romberg. *Come Along* (Nora Bayes > 39th Street, "Peggy Penny," Apr. 8, 1919): But You Can't Believe Them/WM: Blanche Merrill. *Oh, What a Girl!* (Shubert, "Susie Smith," July 28, 1919): Baby/W: Gus Kahn, M: Egbert Van Alstyne — Dainty Little Girl Like You/W: Edgar Smith, M: Charles Jules, Jacques Presburg — Prince Charming/W: Edward Clark, M: Charles Jules, Jacques Presburg.

2390. Muriel De Forrest *The Century Revue* (Century, revue, July 12, 1920): Fig Leaf Number/W: Alfred Bryan, M: Jean Schwartz. *The Midnight Rounders of 1920* (Century roof, revue, CR, Oct. 4, 1920): The Swing; Three Little Marys/W: Alfred Bryan, M: Jean Schwartz.

2391. Lauri de Frece (Mar. 3, 1881–Aug. 25, 1921) B: Liverpool, England. M: FAY COMPTON. Popular comedian of British musicals who died too young of peritonitis. *Tonight's the Night* (Shubert, "Henry," Dec. 24, 1914): Dancing Mad; Land and Water; Too Particular/WM: Paul Rubens, Percy Greenbank.

2392. Marcy DeGonge (May 4, 1957–) B: Newark, NJ. *Cats* (Winter Garden, CR, "Jennyanydots," c 1988): Bustopher Jones; The Old Gumbie Cat/W: T.S. Eliot, M: Andrew Lloyd Webber.

2393. Sydney de Grey (June 16, 1886–June 30, 1941) B: England. *The Girl from Paris* (Wallack's, revival, "Algernon P. Ducie," Jan. 17, 1898): The Festive Continong/W: George Dance, M: Ivan Caryll. *Mr. Wix of Wickham* (Bijou, "Duke of Tadminster," Sept. 19, 1904): Because I Am a Duke/WM: John Wagner, Jerome Kern.

2394. Jossie (Josie) de Guzman *Runaways* (Plymouth, "Lidia," May 13, 1978): Lullaby for Luis; Once Upon a Time; Senoras de la Noche; Song of a Child Prostitute/WM: Elizabeth Swados. *Carmelina* (St. James, "Gia Campbell," Apr. 8, 1979): All That He'd Want Me to Be/W: Alan Jay Lerner, M: Burton Lane. *West Side Story*

(Minskoff, revival, "Maria," Feb. 14, 1980): A Boy Like That; I Feel Pretty; I Have a Love; One Hand, One Heart; Tonight/W: Stephen Sondheim, M: Leonard Bernstein. *Guys and Dolls* (Martin Beck, revival, "Sarah Brown," Apr. 14, 1992): Follow the Fold; If I Were a Bell; I'll Know; I've Never Been in Love Before; Marry the Man Today/WM: Frank Loesser.

2395. Carter DeHaven (Oct. 5, 1886–July 20, 1977) B: Chicago, IL. M: FLORA PARKER, 1907–1928, with whom he sang and danced in vaudeville. Their daughter was GLORIA DE-HAVEN. From 1915 to 1921 the couple appeared in silent movies. *Miss Dolly Dollars* (Knicker-bocker > New Amsterdam, "Guy Gay," Sept. 4, 1905): Dolly Dollars; Life's a Masquerade; The Self-Made Family; She's a Lady with Money/W: Harry B. Smith, M: Victor Herbert. *Hanky-Panky* (Broadway, "Blackie Daw," Aug. 5, 1912): The Lyre Bird and the Jay; Under the Ragtime Flag/W: E. Ray Goetz, M: A. Baldwin Sloane — The Million Dollar Ball/WM: E. Ray Goetz, Irving Berlin. *All Aboard* (44th Street roof garden, revue, "Dick," June 5, 1913): Honey, You Were Made for Me/W: Earl Carroll, M: Jack Glogau — In My Garden of Eden for Two/WM: E. Ray Goetz — Mr. Broadway, U.S.A./WM: E. Ray Goetz, Malvin F. Franklin. *His Little Widows* (Astor, "Pete Lloyd," Apr. 30, 1917): I Want 'Em All; A Wife for Each Day in the Week/W: William Cary Duncan, M: William Schroe-der — Love Me Best of All/WM: ?— My Love, I'm Keeping a Secret/W: Rida Johnson Young, M: William Schroeder.

2396. Charles De Haven *The Passing Show of 1913* (Winter Garden, revue, July 24, 1913): Foolish Cinderella Girl/W: Harold Atteridge, M: Al W. Brown.

2397. Gloria DeHaven (July 23, 1923–) B: Los Angeles, CA. Her parents were CARTER DEHAVEN and FLORA PARKER. She sang with the Bob Crosby and Jan Savitt bands, and appeared in 1940s movie musicals. *Seventh Heaven* (ANTA, "Diane," May 26, 1955): If It's a Dream; Sun at My Window, Love at My Door; Where Is That Someone for Me?/W: Stella Unger, M: Victor Young.

2398. Gerald de la Fontaine *Swingin' the Dream* (Center, "Snug," Nov. 29, 1939): Peace, Brother!; There's Gotta Be a Weddin'/W: Eddie DeLange, M: James Van Heusen.

2399. Jere Delaney (1888–Jan. 2, 1954) *The Greenwich Village Follies of 1919* (Nora Bayes, revue, CR, Sept. 15, 1919): I'm Ashamed to Look the Moon in the Face/W: John Murray Ander-son, M: A. Baldwin Sloane — The Stolen Mel-ody/W: Phil Schwartz, M: Nora Bayes. *Merce-nary Mary* (Longacre, "Patrick O'Brien," Apr. 13, 1925): Cherchez la Femme (Get Your Woman); Just You and I and the Baby/WM: William B. Friedlander, Con Conrad. *A Night in Spain* (44th Street, revue, CR, Nov. 7, 1927): International Vamp/W: Alfred Bryan, M: Jean Schwartz.

2400. Martin Delaney *The Wedding Trip* (Broadway, "Corp. Oscar," Dec. 25, 1911): Here Is the Tunic of a Soldier/W: Harry B. Smith, M: Reginald De Koven.

2401. George De La Pena (1955–) B: New York, NY. M: REBECCA WRIGHT. *The Red Shoes* (Gershwin, "Grisha Ljubov," Dec. 16, 1993): Corps de Ballet; It's a Fairy Tale; The Rag/W: Bob Merrill, M: Jule Styne — Do Svedanya/W: Bob Merrill, Marsha Norman, M: Jule Styne.

2402. Mario De Laval *Carousel* (New York City Center > Majestic, revival, "Jigger Crai-gin," Jan. 25, 1949): Blow High, Blow Low/W: Oscar Hammerstein II, M: Richard Rodgers.

2403. Carmen de Lavallade (Mar. 6, 1931–) New Orleans, LA. *Hot Spot* (Majestic, "Iram," Apr. 19, 1963): Nebraska/W: Martin Charnin, M: Mary Rodgers.

2404. Edwin Delbridge *My Maryland* (Al Jolson, "Dr. Hal Boyd," Sept. 12, 1927): Boys in Gray; The Mocking Bird; Strolling with the One I Love the Best/W: Dorothy Donnelly, M: Sig-mund Romberg.

2405. Lennie Del Duca, Jr. *Marlowe* (Ri-alto, "William Shakespeare," Oct. 12, 1981): Because I'm a Woman; Christopher; Emelia; The Funeral Dirge; Higher Than High/WM: Leo Rost, Jimmy Horowitz.

2406. Don De Leo (June 30, 1904–Aug. 14, 1979) *Billion Dollar Baby* (Alvin, "Jerry Bo-nanza," Dec. 21, 1945): Speaking of Pals/W: Betty Comden, Adolph Green, M: Morton Gould.

2407. Michael DeLeon *South Pacific* (Majes-tic > Broadway, "Jerome," Apr. 7, 1949): Dites-Moi/W: Oscar Hammerstein II, M: Richard Rodgers.

2408. Noel DeLeon *South Pacific* (Majestic > Broadway, "Jerome," Apr. 7, 1949): Dites-Moi/W: Oscar Hammerstein II, M: Richard Rodgers.

2409. Harry Delf (Aug. 28, 1892–Feb. 7, 1964) B: New York, NY. Dancer, playwright and songwriter. *The Midnight Girl* (44th Street, "Francois," Feb. 23, 1914): Love and Victory/ WM: Adolf Philipp, Edward A. Paulton, Jean Briquet. *Hello, Broadway!* (Astor, revue, CR,

"Bum Lung," Mar. 22, 1915): That Old Fashioned Cakewalk/WM: George M. Cohan, Jean Schwartz. *The Cohan Revue of 1916* (Astor, revue, "Billy Holliday," Feb. 9, 1916): The Fair and Warmer Cocktail/WM: George M. Cohan. *The Rainbow Girl* (New Amsterdam, "Ernest Bennett," Apr. 1, 1918): I'll Think of You; Let's Go Down to the Shop; Love's Ever New; Soon We'll Be Seen Upon the Screen/W: Rennold Wolf, M: Louis A. Hirsch. *The Greenwich Village Follies of 1919* (Nora Bayes, revue, c Sept. 15, 1919): The Critics' Blues/W: Philip Bartholomae, John Murray Anderson, M: A. Baldwin Sloane — I'm Ashamed to Look the Moon in the Face/W: John Murray Anderson, M: A. Baldwin Sloane — The Stolen Melody/W: Phil Schwartz, M: Nora Bayes. *Jimmie* (Apollo, "Milton Blum," Nov. 17, 1920): All That I Want; It Isn't Hard to Do; A Little Plate of Soup/W: Oscar Hammerstein II, Otto Harbach, M: Herbert Stothart. *Sun Showers* (Astor, "Jerry Jackson," Feb. 5, 1923): How Do You Doodle?; If the Old Folks Could See Us Now; In the Morning; Sun Showers/WM: Harry Delf.

2410. Chet D'Elia (Nov. 19, 1944–) B: Bridgeport, CT. *The Lieutenant* (Lyceum, "1st General," Mar. 9, 1975): Final Report; Let's Believe in the Captain; Look for the Men with Potential; There's No Other Solution; Twenty-Eight; We've Chosen You, Lieutenant/WM: Gene Curty, Nitra Scharfman, Chuck Strand.

2411. Dorothy Dell (Jan. 30, 1915–June 8, 1934) B: Hattiesburg, MS. She was voted both Miss America and Miss Universe of 1930. One of her few movies was *Little Miss Marker* with Shirley Temple (1934). She was killed in a car accident. *Ziegfeld Follies of 1931* (Ziegfeld, revue, July 1, 1931): Was I?/W: Charles Farrell, M: Chick Endor. *Tattle Tales* (Broadhurst, revue, June 1, 1933): Breaking Up a Rhythm/W: George Waggoner, M: Edward Ward — Sing American Tunes/W: Frank Fay, William Walsh, M: Edward Ward.

2412. Gabriel Dell (Oct. 7, 1920–July 3, 1988) B: Barbados, British West Indies. One of the original Dead End Kids. For several years he was a TV regular on *The Steve Allen Show* (1956). *Ankles Aweigh* (Mark Hellinger, "Spud," Apr. 18, 1955): Here's to Dear Old Us; Walk Like a Sailor/W: Dan Shapiro, M: Sammy Fain. *Can-Can* (New York City Center, revival, "Boris Adzinidzinadze," May 16, 1962): Come Along with Me; If You Loved Me Truly; Never, Never Be an Artist/WM: Cole Porter. *Wonderful Town* (New York City Center, revival, "Chick Clark," Feb. 13, 1963): Conversation Piece (Nice Talk, Nice People)/W: Betty Comden, Adolph Green, M: Leonard Bernstein. *Oklahoma!* (New York City Center, revival, "Ali Hakim," Feb. 27, 1963): It's a Scandal! It's a Outrage!/W: Oscar Hammerstein II, M: Richard Rodgers. *Anyone Can Whistle* (Majestic, "Comtroller Schub," Apr. 4, 1964): I've Got You to Lean On/WM: Stephen Sondheim.

2413. Joseph Dellasorte (May 5, 1940–) B: Yonkers, NY. *Billy* (Billy Rose, "John Thorp," Mar. 22, 1969): Whiskers' Dance/WM: Ron Dante, Gene Allen. *Ari* (Mark Hellinger, "Joab," Jan. 15, 1971): The Saga of the Haganah/W: Leon Uris, M: Walt Smith.

2414. Elaine Delmar *Jerome Kern Goes to Hollywood* (Ritz, revue, Jan. 23, 1986): All the Things You Are; Can I Forget You?; Can't Help Lovin' Dat Man; I've Told Ev'ry Little Star; Ol' Man River; The Song Is You/W: Oscar Hammerstein II, M: Jerome Kern — Bojangles of Harlem; A Fine Romance; I Dream Too Much; Pick Yourself Up; Remind Me/W: Dorothy Fields, M: Jerome Kern — Californ-i-ay/W: E.Y. Harburg, M: Jerome Kern — Day Dreaming/W: Gus Kahn, M: Jerome Kern — Here Comes the Show Boat/W: Billy Rose, M: Maceo Pinkard — I'm Old Fashioned/W: Johnny Mercer, M: Jerome Kern — Long Ago and Far Away; The Show Must Go On/W: Ira Gershwin, M: Jerome Kern — Look for the Silver Lining/W: B.G. DeSylva, M: Jerome Kern — Make Way for Tomorrow/W: E.Y. Harburg, Ira Gershwin, M: Jerome Kern — They Didn't Believe Me/W: Herbert Reynolds, M: Jerome Kern — Till the Clouds Roll By/WM: Jerome Kern, Guy Bolton, P.G. Wodehouse — Who?/W: Oscar Hammerstein II, Otto Harbach, M: Jerome Kern.

2415. John Delmar *Keep Moving* (Forrest, revue, Aug. 23, 1934): Wake Up, Sleepy Moon/W: Jack Scholl, M: Max Rich.

2416. Josephine Del Mar *Meet the People* (Mansfield, revue, Dec. 25, 1940): In Chi-Chi-Castenango/W: Henry Myers, M: Jay Gorney.

2417. Kenny Delmar (Sept. 5, 1910–July 14, 1984) B: Boston, MA. Memorable as Senator Beauregard Claghorn of Allen's Alley on radio's *The Fred Allen Show* (1939). *Texas, Li'l Darlin'* (Mark Hellinger, "Hominy Smith," Nov. 25, 1949): Love Me, Love My Dog; Politics; Texas, Li'l Darlin'; They Talk a Different Language (The Yodel Blues); Whoopin' and a–Hollerin'/W: Johnny Mercer, M: Robert Emmett Dolan.

2418. George Del Monte *Irma La Douce* (Plymouth, "M. Bougne," Sept. 29, 1960): But/Eng. W: Julian More, David Heneker, Monty Norman, M: Marguerite Monnot.

2419. Herbert Delmore *The Vagabond King* (Casino, "Noel Le Jolys," Sept. 21, 1925): Hunting; Nocturne/W: Brian Hooker, M: Rudolf Friml.

2420. Jack De Lon *The Most Happy Fella* (New York City Center, revival, "Herman," Feb. 10, 1959): Big D; I Like Ev'rybody; Standing on the Corner/WM: Frank Loesser. *Street Scene* (New York City Center, revival, "Lippo Fiorentino," Feb. 13, 1960): Ice Cream/W: Langston Hughes, Elmer Rice, M: Kurt Weill. *A Family Affair* (Billy Rose, "Mr. Weaver," Jan. 27, 1962): Harmony; Right Girls/W: James Goldman, William Goldman, M: John Kander. *Jennie* (Majestic, "Abe O'Shaugnessy," Oct. 17, 1963): Born Again; I Believe in Takin' a Chance; When You're Far Away from New York Town/W: Howard Dietz, M: Arthur Schwartz. *Guys and Dolls* (New York City Center, revival, "Nicely-Nicely Johnson," Apr. 28, 1965): Fugue for Tinhorns; Guys and Dolls; The Oldest Established; Sit Down, You're Rockin' the Boat/WM: Frank Loesser. *The Most Happy Fella* (New York City Center, revival, "Herman," May 11, 1966): same as above. *Carousel* (New York City Center, revival, "Enoch Snow," Dec. 15, 1966): Geraniums in the Winder; Mister Snow; A Real Nice Clambake; When the Children Are Asleep/W: Oscar Hammerstein II, M: Richard Rodgers.

2421. George De Long *The Messenger Boy* (Daly's, "Comte Le Fleury," Sept. 16, 1901): Bradshaw's Guide/W: Adrian Ross, M: Ivan Caryll.

2422. Joseph del Puente *Have a Heart* (Liberty, "Yussef," Jan. 11, 1917): Samarkand/W: P.G. Wodehouse, M: Jerome Kern.

2423. Irene Delroy (1898–) B: Bloomington, IL. *Frivolities of 1920* (44th Street, revue, Jan. 8, 1920): Peachie/W: Jack Yellen, M: Albert Gumble. *The Greenwich Village Follies of 1923* (Winter Garden, revue, Sept. 20, 1923): Cock-a-Doodle Doo [Oct. 29, 1923]/W: Cliff Friend, M: Con Conrad — Lovey; Moonlight Kisses/W: John Murray Anderson, Irving Caesar, M: Con Conrad — Where Is My Boy?/WM?. *Vogues of 1924* (Shubert, revue, Mar. 27, 1924): The Belle of the Ball/W: Clifford Grey, M: Herbert Stothart. *Round the Town* (Century roof, revue, May 21, 1924): I Wonder Why the Glow-Worm Winks His Eye at Me/W: Oscar Hammerstein II, M: Herbert Stothart. *The Greenwich Village Follies of 1925* (46th Street > Shubert, revue, Dec. 24, 1925): The Dancing Doctor; Follow Me [Mar. 15, 1926]; You Have Me — I Have You/W: Owen Murphy, M: Harold Levey — Those Knowing Nurses [Mar. 15, 1926]/WM:

Lew Brown, Sidney Clare — Wouldn't You? [Mar. 15, 1926]/WM: Owen Murphy. *Ziegfeld Follies of 1927* (New Amsterdam, revue, Aug. 16, 1927): Ooh, Maybe It's You; Ribbons and Bows/WM: Irving Berlin. *Here's Howe!* (Broadhurst, "Joyce Baxter," May 1, 1928): Imagination; Life as a Twosome; On My Mind a New Love/W: Irving Caesar, M: Joseph Meyer, Roger Wolfe Kahn. *Follow Thru* (46th Street, "Lora Moore," Jan. 9, 1929/Sept. 30, 1929): He's a Man's Man; It's a Great Sport; (If There Were) No More You; You Wouldn't Fool Me, Would You?/W: B.G. DeSylva, Lew Brown, M: Ray Henderson. *Top Speed* (46th Street, "Virginia Rollins," Dec. 25, 1929): I'd Like to Be Liked; Sweeter Than You; We Want You; What Would I Care?/W: Bert Kalmar, M: Harry Ruby. *Anything Goes* (Alvin > 46th Street, CR, "Hope Harcourt," Oct. 7, 1935): All Through the Night; The Gypsy in Me/WM: Cole Porter.

2424. Renee Delting *Molly O'* (Cort, "Mrs. Kean," May 17, 1916): Aesop Was a Very Moral Man/W: Robert B. Smith, M: Carl Woess. *The Magic Melody* (Shubert, "Isabel De Vernon," Nov. 11, 1919): Dream Girl, Give Back My Dream to Me; Lips! Lips! Lips!; Night of Love; Once Upon a Time (The Magic Melody); Two's Company, Three's a Crowd/W: Frederic Arnold Kummer, M: Sigmund Romberg.

2425. Dom De Luise (Aug. 1, 1933–) B: Brooklyn, NY. M: CAROL ARTHUR. Comedy star of the stage, movies and TV. *The Student Gypsy or The Prince of Liederkranz* (54th Street, "Muffin T. Ragamuffin D.D., Ret." Sept. 30, 1963): The Drinking Song; A Gypsy Dance; The Gypsy Life; It's a Wonderful Day to Do Nothing; Merry May; A Woman Is a Woman Is a Woman/WM: Rick Besoyan.

2426. Alice Delysia (Mar. 3, 1888–Feb. 9, 1979) B: Paris, France. Chorus girl, singer and actress, known for her low cut gowns and splendid voice. *Afgar* (Central, "Zaydee," Nov. 8, 1920): Caresses [Dec. 1920]/WM: James V. Monaco — Ceremony of Veils; Garden of Make Believe; Live for Love/W: Douglas Furber, M: Charles Cuvillier — Where Art Thou, Romeo?; Why Don't You?/W: Joseph McCarthy, M: Harry Tierney. *Topics of 1923* (Broadhurst, revue, Nov. 20, 1923): Good Queen Bess; Oh, Alice/W: Tot Seymour, M: Bert Grant — When You Love/W: Harold Atteridge, M: Jean Schwartz.

2427. Peter De Maio B: Hartford, CT. *The Golden Apple* (Alvin, "Silas," Apr. 20, 1954): Come Along, Boys; Helen Is Always Willing; It Was a Glad Adventure/W: John Latouche, M:

Jerome Moross. *Billy* (Billy Rose, "Donald Taff," Mar. 22, 1969): Whiskers' Dance/WM: Ron Dante, Gene Allen.

2428. Alfred De Manby *The Girl from Utah* (Knickerbocker, "Lord Amersham," Aug. 24, 1914): Come Back Little Girl/WM: Augustus Barratt — Dance with Me; Where Has Una Gone?/WM: Paul Rubens, Percy Greenbank.

2429. Carrie De Mar (Apr. 1, 1876–Feb. 29, 1963) M: JOSEPH HART. *Foxy Grandpa* (14th Street, "Polly Bright," Feb. 17, 1902): The Country Club; The Funny Family; Military Charley/WM: Joseph Hart. *The Land of Nod* (New York, "The Chorus Girl," Apr. 1, 1907): Amateur Night/W: George V. Hobart, M: Victor Herbert — The Belle of Bald Head Row/W: Will M. Hough, Frank R. Adams, M: Joseph E. Howard — Sneeze Time/WM: Joseph Hart.

2430. Fleurette De Mar *Foxy Grandpa* (14th Street, "Dorothy Goodman," Feb. 17, 1902): The Country Club; La Parisienne/WM: Joseph Hart. *Paris by Night* (Madison Square roof garden, "Cissy Footlytes," July 2, 1904): The Convivial Girl [July 11, 1904]/W: Henry I. Marshall, M: Robert W. Edwards — I Loves You Lady Deed I Do/WM: Joseph Nathan — Seminole [July 11, 1904]/W: Harry Williams, M: Egbert Van Alstyne — Waltz, Waltz, Waltz/W: John E. Hazzard, M: Lyle Bloodgood.

2431. Frances Demarest M: JOSEPH C. SMITH. *Madame Sherry* (New Amsterdam, "Lulu, ex–Mistigrette," Aug. 30, 1910): Aesthetic Dancing; Every Little Movement (Has a Meaning All Its Own); The Kiss You Gave; The Smile She Means for You; Theophilus; Uncle Says I Mustn't, So I Won't/W: Otto Harbach, M: Karl Hoschna. *Gypsy Love* (Globe, "Ilma," Oct. 17, 1911): Lessons in Love; Love's Sorcery; Matrimony; When I'm Waltzing with You/W: Harry B. Smith, Robert B. Smith, M: Franz Lehar. *The Laughing Husband* (Knickerbocker, "Etelka," Feb. 2, 1914): Forbidden Fruit/W: Arthur Wimperis, M: Edmund Eysler. *The Passing Show of 1914* (Winter Garden > Lyric, revue, June 10, 1914): California [Oct. 5, 1914]; The Midnight Girl at the Midnight Cabaret; Way Down East/W: Harold Atteridge, M: Sigmund Romberg — Out in 'Frisco Town/W: Harold Atteridge, M: Harry Carroll. *The Passing Show of 1915* (Winter Garden, revue, May 29, 1915): (You'd Better See) America First/W: Harold Atteridge, M: Phil Schwartz — I Don't Like the Sea/W: Harold Atteridge, M: William F. Peters — My Hula Maid/W: Harold Atteridge, M: Leo Edwards. *The Blue Paradise* (Casino > 44th Street, "Mrs. Gladys Wynne," Aug. 5,

1915): I'm from Chicago; One Step Into Love/W: Herbert Reynolds, M: Sigmund Romberg — Just Win a Pretty Widow/W: Herbert Reynolds, M: Edmund Eysler. *The Passing Show of 1916* (Winter Garden, revue, June 22, 1916): Let Cupid In/W: Harold Atteridge, M: Otto Motzan — So This Is Paris!/W: Harold Atteridge, M: Harry Tierney. *The Girl from Brazil* (44th Street > Shubert, "Edith Lloyd," Aug. 30, 1916): Heart to Heart/W: Matthew Woodward, M: Robert Winterberg — The Right Brazilian Girl/W: Matthew Woodward, M: Sigmund Romberg. *My Lady's Glove* (Lyric, "Lydia Petrowska," June 18, 1917): Amorous Rose; Love Is for Youth (Prudence Has Fled); Secrecy/W: Edward A. Paulton, M: Oscar Straus — An-ti-ci-pa-tion/WM: ?. *The Royal Vagabond* (Cohan and Harris, "Princess Violetta," Feb. 17, 1919): Messenger Number and Dance/WM: George M. Cohan, Anselm Goetzl — A Wee Bit of Lace/W: George M. Cohan, M: Harry Tierney.

2432. William Demarest (Feb. 27, 1892–Dec. 28, 1983) B: St. Paul, MN. The character actor began in vaudeville and was a professional boxer. He appeared in over 100 movies; on TV he played Uncle Charley O'Casey on the sitcom *My Three Sons* (1965). *Earl Carroll's Sketch Book of 1929* (Earl Carroll > 44th Street > 46th Street, revue, July 1, 1929): Fascinating You/WM: Vincent Rose, Charles Tobias, Henry Tobias, Benee Russell.

2433. Imelda De Martin (Sept. 16, 1936–) B: Dosoldo, Italy. *The Girls Against the Boys* (Alvin, revue, Nov. 2, 1959): I Gotta Have You; Where Did We Go? Out/W: Arnold B. Horwitt, M: Richard Lewine. *The Sound of Music* (Lunt-Fontanne, CR, "Liesel," July 1962): Sixteen, Going on Seventeen/W: Oscar Hammerstein II, M: Richard Rodgers.

2434. Carole Demas (May 26, 1940–) B: Brooklyn, NY. *Grease* (Broadhurst, "Sandy Dumbrowski," June 7, 1972): All Choked Up; It's Raining on Prom Night; Look at Me, I'm Sandra Dee; Summer Nights/WM: Jim Jacobs, Warren Casey.

2435. Ray DeMattis (June 1, 1945–) B: New Haven, CT. *Grease* (Broadhurst, CR, "Roger," c 1974): Mooning; Rock 'n' Roll Party Queen/WM: Jim Jacobs, Warren Casey.

2436. William J. (Will) Deming (Sept. 19, 1870–Sept. 13, 1926) B: Mason, MI. He began his career as an usher at Hooley's Theater in Chicago. *By the Sad Sea Waves* (Grand Opera House, revival, "Algernon Campbell," Mar. 5, 1900): Ragtime Mixes My Brain/W: Harry Bulger, J. Sherrie Mathews, M: Gustav Luders. *Go*

Easy, Mabel (Longacre, "Ted Sparks," May 8, 1922): Girls, Girls, Girls; I Want a Regular Man/ WM: Charles George.

2437. Gertrude Demmler *Nic-Nax of 1926* (Cort, revue, Aug. 2, 1926): When the Sun Kissed the Rose Goodbye/W: Tom Dodd, M: Gitz Rice.

2438. Dolores De Monde *Artists and Models of 1930 [Paris-Riviera Edition]* (Majestic, revue, "Marie," June 10, 1930): L-O-V-E/W: ?, M: Harold Stern, Ernie Golden — My Real Ideal/W: Sammy Lerner, M: Burton Lane.

2439. Jerome Dempsey (Mar. 1, 1929–Aug. 26, 1998) B: St. Paul, MN. *Threepenny Opera* (Vivian Beaumont, revival in new translation, CR, "Tiger Brown," 1976): The Cannon Song/ W: Bertolt Brecht, M: Kurt Weill. *The Mystery of Edwin Drood* (Imperial, "Durdles," Dec. 2, 1985): Off to the Races/WM: Rupert Holmes.

2440. Robert Dempster (Mar. 29, 1883–Oct. 12, 1923) B: Buffalo, NY. *Mlle. Mischief* (Lyric, "Andre Claire," Sept. 28, 1908): Ev'ry Hour Brings Its Flower; Verily, Merrily/W: Sydney Rosenfeld, M: Carl M. Ziehrer. *The King of Cadonia* (Daly's, "Alexis, King of Cadonia," Jan. 10, 1910): Mother and Father/W: M.E. Rourke, M: Jerome Kern. *Betsy* (Herald Square, "Jasper Mallory," Dec. 11, 1911): Composing; There Came a Vision/W: Will B. Johnstone, M: Alexander Johnstone.

2441. Dennis Dengate *The Merry Widow* (New York City Center, revival, "Cascada," Oct. 8, 1944): Women/W: Adrian Ross, M: Franz Lehar.

2442. Anna May Dennehy *Vogues of 1924* (Shubert, revue, Mar. 27, 1924): Three Little Maids/W: Clifford Grey, M: Herbert Stothart.

2443. Barry Dennen (Feb. 22, 1938–) B: Chicago, IL. *Jesus Christ Superstar* (Mark Hellinger, "Pontius Pilate," Oct. 12, 1971): Pilate and Christ; Pilate's Dream; Trial Before Pilate/ W: Tim Rice, M: Andrew Lloyd Webber.

2444. Eileen Dennes *Betty* (Globe, "Estelle," Oct. 3, 1916): On a Saturday Afternoon/W: Adrian Ross, M: Paul Rubens.

2445. Dorothy Dennis B: New York, NY. *All in Fun* (Majestic, revue, Dec. 27, 1940): My Memories Started with You/W: June Sillman, M: Baldwin Bergersen. *New Faces of 1943* (Ritz, revue, Dec. 22, 1942): Animals Are Nice/W: J.B. Rosenberg, M: Lee Wainer — Back to Bundling/ W: Dorothy Sachs, M: Lee Wainer — Richard Crudnut's Charm School/W: June Carroll, John Lund, M: Lee Wainer.

2446. Ronald Dennis (Oct. 2, 1944–) B: Dayton, OH. *A Chorus Line* (Shubert, "Richie,"

Oct. 19, 1975): And.../W: Edward Kleban, M: Marvin Hamlisch.

2447. Winifred Dennis *A Gaiety Girl* (Daly's, revival, "Lady Virginia Forrest," May 7, 1895): High Class Chaperone/W: Harry Greenbank, M: Sidney Jones.

2448. Leslie Denniston (May 19, 1950–) B: San Francisco, CA. *Shenandoah* (Alvin, CR, "Anne," Oct. 12, 1976): Freedom; Violets and Silverbells; We Make a Beautiful Pair/W: Peter Udell, M: Gary Geld. *Happy New Year* (Morosco, "Linda Seton," Apr. 27, 1980): At Long Last Love; Let's Be Buddies; Let's Make It a Night; Once Upon a Time; Red, Hot and Blue; When Your Troubles Have Started/WM: Cole Porter — Boy, Oh, Boy/W: Burt Shevelove, M: Cole Porter. *Copperfield* (ANTA, "Agnes Wickfield," Apr. 13, 1981): Anyone; The Circle Waltz; I Wish He Knew; Villainy Is the Matter/WM: Al Kasha, Joel Hirschhorn.

2449. Reginald Denny (Nov. 20, 1891–June 16, 1967) B: Richmond, Surrey, England. His father was WILLIAM HENRY DENNY. The younger Denny starred in silent films and became a character actor in sound movies, over 200 in all. *The Passing Show of 1919* (Winter Garden, revue, Oct. 23, 1919): Roads of Destiny/W: Harold Atteridge, M: Jean Schwartz. *My Fair Lady* (Mark Hellinger, CR, "Colonel Pickering," Nov. 1957/Feb. 1958): The Rain in Spain; You Did It/W: Alan Jay Lerner, M: Frederick Loewe.

2450. William Henry Denny (Oct. 22, 1853–Aug. 31, 1915) B: Balsall Heath, Birmingham, England. Actor and singer of comic opera and burlesque. *The Tourists* (Majestic, "Loofah," Aug. 25, 1906): Keep on Doing Something/W: R.H. Burnside, M: Gustave Kerker.

2451. Montes de Oca *The Most Happy Fella* (New York City Center, revival, "Giuseppe," May 11, 1966): Abbondanza; Benvenuta; Sposalizio/WM: Frank Loesser.

2452. Daniel De Paolo *The Student Prince* (Broadway, revival, "Lucas," June 8, 1943): Serenade; Student Life; To the Inn We're Marching/W: Dorothy Donnelly, M: Sigmund Romberg.

2453. Valerie De Pena *Man of La Mancha* (Marquis, revival, "Antonia," Apr. 24, 1992): I'm Only Thinking of Him/W: Joe Darion, M: Mitch Leigh.

2454. Harry Depp (Feb. 22, 1883–Mar. 31, 1957) B: St. Louis, MO. *The Pink Lady* (New Amsterdam, "Crapote," Mar. 13, 1911): The Intriguers/W: C.M.S. McLellan, M: Ivan Caryll.

2455. Olive Depp *The Bachelor Belles* (Globe, "Olive," Nov. 7, 1910): The Bachelor

Belles/W: Harry B. Smith, M: Raymond Hubbell.

2456. Lois Deppe *Blackbirds of 1928* (Eltinge, revue, CR, Mar. 25, 1929): I Can't Give You Anything but Love/W: Dorothy Fields, M: Jimmy McHugh. *Great Day!* (Cosmopolitan, "Lijah," Oct. 17, 1929): Great Day; Without a Song/W: Billy Rose, Edward Eliscu, M: Vincent Youmans. *Hello, Paris* (Shubert, "Captain," Nov. 15, 1930): Deep Paradise/W: Charles O. Locke, M: Russell Tarbox — Rosie Road/WM: ?. *Fast and Furious* (New Yorker, revue, Sept. 15, 1931): Frowns/W: Mack Gordon, M: Harry Revel.

2457. Clif de Raita *Dancin'* (Broadhurst, revue, CR, Mar. 13, 1979): Gary Owen/WM: trad. — Was Dog a Doughnut/WM: Cat Stevens.

2458. Frank Derbas *Kiss Me, Kate* (Broadway, revival, "Bill Calhoun" and "Lucentio," Jan. 8, 1952): Bianca; I Sing of Love; Tom, Dick or Harry; We Open in Venice/WM: Cole Porter. *Bells Are Ringing* (Shubert, CR, "Carl"): Mu-Cha-Cha/W: Betty Comden, Adolph Green, M: Jule Styne.

2459. Rubye De Remer (Jan. 9, 1892–Mar. 18, 1984) B: Denver, CO. *Ziegfeld Midnight Frolic [6th Edition]* (New Amsterdam roof, revue, Dec. 29, 1917): Every Girl Is Doing Her Bit Today/W: Clifford Harris, P.H. Valentine, M: James W. Tate — We Are the Bright Lights of Broadway/W: Gene Buck, M: Dave Stamper.

2460. Charles Derickson *The Greenwich Village Follies of 1919* (Nora Bayes, revue, c Sept. 15, 1919): I Want a Daddy Who Will Rock Me to Sleep; Red, Red as the Rose/W: Philip Bartholomae, John Murray Anderson, M: A. Baldwin Sloane — I've a Sweetheart in Each Star/W: Arthur Swanstrom, John Murray Anderson, M: A. Baldwin Sloane. *What's in a Name* (Maxine Elliott, revue, Mar. 19, 1920): Valley of Dreams/W: John Murray Anderson, Jack Yellen, M: Milton Ager. *The Clinging Vine* (Knickerbocker, "Jimmy Manning," Dec. 25, 1922): The Clinging Vine; Homemade Happiness; Lady Luck/W: Zelda Sears, M: Harold A. Levey. *Paradise Alley* (Casino, "Jack Harriman," Mar. 31, 1924): Friendship Leads Us to Love/W: Howard Johnson, M: Adorjan Otvos — Put on the Ritz/W: Howard Johnson, M: Irving Bibo — Tell Me Truly/W: Howard Johnson, M: Carle Carlton — Those Beautiful Chimes; Your Way or My Way/W: Howard Johnson, M: Harry Archer.

2461. Prairie Dern *The Rothschilds* (Lunt-Fontanne, CR, "Hannah Cohen," Aug. 1971): I'm in Love! I'm in Love!/W: Sheldon Harnick, M: Jerry Bock.

2462. Vera De Rosa *The Firefly* (Lyric >

Casino, "Sybil Vandare," Dec. 2, 1912): Call Me Uncle; In Sapphire Seas; A Trip to Bermuda/W: Otto Harbach, M: Rudolf Friml.

2463. Richard Derr (June 15, 1917–May 8, 1992) B: Norristown, PA. Leading man in B movies from 1942. *Plain and Fancy* (Mark Hellinger, "Dan King," Jan. 27, 1955): Take Your Time and Take Your Pick; You Can't Miss It/W: Arnold B. Horwitt, M: Albert Hague.

2464. Cleavant Derricks (May 15, 1953–) B: Knoxville, TN. Twin brother of CLINTON DERRICKS-CARROLL. *Hair* (Biltmore, revival, "Hud," Oct. 5, 1977): Ain't Got No; Colored Spade/W: Gerome Ragni, James Rado, M: Galt MacDermot. *But Never Jam Today* (Longacre, "Caterpiller" and "Cook" and "Tweedledee" and "Seven of Spades," July 31, 1979): All the Same to Me; God Could Give Me Anything; A Real Life Lullabye; They; Twinkle, Twinkle Little Star/WM: Bob Larimer, Bert Keyes. *Dreamgirls* (Imperial, "James Thunder Early," Dec. 20, 1981/Nov. 1983): Ain't No Party; Cadillac Car; Fake Your Way to the Top; Family; I Meant You No Harm; I Want You Baby; It's All Over; Quintette; The Rap; Steppin' to the Bad Side/W: Tom Eyen, M: Henry Krieger. *Big Deal* (Broadway, "Charley," Apr. 10, 1986): Charley, My Boy/WM: Gus Kahn, Ted Fiorito — I'm Sitting on Top of the World/W: Sam M. Lewis, Joe Young, M: Ray Henderson — I've Got a Feelin' You're Foolin'/W: Arthur Freed, M: Nacio Herb Brown — Just a Gigolo/ Eng. W: Irving Caesar, Ger. W: Julius Brammer, M: Leonello Casucci — Pick Yourself Up/ W: Dorothy Fields, M: Jerome Kern — Yes Sir! That's My Baby/W: Gus Kahn, M: Walter Donaldson.

2465. Clinton Derricks-Carroll (May 15, 1953–) B: Knoxville, TN. Twin brother of CLEAVANT DERRICKS. *Your Arms Too Short to Box with God* (Lyceum, revue, Dec. 22, 1976): Can't No Grave Hold My Body Down; Come on Down; Everybody Has His Own Way; We Are the Priests and Elders; We're Gonna Have a Good Time/WM: Alex Bradford. *Dreamgirls* (Imperial, CR, "James Thunder Early"): Ain't No Party; Cadillac Car; Fake Your Way to the Top; Family; I Meant You No Harm; I Want You Baby; Quintette; The Rap; Steppin' to the Bad Side/W: Tom Eyen, M: Henry Krieger.

2466. Clarence Derwent (Mar. 23, 1884–Aug. 6, 1959) B: London, England. Supporting actor on stage for 31 years, he was President of ANTA from 1952 until his death. *Gypsy Lady* (Century, "Baron Pettibois," Sept. 17, 1946): Reality/W: Robert Wright, George Forrest, M: Victor Herbert.

2467. Frank DeSal (Apr. 14, 1943–) B: White Plains, NY. *The Fig Leaves Are Falling* (Broadhurst, "Queen Victoria," Jan. 2, 1969): Light One Candle/W: Allan Sherman, M: Albert Hague. *Bring Back Birdie* (Martin Beck, "Rev. Sun," Mar. 5, 1981): Inner Peace/W: Lee Adams, M: Charles Strouse. *Zorba* (Broadway, revival, "Russian Admiral," Oct. 16, 1983): No Boom Boom; Vive la Difference/W: Fred Ebb, M: John Kander.

2468. Celestine DeSaussure *But Never Jam Today* (Longacre, "Cook," July 31, 1979): A Real Life Lullabye/WM: Bob Larimer, Bert Keyes.

2469. Andre De Shields (Jan. 12, 1946–) B: Baltimore, MD. *The Wiz* (Majestic, "The Wiz," Jan. 5, 1975/Jan. 25, 1977): If You Believe (Believe in Yourself); So You Wanted to Meet the Wizard; Y'all Got It!/WM: Charlie Smalls. *Ain't Misbehavin'* (Longacre, revue, May 9, 1978): Fat and Greasy/WM: Porter Grainger, Charlie Johnson — How Ya Baby?/W: James C. Johnson, M: Fats Waller — I Can't Give You Anything but Love/W: Dorothy Fields, M: Jimmy McHugh — The Ladies Who Sing with a Band/W: George Marion, Jr., M: Fats Waller — 'Tain't Nobody's Biz-ness If I Do/WM: Clarence Williams, Porter Grainger, Graham Prince — That Ain't Right/WM: Nat King Cole, Richard Maltby, Jr., Murray Horwitz. *Stardust* (Biltmore, revue, Feb. 19, 1987): Carolina Rolling Stone/W: Mitchell Parish, M: Eleanor Young, Harry D. Squires — Deep Purple/W: Mitchell Parish, M: Peter DeRose — Dixie After Dark/W: Mitchell Parish, Irving Mills, M: Ben Oakland — Don't Be That Way/W: Mitchell Parish, M: Edgar Sampson, Benny Goodman — Forgotten Dreams/W: Mitchell Parish, M: Leroy Anderson — Midnight at the Onyx/W: Mitchell Parish, M: Will Hudson — Moonlight Serenade/W: Mitchell Parish, M: Glenn Miller — Organ Grinder's Swing/W: Mitchell Parish, Irving Mills, M: Will Hudson — Riverboat Shuffle/W: Mitchell Parish, M: Hoagy Carmichael, Dick Voynow, Irving Mills — Ruby/W: Mitchell Parish, M: Heinz Roemheld — The Scat Song/W: Mitchell Parish, M: Frank Perkins, Cab Calloway — Star Dust/W: Mitchell Parish, M: Hoagy Carmichael — Volare/W: Mitchell Parish, M: Domenico Modugno. *Ain't Misbehavin'* (Longacre, revue, revival, Aug. 15, 1988): same as above.

2470. Alfred DeSio *Donnybrook!* (46th Street, "Gavin Collins," May 18, 1961): The Day the Snow Is Meltin'; Sez I; Wisha Wurra/WM: Johnny Burke. *Kean* (Broadway, "Christie," Nov. 2, 1961): Chime In!; Fracas at Old Drury; Penny Plain, Twopence Colored/WM: Robert Wright,

George Forrest. *She Loves Me* (Eugene O'Neill, "Busboy," Apr. 23, 1963): A Romantic Atmosphere/W: Sheldon Harnick, M: Jerry Bock.

2471. Gaby Deslys (Nov. 4, 1881–Feb. 11, 1920) B: Marseilles, France. A beautiful singing and dancing star with a reputation for scandal. Her American dancing partner was HARRY PILCER; together they popularized a dance called the Gaby Glide. Her life was cut short by consumption. *Vera Violetta* (Winter Garden, "Mme. Adelle de St. Cloche," Nov. 20, 1911): Come and Dance with Me; I've Heard That Before/W: Melville Gideon, M: Louis A. Hirsch — Come Back to Me/W: Harold Atteridge, M: Edmund Eysler. *The Honeymoon Express* (Winter Garden, "Yvonne," Feb. 6, 1913): Bring Back Your Love; When Gaby Did the Gaby Glide; When the Honeymoon Stops Shining; You'll Call the Next Love the First/W: Harold Atteridge, M: Jean Schwartz. *The Belle of Bond Street* (Shubert, "Winnie Harborough," Mar. 30, 1914): It's the Hat and Not the Girl; They Say I'm Frivolous/WM: ?— Mr. Hoggenheimer of Park Lane/W: Adrian Ross, M: Ivan Caryll — The Tango Dip; The Turkey Trotting Boy (Oh! You Turkey Trotter)/W: Harold Atteridge, M: Harry Carroll. *Stop! Look! Listen!* (Globe, revue, "Gaby," Dec. 25, 1915): Everything in America Is Ragtime; I Love to Dance; Take Off a Little Bit; When I'm Out with You; Why Don't They Give Us a Chance?/WM: Irving Berlin.

2472. Florence Desmond (May 31, 1905–Jan. 16, 1993) B: London, England. Actress, singer, dancer and impressionist, she was well known in variety and on radio particularly in England. *This Year of Grace* (Selwyn, revue, Nov. 7, 1928): Little Women; Mother's Complaint/WM: Noel Coward. *If the Shoe Fits* (Century, "Lady Eve," Dec. 5, 1946): I Want to Go Back to the Bottom of the Garden; I'm Not Myself Tonight; In the Morning; Three Questions; With a Wave of My Wand/W: June Carroll, M: David Raksin.

2473. Johnny Desmond (Nov. 14, 1919–Sept. 6, 1985) B: Detroit, MI. A popular singer with orchestras such as Bob Crosby, Gene Krupa and Glenn Miller. Known as Johnny on the Spot, he was featured on radio's *Breakfast Club.*, hosted by Don McNeil and broadcast from Chicago in the 1940s. *Say, Darling* (ANTA, "Rudy Lorraine," Apr. 3, 1958): Chief of Love; The Husking Bee; It's Doom; It's the Second Time You Meet That Matters; Say, Darling; Something's Always Happening on the River; Try to Love Me Just as I Am/W: Betty Comden, Adolph Green,

M: Jule Styne. *Funny Girl* (Winter Garden, CR, "Nick Arnstein," July 5, 1965): I Want to Be Seen with You Tonight; You Are Woman/W: Bob Merrill, M: Jule Styne.

2474. Mona Desmond *It Happened in Nordland* (Lew Fields, CR, "Parthenia Schmitt," Sept. 21, 1905): Jack O'Lantern Girl; The Man Meant Well/W: Glen MacDonough, M: Victor Herbert. *The Better 'Ole* (Greenwich Village > Cort > Booth, "Suzette," Oct. 19, 1918): Tommy/W: James Heard, M: Herman Darewski.

2475. Finita De Soria *Flo Flo* (Cort, "Carmen Carassa," Dec. 20, 1917): In Spain/W: Edward A. Paulton, M: Silvio Hein. *The O'Brien Girl* (Liberty, "Mrs. Hope," Oct. 3, 1921): Learn to Smile/W: Otto Harbach, M: Louis A. Hirsch. *Blossom Time* (Jolson, revival, "Bellabruna," May 19, 1924): Keep It Dark; Let Me Awake; Melody Triste/W: Dorothy Donnelly, M: Sigmund Romberg.

2476. May De Sousa (1882–Aug. 8, 1948) B: Chicago, IL. Her greatest success was in London. *A Skylark* (New York, "Christine Parling," Apr. 4, 1910): Broadway Lament; I Just Can't Wait; I'm Looking for a Little Girl Who's Looking for a Man; Style, Style, Style/W: William B. Harris, Jr., M: Frank Dossert. *Lieber Augustin* (Casino, "Princess Helen," Sept. 3, 1913): Do You Love Me Best?/W: Harry Beswick, M: Leo Fall — If You Were Mine/W: Edgar Smith, M: Leo Fall — Lieber Augustin/W: M.E. Rourke, M: Carl Weber.

2477. Despo (July 13, 1920–) B: Piraeus, Greece. *Ilya Darling* (Mark Hellinger, "Despo," Apr. 11, 1967): I'll Never Lay Down Any More/W: Joe Darion, M: Manos Hadjidakis. *Cabaret* (Broadhurst, CR, "Fraulein Schneider," June 10, 1968): It Couldn't Please Me More; Married; So What?; What Would You Do/W: Fred Ebb, M: John Kander. *A Little Night Music* (Shubert, "Malla," Feb. 25, 1973): The Glamorous Life/WM: Stephen Sondheim.

2478. Rene Detling *The Lilac Domino* (44th Street, "Leonie D'Andorcet," Oct. 28, 1914): Ladies Day; True Love Will Find a Way; What Every Woman Knows (Frocks and Frills)/W: Robert B. Smith, M: Charles Cuvillier.

2479. Donna Devel *Dream with Music* (Majestic, "Kispah," May 18, 1944): The Lion and the Lamb/W: Edward Eager, M: Clay Warnick.

2480. Elise De Vere *The Red Feather* (Lyric, "Mlle Fifine," Nov. 9, 1903): A Lesson in Verse; The Little Milliner; The Tale of a High Born Rooster; Wanda/W: Charles Emerson Cook, M: Reginald De Koven.

2481. Mai de Villiers *The Silver Slipper* (Broadway, "Queen of Venus," Oct. 27, 1902): Invocation of Venus/WM: Leslie Stuart.

2482. Loretta Devine (Aug. 21, 1949–) B: Houston, TX. *Comin' Uptown* (Winter Garden, "Young Mary," Dec. 20, 1979): What Better Time for Love/W: Peter Udell, M: Garry Sherman. *Dreamgirls* (Imperial, "Lorell Robinson," Dec. 20, 1981/Oct. 9, 1984): Ain't No Party; Family; Quintette; The Rap/W: Tom Eyen, M: Henry Krieger. *Gotta Getaway!* (Radio City Music Hall, revue, June 16, 1984): Bubble, Bubble; Once You've Seen a Rainbow/W: Chip Orton, M: Gene Palumbo — Come to the Super Market in Old Peking; I'm Throwing a Ball Tonight/WM: Cole Porter — Gotta Getaway/WM: Glen Roven — Here in Minipoora; Take Good Care of That Lady/WM: Marc Shaiman, Marc Elliot. *Big Deal* (Broadway, "Lilly," Apr. 10, 1986): Button Up Your Overcoat; Life Is Just a Bowl of Cherries/W: B.G. DeSylva, Lew Brown, M: Ray Henderson — I'm Just Wild About Harry/WM: Noble Sissle, Eubie Blake.

2483. Christine DeVito *Cats* (Winter Garden, CR, "Rumpleteazer," c 1992): Mungojerrie and Rumpleteazer/W: T.S. Eliot, M: Andrew Lloyd Webber. *Hello, Dolly!* (Lunt-Fontanne, revival, "Ermengarde," Oct. 19, 1995): Put on Your Sunday Clothes/WM: Jerry Herman.

2484. Karla DeVito (May 29, 1953–) B: Oak Lawn, IL. *Big River: The Adventures of Huckleberry Finn* (Eugene O'Neill, CR, "Mary Jane Wilkes," July 9, 1985): Leavin's Not the Only Way to Go; You Oughta Be Here with Me/WM: Roger Miller.

2485. Ron DeVito *Cats* (Winter Garden, CR, "Rum Tum Tugger," c 1996): Mr. Mistoffolees; Old Deuteronomy; Rum Tum Tugger/W: T.S. Eliot, M: Andrew Lloyd Webber.

2486. Henry De Vitt *The DuBarry* (George M. Cohan, CR, "Prince de Soubise," Dec. 19, 1932): Pantalettes/W: Rowland Leigh, M: Carl Millocker.

2487. Helen Devlin *Let's Face It!* (Imperial, "Dorothy Crowthers," Oct. 29, 1941): I've Got Some Unfinished Business with You/WM: Cole Porter.

2488. John Devlin (Jan. 26, 1937–) B: Cleveland, OH. *Billy* (Billy Rose, "John Claggart, Master-at-Arms," Mar. 22, 1969): The Night and the Sea; Watch Out for Claggart; Work/WM: Ron Dante, Gene Allen.

2489. Sandra Devlin *The Girls Against the Boys* (Alvin, revue, Nov. 2, 1959): I Gotta Have You; Light Travelin' Man/W: Arnold B. Horwitt, M: Albert Hague.

2490. Bessie de Voie *The Show Girl or The Cap of Fortune* (Wallack's, CR, "Lady Betty Pringle," May 1902): By and By/WM: William T. Francis — In Gay Japan/W: D.K. Stevens, M: M.W. Daniels — Reggie's Family Tree; That's the Way of a Sailor/W: D.K. Stevens, M: H.L. Heartz — A Rose and a Lily/W: D.K. Stevens, M: Edward W. Corliss. *Rogers Brothers in Paris* (New Amsterdam, "Clairette Soule," Sept. 5, 1904): The American Minstrels in Paris; Belle of the Silvery Nile/W: George V. Hobart, M: Max Hoffmann. *Rogers Brothers in Ireland* (Liberty > New York, "Hannah Dooley," Sept. 4, 1905): Hannah Dooley; My Irish Maid; St. Patrick's Day/W: George V. Hobart, M: Max Hoffmann. *The Dairymaids* (Criterion, "Winifred," Aug. 26, 1907): Hullo! Little Stranger!/WM: Paul Rubens, Arthur Wimperis. *The Pink Lady* (New Amsterdam, CR, "Desiree," July 24, 1911): By the Saskatchewan/W: C.M.S. McLellan, M: Ivan Caryll.

2491. David Devon *To Live Another Summer, To Pass Another Winter* (Helen Hayes, revue, Oct. 21, 1971): I Wanted to Be a Hero/W: David Paulsen, M: David Krivoshei.

2492. Michael De Vries (Jan. 15, 1951–) B: Grand Rapids, MI. *The Secret Garden* (St. James, "Capt. Albert Lennox," Apr. 25, 1991): A Bit of Earth/W: Marsha Norman, M: Lucy Simon.

2493. Edward Dew (Jan. 29, 1909–) B: Sumner, WA. He began his stage career as a Shakespearean actor. In later Hollywood years, he was a leading man in cowboy movies. *The Red Mill* (Ziegfeld, revival, "The Governor," Oct. 16, 1945): Because You're You; Every Day Is Ladies' Day with Me; Wedding Bells (Wedding Chorus)/W: Henry Blossom, Forman Brown, M: Victor Herbert. *If the Shoe Fits* (Century, "Prince Charming," Dec. 5, 1946): Every Eye; Have You Seen the Countess Cindy?; I Wish; I'm Not Myself Tonight/W: June Carroll, M: David Raksin.

2494. John Dewar (Jan. 24, 1953–) B: Evanston, IL. *Cats* (Winter Garden, CR, "Bustopher Jones" and "Asparagus" and "Growltiger"): Bustopher Jones; Growltiger's Last Stand; Gus; The Theater Cat/W: T.S. Eliot, M: Andew Lloyd Webber.

2495. Earle S. Dewey (June 2, 1881–Feb. 5, 1950) B: Mound City, KS. He left home to join the Lemon Bros. Circus as a tumbler. *Jonica* (Craig, "Barney Norton," Apr. 7, 1930): Gotta Do My Duty/W: Billy Moll, M: Joseph Meyer — Tonight or Never/WM: William B. Friedlander.

2496. Frances Dewey *Shoot the Works!* (George M. Cohan, revue, July 21, 1931): Chirp, Chirp/W: Ira Gershwin, M: Joseph Meyer, Phil Charig — How's Your Uncle?/W: Dorothy Fields, M: Jimmy McHugh — Poor Little Doorstep Baby/W: Max Lief, Nathaniel Lief, M: Michael Cleary. *New Faces of 1934* (Fulton, revue, Mar. 15, 1934): The Byrd Influence/W: June Sillman, Nancy Hamilton, M: Warburton Guilbert — You're My Relaxation/W: Robert Sour, M: Charles M. Schwab.

2497. Fay DeWitt *Pardon Our French* (Broadway, revue, Oct. 5, 1950): I Ought to Know More About You/W: Edward Heyman, M: Victor Young. *Flahooley* (Broadhurst, "Griselda," May 14, 1951): Flahooley; Happy Hunting/W: E.Y. Harburg, M: Sammy Fain. *Vintage '60* (Brooks Atkinson, revue, Sept. 12, 1960): Down in the Streets/WM: Tommy Garlock, Alan Jeffreys. *Oklahoma!* (New York City Center, revival, "Ado Annie Carnes," May 15, 1963): All er Nothin'; The Farmer and the Cowman; I Cain't Say No/W: Oscar Hammerstein II, M: Richard Rodgers.

2498. Josie De Witt (c 1874–July 4, 1905) B: Springfield, IL. M: WILL WEST. *By the Sad Sea Waves* (Herald Square, "Faith Grace," Feb. 21, 1899): Fiddle and I; Honolulu Lady; Military Model/W: J. Sherrie Mathews, Harry Bulger, M: Gustav Luders.

2499. Vinie De Witt *By the Sad Sea Waves* (Grand Opera House, revival, "Rose Flower," Mar. 5, 1900): Soldiers in Love's War/W: Harry Bulger, J. Sherrie Mathews, M: Gustav Luders.

2500. Daisy De Witte *Sunkist* (Globe, revue, "Violet Ray," May 23, 1921): My Sweetie's Smile/WM: Fanchon Wolff, Marco Wolff.

2501. Billy De Wolfe (Feb. 18, 1907–Mar. 5, 1974) B: Wollaston, MA. A comic actor and dancer, he started out in vaudeville and nightclubs. In films from 1943. *Ziegfeld Follies of 1957* (Winter Garden, revue, Mar. 1, 1957): Miss Follies/WM: David Rogers, Colin Romoff. *How to Succeed in Business Without Really Trying* (New York City Center, revival, "J.B. Biggley," Apr. 20, 1966): Been a Long Day; Brotherhood of Man; Grand Old Ivy; Love from a Heart of Gold/WM: Frank Loesser.

2502. Drina De Wolfe *Fad and Folly [orig. Tommy Rot]* (Mrs. Osborn's Playhouse, "Mrs. Immortelle," Nov. 27, 1902): She Read the New York Papers Every Day/W: Paul West, M: John W. Bratton — Try, Try Again/W: Paul West, M: Safford Waters.

2503. Grace de Wolfe *The Girl Who Smiles* (Lyric > Longacre, "Modeste," Aug. 9, 1915): A Breath from Bohemia/WM: Edward A. Paulton, Adolf Philipp, Jean Briquet.

2504. Ward De Wolfe *Her Soldier Boy* (Astor > Lyric > Shubert, "Alfred Appledorp," Dec. 6, 1916): I'd Be Happy Anywhere with You/W: Rida Johnson Young, M: Sigmund Romberg.

2505. Alan Dexter (Oct. 21, 1918–Dec. 19, 1983) B: Seychelles. *The Music Man* (New York City Center, revival, "Charlie Cowell," June 16, 1965): Rock Island/WM: Meredith Willson.

2506. Blanche Deyo M: WALTER JONES. *The Cingalee* (Daly's, "Peggy Sabine," Oct. 24, 1904): The Monkeys/WM: Paul Rubens. *The Social Whirl* (Casino > Majestic, "Germaine du Monde," Apr. 7, 1906): Manicure Song (The Profession of a Manicure)/W: Joseph W. Herbert, M: Gustave Kerker — Run Away, Naughty Man/W: Hugh Morton, M: ?. *The Spring Chicken* (Daly's > New Amsterdam > Daly's, "La Belle Sissi," Oct. 8, 1906): In Seville/W: M.E. Rourke, M: Richard Carle.

2507. Dennis DeYoung (Feb. 18, 1947–) B: Chicago, IL. Vocalist of a group known as Styx. *Jesus Christ Superstar* (Paramount Madison Square Garden, revival, "Pontius Pilate," Jan. 17, 1995): Pilate and Christ; Pilate's Dream; Trial Before Pilate/W: Tim Rice, M: Andrew Lloyd Webber.

2508. Kathye Dezina *Jesus Christ Superstar* (Mark Hellinger, CR, "Mary Magdalene," Mar. 12, 1973): Could We Start Again, Please; Everything's Alright; I Don't Know How to Love Him; Peter's Denial; What's the Buzz/W: Tim Rice, M: Andrew Lloyd Webber.

2509. Lillian D'Honau Sister of MARILYN D'HONAU. *Can-Can* (New York City Center, revival, "Marie," May 16, 1962): If You Loved Me Truly/WM: Cole Porter.

2510. Marilyn D'Honau *Can-Can* (New York City Center, revival, "Celestine," May 16, 1962): If You Loved Me Truly/WM: Cole Porter.

2511. Harold Diamond *Viva O'Brien* (Majestic, "Tom," Oct. 9, 1941): Mozambamba/W: Raymond Leveen, M: Maria Grever.

2512. Jack Diamond Burlesque comedian, partner of JOEY FAYE. *Kiss Me, Kate* (New Century, "Second Man," Dec. 30, 1948): Brush Up Your Shakespeare/WM: Cole Porter.

2513. James Diamond *The Rose of Algeria* (Herald Square, "Bailey Ringling," Sept. 20, 1909): Bohemia, Good-Bye; The Foolish Gardener; The Great White Easiest Way/W: Glen MacDonough, M: Victor Herbert.

2514. Jim Diamond *Lady Fingers* (Vanderbilt > Liberty, "Shadow Martin," Jan. 31, 1929): Follow Master/W: Edward Eliscu, M: Joseph Meyer.

2515. Maurice Diamond *Snapshots of 1921* (Selwyn, revue, CR, July 4, 1921): Dub-Derro (Deburau)/W: Alex Gerber, M: Malvin F. Franklin.

2516. Muni Diamond *Sing for Your Supper* (Adelphi, revue, Apr. 24, 1939): Bonnie Banks/ W: Robert Sour, M: Lee Wainer.

2517. Dolores Dicen *South Pacific* (Majestic > Broadway, CR, "Ngana"): Dites-Moi/W: Oscar Hammerstein II, M: Richard Rodgers.

2518. Evelyn Dickerson *Messin' Around* (Hudson, revue, Apr. 22, 1929): I Don't Love Nobody but You; Roust-Abouts/W: Perry Bradford, M: James P. Johnson.

2519. Jennie Dickerson (c 1855–Aug. 14, 1943) B: Newburgh, NY. *The Girl Who Smiles* (Lyric > Longacre, "Madame Bouliere," Aug. 9, 1915): Join the Families/WM: Edward A. Paulton, Adolf Philipp, Jean Briquet.

2520. Annamary Dickey B: Decatur, IL. She studied opera and debuted at the Metropolitan Opera. *Allegro* (Majestic, "Marjorie Taylor," Oct. 10, 1947): Come Home; A Fellow Needs a Girl; One Foot, Other Foot/W: Oscar Hammerstein II, M: Richard Rodgers. *The King and I* (St. James, CR, "Anna Leonowens," Jan. 1954): Getting to Know You; Hello, Young Lovers; I Whistle a Happy Tune; The Royal Bangkok Academy; Shall I Tell You What I Think of You?; Shall We Dance?/W: Oscar Hammerstein II, M: Richard Rodgers.

2521. Charles Dickson (1860–Dec. 11, 1927) B: New York, NY. *The Girl from Paris* (Herald Square, "Tom Everleigh," Dec. 8, 1896): The Festive Continong; Somebody/W: George Dance, M: Ivan Caryll.

2522. Dorothy Dickson (July 26, 1893–Sept. 25, 1995) B: Kansas City, MO. M: CARL HYSON. In 1921, the actress, singer, dancer moved to London where she became a popular favorite in musicals. *Girl o' Mine* (Bijou, "Betty," Jan. 28, 1918): Every Cloud Is Silver-Lined; I Like to Play with the Boys; Not So Fast/W: Philip Bartholomae, M: Frank Tours. *Rock-a-Bye Baby* (Astor, "Dorothy Manners," May 22, 1918): One, Two, Three; There's No Better Use for Time Than Kissing/W: Herbert Reynolds, M: Jerome Kern. *The Royal Vagabond* (Cohan and Harris, "Carlotta," Feb. 17, 1919): What You Don't Know Won't Hurt You/W: William Cary Duncan, M: Anselm Goetzl. *Lassie* (Nora Bayes, "Lady Gwendolyn Spencer-Hill," Apr. 6, 1920): Boo-Hoo; Flirting; Lady Bird; Skeletons/W: Catherine Chisholm Cushing, M: Hugo Felix.

2523. Crandall Diehl *The Golden Apple* (Alvin, "Agamemnon," Apr. 20, 1954): Come Along, Boys; Helen Is Always Willing; It Was a

Glad Adventure/W: John Latouche, M: Jerome Moross.

2524. Joan Diener (Feb. 24, 1934–) B: Cleveland, OH. *Small Wonder* (Coronet, revue, Sept. 15, 1948): Nobody Told Me/W: Phyllis McGinley, M: Baldwin Bergersen. *Kismet* (Ziegfeld, "Lalume," Dec. 3, 1953): Not Since Ninevah; Rahadlakum/WM: Robert Wright, George Forrest. *Man of La Mancha* (ANTA Washington Square, "Aldonza," Nov. 22, 1965): The Abduction; Aldonza; The Combat; Dulcinea; It's All the Same; Knight of the Woeful Countenance (The Dubbing); What Do You Want of Me?/W: Joe Darion, M: Mitch Leigh. *Cry for Us All* (Broadhurst, "Kathleen Stanton," Apr. 8, 1970): Call in to Her; How Are Ya Since?; That Slavery Is Love; The Verandah Waltz; Who to Love If Not a Stranger/W: William Alfred, Phyllis Robinson, M: Mitch Leigh. *Man of La Mancha* (Vivian Beaumont, revival, "Aldonza," June 22, 1972): same as above. *Home Sweet Homer* (Palace, "Penelope," Jan. 4, 1976): Did He Really Think; I Never Imagined Goodbye; The Rose; The Sorceress/W: Charles Burr, Forman Brown, M: Mitch Leigh. *Man of La Mancha* (Marquis, revival, CR, "Aldonza," June 30, 1992): same as above.

2525. Sharon Dierking *Walking Happy* (Lunt-Fontanne, "Alice Hobson," Nov. 26, 1966): Use Your Noggin/W: Sammy Cahn, M: James Van Heusen.

2526. Burtress Dietch *Cinderella on Broadway* (Winter Garden, revue, CR, July 12, 1920): Cinderella on Broadway; Cindy/W: Harold Atteridge, M: Bert Grant.

2527. Dena Dietrich (Dec. 4, 1928–) B: Pittsburgh, PA. *Here's Where I Belong* (Billy Rose, "Mrs. Tripp," Mar. 3, 1968): Pulverize the Kaiser/W: Alfred Uhry, M: Robert Waldman.

2528. Janette Dietrich *Bombo* (Al Jolson > Winter Garden, "Lois" and "Louello," Oct. 6, 1921): The Globe Trot/W: Harold Atteridge, M: Sigmund Romberg.

2529. Marlene Dietrich (Dec. 27, 1901–May 6, 1992) B: Berlin, Germany. The beautiful, seductive actress and singer started out to be a violinist. Her film career began in Germany in 1923; among others, she is remembered for her role in *The Blue Angel*, directed by Fritz Lang (1930). *Marlene Dietrich* (Lunt-Fontanne, one-person revue, Oct. 9, 1967): Boomerang Baby; Go 'Way from My Window; Look Me Over Closely; White Grass/WM: ? — Everyone's Gone to the Moon/WM: Kenneth King — Falling in Love Again (Can't Help It)/W: Sammy Lerner, M: Frederick Hollander — Honeysuckle Rose/

W: Andy Razaf, M: Fats Waller — I Wish You Love/Eng. W: Albert Beach, M: Charles Trenet — Jonny/W: Edward Heyman, M: Frederick Hollander — The Laziest Gal in Town/WM: Cole Porter — Lili Marlene/Eng. W: Tommie Connor, Ger. W: Hans Leip, M: Norbert Schultze — Lola, Lola/WM: Ray Evans, Jay Livingston — Marie, Marie/W: Harry B. Smith, M: Ludwig Englander — When the World Was Young (Ah, the Apple Trees)/Eng. W: Johnny Mercer, Fr. W: Angela Vannier, M: M. Philippe-Gerard — Where Have All the Flowers Gone?/ WM: Pete Seeger — You're the Cream in My Coffee/W: B.G. DeSylva, Lew Brown, M: Ray Henderson. *Marlene Dietrich* (Mark Hellinger, one-person revue, return engagement, Oct. 3, 1968): same as above.

2530. John Diggs *Carib Song* (Adelphi, "A Friend," Sept. 27, 1945): Can't Stop the Sea/W: William Archibald, M: Baldwin Bergersen. *Love Life* (46th Street, Oct. 7, 1948): Economics/W: Alan Jay Lerner, M: Kurt Weill.

2531. Taye Diggs (Jan. 2, 1972–) B: Rochester, NY. *Rent* (Nederlander, "Benjamin Coffin III," Apr. 29, 1996): Goodbye, Love; Happy New Year; Tune Up; Voice Mail #1; Voice Mail #3; What You Own; You'll See/WM: Jonathan Larson.

2532. William Dillard (c 1912–1995) B: Philadelphia, PA. *Memphis Bound!* (Broadway > Belasco, "Gabriel," May 24, 1945): Trial by Jury/WM: Clay Warnick, Don Walker, based on William S. Gilbert and Arthur Sullivan. *Shuffle Along* (Broadway, "Bugler," May 8, 1952): Bongo-Boola; Jive Drill/W: Noble Sissle, M: Eubie Blake. *My Darlin' Aida* (Winter Garden, "Adam Brown," Oct. 27, 1952): Gotta Live Free; Land of Mine; Master and Slave; Three Stones to Stand On; You're False/W: Charles Friedman, M: Hans Spialek, based on Giuseppe Verdi. *Porgy and Bess* (New York City Center, revival, "Crown," May 6, 1964): A Red-Headed Woman/W: Ira Gershwin, M: George Gershwin — What You Want wid Bess?/W: DuBose Heyward, M: George Gershwin.

2533. Karren Dille *Grease* (Broadhurst, CR, "Betty Rizzo," Dec. 1, 1975): Freddy, My Love; Look at Me, I'm Sandra Dee; There Are Worse Things I Could Do/WM: Jim Jacobs, Warren Casey.

2534. Marjorie Dille *The Threepenny Opera* (Empire, "Jenny Diver," Apr. 13, 1933): Tango Ballad/W: Bertolt Brecht, M: Kurt Weill.

2535. Kaylyn Dillehay *Canterbury Tales* (Rialto, revival, "Molly," Feb. 12, 1980): Beer Is Best (Beer, Beer, Beer)/W: Nevill Coghill, M: Richard Hill, John Hawkins.

2536. Phyllis Diller (July 17, 1917–) B: Lima, OH. A comic and tousled lady, popular in nightclubs and on TV. *Hello, Dolly!* (St. James, CR, "Mrs. Dolly Gallagher Levi," Dec. 26, 1969): Before the Parade Passes By/WM: Lee Adams, Charles Strouse, Jerry Herman — Dancing; Hello, Dolly!; I Put My Hand In; Put on Your Sunday Clothes; So Long, Dearie/WM: Jerry Herman — Motherhood/WM: Bob Merrill, Jerry Herman.

2537. Carol Dilley *Cats* (Winter Garden, CR, "Jennyanydots," Aug. 22, 1994): Bustopher Jones; The Old Gumbie Cat/W: T.S. Eliot, M: Andrew Lloyd Webber.

2538. Dorothy Dilley *Kitty's Kisses* (Playhouse, "Kitty Brown," May 6, 1926): Early in the Morning; I Don't Want Him; Kitty's Kisses; Promise Your Kisses; Two Fellows and a Girl; Whenever I Dream/W: Gus Kahn, M: Con Conrad. *Oh, Earnest!* (Royale, "Cecily Cardew," May 9, 1927): Cecily; Give Me Someone; Let's Pretend; Never Trouble Trouble/W: Francis De Witt, M: Robert Hood Bowers. *Take the Air* (Waldorf, "Lillian Bond [Baby]," Nov. 22, 1927): Japanese Moon; Maybe I'll Baby You; The Wild and Wooly West/W: Gene Buck, M: Dave Stamper — On a Pony for Two/W: Gene Buck, M: James F. Hanley.

2539. Denny Dillon (May 18, 1951–) B: Cleveland, OH. *My One and Only* (St. James, "Mickey," May 1, 1983): Funny Face; I Can't Be Bothered Now/W: Ira Gershwin, M: George Gershwin.

2540. Sandy Dillon B: near Cape Cod, MA. Singer, pianist and recording artist. *Rock 'n Roll! The First 5,000 Years* (St. James, revue, Oct. 24, 1982): Concrete Shoes/WM: Rod Swenson, Chosei Funahara Power — Cry Baby/WM: Norman Meade, Bert Russell.

2541. Gordon Dilworth (May 29, 1913–) B: Brooklyn, NY. *Helen Goes to Troy* (Alvin, "Agamemnon," Apr. 24, 1944): If Menelaus Only Knew It; A Little Chat/W: Herbert Baker, M: Jacques Offenbach, adapted by Eric Wolfgang Korngold. *The Merry Widow* (New York City Center, revival, "Gen. Bardini," Oct. 8, 1944): Women/W: Adrian Ross, M: Franz Lehar. *Paint Your Wagon* (Shubert, "Reuben Sloane," Nov. 12, 1951): I'm on My Way/W: Alan Jay Lerner, M: Frederick Loewe. *My Fair Lady* (Mark Hellinger, "Harry," Mar. 15, 1956): Get Me to the Church on Time; With a Little Bit of Luck/W: Alan Jay Lerner, M: Frederick Loewe. *My Fair Lady* (Mark Hellinger, CR, "Alfred P. Doolittle," Dec. 1961): same as above. *On a Clear Day You Can See Forever* (Mark Hellinger,

"Samuel Welles," Oct. 17, 1965): Ring Out the Bells/W: Alan Jay Lerner, M: Burton Lane. *Walking Happy* (Lunt-Fontanne, "Tubby Wadlow," Nov. 26, 1966): How D'Ya Talk to a Girl; It Might as Well Be Her/W: Sammy Cahn, M: James Van Heusen.

2542. Hubert (Hugh) Dilworth *Bloomer Girl* (Shubert, "Augustus," Oct. 5, 1944): I Got a Song/W: E.Y. Harburg, M: Harold Arlen. *Bloomer Girl* (New York City Center, revival, "Pompey," Jan. 6, 1947): The Eagle and Me; I Got a Song/W: E.Y. Harburg, M: Harold Arlen. *Porgy and Bess* (Ziegfeld, revival, "Jim," Mar. 10, 1953): It Takes a Long Pull to Get There; A Woman Is a Sometime Thing/W: DuBose Heyward, M: George Gershwin.

2543. Donna DiMeo (Mar. 6, 1964–) B: Brooklyn, NY. *Jerome Robbins' Broadway* (Imperial, revue, Feb. 26, 1989): I'm Flying/W: Carolyn Leigh, M: Moose Charlap.

2544. Rita Dimitri (?–June 21, 1997) B: Nice, France. *Can-Can* (Shubert, CR, "La Mome Pistache," 1955): Allez-Vous-En (Go Away); Can-Can; C'est Magnifique; Every Man Is a Stupid Man; I Love Paris; Live and Let Live; Never Give Anything Away/WM: Cole Porter.

2545. Charles Dingle (Dec. 28, 1887–Jan. 19, 1956) B: Wabash, IN. Leading man on stage, notable for his role in *The Little Foxes* (1939), which he reenacted on screen in 1941. *Miss Liberty* (Imperial, "James Gordon Bennett," July 15, 1949): The Most Expensive Statue in the World/WM: Irving Berlin.

2546. Tom Dingle *Hello, Broadway!* (Astor, revue, "Daddy Long Beard," Dec. 25, 1914): Sneaky Steps/WM: George M. Cohan. *Love Birds* (Apollo, "Warrington Knight," Mar. 15, 1921): Carnival Night; When the Cat's Away/W: Ballard Macdonald, M: Sigmund Romberg. *Sun Showers* (Astor, "Tommy Dugan," Feb. 5, 1923): Clip the Coupons; Speak Without Compunction/WM: Harry Delf.

2547. Dene Dinkins *The Fortune Teller* (Al Jolson, revival, "Vaninka," Nov. 4, 1929): Romany Life (Czardas)/W: Harry B. Smith, M: Victor Herbert.

2548. Dante Di Paolo *Along Fifth Avenue* (Broadhurst, revue, Jan. 13, 1949): The Best Time of Day/W: Tom Adair, M: Gordon Jenkins.

2549. Denise DiRenzo *A Chorus Line* (Shubert, CR, "Diana," Feb. 15, 1988): Nothing; What I Did for Love/W: Edward Kleban, M: Marvin Hamlisch.

2550. Sherman Dirkson *Swing It* (Adelphi, "Bob," July 22, 1937): Ain't We Got Love; Rhythm

Is a Racket/W: Cecil Mack, Milton Reddie, M: Eubie Blake.

2551. Bob Dishy B: Brooklyn, NY. *Damn Yankees* (46th Street, CR, "Rocky," Jan. 2, 1956): The Game; Heart/WM: Richard Adler, Jerry Ross. *From A to Z* (Plymouth, revue, Apr. 20, 1960): South American Way/W: Fred Ebb, M: Norman L. Martin. *Can-Can* (New York City Center, revival, "Theophile," May 16, 1962): If You Loved Me Truly; Never, Never Be an Artist/WM: Cole Porter. *Flora, the Red Menace* (Alvin, "Harry Toukarian," May 11, 1965): All I Need (Is One Good Break); Express Yourself; The Flame; Hello, Waves; Not Every Day of the Week; Sign Here/W: Fred Ebb, M: John Kander.

2552. Dean Gus Dittman (c 1931–Jan. 28, 1989) B: Frontenac, Kansas. Singer and actor in theater, radio and movies. *On the Twentieth Century* (St. James, "Oliver Webb," Feb. 19, 1978): Five Zeros; I Rise Again; Never; Sign, Lily, Sign (Sextet)/W: Betty Comden, Adolph Green, M: Cy Coleman.

2553. Tommy Dix (Dec. 6, 1924–) *Best Foot Forward* (Ethel Barrymore, "Chuck Green," Oct. 1, 1941): Buckle Down Winsocki/WM: Hugh Martin, Ralph Blane.

2554. Henry E. Dixey (Jan. 6, 1859–Feb. 25, 1943) B: Boston, MA. M: MARIE NORDSTROM. On the stage in the U.S. for 63 years. After playing the role of Adonis in New York and London, the handsome actor and dancer became a matinee idol and was known as Adonis Dixey. *Hiawatha* (Standard, "Romulus Smith," Feb. 21, 1880): Conspirators Three; Yah! Yoh! Yum!/W: Nathaniel Childs, M: Edward E. Rice. *Adonis* (Bijou, "Adonis," Sept. 4, 1884): He Would Away; A Most Romantic Meeting; Take Me Down the Bay/W: William F. Gill, Henry E. Dixey, M: Edward E. Rice — I'm O'Donohue of Nowhere [Mar. 19, 1885]/W: William F. Gill, M: Edward E. Rice — It's English, You Know [Mar. 19, 1885]/W: H.S. Hewitt, M: Edward E. Rice — The Susceptible Statuette/W: ?, M: Arthur Sullivan. *Adonis* (Star, revival, "Adonis," Nov. 22, 1888): same as above. *The Seven Ages* (Standard, "Bertie Van Loo," Oct. 7, 1889): I'm a Harum Scarum Boy; When We Chance to Meet/W: Henry E. Dixey, M: Edward E. Rice. *Erminie* (Casino, revival, "Ravennes," May 23, 1898): Downy Jailbirds of a Feather/W: Claxson Bellamy, Harry Paulton, M: Edward Jakobowski. *The Burgomaster* (Manhattan, "Peter Stuyvesant," Dec. 31, 1900): Just Keep Cool; The Tale of the Kangaroo/W: Frank Pixley, M: Gustav Luders. *Chu Chin Chow* (Manhattan Opera House > Century, "Ali Baba," Oct. 22,

1917): Any Time's Kissing Time/WM: Frederic Norton — When a Pullet Is Plump It's Tender/W: Oscar Asche, M: Frederic Norton. *The Merry Malones* (Erlanger's, CR, "John Malone," 1928): A Feeling in Your Heart (You'll See a Great Big Beautiful Smile); God Is Good to the Irish; Molly Malone/WM: George M. Cohan.

2555. Adele Dixon (June 3, 1908–Apr. 11, 1992) B: Kensington, England. *Between the Devil* (Imperial, "Claudette Gilbert," Dec. 22, 1937): Celina Couldn't Say No; Don't Go Away, Monsieur; The Gendarme; I See Your Face Before Me/W: Howard Dietz, M: Arthur Schwartz.

2556. Bob Dixon *Redhead* (46th Street, "The Tenor," Feb. 5, 1959): Two Faces in the Dark/W: Dorothy Fields, M: Albert Hague. *The Conquering Hero* (ANTA, "Pfc. O'Dell," Jan. 16, 1961): Five Shots of Whiskey; One Mother Each; Only Rainbows/W: Norman Gimbel, M: Moose Charlap.

2557. Ed Dixon (Sept. 2, 1948–) B: Oklahoma. *King of Schnorrers* (Playhouse, "Belasco," Nov. 28, 1979): I Have Not Lived in Vain/WM: Judd Woldin. *The Three Musketeers* (Broadway, revival, "Cardinal Richelieu," Nov. 11, 1984): Bless My Soul/WM: ?. *Les Miserables* (Broadway, CR, "Thenardier," c 1988/c 1992): Beggars at the Feast; Dog Eats Dog; Master of the House; Thenardier Waltz/W: Herbert Kretzmer, M: Claude-Michel Schonberg. *Cyrano: The Musical* (Neil Simon, "Ragueneau," Nov. 21, 1993): Ragueneau's Patisserie; Rhyming Menu; What a Reward/W: Peter Reeves, Koen Van Dijk, Sheldon Harnick, M: Ad Van Dijk.

2558. Gale Dixon *Coco* (Mark Hellinger, "Noelle," Dec. 18, 1969): A Brand New Dress/W: Alan Jay Lerner, M: Andre Previn.

2559. Harland Dixon (Aug. 10 or 17, 1886–June 27, 1969) B: Toronto, Ontario, Canada. Raised in a strict religious family that frowned on pleasure, he became one of the great eccentric dancers in vaudeville and on Broadway. A partner of JAMES DOYLE, they were known as Doyle and Dixon. He was also JAMES CAGNEY's dance instructor. *The Honeymoon Express* (Winter Garden, "Alfonse," Feb. 6, 1913): I Want a Toy Soldier Man/W: Harold Atteridge, M: Jean Schwartz — The Moving Man/W: ?, M: Al W. Brown. *Dancing Around* (Winter Garden, "Lieut. Tommy," Oct. 10, 1914): Oh, You John/WM: ?— When Tommy Atkins Smiles at All the Girls/W: Harold Atteridge, M: Sigmund Romberg, Harry Carroll. *Stop! Look! Listen!* (Globe, revue, "Frank Steele," Dec. 25, 1915): The Law Must Be Obeyed; A Pair of Ordinary Coons; Stop! Look! Listen/WM: Irving Berlin. *The Cen-*

tury Girl (Century, revue, "Wood B. Rich," Nov. 6, 1916): It Takes an Irishman to Make Love/ WM: Elsie Janis, Irving Berlin. *The Canary* (Globe, "Fleece," Nov. 4, 1918): I Wouldn't Give That for the Man Who Couldn't Dance/WM: Irving Berlin — Take a Chance (Little Girl and Learn to Dance)/W: Harry B. Smith, M: Jerome Kern. *Good Morning, Dearie* (Globe, "Chesty Costello," Nov. 1, 1921): Easy Pickin's; Way Down Town/W: Anne Caldwell, M: Jerome Kern. *Ziegfeld Follies of 1923* (New Amsterdam, revue, Oct. 20, 1923): I'm Bugs Over You/W: Gene Buck, M: Dave Stamper. *Kid Boots* (Earl Carroll > Selwyn, "Menlo Manville," Dec. 31, 1923): The Cake-Eaters' Ball; I'm in My Glory; The Social Observer/W: Joseph McCarthy, M: Harry Tierney. *Oh, Kay!* (Imperial, "Larry Potter," Nov. 8, 1926): Clap Yo' Hands; Don't Ask!; Fidgety Feet/W: Ira Gershwin, M: George Gershwin. *Manhattan Mary* (Apollo, "Bob Sterling," Sept. 26, 1927): It Won't Be Long Now; My Blue Bird's Home Again/W: B.G. DeSylva, Lew Brown, M: Ray Henderson. *Rainbow* (Gallo, "Sergeant Major," Nov. 21, 1928): Hay! Straw!; My Mother Told Me Not to Trust a Soldier/W: Oscar Hammerstein II, M: Vincent Youmans. *Top Speed* (46th Street, "Tad Jordan," Dec. 25, 1929): Dizzy Feet; Fireworks; The Papers; Try Dancing/W: Bert Kalmar, M: Harry Ruby. *A Tree Grows in Brooklyn* (Alvin, "Old Clothes Man" and "Judge," Apr. 19, 1951): That's How It Goes/W: Dorothy Fields, M: Arthur Schwartz.

2560. Jerry Dixon *Once on This Island* (Booth, "Daniel," Oct. 18, 1990): The Ball; Forever Yours; Some Girls/W: Lynn Ahrens, M: Stephen Flaherty.

2561. Lee Dixon (Jan. 22, 1910–Jan. 8, 1953) B: Brooklyn, NY. He appeared in several Warner Bros. musicals. *Higher and Higher* (Shubert, "Mike O'Brien," Apr. 4, 1940): Disgustingly Rich; Lovely Day for a Murder; Morning's at Seven/W: Lorenz Hart, M: Richard Rodgers. *Oklahoma!* (St. James, "Will Parker," Mar. 31, 1943): All er Nothin'; The Farmer and the Cowman; Kansas City/W: Oscar Hammerstein II, M: Richard Rodgers.

2562. MacIntyre Dixon (Dec. 22, 1931–) B: Everett, MA. *Over Here!* (Shubert, "Father," Mar. 6, 1974): The Grass Grows Green (In No Man's Land); Hey Yvette/WM: Richard M. Sherman, Robert B. Sherman. *Beauty and the Beast* (Palace, CR, "Maurice," c 1994): No Matter What/W: Tim Rice, M: Alan Menken.

2563. Marion Dixon *The Magic Melody* (Shubert, "Mlle. Nitouche," Nov. 11, 1919): We

Are the Fixers/W: Frederic Arnold Kummer, M: Sigmund Romberg.

2564. Robert Dixon B: Hartford, CT. *Heaven on Earth* (New Century, "John Bowers," Sept. 16, 1948): Heaven on Earth; Home Is Where the Heart Is; Wedding in the Park; You're So Near (So Near and Yet So Far)/W: Barry Trivers, M: Jay Gorney. *Lend an Ear* (National > Broadhurst, revue, Dec. 16, 1948): Friday Dancing Class; Molly O'Reilly; When Someone You Love Loves You/WM: Charles Gaynor.

2565. Alex Dizen *Les Miserables* (Broadway, CR, "Gavroche"): Look Down/W: Herbert Kretzmer, M: Claude-Michel Schonberg.

2566. George Djimos *Sweet Adeline* (Hammerstein's, "The Jester," Sept. 3, 1929): Oriental Moon/W: Oscar Hammerstein II, M: Jerome Kern.

2567. Dumisani Dlamini (Oct. 23, 1963–) B: Durban, South Africa. *Sarafina!* (Cort, "Crocodile," Jan. 28, 1988): We Will Fight for Our Land/WM: Mbongeni Ngema.

2568. Ntomb'khona Dlamini (c 1971–) B: South Africa. *Sarafina!* (Cort, "Magundane," Jan. 28, 1988): Give Us Power; Mama/WM: Mbongeni Ngema — Talking About Love/WM: Hugh Masekela, Mbongeni Ngema.

2569. Frank Doane *The Mocking Bird* (Bijou, "Jean le Farge," Nov. 10, 1902): From a Different Point of View; Just a Kiss; The Lion and the Mouse/W: Sydney Rosenfeld, M: A. Baldwin Sloane. *Woodland* (New York > Herald Square, "Gen. Rooster," Nov. 21, 1904): The Valley of Hokus Pocus; You Can Never Tell Till You Try/W: Frank Pixley, M: Gustav Luders. *Comin' Thro' the Rye* (Herald Square, "Lord Battersbee," Jan. 9, 1905): When in Love/WM: ?. *The Gay White Way* (Casino, revue, "Favvy Hackettsham," Oct. 7, 1907): A Different Girl Again/ W: Sydney Rosenfeld, M: Ludwig Englander. *The Beauty Spot* (Herald Square, "Chickoree," Apr. 10, 1909): A Prince from Borneo/W: Joseph W. Herbert, M: Reginald De Koven. *Oh! Oh! Delphine* (Knickerbocker > New Amsterdam, "Col. Pomponnet," Sept. 30, 1912): Allaballa Goo-Goo; Hush! Hush! Hush!; Oh, P-P-P-Poor Bouchette; Please Turn Your Backs/W: C.M.S. McLellan, M: Ivan Caryll. *The Girl Behind the Gun* (New Amsterdam, "Col. Servan," Sept. 16, 1918): Happy Family; I Like It; Oh, How Warm It Is Today/W: P.G. Wodehouse, M: Ivan Caryll. *A Lonely Romeo* (Shubert > Casino, "Ichabod Wintergreen," June 10, 1919): Don't Do Anything Till You Hear from Me/W: Robert B. Smith, M: Malvin F. Franklin. *The Yankee Princess* (Knickerbocker, "Primpinette," Oct. 2,

1922): A Husband's Only a Husband/W: B.G. DeSylva, M: Emmerich Kalman. *Go-Go* (Daly's, CR, "Sen. Locksmith," Apr. 16, 1923): I'm Scared of You/W: Alex Rogers, M: C. Luckeyth Roberts. *The Chiffon Girl* (Lyric, "Woolsey," Feb. 19, 1924): The Kind of a Girl for Me; Nineteen Hundred and Eight/WM: Monte Carlo, Alma Sanders. *The Girl Friend* (Vanderbilt, "Arthur Spencer," Mar. 17, 1926): He's a Winner (Sporting Life) (Reporters' Opening); What Is It?/W: Lorenz Hart, M: Richard Rodgers. *She's My Baby* (Globe, "Mr. Hemingway," Jan. 3, 1928): Where Can the Baby Be?/W: Lorenz Hart, M: Richard Rodgers.

2570. George Dobbs *The Red Robe* (Shubert, "Lieut. Roland de Brissac," Dec. 25, 1928): I'll Love Them All to Death; Roll of the Drums; A Soldier of Fortune/W: Harry B. Smith, M: Jean Gilbert. *Broadway Nights* (44th Street, revue, "Duckey Stevens," July 15, 1929): Baby-Doll Dance/W: J. Keirn Brennan, Moe Jaffe, M: Maurie Rubens, Phil Svigals — Hotsy Totsy Hats; White Lights Were Coming/W: Moe Jaffe, M: Sam Timberg, Maurie Rubens. *Three Little Girls* (Shubert, "Franz Walden," Apr. 14, 1930): Annette/W: Harry B. Smith, M: Walter Kollo. *Frederika* (Imperial, "Jung-Stilling," Feb. 4, 1937): The Bane of Man; Jealousy Begins at Home; Out in the Sun/W: Edward Eliscu, M: Franz Lehar.

2571. Frank Dobson *Lady Butterfly* (Globe > Astor, "Fisher," Dec. 22, 1923): The Bad Man Walk; The Booze of Auld Lang Syne/W: Clifford Grey, M: Werner Janssen. *Innocent Eyes* (Winter Garden, revue, "George Tremeres," May 20, 1924): Africa/W: Henry Creamer, M: James F. Hanley — Let's Have a Rattling Good Time/W: Alfred Bryan, M: Jean Schwartz — Love Is Like a Pinwheel/W: Harold Atteridge, Tot Seymour, M: Sigmund Romberg.

2572. Leslie Dockery *Eubie!* (Ambassador, revue, Sept. 20, 1978): Baltimore Buzz; If You've Never Been Vamped by a Brownskin, You've Never Been Vamped at All; Oriental Blues; There's a Million Little Cupids in the Sky/W: Noble Sissle, M: Eubie Blake.

2573. Rory Dodd *Rockabye Hamlet* (Minskoff, "Horatio," Feb. 17, 1976): It Is Done; Swordfight; Twist Her Mind; Why Did He Have to Die?; Your Daddy's Gone Away/WM: Cliff Jones.

2574. Jack Dodds (May 22, 1928–June 2, 1962) B: Ohio. *Kismet* (Ziegfeld, "Akbar," Dec. 3, 1953): Bazaar of the Caravans; He's in Love!; Not Since Ninevah/WM: Robert Wright, George Forrest.

2575. Beth Dodge She and Betty were known as the Dodge Sisters. *A Night in Venice* (Shubert, revue, May 21, 1929): Loose Ankles [Aug. 5, 1929]/W: Moe Jaffe, M: Clay Boland, Maurie Rubens.

2576. Betty Dodge same as BETH DODGE.

2577. Jacqueline Dodge *Billion Dollar Baby* (Alvin, CR, "Miss Texas," June 10, 1946): Who's Gonna Be the Winner?/W: Betty Comden, Adolph Green, M: Morton Gould.

2578. Jerry Dodge (Feb. 1, 1937–Oct. 31, 1974) B: New Orleans, LA. *Hello, Dolly!* (St. James, "Barnaby Tucker," Jan. 16, 1964): Dancing; Put on Your Sunday Clothes/WM: Jerry Herman — Elegance; Motherhood/WM: Bob Merrill, Jerry Herman. *George M!* (Palace, "Jerry Cohan," Apr. 10, 1968): All Aboard for Broadway; Musical Comedy Man; Musical Moon; Twentieth Century Love/WM: George M. Cohan. *George M!* (Palace, CR, "George M. Cohan," Dec. 16, 1968): All Aboard for Broadway; Forty-Five Minutes from Broadway; Give My Regards to Broadway; Harrigan; Musical Comedy Man; My Town; Nellie Kelly I Love You; Over There; So Long, Mary; Twentieth Century Love; The Yankee Doodle Boy; You're a Grand Old Flag/WM: George M. Cohan — I'd Rather Be Right/W: Lorenz Hart, M: Richard Rodgers. *The Desert Song* (Uris, revival, "Benjamin Kidd," Sept. 5, 1973): It; One Good Boy Gone Wrong/New W: Edward Smith, M: Sigmund Romberg. *Mack & Mabel* (Majestic, "Frank Wyman," Oct. 6, 1974): Look What Happened to Mabel/WM: Jerry Herman.

2579. Denny (Dennis) Doherty (Nov. 29, 1941–) B: Halifax, Nova Scotia, Canada. *Man on the Moon* (Little, "President" and "King Can," Jan. 29, 1975): Canis Minor Bolero Waltz; Girls; Mission Control; My Name Is Can; Penthouse of Your Mind/WM: John Phillips.

2580. Lillian Doherty *The Mayor of Tokio* (New York, "Kimono," Dec. 4, 1905): Welcome Oloto/W: Richard Carle, M: William F. Peters.

2581. Lindy Doherty (Aug. 1, 1925–) B: Boston, MA. Actor and singer, part of the musical comedy team Cindy and Lindy. *Top Banana* (Winter Garden, "Cliff Lane," Nov. 1, 1951): Only If You're in Love; Slogan Song (You Gotta Have a Slogan); That's for Sure; Top Banana; You're So Beautiful That.../WM: Johnny Mercer.

2582. Molly Doherty *Kosher Kitty Kelly* (Times Square, "Zella Barnes," June 15, 1925): Why Should a Little Girl Be Lonely? [Sept. 3, 1925]/WM: Leon DeCosta.

2583. Jonathan Dokuchitz *The Who's Tommy* (St. James, "Capt. Walker," Apr. 22, 1993): Christmas; Do You Think It's Alright; Go to the Mirror; I Believe My Own Eyes; There's a Doctor; Twenty-One; We've Won/ WM: Pete Townshend.

2584. Gertrude Dolan *Pom-Pom* (Cohan, CR, "Crevete," Apr. 24, 1916): Mister Love/W: Anne Caldwell, M: Hugo Felix.

2585. Jennie (Janszieka) Dolly (Oct. 25, 1890–June 1, 1941) B: Hungary. M: HARRY FOX, 1914–1920. Twin sister of ROSIE (ROZSIKA) DOLLY. The two were headliners in vaudeville before their stage careers began. Jennie hanged herself, having never fully recovered from an auto accident that scarred her face and nearly killed her. A movie, *The Dolly Sisters* (1945), starring Betty Grable and June Haver, was based on their lives. *A Winsome Widow* (Moulin Rouge, "Jenny," Apr. 11, 1912): Toodle-oodle-oodle on Your Piccolo/WM: S.T. Griffin, Henry Murtagh. *Ziegfeld Follies of 1912* (Moulin Rouge, revue, Oct. 21, 1912): Be My Little Baby Bumble Bee/W: Stanley Murphy, M: Henry I. Marshall. *The Honeymoon Express* (Winter Garden, "Marguerite," Feb. 6, 1913): I Want the Strolling Good; The Same One They Picked for Me/W: Harold Atteridge, M: Jean Schwartz. *Maid in America* (Winter Garden, revue, "The American Cabaret Girl," Feb. 18, 1915): Castles in the Air; Girlie of the Cabaret; Manhattan Mad/W: Harold Atteridge, M: Sigmund Romberg — There Was a Time/W: Alfred Bryan, M: Harry Carroll. *The Greenwich Village Follies of 1924* (Shubert, revue, Sept. 16, 1924): The Dollys and Their Collies; I'm in Love Again [Oct. 13, 1924]; Syncopated Pipes of Pan; Wait for the Moon/ WM: Cole Porter.

2586. Rosie (Rozsika) Dolly (Oct. 25, 1892–Feb. 1, 1970) B: Hungary. M: composer Jean Schwartz. Her twin sister was JENNIE (JANSZIEKA) DOLLY. *A Winsome Widow* (Moulin Rouge, "Rosie," Apr. 11, 1912): same as JENNIE (JANSZIEKA) DOLLY. *Ziegfeld Follies of 1912* (Moulin Rouge, revue, Oct. 21, 1912): same as JENNIE (JANSZIEKA) DOLLY. *Lieber Augustin* (Casino, "Clementine," Sept. 3, 1913): Clementine/WM: ?. *The Whirl of the World* (Winter Garden, revue, "Olivia," Jan. 10, 1914): The Dance of the Fortune Wheel; The Dolly Maxixe; I'll Come Back to You; The Pavlova Gavotte/W: Harold Atteridge, M: Sigmund Romberg. *Hello, Broadway!* (Astor, revue, "Chin Chin," Dec. 25, 1914): That Old Fashioned Cakewalk/WM: George M. Cohan, Jean Schwartz. *The Greenwich Village Follies of 1924*

(Shubert, revue, Sept. 16, 1924): The Dollys and Their Collies; I'm in Love Again [Oct. 13, 1924]; Syncopated Pipes of Pan/WM: Cole Porter.

2587. Dolores (Zitelka Dolores) (c 1890–Nov. 7, 1975) B: London, England. Her real name was Kathleen Mary Rose. *Miss 1917* (Century, revue, Nov. 5, 1917): (Papa Would Persist in Picking) Peaches; Who's Zoo in Girl Land/W: P.G. Wodehouse, M: Jerome Kern — Sammy/W: James O'Dea, M: E.S. Hutchinson. *Sally* (New Amsterdam, "Mrs. Ten Broek," Dec. 21, 1920): This Little Girl/W: Clifford Grey, P.G. Wodehouse, M: Jerome Kern.

2588. Michael Dominico *New Faces of 1952* (Royale, revue, May 16, 1952): Waltzing in Venice/WM: Ronny Graham.

2589. D.L. (David L.) Don (c 1867–Oct. 27, 1949) B: Utica, NY. *The Belle of Bohemia* (Casino, "Phelim McDuffy," Sept. 24, 1900): My Lady in the Moon/W: Harry B. Smith, M: Ludwig Englander. *The Darling of the Gallery Gods [Mid Summer Night's Fancies]* (Crystal Gardens, "Sakkookoo," June 22, 1903): Ida Bell/W: Matthew Woodward, M: Ben M. Jerome — Omi Omai/WM: ? *The Dress Parade [Mid Summer Night's Fancies]* (Crystal Gardens, revue, June 22, 1903): Willie/W: Matthew Woodward, M: Ben M. Jerome. *The Red Mill* (Knickerbocker, "Willem," Sept. 24, 1906): You Can Never Tell About a Woman/W: Henry Blossom, M: Victor Herbert. *The King of Cadonia* (Daly's, "Panix," Jan. 10, 1910): The Blue Bulgarian Band; Lena, Lena/W: M.E. Rourke, M: Jerome Kern.

2590. Jack Donahue (1892–Oct. 1, 1930) B: Charlestown, MA. Brother of JOE DONAHUE. One of the most accomplished tap dancers of his era, he was also a singer, a comic actor and a writer. *Molly Darling* (Liberty, "Chic Jiggs," Sept. 1, 1922): Syncopate/W: Phil Cook, M: Tom Johnstone — When All Your Castles Come Tumbling Down/W: Arthur Francis, M: Milton Schwarzwald — You Know What to Do/W: Phil Cook, M: Tom Johnstone, Milton Schwarzwald. *Be Yourself!* (Sam H. Harris, "Matt McLean," Sept. 3, 1924): The Decent Thing to Do/W: George S. Kaufman, Marc Connelly, M: Lewis E. Gensler — Do It Now; A Good Hand Organ and a Sidewalk's All We Need/WM: ?— Money Doesn't Mean a Thing/W: Ira Gershwin, M: Lewis E. Gensler — Uh-Uh!/W: Ira Gershwin, George S. Kaufman, Marc Connelly, M: Milton Schwarzwald. *Sunny* (New Amsterdam, "Jim Deming," Sept. 22, 1925): Let's Say Goodnight Till It's Morning; When We Get Our Divorce/ W: Otto Harbach, Oscar Hammerstein II, M:

Jerome Kern. *Rosalie* (New Amsterdam, "Bill Delroy," Jan. 10, 1928): Ev'rybody Knows I Love Somebody [Jan. 16, 1928]; Let Me Be a Friend to You/W: Ira Gershwin, M: George Gershwin — Oh Gee! Oh Joy!; Say So!/W: Ira Gershwin, P.G. Wodehouse, M: George Gershwin — Setting Up Exercise/W: P.G. Wodehouse, M: Sigmund Romberg. *Sons o' Guns* (Imperial, "Jimmy Canfield," Nov. 26, 1929): I'm That Way Over You; Why?/W: Arthur Swanstrom, Benny Davis, M: J. Fred Coots.

2591. Joe Donahue (Jan. 3, 1903–) B: Boston, MA. Brother of JACK DONAHUE. *Americana of 1928* (Lew Fields, revue, Oct. 30, 1928): The Ameri-can-can; Hot Pants/W: Irving Caesar, M: Roger Wolfe Kahn — Life as a Twosome/W: Irving Caesar, M: Roger Wolfe Kahn, Joseph Meyer.

2592. Arthur Donaldson (Apr. 5, 1869– Sept. 28, 1955) B: Norsholm, Sweden. In a period of 4 years, he played the Prince of Pilsen 1,345 times. *A Runaway Girl* (Daly's > Fifth Avenue, "Leonello," Aug. 31, 1898): My Kingdom/W: Aubrey Hopwood, Harry Greenbank, M: Ivan Caryll. *The Prince of Pilsen* (Broadway, "Carl Otto, the Prince of Pilsen," Mar. 17, 1903): Biff! Bang!; Pictures in the Smoke; The Tale of the Sea Shell/W: Frank Pixley, M: Gustav Luders.

2593. John Donaldson (?–Nov. 30, 1969) *Orchids Preferred* (Imperial, "Richard Hope, Jr.," May 11, 1937): Boy, Girl, Moon; A Million Dollars/W: Frederick Herendeen, M: Dave Stamper.

2594. Norma Donaldson (July 8, 1928– Nov. 22, 1994) B: New York, NY. *Guys and Dolls* (Broadway, revival, "Miss Adelaide," July 21, 1976): Adelaide's Lament; A Bushel and a Peck; Marry the Man Today; Sue Me; Take Back Your Mink/WM: Frank Loesser.

2595. Ludwig Donath (Mar. 6, 1900–Sept. 29, 1967) B: Vienna, Austria. His career included classical drama, TV and nearly 50 films. *She Loves Me* (Eugene O'Neill, "Zoltan Maraczek," Apr. 23, 1963): Days Gone By/W: Sheldon Harnick, M: Jerry Bock.

2596. Francis X. Donegan *No Other Girl* (Morosco, "Amos Trott," Aug. 13, 1924): The Best in the Trade; Keep the Party Going; Look Out for Us, Broadway/W: Bert Kalmar, M: Harry Ruby. *The City Chap* (Liberty, "Tracy," Oct. 26, 1925): Walking Home with Josie/W: Anne Caldwell, M: Jerome Kern. *The Girl Friend* (Vanderbilt, "Donald Litt," Mar. 17, 1926): I'd Like to Take You Home; Town Hall Tonight; Why Do I?/W: Lorenz Hart, M: Richard Rodgers. *Twinkle Twinkle* (Liberty, CR, "Jack

Wyndham," Apr. 4, 1927): Get a Load of This; I Hate to Talk About Myself; You Know, I Know/W: Harlan Thompson, M: Harry Archer.

2597. Kitty Doner (1895–Aug. 26, 1988) B: Chicago IL. Her mother was NELLIE DONER. A famous male impersonator, Kitty was known as The Best Dressed Man on the American Stage. AL JOLSON romanced her during the time she worked in his shows. In the 1940s she became show director for *Holiday on Ice*; later she auditioned talent for *Ted Mack's Amateur Hour* on TV. *Dancing Around* (Winter Garden, "Pinky Roberts," Oct. 10, 1914): The Dancing Maniacs/WM: ?— Somebody's Dancing with My Girl/W: Harold Atteridge, M: Sigmund Romberg, Harry Carroll. *Robinson Crusoe, Jr.* (Winter Garden, "Suzie Westbury," Feb. 17, 1916): (Go Ahead and) Dance a Little More/W: Harold Atteridge, M: James F. Hanley — Don't Be a Sailor; (You'll Have to) Gallop Some/W: Harold Atteridge, M: Sigmund Romberg — Minstrel Days/W: Harold Atteridge, M: Phil Schwartz. *Sinbad* (Winter Garden > Century > Casino, "Stubb Talmadge," Feb. 14, 1918): The Bedalumbo/W: Harold Atteridge, M: Al Jolson — Our Ancestors; The Rag Lad of Bagdad; Raz-Ma-Taz/W: Harold Atteridge, M: Sigmund Romberg. *The Dancing Girl* (Winter Garden, "Mr. Clark" and "Pinkie" and "Mame," Jan. 24, 1923): Any Little Girl Will Fall; The Bowery of Today; I'm a Devil with the Ladies/W: Harold Atteridge, Irving Caesar, M: Sigmund Romberg — Cuddle Me as We Dance/W: Harold Atteridge, M: Sigmund Romberg.

2598. Nellie Doner (Dec. 15, 1874–) B: London, England. Mother of KITTY DONER. *Wars of the World* (Hippodrome, revue, Sept. 5, 1914): Baby Eyes/WM: Manuel Klein.

2599. Rose Doner Her mother was NELLIE DONER; her sister was KITTY DONER. *The Dancing Girl* (Winter Garden, "Miss Grayson," Jan. 24, 1923): Any Little Girl Will Fall; What Have You to Declare?/W: Harold Atteridge, Irving Caesar, M: Sigmund Romberg — Cuddle Me as We Dance/W: Harold Atteridge, M: Sigmund Romberg.

2600. Ted Doner (1896–1979) Brother of KITTY and ROSE DONER; son of NELLIE DONER. *The Dancing Girl* (Winter Garden, "Mack," Jan. 24, 1923): The Bowery of Today; What Have You to Declare?/W: Harold Atteridge, Irving Caesar, M: Sigmund Romberg — Cuddle Me as We Dance/W: Harold Atteridge, M: Sigmund Romberg. *Innocent Eyes* (Winter Garden, revue, "Jules Dubec," May 20, 1924): Africa/W: Henry Creamer, M: James F. Hanley — Garden of Love/W: Tot Seymour, M: Jean Schwartz — Love Is Like a Pinwheel/W: Harold Atteridge, Tot Seymour, M: Sigmund Romberg. *The Circus Princess* (Winter Garden, "Toni Schlumberger," Apr. 25, 1927): Girls, I Am True to You All; Guarded; I'll Be Waiting; There's Something About You/W: Harry B. Smith, M: Emmerich Kalman — What D'Ya Say?/W: Raymond Klages, M: Jesse Greer.

2601. Gwyda DonHowe (Oct. 20, 1933–) B: Oak Park, IL. *Half a Sixpence* (Broadhurst, CR, "Helen Walsingham"): A Proper Gentleman/WM: David Heneker. *Applause* (Palace, CR, "Karen Richards," Aug. 24, 1970): Fasten Your Seat Belts; Good Friends; Inner Thoughts/W: Lee Adams, M: Charles Strouse. *A Broadway Musical* (Lunt-Fontanne, "Stephanie Bell," Dec. 21, 1978): A Broadway Musical; Lawyers; What You Go Through/W: Lee Adams, M: Charles Strouse.

2602. Brian Donlevy (Feb. 9, 1899–Apr. 6, 1972) B: Portadown County, Armagh, Ireland. M: MARJORIE LANE, 1936–1947. He was brought to the U.S. as an infant. At 13, he was a bugler with the Mexican Punitive Expedition under Gen. Pershing. Comedian and villain, the actor played a wide variety of lead and supporting roles in nearly 100 films. *Rainbow* (Gallo, "Capt. Robert Singleton," Nov. 21, 1928): Virginia/W: Oscar Hammerstein II, M: Vincent Youmans. *Life Begins at 8:40* (Winter Garden, revue, Aug. 27, 1934): Quartet Erotica/W: Ira Gershwin, E.Y. Harburg, M: Harold Arlen.

2603. Michael J. (Mike) Donlin (May 30, 1877–Sept. 23, 1933) B: Peoria, IL or Erie, PA. M: MABEL HITE. *A Certain Party* (Wallack's, "James Barrett," Apr. 24, 1911): Turkey Trot/W: Edgar Smith, M: Tom Kelly.

2604. Berta Donn *Snapshots of 1921* (Selwyn, revue, June 2, 1921): Baby Dollie Walk/WM: Con Conrad. *Sonny* (Cort, "Florence," Aug. 16, 1921): I'm in Love, Dear/W: George V. Hobart, M: Raymond Hubbell. *Sun Showers* (Astor, "May Worthy," Feb. 5, 1923): How Do You Doodle?; In the Morning; On a Moonlight Night; Sun Showers/WM: Harry Delf. *The Magnolia Lady* (Shubert, "Betty Fane," Nov. 25, 1924): I Will Be Good/W: Anne Caldwell, M: Harold A. Levey. *My Maryland* (Al Jolson, "Sue Royce," Sept. 12, 1927): The Bonnie Blue Flag/W: Annie Chambers — Ketchum, M: Harry MacCarthy — Boys in Gray; Ker-choo!; The Mocking Bird; Mr. Cupid; Something Old, Something New/W: Dorothy Donnelly, M: Sigmund Romberg. *There You Are* (George M. Cohan, "Julia Danville [Snooky]," May 16,

1932): The Love Potion/WM: William Heagney, Tom Connell. *Revenge with Music* (New Amsterdam, CR, "Margarita," Feb. 11, 1935): My Father Said; Never Marry a Dancer; Once-in-a-While/W: Howard Dietz, M: Arthur Schwartz.

2605. Henry V. Donnelly (c 1861–Feb. 15, 1910) B: Dayton, OH. *Florodora* (Broadway, revival, "Cyrus W. Gilfain," Mar. 17, 1905): I Want to Marry a Man, I Do/W: Paul Rubens, M: Leslie Stuart — Phrenology; When You're a Millionaire/W: Ernest Boyd-Jones, M: Leslie Stuart. *The Vanderbilt Cup* (Broadway, "Curt Willets," Jan. 16, 1906): If You Were I and I Were You/W: Raymond W. Peck, M: Robert Hood Bowers.

2606. James Donnelly (1865–Apr. 13, 1937) B: Boston, MA. *Keep Kool* (Morosco > Globe > Earl Carroll, revue, May 22, 1924): In They Go, Out They Come; My Calicoquette/W: Paul Gerard Smith, M: Jack Frost. *The Greenwich Village Follies of 1924* (Winter Garden, revue, CR, Dec. 1, 1924): Syncopated Pipes of Pan/WM: Cole Porter.

2607. Jamie Donnelly (1947–) B: Teaneck, NJ. She later became an acting coach in California. *Flora, the Red Menace* (Alvin, "Lulu," May 11, 1965): You Are You/W: Fred Ebb, M: John Kander. *George M!* (Palace, "Ethel Levey," Apr. 10, 1968): I Was Born in Virginia; Push Me Along in My Pushcart; Twentieth Century Love/WM: George M. Cohan. *The Rocky Horror Show* (Belasco, "Popcorn Girl [Trixie]" and "Magenta," Mar. 10, 1975): Science Fiction; Time Warp/WM: Richard O'Brien. *Grease* (Broadhurst, CR, "Jan," c 1974): Freddy, My Love; Mooning/WM: Jim Jacobs, Warren Casey.

2608. Ruth Donnelly (May 17, 1896–Nov. 17, 1982) B: Trenton, NJ. Character actress in movies, playing girlfriends, then motherly types. *Going Up* (Liberty, Dec. 25, 1917): Going Up/W: Otto Harbach, M: Louis A. Hirsch. *As You Were* (Central, revue, "Ethel Nutt," Jan. 27, 1920): Washington Square/W: Cole Porter, E. Ray Goetz, M: Melville Gideon.

2609. Diamond Donner *The District Leader* (Wallack's "Florrie Fenshaw," Apr. 30, 1906): A Heart to Let/WM: Joseph E. Howard.

2610. Tom Donoghue *Les Miserables* (Broadway, CR, "Marius," Sept. 10, 1996): Empty Chairs at Empty Tables; A Heart Full of Love; In My Life; A Little Fall of Rain; Red and Black/W: Herbert Kretzmer, M: Claude-Michel Schonberg.

2611. Marcella Donovan *The Greenwich Village Follies of 1925* (Shubert, revue, CR, Mar.

15, 1926): How Do You Do?/W: Owen Murphy, M: Harold A. Levey — Wouldn't You?/WM: Owen Murphy.

2612. May Donovan see MAY THOMPSON.

2613. Warde Donovan (Feb. 25, 1919–Apr. 16, 1988) B: Los Angeles, CA. *Toplitzky of Notre Dame* (Century, "Angelo," Dec. 26, 1946): Let Us Gather at the Goal Line; Love Is a Random Thing; You Are My Downfall/W: George Marion, Jr., M: Sammy Fain. *The Merry Widow* (New York City Center, revival, "St. Brioche," Apr. 10, 1957): In Marsovia/W: Adrian Ross, M: Franz Lehar.

2614. Gordon Dooley (c 1899–Jan. 23, 1930) B: Altoona, PA. M: MARTHA MORTON. Brother of JOHNNY, RAY and WILLIAM DOOLEY. Their father was a well known circus clown. *Monte Cristo, Jr.* (Winter Garden, "Wilbur," Feb. 12, 1919): Are You Stepping Out Tonight?/W: Harold Atteridge, M: Sigmund Romberg, Jean Schwartz. *The Greenwich Village Follies of 1921* (Shubert, revue, CR, Nov. 14, 1921): Miss Dooley and Mr. Brown/W: Eddie Dowling, Raymond Klages, M: J. Fred Coots. *George White's Scandals of 1925* (Apollo, revue, June 22, 1925): All Alone/WM: Irving Berlin — Lovely Lady/W: B.G. DeSylva, Lew Brown, M: Ray Henderson. *Honeymoon Lane* (Knickerbocker, "Matty Pathe," Sept. 20, 1926): A Little Smile, a Little Sigh/W: Eddie Dowling, M: James F. Hanley.

2615. Johnny Dooley (1887–June 7, 1928) B: Glasgow, Scotland. M: YVETTE RUGEL. Brother of GORDON, RAY and WILLIAM DOOLEY. *The Passing Show of 1917* (Winter Garden, revue, Apr. 26, 1917): The Girl Who Drinks Champagne; Ruth St. Denis/W: Harold Atteridge, M: Sigmund Romberg, Otto Motzan — (I've a) Little Bit of Scotch (in Me)/W: Harold Atteridge, M: Sigmund Romberg. *Listen Lester* (Knickerbocker, "William Penn, Jr.," Dec. 23, 1918): I'd Love To; Show a Little Something New; Sweet Stuff; Two Is Company; When Things Come Your Way; Who Was the Last Girl (You Called by Her First Name)?/W: Harry L. Cort, George E. Stoddard, M: Harold Orlob. *Ziegfeld Follies of 1919* (New Amsterdam, revue, June 16, 1919): I'm the Guy Who Guards the Harem (and My Heart's in My Work)/WM: Irving Berlin — Shimmy Town/W: Gene Buck, M: Dave Stamper. *The Girl in the Spotlight* (Knickerbocker, "Bill Weed," July 12, 1920): Come Across; I Knew Him When; I'll Be There; Oo La La; 'Twas in the Month of June/W: Robert B. Smith, M: Victor Herbert. *Lady But-*

terfly (Globe > Astor, CR, "Alfred Hopper," Feb. 26, 1923): Beautiful Love; The Booze of Auld Lang Syne/W: Clifford Grey, M: Werner Janssen. *Keep Kool* (Morosco > Globe > Earl Carroll, revue, May 22, 1924): The Irish Sheik/W: Paul Gerard Smith, M: Jack Frost.

2616. Ray Dooley (Oct. 30, 1896–Jan. 28, 1984) B: Glasgow, Scotland. M: EDDIE DOWLING. Sister of GORDON, JOHNNY and WILLIAM DOOLEY. The petite performer grew up in Philadelphia. She played babies and obnoxious children before the advent of FANNY BRICE's Baby Snooks. *Hitchy-Koo of 1918* (Globe, revue, June 6, 1918): Let's Play Hookie/WM: E. Ray Goetz, Glen MacDonough. *Ziegfeld Follies of 1919* (New Amsterdam, revue, June 16, 1919): Mandy/WM: Irving Berlin — Shimmy Town/W: Gene Buck, M: Dave Stamper. *The Bunch and Judy* (Globe, "Lizetta" and "Evie Dallas," Nov. 28, 1922): Silenzio; Times Square/W: Anne Caldwell, M: Jerome Kern. *Nifties of 1923* (Fulton, revue, Sept. 25, 1923): When It's Snowing in Hawaii/WM: Frank Crumit. *Sidewalks of New York* (Knickerbocker, "Gertie," Oct. 3, 1927): Playground in the Sky; Wherever You Are/W: Eddie Dowling, M: James F. Hanley. *Thumbs Up!* (St. James, revue, Dec. 27, 1934): Lily Belle May June/W: Earle Crooker, M: Henry Sullivan — My Arab Complex/W: Ballard Macdonald, M: James F. Hanley.

2617. William Dooley (c 1882–Sept. 29, 1921) B: Glasgow, Scotland. Brother of GORDON, JOHNNY and RAY DOOLEY. *Monte Cristo, Jr.* (Winter Garden, "Clarence," Feb. 12, 1919): Are You Stepping Out Tonight?/W: Harold Atteridge, M: Sigmund Romberg, Jean Schwartz.

2618. John Doran *Mecca* (Century, "Abu Yaksan," Oct. 4, 1920): A Fool There Was; Hast Thou Been to Mecca?/W: Oscar Asche, M: Percy E. Fletcher.

2619. Demaris Dore *Present Arms* (Mansfield, "Daisy," Apr. 26, 1928): Crazy Elbows/W: Lorenz Hart, M: Richard Rodgers.

2620. Lynne Dore *Nine-Fifteen Revue* (George M. Cohan, revue, Feb. 11, 1930): Gotta Find a Way to Do It/W: Paul James, M: Roger Wolfe Kahn.

2621. Richard Dore *My Golden Girl* (Nora Bayes > Casino, "Capt. Paul de Bazin," Feb. 2, 1920): Change Partners; A Little Nest for Two; Name the Day/W: Frederic Arnold Kummer, M: Victor Herbert. *Dew Drop Inn* (Astor, "M. Dupont," May 17, 1923): Moonlight Waltz/W: Cyrus D. Wood, M: Alfred Goodman.

2622. Thea Dore *Three Cheers* (Globe, "Floria Farleigh," Oct. 15, 1928): The Americans Are Here/W: B.G. DeSylva, M: Ray Henderson — Because You're Beautiful/W: B.G. DeSylva, Lew Brown, M: Ray Henderson — My Silver Tree/W: Anne Caldwell, M: Raymond Hubbell.

2623. Dorothy Doree *Tattle Tales* (Broadhurst, revue, June 1, 1933): I'll Take an Option on You/W: Leo Robin, M: Ralph Rainger.

2624. Vera Doria (Mar. 20, 1882–June 22, 1957) B: New Zealand. *So Long Letty* (Shubert, "Mrs. Cease," Oct. 23, 1916): Letter Trio/WM: Earl Carroll.

2625. John Dorman (July 19, 1922–) B: Boise, ID. *Guys and Dolls* (New York City Center, revival, "Nicely-Nicely Johnson," May 31, 1955): Fugue for Tinhorns; Guys and Dolls; The Oldest Established; Sit Down, You're Rockin' the Boat/WM: Frank Loesser.

2626. Patricia Dorn *Walk a Little Faster* (St. James, revue, Dec. 7, 1932): Off Again, On Again/Where Have We Met Before?/W: E. Y. Harburg, M: Vernon Duke.

2627. Phyllis Dorne *Almost Crazy* (Longacre, revue, June 20, 1955): Why Not Me?/W: Sam Rosen, M: Ed Scott. *The Vamp* (Winter Garden, "Ticket Girl," Nov. 10, 1955): The Flickers/W: John Latouche, M: James Mundy.

2628. J. Richard (Joseph R.) Dorney *Sharlee* (Daly's, "Jack Vandeveer," Nov. 22, 1923): Broadway Rose; Heart Beats; My Sunshine; Sharlee/W: Alex Rogers, M: C. Luckeyth Roberts.

2629. Marie Doro (May 25, 1882–Oct. 9, 1956) B: Duncannon, PA. Star of silent pictures from 1915 until her retirement in 1922. *The Girl from Kay's* (Herald Square, "Nancy Lowley," Nov. 2, 1903): Smiling Sambo/W: Percy Greenbank, M: Howard Talbot.

2630. Dorothy Dorr (Dec. 23, 1867–) B: Boston, MA. *The Runaways* (Casino, "Josey May," May 11, 1903): How to Write a Comic Opera; In Swell Society/W: Addison Burkhardt, M: Raymond Hubbell.

2631. William Dorriani *Sometime* (Shubert > Casino, "Argentine Singer," Oct. 4, 1918): Spanish Maid (Nina Espagnola)/W: Rida Johnson Young, M: Rudolf Friml. *Tickle Me* (Selwyn, "A Native Boatman," Aug. 17, 1920): The Sun Is Nigh/W: Otto Harbach, Oscar Hammerstein II, M: Herbert Stothart.

2632. John Dorrin (July 17, 1920–) B: Omaha, NE. *Brigadoon* (New York City Center, revival, "Sandy Dean," Mar. 27, 1957): Down on MacConnachy Square/W: Alan Jay Lerner, M: Frederick Loewe. *Gigi* (Uris, "Maitre Duclos," Nov. 13, 1973): The Contract/W: Alan Jay Lerner, M: Frederick Loewe.

2633. Fifi D'Orsay (Apr. 16, 1904–Dec. 2, 1983) B: Montreal, Quebec, Canada. Known as the French Bombshell of 1930s movies, her trademark was the phrase "ooh, la-la." She appeared opposite Will Rogers in her first film, *They Had to See Paris* (1930). *Follies* (Winter Garden, "Solange LaFitte," Apr. 4, 1971): Ah, Paris!/WM: Stephen Sondheim.

2634. Sabry Dorsell *The International Cup* (Hippodrome, "Nancy Gordon," Sept. 3, 1910): Loving/WM: Manuel Klein. *Around the World* (Hippodrome, revue, "Jean Burlington," Sept. 2, 1911): It's a Long Lane That Has No Turning; Salute to the Toreador/WM: Manuel Klein.

2635. Sandra Dorsey (Sept. 28, 1939–) B: Atlanta, GA. *Drat! The Cat!* (Martin Beck, "Emma," Oct. 10, 1965): A Pox Upon the Traitor's Brow; Today Is a Day for a Band to Play/W: Ira Levin, M: Milton Schafer. *On the Town* (Imperial, revival, "Diana Dream," Oct. 31, 1971): Nightclub Song/W: Betty Comden, Adolph Green, M: Leonard Bernstein.

2636. Wisa D'Orso *Mr. President* (St. James, "Princess Kyra," Oct. 20, 1962): The Only Dance I Know (Song for Belly Dancer)/WM: Irving Berlin.

2637. John Dossett *King of Schnorrers* (Playhouse, "David Ben Yonkel," Nov. 28, 1979): Dead; Just for Me; What Do You Do?/WM: Judd Woldin — Tell Me/W: Susan Birkenhead, M: Judd Woldin.

2638. Deborah Dotson *Marilyn* (Minskoff, "Ramona," Nov. 20, 1983): Swing Shift (Miss Parachute)/WM: Beth Lawrence, Norman Thalheimer.

2639. St. Claire Dotson *Hot Rhythm* (Times Square > Waldorf, revue, CR, Sept. 22, 1930): Loving You the Way I Do/W: Jack Scholl, Will Morrissey, M: Eubie Blake.

2640. David Doty *The Best Little Whorehouse Goes Public* (Lunt-Fontanne, "Schmidt," May 10, 1994): Brand New Start/WM: Carol Hall.

2641. J.P. Dougherty (July 25, 1953–) B: Lincoln, IL. *The Three Musketeers* (Broadway, revival, "Innkeeper," Nov. 11, 1984): Gascony Bred/W: Clifford Grey, M: Rudolf Friml.

2642. Bob Douglas *By Jupiter* (Shubert, "Achilles," June 3, 1942): Bottoms Up; For Jupiter and Greece/W: Lorenz Hart, M: Richard Rodgers.

2643. Buddy Douglas (?–2001) *Dream with Music* (Majestic, "Mouse," May 18, 1944): Mouse Meets Girl/W: Edward Eager, M: Clay Warnick.

2644. Larry Douglas (Feb. 17, 1914–Sept. 15,

1996) B: Philadelphia, PA. *What's Up* (National, "Sgt. Willie Klink," Nov. 11, 1943): How Fly Times; My Last Love; You Wash and I'll Dry; You've Got a Hold on Me/W: Alan Jay Lerner, M: Frederick Loewe. *The Duchess Misbehaves* (Adelphi, "Pablo," Feb. 13, 1946): Couldn't Be More in Love; Fair Weather Friends; My Only Romance/W: Gladys Shelley, M: Frank Black. *Hold It!* (National, "Sarge Denton," May 5, 1948): About Face; Down the Well; Heaven Sent; Roll 'Em/W: Sammy Lerner, M: Gerald Marks. *Where's Charley?* (Broadway, CR, "Jack Chesney"): Better Get Out of Here; My Darling, My Darling; The New Ashmoleon Marching Society and Students Conservatory Band/WM: Frank Loesser. *The King and I* (St. James, "Lun Tha," Mar. 29, 1951): I Have Dreamed; We Kiss in a Shadow/W: Oscar Hammerstein II, M: Richard Rodgers. *The Pajama Game* (New York City Center, revival, "Sid Sorokin," May 15, 1957): Hernando's Hideaway; Hey, There; A New Town Is a Blue Town; Once a Year Day; Small Talk; There Once Was a Man/WM: Richard Adler, Jerry Ross.

2645. Norma Douglas *Copper and Brass* (Martin Beck, "Brawn," Oct. 17, 1957): Baby's Baby/W: David Craig, M: David Baker.

2646. Suzzanne Douglas *3 Penny Opera* (Lunt-Fontanne, revival, "Jenny Diver," Nov. 5, 1989): Pimp's Ballad (Tango); Solomon Song/W: Bertolt Brecht, M: Kurt Weill, trans: Michael Feingold. *A Grand Night for Singing* (Criterion Center Stage Right, revue, CR, Dec. 14, 1993): The Gentleman Is a Dope; Hello, Young Lovers; Honey Bun; I Have Dreamed; I Know It Can Happen Again; I'm Gonna Wash That Man Right Outa My Hair; Impossible; It's a Grand Night for Singing; It's Me; Kansas City; A Lovely Night; The Man I Used to Be; My Little Girl (from Soliloquy); So Far; Some Enchanted Evening; That's the Way It Happens; When the Children Are Asleep; When You're Driving Through the Moonlight; Wish Them Well; A Wonderful Guy/W: Oscar Hammerstein II, M: Richard Rodgers.

2647. Walter Douglas *Ginger* (Daly's, "Dick Warewell," Oct. 16, 1923): Beware/W: Frank Stammers, M: Harold Orlob — He Failed to Underwrite a Happy Home; That Ought to Count for Something/W: H.I. Phillips, M: Harold Orlob.

2648. William (Bill) Douglas *Howdy, Mr. Ice!* (Center, revue, June 24, 1948): Forty-eight States; In the Pink; Plenty More Fish in the Sea; Rocked in the Cradle of Jazz; Santa Claus; World's Greatest Show/W: Al Stillman, M: Alan Moran. *Howdy, Mr. Ice of 1950* (Center, revue, May 26, 1949): Big City; Plenty More Fish in the Sea; Rocked in the Cradle of Jazz; We're the Doormen of New York; World's Greatest Show/W: Al Stillman, M: Alan Moran.

2649. Milton (Douglas) Douglass *Padlocks of 1927* (Shubert, revue, CR, Sept. 19, 1927): Hot Heels/W: Billy Rose, Ballard Macdonald, M: Lee David — If I Had a Lover/W: Billy Rose, Ballard Macdonald, M: Henry Tobias. *Good Boy* (Hammerstein's, "Douglass," Sept. 5, 1928): Let's Give a Cheer [Nov. 1928]; Voice of the City/W: Bert Kalmar, M: Harry Ruby, Herbert Stothart. *Melody* (Casino, "Toby," Feb. 14, 1933): The Whole World Loves/W: Irving Caesar, M: Sigmund Romberg.

2650. Nancy Douglass *Bloomer Girl* (Shubert, "Delia," Oct. 4, 1944): Welcome Hinges; When the Boys Come Home/W: E.Y. Harburg, M: Harold Arlen.

2651. Pi Douglass B: Sharon, CT. *The Selling of the President* (Shubert, "Franklin Douglass Pierce" and "Ghoulie," Mar. 22, 1972): Captain Terror; Come-on-a-Good-Life; If You Like People; Sunset/W: Jack O'Brien, M: Bob James.

2652. Stephen Douglass (Sept. 27, 1921–) B: Mt. Vernon, OH. *Carousel* (New York City Center > Majestic, revival, "Billy Bigelow," Jan. 25, 1949): Blow High, Blow Low; The Highest Judge of All; If I Loved You; Soliloquy/W: Oscar Hammerstein II, M: Richard Rodgers. *Make a Wish* (Winter Garden, "Paul Dumont," Apr. 18, 1951): When Does This Feeling Go Away?; Who Gives a Sou?/WM: Hugh Martin. *The Golden Apple* (Alvin, "Ulysses," Apr. 20, 1954): It Was a Glad Adventure; It's the Going Home Together; Store-bought Suit/W: John Latouche, M: Jerome Moross. *The Pajama Game* (St. James, CR, "Sid Sorokin"): Hernando's Hideaway; Hey, There; A New Town Is a Blue Town; Once a Year Day; Small Talk; There Once Was a Man/WM: Richard Adler, Jerry Ross. *Damn Yankees* (46th Street, "Joe Hardy," May 5, 1955): Goodbye, Old Girl; A Man Doesn't Know; Near to You; Two Lost Souls/WM: Richard Adler, Jerry Ross. *Rumple* (Alvin, "Nelson Crandal," Nov. 6, 1957): The First Time I Spoke of You; Gentlemen of the Press; How Do You Say Goodbye?; It's You for Me/W: Frank Reardon, M: Ernest G. Schweikert. *110 in the Shade* (Broadhurst, "File," Oct. 24, 1963): Gonna Be Another Hot Day; A Man and a Woman; Poker Polka; Wonderful Music/W: Tom Jones, M: Harvey Schmidt. *Show Boat* (New York State, revival, "Gaylord Ravenal," July 19, 1966): Only Make Believe; Why Do I Love You; You Are Love/W:

Oscar Hammerstein II, M: Jerome Kern. *I Do! I Do!* (46th Street, CR, "He [Michael]," 1968): All the Dearly Beloved; The Father of the Bride; Good Night; The Honeymoon Is Over; I Do! I Do!; I Love My Wife; Love Isn't Everything; My Cup Runneth Over; Nobody's Perfect; Roll Up the Ribbons; This House; Together Forever; A Well Known Fact; When the Kids Are Married; Where Are the Snows/W: Tom Jones, M: Harvey Schmidt.

2653. Wilfred Douthitt He later became a concert singer named Louis Graveure. *The Lilac Domino* (44th Street, "Count Andre de St. Armand," Oct. 28, 1914): I Call You Back to Me/W: Wilfred Douthitt, M: Ellen Tuckfield — Let the Music Play; Song of the Chimes (Bim Bam); What Is Done You Never Can Undo/W: Robert B. Smith, M: Charles Cuvillier.

2654. Alice Dovey (Aug. 2, 1885–Jan. 11, 1969) B: Plattsmouth, NE. M: JOHN E. HAZZARD. *A Stubborn Cinderella* (Broadway, "Lois," Jan. 25, 1909): Don't Be Anybody's Moon but Mine; Love Me Just Because/W: Will M. Hough, Frank R. Adams, M: Joseph E. Howard. *Old Dutch* (Herald Square, "Liza Streusand," Nov. 22, 1909): I Want a Man to Love Me; My Gypsy Sweetheart; U Dearie/W: George V. Hobart, M: Victor Herbert. *The Summer Widowers* (Broadway, "Celia Carew," June 4, 1910): The Calcium Moon; Gee But I'd Like to Furnish a Flat for You, Dear/W: Glen MacDonough, M: A. Baldwin Sloane. *The Pink Lady* (New Amsterdam, "Angele," Mar. 13, 1911): The Duel; Hide and Seek; My Beautiful Lady; When Love Goes A-Straying/W: C.M.S. McLellan, M: Ivan Caryll. *The Queen of the Movies* (Globe, "Anne Clutterbuck," Jan. 12, 1914): Whistle/W:?, M: Leslie Stuart. *Papa's Darling* (New Amsterdam, "Germaine," Nov. 2, 1914): Edelweiss; Oh, This Love!; Where Shall We Go for Our Honeymoon?; Who Cares!/W: Harry B. Smith, M: Ivan Caryll. *Nobody Home* (Princess > Maxine Elliott, "Violet Brinton," Apr. 20, 1915): Another Little Girl/W: Herbert Reynolds, M: Jerome Kern — The Chaplin Walk/W: Schuyler Greene, M: Otto Motzan, Jerome Kern — You Know and I Know/W: Schuyler Greene, M: Jerome Kern. *Hands Up* (44th Street, "Helene Fudge," July 22, 1915): Cling a Little Closer; Cute Little Summery Time; Tiffany Girl/WM: E. Ray Goetz — Howdy-Do, Goodbye/W: E. Ray Goetz, M: Harold Atteridge — I'm Simply Crazy Over You/W: William Jerome, E. Ray Goetz, M: Jean Schwartz. *Very Good Eddie* (Princess > Casino > 39th Street > Princess, "Elsie Darling," Dec. 23, 1915): Babes in the Wood; Isn't It Great to Be Married?/W: Schuyler Greene, M: Jerome Kern.

2655. Harrison Dowd B: Madison, CT. *Night of Love* (Hudson, "Rudig," Jan. 7, 1941): I'm Thinking of Love; Tonight or Never/W: Rowland Leigh, M: Robert Stolz.

2656. M'el Dowd (Feb. 2, 1940–) B: Chicago, IL. *Camelot* (Majestic, "Morgan Le Fay," Dec. 3, 1960): The Persuasion/W: Alan Jay Lerner, M: Frederick Loewe. *The Sound of Music* (New York City Center, revival, "Elsa Schraeder," Apr. 26, 1967): How Can Love Survive?; No Way to Stop It/W: Oscar Hammerstein II, M: Richard Rodgers.

2657. Helen Dowdy *Show Boat* (Ziegfeld, revival, "Queenie," Jan. 5, 1946): Can't Help Lovin' Dat Man; Queenie's Ballyhoo/W: Oscar Hammerstein II, M: Jerome Kern. *Show Boat* (New York City Center, revival, "Queenie," Sept. 7, 1948): same as above. *Kiss Me, Kate* (New Century, CR, "Hattie"): Another Op'nin', Another Show/WM: Cole Porter. *Mrs. Patterson* (National, "Bessie Bolt," Dec. 1, 1954): I Wish I Was a Bumble Bee/WM: James Shelton.

2658. Doris Dowling (May 15, 1921–) B: Detroit, MI. Notable for character roles in films like *The Lost Weekend* (1945) and *The Blue Dahlia* (1946). *New Faces of 1943* (Ritz, revue, Dec. 22, 1942): Animals Are Nice/W: J.B. Rosenberg, M: Lee Wainer.

2659. Eddie Dowling (Dec. 9, 1892–Feb. 18, 1976) B: Woonsocket, RI. M: RAY DOOLEY. They appeared together in 4 Broadway musicals. *The Velvet Lady* (New Amsterdam, "Mooney," Feb. 13, 1919): Logic; There's Nothing Too Fine for the Finest/W: Henry Blossom, M: Victor Herbert. *Ziegfeld Follies of 1919* (New Amsterdam, revue, June 16, 1919): The Follies Salad/W: Gene Buck, M: Dave Stamper. *Sally, Irene and Mary* (Casino, "Jimmie Dugan," Sept. 4, 1922): How I've Missed You, Mary; Pals; Time Will Tell; Wedding Time/W: Raymond Klages, M: J. Fred Coots. *Sally, Irene and Mary* (Casino, revival, "Jimmie Dugan," Mar. 23, 1925): same as above. *Honeymoon Lane* (Knickerbocker, "Tim Murphy," Sept. 20, 1926): Dreams for Sale/W: Herbert Reynolds, M: James F. Hanley — Little Old New Hampshire; The Little White House (at the End of Honeymoon Lane); The Stone Bridge at Eight/W: Eddie Dowling, M: James F. Hanley — Mary Dear! I Miss You Most of All/W: Henry Creamer, Eddie Dowling, M: James F. Hanley. *Paint Your Wagon* (Shubert, CR, "Ben Rumson," June 1952): I Still See Elisa; Wand'rin Star; Whoop-Ti-Ay!/W: Alan Jay Lerner, M: Frederick Loewe.

2660. Herb Downer *Raisin* (46th Street, "Pastor," Oct. 18, 1973): He Come Down This Morning/W: Robert Brittan, M: Judd Woldin. *Raisin* (46th Street, CR, "Joseph Asagai," c 1974): Alaiyo/W: Robert Brittan, M: Judd Woldin.

2661. Rebecca Downing (Nov. 30, 1962–) B: Birmingham, AL. *Crazy for You* (Sam S. Shubert, CR, "Patsy," c 1995): Slap That Bass/W: Ira Gershwin, M: George Gershwin.

2662. Jerry Downs *Shoot the Works!* (George M. Cohan, revue, July 21, 1931): I Want to Chisel in on Your Heart/W: Max Lief, Nathaniel Lief, M: Michael Cleary.

2663. Johnny Downs (Oct. 10, 1913–June 6, 1994) B: Brooklyn, NY. At age 8 he appeared in the first of the silent film comedies, *Our Gang*, produced by Hal Roach studios and later shown on TV as *Little Rascals*. *Strike Me Pink* (Majestic, revue, Mar. 4, 1933): I Hate to Think That You'll Grow Old, Baby; Strike Me Pink/W: Lew Brown, M: Ray Henderson. *Are You With It?* (New Century, "Wilbur Haskins," Nov. 10, 1945): Nutmeg Insurance; Slightly Perfect; This Is My Beloved/W: Arnold B. Horwitt, M: Harry Revel. *Hold It!* (National, "Bobby Manville," May 5, 1948): About Face; Always You; Buck in the Bank; Heaven Sent; Hold It!/W: Sammy Lerner, M: Gerald Marks.

2664. Charles H. Downz *Americana of 1926* (Belmont, revue, "1st barber in Pan American Quartette," July 26, 1926): Swanee River Melody [added]/W: Al Wilson, M: Charles Weinberg — Thanks Awful/W: Sam M. Lewis, Joe Young, M: Con Conrad — That Lost Barber Shop Chord/W: Ira Gershwin, M: George Gershwin — The Volga Boat Man/W: Dailey Paskman, M: Alexei Archangelsky.

2665. Charles Dox *The Runaways* (Casino, CR, "Diagnosius Fleecem," July 28, 1903): Pretty Maid Adelaide; Tra La La La/W: Addison Burkhardt, M: Raymond Hubbell.

2666. Buddy Doyle (1901–Nov. 9, 1939) *Artists and Models of 1923* (Shubert > Winter Garden, revue, Aug. 20, 1923): Take Me Back to Samoa Some More/W: Cyrus D. Wood, M: Jean Schwartz.

2667. David Doyle (Dec. 1, 1925–Feb. 27, 1997) B: Omaha, NE. Among other TV credits, he played John Bosley in the detective drama *Charlie's Angels* (1976). *South Pacific* (Music Theater of Lincoln Center, revival, "Luther Billis," June 12, 1967): Honey Bun; There Is Nothin' Like a Dame/W: Oscar Hammerstein II, M: Richard Rodgers.

2668. James Doyle Partner of HARLAND DIXON, the two were known as Doyle and Dixon. *The Merry Whirl* (New York, "O.U. Kid," May 30, 1910): The Paris Push; Ring the Wedding Bells/W: Ed Ray, M: Leo Edwards. *The Honeymoon Express* (Winter Garden, "Gaston," Feb. 6, 1913): I Want a Toy Soldier Man/W: Harold Atteridge, M: Jean Schwartz — The Moving Man/W: ?, M: Al W. Brown. *Dancing Around* (Winter Garden, "Lieut. Larry," Oct. 10, 1914): Oh, You John/WM: ?— When Tommy Atkins Smiles at All the Girls/W: Harold Atteridge, M: Sigmund Romberg, Harry Carroll. *Stop! Look! Listen!* (Globe, revue, "Bob Ayers," Dec. 25, 1915): The Law Must Be Obeyed; A Pair of Ordinary Coons; Stop! Look! Listen!/WM: Irving Berlin. *The Century Girl* (Century, revue, "Will B. Rich," Nov. 6, 1916): It Takes an Irishman to Make Love/WM: Elsie Janis, Irving Berlin. *The Canary* (Globe, "Dodge," Nov. 4, 1918): I Wouldn't Give That for the Man Who Couldn't Dance/WM: Irving Berlin — Take a Chance (Little Girl and Learn to Dance/W: Harry B. Smith, M: Jerome Kern. *Wildflower* (Casino, "Alberto," Feb. 7, 1923): Bambalina; Course I Will/W: Otto Harbach, Oscar Hammerstein II, M: Vincent Youmans.

2669. Michael Doyle *Meet the People* (Mansfield, revue, Dec. 25, 1940): A Fellow and a Girl/W: Edward Eliscu, M: Jay Gorney — No Lookin' Back/W: Henry Myers, Edward Eliscu, M: Jay Gorney.

2670. Miriam Doyle *The Maid of the Mountains* (Casino, "Vittoria," Sept. 11, 1918): Husbands and Wives; Over There and Over Here/W: Harry Graham, M: Harold Fraser-Simpson.

2671. Alfred Drake (Oct. 7, 1914–July 25, 1992) B: Brooklyn, NY. One of the most popular singers in Broadway musicals, the baritone debuted on stage in 1933 in the chorus of Gilbert and Sullivan operettas. Years later, he was paid $5,000 a week to star in *Kismet*. *Babes in Arms* (Shubert > Majestic, "Marshall Blackstone," Apr. 14, 1937): Babes in Arms/W: Lorenz Hart, M: Richard Rodgers. *The Two Bouquets* (Windsor, "Albert Parker," May 31, 1938): Against the Stream/WM: trad. — Bashful Lover/W: Eleanor Farjeon, Herb Farjeon, M: C. Moulton — Her Lily-white Hand/W: Eleanor Farjeon, Herb Farjeon, M: Herold — How Can We Bring the Old Folks Round/W: Eleanor Farjeon, Herb Farjeon, M: Henry Smart — What Can I Do?/W: Eleanor Farjeon, Herb Farjeon, M: Samuel Lover, based on What Will You Do, Love? — Yes or No/W: Eleanor Farjeon, Herb Farjeon, M: based on Offenbach. *One for the Money* (Booth, revue,

Feb. 4, 1939): I Only Know; Once Upon a Time; Rhapsody; Send a Boy/W: Nancy Hamilton, M: Morgan Lewis. *The Straw Hat Revue* (Ambassador, revue, Sept. 29, 1939): Four Young People/WM: James Shelton. *Two for the Show* (Booth, revue, Feb. 8, 1940): The All Girl Band; How High the Moon/W: Nancy Hamilton, M: Morgan Lewis. *Oklahoma!* (St. James, "Curly McLain," Mar. 31, 1943): The Farmer and the Cowman; Oh, What a Beautiful Mornin'; Oklahoma; People Will Say We're in Love; Pore Jud; The Surrey with the Fringe on Top/W: Oscar Hammerstein II, M: Richard Rodgers. *Sing Out Sweet Land* (International, revue, "Barnaby Goodchild," Dec. 27, 1944): As I Was Going Along/W: Edward Eager, M: Elie Siegmeister — At Sundown/WM: Walter Donaldson — The Devil and the Farmer's Wife; Little Mohee; Marching Along Down This Road; Wanderin'; Way Down the Ohio/WM: trad.— Hallelujah, I'm a Bum/WM: Harry Kirby McClintock — More Than These; Where/W: Edward Eager, M: John Mundy — My Blue Heaven/W: George Whiting, M: Walter Donaldson — Springfield Mountain (The Pesky Sarpent)/W: poss. Nathan Torrey or Daniel or Jesse Carpenter, M: based on Old Hundred. *The Cradle Will Rock* (Mansfield, revival, "Larry Foreman," Dec. 26, 1947): The Cradle Will Rock; Ex-Foreman; Leaflets; Polyphonic; Stuck Like a Sandwich/WM: Marc Blitzstein. *Kiss Me, Kate* (New Century, "Fred Graham" and "Petruchio," Dec. 30, 1948): I've Come to Wive It Wealthily in Padua; Kiss Me, Kate; So in Love; We Open in Venice; Were Thine That Special Face; Where Is the Life That Late I Led?; Wunderbar/WM: Cole Porter. *The King and I* (St. James, CR, "The King," Apr. 6, 1952/Mar. 1953): A Puzzlement; Shall We Dance?; The Song of the King/W: Oscar Hammerstein II, M: Richard Rodgers. *Kismet* (Ziegfeld, "Hajj," Dec. 3, 1953): And This Is My Beloved; Fate; Gesticulate; The Olive Tree; Rahadlakum; Rhymes Have I/WM: Robert Wright, George Forrest. *Kean* (Broadway, "Edmund Kean," Nov. 2, 1961): Apology?; Civilized People; Domesticity; Elena; The Fog and the Grog; Let's Improvise; Man and Shadow; Service for Service; Sweet Danger; Swept Away; To Look Upon My Love/WM: Robert Wright, George Forrest. *Kismet* (New York State, revival, "Hajj," June 22, 1965): same as above. *Gigi* (Uris, "Honore Lachailles," Nov. 13, 1973): I Remember It Well; I'm Glad I'm Not Young Anymore; It's a Bore; Paris Is Paris Again; Thank Heaven for Little Girls/W: Alan Jay Lerner, M: Frederick Loewe.

2672. Diana Drake *Show Boat* (New York City Center, revival, "Ellie May Chipley," Apr. 8, 1954): Goodbye, My Lady Love/WM: Joseph E. Howard — I Might Fall Back on You; Life Upon the Wicked Stage/W: Oscar Hammerstein II, M: Richard Rodgers. *Hit the Trail* (Mark Hellinger, "Joan," Dec. 2, 1954): Just a Wonderful Time; New Look Feeling; On with the Show; Take Your Time; The Wide Open Spaces/W: Elizabeth Miele, M: Frederico Valerio.

2673. Donna Drake (May 21, 1953–) B: Columbia, SC. *A Chorus Line* (Shubert, CR, "Maggie," Feb. 1977/Apr. 1978): At the Ballet/W: Edward Kleban, M: Marvin Hamlisch. *Sophisticated Ladies* (Lunt-Fontanne, revue, CR, Jan. 5, 1982): Bli-blip/WM: Duke Ellington, Sid Kuller — Hit Me with a Hot Note and Watch Me Bounce/W: Don George, M: Duke Ellington — Imagine My Frustration/WM: Duke Ellington, Billy Strayhorn, Gerald Wilson — Just Squeeze Me/W: Lee Gaines, M: Duke Ellington — Mood Indigo/WM: Duke Ellington, Albany Bigard, Irving Mills. *Wind in the Willows* (Nederlander, "Chief Stoat," Dec. 19, 1985): Evil Weasel; Moving Up in the World; You'll Love It in Jail/WM: Roger McGough, William Perry.

2674. Edwin Drake *The Love Call* (Majestic, CR, "Tim," Nov. 14, 1927): When I Take You All to London/W: Harry B. Smith, M: Sigmund Romberg.

2675. Marty Drake *Hold On to Your Hats* (Shubert, "Radio Aces," Sept. 11, 1940): Don't Let It Get You Down; Then You Were Never in Love; Way Out West Where the West Begins; The World Is in My Arms/W: E.Y. Harburg, M: Burton Lane.

2676. Ronald Drake *Blood Red Roses* (John Golden, "Prince Albert," Mar. 22, 1970): A Garden in the Sun; (O Rock Eternal) Soldier's Prayer/W: John Lewin, M: Michael Valenti.

2677. Susan Drake *Florodora* (New York, CR, "Valleda," Dec. 9, 1901): We Got Up at 8/WM: Leslie Stuart.

2678. Kate Draper *A Day in Hollywood/A Night in the Ukraine* (John Golden > Royale, "Nina," May 1, 1980): Again; Doin' the Production Code; Just Like That; A Night in the Ukraine/W: Dick Vosburgh, M: Frank Lazarus — Just Go to the Movies/WM: Jerry Herman — Too Marvelous for Words/W: Johnny Mercer, M: Richard A. Whiting.

2679. Tamara Drasin see TAMARA.

2680. Inez Draw *Rang-Tang* (Royale, revue, July 12, 1927): Sammy and Topsy/W: Jo Trent, M: Ford Dabney.

2681. Denny Drayson *Heaven on Earth* (New Century, "Punchy," Sept. 16, 1948): Bench in the Park/W: Barry Trivers, M: Jay Gorney.

2682. Thaddius Drayton *Liza* (Daly's, "Dandy," Nov. 27, 1922): Liza/WM: Maceo Pinkard — Lovin' Sam, the Sheik of Alabam'/W: Jack Yellen, M: Milton Ager.

2683. W.P. Dremak (Aug. 2–) B: Akron, OH. *Jesus Christ Superstar* (Mark Hellinger, CR, "Pontius Pilate," July 24, 1972): Pilate and Christ; Pilate's Dream; Trial Before Pilate/W: Tim Rice, M: Andrew Lloyd Webber.

2684. Janis Dremann (Oct. 10, 1913–July 30, 1994) B: Cleveland, OH. *I Married an Angel* (Shubert, "1st Vendeuse" and "Clarinda," May 11, 1938): Angel Without Wings; The Modiste/ W: Lorenz Hart, M: Richard Rodgers.

2685. Louise Dresser (Oct. 5, 1882–Apr. 24, 1965) B: Evansville, IN. M: JACK NORWORTH; JACK GARDNER. She went to Hollywood in 1923, playing character parts in both silent and sound films. She retired from acting in 1937, and helped found the Motion Picture Country House and Hospital where she herself died. *About Town* (Herald Square, "Gertrude Gibson" and "Mrs. Astormont Vanderbell," Oct. 29, 1906): The Gibson Girl; The Same Old Girl/W: Joseph W. Herbert, Raymond Hubbell — I'm Sorry/W: Jack Norworth, M: Albert Von Tilzer. *The Girl Behind the Counter* (Herald Square, "Millie Mostyn," Oct. 1, 1907): Any Time You're Passing By/WM: George Arthurs, C.W. Murphy — I Got to See de Minstrel Show [Dec. 9, 1907]/W: Vincent Bryan, M: Harry Von Tilzer — Much Obliged to You [Nov. 4, 1907]/W: Arthur Anderson, M: Howard Talbot. *The Girls of Gottenburg* (Knickerbocker, "Clementine," Sept. 2, 1908): The Birds in the Trees/ W: Adrian Ross, M: Ivan Caryll — Clementine/W: J.B. Loughrey, M: William T. Francis — Queenie with Her Hair in a Braid/W: John E. Hazzard, M: William T. Francis. *A Matinee Idol* (Daly's > Lyric, "Mrs. Burton," Apr. 28, 1910): Loving Ways/W: A. Seymour Brown, M: Silvio Hein — Put on Your Slippers, You're in for the Night/W: Louise Dresser, E.S.S. Huntington, M: Seymour Furth — Side by Side by the Seaside [June 6, 1910]/WM: ?— Under the Yum-Yum Tree/W: Andrew B. Sterling, M: Harry Von Tilzer. *Hello, Broadway!* (Astor, revue, "Patsy Pygmalion," Dec. 25, 1914): Down by the Erie Canal; Pygmalion Roses/WM: George M. Cohan. *Have a Heart* (Liberty, "Dolly Brabazon," Jan. 11, 1917): Bright Lights; Come Out of the Kitchen/W: P.G. Wodehouse, M: Jerome Kern. *Rock-a-Bye Baby* (Astor, "Aggie," May 22,

1918): According to Dr. Holt; A Kettle Is Singing (The Kettle Song); Little Tune, Go Away; Stitching, Stitching/W: Herbert Reynolds, M: Jerome Kern.

2686. Marie Dressler (Nov. 9, 1869–July 28, 1934) B: Coburg, Ontario, Canada. Daughter of a traveling musician, she played in burlesque, vaudeville and silent film comedies, later starring in MGM comedy-dramas. She is quoted as saying: "I'm too homely for a prima donna and too ugly for a soubrette." She played a leading part in the establishment of Actors Equity. *The Man in the Moon* (New York, "Viola Alum," Apr. 24, 1899): The Timothy D. Sullivan Chowder Party/W: Louis Harrison, Stanislas Stange, M: Gustave Kerker. *The King's Carnival* (New York, revue, "Queen Anne," May 13, 1901): Ragtime Will Be Mah Finish/W: Sydney Rosenfeld, George V. Hobart, M: A. Baldwin Sloane. *Higgledy-Piggledy* (Weber's Music Hall, "Philopena Schnitz," Oct. 20, 1904): A Great Big Girl Like Me; In the Chorus; Mamma's Boarding House/ W: Edgar Smith, M: Maurice Levi. *Twiddle-Twaddle* (Weber's Music Hall, "Matilda Grabfelder," Jan. 1, 1906): Hats; Stories of the Stage; 'Tis Dreadful! 'Tis Astounding; 'Tis Hard to Be a Lady in a Case Like That/W: Edgar Smith, M: Maurice Levi. *Tillie's Nightmare* (Herald Square, "Tillie Blobbs," May 5, 1910): Heaven Will Protect the Working Girl; The Wedding Rehearsal; What I Could do on the Stage/W: Edgar Smith, M: A. Baldwin Sloane. *Roly Poly* (Broadway, "Bijou Fitzsimmons," Nov. 21, 1912): The Prima Donnas; The Zingaras/W: E. Ray Goetz, M: A. Baldwin Sloane.

2687. Charles Drew (c 1846–Nov. 17, 1907) B: Massillon, OH. *The Tattooed Man* (Criterion, "Yussef," Feb. 18, 1907): Take Things Easy; Things We Are Not Supposed to Know/W: Harry B. Smith, M: Victor Herbert.

2688. Don Drew *Earl Carroll's Sketch Book of 1935* (Winter Garden > Majestic, revue, CR, July 1, 1935): Anna Louise of Louisiana/W: Norman Zeno, M: Will Irwin.

2689. Loren Driscoll *Juno* (Winter Garden, "Jerry Devine," Mar. 9, 1959): One Kind Word/WM: Marc Blitzstein.

2690. Donn Driver (c 1923–June 27, 1988) B: Oregon. Dancer, actor, playwright, director. *Show Boat* (New York City Center, revival, CR, "Frank Schultz," May 5, 1954): Goodbye, My Lady Love/WM: Joseph E. Howard — I Might Fall Back on You/W: Oscar Hammerstein II, M: Jerome Kern. *Hit the Trail* (Mark Hellinger, "Jerry," Dec. 2, 1954): Just a Wonderful Time; New Look Feeling; On with the Show; Take

Your Time; The Wide Open Spaces/W: Elizabeth Miele, M: Frederico Valerio. *Finian's Rainbow* (New York City Center, revival, "Og," May 18, 1955): Something Sort of Grandish; When I'm Not Near the Girl I Love/W: E.Y. Harburg, M: Burton Lane.

2691. John S. Driver (Jan. 16, 1947–) B: Erie, PA. *Grease* (Broadhurst, CR, "Roger," c 1974): Mooning; Rock 'n' Roll Party Queen/WM: Jim Jacobs, Warren Casey.

2692. Gregory B. Drotar *Dancin'* (Broadhurst, revue, Mar. 27, 1978/July 24, 1978): Gary Owen/WM: trad. — Was Dog a Doughnut/WM: Cat Stevens.

2693. Hazel Drury *Golden Dawn* (Hammerstein's, "Mombassa Moll," Nov. 30, 1927): Jungle Shadows/W: Oscar Hammerstein II, Otto Harbach, M: Emmerich Kalman, Herbert Stothart.

2694. Patricia Drylie (c 1924–Nov. 11, 1993) B: Toronto, Ontario, Canada. *Ballroom* (Majestic, "Angie," Dec. 14, 1978): One by One/W: Alan Bergman, Marilyn Bergman, M: Billy Goldenberg. *The First* (Martin Beck, "Eunice," Nov. 17, 1981): Is This Year Next Year?/W: Martin Charnin, M: Bob Brush.

2695. Gwen Dubary *The Wedding Trip* (Broadway, "Basile," Dec. 25, 1911): Ah, at Last; Flirtation Duet/W: Harry B. Smith, M: Reginald De Koven.

2696. Bette Dubro *My Darlin' Aida* (Winter Garden, "Jessica Farrow," Oct. 27, 1952 mats.): I Don't Want You; I Want to Pray; Jamboree; Letter Duet; Love Is Trouble; Master and Slave; Me and Lee; The Trial; Why Ain't We Free?/W: Charles Friedman, M: Hans Spialek, based on Giuseppe Verdi.

2697. Maria Duchene *Naughty Marietta* (New York, "Adah," Nov. 7, 1910): Live for Today; 'Neath the Southern Moon/W: Rida Johnson Young, M: Victor Herbert.

2698. Dorceal Duckens *Treemonisha* (Palace, "Luddud," Oct. 21, 1975): Treemonisha in Peril/WM: Scott Joplin.

2699. Dortha Duckworth (Sept. 28, 1905–Nov. 14, 1996) B: Newton, KS. *Oliver!* (Imperial, "Mrs. Bedwin," Jan. 6, 1963): Where Is Love?/WM: Lionel Bart. *Flora, the Red Menace* (Alvin, "The Lady," May 11, 1965): All I Need (Is One Good Break); Palomino Pal/W: Fred Ebb, M: John Kander.

2700. Danielle DuClos (Sept. 29, 1974–) B: Warwick, NY. *Aspects of Love* (Broadhurst, "Jenny Dillingham," Apr. 8, 1990): Falling; The First Man You Remember; Hand Me the Wine and the Dice; Mermaid Song; Other Plea-

sures/W: Don Black, Charles Hart, M: Andrew Lloyd Webber.

2701. Mauricette Ducret *Belmont Varieties* (Belmont, revue, Sept. 26, 1932): No Thank You/W: Mildred Kaufman, M: Alvin Kaufman — That's You; Tu Sais/W: Charles Kenny, M: Serge Walter.

2702. Bernard Dudley (c 1878–Oct. 1964) B: Ireland. *The Merry World* (Imperial, revue, June 8, 1926): Girofle-Girofla/W: Harry B. Smith, M: Charles Lecocq.

2703. Grace Dudley *Florodora* (Casino > New York, CR, "Lady Holyrood"): I Want to Marry a Man, I Do; Tact; When I Leave Town/W: Paul Rubens, M: Leslie Stuart — I've an Inkling/WM: Paul Rubens. *The Girl from Kay's* (Herald Square, "Ellen," Nov. 2, 1903): Bob and Me/W: Claude Aveling, M: Howard Talbot — Tips/W: ?, M: Ivan Caryll.

2704. Harry Dudley *The Ham Tree* (New York, CR, "Bill Peters," Sept. 25, 1905): Sweethearts in Every Town/W: William Jerome, M: Jean Schwartz.

2705. John Dudley *My Lady's Maid* or *Lady Madcap* (Casino, "Lieut. Somerset," Sept. 20, 1906): Flirtation/WM: Percy Greenbank, Paul Rubens.

2706. Tousaint Duers *Hot Rhythm* (Times Square > Waldorf, revue, Aug. 21, 1930): The Penalty of Love/WM: Donald Heywood, Heba Jannath.

2707. John Humbird Duffey *Love's Lottery* (Broadway, "Jack Kite," Oct. 3, 1904): The Sounds We Love to Hear; The Village Recruits/W: Stanislas Stange, M: Julian Edwards. *The Rose Maid* (Globe, "Duke of Barchester," Apr. 22, 1912): I Live for You Alone; Moon, Lovely Moon!; Now His Choice We See; Sweethearts, Wives and Good Fellows (Home of My Heart Good-by); Telephone Song/W: Robert B. Smith, M: Bruno Granichstaedten — A Soldier of Bohemia/W: Raymond W. Peck, M: Robert Hood Bowers. *Sari* (Liberty > New Amsterdam, "Laczi Racz," Jan. 13, 1914): Softly Thro' the Summer Night; Triumphant Youth/W: Catherine Chisholm Cushing, E.P. Heath, M: Emmerich Kalman. *The Three Musketeers* (Manhattan Opera House, "Aramis," May 17, 1921): The Articles of Toilette for a Lady; Now Drink a Glass with Me My Friends; Oh Friendship!; Oh! Who Will Be a Queen!; Yes, I Am Here/WM: Richard W. Temple. *The Chocolate Soldier* (Century, revival, "Maj. Alexius Spiridoff," Dec. 12, 1921): Falling in Love; Never Was There Such a Lover; The Tale of a Coat/W: Stanislaus Stange, M: Oscar Straus. *Sari* (Liberty, revival, "Laczi Racz," Jan. 29, 1930): same as above.

2708. Blanche Duffield *The Baron Trenck* (Casino, "Countess Lydia Von Schwalbenau," Mar. 11, 1912): Angel!; I'm from the Court of the Empress Queen; Incognito; This Handsome Soldier Is Too Bold; Trenck Is My Name; With Song and Cheer/W: Frederick F. Schrader, M: Felix Albini — My Heart's Mine Own/W: Henry Blossom, M: Alfred G. Robyn. *Sari* (Liberty > New Amsterdam, "Juliska Fekete," Jan. 13, 1914): Long Live the King (Vive le Roi); Love Has Wings; Marry Me; Softly Thro' the Summer Night; Triumphant Youth/W: Catherine Chisholm Cushing, E.P. Heath, M: Emmerich Kalman.

2709. Maidie Du Fresne *Americana of 1926* (Belmont, revue, CR, Aug. 30, 1926): Blowin' the Blues Away/W: Ira Gershwin, M: Phil Charig.

2710. Bill Duke (Feb. 26, 1943–) B: Poughkeepsie, NY. Director and actor in movies and TV from 1980. *Ain't Supposed to Die a Natural Death* (Ethel Barrymore, Oct. 20, 1971): I Got the Blood/WM: Melvin Van Peebles.

2711. Jane Dulo (Oct. 13, 1918–May 22, 1994) B: Baltimore, MD. She performed in nightclubs as Jane Dillon. Her many TV credits include *McHale's Navy* (1962) and *Get Smart* (1969). *Are You With It?* (New Century, "Marge Keller," Nov. 10, 1945): Five More Minutes in Bed; Nutmeg Insurance; Send Us Back to the Kitchen/W: Arnold B. Horwitt, M: Harry Revel.

2712. Douglass R. Dumbrille (Oct. 13, 1899–Apr. 2, 1974) B: Hamilton, Ontario, Canada. He went to Hollywood in 1932 where he played gangsters and crooked politicians in more than 200 movies. *Princess Flavia* (Century, "Michael, Duke of Strelsau," Nov. 2, 1925): In Ruritania/W: Harry B. Smith, M: Sigmund Romberg. *The Three Musketeers* (Lyric, "Athos," Mar. 13, 1928): All for One and One for All/W: Clifford Grey, P.G. Wodehouse, M: Rudolf Friml — March of the Musketeers/W: Clifford Grey, M: Rudolf Friml. *Princess Charming* (Imperial, "Ivanoff," Oct. 13, 1930): I'll Be There; One for All/W: Arthur Swanstrom, M: Arthur Schwartz, Albert Sirmay.

2713. Ralph Dumke (July 25, 1899–Jan. 4, 1964) B: South Bend, IN. A football player at Notre Dame, he went into vaudeville, then radio, where he and partner Ed East, calling themselves The Sisters of the Skillet, broadcast humorous advice to housewives on a program called *The Quality Twins* (1928). *The Merry*

Widow (Majestic, revival, "Gen. Bardini," Aug. 4, 1943): Women/W: Adrian Ross, M: Franz Lehar. *Helen Goes to Troy* (Alvin, "Calchas," Apr. 24, 1944): If Menelaus Only Knew It; Tsing-la-la; What Will the Future Say?/W: Herbert Baker, M: Jacques Offenbach, adapted by Eric Wolfgang Korngold. *Mr. Strauss Goes to Boston* (New Century, "Dapper Dan Pepper," Sept. 6, 1945): Down with Sin; For the Sake of Art; Mr. Strauss Goes to Boston/W: Robert Sour, M: Robert Stolz. *Show Boat* (Ziegfeld, revival, "Cap'n Andy Hawks," Jan. 5, 1946): Cap'n Andy's Ballyhoo; Why Do I Love You?/W: Oscar Hammerstein II, M: Jerome Kern.

2714. Daisy Dumont *The Belle of Brittany* (Daly's, "Mlle. Denise de la Vire," Nov. 8, 1909): Little Country Mice; The Old Chateau; Sing to Your Dear One/W: Percy Greenbank, M: Howard Talbot.

2715. Margaret Dumont (Oct. 20, 1889–Mar. 6, 1965) B: Brooklyn, NY. Memorable as a wealthy dowager in the 7 Marx Brothers movies. She also played Mrs. Rhinelander on the TV version of the popular sitcom *My Friend Irma* (1952). *Animal Crackers* (44th Street, "Mrs. Rittenhouse," Oct. 23, 1928): Hooray for Captain Spaulding/WM: Bert Kalmar, Harry Ruby.

2716. Steffi Duna (Feb. 8, 1910–Apr. 22, 1992) B: Budapest, Hungary. M: film actor Dennis O'Keefe. Primarily a dancer, she appeared in a few movies in the 1930s and 40s. *The Threepenny Opera* (Empire, "Polly Peachum," Apr. 13, 1933): Jealousy Duet; Love Duet; Pirate Jenny/W: Bertolt Brecht, M: Kurt Weill.

2717. Brooks Dunbar *The Cradle Will Rock* (Mansfield, Broadway, revival, "Editor Daily," Dec. 26, 1947): Freedom of the Press; Honolulu/WM: Marc Blitzstein.

2718. Dixie Dunbar (Jan. 19, 1915–Aug. 29, 1991) B: Montgomery, AL. Dancer and leading lady of 1930s musical movies. *Life Begins at 8:40* (Winter Garden, revue, Aug. 27, 1934): All the Elks and Masons; Let's Take a Walk Around the Block; You're a Builder — Upper/W: Ira Gershwin, E.Y. Harburg, M: Harold Arlen. *Yokel Boy* (Majestic, "Tiny," July 6, 1939): A Boy Named Lem (and a Girl Named Sue); It's Me Again/W: Lew Brown, Charles Tobias, M: Sam H. Stept.

2719. Cleone Duncan *Anne of Green Gables* (City Center 55th Street, "Lucilla," Dec. 21, 1971): Did You Hear?; General Store/WM: Donald Harron, Norman Campbell.

2720. Doris Duncan *Flossie* (Lyric, "Flossie," June 3, 1924): The First Is Last; Flossie; I'm in Wonderland; Now Is the Time; When Things Go Wrong/W: Ralph Murphy, M: Armand Robi.

2721. Ina Duncan *Runnin' Wild* (Colonial, revue, "Mandy Little," Oct. 29, 1923): Old Fashioned Love/W: Cecil Mack, M: James P. Johnson.

2722. Laura Duncan *Set to Music* (Music Box, revue, Jan. 18, 1939): Debutantes; Mad About the Boy/WM: Noel Coward. *'Tis of Thee* (Maxine Elliott, revue, Oct. 26, 1940): After Tonight/W: Alfred Hayes, M: Al Moss — The Rhythm Is Red an' White an' Blue/W: David Greggory, M: Al Moss.

2723. Rosetta Duncan (Nov. 23, 1900–Dec. 4, 1959) B: Los Angeles, CA. Hugely popular performers of musical comedy, vaudeville and nightclubs, she and VIVIAN DUNCAN were known as the Duncan Sisters. Songwriters, actresses, singers and music publishers, they appeared in the U.S. and in London. Rosetta died in a car accident. *Doing Our Bit* (Winter Garden, revue, Oct. 18, 1917): Old Fashioned Girls/W: Harold Atteridge, M: Sigmund Romberg, Herman Timberg. *She's a Good Fellow* (Globe, "Mazie Moore," May 5, 1919): The Bullfrog Patrol; I've Been Waiting for You All the Time/W: Anne Caldwell, M: Jerome Kern. *Tip Top* (Globe, revue, Oct. 5, 1920): Baby Sister Blues/WM: Henry I. Marshall, Marion Sunshine — Feather Your Nest/WM: James Kendis, James Brockman, Howard Johnson — Humming/W: Louis Breau, M: Ray Henderson — I Want to See My Ida Hoe in Idaho/W: Alex Sullivan, M: Bert Rule — When Shall We Meet Again?/W: Raymond B. Egan, M: Richard A. Whiting. *Topsy and Eva* (Harris, "Topsy," Dec. 23, 1924): Do-Re-Mi; I Never Had a Mammy; Rememb'ring; Um-Um-Da-Da; Uncle Tom's Cabin Blues/WM: Vivian Duncan, Rosetta Duncan — Sweet Onion Time/WM: Sam Coslow. *New Faces of 1936* (Vanderbilt, revue, Oct. 19, 1936): Do-Nuts/W: June Sillman, M: Rev. Hines Rubel.

2724. Sandy Duncan (Feb. 20, 1946–) B: Henderson, TX. M: DON CORREIA. Talented and popular singer and dancer. *The Music Man* (New York City Center, revival, "Zaneeta Shinn," June 16, 1965): Shipoopi/WM: Meredith Willson. *Finian's Rainbow* (New York City Center, revival, "Susan Mahoney," Apr. 5, 1967): When I'm Not Near the Girl I Love/W: E.Y. Harburg, M: Burton Lane. *The Sound of Music* (New York City Center, revival, "Liesel," Apr. 26, 1967): Sixteen, Going on Seventeen/W: Oscar Hammerstein II, M: Richard Rodgers. *Canterbury Tales* (Eugene O'Neill, "Alison" and "Molly" and "May," Feb. 3, 1969): Beer Is Best (Beer, Beer, Beer); I'll Give My Love a Ring;

Pear Tree Quintet; There's the Moon/W: Nevill Coghill, M: Richard Hill, John Hawkins. *The Boy Friend* (Ambassador, revival, "Maisie," Apr. 14, 1970): The Boy Friend; Perfect Young Ladies; The Riviera; Safety in Numbers; Sur La Plage; Won't You Charleston with Me?/WM: Sandy Wilson. *Peter Pan,* or *The Boy Who Wouldn't Grow Up* (Lunt-Fontanne, revival, "Peter Pan," Sept. 6, 1979): I Won't Grow Up; I'm Flying; I've Gotta Crow/W: Carolyn Leigh, M: Moose Charlap — Mysterious Lady; Never Never Land; Ugg-a-Wugg; Wendy/W: Betty Comden, Adolph Green, M: Jule Styne. *Five-Six-Seven-Eight...Dance!* (Radio City Music Hall, revue, June 15, 1983): Cheek to Cheek; It Only Happens When I Dance with You/WM: Irving Berlin — Dance/WM: Paul Jabara — Dance with Me/WM: R. Parker, Jr., David Rubinson — Five-Six-Seven-Eight...Dance!; It's Better with a Band; She Just Loves Las Vegas!/W: David Zippel, M: Wally Harper — I Go to Rio/WM: Peter Allen, Adrienne Anderson — I'm Flying/W: Carolyn Leigh, M: Moose Charlap — I've Got Your Number/W: Carolyn Leigh, M: Cy Coleman — Life Is a Dance/WM: Gavin Christopher — Never Never Land/W: Betty Comden, Adolph Green, M: Jule Styne — Where Did You Learn to Dance?/W: Mack Gordon, M: Josef Myrow — You Mustn't Kick It Around/W: Lorenz Hart, M: Richard Rodgers. *My One and Only* (St. James, "Edith Herbert," Nov. 1, 1984): Blah, Blah, Blah; Boy Wanted; He Loves and She Loves; How Long Has This Been Going On?; I Can't Be Bothered Now; Nice Work If You Can Get It; 'S Wonderful/W: Ira Gershwin, M: George Gershwin.

2725. Todd Duncan (Feb. 12, 1900–Feb. 28, 1998) B: Danville, KY. The singing actor was selected by George Gershwin to originate the role of Porgy. *Porgy and Bess* (Alvin, "Porgy," Oct. 10, 1935): Bess, You Is My Woman Now; I Got Plenty o' Nuttin'; I Loves You, Porgy/W: Ira Gershwin, DuBose Heyward, M: George Gershwin — I'm on My Way; They Pass By Singing; Woman to Lady/W: DuBose Heyward, M: George Gershwin — Oh, Bess, Oh Where's My Bess?/W: Ira Gershwin, M: George Gershwin. *Cabin in the Sky* (Martin Beck, "The Lawd's General," Oct. 25, 1940): The General's Song; Pay Heed/W: John Latouche, M: Vernon Duke. *Porgy and Bess* (Majestic, revival, "Porgy," Jan. 22, 1942): same as above. *Porgy and Bess* (44th Street > New York City Center, revival, "Porgy," Sept. 13, 1943): same as above. *Lost in the Stars* (Music Box, "Stephen Kumalo," Oct. 30, 1949): The Little Grey House; Lost in the Stars; O

Tixo, Tixo, Help Me; The Search; Thousands of Miles/W: Maxwell Anderson, M: Kurt Weill.

2726. Vivian Duncan (June 17, 1902–Sept. 19, 1986) B: Los Angeles, CA. With ROSETTA DUNCAN, they were known as the Duncan Sisters. Nicknamed Jake and Hymie, they performed a yodeling act on stage in 1916; by the 1920s, they were the second highest paid sister act in vaudeville. *Doing Our Bit* (Winter Garden, "Grace Stevens," Oct. 18, 1917): Doing My Bit; Oh, You Sweetie!; Old Fashioned Girls/W: Harold Atteridge, M: Sigmund Romberg, Herman Timberg. *She's a Good Fellow* (Globe, "Betty Blair," May 5, 1919): same as ROSETTA DUNCAN. *Tip Top* (Globe, revue, Oct. 5, 1920): same as ROSETTA DUNCAN. *Topsy and Eva* (Harris, "Eva St. Clare," Dec. 23, 1924): same as ROSETTA DUNCAN. *New Faces of 1936* (Vanderbilt, revue, Oct. 19, 1936): same as ROSETTA DUNCAN.

2727. Mamie Duncan-Gibbs *Jelly's Last Jam* (Virginia, "Hunnie," Apr. 26, 1992): The Chicago Stomp; Good Ole New York; In My Day; Jelly's Jam; Lovin' Is a Lowdown Blues; Somethin' More/W: Susan Birkenhead, M: Jelly Roll Morton — Dr. Jazz/W: Susan Birkenhead, M: Walter Melrose, King Oliver — The Last Rites/ W: Susan Birkenhead, M: Luther Henderson, Jelly Roll Morton. *Cats* (Winter Garden, CR, "Demeter," c 1996): Grizabella, the Glamour Cat; Macavity/W: T.S. Eliot, M: Andrew Lloyd Webber.

2728. Mary Dunckley (Dec. 12, 1910–May 27, 1944) B: New York, NY. *Lovely Lady* (Sam H. Harris, "Marcelle," Dec. 29, 1927): At the Barbecue/W: Harry A. Steinberg, Edward Ward, M: Dave Stamper, Harold A. Levey — The Lost Step; Make Believe You're Happy/W: Cyrus D. Wood, M: Dave Stamper, Harold A. Levey.

2729. Katherine Dunham (June 22, 1910–) B: Chicago, IL. Famous dancer and choreographer, known for her troupe, The Katherine Dunham Dancers. *Cabin in the Sky* (Martin Beck, "Georgia Brown," Oct. 25, 1940): Honey in the Honeycomb; Love Me Tomorrow (But Leave Me Alone Today)/W: John Latouche, M: Vernon Duke. *Carib Song* (Adelphi, "The Woman," Sept. 27, 1945): Basket, Make a Basket; A Girl She Can't Remain; Oh, Lonely One/ W: William Archibald, M: Baldwin Bergersen.

2730. William Dunham *The Passing Show of 1914* (Winter Garden, revue, June 10, 1914): The Moving Picture Glide/W: Harold Atteridge, M: Harry Carroll.

2731. Arthur Dunn (Feb. 3, 1866–Dec. 6, 1932) B: Brooklyn, NY. *The Runaways* (Casino, "Blutch," May 11, 1903): A Kiss for Each Day in the Week; Pretty Maid Adelaide; Tra La La La/W: Addison Burkhardt, M: Raymond Hubbell.

2732. Colleen Dunn *Cats* (Winter Garden, CR, "Cassandra," c 1993): The Old Gumbie Cat/W: T.S. Eliot, M: Andrew Lloyd Webber.

2733. Elaine Dunn *John Murray Anderson's Almanac* (Imperial, revue, Dec. 10, 1953): When Am I Going to Meet Your Mother?; You're So Much a Part of Me/WM: Richard Adler, Jerry Ross. *Catch a Star!* (Plymouth, revue, Sept. 6, 1955): Fly, Little Heart/W: Larry Holofcener, M: Jerry Bock — A Little Traveling Music/W: Paul Francis Webster, Ray Golden, M: Hal Borne — Twist My Arm/W: Paul Francis Webster, M: Sammy Fain. *Flower Drum Song* (St. James, CR, "Linda Low," May 1960): Grant Avenue; I Enjoy Being a Girl; Sunday/W: Oscar Hammerstein II, M: Richard Rodgers. *Pal Joey* (New York City Center, revival, "Gladys Bumps," May 29, 1963): Do It the Hard Way; The Flower Garden of My Heart; Plant You Now, Dig You Later; That Terrific Rainbow; You Mustn't Kick It Around/W: Lorenz Hart, M: Richard Rodgers.

2734. James Dunn (Nov. 2, 1905–Sept. 3, 1967) B: New York, NY. Best remembered for his Oscar winning role as Johnny Nolan in *A Tree Grows in Brooklyn* (1945). *Panama Hattie* (46th Street, "Nick Bullett," Oct. 30, 1940): My Mother Would Love You/WM: Cole Porter.

2735. Johnnie Dunn *Plantation Revue* (48th Street, revue, July 17, 1922): Bugle Call Blues/W: Roy Turk, M: J. Russel Robinson.

2736. Joseph Dunn *Head Over Heels* (George M. Cohan, "Toni," Aug. 29, 1918): Me/W: Edgar Allan Woolf, M: Jerome Kern.

2737. Kathy Dunn *The Sound of Music* (Lunt-Fontanne, "Louisa," Nov. 16, 1959): Do-Re-Mi; Edelweiss; The Lonely Goatherd; So Long, Farewell; The Sound of Music/W: Oscar Hammerstein II, M: Richard Rodgers.

2738. Patricia Dunn (c 1930–May 3, 1990) B: Los Angeles, CA. *Kismet* (Ziegfeld, "Princess of Ababu," Dec. 3, 1953): He's in Love!; Not Since Ninevah; Rahadlakum/WM: Robert Wright, George Forrest.

2739. Robert Dunn *Don't Play Us Cheap!* (Ethel Barrymore, "Mr. Bowser," May 16, 1972): The Book of Life/WM: Melvin Van Peebles.

2740. Vera Dunn (1913–July 11, 2002) *Anything Goes* (Alvin > 46th Street, "Bonnie Letour," Nov. 21, 1934): All Through the Night; Anything Goes; Be Like the Bluebird; Blow, Gabriel, Blow; Buddy, Beware; The Gypsy in Me; I Get a Kick Out of You; Where Are the Men?; You're the Top/WM: Cole Porter.

2741. Irene Dunne (Dec. 20, 1898–Sept. 4, 1990) B: Louisville, KY. A major movie star of the 1930s and 40s. The engaging actress was especially wonderful as Magnolia in *Show Boat* (1936). *The Clinging Vine* (Knickerbocker, "Tessie," Dec. 25, 1922): A Little Bit of Paint/W: Zelda Sears, M: Harold A. Levey. *Lollipop* (Knickerbocker, CR, "Virginia," Mar. 10, 1924): Deep in My Heart; Love in a Cottage; When We Are Married/W: Zelda Sears, M: Vincent Youmans. *The City Chap* (Liberty, "Grace Bartlett," Oct. 26, 1925): The Go-Getter; Like the Nymphs of Spring; No One Knows (How Much I'm in Love); When I Fell in Love with You/W: Anne Caldwell, M: Jerome Kern. *Sweetheart Time* (Imperial, CR, "Violet Stevenson," Mar. 15, 1926): A Girl in Your Arms/W: Irving Caesar, M: Jay Gorney — Sweetheart Time; Who Loves You as I Do?/W: Irving Caesar, M: Joseph Meyer. *Yours Truly* (Shubert, "Diana," Jan. 25, 1927): I Want a Pal; Mayfair/W: Anne Caldwell, M: Raymond Hubbell. *She's My Baby* (Globe, "Polly," Jan. 3, 1928): If I Were You [added]; You're What I Need/W: Lorenz Hart, M: Richard Rodgers. *Luckee Girl* (Casino, "Arlette," Sept. 15, 1928): Chiffon/WM ?—A Flat in Montmartre/WM: Maurice Yvain, Lew Pollack — Friends and Lovers; I Love You So; I'll Take You to the Country; Magic Melody/W: Max Lief, Nathaniel Lief, M: Maurice Yvain.

2742. John Dunsmure *The Viceroy* (Knickerbocker, "Ruffino," Apr. 9, 1900): I See By Your Smile/W: Harry B. Smith, M: Victor Herbert. *Lady Teazle* (Casino, "Snake," Dec. 24, 1904): The Power of the Press; Were I Happily Married/W: John Kendrick Bangs, M: A. Baldwin Sloane. *Happyland* or *The King of Elysia* (Lyric > Casino > Majestic, "Appollus," Oct. 2, 1905): The Black Sheep; Happy Is the Summer's Day; A Soldier of Love/W: Frederick Ranken, M: Reginald De Koven. *The Grand Mogul* (New Amsterdam, "Hon. Josephus Walker," Mar. 25, 1907): Annexation Day/W: Frank Pixley, M: Gustav Luders. *The Young Turk* (New York, "Ammi El Emmun," Jan. 31, 1910): The Sword Is My Sweetheart True/W: Harry Williams, M: Max Hoffmann. *Little Boy Blue* (Lyric, "Earl of Goberdeen," Nov. 27, 1911): The Crystal Ball/W: Grant Stewart, M: Henry Bereny — Sandy McDougal/WM: Edward A. Paulton — When the Mists o' the Night [Feb. 19, 1912]/W: Edward A. Paulton, M: Arthur Weld — You're Very Like Your Sister, Dear/W: Edward A. Paulton, M: Henry Bereny. *Somebody's Sweetheart* (Central >

Casino, "Ben Hud," Dec. 23, 1918): Follow Me; On Wings of Doubt; Sultana/W: Alonzo Price, M: Antonio Bafunno — It Gets Them All/W: Arthur Hammerstein, M: Herbert Stothart. *The Chocolate Soldier* (Century, revival, "Col. Kasimir Popoff," Dec. 12, 1921): The Tale of a Coat/W: Stanislaus Stange, M: Oscar Straus. *The Love Song* (Century, "Col. Bugeaud," Jan. 13, 1925): March On; When the Drum Beat Calls to Glory/W: Harry B. Smith, M: Edward Kunneke, Jacques Offenbach. *The Chocolate Soldier* (Jolson, revival, "Col. Kasimir Popoff," Jan. 27, 1930): same as above. *Gypsy Blonde* (Lyric, "Devilshoof," June 25, 1934): The Broad Highway; Comrade Your Hand; Silence/W: Frank Gabrielson, M: Michael Balfe.

2743. Ethel Dunton *Broadway Nights* (44th Street, revue, "Doris Williams," July 15, 1929): Come Hit Your Baby/W: Moe Jaffe, M: Sam Timberg, Maurie Rubens.

2744. William DuPree *Carmen Jones* (New York City Center, revival, "Joe," May 31, 1956): Dere's a Cafe on de Corner; Dis Flower; If You Would Only Come Away; You Talk Jus' Like My Maw/W: Oscar Hammerstein II, M: Georges Bizet.

2745. Ann Duquesnay *The Wiz* (Lunt-Fontanne, revival, "Glinda," May 24, 1984): If You Believe (Believe in Yourself); A Rested Body Is a Rested Mind/WM: Charlie Smalls. *Jelly's Last Jam* (Virginia, "Gran Mimi," Apr. 26, 1992): Get Away, Boy/W: Susan Birkenhead, M: Luther Henderson — Lonely Boy Blues/WM: trad.

2746. Edward Durand (1871–July 21, 1936) B: France. *Katinka* (44th Street > Lyric, "Arif Bey," Dec. 23, 1915): Skidiskischatch/W: Otto Harbach, M: Rudolf Friml.

2747. Jack Durant (Apr. 12, 1905–Jan. 7, 1984) B: New York, NY. *Pal Joey* (Ethel Barrymore, "Ludlow Lowell," Dec. 25, 1940): Do It the Hard Way; Plant You Now, Dig You Later/W: Lorenz Hart, M: Richard Rodgers. *The Girl from Nantucket* (Adelphi, "Dick Oliver," Nov. 8, 1945): Hooray for Nicoletti/W: Kay Twomey, Burt Milton, M: Jacques Belasco — I Love That Boy/W: Kay Twomey, M: Jacques Belasco — Magnificent Failure/WM: Hughie Prince, Dick Rogers — When a Hick Chick Meets a City Slicker/W: Burt Milton, M: Jacques Belasco. *Pal Joey* (New York City Center, revival, "Ludlow Lowell," May 29, 1963): same as above.

2748. Jimmy Durante (Feb. 10, 1893–Jan. 29, 1980) B: New York, NY. The inimitable comic actor, singer, pianist, songwriter started out to be a photo engraver. By age 14 he was known as Ragtime Jimmy. His vaudeville partners were LOU CLAYTON and EDDIE JACKSON. *Show Girl* (Ziegfeld, "Snozzle," July 2, 1929): Can Broadway Do Without Me?; I Ups to Him and He Ups to Me; I'm Jimmy, the Well Dressed Man/WM: Jimmy Durante — Spain/W: Gus Kahn, M: Isham Jones. *The New Yorkers* (Broadway, "Jimmie Deegan," Dec. 8, 1930): Data; The Hot Patata; Money; Sheikin Fool; Wood/WM: Jimmy Durante — Venice/WM: Cole Porter. *Strike Me Pink* (Majestic, revue, Mar. 4, 1933): A Bit of Temperament; Dinner at Ten; Hollywood, Park Avenue and Broadway; On Any Street; Ooh, I'm Thinking/W: Lew Brown, M: Ray Henderson. *Jumbo* (Hippodrome, "Claudius B. Bowers," Nov. 16, 1935): Laugh; Women/W: Lorenz Hart, M: Richard Rodgers. *Red, Hot and Blue!* (Alvin, "Policy Pinkie," Oct. 29, 1936): A Little Skipper from Heaven Above/WM: Cole Porter. *Stars in Your Eyes* (Majestic, "Bill," Feb. 9, 1939): He's Goin' Home; It's All Yours; Self-Made Man; Terribly Attractive/W: Dorothy Fields, M: Arthur Schwartz. *Keep Off the Grass* (Broadhurst, revue, May 23, 1940): A Fugitive from Esquire/W: Howard Dietz, M: Jimmy McHugh — Rhett, Scarlett, Ashley/W: Al Dubin, M: Jimmy McHugh.

2749. Lillian Durkin *Ed Wynn Carnival* (New Amsterdam, revue, Apr. 5, 1920): Sphinx of the Desert; When I Was Small/WM: Ed Wynn.

2750. Charles Durning (Feb. 28, 1933–) B: Highland Falls, NY. On the TV sitcom *Evening Shade* (1990), he was Dr. Harlan Elldridge. *Drat! The Cat!* (Martin Beck, "Pincer," Oct. 10, 1965): Drat! The Cat!; A Pox Upon the Traitor's Brow; Today Is a Day for a Band to Play/W: Ira Levin, M: Milton Schafer. *Pousse Cafe* (46th Street, "Maurice," Mar. 18, 1966): The Good Old Days/W: Marshall Barer, M: Duke Ellington.

2751. Jean Du Shon *Blues in the Night* (Rialto, "Woman #3," June 2, 1982): Am I Blue?/W: Grant Clarke, M: Harry Akst — Blues in the Night/W: Johnny Mercer, M: Harold Arlen — Dirty No Gooder Blues; It Makes My Love Come Down; Wasted Life Blues/WM: Bessie Smith — I Gotta Right to Sing the Blues/W: Ted Koehler, M: Harold Arlen — Kitchen Man/WM: Andy Razaf, Alex Belledna — New Orleans Hop Scop Blues/WM: George W. Thomas — Nobody Knows You When You're Down and Out/WM: Jimmy Cox — Take It Right Back/WM: H. Grey — Take Me for a Buggy Ride/WM: Wesley Wilson.

2752. Robert DuSold (June 7, 1959–) B: Waukesha, WI. *Les Miserables* (Broadway, CR, "Javert"): Soliloquy; Stars/W: Herbert Kretzmer, M: Claude-Michel Schonberg.

2753. Nancy Dussault (June 30, 1936–) B: Pensacola, FL. *The Cradle Will Rock* (New York City Center, revival, "Sister Mister," Feb. 11, 1960): Croon-Spoon; Honolulu; Let's Do Something/WM: Marc Blitzstein. *Do Re Mi* (St. James, "Tilda Mullen," Dec. 26, 1960): Ambition; Cry Like the Wind; Fireworks; Make Someone Happy; What's New at the Zoo?/W: Betty Comden, Adolph Green, M: Jule Styne. *The Sound of Music* (Lunt-Fontanne, CR, "Maria Rainer," Sept. 1962): Do-Re-Mi; Edelweiss; The Lonely Goatherd; My Favorite Things; An Ordinary Couple; Sixteen, Going on Seventeen; So Long, Farewell; The Sound of Music/W: Oscar Hammerstein II, M: Richard Rodgers. *Bajour* (Shubert, "Emily Kirsten," Nov. 23, 1964/Feb. 28, 1965): Bajour; I Can; Living Simply; Love Is a Chance; Must It Be Love?; Where Is the Tribe for Me?; Words, Words, Words/WM: Walter Marks. *Carousel* (New York City Center, revival, "Carrie Pipperidge," Dec. 15, 1966): June Is Bustin' Out All Over; Mister Snow; A Real Nice Clambake; When the Children Are Asleep; You're a Queer One, Julie Jordan/W: Oscar Hammerstein II, M: Richard Rodgers. *Finian's Rainbow* (New York City Center, revival, "Sharon McLonergan," Apr. 5, 1967): How Are Things in Glocca Morra?; If This Isn't Love; Look to the Rainbow; Old Devil Moon; Something Sort of Grandish; That Great Come-and-Get-It Day/W: E.Y. Harburg, M: Burton Lane. *Into the Woods* (Martin Beck, CR, "Witch," Dec. 13, 1988/May 27, 1989): Children Will Listen; Lament (Children Won't Listen); Last Midnight; Stay with Me; Your Fault/WM: Stephen Sondheim.

2754. Laura Dean Dutton B: Boston, MA. *New Faces of 1943* (Ritz, revue, Dec. 22, 1942): Animals Are Nice; Yes, Sir, I've Made a Date/W: J.B. Rosenberg, M: Lee Wainer — Hey, Gal!; New Shoes/W: June Carroll, M: Will Irwin — Love, Are You Raising Your Head Again?/W: June Carroll, M: Lee Wainer.

2755. Josephine Duval *Mayflowers* (Forrest, "Gypsy's Daughter," Nov. 24, 1925): Oh! Sam/W: Clifford Grey, M: J. Fred Coots, Maurie Rubens — Put Your Troubles in a Candy Box/W: Clifford Grey, M: J. Fred Coots — Whoa, Emma!/W: Clifford Grey, M: Edward Kunneke.

2756. George Dvorsky (May 11, 1959–) B: Greensburg, PA. *Marilyn* (Minskoff, "Jim Dougherty," Nov. 20, 1983): Jimmy Jimmy/

WM: Jeanne Napoli, Doug Frank. *Gentlemen Prefer Blondes* (Lyceum, revival, "Henry Spofford," Apr. 10, 1995): Homesick Blues; Just a Kiss Apart; A Ride on a Rainbow/W: Leo Robin, M: Jule Styne.

2757. Mabel Dwight *Sporting Days* and *Battle in the Skies* (Hippodrome, CR, "Kitty Vanderveer," Feb. 22, 1909): When the Circus Comes to Town/WM: Manuel Klein. *A Trip to Japan* (Hippodrome, CR, "Dolly Dixon," Sept. 4, 1909): Meet Me Where the Lanterns Glow/WM: Manuel Klein.

2758. James Dybas (Feb. 7, 1944–) B: Chicago, IL. *Do I Hear a Waltz?* (46th Street, "Vito," Mar. 18, 1965): Here We Are Again/W: Stephen Sondheim, M: Richard Rodgers. *Pacific Overtures* (Winter Garden, "Old Man," Jan. 11, 1976): Someone in a Tree/WM: Stephen Sondheim.

2759. Melissa Dye (Apr. 15–) B: De Kalb, IL. *Grease* (Eugene O'Neill, revival, CR, Sandy Dumbrowski"): It's Raining on Prom Night; Look at Me, I'm Sandra Dee; Rydell Fight Song; Since I Don't Have You; Summer Nights/WM: Jim Jacobs, Warren Casey.

2760. James Dyer *Messin' Around* (Hudson, revue, Apr. 22, 1929): I Don't Love Nobody but You/W: Perry Bradford, M: James P. Johnson.

2761. James Dyso *The Sun Dodgers* (Broadway, "Officer Muldoon," Nov. 30, 1912): Two Heads Are Better Than One/W: E. Ray Goetz, M: A. Baldwin Sloane.

2762. Ronald (Ronnie) Dyson (June 5, 1950–Nov. 10, 1990) B: Washington, DC. *Hair* (Biltmore, "Ron," Apr. 29, 1968): Abie Baby; Aquarius/W: Gerome Ragni, James Rado, M: Galt MacDermot.

2763. Daisy Eagan (Nov. 4, 1979–) B: Brooklyn, NY. *Les Miserables* (Broadway, CR, "Young Cosette," Apr. 1990): Castle on a Cloud/W: Herbert Kretzmer, M: Claude-Michel Schonberg. *The Secret Garden* (St. James, "Mary Lennox," Apr. 25, 1991): Come Spirit, Come Charm; The Girl I Mean to Be; I Heard Someone Crying; It's a Maze; Letter Song; Opening Dream; Show Me the Key; Storm II; Wick/W: Marsha Norman, M: Lucy Simon.

2764. Berry Earle *A la Carte* (Martin Beck, revue, Aug. 17, 1927): Kangaroo/W: Henry Creamer, M: James P. Johnson.

2765. Edward Earle (Dec. 20, 1929–) B: Santa Barbara, CA. *Musical Chairs* (Rialto, "Brown Suit," May 14, 1980): Musical Chairs/WM: Tom Savage. *Charlie and Algernon* (Helen Hayes, "Dr. Strauss," Sept. 14, 1980): Everything Was Perfect; Have I the Right?; Some Bright Morning/W: David Rogers, M: Charles Strouse.

2766. Florence Earle (?–Apr. 4, 1942) B: Madrid, Spain. M: GEORGE RICHARDS. *Talk About Girls* (Waldorf, "Mrs. Alden," June 14, 1927): Home Town/W: Irving Caesar, M: Harold Orlob.

2767. Hamilton Earle *The Quaker Girl* (Park, CR, "Prince Carlo," 1912): Come to the Ball/W: Adrian Ross, M: Lionel Monckton.

2768. Rosa Earle *Babette* (Broadway, "Margot," Nov. 16, 1903): There Once Was an Owl/W: Harry B. Smith, M: Victor Herbert.

2769. Virginia Earle (Aug. 6, 1873–Sept. 21, 1937) B: Cincinnati, OH. *The Geisha* (Daly's, CR, "Molly Seamore," Dec. 12, 1896): Chon Kina; The Interfering Parrot; The Toy Duet/W: Harry Greenbank, M: Sidney Jones — The Toy Monkey/W: Harry Greenbank, M: Lionel Monckton. *A Runaway Girl* (Daly's > Fifth Avenue, "Winifred Grey," Aug. 31, 1898): The Boy Guessed Right/WM: Lionel Monckton — The Cigarette Song/W: Aubrey Hopwood, M: Lionel Monckton — No One in the World Like You/W: Aubrey Hopwood, M: Alfred D. Cammeyer — The Singing Girl/W: Aubrey Hopwood, Harry Greenbank, M: Ivan Caryl. *The Casino Girl* (Casino, "Percy Harold Ethelbert Frederick Cholmondley," Mar. 19, 1900): Descriptive Song; The Way Actresses Are Made/W: Harry B. Smith, M: Harry T. MacConnell — Down de Lover's Lane/W: Paul Laurence Dunbar, M: Will Marion Cook. *The Belle of Bohemia* (Casino, "Katie," Sept. 24, 1900): Mlle. Zizi; My Lady in the Moon; Pretty Kitty McGuire; Tell Me When I Shall Find Him; What Eve Said to Adam; The Wishing Cap/W: Harry B. Smith, M: Ludwig Englander. *Florodora* (Winter Garden, CR, "Lady Holyrood," Jan. 27, 1902): I Want to Marry a Man, I Do; Tact; When I Leave Town/W: Paul Rubens, M: Leslie Stuart — I've an Inkling/WM: Paul Rubens. *Sergeant Kitty* (Daly's, "Kitty La Tour," Jan. 18, 1904): I Have Thought of a Scheme; Love; Love Laughs at Locksmiths; Oh, Kitty; A Postillion's Life; We Are a Gallant Regiment; What Is a Poor Girl to Do; You Never Know What's Going to Happen Next (Strange Things Happen Every Day)/W: R.H. Burnside, M: A. Baldwin Sloane. *In Newport* (Liberty, "Viola Cartwright," Dec. 26, 1904): Don't Go Too Dangerously Nigh; Peggy Is a New Yorker Now; Stockings; Zel, Zel/W: Bob Cole, James Weldon Johnson, M: J. Rosamond Johnson. *Lifting the Lid* (New Amsterdam roof, "Bessie Otis Adams," June 5, 1905): Baa, Baa, Black Sheep; Over Sunday/W: James O'Dea; M: William C. Polla. *The Geisha* (44th Street, revival, CR, "Molly Seamore," Apr. 30,

1913): Chon Kina; The Interfering Parrot; The Toy Duet/W: Harry Greenbank, M: Sidney Jones.

2770. Candice Earley (Aug. 18, 1950–) B: Ft. Hood, TX. *Grease* (Broadhurst, CR, "Sandy Dumbrowski," June 17, 1975): All Choked Up; It's Raining on Prom Night; Look at Me, I'm Sandra Dee; Summer Nights/WM: Jim Jacobs, Warren Casey.

2771. Gertrude Early *Miss Millions* (Punch and Judy, "Rosie," Dec. 9, 1919): Hustle and Bustle Around/W: R.H. Burnside, M: Raymond Hubbell.

2772. Myles Eason (May 7, 1915–Jan. 8, 1977) B: Tatura, Victoria., Australia. *My Fair Lady* (New York City Center, revival, "Henry Higgins," May 20, 1964): A Hymn to Him; I'm an Ordinary Man; I've Grown Accustomed to Her Face; The Rain in Spain; Why Can't the English?; You Did It/W: Alan Jay Lerner, M: Frederick Loewe.

2773. Randall Easterbrook (Jan. 15, 1951–) B: Peoria, IL. *Hair* (Biltmore, revival, "Claude," Oct. 5, 1977): Hair; I Got Life; Let the Sunshine In (The Flesh Failures); Manchester; Where Do I Go/W: Gerome Ragni, James Rado, M: Galt MacDermot. *Musical Chairs* (Rialto, "Brad," May 14, 1980): Every Time the Music Starts/WM: Tom Savage.

2774. Dickinson Eastham *South Pacific* (Majestic, "Seabee Richard West," Apr. 7, 1949): There Is Nothin' Like a Dame/W: Oscar Hammerstein II, M: Richard Rodgers.

2775. Gretchen Eastman *Iole* (Longacre, "Aphrodite," Dec. 29, 1913): Back to Nature; Nude Descending a Staircase; Think of That/WM: ?— None but the Brave Deserve the Fair/W: Will M. Hough, Frank Adams, M: Joseph E. Howard — Oh Precious Thoughts/W: Robert W. Chambers, M: William F. Peters. *The Road to Mandalay* (Park, "Yvette," Mar. 1, 1916): Back to Paris; Imagination; Shadows/W: William J. McKenna, M: Oreste Vessella. *The Grass Widow* (Liberty > Princess, "Colette," Dec. 3, 1917): Dance with Me; The Grass Widow; Somewhere There's Someone for Me; When the Saxophone Is Playing/W: Channing Pollock, Rennold Wolf, M: Louis A. Hirsch. *The Greenwich Village Follies of 1921* (Shubert, revue, CR, Nov. 14, 1921): That Reminiscent Melody/W: John Murray Anderson, Jack Yellen, M: Milton Ager.

2776. Joan Eastman (c 1937–Aug. 24, 1969) *Stop the World— I Want to Get Off* (Shubert, CR, "Evie Littlechap" and "Anya" and "Ilse" and "Ginnie," July 22, 1963/Nov. 4, 1963): All American; Family Fugue; Glorious Russian; Meilinki Meilchik; Nag! Nag! Nag!; Someone Nice Like You; Typically English; Typische Deutsche/WM: Leslie Bricusse, Anthony Newley.

2777. Julia Eastman *Rogers Brothers in London* (Knickerbocker, "Mabel Strong," Sept. 7, 1903): Mr. Breezy/W: Ed Gardenier, M: Melville Ellis. *Rogers Brothers in Ireland* (Liberty > New York, "Sheila Rhue," Sept. 4, 1905): When I Rode on the Choo Choo Cars/W: George V. Hobart, M: Max Hoffmann.

2778. Sheena Easton (Apr. 27, 1959–) B: Glasgow, Scotland. Pop singer with a number of hit songs, most notably, "Morning Train" WM: Florrie Palmer, 1981. On TV she played Sonny's wife on the drama *Miami Vice* (1987). *Man of La Mancha* (Marquis, revival, "Aldonza," Apr. 24, 1992): The Abduction; Aldonza; The Combat; Dulcinea; It's All the Same; Knight of the Woeful Countenance (The Dubbing); What Do You Want of Me?/W: Joe Darion, M: Mitch Leigh. *Grease* (Eugene O'Neill, revival, CR, "Betty Rizzo"): Greased Lightnin'; Look at Me, I'm Sandra Dee; There Are Worse Things I Could Do/WM: Jim Jacobs, Warren Casey.

2779. Gini Eastwood *Hard Job Being God* (Edison, "Sarah" and "Jacob's Wife" and "Susanna" and "Moabite" and "Judean," May 15, 1972): Famine; Festival; Hail, David; A Psalm of Peace; Ruth; Wherever You Go/WM: Tom Martel.

2780. Doris Eaton (Mar. 14, 1904–) B: Norfolk, VA. Sister of MARY EATON and PEARL EATON. Between 1936 and 1968 she was a dance teacher with the Arthur Murray Studios. At the age of 88, she graduated from Oklahoma University. *No Other Girl* (Morosco, "Molly Lane," Aug. 13, 1924): Day Dreams; I Know That I Love You; Molly/W: Bert Kalmar, M: Harry Ruby. *Big Boy* (44th Street, CR, "Annabelle Bedford," Nov. 30, 1925): Born and Bred in Old Kentucky; The Dance from Down Yonder; Tap the Toe; True Love/W: B.G. DeSylva, M: Joseph Meyer, James F. Hanley. *Cross My Heart* (Knickerbocker, "Elsie Gobble," Sept. 17, 1928): Come Along Sunshine; Dream Sweetheart; Good Days and Bad Days; Sold/W: Joseph McCarthy, M: Harry Tierney.

2781. Mary Eaton (1901–Oct. 10, 1948) B: Norfolk, VA. Sister of DORIS EATON and PEARL EATON. She appeared in several movies, most notably *Cocoanuts* (1929) and *Glorifying the American Girl* (1929). *Ziegfeld Follies of 1920* (New Amsterdam, revue, June 22, 1920): Mary and Doug/W: Gene Buck, M: Dave Stamper — When the Right One Comes Along/W:

Gene Buck, M: Victor Herbert. *Ziegfeld Follies of 1921* (Globe, revue, June 21, 1921): Now I Know/W: Grant Clarke, M: James V. Monaco. *Ziegfeld Follies of 1922* (New Amsterdam, revue, June 5, 1922): Throw Me a Kiss/W: Gene Buck, M: Louis A. Hirsch, Dave Stamper. *Kid Boots* (Earl Carroll > Selwyn, "Polly Pendleton," Dec. 31, 1923): Along the Old Lake Trail; If Your Heart's in the Game; A Play-Fair Man!; Some One Loves You After All; Win for Me/W: Joseph McCarthy, M: Harry Tierney. *Lucky* (New Amsterdam, "Lucky," Mar. 22, 1927): Dancing the Devil Away; Lucky/W: Otto Harbach, Bert Kalmar, M: Harry Ruby — Once in a Blue Moon/W: Anne Caldwell, M: Jerome Kern — Spring Is Here/WM: ?— That Little Something; When the Bo-Tree Blossoms Again/W: Bert Kalmar, Harry Ruby, M: Jerome Kern. *The 5 O'Clock Girl* (44th Street, "Patricia Brown," Oct. 10, 1927): Lonesome Romeos; Thinking of You; Up in the Clouds; Who Did? You Did/W: Bert Kalmar, M: Harry Ruby.

2782. Pearl Eaton (1898–?) Sister of DORIS EATON and MARY EATON. M: Oscar Levant's brother, Harry. Pearl was the first of the 3 Eaton sisters hired by Flo Ziegfeld to be a featured dancer in the *Follies*. She later became a dance director in Hollywood. *Tick-Tack-Toe* (Princess, revue, Feb. 13, 1920): A Double Order of Chicken; My Manicure Maids; Tell Me, Kind Spirit/WM: Herman Timberg. *She's My Baby* (Globe, "Pearl," Jan. 3, 1928): I Need Some Cooling Off; This Goes Up (Smile) (Keep Your Eye on Me); Wasn't It Great? (It's All Over Now); Where Can the Baby Be?/W: Lorenz Hart, M: Richard Rodgers.

2783. Sally Eaton (Aug. 6, 1947–) B: Illinois. *Hair* (Biltmore, "Jeanie," Apr. 29, 1968): Air/W: Gerome Ragni, James Rado, M: Galt MacDermot.

2784. Cheryl Ebarb *The Best Little Whorehouse in Texas* (46th Street > Eugene O'Neill, CR, "Shy," c 1980): Girl, You're a Woman/WM: Carol Hall.

2785. Christine Ebersole (Feb. 21, 1953–) B: Park Forest, IL. *Oklahoma!* (Palace, revival, "Ado Annie Carnes," Dec. 13, 1979): All er Nothin'; The Farmer and the Cowman; I Cain't Say No/W: Oscar Hammerstein II, M: Richard Rodgers. *Camelot* (New York State, revival, "Queen Gueneevere," July 8, 1980): Before I Gaze at You Again; Camelot; I Loved You Once in Silence; The Jousts; The Lusty Month of May; The Simple Joys of Maidenhood; What Do the Simple Folk Do?/W: Alan Jay Lerner, M: Frederick Loewe. *Harrigan 'n Hart* (Longacre, "Gerta

Granville," Jan. 31, 1985): Girl of the Mystic Star; Silly Boy/WM: ?— I Need This One Chance; What You Need Is a Woman/W: Peter Walker, M: Max Showalter.

2786. Buddy Ebsen (Apr. 2, 1908–) B: Belleville, IL. Brother of VILMA EBSEN, with whom he danced in nightclubs and on road tours. He appeared in comic movie musical roles from 1936, and in Westerns. On TV he played Jud Clampett on the popular sitcom *The Beverly Hillbillies* (1962) and was the star of the detective series *Barnaby Jones* (1973). *Yokel Boy* (Majestic, "Elmer Whipple," July 6, 1939): I Know I'm Nobody/W: Lew Brown, Charles Tobias, M: Sam H. Stept. *Show Boat* (Ziegfeld, revival, "Frank Schultz," Jan. 5, 1946): Goodbye, My Lady Love/WM: Joseph E. Howard.

2787. Vilma Ebsen Sister of BUDDY EBSEN. *Between the Devil* (Imperial, "Annabelle Scott," Dec. 22, 1937): Five O'Clock; I'm Against Rhythm; You Have Everything/W: Howard Dietz, M: Arthur Schwartz.

2788. Maude Eburne (Nov. 10, 1875–Oct. 8, 1960) B: Canada. In movies from 1930, she specialized in snoopy neighbors and disapproving matrons. *The Canary* (Globe, "Mary Ellen," Nov. 4, 1918): You're So Beautiful/WM: Irving Berlin. *Love Dreams* (Times Square > Apollo, "Hildegard," Oct. 10, 1921): Reputation/W: Oliver Morosco, M: Werner Janssen. *Great Day!* (Cosmopolitan, "Mazie Brown," Oct. 17, 1929): The Wedding Bells Ring On/W: Billy Rose, Edward Eliscu, M: Vincent Youmans.

2789. Helyn (Helen) Eby-Rock (July 18, 1896–July 20, 1979) B: Pennsylvania. M: WILLIAM ROCK. After her husband died, she became the sidekick of JACK HALEY in vaudeville. They played the Palace in 1925. *The City Chap* (Liberty, "Miss Sperry," Oct. 26, 1925): The Fountain of Youth/W: Anne Caldwell, M: Jerome Kern. *Honeymoon Lane* (Knickerbocker, "Mazie Buck," Sept. 20, 1926): Chorus Picking Time on Broadway/W: Eddie Dowling, M: James F. Hanley.

2790. T. Wilmot Eckert *A Pullman Palace Car* (Haverley's Lyceum, "Detective in Disguise," Nov. 3, 1879): 'Tis Time to Say Good Night/W: ?, M: Alfred Cellier.

2791. Billy Eckhard *Happy* (Daly's, CR, "Teddy," Feb. 6, 1928): Hitting on High; Mad About You/W: Earle Crooker, McElbert Moore, M: Frank Grey.

2792. Lois Eckhart *George White's Scandals of 1936* (New Amsterdam, revue, Dec. 25, 1935): Cigarette; I'm the Fellow Who Loves You/W: Jack Yellen, M: Ray Henderson.

2793. Robert Ecton *Rhapsody in Black* (Sam H. Harris, revue, May 4, 1931): Great Gettin' Up Mornin'/WM: trad. — St. Louis Blues/WM: W.C. Handy.

2794. Jack Eddleman (Sept. 7, 1933–) B: Weatherford, TX. *Hot Spot* (Majestic, "Deva," Apr. 19, 1963): Smiles/W: Martin Charnin, M: Mary Rodgers. *The Girl Who Came to Supper* (Broadway, "Tony Morelli," Dec. 8, 1963): Swing Song/WM: Noel Coward.

2795. Gregg Edelman (Sept. 12, 1958–) B: Chicago, IL. M: CAROLEE CARMELLO. *Cabaret* (Imperial, revival, "Clifford Bradshaw," Oct. 22, 1987): Perfectly Marvelous; Why Should I Wake Up?/W: Fred Ebb, M: John Kander. *Anything Goes* (Vivian Beaumont, revival, CR, "Billy Crocker," May 16, 1989): All Through the Night; Easy to Love; It's Delovely; You're the Top/WM: Cole Porter. *City of Angels* (Virginia, "Stine," Dec. 11, 1989): Double Talk; Funny; You're Nothing Without Me/W: David Zippel, M: Cy Coleman. *Cats* (Winter Garden, CR, "Bustopher Jones" and "Asparagus" and "Growltiger"): Bustopher Jones; Growltiger's Last Stand; Gus: The Theater Cat/W: T.S. Eliot, M: Andrew Lloyd Webber. *Anna Karenina* (Circle in the Square, "Constantine Levin," Aug. 26, 1992): In a Room; On a Train; That Will Serve Her Right; Would You?/W: Peter Kellogg, M: Daniel Levine. *Falsettos* (John Golden, revival, CR, "Marvin," June 1, 1993): The Chess Game; Everyone Hates His Parents; Everyone Tells Jason to See a Psychiatrist; Father to Son; The Fight; Four Jews in a Room Bitching; I Never Wanted to Love You; Jason's Therapy; Love Is Blind; March of the Falsettos; Marvin at the Psychiatrist; Marvin Hits Trina; Something Bad Is Happening; This Had Better Come to a Stop; Thrill of First Love; A Tight Knit Family; Unlikely Lovers; What More Can I Say?; What Would I Do?/WM: William Finn.

2796. Herbert (Herb) Edelman (Nov. 5, 1930–July 21, 1996) B: Brooklyn, NY. He worked extensively on TV, in sitcoms such as *Ladies' Man* (1980), *9 to 5* (1982) and *The Golden Girls* (1985). *Bajour* (Shubert, "The King of Newark," Nov. 23, 1964): Honest Man/WM: Walter Marks.

2797. Sandy Edgerton *Crazy for You* (Sam S. Shubert, CR, "Irene Roth"): Naughty Baby/W: Ira Gershwin, Desmond Carter, M: George Gershwin.

2798. Connie Ediss (Aug. 11, 1871–Apr. 18, 1934) B: Brighton, Sussex, England. Leading comedienne of the Gaiety Theater period of British musicals. *The Shop Girl* (Palmer's, "Ada Smith," Oct. 28, 1895): Foundlings Are We/W: H.J.W. Dam, M: Ivan Caryll. *The Girl Behind the Counter* (Herald Square, "Mrs. Henry Schniff," Oct. 1, 1907): Ah! Eh! Oh! [Dec. 9, 1907]/W: Arthur Wimperis, M: Walter Davidson — Now I've Married a Millionaire/W: J.P. Harrington, M: James W. Tate — When I Was in the Chorus at the Gaiety [Nov. 4, 1907]/WM: Arthur Wimperis, Walter Davidson, Harry Von Tilzer. *The Arcadians* (Liberty > Knickerbocker, "Mrs. Smith," Jan. 17, 1910): Somewhere/W: Arthur Wimperis, M: Lionel Monckton. *The Girl on the Film* (44th Street, "Euphemia Knox," Dec. 29, 1913): On the Ground; You Don't See It but It's There/W: Adrian Ross, M: Walter Kollo, Willie Bredschneider. *Suzi* (Casino > Shubert, "Lina Balzer," Nov. 3, 1914): The Match Makers; Secrets/W: Otto Harbach, M: Aladar Renyi — Teenie-Eenie-Weenie/W: Otto Harbach, M: Paul Lincke.

2799. Edloe (Apr. 1943–) B: Baltimore, MD. *Hello, Dolly!* (St. James, CR, "Ermengarde," c 1968): Put On Your Sunday Clothes/WM: Jerry Herman. *Via Galactica* (Uris, "April," Nov. 28, 1972): Different; Oysters; Terre Haute High/W: Christopher Gore, M: Galt MacDermot.

2800. Wendy Edmead (July 6, 1956–) B: New York, NY. *Stop the World — I Want to Get Off* (New York State, revival, "Susan Littlechap," Aug. 3, 1978): Family Fugue; Nag! Nag! Nag!/WM: Leslie Bricusse, Anthony Newley. *Dancin'* (Broadhurst, revue, CR, Nov. 2, 1978): Dixie/WM: Daniel Decatur Emmett — Here You Come Again/WM: Barry Mann, Cynthia Weil. *Cats* (Winter Garden, "Demeter," Oct. 7, 1982): Grizabella, the Glamour Cat; Macavity/W: T.S. Eliot, M: Andrew Lloyd Webber.

2801. Grace Edmond (?–June 19, 1936) *Oh! Oh! Delphine* (Knickerbocker > New Amsterdam, "Delphine," Sept. 30, 1912): Can We Forget?; Hush! Hush! Hush!; Oh! Oh! Delphine; The Quarrel; Why Shouldn't You Tell Me That?/W: C.M.S. McLellan, M: Ivan Caryll. *Some Night* (Harris, "Marjorie," Sept. 23, 1918): Can't You See?; Something That Money Can't Buy/WM: Harry Delf.

2802. Christopher Edmonds *The Human Comedy* (Royale, "Thief," Apr. 5, 1984): Give Me All the Money/W: William Dumaresq, M: Galt MacDermot.

2803. Florence Edney (June 2, 1879–Nov. 24, 1950) B: London, England. Popular actress in England and the U.S. On the radio soap *Amanda of Honeymoon Hill* (1940), she played Aunt Maisie, "the wise old woman of the valley."

My Best Girl (Park, "Mrs. Wellington Bolliver," Sept. 12, 1912): Howdy-Do/W: Clifton Crawford, M: A. Baldwin Sloane.

2804. May Edouin (?–Sept. 1944) Daughter of WILLIE EDOUIN. *Florodora* (Casino > New York, "Angela Gilfain," Nov. 10, 1900): Galloping/W: Ernest Boyd-Jones, M: Leslie Stuart — Willie Was a Gay Boy/W: Alfred Murray, M: ?.

2805. Willie Edouin (Jan. 1, 1846–Apr. 14, 1908) B: Brighton, Sussex, England. M: ALICE ATHERTON. Father of MAY EDOUIN. One of the most popular comedic actors of his time in Britain and the U.S. *Hiawatha* (Standard, "William Penn Brown," Feb. 21, 1880): Conspirators Three; Yah! Yoh! Yum!/W: Nathaniel Childs, M: Edward E. Rice. *Florodora* (Casino > New York > Winter Garden, "Anthony Tweedlepunch," Nov. 10, 1900): I Want to Marry a Man, I Do/W: Paul Rubens, M: Leslie Stuart — When We're on the Stage/WM: ?.

2806. Paula Edwardes (Sept. 29, 1878–) B: Boston, MA. Broadway soubrette whose very successful stage career began at age 13 and ended with a nervous breakdown. *A Runaway Girl* (Daly's > Fifth Avenue, "Carmencita," Aug. 31, 1898): Barcelona/W: Aubrey Hopwood, Harry Greenbank, M: Ivan Caryll — Society (Oh! I Love Society)/W: Harry Greenbank, M: Lionel Monckton. *A Runaway Girl* (Daly's, revival, "Carmencita," Apr. 23, 1900): same as above. *The Defender* (Herald Square, "Jellie Canvas," July 3, 1902): Good Night; Heart-to-Heart Talks; Houp-La/W: Allen Lowe, M: Charles Denee. *Winsome Winnie* (Casino, "Winnie Walker," Dec. 1, 1903): Everything Is Big in Chicago; Heroes; I Don't Remember That; Sing Song Lee; They're Looking for Me/W: Frederick Ranken, M: Gustave Kerker — Miss Walker of Kalamazoo/WM: Harry Paulton, Edward Jakobowski. *The Princess Beggar* (Casino, "Elaine," Jan. 7, 1907): All Hail the Queen!; Chimes of Long Ago; Madrigal; A Sad, Sad World; When It's Raining/W: Edward A. Paulton, M: Alfred G. Robyn — Wouldn't You Like to Learn to Love Me?/WM: Edward Montagu.

2807. Alan Edwards (June 3, 1892–May 8, 1954) B: New York, NY. *Love o' Mike* (Shubert > Maxine Elliott, "Bruce Grant," Jan. 15, 1917): Don't Tempt Me; Lulu; We'll See/W: Harry B. Smith, M: Jerome Kern. *Her Family Tree* (Lyric > Shubert, Dec. 27, 1920): As We Sow, So Shall We Reap; The Gold-Diggers; A Romantic Knight/WM: Seymour Simons. *Snapshots of 1921* (Selwyn, revue, June 2, 1921): Rendezvous/W: Sidney D. Mitchell, M: Leopold Godowsky. *The*

Gingham Girl (Earl Carroll, "Harrison Bartlett," Aug. 28, 1922): Tell Her While the Waltz Is Playing/W: Neville Fleeson, M: Albert Von Tilzer. *Poppy* (Apollo, "William Van Wyck," Sept. 3, 1923): The Girl I've Never Met/W: Anne Caldwell, M: Ivan Caryll — Poppy Dear; Two Make a Home/W: Dorothy Donnelly, M: Stephen Jones, Arthur Samuels. *Lady, Be Good!* (Liberty, "Jack Robinson," Dec. 1, 1924): So Am I/W: Ira Gershwin, M: George Gershwin. *Twinkle Twinkle* (Liberty, "Richard Grey," Nov. 16, 1926): Sweeter Than You/W: Bert Kalmar, M: Harry Ruby — Twinkle Twinkle/W: Harlan Thompson, M: Harry Archer. *The Merry Malones* (Erlanger's, "Joe Thompson" and "Joe Westcott," Sept. 26, 1927): Like a Little Ladylike Lady Like You; Like the Wandering Minstrel; To Heaven on the Bronx Express/WM: George M. Cohan. *Three Cheers* (Globe, "Barry Vance," Oct. 15, 1928): Maybe This Is Love; Pompanola/W: B.G. DeSylva, Lew Brown, M: Ray Henderson — Two Boys/W: B.G. DeSylva, M: Ray Henderson. *Simple Simon* (Ziegfeld, "Tony Prince" and "Prince Charming," Feb. 18, 1930): I Can Do Wonders with You; Send for Me/W: Lorenz Hart, M: Richard Rodgers.

2808. Carrie Edwards *Strut Miss Lizzie* (Times Square, revue, June 19, 1922): Hoola from Coney Isle/WM: Henry Creamer, Turner Layton.

2809. Charles Edwards (Sept. 1, 1898–Apr. 18, 1978) B: Rhode Island. *Kissing Time* (Lyric, "Paul Pommery," Oct. 11, 1920): Keep a Fox Trot for Me/W: ?, M: Ivan Caryll — Mimi Jazz/WM: ?.

2810. Cliff Edwards (June 14, 1895–July 17, 1971) B: Hannibal, MO. Known as Ukelele Ike, the singer and actor sold over 74 million records and appeared in more than 100 movies. He was the voice of Jiminy Cricket in Walt Disney's animated film, *Pinocchio* (1939), and introduced the Oscar winning song "When You Wish Upon a Star." He died alone and penniless. *The Mimic World* (Century roof, revue, Aug. 17, 1921): The Moth and the Flame/W: George Taggart, M: Max S. Witt — When the Statues Come to Life/W: Howard Johnson, M: Archie Gottler. *Lady, Be Good!* (Liberty, "Jeff," Dec. 1, 1924): Fascinating Rhythm; Little Jazz Bird/W: Ira Gershwin, M: George Gershwin — Insufficient Sweetie [added]/WM: Cliff Edwards, Wells — Who Takes Care of the Caretaker's Daughter (While the Caretaker's Busy Taking Care)?/WM: Chick Endor. *Sunny* (New Amsterdam, "Sam," Sept. 22, 1925): Just a Little Thing Called Rhythm/WM: Edward Ward, Chick Endor —

Paddlin' Madelin' Home/WM: Harry Woods. *George White's Scandals of 1936* (New Amsterdam, revue, Dec. 25, 1935): Anything Can Happen [Mar. 23, 1936]/W: Jack Yellen, Ballard Macdonald, M: Ray Henderson — The Buxom Mrs. Bascom; I'm the Fellow Who Loves You [Mar. 23, 1936]/W: Jack Yellen, M: Ray Henderson.

2811. Eugene Edwards *It's So Nice to Be Civilized* (Martin Beck, "Rev. Williams," June 3, 1980): When I Rise/WM: Micki Grant.

2812. Gloria Edwards (Aug. 7, 1944–Feb. 12, 1988) B: California. M: DICK ANTHONY WILLIAMS. *Ain't Supposed to Die a Natural Death* (Ethel Barrymore, Oct. 20, 1971): Coolest Place in Town/WM: Marvin Van Peebles.

2813. Gordon Edwards *Bless You All* (Mark Hellinger, revue, Dec. 14, 1950): Don't Wanna Write About the South/WM: Harold Rome.

2814. Irving Edwards *The Merry World* (Imperial, revue, June 8, 1926): Deauville/WM: Herman Hupfeld — Military Charleston/WM: ?— Tallahassee/WM: B.G. DeSylva, C. Luckyeth Roberts.

2815. Jack Edwards *Merry-Go-Round* (Klaw, revue, May 31, 1927): Sentimental Silly; Something Tells Me/W: Howard Dietz, Morrie Ryskind, M: Henry Souvaine, Jay Gorney.

2816. Kent (Kenneth) Edwards (c 1918–Aug. 7, 1993) *New Faces of 1943* (Ritz, revue, Dec. 22, 1942): Animals Are Nice/W: J.B. Rosenberg, M: Lee Wainer — Hey, Gal!/W: June Carroll, M: Will Irwin — Land of Rockefellera/W: John Lund, M: Lee Wainer — Richard Crudnut's Charm School/W: June Carroll, John Lund, M: Lee Wainer. *Song of Norway* (Imperial, "Einar," Aug. 21, 1944): Freddy and His Fiddle/WM: Robert Wright, George Forrest, based on Edvard Grieg.

2817. Lou Edwards *The Mimic World* (Century roof, revue, Aug. 17, 1921): The Moth and the Flame/W: George Taggart, M: Max S. Witt.

2818. Marcelle Edwards *Earl Carroll's Vanities of 1932* (Broadway, revue, CR, Oct. 10, 1932): I Gotta Right to Sing the Blues/W: Ted Koehler, M: Harold Arlen.

2819. Maurice Edwards *Happy as Larry* (Coronet, "1st Tailor," Jan. 6, 1950): And So He Died; The Dirty Dog; Give the Doctor the Best in the House; He's a Bold Rogue; Oh, Mrs. Larry; Without a Stitch/W: Donagh MacDonagh, M: Mischa Portnoff, Wesley Portnoff. *The Golden Apple* (Alvin, "Nestor," Apr. 20, 1954): Come Along, Boys; Helen Is Always Willing; It Was a Glad Adventure/W: John Latouche, M: Jerome Moross.

2820. Neely Edwards (Sept. 16, 1883–July 10, 1965) B: Delphos, Ohio. *Ned Wayburn's Town Topics* (Century, revue, "Ben Zine," Sept. 23, 1915): The Oskaloosa Pets/W: Robert B. Smith, M: Harold Orlob.

2821. Penny Edwards (Aug. 24, 1928–Aug. 26, 1998) B: Jackson Heights, NY. At age 15 she appeared in *The Ziegfeld Follies*. In the 1940s and 50s she made Hollywood Westerns, several with Roy Rogers. *The Duchess Misbehaves* (Adelphi, "Mariposa," Feb. 13, 1946): Couldn't Be More in Love; Fair Weather Friends; The Honeymoon Is Over/W: Gladys Shelley, M: Frank Black.

2822. Randall Edwards (June 15, 1955–) B: Atlanta, GA. *Legs Diamond* (Mark Hellinger, "Kiki Roberts," Dec. 26, 1988): I Was Made for Champagne; The Man Nobody Could Love; Now You See Me, Now You Don't; Only Steal from Thieves; Tropicabana Rhumba/WM: Peter Allen.

2823. Sam Edwards (c 1851–May 2, 1921) B: San Francisco, CA. *See America First* (Maxine Elliott, "Sen. Huggins," Mar. 28, 1916): See America First/WM: T. Lawrason Riggs, Cole Porter.

2824. Sarah Edwards (Oct. 11, 1881–Jan. 7, 1965) B: South Wales, UK. M: VERNON JACOBSON. *Princess Virtue* (Central, "Mrs. Demarest," May 4, 1921): Voices of Youth/WM: Gitz Rice, B.C. Hilliam *The Merry Malones* (Erlanger's, "Helen Malone," Sept. 26, 1927): Gip-Gip; Molly Malone/WM: George M. Cohan.

2825. Snitz Edwards (Jan. 1, 1862–May 1, 1937) B: Budapest, Hungary. *The Ballet Girl* (Manhattan, "Kopsdoppen," Dec. 21, 1897): Janken and Mieken/W: Adrian Ross, M: Carl Kiefert — My Dickey Say Nodings at All/W: ?, M: Sebastian Hiller. *The Silver Slipper* (Broadway, "Sir Victor Shallamar," Oct. 27, 1902): Tonight's the Night/W: W.H. Risque, M: Leslie Stuart. *High Jinks* (Lyric > Casino, "Fritz Denkmahl," Dec. 10, 1913): I Know Your Husband Very Well/W: Otto Harbach, M: Rudolf Friml.

2826. Thelma Edwards *Just Fancy* (Casino, "Jill" and "Kay," Oct. 11, 1927): Ain't Love Grand; Dressed Up for Your Sunday Beau; Shake, Brother!; You Came Along/W: Leo Robin, M: Joseph Meyer, Phil Charig.

2827. Thomas Edwards *South Pacific* (New York City Center, revival, "Marine Cpl. Hamilton Steeves," Apr. 13, 1961): There Is Nothin' Like a Dame/W: Oscar Hammerstein II, M: Richard Rodgers.

2828. Gerome Edwardy *Monte Carlo* (Herald Square, "Suzanne," Mar. 21, 1898): The Duties of a Ladies' Maid; The Use of French/W: Harry Greenbank, M: Howard Talbot.

2829. Susan Egan (Feb. 18, 1970–) B: Long Beach, CA. *Beauty and the Beast* (Palace, "Belle," Apr. 18, 1994): Belle; Something There/W: Howard Ashman, M: Alan Menken — Home; Me; No Matter What; Transformation/W: Tim Rice, M: Alan Menken.

2830. Jane Egbert *The Love Call* (Majestic, "Lena Keller," Oct. 24, 1927): I Live, I Die for You; Tony, Tony, Tony/W: Harry B. Smith, M: Sigmund Romberg.

2831. Lucy Egerton *The White Fawn* (Niblo's Garden, "Prince Leander," Jan. 17, 1868): Prince Leander Is My Name; Waking at Early Dawn/W: James Mortimer, M: Edward Mollenhauer.

2832. Marta (Eggerth) Eggert (Apr. 17, 1912–) B: Budapest, Hungary. M: JAN KIEPURA. She starred in filmed operettas in Austria and Germany during the 1930s. *Higher and Higher* (Shubert, "Minnie Sorenson," Apr. 4, 1940): Ev'ry Sunday Afternoon; From Another World; How's Your Health?; Nothing but You/W: Lorenz Hart, M: Richard Rodgers. *The Merry Widow* (Majestic, revival, "Sonia Sadoya, the Widow," Aug. 4, 1943): I Love You So (The Merry Widow Waltz); In Marsovia; Vilia/W: Adrian Ross, M: Franz Lehar — Kuiawiak/W: Jan Kiepura, M: Henri Wieniawski. *The Merry Widow* (New York City Center, revival, "Sonia, the Widow," Oct. 8, 1944): I Love You So (The Merry Widow Waltz); In Marsovia; Vilia/W: Adrian Ross, M: Franz Lehar. *Polonaise* (Alvin, "Marisha," Oct. 6, 1945): Autumn Songs; I Wonder as I Wander; Just for Tonight; Now I Know Your Face by Heart/W: John Latouche, M: Bronislau Kaper, based on Frederic Chopin — The Next Time I Care; Stranger/W: John Latouche, M: Bronislau Kaper. *The Merry Widow* (New York City Center, revival, "Sonia, the Widow," Apr. 10, 1957): same as above.

2833. John Ehrle *Fine and Dandy* (Erlanger's, "Edgar Little," Sept. 23, 1930): Can This Be Love?; Wheels of Steel/W: Paul James, M: Kay Swift. *Face the Music* (44th Street, return engagement, "Rodney St. Clair," Jan. 31, 1933): Drinking Song; My Rhinestone Girl/WM: Irving Berlin.

2834. Anita Ehrler *Jerry's Girls* (St. James, revue, Dec. 18, 1985): It Takes a Woman; It's Today; La Cage Aux Folles; Mame; That's How Young I Feel; We Need a Little Christmas/WM: Jerry Herman.

2835. Jon Ehrlich *Big River: The Adventures*

of Huckleberry Finn (Eugene O'Neill, CR, "Huckleberry Finn," Apr. 21, 1987): I, Huckleberry, Me; Leavin's Not the Only Way to Go; Muddy Water; River in the Rain; Waitin' for the Light to Shine; When the Sun Goes Down in the South; Worlds Apart/WM: Roger Miller.

2836. Ethyl Eichelberger (July 17, 1945– Aug. 12, 1990) B: Pekin, IL. *3 Penny Opera* (Lunt-Fontanne, revival, "Ballad Singer," Nov. 5, 1989): Ballad of Mack the Knife (Moritat)/W: Bertolt Brecht, M: Kurt Weill, trans: Michael Feingold.

2837. Jill Eikenberry (Jan. 21, 1947–) B: New Haven, CT. She played Ann Kelsey on the TV legal drama *L.A. Law* (1986). *Onward Victoria* (Martin Beck, "Victoria Woodhull," Dec. 14, 1980): The Age of Brass; Another Life; Beecher's Defense; Changes; I Depend on You; Love and Joy; Magnetic Healing; Read It in the Weekly; A Taste of Forever; Unescorted Women; Victoria's Banner; You Cannot Drown the Dreamer/W: Charlotte Anker, Irene Rosenberg, M: Keith Herrmann.

2838. Janet Eilber (July 27, 1951–) B: Detroit, MI. *Dancin'* (Broadhurst, revue, CR, May 13, 1980): Pack Up Your Troubles in Your Old Kit Bag (and Smile, Smile, Smile)/W: George Asaf, M: Felix Powell.

2839. George Eising *Sally, Irene and Mary* (44th Street, revival, "Rodman Jones," Mar. 23, 1925): Until You Say Yes/W: Raymond Klages, M: J. Fred Coots.

2840. David Eisler (c 1956–Feb. 16, 1992) *Brigadoon* (New York State, revival, "Charlie Dalrymple," Feb. 28, 1986): Come to Me, Bend to Me; From This Day On; I'll Go Home with Bonnie Jean/W: Alan Jay Lerner, M: Frederick Loewe. *Brigadoon* (New York State, revival, "Charlie Dalrymple," Nov. 7, 1991): Come to Me, Bend to Me; I'll Go Home with Bonnie Jean/W: Alan Jay Lerner, M: Frederick Loewe.

2841. Mabel Elaine *Ned Wayburn's Town Topics* (Century, revue, Sept. 23, 1915): Cotton Blossom Serenade/W: Thomas Gray, M: Harold Orlob. *Hello, Alexander* (44th Street, "Eczema Johnson," Oct. 7, 1919): Ghost of Old Black Joe; Swanee Glide/W: Alfred Bryan, M: Jean Schwartz — Yazoo Rag/WM: ?. *Red Pepper* (Shubert, "Lilly Rose," May 29, 1922): Bugaboo/WM: Howard E. Rogers, Albert Gumble, Owen Murphy — Levee Land; Strut Your Stuff/W: Howard E. Rogers, M: Albert Gumble. *Lovely Lady* (Sam H. Harris, CR, "Parthenia," Apr. 9, 1928): At the Barbecue/W: Harry A. Steinberg, Eddie Ward, M: Dave Stamper, Harold A. Levey. *Boom-Boom* (Casino, CR, "Tilly Mc-

Guire," Feb. 25, 1929): Be That Way; He's Just My Ideal; We're Going to Make Boom-Boom; What a Girl/W: Mann Holiner, J. Keirn Brennan, M: Werner Janssen.

2842. Mildred Elaine M: CHARLES MC-NAUGHTON. *The Little Cafe* (New Amsterdam, CR, "Gaby Gaufrette," Feb. 16, 1914): Just Because It's You; So I Smile; Thy Mouth Is a Rose/W: C.M.S. McLellan, M: Ivan Caryll.

2843. Charlie Elbey *Ned Wayburn's Gambols* (Knickerbocker, revue, Jan. 15, 1929): I Bring My Girls Along/W: Clifford Grey, M: Walter G. Samuels.

2844. Althea Elder *I Married an Angel* (Shubert, "Florabella," May 11, 1938): Angel Without Wings/W: Lorenz Hart, M: Richard Rodgers. *Jackpot* (Alvin, "Peggy," Jan. 13, 1944): The Last Long Mile/W: Howard Dietz, M: Vernon Duke. *Billion Dollar Baby* (Alvin, "Miss Texas," Dec. 21, 1945): Who's Gonna Be the Winner?/W: Betty Comden, Adolph Green, M: Morton Gould. *Three to Make Ready* (Adelphi, revue, Mar. 7, 1946): Barnaby Beach/W: Nancy Hamilton, M: Morgan Lewis.

2845. Mike Eldred *Jesus Christ Superstar* (Paramount Madison Square Garden, revival, "Peter," Jan. 17, 1995): The Arrest; Could We Start Again, Please; Peter's Denial/W: Tim Rice, M: Andrew Lloyd Webber.

2846. Edith Eldridge *The Defender* (Herald Square, "Winsome," July 3, 1902): Love Is Queen of the Sea/W: Allen Lowe, M: Charles Denee.

2847. June Eldridge *The Passing Show of 1914* (Lyric, revue, CR, Oct. 5, 1914): The Girl of Today/W: Harold Atteridge, M: Sigmund Romberg — Kitty MacKay; You're Just a Little Better (Than the One I Thought Was Best)/W: Harold Atteridge, M: Harry Carroll — That Bohemian Rag/W: Lou Havez, M: Gus Edwards, Louis Silvers.

2848. Helen Eley *The Passing Show of 1915* (Winter Garden, revue, May 29, 1915): Gamble on Me!; The Peasant Girl/W: Harold Atteridge, M: Leo Edwards. *Battling Buttler* (Selwyn, "Mrs. Alfred Buttler," Oct. 8, 1923): Apples, Bananas and You/W: Ballard Macdonald, M: Walter L. Rosemont.

2849. Taina Elg (Mar. 9, 1930–) B: Impilahti, Finland. She trained as a ballet dancer with the National Opera Company in Finland and with the Sadler's Wells Ballet. In the 1950s, she appeared in several international films. *Look to the Lilies* (Lunt-Fontanne, "Sister Albertine," Mar. 29, 1970): Casamagordo, New Mexico; Follow the Lamb; Gott Is Gut; Himmlisher Vater; I Admire You Very Much Mr. Schmidt; Look to the Lilies; One Little Brick at a Time; Them and They/W: Sammy Cahn, M: Jule Styne. *Where's Charley?* (Circle in the Square, revival, "Donna Lucia D'Alvadorez," Dec. 20, 1974): Lovelier Than Ever/WM: Frank Loesser. *The Utter Glory of Morrissey Hall* (Mark Hellinger, "Mrs. Delmonde," May 13, 1979): Morning; Oh, Sun/WM: Clark Gesner. *Nine* (46th Street, "Guido's Mother," May 9, 1982): Nine/WM: Maury Yeston.

2850. Claire Elgin *Earl Carroll's Vanities of 1923* (Earl Carroll, revue, CR, July 16, 1923): Get in a Bathing Suit; Jazzmania/WM: Earl Carroll.

2851. Grace Elhew *The Greenwich Village Follies of 1925* (Shubert, revue, Mar. 15, 1926): How Do You Do?/W: Owen Murphy, M: Harold A. Levey.

2852. Alix Elias *Hello, Dolly!* (St. James, CR, "Minnie Fay," Apr. 1967): Dancing/WM: Jerry Herman — Elegance; Motherhood/WM: Bob Merrill, Jerry Herman. *Two Gentlemen of Verona* (St. James, "Lucetta," Dec. 1, 1971): Don't Have the Baby; Follow the Rainbow; Land of Betrayal; Love, Is That You?; Two Gentlemen of Verona/W: John Guare, M: Galt MacDermot.

2853. Sylvia Elias *Princess Virtue* (Central, "Maxine," May 4, 1921): Moonlight/WM: Gitz Rice, B.C. Hilliam.

2854. Tom Elias *Cleavage* (Playhouse, June 23, 1982): All the Lovely Ladies; Living in Sin; The Thrill of the Chase/WM: Buddy Sheffield.

2855. Kate Elinore (Dec. 2, 1876–Dec. 30, 1924) B: Brooklyn, NY. *Naughty Marietta* (New York, "Lizette," Nov. 7, 1910): If I Were Anybody Else but Me; The Sweet Bye-and-Bye/W: Rida Johnson Young, M: Victor Herbert.

2856. David Elledge (July 27, 1957–) B: Omak, WA. *Grand Hotel* (Martin Beck, "Werner Holst," Nov. 12, 1989): Some Have, Some Have Not/WM: Robert Wright, George Forrest, Maury Yeston.

2857. Sandy Ellen *Drat! The Cat!* (Martin Beck, "Emma," Oct. 10, 1965): A Pox Upon the Traitor's Brow; Today Is a Day for a Band to Play/W: Ira Levin, M: Milton Schafer.

2858. Yvonne Elliman (Dec. 29, 1951–) B: Honolulu, Hawaii. *Jesus Christ Superstar* (Mark Hellinger, "Mary Magdalene," Oct. 12, 1971): Could We Start Again, Please; Everything's Alright; I Don't Know How to Love Him; Peter's Denial; What's the Buzz/W: Tim Rice, M: Andrew Lloyd Webber.

2859. Marita Ellin *Allez-Oop* (Earl Carroll, revue, CR, Oct. 3, 1927): In the Heart of

Spain/W: Leo Robin, M: Phil Charig, Richard Myers.

2860. Desiree Ellinger (Oct. 7, 1893–Apr. 30, 1951) B: Manchester, England. International star of the stage for 20 years. In 1925, she flew from Boston to New York in an open cockpit biplane to take over for the ailing MARY ELLIS in *Rose-Marie*. *Rose-Marie* (Imperial, CR, "Rose-Marie La Flamme," June 1925): I Love Him; Indian Love Call; Lak Jeem; Pretty Things; Rose-Marie/W: Otto Harbach, Oscar Hammerstein II, M: Rudolf Friml — The Minuet of the Minute/W: Otto Harbach, Oscar Hammerstein II, M: Herbert Stothart. *Song of the Flame* (44th Street, CR, "Aniuta," June 1926): The Cossack Love Song (Don't Forget Me); Song of the Flame/W: Otto Harbach, Oscar Hammerstein II, M: George Gershwin, Herbert Stothart — The Signal/W: Otto Harbach, Oscar Hammerstein II, M: George Gershwin — Wander Away/ W: Otto Harbach, Oscar Hammerstein II, M: Herbert Stothart. *The Wild Rose* (Martin Beck, "Princess Elise," Oct. 20, 1926): The Coronation; It Was Fate; Lady of the Rose; We'll Have a Kingdom; Wild Rose/W: Otto Harbach, Oscar Hammerstein II, M: Rudolf Friml — L'Heure d'Or (One Golden Hour)/W: Otto Harbach, J.B. Kantor, M: Rudolf Friml. *Cherry Blossoms* (44th Street > Cosmopolitan, "Yo-San" and "O-Yuki-San,' Mar. 28, 1927): Duet; Legend Song; Romance/W: Harry B. Smith, M: Sigmund Romberg—'Neath the Cherry Blossom Moon/ W: J. Keirn Brennan, M: Will Ortman. *Kiss Me* (Lyric, "Doris Durant [Dodo]," July 18, 1927): Dodo; If You'll Always Say Yes; Kiss Me!; Pool of Love; Rose of Iran; Sleeping Beauty's Dream; You in Your Room, I in Mine/W: Derick Wulff, M: Winthrop Cortelyou.

2861. Mercedes Ellington (Feb. 9, 1949–) B: New York, NY. Granddaughter of Duke Ellington. *Sophisticated Ladies* (Lunt-Fontanne, revue, Mar. 1, 1981): Caravan/W: Irving Mills, M: Juan Tizol, Duke Ellington — Hey Baby/ WM: Duke Ellington.

2862. Jessie Elliott *Alive and Kicking* (Winter Garden, revue, Jan. 17, 1950): I'm All Yours/ W: Mike Stuart, Ray Golden, M: Leo Schumer.

2863. John Elliott *Hooray for What!* (Winter Garden, revue, CR, Mar. 28, 1938): Life's a Dance/W: E.Y. Harburg, M: Harold Arlen.

2864. Leonard Elliott (Nov. 23, 1905–Dec. 31, 1989) *Right This Way* (46th Street, "Bomboski," Jan. 4, 1938): Soapbox Sillies/W: Marianne Brown Waters, M: Bradford Greene. *Dream with Music* (Majestic, "Sinbad," May 18, 1944): Give, Sinbad, Give; Mr. and Mrs. Wrong;

Relax and Enjoy It/W: Edward Eager, M: Clay Warnick. *Marinka* (Winter Garden > Ethel Barrymore, "Francis," July 18, 1945): Cab Song; Treat a Woman Like a Drum; Young Man Danube/W: George Marion, Jr., M: Emmerich Kalman.

2865. Patricia Elliott (July 21, 1942–) B: Gunnison, CO. *A Little Night Music* (Shubert, "Countess Charlotte Malcolm," Feb. 25, 1973): Every Day a Little Death/WM: Stephen Sondheim.

2866. Robert Elliott (Oct. 9, 1879–Nov. 15, 1951) B: Ohio. Irish leading man in silent films from 1917. *A Country Girl* (Herald Square, revival, "The Rajah of Bhong," May 29, 1911): Peace! Peace!; The Rajah of Bhong/W: Adrian Ross, M: Lionel Monckton.

2867. Scott Elliott *Ain't Broadway Grand* (Lunt-Fontanne, "Wally Farfle," Apr. 18, 1993): Ain't Broadway Grand/W: Lee Adams, M: Mitch Leigh.

2868. Shawn Elliott B: Puerto Rico. M: DONNA MURPHY. *Jacques Brel Is Alive and Well and Living in Paris* (Town Hall, revue, revival, Feb. 19, 1981): Alone; Bachelor's Dance/ Eng. W: Eric Blau, M: Jacques Brel — The Bulls/ Eng. W: Eric Blau, Mort Shuman, M: Jacques Brel, Gerard Jouannest, Jean Corti — Fannette; Girls and Dogs; The Middle Class; The Statue/ Eng. W: Eric Blau, Mort Shuman, M: Jacques Brel. *City of Angels* (Virginia, "Munoz," Dec. 11, 1989): All Ya Have to Do Is Wait/W: David Zippel, M: Cy Coleman.

2869. Stephen Elliott (Nov. 27, 1920–) B: New York, NY. His TV credits include *Falcon Crest* (1981), *Dallas* (1985) and *Chicago Hope* (1994). *Georgy* (Winter Garden, "James Leamington," Feb. 26, 1970): Georgy; Sweet Memory; That's How It Is/W: Carole Bayer Sager, M: George Fischoff.

2870. Anita Ellis (Apr. 1920–) B: Montreal, Canada. Sister of LARRY KERT. Vocalist on radio's *The Edgar Bergen/Charlie McCarthy Show; The Jack Carson Show* (1943); *The Red Skelton Show* (1945). *Flower Drum Song* (St. James, "Night Club Singer," Dec. 1, 1958): Fan Tan Fannie/W: Oscar Hammerstein II, M: Richard Rodgers.

2871. Antonia Ellis (Apr. 30, 1944–) B: Newport, Isle of Wight. *Pippin* (Imperial, CR, "Fastrada," Jan. 5, 1976): Spread a Little Sunshine/WM: Stephen Schwartz. *Mail* (Music Box, "Sandi," Apr. 14, 1988): Don't Count on It; It's Just a Question of Technique; One Lost Weekend; Publish Your Book/W: Jerry Colker, M: Michael Rupert.

2872. Joan Ellis *The Best Little Whorehouse in Texas* (46th Street, "Shy," June 19, 1978): Girl, You're a Woman/WM: Carol Hall.

2873. Larry Ellis (July 28, 1939–) B: New York, NY. *Frank Merriwell, or Honor Challenged* (Longacre, "Frank Merriwell," Apr. 24, 1971): The Fallin'-Out-of-Love Rag; Howdy, Mr. Sunshine; In Real Life; Inza; Look for the Happiness Ahead; The Pure in Heart/WM: Larry Frank, Skip Redwine. *No, No, Nanette* (46th Street, revival, CR, "Billy Early"): The Call of the Sea; You Can Dance with Any Girl at All/W: Irving Caesar, M: Vincent Youmans — Take a Little One-Step/W: Zelda Sears, M: Vincent Youmans — Telephone Girlie/W: Otto Harbach, M: Vincent Youmans.

2874. Mary Ellis (June 15, 1897–Jan. 30, 2003) B: New York, NY. Soprano and dramatic actress on Broadway and the London stages, in movies and TV. At age 18, she sang with the Metropolitan Opera for the first time. She moved to London in 1930. *Rose-Marie* (Imperial, "Rose-Marie La Flamme," Sept. 2, 1924): I Love Him; Indian Love Call; Lak Jeem; Pretty Things; Rose-Marie/W: Otto Harbach, Oscar Hammerstein II, M: Rudolf Friml — The Minuet of the Minute/W: Otto Harbach, Oscar Hammerstein II, M: Herbert Stothart.

2875. Maurice Ellis (May 11, 1905–) B: Providence, RI. *The Hot Mikado* (Broadhurst, "Pooh-Bah," Mar. 23, 1939): The Flowers That Bloom in the Spring; So Pardon Us; Young Men Despair/W: William S. Gilbert, M: Arthur Sullivan. *Early to Bed* (Broadhurst, "Gendarme," June 17, 1943): Slightly Less Than Wonderful/W: George Marion, Jr., M: Fats Waller. *Seventeen* (Broadhurst, "Genesis," June 21, 1951): I Could Get Married Today/W: Kim Gannon, M: Walter Kent.

2876. Melville Ellis (c 1879–Apr. 4, 1917) B: Phoenix, AZ. In 1913 he worked as pianist and costume and set designer for IRENE BORDONI on her vaudeville tour of the Orpheum circuit. *The Toreador* (Knickerbocker, "Augustus Traill," Jan. 6, 1902): Away to Espana/W: Adrian Ross, M: Ivan Caryll. *Fritz in Tammany Hall* (Herald Square, "Grant Bellyne," Oct. 16, 1905): My Irish Daisy/W: William Jerome, M: Jean Schwartz. *The Orchid* (Herald Square, "Dr. Ronald Fausset," Apr. 8, 1907): Oh, Mr. Registrar!/W: Percy Greenbank, M: Lionel Monckton. *The Honeymoon Express* (Winter Garden, "Dr. D'Zuvray," Feb. 6, 1913): Bring Back Your Love/W: Harold Atteridge, M: Jean Schwartz. *Dancing Around* (Winter Garden, "John Elliot," Oct. 10, 1914): The Broadway Triangle/WM: ?.

2877. Scott Ellis (Apr. 19, 1957–) B: Washington, DC. *Musical Chairs* (Rialto, "Sally's Boyfriend," May 14, 1980): Sally/WM: Tom Savage. *The Rink* (Martin Beck, "Sugar" and "Danny," Feb. 9, 1984): All the Children in a Row; Not Enough Magic/W: Fred Ebb, M: John Kander.

2878. Sheila Ellis *Your Arms Too Short to Box with God* (Lyceum, revue, Dec. 22, 1976): The Band; Come on Down; Just a Little Bit of Jesus Goes a Long Way/WM: Alex Bradford. *But Never Jam Today* (Longacre, "Five of Spades" and "Cook," July 31, 1979): God Could Give Me Anything; A Real Life Lullabye; They/WM: Bob Larimer, Bert Keyes.

2879. Toni Ellis *Blackbirds of 1933-34* (Apollo, revue, Dec. 2, 1933): Your Mother's Son-in-Law/W: Mann Holiner, M: Alberta Nichols.

2880. Dorothy Ellsworth *Let's Go* (Fulton, revue, Mar. 9, 1918): The Flower Garden Girls/WM: ?— The Newspaper Girl/WM: E. Ray Goetz.

2881. Grace Ellsworth *Canary Cottage* (Morosco, "Mrs. Hugg," Feb. 5, 1917): Such a Chauffeur/WM: Earl Carroll.

2882. Harry Ellsworth *The Dream Girl* (Ambassador, CR, "Bobby Thompkins," Oct. 20, 1924): Making a Venus; Stop, Look and Listen/W: Rida Johnson Young, M: Victor Herbert — Saxophone Man/W: Harold Atteridge, M: Sigmund Romberg.

2883. Lucille Elmore *Stepping Stones* (Globe, "Mary," Nov. 6, 1923): Little Angel Cake/W: Anne Caldwell, M: Jerome Kern. *Stepping Stones* (Globe, revival, "Mary," Sept. 1, 1924): same as above.

2884. Marion Elmore *Hiawatha* (Standard, "Mrs. Lo," Feb. 21, 1880): It Was Many Years Ago; A Marriageable Daughter/W: Nathaniel Childs, M: Edward E. Rice.

2885. Steve Elmore (July 12, 1936–) B: Niangua, MO. *Company* (Alvin, "Paul," Apr. 26, 1970): Getting Married Today; Have I Got a Girl for You/WM: Stephen Sondheim. *Sondheim: A Musical Tribute* (Shubert, revue, Mar. 11, 1973): Getting Married Today/WM: Stephen Sondheim. *42nd Street* (CR, "Julian Marsh," Jan. 15, 1985): 42nd Street; Lullaby of Broadway/W: Al Dubin, M: Harry Warren.

2886. Julian Eltinge (May 14, 1881–Mar. 7, 1941) B: Newtonville, MA. This famous female impersonator was called the Mr. Lillian Russell of his day. In 1910 a Broadway theater was named after him; 9 years later he was reputed to be worth a quarter of a million dollars. In 1928 he retired to a California ranch. The year after his death, the Eltinge Theater was converted into a movie house. *The Fascinating Widow* (Liberty, "Hal Blake," Sept. 11, 1911): Don't Take Your Beau to the Seashore/W: E. Ray Goetz, M: Irving Berlin — The Fascinating Widow/W: E. Ray Goetz, M: Kerry Mills — I'm to Be a Blushing Bride; The Ragtime College Girl/W: Sam M. Lewis, M: Kerry Mills. *Cousin Lucy* (George M. Cohan, "Jerry Jackson," Aug. 27, 1915): Mam'-selle Lucette/W: Edward Madden, M: Percy Wenrich — Society; Those Come Hither Eyes; Two Heads Are Better Than One/W: Schuyler Greene, M: Jerome Kern.

2887. Edmund Elton (Feb. 5, 1871–Jan. 4, 1952) B: England. *The Desert Song* (Casino, "Gen. Birabeau," Nov. 30, 1926): All Hail to the General/W: Otto Harbach, Oscar Hammerstein II, M: Sigmund Romberg.

2888. June Elvidge (June 30, 1893–May 1, 1965) B: St. Paul, MN. In movies in the 1910s and 1920s. *The Girl in the Spotlight* (Knickerbocker, "Nina Romaine," July 12, 1920): I Love the Ground You Walk On/W: Robert B. Smith, M: Victor Herbert.

2889. Edgar Atchinson Ely *Madame Troubadour* (39th Street, "Joseph," Oct. 10, 1910): Don't Be Rash; Tra-la-la, Etcetera/W: Joseph W. Herbert, M: Felix Albini.

2890. Stephanie Ely *My One and Only* (St. James, CR, "Edith Herbert," Jan. 3, 1984): Blah, Blah, Blah; Boy Wanted; He Loves and She Loves; How Long Has This Been Going On?; I Can't Be Bothered Now; Nice Work If You Can Get It; 'S Wonderful/W: Ira Gershwin, M: George Gershwin.

2891. Ruby Elzy (1909–June 27, 1943) B: Bontotoc, MS. *Fast and Furious* (New Yorker, revue, Sept. 15, 1931): So Lonesome/WM: J. Rosamond Johnson, Joe Jordan — Where's My Happy Ending?/W: Mack Gordon, Harold Adamson, M: Harry Revel. *Porgy and Bess* (Alvin, "Serena," Oct. 10, 1935): My Man's Gone Now/W: DuBose Heyward, M: George Gershwin — Oh, Bess, Oh Where's My Bess?/W: DuBose Heyward, Ira Gershwin, M: George Gershwin. *John Henry* (44th Street, "Julie Anne," Jan. 10, 1940): I've Trampled All Over; Lullaby/W: Roark Bradford, M: Jacques Wolfe. *Porgy and Bess* (Majestic, revival, "Serena," Jan. 22, 1942): My Man's Gone Now; Time and Time Again/W: DuBose Heyward, M: George Gershwin.

2892. Terrence Emanuel *Hello, Dolly!* (Minskoff, revival, "Cornelius Hackl," Nov. 6, 1975): Dancing; Hello, Dolly!; It Only Takes a Mo-

ment; Put on Your Sunday Clothes/WM: Jerry Herman — Elegance; Motherhood/WM: Bob Merrill, Jerry Herman.

2893. Dorothy Embry *Hummin' Sam* (New Yorker, "Esmaraldae," Apr. 8, 1933): If I Didn't Have You; I'll Be True, but I'll Be Blue/WM: Alexander Hill.

2894. Nellie Emerald *Sergeant Kitty* (Daly's, "Suzette," Jan. 18, 1904): Cupid's Cure/W: R.H. Burnside, M: A. Baldwin Sloane.

2895. Hope Emerson (Oct. 29, 1897–Aug. 24, 1960) B: Hawarden, IA. Six feet two and weighing nearly 200 pounds, she found herself cast as killers and jail matrons in Hollywood movies. On the TV sitcom *I Married Joan* (1952) she played Minerva Parker; on the detective drama *Peter Gunn* (1958) she was Mother. *Smiling Faces* (Shubert, "Amy Edwards," Aug. 30, 1932): Can't Get Rid of Me; It's Just an Old Spanish Custom; Poor Little, Shy Little, Demure Little Me/W: Mack Gordon, M: Harry Revel. *Street Scene* (Adelphi, "Emma Jones," Jan. 9, 1947): Ain't It Awful, the Heat?; Get a Load of That; Ice Cream; When a Woman Has a Baby/W: Langston Hughes, Elmer Rice, M: Kurt Weill.

2896. Lillian Emerson B: Fayetteville, NC. *Tell Her the Truth* (Cort, "Gwen," Oct. 28, 1932): Happy the Day; That's Fine/W: R.P. Weston, Bert Lee, M: Joseph Tunbridge, Jack Waller. *Say When* (Imperial, "Ellen," Nov. 8, 1934): Isn't It June?; It Must Have Been the Night; When Love Comes Swinging Along/W: Ted Koehler, M: Ray Henderson.

2897. Louie Emery *Lassie* (Nora Bayes, "Mrs. McNab," Apr. 6, 1920): Barrin' o' the Door/W: Catherine Chisholm Cushing, M: Hugo Felix.

2898. Rick Emery (c 1953–Apr. 7, 1992) *Musical Chairs* (Rialto, "Tuxedo," May 14, 1980): Musical Chairs; There You Are/WM: Tom Savage.

2899. Jarrod Emick (July 2, 1969–) B: Ft. Eustas, VA. *Miss Saigon* (Broadway, CR, "Chris"): The Ceremony; The Confrontation; The Guilt Inside Your Head; The Last Night of the World; Sun and Moon; The Telephone; Why God Why/W: Richard Maltby, Jr., Alain Boublil, M: Claude-Michel Schonberg. *Damn Yankees* (Marquis, revival, "Joe Hardy," Mar. 3, 1994): Goodbye, Old Girl; A Man Doesn't Know; Near to You; Shoeless Joe from Hannibal, MO./WM: Richard Adler, Jerry Ross.

2900. Ivor Emmanuel (1927–) B: Pontrhydyfen, Wales, UK. *A Time for Singing* (Broadway, "David Griffith," May 21, 1966): And the

Mountains Sing Back; How Green Was My Valley; Let Me Love You; Someone Must Try; That's What Young Ladies Do; There Is Beautiful You Are; What a Party/WM: Gerald Freedman, John Morris.

2901. Dorothy L. Emmerson B: Kyoto, Japan. *The Education of H*Y*M*A*N* K*A*P*-L*A*N* (Alvin, "Eileen Higby," Apr. 4, 1968): A Dedicated Teacher/WM: Paul Nassau, Oscar Brand.

2902. Joseph K. Emmet (Mar. 13, 1841–June 15, 1891) B: St. Louis, MO. An actor who used Dutch dialect humor; a singer, songwriter and musician, Emmet became a hugely popular comic star of his day. *The New Fritz, Our Cousin German* (Standard, "Fritz Von Vonderblinkinstoffen," Apr. 22, 1878): Climb Up, Climb Up; Do You Love Me?; Emmet's Lullaby (Brother's Lullaby); Meet Me at the Garden Gate; Oh, Don't Tickle Me; Oh, He Hit Me in de Nose; Sauerkraut Receipt; Schneider, How You Vas?; She Fainted Away in My Arms; Wake Out/WM: Joseph K. Emmet. *Fritz Among the Gypsies* (14th Street, "Fritz," Jan. 1, 1883): Sweet Violets/WM: Joseph K. Emmet. *Fritz in Ireland* (Park, "Fritz Schultz," Nov. 3, 1897): The Bells Are Ringing; Emmet's Cuckoo Song; Emmet's Lullaby (Brother's Lullaby); Emmet's Swell Song; I Know What Love Is; The Love of the Shamrock; Wilheinderick Strauss/WM: Joseph K. Emmet.

2903. Grace Emmons *The Wedding Trip* (Broadway, "Candide," Dec. 25, 1911): The Family Council/W: Harry B. Smith, M: Reginald De Koven.

2904. Georgia Engel (July 28, 1948–) B: Washington, DC. Most fondly remembered as Georgette on the TV sitcom *The Mary Tyler Moore Show* (1973). *Hello, Dolly!* (St. James, CR, "Minnie Fay," Dec. 26, 1969): Dancing/WM: Jerry Herman — Elegance; Motherhood/WM: Bob Merrill, Jerry Herman. *My One and Only* (St. James, CR, "Mickey," Nov. 1, 1984): Funny Face; I Can't Be Bothered Now/W: Ira Gershwin, M: George Gershwin.

2905. Cecil Engelheart *A Princess of Kensington* (Broadway, "Joy," Aug. 31, 1903): Love in a Cottage; Seven O'Clock in the Morning; Who That Knows How I Love You, Love/W: Basil Hood, M: Edward German. *The Medal and the Maid* (Broadway, "Josephine," Jan. 11, 1904): Come, Kind Gentlemen; Hide and Seek; Who'll Buy My Flowers?/W: Charles H. Taylor, M: Sidney Jones.

2906. Paul England (June 17, 1893–Nov. 21, 1968) B: London, England. *Where's Charley?* (St James > Broadway, "Sir Francis Chesney," Oct.

11, 1948): The New Ashmoleon Marching Society and Students Conservatory Band/WM: Frank Loesser.

2907. Violet Englefield (c 1886–Mar. 22, 1946) B: England. *Sky High* (Shubert > Winter Garden > Casino, "Mrs. Horridge," Mar. 2, 1925): Gossiping/WM: ?.

2908. Anna English *Simply Heavenly* (Playhouse, "Zarita," Aug. 20, 1957): Let Me Take You for a Ride; Let's Ball Awhile; Look for the Morning Star; The Men in My Life/W: Langston Hughes, M: David Martin.

2909. Cory English *Hello, Dolly!* (Lunt-Fontanne, revival, "Barnaby Tucker," Oct. 19, 1995): Dancing; Put on Your Sunday Clothes/WM: Jerry Herman — Elegance; Motherhood/WM: Bob Merrill, Jerry Herman. *A Funny Thing Happened on the Way to the Forum* (St. James, revival, "A Protean," Apr. 18, 1996): Bring Me My Bride; Comedy Tonight/WM: Stephen Sondheim.

2910. Genora English *Swing It* (Adelphi, "Mame," July 22, 1937): Huggin' and Muggin'; It's the Youth in Me/W: Cecil Mack, Milton Reddie, M: Eubie Blake. *Sing for Your Supper* (Adelphi, revue, Apr. 24, 1939): Opening Night/W: Robert Sour, M: Lee Wainer.

2911. Lois Englund *A Chorus Line* (Shubert, CR, "Val," July 1978): And...; Dance: Ten, Looks: Three/W: Edward Kleban, M: Marvin Hamlisch.

2912. Patricia Englund *Angel* (Minskoff, "Madame Victoria," May 10, 1978): I Can't Believe It's You/W: Peter Udell, M: Gary Geld.

2913. John (Jon) Engstrom B: Fresno, CA. *The Pajama Game* (Lunt-Fontanne, revival, "2nd Helper," Dec. 9, 1973): Steam Heat/WM: Richard Adler, Jerry Ross.

2914. Luce Ennis *The Merry Widow* (New York State Theater, revival, "Sylvanie, Mme. Khadja," Aug. 17, 1964): When in France/W: Forman Brown, M: Franz Lehar.

2915. Winston George Enriques *House of Flowers* (Alvin, "Do," Dec. 30, 1954): Smellin' of Vanilla (Bamboo Cage)/WM: Truman Capote, Harold Arlen.

2916. Boni Enten (Feb. 20, 1947–) B: Baltimore, MD. *The Rocky Horror Show* (Belasco, "Columbia," Mar. 10, 1975): Eddie's Teddy; Time Warp/WM: Richard O'Brien. *Pal Joey* (Circle in the Square, revival, "Linda English," June 27, 1976): I Could Write a Book; Take Him/W: Lorenz Hart, M: Richard Rodgers.

2917. Jules Epailly (Oct. 10, 1886–Apr. 29, 1967) B: France. *Princess Virtue* (Central, "Gautier," May 4, 1921): Clothes/WM: Gitz Rice,

B.C. Hilliam. *Lovely Lady* (Sam H. Harris, "Francois," Dec. 29, 1927): Decoys/W: Cyrus D. Wood, M: Dave Stamper, Harold A. Levey.

2918. Phil Eppens *Naughty-Naught ['00]* (American Music Hall, "Stub," Jan. 23, 1937): Coney by the Sea/W: Ted Fetter, M: Richard Lewine.

2919. Alvin Epstein (May 14, 1925–) B: New York, NY. *From A to Z* (Plymouth, revue, Apr. 20, 1960): South American Way/W: Fred Ebb, M: Norman L. Martin. *No Strings* (54th Street, "Luc Delbert," Mar. 15, 1962): Be My Host; La, La, La/WM: Richard Rodgers. *A Kurt Weill Cabaret* (Bijou, revue, Nov. 5, 1979/Mar. 22, 1980): Alabama Song; Duet, Herr Jakob Schmidt/W: Bertolt Brecht, M: Kurt Weill — Ballad of Mack the Knife (Moritat)/Ger. W: Bertolt Brecht, Eng. W: Marc Blitzstein, M: Kurt Weill — Ballad of Sexual Slavery/W: George Tabori, M: Kurt Weill — Ballad of the Pimp and the Whore; Kanonensong/W: Marc Blitzstein, M: Kurt Weill — Eating/W: Arnold Weinstein, M: Kurt Weill — The Life That We Lead; Sailor's Tango/W: Will Holt, M: Kurt Weill — The Saga of Jenny/W: Ira Gershwin, M: Kurt Weill — September Song/W: Maxwell Anderson, M: Kurt Weill — That's Him/W: Ogden Nash, M: Kurt Weill. *3 Penny Opera* (Lunt-Fontanne, revival, "Jonathan Jeremiah Peachum," Nov. 5, 1989): Peachum's Morning Hymn; Song of Futility; Why-Can't-They Song/W: Bertolt Brecht, M: Kurt Weill, trans: Michael Feingold.

2920. Pierre Epstein (July 27, 1930–) B: Toulouse, France. *Bajour* (Shubert, CR, "The King of Newark," May 17, 1965): Honest Man/WM: Walter Marks.

2921. Eddie Ericksen *Donnybrook!* (46th Street, "An Irish Boy," May 18, 1961): The Day the Snow Is Meltin'/WM: Johnny Burke.

2922. Leif Erickson (Oct. 27, 1911–Jan. 29, 1986) B: Alameda, California. M: actress Frances Farmer; they later divorced. The singer and actor appeared in more than 75 movies. On the radio he was Richard Rhinelander on the sitcom *My Friend Irma* (1947). On TV he played Big John Cannon in the Western *The High Chaparral* (1967). *Higher and Higher* (Shubert, "Patrick O'Toole," Apr. 4, 1940): Ev'ry Sunday Afternoon; How's Your Health?; Nothing but You/W: Lorenz Hart, M: Richard Rodgers.

2923. Aimee Erlich *Little Nemo* (New Amsterdam, "Little Princess," Oct. 20, 1908): In Happy Slumberland; Won't You Be My Playmate?/W: Harry B. Smith, M: Victor Herbert.

2924. Peter Ermides *The Who's Tommy* (St. James, CR, "Tommy" c 1994): Amazing Journey; I'm Free; Listening to You; Pinball Wizard; See Me, Feel Me; Sensation; Welcome; We're Not Going to Take It/WM: Pete Townshend.

2925. Arthur (Earnest) Ernest *His Honor the Mayor* (New York > Wallack's, "Jack Thayer," May 28, 1906): She's All My Own (Mary Ann)/W: Charles J. Campbell, Ralph Skinner, M: Julian Edwards.

2926. Leila Ernst (July 28, 1922–) B: Jaffrey, NH. *Too Many Girls* (Imperial, "Tallulah Lou," Oct. 18, 1939): Spic and Spanish/W: Lorenz Hart, M: Richard Rodgers. *Pal Joey* (Ethel Barrymore > Shubert > St. James, "Linda English," Dec. 25, 1940): I Could Write a Book; Take Him/W: Lorenz Hart, M: Richard Rodgers. *If the Shoe Fits* (Century, "Cinderella," Dec. 5, 1946): I Wish; I'm Not Myself Tonight; In the Morning; This Is the End of the Story; Three Questions; With a Wave of My Wand/W: June Carroll, M: David Raksin.

2927. Melissa Errico (Mar. 23, 1970–) B: New York, NY. *Anna Karenina* (Circle in the Square, "Princess Kitty Scherbatsky," Aug. 26, 1992): How Awful; How Many Men?; In a Room; Mazurka; Would You?/W: Peter Kellogg, M: Daniel Levine. *My Fair Lady* (Virginia, revival, "Eliza Doolittle," Dec. 9, 1993): I Could Have Danced All Night; Just You Wait; The Rain in Spain; Show Me; Without You; Wouldn't It Be Loverly?/W: Alan Jay Lerner, M: Frederick Loewe.

2928. Leon Errol (July 3, 1881–Oct. 12, 1951) B: Sydney, Australia. The comic actor with the twitching face and rubbery legs appeared in dozens of films from 1924 until his death from a heart attack. *Ziegfeld Follies of 1911* (Jardin de Paris, revue, June 26, 1911): My Beautiful Lady/W: C.M.S. McLellan, M: Ivan Caryll — Texas Tommy Swing/WM: Sid Brown, Val Harris. *A Winsome Widow* (Moulin Rouge, "Ben Gay," Apr. 11, 1912): Teach Me Everything You Know/W: ?, M: Raymond Hubbell. *Ziegfeld Follies of 1912* (Moulin Rouge, revue, Oct. 21, 1912): Good Old Circus Band/W: Harry B. Smith, M: Raymond Hubbell. *Ziegfeld Follies of 1915* (New Amsterdam, revue, June 21, 1915): Twenty Years Ago/W: ?, M: Louis A. Hirsch. *Hitchy-Koo of 1917* (Cohan and Harris > Liberty > 44th Street, revue, June 7, 1917): Ghosts/WM: ?— Jim Jam Gems [Aug. 6, 1917]/WM: E. Ray Goetz. *Sally* (New Amsterdam, "Connie," Dec. 21, 1920): The Schnitza Komisski/W: Clifford Gray, M: Jerome Kern. *Louis the 14th* (Cosmopolitan, "Louie Ketchup," Mar. 3, 1925): Follow the Rajah; Taking a Wife/W: Arthur Wimperis, M: Sigmund Romberg. *Yours Truly* (Shubert,

"Truly," Jan. 25, 1927): Don't Shake My Tree/W: Anne Caldwell, M: Raymond Hubbell.

2929. Martha Errolle *Night of Love* (Hudson, "Madi Linden," Jan. 7, 1941): Chiquitin Trio; I'm Thinking of Love; My Loved One; Streamlined Pompadour/W: Rowland Leigh, M: Robert Stolz. *Park Avenue* (Shubert, "Mrs. Elsa Crowell," Nov. 4, 1946): Don't Be a Woman If You Can; Hope for the Best; There's Nothing Like Marriage for People/W: Ira Gershwin, M: Arthur Schwartz.

2930. Ralph Errolle *The Spring Maid* (Liberty, "Baron Rudi," Dec. 26, 1910): The Fountain Fay Protective Institution, Limited/W: Robert B. Smith, M: Heinrich Reinhardt — Take Me Dear/W: Robert B. Smith, M: Robert Hood Bowers. *The Nightingale* (Jolson, "Capt. Rex Gurnee," Jan. 3, 1927): Homeland; May Moon/ W: P.G. Wodehouse, M: Armand Vecsey.

2931. Elsa Ersias *Moonlight* (Longacre, "Suzanne Franklyn," Jan. 30, 1924): The Daffydill; How Can a Lady Be Certain?; Turn on the Popular Moon/W: William B. Friedlander, M: Con Conrad — How Do I Know He Loves Me?/ WM: William B. Friedlander. *Louie the 14th* (Cosmopolitan, "Countess Zichky," Oct. 12, 1925): Give a Little, Get a Little Kiss/W: Irving Caesar, M: Sigmund Romberg.

2932. Barbara Erwin (June 30, 1937–) B: Boston, MA. *Annie* (Alvin, "Lily," Apr. 21, 1977/May 29, 1979): Easy Street/W: Martin Charnin, M: Charles Strouse. *Gypsy* (St. James, revival, "Tessie Tura," Nov. 16, 1989): You Gotta Have a Gimmick/W: Stephen Sondheim, M: Jule Styne. *Gypsy* (Marquis, return engagement of revival, "Tessie Tura," Apr. 28, 1991): same as above.

2933. Frank Erwin *The Love Call* (Majestic, "Joe," Oct. 24, 1927): When I Take You All to London/W: Harry B. Smith, M: Sigmund Romberg.

2934. Stuart Erwin (Feb. 14, 1902–Dec. 21, 1967) B: Squaw Valley, CA. He appeared in more than 100 movies. In 1950 he played himself as a blunderbuss dad on the popular sitcom *The Stu Erwin Show*. *Great to Be Alive* (Winter Garden, "Woodrow Twigg," Mar. 23, 1950): Headin' for a Weddin'/W: Walter Bullock, M: Abraham Ellstein.

2935. Charles Esdale (c 1873–July 10, 1937) *See-Saw* (Cohan, "Jephson," Sept. 23, 1919): I'll Take Care of Him/W: Earl Derr Biggers, M: Louis A. Hirsch.

2936. Drew Eshelman (Oct. 12, 1946–) B: Long Beach, CA. *Les Miserables* (Broadway, CR, "Thenardier"): Beggars at the Feast; Dog Eats Dog; Master of the House; Thenardier Waltz/ W: Herbert Kretzmer, M: Claude-Michel Schonberg.

2937. Sidonie Espero *Kitty Darlin'* (Casino, "Lady Bab Flyte," Nov. 7, 1917): I Want a Man Who's Gentle/WM: ?— Spread the News/W: P.G. Wodehouse, M: Rudolf Friml. *The Maid of the Mountains* (Casino, "Teresa," Sept. 11, 1918): Farewell; Love Will Find a Way/W: Harry Graham, M: Harold Fraser-Simpson — My Life Is Love; A Paradise for Two; When You're in Love/W: Clifford Harris, Arthur Valentine, M: James W. Tate. *Honey Girl* (Cohan and Harris, "Carmencita," May 3, 1920): Can I Find a Toreador?; Myltyl and Tyltyl (The Bluebird Song)/ W: Neville Fleeson, M: Albert Von Tilzer. *The Gingham Girl* (Earl Carroll, CR, "Sonya Maison," Mar. 5, 1923): Down Greenwich Village Way; The Wonderful Thing We Call Love/W: Neville Fleeson, M: Albert Von Tilzer.

2938. Giancarlo Esposito (Apr. 26, 1958–) B: Copenhagen, Denmark. *Lost in the Stars* (Imperial, revival, "Alex," Apr. 18, 1972): Big Mole/W: Maxwell Anderson, M: Kurt Weill. *Seesaw* (Uris, "Julio Gonzales," Mar. 18, 1973): Spanglish/W: Dorothy Fields, M: Cy Coleman.

2939. Viola Essen (Aug. 11, 1925–Jan. 16, 1970) B: St. Louis, MO. *Follow the Girls* (44th Street, CR, "Betty Deleaninnion," Feb. 11, 1945): Where You Are/W: Dan Shapiro, Milton Pascal, M: Phil Charig.

2940. Carl Esser *Half a Sixpence* (Broadhurst, CR, "Sid Pornick"): All in the Cause of Economy; Flash! Bang! Wallop!; If the Rain's Got to Fall; The Party's on the House; A Proper Gentleman/WM: David Heneker.

2941. Fred Essler (Feb. 13, 1895–Jan. 17, 1973) B: Vienna, Austria-Hungary. *From Vienna* (Music Box, revue, June 20, 1939): Salzburg Puppet-Show/W: Lothar Metzl, Werner Michel, Eva Franklin, M: Otto Andreas.

2942. Eleanore E'Stelle *The Merry Whirl* (New York, "Jacqueline," May 30, 1910): The Paris Push/W: Ed Ray, M: Leo Edwards.

2943. Suellen Estey (Nov. 21–) B: Mason City, IA. *The Selling of the President* (Shubert, "Bonnie Sue Taylor," Mar. 22, 1972): If You Like People; Mason Cares; Terminex/W: Jack O'Brien, M: Bob James. *Barnum* (St. James, CR, "Chairy Barnum," Jan. 19, 1982): Black and White; The Colors of My Life; I Like Your Style; One Brick at a Time/W: Michael Stewart, M: Cy Coleman. *Barnum* (St. James, CR, "Jenny Lind," Jan. 26, 1982): Love Makes Such Fools of Us All/W: Michael Stewart, M: Cy Coleman. *Sweeney Todd* (Circle in the Square, revival,

"Beggar Woman," Sept. 14, 1989): Ah, Miss; God, That's Good; Johanna; No Place Like London; Wait/WM: Stephen Sondheim.

2944. Dorothy Etheridge *Music in My Heart* (Adelphi, "Natuscha," Oct. 2, 1947): Gossip; Natuscha/W: Forman Brown, M: Franz Steininger, based on Peter I. Tchaikovsky.

2945. Ruth Etting (Nov. 23, 1896–Sept. 24, 1978) B: David City, NE. Billed as The Sweetheart of Song, the singer-actress performed in 1930s movies, in nightclubs and on the radio. Doris Day portrayed her in the 1955 film *Love Me or Leave Me,* the story of her career and her marriage to mobster Martin Snyder, aka Moe the Gimp. *Ziegfeld Follies of 1927* (New Amsterdam, revue, Aug. 16, 1927): Jimmy; Shaking the Blues Away; Tickling the Ivories/WM: Irving Berlin. *Whoopee* (New Amsterdam, "Leslie Daw," Dec. 4, 1928): Gypsy Joe; The Gypsy Song; Love Me or Leave Me/W: Gus Kahn, M: Walter Donaldson. *Nine-Fifteen Revue* (George M. Cohan, revue, Feb. 11, 1930): Gee I'm So Good, It's Too Bad; Get Happy/W: Ted Koehler, M: Harold Arlen — How Would a City Girl Know?; Up Among the Chimney Pots/W: Paul James, M: Kay Swift — You Will Never Know/W: Paul James, M: Vincent Youmans. *Simple Simon* (Ziegfeld, "Sal," Feb. 18, 1930): Happy Days and Lonely Nights [Apr. 1930]/W: Billy Rose, M: Fred Fisher — I Still Believe in You; Ten Cents a Dance/W: Lorenz Hart, M: Richard Rodgers — Love Me or Leave Me [Apr. 1930]/W: Gus Kahn, M: Walter Donaldson. *Ziegfeld Follies of 1931* (Ziegfeld, revue, July 1, 1931): Cigarettes, Cigars!/W: Mack Gordon, M: Harry Revel — Shine On, Harvest Moon/WM: Jack Norworth, Nora Bayes.

2946. Robert Evan *Les Miserables* (Broadway, CR, "Jean Valjean," Sept. 10, 1996): Bring Him Home; Come to Me; In My Life; Soliloquy; Thenardier Waltz; Who Am I?/W: Herbert Kretzmer, M: Claude-Michel Schonberg.

2947. Ed Evanko B: Winnipeg, Canada. *Canterbury Tales* (Eugene O'Neill, "Squire" and "Nicholas" and "Alan" and "Damian," Feb. 3, 1969): Beer Is Best (Beer, Beer, Beer); I Am All A-Blaze; I Have a Noble Cock; I'll Give My Love a Ring; Pear Tree Quintet; There's the Moon/W: Nevill Coghill, M: Richard Hill, John Hawkins. *Rex* (Lunt-Fontanne, "Mark Smeaton," Apr. 25, 1976): The Chase; Elizabeth; No Song More Pleasing/W: Sheldon Harnick, M: Richard Rodgers.

2948. Bobby Evans *Blackbirds of 1939* (Hudson, revue, Feb. 11, 1939): Name It and It's Yours/WM: Mitchell Parish, Abner Silver,

Sammy Fain — Swing Struck/W: Irving Taylor, M: Vic Mizzy.

2949. Bonnie Evans *Kismet* (Ziegfeld, "Princess of Ababu," Dec. 3, 1953): He's in Love!; Not Since Ninevah; Rahadlakum/WM: Robert Wright, George Forrest.

2950. Charles E. Evans (c 1867–Apr. 21, 1953) *The Sho-Gun* (Wallack's, "William Henry Spangle," Oct. 10, 1904): The Games We Used to Play; The Irrepressible Yank; Love, You Must Be Blind/W: George Ade, M: Gustav Luders.

2951. Damon Evans (Nov. 24, 1949–) B: Baltimore, MD. He played Lionel Jefferson on the TV sitcom *The Jeffersons* (1975). *The Me Nobody Knows* (Longacre, CR, "Lloyd," Nov. 1971): Black; The Horse; Jail-Life Walk; War Babies; What Happens to Life/W: Will Holt, M: Gary William Friedman. *Via Galactica* (Uris, "Hels," Nov. 28, 1972): The Other Side of the Sky; Oysters/W: Christopher Gore, M: Galt MacDermot.

2952. David Evans *A Funny Thing Happened on the Way to the Forum* (Alvin, "A Protean," May 8, 1962): Bring Me My Bride; Comedy Tonight/WM: Stephen Sondheim.

2953. Edith Evans *Tattle Tales* (Broadhurst, revue, June 1, 1933): Harlem Lullaby/WM: Willard Robison, Margot Millham.

2954. Ella Evans *Oh, What a Girl!* (Shubert, "Ella Evans," July 28, 1919): Oh That Shimmy!/W: Edward Clark, M: Charles Jules, Jacques Presburg.

2955. George (Honey Boy) Evans (Mar. 10, 1870–Mar. 12, 1915) B: Pontotlyn, Wales. Famous blackface minstrel and comedian, known as Honey Boy after his song "I'll Be True to My Honey Boy." *Cohan and Harris Minstrels* (New York, revue, Aug. 3, 1908): Kiss Your Minstrel Boy Goodbye/W: William Jerome, M: Jean Schwartz.

2956. Greek Evans *Eileen* (Shubert, "Shaun Dhu," Mar. 19, 1917): Free Trade and a Misty Moon/W: Henry Blossom, M: Victor Herbert. *Toot-Toot!* (George M. Cohan, "Capt. Jones" and "Peter Deerfoot," Mar. 11, 1918): Indian Fox Trot/W: Berton Braley, M: Jerome Kern — The Last Long Mile (Plattsburg Marching Song)/WM: Emil Breitenfeld. *Blossom Time* (Jolson, revival, "Franz Schubert," May 19, 1924): Moment Musicale; My Springtime Thou Art; Serenade; Song of Love; Tell Me, Daisy/W: Dorothy Donnelly, M: Sigmund Romberg. *The Student Prince [in Heidelberg]* (Al Jolson, "Dr. Engel," Dec. 2, 1924): Golden Days; Student Life/W: Dorothy Donnelly, M: Sigmund Romberg. *Song of the Flame* (44th Street, "Konstantin," Dec. 30, 1925): Far Away; Song of the Flame/W: Otto Harbach, Oscar Hammerstein II, M: George Gershwin, Herbert Stothart — Tartar; Wander Away/W: Otto Harbach, Oscar Hammerstein II, M: Herbert Stothart. *Yours Truly* (Shubert, "Chang," Jan. 25, 1927): Dawn of Dreams; Lotus Flower/W: Anne Caldwell, M: Raymond Hubbell. *Enchanted Isle* (Lyric, "Bob Sherill," Sept. 19, 1927): Close in Your Arms; Could I Forget?; Dream Girl; Enchanted Castle; Voice of the High Sierras/WM: Ida Hoyt Chamberlain. *Take the Air* (Waldorf, "Capt. Halliday," Nov. 22, 1927): Just Like a Wild, Wild Rose; Wings/W: Gene Buck, M: Dave Stamper. *Music in May* (Casino, "Karl von Dorn," Apr. 1, 1929): The Glory of Spring; I Found a Friend/W: J. Keirn Brennan, M: Maurie Rubens. *Robin Hood* (Jolson, revival, "Little John," Nov. 18, 1929): Brown October Ale; Come the Bowmen in Lincoln Green; O, See the Lambkins Play!/W: Harry B. Smith, M: Reginald De Koven. *The Serenade* (Jolson, revival, "Carlo Alvarado," Mar. 4, 1930): Don Jose of Sevilla; I Love Thee, I Adore Thee; With Cracking of Whip and Rattle of Spur/W: Harry B. Smith, M: Victor Herbert. *East Wind* (Manhattan, "Monsieur Granier," Oct. 27, 1931): It's a Wonderful World; When You Are Young/W: Oscar Hammerstein II, M: Sigmund Romberg.

2957. Harry Evans *Cross My Heart* (Knickerbocker, "Maxie Squeeze," Sept. 17, 1928): Come Along Sunshine; Such Is Fame/W: Joseph McCarthy, M: Harry Tierney.

2958. Harvey Evans (Jan. 7, 1941–) B: Cincinnati, OH. *Hello, Dolly!* (St. James, CR, "Barnaby Tucker," July 1967): Dancing; Put on Your Sunday Clothes/WM: Jerry Herman — Elegance; Motherhood/WM: Bob Merrill, Jerry Herman. *George M!* (Palace, "Sam Harris," Apr. 10, 1968): All Our Friends; So Long, Mary/WM: George M. Cohan. *The Boy Friend* (Ambassador, revival, "Bobby Van Husen," Apr. 14, 1970): The Riviera; Safety in Numbers; Sur La Plage; Won't You Charleston with Me?/WM: Sandy Wilson. *Follies* (Winter Garden, "Young Buddy," Apr. 4, 1971): Waiting for the Girls Upstairs/WM: Stephen Sondheim. *Sondheim: A Musical Tribute* (Shubert, revue, Mar. 11, 1973): Me and My Town; Your Eyes Are Blue/WM: Stephen Sondheim. *Sextet* (Bijou, "Kenneth," Mar. 3, 1974): Hi; Keep on Dancing; Spunk; Women and Men/W: Lee Goldsmith, M: Lawrence Hurwit.

2959. Karen Evans *Runaways* (Plymouth, "Deidre," May 13, 1978): Lullaby from Baby to Baby; Where Are Those People Who Did Hair?/WM: Elizabeth Swados.

2960. L. Barton Evans *Earl Carroll's Vanities of 1923* (Earl Carroll, revue, CR, Dec. 17, 1923): The Band Plays Home Sweet Home/ WM: Earl Carroll — A Girl Is Like Sunshine/W: Roy Turk, M: William Daly.

2961. Lyle Evans *The Desert Song* (Casino, "Ali Ben Ali," Nov. 30, 1926): Let Love Go/W: Otto Harbach, Oscar Hammerstein II, M: Sigmund Romberg. *The New Moon* (Imperial > Casino, "Besac," Sept. 19, 1928): A Chanty; Funny Little Sailor Man; Love Is Quite a Simple Thing/W: Oscar Hammerstein II, M: Sigmund Romberg.

2962. Maurice Evans (June 3, 1901–Mar. 12, 1989) B: Dorchester, Dorset, England. He came to the U.S. in 1935 to be Romeo opposite Katharine Cornell's Juliet. The great Shakespearian actor later played an ape in the movie *Planet of the Apes* (1968). *Tenderloin* (46th Street, "The Reverend Dr. Brock," Oct. 17, 1960): The Army of the Just; Dear Friend; Dr. Brock; Good Clean Fun; How the Money Changes Hands; What's in It for You?/W: Sheldon Harnick, M: Jerry Bock.

2963. Rex Evans (Apr. 13, 1903–Apr. 3, 1969) B: Southport, England. The British character actor often played butlers in Hollywood. *Gentlemen Prefer Blondes* (Ziegfeld, "Sir Francis Beekman," Dec. 8, 1949): It's Delightful Down in Chile/W: Leo Robin, M: Jule Styne.

2964. Tempe Evans *Fiddlers Three* (Cort, "Giorgio," Sept. 3, 1918): Proud Little Pages/W: William Cary Duncan, M: Alexander Johnstone.

2965. Virginia Evans *Hanky-Panky* (Broadway, "Iona Carr," Aug. 5, 1912): The Million Dollar Ball/WM: E. Ray Goetz, Irving Berlin.

2966. Warwick Evans *Blood Brothers* (Music Box, "Narrator," Apr. 25, 1993): Light Romance; Madman; Shoes Upon the Table/WM: Willy Russell.

2967. Wilbur Evans (Aug. 5, 1905–May 31, 1987) B: Philadelphia, PA. *Mexican Hayride* (Winter Garden, "David Winthrop," Jan. 28, 1944): The Good Will Movement; I Love You/WM: Cole Porter. *Up in Central Park* (Century, "John Matthews," Jan. 27, 1945): April Snow; The Big Back Yard; Close As Pages in a Book; It Doesn't Cost You Anything to Dream; Rip Van Winkle; When She Walks in the Room/W: Dorothy Fields, M: Sigmund Romberg. *By the Beautiful Sea* (Majestic, "Dennis Emery," Apr. 8, 1954): Alone Too Long; More Love Than Your Love/W: Dorothy Fields, M: Arthur Schwartz. *Man of La Mancha* (ANTA Washington Square, CR, "The Innkeeper," Apr. 11, 1967): Knight of the Woeful Countenance

(The Dubbing)/W: Joe Darion, M: Mitch Leigh.

2968. Willie Evans *Cheer Up* (Hippodrome, revue, Aug. 23, 1917): When Old New York Goes Dry/WM: Benjamin Hapgood Burt.

2969. Frances Everett *Swing It* (Adelphi, "Sadie," July 22, 1937): Ain't We Got Love/W: Cecil Mack, Milton Reddie, M: Eubie Blake.

2970. Tanya Everett (c 1948–) *Fiddler on the Roof* (Imperial, "Chava," Sept. 22, 1964): Matchmaker, Matchmaker/W: Sheldon Harnick, M: Jerry Bock.

2971. Rex Everhart (June 13, 1920–Mar. 13, 2000) B: Watseka, IL. *Skyscraper* (Lunt-Fontanne, "Stanley," Nov. 13, 1965): Haute Couture; Local 403 (The Socially Conscious Civic Minded Iron Workers Union)/W: Sammy Kahn, M: James Van Heusen. *1776* (46th Street, CR, "Benjamin Franklin"): But, Mr. Adams; The Egg; He Plays the Violin; The Lees of Old Virginia/WM: Sherman Edwards. *Chicago* (46th Street, CR, "Amos Hart," Feb. 20, 1976/Sept. 1976): Mr. Cellophane/W: Fred Ebb, M: John Kander. *Woman of the Year* (Palace, "Maury," Mar. 29, 1981): One of the Boys/W: Fred Ebb, M: John Kander. *Anything Goes* (Vivian Beaumont, revival, "Elisha Whitney," Oct. 19, 1987): I Want to Row on the Crew/WM: Cole Porter.

2972. Larry Evers *Dream with Music* (Majestic, "Guard," May 18, 1944): Battle of the Genie/W: Edward Eager, M: Clay Warnick.

2973. Paul Everton (Sept. 19, 1868–Feb. 26, 1948) B: New York, NY. *Kid Boots* (Earl Carroll > Selwyn, "Herbert Pendleton," Dec. 31, 1923): Down 'Round the 19th Hole/W: Joseph McCarthy, M: Harry Tierney. *A Connecticut Yankee* (Vanderbilt, "King Arthur of Britain," Nov. 3, 1927): At the Round Table (Knight's Opening)/W: Lorenz Hart, M: Richard Rodgers.

2974. Robert Evett (Oct. 16, 1874–Jan. 16, 1949) B: Warwickshire, England. London's star operetta tenor of the early 1900s. He later became a producer of musicals. *The Doll Girl* (Globe, "Tiborius," Aug. 25, 1913): If We Were on Our Honeymoon (Railway Duet); Will It All End in Smoke?/W: Harry B. Smith, M: Jerome Kern — It Is I; Rosalilla of Sevilla/W: Harry B. Smith, M: Leo Fall. *Suzi* (Casino > Shubert, "Stephan," Nov. 3, 1914): Angling [Nov. 30, 1914]; A Fascinating Night; I'll Not Let Love Disparage Marriage [Nov. 9, 1914]; It Thrills! It Thrills!; 'Twas in a Garden/W: Otto Harbach, M: Aladar Renyi.

2975. William Eville *Pom-Pom* (Cohan, "Macache," Feb. 28, 1916): Zim-Zim/W: Anne Caldwell, M: Hugo Felix.

2976. Lois Ewell *The Merry Widow* (New Amsterdam, "Natalie, Baroness Popoff," Oct. 21, 1907): A Dutiful Wife; Oh, Say No More/W: Adrian Ross, M: Franz Lehar. *The Merry Widow* (New Amsterdam, CR, "Sonia," Mar. 18, 1908): I Love You So (The Merry Widow Waltz); In Marsovia; The Silly Cavalier; Vilia/W: Adrian Ross, M: Franz Lehar.

2977. Tom Ewell (Apr. 29, 1909–Sept. 12, 1994) B: Owensboro, KY. The actor, who started out to become a lawyer, won a Tony for *The Seven Year Itch*, which he later played on screen opposite Marilyn Monroe. *Sunny River* (St. James, "Daniel Marshall," Dec. 4, 1941): Bundling; The Butterflies and the Bees; The Duello; She Got Him/W: Oscar Hammerstein II, M: Sigmund Romberg.

2978. William Eythe (Apr. 7, 1918–Jan. 26, 1957) B: Mars, PA. A featured player in 13 movies in the 1940s, including *The Ox-Bow Incident, The Song of Bernadette* and *The House on 92nd Street*. He became an alcoholic and died of acute hepatitis. *Lend an Ear* (National > Broadhurst, revue, Dec. 16, 1948): The Gladiola Girl; I'll Be True to You; In Our Teeny Little Weeny Nest; Neurotic You and Psychopathic Me; Where Is the She for Me?/WM: Charles Gaynor. *The Liar* (Broadhurst, "Lelio Bisognosi," May 18, 1950): A Jewel of a Duel; The Liar's Song; Out of Sight, Out of Mind; Supper Trio; Truth; What's in a Name?/W: Edward Eager, M: John Mundy.

2979. Nanette Fabray (Oct. 27, 1920–) B: San Diego, CA. Actress and singer of stage, screen, radio and TV. She began her career in vaudeville with FANCHON and MARCO, and starred on radio's *Charlie Chan* series and *Our Gang* comedies. Among her TV roles she was Ann Victor in *Caesar's Hour* (1954) and Grandma Katherine Romano in *One Day at a Time* (1979). *Let's Face It!* (Imperial, "Jean Blanchard," Oct. 29, 1941): Ace in the Hole; Farming; I've Got Some Unfinished Business with You; You Irritate Me So/WM: Cole Porter. *By Jupiter* (Shubert, CR, "Antiope," Jan. 1943): Bottoms Up; Careless Rhapsody; Here's a Hand; Nobody's Heart (Belongs to Me)/W: Lorenz Hart, M: Richard Rodgers. *My Dear Public* (46th Street, revue, "Jean," Sept. 9, 1943): Feet on the Sidewalk (Head in the Sky)/WM: Sammy Lerner, Gerald Marks — I Love to Sing the Words (While We're Dancing); This Is Our Private Love Song/WM: Sammy Lerner, Gerald Marks, Irving Caesar — May All Our Children Have Rhythm/WM: ?. *Jackpot* (Alvin, "Sally Madison," Jan. 13, 1944): Blind Date; It Was Nice Knowing You; The Last Long Mile; What Happened?/W: Howard Dietz, M: Vernon Duke. *Bloomer Girl* (Shubert, CR, "Evelina Applegate"): Evelina; It Was Good Enough for Grandma; Lullaby (Satin Gown and Silver Shoe); The Rakish Young Man with the Whiskers; Right as the Rain; Welcome Hinges/W: E.Y. Harburg, M: Harold Arlen. *Bloomer Girl* (New York City Center, revival, "Evelina Applegate," Jan. 6, 1947): same as above. *High Button Shoes* (New Century, "Sara Longstreet," Oct. 9, 1947): I Still Get Jealous; Papa, Won't You Dance with Me?; She's Right (Security)/W: Sammy Cahn, M: Jule Styne. *Love Life* (46th Street, "Susan Cooper," Oct. 7, 1948): Green-Up Time; Here I'll Stay; Progress/W: Alan Jay Lerner, M: Kurt Weill. *Arms and the Girl* (46th Street, "Jo Kirkland," Feb. 2, 1950): A Cow and a Plough and a Frau; A Girl with a Flame; He Will Tonight; I'll Never Learn; Plantation in Philadelphia; That's My Fella; You Kissed Me/W: Dorothy Fields, M: Morton Gould. *Make a Wish* (Winter Garden, "Janette," Apr. 18, 1951): I Wanna Be Good 'n' Bad; Over and Over; Tonight You Are in Paree; What I Was Warned About; Who Gives a Sou?/WM: Hugh Martin — Make a Wish; Take Me Back to Texas with You/W: Timothy Gray, M: Hugh Martin. *Mr. President* (St. James, "Nell Henderson," Oct. 20, 1962): The First Lady; Glad to Be Home; I'm Gonna Get Him; In Our Hide-Away; Is He the Only Man in the World?; Laugh It Up; Let's Go Back to the Waltz; They Love Me; You Need a Hobby/WM: Irving Berlin.

2980. Manolo Fabregas (c 1921–Feb. 5, 1996) B: Mexico. Member of a theatrical family, he appeared in Mexican films from the 1930s. *The King and I* (New York City Center, revival, "The King," June 12, 1963): A Puzzlement; Shall We Dance?; Song of the King/W: Oscar Hammerstein II, M: Richard Rodgers.

2981. Amanda Fabris *Erminie* (Broadway, revival, "Erminie de Pontvert," Oct. 3, 1893): At Midnight on My Pillow Lying; Dear Mother, in Dreams I See Her/W: Claxson Bellamy, Harry Paulton, M: Edward Jakobowski.

2982. Aldo Fabrizi (Nov. 1, 1905–Apr. 2, 1990) B: Rome, Italy. Actor, director and writer, he began as a music hall comedian. His performance as the priest in Rossellini's film *Open City* (1945) led to international fame. *Rugantino* (Mark Hellinger, "Mastro Titta," Feb. 6, 1964): A House Is Not the Same Without a Woman; Just Stay Alive; Roma; The Saltarello/Eng. W: Alfred Drake, Ital. W: Pietro Garinei, Sandro Giovannini, M: Armando Trovaioli.

2983. Joan Fagan *Donnybrook!* (46th Street,

"Ellen Roe Danaher," May 18, 1961): For My Own; He Makes Me Feel I'm Lovely; I Have My Own Way; Sez I/WM: Johnny Burke. *110 in the Shade* (Broadhurst, CR, "Lizzie Curry," Apr. 23, 1964): Is It Really Me?; Love, Don't Turn Away; A Man and a Woman; Old Maid; Raunchy; Simple Little Things; Wonderful Music; You're Not Foolin' Me/W: Tom Jones, M: Harvey Schmidt.

2984. Thelma Fair *When Johnny Comes Marching Home* (New York, "Amelia Graham," Dec. 16, 1902): Good Day, Yankees!; I Could Waltz On Forever; Marry the Man and Be Merry/W: Stanislaus Stange, M: Julian Edwards. *Mr. Wix of Wickham* (Bijou, "Lady Betty," Sept. 19, 1904): Cupid's Garden/WM: Max C. Eugene — Raindrops/WM: George Everard.

2985. Spring Fairbank (Mar. 15, 1941–) B: Chicago, IL. *Very Good Eddie* (Booth, revival, "Mrs. Georgina Kettle," Dec. 21, 1975): Isn't It Great to Be Married/W: Schuyler Greene, M: Jerome Kern.

2986. Madeleine Fairbanks (Nov. 15, 1900–Jan. 15, 1989) B: New York, NY. With her look-alike sister Marion, they were known as the Fairbanks Twins. Starting in show business as children, the two made hundreds of silent movies between 1913 and 1917. *Ziegfeld Follies of 1918* (New Amsterdam > Globe, revue, June 18, 1918): When I'm Looking at You/W: Gene Buck, M: Dave Stamper. *Two Little Girls in Blue* (George M. Cohan, "Dolly Sartoris," May 3, 1921): Just Like You/W: Ira Gershwin, M: Paul Lannin — Two Little Girls in Blue; You Started Something/W: Ira Gershwin, M: Vincent Youmans. *Hassard Short's Ritz Revue* (Ritz > Winter Garden, revue, Sept. 17, 1924): The Little Black Cat/W: Anne Caldwell, M: Raymond Hubbell — When You and I Were Dancing/W: Graham John, M: H.M. Tennant. *Mercenary Mary* (Longacre, "Edith Somers," Apr. 13, 1925): Honey, I'm in Love with You; Over a Garden Wall/WM: William B. Friedlander, Con Conrad. *George White's Scandals of 1926* (Apollo, revue, June 14, 1926): My Jewels/W: B.G. DeSylva, Lew Brown, M: Ray Henderson. *Oh, Kay!* (Imperial, "Dolly Ruxton," Nov. 8, 1926): Don't Ask!/W: Ira Gershwin, M: George Gershwin. *Allez-Oop* (Earl Carroll, revue, Aug. 2, 1927): Doin' the Gorilla/W: Leo Robin, M: Phil Charig, Richard Myers. *Happy* (Earl Carroll > Daly's, "Lorelei Lynn," Dec. 5, 1927): Black Sheep; Happy; Lorelei; Mad About You; The Serpentine; Sunny Side of You; The Younger Generation/W: Earle Crooker, McElbert Moore, M: Frank Grey.

2987. Marion Fairbanks (Nov. 15, 1900–Sept. 20, 1973) B: New York, NY. Twin of MADELEINE FAIRBANKS. *Ziegfeld Follies of 1918* (New Amsterdam > Globe, revue, June 18, 1918): same as above. *Two Little Girls in Blue* (George M. Cohan, "Polly Sartoris," May 3, 1921): Oh Me! Oh My! (Oh You); Two Little Girls in Blue; Who's Who with You?/W: Ira Gershwin, M: Vincent Youmans. *George White's Scandals of 1926* (Apollo, revue, June 14, 1926): same as above. *Oh, Kay!* (Imperial, "Phil Ruxton," Nov. 8, 1926): Don't Ask!; Fidgety Feet/W: Ira Gershwin, M: George Gershwin.

2988. Nola Fairbanks *Icetime of 1948* (Center, revue, May 28, 1947): Breaking the Ice/WM: Al Stillman, Paul McGrane — Lillian Russell/WM: James Littlefield, John Fortis. *Howdy, Mr. Ice!* (Center, revue, June 24, 1948): Cradle of Jazz; I Only Wish I Knew; In the Pink; Plenty More Fish in the Sea; Santa Claus; World's Greatest Show/W: Al Stillman, M: Alan Moran. *Howdy, Mr. Ice of 1950* (Center, revue, May 26, 1949): Big City; I Only Wish I Knew; Plenty More Fish in the Sea; World's Greatest Show; You Was/W: Al Stillman, M: Alan Moran.

2989. Andrew Fairchild *How Come?* (Apollo, "Deacon Long Tack," Apr. 16, 1923): Count Your Money/WM: Ben Harris, Henry Creamer, Will Vodery.

2990. Judith Fairfield *Rose-Marie* (Imperial, CR, "Lady Jane," Nov. 1925): One Man Woman; Only a Kiss; Why Shouldn't We?/W: Otto Harbach, Oscar Hammerstein II, M: Herbert Stothart.

2991. Harry Fairleigh *The Yankee Consul* (Broadway > Wallack's, "Lieut. Commander Jack Morrell," Feb. 22, 1904): Cupid Has Found My Heart; Oh, Glad Is the Life of a Sailor at Sea/W: Henry Blossom, M: Alfred G. Robyn. *Woodland* (New York > Herald Square, "Robin Redbreast," Nov. 21, 1904): Dainty Little Ingenue/W: Frank Pixley, M: Gustav Luders. *The Vanderbilt Cup* (Broadway, CR, "Dexter Joyce," Feb. 12, 1906): So I've Been Told; Somewhere in the World (There's a Little Girl for Me)/W: Raymond W. Peck, M: Robert Hood Bowers. *The Top o' the World* (Majestic > Casino, "Shellman," Oct. 19, 1907): Cupid and You and I/WM: Manuel Klein — Where Fate Shall Guide/W: James O'Dea, M: Anne Caldwell. *A Waltz Dream* (Broadway, "Lieut. Montschi," Jan. 27, 1908): Love's Roundelay/W: Joseph W. Herbert, M: Oscar Straus. *A Waltz Dream* (Broadway, CR, "Lieut. Niki," Feb. 24, 1908): The Family's Ancient Tree; Love Cannot Be Bought; Love's Roundelay; Sweetest Maid of All; Two Is Plenty/

W: Joseph W. Herbert, M: Oscar Straus — I Love and the World Is Mine/W: Florence Earle Coates, M: Charles Gilbert Spross. *The Gay Hussars* (Knickerbocker, CR, "Capt. Von Lorenty," Aug. 16, 1909): Love Is a Traitor; Vagrant Fancies/W: Grant Stewart, M: Emmerich Kalman. *A Skylark* (New York, "Tom Randolph," Apr. 4, 1910): Broadway Lament; I Just Can't Wait; I'm Looking for a Little Girl Who's Looking for a Man/W: William B. Harris, Jr., M: Frank Dossert. *My Best Girl* (Park, "Capt. Robert Denton, U.S.A.," Sept. 12, 1912): Howdy-Do/W: Clifton Crawford, M: A. Baldwin Sloane — Love and the Automobile/W: Rennold Wolf, M: Augustus Barratt.

2992. Sandy Faison *Annie* (Alvin, "Grace Farrell," Apr. 21, 1977): Annie; I Think I'm Gonna Like It Here; A New Deal for Christmas; N.Y.C.; You Won't Be an Orphan for Long/W: Martin Charnin, M: Charles Strouse. *Charlie and Algernon* (Helen Hayes, "Alice Kinnian," Sept. 14, 1980): Have I the Right?; Hey Look at Me; I Got a Friend; No Surprises; Now; Reading; Some Bright Morning; Whatever Time There Is/W: David Rogers, M: Charles Strouse. *Is There Life After High School?* (Ethel Barrymore, revue, May 7, 1982): Fran and Janie; Second Thoughts/WM: Craig Carnelia.

2993. Lola Falana (Sept. 11, 1943–) B: Philadelphia, PA. Entertainer known for spectacular Las Vegas shows. *Golden Boy* (Majestic, "Lola," Oct. 20, 1964): This Is the Life/W: Lee Adams, M: Charles Strouse. *Doctor Jazz* (Winter Garden, "Edna Mae Sheridan," Mar. 19, 1975): All I Want Is My Black Baby Back; Evolution Papa; Free and Easy; I've Got Elgin Watch Movements in My Hips; Juba Dance; Look Out for Lil/WM: Buster Davis — I Love It/W: E. Ray Goetz, M: Harry Von Tilzer.

2994. Helen Falconer (?–May 30, 1968) M: songwriter Gene Buck. *The Lady of the Slipper* (Globe, "Clara," Oct. 28, 1912): Fond of the Ladies/W: James O'Dea, M: Victor Herbert. *Chin-Chin* (Globe, "Violet Bond," Oct. 20, 1914): Love Moon/W: Anne Caldwell, M: Ivan Caryll. *Jack O'Lantern* (Globe, "Cicely," Oct. 16, 1917): Knit, Knit; A Sweetheart of My Own/W: Anne Caldwell, R.H. Burnside, M: Ivan Caryll — Wait Till the Cows Come Home/W: Anne Caldwell, M: Ivan Caryll.

2995. Eleanor Falk *A Chinese Honeymoon* (Casino, CR, "Mrs. Pineapple"): The A La Girl/W: George Dance, M: Howard Talbot — My Little Hong Kong Baby [Sept. 1, 1902]/W: Paul West, M: John W. Bratton.

2996. Willy Falk (July 21–) B: New York,

NY. *Miss Saigon* (Broadway, "Chris," Apr. 11, 1991): The Ceremony; The Confrontation; The Guilt Inside Your Head; The Last Night of the World; Sun and Moon; The Telephone; Why God Why?/W: Richard Maltby, Jr., Alain Boublil, M: Claude-Michel Schonberg.

2997. Patricia Falkenhain (Dec. 3, 1926–) B: Atlanta, GA. *The Utter Glory of Morrissey Hall* (Mark Hellinger, "Foresta Studley," May 13, 1979): Proud, Erstwhile, Upright, Fair; Way Back When/WM: Clark Gesner.

2998. Eva Fallon *The Student King* (Garden, "Fantine," Dec. 25, 1906): Pray Pretty Maid; Would You Like a Little Girl Like Me/W: Frederick Ranken, Stanislaus Stange, M: Reginald De Koven. *The Yankee Tourist* (Astor, "Chief Steward," Aug. 12, 1907): Stewards' Song; Wouldn't You Like to Have Me for a Sweetheart?/W: Wallace Irwin, M: Alfred G. Robyn. *Three Twins* (Majestic, CR, "Kate Armitage," Feb. 8, 1909): Cuddle Up a Little Closer, Lovey Mine; Good Night, Sweetheart, Good Night; The Little Girl Up There/W: Otto Harbach, M: Karl Hoschna. *The Bachelor Belles* (Globe, "Daphne Brooks," Nov. 7, 1910): She Trimmed Them Oh So Neatly; You've Been Kissing the Blarney Stone/W: Harry B. Smith, M: Raymond Hubbell. *The Purple Road* (Liberty > Casino, "Kathi," Apr. 7, 1913): Feed Me with Love/W: Fred DeGresac, William Cary Duncan, M: Heinrich Reinhardt — When Someone Marries Me/WM: ? — Wicked Little Chichis/W: Fred DeGresac, William Cary Duncan, M: William F. Peters. *Hop o' My Thumb* (Manhattan Opera House, "Mirabelle," Nov. 26, 1913): Come and Watch the Moon with Me; The Forest Bird; Take a Little Perfume; Those Days of Long Ago/W: Sydney Rosenfeld, M: Manuel Klein. *The Midnight Girl* (44th Street, "Lucille," Feb. 23, 1914): Dolly/WM: Adolf Philipp, Edward A. Paulton, Jean Briquet. *The Princess Pat* (Cort, "Grace Holbrook," Sept. 29, 1915): For Better or for Worse; I'd Like to Have You Around; In a Little World for Two; Make Him Guess; When a Girl's About to Marry/W: Henry Blossom, M: Victor Herbert. *Somebody's Sweetheart* (Central > Casino, "Helen Williams," Dec. 23, 1918): In the Old Fashioned Way; Spain/W: Arthur Hammerstein, M: Herbert Stothart.

2999. Peter Falzone *The Yearling* (Alvin, "Fodder-Wing," Dec. 10, 1965): Boy Talk; Some Day I'm Gonna Fly/W: Herbert Martin, M: Michael Leonard.

3000. Marie Fanchonetti *Tillie's Nightmare* (Herald Square, "Miss Thompson," May 5, 1910): The Shopping Glide/W: Edgar Smith, M:

A. Baldwin Sloane. *High Jinks* (Casino, CR, "Chi-Chi," June 8, 1914): The Bubble; Chi-Chi/W: Otto Harbach, M: Rudolf Friml. *The Girl Who Smiles* (Lyric > Longacre, "Pauline Legarde," Aug. 9, 1915): Baby Mine; Dance Me Goodbye; A Honeymoon in May; Oh Pauline/WM: Edward A. Paulton, Adolf Philipp, Jean Briquet.

3001. Shannon Fanning *Grease* (Broadhurst, CR, "Sandy Dumbrowski"): All Choked Up; It's Raining on Prom Night; Look at Me, I'm Sandra Dee; Summer Nights/WM: Jim Jacobs, Warren Casey.

3002. Felix Fantus *A Knight for a Day* (Wallack's, CR, "Marceline," Jan. 20, 1908): The Bold Banditti; Marceline's Meat Sauce/W: Robert B. Smith, M: Raymond Hubbell.

3003. Constance Farber *Sinbad* (Winter Garden > Century > Casino, "Tessie Verdear," Feb. 14, 1918): I Hail from Cairo/W: Harold Atteridge, M: Sigmund Romberg — Where Do They Get Those Guys?/W: Alfred Bryan, Jack Yellen, M: Albert Gumble. *The Greenwich Village Follies of 1920* (Shubert, revue, Jan. 3, 1921): A Broadway Cinderella/W: Harry Carroll, M: Ballard Macdonald.

3004. Irene Farber *Sinbad* (Winter Garden > Century > Casino, "Jeanette Verdear," Feb. 14, 1918): Love Ahoy!/W: Harold Atteridge, M: Sigmund Romberg.

3005. Arthur Faria (Nov. 24, 1944–) B: Fall River, MA. *The Boy Friend* (Ambassador, revival, "Pierre," Apr. 14, 1970): The Boy Friend; It's Nicer in Nice; The Riviera; Safety in Numbers; Sur La Plage/WM: Sandy Wilson.

3006. Michael J. Farina (Aug. 22, 1958–) B: Bronx, NY. *My Fair Lady* (Virginia, revival, "Jamie," Dec. 9, 1993): Get Me to the Church on Time; With a Little Bit of Luck/W: Alan Jay Lerner, M: Frederick Loewe.

3007. Karl Farkas (Oct. 28, 1893–May 16, 1971) B: Vienna, Austria. *The Merry Widow* (New York City Center, revival, "Baron Popoff," Oct. 8, 1944): Women/W: Adrian Ross, M: Franz Lehar.

3008. Maurice Farkoa (Apr. 24, 1864–Mar. 21, 1916) B: Smyrna, Turkey. *Dream City* (Weber's, "Henri D'Absinthe," Dec. 25, 1906): Nancy, I Fancy You; Ta Ta, My Dainty Little Darling [Mar. 18, 1907]/W: Edgar Smith, M: Victor Herbert. *Tonight's the Night* (Shubert, "Pedro," Dec. 24, 1914): I'm a Millionaire; Pink and White; You Must Not Flirt with Me/WM: Paul Rubens, Percy Greenbank. *Miss Information* (George M. Cohan, "Francois Fychere," Oct. 5, 1915): Banks of the Wye/W: Frederick

Edward Weatherly, M: Frank Tours — Constant Lover/W: Arthur Wimperis, M: Herman Finck.

3009. J.J. Farley *The Gospel at Colonus* (Lunt-Fontanne, Mar. 24, 1988): Stop, Do Not Go On/W: Lee Breuer, M: Bob Telson.

3010. Tekla Farm *Love's Lottery* (Broadway, "Molly Muggins," Oct. 3, 1904): Behold Our Lady Great; Holiday Joys; Song of the Tub; The Village Recruits/W: Stanislas Stange, M: Julian Edwards.

3011. John Farman *A Hero Is Born* (Adelphi, "Gaston" and "Singing Escort," Oct. 1, 1937): The Best Dance of All; The Secret of Success/W: Agnes Morgan, M: A. Lehman Engel.

3012. Matt Farnsworth (Aug. 16, 1978–) B: Chicago, IL. *Cats* (Winter Garden, CR, "Munkustrap," c 1996): The Awefull Battle of the Pekes and Pollicles; The Marching Songs of the Pollicle Dogs; Old Deuteronomy/W: T.S. Eliot, M: Andrew Lloyd Webber.

3013. Ralph Farnsworth (c 1923–Feb. 24, 1994) *Man of La Mancha* (CR, "The Padre," July 6, 1970): I'm Only Thinking of Him; The Psalm; To Each His Dulcinea (To Every Man His Dream)/W: Joe Darion, M: Mitch Leigh.

3014. Franklyn (Frank) Farnum (June 5, 1876–July 4, 1961) B: Boston, MA. Leading man of silent Westerns. He appeared in over 1,000 movies. *Somewhere Else* (Broadway, "Rocky Rixon," Jan. 20, 1913): If I Kissed You; Well, Fellows, I Guess We're Here/W: Avery Hopwood, M: Gustav Luders. *Padlocks of 1927* (Shubert, revue, CR, Sept. 19, 1927): The Tap Tap/W: Billy Rose, Ballard Macdonald, M: Jesse Greer.

3015. Jamie Farr (July 1, 1934–) B: Toledo, OH. *Guys and Dolls* (Martin Beck, revival, CR, "Nathan Detroit," Mar. 15, 1994): The Oldest Established; Sue Me/WM: Frank Loesser.

3016. Kimberly Farr (Oct. 16, 1948–) B: Chicago, IL. *Mother Earth* (Belasco, revue, Oct. 19, 1972): Corn on the Macabre/WM: Ron Thronson, Roger Ailes, Ray Golden — Ecology Waltz/W: Ray Golden, M: Toni Shearer. *Going Up* (John Golden, revival, "Grace Douglas," Sept. 16, 1976): If You Look in Her Eyes; Kiss Me; (Everybody Ought to Know How to Do) The Tickle Toe/W: Otto Harbach, M: Louis A. Hirsch — I'll Think of You/W: Rennold Wolf, M: Louis A. Hirsch. *Happy New Year* (Morosco, "Julia Seaton," Apr. 27, 1980): At Long Last Love; I Am Loved; Ours; Ridin' High/WM: Cole Porter.

3017. Tony Farrar *New Faces of 1943* (Ritz, revue, Dec. 22, 1942): Animals Are Nice/W: J.B. Rosenberg, M: Lee Wainer.

3018. Isabelle Farrell *13 Daughters* (54th Street, "Cecilia," Mar. 2, 1961): Puka Puka Pants/WM: Eaton Magoon, Jr.

3019. James Farrell *Ziegfeld Follies of 1936-1937* (Winter Garden, revue, Sept. 14, 1936): Midnight Blue/W: Edgar Leslie, M: Joe Burke — Time Marches On/W: Ira Gershwin, M: Vernon Duke. *Banjo Eyes* (Hollywood, "The Captain," Dec. 25, 1941): We Did It Before (and We Can Do It Again)/WM: Charles Tobias, Cliff Friend.

3020. James Patrick Farrell III *Dude* (Broadway, "Zero," Oct. 9, 1972): The Days of This Life; Talk to Me About Love/W: Gerome Ragni, M: Galt MacDermot.

3021. Margaret Farrell *Miss Princess* (Park, "Hypatia Caldwell," Dec. 23, 1912): Behind the Scenes/W: Will Johnstone, M: Alexander Johnstone.

3022. Marguerite Farrell (c 1889–Jan. 26, 1951) *The American Maid* (Broadway, "Rose Green," Mar. 3, 1913): Cheer Up; My Love Is a Blower; Sweetheart; We Chant a Song of Labor; When You Change Your Name to Mine; With Pleasure/W: Leonard Liebling, M: John Philip Sousa. *Step This Way* (Shubert > Astor, May 29, 1916): If I Knock the L Out of Kelly (It Would Still Be Kelly to Me)/W: Sam M. Lewis, Joe Young, M: Bert Grant — When You Drop Off at Cairo, Illinois/W: E. Ray Goetz, M: Cliff Hess.

3023. Tommy Farrell (Oct. 7, 1921–) B: Hollywood, CA. *Barefoot Boy with Cheek* (Martin Beck, "Muskie Pike," Apr. 3, 1947): Alice in Boogieland; There's Lots of Things You Can Do with Two (But Not with Three)/W: Sylvia Dee, M: Sidney Lippman.

3024. Walter Farrell *The Conquering Hero* (ANTA, "Pfc. Doyle," Jan. 16, 1961): Five Shots of Whiskey; One Mother Each; Only Rainbows/W: Norman Gimbel, M: Moose Charlap.

3025. Albert Farrington *The Chaperons* (New York > New York roof, "Tom Schuyler," June 5, 1902): We're All Good Fellows/W: Frederick Ranken, M: Isidore Witmark.

3026. Frank Farrington (July 8, 1873–May 27, 1924) B: Brixton, England. *Miss Millions* (Punch and Judy, "Bates," Dec. 9, 1919): Cutest Little House; Hustle and Bustle Around/W: R.H. Burnside, M: Raymond Hubbell.

3027. Dolores Farris *Oh, Please!* (Fulton, "Ruth King," Dec. 17, 1926): Snappy Show in Town; I'm Waiting for a Wonderful Girl/W: Anne Caldwell, M: Vincent Youmans.

3028. Edna Fassett *Mlle, Modiste* (Knickerbocker, "Fanchette," Dec. 25, 1905): When the Cat's Away, the Mice Will Play/W: Henry Blossom, M: Victor Herbert.

3029. Jay Fassett (Nov. 13, 1889–Feb. 1973) B: Elmira, NY. *Bunk of 1926* (Heckscher, revue, Feb. 16, 1926): A Geisha Legend; You Told Me That You Loved Me, but You Never Told Me Why/W: Percy Waxman, M: Gene Lockhart.

3030. Worthe Faulkner *Kitty Darlin'* (Casino, "Capt. Dennis O'Hara," Nov. 7, 1917): Dear Old Dublin/W: P.G. Wodehouse, M: Rudolf Friml — Kitty Darlin'/W: Otto Harbach, M: Rudolf Friml. *Marjolaine* (Broadhurst, "John Sayle, Tenth Baron Otford," Jan. 24, 1922): Stars of Your Eyes; Syringa Tree/W: Brian Hooker, M: Hugo Felix. *The Magic Ring* (Liberty, "Abdullah," Oct. 1, 1923): Abdullah's Farewell; The Love Song (of Yesterday)/W: Zelda Sears, M: Harold A. Levey. *The Magnolia Lady* (Shubert, "Jefferson Page," Nov. 25, 1924): The Magic Hour; On the Washington Train; Phantoms of the Ballroom; Three Little Girls/W: Anne Caldwell, M: Harold A. Levey. *Honeymoon Lane* (Knickerbocker, "Dream Man," Sept. 20, 1926): Dreams for Sale/W: Herbert Reynolds, M: James F. Hanley.

3031. Florence Faun *The New Yorkers* (Edyth Totten, revue, Mar. 10, 1927): Romany/W: Henry Myers, M: Arthur Schwartz.

3032. Lotta Faust (Feb. 8, 1880–Jan. 25, 1910) B: New York, NY. M: RICHIE LING. *The Belle of Bohemia* (Casino, "Carrie Van Cortlandt," Sept. 24, 1900): Always Make Allowances for Love/W: Harry B. Smith, M: Ludwig Englander. *The Liberty Belles* (Madison Square, "Teresa Corsini," Sept. 30, 1901): Lesson Book Song/W: ?, M: Aimee Lachaume. *The Wizard of Oz* (Majestic, CR, "Tryxie Trifle," Feb. 2, 1903): Sammy/W: James O'Dea, M: Edward Hutchinson — When the Circus Comes to Town/W: James O'Dea, M: Bob Adams. *Wonderland* (Majestic, "Hildegarde Figgers," Oct. 24, 1905): Popular Pauline/W: Glen MacDonough, M: Victor Herbert. *The White Hen* (Casino, "Lisa Sommer," Feb. 16, 1907): Everything Is Higher Nowadays/W: Paul West, M: Gustave Kerker — Smile, Smile, Smile/W: Louis Mann, M: Martin Brown. *The Girl Behind the Counter* (Herald Square, "Ninette Valois," Oct. 1, 1907): The Band Box Girl/W: Edgar Selden, M: Seymour Furth — When You Steal a Kiss or Two (Making Love)/WM: Kenneth S. Clark. *The Mimic World* (Casino, revue, "Mlle. Ou La La," July 9, 1908): Mademoiselle/WM: ? — Phoebe Snow/W: Paul West, M: Herman Wade — When Johnny Comes Marching Home from College Again/W: E. Ray Goetz, M: Louis A. Hirsch. *The Midnight Sons* (Broadway, "Merri Murray," May 22, 1909): Carmen the Second; The Soubrette's

Secret/W: Glen MacDonough, M: Raymond Hubbell.

3033. Edward M. Favor (c 1856–Jan. 10, 1936) *The Blue Moon* (Casino, "Maj. Vivian Callabone," Nov. 3, 1906): All My Girls/WM: Collin Davis — Burmah Girl; Major's Song/WM: Percy Greenbank, Paul Rubens, Howard Talbot. *The Girls of Holland* (Lyric, "Little Snowdrop," Nov. 18, 1907): Why Is It?/W: Stanislaus Stange, M: Reginald De Koven.

3034. Allen Fawcett (1947–) B: Schenectady, NY. *Joseph and the Amazing Technicolor Dreamcoat* (Royale, revival, CR, "Joseph," June 24, 1982): Any Dream Will Do; The Brothers Came to Egypt; Close Ev'ry Door to Me; A Coat of Many Colors; Go, Go, Go, Joseph; Grovel, Grovel; Jacob and Sons; Jacob in Egypt; Joseph All the Time; Joseph's Dreams; Pharaoh's Dream Explained; Potiphar; Stone the Crows; Who's the Thief/W: Tim Rice, M: Andrew Lloyd Webber.

3035. Frank Fay (Nov. 17, 1897–Sept. 25, 1961) B: San Francisco, CA. M: FRANCES WHITE; movie star Barbara Stanwyck, two of his several wives. The headliner vaudeville performer and monologist with the sharp tongue and acid wit made many enemies due to his arrogance and drinking bouts. The role of Elwood P. Dowd in *Harvey*, which he played over 2,000 times, revived his sagging career in 1944. *Girl o' Mine* (Bijou, "Jack," Jan. 18, 1918): The Birdies in the Trees; It's the Woman Who Pays; Rug Snug; Today Is the Day/W: Philip Bartholomae, M: Frank Tours. *Oh, What a Girl!* (Shubert, "Bill Corcoran," July 28, 1919): Could You Teach Me?; Get Him Up; Oh That Shimmy!/W: Edward Clark, M: Charles Jules, Jacques Presburg — Dainty Little Girl Like You/W: Edgar Smith, M: Charles Jules, Jacques Presburg. *Jim Jam Jems* (Cort, "Johnny Case," Oct. 4, 1920): Don't Let Me Catch You Falling in Love; Jim Jam Jems; When the Right Little Girl Comes Along/W: Harry L. Cort, George E. Stoddard, M: James F. Hanley. *Frank Fay's Fables* (Park, revue, Feb. 6, 1922): It's a Pop, Pop, Popular Song/WM: Frank Fay, Clarence Gaskill. *Harry Delmar's Revels* (Shubert, revue, Nov. 28, 1927): Me and My Shadow/W: Billy Rose, M: Al Jolson, Dave Dreyer — My Rainbow/W: Jeanne Hackett, M: Lester Lee. *Tattle Tales* (Broadhurst, revue, June 1, 1933): Hang Up Your Hat on Broadway/W: George Waggoner, M: Edward Ward — I'll Take an Option on You/W: Leo Robin, M: Ralph Rainger.

3036. Hugh Fay (June 9, 1882–Dec. 4, 1926) B: New York, NY. *Three Twins* (Majestic,

CR, "Ned Moreland," Feb. 8, 1909): Little Miss Up-to-Date/W: Otto Harbach, M: Karl Hoschna.

3037. Olive Fay *Woof, Woof* (Royale, "Chotsy," Dec. 25, 1929): I Like It; Satanic Strut; Topple Down/WM: Eddie Brandt, Edward Pola.

3038. Alice Faye (May 5, 1912–May 9, 1998) B: New York, NY. M: singer Tony Martin; comedian Phil Harris. The actress-singer-dancer began on stage at age 7 and went on to become a megastar of 1930s and 40s movie musicals. She and husband Harris had their own very popular radio sitcom in the 1940s and 50s. *Good News* (St. James, revival, "Prof. Kenyon," Dec. 23, 1974): The Best Things in Life Are Free; Good News; I Want to Be Bad; Life Is Just a Bowl of Cherries; The Professor and the Students; Together; You're the Cream in My Coffee/W: B.G. DeSylva, Lew Brown, M: Ray Henderson.

3039. Denise Faye *Swinging on a Star* (Music Box, revue, Oct. 22, 1995): Annie Doesn't Live Here Anymore/W: Johnny Burke, Joe Young, M: Harold Spina — Chicago Style; Imagination; Like Someone in Love; Personality; When Stanislaus Got Married; You Don't Have to Know the Language/W: Johnny Burke, M: James Van Heusen — One, Two, Button Your Shoe/W: Johnny Burke, M: Arthur Johnston — What's New?/W: Johnny Burke, M: Bob Haggart — You're Not the Only Oyster in the Stew/W: Johnny Burke, M: Harold Spina.

3040. Herbie Faye (Feb. 2, 1899–June 28, 1980) He played Pvt. Sam Fender on the TV sitcom *The Phil Silvers Show* (1955). *Top Banana* (Winter Garden, "Moe," Nov. 1, 1951): O.K. for TV; Slogan Song (You Gotta Have a Slogan); Top Banana/WM: Johnny Mercer.

3041. Joey Faye (July 12, 1910–Apr. 26, 1997) B: New York, NY. Partner of JACK DIAMOND. In the 1930s he starred at Minsky's burlesque theater. *Allah Be Praised!* (Adelphi, "Youssouf," Apr. 20, 1944): Let's Go Too Far/W: George Marion, Jr., M: Don Walker. *The Duchess Misbehaves* (Adelphi, "Goya," Feb. 13, 1946): Broadminded; Ole Ole/W: Gladys Shelley, M: Frank Black. *High Button Shoes* (New Century, "Mr. Pontdue," Oct. 9, 1947): He Tried to Make a Dollar; Nobody Ever Died for Dear Old Rutgers; You're My Girl/W: Sammy Cahn, M: Jule Styne. *High Button Shoes* (New Century, CR, "Harrison J. Floy," May 1949): Can't You Just See Yourself?; He Tried to Make a Dollar; Nobody Ever Died for Dear Old Rutgers; On a Sunday by the Sea; There's Nothing Like a Model; You're My Girl/W: Sammy Cahn, M: Jule Styne. *Top Banana* (Winter Garden,

"Pinky," Nov. 1, 1951): O.K. for TV; Slogan Song (You Gotta Have a Slogan); Top Banana/WM: Johnny Mercer. *Little Me* (Lunt-Fontanne, "Bernie Buchsbaum," Nov. 17, 1962): To Be a Performer/W: Carolyn Leigh, M: Cy Coleman. *Guys and Dolls* (New York City Center, revival, "Benny Southstreet," Apr. 28, 1965): Fugue for Tinhorns; Guys and Dolls; The Oldest Established/WM: Frank Loesser. *Man of La Mancha* (Martin Beck, CR, "Sancho Panza," Nov. 1, 1968): The Combat; Golden Helmet; I Really Like Him; Knight of the Woeful Countenance (The Dubbing); A Little Gossip; Man of La Mancha (I, Don Quixote)/W: Joe Darion, M: Mitch Leigh. *70, Girls, 70* (Broadhurst, Apr. 15, 1971): Broadway, My Street; See the Light/W: Fred Ebb, M: John Kander. *Grind* (Mark Hellinger, "Solly," Apr. 16, 1985): Cadava; Timing/W: Ellen Fitzhugh, M: Larry Grossman.

3042. Greta Fayne *Ziegfeld Follies of 1924-1925* (New Amsterdam, revue, CR, Jan. 26, 1925): The Great Wide Open Spaces/W: Gene Buck, M: Dave Stamper — The Old Town Band/W: Joseph McCarthy, M: Harry Tierney.

3043. Leslie Feagan (Jan. 9, 1951–) B: Hinckley, OH. *Guys and Dolls* (Martin Beck, revival, "Calvin," Apr. 14, 1992): Follow the Fold/WM: Frank Loesser.

3044. Clifford Fearl B: New York, NY. *Flahooley* (Broadhurst, "Citizen of Capsulanti," May 14, 1951): Sing the Merry/W: E.Y. Harburg, M: Sammy Fain. *Mame* (Winter Garden, "Uncle Jeff," May 24, 1966): The Fox Hunt/WM: Jerry Herman. *Jimmy* (Winter Garden, "Warrington Brock," Oct. 23, 1969): It's a Nice Place to Visit; They Never Proved a Thing/WM: Bill Jacob, Patti Jacob. *My Fair Lady* (Uris, revival, "Jamie," Aug. 18, 1981): Get Me to the Church on Time; With a Little Bit of Luck/W: Alan Jay Lerner, M: Frederick Loewe.

3045. Peggy Fears (June 1, 1903–Aug. 24, 1994) B: New Orleans, LA. *Morris Gest Midnight Whirl* (Century Grove, revue, Dec. 27, 1919): Limehouse Nights/W: B.G. DeSylva, John Henry Mears, M: George Gershwin. *Ziegfeld's American Revue of 1926 aka No Foolin'* (Globe, revue, June 24, 1926): Florida, the Moon and You/W: Gene Buck, M: Rudolf Friml — Wasn't It Nice?/W: Irving Caesar, M: Rudolf Friml. *Rufus Le Maire's Affairs* (Majestic, revue, Mar. 28, 1927): Dancing by Moonlight; Down Where the Morning Glories Twine; The Mirror Never Lies; Wandering Through Dreamland/W: Ballard Macdonald, M: Martin Broones.

3046. Tovah Feldshuh (Dec. 27, 1952–) B:

New York, NY. Popular cabaret performer. *Sarava* (Mark Hellinger, "Flor," Feb. 23, 1979): Hosanna; Muito Born; Nothing's Missing; Play the Queen; Sarava; Vadinho Is Gone; Which Way Do I Go?/W: N. Richard Nash, M: Mitch Leigh.

3047. Seymour Felix (Oct. 23, 1892–Mar. 16, 1961) B: New York, NY. Choreographer and dance director. *The Mimic World* (Casino, revue, CR, "George M. Cohan," July 9, 1908): All the Stars and Stripes Belong to Me/WM: ?.

3048. Blanche Fellows *New Faces of 1943* (Ritz, revue, CR, Jan. 24, 1943): Animals Are Nice; Yes, Sir, I've Made a Date/W: J.B. Rosenberg, M: Lee Wainer — Hey, Gal!; New Shoes/W: June Carroll, M: Will Irwin — Love, Are You Raising Your Head Again?/W: June Carroll, M: Lee Wainer — Richard Crudnut's Charm School/W: June Carroll, John Lund, M: Lee Wainer.

3049. Don Fellows (Dec. 2, 1922–) B: Salt Lake City, UT. *South Pacific* (Majestic, "Lieut. Buzz Adams," Apr. 7, 1949): There Is Nothin' Like a Dame/W: Oscar Hammerstein II, M: Richard Rodgers. *South Pacific* (Majestic, CR, "Seabee Richard West," c 1952): same as above.

3050. Edith Fellows (May 20, 1923–) B: Boston, MA. Starting as a child star she appeared in hundreds of movies for Columbia, Paramount, Warner Brothers, Monogram and Republic studios. *Marinka* (Ethel Barrymore, CR, "Marinka," Nov. 4, 1945): If I Never Waltz Again; My Prince Came Riding; One Last Love Song; Sigh by Night; Treat a Woman Like a Drum; Turn on the Charm/W: George Marion, Jr., M: Emmerich Kalman. *Louisiana Lady* (New Century, "Marie-Louise," June 4, 1947): I Want to Live, I Want to Love; Just a Bit Naive; That's Why I Want to Go Home; When You Are Close to Me/W: Monte Carlo, M: Alma Sanders.

3051. Harry Fender *Shubert Gaieties of 1919* (44th Street, revue, July 14, 1919): Freedom of the C's; My Beautiful Tiger Girl/W: Alfred Bryan, M: Jean Schwartz. *Florodora* (Century, revival, "Capt. Arthur Donegal," Apr. 5, 1920): Come to St. George's/WM: Leslie Stuart — The Fellow Who Might/W: Ernest Boyd-Jones, M: Leslie Stuart — I Want to Be a Military Man/W: Frank Clement, M: Leslie Stuart. *The Last Waltz* (Century, "Baron Ippolith," May 10, 1921): A Baby in Love/W: Harold Atteridge, M: Ralph Benatzky, Alfred Goodman. *Lady in Ermine* (Ambassador, "Count Adrian Beltrami," Oct. 2, 1922): Childhood Days; Little Boy/WM: ?— The Lady in Ermine/W: Cyrus D. Wood, M: Alfred Goodman. *Adrienne* (George M. Cohan, "Stephen Hayes," May 28, 1923): Cheer Up;

Love Is All/W: A. Seymour Brown, M: Albert Von Tilzer. *Kid Boots* (Earl Carroll > Selwyn, "Tom Sterling," Dec. 31, 1923): If Your Heart's in the Game; A Play-Fair Man!; Polly Put the Kettle On; The Same Old Way/W: Joseph McCarthy, M: Harry Tierney. *Louie the 14th* (Cosmopolitan, "Capt. William Brent, A.E.F.," Mar. 3, 1925): Edelweiss [June 1, 1925]/W: Clifford Grey, M: Sigmund Romberg — Homeland; True Hearts; Wayside Flower/W: Arthur Wimperis, M: Sigmund Romberg.

3052. Jeff Fenholt *Jesus Christ Superstar* (Mark Hellinger, "Jesus of Nazareth," Oct. 12, 1971): The Arrest; The Crucifixion; Everything's Alright; Gethsemane; Hosanna; I Don't Know How to Love Him; The Last Supper; Pilate and Christ; Poor Jerusalem; Strange Thing Mystifying; The Temple; Trial Before Pilate; What's the Buzz/W: Tim Rice, M: Andrew Lloyd Webber.

3053. John Fennessy *Grease* (Broadhurst, CR, "Kenickie"): Greased Lightnin'/WM: Jim Jacobs, Warren Casey.

3054. Mildred Fenton On radio she produced a quiz show called *Detect and Collect* (1945). *Leave It to Me!* (Imperial, CR, "Dolly Winslow," Sept. 4, 1939): My Heart Belongs to Daddy; When All's Said and Done/WM: Cole Porter.

3055. Bill Ferguson *Small Wonder* (Coronet, revue, Sept. 15, 1948): Nobody Told Me/W: Phyllis McGinley, M: Baldwin Bergersen.

3056. Elsie Ferguson (Aug. 19, 1883–Nov. 15, 1961) B: New York, NY. Married 4 times and once called "the most beautiful girl on the American and British stage," she went to Hollywood and appeared in silent melodramas from 1917 to 1927. *The Liberty Belles* (Madison Square, "Marian Morris," Sept. 30, 1901): Lesson Book Song/W: ?, M: Aimee Lachaume. *Miss Dolly Dollars* (Knickerbocker > New Amsterdam, "Celeste," Sept. 4, 1905): Life's a Masquerade/W: Harry B. Smith, M: Victor Herbert.

3057. Gail Mae Ferguson *Dancin'* (Broadhurst, revue, CR, Dec. 31, 1979): Was Dog a Doughnut/WM: Cat Stevens — When Johnny Comes Marching Home/WM: Patrick Sarsfield Gilmore.

3058. Jean Ferguson *Peg o' My Dreams* (Al Jolson, "Fay," May 5, 1924): Right O; Shy Little Irish Smile/W: Anne Caldwell, M: Hugo Felix. *Hassard Short's Ritz Revue* (Winter Garden, revue, CR, Feb. 2, 1925): Broadway's Boudoir/W: Anne Caldwell, M: Frank Tours.

3059. Myrtle Ferguson *Topsy and Eva* (Harris, "Ophelia St. Clare," Dec. 23, 1924): Do-Re-Mi/WM: Vivian Duncan, Rosetta Duncan.

3060. W.J. Ferguson (1845–May 4, 1930) B: Baltimore, MD. *Florodora* (Casino > New York, CR, "Anthony Tweedlepunch," Jan. 28, 1901): I Want to Marry a Man, I Do/W: Paul Rubens, M: Leslie Stuart — When We're on the Stage/ WM: ?. *The Show Girl or The Cap of Fortune* (Wallack's, "Lord Cadawallader Dyce," May 5, 1902): Advice; The Family Ghost; Reggie's Family Tree; That's the Way of a Sailor/W: D.K. Stevens, M: H.L. Heartz. *The Little Whopper* (Casino, "Oliver Butts," Oct. 13, 1919): 'Round the Corner/W: Otto Harbach, Bide Dudley, M: Rudolf Friml.

3061. Danielle Ferland (Jan. 31, 1971–) B: Derby, CT. *Sunday in the Park with George* (Booth, "Louise," May 2, 1984): The Day Off/ WM: Stephen Sondheim. *Into the Woods* (Martin Beck, "Little Red Ridinghood," Nov. 5, 1987): Hello, Little Girl; I Know Things Now; No One Is Alone; Your Fault/WM: Stephen Sondheim.

3062. Harry Fern *Girlies* (New Amsterdam, "Bud Washington," June 13, 1910): Barber Shop Chord [June 20, 1910]/W: Harry Williams, M: Egbert Van Alstyne. *Toot-Toot!* (George M. Cohan, "Porter," Mar. 11, 1918): It's Immaterial to Me/W: Berton Braley, M: Jerome Kern.

3063. Jose Fernandez (Aug. 19, 1948–) B: Havana, Cuba. *The Me Nobody Knows* (Helen Hayes > Longacre, "Carlos," Dec. 18, 1970): How I Feel; The Tree/W: Will Holt, M: Gary William Friedman.

3064. Gina Ferrall *Les Miserables* (Broadway, CR, "Mme. Thenardier," c 1993): Beggars at the Feast; Master of the House; Thenardier Waltz/ W: Herbert Kretzmer, M: Claude-Michel Schonberg.

3065. Cliff Ferre (June 18, 1920–) B: Waitsfield, VT. *Dance Me a Song* (Royale, revue, Jan. 20, 1950): It's the Weather/WM: James Shelton.

3066. Andy Ferrell (Sept. 1950–) B: Wilson, NC. *Canterbury Tales* (Rialto, revival, "John," Feb. 12, 1980): Beer Is Best (Beer, Beer, Beer)/W: Nevill Coghill, M: Richard Hill, John Hawkins.

3067. Jose Ferrer (Jan. 8, 1909–Jan. 26, 1992) B: Santurce, Puerto Rico. M: actress Uta Hagen; singer Rosemary Clooney. Actor, director and producer of stage, screen and TV. Some of his great stage roles included Shakespeare's Iago and Richard III and Edmond Rostand's Cyrano de Bergerac. *Let's Face It!* (Imperial, CR, "Jerry Walker," Jan. 1943): Baby Games; Ev'rything I Love; Farming; I Hate You, Darling; Let's Not Talk About Love/WM: Cole Porter —

A Fairy Tale; Melody in 4-F/W: Sylvia Fine, M: Max Liebman. *The Girl Who Came to Supper* (Broadway, "The Grand Duke Charles, Prince Regent of Carpathia," Dec. 8, 1963): Coronation Chorale (Westminster Abbey); Curt, Clear and Concise; I'll Remember Her; Lonely; Middle Age; My Family Tree; Soliloquies; This Time It's True Love/WM: Noel Coward. *Man of La Mancha* (ANTA Washington Square, CR, "Don Quixote," May 28, 1966/Apr. 11, 1967): The Combat; Dulcinea; Golden Helmet; The Impossible Dream (The Quest); Man of La Mancha (I, Don Quixote)/W: Joe Darion, M: Mitch Leigh.

3068. Pat Ferrier *Redhead* (46th Street, "Tilly," Feb. 5, 1959): We Loves Ya, Jimey/W: Dorothy Fields, M: Albert Hague.

3069. Mabel Ferry *Baron Trenck* (Casino, "Anna," Mar. 11, 1912): Cupid Is a Cruel Master/W: Henry Blossom, M: Alfred G. Robyn. *Ziegfeld Midnight Frolic [4th Edition]* (New Amsterdam roof, revue, Oct. 3, 1916): My Midnight Belle/W: Gene Buck, M: Dave Stamper. *Ziegfeld Midnight Frolic [7th Edition]* (New Amsterdam roof, revue, Aug. 19, 1918): The Motor Girl/W: Gene Buck, M: Dave Stamper. *Ziegfeld Nine O'Clock Revue and Midnight Frolic* (New Amsterdam roof, revue, Dec. 9, 1918): Won't You Play the Game?/W: Gene Buck, M: Dave Stamper. *Glory* (Vanderbilt, "Myrtie Brown," Dec. 25, 1922): Saw Mill River Road; The Upper Crust/W: Joseph McCarthy, M: Harry Tierney — When the Curfew Rings at Nine/WM: Al W. Brown. *Adrienne* (George M. Cohan, "Grace Clayton," May 28, 1923): Dance with Me; The Hindoo Hop; Just a Pretty Little Home; Live While You're Here/W: A. Seymour Brown, M: Albert Von Tilzer.

3070. Stephen Ferry *Kismet* (Ziegfeld, "Wazir's Guard," Dec. 3, 1953): Was I Wazir?/WM: Robert Wright, George Forrest.

3071. Michael Fesco (May 24, 1936–) B: Oxford, MA. *New Faces of 1962* (Alvin, revue, Feb. 1, 1962): I Want You to Be the First to Know/W: June Carroll, M: Arthur Siegel.

3072. Stepin Fetchit (May 30, 1892–Nov. 19, 1985) B: Key West, FL. His real name was Lincoln Theodore Maurie Andrew Perry, the first black actor to be hugely successful in Hollywood in the 1920s and 30s, by playing a comic stereotype of the time. In 1978 he was elected into the Black Filmmakers Hall of Fame. *Walk with Music* (Ethel Barrymore, "Chesterfield," June 4, 1940): Everything Happens to Me/W: Johnny Mercer, M: Hoagy Carmichael.

3073. Edward Fetherston (Sept. 9, 1896–

June 12, 1965) B: New York, NY. *Flossie* (Lyric, "Chummy," June 3, 1924): The Battle Cry of Freedom; The First Is Last; Walla Walla/W: Ralph Murphy, M: Armand Robi.

3074. Ted Fetter (June 10, 1907–Mar. 13, 1996) B: Ithaca, NY. A successful lyric writer, he later became a TV executive. *The Garrick Gaieties of 1930* (Guild, revue, June 4, 1930): Johnny Wanamaker/W: Paul James, M: Kay Swift.

3075. Carol Field *Catch a Star!* (Plymouth, revue, Sept. 6, 1955): One Hour Ahead of the Posse/W: Ray Golden, Dave Ormont, M: Phil Charig.

3076. Grace Field *It Happened in Nordland* (Lew Fields, "Nadine," Dec. 5, 1904): The Matinee Maid/W: Glen MacDonough, M: Victor Herbert. *The Little Cherub* (Criterion, CR, "Lady Rosa Congress," Oct. 22, 1906): Dear Little Girls; Olympian Octet; Pierrot and Pierrette/W: Owen Hall, M: Ivan Caryll — I Should So Love to Be a Boy/W: C.H. Bovill, M: Frank Tours. *The Red Petticoat* (Daly's > Broadway, "Dora," Nov. 13, 1912): Little Golden Maid; A Prisoner of Love/W: Paul West, M: Jerome Kern — Oh, You Wonderful Spring/W: M.E. Rourke, M: Jerome Kern. *Lieber Augustin* (Casino, "Anna," Sept. 3, 1913): Anna, What's Wrong?/W: Scott Craven, M: Leo Fall — Do You Love Me Best?/W: Harry Beswick, M: Leo Fall. *Molly O'* (Cort, "Josette," May 17, 1916): Isn't That Like a Man!; Marry Me and See; One Way of Doing It/W: Robert B. Smith, M: Carl Woess. *The Kiss Burglar* (Cohan, "Mrs. E. Chatterton-Pym," May 9, 1918): The Little Black Sheep; One Day/W: Glen MacDonough, M: Raymond Hubbell.

3077. Robert Field see ROBERT ROUNSEVILLE.

3078. May Fielding *The Royal Middy* (Daly's, "Marie Francesca, Queen of Portugal," Jan. 28, 1880): Again Enfolded Within Thine Arms; In Woman's Heart Alone; The Mask; Of All the Fine Fellows That Sail on the Sea; To Our Flag/W: F. Zell, M: Richard Genee. *Cinderella at School* (Daly's, "Niobe Marsh," Mar. 5, 1881): Farewell; The Linnet in the Tree; Maiden Fair Awake to Me; Poor Cinderella; 'Tis Not Becoming in a Maiden; Why Am I So Sad Today?; You Are an Orphan/WM: Woolson Morse.

3079. Al Fields *The Runaways* (Casino, "Diagnosius Fleecem," May 11, 1903): Pretty Maid Adelaide; Tra La La La/W: Addison Burkhardt, M: Raymond Hubbell.

3080. Amelia Fields *Dolly Varden* (Herald Square, "Lady Alice," Jan. 27, 1902): Brides and Grooms; For the Benefit of Man; Loveable Love; Swing My Pretty One/W: Stanislaus Stange, M: Julian Edwards. *A Princess of Kensington* (Broadway, "Nell Reddish," Aug. 31, 1903): Oh! What Is Woman's Duty/W: Basil Hood, M: Edward German.

3081. Benny Fields (June 14, 1894–Aug. 16, 1959) B: Milwaukee, WI. M: BLOSSOM SEELEY. They were partners for 33 years, and popular headliners at the Palace. Considered an early crooner, he sang in an easygoing style, contrasting with his wife's powerful delivery. The Paramount movie *Somebody Loves Me* (1952), with Betty Hutton and Ralph Meeker, was the possibly less than accurate story of their lives together. *The Greenwich Village Follies of 1928* (Winter Garden, revue, Apr. 9, 1928): Golden Gate; Slaves of Broadway/W: Max Lief, Nathaniel Lief, M: Maurie Rubens — What's the Reason?/W: Harold Atteridge, M: Maurie Rubens.

3082. Chip Fields *Hello, Dolly!* (Minskoff, revival, "Minnie Fay," Nov. 6, 1975): Dancing/WM: Jerry Herman — Elegance; Motherhood/WM: Bob Merrill, Jerry Herman.

3083. Clare Fields *The Best Little Whorehouse in Texas* (46th Street > Eugene O'Neill, CR, "Beatrice," c 1980): Hard-Candy Christmas/WM: Carol Hall.

3084. Eddie Fields (?–May 1962) *Strut Miss Lizzie* (Times Square, revue, June 19, 1922): Mandy/WM: Henry Creamer, Turner Layton.

3085. Joe Fields (Jan. 23, 1935–) B: Uniontown, AL. *Ain't Supposed to Die a Natural Death* (Ethel Barrymore, Oct. 20, 1971): Mirror Mirror on the Wall/WM: Melvin Van Peebles.

3086. Lew Fields (Jan. 1, 1867–July 20, 1941) B: New York, NY. Father of songwriter Dorothy Fields. Very successful comic actor, manager, producer and librettist. Childhood friend and vaudeville partner of JOE WEBER, they were known as Weber and Fields. *Hurly-Burly* (Weber and Fields Music Hall, "Herr Bierheister," Sept. 8, 1898): A Loidy Wot Is Studyin' for the Stoige/W: Harry B. Smith, Edgar Smith, M: John Stromberg. *It Happened in Nordland* (Lew Fields, "Hubert," Dec. 5, 1904): Beatrice Barefacts/W: Glen MacDonough, M: Victor Herbert. *Blue Eyes* (Casino, "Peter Van Dam," Feb. 21, 1921): When Gentlemen Disagree/W: Zeke Meyers, M: I.B. Kornblum.

3087. Sally Fields *The Dancing Girl* (Winter Garden, "Eliza," Jan. 24, 1923): That American Boy of Mine/W: Irving Caesar, M: George Gershwin — Way Down in Pago Pago/W: Harold Atteridge, Carley Mills, M: Sigmund Romberg.

3088. W.C. Fields (Jan. 29, 1880–Dec. 25, 1946) B: Philadelphia, PA. The legendary comic star of burlesque, vaudeville, stage and movies began at about 14 as a juggler. *Poppy* (Apollo, "Prof. Eustace McGargle," Sept. 3, 1923): Kadoola Kadoola/W: Dorothy Donnelly, M: Stephen Jones, Arthur Sam- uels.

3089. Oscar L. Figman (1882–July 18, 1930) *A Female Drummer* (Star > Manhattan, "Corset Staye," Dec. 26, 1898): The Swellest Thing/W: Charles E. Blaney, M: Frank David. *Flo Flo* (Cort, "Robert Simpson," Dec. 20, 1917): Business Is Business; Don't Trust Them; If It Wasn't for My Wife and Family; Lingerie; A Wonderful Creature/W: Edward A. Paulton, M: Silvio Hein. *Peg o' My Dreams* (Al Jolson, "Jarvis," May 5, 1924): The Gap in the Hedge/W: Anne Caldwell, M: Hugo Felix.

3090. Rona Figueroa (Mar. 30, 1972–) B: San Francisco, CA. *Miss Saigon* (Broadway, CR, "Kim," c 1993): Back in Town; The Ceremony; The Guilt Inside Your Head; I Still Believe; I'd Give My Life for You; The Last Night of the World; Little God of My Heart; The Movie in My Mind; Please; Room 317; Sun and Moon; You Will Not Touch Him/W: Richard Maltby, Jr., Alain Boublil, M: Claude-Michel Schonberg.

3091. Tammie Fillhart *The Happy Time* (Broadway, "Sylvie," Jan. 18, 1968): Catch My Garter; The Life of the Party; Tomorrow Morning/W: Fred Ebb, M: John Kander.

3092. Clyde Fillmore (Oct. 25, 1876–Dec. 19, 1946) B: McConnelsville, OH. *Too Many Girls* (Imperial, "Harvey Casey," Oct. 18, 1939): Pottawatomie/W: Lorenz Hart, M: Richard Rodgers.

3093. Karen Fineman *City of Angels* (Virginia, CR, "Mallory Kingsley," Mar. 1991): Lost and Found/W: David Zippel, M: Cy Coleman.

3094. Charles Finin *The Merry Malones* (Erlanger's, "Charlie Malone," Sept. 26, 1927): The Honor of the Family; Our Own Way of Going Along (If You Like Coffee and I Like Tea)/WM: George M. Cohan.

3095. John Fink *1776* (46th Street, CR, "Thomas Jefferson," May 30, 1969): But, Mr. Adams; The Egg/WM: Sherman Edwards. *1776* (46th Street, CR, "Edward Rutledge"): Molasses to Rum/WM: Sherman Edwards.

3096. Genevieve Finlay *A Country Girl* (Daly's, "Princess Mehelaneh of Bhong," Sept. 22, 1902): Under the Deodar/W: Adrian Ross, M: Lionel Monckton. *The Cingalee* (Daly's, "Nanoya," Oct. 24, 1904): My Cinnamon Tree/ W: Adrian Ross, M: Lionel Monckton. *A Coun-*

try Girl (Herald Square, revival, "Princess Mehelaneh of Bhong," May 29, 1911): The Rajah of Bhong; Under the Deodar/W: Adrian Ross, M: Lionel Monckton — Sloe Eyes/WM: Paul Rubens.

3097. Vera Finlay *Bright Eyes* (New York, "Mrs. Hunter-Chase," Feb. 28, 1910): The Mood You Are In/W: Otto Harbach, M: Karl Hoschna.

3098. Flora Finlayson (?–Aug. 18, 1896) B: Scotland. *Robin Hood* (Standard, CR, "Allan-a-Dale," Oct. 1, 1891): The Bells of St. Swithins; Come the Bowmen in Lincoln Green; In Sherwood Forest; The Legend of the Chimes; Milkmaid's Song/W: Harry B. Smith, M: Reginald De Koven — Oh, Promise Me/W: Clement Scott, M: Reginald De Koven.

3099. Gracie Finley *Anne of Green Gables* (City Center 55th Street, "Anne Shirley," Dec. 21, 1971): The Facts; Gee I'm Glad I'm No One Else but Me; Humble Pie; I'll Show Him; Kindred Spirits; Oh Mrs. Lynde!; We Clearly Requested; Where Did the Summer Go To?; Wondrin'/WM: Donald Harron, Norman Campbell.

3100. Marjorie Finley *Sunny Days* (Imperial, "Nanine," Feb. 8, 1928): A Belle, a Beau and a Boutonniere; One Sunny Day/W: Clifford Grey, William Cary Duncan, M: Jean Schwartz.

3101. Patte Finley B: Asheville, NC. *Hello, Dolly!* (St. James, CR, "Irene Molloy," Aug. 9, 1965): Dancing; It Only Takes a Moment; Ribbons Down My Back/WM: Jerry Herman — Elegance; Motherhood/WM: Bob Merrill, Jerry Herman.

3102. Carrie Finnell A burlesque stripper in the 1920s, she was billed as The Girl with the Million Dollar Legs and introduced the tassel to the art of striptease. *Star and Garter* (Music Box, revue, June 24, 1942): Don't Take On More Than You Can Do/WM: Irving Gordon, Alan Roberts, Jerome Brainin — Turkish Oomph [Aug. 30, 1942]/W: Jerry Seelen, M: Lester Lee.

3103. Mary Finney (Sept. 30, 1906–Feb. 26, 1973) B: Spokane, WA. She was a secretary for the last 5 years of her life. *Happy Hunting* (Majestic, "Maud Foley," Dec. 6, 1956): Wedding-of-the-Year Blues/W: Matt Dubey, M: Harold Karr.

3104. Angelina Fiordellisi (Mar. 15, 1955–) B: Detroit, MI. *Zorba* (Broadway, revival, "Crow," Oct. 16, 1983): The Crow/W: Fred Ebb, M: John Kander.

3105. Elizabeth Firth *The Siren* (Knickerbocker, "Clarisse," Aug. 28, 1911): Wallflower Sweet/W: Harry B. Smith, M: Leo Fall.

3106. Bertie Fisch *Adonis* (Bijoux, "Lady

Nattie," Sept. 4, 1884): We Are the Duchess' Daughters/W: William F. Gill, Henry E. Dixey, M: Edward E. Rice.

3107. Alice Fischer (Jan. 16, 1869–June 23, 1947) B: Terre Haute, IN. *Piff! Paff!! Pouf!!!* (Casino, "Mrs. Lillian Montague," Apr. 2, 1904): We Really Ought to Be Married/W: William Jerome, M: Jean Schwartz. *Funabashi* (Casino, "Nan Livingston," Jan. 6, 1908): I Walked Around/W: Vincent Rose, Ted Snyder, M: Safford Waters.

3108. Robert C. Fischer (May 28, 1881–Mar. 11, 1973) B: Danzig, Germany. *Sweet Adeline* (Hammerstein's, "Emil Schmidt," Sept. 3, 1929): 'Twas Not So Long Ago/W: Oscar Hammerstein II, M: Jerome Kern. *May Wine* (St. James, "Josef," Dec. 5, 1935): I Built a Dream One Day/W: Oscar Hammerstein II, M: Sigmund Romberg.

3109. Charles Fisher (1816–1891) B: England. Imporant and well respected stage actor in Britain and the U.S. *The Royal Middy* (Daly's, "Capt. Norberto," Jan. 28, 1880): Sword in Hand, Man to Man/W: F. Zell, M: Richard Genee.

3110. Grace Fisher *The Show of Wonders* (Winter Garden, revue, Oct. 26, 1916): Get a Girlie/W: Harold Atteridge, M: Herman Timberg — Girls Prepare/W: Harold Atteridge, M: Sigmund Romberg — Naughty, Naughty, Naughty/ W: Joe Goodwin, William Tracey, M: Nat Vincent. *The Love Mill* (48th Street, "Mrs. Carter-Beaumont," Feb. 7, 1918): Down the Bridal Path of Love; I Loved Him for He Loved the Love That I Loved; The Love Mill; Why Can't It All Be a Dream?/W: Earl Carroll, M: Alfred Francis. *The Royal Vagabond* (Cohan and Harris, "Princess Helena," Feb. 17, 1919): In a Kingdom of Our Own/WM: George M. Cohan — Royalty/WM: George M. Cohan, Anselm Goetzl — When the Cherry Blossoms Fall (Love Is Love)/W: Stephen Ivor Szinnyey, William Cary Duncan, M: Anselm Goetzl.

3111. Harry E. Fisher (c 1868–May 28, 1923) B: Bristol, England. The comedian, part of the vaudeville team of Fisher and Carroll, came to the U.S. about 1888. *It Happened in Nordland* (Lew Fields, "Baron Sparta," Dec. 5, 1904): Slippery James/W: Glen MacDonough, M: Victor Herbert.

3112. Irving Fisher (c 1886–Feb. 4, 1959) *The Century Girl* (Century, revue, "Howell Lauder," Nov. 6, 1916): Alice in Wonderland/ WM: Irving Berlin — When Uncle Sam Rules the Wave/W: Henry Blossom, M: Victor Herbert. *Ziegfeld Follies of 1917* (New Amsterdam,

revue, June 12, 1917): Just Because You're You/W: Gene Buck, M: Jerome Kern — My Arabian Maid/W: Gene Buck, M: Raymond Hubbell. *Sally* (New Amsterdam, "Blair Farquar," Dec. 21, 1920): Sally (Dear Little Girl)/W: Clifford Grey, M: Jerome Kern — Whip-Poor-Will/W: B.G. DeSylva, M: Jerome Kern. *Ziegfeld Follies of 1924–1925* (New Amsterdam, revue, June 24, 1924): Adoring You/W: Joseph McCarthy, M: Harry Tierney — The Beauty Contest/W: Joseph McCarthy, M: Harry Tierney, Victor Herbert — Ever Lovin' Bee [Jan. 26, 1925]; Lonely Little Melody/W: Gene Buck, M: Dave Stamper — I'd Like to be a Gardener in a Garden of Girls [Aug. 3, 1925]; I'd Like to Corral a Gal; In the Shade of the Alamo [Aug. 3, 1925]; Montmartre/W: Gene Buck, M: Raymond Hubbell — Someone, Someday, Somewhere [Mar. 10, 1925]/W: Gene Buck, M: Rudolf Friml — Titina/W: Gene Buck, M: Leo Daniderff — You're My Happy Ending/W: Gene Buck, M: James F. Hanley. *Ziegfeld's American Revue of 1926 aka No Foolin'* (Globe, revue, June 24, 1926): Florida, the Moon and You; I Want a Girl to Call My Own/W: Gene Buck, M: Rudolf Friml — Poor Little Marie/W: Gene Buck, M: James F. Hanley, Billy Rose. *Luckee Girl* (Casino, "Lucien De Gravere," Sept. 15, 1928): A Flat in Montmartre/WM: Maurice Yvain, Lew Pollack — I Love You So/W: Max Lief, Nathaniel Lief, M: Maurice Yvain.

3113. J.J. Fisher *The Good Mister Best* (Garrick, "Ed Kauffman" and "Capt. Watchhalle," Aug. 30, 1897): Zim Boom Ta-ra/W: John J. McNally, M: ?.

3114. Joely Fisher (Oct. 29, 1967–) B: Burbank, CA. Daughter of singers Connie Stevens and Eddie Fisher. *Grease* (Eugene O'Neill, revival, CR, "Betty Rizzo," c 1994): Greased Lightnin'; Look at Me, I'm Sandra Dee; There Are Worse Things I Could Do/WM: Jim Jacobs, Warren Casey.

3115. Lola Fisher *My Fair Lady* (Mark Hellinger, CR, "Eliza Doolittle," Aug. 14, 1956): I Could Have Danced All Night; Just You Wait; The Rain in Spain; Show Me; Without You; Wouldn't It Be Loverly?/W: Alan Jay Lerner, M: Frederick Loewe. *Fiorello!* (New York City Center, revival, "Thea LaGuardia," June 13, 1962): 'Til Tomorrow; When Did I Fall in Love?/W: Sheldon Harnick, M: Jerry Bock.

3116. Sallie Fisher (Aug. 10, 1880–June 8, 1950) B: Wyoming. *Sergeant Brue* (Knickerbocker, "Aurora," Apr. 24, 1905): Dearie/WM: Clare Kummer. *The Man from Now* (New Amsterdam, "Dora," Sept. 3, 1906): Astronomy/ WM: ? — Coaxing/W: ?, M: Bernard Rolt — The

Dainty Music Maid; The Only Way to Love (Love's Lesson)/WM: Manuel Klein. *The Tatooed Man* (Criterion, "Leila," Feb. 18, 1907): The Floral Wedding; The Land of Dreams; Watch the Professor/W: Harry B. Smith, M: Victor Herbert. *A Knight for a Day* (Wallack's, "Muriel Oliver," Dec. 16, 1907): Garden of Dreams [Mar. 16, 1908]; My Very Own/WM: Clare Kummer — Life Is a See-Saw; The Little Girl in Blue/W: Robert B. Smith, M: Raymond Hubbell. *A Stubborn Cinderella* (Broadway, "Lady Leslie," Jan. 25, 1909): Don't Be Cross with Me; When You First Kiss the Last Girl You Love/W: Will M. Hough, Frank R. Adams, M: Joseph E. Howard. *Modest Suzanne* (Liberty, "Suzanne," Jan. 1, 1912): All the World Loves a Lover; Confidence; Father and Son; A Model Married Pair [Jan. 8, 1912]; Paris; Suzanne, Suzanne/W: Robert B. Smith, M: Jean Gilbert. *The Woman Haters* (Astor, "Maria Wilton," Oct. 7, 1912): He Will Take Me to His Heart/W: M.E. Rourke, M: Edmund Eysler — The Jag of Joy; The Letters That Never Were Written/W: George V. Hobart, M: Edmund Eysler. *Eva* (New Amsterdam, "Eva," Dec. 30, 1912): A Cinderella Duet; Love Is a Pilgrim/W: Glen Mac-Donough, M: Franz Lehar. *Watch Your Step* (New Amsterdam, revue, "Ernesta Hardacre," Dec. 8, 1914): Play a Simple Melody; What Is Love?/WM: Irving Berlin.

3117. George Fiske *The Isle of Spice* (Majestic, "Lieut. Harold Katchall," Aug. 23, 1904): Star of Fate/W: George E. Stoddard, M: Paul Schindler — Uncle Sam's Marines; You and I/W: Allen Lowe, M: Paul Schindler, Ben M. Jerome.

3118. Virginia Fissinger *Doing Our Bit* (Winter Garden, revue, "Virginia," Oct. 18, 1917): Fiesta; Hello, Miss Tango!; Mister Rag and I/W: Harold Atteridge, M: Sigmund Romberg, Herman Timberg. *Monte Cristo, Jr.* (Winter Garden, "Virginia," Feb. 12, 1919): Festive Nights; Monte Cristo/W: Harold Atteridge, M: Sigmund Romberg, Jean Schwartz.

3119. Robert Fitch (Apr. 29, 1934–) B: Santa Cruz, CA. *Lorelei or Gentlemen Still Prefer Blondes* (Palace, "Robert Lemanteur," Jan. 27, 1974): Mamie Is Mimi/W: Leo Robin, M: Jule Styne — Miss Lorelei Lee/W: Betty Comden, Adolph Green, M: Jule Styne. *Mack and Mabel* (Majestic, "Wally," Oct. 6, 1974): Look What Happened to Mabel/WM: Jerry Herman. *Annie* (Alvin, "Rooster Hannigan," Apr. 21, 1977): Easy Street/W: Martin Charnin, M: Charles Strouse. *Do Black Patent Leather Shoes Really Reflect Up?* (Alvin, "Father O'Reilly," May 27, 1982): Patron Saints/WM: James Quinn, Alaric

Jans. *The Will Rogers Follies* (Palace, CR, "Clem Rogers," c 1992): It's a Boy!; Will-a-Mania/W: Betty Comden, Adolph Green, M: Cy Coleman.

3120. Mark Fite (Jan. 24, 1954–) B: Race-land, LA. *Cleavage* (Playhouse, June 23, 1982): Just Another Song; Puberty; Reprise Me; The Thrill of the Chase/WM: Buddy Sheffield.

3121. Kathy Fitzgerald *Swinging on a Star* (Music Box, revue, Oct. 22, 1995): Apalachicola; Chicago Style; Here's That Rainy Day; His Rocking Horse Ran Away; Pakistan; Personality; Road to Morocco; What Does It Take to Make You Take to Me?; You Danced with Dynamite/W: Johnny Burke, M: James Van Heusen — Shadows on the Swanee/W: Johnny Burke, Joe Young, M: Harold Spina — You're Not the Only Oyster in the Stew/W: Johnny Burke, M: Harold Spina.

3122. Lillian Fitzgerald (?–July 9, 1947) B: New York, NY. *Ed Wynn Carnival* (New Amsterdam, revue, "Miss Perrin," Apr. 5, 1920): The Palmy Days/WM: Ed Wynn. *Bye, Bye Barbara* (National, "Paulette," Aug. 25, 1924): Amusing Myself; Quaint Little House for Two/WM: Monte Carlo, Alma Sanders. *Americana of 1932* (Shubert, revue, Oct. 5, 1932): Whistling for a Kiss/W: E.Y. Harburg, Johnny Mercer, M: Richard Myers.

3123. W.H. Fitzgerald *The Viceroy* (Knickerbocker, "Barabino," Apr. 9, 1900): On My Nuptial Day; One Fellow's Joy Is Another Fellow's Woe; A Sailor's Life/W: Harry B. Smith, M: Victor Herbert.

3124. Dave Fitzgibbon *Wake Up and Dream* (Selwyn, revue, CR, Jan. 6, 1930): Looking at You/WM: Cole Porter. *Walk a Little Faster* (St. James, revue, Dec. 7, 1932): Speaking of Love/W: E.Y. Harburg, M: Vernon Duke.

3125. Dorothy Fitzgibbon *Say When* (Morosco, "Diana Wynne," June 26, 1928): Little White Lies/W: Helen Wallace, M: Arthur Sheekman — My One Girl/WM: W. Franke Harling — No Room for Anybody in My Heart but You/W: Max Lief, Nathaniel Lief, M: Ray Perkins. *The Third Little Show* (Music Box, revue, June 1, 1931): Say the Word/W: Harold Adamson, M: Burton Lane. *Walk a Little Faster* (St. James, revue, Dec. 7, 1932): Speaking of Love/W: E.Y. Harburg, M: Vernon Duke.

3126. Eleanor Fitzhugh *Under Many Flags* (Hippodrome, revue, CR, Oct. 7, 1912): Fishing/WM: Manuel Klein.

3127. Jack Fitzhugh *My Best Girl* (Park, CR, "Private Stuart," Oct. 28, 1912): I'm Smiling at de Moon Dat Smiles at You/W: Channing Pollock, Rennold Wolf, M: Augustus Barratt.

3128. Venita Fitzhugh (c 1895–Jan. 1, 1920) *The Enchantress* (New York, "Princess Stephanie," Oct. 19, 1911): When the Right Man Sings Tra La/W: Harry B. Smith, M: Victor Herbert. *All Aboard* (44th Street roof garden, revue, "Alice Brown," June 5, 1913): Over the Ocean; Tulip Time/WM: E. Ray Goetz, Malvin F. Franklin. *The Marriage Market* (Knickerbocker, "Mariposa Gilroy," Sept. 22, 1913): Compliments; Hand in Hand; June Is in the Air/W: Arthur Anderson, M: Victor Jacobi — Little Gray Home in the West [Sept. 29, 1913]/W: D. Eardley-Wilmot, M: Hermann Lohr — Oh, How Near and Yet How Far/W: Adrian Ross, M: Victor Jacobi. *The Laughing Husband* (Knickerbocker, "Dolly," Feb. 2, 1914): Bought and Paid For; You're Here and I'm Here/W: Harry B. Smith, M: Jerome Kern. *The Girl from Utah* (Knickerbocker, CR, "Dora Manners," Sept. 30, 1914): The Music of Love; Where Has Una Gone?/W: Percy Greenbank, M: Paul Rubens — Only to You/WM: Paul Rubens — When We Meet the Mormon?/WM: ?—*A World of Pleasure* (Winter Garden, revue, Oct. 14, 1915): I Could Go Home to a Girlie Like You; Take Me Home with You/W: Harold Atteridge, M: Sigmund Romberg.

3129. Allen Fitzpatrick (Jan. 31, 1955–) B: Boston, MA. *Gentlemen Prefer Blondes* (Lyceum, revival "Gus Esmond," Apr. 10, 1995): Bye Bye Baby; Gentlemen Prefer Blondes; Homesick Blues/W: Leo Robin, M: Jule Styne.

3130. Edmund Fitzpatrick *Blossom Time* (Century, CR, "Von Schwind," Nov. 20, 1922): Keep It Dark; My Springtime Thou Art; Serenade/W: Dorothy Donnelly, M: Sigmund Romberg.

3131. Nanette Flack *Sporting Days and Battle in the Skies* (Hippodrome, "Mary Seymour" and "Alice Gedison," Sept. 5, 1908): I'm Looking for a Sweetheart and I Think You'll Do [Feb. 22, 1909]/W: R.H. Burnside, M: Manuel Klein — Love Is King/WM: Manuel Klein. *A Trip to Japan* (Hippodrome, "O Kosan," Sept. 4, 1909): Fair Flower of Japan/WM: Manuel Klein. *The International Cup* (Hippodrome, "Mme. Giradot," Sept. 3, 1910): The Sons of Every Nation Are Americans Today/WM: Manuel Klein. *When Johnny Comes Marching Home* (New Amsterdam > Manhattan Opera House, revival, "Kate Pemberton," May 7, 1917): Fairyland; Katie, My Southern Rose; Love's Night; Spring, Sweet Spring; The Suwanee River; Who Knows?/W: Stanislaus Stange, M: Julian Edwards. *Good Times* (Hippodrome, revue, Aug. 9, 1920): Sing a Serenade [Aug. 24, 1920]; You're Just Like a Rose/W: R.H. Burn-side, M: Raymond Hubbell. *Better Times* (Hippodrome, revue, Sept. 2, 1922): Just a Fan; My Golden Dream Ship/W: R.H. Burnside, M: Raymond Hubbell. *Hello, Lola* (Eltinge, "Mrs. Baxter," Jan. 12, 1926): Lullaby/W: Dorothy Donnelly, M: William B. Kernell.

3132. Niki Flacks (Apr. 7, 1943–) B: Daytona Beach, FL. *Candide* (Broadway, revival, CR, "Old Lady," July 3, 1975): The Best of All Possible Worlds; I Am Easily Assimilated/WM: Leonard Bernstein.

3133. Fannie Flagg (Sept. 21, 1941–) B: Birmingham, AL. Among her many TV appearances she played Dick Van Dyke's sister on *The New Dick Van Dyke Show* (1971). *The Best Little Whorehouse in Texas* (46th Street, CR, "Mona Stangley," May 12, 1980): Bus from Amarillo; Girl, You're a Woman; A Li'l Ole Bitty Pissant Country Place; No Lies; 20 Fans/WM: Carol Hall.

3134. Edward Flanagan (c 1880–Aug. 18, 1925) B: St. Louis, MO. *Ned Wayburn's Town Topics* (Century, revue, "Car Bona," Sept. 23, 1915): The Oskaloosa Pets/W: Robert B. Smith, M: Harold Orlob.

3135. Michael Flanders (Mar. 1, 1922–Apr. 15, 1975) B: London, England. Actor, lyricist, humorist. Broadcaster with BBC radio, 1948-75. After contracting polio in the Navy during WWII and facing life in a wheelchair, he decided against becoming an actor and turned to writing for the theater, radio and TV. His partner in this endeavor was DONALD SWANN. *At the Drop of a Hat* (Golden, revue, Oct. 8, 1959): Design for Living; A Gnu; Hippopotamus; The Hog Beneath the Skin; In the Bath; Judgment of Paris; Kokoraki; Madeira, M'Dear?; Misalliance; The Reluctant Cannibal; Sea Fever; Song of Reproduction; A Song of the Weather; Transport of Delight; Tried by the Centre Court; The Wompom/WM: Michael Flanders, Donald Swann — Down Below [Mar. 28, 1960]; The Youth of the Heart/W: Sidney Carter, M: Donald Swann — Greensleeves/WM: unknown. *At the Drop of Another Hat* (Booth, revue, Dec. 27, 1966): All Gall; Armadillo Idyll; Food for Thought; The Gas Man Cometh; Horoscope; Los Olivadados; Motor Perpetuo; P** P* B**** B** D******; Prehistoric Complaint; Sloth; Slow Train; A Song of Patriotic Prejudice; Thermodynamic Duo; Twenty Tons of TNT; Twice Shy/WM: Michael Flanders, Donald Swann — Bilbo's Song/W: J.R.R. Tolkien, M: Donald Swann — Ill Wind/W: Michael Flanders, M: Wolfgang Amadeus Mozart — In the Desert/WM: Donald Swann.

3136. Louisa Flaningam (May 5, 1945–) B: Chester, SC. *The Magic Show* (Cort, CR, "Charmin," Mar. 1976): Charmin's Lament; The Goldfarb Variations; Sweet, Sweet, Sweet/WM: Stephen Schwartz. *The Most Happy Fella* (Majestic, revival, "Cleo," Oct. 11, 1979): Big D; Happy to Make Your Acquaintance; I Like Ev'rybody; Ooh! My Feet!/WM: Frank Loesser. *Guys and Dolls* (Martin Beck, revival, CR, "Agatha," c 1993): Follow the Fold/WM: Frank Loesser.

3137. Gary Flannery *Dancin'* (Broadhurst, revue, CR, Jan. 30, 1979): Easy; If It Feels Good, Let It Ride/WM: Carol Bayer Sager, Melissa Manchester — Was Dog a Doughnut/WM: Cat Stevens.

3138. Robert Flavelle *The Golden Apple* (Alvin, "Diomede," Apr. 20, 1954): Come Along, Boys; Helen Is Always Willing; It Was a Glad Adventure/W: John Latouche, M: Jerome Moross.

3139. Lucille Flaven *The French Maid* (Herald Square, CR, "Dorothy Travers [Dolly]," Feb. 14, 1898): Charity's Useful Disguise/W: Basil Hood, M: Walter Slaughter — You Can Read It in My Eyes/W: Henry Norman, M: Herman Perlet.

3140. Tim Flavin *Happy New Year* (Morosco, "Thompson," Apr. 27, 1980): Let's Make It a Night/WM: Cole Porter.

3141. Tom Fleetwood *The Yearling* (Alvin, "Millwheel Forrester," Dec. 10, 1965): What a Happy Day/W: Herbert Martin, M: Michael Leonard.

3142. Blanche Fleming *The Garrick Gaieties of 1926* (Garrick, revue, May 10, 1926): Keys to Heaven/W: Lorenz Hart, M: Richard Rodgers. *Merry-Go-Round* (Klaw, revue, May 31, 1927): Sentimental Silly; Tampa/W: Howard Dietz, Morrie Ryskind, M: Henry Souvaine, Jay Gorney.

3143. Claude Fleming (Feb. 22, 1884–Mar. 24, 1952) B: Sydney, New South Wales, Australia. *Pretty Mrs. Smith* (Casino, "Frank Smith," Sept. 21, 1914): Let Bygones Be Bygones; The Plain Ol' Name o' Smith/W: Earl Carroll, M: Alfred G. Robyn — Love Has Come to Live in Our House/W: Oliver Morosco, M: Henry James. *Robinson Crusoe, Jr.* (Winter Garden, "Hiram Westbury," Feb. 17, 1916): Simple Life/W: Harold Atteridge, M: Sigmund Romberg — Where Did Robinson Crusoe Go with Friday on Saturday Night?/W: Sam M. Lewis, Joe Young, M: George W. Meyer.

3144. Cynthia Fleming *A Chorus Line* (Shubert, CR, "Kristine"): Sing!/W: Edward Kleban, M: Marvin Hamlisch. *A Chorus Line* (Shubert, CR, "Sheila," Nov. 1986): At the Ballet/W: Edward Kleban, M: Marvin Hamlisch.

3145. Daisy Fleming *Strut Miss Lizzie* (Times Square, revue, June 19, 1922): Breakin' the Leg/WM: Henry Creamer, Turner Layton.

3146. Eugene Fleming (Apr. 26, 1961–) B: Richmond, VA. *A Chorus Line* (Shubert, CR, "Richie," Sept. 1984): And…/W: Edward Kleban, M: Marvin Hamlisch. *The Tap Dance Kid* (Broadhurst, CR, "Dipsey Bates," July 9, 1985): Class Act; Dance If It Makes You Happy; Fabulous Feet; Man in the Moon; My Luck Is Changing; Tap Tap/W: Robert Lorick, M: Henry Krieger. *The High Rollers Social and Pleasure Club* (Helen Hayes, revue, "Jester," Apr. 21, 1992): Challenge Dance; Chicken Shack Boogie; Don't You Feel My Leg; Ooh Poo Pa Doo; Tu Way Pocky Way/WM: ?— I Like It Like That/WM: Chris Kenner, Alan Toussaint — Jambalaya/WM: Hank Williams. *Swinging on a Star* (Music Box, revue, Oct. 22, 1995): Ain't It a Shame About Mame; Doctor Rhythm; Don't Let That Moon Get Away/W: Johnny Burke, M: James V. Monaco — Annie Doesn't Live Here Anymore/W: Johnny Burke, Joe Young, M: Harold Spina — Chicago Style; Imagination; Pakistan; Thank Your Lucky Stars and Stripes; When Stanislaus Got Married/W: Johnny Burke, M: James Van Heusen — Irresistible/W: Johnny Burke, M: Harold Spina — Misty/W: Johnny Burke, M: Erroll Garner — Whoopsie Daisy Day/WM: Johnny Burke.

3147. John Fleming *Of V We Sing* (Concert, revue, Feb. 11, 1942): Juke Box/W: Alfred Hayes, M: Alex North — Red, White and Blues [Mar. 10, 1942]/WM: Lewis Allan.

3148. Juanita Fleming *The Wiz* (Lunt-Fontanne, revival, "Addaperle," May 24, 1984): He's the Wizard/WM: Charlie Smalls.

3149. Robert Fleming *Lady Fingers* (Vanderbilt > Liberty, "Masters," Jan. 31, 1929): The Life of a Nurse/W: Edward Eliscu, M: Joseph Meyer.

3150. Suzanne Fleming *Manhattan Mary* (Apollo, "A Society Bud" and "Tiny Forsythe," Sept. 26, 1927): It Won't Be Long Now; My Blue Bird's Home Again/W: B.G. DeSylva, Lew Brown, M: Ray Henderson.

3151. Una Fleming *The Velvet Lady* (New Amsterdam, "Una," Feb. 3, 1919): I've Danced to Beat the Band/W: Henry Blossom, M: Victor Herbert. *The Sweetheart Shop* (Knickerbocker, "Peggy," Aug. 31, 1920): The Dresden China Belle/W: Anne Caldwell, M: Hugo Felix. *Her Family Tree* (Lyric, Dec. 27, 1920): I Love You; A Romantic Knight/WM: Seymour Simons.

3152. Bill Fletcher (1922–) *The Student Gypsy or The Prince of Liederkranz* (54th Street, "Gryphon Allescu," Sept. 30, 1963): A Gypsy Dance/WM: Rick Besoyan.

3153. Bramwell Fletcher (Feb. 20, 1904–June 22, 1988) B: Bradford, Yorkshire, England. The actor of stage, screen and TV began as a clerk with an insurance company in London. *Maggie* (National, "Alick Wylie," Feb. 18, 1953): The New Me; Thimbleful; The Train with the Cushioned Seats/WM: William Roy. *My Fair Lady* (Mark Hellinger, CR, "Henry Higgins," Aug. 25, 1958): A Hymn to Him; I'm an Ordinary Man; I've Grown Accustomed to Her Face; The Rain in Spain; Why Can't the English?; You Did It/W: Alan Jay Lerner, M: Frederick Loewe.

3154. Jack Fletcher (Apr. 21, 1921–Feb. 15, 1990) B: Forest Hills, NY. *Can-Can* (New York City Center, revival, "Etienne," May 16, 1962): If You Loved Me Truly; Never, Never Be an Artist/WM: Cole Porter. *Ben Franklin in Paris* (Lunt-Fontanne, "Pedro Count de Aranda," Oct. 27, 1964): God Bless the Human Elbow/W: Sidney Michaels, M: Mark Sandrich, Jr. *Drat! The Cat!* (Martin Beck, "Lucius Van Guilder," Oct. 10, 1965): Dancing with Alice; Drat! The Cat!; It's Your Fault/W: Ira Levin, M: Milton Schafer. *Wonderful Town* (New York City Center, revival, "Frank Lippencott," May 17, 1967): Conversation Piece (Nice Talk, Nice People)/W: Betty Comden, Adolph Green, M: Leonard Bernstein. *Lorelei or Gentlemen Still Prefer Blondes* (Palace, "Lord Francis Beekman," Jan. 27, 1974): It's Delightful Down in Chile/W: Leo Robin, M: Jule Styne. *Sugar Babies* (Mark Hellinger, revue, "Jack," Oct. 8, 1979): Let Me Be Your Sugar Baby/WM: Arthur Malvin.

3155. Juanita Fletcher *When Johnny Comes Marching Home* (New Amsterdam > Manhattan Opera House, revival, "Cordelia Allen," May 7, 1917): But They Didn't; I Could Waltz On Forever; 'Twas Down in the Garden of Eden; While You're Thinking/W: Stanislaus Stange, M: Julian Edwards — My Father Fights for Uncle Sam/WM: ?. *Kitty Darlin'* (Casino, "Lady Julia Standish," Nov. 7, 1917): You'll See/W: P.G. Wodehouse, M: Rudolf Friml. *Apple Blossoms* (Globe, "Polly," Oct. 7, 1919): Brothers/W: William Le Baron, M: Victor Jacobi. *Little Miss Charity* (Belmont, "Angel Butterfield," Sept. 2, 1920): Crinoline Girl; Eyes of Youth; I Think So, Too; Step Inside; That Certain Something; When Love Comes to Your Heart; A Woman's Touch/W: Edward Clark, M: S.R. Henry, M. Savin.

3156. Neil Fletcher *Parisiana* (Edyth Totten, revue, Feb. 9, 1928): Maybe/WM: Vincent Valentini.

3157. Susann Fletcher (Sept. 7, 1955–) B: Wilmington, DE. *The Best Little Whorehouse in Texas* (46th Street, CR, "Angel"): Hard-Candy Christmas/WM: Carol Hall. *Jerome Robbins' Broadway* (Imperial, revue, Feb. 26, 1989): Sunrise, Sunset/W: Sheldon Harnick, M: Jerry Bock — You Gotta Have a Gimmick/W: Stephen Sondheim, M: Jule Styne. *The Goodbye Girl* (Marquis, "Donna," Mar. 4, 1993): Richard Interred; Too Good to Be Bad (2 Good 2 B Bad)/W: David Zippel, M: Marvin Hamlisch.

3158. Douglas Flint *Mr. Wix of Wickham* (Bijou, "Potter," Sept. 19, 1904): Rub a Dub/WM: Jerome Kern.

3159. Jay C. Flippen (Mar. 6, 1898–Feb. 3, 1971) B: Little Rock, AR. A vaudeville comedian, especially popular in blackface. Later he was a character actor in movies and TV and a radio emcee. *Hello, Lola* (Eltinge, "Genesis," Jan. 12, 1926): Five Foot Two; In the Dark; Sophie; That Certain Party/W: Dorothy Donnelly, M: William B. Kernell.

3160. Leila Florentino (Aug. 12–) B: Philippines. *Miss Saigon* (Broadway, CR, "Kim," Mar. 16, 1992): Back in Town; The Ceremony; The Guilt Inside Your Head; I Still Believe; I'd Give My Life for You; The Last Night of the World; Little God of My Heart; The Movie in My Mind; Please; Room 317; Sun and Moon; You Will Not Touch Him/W: Richard Maltby, Jr., Alain Boublil, M: Claude-Michel Schonberg.

3161. Joseph Florestano *Bloomer Girl* (Shubert, "2nd Deputy," Oct. 5, 1944): Simon Legree/W: E.Y. Harburg, M: Harold Arlen.

3162. Martha Flowers *Porgy and Bess* (New York City Center, revival, "Bess," May 17, 1961): Bess, You Is My Woman Now; I Loves You, Porgy/W: DuBose Heyward, Ira Gershwin, M: George Gershwin — Leavin' Fo' de Promis' Land; What You Want wid Bess?/W: DuBose Heyward, M: George Gershwin — There's a Boat Dat's Leavin' Soon for New York/W: Ira Gershwin, M: George Gershwin.

3163. Estelle Floyd *My Magnolia* (Mansfield, revue, "Lulu Belle," July 8, 1926): Laugh Your Blues Away; Sweet Popopper/W: Alex Rogers, M: C. Luckeyth Roberts.

3164. Paul Floyd *Messin' Around* (Hudson, revue, Apr. 22, 1929): Circus Time/W: Perry Bradford, M: James P. Johnson.

3165. Eddie Flynn *Hello, Alexander* (44th Street, "Spike Murphy," Oct. 7, 1919): Pantomime Baseball/W: Alfred Bryan, M: Jean Schwartz.

3166. Elinor Flynn (Mar. 17, 1910–July 4, 1938) B: Chicago, IL. *Fools Rush In* (Playhouse, revue, Dec. 25, 1934): Let's Hold Hands/W: June Sillman, M: Richard Lewine.

3167. J. Lee Flynn *State Fair* (Music Box, "Clay," Mar. 27, 1996): More Than Just a Friend/WM: Richard Rodgers.

3168. Kitty Flynn *Sally, Irene and Mary* (Casino, "Irene," Sept. 4, 1922): Opportunity; Stage Door Johnnies; Wedding Time/W: Raymond Klages, M: J. Fred Coots.

3169. Marie Flynn *When Dreams Come True* (Lyric > 44th Street, "Beth," Aug. 18, 1913): Dear World; Dream Waltz; Giddy Up, Giddy Up, Dearie; Who's the Little Girl?; Y-O-U, Dear, Y-O-U/W: Philip Bartholomae, M: Silvio Hein. *You're in Love* (Casino, "Georgiana Payton," Feb. 6, 1917): He Will Understand/W: Otto Harbach, M: Rudolf Friml—I'm Only Dreaming; Love Land; Things That They Must Not Do; A Year Is a Long, Long Time; You're in Love/W: Otto Harbach, Edward Clark, M: Rudolf Friml. *The Velvet Lady* (New Amsterdam, "Ottilie Howell," Feb. 3, 1919): Come Be My Wife; Fair Honeymoon; Throwing the Bull/W: Henry Blossom, M: Victor Herbert.

3170. Martha Flynn *The Music Man* (Majestic, "Mrs. Squires," Dec. 19, 1957): It's You; Pick-a-Little, Talk-a-Little/WM: Meredith Willson.

3171. Tom Flynn *The Who's Tommy* (St. James, "News Vendor," Apr. 22, 1993): Miracle Cure/WM: Pete Townshend.

3172. Merwin Foard *Les Miserables* (Broadway, CR, "Javert," c 1994): Soliloquy; Stars/W: Herbert Kretzmer, M: Claude-Michel Schonberg.

3173. Brian Foley *1776* (46th Street, CR, "Thomas Jefferson," Jan. 15, 1971): But, Mr. Adams; The Egg/WM: Sherman Edwards.

3174. Chotzi Foley *Gypsy* (Broadway, "Electra," May 21, 1959): You Gotta Have a Gimmick/W: Stephen Sondheim, M: Jule Styne.

3175. Cynthia Foley *Stepping Stones* (Globe, revival, "Richard," Sept. 1, 1924): Little Angel Cake/W: Anne Caldwell, M: Jerome Kern. *Three Cheers* (Globe, "Ermyntrude," Oct. 15, 1928): Because You're Beautiful; Pompanola/W: B.G. DeSylva, Lew Brown, M: Ray Henderson.

3176. Ellen Foley (June 5, 1951–) B: St. Louis, MO. Rock n' roll singer. *Hair* (Biltmore, revival, "Sheila," Oct. 5, 1977): Easy to Be Hard; Good Morning, Starshine; I Believe in Love; Let the Sunshine In (The Flesh Failures)/W: Gerome Ragni, James Rado, M: Galt MacDermot. *Me and My Girl* (Marquis, revival, CR, "Sally

Smith," Feb. 23, 1988): Hold My Hand/W: Harry Graham, M: Maurice Elwin, Noel Gay — The Lambeth Walk; Me and My Girl; Take It on the Chin/W: L. Arthur Rose, Douglas Furber, M: Noel Gay — Once You Lose Your Heart/WM: Noel Gay. *Into the Woods* (Martin Beck, CR, "Witch," Aug. 1, 1989): Children Will Listen; Lament (Children Won't Listen); Last Midnight; Stay with Me; Your Fault/WM: Stephen Sondheim.

3177. John Foley *Pump Boys and Dinettes* (Princess, "Jackson," Feb. 4, 1982): Mona/WM: Jim Wann.

3178. Louis B. Foley *Rogers Brothers in Paris* (New Amsterdam, "Leo," Sept. 5, 1904): Kindness/W: George V. Hobart, M: Max Hoffmann.

3179. Dorothy Follis (1892–Aug. 15, 1923) B: Newark, NJ. *The Rose Maid* (Globe, "Gwendolen Bruce," Apr. 22, 1912): The American Heiress; One Waltz, Only One Waltz/W: Robert B. Smith, M: Bruno Granichstaedten.

3180. Nellie Follis *The Chaperons* (New York > New York roof, "Violet Smilax," June 5, 1902): The Little Maid Who Couldn't Say No/W: Frederick Ranken, M: Isidore Witmark.

3181. Gene Fontaine *Smile at Me* (Fulton, revue, Aug. 23, 1935): Fiesta in Madrid/WM: Edward J. Lambert, Gerald Dolin — I'm Dreaming While We're Dancing; Smile at Me/WM: Edward J. Lambert.

3182. Luther Fontaine (Apr. 14, 1947–) B: Kansas City, KS. *The First* (Martin Beck, "Junkyard Jones," Nov. 17, 1981): The National Pastime (This Year's Nigger)/W: Martin Charnin, M: Bob Brush.

3183. Char Fontane B: Los Angeles, CA. *Grease* (Broadhurst, CR, "Marty"): Freddy, My Love/WM: Jim Jacobs, Warren Casey.

3184. Gladys Fooshee Sister of SYBIL FOOSHEE. *Red Pepper* (Shubert, "Babe Stringer," May 29, 1922): Chickens; Ginger; Strong for Girls/WM: Howard E. Rogers, Albert Gumble, Owen Murphy. *The Passing Show of 1922* (Winter Garden, revue, Sept. 20, 1922): Orphans of the Storm/W: Harold Atteridge, M: Alfred Goodman.

3185. Sybil Fooshee *Red Pepper* (Shubert, "Billie Bull," May 29, 1922): same as GLADYS FOOSHEE. *The Passing Show of 1922* (Winter Garden, revue, Sept. 20, 1922): same as GLADYS FOOSHEE.

3186. Gene Foote (Oct. 30, 1936–) B: Johnson City, TN. *Chicago* (46th Street, "Aaron," June 3, 1975): Me and My Baby/W: Fred Ebb, M: John Kander.

3187. Dick Foran (June 18, 1910–Aug. 10,

1979) B: Flemington, NJ. His father was Sen. Arthur F. Foran of NJ. He began his career as a singer and band leader. At Warner Brothers he played singing cowboys and the nice guy who loses the girl. *A Connecticut Yankee* (Martin Beck, revival, "Lieut. Martin Barrett, U.S.N.," Nov. 17, 1943): Can't You Do a Friend a Favor?; My Heart Stood Still; Thou Swell; You Always Love the Same Girl/W: Lorenz Hart, M: Richard Rodgers.

3188. Ben Forbes *The Girl in the Spotlight* (Knickerbocker, "Frank Marvin," July 12, 1920): I Cannot Sleep Without Dreaming of You; It Would Happen Anyway; Somewhere I Know There's a Girl for Me/W: Robert B. Smith, M: Victor Herbert.

3189. Brenda Forbes (Jan. 14, 1908–Sept. 11, 1996) B: London, England. Her brother was RALPH FORBES; their mother, Mary Forbes, was a star of the British stage. *One for the Money* (Booth, revue, Feb. 4, 1939): I Hate Spring [added]/W: Nancy Hamilton, M: Martha Caples. *Two for the Show* (Booth, revue, Feb. 8, 1940): This "Merry" Christmas/W: Nancy Hamilton, M: Morgan Lewis. *Three to Make Ready* (Adelphi, revue, Mar. 7, 1946): And Why Not I?/W: Nancy Hamilton, M: Morgan Lewis. *Darling of the Day* (George Abbott, "Lady Vale," Jan. 27, 1968): Panache/W: E.Y. Harburg, M: Jule Styne.

3190. Donna Liggitt Forbes (Sept. 9, 1947–) B: Wilson, NC. *Hurry, Harry* (Ritz, "Melina" and "Native No. 2," Oct. 12, 1972): Africa Speaks; When a Man Cries/W: David Finkle, M: Bill Weeden.

3191. Edward Forbes (?–May 15, 1969) *A Hero Is Born* (Adelphi, "Chief Steward," Oct. 1, 1937): A Love-Lorn Maid; Tra La La/W: Agnes Morgan, M: A. Lehman Engel.

3192. Harold Forbes *The American Idea* (New York, "Charlie Sullivan," Oct. 5, 1908): Brothers and Sisters; That's Some Love/WM: George M. Cohan. *The Girl of My Dreams* (Criterion, "Pidgeon Williams," Aug. 7, 1911): Dearest Little Marionette; Every Girlie Loves Me but the Girl I Love; Something Very Mysterious/W: Otto Harbach, M: Karl Hoschna.

3193. Jean Forbes *Robinson Crusoe, Jr.* (Winter Garden, Feb. 17, 1916): When You're Starring in the Movies/W: Harold Atteridge, M: Sigmund Romberg.

3194. Ralph Forbes (Sept. 30, 1902–Mar. 31, 1951) B: London, England. M: RUTH CHATTERTON. Brother of BRENDA FORBES. He made more than 50 films; his first in the U.S. was the silent *Beau Geste* (1926). *The*

Magnolia Lady (Shubert, "Kenneth Craig," Nov. 25, 1924): The French Lesson; Moon Man/W: Anne Caldwell, M: Harold A. Levey.

3195. Anna Ford *A Matinee Idol* (Daly's > Lyric, "Marie," Apr. 28, 1910): I Want to Wed a Soldier Boy [May 2, 1910]; She's the Only Girl for Me/W: E. Ray Goetz, A. Seymour Brown, M: Silvio Hein.

3196. Chip Ford *Shenandoah* (Alvin, "Gabriel," Jan. 7, 1975): Freedom; Why Am I Me?/W: Peter Udell, M: Gary Geld.

3197. Clebert Ford (Jan. 29, 1932–) B: Brooklyn, NY. *Ain't Supposed to Die a Natural Death*, Oct. 20, 1971): Catch That on the Corner/WM: Melvin Van Peebles.

3198. David Ford (Oct. 30, 1929–Aug. 7, 1983) B: La Jolla, CA. He appeared on TV soaps *Search for Tomorrow* (1951) and *Dark Shadows* (1966). *1776* (46th Street, CR, "John Dickinson," July 1970): Cool, Cool, Considerate Men/WM: Sherman Edwards.

3199. George Ford M: HELEN FORD. He produced some of his wife's shows, such as *Dearest Enemy*. *The Passing Show of 1913* (Winter Garden, revue, July 24, 1913): Reflections/W: Harold Atteridge, M: Jean Schwartz.

3200. Helen Ford (June 6, 1894–Jan. 19, 1982) B: Troy, NY. M: GEORGE FORD. *Sometime* (Casino, CR, "Enid Vaughn," Mar. 24, 1919): Baby Doll; Sometime/W: Rida Johnson Young, M: Rudolf Friml. *Always You* (Central, "Toinette Fontaine," Jan. 5, 1920): Always You; Same Old Places; Syncopated Heart/W: Oscar Hammerstein II, M: Herbert Stothart. *The Sweetheart Shop* (Knickerbocker, "Natalie Blythe," Aug. 31, 1920): Didn't You?/W: Anne Caldwell, M: Hugo Felix — Waiting for the Sun to Come Out/W: Arthur Francis, M: George Gershwin. *For Goodness Sake* (Lyric, "Marjorie Leeds," Feb. 20, 1922): Every Day/W: Arthur Jackson, M: William Daly — Greatest Team of All; When Somebody Cares/W: Arthur Jackson, M: Paul Lannin, William Daly — Someone/W: Ira Gershwin, M: George Gershwin. *The Gingham Girl* (Earl Carroll, "Mary Thompson," Aug. 28, 1922): As Long As I Have You; Love and Kisses; The Twinkle in Your Eye/W: Neville Fleeson, M: Albert Von Tilzer. *Helen of Troy, New York* (Selwyn > Times Square, "Helen McGuffey," June 19, 1923): Cry Baby; Helen of Troy, New York; It Was Meant to Be; A Little Bit of Jazz; Look for the Happy Ending; We'll Have a Model Factory/W: Bert Kalmar, M: Harry Ruby. *No Other Girl* (Morosco, "Hope Franklin," Aug. 13, 1924): The Best in the Trade; I Would Rather Dance a Waltz; In the Corner of My Mind; No Other Girl/W: Bert Kalmar, M: Harry Ruby. *Dearest Enemy* (Knickerbocker, "Betsy Burke," Sept. 18, 1925): Bye and Bye; Here in My Arms (It's Adorable); Here's a Kiss; I'd Like to Hide It/W: Lorenz Hart, M: Richard Rodgers. *Peggy-Ann* (Vanderbilt, "Peggy-Ann Barnes," Dec. 27, 1926): I'm So Humble; In His Arms; A Little Birdie Told Me So; Maybe It's Me; A Tree in the Park; Where's That Rainbow?/W: Lorenz Hart, M: Richard Rodgers. *Chee-Chee* (Mansfield, "Chee-Chee," Sept. 25, 1928): Dear, Oh Dear; I Must Love You/W: Lorenz Hart, M: Richard Rodgers. *Great Lady* (Majestic, "Freelove Clark," Dec. 1, 1938): I Never Saw a King Before; Sisters Under the Skin; Sweet William/W: Earle Crooker, M: Frederick Loewe.

3201. Marion Ford *The Grass Widow* (Liberty > Princess, "Betty," Dec. 3, 1917): All the Girls Have Got a Friend in Me; C.D.Q./W: Channing Pollock, Rennold Wolf, M: Louis A. Hirsch.

3202. Marjorie Ford *Blossom Time* (46th Street, revival, "Fritzi," Dec. 26, 1938): Love Is a Riddle; Peace to My Lonely Heart; Three Little Maids/W: Dorothy Donnelly, M: Sigmund Romberg.

3203. Phil Ford M: partner and performer MIMI HINES. *Funny Girl* (Winter Garden, CR, "Eddie Ryan," Dec. 1965): Find Yourself a Man; If a Girl Isn't Pretty; Who Taught Her Everything?/W: Bob Merrill, M: Jule Styne.

3204. Richard Ford *The Grand Street Follies of 1928* (Booth, revue, May 28, 1928): Briny Blues/W: Agnes Morgan, M: Serge Walter — Just a Little Love Song/WM: Max Ewing.

3205. Robert F. Ford *My Princess* (Shubert, "Peter Loomis," Oct. 6, 1927): Dear Girls, Goodbye; The Glorious Chase; My Passion Flower/W: Dorothy Donnelly, M: Sigmund Romberg.

3206. Ruth Ford (July 7, 1912–) B: Hazelhurst, MS. M: ZACHARY SCOTT. *The Grass Harp* (Martin Beck, "Verena Talbo," Nov. 2, 1971): What Do I Do Now?/W: Kenward Elmslie, M: Claibe Richardson.

3207. Hal Forde (c 1877–Dec. 4, 1955) B: Ireland. *The Enchantress* (New York, "Prince Ivan of Zergovia," Oct. 19, 1911): The Last Little Girl Is You; One Word from You; Rose, Lucky Rose/W: Harry B. Smith, M: Victor Herbert. *Adele* (Longacre > Harris, "Baron Charles de Chantilly," Aug. 28, 1913): Adele; A Honeymoon with You; Yours for Me and Mine for You/WM: Paul Herve, Edward A. Paulton, Adolf Philipp, Jean Briquet — The Clock Is Striking Ten; Close

Your Eyes; Like Swallow Flying; Matter of Opinion; Paris! Goodbye!; Strawberries and Cream; A Waste of Time to Plan/WM: Edward A. Paulton, Adolf Philipp, Jean Briquet. *Maid in America* (Winter Garden, revue, "John Gray," Feb. 18, 1915): Garden of Paradise; It Is All for You/W: Harold Atteridge, M: Sigmund Romberg. *The Girl from Brazil* (44th Street > Shubert, "Carl Cederstol," Aug. 30, 1916): The Financial Viking/WM: ?— Heart to Heart/W: Matthew Woodward, M: Robert Winterberg — Oh You Lovely Ladies/W: Matthew Woodward, M: Sigmund Romberg. *Oh, Boy!* (Princess > Casino, "Jim Marvin," Feb. 20, 1917): The First Day of May; Flubby Dub; Koo-La-Loo; Let's Make a Night of It; Nesting Time in Flatbush/W: P.G. Wodehouse, M: Jerome Kern — A Package of Seeds/W: Herbert Reynolds, P.G. Wodehouse, M: Jerome Kern. *Molly Darling* (Liberty, "Chauncey Chesbro," Sept. 1, 1922): Mellow Moon; There's an Eve in Ev'ry Garden/W: Phil Cook, M: Tom Johnstone. *Oh, Ernest!* (Royale, "Hon. John Worthing, J.P.," May 9, 1927): Ancestry; Cupid's College; He Knows Where the Rose Is in Bloom; Never Trouble Trouble; Taken by Surprise; There's a Muddle/W: Francis De Witt, M: Robert Hood Bowers. *The Houseboat on the Styx* (Liberty, "Sir Walter Raleigh," Dec. 25, 1928): The Fountain of Youth; The Houseboat on the Styx; Men of Hades; Someone Like You/W: Monte Carlo, M: Alma Sanders. *The Merry Widow* (Erlanger's, revival, "Baron Popoff," Sept. 14, 1931): Women/W: Adrian Ross, M: Franz Lehar. *As Thousands Cheer* (Music Box, revue, Sept. 30, 1933): Majestic Sails at Midnight/WM: Irving Berlin.

3208. Stanley H. Forde (Feb. 9, 1878–Jan. 28, 1929) B: Buffalo, NY. *The Medal and the Maid* (Broadway, "Darien," Jan. 11, 1904): The Philosophic Brigand/W: Charles H. Taylor, M: Sidney Jones. *Woodland* (New York > Herald Square, "Judge Owl," Nov. 21, 1904): At Night, At Night; The Valley of Hokus-Pocus/W: Frank Pixley, M: Gustav Luders. *The Princess Beggar* (Casino, "Baron Lombardo," Jan. 7, 1907): I Don't Love You; I Want It All; Madrigal/W: Edward A. Paulton, M: Alfred G. Robyn. *The Talk of New York* (Knickerbocker, "Dudley Wilcox," Dec. 3, 1907): Drink with Me; Follow Your Uncle Dudley/WM: George M. Cohan. *Modest Suzanne* (Liberty, "Baron Dauvray," Jan. 1, 1912): The Return; Suzanne, Suzanne; Virtue Is Its Own Reward/W: Robert B. Smith, M: Jean Gilbert. *Nothing but Love* (Lyric, "Commodore Marbury," Oct. 14, 1919): It's Not What You Say/W: Frank Stammers, M: Harold Orlob. *Jim*

Jam Jems (Cort, "Cyrus Ward," Oct. 4, 1920): I've Always Been Fond of Babies (That's Why I'm in Love with You); The Magic Kiss; Show Me the Town/W: Harry L. Cort, George E. Stoddard, M: James F. Hanley—Poor Old Florodora Girl/W: Ballard Macdonald, M: James F. Hanley. *Castles in the Air* (Selwyn, "Philip Rodman," Sept. 6, 1926): The Singer's Career, Ha! Ha!/W: Raymond W. Peck, M: Percy Wenrich.

3209. Marcel Forestieri *Bring Back Birdie* (Martin Beck, "Mayor C.B. Townsend," Mar. 5, 1981): You Can Never Go Back/W: Lee Adams, M: Charles Strouse.

3210. Ted Forlow (Apr. 29, 1931–) B: Independence, MO. *Man of La Mancha* (Vivian Beaumont, revival, "Anselmo," June 22, 1972): Little Bird, Little Bird/W: Joe Darion, M: Mitch Leigh. *Man of La Mancha* (Palace, revival, "The Barber," Sept. 15, 1977): Barber's Song; Golden Helmet/W: Joe Darion, M: Mitch Leigh. *Man of La Mancha* (Marquis, revival, "The Barber," Apr. 24, 1992): same as above.

3211. Hilda Forman B: Tennessee. Sister of LOUISE and MAXINE FORMAN. *America's Sweetheart* (Broadhurst, "Georgia," Feb. 10, 1931): Sweet Geraldine; Tennessee Dan/W: Lorenz Hart, M: Richard Rodgers.

3212. Louise Forman B: Tennessee. *America's Sweetheart* (Broadhurst, "Georgiana," Feb. 10, 1931): same as HILDA FORMAN.

3213. Maxine Forman B: Tennessee. *America's Sweetheart* (Broadhurst, "Georgette," Feb. 10, 1931): same as HILDA FORMAN.

3214. Joseph Anthony Foronda (Jan. 17, 1954–) B: Fairbanks, AK. *Shogun: The Musical* (Marquis, "Lord Buntaro," Nov. 20, 1990): Cha-No-Yu; How Nice to See You/W: John Driver, M: Paul Chihara. *Miss Saigon* (Broadway, CR, "The Engineer," Nov. 11, 1996): The American Dream; Back in Town; The Heat Is On in Saigon; If You Want to Die in Bed; The Morning of the Dragon; The Telephone; What a Waste/W: Richard Maltby, Jr., Alain Boublil, M: Claude-Michel Schonberg.

3215. Almyra Forrest *The Prince of Pilsen* (Broadway, CR, "Edith Adams," July 6, 1903): The Field and Forest; The Message of the Violet; We Know It's Wrong to Flirt/W: Frank Pixley, M: Gustav Luders. *The Prince of Pilsen* (New York, revival, "Edith Adams," Apr. 3, 1905): same as above. *The Gingerbread Man* (Liberty > New York, "Mazie Bon-Bon," Dec. 25, 1905): Beautiful Land of Bon-Bon/W: Frederick Ranken, M: A. Baldwin Sloane.

3216. Arthur Forrest (Aug. 16, 1859–May 14, 1933) B: Bayreuth, Bavaria. *The Enchantress* (New York, "Ozir," Oct. 19, 1911): All Your Own Am I/W: Harry B. Smith, M: Victor Herbert.

3217. June Forrest *Great Lady* (Majestic, "Waitress," Dec. 1, 1938): Madame Is at Home/W: Earle Crooker, M: Frederick Loewe.

3218. Paul Forrest (July 2, 1923–) B: Philadelphia, PA. *Jimmy* (Winter Garden, "Antonio Viscelli," Oct. 23, 1969): It's a Nice Place to Visit; They Never Proved a Thing/WM: Bill Jacob, Patti Jacob. *The First* (Martin Beck, "Sorrentino," Nov. 17, 1981): Is This Year Next Year?/W: Martin Charnin, M: Bob Brush.

3219. Steve Forrest (Sept. 29, 1924–) B: Huntsville, TX. Brother of movie actor Dana Andrews. He appeared in movies and radio. On TV he played Ben Stivers/Wes Parmalee in the drama *Dallas* (1986). *The Body Beautiful* (Broadway, "Bob," Jan. 23, 1958): All of These and More; Pfft!/W: Sheldon Harnick, M: Jerry Bock.

3220. Undine Forrest *Catch a Star!* (Plymouth, revue, Sept. 6, 1955): The Story of Alice/W: Larry Holofcener, M: Jerry Bock.

3221. Hattie Forsythe *The Belle of Mayfair* (Daly's, "Lady Lucille," Dec. 3, 1906): Eight Little Debutantes Are We/W: William Caine, M: Leslie Stuart.

3222. Henderson Forsythe (Sept. 11, 1917–) B: Macon, MO. *The Best Little Whorehouse in Texas* (46th Street, "Sheriff Ed Earl Dodd," June 19, 1978/Jan. 29, 1979): Good Old Girl/WM: Carol Hall. *110 in the Shade* (New York State, revival, "H.C. Curry," July 18, 1992): Lizzie's Comin' Home; Poker Polka/W: Tom Jones, M: Harvey Schmidt.

3223. George K. Fortescque (c 1848–Jan 13, 1914) B: Manchester, Lancastershire, England. *Evangeline, or The Belle of Arcadia* (Daly's, revival, "Catherine," June 4, 1877): We Are Off to Seek for Eva/W: J. Cheever Goodwin, M: Edward E. Rice. *San Toy* (Daly's, "Yen-How," Oct. 1, 1900): I Mean to Introduce It into China/WM: ?—Six Little Wives/W: Edward Morton, M: Sidney Jones.

3224. Robert Fortier B: California. *Pal Joey* (Broadhurst, revival, "Victor," Jan. 3, 1952): Happy Hunting Horn; That Terrific Rainbow/W: Lorenz Hart, M: Richard Rodgers. *Me and Juliet* (Majestic, "Jim," May 28, 1953): We Deserve Each Other/W: Oscar Hammerstein II, M: Richard Rodgers.

3225. Daniel Fortus (Jan. 6, 1953–May 19, 1984) B: Brooklyn, NY. *Minnie's Boys* (Imperial, "Adolph Marx [Harpo]," Mar. 26, 1970): The Act; Be Happy; Four Nightingales; If You

Wind Me Up; Mama, a Rainbow; More Precious Far; The Smell of Christmas; Where Was I When They Passed Out Luck?; You Don't Have to Do It for Me/W: Hal Hackady, M: Larry Grossman. *Molly* (Alvin, "Sammy," Nov. 1, 1973): In Your Eyes/W: Mack David, M: Jerry Livingston.

3226. Harlan S. Foss (c 1941–Aug. 17, 1991) *Man on the Moon* (Little, "Dr. Bomb," Jan. 29, 1975): Family of Man; Mission Control; Sunny Moon/WM: John Phillips.

3227. Bob Fosse (June 23, 1927–Sept. 23, 1987) B: Chicago, IL. M: JOAN MC-CRACKEN; GWEN VERDON. Brilliant dancer, choreographer and director. *Dance Me a Song* (Royale, revue, Jan. 20, 1950): It's the Weather/WM: James Shelton. *Pal Joey* (New York City Center, revival, "Joey Evans," May 31, 1961): Den of Iniquity; Happy Hunting Horn; I Could Write a Book; Pal Joey (What Do I Care for a Dame?); You Mustn't Kick It Around/W: Lorenz Hart, M: Richard Rodgers. *Pal Joey* (New York City Center, revival, "Joey Evans," May 29, 1963): same as above.

3228. Isabella Fosta *Artists and Models of 1923* (Shubert > Winter Garden, revue, CR, Oct. 15, 1923): Flower of the Woodland/W: Cyrus D. Wood, Harold Atteridge, M: Jean Schwartz — Somehow/W: Cyrus D. Wood, M: Jean Schwartz.

3229. Allen K. Foster (1879–Nov. 2, 1937) B: Halifax, Nova Scotia, Canada. Dancer, director and choreographer. *Comin' Thro' the Rye* (Herald Square, "Flip," Jan. 9, 1906): I Don't Want to Be a Sailor/WM: ?.

3230. Charles B. Foster *Three Showers* (Harris > Plymouth, "Harrison Green," Apr. 5, 1920): You May Be the World to Your Mother/W: Henry Creamer, M: Turner Layton.

3231. Claiborne Foster (Apr. 15, 1900–) B: Shreveport, LA. *Miss Daisy* (Shubert > Lyric, "Sally Smith," Sept. 9, 1914): Dreams! Oh Dreams!; Kissing; My Little Queen Bee; Pierrot's Ball; Tea Leaves; Youth/W: Philip Bartholomae, M: Silvio Hein.

3232. Hunter Foster (c 1970–) M: JENNIFER CODY. *Grease* (Eugene O'Neill, revival, "Roger," May 11, 1994): Mooning/WM: Jim Jacobs, Warren Casey.

3233. Leesa Foster *Porgy and Bess* (New York City Center, revival, "Bess," May 17, 1961): Bess, You Is My Woman Now; I Loves You, Porgy/W: DuBose Heyward, Ira Gershwin, M: George Gershwin — Leavin' fo' de Promis' Land; What You Want wid Bess?/W: DuBose Heyward, M: George Gershwin — There's a Boat Dat's Leavin'

Soon for New York/W: Ira Gershwin, M: George Gershwin.

3234. Lora Foster *Ziegfeld Follies of 1927* (New Amsterdam, revue, Aug. 16, 1927): It All Belongs to Me/WM: Irving Berlin.

3235. Louise Foster *Miss Princess* (Park, "Countess Matilda," Dec. 23, 1912): Behind the Scenes/W: Will Johnstone, M: Alexander Johnstone.

3236. Mark Fotopoulos *Harrigan 'n Hart* (Longacre, "Johnny Wild," Jan. 31, 1985): Ada with the Golden Hair; The Old Barn Floor; The Skidmore Fancy Ball/W: Edward Harrigan, M: Dave Braham. *Cats* (Winter Garden, CR, "Munkustrap"): The Awefull Battle of the Pekes and Pollicles; The Marching Songs of the Pollicle Dogs; Old Deuteronomy/W: T.S. Eliot, M: Andrew Lloyd Webber.

3237. Clarence Fountain *The Gospel at Colonus* (Lunt-Fontanne, "Oedipus," Mar. 24, 1988): All My Heart's Desire; Lift Me Up; A Voice Foretold/W: Lee Breuer, M: Bob Telson.

3238. Thomas Jefferson Fouse, Jr. *Your Arms Too Short to Box with God* (Lyceum, revue, Dec. 22, 1976): Do You Know Jesus?; Everybody Has His Own Way; He's a Wonder; I Know I Have to Leave Here; It Was Alone/WM: Alex Bradford.

3239. Beth Fowler (Nov. 1, 1940–) B: New Jersey. *A Little Night Music* (Shubert, "Mrs. Segstrom," Feb. 25, 1973): Perpetual Anticipation/WM: Stephen Sondheim. *Peter Pan, or The Boy Who Wouldn't Grow Up* (Lunt-Fontanne, revival, "Mrs. Darling," Sept. 6, 1979): Tender Shepherd/W: Carolyn Leigh, M: Moose Charlap. *Baby* (Ethel Barrymore, "Arlene MacNally," Dec. 4, 1983): And What If We Had Loved Like That; Baby, Baby, Baby; I Want It All; The Plaza Song; We Start Today/W: Richard Maltby, Jr., M: David Shire. *Take Me Along* (Martin Beck, revival, "Lily Miller," Apr. 14, 1985): But Yours; I Get Embarrassed; Knights on White Horses; Oh, Please; Promise Me a Rose; We're Home/WM: Bob Merrill. *Teddy & Alice* (Minskoff, "Edith Roosevelt," Nov. 12, 1987): Battlelines; Charge; The Coming-Out Party; The Fourth of July; Private Thoughts; This House; Wave the Flag/W: Hal Hackady, M: John Philip Sousa, Richard Kapp. *Sweeney Todd* (Circle in the Square, revival, "Mrs. Lovett," Sept. 14, 1989): By the Sea; God, That's Good; A Little Priest; My Friends; Not While I'm Around; Parlor Songs; Pirelli's Miracle Elixir; Poor Thing; Wait; The Worst Pies in London/WM: Stephen Sondheim. *Beauty and the Beast* (Palace, "Mrs. Potts," Apr. 18, 1994/c 1996): Be Our Guest; Beauty and the Beast; Human Again; Something There/ W: Howard Ashman, M: Alan Menken — Home/W: Tim Rice, M: Alan Menken.

3240. Charles Fowler *Melody* (Casino, "Bob," Feb. 14, 1933): The Whole World Loves/W: Irving Caesar, M: Sigmund Romberg.

3241. Steve Fowler *Starlight Express* (Gershwin, "Poppa," Mar. 15, 1987): Belle; I Am the Starlight; Poppa's Blues; Race Two/W: Richard Stilgoe, M: Andrew Lloyd Webber.

3242. Bertram Fox (Aug. 8, 1881–Jan. 24, 1946) B: Stamford, CT. Composer, singer, teacher. *The Enchantress* (New York, "Prince Zepi," Oct. 19, 1911): When the Right Man Sings Tra-la/W: Harry B. Smith, M: Victor Herbert.

3243. Della Fox (Oct. 13, 1871–June 16, 1913) B: St. Louis, MO. M: DE WOLF HOPPER. The petite blonde soubrette began at age 7 in the chorus of Gilbert and Sullivan's *H.M.S. Pinafore. Wang* (Broadway, "Mataya," May 4, 1891): Ask the Man in the Moon; Baby, Baby, Dance My Darling Baby; No Matter What Others May Say; A Pretty Girl, a Summer Night; Where Are You Going, My Pretty Maid?/W: J. Cheever Goodwin, M: Woolson Morse — Tizan, My Maid of Hindoostan/W: George Lieb, M: Leo Friedman. *Rogers Brothers in Central Park* (Victoria, "Belle Money," Sept. 17, 1900): If Cabby Told Half What He Knows/W: J. Cheever Goodwin, M: Maurice Levi.

3244. Dulce Fox *The Cradle Will Rock* (Windsor > Mercury, "Sister Mister," Jan. 3, 1938): Croon-Spoon; Honolulu; Let's Do Something/WM: Marc Blitzstein.

3245. Franklyn Fox (c 1894–Nov. 2, 1967) B: England. *Caviar* (Forrest, "Carol," June 7, 1934): Here's to You/W: Edward Heyman, M: Harden Church.

3246. Harry Fox (May 25, 1882–July 23, 1959) B: Pomona, CA. M: JENNIE DOLLY, 1914-1920; FLORRIE MILLERSHIP. *The Passing Show of 1912* (Winter Garden, revue, July 22, 1912): Ida/WM: ?. *The Honeymoon Express* (Winter Garden, "Pierre," Feb. 6, 1913): Our Little Cabaret Up Home; The Same One They Picked for Me; That Is the Life for Me/W: Harold Atteridge, M: Jean Schwartz. *Maid in America* (Winter Garden, revue, "The American Made Comedian," Feb. 18, 1915): There Was a Time/ W: Alfred Bryan, M: Harry Carroll. *Stop! Look! Listen!* (Globe, revue, "Abel Conner," Dec. 25, 1915): And Father Wanted Me to Learn a Trade; I Love a Piano; Stop! Look! Listen!/WM: Irving Berlin. *Oh, Look!* (Vanderbilt, "Stephen Baird," Mar. 7, 1918): I Think You're Absolutely Wonderful (What Do You Think of Me?); A Kiss for

Cinderella; Typical Topical Tunes; We Will Live for Love and Love Alone/W: Joseph McCarthy, M: Harry Carroll — I'm Always Chasing Rainbows/W: Joseph McCarthy, M: Harry Carroll, based on Frederic Chopin. *Round the Town* (Century roof, revue, May 21, 1924): It's Good for You to Exercise Your Mind/W: Dorothy Parker, M: Arthur Samuels — Save a Kiss for Rainy Weather/W: Raymond B. Egan, M: Richard A. Whiting, Will Ortman. *George White's Scandals of 1925* (Apollo, revue, June 22, 1925): Even As You and I; What a World This Would Be/W: B.G. DeSylva, Lew Brown, M: Ray Henderson.

3247. Robert Fox (Oct. 21, 1949–) B: San Francisco, CA. Formerly ROBERT BACIGALUPI. *The Robber Bridegroom* (Harkness, "Goat," Oct. 7, 1975): Poor Tied Up Darlin'/W: Alfred Uhry, M: Robert Waldman. *Camelot* (New York State, revival, "Mordred," July 8, 1980): Fie on Goodness; The Seven Deadly Virtues/W: Alan Jay Lerner, M: Frederick Loewe.

3248. Earle A. Foxe (Dec. 25, 1891–Dec. 10, 1973) B: Oxford, OH. *Princess Virtue* (Central, "Carre," May 4, 1921): Clothes; Eight Little Nobodys; Life Is All Sunshine with You/WM: Gitz Rice, B.C. Hilliam.

3249. Eddie Foy, Sr. (Mar. 9, 1854–Feb. 16, 1928) B: New York, NY. Father of EDDIE FOY, JR. The singer-dancer-comedian was a popular favorite in vaudeville and on Broadway. He had 11 children; 7 survived, performing on stage as a family. He was portrayed by Bob Hope in the 1955 movie, *The Seven Little Foys. An Arabian Girl and Forty Thieves* (Herald Square, "Cassim D'Artagnan," Apr. 29, 1899): Hoo-doo-doo-doo-man; Pictures/W: J. Cheever Goodwin, M:?. *The Strollers* (Knickerbocker, "Kamfer," June 24, 1901): I'm Tired/W: William Jerome, M: Jean Schwartz. *The Wild Rose* (Knickerbocker, "Paracelsus Noodle," May 5, 1902): I'm Unlucky/W: William Jerome, M: Jean Schwartz — They Were All Doing the Same/ WM: Ren Shields. *Mr. Bluebeard* (Knickerbocker, "Sister Anne," Jan. 21, 1903): Hamlet Was a Melancholy Dane/W: William Jerome, M: Jean Schwartz. *Piff! Paff!! Pouf!!!* (Casino, "Peter Pouffle," Apr. 2, 1904): The Ghost That Never Walked; I'm So Happy/W: William Jerome, M: Jean Schwartz. *The Earl and the Girl* (Casino, "Jim Cheese," Nov. 4, 1905): One Night Only/W: Percy Greenbank, M: Ivan Caryll — Would You Like to Change from Miss to Mrs.? [Jan. 15, 1906]/W: Addison Burkhardt, M: Albert Von Tilzer. *The Orchid* (Herald

Square > Casino, "Artie Choke," Apr. 8, 1907): And They Say He Went to College/W: Edward P. Moran, M: Seymour Furth — He Goes to Church on Sunday/W: Vincent Bryan, M: E. Ray Goetz. *Mr. Hamlet of Broadway* (Casino, "Joey Wheeze," Dec. 23, 1908): Everything Depends on Money/WM: ? — None of Them's Got Anything on Me/W: William Jerome, M: Jean Schwartz — When I Was a Kid Like You/W: Edward Madden, M: Ben M. Jerome. *Up and Down Broadway* (Casino, revue, July 18, 1910): Go on Your Mission; Have a Smile with Momus; I'm the Ghost of Kelly/W: William Jerome, M: Jean Schwartz — I'm the Lily/W: Junie McCree, M: Albert Von Tilzer. *Over the River* (Globe, "Madison Parke," Jan. 8, 1912): Mexico; When There's No Light at All/WM: John L. Golden — New York Isn't Such a Bad Old Town/W: William Jerome, M: Jean Schwartz.

3250. Eddie Foy, Jr. (Feb. 4, 1905–July 15, 1983) B: New Rochelle, NY. One of the 7 little Foys. On screen, he played his father, EDDIE FOY, SR., in *Lillian Russell* (1940), *Wilson* (1944) and *Yankee Doodle Dandy* (1944). He repeated his Broadway role in the 1957 film adaptation of *Pajama Game*. *Show Girl* (Ziegfeld, "Denny Kerrigan," July 2, 1929): So Are You!/W: Ira Gershwin, Gus Kahn, M: George Gershwin. *Ripples* (New Amsterdam, "Corp. Jack Sterling," Feb. 11, 1930): Babykins; There's Nothing Wrong with a Kiss/W: Irving Caesar, Graham John, M: Oscar Levant — Big Brother to Me [Mar. 24, 1930]/W: Howard Dietz, M: Arthur Schwartz — Talk with Your Heel and Your Toe/W: Irving Caesar, M: Oscar Levant — We Never Sleep/W: Irving Caesar, Graham John, M: Oscar Levant, Albert Sirmay. *Smiles* (Ziegfeld, "Gilbert Stone," Nov. 18, 1930): Hotcha Ma Chotch/W: Harold Adamson, Clifford Grey, M: Vincent Youmans — Why Ain't I Home?/W: Ring Lardner, M: Vincent Youmans — You're Driving Me Crazy [Dec. 1930]/WM: Walter Donaldson. *The Cat and the Fiddle* (Globe, "Alexander Sheridan," Oct. 15, 1931): Try to Forget/W: Otto Harbach, M: Jerome Kern. *Orchids Preferred* (Imperial, "Bubbles Wilson," May 11, 1937): Eddy-Mac; I'm Leaving the Bad Girls for Good; Paying Off; Strictly Confidential/W: Frederick Herendeen, M: Dave Stamper. *The Red Mill* (Ziegfeld, revival, "Kid Conner," Oct. 16, 1945): The Streets of New York (In Old New York); Whistle It/W: Henry Blossom, M: Victor Herbert. *The Pajama Game* (St. James, "Hines," May 13, 1954): I'll Never Be Jealous Again; The Pajama Game; Think of the Time I Save/WM: Richard Adler, Jerry Ross. *Rumple* (Alvin, "Rumple,"

Nov. 6, 1957): In Times Like These; Oblivia; Peculiar State of Affairs; Wish/W: Frank Reardon, M: Ernest G. Schweikert. *Donnybrook!* (46th Street, "Mikeen Flynn," May 18, 1961): Dee-lightful Is the Word; I Wouldn't Bet One Penny; Wisha Wurra/WM: Johnny Burke.

3251. Gloria Foy (Oct. 25, 1913–Feb. 27, 1977) B: Lima, OH. *What's in a Name?* (Maxine Elliott, revue, Mar. 19, 1920): Strike!; Without Kissing, Love Isn't Love [Mar. 22, 1920]/W: John Murray Anderson, Jack Yellen, M: Milton Ager. *Up She Goes* (Playhouse, "Alice Cook," Nov. 6, 1922): Journey's End; Let's Kiss; The Strike; Tyup (Hitch Your Wagon to a Star); Up with the Stars; We're Nearing the Day/W: Joseph McCarthy, M: Harry Tierney. *Round the Town* (Century roof, revue, May 21, 1924): Poor Little Wallflower/W: Ned Wever, M: Alfred Nathan — Save a Kiss for Rainy Weather/W: Raymond B. Egan, M: Richard A. Whiting, Will Ortman. *Betty Lee* (44th Street, "Betty Lee," Dec. 25, 1924): Athletic Boy; Cheer, Girls, Cheer; The Daily Dozen/W: Otto Harbach, Irving Caesar, M: Louis A. Hirsch, Con Conrad — Betty Lee; Sweet Arabian Dreams/W: Otto Harbach, Irving Caesar, M: Louis A. Hirsch — I'm Going to Dance at Your Wedding/W: Irving Caesar, M: Con Conrad. *The Circus Princess* (Winter Garden, "Fritzi Burgstaller, alias Mabel Gibson," Apr. 25, 1927): I Like the Boys; I'll Be Waiting; There's Something About You/W: Harry B. Smith, M: Emmerich Kalman — What D'Ya Say?/W: Raymond Klages, M: Jesse Greer.

3252. Hope Foye *Dance Me a Song* (Royale, revue, Jan. 20, 1950): I'm the Girl; Lilac Wine/WM: James Shelton.

3253. Richard France (Jan. 6, 1930–) B: Chicago, IL. *Seventeen* (Broadhurst, "Lester," June 21, 1951): The Hoosier Way; Reciprocity; Summertime Is Summertime; Things Are Gonna Hum This Summer; Weatherbee's Drug Store/W: Kim Gannon, M: Walter Kent. *By the Beautiful Sea* (Majestic, "Mickey Powers," Apr. 8, 1954): Good Time Charlie; Old Enough to Love/W: Dorothy Fields, M: Arthur Schwartz. *Kiss Me, Kate* (New York City Center, revival, "Bill Calhoun" and "Lucentio," May 9, 1956): Bianca; I Sing of Love; Tom, Dick or Harry; We Open in Venice/WM: Cole Porter. *Annie Get Your Gun* (New York City Center, revival, "Tommy Keeler," Feb. 19, 1958): I'll Share It All with You; Who Do You Love, I Hope/WM: Irving Berlin. *The Girls Against the Boys* (Alvin, revue, Nov. 2, 1959): I Gotta Have You; Where Did We Go? Out/W: Arnold B. Horwitt, M: Richard Lewine — Light Travelin' Man/W:

Arnold B. Horwitt, M: Albert Hague. *Show Boat* (New York City Center, revival, "Frank Schultz," Apr. 12, 1961): Goodbye, My Lady Love/WM: Joseph E. Howard. *Fiorello!* (New York City Center, revival, "Neil," June 13, 1962): On the Side of the Angels/W: Sheldon Harnick, M: Jerry Bock. *Oklahoma!* (New York City Center, revival, "Will Parker," Feb. 27, 1963): All er Nothin'; The Farmer and the Cowman; Kansas City/W: Oscar Hammerstein II, M: Richard Rodgers. *Oklahoma!* (New York City Center, revival, "Will Parker," May 15, 1963): same as above. *What Makes Sammy Run?* (54th Street, "Tracy Clark," Feb. 27, 1964): Paint a Rainbow/WM: Ervin Drake. *Oklahoma!* (New York City Center, revival, "Will Parker," Dec. 15, 1965): same as above. *Wonderful Town* (New York City Center, revival, "Chick Clark," May 17, 1967): Conversation Piece (Nice Talk, Nice People)/W: Betty Comden, Adolph Green, M: Leonard Bernstein. *Carnival!* (New York City Center, revival, "Marco the Magnificent," Dec. 12, 1968): It Was Always You; Magic, Magic; Sword, Rose and Cape/WM: Bob Merrill.

3254. Corrine (Francis) Frances *The Little Cherub* (Criterion, "Lady Isobel Congress," Aug. 6, 1906): Dear Little Girls; Olympian Octet/W: Owen Hall, M: Ivan Caryll — I Should So Love to Be a Boy/W: C.H. Bovill, M: Frank Tours. *The Passing Show of 1913* (Winter Garden, revue, July 24, 1913): Inauguration Day; Romance Land/W: Harold Atteridge, M: Al W. Brown — That Good Old Fashioned Cakewalk/W: Harold Atteridge, M: Jean Schwartz.

3255. Sergio Franchi (Apr. 6, 1926–May 1, 1990) B: Cremona, Italy. Brother of DANA VALERY. Singer in nightclubs, on TV and 25 record albums. *Do I Hear a Waltz?* (46th Street, "Renato Di Rossi," Mar. 18, 1965): Bargaining; Perfectly Lovely Couple; Someone Like You; Stay; Take the Moment; Thank You So Much; Thinking/W: Stephen Sondheim, M: Richard Rodgers. *Nine* (46th Street, CR, "Guido Contini," May 9, 1983): The Bells of St. Sebastian; The Grand Canal; Guido's Song; I Can't Make This Movie; Long Ago; A Man Like You; Nine; Only with You; Unusual Way/WM: Maury Yeston.

3256. Anne Francine (Aug. 8, 1917–Dec. 3, 1999) B: Philadelphia, PA. *Mame* (Winter Garden, CR, "Vera Charles," July 10, 1967/Sept. 23, 1968): Bosom Buddies; The Man in the Moon/WM: Jerry Herman. *A Broadway Musical* (Lunt-Fontanne, "Shirley Wolfe," Dec. 21, 1978): A Broadway Musical; Yenta Power/W: Lee Adams, M: Charles Strouse. *Mame* (Gershwin,

revival, "Vera Charles," July 24, 1983): same as above.

3257. Alma Francis *Eva* (New Amsterdam, "Pipsi Paquerette," Dec. 30, 1912): The Imp of Montmartre; The Quarrel; The Starlight Guards; The Up-to-Date Troubador/W: Glen MacDonough, M: Franz Lehar. *The Little Cafe* (New Amsterdam, "Yvonne," Nov. 10, 1913): I Love the Little Cafe; I Wonder Whom I'll Marry; This Gay Paree/W: C.M.S. McLellan, M: Ivan Caryll.

3258. Arlene Francis (Oct. 20, 1907–May 31, 2001) B: Boston, MA. M: MARTIN GABEL. For many years the actress was a popular personality on radio and TV. *Gigi* (Uris, CR, "Aunt Alicia," Jan. 24, 1974): The Contract; It's a Bore/W: Alan Jay Lerner, M: Frederick Loewe.

3259. Carl D. Francis *Padlocks of 1927* (Shubert, revue, July 5, 1927): Hot Heels; That Stupid Melody/W: Billy Rose, Ballard Macdonald, M: Lee David. *Sidewalks of New York* (Knickerbocker, "Hon. Percival Short," Oct. 3, 1927): Just a Little Smile from You; Wherever You Are/W: Eddie Dowling, M: James F. Hanley. *Billie* (Erlanger's, "Peter Pembroke," Oct. 1, 1928): Bluff/WM: George M. Cohan. *Top Speed* (46th Street, CR, "Tad Jordan," Feb. 17, 1930): Dizzy Feet; Fireworks; The Papers; Try Dancing/W: Bert Kalmar, M: Harry Ruby.

3260. Carrie Francis *The Good Mister Best* (Garrick, "Hattie," Aug. 30, 1897): Puff, Puff/W: John J. McNally, M: ?.

3261. Dick Francis (c 1889–Apr. 11, 1949) B: Derby, England. *This Year of Grace* (Selwyn, revue, Nov. 7, 1928): Chauve-Souris; Lilac Time [Feb. 25, 1929]/WM: Noel Coward.

3262. Dorothy Francis *The Merry Widow* (Knickerbocker, revival, "Natalie, Baroness Popoff," Sept. 5, 1921): A Dutiful Wife; Love in My Heart; Oh, Say No More/W: Adrian Ross, M: Franz Lehar. *The Love Song* (Century, "Eugenie De Montijo," Jan. 13, 1925): Fair Land of Dreaming; The Love Song (Remember Me)/W: Harry B. Smith, M: Edward Kunneke — He Writes a Song; Only a Dream/W: Harry B. Smith, M: Jacques Offenbach. *Sunny* (New Amsterdam, "Marcia Manners," Sept. 22, 1925): Sunshine/W: Otto Harbach, Oscar Hammerstein II, M: Jerome Kern. *Criss Cross* (Globe, "Yasmini," Oct. 12, 1926): Dear Algerian Land; Dreaming of Allah; The Portrait Parade; Rose of Delight/W: Anne Caldwell, Otto Harbach, M: Jerome Kern — In Araby with You/W: Otto Harbach, Oscar Hammerstein II, M: Jerome Kern.

3263. Emma Francis *Rogers Brothers in*

Washington (Knickerbocker, "Margy," Sept. 2, 1901): The Game of Love/W: Harry B. Smith, M: Maurice Levi. *Buster Brown* (Majestic, CR, "Susie Sweet," Mar. 22, 1905): Bo-Peep; Sue, Sue I Love You/W: Paul West, M: John W. Bratton.

3264. Eva Francis *Woodland* (New York > Herald Square, "Lieut. Sparrow," Nov. 21, 1904): Clear the Way/W: Frank Pixley, M: Gustav Luders. *Dream City* (Weber's, "Gladys," Dec. 25, 1906): Down a Shady Lane/W: Edgar Smith, M: Victor Herbert. *The Soul Kiss* (New York, "Lucia," Jan. 28, 1908): The Dollar Sign/W: Jessie Villars, M: Fleta Jan Brown. *The Soul Kiss* (New York, CR, "Suzette," Mar. 2, 1908): Any Old Place in the World with You; Let's Pretend/W: Harry B. Smith, M: Maurice Levi. *The Yankee Girl* (Herald Square, "Dolly Dean," Feb. 10, 1910): Where's Mama?/W: George V. Hobart, M: Silvio Hein.

3265. Helen Francis *Tangerine* (Casino, CR, "Mildred Floyd," Apr. 10, 1922): Man Is the Lord of It All/W: Carle Carlton, M: Jean Schwartz.

3266. James Francis-Robertson (c 1869–May 18, 1942) B: Weymouth, England. *No Other Girl* (Morosco, "Obadiah Bingle," Aug. 13, 1924): Look Out for Us, Broadway/W: Bert Kalmar, M: Harry Ruby.

3267. Nelly Franck *Reunion in New York* (Little, revue, Feb. 21, 1940): Where Is My Homeland/W: Werner Michel, August Spectorsky, M: Nelly Franck.

3268. Virginia Franck *Treasure Girl* (Alvin, "Mary Grimes," Nov. 8, 1928): Got a Rainbow/W: Ira Gershwin, M: George Gershwin.

3269. Don Francks (Feb. 28, 1932–) B: Vancouver, Canada. He appeared in the movie version of *Finian's Rainbow* (1968). *Kelly* (Broadhurst, "Hop Kelly," Feb. 6, 1965): Ballad to a Brute; I'm Gonna Walk Right Up to Her; Me and the Elements; A Moment Ago; (I'll) Never Go There Anymore; Ode to the Bridge; Simple Ain't Easy/W: Eddie Lawrence, M: Moose Charlap.

3270. Arlyne Frank B: Minneapolis, MN. *Touch and Go* (Broadhurst > Broadway, revue, Oct. 13, 1949): Under the Sleeping Volcano/W: Walter Kerr, Jean Kerr, M: Jay Gorney. *The Music Man* (Majestic, CR, "Marian Paroo," June 1959): Goodnight, My Someone; My White Knight; Piano Lesson; Seventy-Six Trombones; Shipoopi; Till There Was You; Will I Ever Tell You?/WM: Meredith Willson.

3271. Dorothy (Dottie) Frank (July 8, 1942–) B: St. Louis, MO. *Different Times* (ANTA, "Marianne" and "Hattie Verne," May 1, 1972): I Miss Him; Marianne/WM: Michael Brown. *Irene* (Minskoff, revival, CR, "Jane Burke"): The Great Lover Tango/W: Otis Clements, M: Charles Gaynor — We're Getting Away with It/W: Joseph McCarthy, M: Harry Tierney.

3272. Bessie Franklin *The Motor Girl* (Lyric, "Mrs. Arthur Dare," June 15, 1909): Coffee and Cheese/W: Charles J. Campbell, M: Julian Edwards.

3273. Bonnie Franklin (Jan. 6, 1944–) B: Santa Monica, CA. She played the lead character, Ann Romano Royer, on the TV series *One Day at a Time* (1975). *Applause* (Palace, "Bonnie," Mar. 30, 1970/June 21, 1971/Nov. 22, 1971): Applause; She's No Longer a Gypsy/W: Lee Adams, M: Charles Strouse.

3274. Frederic Franklin (June 13, 1914–) B: Liverpool, England. *Song of Norway* (Imperial, "Freddy," Aug. 21, 1944): Freddy and His Fiddle/WM: Robert Wright, George Forrest, based on Edvard Grieg.

3275. Irene Franklin (June 13, 1876–June 16, 1941) B: St. Louis, MO. After a career in vaudeville, the theater and movies, and as a song writer with husband Burton Green, she died penniless at the Actors Fund Home in Englewood, NJ. *The Orchid* (Herald Square, "Josephine Zaccary," Apr. 8, 1907): I Must Propose to You/WM: Paul Rubens — Oh, Mr. Registrar!/W: Percy Greenbank, M: Lionel Monckton. *The Summer Widowers* (Broadway, "Claribel Clews," June 4, 1910): I Knew Her When; Miss Dennett/W: Irene Franklin, M: Burton Green. *Hands Up* (44th Street, "Violet Lavender," July 22, 1915): You Can't Fool a New York Kid/W: Irene Franklin, M: Burton Green. *The Passing Show of 1917* (Winter Garden, revue, Apr. 26, 1917): The Awkward Age; The Chorus Girl; Same Old Song; The Telephone Girl/W: Harold Atteridge, M: Sigmund Romberg, Otto Motzan. *The Greenwich Village Follies of 1921* (Shubert, revue, Aug. 31, 1921): Broadway Wedding Bells/WM: ?. *Sweet Adeline* (Hammerstein's, "Lulu Ward," Sept 3, 1929): Indestructible Kate/W: Irene Franklin, M: Jerry Jamagin — My Husband's First Wife/W: Irene Franklin, M: Jerome Kern — Naughty Boy/W: Oscar Hammerstein II, M: Jerome Kern.

3276. Lee Franklin *The Rothschilds* (Lunt-Fontanne, "Young Amshel Rothschild," Oct. 19, 1970): Sons/W: Sheldon Harnick, M: Jerry Bock.

3277. Nancy Franklin B: New York, NY. *Charlie and Algernon* (Helen Hayes, "Mrs. Donner," Sept. 14, 1980): Jelly Donuts and Chocolate Cake; Somebody New/W: David Rogers, M: Charles Strouse.

3278. Nony Franklin (?–July 20, 1965) *Sweethearts* (Shubert, revival, "Corinne," Jan. 21, 1947): Every Lover Must Meet His Fate; Game of Love; Sweethearts/W: Robert B. Smith, M: Victor Herbert.

3279. Tony Franklin *Dreamgirls* (Imperial, "Wayne," Dec. 20, 1981): Steppin' to the Bad Side/W: Tom Eyen, M: Henry Krieger. *Dreamgirls* (Imperial, CR, "C.C. White," Jan. 1984): Cadillac Car; Family; I Miss You Old Friend; Quintette; The Rap; Steppin' to the Bad Side/W: Tom Eyen, M: Henry Krieger.

3280. William Franklin (Aug. 18, 1906–?) B: Shaw, MS. *Porgy and Bess* (New York City Center, revival, CR, "Porgy," Feb. 7, 1944): Bess, You Is My Woman Now; I Got Plenty o' Nuttin'; I Loves You Porgy/W: Ira Gershwin, DuBose Heyward, M: George Gershwin — I'm on My Way; They Pass By Singing; Woman to Lady/W: DuBose Heyward, M: George Gershwin — Oh, Bess, Oh Where's My Bess?/W: Ira Gershwin, M: George Gershwin. *Carib Song* (Adelphi, "The Husband," Sept. 27, 1945): This Woman; Today I Is So Happy; Water Movin' Slow; You Know, Oh Lord/W: William Archibald, M: Baldwin Bergersen.

3281. Laurie Franks (Aug. 14, 1929–) B: Lucasville, OH. *Anya* (Ziegfeld, "Olga," Nov. 29, 1965): That Prelude!/WM: Robert Wright, George Forrest. *The Utter Glory of Morrissey Hall* (Mark Hellinger, "Teresa Winkle," May 13, 1979): You Will Know When the Time Has Arrived/WM: Clark Gesner. *The Human Comedy* (Royale, "Miss Hicks," Apr. 5, 1984): The Assyrians/W: William Dumaresq, M: Galt MacDermot.

3282. Gina Franz *The Utter Glory of Morrissey Hall* (Mark Hellinger, "Vickers," May 13, 1979): Lost; You Will Know When the Time Has Arrived/WM: Clark Gesner.

3283. Joy Franz (1944–) B: Modesto, CA. *Pippin* (Imperial, CR, "Catherine," Feb. 10, 1976): Kind of Woman; Love Song/WM: Stephen Schwartz. *Musical Chairs* (Rialto, "Janet," May 14, 1980): Other People; What I Could Have Done Tonight/WM: Tom Savage.

3284. Carlotta Franzell B: Detroit, MI. *Carmen Jones* (Broadway, "Cindy Lou," Dec. 2, 1943): My Joe; You Talk Jus' Like My Maw/W: Oscar Hammerstein II, M: Georges Bizet.

3285. Leslie Franzos *Sherry!* (Alvin, "Ginger," Mar. 27, 1967): The Fred Astaire Affair/W: James Lipton, M: Laurence Rosenthal.

3286. Alec Fraser (Feb. 16, 1884–June 20, 1956) B: Fife, Scotland. Singer and actor. Brother-in-law of HUNTLEY WRIGHT. *The Vagabond King* (Casino, CR, "Francois Villon," July 1926): Love Me Tonight; Only a Rose; Song of the Vagabonds; Tomorrow/W: Brian Hooker, M: Rudolf Friml.

3287. Alison Fraser (July 8, 1955–) B: Natick, MA. *The Mystery of Edwin Drood* (Imperial, CR, "Helena Landless," Aug. 13, 1986): Ceylon; Moonfall; No Good Can Come from Bad/WM: Rupert Holmes. *Romance Romance* (Helen Hayes, "Josefine Weninger" and "Monica," May 1, 1988): Goodbye, Emil; Great News; How Did I End Up Here?; I'll Always Remember the Song; It's Not Too Late; The Little Comedy; The Night It Had to End; Now; Oh, What a Performance!; Plans A & B; A Rustic Country Inn; Yes, It's Love/W: Barry Harman, M: Keith Herrmann. *The Secret Garden* (St. James, "Martha," Apr. 25, 1991): Come Spirit, Come Charm; A Fine White Horse; Hold On; Letter Song/W: Marsha Norman, M: Lucy Simon.

3288. Ann Fraser B: Winnetka, IL. *Brigadoon* (New York City Center, revival, "Meg Brockie," May 30, 1962): Down on MacConnachy Square; The Love of My Life; My Mother's Weddin' Day/W: Alan Jay Lerner, M: Frederick Loewe. *Brigadoon* (New York City Center, revival, "Meg Brockie," Jan. 30, 1963): same as above. *Oklahoma!* (New York City Center, revival, "Ado Annie Carnes," Feb. 27, 1963): All er Nothin'; The Farmer and the Cowman; I Cain't Say No/W: Oscar Hammerstein II, M: Richard Rodgers.

3289. Douglass Fraser *Jesus Christ Superstar* (Paramount Madison Square Garden, revival, "King Herod," Jan. 17, 1995): King Herod's Song/W: Tim Rice, M: Andrew Lloyd Webber.

3290. Jane Fraser *Pal Joey* (Ethel Barrymore > Shubert > St. James, "Terry," Dec. 25, 1940): Happy Hunting Horn/W: Lorenz Hart, M: Richard Rodgers.

3291. Margaret Fraser *The Catch of the Season* (Daly's, "Hon. Honoria Bedford," Aug. 28, 1905): Cigarette/W: Charles H. Taylor, M: Herbert E. Haines, Evelyn Baker.

3292. Ronald Fraser (Apr. 11, 1930–Mar. 13, 1997) B: Ashton-under-Lyme, England. Character actor of movies and TV. *La Grosse Valise* (54th Street, "Jean-Loup Roussel," Dec. 14, 1965): A Big One; C'est Defendu; For You; Happy Song; La Grosse Valise; Slippy Sloppy Shoes; Spanish Dance; Xanadu/W: Harold Rome, M: Gerard Calvi.

3293. Sudworth Fraser *The Merry World* (Imperial, revue, June 8, 1926): Love's Call/

W: Clifford Grey, M: J. Fred Coots, Maurie Rubens.

3294. Diane Fratantoni (Mar. 29, 1956–) B: Wilmington, DE. M: BRIAN SUTHER-LAND. *A Chorus Line* (Shubert, CR, "Diana," Sept. 1979/June 1982): Nothing; What I Did for Love/W: Edward Kleban, M: Marvin Hamlisch. *She Loves Me* (Roundabout, revival, CR, "Amalia Balash," Sept. 28, 1993): Dear Friend; I Don't Know His Name; Ice Cream; No More Candy; Three Letters; Where's My Shoe?; Will He Like Me?/W: Sheldon Harnick, M: Jerry Bock. *Cats* (Winter Garden, CR, "Grizabella"): Grizabella, the Glamour Cat/W: T.S. Eliot, M: Andrew Lloyd Webber — Memory/W: Trevor Nunn, based on T.S. Eliot, M: Andrew Lloyd Webber.

3295. James Frawley (1937–) B: Houston, TX. *Anyone Can Whistle* (Majestic, "Chief Magruder," Apr. 4, 1964): I've Got You to Lean On/WM: Stephen Sondheim.

3296. Paul Frawley (June 2, 1889–Jan. 21, 1973) Brother of WILLIAM FRAWLEY. *Odds and Ends of 1917* (Bijou, revue, Nov. 19, 1917): Give Me an Old Fashioned Girlie/W: Bide Dudley, Jack Norworth, M: James Byrnes — When I Wave My Flag/W: R.P. Weston, M: Jack Norworth. *Come Along* (Nora Bayes > 39th Street, "Tom McManus," Apr. 8, 1919): Mother Dear; Thoughts; When You Are Happy/WM: John L. Nelson. *Three Showers* (Harris > Plymouth, "Peter Fitzhugh," Apr. 5, 1920): How Wonderful You Are; It Must Be Love; Open Your Heart; Where Is the Love?/W: Henry Creamer, M: Turner Layton. *Kissing Time* (Lyric, "Robert Perronet," Oct. 11, 1920): Absolutely Certain/W: ?, M: Ivan Caryll — As Long as the World Goes Round (Tra-La-La); Bill and Coo; Kikerikee; Love's Telephone/W: George V. Hobart, M: Ivan Caryll — It's the Nicest Sort of Feeling (Ting-a-ling-a-ling)/W: Irving Caesar, M: William Daly — Kissing Time/W: Irving Caesar, M: Ivan Caryll. *Music Box Revue of 1921* (Music Box, revue, Sept. 22, 1921): Say It with Music/WM: Irving Berlin. *Helen of Troy, New York* (Selwyn > Times Square, "David Williams," June 23, 1923/Aug. 13, 1923): It Was Meant to Be; Look for the Happy Ending; We'll Have a Model Factory/W: Bert Kalmar, M: Harry Ruby. *Sunny* (New Amsterdam, "Tom Warren," Sept. 22, 1925): Sunny; Who?/W: Otto Harbach, Oscar Hammerstein II, M: Jerome Kern. *Piggy* (Royale, "Guy Hoggenheimer," Jan. 11, 1927): Ding Dong Dell (Spells I Love You); I Need a Little Bit, You Need a Little Bit (A Little Bit of Love); It Just Had to Happen/W: Lew Brown, M: Cliff Friend. *Manhattan Mary* (Apollo, "Jimmy

Moore," Sept. 26, 1927): Manhattan Mary; Nothing but Love/W: B.G. DeSylva, Lew Brown, M: Ray Henderson. *Treasure Girl* (Alvin, "Neil Forrester," Nov. 8, 1928): Feeling I'm Falling; I Don't Think I'll Fall in Love Today; Place in the Country/W: Ira Gershwin, M: George Gershwin. *Top Speed* (46th Street, "Gerry Brooks," Dec. 25, 1929): I'd Like to Be Liked; Sweeter Than You; What Would I Care?/W: Bert Kalmar, M: Harry Ruby. *Here Goes the Bride* (46th Street, "Tony Doyle," Nov. 3, 1931): It Means So Little to You/W: Edward Heyman, M: Richard Myers — My Sweetheart 'Tis of Thee/W: Edward Heyman, M: Johnny Green.

3297. William Frawley (Feb. 26, 1887–Mar. 3, 1966) B: Burlington, IA. Brother of PAUL FRAWLEY, with whom he sang and danced in vaudeville. He appeared in over 100 films, usually in comic roles. Best remembered on TV as Fred Mertz in *I Love Lucy* (1951) and Bub O'Casey in *My Three Sons* (1960). *Merry, Merry* (Vanderbilt, "J. Horatio Diggs," Sept. 24, 1925): Oh, Wasn't It Lovely?; We Were a Wow/W: Harlan Thompson, M: Harry Archer. *Bye, Bye, Bonnie* (Ritz > Cosmopolitan, "Butch Hogan," Jan. 13, 1927): I Like to Make It Cozy/W: Neville Fleeson, M: Albert Von Tilzer. *Talk About Girls* (Waldorf, "Henry Quill," June 14, 1927): Oo, How I Love You/W: Irving Caesar, M: Harold Orlob. *Sons o' Guns* (Imperial, "Hobson," Nov. 26, 1929): Over Here/W: Arthur Swanstrom, Benny Davis, M: J. Fred Coots. *Tell Her the Truth* (Cort, "Mr. Parkin," Oct. 28, 1932): Horrortorio!; Sing, Brothers!/W: R.P. Weston, Bert Lee, M: Joseph Tunbridge, Jack Waller.

3298. E. Lovatt Frazer *Fad and Folly [orig. Tommy Rot]* (Mrs. Osborn's Playhouse, "Tommy Rottingham," Nov. 27, 1902): Doing Well/W: Paul West, M: Safford Waters — She'll Do/WM: Jackson Gowraud.

3299. Charlotte Frazier *Company* (Alvin, CR, "Susan," Mar. 29, 1971): Poor Baby/WM: Stephen Sondheim.

3300. Grenoldo Frazier *Hello, Dolly!* (Minskoff, revival, "Barnaby Tucker," Nov. 6, 1975): Dancing; Put on Your Sunday Clothes/WM: Jerry Herman — Elegance; Motherhood/WM: Bob Merrill, Jerry Herman.

3301. Fred Frear *The Sultan of Sulu* (Wallack's, "Hadji Tantong," Dec. 29, 1902): Since I First Met You/W: George Ade, M: Alfred G. Wathall. *The Mayor of Tokio* (New York, "Kow Tow," Dec. 4, 1905): Cruising Home; Is Marriage a Failure?; The Mayor of Tokio/W: Richard Carle, M: William F. Peters. *Rob Roy* (Liberty, revival, "Tammas MacSorlie," Sept. 15, 1913): My True Love Is a Shepherdess/W: Harry B. Smith, M: Reginald De Koven.

3302. Helena Frederick (c 1882–Nov. 19, 1926) *The Tenderfoot* (New York, "Marion Worthington," Feb. 22, 1904): Fascinating Venus; Only a Kiss/W: Richard Carle, M: H.L. Heartz.

3303. Pauline Frederick (Aug. 12, 1883–Sept. 19, 1938) B: Boston, MA. She had 5 husbands. An early star of silent pictures from her debut in *Bella Donna* (1915), she later became an important Broadway actress. She died of asthma. *A Princess of Kensington* (Broadway, "Titania," Aug. 31, 1903): From Where the Scotch Mountains/W: Basil Hood, M: Edward German. *It Happened in Nordland* (Lew Fields, CR, "Katherine Peepfogle," Oct. 16, 1905): Bandanna Land; Beatrice Barefacts; Commanderess-in-Chief; The Coon Banshee/W: Glen MacDonough, M: Victor Herbert.

3304. Vicki Frederick (1954–) B: Georgia. *A Chorus Line* (Shubert, CR, "Cassie," Feb. 9, 1977): The Music and the Mirror/W: Edward Kleban, M: Marvin Hamlisch. *Dancin'* (Broadhurst, revue, Mar. 27, 1978/Sept. 12, 1978/Jan. 16, 1979): Here You Come Again/WM: Barry Mann, Cynthia Weil — Pack Up Your Troubles in Your Old Kit Bag (and Smile, Smile, Smile)/W: George Asaf, M: Felix Powell — Stouthearted Men/W: Oscar Hammerstein II, M: Sigmund Romberg — Was Dog a Doughnut/WM: Cat Stevens — When Johnny Comes Marching Home/WM: Patrick Sarsfield Gilmore.

3305. Anna Fredericks *Some Night* (Harris, "Daisy," Sept. 23, 1918): Everything Is Going Higher; I'll Be Waiting for You; Something That Money Can't Buy; When We Are Married/WM: Harry Delf.

3306. Arline Fredericks *Nothing but Love* (Lyric, "Mrs. Maud Winchester," Oct. 14, 1919): It's Not What You Say; Wonderful Man/W: Frank Stammers, M: Harold Orlob.

3307. Charles Fredericks *Strut Miss Lizzie* (Times Square, revue, June 19, 1922): Buzz Mirandy; Crooning; I Love Sweet Angeline; Mandy; Wyoming Lullaby/WM: Henry Creamer, Turner Layton.

3308. Charles Fredericks (Sept. 5, 1918–May 14, 1970) B: Columbus, MS. He spent 10 years in vaudeville and nightclubs before his Broadway debut in 1946. *Show Boat* (Ziegfeld, revival, "Gaylord Ravenal," Jan. 5, 1946): Make Believe; Why Do I Love You?; You Are Love/W: Oscar Hammerstein II, M: Jerome Kern. *Music in My Heart* (Adelphi, "Capt. Nicholas Gregorovitch," Oct. 2, 1947): Am I Enchanted; Love

Is a Game for Soldiers; Love Is the Sovereign of My Heart; Once Upon a Time; Song of the Troika; Stolen Kisses; Three's a Crowd/W: Forman Brown, M: Franz Steininger, based on Peter I. Tchaikovsky.

3309. Chester Fredericks *Florida Girl* (Lyric, "Gregory," Nov. 2, 1925): Beautiful Sea; Skipper/W: Paul Porter, Benjamin Hapgood Burt, M: Milton Suskind. *Gay Paree* (Winter Garden, revue, Nov. 9, 1926): Bad Little Boy with Dancing Legs/WM: ?.

3310. Lydia Fredericks *Touch and Go* (Broadhurst > Broadway, revue, Oct. 13, 1949): Under the Sleeping Volcano/W: Walter Kerr, Jean Kerr, M: Jay Gorney. *The Girl in Pink Tights* (Mark Hellinger, "Nellie," Mar. 5, 1954): You've Got to Be a Little Crazy/W: Leo Robin, M: Sigmund Romberg.

3311. Louie Freear (Nov. 26, 1872–Mar. 23, 1939) B: London, England. Comic actress of variety, Shakespeare and musical comedy in London and the U.S. *The Man in the Moon* (New York, "Liza Ellen," Apr. 24, 1899): 'E Didn't Know Just W'at to Say/W: Walter Ford, M: John W. Bratton — The Flat on the Opposite Side/W: Louis Harrison, Stanislas Stange, M: Gustave Kerker — Perhaps I Will, Perhaps I Won't; She Just Walks On/WM: ?.

3312. Cassius Freeborn *Hitchy-Koo of 1920* (New Amsterdam, revue, Oct. 19, 1920): Old New York/W: Glen MacDonough, Anne Caldwell, M: Jerome Kern.

3313. Bert Freed (Nov. 3, 1919–Aug. 2, 1994) B: Bronx, NY. Character actor who appeared in more than 75 movies and 200 TV shows. *The Day Before Spring* (National, "Bill Tomkins," Nov. 22, 1945): Friends to the End/W: Alan Jay Lerner, M: Frederick Loewe.

3314. Sam Freed (Aug. 29, 1948–) B: York, PA. *Candide* (Broadway, revival, "Maximilian," Mar. 10, 1974): The Best of All Possible Worlds; Life Is Happiness Indeed/W: Stephen Sondheim, M: Leonard Bernstein.

3315. Vinton Freedley (Nov. 5, 1891–June 5, 1969) B: Philadelphia, PA. He produced musicals with Alex A. Arons, 1923–1934. In 1928 they built the Alvin Theater on Broadway. In the 1940s he was president of ANTA, the American National Theater and Academy. *Miss Millions* (Punch and Judy, "Jack Honeydew," Dec. 9, 1919): I Know That I'm in Love with You; If You'll Just Wait a Little While/W: R.H. Burnside, M: Raymond Hubbell. *For Goodness Sake* (Lyric, "Jefferson Dangerfield," Feb. 20, 1922): Every Day/W: Arthur Jackson, M: William Daly — The French Pastry Walk/W: Arthur

Jackson, Ira Gershwin, M: Paul Lannin, William Daly — Greatest Team of All; When Somebody Cares/W: Arthur Jackson, M: Paul Lannin, William Daly — Someone/W: Ira Gershwin, M: George Gershwin. *Elsie* (Vanderbilt, "Harry Hammond," Apr. 2, 1923): Honeymoon Home/ WM: Monte Carlo, Alma Sanders — My Crinoline Girl; Two Hearts in Tune/WM: Noble Sissle, Eubie Blake.

3316. Gladys Freeland *Fast and Furious* (New Yorker, revue, Sept. 15, 1931): So Lonesome/WM: J. Rosamond Johnson, Joe Jordan.

3317. Al Freeman, Jr. (Mar. 21, 1934–) B: San Antonio, TX. A regular on the daytime soap *One Life to Live* ; in movies from 1964. *Look to the Lilies* (Lunt-Fontanne, "Homer Smith," Mar. 29, 1970): Does It Really Matter; Don't Talk About God; First Class Number One Bum; Follow the Lamb; I, Yes, Me, That's Who; I'd Sure Like to Give It a Shot; One Little Brick at a Time; Some Kind of Man; There Comes a Time/W: Sammy Cahn, M: Jule Styne.

3318. Arny Freeman (Aug. 28, 1908–Feb. 13, 1986) B: Chicago, IL. *Hot Spot* (Majestic, "The Nadir of D'hum," Apr. 19, 1963): A Little Trouble Goes a Long, Long Way/W: Martin Charnin, M: Mary Rodgers. *Working* (46th Street, "Joe Zutty," May 14, 1978): Joe/WM: Craig Carnelia.

3319. Cheryl Freeman *The Who's Tommy* (St. James, "Gypsy," Apr. 22, 1993): Acid Queen/WM: Pete Townshend.

3320. Damita Jo Freeman *Platinum* (Mark Hellinger, "Damita," Nov. 12, 1978): Platinum Dreams; Ride Baby Ride; Sunset/W: Will Holt, M: Gary William Friedman.

3321. Grace Freeman *Rogers Brothers in Washington* (Knickerbocker, CR, "Maude Braley," Oct. 9, 1901): Watermelon Party/W: Harry B. Smith, M: Maurice Levi. *A Country Girl* (Daly's, "Marjorie Joy," Sept. 22, 1902): Boy and Girl/W: Adrian Ross, M: Lionel Monckton — Coo/W: Percy Greenbank, M: Paul Rubens. *The Girl from Kay's* (Herald Square, CR, "Norah Chalmers,"1903): Bride's Song/WM: Bernard Rolt — Semi-Detached/W: Adrian Ross, M: Ivan Caryll. *A Country Girl* (Herald Square, revival, "Marjorie Joy," May 29, 1911): same as above.

3322. Howard Freeman (Dec. 9, 1899–Dec. 11, 1967) B: Helena, MT. Comic character actor in movies from 1943. *Hot Spot* (Majestic, "Sumner Tubb, Sr.," Apr. 19, 1963): I Had Two Dregs/W: Martin Charnin, M: Mary Rodgers.

3323. Irving Freeman *You'll See Stars* (Maxine Elliott, revue, "Walter Winchell," Dec. 29,

1942): All You Have to Do Is Stand There/W: Herman Timberg, M: Leo Edwards.

3324. John Freeman *The Passing Show of 1914* (Winter Garden, revue, June 10, 1914): The Moving Picture Glide/W: Harold Atteridge, M: Harry Carroll.

3325. Jonathan Freeman (Feb. 5, 1950–) B: Bay Village, OH. *She Loves Me* (Roundabout, revival, "Headwaiter," June 10, 1993): A Romantic Atmosphere/W: Sheldon Harnick, M: Jerry Bock. *How to Succeed in Business Without Really Trying* (Richard Rodgers, revival, "Bert Bratt," Mar. 23, 1995): A Secretary Is Not a Toy/WM: Frank Loesser.

3326. Morgan Freeman (June 1, 1937–) B: Memphis, TN. Notable for the film *Driving Miss Daisy* (1989). *Hello, Dolly!* (St. James, CR, "Rudolph," Nov. 12, 1967): Hello, Dolly!/WM: Jerry Herman. *The Gospel at Colonus* (Lunt-Fontanne, "Messenger," Mar. 24, 1988): All My Heart's Desire; Who Is This Man?/W: Lee Breuer, M: Bob Telson.

3327. Stu Freeman *Hard Job Being God* (Edison, "Moses" and "David" and "Moabite," May 15, 1972): The Eleven Commandments; Hail, David; Moses' Song; Passover; Ruth; The Ten Plagues; A Very Lonely King/WM: Tom Martel.

3328. W.S. Freeman *Funabashi* (Casino, "William Harrison," Jan. 6, 1908): The Girl Behind the Man Behind the Gun/WM: Safford Waters.

3329. Yvette Freeman (Oct. 1, 1950–) B: Chester, PA. *Ain't Misbehavin'* (Longacre, revue, CR, Sept. 24, 1979): Cash for Your Trash/W: Ed Kirkeby, M: Fats Waller — Find Out What They Like; Honeysuckle Rose/W: Andy Razaf, M: Fats Waller — It's a Sin to Tell a Lie/WM: Billy Mayhew — I've Got a Feeling I'm Falling/ W: Billy Rose, M: Fats Waller, Harry Link — Lounging at the Waldorf/W: Richard Maltby, Jr., M: Fats Waller — Mean to Me/WM: Roy Turk, Fred E. Ahlert — When the Nylons Bloom Again/W: George Marion, Jr., M: Fats Waller.

3330. Benny Freigh *Snow White and the Seven Dwarfs* (Radio City Music Hall, "Grumpy," Oct. 18, 1979/Jan. 11, 1980): Bluddle-uddle-um-dum (The Washing Song); The Dwarf's Yodel Song (The Silly Song); Heigh-Ho/W: Larry Morey, M: Frank Churchill.

3331. Dorothea Freitag *70, Girls, 70* (Broadhurst, Apr. 15, 1971): Hit It, Lorraine/W: Fred Ebb, M: John Kander.

3332. Arthur French (Feb. 22, 1949–) B: New York, NY. *Ain't Supposed to Die a Natural Death* (Ethel Barrymore, Oct. 20, 1971): Heh

Heh (Chuckle); Just Don't Make No Sense/WM: Melvin Van Peebles.

3333. Harold French (Apr. 23, 1897–Oct. 19, 1997) B: London, England. Film and stage director. *By the Way* (Gaiety > Central, revue, Dec. 28, 1925): In the Same Way I Love You/W: Eric Little, M: H.M. Tennant — What Can They See in Dancing?/W: Graham John, M: Vivian Ellis.

3334. Henri French (Dec. 25, 1876–?) B: Brussels, Belgium. Known as Henri the Great. *His Honor the Mayor* (Wallack's, "R. La Carte," May 28, 1906): Come Take a Skate with Me/WM: R. Browne, Gus Edwards.

3335. Hugh French (Jan. 30, 1910–Nov. 2, 1976) B: London, England. *Set to Music* (Music Box, revue, Jan. 18, 1939): Never Again; The Party's Over Now; The Stately Homes of England; Three White Feathers/WM: Noel Coward.

3336. Leslie French (Apr. 23, 1904–Jan. 21, 1999) B: Bromley, Kent, England. Actor, singer, dancer, choreographer, he often broadcast for the B.B.C. *The Two Bouquets* (Windsor, "Edward Gill," May 31, 1938): Dearest Miss Bell/W: Eleanor Farjeon, Herb Farjeon, M: trad. — Dearest Miss Flo/W: Eleanor Farjeon, Herb Farjeon, M: trad., based on All Around the Ring — A Health to Dear Mama/W: Eleanor Farjeon, Herb Farjeon, M: trad., based on Schneider, How Was You — How Can We Bring the Old Folks Round/W: Eleanor Farjeon, Herb Farjeon, M: Henry Smart — A Little Champagne for Papa/W: Eleanor Farjeon, Herb Farjeon, M: trad., based on The Bells They Are Ringing for Sarah — The White and the Pink/W: Eleanor Farjeon, Herb Farjeon, M: Planquette, based on Heave Ho! — The Youth Who Sows/W: Eleanor Farjeon, Herb Farjeon, M: trad., based on My Heart Is Like a Silent Lute.

3337. Bob Freschi *The Most Happy Fella* (Booth, revival, "Clem," Feb. 13, 1992): Standing on the Corner/WM: Frank Loesser.

3338. Elbert Fretwell *The Maids of Athens* (New Amsterdam, "Capt. William Penn Harris," Mar. 18, 1914): Ah Yes, I Am in Love; Bid Me Forget/W: Carolyn Wells, M: Franz Lehar — Our Glorious Stripes and Stars/W: Carolyn Wells, M: Paul Kerr.

3339. Leonard Frey (Sept. 4, 1938–Aug. 24, 1988) B: Brooklyn, NY. *Fiddler on the Roof* (Imperial, "Mendel," Sept. 22, 1964): Anatevka/W: Sheldon Harnick, M: Jerry Bock. *Fiddler on the Roof* (Imperial, CR, "Motel," Aug. 1965): Miracle of Miracles/W: Sheldon Harnick, M: Jerry Bock. *Fiddler on the Roof* (Imperial,

CR, "Perchik"): Now I Have Everything/W: Sheldon Harnick, M: Jerry Bock. *A Kurt Weill Cabaret* (Bijou, revue, CR, Feb. 11, 1980): Alabama Song; Duet, Herr Jakob Schmidt/W: Bertolt Brecht, M: Kurt Weill — Ballad of Mack the Knife (Moritat)/Ger. W: Bertolt Brecht, Eng. W: Marc Blitzstein, M: Kurt Weill — Ballad of Sexual Slavery/W: George Tabori, M: Kurt Weill — Ballad of the Pimp and the Whore; Kanonensong/W: Marc Blitzstein, M: Kurt Weill — Eating/W: Arnold Weinstein, M: Kurt Weill — The Life That We Lead; Sailor's Tango/W: Will Holt, M: Kurt Weill — The Saga of Jenny/W: Ira Gershwin, M: Kurt Weill — September Song/W: Maxwell Anderson, M: Kurt Weill — That's Him/W: Ogden Nash, M: Kurt Weill.

3340. Nathaniel Frey (Aug. 3, 1913–Nov. 7, 1970) B: New York, NY. *Wonderful Town* (Winter Garden, "Policeman," Feb. 25, 1953): My Darlin' Eileen/W: Betty Comden, Adolph Green, M: Leonard Bernstein. *Damn Yankees* (46th Street, "Smokey," May 5, 1955): The Game; Heart/WM: Richard Adler, Jerry Ross. *Damn Yankees* (46th Street, CR, "Applegate," Mar. 1957): Not Meg; Those Were the Good Old Days/WM: Richard Adler, Jerry Ross. *Goldilocks* (Lunt-Fontanne, "Pete," Oct. 11, 1958): Bad Companions; Two Years in the Making/W: Joan Ford, Walter Kerr, Jean Kerr, M: Leroy Anderson. *Fiorello!* (Broadhurst, "Morris Cohen," Nov. 23, 1959): Marie's Law; On the Side of the Angels/W: Sheldon Harnick, M: Jerry Bock. *She Loves Me* (Eugene O'Neill, "Ladislav Sipos," Apr. 23, 1963): Good Morning, Good Day; Goodbye, Georg; Perspective; Sounds While Selling; Thank You, Madam/W: Sheldon Harnick, M: Jerry Bock. *The Education of H*Y*M*A*N K*A*P*L*A*N* (Alvin, "Sam Pinsky," Apr. 4, 1968): All American; Spring in the City/WM: Paul Nassau, Oscar Brand.

3341. William Frey (?–Feb. 20, 1988) *Starlight Express* (Gershwin, "Turnov," Mar. 15, 1987): Race One/W: Richard Stilgoe, M: Andrew Lloyd Webber.

3342. Howard Fried *The Cradle Will Rock* (New York City Center, revival, "Prof. Scoot," Feb. 11, 1960): Do I Have to Say?/WM: Marc Blitzstein.

3343. Ray Friedeck *A Christmas Carol* (Madison Square Garden, return engagement, "Fezziwig," Nov. 2, 1996): Mr. Fezziwig's Annual Christmas Ball/W: Lynn Ahrens, M: Alan Menken.

3344. Kate Friedlich Niece of playwright and screenwriter George S. Kaufman. *Small*

Wonder (Coronet, revue, Sept. 15, 1948): No Time/W: Phyllis McGinley, M: Baldwin Bergersen.

3345. Stella Friend She sang on Fred Waring's radio variety show with a group calling itself Stella and the Fellas. *The New Yorkers* (Broadway, "Girl Friend," Dec. 8, 1930): Love for Sale/WM: Cole Porter.

3346. Andrea Frierson *The Me Nobody Knows* (Longacre, CR, "Rhoda," Nov. 1971): Black; Robert, Alvin, Wendell and Jo Jo; Something Beautiful/W: Will Holt, M: Gary William Friedman. *Once on This Island* (Booth, "Erzulie," Oct. 18, 1990): And the Gods Heard Her Prayer; Forever Yours; The Human Heart/W: Lynn Ahrens, M: Stephen Flaherty. *A Christmas Carol* (Paramount Madison Square Garden, "Blind Hag" and "Scrooge's Mother," Dec. 1, 1994): God Bless Us, Every One; Nothing to Do with Me/W: Lynn Ahrens, M: Alan Menken.

3347. Andrew Frierson *Street Scene* (New York City Center, revival, "Henry Davis," Feb. 13, 1960): I Got a Marble and a Star; Ice Cream/W: Langston Hughes, Elmer Rice, M: Kurt Weill. *Show Boat* (New York City Center, revival, "Joe," Apr. 12, 1961): Can't Help Lovin' Dat Man; Ol' Man River/W: Oscar Hammerstein II, M: Jerome Kern.

3348. George Frierson *The Garrick Gaieties of 1926* (Garrick, revue, May 10, 1926): Keys to Heaven/W: Lorenz Hart, M: Richard Rodgers.

3349. Trixie Friganza (Nov. 29, 1870–Feb. 27, 1955) B: Grenola, KS. Often billed as Broadway's Favorite Champagne Girl. A large woman with a self-deprecating sense of humor, she spoke of her size as a "perfect forty-six." *The Chaperons* (New York > New York roof, "Aramanthe Dedincourt," June 5, 1902): Flowers; The Man Behind the Scenes/W: Frederick Ranken, M: Isidore Witmark. *The Prince of Pilsen* (Broadway, CR, "Mrs. Madison Crocker," Apr. 6, 1903): The American Girl (Song of the Cities); Floral Fete (Our Floral Queen); A Season at the Shore; The Widow/W: Frank Pixley, M: Gustav Luders. *The Darling of the Gallery Gods [Mid Summer Night's Fancies]* (Crystal Gardens, "Whoa San," June 22, 1903): Ida Bell; Whoa San/W: Matthew Woodward, M: Ben M. Jerome — My Japanese Baby/W: Arthur Ambrose, M: A. Baldwin Sloane. *The Dress Parade [Mid Summer Night's Fancies]* (Crystal Gardens, revue, June 22, 1903): Ella/W: Nicholas Biddle, M: Ben M. Jerome. *The Sho-Gun* (Wallack's, CR, "Omee-Omi," Feb. 2, 1905): Love, You Must Be Blind; The Man She'll Never Meet/W: George Ade, M: Gustav Luders. *Higgledy Pig-*

gledy (Weber's Music Hall, CR, "Mimi de Chartreuse," Mar. 6, 1905): Game of Love; Nancy Clancy/W: Edgar Smith, M: Maurice Levi. *Twiddle-Twaddle* (Weber's Music Hall, "Mrs. Jack Van Shaik," Jan. 1, 1906): Hats; Society Buds; 'Tis Dreadful! 'Tis Astounding/W: Edgar Smith, M: Maurice Levi. *The Orchid* (Herald Square > Casino, "Caroline Vokins," Apr. 8, 1907): Fancy Dress/W: Adrian Ross, M: Lionel Monckton — No Wedding Bells for Me/W: Edward P. Moran, Will Heelan, M: Seymour Furth — A Perfect Lady/W: Harold Atteridge, M: Hugo Frey. *The American Idea* (New York, "Mrs. William Waxtapper," Oct. 5, 1908): Cohan's Pet Names (That's the Pet Name for Me); They Always Follow Me/WM: George M. Cohan. *The Passing Show of 1912* (Winter Garden, revue, July 22, 1912): All the World Is Madly Prancing; The Metropolitan Squawktette/W: Harold Atteridge, M: Louis A. Hirsch. *Ned Wayburn's Town Topics* (Century, revue, "Mrs. Albany Dayline," Sept. 23, 1915): Brazilian Jubilee/WM: ?— The Old Are Getting Younger Every Day; Put It Over/W: Robert B. Smith, M: Harold Orlob. *Canary Cottage* (Morosco, "Blanche Moss," Feb. 5, 1917): Follow the Cook; The More I See of Men the More I Love My Dog/WM: Earl Carroll. *Murray Anderson's Almanac* (Erlanger's, revue, Aug. 14, 1929): Getting Into the Talkies/WM: Neville Fleeson — I May Be Wrong (But I Think You're Wonderful)/W: Harry Ruskin, M: Henry Sullivan.

3350. Al Frisco *Pansy* (Belmont, "James," May 14, 1929): Gettin' Together/WM: Maceo Pinkard.

3351. Joe Frisco (Nov. 4, 1889–Feb. 16, 1958) B: Milan, IL. A dancing comedian whose trademarks were a derby hat, a cigar and a stutter. *Earl Carroll's Vanities of 1928* (Earl Carroll, revue, Aug. 6, 1928): Getting the Beautiful Girls/W: Ned Washington, George Whiting, M: Michael Cleary, Joe Burke.

3352. Marguerite L. Fritts *The Grass Widow* (Liberty > Princess, "Lucille," Dec. 3, 1917): The Grass Widow/W: Channing Pollock, Rennold Wolf, M: Louis A. Hirsch.

3353. Rico Froelich *The Most Happy Fella* (Imperial > Broadway, "Pasquale," May 3, 1956): Abbondanza; Benvenuta; Sposalizio/WM: Frank Loesser. *Juno* (Winter Garden, "Sullivan," Mar. 9, 1959): It's Not Irish; We Can Be Proud/WM: Marc Blitzstein. *Something More!* (Eugene O'Neill, "Joe Santini" and "Policeman," Nov. 10, 1964): Bravo, Bravo, Novelisto; Don't Make a Move/W: Marilyn Bergman, Alan Bergman, M: Sammy Fain.

3354. Jane Froman (Nov. 10, 1907–Apr. 22, 1980) B: St. Louis, MO. The movie *With a Song in My Heart* (1952) starring Susan Hayward, tells the story of Froman's comeback following a nearly fatal plane crash. *Ziegfeld Follies of 1934* (Winter Garden, revue, Jan. 4, 1934): Green Eyes/W: E.Y. Harburg, M: Robert Emmett Dolan — The House Is Haunted (By the Echo of Your Last Goodbye)/W: Billy Rose, M: Basil G. Adlam — Moon About Town/W: E.Y. Harburg, M: Dana Suesse — Suddenly/W: E.Y. Harburg, Billy Rose, M: Vernon Duke — What Is There to Say?/W: E.Y. Harburg, M: Vernon Duke — You Oughta Be in Pictures/W: Edward Heyman, M: Dana Suesse. *Keep Off the Grass* (Broadhurst, revue, May 23, 1940): Clear Out of This World; Look Out for My Heart; This Is Spring; This Is Winter/W: Al Dubin, M: Jimmy McHugh — Two in a Taxi/W: Howard Dietz, M: Jimmy McHugh. *Artists and Models of 1943* (Broadway, revue, Nov. 5, 1943): Let's Keep It That Way/W: Milton Berle, Ervin Drake, M: Abner Silver — My Heart Is on a Binge; Swing Low, Sweet Harriet; You Are Romance/W: Milton Pascal, Dan Shapiro, M: Phil Charig.

3355. Albert Froom *The Tourists* (Majestic, CR, "Loofah," Sept. 24, 1906): Keep on Doing Something/W: R.H. Burnside, M: Gustave Kerker.

3356. Alfred Froom *Billie* (Erlanger's, "Grover Sheldon," Oct. 1, 1928): Bluff/WM: George M. Cohan.

3357. George B. Frothingham (Apr. 12, 1844–Jan. 19, 1915) B: Boston, MA. *Robin Hood* (Standard, "Friar Tuck," Sept. 28, 1891): O, See the Lambkins Play!/W: Harry B. Smith, M: Reginald De Koven. *The Knickerbockers* (Garden, "Burgomaster Dietrick Schermerhorn," May 29, 1893): Sing Your Merriest Lays/W: Harry B. Smith, M: Reginald De Koven. *The Serenade* (Knickerbocker, "Gomez," Mar. 16, 1897): Dreaming, Dreaming/W: Harry B. Smith, M: Victor Herbert. *The Viceroy* (Knickerbocker, "Bastroco," Apr. 9, 1900): A Sailor's Life; With Military Pomp/W: Harry B. Smith, M: Victor Herbert. *Robin Hood* (New Amsterdam, revival, "Friar Tuck," May 6, 1912): Roundelay/W: Harry B. Smith, M: Reginald De Koven.

3358. Romaine Fruge (Mar. 4, 1959–) B: Los Angeles, CA. *Big River: The Adventures of Huckleberry Finn* (Eugene O'Neill, CR, "Huckleberry Finn," c 1986): I, Huckleberry, Me; Leavin's Not the Only Way to Go; Muddy Water; River in the Rain; Waitin' for the Light to Shine; When the Sun Goes Down in the South; Worlds Apart/WM: Roger Miller.

3359. Ray Fry (Feb. 22, 1923–) B: Hebron, IN. *The Cradle Will Rock* (Mansfield > Broadway, revival, "Prof. Scoot," Dec. 26, 1947): Do I Have to Say?/WM: Marc Blitzstein.

3360. Willard Charles Fry *Just Fancy* (Casino, "A Gentlemanly Highwayman," Oct. 11, 1927): I'm a Highway Gentleman/W: Leo Robin, M: Joseph Meyer, Phil Charig.

3361. David Frye *The Most Happy Fella* (New York State, revival, "Jake," Sept. 4, 1991): Standing on the Corner/WM: Frank Loesser.

3362. Dwight Frye (Feb. 22, 1899–Nov. 7, 1943) B: Salina, KS. M: LAURA LEE. Movie character actor of thrillers and chillers from 1927. *Sitting Pretty* (Fulton, "Horace," Apr. 8, 1924): Bongo on the Congo; Dear Old Fashioned Prison of Mine (Tulip Time in Sing Sing); Mr. and Mrs. Rorer/W: P.G. Wodehouse, M: Jerome Kern.

3363. Edward Frye *Swing It* (Adelphi, "Capt. Jake Frye," July 22, 1937): Blah, Blah, Blah/W: Ira Gershwin, M: George Gershwin — Captain, Mate and Crew/W: Cecil Mack, Milton Reddie, M: Eubie Blake.

3364. Jason Fuchs (Mar. 5, 1986–) B: New York, NY. *A Christmas Carol* (Paramount Madison Square Garden, "Jonathan," Dec. 1, 1994): Nothing to Do with Me; The Years Are Passing By/W: Lynn Ahrens, M: Alan Menken. *A Christmas Carol* (Paramount Madison Square Garden > Madison Square Garden, return engagements, "Jonathan," Nov. 20, 1995 > Nov. 22, 1996): London Town Carol; Street Song/W: Lynn Ahrens, M: Alan Menken. *A Christmas Carol* (Madison Square Garden, return engagement, "Jonathan," Nov. 22, 1996): same as 1995.

3365. Edward (Eddie) Fuller (c 1912–Jan. 22, 1979) B: Newburg, MO. *The Cradle Will Rock* (Windsor > Mercury, "Yasha," Jan. 3, 1938): Art for Art's Sake; Ask Us Again; The Rich/WM: Marc Blitzstein. *Sing for Your Supper* (Adelphi, revue, Apr. 24, 1939): At Long Last; Oh, Boy Can We Deduct/W: Robert Sour, M: Lee Wainer.

3366. Lorenzo Fuller *Finian's Rainbow* (46th Street, "2nd Passion Pilgrim Gospeler," Jan. 10, 1947): The Begat/W: E.Y. Harburg, M: Burton Lane. *Kiss Me, Kate* (New Century, "Paul," Dec. 30, 1948): Too Darn Hot/WM: Cole Porter.

3367. Mollie Fuller *Adonis* (Bijoux, "Lady Pattie," Sept. 4, 1884): We Are the Duchess' Daughters/W: William F. Gill, Henry E. Dixey, M: Edward E. Rice.

3368. Penny Fuller (July 21, 1940–) B: Durham, NC. *Cabaret* (Broadhurst, CR, "Sally

Bowles"): Cabaret; Don't Tell Mama; Perfectly Marvelous; Why Should I Wake Up?/W: Fred Ebb, M: John Kander. *Applause* (Palace, "Eve Harrington," Mar. 30, 1970/May 3, 1971): The Best Night of My Life; One Halloween/W: Lee Adams, M: Charles Strouse. *Rex* (Lunt-Fontanne, "Anne Boleyn" and "Princess Elizabeth," Apr. 25, 1976): Away from You; Christmas at Hampton Court; In Time; The Masque; The Wee Golden Warrior/W: Sheldon Harnick, M: Richard Rodgers.

3369. Rosalinde Fuller (Feb. 16, 1901–Sept. 15, 1982) B: Portsmouth, England. Known as a folksinger in England, she came to the U.S. in 1914. In 1919, she entertained American troops in France. After 1921 she began to act in the classics, such as Shakespeare, Shaw and Chekov. *What's in a Name?* (Maxine Elliott, revue, Mar. 19, 1920): My Bridal Veil [Mar. 22, 1920]; A Young Man's Fancy (Music Box Song)/W: John Murray Anderson, Jack Yellen, M: Milton Ager. *The Greenwich Village Follies of 1921* (Shubert, revue, Aug. 31, 1921): Oh, Heigh-Ho! [Sept. 26, 1921]; Snow Flake [Sept. 26, 1921]; When Dreams Come True/W: John Murray Anderson, Arthur Swanstrom, M: Carey Morgan — That Reminiscent Melody [Nov. 14, 1921]; A Young Man's Fancy (Music Box Song) [Nov. 14, 1921]/W: John Murray Anderson, Jack Yellen, M: Milton Ager — Three O'Clock in the Morning/W: Dorothy Terris, M: Julian Robledo.

3370. Maude Fulton (May 14, 1881–Nov. 10, 1950) B: El Dorado, KS. M: ROBERT H. OBER. She began as a stenographer and telegraph operator, later becoming known as a writer of stories, plays and films. *The Orchid* (Herald Square > Casino, "Thisbe," Apr. 8, 1907): The Lady Secretary/WM: ?— Liza Ann (A Yorkshire Idyll)/W: Leslie Mayne, M: Lionel Monckton — Promenade des Anglaise/W: Adrian Ross, M: Ivan Caryll. *Funabashi* (Casino, "Macy Bloomingdale Saks," Jan. 6, 1908): I Walked Around/W: Vincent Rose, Ted Snyder, M: Safford Waters — I'd Guess You/W: Carolyn Wells, M: Safford Waters — I've Been Discharged by Them All/W: Paul West, M: Safford Waters.

3371. Maud Furniss *A Chinese Honeymoon* (Casino, CR, "Mrs. Pineapple," Sept. 1, 1902): The A la Girl/W: George Dance, M: Howard Talbot.

3372. Jim Fyfe (Sept. 27, 1958–) B: Camden, NJ. *Legs Diamond* (Mark Hellinger, "Moran," Dec. 26, 1988): Charge It to A.R./WM: Peter Allen.

3373. Martin Gabel (June 19, 1912–May 22, 1986) B: Philadelphia, PA. M: ARLENE FRAN-

CIS, with whom he often appeared on the TV panel quiz *What's My Line?* On radio, the actor played Dr. John Wayne on the 15 minute weekday soap *Big Sister* (1936); he was Neil Williams on *The Easy Aces* (1939). *Baker Street* (Broadway > Martin Beck, "Professor Moriarty," Feb. 16, 1965): I Shall Miss You, Holmes/W: Sheldon Harnick, M: Jerry Bock.

3374. June Gable (June 5, 1945–) B: New York, NY. On TV she was Det. Baptista on *Barney Miller* (1976); and a regular on *Laugh-In* (1979). *Candide* (Broadway, revival, "Old Lady," Mar. 10, 1974): The Best of All Possible Worlds/W: Stephen Sondheim, M: Leonard Bernstein — I Am Easily Assimilated/WM: Leonard Bernstein.

3375. Eva Gabor (Feb. 11, 1919–1995) B: Budapest, Hungary. On TV's *Green Acres* (1965), she was EDDIE ALBERT's wife. *Tovarich* (Broadway, CR, "Tatiana," Oct. 21, 1963): All for You; I Know the Feeling; Make a Friend; The Only One; Wilkes-Barre, Pa.; You Love Me/W: Anne Crosswell, M: Lee Pockriss — You'll Make an Elegant Butler (I'll Make an Elegant Maid)/WM: Joan Javits, Philip Springer.

3376. John Gabriel (May 25, 1931–) B: Niagara Falls, NY. *Applause* (Palace, CR, "Bill Sampson," May 1, 1972): Fasten Your Seat Belts; One of a Kind; Think How It's Gonna Be/W: Lee Adams, M: Charles Strouse.

3377. Master Gabriel (June 19, c 1877–Sept. 2, 1929) B: New York, NY. A so-called midget whose real name was Gabriel Wiegel. *Buster Brown* (Majestic, "Buster Brown," Jan. 24, 1905): Bo-Peep; Buster's Chums; Resolved/W: Paul West, M: John W. Bratton. *Little Nemo* (New Amsterdam, "Little Nemo," Oct. 20, 1908): I Guess I Talk Too Much; In Happy Slumberland; Won't You Be My Playmate?/W: Harry B. Smith, M: Victor Herbert. *Letty Pepper* (Vanderbilt, "Billy," Apr. 10, 1922): I Love to Dance/W: Leo Wood, Irving Bibo, M: Werner Janssen — You Teach Me/W: Ballard Macdonald, M: James F. Hanley.

3378. Ida Gabrielle *The Office Boy* (Victoria, "Florine," Nov. 2, 1903): After Business Hours/W: Harry B. Smith, M: Ludwig Englander.

3379. Frank Gaby (1896–Feb. 12, 1945) *Artists and Models of 1924* (Astor > Casino, revue, Oct. 15, 1924): Off to Greenwich Village/WM: ?— What a Beautiful Face Will Do/W: ?, M: Sigmund Romberg. *Gay Paree* (Winter Garden, revue, Nov. 9, 1926): There Never Was a Town Like Paris/W: Mann Holiner, M: Alberta Nichols.

3380. Nadine Gae *Ziegfeld Follies of 1943* (Winter Garden, revue, Apr. 1, 1943): Hold That Smile/W: Jack Yellen, M: Ray Henderson.

3381. Mary Gaebler (May 4, 1951–) B: Davenport, IA. *The Music Man* (City Center 55th Street, revival, "Maud Dunlop," June 5, 1980): It's You; Pick-a-Little, Talk-a-Little/WM: Meredith Willson.

3382. Truman (Trueman) Gaige *Blossom Time* (Ambassador, revival, "Erkman," Mar. 23, 1931): Love Is a Riddle/W: Dorothy Donnelly, M: Sigmund Romberg. *Bitter Sweet* (44th Street, revival, "Mr. Proutie," May 7, 1934): The Last Dance; Tarara Boom-de-Ay/WM: Noel Coward. *Gigi* (Uris, "Manuel," Nov. 13, 1973): It's a Bore/W: Alan Jay Lerner, M: Frederick Loewe.

3383. Mme. Gaillard *Mlle. Modiste* (Globe, revival, "Mme. Cecelie," May 26, 1913): When the Cat's Away, the Mice Will Play/W: Henry Blossom, M: Victor Herbert.

3384. Boyd Gaines (May 11, 1953–) B: Atlanta, GA. He played dental student Mark Royer on the TV sitcom *One Day at a Time* (1981). *She Loves Me* (Roundabout, revival, "Georg Nowack," June 10, 1993): Good Morning, Good Day; She Loves Me; Sounds While Selling; Three Letters; Tonight at Eight; Where's My Shoe?/W: Sheldon Harnick, M: Jerry Bock.

3385. Davis Gaines (Jan. 21, 1955–) B: Orlando, FL. *The Phantom of the Opera* (Majestic, CR, "Raoul, Vicomte de Chagny," Mar. 12, 1990): All I Ask of You; Bravo, Bravo; Little Lotte; The Mirror; Notes; Prima Donna; Raoul, I've Been There; Think of Me; Twisted Every Way; Wandering Child; Why Have You Brought Me Here/W: Charles Hart, Richard Stilgoe, M: Andrew Lloyd Webber. *The Phantom of the Opera* (Majestic, CR, "The Phantom of the Opera," c 1993): All I Ask of You; Bravo, Bravo; I Remember; Little Lotte; The Mirror; The Music of the Night; Notes; The Point of No Return; Prima Donna; Stranger Than You Dreamt It; Twisted Every Way; Wandering Child/W: Charles Hart, Richard Stilgoe, M: Andrew Lloyd Webber — The Phantom of the Opera/W: Mike Batt, Richard Stilgoe, M: Andrew Lloyd Webber.

3386. Marjorie Gaines *Mystery Moon* (Royale, "Pearl Lindy," June 23, 1930): Clean Out the Corner; Milkmaids of Broadway; Pepper and Salt/WM: Monte Carlo, Alma Sanders.

3387. Charles Galagher *The Baron Trenck* (Casino, "Alla Wanja," Mar. 11, 1912): We're Bold, Bad Bandits All/W: Frederick F. Schrader, M: Felix Albini. *Robin Hood* (Jolson, revival, "Will Scarlet," Nov. 18, 1929): The Armorers'

Song; Come the Bowmen in Lincoln Green; O, See the Lambkins Play!; The Tailor and the Crow (Jet Black Crow)/W: Harry B. Smith, M: Reginald De Koven. *The Serenade* (Jolson, revival, "Romero," Mar. 4, 1930): The Monk and the Maid; Song of the Carbine/W: Harry B. Smith, M: Victor Herbert.

3388. Tom Galantich B: Brooklyn, NY. *City of Angels* (Virginia, "Officer Pasco," Dec. 11, 1989): All Ya Have to Do Is Wait/W: David Zippel, M: Cy Coleman. *City of Angels* (Virginia, CR, "Stone"): Double Talk; Ev'rybody's Gotta Be Somewhere; The Tennis Song; With Every Breath I Take; You're Nothing Without Me/W: David Zippel, M: Cy Coleman.

3389. Anthony Galde *Prince of Central Park* (Belasco, "Elmo," Nov. 9, 1989): Follow the Leader; I Fly by Night; They Don't Give You Life at Sixteen/W: Gloria Nissenson, M: Don Sebesky.

3390. Andy Gale B: New York, NY. *Rags* (Mark Hellinger, "Homesick Immigrant," Aug. 21, 1986): I Remember/W: Stephen Schwartz, M: Charles Strouse.

3391. Charles Gale *Sidewalks of New York* (Knickerbocker, "Whitey," Oct. 3, 1927): Way Down Town/W: Eddie Dowling, M: James F. Hanley.

3392. Roberta Gale (Oct. 18, 1914–) B: Pittsburgh, PA. *The New Yorkers* (Edyth Totten, revue, Mar. 10, 1927): Pretty Little So-and-So/W: Henry Myers, M: Edgar Fairchild — Triangle/W: Henry Myers, M: Charles M. Schwab.

3393. Victory Gale *The Sultan of Sulu* (Wallack's, "Galula," Dec. 29, 1902): Since I First Met You/W: George Ade, M: Alfred G. Wathall.

3394. Warren Galjour *Wonderful Town* (Winter Garden, "Guide" and "Associate Editor" and "Policeman," Feb. 25, 1953): Christopher Street; My Darlin' Eileen; What a Waste/W: Betty Comden, Adolph Green, M: Leonard Bernstein.

3395. Betty Gallagher *Happy Go Lucky* (Liberty, "Mable Holly," Sept. 30, 1926): It's In, It's Out; You're the Fellow the Fortune Teller Told Me All About/W: Helena Evans, M: Lucien Denni. *Princess Charming* (Imperial, "Marie," Oct. 13, 1930): Take a Letter to the King/W: Arthur Swanstrom, M: Arthur Schwartz, Albert Sirmay.

3396. Charles E. Gallagher *The Fortune Teller* (Al Jolson, revival, "Sandor," Nov. 4, 1929): Gypsy Love Song (Slumber On, My Little Gypsy Sweetheart); Ho! Ye Townsmen; Romany Life (Czardas)/W: Harry B. Smith, M: Victor Herbert.

3397. Dan Gallagher B: Philadelphia, PA. *The Vagabond King* (Shubert, revival, "Noel of Anjou," June 29, 1943): Hunting; Nocturne/W: Brian Hooker, M: Rudolf Friml. *Bloomer Girl* (Shubert, "Hiram Crump," Oct. 5, 1944): The Farmer's Daughter; Welcome Hinges/W: E.Y. Harburg, M: Harold Arlen.

3398. David Gallagher (Feb. 9, 1985–) B: College Point, NY. *A Christmas Carol* (Paramount Madison Square Garden, "Scrooge at 8," Dec. 1, 1994): God Bless Us, Every One/W: Lynn Ahrens, M: Alan Menken.

3399. Ed Gallagher (1873–May 28, 1929) B: San Francisco, CA. Vaudeville and musical comedy partner of AL SHEAN. *The Rose Maid* (Globe, "Dennis," Apr. 22, 1912): Money Talks; Telephone Song/W: Robert B. Smith, M: Bruno Granichstaedten. *Ziegfeld Follies of 1922* (New Amsterdam, revue, June 5, 1922): Mister Gallagher and Mister Shean/WM: Ed Gallagher, Al Shean.

3400. Frank Gallagher M: LUCY WESTON. *Babes in Toyland* (Jolson, revival, "Alan," Dec. 23, 1929): Before and After; Fioretta; Go to Sleep, Slumber Deep; I Can't Do the Sum; Song of the Poet (Rock-a-Bye Baby)/W: Glen Mac-Donough, M: Victor Herbert.

3401. Helen Gallagher (July 19, 1926–) B: Brooklyn, NY. She won an Emmy for the TV soap *Ryan's Hope* (1976). *Seven Lively Arts* (Ziegfeld, revue, CR, Dec. 1944): Hence, It Don't Make Sense/WM: Cole Porter. *Touch and Go* (Broadhurst > Broadway, revue, Oct. 13, 1949): Easy Does It/W: Walter Kerr, Jean Kerr, M: Jay Gorney. *Make a Wish* (Winter Garden, "Poupette," Apr. 18, 1951): I'll Never Make a Frenchman Out of You; Take Me Back to Texas with You/W: Timothy Gray, M: Hugh Martin — Suits Me Fine; That Face!; Who Gives a Sou?/WM: Hugh Martin. *Pal Joey* (Broadhurst, revival, "Gladys Bumps," Jan. 3, 1952): The Flower Garden of My Heart; Plant You Now, Dig You Later; That Terrific Rainbow; You Mustn't Kick It Around/W: Lorenz Hart, M: Richard Rodgers. *Hazel Flagg* (Mark Hellinger, "Hazel Flagg," Feb. 11, 1953): I Feel Like I'm Gonna Live Forever; I'm Glad I'm Leaving; Laura De Maupassant; My Wild Imagination [May 16, 1953]; The World Is Beautiful Today; You're Gonna Dance with Me, Willie/W: Bob Hilliard, M: Jule Styne. *Guys and Dolls* (New York City Center, revival, "Miss Adelaide," Apr. 20, 1955): Adelaide's Lament; A Bushel and a Peck; Marry the Man Today; Sue Me; Take Back Your Mink/WM: Frank Loesser. *Finian's Rainbow* (New York City Center, revival, "Sharon

McLonergan," May 18, 1955): How Are Things in Glocca Morra?; If This Isn't Love; Look to the Rainbow; Old Devil Moon; Something Sort of Grandish; That Great Come-and-Get-It Day; When the Idle Poor Become the Idle Rich/W: E.Y. Harburg, M: Burton Lane. *The Pajama Game* (St. James, CR, "Gladys," June 1955): Her Is; Hernando's Hideaway; Steam Heat/WM: Richard Adler, Jerry Ross. *Brigadoon* (New York City Center, revival, "Meg Brockie," Mar. 27, 1957): Down on MacConnachy Square; The Love of My Life; My Mother's Weddin' Day/W: Alan Jay Lerner, M: Frederick Loewe. *Portofino* (Adelphi, "Kitty," Feb. 21, 1958): Here I Come/W: Richard Ney, M: Louis Bellson, Will Irwin — I'm in League with the Devil/W: Richard Ney, M: Will Irwin — Isn't It Wonderful?/W: Richard Ney, M: Louis Bellson. *Oklahoma!* (New York City Center, revival, "Ado Annie Carnes," Mar. 19, 1958): All er Nothin'; The Farmer and the Cowman; I Cain't Say No/W: Oscar Hammerstein II, M: Richard Rodgers. *Sweet Charity* (Palace, "Nickie," Jan. 29, 1966): Baby, Dream Your Dream; Big Spender; I Love to Cry at Weddings; There's Gotta Be Something Better Than This/W: Dorothy Fields, M: Cy Coleman. *Sweet Charity* (Palace, CR, "Charity Hope Valentine," July 11, 1966): Charity's Soliloquy; If My Friends Could See Me Now; I'm a Brass Band; I'm the Bravest Individual; There's Gotta Be Something Better Than This; Where Am I Going?; You Should See Yourself/W: Dorothy Fields, M: Cy Coleman. *Mame* (Winter Garden, CR, "Agnes Gooch," Apr. 29, 1968): Gooch's Song; St. Bridget; We Need a Little Christmas/WM: Jerry Herman. *Cry for Us All* (Broadhurst, "Bessie Legg," Apr. 8, 1970): Swing Your Bag/W: Alfred Robinson, Phyllis Robinson, M: Mitch Leigh. *No, No, Nanette* (46th Street, revival, "Lucille Early," Jan. 19, 1971): Take a Little One-Step/W: Zelda Sears, M: Vincent Youmans — Too Many Rings Around Rosie; Where-Has-My-Hubby-Gone? Blues; You Can Dance with Any Girl at All/W: Irving Caesar, M: Vincent Youmans. *Sugar Babies* (Mark Hellinger, revue, CR, Sept. 21, 1981): Don't Blame Me; I Can't Give You Anything but Love; On the Sunny Side of the Street/W: Dorothy Fields, M: Jimmy McHugh — Down at the Gaiety Burlesque; Every Day Another Tune; Goin' Back to New Orleans; Mr. Banjo Man/WM: Arthur Malvin — I Feel a Song Comin' On/WM: Dorothy Fields, Jimmy McHugh, George S. Oppenheimer — I'm Shooting High/W: Ted Koehler, M: Jimmy McHugh — In Louisiana/W: Arthur Malvin, M: Jimmy McHugh — When

You and I Were Young, Maggie Blues/W: Jack Frost, M: Jimmy McHugh.

3402. Juliana Gallagher *Street Scene* (Adelphi, "Mary Hildebrand," Jan. 9, 1947): Catch Me If You Can/W: Langston Hughes, Elmer Rice, M: Kurt Weill.

3403. Peter Gallagher (Aug. 19, 1955–) B: Armonk, NY. In movies from 1980. *Grease* (Broadhurst, CR, "Danny Zuko"): All Choked Up; Alone at a Drive-In Movie; Summer Nights/WM: Jim Jacobs, Warren Casey. *A Doll's Life* (Mark Hellinger, "Otto," Sept. 23, 1982): Loki and Baldur; Stay with Me, Nora; There She Is; A Woman Alone/W: Betty Comden, Adolph Green, M: Larry Grossman. *Guys and Dolls* (Martin Beck, revival, "Sky Masterson," Apr. 14, 1992): I'll Know; I've Never Been in Love Before; Luck Be a Lady; My Time of Day/WM: Frank Loesser.

3404. Richard (Skeets) Gallagher (July 28, 1891–May 22, 1955) B: Terre Haute, IN. M: PAULINE MASON. A song and dance man in vaudeville, he appeared in Hollywood talking pictures from 1928. *Up in the Clouds* (Lyric, "Bud Usher," Jan. 2, 1922): Friends; Jean; The Last Girl Is the Best Girl/W: Will B. Johnstone, M: Tom Johnstone. *Up She Goes* (Playhouse, "Frank Andrews," Nov. 6, 1922): Let's Kiss; Settle Down, Travel 'Round; Takes a Heap of Love; Tyup (Hitch Your Wagon to a Star); We'll Do the Riviera/W: Joseph McCarthy, M: Harry Tierney. *Marjorie* (Shubert, "Eph Daw," Aug. 11, 1924): Good Things and Bad Things; Super-Sheik/W: Harold Atteridge, M: Sigmund Romberg — Nature/W: Harold Atteridge, M: Herbert Stothart — Popularity/W: Harold Atteridge, M: Stephen Jones — Shuffle Your Troubles Away/W: Henry Creamer, M: James F. Hanley. *The Magnolia Lady* (Shubert, "Peter Ravenel," Nov. 25, 1924): A la Gastronome; I Will Be Good; Liza Jane; When the Bell Goes Ting-a-Ling-Ling/W: Anne Caldwell, M: Harold A. Levey. *The City Chap* (Liberty, "Nat Duncan," Oct. 26, 1925): If You Are As Good As You Look; No One Knows (How Much I'm in Love); Sympathetic Someone; Walking Home with Josie; When I Fell in Love with You/W: Anne Caldwell, M: Jerome Kern — Journey's End/W: P.G. Wodehouse, M: Jerome Kern. *Lucky* (New Amsterdam, "Teddy Travers," Mar. 22, 1927): By the Light of the Silvery Moon/W: Edward Madden, M: Gus Edwards — Spring Is Here; Without Thinking of You/WM: ?.

3405. Robert Gallagher (Aug. 28, 1920–) B: Chicago, IL. *Two on the Aisle* (Mark Hellinger, revue, July 19, 1951): Show Train/

W: Betty Comden, Adolph Green, M: Jule Styne.

3406. John Gallaudet (Aug. 25, 1903–Nov. 5, 1983) *The Gang's All Here* (Imperial, "Hector Winterbottom," Feb. 18, 1931): Baby Wanna Go Bye-Bye with You; Gypsy Rose; It Always Takes Two/W: Owen Murphy, Robert A. Simon, M: Lewis E. Gensler.

3407. Katherine Gallimore *Angela* (Ambassador, "Bijou," Dec. 3, 1928): Bundle of Love; Don't Forget Your Etiquette; Oui, Oui!!; The Regal Romp; Tally-Ho/W: Mann Holiner, M: Alberta Nichols.

3408. John Gallogly (Aug. 23, 1952–) B: Providence RI. *The Utter Glory of Morrissey Hall* (Mark Hellinger, "Charles Hill," May 13, 1979): The Letter; You Would Say/WM: Clark Gesner.

3409. Goodie Galloway *Cherry Blossoms* (44th Street > Cosmopolitan, "O-Dam-San," Mar. 28, 1927): If You Know What I Think/W: Harry B. Smith, M: Sigmund Romberg.

3410. Jane Galloway (Feb. 27, 1950–) B: St. Louis, MO. *Little Johnny Jones* (Alvin, revival, "Florabelle Fly," Mar. 21, 1982): American Ragtime; Goodbye Flo; Oh, You Wonderful Boy/WM: George M. Cohan.

3411. Katherine Galloway *Molly O'* (Cort, "Molly O'Malley," May 17, 1916): Champagne and Laughter; Love Is an Art; The Voice of Love; When Fortune Smiles on You/W: Robert B. Smith, M: Carl Woess. *He Didn't Want to Do It* (Broadhurst, "Paula Wainwright," Aug. 20, 1918): It's the Scotch; The Song of the Trees; The Song of the World/W: George Broadhurst, M: Silvio Hein.

3412. Leata Galloway *Dude* (Broadway, "Nero," Oct. 9, 1972): A Song to Sing; You Can Do Nothing About It/W: Gerome Ragni, M: Galt MacDermot. *Rockabye Hamlet* (Minskoff, "Gertrude," Feb. 17, 1976): All My Life; Laertes Coercion; The Last Blues; Midnight Mass; Set It Right; Shall We Dance; Swordfight; Tis Pity, Tis True; The Wedding/WM: Cliff Jones. *The Human Comedy* (Royale, "Diana Steed," Apr. 5, 1984): The Birds in the Trees; I've Known a Lot of Guys; A Lot of Men/W: William Dumaresq, M: Galt MacDermot.

3413. Louise Galloway (c 1879–Oct. 10, 1949) B: Marshall, MI. *The Clinging Vine* (Knickerbocker, "Mrs. Anthony Allen," Dec. 25, 1922): Grandma/W: Zelda Sears, M: Harold A. Levey. *Rainbow Rose* (Forrest, "Martha," Mar. 16, 1926): We Want Our Breakfast/WM: Owen Murphy, Harold A. Levey.

3414. Selby Galloway *The Merry World* (Imperial, revue, June 8, 1926): Dancing Jim/W:

Donovan Parsons, M: Marc Anthony — Deauville/WM: Herman Hupfeld — Military Charleston [June 14, 1926]/WM: ?.

3415. John Galludet *Here Goes the Bride* (46th Street, "Roger Loring," Nov. 3, 1931): It's My Nature; One Second of Sex/W: Edward Heyman, M: Johnny Green.

3416. Laurie Gamache (Sept. 25, 1959–) B: Mayville, ND. *A Chorus Line* (Shubert, CR, "Cassie," May 18, 1987): The Music and the Mirror/W: Edward Kleban, M: Marvin Hamlisch.

3417. Marcelo Gamboa (Apr. 2, 1939–) B: Buenos Aires, Argentina. *The Boy Friend* (Ambassador, revival, "Marcel," Apr. 14, 1970): The Boy Friend; It's Nicer in Nice; The Riviera; Safety in Numbers; Sur la Plage/WM: Sandy Wilson.

3418. Florence Gammage *Florodora* (New York, CR, "Valleda"): We Got Up at 8/WM: Leslie Stuart.

3419. Lynne Gannaway *Candide* (Broadway, revival, "Penitente" and "Cartagenian" and "Houri," Mar. 10, 1974): O Miserere/W: Richard Wilbur, M: Leonard Bernstein.

3420. James Gannon *Camelot* (Majestic, "Sir Sagramore," Dec. 3, 1960): Then You May Take Me to the Fair/W: Alan Jay Lerner, M: Frederick Loewe. *Donnybrook!* (46th Street, "Matthew Gilbane," May 18, 1961): Sez I; Wisha Wurra/WM: Johnny Burke.

3421. Jack Gansert *Marinka* (Winter Garden > Ethel Barrymore, "Lieut. Palafy," July 18, 1945): Treat a Woman Like a Drum; Young Man Danube/W: George Marion, Jr., M: Emmerich Kalman.

3422. Henry Gant *The Red Moon* (Majestic, "Bill Gibson," May 3, 1909): Keep on Smilin'/W: Bob Cole, M: J. Rosamond Johnson.

3423. Carl Gantvoort (1883–Sept. 28, 1935) B: Bowling Green, KY. *Robin Hood* (New Amsterdam, revival, "Little John," May 6, 1912): Brown October Ale; Roundelay/W: Harry B. Smith, M: Reginald De Koven. *The Geisha* (44th Street, revival, "Reginald Fairfax," Mar. 27, 1913): Kissing Duet; Star of My Soul; The Toy Duet; We Are Going to Call on the Marquis/W: Harry Greenbank, M: Sidney Jones. *Iole* (Longacre, "George Wayne," Dec. 29, 1913): If Dreams Come True; To Rent, to Let/WM: ?— Iole; Why Do You Think I Love You So?/W: Robert W. Chambers, M: William F. Peters— None but the Brave Deserve the Fair/W: Will M. Hough, Frank R. Adams, M: Joseph E. Howard. *Pom-Pom* (Cohan, "Bertrand," Feb. 28, 1916): Kiss Me; Only One Hour; Ships in the Night/W: Anne Caldwell, M: Hugo Felix. *The Riviera Girl* (New Amsterdam, "Victor de Berryl," Sept. 24, 1917): Half a Married Man; Life's a Tale; Will You Forget?/W: P.G. Wodehouse, M: Emmerich Kalman— Man, Man, Man/W: Bob Cole, M: J. Rosamond Johnson. *The Maid of the Mountains* (Casino, "Beppo," Sept. 11, 1918): Dividing the Spoils/W: Clifford Harris, M: Harold Fraser-Simpson— I Don't Care; Live for Today; My Life Is Love; Though Curs May Quail/W: Harry Graham, M: Harold Fraser-Simpson— A Paradise for Two/W: Clifford Harris, Arthur Valentine, M: James W. Tate. *Little Simplicity* (Astor > 44th Street, "Alan Van Cleve," Nov. 4, 1918): Days of Youth; Hush! Hush!; I Cannot Leave You; Learning to Love; National Air's Medley; A Voice Calling Me; You Don't Know/W: Rida Johnson Young, M: Augustus Barratt.

3424. Victor Garber (Mar. 16, 1949–) B: London, Ontario, Canada. On TV he was Dennis Widmer in *The Days and Nights of Molly Dodd* (1987). *Sweeney Todd, the Demon Barber of Fleet Street* (Uris, "Anthony Hope," Mar. 1, 1979): Ah, Miss; City on Fire!; Kiss Me; No Place Like London/WM: Stephen Sondheim. *Little Me* (Eugene O'Neill, revival, "Noble Eggleston" and "Val du Val" and "Fred Poitrine," Jan. 21, 1982): Boom-Boom (Le Grand Boom-Boom); I Love You (As Much as I Am Able); Real Live Girl/W: Carolyn Leigh, M: Cy Coleman. *Damn Yankees* (Marquis, revival, "Applegate," Mar. 3, 1994): Those Were the Good Old Days; Two Lost Souls/WM: Richard Adler, Jerry Ross.

3425. Betty Garde (Sept. 19, 1905–Dec. 25, 1989) B: Philadelphia, PA. She worked extensively in radio where she was Belle in the 15 minute weekday comedy soap *Lorenzo Jones and His Wife Belle* (1937). On TV she played Aggie Larkin in the sitcom *The Real McCoys* (1959). *Oklahoma!* (St. James, "Aunt Eller Murphy," Mar. 31, 1943): The Farmer and the Cowman; Kansas City; Oklahoma!; The Surrey with the Fringe on Top/W: Oscar Hammerstein II, M: Richard Rodgers. *Oklahoma!* (New York City Center, revivals, "Aunt Eller Murphy," Mar. 19, 1958/Feb. 27, 1963/May 15, 1963): same as above.

3426. Tess Gardella (c 1898–Jan. 3, 1950) B: Wilkes-Barre, PA. Producer Lew Leslie brought her into vaudeville, put her in blackface and renamed her Aunt Jemima. She was the first Jemima on the radio variety *Aunt Jemima Show* (1929). *Show Boat* (Ziegfeld, "Queenie," Dec. 27, 1927): Can't Help Lovin' Dat Man; C'mon

Folks (Ballyhoo); Hey, Feller/W: Oscar Hammerstein II, M: Jerome Kern. *Show Boat* (Casino, return engagement, "Queenie," May 19, 1932): same as above.

3427. Vincent Gardenia (Jan. 7, 1922–Dec. 9, 1992) B: Naples, Italy. At 5 he began acting with his father's troupe, the Gennaro Gardenia Company. On TV he played Frank Lorenzo in *All in the Family* (1973). *Ballroom* (Majestic, "Alfred Rossi," Dec. 14, 1978): I Love to Dance/ W: Alan Bergman, Marilyn Bergman, M: Billy Goldenberg.

3428. Arline Gardiner *Americana of 1926* (Belmont, revue, July 26, 1926): Just Lovin'/W: J.P. McEvoy, M: Henry Souvaine — Sunny Disposish/W: Ira Gershwin, M: Phil Charig.

3429. Edgar Gardiner *I'll Say She Is* (Casino, "Thief," May 19, 1924): Break Into Your Heart; Pretty Girl; Wall Street Blues/W: Will B. Johnstone, M: Tom Johnstone. *Americana of 1926* (Belmont, revue, July 26, 1926): Just Lovin'/W: J.P. McEvoy, M: Henry Souvaine — Sunny Disposish/W: Ira Gershwin, M: Phil Charig. *Allez-Oop* (Earl Carroll, revue, Aug. 2, 1927): Blow Hot and Heavy; Doin' the Gorilla; Hoof, Hoof/ W: Leo Robin, M: Phil Charig, Richard Myers. *Rain or Shine* (George M. Cohan, "Harry," Feb. 9, 1928): Oh, Baby!/WM: Owen Murphy — Who's Goin' to Get You?/W: Jack Yellen, M: Milton Ager.

3430. Frank Gardiner *Oh, Kay!* (Imperial, "Judge Appleton," Nov. 8, 1926): Bride and Groom/W: Ira Gershwin, M: George Gershwin.

3431. James W. (Jimmy) Gardiner (c 1919–Nov. 6, 1976) *Early to Bed* (Broadhurst, "Wilbur," June 17, 1943): Get Away, Young Man/W: George Marion, Jr., M: Fats Waller.

3432. Reginald Gardiner (Feb. 27, 1903– July 7, 1980) B: Wimbledon, Surrey, England. M: WYN RICHMOND. He came to the U.S. in 1935, and appeared in numerous movies in Britain and the U.S. *The Show Is On* (Winter Garden, revue, Dec. 25, 1936): Rhythm/W: Lorenz Hart, M: Richard Rodgers. *My Fair Lady* (New York City Center, revival, "Alfred P. Doolittle," May 20, 1964): Get Me to the Church on Time; With a Little Bit of Luck/W: Alan Jay Lerner, M: Frederick Loewe.

3433. Ann Gardner B: Iowa City, IA. *Canterbury Tales* (Eugene O'Neill, "Prioress" and "Proserpina," Feb. 3, 1969): Love Will Conquer All; Pear Tree Quintet/W: Nevill Coghill, M: Richard Hill, John Hawkins.

3434. Bert Gardner *A Night in Spain* (44th Street, revue, May 3, 1927): International Vamp/ W: Alfred Bryan, M: Jean Schwartz.

3435. Jack Gardner (c 1873–Sept. 30, 1950) B: Louisville, KY. M: LOUISE DRESSER, with whom he played in vaudeville. *The Belle of Mayfair* (Daly's, "Hugh Meredith," Dec. 3, 1906): Come to St. George's; Hello! Come Along Girls; I Know a Girl/WM: Leslie Stuart. *The Talk of New York* (Knickerbocker, "Joe Wilcox," Dec. 3, 1907): I Want the Whole World to Know I Love You; When We Are M-a-double-r-i-e-d/WM: George M. Cohan. *The Yankee Prince* (Knickerbocker, "Whiteside Webster," Apr. 20, 1908): I'm Awfully Strong for You; Money; Showing the Yankees London Town; Villains in the Play/WM: George M. Cohan. *Fluffy Ruffles* (Criterion, "Herbert Henshaw," Sept. 7, 1908): I Love to Sit and Look at You/W: Edward Madden, M: Pat Rooney — In Love's Bouquet/WM: Edwin S. Brill. *The Chocolate Soldier* (Lyric > Herald Square > Lyric > Casino, "Lieut. Bumerli," Sept. 13, 1909): The Chocolate Soldier; The Letter Song; Seek the Spy; Sympathy; The Tale of a Coat; That Would Be Lovely/W: Stanislaus Stange, M: Oscar Straus. *Madame Sherry* (New Amsterdam, "Edward Sherry, ex-Anatole," Aug. 30, 1910): The Birth of Passion; I Want to Play House with You; The Smile She Means for You; Theophilus/W: Otto Harbach, M: Karl Hoschna.

3436. Lynn Gardner *What's Up?* (National, "Margaret," Nov. 11, 1943): Joshua; My Last Love; Three Girls in a Boat; You Wash and I'll Dry; You've Got a Hold on Me/W: Alan Jay Lerner, M: Frederick Loewe.

3437. Rita Gardner *A Family Affair* (Billy Rose, "Sally Nathan," Jan. 27, 1962): Anything for You; Every Girl Wants to Get Married; There's a Room in My House/W: James Goldman, William Goldman, M: John Kander. *Pal Joey* (New York City Center, revival, "Linda English," May 29, 1963): I Could Write a Book; Take Him/W: Lorenz Hart, M: Richard Rodgers. *Ben Franklin in Paris* (Lunt-Fontanne, CR, "Janine Nicolet," Nov. 30, 1964): When I Dance with the Person I Love; You're in Paris/W: Sidney Michaels, M: Mark Sandrich, Jr. *1776* (46th Street, CR, "Abigail Adams," Oct. 19, 1971): Till Then; Yours, Yours, Yours/WM: Sherman Edwards.

3438. David Garfield (Feb. 6, 1941–1994) B: Brooklyn, NY. *Fiddler on the Roof* (Imperial, CR, "Motel," Mar. 1967): Miracle of Miracles/W: Sheldon Harnick, M: Jerry Bock. *The Rothschilds* (Lunt-Fontanne, "Solomon Rothschild," Oct. 19, 1970): Bonds; Everything; Rothschild & Sons/W: Sheldon Harnick, M: Jerry Bock.

3439. Terese Gargiulo *Cleavage* (Playhouse,

June 23, 1982): Lead 'Em Around by the Nose; Only Love; Reprise Me; Surprise Me/WM: Buddy Sheffield.

3440. Jacki Garland *The Happy Time* (Broadway, "Lizette," Jan. 18, 1968): Catch My Garter; The Life of the Party; Tomorrow Morning/W: Fred Ebb, M: John Kander.

3441. Judy Garland (June 10, 1922–June 22, 1969) B: Grand Rapids, MN. Mother of LIZA MINNELLI and LORNA LUFT. The inimitable Garland will never be forgotten, for her movie role as Dorothy in *The Wizard of Oz* (1939), and for all the subsequent movie musicals that made her a megastar. *Judy Garland at Home at the Palace* (Palace, revue, July 31, 1967): For Me and My Gal/W: Edgar Leslie, E. Ray Goetz, M: George W. Meyer — I Feel a Song Comin' On/W: Dorothy Fields, George S. Oppenheimer, M: Jimmy McHugh — I Loved Him, but He Didn't Love Me/WM: Cole Porter — Me and My Shadow/W: Billy Rose, M: Al Jolson, Dave Dreyer — Over the Rainbow/W: E.Y. Harburg, M: Harold Arlen — Rockabye Baby/WM: ? — That's Entertainment/W: Harold Dietz, M: Arthur Schwartz — Together/W: B.G. DeSylva, Lew Brown, M: Ray Henderson — The Trolley Song/WM: Hugh Martin, Ralph Blane — You Made Me Love You (I Didn't Want to Do It)/W: Joseph McCarthy, M: James V. Monaco.

3442. Patricia Garland *A Chorus Line* (Shubert, "Judy," Oct. 19, 1975): And.../W: Edward Kleban, M: Marvin Hamlisch.

3443. David Garlick *Oliver!* (Mark Hellinger, revival, "The Artful Dodger," Apr. 29, 1984): Consider Yourself; I'd Do Anything; It's a Fine Life/WM: Lionel Bart.

3444. Jay Garner *1776* (46th Street, CR, "Benjamin Franklin," July 12, 1971): But, Mr. Adams; The Egg; He Plays the Violin; The Lees of Old Virginia/WM: Sherman Edwards. *Goodtime Charley* (Palace, "Archbishop," Mar. 3, 1975): Confessional/W: Hal Hackady, M: Larry Grossman. *The Best Little Whorehouse in Texas* (46th Street, "Governor" and "Traveling Salesman" and "Scruggs," June 19, 1978/Aug.13, 1979): The Sidestep; Texas Has a Whorehouse in It; 20 Fans/WM: Carol Hall. *La Cage aux Folles* (Palace, "Edouard Dindon," Aug. 21, 1983): Cocktail Counterpoint/WM: Jerry Herman. *Me and My Girl* (Marquis, revival, CR, "Sir John Tremayne," Jan. 31, 1989): Love Makes the World Go Round/WM: Noel Gay. *Hello, Dolly!* (Lunt-Fontanne, revival, "Horace Vandergelder," Oct. 19, 1995): Before the Parade Passes By/WM: Lee Adams, Charles Strouse,

Jerry Herman — Hello, Dolly!; It Takes a Woman/WM: Jerry Herman — Motherhood/WM: Bob Merrill, Jerry Herman.

3445. Luvenia Garner *Porgy and Bess* (Radio City Music Hall, revival, "Clara," Apr. 7, 1983): Summertime/W: DuBose Heyward, M: George Gershwin.

3446. Ward Garner *Sleepy Hollow* (St. James, "Hendrick," June 3, 1948): You've Got That Kind of Face/W: Ruth Hughes Aarons, Miriam Battista, Russell Maloney, M: George Lessner.

3447. Chip Garnett (May 8, 1953–) B: New Kensington, PA. *Bubbling Brown Sugar* (ANTA, "Jim" and "Male Nightclub Singer," Mar. 2, 1976): It Don't Mean a Thing/W: Irving Mills, M: Duke Ellington — Love Will Find a Way/WM: Noble Sissle, Eubie Blake — Sophisticated Lady/W: Mitchell Parish, Irving Mills, M: Duke Ellington.

3448. Pauline Garon (Sept. 9, 1901–Aug. 30, 1965) B: Montreal, Quebec, Canada. *Buddies* (Selwyn, "Babette," Oct. 27, 1919): Italie/WM: B.C. Hilliam.

3449. Betty Garrett (May 23, 1919–) B: St. Joseph, MO. M: movie actor LARRY PARKS. On TV she played Irene Lorenzo, wife of VICTOR GARDENIA, on the sitcom *All in the Family* (1973); and landlady Mrs. Edna Babish De Fazio on *LaVerne and Shirley* (1976). Her movie career was disrupted by the MacCarthy hearings in the 1950s. *Of V We Sing* (Concert, revue, Feb. 11, 1942): Don't Sing Solo/W: Roslyn Harvey, M: George Kleinsinger — Juke Box/W: Alfred Hayes, M: Alex North — Queen Esther/W: Beatrice Goldsmith, M: George Kleinsinger — Sisters Under the Skin/W: Sylvia Marks, M: Baldwin Bergersen. *Let Freedom Sing* (Longacre, revue, Oct. 5, 1942): Be Calm; Give a Viva!; History Eight to the Bar; Johnny Is a Hoarder; Of the People Stomp/WM: Harold Rome. *Something for the Boys* (Alvin, "Mary-Frances," Jan. 7, 1943): I'm in Love with a Soldier Boy/WM: Cole Porter. *Jackpot* (Alvin, "Sgt. Maguire," Jan. 13, 1944): He's Good for Nothing but Me; (I'm in Love with) My Top Sergeant; Sugarfoot; There Are Yanks (from the Banks of the Wabash)/W: Howard Dietz, M: Vernon Duke. *Laffing Room Only* (Winter Garden, revue, Dec. 23, 1944): Go Down to Boston Harbor; The Steps of the Capitol; Stop That Dancing; Sunny California; This Is as Far as I Go/WM: Burton Lane. *Call Me Mister* (National > Plymouth, revue, Apr. 18, 1946): Military Life (The Jerk Song); South America, Take It Away; Surplus Blues (Little Surplus Me); Yuletide, Park Avenue/WM: Harold Rome. *Bells Are Ringing*

(Shubert, CR, "Ella Peterson," 2 weeks in 1958): Better Than a Dream; Drop That Name; Hello, Hello There!; I'm Goin' Back; Is It a Crime?; It's a Perfect Relationship; Just in Time; Long Before I Knew You; Mu-Cha-Cha; The Party's Over/ W: Betty Comden, Adolph Green, M: Jule Styne. *Beg, Borrow or Steal* (Martin Beck, "Clara," Feb. 10, 1960): Don't Stand Too Close to the Picture; I Can't Stop Talking; It's All in Your Mind; Let's Be Strangers Again; No One Knows Me; Presenting Clara Spencer; Think; You've Got Something to Say/W: Bud Freeman, M: Leon Prober. *Meet Me in St. Louis* (Gershwin, "Katie," Nov. 2, 1989): Ghosties and Ghoulies and Things That Go Bump in the Night; A Touch of the Irish/WM: Hugh Martin, Ralph Blane.

3450. Bob Garrett (Mar. 2, 1947–) B: New York, NY. *Grease* (Broadhurst, CR, "Teen Angel," c 1974): Beauty School Dropout; Born to Hand-Jive/WM: Jim Jacobs, Warren Casey.

3451. Harrison Garrett *My Best Girl* (Park, "Harry Perkins," Sept. 12, 1912): Love and the Automobile/W: Rennold Wolf, M: Augustus Barratt. *When Johnny Comes Marching Home* (New Amsterdam > Manhattan Opera House, revival, "Capt. Geoffry Martin," May 7, 1917): 'Twas Down in the Garden of Eden/W: Stanislaus Stange, M: Julian Edwards.

3452. Joy Garrett (Mar. 2, 1945–Feb. 11, 1993) Ft. Worth, TX. She appeared on the TV soap *Young and Restless* for 7 years. *Inner City* (Ethel Barrymore, revue, Dec. 19, 1971): The Brave Old City of New York; The Hooker; Summer Nights/W: Eve Merriam, M: Helen Miller.

3453. Kelly Garrett (Mar. 25, 1948–) B: Chester, PA. She was a vocalist on TV's *Your Hit Parade* (1974). *Mother Earth* (Belasco, revue, Oct. 19, 1972): Corn on the Macabre/WM: Ron Thronson, Roger Ailes, Ray Golden — Mother Earth; Sail On Sweet Universe; Talons of Time; Tiger! Tiger!; Too Many Old Ideas/W: Ron Thronson, M: Toni Shearer. *The Night That Made America Famous* (Ethel Barrymore, revue, Feb. 26, 1975): As I Grow Older; I'm a Wonderfully Wicked Woman; It's My Day; Maxie; Peace Teachers; Taxi; Too Much World/WM: Harry Chapin.

3454. Lloyd Garrett *George White's Scandals of 1920* (Globe, revue, June 7, 1920): Idle Dreams; On My Mind the Whole Night Long/W: Arthur Jackson, M: George Gershwin. *George White's Scandals of 1921* (Liberty, revue, July 11, 1921): Drifting Along with the Tide/W: Arthur Jackson, M: George Gershwin.

3455. Elsa Garrette *The Girl Who Smiles* (Lyric > Longacre, "Yvonne," Aug. 9, 1915): A Breath from Bohemia/WM: Edward A. Paulton, Adolf Philipp, Jean Briquet. *When Johnny Comes Marching Home* (New Amsterdam > Manhattan Opera House, revival, "Amelia Thropp," May 7, 1917): I Could Waltz On Forever/W: Stanislaus Stange, M: Julian Edwards.

3456. Beulah Garrick (June 12, 1921–) B: Nottingham, England. *Juno* (Winter Garden, "Miss Quinn," Mar. 9, 1959): You Poor Thing/ WM: Marc Blitzstein. *Funny Girl* (Winter Garden or Majestic, CR, "Mrs. Strakosh," c 1965): Find Yourself a Man; If a Girl Isn't Pretty/W: Bob Merrill, M: Jule Styne. *Copperfield* (ANTA, "Mrs. Heep," Apr. 13, 1981): 'Umble; Villainy Is the Matter/WM: Al Kasha, Joel Hirschhorn.

3457. Helena Collier Garrick (?–Dec. 9, 1954) *Hokey-Pokey; and Bunty, Bulls and Strings* (Broadway, "Clorinda McCann," Feb. 8, 1912): On the Stage/W: E. Ray Goetz, M: A. Baldwin Sloane, William T. Francis. *Roly Poly* (Weber and Fields, CR, "Bijou Fitzsimmons," Dec. 23, 1912): The Prima Donnas; The Zingaras/W: E. Ray Goetz, M: A. Baldwin Sloane.

3458. John Garrick (Aug. 31, 1902–1966) B: Brighton, England. He worked in a bank before starting in variety. He made movies in the U.S. and England from 1929, often playing the other man. *A Little Racketeer* (44th Street, "Dick Barrison," Jan. 18, 1932): Danger If I Love You; You and I Could Be Just Like That/W: Edward Eliscu, M: Henry Sullivan — Mr. Moon/W: Lupin Fein, Moe Jaffe, M: Lee Wainer — Starry Sky/W: Edward Eliscu, M: Dimitri Tiomkin. *Face the Music* (New Amsterdam, CR, "Pat Mason, Jr.," May 30, 1932): I Say It's Spinach; Let's Have Another Cup of Coffee; Manhattan Madness; On a Roof in Manhattan; Soft Lights and Sweet Music/WM: Irving Berlin.

3459. David Garrison (June 30, 1952–) B: Long Branch, NJ. On the TV sitcom *Married....with Children* (1987) he played Steve Rhodes. *A History of the American Film* (ANTA, revue, "Minstrel" and "David," Mar. 30, 1978): Isn't It Fun to Be in the Movies; Minstrel Song; Ostende Nobis Tosca/W: Christopher Durang, M: Mel Marvin. *A Day in Hollywood/A Night in the Ukraine* (John Golden, "Serge B. Samovar," May 1, 1980): Doin' the Production Code; Famous Feet; Natasha; A Night in the Ukraine; Samovar the Lawyer/W: Dick Vosburgh, M: Frank Lazarus — Japanese Sandman/W: Raymond B. Egan, M: Richard A. Whiting — Just Go to the Movies/WM: Jerry Herman.

3460. Marion Garson *Mother Goose* (New

Amsterdam, "Maud," Dec. 2, 1903): Pansy Faces/WM: William H. Penn. *The Rich Mr. Hoggenheimer* (Wallack's, "Amy Leigh," Oct. 22, 1906): Any Old Time at All/W: William Jerome, M: Jean Schwartz — Au Revoir My Little Hyacinth [Oct. 29, 1906]/W: A.E. Sidney Davis, M: Herman Darewski. *Ziegfeld Follies of 1909* (Jardin de Paris, New York roof, revue, CR, Sept. 6, 1909): I Wish I Was a Boy and I Wish I Was a Girl (I'm Glad I'm a Boy and I'm Glad I'm a Girl)/WM: Nora Bayes, Jack Norworth — Linger Longer Lingerie; Love in the Springtime/W: Harry B. Smith, M: Maurice Levi — Up! Up! Up! in My Aeroplane/W: Edward Madden, M: Gus Edwards.

3461. Edward (Eddie) Garvie (Oct. 30, 1866–Feb. 17, 1939) B: Meriden, CT. *Hodge, Podge & Co.* (Madison Square, "I. Hyde," Oct. 23, 1900): The Town Folks Will Be Pleased/W: Walter Ford, M: John W. Bratton. *The Maid and the Mummy* (New York, "Bolivar," July 25, 1904): I'm So Dizzy; Peculiar Julia/WM: Richard Carle — Sad Experiences/W: Richard Carle, M: Robert Hood Bowers. *The White Cat* (New Amsterdam, CR, "King Hardluck the 13th," Nov. 13, 1905): Graft/W: Harry B. Smith, M: Ludwig Englander. *The Princess Beggar* (Casino, "King Otto XXX of Vagaria," Jan. 7, 1907): All Hail the Queen!; I Don't Love You; It's All the Same to Me; A Sad, Sad World; Waiting for Me/W: Edward A. Paulton, M: Alfred G. Robyn. *The Belle of Brittany* (Daly's, "Poquelin," Nov. 8, 1909): The Old Chateau/W: Percy Greenbank, M: Howard Talbot. *A Skylark* (New York, "Casey," Apr. 4, 1910): I Just Can't Wait/W: William B. Harris, Jr., M: Frank Dossert. *The Fascinating Widow* (Liberty, "Lankton Wells," Sept. 11, 1911): Put Your Arms Around Me Honey/W: Sam M. Lewis, M: Kerry Mills. *When Dreams Come True* (Lyric > 44th Street, "Hercules Strong," Aug. 18, 1913): Come Along to the Movies; It's Great to Be a Wonderful Detective; Love Is Such a Funny Little Feeling; Minnie, Ha Ha/W: Philip Bartholomae, M: Silvio Hein. *Toot-Toot!* (George M. Cohan, "Mr. Wellington," Mar. 11, 1918): Quarrel and Part/W: Berton Braley, M: Jerome Kern. *Listen Lester* (Knickerbocker, "Col. Rufus Dodge," Dec. 23, 1918): Who Was the Last Girl (You Called by Her First Name)?/W: Harry L. Cort, George E. Stoddard, M: Harold Orlob.

3462. Harold Gary (May 7, 1906–Jan. 21, 1984) B: New York, NY. *Billion Dollar Baby* (Alvin, CR, "Dapper Welch," June 10, 1946): Speaking of Paris/W: Betty Comden, Adolph Green, M: Morton Gould. *Let It Ride!* (Eugene

O'Neill, "Harry," Oct. 12, 1961): Broads Ain't People; If Flutterby Wins/WM: Jay Livingston, Ray Evans.

3463. Ted Gary *Babes in Arms* (Shubert > Majestic, "Ted," Apr. 14, 1937): You Are So Fair/W: Lorenz Hart, M: Richard Rodgers. *Stars in Your Eyes* (Majestic, "Assistant Director," Feb. 9, 1939): Never a Dull Moment/W: Dorothy Fields, M: Arthur Schwartz.

3464. Willard Gary *Two for the Show* (Booth, revue, Feb. 8, 1940): That Terrible Tune/W: Nancy Hamilton, M: Morgan Lewis.

3465. Ronald Garza *Starlight Express* (Gershwin, "Rocky III," Mar. 15, 1987): Belle; Poppa's Blues; Right Place, Right Time/W: Richard Stilgoe, M: Andrew Lloyd Webber.

3466. Marie Gaspar *What's in a Name?* (Maxine Elliott, revue, Mar. 19, 1920): Rap Tap-a-Tap/W: John Murray Anderson, Jack Yellen, M: Milton Ager.

3467. Eddie Gasper *West Side Story* (Winter Garden, revival, "Snowboy," Apr. 27, 1960): Gee, Officer Krupke!/W: Stephen Sondheim, M: Leonard Bernstein. *Sweet Charity* (Palace, "Brother Eddie," Jan. 29, 1966): The Rhythm of Life/W: Dorothy Fields, M: Cy Coleman.

3468. William (Billy) Gaston *The Rose of Algeria* (Herald Square, "Bailey Sells," Sept. 20, 1909): The Foolish Gardener; The Great White Easiest Way/W: Glen MacDonough, M: Victor Herbert. *He Came from Milwaukee* (Casino, CR, "Bruce Chetwynde," Aug. 28, 1911): Merry Wedding Bells; There's an Aeroplane Air About You; When We Are Married to You and Me; The Zinga-Zulu Man/W: Edward Madden, M: Ben M. Jerome, Louis A. Hirsch.

3469. Earl Gates *Roly-Boly Eyes* (Knickerbocker, "Buddie Montrose," Sept. 25, 1919): A Bungalow for Two; I Want a Man; When Dancing's a Profession; When They Do the Dippy Doodlums/W: Edgar Allen Woolf, M: Eddy Brown, Louis Gruenberg.

3470. Ruth Gates (Oct. 28, 1888–May 23, 1966) B: Denton, TX. The actress of the stage, radio and TV was a niece of Edwin Booth and a protege of David Belasco. For many years before she died, she lived at the Royalton Hotel in NYC. *Show Boat* (New York City Center, revival, "Parthy Ann Hawks," Sept. 7, 1948): Why Do I Love You?/W: Oscar Hammerstein II, M: Jerome Kern.

3471. Marjorie Gateson (Jan. 17, 1897–Apr. 17, 1977) B: Brooklyn, NY. The distinguished character actress appeared in more than 100 movies. On TV she was Mother Barbour on *One Man's Family* (1949), originally a radio soap; then she played Grace Tyrell on *The Secret Storm* (1956). *Have a Heart* (Liberty, "Lizzie," Jan. 11, 1917): I'm So Busy/W: Schuyler Greene, P.G. Wodehouse, M: Jerome Kern — You Said Something/W: P.G. Wodehouse, M: Jerome Kern. *Her Soldier Boy* (Lyric > Shubert, CR, "Amy Lee," Apr. 30, 1917): Home Again/W: Augustus Barratt, M: Sigmund Romberg — Military Stamp/ WM: Clifton Crawford — Pack Up Your Troubles in Your Old Kit Bag (and Smile, Smile, Smile)/W: George Asaf, M: Felix Powell. *Fancy Free* (Astor, "Pinkie Pestlewaite," Apr. 11, 1918): Tinkle-Inkle-Inkle/WM: Augustus Barratt. *Little Simplicity* (Astor > 44th Street, "Lulu Clavelin," Nov. 4, 1918): Boom a Rang; Days of Youth; Maybe You'll Look Good to Me; National Air's Medley/W: Rida Johnson Young, M: Augustus Barratt. *Shubert Gaieties of 1919* (44th Street, revue, July 14, 1919): Cherry Blossom Lane; I've Made Up My Mind to Mind a Maid Made Up Like You/W: Alfred Bryan, M: Jean Schwartz — This Is the Day/W: Blanche Merrill, M: M.K. Jerome — What Are We Going to Do?/WM: ?. *Little Miss Charity* (Belmont, "Amy Shirley," Sept. 2, 1920): Dance Me Around; Poor Workingman; Revenge; That Certain Something; A Woman's Touch/W: Edward Clark, M: S.R. Henry, M. Savin. *The Rose Girl* (Ambassador, "Fleurette," Feb. 11, 1921): My Old New Jersey Home/W: Ballard Macdonald, M: Nat Vincent — Quarrel Number; The Rose Girl Blues; That's Me; When Our Sundays Are Blue; When That Somebody Comes/W: William Cary Duncan, M: Anselm Goetzl. *The Love Letter* (Globe, "Countess Irma," Oct. 4, 1921): Any Girl; Scandal Town/W: William Le Baron, M: Victor Jacobi — Man, Man, Man/W: P.G. Wodehouse, M: Emmerich Kalman. *For Goodness Sake* (Lyric, "Vivian Reynolds," Feb. 20, 1922): Hubby [Mar. 31, 1922]; When You're in Rome/W: Arthur Jackson, M: Paul Lannin, William Daly — Tra-La-La/W: Ira Gershwin, M: George Gershwin. *Lady Butterfly* (Globe, "Enid Crawford," Jan. 22, 1923): Don't Tell the Old Home Town [Feb. 26, 1923]; Kiss Time; Lady Butterfly; My Cottage in Sunshine Lane/ W: Clifford Grey, M: Werner Janssen. *Sweet Little Devil* (Astor > Central, "Joyce West," Jan. 21, 1924): The Matrimonial Handicap; Strike, Strike, Strike; System/W: B.G. DeSylva, M: George Gershwin. *Oh, Ernest!* (Royale, "Hon. Gwendolen Fairfax," May 9, 1927): Cupid's College; He Knows Where the Rose Is in Bloom; Never Trouble Trouble; Taken by Surprise/W: Francis De Witt, M: Robert Hood Bowers. *Show Boat* (New York City Center, revival, "Parthy

Ann Hawks," Apr. 8, 1954): Why Do I Love You?/W: Oscar Hammerstein II, M: Jerome Kern.

3472. Margaret Gathright *The Girls Against the Boys* (Alvin, revue, Nov. 2, 1959): Light Travelin' Man/W: Arnold B. Horwitt, M: Albert Hague.

3473. Larry Gatlin (May 2, 1948–) B: Seminole, TX. The singer and songwriter was lead singer in the country pop group called the Gatlin Brothers in the 1970s. *The Will Rogers Follies* (Palace, CR, "Will Rogers," Feb. 16, 1993): The Big Time; Favorite Son; Give a Man Enough Rope; Marry Me Now; Never Met a Man I Didn't Like; Presents for Mrs. Rogers; So Long Pa; Will-a-Mania/W: Betty Comden, Adolph Green, M: Cy Coleman.

3474. Hazel Gaudreau *I'll Say She Is* (Casino, "Hazel," May 19, 1924): Wall Street Blues/ W: Will B. Johnstone, M: Tom Johnstone.

3475. Warner Gault *The Broadway Whirl* (Times Square, revue, June 8, 1921): All Girls Are Like the Rainbow/W: Joseph McCarthy, B.G. DeSylva, M: Harry Tierney. *Footlights* (Lyric, revue, CR, "Billy Bamper," Sept. 19, 1927): The Ducks Call It Luck/WM: Harry Denny — I Adore You/WM: Ballard Macdonald, Sam Coslow, Rene Mercier — Sahara Moon/ WM: Harry Denny, Dave Ringle.

3476. Katherine Gauthier *The Grand Street Follies of 1929* (Booth, revue, "Columbine," May 1, 1929): I Need You So/W: David Goldberg, Howard Dietz, M: Arthur Schwartz.

3477. Dick Gautier (1939–) He played Hymie, the robot, on TV's *Get Smart* (1966). *Bye Bye Birdie* (Martin Beck, "Conrad Birdie," Apr. 14, 1960): Honestly Sincere; A Lot of Livin' to Do; One Last Kiss/W: Lee Adams, M: Charles Strouse.

3478. John Gavin (Apr. 8, 1932–) B: Los Angeles, CA. M: CONSTANCE TOWERS. He appeared in movies and on TV from 1957. From 1971 to 1973 he was President of the Screen Actors Guild; from 1981 to 1986 he was U.S. Ambassador to Mexico. *Seesaw* (Uris, CR, "Jerry Ryan," June 18, 1973): Chapter 54, Number 1909; In Tune; My City; Spanglish; We've Got It; You're a Lovable Lunatic/W: Dorothy Fields, M: Cy Coleman.

3479. Igors Gavon (Nov. 14, 1937–) B: Latvia. *Hello, Dolly!* (St. James, "Ambrose Kemper," Jan. 16, 1964): Come and Be My Butterfly; Put on Your Sunday Clothes/WM: Jerry Herman. *Billy* (Billy Rose, "Boyer," Mar. 22, 1969): The Fiddlers' Green/WM: Ron Dante, Gene Allen.

3480. William Gaxton (Dec. 2, 1889–Feb. 12, 1963) B: San Francisco, CA. M: MADELEINE CAMERON. The popular singer and comedian began in vaudeville at 15. *A Connecticut Yankee* (Vanderbilt, "Martin," Nov. 3, 1927): My Heart Stood Still; Thou Swell/W: Lorenz Hart, M: Richard Rodgers. *Fifty Million Frenchmen* (Lyric, "Peter Forbes," Nov. 27, 1929): Do You Want to See Paris?; You Do Something to Me; You Don't Know Paree/WM: Cole Porter. *Of Thee I Sing* (Music Box, "John P. Wintergreen," Dec. 26, 1931): A Kiss for Cinderella; Of Thee I Sing; Prosperity Is Just Around the Corner; Some Girls Can Bake a Pie; Who Cares?/W: Ira Gershwin, M: George Gershwin. *Let 'Em Eat Cake* (Imperial, "John P. Wintergreen," Oct. 21, 1933): Double Dummy Drill; The General's Gone to a Party; A Hell of a Hole; It Isn't What You Did (It's What You Didn't Do); Let 'Em Eat Cake; Mine; On and On and On; Who's the Greatest...?/W: Ira Gershwin, M: George Gershwin. *Anything Goes* (Alvin > 46th Street, "Billy Crocker," Nov. 21, 1934): All Through the Night; I Get a Kick Out of You; You're the Top/WM: Cole Porter. *White Horse Inn* (Center, "Leopold," Oct. 1, 1936): Goodbye, Au Revoir, Auf Wiedersehn/W: Irving Caesar, M: Eric Coates — I Cannot Live Without Your Love; Market Day in the Village/W: Irving Caesar, M: Ralph Benatzky. *Leave It to Me!* (Imperial, "Buckley Joyce Thomas," Nov. 9, 1938): Far Away; From Now On; We Drink to You, J.H. Brody; When All's Said and Done/WM: Cole Porter. *Louisiana Purchase* (Imperial, "Jim Taylor," May 28, 1940): Fools Fall in Love; Outside of That I Love You; Sex Marches On/WM: Irving Berlin. *Nellie Bly* (Adelphi, "Frank Jordan," Jan. 21, 1946): All Around the World; Harmony; Just My Luck; Sky High; Start Dancing; You May Not Love Me [Jan. 28, 1946]/W: Johnny Burke, M: James Van Heusen.

3481. Maisie Gay (Jan. 7, 1883–Sept. 13, 1945) B: London, England. *Sybil* (Liberty, "Margot," Jan. 10, 1916): At a Grand Hotel; A Cup of Tea; Following the Drum/W: Harry Graham, M: Victor Jacobi. *Pins and Needles* (Shubert, revue, Feb. 1, 1922): The Gypsy Warned Me/WM: ?.

3482. Gregory Gaye (1900–1993) Character actor in movies from 1936. *Through the Years* (Manhattan, "Capt. Moreau," Jan. 28, 1932): Drums in My Heart/W: Edward Heyman, M: Vincent Youmans.

3483. Echlin Gayer (1878–Feb. 14, 1926) B: England. *Fiddlers Three* (Cort, "Reginald Denby, Lord Duffer," Sept. 3, 1918): Don't You Think You'll Miss Me?; It Was All on Account of Nipper!; Just a Slip of the Tongue/W: William Cary Duncan, M: Alexander Johnstone.

3484. Diana Gaylen *I Married an Angel* (Shubert, "Arabella," May 11, 1938): Angel Without Wings/W: Lorenz Hart, M: Richard Rodgers.

3485. Bobby Gaylor *The Wizard of Oz* (Majestic, "Oz, the Wonderful Wizard," Jan. 20, 1903): Connemara Christening/W: Edgar Smith, M: A. Baldwin Sloane — On a Pay Night Evening/W: Paul West, M: Bruno Schilinski.

3486. George Gaynes (May 3, 1917–) B: Helsinki, Finland. M: ALLYN ANN MCLERIE. Formerly known as GEORGE JONGEYANS. His parents were of Dutch and Russian ancestry. When WWII broke out he escaped to England from Italy, where he was studying for an operatic career, and joined the Royal Dutch Navy. Among TV credits, the character actor played Arthur Feldman on *The Days and Nights of Molly Dodd* (1989). *Out of This World* (New Century, "Jupiter," Dec. 21, 1950): Hark to the Song of the Night; I Jupiter, I Rex/WM: Cole Porter. *Wonderful Town* (Winter Garden, "Robert Baker," Feb. 25, 1953): Conversation Piece (Nice Talk, Nice People); It's Love; A Quiet Girl; What a Waste/W: Betty Comden, Adolph Green, M: Leonard Bernstein. *The Beggar's Opera* (New York City Center, revival, "Mr. Lockit," Mar. 13, 1957): In the Days of My Youth; Is Then His Fate Decreed, Sir?; Through All the Employments of Life; 'Tis Woman That Seduces All Mankind/WM: John Gay. *Can-Can* (New York City Center, revival, "Judge Aristide Forestier," May 16, 1962): C'est Magnifique; I Am in Love; It's All Right with Me/WM: Cole Porter.

3487. Leslie Gaze *All for the Ladies* (Lyric, CR, "Hector Renaud," Apr. 5, 1913): I'd Like to Have a Little Girl Like You Like Me; The Sunday Dress Parade; Women, Women!/W: Henry Blossom, M: Alfred G. Robyn. *Iole* (Longacre, "Stuyvesant Briggs," Dec. 29, 1913): I Wonder Why/W: Robert W. Chambers, M: William F. Peters — If Dreams Come True; To Rent, to Let/WM: ? — None but the Brave Deserve the Fair/ W: Will M. Hough, Frank R. Adams, M: Joseph E. Howard.

3488. Luella Gear (Sept. 5, 1897–Apr. 3, 1980) B: New York, NY. *Love o' Mike* (Shubert > Maxine Elliott, "Luella," Jan. 15, 1917): Drift with Me/W: Harry B. Smith, M: Jerome Kern. *Elsie* (Vanderbilt, "Margery Hammond," Apr. 2, 1923): Baby Bunting; Everybody's Struttin' Now/WM: Noble Sissle, Eubie Blake. *Poppy*

(Apollo, "Mary Delafield," Sept. 3, 1923): Alibi Baby/W: Howard Dietz, M: Arthur Samuels — A Picnic Party with You/W: Dorothy Donnelly, M: John C. Egan — What Do You Do Sunday, Mary?/W: Irving Caesar, M: Stephen Jones. *Queen High* (Ambassador, "Florence Cole," Sept. 7, 1926): Beautiful Baby/W: B.G. DeSylva, M: James F. Hanley — Gentlemen Prefer Blondes; You'll Never Know/W: B.G. DeSylva, M: Lewis E. Gensler. *The Optimists* (Casino de Paris, revue, Jan. 30, 1928): (I Promise I'll Be) Practically True to You/W: Clifford Grey, M: Melville Gideon — We All Play the Grand Piano/WM: ?. *Ups-A-Daisy!* (Shubert, "Ethel Billings," Oct. 8, 1928): A Great Little Guy/W: Robert A. Simon, M: Lewis E. Gensler — Oh, How Happy We'll Be; Oh, How I Miss You Blues!/W: Robert A. Simon, Clifford Grey, M: Lewis E. Gensler. *Gay Divorce* (Ethel Barrymore > Shubert, "Hortense," Nov. 29, 1932): I Still Love the Red, White and Blue; Mister and Missus Fitch/WM: Cole Porter. *Life Begins at 8:40* (Winter Garden, revue, Aug. 27, 1934): C'est la Vie; I Couldn't Hold My Man; Life Begins at City Hall (Beautifying the City); My Paramount-Publix-Roxy Rose/W: Ira Gershwin, E.Y. Harburg, M: Harold Arlen. *On Your Toes* (Imperial > Majestic, "Peggy Porterfield," Apr. 11, 1936): The Heart Is Quicker Than the Eye; There's a Small Hotel; Too Good for the Average Man/W: Lorenz Hart, M: Richard Rodgers. *The Streets of Paris* (Broadhurst, revue, June 19, 1939): Doin' the Chamberlain/W: Al Dubin, M: Jimmy McHugh — The French Have a Word for It/WM: Harold Rome. *Crazy with the Heat* (44th Street, revue, Jan. 14, 1941): I'm a Bundle from Britain [added]/WM: Lois Long, Don Thorburn — Yacht Song/WM: Walter Nones. *Count Me In* (Ethel Barrymore, "Mama," Oct. 8, 1942): On Leave for Love/WM: Ann Ronell. *My Romance* (Shubert > Adelphi, "Octavia Fotheringham," Oct. 19, 1948): Little Emmaline/W: Rowland Leigh, M: Sigmund Romberg.

3489. Arthur Geary *My Lady's Glove* (Lyric, "Lieut. Jureau," June 18, 1917): Amorous Rose; Since Today Our Colonel's Mating/W: Edward A. Paulton, M: Oscar Straus — Do Buy Some Candy, Sir; Keep Repeating It; Look Before You Leap/W: Edward A. Paulton, M: Sigmund Romberg. *The Star Gazer* (Plymouth, "Lieut. Claydown," Nov. 26, 1917): My Heart Is Like a Bird in May/W: Matthew C. Woodward, M: Franz Lehar. *Everything* (Hippodrome, Aug. 22, 1918): Follow the Flag/W: R.H. Burnside, M: Raymond Hubbell — (Come to) The Land of Romance/W: John L. Golden, M: James Tate.

Happy Days (Hippodrome, revue, Aug. 23, 1919): Life's a Race; My Sing Song Girl; Somewhere There's Some Girl/W: R.H. Burnside, M: Raymond Hubbell. *Good Times* (Hippodrome, revue, Aug. 9, 1920): Colorland; The Land I Love; You Can't Beat the Luck of the Irish/W: R.H. Burnside, M: Raymond Hubbell. *Blossom Time* (Jolson, revival, "Baron Franz Schober," May 19, 1924): Let Me Awake; Love Is a Riddle; Only One Love Ever Fills the Heart; Serenade/W: Dorothy Donnelly, M: Sigmund Romberg. *Countess Maritza* (Shubert, "Lazlo," Sept. 18, 1926): Hola, Follow, Follow Me (Song of Greeting)/W: Harry B. Smith, M: Emmerich Kalman.

3490. Lottie Gee *Shuffle Along of 1921* (63rd Street Music Hall, "Jessie Williams," May 23, 1921): Everything Reminds Me of You; Gypsy Blues; I'm Just Wild About Harry; Love Will Find a Way/W: Noble Sissle, M: Eubie Blake.

3491. Will Geer (Mar. 9, 1902–Apr. 22, 1978) B: Frankfort, IN. He studied botany at the U. of Chicago, and wrote a book about the plants mentioned in Shakespeare's plays. He won an Emmy for his role as Grandpa on *The Waltons* (1972). *The Cradle Will Rock* (Windsor > Mercury, "Mr. Mister," Jan. 3, 1938): Freedom of the Press; Honolulu/WM: Marc Blitzstein. *The Cradle Will Rock* (Mansfield > Broadway, revival, "Mr. Mister," Dec. 26, 1947): Ex-Foreman; Freedom of the Press; Honolulu; Lovely Morning; Polyphonic/WM: Marc Blitzstein. *The Vamp* (Winter Garden, "Uncle Garvey," Nov. 10, 1955): Keep Your Nose to the Grindstone/W: John Latouche, M: James Mundy. *110 in the Shade* (Broadhurst, "H.C. Curry," Oct. 24, 1963): Lizzie's Coming Home; Poker Polka; Raunchy/W: Tom Jones, M: Harvey Schmidt.

3492. Georgyn Geetlein *Two Gentlemen of Verona* (St. James, "Vissi D'Amore," Dec. 1, 1971): Love, Is That You?/W: John Guare, M: Galt MacDermot.

3493. Deborah Geffner (Aug. 26, 1952–) B: Pittsburgh, PA. *A Chorus Line* (Shubert, CR, "Kristine," Oct. 1976/Jan. 1979): Sing!/W: Edward Kleban, M: Marvin Hamlisch.

3494. Jody Gelb (Mar. 11–) B: Cincinnati, OH. *The Who's Tommy* (St. James, "Minister's Wife," Apr. 22, 1993): Christmas/WM: Pete Townshend.

3495. Steven Gelfer (Feb. 21, 1949–) B: Brooklyn, NY. *Cats* (Winter Garden, CR, "Mungojerrie"): Mungojerrie and Rumpleteazer/W: T.S. Eliot, M: Andrew Lloyd Webber.

3496. Becky Gelke (Feb. 17, 1953–) B: Ft. Knox, KY. *The Best Little Whorehouse in Texas*

(46th Street, "Ruby Rae," June 19, 1978): Hard-Candy Christmas/WM: Carol Hall. *The Best Little Whorehouse in Texas* (46th Street, CR, "Ginger," c 1980): same as above. *The Best Little Whorehouse in Texas* (46th Street > Eugene O'Neill, CR, "Doatsey Mae," Nov. 24, 1980): Doatsey Mae; Texas Has a Whorehouse in It/WM: Carol Hall.

3497. Rhoda Gemignani (Oct. 21, 1940–) B: San Francisco, CA. *Cabaret* (Broadhurst, CR, "Fraulein Kost," c 1968): Tomorrow Belongs to Me/W: Fred Ebb, M: John Kander.

3498. Adeline Genee (Jan. 6, 1875–Apr. 23, 1970) B: Aarhus, Denmark. A ballerina, she appeared at the Palace in 1914. *The Silver Star* (New Amsterdam, "Adeline Genee," Nov. 1, 1909): The Silver Star/W: Harry B. Smith, M: Albert Gumble. *The Bachelor Belles* (Globe, "Adeline Genee," Nov. 7, 1910): Roses and Butterflies; Song of the Fashions/W: Harry B. Smith, M: Raymond Hubbell.

3499. Edmond Genest (Oct. 27, 1943–) B: Boston, MA. *Onward Victoria* (Martin Beck, "Theodore Tilton," Dec. 14, 1980): The Age of Brass; Curiosity; Read It in the Weekly; A Taste of Forever/W: Charlotte Anker, Irene Rosenberg, M: Keith Herrmann.

3500. Genevieve She was a frequent and charming visitor to the *Jack Paar Show* (1958). *Can-Can* (New York City Center, revival, "La Mome Pistache," May 16, 1962): Allez-Vous-En (Go Away); Can-Can; C'est Magnifique; I Love Paris; Live and Let Live; Never Give Anything Away/WM: Cole Porter.

3501. Livia Genise (Oct. 15, 1949–) B: Brooklyn, NY. *Grease* (Broadhurst, CR, "Betty Rizzo"): Freddy, My Love; Look at Me, I'm Sandra Dee; There Are Worse Things I Could Do/WM: Jim Jacobs, Warren Casey.

3502. Peter Gennaro (?–Sept. 28, 2000) B: New Orleans, LA. Dancer and choreographer with many TV variety show credits in the 1950s. *The Pajama Game* (St. James, "Worker," May 13, 1954): Steam Heat/WM: Richard Adler, Jerry Ross. *Bells Are Ringing* (Shubert, "Carl," Nov. 29, 1956): Mu-Cha-Cha/W: Betty Comden, Adolph Green, M: Jule Styne.

3503. Alice Gentle (1885 –Feb. 28, 1958) B: Chatsworth, IL. Mother of GEORGE MAC-FARLANE. The soprano sang with opera companies in the U.S. and Europe. *All for the Ladies* (Lyric, "Georgette Clemente," Dec. 30, 1912): (I Live But) In Dreams Alone; The Sunday Dress Parade/W: Henry Blossom, M: Alfred G. Robyn.

3504. Norma Gentner *The Firebrand of Flo-*

rence (Alvin, "Columbina," Mar. 22, 1948): Come to Florence (Civic Song); Dizzily, Busily/W: Ira Gershwin, M: Kurt Weill.

3505. Minnie Gentry (c 1916–May 6, 1993) B: Virginia. *Ain't Supposed to Die a Natural Death* (Ethel Barrymore, Oct. 20, 1971): Put a Curse on You/WM: Melvin Van Peebles.

3506. Stephen Geoffreys (Nov. 22, 1964–) B: Cincinnati, OH. *The Human Comedy* (Royale, "Homer Macauley," Apr. 5, 1984): Cocoanut Cream Pie; Dear Brother; Everything Is Changed; Happy Anniversary; Happy Birthday; I Can Carry a Tune; Mr. Grogan, Wake Up; Noses; We're a Little Family; What Am I Supposed to Do?; When I Am Lost; You're a Little Young for the Job/W: William Dumaresq, M: Galt MacDermot.

3507. Betty George *Heaven on Earth* (New Century, "Officer Blandings," Sept. 16, 1948): In the Back of a Hack/W: Barry Trivers, M: Jay Gorney.

3508. Martha George *The Gay Musician* (Wallack's, "Matilda Yager," May 18, 1908): At Last I Hold You; I Want to Be Your Baby Boy; That Melody/W: Charles J. Campbell, M: Julian Edwards.

3509. Yvonne Georges *The Greenwich Village Follies of 1922* (Shubert, revue, Sept. 12, 1922): Parisian Nights/W: Irving Caesar, John Murray Anderson, M: Louis A. Hirsch.

3510. Florence Gerald (?–1942) *Nearly a Hero* (Casino, CR, "Mrs. Doolittle," Mar. 9, 1908): Bridge/WM: ?.

3511. May Gerald *Happy Days* (Hippodrome, revue, Aug. 23, 1919): Don't You Remember Those School Days?/W: R.H. Burnside, M: Raymond Hubbell.

3512. Danny Gerard (May 29, 1977–) B: New York, NY. He played Alan Silver, age 14, on the TV comedy-drama *Brooklyn Bridge* (1991). *Into the Light* (Neil Simon, "Mathew Prescott," Oct. 22, 1986): Be There; Trading Solos; Wishes/W: John Forster, M: Lee Holdridge. *Les Miserables* (Broadway, CR, "Gavroche," c 1987): Look Down/W: Herbert Kretzmer, M: Claude-Michel Schonberg.

3513. Dixie Gerard *The Big Show* (Hippodrome, revue, Aug. 31, 1916): We'll Stand By Our Country/W: R.H. Burnside, John L. Golden, M: Raymond Hubbell.

3514. Will Gerard *Marilyn* (Minskoff, "Arthur Miller," Nov. 20, 1983): In Disguise/WM: Doug Frank.

3515. Bill Gerber *Promises, Promises* (Shubert, CR, "Chuck Baxter," Nov. 8, 1971): A Fact Can Be a Beautiful Thing; Half as Big as Life;

I'll Never Fall in Love Again; It's Our Little Secret; Promises, Promises; She Likes Basketball; Upstairs; You'll Think of Someone; A Young Pretty Girl Like You/W: Hal David, M: Burt Bacharach.

3516. Billie Gerber *Murray Anderson's Almanac* (Erlanger's, revue, Aug. 14, 1929): I Can't Remember the Words/W: Jack Yellen, M: Milton Ager, Henry Cabot Lodge — Same Old Moon/W: Clifford Orr, John Murray Anderson, M: Henry Sullivan.

3517. Jonathan S. Gerber *The News* (Helen Hayes, "Feature Editor," Nov. 7, 1985): The Contest/WM: Paul Schierhorn.

3518. Elizabeth Gergely *Her Soldier Boy* (Astor > Lyric > Shubert, "Elsje," Dec. 6, 1916): Amsterdam/WM: Augustus Barratt. *The Student Prince* (Majestic, revival, "Kathie," Jan. 29, 1931): Come Boys, Let's All Be Gay, Boys (Students' March Song); Deep in My Heart, Dear; Student Life; To the Inn We're Marching/W: Dorothy Donnelly, M: Sigmund Romberg.

3519. Alfred Gerrard *The Velvet Lady* (New Amsterdam, "Ned Pembroke," Feb. 3, 1919): Fair Honeymoon; I've Danced to Beat the Band; Little Boy and Girl; Throwing the Bull/W: Henry Blossom, M: Victor Herbert. *Mary* (Knickerbocker, "Tommy Boyd," Oct. 18, 1920): Anything You Want to Do, Dear; Don't Fall Until You've Seen Them All; Money, Money, Money; That Might Have Satisfied Grandma; Tom, Tom, Toddle; We'll Have a Wonderful Party; When a Woman Exits Laughing/W: Otto Harbach, M: Louis A. Hirsch. *Sally, Irene and Mary* (Casino, "Clarence Edwards," Sept. 4, 1922): Opportunity; Stage Door Johnnies; Wedding Time/W: Raymond Klages, M: J. Fred Coots. *Betty Lee* (44th Street, "Berkley Fresno," Dec. 25, 1924): Athletic Boy; Give Him Your Sympathy/W: Otto Harbach, Irving Caesar, M: Louis A. Hirsch, Con Conrad — I'm Going to Dance at Your Wedding/W: Irving Caesar, M: Con Conrad.

3520. Theodora Gerrard *Havana* (Casino, CR, "Pepita," Apr. 19, 1909): The Yacht/W: Adrian Ross, M: Leslie Stuart.

3521. Frances (Frankie) Gershwin (Dec. 26, 1906–Jan. 18, 1999) B: New York, NY. Singing and dancing sister of George and Ira Gershwin. *Merry-Go-Round* (Klaw, revue, CR, July 18, 1927): Cider Ella/W: ?, M: Gene Salzer. *Americana of 1928* (Lew Fields, revue, Oct. 30, 1928): Hot Pants/W: Irving Caesar, M: Roger Wolfe Kahn — Life as a Twosome/W: Irving Caesar, M: Roger Wolfe Kahn, Joseph Meyer.

3522. John Gerstad (Sept. 3, 1924–Dec. 1,

1981) B: Boston, MA. Actor, director, producer, playwright. *Come Summer* (Lunt-Fontanne, "Labe Pratt," Mar. 18, 1969): Moonglade/W: Will Holt, M: David Baker.

3523. Mara Getz *Mail* (Music Box, "Dana," Apr. 14, 1988): Crazy World; Hit the Ground Running; It's Getting Harder to Love You; One Lost Weekend; Pages of My Diary; Where Am I?; Where Are You?/W: Jerry Colker, M: Michael Rupert.

3524. Stuart Getz *Mame* (Winter Garden, CR, "Patrick Dennis, age 10," May 8, 1967): The Fox Hunt; Mame; My Best Girl; St. Bridget; We Need a Little Christmas/WM: Jerry Herman.

3525. Tamara Geva (Mar. 17, 1906–Dec. 9, 1997) B: St. Petersburg, Russia. M: George Balanchine, dancer and choreographer. She was trained as a ballet dancer in Russia. *Three's a Crowd* (Selwyn, revue, Oct. 15, 1930): Talkative Toes/W: Howard Dietz, M: Vernon Duke. *Flying Colors* (Imperial, revue, Sept. 15, 1932): All's Well; Louisiana Hayride; Riding Habit; Two-Faced Woman [added]/W: Howard Dietz, M: Arthur Schwartz. *Right This Way* (46th Street, "Mimi Chester," Jan. 4, 1938): Don't Listen to Your Heart; Right This Way/W: Marianne Brown Waters, M: Bradford Greene — I Can Dream, Can't I?; I Love the Way We Fell in Love; I'll Be Seeing You/W: Irving Kahal, M: Sammy Fain.

3526. Steve Geyer *Grease* (New York City Center, return engagement, "Kenickie," Nov. 29, 1996): Greased Lightnin'; Rock 'n' Roll Party Queen/WM: Jim Jacobs, Warren Casey. *Grease* (Eugene O'Neill, revival, CR, "Kenickie," c 1996): same as above.

3527. Kurnar Ghoshal *Golden Dawn* (Hammerstein's, "Hasmali," Nov. 30, 1927): Mulunghu Thabu/W: Oscar Hammerstein II, M: Emmerich Kalman, Herbert Stothart.

3528. Alice Ghostley (Aug. 14, 1926–) B: Eve, MO. On TV she played Bernice Clifton on the sitcom *Designing Women* (1987) and Irma Wallingsford on *Evening Shade* (1992). *New Faces of 1952* (Royale, revue, May 16, 1952): Boston Beguine/WM: Sheldon Harnick — Take Off the Mask/WM: Alice Ghostley, Ronny Graham. *Shangri-La* (Winter Garden, "Miss Brinklow," June 13, 1956): I'm Just a Little Bit Confused; What Every Old Girl Should Know/W: Jerome Lawrence, Robert E. Lee, M: Harry Warren. *Annie* (Alvin, CR, "Miss Hannigan," Aug. 15, 1978/Jan. 29, 1980/Oct. 8, 1980): Easy Street; Little Girls/W: Martin Charnin, M: Charles Strouse.

3529. Andy Gibb (Mar. 5, 1958–Mar. 10,

1988) B: Manchester, England. Younger brother singer- songwriter of rock group The Bee Gees, with successful career of his own. *Joseph and the Amazing Technicolor Dreamcoat* (Royale, revival, CR, "Joseph," Dec. 1, 1982): Any Dream Will Do; The Brothers Came to Egypt; Close Ev'ry Door to Me; A Coat of Many Colors; Go, Go, Go, Joseph; Grovel, Grovel; Jacob and Sons; Jacob in Egypt; Joseph All the Time; Joseph's Dreams; Pharaoh's Dream Explained; Potiphar; Stone the Crows; Who's the Thief?/W: Tim Rice, M: Andrew Lloyd Webber.

3530. Nancy Gibbs (?–Oct. 31, 1955) B: Wales. *The Whirl of New York* (Winter Garden, "Violet Gray," June 13, 1921): Follow On; I Do, So There!; The Purity Brigade/W: Hugh Morton, M: Gustav Kerker — Gee, I Wish I Had a Girl Like You/W: Cliff Friend, M: Lew Pollack, Al Goodman — I Know That I'm in Love/W: Sidney D. Mitchell, M: Lew Pollack, Al Goodman. *Artists and Models of 1923* (Shubert > Winter Garden, revue, CR, Sept. 3, 1923): Flower of the Woodland/W: Cyrus D. Wood, Harold Atteridge, M: Jean Schwartz — Somehow/W: Cyrus D. Wood, M: Jean Schwartz. *Artists and Models of 1924* (Astor > Casino, revue, Oct. 15, 1924): Always the Same/W: ?, M: Sigmund Romberg — Behind Milady's Fan; My Lily Maid/WM: ? — Good Night/WM: Leo Wood, Irving Bibo, Con Conrad. *Nic-Nax of 1926* (Cort, revue, Aug. 2, 1926): For a Girl (Boy) Like You/W: Joe Goodwin, M: Gitz Rice — I Have Forgotten You Almost/W: Anna Fitziu, M: Gitz Rice — In Old Rangoon/WM: Gitz Rice — Without the One You Love/WM: Gitz Rice, Werner Janssen.

3531. Sheila Gibbs (Feb. 16, 1947–) B: New York, NY. *Two Gentlemen of Verona* (St. James, "Milkmaid," Dec. 1, 1971): Milkmaid/W: John Guare, M: Galt MacDermot. *Runaways* (Plymouth, "Mocha," May 13, 1978): We Are Not Strangers/WM: Elizabeth Swados. *Once on This Island* (Booth, "Mama Euralie," Oct. 18, 1990): One Small Girl; A Part of Us; Pray; Ti Moune/W: Lynn Ahrens, M: Stephen Flaherty.

3532. David Warren Gibson *Sweet Charity* (Minskoff, revival, "Dark Glasses," Apr. 27, 1986): You Should See Yourself/W: Dorothy Fields, M: Cy Coleman.

3533. Debbie Gibson (Apr. 31, 1970–) B: Merrick, NY. Young singer and songwriter with hit rock album "Out of the Blue" (1988). *Les Miserables* (Broadway, CR, "Eponine," Jan. 7, 1992/Mar. 29, 1992): A Heart Full of Love; In My Life; A Little Fall of Rain; On My Own/W: Herbert Kretzmer, M: Claude-Michel Schonberg.

3534. Judy Gibson (Sept. 11, 1947–) B: Trenton, NJ. *Rockabye Hamlet* (Minskoff, "Playeress" and "Honeybelle Huckster," Feb. 17, 1976): He Got It in the Ear; Something's Rotten in Denmark; The Wart Song/WM: Cliff Jones.

3535. Madeline Gibson (1909– ?) B: London, England. *This Year of Grace* (Selwyn, revue, Nov. 7, 1928): Little Women; Mary Make Believe; A Room with a View; Teach Me to Dance Like Grandma/WM: Noel Coward.

3536. Scott Gibson *Porgy and Bess* (New York City Center, revival, "Jim," May 17, 1961): It Takes a Long Pull to Get There; A Woman Is a Sometime Thing/W: DuBose Heyward, M: George Gershwin.

3537. Virginia Gibson (Apr. 9, 1926–) B: St. Louis, MO. On TV she appeared in comic sketches on *The Johnny Carson Show* (1955) and as a vocalist on *Your Hit Parade* (1957). *Happy Hunting* (Majestic, "Beth Livingstone," Dec. 6, 1956): Don't Tell Me; If'n; Mutual Admiration Society; A New-Fangled Tango/W: Matt Dubey, M: Harold Karr.

3538. William L. Gibson *A World of Pleasure* (Winter Garden, revue, Oct. 14, 1915): Fifth Avenue/W: Harold Atteridge, M: Sigmund Romberg.

3539. Frances Gibsone *Piff! Paff!! Pouf!!!* (Casino, CR, "Rose Melon," May 16, 1904): Goodnight, My Own True Love/W: William Jerome, Stanislaus Stange, M: Jean Schwartz — Love, Love, Love; We Really Ought to Be Married/W: William Jerome, M: Jean Schwartz — My Unkissed Man/W: Stanislaus Stange, M: Jean Schwartz.

3540. Melville Gideon (May 21, 1884–Nov. 11, 1933) B: New York, NY. Performer, producer and composer. *The Optimists* (Casino de Paris, revue, Jan. 30, 1928): Amapu/W: Edward Knoblock, M: Melville Gideon — Little Lacquer Lady/W: Clifford Seyler, M: Melville Gideon.

3541. Elvira Giersdorf With IRENE and RAE they were known as The Giersdorf Sisters. In 1936 they sang on the radio program *Johnny Presents,* sponsored by Philip Morris Cigarettes. *Hello, Daddy* (Mansfield > George M. Cohan > Erlanger's, "Gertrude," Dec. 26, 1928): As Long as We're in Love/W: Dorothy Fields, M: Jimmy McHugh.

3542. Irene Giersdorf *Hello, Daddy* (Mansfield > George M. Cohan > Erlanger's, "Helene," Dec. 26, 1928): same as ELVIRA GIERSDORF.

3543. Rae Giersdorf *A la Carte* (Martin Beck, revue, Aug. 17, 1927): Give Trouble the Air/W: Leo Robin, M: Louis Alter. *Hello, Daddy*

(Mansfield > George M. Cohan > Erlanger's, "Marguerite," Dec. 26, 1928): As Long as We're in Love/W: Dorothy Fields, M: Jimmy McHugh.

3544. Gordon Gifford *My Dear Public* (46th Street, revue, "Gordon," Sept. 9, 1943): My Dear Public/WM: ?— Pipes of Pan Americana/W: Irving Caesar, M: Gerald Marks.

3545. Julia Gifford *When Johnny Comes Marching Home* (New York, "Robert Pemberton," Dec. 16, 1902): The Suwanee River/W: Stanislaus Stange, M: Julian Edwards. *When Johnny Comes Marching Home* (New Amsterdam > Manhattan Opera House, revival, "Robert Pemberton, May 7, 1917): same as above.

3546. Elaine Giftos (Jan. 24, 1945–) B: Pittsfield, MA. *New Faces of 1968* (Booth, revue, May 2, 1968): Something Big/W: David Axelrod, M: Sam Pottle.

3547. Melinda Gilb *Singin' in the Rain* (Gershwin, "Singer," July 2, 1985): Temptation/W: Arthur Freed, M: Nacio Herb Brown.

3548. Alan Gilbert (Nov. 14–) B: Schenectady, NY. A writer and TV producer, he started out in vaudeville and as an emcee on radio. *Bloomer Girl* (Shubert, "Male Soloist," Oct. 5, 1944): Man for Sale/W: E.Y. Harburg, M: Harold Arlen. *South Pacific* (Majestic > Broadway, "Yeoman Herbert Quale," Apr. 7, 1949): There Is Nothin' Like a Dame/W: Oscar Hammerstein II, M: Richard Rodgers. *The Most Happy Fella* (Imperial > Broadway, "Clem," May 3, 1956): Standing on the Corner/WM: Frank Loesser.

3549. Bert Gilbert *The Maids of Athens* (New Amsterdam, Mar. 18, 1914): The Clever Detective/W: Carolyn Wells, M: Charles J. Anditzer. *Sari* (New Amsterdam, CR, "Cadeaux," May 11, 1914): Paris? (Oh My! Yes Dear)/W: Catherine Chisholm Cushing, E.P. Heath, M: Emmerich Kalman. *China Rose* (Martin Beck, CR, "Hi," Mar. 16, 1925): I'm Hi, I'm Lo; I'm No Butterfly/W: Harry Cort, George E. Stoddard, M: A. Baldwin Sloane.

3550. Billy Gilbert (Sept. 12, 1893–Sept. 23, 1971) B: Louisville, KY. The comic actor was also a producer and director. He appeared in more than 100 movies from 1929. In 1937 he created the character of Sneezy in Walt Disney's *Snow White and the Seven Dwarfs*. *The Chocolate Soldier* (Century, revival, "Col. Kasimir Popoff," Mar. 12, 1947): Just a Connoisseur; The Tale of a Coat; Thank the Lord the War Is Over/W: Stanislaus Stange, M: Oscar Straus. *Buttrio Square* (New Century, "Pappa Mario," Oct. 14, 1952): I'm Gonna Be a Pop/W: Gen Genovese,

M: Fred Stamer. *Fanny* (Majestic, CR, "Panisse," c 1955): Cold Cream Jar Song; Never Too Late for Love; Panisse and Son; To My Wife; Welcome Home/WM: Harold Rome.

3551. Elsie Gilbert *Just a Minute* (Century, CR, "Helen," Dec. 10, 1928): Heigh-Ho Cheerio; You'll Kill 'Em/W: Walter O'Keefe, M: Harry Archer.

3552. Jody Gilbert (Mar. 18, 1916–1979) B: Ft. Worth, TX. She played Rosa on the radio sitcom *Life with Luigi* (1948). *If the Shoe Fits* (Century, "Mistress Spratt," Dec. 5, 1946): I Wish/W: June Carroll, M: David Raksin.

3553. John Charles Gilbert *The Count of Luxembourg* (Jolson's, revival, "Anatole Brissard," Feb. 17, 1930): Bohemia/W: Basil Hood, M: Franz Lehar — A Carnival for Life; In Society/W: Adrian Ross, M: Franz Lehar. *Blossom Time* (Ambassador, revival, "Franz Schubert," Mar. 23, 1931): Lonely Heart; Moment Musicale; My Springtime Thou Art; Serenade; Song of Love; Tell Me, Daisy/W: Dorothy Donnelly, M: Sigmund Romberg.

3554. Mrs. G.H. Gilbert (1821–Nov. or Dec. 1904) B: England. Her birth name was Anne Hartley. An actress and dancer, she lived in the U.S. with her actor and dancer husband, whom she married in 1846. Her specialty was elderly comic ladies. *Cinderella at School* (Daly's, "Zenobia Tropics," Mar. 5, 1881): A Cotton Cloth Ghost/WM::Woolson Morse.

3555. Myrtle Gilbert *Hanky-Panky* (Broadway, "Dopie Wriggle," Aug. 5, 1912): The Lyre Bird and the Jay; Tennis; Where the Edelweiss Is Blooming/W: E. Ray Goetz, M: A. Baldwin Sloane. *The Pleasure Seekers* (Winter Garden, revue, "Marcelline," Nov. 3, 1913): I've Got a Little Chalet in the Valley/WM: E. Ray Goetz, Bert Grant — There's a Lot of Pretty Little Things in Paris/WM: E. Ray Goetz.

3556. Newton R. Gilchrist *State Fair* (Music Box, "Hank Munson," Mar. 27, 1996): More Than Just a Friend/WM: Richard Rodgers.

3557. Rebecca Gilchrist (June 10, 1948–) B: Parkersburg, WV. *Grease* (Broadhurst, CR, "Jan," c 1974): Freddy, My Love; Mooning/WM: Jim Jacobs, Warren Casey.

3558. Harry Gilfoil *The Liberty Belles* (Madison Square, "Uncle Jasper Pennyfeather," Sept. 30, 1901): Oh, What a Lovely Dream!/W: Andrew B. Sterling, George Totten Smith, Edward P. Moran, M: Harry Von Tilzer. *The Pearl and the Pumpkin* (Broadway, CR, "McGinty, the Ancient Mariner," Oct. 2, 1905): Fol-de-iddley-ido; It Is the English; My Combination Girl; Sitting on the Starboard Tack; We'll

Hang Together/W: Paul West, M: John W. Bratton. *The Yankee Girl* (Herald Square, "Willie Wiggs," Feb. 10, 1910): Where's Mama?/W: George V. Hobart, M: Silvio Hein. *The Wall Street Girl* (Cohan, "James Green," Apr. 15, 1912): I Can Drink/WM: Benjamin Hapgood Burt.

3559. Jack Gilford (July 25, 1907–June 4, 1990) B: Brooklyn, NY. Comic character actor in films and TV whose career was interrupted for a decade in 1956 by Sen. Joseph McCarthy's hearings. *Alive and Kicking* (Winter Garden, revue, Jan. 17, 1950): What a Delightful Day/W: Ray Golden, Paul Francis Webster, M: Sammy Fain. *Once Upon a Mattress* (Alvin > Winter Garden > Cort > St. James, "The King," Nov. 25, 1959): Man to Man Talk; The Minstrel, the Jester and I; Normandy/W: Marshall Barer, M: Mary Rodgers. *A Funny Thing Happened on the Way to the Forum* (Alvin, "Hysterium," May 8, 1962): Everybody Ought to Have a Maid; I'm Calm; Lovely/WM: Stephen Sondheim. *Cabaret* (Broadhurst, "Herr Schultz," Nov. 20, 1966): It Couldn't Please Me More; Married; Meeskite/W: Fred Ebb, M: John Kander. *No, No, Nanette* (46th Street, revival, "Jimmy Smith," Jan. 19, 1971): I Want to Be Happy/W: Irving Caesar, M: Vincent Youmans.

3560. Frank Gill, Jr. (Dec. 17, 1907–July 11, 1970) B: Illinois. The comic appeared on Joe E. Brown's radio show (1938). In later years, he became a writer for the screen and TV. *Just Fancy* (Casino, "Juan Hernandez," Oct. 11, 1927): Mi Chiquita/W: Leo Robin, M: Joseph Meyer, Phil Charig.

3561. Ray Gill (Aug. 1, 1950–Sept. 27, 1992) B: Bayonne, NJ. *The First* (Martin Beck, "Clyde Sukeforth," Nov. 17, 1981): Is This Year Next Year?; It Ain't Gonna Work!/W: Martin Charnin, M: Bob Brush.

3562. Meg Gillentine *Cats* (Winter Garden, CR, "Cassandra," c 1996): The Old Gumbie Cat/W: T.S. Eliot, M: Andrew Lloyd Webber.

3563. Anita Gillette (Aug. 16, 1936–) B: Baltimore, MD. On TV she played Dr. Emily Hanover on the police drama *Quincy, M.E.* (1982). *Carnival!* (Imperial, CR, "Lili," 10 days during run): Beautiful Candy; I Hate Him; Magic, Magic; Mira (Can You Imagine That?); The Rich (Puppet Song); A Very Nice Man; Yes, My Heart; Yum Ticky-Ticky Tum Tum (Puppet Song)/WM: Bob Merrill. *All American* (Winter Garden, "Susan," Mar. 19, 1962): I Couldn't Have Done It Alone; I've Just Seen Him; Nightlife/W: Lee Adams, M: Charles Strouse. *Mr. President* (St. James, "Leslie Henderson," Oct. 20, 1962): Empty Pockets Filled with Love; I'm Gonna Get Him; Is He the Only Man in the World?; Laugh It Up; Pigtails and Freckles; The Secret Service; The Washington Twist/WM: Irving Berlin. *Kelly* (Broadhurst, "Angela Crane," Feb. 6, 1965): Ballad to a Brute; A Moment Ago; (I'll) Never Go There Anymore/W: Eddie Lawrence, M: Moose Charlap. *Guys and Dolls* (New York City Center, revival, "Sarah Brown," Apr. 28, 1965): Follow the Fold; If I Were a Bell; I'll Know; I've Never Been in Love Before; Marry the Man Today/WM: Frank Loesser. *Cabaret* (Broadway, CR, "Sally Bowles," Nov. 4, 1968): Cabaret; Don't Tell Mama; Perfectly Marvelous; Why Should I Wake Up?/W: Fred Ebb, M: John Kander. *Jimmy* (Winter Garden, "Betty Compton," Oct. 23, 1969): Jimmy; Oh, Gee!; One in a Million; The Squabble Song; That Old Familiar Ring; The Walker Walk/WM: Bill Jacob, Patti Jacob.

3564. Bobby Gillette *Shoot the Works!* (George M. Cohan, revue, July 21, 1931): Let's Go Out in the Open Air/WM: Ann Ronell — My Heart's a Banjo/W: E.Y. Harburg, M: Jay Gorney.

3565. Priscilla Gillette (Nov. 27, 1925–) B: Tenafly, NJ. *Regina* (46th Street, "Alexandra Giddens," Oct. 31, 1949): What Will It Be?/WM: Marc Blitzstein. *Out of This World* (New Century, "Helen," Dec. 21, 1950): I Am Loved; No Lover; Use Your Imagination; What Do You Think About Men?/WM: Cole Porter. *The Golden Apple* (Alvin, "Penelope" and "Circe," Apr. 20, 1954): Circe, Circe; It's the Going Home Together; My Love Is on the Way; Windflowers (When We Were Young)/W: John Latouche, M: Jerome Moross.

3566. Ruth Gillette (1907–May 13, 1994) *Gay Paree* (Shubert, revue, Aug. 18, 1925): The Glory of the Morning Sunshine; Wedgewood Maid/WM: ? — Venetian Nights/WM: Clarence Gaskill. *The Merry World* (Imperial, revue, CR, July 12, 1926): Beauty Adorned/W: Clifford Grey, M: J. Fred Coots, Maurie Rubens — Girofle-Girofla/W: Harry B. Smith, M: Charles Lecocq — Heroes of Yesterday/WM: ? — Whispering Trees/W: Herbert Reynolds, M: J. Fred Coots — You and I (in Old Versailles)/W: B.G. DeSylva, M: George Gershwin, Jack Green. *Babes in Toyland* (Jolson, revival, "Tom Tom," Dec. 23, 1929): Never Mind, Bo Peep, You Will Find Your Sheep; Toyland/W: Glen MacDonough, M: Victor Herbert. *Babes in Toyland* (Imperial, revival, "Tom Tom," Dec. 22, 1930): same as above. *70, Girls, 70* (Broadhurst, Apr. 15, 1971): You and I, Love/W: Fred Ebb, M: John Kander.

3567. Viola Gillette (Oct. 7–Apr. 1, 1956) B: Salt Lake City, UT. *The Sleeping Beauty and the Beast* (Broadway, "Prince Charming," Nov. 4, 1901): Come Out Dinah, on the Green (Darkey Serenade)/W: Bob Cole, James Weldon Johnson, M: J. Rosamond Johnson — A Dream That Never Comes True/W: J. Cheever Goodwin, M: Frederic Solomon. *Mother Goose* (New Amsterdam, "Colin," Dec. 2, 1903): The Time to Love/ W: George V. Hobart, M: Frederic Solomon. *The Beauty Spot* (Herald Square, "Nichette," Apr. 10, 1909): The Ballerina; Boys Will Be Boys; Kissing [May 17, 1909]; Ode to Aphrodite/ W: Joseph W. Herbert, M: Reginald De Koven. *Lieber Augustin* (Casino, "Capt. Pips," Sept. 3, 1913): Why Do They All Make Love to Me?/ WM: Dick Temple. *Hop o' My Thumb* (Manhattan Opera House, "Hilario," Nov. 26, 1913): Come and Watch the Moon with Me; A Happy Noble Outlaw Band; Those Days of Long Ago/W: Sydney Rosenfeld, M: Manuel Klein. *Caroline* (Ambassador, "Mrs. Calhoun," Jan. 31, 1923): Will o' the Wisp/W: Harry B. Smith, M: Edward Kunneke. *Rainbow Rose* (Forrest, "Mrs. Barrett," Mar. 16, 1926): Dreams/WM: Harold A. Levey, Owen Murphy.

3568. Ida Gilliams *Cats* (Winter Garden, CR, "Cassandra," May 22, 1995): The Old Gumbie Cat/W: T.S. Eliot, M: Andrew Lloyd Webber.

3569. Helen Gilligan *Rain or Shine* (George M. Cohan, CR, "Mary Wheeler," July 2, 1928): Circus Days; Forever and Ever; Glad Tidings; Rain or Shine; Who's Goin' to Get You?/W: Jack Yellen, M: Milton Ager.

3570. Helen Gilliland (Jan. 31, 1897–) B: Belfast, Ireland. *The Red Robe* (Shubert, "Renee de Cocheforet," Dec. 25, 1928): Home of Mine; I Plead, Dear Heart; Only a Smile; Where Love Grows/W: Harry B. Smith, M: Jean Gilbert.

3571. Claude Gillingwater (Aug. 2, 1870–Nov. 1, 1939) B: St. Louis, MO. From 1913 to 1917 he starred in plays he had written himself. He appeared in 27 films as a comedian and character actor from 1931. A lingering illness caused him to end his life with a gunshot. *Mlle. Modiste* (Knickerbocker, "Hiram Bent," Dec. 25, 1905): The Keokuk Kulture Klub/W: Henry Blossom, M: Victor Herbert. *Mlle. Modiste* (Globe, revival, "Hiram Bent," May 26, 1913): same as above.

3572. James Gillis *Babes in Arms* (Shubert > Majestic, "Jimmy," Apr. 14, 1937): Imagine; Way Out West (on West End Avenue)/W: Lorenz Hart, M: Richard Rodgers.

3573. Margalo Gillmore (May 31, 1897– 1986) B: London, England. *Peter Pan* (Winter Garden, "Mrs. Darling," Oct. 20, 1954): Tender Shepherd/W: Carolyn Leigh, M: Moose Charlap.

3574. Mabelle (Mabel) Gilman (1880–?) *The Geisha* (Daly's, revival, "Molly Seamore," Mar. 21, 1898): Chon Kina; The Interfering Parrot; The Toy Duet/W: Harry Greenbank, M: Sidney Jones. *A Runaway Girl* (Daly's > Fifth Avenue, "Alice," Aug. 31, 1898): The Pickaninnies/W: Aubrey Hopwood, M: Ivan Caryll. *In Gay Paree* (Casino, "Louisette," Mar. 20, 1899): Tootsie Wootsie Woo/W: Grant Stewart, M: Ludwig Englander. *The Casino Girl* (Casino, "Laura Lee," Mar. 19, 1900): Mam'selle/W: Harry B. Smith, M: Arthur Nevin — Romance [Apr. 9, 1900]/W: Harry B. Smith, M: Will Marion Cook — The Way Actresses Are Made/ W: Harry B. Smith, M: Harry T. MacConnell. *The Mocking Bird* (Bijou, "Yvette Millet," Nov. 10, 1902): If You Couldn't Change Your Mind; Just a Kiss; The Lion and the Mouse; Sly Musette; What's the Matter with the Moon Tonight?/W: Sydney Rosenfeld, M: A. Baldwin Sloane.

3575. Toni Gilman She was a panelist on the TV quiz show *Down You Go* (1951). *Beat the Band* (46th Street, "Willow Willoughby," Oct. 14, 1942): I'm Physical, You're Cultured/W: George Marion, Jr., M: Johnny Green.

3576. Charles Gilmore *Ziegfeld Follies of 1912* (Moulin Rouge, revue, Oct. 21, 1912): Hurry Little Children; Sunday Morn/W: Edward Harrigan, M: Dave Braham.

3577. Jeannette (Janette) Gilmore *Florida Girl* (Lyric, "Marcelle," Nov. 2, 1925): Daphne; Lady of My Heart/W: Paul Porter, Benjamin Hapgood Burt, M: Milton Suskind. *Oh, Kay!* (Imperial, "Peggy," Nov. 8, 1926): Clap Yo' Hands/W: Ira Gershwin, M: George Gershwin.

3578. Susan Gilmour *Les Miserables* (Broadway, CR, "Fantine," c 1993): Come to Me; I Dreamed a Dream/W: Herbert Kretzmer, M: Claude-Michel Schonberg.

3579. Betty Gilpatrick *Laffing Room Only* (Winter Garden, revue, CR, Feb. 4, 1945): Hooray for Anywhere; The Steps of the Capitol; Stop That Dancing/WM: Burton Lane. *Call Me Mister* (National > Plymouth, revue, Apr. 18, 1946): Military Life (The Jerk Song)/WM: Harold Rome.

3580. Winifred Gilraine *Mary's Lamb* (New York, "Weenie," May 25, 1908): We're Hollandaise/WM: Richard Carle.

3581. John Gilroy (Feb. 5, 1872–May 8, 1937) B: New York, NY. M: MAMIE GILROY.

The Darling of the Gallery Gods [Mid Summer Night's Fancies] (Crystal Gardens, "Dandy Doo," June 22, 1903): Ida Bell/W: Matthew Woodward, M: Ben M. Jerome. *The Dress Parade [Mid Summer Night's Fancies]* (Crystal Gardens, revue, June 22, 1903): The Marriage of the Daffodil and Daisy/W: Nicholas Biddle, M: Ben M. Jerome.

3582. Mamie Gilroy (1877–Aug. 8, 1904) B: New York, NY. M: JOHN GILROY. *The Darling of the Gallery Gods [Mid Summer Night's Fancies]* (Crystal Gardens, "Rosy Dawn," June 22, 1903): Ida Bell; Oshi Dori/W: Matthew Woodward, M: Ben M. Jerome. *The Dress Parade [Mid Summer Night's Fancies]* (Crystal Gardens, revue, June 22, 1903): Down Where Two Lovers Sat/W: John Gilroy, M: Ben M. Jerome.

3583. Harriette Gimbel *The Greenwich Village Follies of 1920* (Shubert, revue, Jan. 3, 1921): At the Krazy Kat's Ball/W: Arthur Swanstrom, John Murray Anderson, M: A. Baldwin Sloane. *The Greenwich Village Follies of 1922* (Shubert, revue, Sept. 12, 1922): Beautiful Girls/W: Bert Kalmar, M: Harry Ruby — A Kiss from a Red-Headed Miss/W: Irving Caesar, John Murray Anderson, M: Louis A. Hirsch. *Artists and Models of 1923* (Shubert > Winter Garden, revue, Aug. 20, 1923): Johnnie/W: Cyrus D. Wood, Harold Atteridge, M: Jean Schwartz — Say It with a Ukelele [Feb. 4, 1924]/WM: Art Conrad — Take Me Back to Samoa Some More/W: Cyrus D. Wood, M: Jean Schwartz.

3584. Hermione Gingold (Dec. 9, 1897–May 24, 1987) B: London, England. Fine comedienne and character actress, notable as the grandmother in the film *Gigi* (1958). *John Murray Anderson's Almanac* (Imperial, revue, Dec. 10, 1953): Which Witch?/W: Allan Melville, M: Charles Zwar. *First Impressions* (Alvin, "Mrs. Bennet," Mar. 19, 1959): As Long as There's a Mother; Five Daughters; Have You Heard the News?; A House in Town; Let's Fetch the Carriage; Wasn't It a Simply Lovely Wedding?/WM: Robert Goldman, Glenn Paxton, George David Weiss. *From A to Z* (Plymouth, revue, Apr. 20, 1960): The Best Gold/WM: Jerry Herman — Four for the Road/W: Fred Ebb, Lee Goldsmith, M: Paul Klein. *Milk and Honey* (Martin Beck, CR, "Clara Weiss," Sept. 4, 1962): Chin Up, Ladies; Hymn to Hymie/WM: Jerry Herman. *A Little Night Music* (Shubert, "Madame Armfeldt," Feb. 25, 1973): The Glamorous Life; Liaisons/WM: Stephen Sondheim.

3585. Sophie Ginn *The Cradle Will Rock* (New York City Center, revival, "Sadie Polock," Feb. 11, 1960): Gus and Sadie Love Song/WM: Marc Blitzstein.

3586. Eddie Girard (c 1868–Dec. 10, 1946) B: Paterson, NJ. *The City Chap* (Liberty, "Watty," Oct. 26, 1925): The City Chap; Walking Home with Josie/W: Anne Caldwell, M: Jerome Kern.

3587. Harry Girard *Dolly Varden* (Herald Square, CR, "Capt. Richard Belleville," Apr. 28, 1902): An Aural Understanding; Brides and Grooms; Dolly Varden; I'm Twirling, Whirling; To Be with Thee; What Love Means/W: Stanislaus Stange, M: Julian Edwards. *Dolly Varden* (Victoria, return engagement, "Capt. Richard Belleville," Sept. 22, 1902): same as above. *The Alaskan* (Knickerbocker, "Richard Atwater," Aug. 12, 1907): Arlee; Rainbow and the Thistle; Song of the Riffles; Veasy Drew/W: Joseph Blethen, M: Harry Girard.

3588. Henry Girard *San Toy* (Daly's, "Lieut. Harvey Tucker," Oct. 1, 1900): We'll Keep the Feast in Pynka Pong/W: Harry Greenbank, Adrian Ross, M: Sidney Jones.

3589. Paulette Girard *The Boy Friend* (Royale, "Hortense," Sept. 30, 1954): Perfect Young Ladies/WM: Sandy Wilson.

3590. Marion Giroux *Adonis* (Star, revival, "Lady Hattie," Nov. 22, 1888): We Are the Duchess' Daughters/W: William F. Gill, Henry E. Dixey, M: Edward E. Rice.

3591. Howard Girven *Billy* (Billy Rose, "Smithy," Mar. 22, 1969): Chanty/WM: Ron Dante, Gene Allen.

3592. Lillian Gish (Oct. 14, 1893–Feb. 27, 1993) B: Springfield, OH. One of the most popular actresses of her time, she appeared on stage from the age of 5, on screen from 1912 at Biograph, where she made 40 films with director D.W. Griffith. *Anya* (Ziegfeld, "Dowager Empress," Nov. 29, 1965): Little Hands/WM: Robert Wright, George Forrest. *A Musical Jubilee* (St. James, revue, Nov. 13, 1975): I Didn't Raise My Boy to Be a Soldier/W: Alfred Bryan, M: Al Piantadosi — I Wanna Be Loved by You/W: Bert Kalmar, M: Harry Ruby, Herbert Stothart — Moonstruck/WM: Ivan Caryll, Lionel Monckton — 'S Wonderful/W: Ira Gershwin, M: George Gershwin.

3593. Murray Gitlin (c 1927–June 22, 1994) *The Golden Apple* (Alvin, "Bluey," Apr. 20, 1954): Come Along, Boys; Helen Is Always Willing; It Was a Glad Adventure/W: John Latouche, M: Jerome Moross.

3594. Roy Giusti (Feb. 10, 1894–Nov. 15, 1969) B: San Francisco, CA. *Earl Carroll's Vanities of 1923* (Earl Carroll, revue, July 5, 1923): The Band Plays Home Sweet Home; The Birth of a New Revue/WM: Earl Carroll — A Girl

Is Like Sunshine/W: Roy Turk, M: William Daly.

3595. George Givot (1903–June 7, 1984) B: Omaha, NE. The comic actor and master of dialects started out in vaudeville and radio, appearing in movies from 1933. *Earl Carroll's Sketch Book of 1929* (Earl Carroll > 44th Street > 46th Street, revue, July 1, 1929): Kinda Cute; Papa Likes a Hot Papoose/W: E.Y. Harburg, M: Jay Gorney. *Pardon My English* (Majestic, "Michael Bramleigh," Jan. 20, 1933): Isn't It a Pity?; Luckiest Man in the World; Pardon My English; Tonight/W: Ira Gershwin, M: George Gershwin. *Mexican Hayride* (Winter Garden, "Lombos Campos," Jan. 28, 1944): Count Your Blessings/WM: Cole Porter. *Do Re Mi* (St. James, "Skin Demopoulos," Dec. 26, 1960): It's Legitimate/W: Betty Comden, Adolph Green, M: Jule Styne.

3596. Hazel Gladstone *The Magic Ring* (Liberty, "Singing Girl," Oct. 1, 1923): Keepsakes/W: Zelda Sears, M: Harold A. Levey.

3597. Darel Glaser (Jan. 12, 1957–) B: Chicago, IL. *Cry for Us All* (Broadhurst, "Flylegs," Apr. 8, 1970): The Broken Heart or The Wages of Sin; The Cruelty Man; Home Free All; I Lost It; See No Evil/W: William Alfred, Phyllis Robinson, M: Mitch Leigh.

3598. Lulu Glaser (June 2, 1872–Sept. 5, 1958) B: Allegheny City, PA. M: RALPH HERZ; THOMAS G. RICHARDS. When the leading lady of *The Lion Tamer* (1891) was taken ill, her understudy, Lulu Glaser, took over and became a star. She retired to her home in Weston, CT. in 1918. *Cyrano de Bergerac* (Knickerbocker, "Roxane," Sept. 18, 1899): I Am a Court Coquette; I Must Marry a Handsome Man; I Wonder; Let the Sun of Thine Eyes; Over the Mountains; Since I Am Not for Thee; Waltz Song/W: Harry B. Smith, M: Victor Herbert. *Dolly Varden* (Herald Square, "Dolly Varden," Jan. 27, 1902): An Aural Understanding; Brides and Grooms; The Cannibal Maid; For the Benefit of Man; I'm Twirling, Whirling; The Lay of the Jay; What Love Means/W: Stanislaus Stange, M: Julian Edwards. *Miss Dolly Dollars* (Knickerbocker > New Amsterdam, "Dorothy Gay [Dolly Dollars]," Sept. 4, 1905): An American Heiress; It's All in the Book You Know (Ollendorf Duet); Just Get Out and Walk; The Moth and the Moon; Queen of the Ring/W: Harry B. Smith, M: Victor Herbert. *Lola from Berlin* (Liberty, "Lotchen von Breckenhaussett [Lola]," Sept. 16, 1907): Altdeutscher Leibersreim; Beneath the Moon; Madchenlied; Poor Little Foolish Man; There's Not Another Girlie

in the World Like You; Unter den Linden, in Germany/W: William Jerome, M: Jean Schwartz. *Mlle. Mischief* (Lyric, "Rosette," Sept. 28, 1908): The Joy Duet; She Knew a Thing or Two; A Single Day; Sweetheart; Verily, Merrily/W: Sydney Rosenfeld, M: Carl M. Ziehrer. *The Girl and the Kaiser* (Herald Square, "Christ'l," Nov. 22, 1910): At Court; Hungarian Rhythmic Air; Laughing and Happy Am I; With a Glance Demure/W: Leonard Liebling, M: Georges Jarno.

3599. William Glaser *Lola from Berlin* (Liberty, "Billy Needham," Sept. 16, 1907): I Think of You the Whole Year Round/W: William Jerome, M: Jean Schwartz.

3600. David Glassford (Apr. 17, 1866–Oct. 17, 1935) B: Sydney, New South Wales, Australia. *Lassie* (Nora Bayes, "Lord Inglehart," Apr. 6, 1920): Skeletons/W: Catherine Chisholm Cushing, M: Hugo Felix.

3601. William Glassman (1945–) B: Boston, MA. *The Music Man* (New York City Center, revival, "Tommy Djilas," June 16, 1965): Shipoopi/WM: Meredith Willson.

3602. Stephen Glavin *The Mystery of Edwin Drood* (Imperial, "Deputy," Dec. 2, 1985): Off to the Races/WM: Rupert Holmes.

3603. Helen Gleason (Jan. 1, 1867–Aug. 27, 1955) B: California. *Frederika* (Imperial, "Frederika," Feb. 4, 1937): I Asked My Heart; One; Stormy Love; Why Did He Kiss My Heart Awake?/W: Edward Eliscu, M: Franz Lehar. *Night of Love* (Hudson, "Nella Vago," Jan. 7, 1941): I'm Thinking of Love; Loosen Up; The One Man I Need; Serenade for You; Tonight or Never; Without You/W: Rowland Leigh, M: Robert Stolz.

3604. Jackie Gleason (Feb. 26, 1916–June 24, 1987) B: Brooklyn, NY. One of the great comics of his time, he was also a serious actor. Best remembered as Ralph Cramden in the TV classic sitcom *The Honeymooners* (1955). *Keep Off the Grass* (Broadhurst, revue, May 23, 1940): The Cabby's Serenade/W: Al Dubin, M: Jimmy McHugh — On the Old Park Bench/W: Howard Dietz, M: Jimmy McHugh. *Artists and Models of 1943* (Broadway, revue, Nov. 5, 1943): North Dakota, South Dakota, Minnesota Moon; Way Up North in Dixie/W: Milton Pascal, Dan Shapiro, M: Phil Charig. *Follow the Girls* (New Century > 44th Street, "Goofy Gale," Apr. 8, 1944): A Tree That Grows in Brooklyn; You're Perf/W: Milton Pascal, Dan Shapiro, M: Phil Charig. *Take Me Along* (Shubert, "Uncle Sid," Oct. 22, 1959): But Yours; I Get Embarrassed; Little Green Snake; Promise Me a Rose; Sid Ol' Kid; Take Me Along/WM: Bob Merrill.

3605. James Gleason (May 23, 1886–Apr. 12, 1959) B: New York, NY. Born in a boarding house to a theatrical family, the versatile character actor appeared in plays from childhood and in films from 1930. *Tangerine* (Casino, CR, "Fred Allen," Nov. 14, 1921): It's Great to Be Married (and Lead a Single Life)/W: Howard Johnson, M: Monte Carlo, Alma Sanders, Carle Carlton — Love Is a Business; South Sea Island Blues/W: Howard Johnson, M: Monte Carlo, Alma Sanders — Man Is the Lord of It All/W: Carle Carlton, M: Jean Schwartz.

3606. Joanna Gleason (June 2, 1950–) B: Toronto, Canada. *I Love My Wife* (Ethel Barrymore, "Monica," Apr. 17, 1977): Lovers on Christmas Eve; Married Couple Seeks Married Couple; Monica; Someone Wonderful I Missed/W: Michael Stewart, M: Cy Coleman. *Into the Woods* (Martin Beck, "Baker's Wife," Nov. 5, 1987/May 23, 1989): Any Moment (Anything Can Happen in the Woods); It Takes Two (You're Different in the Woods); Maybe They're Magic (Magic Beans); Moments in the Woods; A Very Nice Prince/WM: Stephen Sondheim. *Nick and Nora* (Marquis, "Nora Charles," Dec. 8, 1991): As Long as You're Happy; A Busy Night at Lorraine's; Is There Anything Better Than Dancing?; Let's Go Home; May the Best Man Win; Swell/W: Richard Maltby, Jr., M: Charles Strouse.

3607. Thomas (Tommy) Gleason (Feb. 11, 1915–) B: South Bend, IN. *Let's Face It!* (Imperial, "Royal Guard," Oct. 29, 1941): Let's Face It; A Little Rumba Numba/WM: Cole Porter. *South Pacific* (Majestic > Broadway, "Sgt. Kenneth Johnson," Apr. 7, 1949): There Is Nothin' Like a Dame/W: Oscar Hammerstein II, M: Richard Rodgers. *By the Beautiful Sea* (Majestic, "Diabolo," Apr. 8, 1954): Hooray for George the Third/W: Dorothy Fields, M: Arthur Schwartz.

3608. Robert Gleckler (Jan. 11, 1887–Feb. 25, 1939) B: Pierre, SD. *Hot-cha!* (Ziegfeld, "Jose Diaz," Mar. 8, 1932): Jose, Can't You See!/W: Lew Brown, M: Ray Henderson.

3609. Cunningham Glen *Bitter Sweet* (Ziegfeld, "Vernon Craft," Nov. 5, 1929): Green Carnation/WM: Noel Coward.

3610. Hazel Glen *Stepping Stones* (Globe, revival, "Lupina," Sept. 1, 1924): Babbling Babette; Because You Love the Singer; Once in a Blue Moon; Our Lovely Rose/W: Anne Caldwell, M: Jerome Kern.

3611. Ernest Glendinning (Feb. 19, 1884–May 17, 1936) B: Ulverston, Lancaster, England. In the U.S. from 1900. *The Honeymoon Express* (Winter Garden, "Henri Dubonet," Feb. 6, 1913): Bring Back Your Love; The Ragtime Express/W: Harold Atteridge, M: Jean Schwartz. *Sonny* (Cort, "Joe Marden," Aug. 16, 1921): Dream; My Dear Old Chum/W: George V. Hobart, M: Raymond Hubbell. *Moonlight* (Longacre, "Peter Darby," Jan. 30, 1924): Aren't We All?; Honeymoon Blues; In a Bungalow; On Such a Night/W: William B. Friedlander, M: Con Conrad.

3612. Ralph Glenmore *A Chorus Line* (Shubert, CR, "Richie," June 1980): And.../W: Edward Kleban, M: Marvin Hamlisch.

3613. Daphne Glenne *The Quaker Girl* (Park, "Princess Mathilde," Oct. 23, 1911): A Runaway Match; Wonderful/W: Adrian Ross, M: Lionel Monckton.

3614. Michael Glenn-Smith (July 2, 1945–) B: Abilene, TX. *Celebration* (Ambassador, "Orphan," Jan. 22, 1969): Celebration; Fifty Million Years Ago; I'm Glad to See You've Got What You Want; Love Song; My Garden; Orphan in the Storm; Winter and Summer/W: Tom Jones, M: Harvey Schmidt.

3615. Shaun Glenville (May 16, 1884–Dec. 28, 1968) B: Dublin, Ireland. M: DOROTHY WARD. His mother managed the Abbey Theater in Dublin. The comedian, a favorite in pantomime, made his first trip onstage at the age of 2 weeks. *Phoebe of Quality Street* (Shubert, "Sgt. Terence O'Toole," May 9, 1921): Is It Safe to Depend on the Irish?; O'Toole/W: Edward Delaney Dunn, M: Walter Kollo — Let's Make Up/W: Mrs. Edward Delaney Dunn, M: Walter Kollo. *The Whirl of New York* (Winter Garden, "Doc Sniffkins," June 13, 1921): Dancing Fool/W: Harry B. Smith, Francis Wheeler, M: Ted Snyder.

3616. Eleanor Glockner *Guys and Dolls* (Martin Beck, revival, "Agatha," Apr. 14, 1992): Follow the Fold/WM Frank Loesser.

3617. Adelaide Gloria *The Rise of Rosie O'Reilly* (Liberty, "Mrs. Casparoni," Dec. 25, 1923): Love Dreams/WM: George M. Cohan.

3618. Albert Gloria *The Rise of Rosie O'Reilly* (Liberty, "Casparoni," Dec. 25, 1923): The Arrival of the Plot; Love Dreams/WM: George M. Cohan.

3619. Rosemary Glosz *The Prince of Pilsen* (Broadway, CR, "Edith Adams," May 25, 1903): The Field and Forest; The Message of the Violet; We Know It's Wrong to Flirt/W: Frank Pixley, M: Gustav Luders. *The Merry Widow* (New Amsterdam, CR, "Sonia," June 22, 1908): I Love You So (The Merry Widow Waltz); In Marsovia; Silly Cavalier; Vilia/W: Adrian Ross, M: Franz Lehar.

3620. Bill Glover *Finian's Rainbow* (New York City Center, revival, "2nd Passion Pilgrim Gospeler," Apr. 27, 1960): The Begat/W: E.Y. Harburg, M: Burton Lane. *Trumpets of the Lord* (Brooks Atkinson, revival, "Singer," Apr. 29, 1969): In His Care/WM: based on gospel hymn.

3621. Ralph Glover *Big Boy* (44th Street, CR, "Jack Bedford," Aug. 24, 1925): The Dance from Down Yonder; Tap the Toe/W: B.G. DeSylva, M: Joseph Meyer, James F. Hanley.

3622. Savion Glover (Nov. 19, 1973–) B: Newark, NJ. *The Tap Dance Kid* (Broadhurst, CR, "Willie Sheridan," Nov. 1984): Crosstown; Dance If It Makes You Happy; Dancing Is Everything; Someday; Tap Tap; They Never Hear What I Say/W: Robert Lorick, M: Henry Krieger. *Jelly's Last Jam* (Virginia, "Young Jelly," Apr. 26, 1992): The Creole Way; Get Away, Boy; Street Scene/W: Susan Birkenhead, M: Luther Henderson — Lonely Boy Blues/WM: trad.— The Whole World's Waitin' to Sing Your Song/ W: Susan Birkenhead, M: Jelly Roll Morton.

3623. Arnold Gluck *The Greenwich Village Follies of 1925* (Shubert, revue, CR, Mar. 15, 1926): White Cargo/WM: ?— Wouldn't You?/ WM: Owen Murphy.

3624. Joanna Glushak (May 27, 1958–) B: New York, NY. *Sunday in the Park with George* (Booth, CR, "Dot" and "Marie," Aug. 27, 1984): Children and Art; Color and Light; Everybody Loves Louis; Move On; Sunday in the Park with George; We Do Not Belong Together/WM: Stephen Sondheim.

3625. Rita Glynde *Murray Anderson's Almanac* (Erlanger's, revue, Aug. 14, 1929): The Polka Dot/W: Clifford Orr, M: Henry Sullivan — Tiller, Foster, Hoffman, Hale and Albertina Rasch/W: Henry Myers, M: Henry Sullivan.

3626. Carlin Glynn (Feb. 19, 1940–) B: Cleveland, OH. *The Best Little Whorehouse in Texas* (46th Street, "Mona Stangley," June 19, 1978/Aug. 20, 1979/Mar. 10, 1982): Bus from Amarillo; Girl, You're a Woman; A Li'l Ole Bitty Pissant Country Place; No Lies; 20 Fans/WM: Carol Hall.

3627. Celia Glynn *By the Way* (Gaiety > Central, revue, Dec. 28, 1925): I Was Meant for Someone [Apr. 19, 1926]/WM: Ballard Macdonald, James F. Hanley — In the Same Way I Love You/W: Eric Little, M: H.M. Tennant — No One's Ever Kissed Me/W: Ronald Jeans, M: Philip Braham — What Can They See in Dancing?/W: Graham John, M: Vivian Ellis.

3628. Stacia Goad *Starlight Express* (Gershwin, CR, "Ashley," c 1987): Engine of Love/W: Peter Reeves, Richard Stilgoe, M: Andrew Lloyd

Webber — Lotta Locomotion; Pumping Iron; Race Two; Rolling Stock; U.N.C.O.U.P.L.E.D./ W: Richard Stilgoe, M: Andrew Lloyd Webber.

3629. George Gobel (May 20, 1919–Feb. 24, 1991) B: Chicago, IL. The affable TV comedian started out when he was a boy, singing on radio. Best remembered for *The George Gobel Show* (1954). *Let It Ride!* (Eugene O'Neill, "Erwin," Oct. 12, 1961): Broads Ain't People; He Needs You; Hey, Jimmy, Joe, John, Jack; His Own Little Island; If Flutterby Wins; I'll Learn Ya/WM: Jay Livingston, Ray Evans.

3630. Len Gochman *How to Succeed in Business Without Really Trying* (New York City Center, revival, "J. Pierpont Finch," Apr. 20, 1966): Been a Long Day; Brotherhood of Man; The Company Way; Grand Old Ivy; How To; I Believe in You; Rosemary/WM: Frank Loesser. *Finian's Rainbow* (New York City Center, revival, "Og," Apr. 5, 1967): Something Sort of Grandish; When I'm Not Near the Girl I Love/ W: E.Y. Harburg, M: Burton Lane.

3631. Ann Goddard *Sweet and Low* (44th Street, revue, CR, Feb. 9, 1931): For I'm in Love Again/W: Mort Dixon, Billy Rose, M: Mischa Spoliansky.

3632. Willoughby Goddard (July 4, 1926–) B: Bicester, England. *Oliver!* (Imperial, "Mr. Bumble," Jan. 6, 1963): Boy for Sale; I Shall Scream; Oliver!; That's Your Funeral/WM: Lionel Bart.

3633. Arthur Godfrey (Aug. 31, 1903–Mar. 16, 1983) B: New York, NY. Popular folksy entertainer with his own shows on radio and TV from the 1930s. For a time he was the most influential man in broadcasting. *Three to Make Ready* (Adelphi, revue, Mar. 7, 1946): A Lovely Lazy Kind of Day/W: Nancy Hamilton, M: Morgan Lewis.

3634. Carrie Godfrey *Adonis* (Bijoux, "Artea," Sept. 4, 1884): Golden Chains/W: J. Cheever Goodwin, M: Edward E. Rice.

3635. Dorothy Godfrey *The Lady in Red* (Lyric, "Marjorie Cole," May 12, 1919): Garibaldi Band; A Little Bit of Scotch; Pretty Little Girls Like You/W: Anne Caldwell, M: Richard Winterberg.

3636. Lynnie Godfrey (Sept. 11, 1952–) B: New York, NY. *Eubie!* (Ambassador, revue, Sept. 20, 1978): Daddy; If You've Never Been Vamped by a Brownskin, You've Never Been Vamped at All; I'm Craving for That Kind of Love; I'm Just Wild About Harry/W: Noble Sissle, M: Eubie Blake.

3637. Inez Goetz *Lew Leslie's International Revue* (Majestic, revue, CR, Mar. 17, 1930): Big

Papoose Is on the Loose/W: Dorothy Fields, M: Jimmy McHugh.

3638. Charles Goff *My Fair Lady* (New York City Center, revival, "Harry," June 13, 1968): Get Me to the Church on Time; With a Little Bit of Luck/W: Alan Jay Lerner, M: Frederick Loewe. *The Red Shoes* (Gershwin, "Dmitri," Dec. 16, 1993): It's a Fairy Tale/W: Bob Merrill, M: Jule Styne.

3639. Helen Goff *A World of Pleasure* (Winter Garden, revue, CR, Jan. 3, 1916): The Melting Pot/W: Harold Atteridge, M: Sigmund Romberg.

3640. Herbert Goff *Elsie Janis and Her Gang* (Gaiety, revue, Jan. 16, 1922): Love in the Springtime Is Not What It Used to Be/W: Elsie Janis, M: George S. Hirst. *I'll Say She Is* (Casino, CR, "Chief," Nov. 17, 1924): I'm Saving You for a Rainy Day; Only You; Pretty Girl/W: Will B. Johnstone, M: Tom Johnstone. *Kitty's Kisses* (Playhouse, CR, "Robert Mason," Sept. 27, 1926): I'm in Love/W: Gus Kahn, Otto Harbach, M: Con Conrad — Kitty's Kisses; Whenever I Dream/W: Gus Kahn, M: Con Conrad. *The Great Waltz* (Center, return engagement, CR, "Capt. Boris Androff," Sept. 9, 1935): Love's Never Lost/W: Desmond Carter, M: Johann Strauss.

3641. Jerry Goff *Strike Up the Band* (Times Square, "Jim Townsend," Jan. 14, 1930): He Knows Milk; Soon; Strike Up the Band; A Typical Self-Made American/W: Ira Gershwin, M: George Gershwin.

3642. Al Gold *Shoot the Works!* (George M. Cohan, revue, July 21, 1931): Chirp, Chirp/W: Ira Gershwin, M: Joseph Meyer, Phil Charig — How's Your Uncle?/W: Dorothy Fields, M: Jimmy McHugh.

3643. Annabelle Gold *Pipe Dream* (Shubert, "Sonya," Nov. 30, 1955): A Lopsided Bus/W: Oscar Hammerstein II, M: Richard Rodgers.

3644. Belle Gold (Nov. 21, 1882–Feb. 27, 1953) B: Macon, GA. *The Ham Tree* (New York, "Desdemona," Aug. 28, 1905): Desdie, My Desdemona/W: William Jerome, M: Jean Schwartz.

3645. David Gold (Feb. 2, 1929–) B: New York, NY. *Drat! The Cat!* (Martin Beck, "Roger Purefoy," Oct. 10, 1965): My Son, Uphold the Law/W: Ira Levin, M: Milton Schafer. *The Education of H*Y*M*A*N K*A*P*L*A*N* (Alvin, "Reuben Plonsky," Apr. 4, 1968): Spring in the City/WM: Paul Nassau, Oscar Brand. *On Your Toes* (Virginia, revival, CR, "Sergei Alexandrovitch," Aug. 30, 1983): Quiet Night; Too Good for the Average Man/W: Lorenz Hart, M: Richard Rodgers.

3646. Diana Goldberg *The President's Daughter* (Billy Rose, "Minke," Nov. 3, 1970): I Have What You Want; We Two; Welcome, Mr. Golden!; Women's Liberation/W: Jacob Jacobs, M: Murray Rumshinsky.

3647. Hanan Goldblatt *To Live Another Summer, To Pass Another Winter* (Helen Hayes, revue, Oct. 21, 1971): I Wanted to Be a Hero; Sorry We Won/W: David Paulsen, M: David Krivoshei — To Live Another Summer, To Pass Another Winter/W: David Paulsen, M: Dov Seltzer.

3648. Jeff Goldblum (Oct. 22, 1952–) B: Pittsburgh, PA. Leading man in movies, often as a science-fictional scientist. *The Moony Shapiro Songbook* (Morosco, revue, May 3, 1981): Climbin'; Happy Hickory; I Found Love; I'm Gonna Take Her Home to Momma; Je Vous Aime, Milady; Messages; Nostalgia; A Storm in My Heart; Talking Picture Show/W: Julian More, M: Monty Norman.

3649. Annie Golden (Oct. 19, 1951–) B: Brooklyn, NY. *Leader of the Pack* (Ambassador, "Annie Golden," Apr. 8, 1985): Baby, I Love You; Be My Baby; I Can Hear Music/WM: Jeff Barry, Ellie Greenwich, Phil Spector — Leader of the Pack/WM: Jeff Barry, Ellie Greenwich, George Morton — Maybe I Know/WM: Jeff Barry, Ellie Greenwich — We're Gonna Make It (After All)/WM: Ellie Greenwich.

3650. Jay Golden *Broadway Sho-Window* (Broadway, revue, CR, Apr. 19, 1936): Poverty Row or Luxury Lane/W: Howard Johnson, M: Gus Edwards.

3651. Neil Golden *Earl Carroll's Vanities of 1928* (Earl Carroll, revue, CR, Dec. 10, 1928): The Dryad/WM: George Bagby, G. Romilli — Pretty Girl/W: Grace Henry, M: Morris Hamilton.

3652. Richard Golden (July 6, 1854–Aug. 9, 1909) B: Bangor, ME. *The Fortune Teller* (Wallack's, "Fresco," Sept. 26, 1898): Signor Monsieur Muldoni/W: Harry B. Smith, M: Victor Herbert. *The Tourists* (Majestic, "Timothy Todd," Aug. 25, 1906): That's the Time; When You Take a Trip/W: R.H. Burnside, M: Gustave Kerker.

3653. Ricky Paull Goldin (Jan. 5, 1968–) B: San Francisco, CA. *Grease* (Eugene O'Neill, revival, "Danny Zuko," May 11, 1994): Alone at a Drive-In Movie; Summer Nights/WM: Jim Jacobs, Warren Casey.

3654. Charles Goldner (Dec. 7, 1900–Apr. 15, 1955) B: Vienna, Austria. The character actor moved to Britain in the 1930s. *The Girl in Pink Tights* (Mark Hellinger, "Maestro Gallo," Mar.

5, 1954): I Promised Their Mothers; Love Is the Funniest Thing/W: Leo Robin, M: Sigmund Romberg.

3655. Merwin Goldsmith (Aug. 7, 1937–) B: Detroit, MI. *Rex* (Lunt-Fontanne, "Comus," Apr. 25, 1976): The Chase/W: Sheldon Harnick, M: Richard Rodgers. *Ain't Broadway Grand* (Lunt-Fontanne, "Jaeger," Apr. 18, 1993): Ain't Broadway Grand; Lindy's/W: Lee Adams, M: Mitch Leigh.

3656. John H. Goldsworthy (Apr. 28, 1884–July 10, 1958) B: England. *The Queen of the Movies* (Globe, "Baron Victor de Gardennes," Jan. 12, 1914): Forgive and Forget; Who Is to Know?/W: Edward A. Paulton, M: Jean Gilbert. *The Dancing Duchess* (Casino, "Capt. Carl Czardis," Aug. 20, 1914): Danube So Blue; I Like You; Love Is a Summer's Morning/W: R.H. Burnside, M: Milton Lusk — Nay, Nay Pauline/W: Jennings Cox, M: Emerson Foote. *See America First* (Maxine Elliott, "Cecil, Duke of Pendragon," Mar. 28, 1916): Damsel, Damsel (Prithee, Come Crusading with Me); Ever and Ever Yours; I've a Shooting Box in Scotland; To Follow Every Fancy/WM: T. Lawrason Riggs, Cole Porter. *The Girl from Brazil* (44th Street > Shubert, "Baron Heinz von Reedigan," Aug. 30, 1916): I'll Be Your Own Romeo/W: Matthew Woodward, M: Robert Winterberg — My Senorita; Oh You Lovely Ladies; Stolen Kisses/W: Matthew Woodward, M: Sigmund Romberg. *Rambler Rose* (Empire, "Gerald Morton," Sept. 10, 1917): Dream! Dream!/W: Harry B. Smith, M: Victor Jacobi. *The Royal Vagabond* (Cohan and Harris, "Col. Ivan Petroff," Feb. 17, 1919): In a Kingdom of Our Own/WM: George M. Cohan — When the Cherry Blossoms Fall (Love Is Love)/W: Stephen Ivor Szinnyey, William Cary Duncan, M: Anselm Goetzl.

3657. Wanda Goll *Hello, Daddy* (Mansfield > George M. Cohan > Erlanger's, "Helen," Dec. 26, 1928): Futuristic Rhythm/W: Dorothy Fields, M: Jimmy McHugh.

3658. Georgia Gomez *Mr. Lode of Koal* (Majestic, "Kinklets," Nov. 1, 1909): The Harbor of Lost Dreams/W: Alex Rogers, M: Bert Williams.

3659. Lillian Gonne *The Passing Show of 1913* (Winter Garden, revue, July 24, 1913): Ragging the Nursery Rhymes; Whistling Cowboy Joe/WM: Al W. Brown.

3660. Ernesto Gonzalez (Apr. 8, 1940–) B: San Juan, Puerto Rico. *Ride the Winds* (Bijou, "Sensei Takuan," May 16, 1974): Flower Song; Remember That Day/WM: John Driver.

3661. Guillermo Gonzalez *Cats* (Winter Garden, CR, "Mungojerrie"): Mungojerrie and Rumpleteazer/W: T.S. Eliot, M: Andrew Lloyd Webber.

3662. Jack Good *Hello, Paris* (Shubert, "Ross Peters," Nov. 15, 1930): Dance Your Troubles Away; Heavenly Days [Nov. 24, 1930]; Pack Your Suitcase with Love [Nov. 24, 1930]; Paris; You Made a Hit with Me [Nov. 24, 1930]/WM: ?. *Face the Music* (New Amsterdam, "Joe," Feb. 17, 1932): I Don't Want to Be Married; You Must Be Born with It/WM: Irving Berlin. *Face the Music* (44th Street, return engagement, "Joe," Jan. 31, 1933): same as above. *The Show Is On* (Winter Garden, revue, CR, Sept. 18, 1937): Little Old Lady/W: Stanley Adams, M: Hoagy Carmichael — What Has He Got?/W: Ted Fetter, M: Vernon Duke.

3663. Jack Goode (June 2, 1908–June 24, 1971) B: Columbus, OH. *The Desert Song* (New York City Center, revival, "Bennie Kidd," Jan. 8, 1946): It; One Good Man Gone Wrong/W: Otto Harbach, Oscar Hammerstein II, M: Sigmund Romberg. *Gypsy Lady* (Century, "Fresco," Sept. 17, 1946): The Facts of Life Backstage; My First Waltz; Pantomime; Piff Paff; Reality; Young Lady a la Mode/W: Robert Wright, George Forrest, M: Victor Herbert. *Sally* (Martin Beck, revival, "Otis Hooper," May 6, 1948): Bungalow in Quogue/W: P.G. Wodehouse, M: Jerome Kern — The Church 'Round the Corner/W: Clifford Grey, P.G. Wodehouse, M: Jerome Kern. *The Pajama Game* (St. James, CR, "Hines," Sept. 1956): I'll Never Be Jealous Again; The Pajama Game; Think of the Time I Save/WM: Richard Adler, Jerry Ross. *Hello, Dolly!* (St. James, CR, "Horace Vandergelder," Mar. 28, 1970): Before the Parade Passes By/WM: Lee Adams, Charles Strouse, Jerry Herman — Hello, Dolly!; It Takes a Woman; So Long, Dearie/WM: Jerry Herman — Motherhood/WM: Bob Merrill, Jerry Herman.

3664. Danzi Goodell *The City Chap* (Liberty, Oct. 26, 1925): The Fountain of Youth/W: Anne Caldwell, M: Jerome Kern.

3665. Neila Goodelle *The Garrick Gaieties of 1930* (Guild, revue, return engagement, Oct. 16, 1930): Lazy Levee Loungers/WM: Willard Robison — There Ain't No Love; Unaccustomed As I Am/W: E.Y. Harburg, M: Vernon Duke. *The Only Girl* (44th Street, revival, "Patricia La Montrose [Patsy]," May 21, 1934): Here's How; Here's to the Land We Love, Boys!; The More I See of Others, Dear, the Better I Love You; Personality; You Have to Have a Part to Make a Hit/W: Henry Blossom, M: Victor Herbert. *The Illustrators' Show* (48th Street, revue, Jan. 22,

1936): Bang, the Bell Rang!; If You Didn't Love Me Who Else Would; Wild Trumpets and Crazy Piano (Got a Guy to Forget)/W: Frank Loesser, M: Irving Actman — Just for Tonight/WM: Charlotte Kent — A Waltz Was Born in Vienna/W: Earle Crooker, M: Frederick Loewe.

3666. Joseph Gooderowe *San Toy* (Daly's, "Fo-Hop," Oct. 1, 1900): When You Are Wed to Me/W: Harry Greenbank, Adrian Ross, M: Sidney Jones.

3667. Ernest Goodhart *Blossom Time* (46th Street, revival, "Erkman," Dec. 26, 1938): Love Is a Riddle/W: Dorothy Donnelly, M: Sigmund Romberg.

3668. Helen Goodhue *Hello Yourself!!!!* (Casino, "Big Bertha," Oct. 30, 1928): Daily Dozen; He-Man/W: Leo Robin, M: Richard Myers.

3669. Sally Gooding *Keep Moving* (Forrest, revue, Aug. 23, 1934): Midtown; Superstition/W: Jack Scholl, M: Max Rich.

3670. Marvin Goodis A member of the U.S. Army in WW II. *This Is the Army* (Broadway, revue, July 4, 1942): Mandy/WM: Irving Berlin.

3671. Davis Goodman *Topsy and Eva* (Harris, "Gee Gee," Dec. 23, 1924): Kiss Me/WM: Vivian Duncan, Rosetta Duncan.

3672. Dody Goodman (Oct. 28, 1915–) B: Columbus, OH. Actress and dancer with an offbeat comedic flair. Probably best remembered for her appearances on Jack Paar's late night TV show. *Fiorello!* (New York City Center, revival, "Dora," June 13, 1962): I Love a Cop; Unfair/W: Sheldon Harnick, M: Jerry Bock. *Lorelei or Gentlemen Still Prefer Blondes* (Palace, "Mrs. Ella Spofford," Jan. 27, 1974): It's High Time; Keeping Cool with Coolidge/W: Leo Robin, M: Jule Styne — Miss Lorelei Lee/W: Betty Comden, Adolph Green, M: Jule Styne. *Grease* (Eugene O'Neill, revival, CR, "Miss Lynch"): Alma Mater; Born to Hand-Jive/WM: Jim Jacobs, Warren Casey.

3673. John Goodman (June 20, 1952–) B: St. Louis, MO. He was Roseanne's husband, Dan Conner, in the TV sitcom *Roseanne* (1988). *Big River: The Adventures of Huckleberry Finn* (Eugene O'Neill, "Pap Finn," Apr. 25, 1985): Guv'ment/WM: Roger Miller.

3674. Lee Goodman (c 1924–Feb. 6, 1988) *Carnival in Flanders* (New Century, "Innkeeper," Sept. 8, 1953): Ring the Bell; You're Dead!/W: Johnny Burke, M: James Van Heusen. *How to Succeed in Business Without Really Trying* (New York City Center, revival, "Bud Frump," Apr. 20, 1966): Been a Long Day; Brotherhood of Man; Coffee Break; The Company Way; I

Believe in You; A Secretary Is Not a Toy/WM: Frank Loesser. *Company* (Alvin, CR, "David," Mar. 29, 1971/Oct. 25, 1971): Have I Got a Girl for You; Sorry-Grateful/WM: Stephen Sondheim. *So Long, 174th Street* (Harkness, "Papa," Apr. 27, 1976): If You Want to Break Your Father's Heart; My Son the Druggist/WM: Stan Daniels.

3675. Carol Goodner (May 30, 1904–) B: New York, NY. *Let's Face It!* (Imperial, CR, "Maggie Watson," July 1942 or Aug. 17, 1942): Baby Games; A Lady Needs a Rest; Let's Not Talk About Love/WM: Cole Porter.

3676. Mamie Goodrich *Buster Brown* (Majestic, "Gladys O'Flynn," Jan. 24, 1905): Oh Gladys/W: Paul West, M: John W. Bratton.

3677. Don Goodspeed (Apr. 1, 1958–) B: Truro, NS, Canada. *Aspects of Love* (Broadhurst, "Hugo Le Muenier," Apr. 8, 1990): Hand Me the Wine and the Dice/W: Don Black, Charles Hart, M: Andrew Lloyd Webber.

3678. Doris Goodwin *Three Twins* (Herald Square > Majestic, CR, "Kate Armitage," Nov. 30, 1908): Cuddle Up a Little Closer, Lovey Mine; Good Night, Sweetheart, Good Night; The Little Girl Up There/W: Otto Harbach, M: Karl Hoschna. *The Young Turk* (New York, "Mirza," Jan. 31, 1910): I'll Be Happy Too; The Parisian Glide; Under the Oriental Moon/W: Harry Williams, M: Max Hoffmann. *Madame Troubadour* (Lyric > 39th Street, "Martine," Oct. 10, 1910): The Chimes Number/W: Joseph W. Herbert, M: Felix Albini.

3679. Gloria Goodwin *Love o' Mike* (Shubert > Maxine Elliott, "Gloria," Jan. 15, 1917): Look in the Book; Lulu/W: Harry B. Smith, M: Jerome Kern. *The Melting of Molly* (Broadhurst, "Dot Carter," Dec. 30, 1918): Dancing School; Floating Down a Moonlight Stream; I Want My Husband When I Wed; Jazz, How I Love to Hear It/W: Cyrus D. Wood, M: Sigmund Romberg — Jazz All Your Troubles Away/W: Augustus Barratt, M: Sigmund Romberg.

3680. Ruth Goodwin *Oh, Please!* (Fulton, CR, "Clarice Cartier," Feb. 14, 1927): I'm Waiting for a Wonderful Girl; Snappy Show in Town/W: Anne Caldwell, M: Vincent Youmans. *Lovely Lady* (Sam H. Harris, "Celeste," Dec. 29, 1927): At the Barbecue/W: Harry A. Steinberg, Edward Ward, M: Dave Stamper, Harold A. Levey — The Lost Step; Make Believe You're Happy/W: Cyrus D. Wood, M: Dave Stamper, Harold A. Levey.

3681. Thelma Goodwin *Three Little Girls* (Shubert, "Charlotte," Apr. 14, 1930): Doll Song/W: Harry B. Smith, M: Walter Kollo.

3682. Bernard Gorcey (1888–Sept. 11, 1955) B: Switzerland. In the role of Isaac Cohen, Gorcey was one of the original cast of the play *Abie's Irish Rose*, which opened at the Fulton Theater on Broadway on May 23, 1922, and in spite of critical sneering and other obstacles along the way, ran for 2,327 performances. *High Jinks* (Casino, CR, "Fritz Denkmahl," June 8, 1914): I Know Your Husband Very Well/W: Otto Harbach, M: Rudolf Friml. *Katinka* (44th Street > Lyric, "Herr Knopf," Dec. 23, 1915): Skidis-kischatch/W: Otto Harbach, M: Rudolf Friml. *Song of the Flame* (44th Street, "Count Boris," Dec. 30, 1925): I Want Two Husbands/W: Otto Harbach, Oscar Hammerstein II, M: Herbert Stothart.

3683. Anna Belle Gordon *Marrying Mary* (Daly's, "Miss Smith," Aug. 27, 1906): Old Reliable Jokes/W: Benjamin Hapgood Burt, M: Silvio Hein.

3684. Bert Gordon (Apr. 8, 1895–Nov. 30, 1974) B: New York, NY. From about 1935, the comedian played a character called The Mad Russian on Eddie Cantor's radio show. *Hold On to Your Hats* (Shubert, "Concho," Sept. 11, 1940): Down on the Dude Ranch/W: E.Y. Harburg, M: Burton Lane.

3685. Bruce Gordon (1916–) B: Massachusetts. On TV he was Frank Nitti in *The Untouchables* (1959) and Gus Chernak in *Peyton Place* (1965). *Nowhere to Go but Up* (Winter Garden, "Anthony Baiello," Nov. 10, 1962): Dear Mom; Follow the Leader Septet; Take Me Back; Yes, Mr. Baiello/W: James Lipton, M: Sol Berkowitz.

3686. Carl Gordon (Jan. 20, 1932–) B: Richmond, VA. *Ain't Supposed to Die a Natural Death* (Ethel Barrymore, Oct. 20, 1971): You Gotta be Holdin' Out Five Dollars on Me/WM: Melvin Van Peebles.

3687. Carolyn Gordon *San Toy* (Daly's, CR, "Dudley," Mar. 18, 1901): The Lady's Maid/W: Harry Greenbank, Adrian Ross, M: Lionel Monckton — Pletty Little Chinee; Samee Gamee; We'll Keep the Feast in Pynka Pong/W: Harry Greenbank, Adrian Ross, M: Sidney Jones — Rhoda and Her Pagoda/W: Adrian Ross, M: Lionel Monckton.

3688. Donald Gordon *Bitter Sweet* (Ziegfeld, "Marquis of Steere" and "Duke of Tenterden," Nov. 5, 1929): The Last Dance; Tarara Boom-de-Ay/WM: Noel Coward.

3689. Eleanor Gordon *The Velvet Lady* (New Amsterdam, "Miss Winnacker [Auntie]," Feb. 3, 1919): Throwing the Bull/W: Henry Blossom, M: Victor Herbert. *The Little Blue Devil* (Central, "Mrs. Lewellyn," Nov. 3, 1919):

Shimmy-Shaking Love/W: Harold Atteridge, M: Harry Carroll.

3690. Elsie Gordon Known as The Girl with 100 Voices. *He Didn't Want to Do It* (Broadhurst, "Wilda Wood," Aug. 20, 1918): The Spirit of the Carnival; You're the Only One for Me/W: George Broadhurst, M: Silvio Hein.

3691. Frances Gordon *Moonshine* (Liberty, "Lady Gweneth," Oct. 30, 1905): How Happy Would This Chappie Be/W: George V. Hobart, M: Silvio Hein — A Hundred Years from Now/W: George V. Hobart, Edwin Milton Royle, M: Silvio Hein. *The Pink Lady* (New Amsterdam, CR, "Desiree," Sept. 9, 1912): By the Saskatchewan/W: C.M.S. McLellan, M: Ivan Caryll.

3692. Gary Gordon *The Golden Apple* (Alvin, "Doc MacCahan," Apr. 20, 1954): Come Along, Boys; Helen Is Always Willing; It Was a Glad Adventure/W: John Latouche, M: Jerome Moross.

3693. Hayes Gordon (Feb. 25, 1920–Oct. 19, 1999) B: Boston, MA. Founder of the Ensemble Theater in Australia. *Sleepy Hollow* (St. James, "Brom Van Brunt [Bones]," June 3, 1948): The Englishman's Head; Here and Now; I Still Have Plenty to Learn; Pedro, Ichabod/W: Miriam Battista, Russell Maloney, M: George Lessner — I'm Lost/W: Ruth Hughes Aarons, M: George Lessner. *Small Wonder* (Coronet, revue, Sept. 15, 1948): Ballad for Billionaires/W: Burt Shevelove, M: Albert Selden — Nobody Told Me/W: Phyllis McGinley, M: Baldwin Bergersen.

3694. Jeanne Gordon *On the Town* (Adelphi, "Spanish Singer," Dec. 28, 1944): I'm Blue/W: Betty Comden, Adolph Green, M: Leonard Bernstein.

3695. Kitty Gordon (Apr. 22, 1878–May 26, 1974) B: Folkestone, Kent, England. M: JACK WILSON, one of 4 husbands. *The Girl and the Wizard* (Casino, "Murietta," Sept. 27, 1909): The Black Butterfly; Song of the Heart/W: Edward Madden, M: Julian Edwards — By the Blue Lagoon/W: Percival Knight, M: Jerome Kern — Military Mary Ann/W: Edward Madden, M: Louis A. Hirsch — Opera Comique [Nov. 1, 1909]; When I Sang Toreador/WM: Melville Gideon — True Blue/W: Glen MacDonough, M: Raymond Hubbell. *Alma, Where Do You Live?* (Weber's, "Alma," Sept. 26, 1910): Alma; Boogie Boo; Childhood Days; Kiss Me, My Love; The Land of Beautiful Dreams; Sail Home/W: George V. Hobart, M: Adolf Philipp. *La Belle Paree* (Winter Garden, "Lady Guff Jordon," Mar. 10, 1911): Monte Carlo Moon/W: Edward Madden, M: Frank Tours. *The En-*

chantress (New York, "Vivien Savary," Oct. 19, 1911): All Your Own Am I; One Word from You; Rose, Lucky Rose; To the Land of My Own Romance/W: Harry B. Smith, M: Victor Herbert. *A World of Pleasure* (Winter Garden, revue, Oct. 14, 1915): Down in Catty Corner; Fascination; The Girl of the Fan; In the War Against Men/W: Harold Atteridge, M: Sigmund Romberg.

3696. Mackenzie Gordon *The Silver Slipper* (Broadway, "Donald Gregor," Oct. 27, 1902): Because I Love You Dear/W: W.H. Risque, M: Leslie Stuart — Two Eyes of Blue/W: Charles H. Taylor, M: Leslie Stuart.

3697. Noel Gordon *Kiss Me, Kate* (New Century, "First Suitor," Dec. 30, 1948): Tom, Dick or Harry/WM: Cole Porter.

3698. Phyllis Gordon *Up and Down Broadway* (Casino, revue, July 18, 1910): Come Down to Earth, My Dearie; Go on Your Mission; I Am Melpomene/W: William Jerome, M: Jean Schwartz — When Sist' Tetrazin' Met Cousin Carus/WM: Edward Madden, Louis A. Hirsch, Melville Gideon.

3699. Roy Gordon (Jan. 15, 1896–Oct. 12, 1978) *The Sweetheart Shop* (Knickerbocker, "Gideon Blount," Aug. 31, 1920): The Sweetheart Shop/W: Anne Caldwell, M: Hugo Felix. *Princess Charming* (Imperial, "Baron Sigman," Oct. 13, 1930): Take a Letter to the King/W: Arthur Swanstrom, M: Arthur Schwartz, Albert Sirmay.

3700. William C. Gordon *The Clinging Vine* (Knickerbocker, "Bascom," Dec. 25, 1922): Spring Fever/W: Zelda Sears, M: Harold A. Levey.

3701. Zoe Gordon *Bitter Sweet* (Ziegfeld, "Lotte," Nov. 5, 1929): Ladies of the Town/WM: Noel Coward.

3702. Edward Gore *The Toreador* (Knickerbocker, "Gov. of Villaya," Jan. 6, 1902): The Governor of Villaya/W: Adrian Ross, M: Ivan Caryll.

3703. Ili Gorlizki *To Live Another Summer, To Pass Another Winter* (Helen Hayes, revue, Oct. 21, 1971): Noah's Ark/W: David Paulsen, M: Dov Seltzer — Sorry We Won/W: David Paulsen, M: David Krivoshei — What Are the Basic Things?/W: Lillian Burstein, M: Dov Seltzer.

3704. Bob Gorman (Dec. 30, 1928–Oct. 11, 1988) B: Peoria, TN. Performer, pianist and singing coach. *Gantry* (George Abbott, "Trosper," Feb. 14, 1970): Foresight/W: Fred Tobias, M: Stanley Lebowsky.

3705. Julia Gorman *George White's Scandals*

of 1931 (Apollo, revue, Sept. 14, 1931): Back from Hollywood/W: Lew Brown, M: Ray Henderson.

3706. Michael Gorman *A Chorus Line* (Shubert, CR, "Bobby," Aug. 1980): And…/W: Edward Kleban, M: Marvin Hamlisch.

3707. Eydie Gorme (Aug. 16, 1932–) B: Bronx, NY. M: STEVE LAWRENCE. *Golden Rainbow* (Shubert, "Judy Harris," Feb. 4, 1968): All in Fun; Desert Moon; For Once in Your Life; He Needs Me Now; How Could I Be So Wrong; It's You Again; Taking Care of You; We Got Us/WM: Walter Marks.

3708. Ruth Gormly *Broadway Nights* (44th Street, revue, "Boots McAllister," July 15, 1929): Come Hit Your Baby; Hotsy Totsy Hats; White Lights Were Coming/W: Moe Jaffe, M: Sam Timberg, Maurie Rubens.

3709. Edyta Gorniak *Metro* (Minskoff, "Edyta," Apr. 16, 1992): Waiting/Eng. W: Mary Bracken Phillips, M: Janusz Stoklosa.

3710. Maggy Gorrill (Feb. 19, 1952–) B: Long Island City, NY. *Peter Pan, or The Boy Who Wouldn't Grow Up* (Lunt-Fontanne, revival, "Liza," Sept. 6, 1979): I've Gotta Crow/W: Carolyn Leigh, M: Moose Charlap.

3711. Frank Gorshin (Apr. 5, 1933–) B: Pittsburgh, PA. He played the Riddler in TV's *Batman* series (1965). *Jimmy* (Winter Garden, "Jimmy Walker," Oct. 23, 1969): The Darlin' of New York; Life Is a One-Way Street; The Little Woman; One in a Million; Our Jimmy; Riverside Drive; The Squabble Song; That Old Familiar Ring; They Never Proved a Thing; The Walker Walk; What's Out There for Me?; Will You Think of Me Tomorrow?/WM: Bill Jacob, Patti Jacob.

3712. Virginia Gorski (Apr. 9, 1926–) B: St. Louis, MO. *Billion Dollar Baby* (Alvin, CR, "Maribelle Jones," June 10, 1946): Bad Timing; Dreams Come True; Faithless; A Life with Rocky; A Lovely Girl; Who's Gonna Be the Winner?/W: Betty Comden, Adolph Green, M: Morton Gould. *Look Ma, I'm Dancin'* (Adelphi, "Snow White," Jan. 29, 1948): The Little Boy Blues; Shauny O'Shay/WM: Hugh Martin. *Along Fifth Avenue* (Broadhurst, revue, Jan. 13, 1949): Fifth Avenue/W: Tom Adair, M: Gordon Jenkins.

3713. Robert Goss *The Merry Widow* (New York State Theater, revival, "Chevalier St. Brioche," Aug. 17, 1964): When in France; Who Knows the Way to My Heart?; Women/W: Forman Brown, M: Franz Lehar.

3714. Louis (Lou) Gossett (May 27, 1936–) B: Brooklyn, NY. The popular screen and TV actor once played basketball for the NY Knicks.

The Zulu and the Zayda (Cort, "Paulus," Nov. 10, 1965): It's Good to Be Alive; Zulu Love Song (Wait for Me)/WM: Harold Rome.

3715. Ruth Gottschall (Apr. 14, 1957–) B: Wilmington, DE. *Prince of Central Park* (Belasco, "Young Margie," Nov. 9, 1989): We Were Dancing/W: Gloria Nissenson, M: Don Sebesky.

3716. Berni Gould *By Jupiter* (Shubert, "Homer," June 3, 1942): Bottoms Up/W: Lorenz Hart, M: Richard Rodgers. *Let Freedom Sing* (Longacre, revue, Oct. 5, 1942): Mittel-Europa/W: Henry Myers, Edward Eliscu, M: Jay Gorney.

3717. Billy Gould (c 1869–Feb. 1, 1950) B: New York, NY. Song and dance man. One of his partners was VALESKA SURATT. *Maid in America* (Winter Garden, revue, CR, "The Made in America Song Writer" and "John Gray," May 17, 1915): Dancing Around the U.S.A./W: Jack Yellen, M: Harry Carroll, George L. Cobb — Garden of Paradise; (It Is All for You) Only for You; The Times Square Arguments/W: Harold Atteridge, M: Sigmund Romberg — Made in the U.S.A./W: Harold Atteridge, M: Harry Carroll.

3718. Edith (Kelly) Gould see EDITH KELLY.

3719. Elliott Gould (Aug. 29, 1938–) B: Brooklyn, NY. M: BARBRA STREISAND, 1963 to1966. In movies and TV from 1966. *Irma La Douce* (Plymouth, CR, "Polyte-Le-Mou"): But; The Freedom of the Seas; From a Prison Cell; Le Grisbi Is le Root of le Evil in Man; Sons of France; That's a Crime; There Is Only One Paris for That/W: Julian More, David Heneker, Monty Norman, M: Marguerite Monnot. *I Can Get It for You Wholesale* (Shubert, "Harry Bogen," Mar. 22, 1962): Ballad of the Garment Trade; Eat a Little Something; The Family Way; A Funny Thing Happened (On My Way to Love); A Gift Today (The Bar Mitzvah Song); Momma, Momma; The Sound of Money; The Way Things Are; When Gemini Meets Capricorn/WM: Harold Rome. *Drat! The Cat!* (Martin Beck, "Bob Purefoy," Oct. 10, 1965): Dancing with Alice; Deep in Your Heart; Holmes and Watson; Let's Go; Purefoy's Lament; She Touched Me; She's Roses; Wild and Reckless/W: Ira Levin, M: Milton Schafer.

3720. Jay Gould *Tick-Tack-Toe* (Princess, revue, Feb. 13, 1920): Hoppy Poppy Queen; I'd Like to Know Why I Fell in Love with You; Love Is a Game of Cards; My Manicure Maids; Playing for the Girl; Shimmy All the Blues Away/WM: Herman Timberg. *The Broadway Whirl* (Times Square > Selwyn, revue, June 8, 1921):

The Broadway Whirl/W: Joseph McCarthy, M: Harry Tierney — Limehouse Nights/W: B.G. DeSylva, John Henry Mears, M: George Gershwin — Stars of Broadway/WM: ?. *Molly Darling* (Liberty, "Archie Ames," Sept. 1, 1922): Contrary Mary; Dear Little Gad-About; Don't Tag Along/W: Phil Cook, M: Tom Johnstone. *Topics of 1923* (Broadhurst, revue, Nov. 20, 1923): Doing the Apache/W: Harold Atteridge, M: Sigmund Romberg — The Jazz Wedding/WM: ?. *Plain Jane* (New Amsterdam, "Dick Kingsley," May 12, 1924): Along the Road to Love; A Playhouse Planned for You; Someone Like You [May 19, 1924]; When the Whistle Blows/W: Phil Cook, M: Tom Johnstone.

3721. Rita Gould *Ziegfeld Follies of 1914* (New Amsterdam, revue, June 1, 1914): I've Got Him Now!/W: Gene Buck, M: Dave Stamper — Rock Me in the Cradle of Love [June 8, 1914]/WM: J. Leubrie Hill. *Maid in America* (Winter Garden, revue, CR, "Nettie, Belle of the Broadway Knitting Club," Apr. 12, 1915): The Stolen Melody/WM: Harold Atteridge, Phil Schwartz, Nora Bayes — There's a Little Bit of Everything on Broadway/WM: Leo Edwards — When Grandma Was a Little Girl Like Me/W: James O'Dea, M: Anne Caldwell.

3722. William Gould *The Runaways* (Casino, "Dave Budd," May 11, 1903): The Maiden and the Jay/WM: William Gould — Miss Susanna from Urbana/W: Addison Burkhardt, M: Raymond Hubbell. *Hip! Hip! Hooray!* (Music Hall, revue, "Punch Hardy," Oct. 10, 1907): In Philadelphia/W: Whitford Watson, M: Gus Edwards — Put Me Amongst the Girls/W: George Arthurs, M: C.W. Murphy.

3723. Robert Goulet (Nov. 26, 1933–) B: Lawrence, MA. Popular, enduring singer and actor of the stage and TV. *Camelot* (Majestic, "Sir Lancelot," Dec. 3, 1960): C'est Moi; If Ever I Would Leave You/W: Alan Jay Lerner, M: Frederick Loewe. *The Happy Time* (Broadway, "Jacques Bonnard," Jan. 18, 1968): Among My Yesterdays; Being Alive; A Certain Girl; The Happy Time; I Don't Remember You; Please Stay; Seeing Things; Tomorrow Morning/W: Fred Ebb, M: John Kander. *Camelot* (Gershwin, revival, "King Arthur," June 21, 1993): Camelot; How to Handle a Woman; I Wonder What the King Is Doing Tonight; The Jousts; What Do the Simple Folk Do?/W: Alan Jay Lerner, M: Frederick Loewe.

3724. John Gourlay (?–Nov. 15, 1906) *The French Maid* (Herald Square, "Adm. Sir Hercules Hawser, K.C.B.," Sept. 27, 1897): It's Ever My Endeavor/W: Basil Hood, M: Walter Slaughter.

3725. Harry Goz (June 23, 1932–) B: St. Louis, MO. *Fiddler on the Roof* (Imperial, CR, "Lazar Wolf," July 1967): Anatevka; To Life/W: Sheldon Harnick, M: Jerry Bock. *Fiddler on the Roof* (Imperial, CR, "Tevye," Aug. 14, 1967/Nov. 6, 1967/Sept. 8, 1969): Anatevka; Do You Love Me?; If I Were a Rich Man; Sabbath Prayer; Sunrise, Sunset; The Tailor, Motel Kamzoil; To Life; Tradition/W: Sheldon Harnick, M: Jerry Bock. *Two by Two* (Imperial, "Shem," Nov. 10, 1970/Feb. 18, 1971): As Far as I'm Concerned; Put Him Away; You Have Got to Have a Rudder on the Ark/W: Martin Charnin, M: Richard Rodgers. *Two by Two* (Imperial, CR, "Noah," Feb. 5, 1971): The Covenant; Hey, Girlie; Ninety Again!; Poppa Knows Best; Something, Somewhere; Two by Two; When It Dries; Why Me?; You; You Have Got to Have a Rudder on the Ark/W: Martin Charnin, M: Richard Rodgers. *Chess* (Imperial, "Molokov," Apr. 28, 1988): Let's Work Together; A Model of Decorum & Tranquility; U.S. Versus U.S.S.R./W: Tim Rice, M: Benny Anderson, Bjorn Ulvaeus.

3726. Jason Graae (May 15, 1958–) B: Chicago, IL. *Do Black Patent Leather Shoes Really Reflect Up?* (Alvin, "Louis Schlang," May 27, 1982): Doo-Waa, Doo-Wee/WM: James Quinn, Alaric Jans. *Stardust* (Biltmore, revue, Feb. 19, 1987): Belle of the Ball; Forgotten Dreams; Sleigh Ride; The Syncopated Clock/W: Mitchell Parish, M: Leroy Anderson — Carolina Rolling Stone/W: Mitchell Parish, M: Eleanor Young, Harry D. Squires — Deep Purple/W: Mitchell Parish, M: Peter DeRose — Does Your Heart Beat for Me?/W: Mitchell Parish, M: Russ Morgan, Arnold Johnson — Moonlight Serenade/W: Mitchell Parish, M: Glenn Miller — Organ Grinder's Swing/W: Mitchell Parish, Irving Mills, M: Will Hudson — Riverboat Shuffle/W: Mitchell Parish, M: Hoagy Carmichael, Dick Voynow, Irving Mills — Sidewalks of Cuba/WM: Mitchell Parish, Irving Mills, Ben Oakland — Star Dust/W: Mitchell Parish, M: Hoagy Carmichael — Volare/W: Mitchell Parish, M: Domenico Modugno — Wealthy, Shmelthy, as Long as You're Healthy; You're So Indiff'rent/W: Mitchell Parish, M: Sammy Fain. *Falsettos* (John Golden, revival, CR, "Mendel," June 4, 1993): Canceling the Bar Mitzvah; Everyone Hates His Parents; The Fight; Four Jews in a Room Bitching; The Games I Play; I Never Wanted to Love You; Jason's Therapy; Love Is Blind; Making a Home; March of the Falsettos; A Marriage Proposal; Marvin at the Psychiatrist; Marvin Hits Trina; Please Come to My House; This Had Better Come to a Stop; A Tight Knit Family/

WM: William Finn. *A Grand Night for Singing* (Criterion Center Stage Right, revue, Nov. 17, 1993): All at Once You Love Her; Don't Marry Me; Hello, Young Lovers; Honey Bun; I Have Dreamed; I Know It Can Happen Again; Impossible; It's a Grand Night for Singing; It's Me; Kansas City; Love, Look Away; A Lovely Night; The Man I Used to Be; Maria; My Little Girl (from Soliloquy); Shall We Dance?; So Far; Some Enchanted Evening; The Surrey with the Fringe on Top; That's the Way It Happens; When the Children Are Asleep; When You're Driving Through the Moonlight; Wish Them Well/W: Oscar Hammerstein II, M: Richard Rodgers.

3727. Ariel Grabber *Starmites* (Criterion Center Stage Right, "Shak Graa," Apr. 27, 1989): Immolation/WM: Barry Keating.

3728. Betty Grable (Dec. 18, 1916–July 3, 1973) B: St. Louis, MO. M: film star Jackie Coogan, 1937–1940; musician Harry James, 1943–1965. Mega-moviestar Grable, with her long legs and delicate complexion, was the pin-up girl of World War II. *Du Barry Was a Lady* (46th Street, "Alice Barton" and "Alisande," Dec. 6, 1939): Ev'ry Day a Holiday; Katie Went to Haiti; Well, Did You Evah!/WM: Cole Porter. *Hello, Dolly!* (St. James, CR, "Mrs. Dolly Gallagher Levi," June 12, 1967): Before the Parade Passes By/WM: Lee Adams, Charles Strouse, Jerry Herman — Dancing; Hello, Dolly!; I Put My Hand In; Put on Your Sunday Clothes; So Long, Dearie/WM: Jerry Herman — Motherhood/WM: Bob Merrill, Jerry Herman.

3729. Barbara Grace *Queen High* (Ambassador, "Kitty," Sept. 7, 1926): Beautiful Baby/W: B.G. DeSylva, M: James F. Hanley — Everything Will Happen for the Best; It Pays to Advertise; The Weaker Sex; Who'll Mend a Broken Heart?/W: B.G. DeSylva, M: Lewis E. Gensler.

3730. Frank Grace With JOHN (JOHNNY; JOHNNIE) BERKES, they were known as Grace and Berkes. *Robinson Crusoe, Jr.* (Winter Garden, Feb. 17, 1916): (Go Ahead and) Dance a Little More/W: Harold Atteridge, M: James F. Hanley — Don't Be a Sailor; Happy Hottentots/W: Harold Atteridge, M: Sigmund Romberg. *Sinbad* (Winter Garden > Century > Casino, Feb. 14, 1918): The Bedalumbo/W: Harold Atteridge, M: Al Jolson — Love Ahoy!; The Rag Lad of Bagdad; Raz-Ma-Taz/W: Harold Atteridge, M: Sigmund Romberg. *The Passing Show of 1921* (Winter Garden, revue, Dec. 29, 1920): The Dancing Blues; I'm Oriental [May 2, 1921]/W: Harold Atteridge, M: Lew Pollack — The Sweetest Melody/WM: Abner Silver.

3731. Monica Lee Gradischek *Grease* (Eugene O'Neill, revival, CR, "Frenchy," c 1994): Beauty School Dropout/WM: Jim Jacobs, Warren Casey.

3732. Lottie Grady *Mr. Lode of Koal* (Majestic, "Mysteria," Nov. 1, 1909): Mum's the Word, Mr. Moon/W: Alex Rogers, M: J. Leubrie Hill.

3733. Douglas Graeme-Brooke *Bitter Sweet* (Ziegfeld, "Mr. Proutie," Nov. 5, 1929): The Last Dance; Tarara Boom-de-Ay/WM: Noel Coward.

3734. Ilene Graff (Feb. 28–) B: New York, NY. *Grease* (Broadhurst, CR, "Sandy Dumbrowski," Mar. 1973): All Choked Up; It's Raining on Prom Night; Look at Me, I'm Sandra Dee; Summer Nights/WM: Jim Jacobs, Warren Casey. *I Love My Wife* (Ethel Barrymore, "Cleo," Apr. 17, 1977): Love Revolution; Married Couple Seeks Married Couple; Sexually Free; Someone Wonderful I Missed/W: Michael Stewart, M: Cy Coleman.

3735. Randy Graff (May 23, 1955–) B: Brooklyn, NY. *Les Miserables* (Broadway, "Fantine," Mar. 12, 1987): Come to Me; I Dreamed a Dream/W: Herbert Kretzmer, M: Claude-Michel Schonberg. *City of Angels* (Virginia, "Oolie" and "Donna," Dec. 11, 1989): The Buddy System; What You Don't Know About Women; You Can Always Count on Me/W: David Zippel, M: Cy Coleman. *Falsettos* (John Golden, revival, CR, "Trina," Apr. 12, 1993): Canceling the Bar Mitzvah; Everyone Hates His Parents; Everyone Tells Jason to See a Psychiatrist; The Fight; The Games I Play; Holding to the Ground; I Never Wanted to Love You; I'm Breaking Down; Jason's Therapy; Love Is Blind; Making a Home; A Marriage Proposal; Marvin Hits Trina; Please Come to My House; This Had Better Come to a Stop; Trina's Song/WM: William Finn.

3736. Todd Graff (Oct. 22, 1959–) B: New York, NY. *Baby* (Ethel Barrymore, "Danny Hooper," Dec. 4, 1983): At Night She Comes Home to Me; Baby, Baby, Baby; Fatherhood Blues; I Chose Right; Two People in Love; We Start Today; What Could Be Better?/W: Richard Maltby, Jr., M: David Shire.

3737. Gloria Grafton She also played the role of Mickey Considine on the spectacular but unsuccesful radio version of *Jumbo*, known as *The Jumbo Fire Chief Program* (1935). On the first broadcast she introduced the song "My Romance" with DONALD NOVIS. *The Second Little Show* (Royale, revue, Sept. 2, 1930): My Intuition; You're the Sunrise/W: Howard Dietz, M: Arthur Schwartz — Tired of Love/W: Ted

Fetter, M: Del Cleveland. *Jumbo* (Hipppodrome, "Mickey Considine," Nov. 16, 1935): The Circus Wedding; Little Girl Blue; The Most Beautiful Girl in the World; My Romance/W: Lorenz Hart, M: Richard Rodgers.

3738. Beatrice Graham *Who's Who* (Hudson, revue, Mar. 1, 1938): It's You I Want/W: Al Stillman, M: Paul McGrane.

3739. Deborah Graham (Jan. 20, 1959–) B: Speedway, IN. *Romance Romance* (Helen Hayes, "Barb," May 1, 1988): Let's Not Talk About It; My Love for You; Small Craft Warnings; Think of the Odds/W: Barry Harman, M: Keith Herrmann.

3740. Edward Graham *Earl Carroll's Vanities of 1928* (Earl Carroll, revue, Aug. 6, 1928): Painting a Vanities Girl/WM: Ernie Golden.

3741. Elizabeth Graham *Porgy and Bess* (Uris, revival, "Clara," Sept. 25, 1976): Summertime/W: DuBose Heyward, M: George Gershwin.

3742. Frederick (Fred) Graham *The Little Cafe* (New Amsterdam, "Baron Tombola," Nov. 10, 1913): The Beauty Contest/W: C.M.S. McLellan, M: Ivan Caryll. *See-Saw* (Cohan, "Harkins," Sept. 23, 1919): When You Come Near I Feel All of a Ooh!/W: Earl Derr Biggers, M: Louis A. Hirsch. *Up She Goes* (Playhouse, "Uncle Bob Bennett," Nov. 6, 1922): Bobbin' About; Tyup (Hitch Your Wagon to a Star)/W: Joseph McCarthy, M: Harry Tierney.

3743. George M. Graham *The Belle of Brittany* (Daly's, "Compte Victoire de Casserole," Nov. 8, 1909): The Old Chateau/W: Percy Greenbank, M: Howard Talbot, Marie Horne.

3744. June Graham *Heaven on Earth* (New Century, "A Lover," Sept. 16, 1948): Heaven on Earth/W: Barry Trivers, M: Jay Gorney.

3745. R.E. Graham *Florodora* (Casino > New York, "Cyrus W. Gilfain," Nov. 10, 1900): I Want to Marry a Man, I Do/W: Paul Rubens, M: Leslie Stuart — Phrenology; When You're a Millionaire/W: Ernest Boyd-Jones, M: Leslie Stuart. *Piff! Paff!! Pouf!!!* (Casino, CR, "August Melon," Aug. 8, 1904): Cordelia Malone; Dear Old Manhattan Isle; For You; I Don't Want Any Wurzburger/W: William Jerome, M: Jean Schwartz. *My Lady's Maid or Lady Madcap* (Casino, "Bill Stratford," Sept. 20, 1906): Flirtation; We Get There Just the Same/WM: Percy Greenbank, Paul Rubens. *The Rose Maid* (Globe, "Sir John Portman," Apr. 22, 1912): The Happy Family/W: Robert B. Smith, M: Bruno Granichstaedten.

3746. Rachael Graham *Meet Me in St. Louis* (Gershwin, "Agnes Smith," Nov. 2, 1989): Be

Anything but a Girl; Ghosties and Ghoulies and Things That Go Bump in the Night/WM: Hugh Martin, Ralph Blane.

3747. Ronald Graham (1913–July 4, 1950) B: Hamilton, Scotland. *Virginia* (Center, "Col. Richard Fairfax," Sept. 2, 1937): If You Were Someone Else/W: Al Stillman, M: Arthur Schwartz — You and I Know/W: Al Stillman, Laurence Stallings, M: Arthur Schwartz. *The Boys from Syracuse* (Alvin, "Antipholus of Ephesus," Nov. 23, 1938): Come with Me; The Shortest Day of the Year/W: Lorenz Hart, M: Richard Rodgers. *The Boys from Syracuse* (Alvin, CR, "Antipholus of Syracuse," May 1939): Dear Old Syracuse; This Can't Be Love; You Have Cast Your Shadow on the Sea/W: Lorenz Hart, M: Richard Rodgers. *Du Barry Was a Lady* (46th Street > Royale, "Alex Barton" and "Alexandre," Dec. 6, 1939): Do I Love You?; It Was Written in the Stars/WM: Cole Porter. *By Jupiter* (Shubert, "Theseus," June 3, 1942): Careless Rhapsody; The Gateway of the Temple of Minerva; Here's a Hand; Wait Till You See Her/W: Lorenz Hart, M: Richard Rodgers. *Dream with Music* (Majestic, "Michael" and "Aladdin," May 18, 1944): Baby, Don't Count on Me; Come with Me; The Moon Song/W: Edward Eager, M: Clay Warnick.

3748. Ronny Graham (Aug. 26, 1919–July 4, 1998) B: Philadelphia, PA. Comic actor and screenwriter. He played Rev. Bemis on the TV sitcom *Chico and the Man* (1975). *New Faces of 1952* (Royale, revue, May 16, 1952): Take Off the Mask/WM: Alice Ghostley, Ronny Graham. *Something More!* (Eugene O'Neill, "Monte Checkovitch," Nov. 10, 1964): Church of My Choice; Grazie Per Niente; Life Is Too Short/W: Marilyn Bergman, Alan Bergman, M: Sammy Fain — Jaded, Degraded Am I!/W: Marilyn Bergman, Alan Bergman, M: Jule Styne.

3749. Nellie Graham-Dent *The Little Whopper* (Casino, "Miss Granville," Oct. 13, 1919): Oh! What a Little Whopper/W: Otto Harbach, Bide Dudley, M: Rudolf Friml. *Just Because* (Earl Carroll, "Mrs. Bennett," Mar. 22, 1922): Widow's Blues/W: Helen S. Woodruff, M: Madelyn Sheppard.

3750. Sidney Grammer *Conversation Piece* (44th Street, "Mr. Hailsham," Oct. 23, 1934): Regency Rakes/WM: Noel Coward.

3751. Albert Gran (Aug. 4, 1862–Dec. 16, 1932) B: Bergen, Norway. *The King of Cadonia* (Daly's, "Gen. Bonski," Jan. 10, 1910): Time for the King/W: Adrian Ross, M: Sidney Jones.

3752. Marjorie Graner *Pal Joey* (New York City Center, revival, "The Kid," May 31, 1961):

You Mustn't Kick It Around/W: Lorenz Hart, M: Richard Rodgers.

3753. Farley Granger (July 1, 1925–) B: San Jose, CA. *First Impressions* (Alvin, "Fitzwilliam Darcy," Mar. 19, 1959): A Gentleman Never Falls Wildly in Love; The Heart Has Won the Game; I Suddenly Find You Agreeable; A Perfect Evening/WM: Robert Goldman, Glenn Paxton, George Weiss. *The King and I* (New York City Center, revival, "The King," May 11, 1960): A Puzzlement; Shall We Dance?; Song of the King/W: Oscar Hammerstein II, M: Richard Rodgers.

3754. Michael Granger (May 14, 1923–) B: Kansas City, MO. *Fiddler on the Roof* (Imperial, "Lazar Wolf," Sept. 22, 1964): Anatevka; To Life/W: Sheldon Harnick, M: Jerry Bock.

3755. Seth Granger (Oct. 17, 1974–) *Teddy & Alice* (Minskoff, "Kermit Roosevelt," Nov. 12, 1987): Charge; Private Thoughts/W: Hal Hackady, M: John Philip Sousa, Richard Kapp.

3756. Al Grant *Nancy Brown* (Bijou, "Noah Little," Feb. 16, 1903): I'm Glad I'm Not Methusalem/WM: Eugene Ellsworth — The Katy-did, the Cricket and the Frog/W: J. Rosamond Johnson, M: Bob Cole.

3757. Cary Grant see ARCHIE LEACH.

3758. Douglas Grant *The Me Nobody Knows* (Helen Hayes, "Benjamin," Dec. 18, 1970): Black; Flying Milk and Runaway Plates/W: Will Holt, M: Gary William Friedman.

3759. Micki Grant (June 30–) B: Chicago, IL. *Don't Bother Me, I Can't Cope* (Playhouse, revue, Apr. 19, 1972): I Gotta Keep Movin'; It Takes a Whole Lot of Human Feeling; Questions; So Little Time; Thank Heaven for You; Time Brings About a Change; You Think I Got Rhythm?/WM: Micki Grant.

3760. Sean Grant (July 13, 1966–) B: Brooklyn, NY. *Starlight Express* (Gershwin, "Rocky II," Mar. 15, 1987): Belle; Poppa's Blues; Right Place, Right Time/W: Richard Stilgoe, M: Andrew Lloyd Webber.

3761. Sterling Grant *Messin' Around* (Hudson, revue, Apr. 22, 1929): Sorry That I Strayed Away from You/W: Perry Bradford, M: James P. Johnson. *Change Your Luck* (George M. Cohan, "Romeo Green," June 6, 1930): Honesty; I'm Honest; What Have I Done?; You Should Know/WM: James C. Johnson.

3762. Sydney Grant (Feb. 20, 1873–July 12, 1953) B: Boston, MA. *The Passing Show of 1912* (Winter Garden, revue, July 22, 1912): It's All Over Now; Modern Love/W: Harold Atteridge, M: Louis A. Hirsch — The Philadelphia Drag/WM: Harold Orlob. *The Man with Three Wives*

(Weber and Fields, "Wendelin," Jan. 23, 1913): Hello, Hello/W: Harold Atteridge, M: Al W. Brown — Tootsie, Wootsie/W: Paul M. Potter, Harold Atteridge, M: Franz Lehar. *The Passing Show of 1913* (Winter Garden, revue, July 24, 1913): I Must Have My Way/WM: ?. *Pretty Mrs. Smith* (Casino, "Bobby Jones," Sept. 21, 1914): The Bensonhurst Gavotte; The Plain Ol' Name o' Smith/W: Earl Carroll, M: Alfred G. Robyn — Mrs. Sippi You're a Grand Old Girl/W: William (Billy) Gould, M: Belle Ashlyn. *So Long Letty* (Shubert, "Tommy Robbins," Oct. 23, 1916): Aloha; So Long Letty/WM: Earl Carroll. *The Little Whopper* (Casino, "George Emmett," Oct. 13, 1919): I Have a Date; Snap Your Fingers; We May Meet Again/W: Otto Harbach, Bide Dudley, M: Rudolf Friml. *Flossie* (Lyric, "Archie," June 3, 1924): The Battle Cry of Freedom; I'm in Wonderland; Poogie-Woo; When Things Go Wrong/W: Ralph Murphy, M: Armand Robi.

3763. Bernard Granville (July 4, 1886–Oct. 5, 1936) B: Chicago, IL. He was the father of actress and producer Bonita Granville. *A Winsome Widow* (Moulin Rouge, CR, "Rashleigh Gay," July 1, 1912): Oh, You Fascinating Girl/W: Frank Tinney, Sidney Jones, M: Fred Strasser. *Ziegfeld Follies of 1912* (Moulin Rouge, revue, Oct. 21, 1912): Beautiful Girl/W: John E. Hazzard, M: Raymond Hubbell — Dip, Dip, Dip; Follow the Circus Band; Yodel Song; You Gotta Keep Movin' and Dance (You Gotta Keep A-Goin')/W: Harry B. Smith, M: Raymond Hubbell. *The Whirl of the World* (Winter Garden, revue, "Jack Phillips," Jan. 10, 1914): A Dancing Romeo; Early Hours of the Morn/W: Harold Atteridge, M: Sigmund Romberg — The Twentieth Century Rag/WM: Henry Lehman. *The Passing Show of 1914* (Winter Garden, revue, June 10, 1914): The Eagle Rock; Good Old Levee Days; You're Just a Little Bit Better (Than the One I Thought Was Best)/W: Harold Atteridge, M: Harry Carroll. *Dancing Around* (Winter Garden, "Lieut. Hartley," Oct. 10, 1914): The Broadway Triangle; The Call to the Colors; Oh, You John/WM: ?— It's a Long Way to Tipperary/WM: Jack Judge, Harry H. Williams — My Lady of the Telephone/W: Harold Atteridge, M: Jean Gilbert — My Rainbow Beau/W: Harold Atteridge, M: Sigmund Romberg. *Ziegfeld Follies of 1915* (New Amsterdam, revue, June 21, 1915): A Girl for Each Month of the Year/W: Rennold Wolf, Channing Pollack, M: Louis A. Hirsch — Hello, Frisco! (I Called You Up to Say Hello!); My Radium Girl/W: Gene Buck, M: Louis A. Hirsch — We'll Build a Little Home in the U.S.A./W: Ward Wesley, M: Charles Elbert. *Ziegfeld Follies of 1916* (New Amsterdam, revue, June 12, 1916): Goodbye, Dear Old Bachelor Days; I Left Her on the Beach at Honolulu/W: Gene Buck, M: Louis A. Hirsch — Have a Heart; My Lady of the Nile/W: Gene Buck, M: Jerome Kern — In Florida Among the Palms [July 31, 1916]/WM: Irving Berlin. *The Little Blue Devil* (Central, "Augustus Rollett," Nov. 3, 1919): Cuckoo Town; Just a Kiss; Shimmy-Shaking Love; A Stroller in Dreamland/W: Harold Atteridge, M: Harry Carroll — Omar Khayyam/W: Harold Atteridge, M: Sigmund Romberg. *Morris Gest Midnight Whirl* (Century Grove, revue, Dec. 27, 1919): The League of Nations (Depend on Beautiful Clothes); Poppyland/W: B.G. DeSylva, John Henry Mears, M: George Gershwin. *Ziegfeld Follies of 1920* (New Amsterdam, revue, June 22, 1920): Any Place Would Be Wonderful with You; Sunshine and Shadows/W: Gene Buck, M: Dave Stamper — Bells; The Syncopated Vamp/WM: Irving Berlin — My Midnight Frolic Girl [June 28, 1920]/WM: Art Hickman, Ben Black. *Frank Fay's Fables* (Park, revue, Feb. 6, 1922): Arms of the China Wall; Columbus Wouldn't Know Columbus Circle as It Is Today; My Land; Oh, What a Happy Day; Two Are One (You Need Two Souls but One Thought/WM: Frank Fay, Clarence Gaskill. *Go-Go* (Daly's, "Jack Locksmith," Mar. 12, 1923): Go-Go Bug; Isabel; Rosetime and You/W: Alex Rogers, M: C. Luckeyth Roberts. *Earl Carroll's Vanities of 1923* (Earl Carroll, revue, CR, Sept. 10, 1923): Chasing Little Rainbows; Cretonne Girl; Mr. Wagner's Wedding March; When the Snowflakes Fall/WM: Earl Carroll. *Castles in the Air* (Selwyn, "Monty Blair," Sept. 6, 1926): Baby; Girls and the Gimmies; I Would Like to Fondle You; The Other Fellow's Girl/W: Raymond Peck, M: Percy Wenrich. *All the King's Horses* (Imperial, CR, "Con Conley," Mar. 1934): (I've Gone) Nuts Over You; Ouch; Tamboree/W: Frederick Herendeen, M: Edward A. Horan.

3764. Thomas Graves (?–Dec. 21, 1915) B: London, England. *The Man with Three Wives* (Weber and Fields, CR, "Baron Pickford," Mar. 3, 1913): Man Is Faithful Till He's Caught; Vengeance; We Are Free/W: Paul M. Potter, Harold Atteridge, M: Franz Lehar.

3765. Yolanda Graves *Honky Tonk Nights* (Biltmore, "Ruby Bush," Aug. 7, 1986): Roll with the Punches; The Sampson Beauties/W: Ralph Allen, David Campbell, M: Michael Valenti.

3766. Jan Graveson *Blood Brothers* (Music

Box, "Linda," Apr. 25, 1993): Kids Game/WM: Willy Russell.

3767. Debbie (Shapiro) Gravitte (Sept. 29, 1954–) B: Los Angeles, CA. *Blues in the Night* (Rialto, "Woman #2," June 2, 1982): Am I Blue?/ W: Grant Clarke, M: Harry Akst — Blues in the Night/W: Johnny Mercer, M: Harold Arlen — Copenhagen/W: Walter Melrose, M: Charlie Davis — I Gotta Right to Sing the Blues/W: Ted Koehler, M: Harold Arlen — It Makes My Love Come Down/WM: Bessie Smith — I've Got a Date with a Dream/W: Mack Gordon, M: Harry Revel — Nobody Knows You When You're Down and Out/WM: Jimmy Cox — Take It Right Back/WM: H. Grey — Willow Weep for Me/WM: Ann Ronell. *Zorba* (Broadway, revival, "The Woman," Oct. 16, 1983): The Bend of the Road; The Butterfly; The Crow; Grandpapa; Life Is; Only Love; That's a Beginning; The Top of the Hill; Why Can't I Speak/W: Fred Ebb, M: John Kander. *Jerome Robbins' Broadway* (Imperial, revue, Feb. 26, 1989): America/W: Stephen Sondheim, M: Leonard Bernstein — Mr. Monotony/WM: Irving Berlin — Papa, Won't You Dance with Me?/W: Sammy Cahn, M: Jule Styne — Ya Got Me/W: Betty Comden, Adolph Green, M: Leonard Bernstein — You Gotta Get a Gimmick/W: Stephen Sondheim, M: Jule Styne. *Ain't Broadway Grand* (Lunt-Fontanne, "Gypsy Rose Lee," Apr. 18, 1993): Girls Ahoy!; It's Time to Go; Maybe, Maybe Not/W: Lee Adams, M: Mitch Leigh.

3768. Adrienne Gray *Sing Out Sweet Land* (International, revue, "Farm Girl," Dec. 27, 1944): Hardly Think I Will/WM: trad.

3769. Alexander Gray (1902–1975) In 1931 the baritone sang with Nat Shilkret's studio band on the CBS radio program *The Chesterfield Quarter Hour. Ziegfeld Follies of 1922* (New Amsterdam, revue, CR, Oct. 2, 1922): List'ning on Some Radio/W: Gene Buck, M: Louis A. Hirsch, Dave Stamper. *Ziegfeld Follies of 1922 [Summer Edition]* (New Amsterdam, revue, July 16, 1923): Bring on the Girls/W: Gene Buck, M: Victor Herbert — List'ning on Some Radio; 'Neath the South Sea Moon/W: Gene Buck, M: Louis A. Hirsch, Dave Stamper — Songs I Can't Forget/W: Gene Buck, M: Louis A. Hirsch. *Annie Dear* (Times Square, "Wilbur Jennings," Nov. 4, 1924): Help, Help, Help/WM: Clare Kummer — Louwanna/W: Clifford Grey, M: Sigmund Romberg, Jean Schwartz — The Only Girl/W: Arthur Wimperis, M: Sigmund Romberg. *Tell Me More!* (Gaiety, "Kenneth Dennison," Apr. 13, 1925): Tell Me More!; Three Times a Day/W: Ira Gershwin, B.G. DeSylva,

M: George Gershwin. *The Merry World* (Imperial, revue, June 8, 1926): Golden Gates of Happiness/W: Clifford Grey, M: J. Fred Coots — Whispering Trees/W: Herbert Reynolds, M: J. Fred Coots — White Rose, Red Rose/WM: R. Moreiti. *Naughty Riquette* (Cosmopolitan, "Gaston Riviere," Sept. 13, 1926): I May/W: Harry B. Smith, M: Maurie Rubens, Kendall Burgess — Make Believe You're Mine; Two Are Company/W: Harry B. Smith, M: Oscar Straus. *The Desert Song* (Casino, CR, "Red Shadow" and "Pierre Birabeau," June 1927): The Desert Song; Farewell; I Want a Kiss; One Alone; The Riff Song; Then You Will Know/W: Otto Harbach, Oscar Hammerstein II, M: Sigmund Romberg. *John Henry* (44th Street, "Billie Bob Russell," Jan. 10, 1940): The Captain's Song/W: Roark Bradford, M: Jacques Wolfe. *Blossom Time* (Ambassador, revival, "Franz Schubert," Sept. 4, 1943): Lonely Heart; My Springtime Thou Art; Serenade; Song of Love; Tell Me, Daisy/W: Dorothy Donnelly, M: Sigmund Romberg.

3770. Bessie Gray *The Kiss Burglar* (Broadhurst > Nora Bayes, revival, "Tissie Baltimore," Mar. 17, 1919): On the Shimmering, Glimmering Nile/W: Glen MacDonough, M: Raymond Hubbell.

3771. Charles Gray (July 15, 1960–Mar. 2, 2000) Annapolis, MD. *Grease* (Eugene O'Neill, revival, CR, "Teen Angel," c 1994): Beauty School Dropout/WM: Jim Jacobs, Warren Casey.

3772. Dolores Gray (June 7, 1924–June 26, 2002) B: Chicago, IL. She sang in nightclubs and cabaret and on Rudy Vallee's radio program. In 1945 she had her own radio program. *Seven Lively Arts* (Ziegfeld, revue, Dec. 7, 1944): Is It the Girl? (Or Is It the Gown?)/WM: Cole Porter. *Are You With It?* (New Century, "Bunny La Fleur," Nov. 10, 1945): Are You With It?; In Our Cozy Little Cottage of Tomorrow; You Gotta Keep Saying No/W: Arnold B. Horwitt, M: Harry Revel. *Two on the Aisle* (Mark Hellinger, revue, July 19, 1951): Catch Our Act at the Met; Give a Little, Get a Little; Hold Me, Hold Me, Hold Me; How Will He Know?; If You Hadn't but You Did; There Never Was a Baby Like My Baby/W: Betty Comden, Adolph Green, M: Jule Styne. *Carnival in Flanders* (New Century, "Cornelia," Sept. 8, 1953): For a Moment of Your Love; Here's That Rainy Day; How Far Can a Lady Go?; I'm One of Your Admirers; It's a Fine Old Institution; It's an Old Spanish Custom; A Seventeen Gun Salute; The Stronger Sex/W: Johnny Burke, M: James Van Heusen. *Destry Rides Again* (Imperial, "Frenchy," Apr. 23, 1959):

Anyone Would Love You; Fair Warning; I Hate Him; I Know Your Kind; I Say Hello; Ladies; Once Knew a Fella; Ring on the Finger/WM: Harold Rome. *Sherry!* (Alvin, "Lorraine Sheldon," Mar. 27, 1967): Christmas Eve Broadcast; Listen Cosette; Proposal Duet; Putty in Your Hands; Sherry/W: James Lipton, M: Laurence Rosenthal. *42nd Street* (Winter Garden, CR, "Dorothy Brock," June 17, 1986): About a Quarter to Nine; I Know Now; Shadow Waltz; You're Getting to Be a Habit with Me/W: Al Dubin, M: Harry Warren — Getting Out of Town/W: Mort Dixon, M: Harry Warren.

3773. Edward Earl (Eddie) Gray (1898– Sept. 15, 1969) B: London, England. Known as Monsewer Eddie Gray. *Three Showers* (Harris > Plymouth, Apr. 5, 1920): You May Be the World to Your Mother/W: Henry Creamer, M: Turner Layton.

3774. Gilda Gray (Oct. 24, 1900–Dec. 22, 1959) B: Cracow, Poland. Star of musical comedy, cabaret and silent pictures. She introduced the shimmy, a hugely popular dance of the 1920s. *Shubert Gaieties of 1919* (44th Street, revue, July 14, 1919): Beale Street Blues/WM: W.C. Handy. *Hello, Alexander* (44th Street, Nov. 3, 1919): same as above. *Snapshots of 1921* (Selwyn, revue, June 2, 1921): The Baby Blues; Futuristic Melody/W: E. Ray Goetz, M: George Gershwin. *Ziegfeld Follies of 1922* (New Amsterdam, revue, June 5, 1922): Come Along [June 12, 1922]/W: Henry Creamer, M: Turner Layton — It's Getting Dark on Old Broadway; 'Neath the South Sea Moon/W: Gene Buck, M: Louis A. Hirsch, Dave Stamper. *Ziegfeld Follies of 1922 [Summer Edition]* (New Amsterdam, revue, July 16, 1923): It's Getting Dark on Old Broadway; 'Neath the South Sea Moon/W: Gene Buck, M: Louis A. Hirsch, Dave Stamper.

3775. Gordon Gray *Fiddler on the Roof* (Imperial, CR, "Perchik," Aug. 1965): Now I Have Everything/W: Sheldon Harnick, M: Jerry Bock.

3776. Helen Gray *Nine-Fifteen Revue* (George M. Cohan, revue, Feb. 11, 1930): How Would a City Girl Know?/W: Paul James, M: Kay Swift — Ta Ta, Ol' Bean/W: Edward Eliscu, M: Manning Sherwin. *The Second Little Show* (Royale > Shubert, revue, Sept. 2, 1930): What a Case I've Got on You!/W: Howard Dietz, M: Arthur Schwartz.

3777. Kevin Gray (Feb. 25, 1958–) B: Westport, CT. *Chu Chem* (Ritz, "Prince," Mar. 17, 1989): I'll Talk to Her; Love Is; The River; Shame on You; We Dwell in Our Hearts; You'll Have to Change/W: Jim Haines, Jack Wohl, M:

Mitch Leigh. *The Phantom of the Opera* (Majestic, CR, "Raoul, Vicomte de Chagny," Sept. 18, 1990): All I Ask of You; Bravo, Bravo; Little Lotte; The Mirror; Notes; Prima Donna; Raoul, I've Been There; Think of Me; Twisted Every Way; Wandering Child; Why Have You Brought Me Here/W: Charles Hart, Richard Stilgoe, M: Andrew Lloyd Webber. *The Phantom of the Opera* (Majestic, CR, "The Phantom of the Opera"): All I Ask of You; Bravo, Bravo; I Remember; Little Lotte; The Mirror; The Music of the Night; Notes; Prima Donna; The Point of No Return; Stranger Than You Dreamt It; Twisted Every Way; Wandering Child/W: Charles Hart, Richard Stilgoe, M: Andrew Lloyd Webber — The Phantom of the Opera/W: Mike Batt, Richard Stilgoe, M: Andrew Lloyd Webber.

3778. Lawrence Gray (c 1899–Feb. 2, 1970) *The Laugh Parade* (Imperial, revue, Nov. 2, 1931): Ooh! That Kiss; You're My Everything/W: Mort Dixon, Joe Young, M: Harry Warren.

3779. Margery Gray *Tenderloin* (46th Street, "Margie" and "Prostitute," Oct. 17, 1960): The Picture of Happiness; Reform/W: Sheldon Harnick, M: Jerry Bock. *Tovarich* (Broadway, "Helen Davis," Mar. 18, 1963): Make a Friend; No! No! No!; Stuck with Each Other; Uh-Oh!/W: Anne Crosswell, M: Lee Pockriss.

3780. Maude Gray *The Never Homes* (Broadway, "Annie Key," Oct. 5, 1911): I'm All for You; Just a Little Bit of Lingerie/W: E. Ray Goetz, M: A. Baldwin Sloane. *The Sun Dodgers* (Broadway, "Trixie Turner," Nov. 30, 1912): At the Picture Show/WM: E. Ray Goetz, Irving Berlin — Ginger; Rag Me Around/W: E. Ray Goetz, M: A. Baldwin Sloane. *The Fortune Teller* (Century roof, revival, "Irma," Sept. 29, 1923): Always Do as People Say You Should; Gypsy Love Song (Slumber On, My Little Gypsy Sweetheart); Serenade/W: Harry B. Smith, M: Victor Herbert.

3781. Michael Gray (?–Mar. 19, 1988) *Your Arms Too Short to Box with God* (Lyceum, revue, Dec. 22, 1976): Come on Down; Everybody Has His Own Way; We Are the Priests and Elders/WM: Alex Bradford.

3782. Oliver Gray (Aug. 29, 1928–) B: Bournemouth, England. *Kean* (Broadway, "Prince of Wales," Nov. 2, 1961): The Social Whirl/WM: Robert Wright, George Forrest.

3783. Roger Gray (May 26, 1887–Jan. 20, 1959) B: Omaha, NE. *The Royal Vagabond* (Cohan and Harris, "Marcel," Feb. 17, 1919): Opera, Comic Opera/WM: George M. Cohan — Talk, Talk, Talk [Feb. 24, 1919]/W: William Cary Duncan, M: Anselm Goetzl. *Little Jessie James* (Longacre, "William J. Pierce," Aug. 15, 1923): The Blue Bird/W: Harlan Thompson, M: Harry Archer. *My Girl* (Vanderbilt, "Pinkie," Nov. 24, 1924): Fifteen Minutes a Day/W: Harlan Thompson, M: Harry Archer.

3784. Kathryn Grayson (Feb. 9, 1921–) B: Winston-Salem, NC. M: JOHNNY JOHNSTON. The movie star with the lovely soprano voice was studying opera when MGM talent scouts heard her on Eddie Cantor's radio program. Her first movie was *Andy Hardy's Private Secretary* (1941). *Camelot* (Majestic, CR, "Queen Guenevere," Oct. 22, 1962): Before I Gaze at You Again; Camelot; I Loved You Once in Silence; The Jousts; The Lusty Month of May; The Simple Joys of Maidenhood; Then You May Take Me to the Fair; What Do the Simple Folk Do?/W: Alan Jay Lerner, M: Frederick Loewe.

3785. Milt Grayson *Raisin* (46th Street, CR, "Pastor," c 1974): He Come Down This Morning/W: Robert Brittan, M: Judd Woldin.

3786. Robin Grean *Platinum* (Mark Hellinger, "Robin," Nov. 12, 1978): Platinum Dreams; Ride Baby Ride; Sunset/W: Will Holt, M: Gary William Friedman.

3787. Adolph Green (Dec. 2, 1915–Oct. 24, 2002) B: New York, NY. M: PHYLLIS NEWMAN. Lyric and book writer and actor; with partner BETTY COMDEN, notable for a string of Broadway musical hits. *On the Town* (Adelphi, "Ozzie," Dec. 28, 1944): Carried Away; New York, New York; Some Other Time; Ya Got Me/W: Betty Comden, Adolph Green, M: Leonard Bernstein.

3788. Brian Lane Green (Mar. 9, 1962–) *Big River: The Adventures of Huckleberry Finn* (Eugene O'Neill, CR, "Huckleberry Finn," Oct. 21, 1986): I, Huckleberry, Me; Leavin's Not the Only Way to Go; Muddy Water; River in the Rain; Waitin' for the Light to Shine; When the Sun Goes Down in the South; Worlds Apart/WM: Roger Miller. *Starmites* (Criterion Center Stage Right, "Spacepunk," Apr. 27, 1989): Afraid of the Dark; Immolation; Love Duet; Milady; Starmites/WM: Barry Keating.

3789. Chuck Green *Ziegfeld Follies of 1957* (Winter Garden, revue, Mar. 1, 1957): Miss Follies/WM: David Rogers, Colin Romoff.

3790. Cora Green *Strut Miss Lizzie* (Times Square, revue, June 19, 1922): Brother-in-Law Dan; Hoola from Coney Isle; I Love Sweet Angeline; In Yama; Jazz Blues/WM: Henry Creamer, Turner Layton. *Dixie to Broadway* (Broadhurst, revue, Oct. 29, 1924): Dixie Wildflowers; Hanging Around; He Only Comes to See Me Once in a While (But Oh That Once in a While)/W: Grant Clarke, Roy Turk, M: George W. Meyer, Arthur Johnston.

3791. Daisy (Greene) Green *Nearly a Hero* (Casino, "Marie," Feb. 24, 1908): The Walking Tour/WM: ?. *Havana* (Casino, CR, "Pepita," May 24, 1909): The Yacht/W: Adrian Ross, M: Leslie Stuart.

3792. Darren Green *Raisin* (46th Street, CR, "Travis Younger," Nov. 1974): He Come Down This Morning; Sidewalk Tree/W: Robert Brittan, M: Judd Woldin.

3793. David Green (June 16, 1942–) B: Cleveland, OH. *Teddy & Alice* (Minskoff, "J.P. Morgan," Nov. 12, 1987): Election Eve; Wave the Flag/W: Hal Hackady, M: John Philip Sousa, Richard Kapp.

3794. Eddie Green (c 1901–Sept. 1950) B: Baltimore, MD. On radio's *Duffy's Tavern* he was Eddie, the wisecracking waiter (1940); on *Amos 'n' Andy* he played Stonewall, the crooked lawyer (after 1943). *Hot Chocolates* (Hudson, revue, June 20, 1929): The Unloaded Gun/WM: ?. *The Hot Mikado* (Broadhurst, "Ko-Ko," Mar. 23, 1939): Behold the Lord High Executioner; The Flowers That Bloom in the Spring; Here's a How-de-do; I've Got a Little List; Titwillow/W: William S. Gilbert, M: Arthur Sullivan.

3795. Ethel Green *The Rose of Algeria* (Herald Square, "Millicent Madison, M.D.," Sept. 20, 1909): Ask Her While the Band Is Playing/W: Vincent Bryan, M: Victor Herbert— Bohemia, Good-Bye; The Great White Easiest Way; You'll Feel Better Then/W: Glen MacDonough, M: Victor Herbert. *A Matinee Idol* (Daly's > Lyric, "Lucy Gray," Apr. 28, 1910): I Will Always Love You, Dear; Little Lady in the Moon; Won't You Let Me Build a Nest for You (The Robin and the Wren)/W: A. Seymour Brown, M: Silvio Hein — A Yankee Romeo/W: E. Ray Goetz, M: Silvio Hein. *Dr. Deluxe* (Knickerbocker, "Margie Melville," Apr. 17, 1911): For Every Boy That's Lonely There's a Girl That's Lonely Too/W: Otto Harbach, M: Karl Hoschna.

3796. Frank Green *Bells Are Ringing* (Shubert, "Singer at Night Club," Nov. 29, 1956): The Midas Touch/W: Betty Comden, Adolph Green, M: Jule Styne.

3797. H.F. Green *New Girl in Town* (46th Street, "Seaman," May 14, 1957): Roll Yer Socks Up/WM: Bob Merrill.

3798. James Green *Strut Miss Lizzie* (Times Square, revue, June 19, 1922): When You Look in the Eyes of a Mule/WM: Henry Creamer, Turner Layton.

3799. Jane Green *The Midnight Rounders of 1920* (Century roof, revue, July 12, 1920): Romantic Blues/W: Harold Atteridge, M: Bert Grant. *Cinderella on Broadway* (Winter Garden, revue, CR, July 12, 1920): same as above. *The Greenwich Village Follies of 1923* (46th Street > Shubert, revue, Dec. 24, 1925): Go South/W: Owen Murphy, M: Richard Myers — Whistle Away Your Blues/W: Leo Robin, M: Richard Myers.

3800. Marion Green (Mar. 8, 1890–Mar. 17, 1956) B: Janesville, IA. A concert and oratorio singer, he debuted with the Chicago Symphony Orchestra at 18. *Monsieur Beaucaire* (New Amsterdam, "Monsieur Beaucaire," Dec. 11, 1919): English Maids; Gold and Blue and White; Lightly, Lightly; Red Rose; Say No More; Under the Moon/W: Adrian Ross, M: Andre Messager. *The Rose of Stamboul* (Century, "Achmed Bey," Mar. 7, 1922): Rose of Stamboul; Waltz Duet; With Papers Duly Signed/W: Harold Atteridge, M: Sigmund Romberg. *Greenwich Village Follies of 1923* (Winter Garden, revue, Sept. 20, 1923): Conchita/W: ?, M: Lewis E. Gensler. *Annie Dear* (Times Square, "John Rawson," Nov. 4, 1924): Come to My Party; I Want to Be Loved/WM: Clare Kummer — The Only Girl/ W: Arthur Wimperis, M: Sigmund Romberg — Whisper to Me/W: Clifford Grey, M: Sigmund Romberg.

3801. Martyn Green (Apr. 22, 1899–Feb. 8, 1975) B: London, England. Principal comedian with the D'Oyly Carte Opera Company, producer of Gilbert and Sullivan operas. He moved to New York in 1953. In 1959 he lost a leg in an accident, but continued to work afterward. *Shangri-La* (Winter Garden, "Chang," June 13, 1956): The Beetle Race; What Every Old Girl Should Know/W: Jerome Lawrence, Robert E. Lee, M: Harry Warren.

3802. Mitzi Green (Oct. 22, 1920–May 24, 1969) B: Bronx, NY. Daughter of vaudevillians JOE KENO and ROSIE GREEN, she was a child actress in early talking pictures and *Our Gang* short films. *Babes in Arms* (Shubert > Majestic, "Billie Smith," Apr. 14, 1937): All at Once; Babes in Arms; The Lady Is a Tramp; My Funny Valentine; Where or When/W: Lorenz Hart, M: Richard Rodgers. *Walk with Music* (Ethel Barrymore, "Rhoda Gibson," June 4, 1940): Break It Up, Cinderella; Ooh! What You Said; Today I Am a Glamour Girl; Way Back in 1939 A.D.; What'll They Think of Next/W: Johnny Mercer, M: Hoagy Carmichael. *Let Freedom Sing* (Longacre, revue, Oct. 5, 1942): Fraught/WM: Marc Blitzstein — Grandpa Guer-

rilla/W: Hy Zaret, M: Walter Kent — I Did It for Defense; The Lady Is a WAAC/WM: Harold Rome — The Little Things We Like/W: Roslyn Harvey, M: Lou Cooper. *Billion Dollar Baby* (Alvin, "Georgia Motley," Dec. 21, 1945): Broadway Blossom; Havin' a Time; A Lovely Girl; There I'd Be/W: Betty Comden, Adolph Green, M: Morton Gould.

3803. Rosie Green M: JOE KENO. Mother of MITZI GREEN. *The American Idea* (New York, "Vera," Oct. 5, 1908): The Gendarme's Dance/WM: George M. Cohan. *The Whirl of New York* (Winter Garden, "Mamie Clancy," June 13, 1921): The Belle of New York/W: Hugh Morton, M: Gustav Kerker.

3804. Ruby Green *Set to Music* (Music Box, revue, Jan. 18, 1939): Debutantes/WM: Noel Coward.

3805. Solomon Earl Green *House of Flowers* (Alvin, "Don't," Dec. 30, 1954): Smellin' of Vanilla (Bamboo Cage)/WM: Truman Capote, Harold Arlen.

3806. Teddy Green *Baker Street* (Broadway > Martin Beck, "Wiggins," Feb. 16, 1965): Leave It to Us, Guv; Roof Space/WM: Marian Grudeff, Raymond Jessel. *Darling of the Day* (George Abbott, "Alf," Jan. 27, 1968): A Gentleman's Gentleman; It's Enough to Make a Lady Fall in Love; Money, Money, Money; Not on Your Nellie; What Makes a Marriage Merry/W: E.Y. Harburg, M: Jule Styne.

3807. Mitchell Greenberg (Sept. 19, 1950–) B: Brooklyn, NY. *Marilyn* (Minskoff, "Agent," Nov. 20, 1983): Uh-Huh/WM: Beth Lawrence, Norman Thalheimer. *3 Penny Opera* (Lunt-Fontanne, revival, "Crook-Finger Jack," Nov. 5, 1989): Wedding Song/W: Bertolt Brecht, M: Kurt Weill, trans: Michael Feingold. *Ain't Broadway Grand* (Lunt-Fontanne, "Murray Pearl," Apr. 18, 1993): Ain't Broadway Grand; They'll Never Take Us Alive/W: Lee Adams, M: Mitch Leigh.

3808. Allan Greene *Just Fancy* (Casino, "3rd Alderman," Oct. 11, 1927): Two Loving Arms/ W: Leo Robin, M: Joseph Meyer, Phil Charig.

3809. Billy M. Greene (c 1897–1973) *Bye, Bye Barbara* (National, "Chin Lee," Aug. 25, 1924): China/WM: Monte Carlo, Alma Sanders.

3810. Ellen Greene (Feb. 22–) B: Brooklyn, NY. *The Threepenny Opera* (Vivian Beaumont, revival, "Jenny Towler," May 1, 1976): Ballad of Immoral Earnings; Pirate Jenny; Solomon Song; What Keeps Mankind Alive?/W: Bertolt Brecht, M: Kurt Weill, trans: Ralph Manheim, John Willett.

3811. Frank Greene *Lifting the Lid* (New

Amsterdam roof, "George Stonefellow," June 5, 1905): My Syndi-Kate (Cindy Kate)/W: William Jerome, M: Jean Schwartz. *The Dancing Girl* (Winter Garden, "Mr. Robinson," Jan. 24, 1923): Venetian Carnival/W: Harold Atteridge, Irving Caesar, M: Sigmund Romberg. *Rose-Marie* (Imperial, "Edward Hawley," Sept. 2, 1924): I Love Him; Rose-Marie/W: Otto Harbach, Oscar Hammerstein II, M: Rudolf Friml. *Lovely Lady* (Sam H. Harris, "Lord Islington," Dec. 29, 1927): Decoys/W: Cyrus D. Wood, M: Dave Stamper, Harold A. Levey.

3812. Jane Greene *Nifties of 1923* (Fulton, revue, Sept. 25, 1923): Calico Days/WM: Noble Sissle, Ray Perkins, Eubie Blake.

3813. Jeanne Greene (c 1906–Apr. 14, 1975) B: New York, NY. *Bunk of 1926* (Broadhurst, revue, Apr. 26, 1926): A Modest Little Thing/WM: Gene Lockhart.

3814. Ruby Greene *Fast and Furious* (New Yorker, revue, Sept. 15, 1931): So Lonesome/WM: J. Rosamond Johnson, Joe Jordan.

3815. Sam Greene *Ben Franklin in Paris* (Lunt-Fontanne, "Captain Wickes," Oct. 27, 1964): I Love the Ladies/W: Sidney Michaels, M: Mark Sandrich, Jr.

3816. Debra Greenfield *Marlowe* (Rialto, "Audrey Walsingham," Oct. 12, 1981): The Ends Justify the Means/WM: Leo Rost, Jimmy Horowitz.

3817. Edward Greenhalgh *Foxy* (Ziegfeld, "Buzzard," Feb. 16, 1964): Money Isn't Everything/W: Johnny Mercer, M: Robert Emmett Dolan.

3818. Augusta Greenleaf *The Red Mill* (Knickerbocker, "Gretchen Van Borkem," Sept. 24, 1906): In the Isle of Our Dreams; Moonbeams/W: Henry Blossom, M: Victor Herbert.

3819. R. Eddie Greenlee *Liza* (Daly's, "Ras Johnson," Nov. 27, 1922): Lovin' Sam, the Sheik of Alabam'/W: Jack Yellen, M: Milton Ager — My Creole Girl/WM: Nat Vincent, Maceo Pinkard.

3820. Sydney Greenstreet (Dec. 27, 1879– Jan. 19, 1954) B: Sandwich, Kent, England. One of the great movie villains. After high school he went to Ceylon to learn the tea business; at night he memorized Shakespeare. His movie debut at age 62 was in *The Maltese Falcon* (1941). *Lady Billy* (Liberty, "Bateson," Dec. 14, 1920): Historic Huzzies; The Worm's Revenge/W: Zelda Sears, M: Harold A. Levey. *The Magic Ring* (Liberty, "Henry Brockway," Oct. 1, 1923): Education; Keepsakes; When the Organ Plays/W: Zelda Sears, M: Harold A. Levey. *The Madcap* (Royale, "Lord Clarence Steeple," Jan. 31, 1928):

Buy Your Way; Honeymooning Blues; Old Enough to Marry/W: Clifford Grey, M: Maurie Rubens. *Roberta* (New Amsterdam, "Lord Henry Delves," Nov. 18, 1933): Let's Begin/W: Otto Harbach, M: Jerome Kern.

3821. Ellie Greenwich (Oct. 23, 1940–) B: Brooklyn, NY. M: songwriter Jeff Barry, 1962– 1965. Writer of a string of 1960s song hits, many with Barry. *Leader of the Pack* (Ambassador, "Ellie Greenwich," Apr. 8, 1985): Da Doo Ron Ron; What a Guy/WM: Jeff Barry, Ellie Greenwich, Phil Spector — Maybe I Know/WM: Jeff Barry, Ellie Greenwich — We're Gonna Make It (After All)/WM: Ellie Greenwich.

3822. Barrett Greenwood *Girl o' Mine* (Bijou, "Charlie," Jan. 28, 1918): Changing Styles [Mar. 4, 1918]; Every Cloud Is Silver-Lined; Fatal Step [Mar. 4, 1918]; It's the Woman Who Pays; Not So Fast; Saturday Night; The Winning Race/W: Philip Bartholomae, M: Frank Tours. *Fifty-Fifty, Ltd.* (Comedy, "Kenneth Patterson," Oct. 27, 1919): Along the Hudson; Without a Beautiful Girl/WM: Arthur Swanstrom, Carey Morgan — Every Little Girlie Has a Way of Her Own; Honey Bunch; Silence of Love/WM: Leon De Costa. *Love Birds* (Apollo, "Hal Sterling," Mar. 15, 1921): Carnival Night; Is It Hard to Guess?; Let's Pretend/W: Ballard Macdonald, M: Sigmund Romberg. *Red Pepper* (Shubert, "Richard Pitney," May 29, 1922): In the Starlight; Wedding Bells; Wedding Day/WM: Howard E. Rogers, Albert Gumble, Owen Murphy — It Must Be You/W: Howard E. Rogers, M: Albert Gumble, Herman Paley. *Little Nellie Kelly* (Liberty, "Jack Lloyd," Nov. 13, 1922): Over the Phone (Telephone Song)/WM: George M. Cohan. *Be Yourself!* (Sam H. Harris, "David Robinson," Sept. 3, 1924): A Good Hand Organ and a Sidewalk's All We Need/ WM: ? — I Came Here/W: Ira Gershwin, George S. Kaufman, Marc Connelly, M: Lewis E. Gensler — Money Doesn't Mean a Thing/W: Ira Gershwin, M: Lewis E. Gensler — My Road/W: George S. Kaufman, Marc Connelly, M: Lewis E. Gensler.

3823. Charlotte Greenwood (June 25, 1890–Jan. 18, 1978) B: Philadelphia, PA. Tall, leggy character actress turned comedienne of vaudeville, stage and screen. Best known to movie buffs as Aunt Eller in *Oklahoma!* (1956). *The Passing Show of 1912* (Winter Garden, revue, July 22, 1912): Girlish Laughter; It's All Over Now; The Kangaroo Hop; Modern Love/W: Harold Atteridge, M: Louis A. Hirsch. *The Man with Three Wives* (Weber and Fields, "Sidonie," Jan. 23, 1913): Hello, Hello/W: Harold Atteridge, M: Al W. Brown — Tootsie-Wootsie/W: Paul M. Potter, Harold Atteridge, M: Franz Lehar. *The Passing Show of 1913* (Winter Garden, revue, July 24, 1913): Heaven Will Protect the Working Girl/W: Edgar Smith, M: A. Baldwin Sloane — I Must Have My Way/WM: ?. *Pretty Mrs. Smith* (Casino, "Letitia Proudfoot," Sept. 21, 1914): The Bensonhurst Gavotte/W: Earl Carroll, M: Alfred G. Robyn — Long, Lean, Lanky Letty/WM: Sydney Grant — Mrs. Sippi You're a Grand Old Girl/W: Billy Gould, M: Belle Ashlyn. *So Long Letty* (Shubert, "Letty Robbins," Oct. 23, 1916): Here Come the Married Men; On a Beautiful Beach; So Long Letty/WM: Earl Carroll. *Linger Longer Letty* (Fulton, "Letty Larkin," Nov. 20, 1919): Let's Pretend/W: Bernard Grossman, M: Alfred Goodman — Linger Longer Letty/W: Oliver Morosco, M: Alfred Goodman — Oh, by Jingo! Oh, by Gee! (You're the Only Girl for Me)/W: Lew Brown, M: Albert Von Tilzer — A Twentieth Century Lullaby/W: Bernard Grossman, George Yoerger, M: Alfred Goodman. *Letty Pepper* (Vanderbilt, "Letty Pepper," Apr. 10, 1922): Blue Bird Blues; Lavender and Lace; Ray of Sunshine/W: Leo Wood, Irving Bibo, M: Werner Janssen — Long, Lean, Lanky Letty Pepper/WM: ? — You Teach Me/W: Ballard Macdonald, M: James F. Hanley. *Music Box Revue of 1922* (Music Box, revue, Oct. 23, 1922): I'm Looking for a Daddy Long Legs; Too Many Boys/WM: Irving Berlin. *Hassard Short's Ritz Revue* (Ritz > Winter Garden, revue, Sept. 17, 1924): I Long to Belong/W: Owen Murphy, M: Jay Gorney — A Perfect Day; Too Tall/W: Harry Ruskin, May Tully, M: Martin Broones — Scandal, and a Cup of Tea/W: Kenneth Webb, M: Roy Webb. *Out of This World* (New Century, "Juno," Dec. 21, 1950): Cherry Pies Ought to Be You; Climb Up the Mountain; I Got Beauty; I Sleep Easier Now; Nobody's Chasing Me; What Do You Think About Men?/WM: Cole Porter.

3824. Julie Gregg (Jan. 24, 1944–) B: Niagara Falls, NY. *The Happy Time* (Broadway, "Laurie Mannon," Jan. 18, 1968): I Don't Remember You; Seeing Things/W: Fred Ebb, M: John Kander.

3825. Mitchell Gregg (Jan. 15, 1921–) B: New York, NY. *Music in the Air* (Ziegfeld, revival, "Karl Reder," Oct. 8, 1951): I've Told Ev'ry Little Star; Prayer (Our Journey May Be Long); We Belong Together/W: Oscar Hammerstein II, M: Jerome Kern. *Say, Darling* (ANTA, "Rex Dexter," Apr. 3, 1958): Dance Only with Me; Say, Darling; Something's Always Happening on the River/W: Betty Comden, Adolph

Green, M: Jule Styne. *The Unsinkable Molly Brown* (Winter Garden, "Prince DeLong," Nov. 3, 1960): Bon Jour (The Language Song); Dolce Far Niente; Happy Birthday, Mrs. J.J. Brown/WM: Meredith Willson. *No Strings* (54th Street, "Louis dePourtal," Mar. 15, 1962): The Man Who Has Everything/WM: Richard Rodgers.

3826. Feleshe Gregorio *Chu Chin Chow* (Manhattan Opera House > Century, "Baba Mustafa," Oct. 22, 1917): The Cobbler's Song/W: Oscar Asche, M: Frederic Norton.

3827. George Gregory *The Dairymaids* (Criterion, "Sam Brudenell," Aug. 26, 1907): Poaching/W: ?, M: Paul Rubens.

3828. Gilbert Gregory *By the Sad Sea Waves* (Herald Square, "Prof. Wagner Flat" and "John Phillips," Feb. 21, 1899): Buttercups and Daisies/WM: J. Sherrie Mathews, Harry Bulger. *The Isle of Spice* (Majestic, "Slubsy Mackinaw," Aug. 23, 1904): Silly Sailors/W: George E. Stoddard, M: Paul Schindler. *The Man from Now* (New Amsterdam, "Eli Beasley," Sept. 3, 1906): I Want to Go Home Now/W: Vincent Bryan, M: Manuel Klein.

3829. Heathe Gregory *Love's Lottery* (Broadway, "Tom Ryder," Oct. 3, 1904): Holiday Joys; The Sounds We Love to Hear; The Village Recruits/W: Stanislas Stange, M: Julian Edwards.

3830. John Gregory *Under the Counter* (Shubert, "Lieut. Cmdr. Hugo Conway, RNVR," Oct. 3, 1947): Ai Yi Yi/W: Harold Purcell, M: Manning Sherwin.

3831. Michael Scott Gregory (Mar. 13, 1962–Feb. 25, 1992) B: Ft. Lauderdale, FL. *Sophisticated Ladies* (Lunt-Fontanne, revue, CR, Jan. 5, 1982): Caravan/W: Irving Mills, M: Juan Tizol, Duke Ellington — Drop Me Off in Harlem/W: Nick Kenny, M: Duke Ellington — I Love You Madly; I've Got to Be a Rug Cutter/WM: Duke Ellington — Imagine My Frustration/WM: Duke Ellington, Billy Strayhorn, Gerald Wilson — It Don't Mean a Thing/W: Irving Mills, M: Duke Ellington — Perdido/W: Hans Lengsfelder, Ervin Drake, M: Juan Tizol. *Starlight Express* (Gershwin, "Dustin," Mar. 15, 1987): Belle; Final Selection; Race Two/W: Richard Stilgoe, M: Andrew Lloyd Webber. *Cats* (Winter Garden, CR, "Skimbleshanks," during run): Skimbleshanks/W: T.S. Eliot, M: Andrew Lloyd Webber. *Cats* (Winter Garden, CR, "Mistoffolees"): The Invitation to the Jellicle Ball; Mr. Mistoffolees; Mungojerrie and Rumpleteazer/W: T.S. Eliot, M: Andrew Lloyd Webber.

3832. Paul Gregory *Golden Dawn* (Hammerstein's, "Steve Allen," Nov. 30, 1927): Dawn/W: Oscar Hammerstein II, Otto Harbach, M: Robert Stolz, Herbert Stothart — Here in the Dark/W: Oscar Hammerstein II, Otto Harbach, M: Emmerich Kalman, Herbert Stothart. *Whoopee* (New Amsterdam, "Wanenis," Dec. 4, 1928): Here's to the Girl of My Heart; I'm Bringing a Red, Red Rose/W: Gus Kahn, M: Walter Donaldson. *Smiles* (Ziegfeld, "Dick," Nov. 18, 1930): Here's a Day to Be Happy/W: Harold Adamson, Clifford Grey, M: Vincent Youmans — Time on My Hands/W: Harold Adamson, Mack Gordon, M: Vincent Youmans.

3833. Quentin Gregory *Messin' Around* (Hudson, revue, Apr. 22, 1929): I Don't Love Nobody but You/W: Perry Bradford, M: James P. Johnson.

3834. Algernon Greig *Eileen* (Shubert, "Sir Reggie Stribling," Mar. 19, 1917): If Eve Had Left the Apple on the Bough/W: Henry Blossom, M: Victor Herbert.

3835. Robert Greig (Dec. 27, 1880–June 27, 1958) B: Melbourne, Australia. The portly butler in many movies. *Animal Crackers* (44th Street, "Hives," Oct. 23, 1928): Hooray for Captain Spaulding/WM: Bert Kalmar, Harry Ruby.

3836. Travis Jordan Greisler *The Who's Tommy* (St. James, CR, "Tommy, age 10," c 1994): Listening to You/WM: Pete Townshend.

3837. Ben S. Grennell *Marrying Mary* (Daly's, "M. Archambeau," Aug. 27, 1906): Is There Anyone Here by the Name of Smith?/W: Benjamin Hapgood Burt, M: Silvio Hein.

3838. Edith Gresham (c 1897–Dec. 31, 1976) B: New York, NY. Daughter of HERBERT GRESHAM. Actress of stage, radio and TV. *Oklahoma!* (St. James, CR, "Aunt Eller Murphy, Jan. 1948): The Farmer and the Cowman; Kansas City; Oklahoma!; The Surrey with the Fringe on Top/W: Oscar Hammerstein II, M: Richard Rodgers.

3839. Herbert Gresham (c 1854–Feb. 23, 1921) B: London, England. Father of EDITH GRESHAM. *Adonis* (Bijoux, "Marquis de Baccarat," Sept. 4, 1884): Go Basest Lord/W: William F. Gill, Henry E. Dixey, M: Edward E. Rice. *Adonis* (Star, revival, "Marquis de Baccarat," Nov. 22, 1888): same as above. *The Geisha* (Daly's, "Dick Cunningham," Sept. 9, 1896): The Dear Little Jappy-jap-jappy; Here They Come/W: Harry Greenbank, M: Sidney Jones. *A Runaway Girl* (Daly's > Fifth Avenue, "Prof. Tamarind," Aug. 31, 1898): Barcelona/W: M: Ivan Caryll.

3840. May Greville *The Vanderbilt Cup*

(New York, CR, "Mrs. Herkimer," Jan. 28, 1907): The Fatal Curse of Beauty/W: Raymond Peck, M: Robert Hood Bowers.

3841. Joel Grey (Apr. 11, 1932–) B: Cleveland, OH. M: JO WILDER. *Stop the World—I Want to Get Off* (Shubert, CR, "Littlechap," Nov. 4, 1963): All American; Family Fugue; Glorious Russian; Gonna Build a Mountain; I Wanna Be Rich; Lumbered; Meilinki Meilchick; Mumbo Jumbo; Nag! Nag! Nag!; Once in a Lifetime; Someone Nice Like You; Typically English; Typische Deutsche; What Kind of Fool Am I?/WM: Leslie Bricusse, Anthony Newley. *Half a Sixpence* (Broadhurst, CR, "Arthur Kipps"): All in the Cause of Economy; Flash! Bang! Wallop!; Half a Sixpence; If the Rain's Got to Fall; Long Ago; Money to Burn; The Party's on the House; A Proper Gentleman; She's Too Far Above Me/WM: David Heneker. *Cabaret* (Broadhurst, "Master of Ceremonies," Nov. 20, 1966/Sept. 25, 1967): If You Could See Her; The Money Song; Tomorrow Belongs to Me; Two Ladies; Wilkommen/W: Fred Ebb, M: John Kander. *George M!* (Palace, "George M. Cohan," Apr. 10, 1968/Dec. 23, 1968): All Aboard for Broadway; Forty-Five Minutes from Broadway; Give My Regards to Broadway; Harrigan; Musical Comedy Man; My Town; Nellie Kelly I Love You; Over There; So Long, Mary; Twentieth Century Love; The Yankee Doodle Boy; You're a Grand Old Flag/WM: George M. Cohan — I'd Rather Be Right/W: Lorenz Hart, M: Richard Rodgers. *Goodtime Charley* (Palace, "Charley," Mar. 3, 1975): Bits and Pieces; Born Lover; Coronation; Goodtime Charley; I Leave the World; Why Can't We All Be Nice?; You Still Have a Long Way to Go/W: Hal Hackady, M: Larry Grossman. *The Grand Tour* (Palace, "S.L. Jacobowsky," Jan. 11, 1979): I'll Be Here Tomorrow; Marianne; Mrs. S.L. Jacobowsky; One Extraordinary Thing; Wedding Conversation; We're Almost There; You I Like/WM: Jerry Herman. *Cabaret* (Imperial, revival, "Master of Ceremonies," Oct. 22, 1987): same as above. *Chicago* (Richard Rodgers, revival, "Amos Hart," Nov. 14, 1996): Mister Cellophane/W: Fred Ebb, M: John Kander.

3842. Justine Grey *Angel Face* (Knickerbocker, CR, "Pearl," Jan. 26, 1920): My Idea of Something to Go Home To/W: Robert B. Smith, M: Victor Herbert.

3843. Madeleine Grey *Enchanted Isle* (Lyric, "Mrs. Stewart Haverhill-Smith," Sept. 19, 1927): What a Jamboree!/WM: Ida Hoyt Chamberlain.

3844. Minerva Grey *The Girl in the Spot-*

light (Knickerbocker, "Bess," July 12, 1920): Come Across; I'll Be There/W: Robert B. Smith, M: Victor Herbert.

3845. William Daniel Grey *Jesus Christ Superstar* (Longacre, revival, "Jesus of Nazareth," Nov. 23, 1977): The Arrest; The Crucifixion; Everything's Alright; Gethsemane; Hosanna; I Don't Know How to Love Him; The Last Supper; Pilate and Christ; Poor Jerusalem; Strange Thing Mystifying; The Temple; Trial Before Pilate; What's the Buzz/W: Tim Rice, M: Andrew Lloyd Webber.

3846. Marie Louise Gribben *The Auto Race* (Hippodrome, "Virginia Carter," Nov. 25, 1907): Sweet Is the Perfume of Summer Flowers/WM: Manuel Klein.

3847. David Alan Grier (June 30, 1955–) B: Detroit, MI. In movies from 1983, and a cast member of the comedy variety TV show *In Living Color* (1990). *The First* (Martin Beck, "Jackie Robinson," Nov. 17, 1981): The First; It's a Beginning; The National Pastime (This Year's Nigger); Will We Ever Know Each Other; You Do-Do-Do-It Good!/W: Martin Charnin, M: Bob Brush. *Dreamgirls* (Imperial, CR, "James Thunder Early," Mar. 1984): Ain't No Party; Cadillac Car; Fake Your Way to the Top; Family; I Meant You No Harm; I Want You Baby; Quintette; The Rap; Steppin' to the Bad Side/ W: Tom Eyen, M: Henry Krieger.

3848. Joe Grifasi (June 14, 1944–) B: Buffalo, NY. *Happy End* (Martin Beck, revival, "Capt. Hannibal Jackson," May 7, 1977): Brother, Give Yourself a Shove; Don't Be Afraid; In Our Childhood's Bright Endeavor; Lieutenants of the Lord; The Liquor Dealer's Dream; March Ahead/W: Bertolt Brecht, M: Kurt Weill. *The Mystery of Edwin Drood* (Imperial, "Bazzard," Dec. 2, 1985): No Good Can Come from Bad/WM: Rupert Holmes.

3849. Ethel Griffies (Apr. 26, 1878–Sept. 9, 1975) B: Sheffield, Yorkshire, England. The character actress was on stage from age 2 and appeared in more than 100 films. *Miss Liberty* (Imperial, "Countess," July 15, 1949): Only for Americans/WM: Irving Berlin.

3850. Merv Griffin (July 6, 1925–) B: San Mateo, CA. Singer and emcee on radio and TV; owner of hotels and nightclubs. *Finian's Rainbow* (New York City Center, revival, "Woody Mahoney," May 18, 1955): If This Isn't Love; Look to the Rainbow; Old Devil Moon; That Great Come and Get It Day/W: E.Y. Harburg, M: Burton Lane.

3851. Thomas Griffin *South Pacific* (Majestic > Broadway, CR, "Jerome," c 1952): Dites-Moi/W: Oscar Hammerstein II, M: Richard Rodgers.

3852. Victor Griffin *Ballroom* (Majestic, "Harry the Noodle," Dec. 14, 1978): Goodnight Is Not Goodbye/W: Alan Bergman, Marilyn Bergman, M: Billy Goldenberg.

3853. Wee Griffin *The Prince of Pilsen* (Jolson, revival, "Jimmy," Jan. 13, 1930): Keep It Dark/W: Frank Pixley, M: Gustav Luders. *The Count of Luxembourg* (Jolson, revival, "Mimi," Feb. 17, 1930): Rootsie-Pootsie/W: Adrian Ross, Basil Hood, M: Franz Lehar.

3854. William (Bill) Griffis (July 12, 1917– Apr. 13, 1998) B: Hollywood, CA. He worked frequently in radio in the 1940s. *The Cradle Will Rock* (New York City Center, revival, "Harry Druggist," Feb. 11, 1960): Polyphonic; Summer Weather/WM: Marc Blitzstein. *Here's Love* (Shubert, "Tammany O'Halloran," Oct. 3, 1963): My State, My Kansas, My Home/WM: Meredith Willson. *Oklahoma!* (Music Theater of Lincoln Center, revival, "Andrew Carnes," June 23, 1969): The Farmer and the Cowman/W: Oscar Hammerstein II, M: Richard Rodgers. *Jimmy* (Winter Garden, "Al Smith," Oct. 23, 1969): The Darlin' of New York; The Little Woman; Our Jimmy/WM: Bill Jacob, Patti Jacob. *Over Here!* (Shubert, "Rankin," Mar. 6, 1974): The Grass Grows Green (in No Man's Land); Hey, Yvette!/WM: Richard M. Sherman, Robert B. Sherman.

3855. Andy Griffith (June 1, 1926–) B: Mt. Airy, NC. Comic actor best remembered for TV's long running *Andy Griffith Show* (1960) and for *Matlock* (1986). *Destry Rides Again* (Imperial, "Destry," Apr. 23, 1959): Anyone Would Love You; Ballad of a Gun; Once Knew a Fella; Only Time Will Tell; Tomorrow Morning/WM: Harold Rome.

3856. Billy Griffith *The Red Mill* (Ziegfeld, revival, "Pennyfeather," Oct. 16, 1945): When You're Pretty and the World Is Fair/W: Henry Blossom, M: Victor Herbert.

3857. Eleanor Griffith *Poor Little Ritz Girl* (Central, "Barbara Arden," July 28, 1920): All You Need to Be a Star; Love Will Call; You Can't Fool Your Dreams/W: Lorenz Hart, M: Richard Rodgers. *Ziegfeld Midnight Frolic [11th Edition] aka Ziegfeld New Midnight Frolic* (New Amsterdam roof, revue, Feb. 9, 1921): Gondolier/W: Ballard Macdonald, M: Dave Stamper — Rose of My Heart/W: Weston Wilson, M: Neil Moret. *The Last Waltz* (Century, "Babuschka," May 10, 1921): A Baby in Love/W: Harold Atteridge, M: Ralph Benatzky, Alfred Goodman. *Springtime of Youth* (Broadhurst, "Polly Baxter," Oct. 26,

1922): Find the Right Girl; Just Like a Doll; Pretty Polly/W: Cyrus D. Wood, M: Sigmund Romberg. *Mercenary Mary* (Longacre, "Mary Skinner," Apr. 13, 1925): I've Got to Be a Chaste Woman; Mercenary Mary/WM: William B. Friedlander, Con Conrad.

3858. Peter Griffith (Oct. 23, 1933–) B: Baltimore, MD. *Street Scene* (Adelphi, "Willie Maurrant," Jan. 9, 1947): Catch Me If You Can/W: Langston Hughes, Elmer Rice, M: Kurt Weill.

3859. William Griffith *Lady Fingers* (Vanderbilt > Liberty, "Dr. Jasper," Jan. 31, 1929): Follow Master/W: Edward Eliscu, M: Joseph Meyer.

3860. Harry Griffiths *Hip-Hip Hooray* (Hippodrome, revue, "The Jaunty Juvenile," Sept. 30, 1915): The Land of Love and Roses/W: John L. Golden, M: Raymond Hubbell.

3861. Rollin Grimes, Jr. *90 in the Shade* (Knickerbocker, "Peter," Jan. 25, 1915): Courtship de Dance; Peter Pan/WM: ?. *Daffy Dill* (Apollo, "Harry Jones," Aug. 22, 1922): Fair Enough/W: Oscar Hammerstein II, M: Herbert Stothart. *My Maryland* (Al Jolson, "Edgar Strong," Sept. 12, 1927): Boys in Gray; The Mocking Bird; Strolling with the One I Love the Best/W: Dorothy Donnelly, M: Sigmund Romberg. *My Maryland* (Al Jolson, CR, "Jack Negly," Mar. 26, 1928): Won't You Marry Me?/W: Dorothy Donnelly, M: Sigmund Romberg.

3862. Tammy Grimes (Jan. 30, 1934–) B: Lynn, MA. M: CHRISTOPHER PLUMMER, 1956-1960. In 1955 she made her professional debut, replacing Kim Stanley in the play *Bus Stop*. *The Cradle Will Rock* (New York City Center, revival, "Moll," Feb. 11, 1960): I'm Checkin' Home Now; Nickel Under the Foot; Polyphonic; So That's the Way/WM: Marc Blitzstein. *The Unsinkable Molly Brown* (Winter Garden, "Molly Tobin," Nov. 3, 1960): Are You Sure?; Bea-u-ti-ful People of Denver; Belly Up to the Bar, Boys; Bon Jour (The Language Song); Chick-a-pen; Colorado, My Home; Dolce Far Niente; I Ain't Down Yet; My Own Brass Bed/WM: Meredith Willson. *High Spirits* (Alvin, "Elvira," Apr. 7, 1964): Faster Than Sound; Forever and a Day; Home Sweet Heaven; I Know Your Heart; Something Tells Me; What in the World Did You Want?; You'd Better Love Me/WM: Hugh Martin, Timothy Gray. *A Musical Jubilee* (St. James, revue, Nov. 13, 1975): Der Shimmy/W: ?, M: Emmerich Kalman — Find Me a Primitive Man/WM: Cole Porter — How Jazz Was Born/W: Andy Razaf, Henry Creamer, M: Fats Waller — I Wanna Be Loved by You/W:

Bert Kalmar, M: Harry Ruby, Herbert Stothart — I'm Just Wild About Harry/W: Noble Sissle, M: Eubie Blake — It's a Long Way to Tipperary/WM: Jack Judge, Harry H. Williams — Liza/W: Gus Kahn, Ira Gershwin, M: George Gershwin — Poor Little Rich Girl/WM: Noel Coward — Sweet Betsy from Pike/W: John A. Stone, M: ?— They Didn't Believe Me/W: Herbert Reynolds, M: Jerome Kern — Totem Tom-Tom/W: Otto Harbach, Oscar Hammerstein II, M: Rudolf Friml — We're Blase/W: Bruce Sievier, M: Ord Hamilton. *42nd Street* (Winter Garden, "Dorothy Brock," Aug. 25, 1980): About a Quarter to Nine; I Know Now; Shadow Waltz; You're Getting to Be a Habit with Me/W: Al Dubin, M: Harry Warren — Getting Out of Town/W: Mort Dixon, M: Harry Warren.

3863. Taryn Grimes *Take Me Along* (Martin Beck, revival, "Muriel Macomber," Apr. 14, 1985): I Would Die; Nine O'Clock/WM: Bob Merrill.

3864. Lores Grimm *Fifty Miles from Boston* (Garrick, "Eddie Moseley," Feb. 3, 1908): The Boys Who Fight the Flames/WM: George M. Cohan.

3865. Jack Grinnage *The Billy Barnes People* (Royale, revue, June 13, 1961): Damn Alot; I Like You; If It Wasn't for People/WM: Billy Barnes.

3866. Ben F. Grinnell *Madame Sherry* (New Amsterdam, CR, Phillippe," Oct. 24, 1910): The Other Fellow/W: Otto Harbach, M: Karl Hoschna.

3867. Frank Grinnell *Bitter Sweet* (44th Street, revival, "Bertram Sellick" and "Duke of Tenterden," May 7, 1934): Green Carnation; The Last Dance; Tarara Boom-de-Ay/WM: Noel Coward.

3868. Frank Griso *A Time for Singing* (Broadway, "Huw Morgan," May 21, 1966): Tell Her; Why Would Anyone Want to Get Married/WM: Gerald Freedman, John Morris.

3869. Reri Grist (c 1932–) B: New York, NY. The internationally known soprano made her operatic debut in 1959. *Carmen Jones* (New York City Center, revival, "Cindy Lou," May 31, 1956): My Joe; You Talk Just Like My Maw/W: Oscar Hammerstein II, M: Georges Bizet. *West Side Story* (Winter Garden, "Consuelo," Sept. 26, 1957): Somewhere/W: Stephen Sondheim, M: Leonard Bernstein.

3870. Grace Griswold (c 1872–June 13, 1927) B: Ashtabula, OH. *The Vanderbilt Cup* (Broadway > New York, "Mrs. Filestrom," Jan. 16, 1906): The Fatal Curse of Beauty/W: Raymond Peck, M: Robert Hood Bowers.

3871. George Grizzard (Apr. 1, 1928–) B:

Roanoke Rapids, VA. *Noel Coward's Sweet Potato* (Ethel Barrymore, revue, Sept. 29, 1968): A Bar on the Piccola Marina; I Wonder What Happened to Him; Mad Dogs and Englishmen; Men About Town; Mrs. Worthington; Useless Useful Phrases/WM: Noel Coward.

3872. Steve Grober *Shenandoah* (Alvin, CR, "Robert, the boy," Aug. 16, 1976): Why Am I Me?/W: Peter Udell, M: Gary Geld.

3873. Dorris Groday *Free for All* (Manhattan, "Joan Summer," Sept. 8, 1931): Just Eighteen; Living in Sin/W: Oscar Hammerstein II, M: Richard A. Whiting.

3874. Gordon Grody *The Lieutenant* (Lyceum, "Defense Attorney," Mar. 9, 1975): Damned No Matter How He Turned/WM: Gene Curty, Nitra Scharfman, Chuck Strand.

3875. Cris Groenendaal (Feb. 17, 1948–) B: Erie, PA. *Sweeney Todd, the Demon Barber of Fleet Street* (Uris, CR, "Anthony Hope," Aug. 1979): Ah, Miss; City on Fire!; Kiss Me; No Place Like London/WM: Stephen Sondheim. *Sunday in the Park with George* (Booth, "Louis," May 2, 1984): The Day Off/WM: Stephen Sondheim. *Sunday in the Park with George* (Booth, CR, "George," Jan. 15, 1985): Beautiful; Color and Light; The Day Off; Finishing the Hat; Lesson #8; Move On; Putting It Together; We Do Not Belong Together/WM: Stephen Sondheim. *The Phantom of the Opera* (Majestic, "Monsieur Andre," Jan. 26, 1988): Notes; Prima Donna; Twisted Every Way/W: Charles Hart, Richard Stilgoe, M: Andrew Lloyd Webber. *The Phantom of the Opera* (Majestic, CR, "The Phantom of the Opera," Mar. 20, 1989): All I Ask of You; Bravo, Bravo; I Remember; Little Lotte; The Mirror; The Music of the Night; Notes; Prima Donna; The Point of No Return; Stranger Than You Dreamt It; Twisted Every Way; Wandering Child/W: Charles Hart, Richard Stilgoe, M: Andrew Lloyd Webber — The Phantom of the Opera/W: Mike Batt, Richard Stilgoe, M: Andrew Lloyd Webber. *A Funny Thing Happened on the Way to the Forum* (St. James, revival, "Miles Gloriosus," Apr. 18, 1996): Bring Me My Bride; Comedy Tonight/WM: Stephen Sondheim.

3876. Harry Groener (Sept. 10, 1951–) B: Augsburg, Germany. *Oklahoma!* (Palace, revival, "Will Parker," Dec. 13, 1979): All er Nothin'; The Farmer and the Cowman; Kansas City/W: Oscar Hammerstein II, M: Richard Rodgers. *Oh, Brother!* (ANTA, "Western Mousada," Nov. 10, 1981): Everybody Calls Me by My Name; O.P.E.C. Maiden/W: Donald Driver, M: Michael Valenti. *Is There Life After High School?*

(Ethel Barrymore, revue, May 7, 1982): Beer; Things I Learned in High School; Thousands of Trumpets/WM: Craig Carnelia. *Cats* (Winter Garden, "Munkustrap," Oct. 7, 1982): The Awefull Battle of the Pekes and Pollicles; The Marching Songs of the Pollicle Dogs; Old Deuteronomy/W: T.S. Eliot, M: Andrew Lloyd Webber. *Harrigan 'n Hart* (Longacre, "Edward Harrigan," Jan. 31, 1985): Dip Me in the Golden Sea; I Love to Follow a Band; She's Our Gretel; Wonderful Me/WM: ?— Maggie Murphy's Home; The Mulligan Guard; Such an Education Has My Mary Ann/W: Edward Harrigan, M: David Braham — Something New, Something Different; That's My Partner; We'll Be There/W: Peter Walker, M: Max Showalter. *Sunday in the Park with George* (Booth, CR, "George," Apr. 23, 1985): Beautiful; Color and Light; The Day Off; Finishing the Hat; Lesson #8; Move On; Putting It Together; We Do Not Belong Together/WM: Stephen Sondheim. *Crazy for You* (Sam S. Shubert, "Bobby Child," Feb. 19, 1992): Could You Use Me?; Embraceable You; I Can't Be Bothered Now; I Got Rhythm; K-ra-zy for You; Nice Work If You Can Get It; Shall We Dance?; Slap That Bass; Stiff Upper Lip; They Can't Take That Away from Me; Things Are Looking Up; What Causes That?/W: Ira Gershwin, M: George Gershwin.

3877. Oscar Grogan *You Said It* (46th Street, "Eddie Brown," Jan. 19, 1931): While You Are Young/W: Jack Yellen, M: Harold Arlen.

3878. Ernest Groh *The Maid and the Mummy* (New York, CR, "Don Romero de Cabanos," Aug. 8, 1904): Flo; Sad Experiences/W: Richard Carle, M: Robert Hood Bowers.

3879. Katarzyna Groniec *Metro* (Minskoff, "Anka," Apr. 16, 1992): Dreams Don't Die; Love Duet; Love Duet II; Waiting; Windows/Eng. W: Mary Bracken Phillips, M: Janusz Stoklosa.

3880. Helen Groody Sister of LOUISE GROODY. *Frank Fay's Fables* (Park, revue, Feb. 6, 1922): The Merry Little Widows; Oh, What a Happy Day; That Swanee River Melody/WM: Frank Fay, Clarence Gaskill. *Glory* (Vanderbilt, "Lucy Ann Willing," Dec. 25, 1922): Saw Mill River Road/W: Joseph McCarthy, M: Harry Tierney — When the Curfew Rings at Nine/WM: Al W. Brown.

3881. Louise Groody (Mar. 26, 1897–Sept. 16, 1961) B: Waco, TX. M: WILLIAM HARRIGAN. Sister of HELEN GROODY. The bright, lively musical comedy star began her career in 1915 as a cabaret dancer in New York. *Around the Map* (New Amsterdam, revue, "Gladiola," Nov. 1, 1915): There's One Thing That a Coon

Can Do/W: C.M.S. McLellan, M: Louis A. Hirsch. *Toot-Toot!* (George M. Cohan, "Mrs. Walter Colt," Mar. 11, 1918): Runaway Colts/W: Berton Braley, M: Jerome Kern. *Fiddlers Three* (Cort, "Gilda Varelli," Sept. 3, 1918): Don't You Think You'll Miss Me?; For Love; Rap, Rap, Rap/W: William Cary Duncan, M: Alexander Johnstone. *The Night Boat* (Liberty, "Barbara," Feb. 2, 1920): Don't You Want to Take Me?; A Heart for Sale; I'd Like a Lighthouse; Some Fine Day; Whose Baby Are You?/W: Anne Caldwell, M: Jerome Kern — Good Night Boat/W: Anne Caldwell, Frank Craven, M: Jerome Kern. *Good Morning, Dearie* (Globe, "Rose-Marie," Nov. 1, 1921): Blue Danube Blues; Good Morning, Dearie; Niagara Falls; Rose-Marie; Way Down Town/W: Anne Caldwell, M: Jerome Kern. *One Kiss* (Fulton, "Eva," Nov. 27, 1923): Gentlemen; Is That So!; London Town; Up There; When We Are Married; Your Lips/W: Clare Kummer, M: Maurice Yvain. *No! No! Nanette* (Globe, "Nanette," Sept. 16, 1925): I Want to Be Happy; Tea for Two/W: Irving Caesar, M: Vincent Youmans — I'm Waiting for You; No, No, Nanette/W: Otto Harbach, M: Vincent Youmans. *Hit the Deck* (Belasco, "Loo-Loo Martin," Apr. 25, 1927): Harbor of My Heart; If He'll Come Back to Me; Join the Navy!; Loo-Loo/W: Clifford Grey, Leo Robin, M: Vincent Youmans — Sometimes I'm Happy/W: Irving Caesar, M: Vincent Youmans.

3882. Vera Grosset *The Kiss Burglar* (Broadhurst > Nora Bayes, revival, "Pinkie Doolittle," Mar. 17, 1919): He Loves Me, He Loves Me Not/W: Glen MacDonough, M: Raymond Hubbell. *Oh, What a Girl!* (Shubert, "Lola Chappelle," July 28, 1919): Get Him Up/W: Edward Clark, M: Charles Jules, Jacques Presburg. *Broadway Brevities of 1920* (Winter Garden, revue, Sept. 29, 1920): Won't You Let Me Take a Picture of You?/WM: ?.

3883. Henry Grossman (Oct. 11, 1938–) B: New York, NY. *Grand Hotel* (Martin Beck, "Ernest Schmidt," Nov. 12, 1989): Some Have, Some Have Not/WM: Robert Wright, George Forrest, Maury Yeston.

3884. George Grossmith, Jr. (May 11, 1874– June 6, 1935) B: London, England. Brother of LAWRENCE GROSSMITH. The musical comedy star of Britain and the U.S. was the first chairman of Alexander Korda's production company, London Films. *The Shop Girl* (Palmer's, "Bertie Boyd," Oct. 28, 1895): Beautiful Bountiful Bertie/W: George Grossmith, M: Lionel Monckton. *The School Girl* (Daly's > Herald Square, "Sir Ormsby St. Ledger," Sept. 1, 1904):

Belinda on the Line/W: Paul Rubens, M: Leslie Stuart — Florrie; Old English Cake Walk; Real Town Lady/WM: Paul Rubens — Jingles, Jokes and Rhymes [Oct. 31, 1904]/WM: Benjamin Hapgood Burt — My Cosey Corner Girl/W: Charles Noel Douglas, M: John W. Bratton — We Want to Be Simpler/WM: Leslie Stuart. *Fluffy Ruffles* (Criterion, "Hon. Augustus Traddles," Sept. 7, 1908): Dining Out/W: George Grossmith, M: Jerome Kern — Sweetest Girl, Silly Boy, I Love You (Reckless Boy, I Love You)/W: Wallace Irwin, M: Jerome Kern — There's Something Rather Odd About Augustus/W: C.H. Bovill, M: Jerome Kern. *The Girl on the Film* (44th Street, "Max Daly," Dec. 29, 1913): Ah! Che Vedo/WM: ?— Down by the Country Side; In Bond Street/W: Adrian Ross, M: Walter Kollo — Oh! If You Were a Girl; Tommy Won't You Teach Me How to Tango/W: Adrian Ross, M: Albert Sirmay. *Tonight's the Night* (Shubert, "Hon. Dudley Mitten," Dec. 24, 1914): Boots and Shoes; Dancing Mad; I Could Love You If I Tried; The Only Way/WM: Paul Rubens, Percy Greenbank. *Princess Charming* (Imperial, "King Christian II of Elyria," Oct. 13, 1930): I'll Be There; A Wonderful Thing for the King/W: Arthur Swanstrom, M: Arthur Schwartz, Albert Sirmay. *Meet My Sister* (Shubert, "Marquis de Chatelard," Dec. 30, 1930): I Like You/W: Mack Gordon, M: Harry Revel.

3885. Lawrence Grossmith (Mar. 29, 1877– Feb. 21, 1944) B: London, England. M: CORALIE BLYTHE. Brother of GEORGE GROSSMITH, JR. *About Town* (Herald Square, CR, "The Duke of Blushington," Oct. 29, 1906): Dinner Time [Nov. 15, 1906]/WM: Addison Burkhardt — The Piccadilly Crawl/W: Addison Burkhardt, M: Melville Ellis. *Nobody Home* (Princess > Maxine Elliott, "Freddy Popple," Apr. 20, 1915): Beautiful, Beautiful Bed/W: Lawrence Grossmith, M: C.W. Murphy, Dan Lipton. *Flora Bella* (Casino > 44th Street, "Count Sergiey Weronzeff," Sept. 11, 1916): Adam; On to Petrograd/W: Percy Waxman, M: Charles Cuvillier — Creep, Creep, the World's Asleep/W: Victor Schertzinger, M: Milton Schwarzwald. *Love o' Mike* (Shubert > Maxine Elliott, "Capt. Lord Michael Kildare," Jan. 15, 1917): It Wasn't My Fault/W: Herbert Reynolds, M: Jerome Kern — Lulu; Moo Cow/W: Harry B. Smith, M: Jerome Kern.

3886. Guy Grosso *La Grosse Valise* (54th Street, "Pepito," Dec. 14, 1965): A Big One; C'est Defendu; Happy Song/W: Harold Rome, M: Gerard Calvi.

3887. James David Grout (Oct. 22, 1927–)

B: London, England. *Half a Sixpence* (Broadhurst, "Chitterlow," Apr. 25, 1965): Flash! Bang! Wallop!/WM: David Heneker.

3888. Betty Ann Grove *George M!* (Palace, "Nellie Cohan," Apr. 10, 1968): All Aboard for Broadway; Musical Comedy Man; Musical Moon; Twentieth Century Love/WM: George M. Cohan. *I Remember Mama* (Majestic, "Aunt Sigrid," May 31, 1979): Uncle Chris/W: Raymond Jessel, M: Richard Rodgers. *On Your Toes* (Virginia, revival, "Lil Dolan," Mar. 6, 1983): Two-a-Day for Keith/W: Lorenz Hart, M: Richard Rodgers.

3889. Stanley Grover (Mar. 28, 1926–Aug. 24, 1997) B: Woodstock, IL. *13 Daughters* (54th Street, "Willoughby," Mar. 2, 1961): My Pleasure/WM: Eaton Magoon, Jr. *South Pacific* (New York City Center, revival, "Lieut. Joseph Cable, U.S.M.C.," Apr. 13, 1961): Bali Ha'i; Younger Than Springtime; You've Got to Be Carefully Taught/W: Oscar Hammerstein II, M: Richard Rodgers. *Let It Ride!* (Eugene O'Neill, "Carver," Oct. 12, 1961): Love Let Me Know; Who's Doing What to Erwin?/WM: Jay Livingston, Ray Evans. *Mr. President* (St. James, "Charley Wayne," Oct. 20, 1962): Meat and Potatoes/WM: Irving Berlin. *Finian's Rainbow* (New York City Center, revival, "Woody Mahoney," Apr. 5, 1967): If This Isn't Love; Look to the Rainbow; Old Devil Moon; That Great Come-and-Get-It Day/W: E.Y. Harburg, M: Burton Lane. *The King and I* (New York City Center, revival, "Lun Tha," May 23, 1968): I Have Dreamed; We Kiss in a Shadow/W: Oscar Hammerstein II, M: Richard Rodgers. *Company* (Alvin, CR, "Larry," Mar. 29, 1971): Have I Got a Girl for You; Sorry-Grateful/WM: Stephen Sondheim. *The Desert Song* (Uris, revival, "Capt. Paul Fontaine," Sept. 5, 1973): I Want a Kiss; Margot; Soft as a Pigeon/W: Otto Harbach, Oscar Hammerstein II, M: Sigmund Romberg.

3890. Charlotte Groves *The Sultan of Sulu* (Wallack's, "Miss Dorchester," Dec. 29, 1902): The Peachy Teacher; Ten Little Gentlemen of Spooney Town/W: George Ade, M: Alfred G. Wathall.

3891. Lillie Grubb (?–1890) *Adonis* (Bijoux, "Talamea," Sept. 4, 1884): Golden Chains/W: J. Cheever Goodwin, M: Edward E. Rice — The Wall Street Broker [Mar. 19, 1885]/W: H.S. Hewitt, M: Edward E. Rice.

3892. Michael Gruber *A Chorus Line* (Shubert, CR, "Mike," Jan. 16, 1989): I Can Do That/W: Edward Kleban, M: Marvin Hamlisch. *Cats* (Winter Garden, CR, "Munkustrap"): The Awefull Battle of the Pekes and Pollicles; The Marching Songs of the Pollicle Dogs; Old Deuteronomy/W: T.S. Eliot, M: Andrew Lloyd Webber.

3893. Allan Gruet (Mar. 22, 1945–) B: Paterson, NJ. *The Rothschilds* (Lunt-Fontanne, "Kalman Rothschild," Oct. 19, 1970): Bonds; Everything; Rothschild & Sons/W: Sheldon Harnick, M: Jerry Bock.

3894. Adam Grupper *Guys and Dolls* (Martin Beck, revival, CR, "Benny Southstreet," c 1993): Fugue for Tinhorns; Guys and Dolls; The Oldest Established/WM: Frank Loesser.

3895. Harry Guardino (Dec. 23, 1925–July 17, 1995) B: Brooklyn, NY. *Anyone Can Whistle* (Majestic, "J. Bowden Hapgood," Apr. 4, 1964): Come Play Wiz Me; Everybody Says Don't; Simple; With So Little to Be Sure Of/WM: Stephen Sondheim. *Woman of the Year* (Palace, "Sam Craig," Mar. 29, 1981/Dec. 15, 1981): The Poker Game; See You in the Funny Papers; Shut Up, Gerald; So What Else Is New?; Sometimes a Day Goes By; Table Talk; The Two of Us; We're Gonna Work It Out/W: Fred Ebb, M: John Kander.

3896. Michael Guarnera *Jesus Christ Superstar* (Paramount Madison Square Garden, revival, "2nd Priest," Jan. 17, 1995): This Jesus Must Die/W: Tim Rice, M: Andrew Lloyd Webber.

3897. Elna Gudrun *The Merry World* (Imperial, revue, June 8, 1926): Deauville/WM: Herman Hupfeld — Military Charleston [July 12, 1926]; Tallahassee [July 12, 1926]/WM: ?.

3898. Jean Guelis *The Firebrand of Florence* (Alvin, "Arlecchino," Mar. 22, 1945): Come to Florence (Civic Song); Dizzily, Busily/W: Ira Gershwin, M: Kurt Weill.

3899. Laura Guerite *Mr. Wix of Wickham* (Bijou, "Madame Marie," Sept. 19, 1904): Bluff; Her First Can Can; Waiting for You/WM: John Wagner, Jerome Kern. *The Orchid* (Herald Square > Casino, "Zelie Homberg," Apr. 8, 1907): Come Along with Me/W: Adrian Ross, M: Lionel Monckton. *The Gay White Way* (Casino, revue, "Anna Held," Oct. 7, 1907): The Broadway Show/WM: ? — If You Must Make Eyes at Someone/W: Leo Wood, Matt Woodward, M: Leo Edwards — Tiddley-Om-Pom [Oct. 21, 1907]/WM: Leigh, Powell. *The Mimic World* (Casino, revue, CR, "Mlle Ou La La," Aug. 24, 1908): Mademoiselle/WM: ?. *Mr. Hamlet of Broadway* (Casino, "Mrs. Daisy Stringer," Dec. 23, 1908): Beautiful Eyes/W: George Whiting, Carter De Haven, M: Ted Snyder — The Hornpipe Rag/W: Edward Madden, M: Ben M. Jerome — Won't You Harmonize with Me?/W: George Arthurs, M: C.W. Murphy. *A Broken Idol* (Herald Square, "Mlle. Marie de Deau," Aug. 16, 1909): Marie/W: Harry Williams, M: Egbert Van Alstyne — Yankee Land/W: George V. Hobart, M: Victor Herbert.

3900. Alvaleta Guess (1955–Sept. 2, 1996) B: Kansas City, MO. *Swinging on a Star* (Music Box, revue, Oct. 22, 1995): Annie Doesn't Live Here Anymore; Shadows on the Swanee/W: Johnny Burke, Joe Young, M: Harold Spina — Doctor Rhythm/W: Johnny Burke, M: James V. Monaco — Irresistible; You're Not the Only Oyster in the Stew/W: Johnny Burke, M: Harold Spina — It Could Happen to You; Sunday, Monday or Always; When Stanislaus Got Married/W: Johnny Burke, M: James Van Heusen — Whoopsie Daisy Day/WM: Johnny Burke.

3901. Georges Guetary (Feb. 8, 1915–Sept. 13, 1997) B: Alexandria, Egypt. Best remembered for singing and dancing in the film *An American in Paris (1951). Arms and the Girl* (46th Street, "Franz," Feb. 2, 1950): A Cow and a Plough and a Frau; I Like It Here; I'll Never Learn; Plantation in Philadelphia; She's Exciting/W: Dorothy Fields, M: Morton Gould. *Portofino* (Adelphi, "Nicky," Feb. 21, 1958): Isn't It Wonderful?; It Might Be Love; New Dreams for Old; Portofino; Why Not for Marriage?/W: Richard Ney, M: Louis Bellson — No Wedding Bells for Me/W: Richard Ney, M: Will Irwin — That's Love/WM: Richard Ney — Under a Spell/W: Sheldon Harnick, M: Louis Bellson, Will Irwin.

3902. George Guidall (June 7, 1938–) B: Plainfield, NJ. *The President's Daughter* (Billy Rose, "Sam Golden," Nov. 3, 1970): Everything Is Possible in Life; What More Do I Need?/W: Jacob Jacobs, M: Murray Rumshinsky.

3903. Kristina Marie Guiguet *The Phantom of the Opera* (Majestic, CR, "Mme. Giry," c 1993): Magical Lasso; Notes; Prima Donna; Twisted Every Way/W: Charles Hart, Richard Stilgoe, M: Andrew Lloyd Webber.

3904. Nanette Guilford At 17, she debuted at the Metropolitan Opera. *Cavier* (Forrest, "Elena," June 7, 1934): Dream Kingdom; Gypsy; Here's to You; Prince Charming; Your Prince Was Not So Charming/W: Edward Heyman, M: Harden Church.

3905. Robert Guillaume (Nov. 30, 1930–) B: St. Louis, MO. The leading man and comedian began as an opera singer. On TV he appeared as Benson on the sitcom *Soap* (1977) and as Benson DuBois in *Benson* (1979), its spinoff. *Kwamina* (54th Street, "Ako," Oct. 23, 1961): The Cocoa Bean Song; Nothing More to

Look Forward To/WM: Richard Adler. *Porgy and Bess* (New York City Center, revival, "Sportin' Life," May 6, 1964): I Ain't Got No Shame/W: Ira Gershwin, DuBose Heyward, M: George Gershwin — It Ain't Necessarily So; There's a Boat Dat's Leavin' Soon for New York/W: Ira Gershwin, M: George Gershwin — A Woman Is a Sometime Thing/W: DuBose Heyward, M: George Gershwin. *Purlie* (Broadway, CR, "Purlie," Oct. 4, 1971): Down Home; The Harder They Fall; New-Fangled Preacher Man/W: Peter Udell, M: Gary Geld. *Purlie* (Billy Rose, revival, "Purlie," Dec. 27, 1972): same as above. *Guys and Dolls* (Broadway, revival, "Nathan Detroit," July 21, 1976): The Oldest Established; Sue Me/WM: Frank Loesser.

3906. Texas Guinan (1884–Nov. 5, 1933) B: Waco, TX. A singer in vaudeville, but best known as a nightclub hostess and entertainer in the 1920s. Betty Hutton played her in the movie *Incendiary Blonde* (1945). *Hop o' My Thumb* (Manhattan Opera House, "Zaza, the Queen," Nov. 26, 1913): For a Girl Has Her Living to Make/W: Sydney Rosenfeld, M: Manuel Klein. *Padlocks of 1927* (Shubert, revue, July 5, 1927): Here I Am; It's Tough to Be a Hostess/W: Billy Rose, Ballard Macdonald, M: Lee David — String Along with Texas/W: Billy Rose, Ballard Macdonald, M: ? — Texas and Barnum and Cohan/W: Billy Rose, Ballard Macdonald, M: Jesse Greer.

3907. Raymond Guion (Aug. 13, 1908–May 3, 1998) B: New York, NY. After 1931, when he began appearing in films, the actor was known as GENE RAYMOND. M: star of movie musicals Jeanette MacDonald, 1937–1965. *Say When* (Morosco, "Michael Graham," June 26, 1928): How About It?/W: Raymond Klages, M: Jesse Greer — Who's the Boy?/W: Max Lief, Nathaniel Lief, M: Ray Perkins.

3908. Carmen Guiterrez *West Side Story* (Winter Garden, "Teresita," Sept. 26, 1957): I Feel Pretty/W: Stephen Sondheim, M: Leonard Bernstein.

3909. Laurence Guittard (July 16, 1939–) B: San Francisco, CA. *Man of La Mancha* (ANTA Washington Square, CR, "Don Quixote," May 22, 1968 matinees): The Combat; Dulcinea; Golden Helmet; The Impossible Dream (The Quest); Man of La Mancha (I, Don Quixote)/W: Joe Darion, M: Mitch Leigh. *A Little Night Music* (Shubert, "Count Carl-Magnus Malcolm," Feb. 25, 1973): In Praise of Women; It Would Have Been Wonderful/WM: Stephen Sondheim. *Sondheim: A Musical Tribute* (Shubert, revue, Mar. 11, 1973): We're Gonna

Be All Right/W: Stephen Sondheim, M: Richard Rodgers. *Oklahoma!* (Palace, revival, "Curly McLain," Dec. 13, 1979): The Farmer and the Cowman; Oh, What a Beautiful Mornin'; Oklahoma!; People Will Say We're in Love; Pore Jud; The Surrey with the Fringe on Top/W: Oscar Hammerstein II, M: Richard Rodgers. *The Sound of Music* (New York State, revival, "Capt. Georg Von Trapp," Mar. 8, 1990): Do-Re-Mi; Edelweiss; How Can Love Survive?; No Way to Stop It; An Ordinary Couple; So Long, Farewell; The Sound of Music/W: Oscar Hammerstein II, M: Richard Rodgers. *Man of La Mancha* (Marquis, revival, CR, "Don Quixote," June 30, 1992): same as above.

3910. David Gunderman *A Change in the Heir* (Edison, "Nicholas," Apr. 29, 1990): Shut Up and Dance/W: George H. Gorham, M: Dan Sticco.

3911. Nicholas Gunn (Aug. 28, 1947–) B: Brooklyn, NY. *The Mystery of Edwin Drood* (Imperial, "Shade of Jasper," Dec. 2, 1985): Ceylon/WM: Rupert Holmes.

3912. Louise Gunning (Apr. 1, 1879–July 24, 1960). *Rogers Brothers in Wall Street* (Victoria, "Patrice Rafferty," Sept. 18, 1899): The Belle of Murray Hill/W: Willis Clark, M: Maurice Levi. *Mr. Pickwick* (Herald Square, "Arabella," Jan. 19, 1903): The Forest Air; The Lay of the Merry Ha! Ha!; Love; The Story of the Rainbow/W: Grant Stewart, M: Manuel Klein — Speak Low/W: Hermann Klein, M: Manuel Klein. *The Office Boy* (Victoria, "Euphemia," Nov. 2, 1903): Because He Told Me So; If I Were the Bride of a Soldier; A Maiden's Heart; Signs; Will You Be My Hero, Noble Sir?/W: Harry B. Smith, M: Ludwig Englander. *Love's Lottery* (Broadway, "Laura Skeffington," Oct. 3, 1904): Behold Our Lady Great; Cupid's a Lad; A Glimpse of Eden; Holiday Joys; The Honeymoon; The Temptation; What Art Thou?/W: Stanislas Stange, M: Julian Edwards. *The White Hen* (Casino, "Pepi Gloeckner," Feb. 16, 1907): At Last We're All Alone, Dear; Follow, Follow, Follow; Printemps; That's Why the Danube Was Blue/W: Paul West, M: Gustave Kerker. *Tom Jones* (Astor, "Sophia," Nov. 11, 1907): Beguile, Beguile, with Music Sweet; Dream O'Day Jill; Here's a Paradox for Lovers; I Wonder; Wisdom Says Festina Lente/W: Charles M. Taylor, M: Edward German. *Marcelle* (Casino, "Marcelle," Oct. 1, 1908): Far, Far Away (Memories Fond and True); The Message of the Red, Red Rose; My Own Paree/W: Frank Pixley, M: Gustav Luders. *The Balkan Princess* (Herald Square > Casino, "Princess Stephanie of Balaria," Feb. 9,

1911): Don't Let's Meet Again; I Like You All; Wonderful World/WM: Arthur Wimperis, Paul Rubens — When the Sunshine of Springtime/W: C.B. Lacy, M: Harry Gilbert. *The American Maid* (Broadway, "Annabel Vandeveer," Mar. 3, 1913): Cheer Up; The Crystal Lute; The Matrimonial Mart; Sweetheart; This Is My Busy Day/W: Leonard Liebling, M: John Philip Sousa.

3913. Bob Gunton (Nov. 15, 1945–) B: Santa Monica, CA. *Working* (46th Street, "Frank Decker," May 14, 1978): Brother Trucker/WM: James Taylor — Fathers and Sons/WM: Stephen Schwartz. *King of Hearts* (Minskoff, "Raoul," Oct. 22, 1978): King of Hearts; Le Grand Cirque de Provence; Nothing, Only Love/W: Jacob Brackman, M: Peter Link. *Evita* (Broadway, "Peron," Sept. 25, 1979): The Art of the Possible; Dice Are Rolling; I'd Be Surprisingly Good for You; A New Argentina; On the Balcony of the Casa Rosada; Rainbow Tour; She Is a Diamond/W: Tim Rice, M: Andrew Lloyd Webber. *Big River: The Adventures of Huckleberry Finn* (Eugene O'Neill, "The King," Apr. 25, 1985): When the Sun Goes Down in the South/WM: Roger Miller. *Roza* (Royale, "Lola," Oct. 1, 1987): Different; Don't Make Me Laugh; Get the Lady Dressed; Lola's Ceremony; Yussef's Visit/W: Julian More, M: Gilbert Becaud. *Sweeney Todd* (Circle in the Square, revival, "Sweeney Todd," Sept. 14, 1989): By the Sea; Epiphany; God, That's Good; The Judge's Return; A Little Priest; My Friends; No Place Like London; Pirelli's Miracle Elixir; Pretty Women/WM: Stephen Sondheim.

3914. Dennis Gurney *The Prince of Pilsen* (Jolson, revival, "Arthur St. John Wilberforce, Lord Somerset," Jan. 13, 1930): Artie; The Widow/W: Frank Pixley, M: Gustav Luders.

3915. Jonathan Guss *The Most Happy Fella* (New York State, revival, "Al," Sept. 4, 1991): Standing on the Corner/WM: Frank Loesser.

3916. Barrington Guy *Blackbirds of 1928* (Eltinge, revue, CR, May 27, 1929): I Can't Give You Anything but Love/W: Dorothy Fields, M: Jimmy McHugh. *Black Rhythm* (Comedy, "Sunny," Dec. 19, 1936): Emaline/WM: Donald Heywood.

3917. Jasmine Guy She played Whitley Gilbert on the TV sitcom *A Different World* (1987). *Leader of the Pack* (Ambassador, "Mickey," Apr. 8, 1985): Jivette Boogie Beat/WM: Ellie Greenwich. *Grease* (Eugene O'Neill, revival, CR, "Betty Rizzo"): Greased Lightnin'; Look at Me, I'm Sandra Dee; There Are Worse Things I Could Do/WM: Jim Jacobs, Warren Casey.

3918. Charles Guyer *The Show Girl or The Cap of Fortune* (Wallack's, "Jhonnie Jhones," May 5, 1902): Adeline/W: D.K. Stevens, M: Edward W. Corliss — Invocation to Pie; We Are Trying to Support Our Only Mother/W: D.K. Stevens, M: M.W. Daniels.

3919. Sheila Guyse *Memphis Bound!* (Broadway > Belasco, "Lily Valentine," May 24, 1945): Love or Reason; The Nightingale, the Moon and I; Old Love and Brand New Love; Sorry Her Lot/WM: Clay Warnick, Don Walker, based on William S. Gilbert and Arthur Sullivan. *Lost in the Stars* (Music Box, "Linda," Oct. 30, 1949): Who'll Buy?/W: Maxwell Anderson, M: Kurt Weill.

3920. Jack Gwillim (Dec. 15, 1915–July 2, 2001) B: Canterbury, England. *My Fair Lady* (Uris, revival, "Colonel Pickering," Aug. 18, 1981): The Rain in Spain; You Did It/W: Alan Jay Lerner, M: Frederick Loewe.

3921. Fred Gwynne (July 10, 1926–July 2, 1993) B: New York, NY. Comically and endearingly ghoulish character actor. From 1955-1960 he wrote advertising copy for the J. Walter Thompson agency. Best known for such TV sitcom roles as Officer Francis Muldoon in *Car 54, Where Are You?* (1961) and Herman Munster in *The Munsters* (1964). *Irma La Douce* (Plymouth, "Polyte-Le-Mou," Sept. 29, 1960): But; The Freedom of the Seas; From a Prison Cell; Le Grisbi Is le Root of le Evil in Man; Sons of France; That's a Crime; There Is Only One Paris for That/W: Julian More, David Heneker, Monty Norman, M: Marguerite Monnot. *Here's Love* (Shubert, "Marvin Shellhammer," Oct. 3, 1963): My State, My Kansas, My Home; Pine Cones and Holly Berries; The Plastic Alligator/WM: Meredith Willson. *Angel* (Minskoff, "W.O. Gant," May 10, 1978): Fingers and Toes; Gant's Waltz; I Can't Believe It's You; Tomorrow I'm Gonna Be Old/W: Peter Udell, M: Gary Geld.

3922. Paul Gyngell (Jan. 26, 1963–) B: Church Village, South Wales. *Carrie* (Virginia, "Tommy," May 12, 1988): Do Me a Favor; Don't Waste the Moon; Heaven/W: Dean Pitchford, M: Michael Gore.

3923. Alisa Gyse (1960–) B: Chicago, IL. *Uptown…It's Hot!* (Lunt-Fontanne, revue, Jan. 29, 1986): Amazing Grace/WM: Rev. John Newton — Be My Baby/WM: Jeff Barry, Ellie Greenwich, Phil Spector — Body and Soul/W: Edward Heyman, Robert Sour, Frank Eyton, M: Johnny Green — Ill Wind; Stormy Weather/W: Ted Koehler, M: Harold Arlen — Old Landmark/WM: M.A. Brunner — When Your Lover Has Gone/WM: E.A. Swan — Why Do Fools Fall in Love?/WM: Frank Lymon, Morris Levy. *Dreamgirls* (Ambassador, revival, "Deena Jones," June 28, 1987): Family; Hard to Say Goodbye, My Love; I'm Somebody; One Night Only; Only the Beginning; Quintette; When I First Saw You/W: Tom Eyen, M: Henry Krieger.

3924. Dolly Haas (Apr. 29, 1910–Sept. 16, 1994) B: Hamburg, Germany. M: artist Al Hirschfeld. Popular German film star of the early 1930s. *Lute Song* (New York City Center, revival, "Tchao-Ou-Niang, the wife," Mar. 12, 1959): Bitter Harvest; Chinese Market Place; Monkey See, Monkey Do; Mountain High, Valley Low; Vision Song; Where You Are/W: Bernard Hanighen, M: Raymond Scott.

3925. Hugo Haas (Feb. 19, 1901–Dec. 1, 1968) B: Brno, Czechoslovakia. Member of the State Theater in Prague. Film writer, producer, director, actor in Hollywood from 1939. His New York stage debut was in 1941. *Magdalena* (Ziegfeld, "Gen. Carabana," Sept. 20, 1948): The Civilized People; Come to Colombia; Travel, Travel, Travel/W: Robert Wright, George Forrest, M: Heitor Villa-Lobos.

3926. Linda Haberman *Dancin'* (Broadhurst, revue, CR, May 1979): Gary Owen/WM: trad.

3927. Pearl Hacker *Touch and Go* (Broadhurst > Broadway, revue, Oct. 13, 1949): Under the Sleeping Volcano/W: Walter Kerr, Jean Kerr, M: Jay Gorney.

3928. Buddy Hackett (Aug. 31, 1924–) B: Brooklyn, NY. His career as a stand-up comic and actor began in the Borscht Belt in the Catskill Mountains. He was a frequent guest on TV's late night *Jack Paar Show* (1958). *I Had a Ball* (Martin Beck, "Garside," Dec. 15, 1964): Can It Be Possible?; Dr. Freud; You Deserve Me/WM: Jack Lawrence, Stan Freeman.

3929. Dolly Hackett *The Passing Show of 1916* (Winter Garden, revue, June 22, 1916): The Making of a Girl/W: Harold Atteridge, M: George Gershwin, Sigmund Romberg — Pretty Baby/W: Gus Kahn, M: Tony Jackson, Egbert Van Alstyne. *The Passing Show of 1921* (Winter Garden, revue, Dec. 29, 1920): Ta-Voo (Ta-Hoo); When There's No One to Love/W: Harold Atteridge, M: Jean Schwartz — You May Be a Bad Man/WM: ?. *Make It Snappy* (Winter Garden, revue, Apr. 13, 1922): (Tell Me What's the Matter) Loveable Eyes; When the Wedding Chimes Are Ringing/W: Harold Atteridge, M: Jean Schwartz.

3930. Hal Hackett (Aug. 24, 1924–Dec. 4, 1967) B: Sleepy-Eye, MN. *Kismet* (Ziegfeld,

"Second Policeman," Dec. 3, 1953): He's in Love!; Was I Wazir?/WM: Robert Wright, George Forrest.

3931. Jeanne (Janette; Jeanette) Hackett (1888–Aug. 16, 1979) B: New York, NY. M: Harry Delmar, with whom she teamed in vaudeville; JOHN STEEL, 1930. She was a dancer and choreographer. *Harry Delmar's Revels* (Shubert, revue, CR, Dec. 26, 1927): If You Have Troubles Laugh Them Away (Laff 'Em Away)/WM: Lester Lee.

3932. Joan Hackett (Mar. 1, 1933–Oct. 8, 1983) B: New York, NY. Character actress of stage, screen and TV. *Park* (John Golden, "Young Woman," Apr. 22, 1970): Bein' a Kid; Hello Is the Way Things Begin; I Want It Just to Happen/W: Paul Cherry, M: Lance Mulcahy.

3933. Jonathan Hadary (Oct. 11, 1948–) B: Chicago, IL. *Gypsy* (St. James, revival, "Herbie," Nov. 16, 1989): Small World; Together Wherever We Go; You'll Never Get Away from Me/W: Stephen Sondheim, M: Jule Styne. *Gypsy* (Marquis, return engagement of revival, "Herbie," Apr. 28, 1991): same as above. *Guys and Dolls* (Martin Beck, revival, CR, "Nathan Detroit," May 17, 1993): The Oldest Established; Sue Me/WM: Frank Loesser.

3934. Tom Hadaway *The Messenger Boy* (Daly's, "Prof. Phunckwitz," Sept. 16, 1901): Bradshaw's Guide/W: Adrian Ross, M: Ivan Caryll.

3935. Peggy (Phebe) Hagan *Applause* (Palace, CR, "Karen Richards," Dec. 13, 1971/May 1, 1972): Fasten Your Seat Belts; Good Friends; Inner Thoughts/W: Lee Adams, M: Charles Strouse.

3936. Chris Hagen *Mame* (Winter Garden, CR, "Patrick Dennis, age 10"): The Fox Hunt; Mame; My Best Girl; St. Bridget; We Need a Little Christmas/WM: Jerry Herman.

3937. Fan Haggerty *Head Over Heels* (George M. Cohan, "Miss Graham," Aug. 29, 1918): With Type a-Ticking/W: Edgar Allan Woolf, M: Jerome Kern.

3938. George Haggerty B: New York, NY. In vaudeville, he acted as a stooge to FRANK FAY in an act at the Palace in 1924. *Hello Yourself!!!!* (Casino, "Cicero," Oct. 30, 1928): Tired of It All/W: Leo Robin, M: Richard Myers. *You Said It* (46th Street, "Willoughby Weatherby Pinkham," Jan. 19, 1931): You'll Do/W: Jack Yellen, M: Harold Arlen.

3939. Emma Haig (Jan. 21, 1898–June 9, 1939) B: Philadelphia, PA. A popular dancer in vaudeville, described by Variety as "a whirlwind of speed, a gifted kicker, and a tireless wonder."

Unfortunately for her singing, she had a noticeable lisp. *Miss 1917* (Century, revue, Nov. 5, 1917): A Dancing M.D./W: P.G. Wodehouse, M: Jerome Kern — Dinah/W: Sam M. Lewis, Joe Young, M: Harry Akst. *Music Box Revue of 1921* (Music Box, revue, Sept. 22, 1921): Dancing the Seasons Away/WM: Irving Berlin. *Our Nell* (Nora Bayes, "Angeline Weems," Dec. 4, 1922): The Cooney County Fair; Walking Home with Angeline/W: Brian Hooker, M: George Gershwin — Names I Love to Hear/W: Brian Hooker, M: George Gershwin, William Daly. *The Rise of Rosie O'Reilly* (Liberty, "Cutie Magee," Dec. 25, 1923): Keep A-Countin' Eight; My Gang/WM: George M. Cohan. *Tell Me More!* (Gaiety, "Bonnie Reeves," Apr. 13, 1925): Baby!; Ukelele Lorelei/W: Ira Gershwin, B.G. DeSylva, M: George Gershwin.

3940. Marian Hailey (Feb. 1, 1941–) B: Portland, OR. *Company* (Alvin, CR, "Amy," May 13, 1971): Getting Married Today; Poor Baby/WM: Stephen Sondheim.

3941. William Hain *The DuBarry* (George M. Cohan, "Rene la Vallery," Nov. 22, 1932): If I Am Dreaming; The Road to Happiness; Without Your Love/W: Rowland Leigh, M: Carl Millocker. *Roberta* (New Amsterdam, "Ladislaw," Nov. 18, 1933): The Touch of Your Hand/W: Otto Harbach, M: Jerome Kern.

3942. A. Larry Haines (Aug. 3, 1917–) B: Mt. Vernon, NY. *Promises, Promises* (Shubert, "Dr. Dreyfuss," Dec. 1, 1968): A Young Pretty Girl Like You/W: Hal David, M: Burt Bacharach.

3943. Helen Haines *Peg o' My Dreams* (Al Jolson, "Muriel," May 5, 1924): Right-O; Shy Little Irish Smile/W: Anne Caldwell, M: Hugo Felix.

3944. Mitzi Hajos (Apr. 27, 1891–) B: Budapest, Hungary. M: BOYD MARSHALL. The singer and dancer came to the U.S. in 1909, working in cabaret and vaudeville. Her role in *Sari* made her a star. From about 1920, she was billed as MITZI. *Sari* (Liberty > New Amsterdam, "Sari Racz," Jan. 13, 1914): Ha-za-za; Long Live the King (Vive le Roi); Love's Own Sweet Song (Sari Waltz); Pick a Husband; There's No Place Like Home with You; Triumphant Youth/W: C.C.S. Cushing, E.P. Heath, M: Emmerich Kalman. *Pom-Pom* (Cohan, "Paulette" and "Pom-Pom, the Pickpocket," Feb. 28, 1916): The Circus in the Moon; Evelyn; In the Dark; Kiss Me; Pom-Pom; You Shall Not Go/W: Anne Caldwell, M: Hugo Felix. *Head Over Heels* (George M. Cohan, "Mitzi Bambinetti," Aug. 29, 1918): All the World Is Swaying; The Big

Show; Funny Little Something; Head Over Heels; Mitzi's Lullaby; Vorderveele/W: Edgar Allan Woolf, M: Jerome Kern — Every Bee Has a Bud of Its Own/W: Edgar Allan Woolf, M: Harold A. Levey. *Lady Billy* (Liberty, "Countess Antonia Celestina-Elizabeta-Selana-Wilhelmina of Pardove [Master Billy]," Dec. 14, 1920): Come to Arcady; Goodbye, Goodbye; Historic Huzzies; If; Just Plant a Kiss; The Legend/W: Zelda Sears, M: Harold A. Levey. *The Magic Ring* (Liberty, "Polly Church," Oct. 1, 1923): Education; Famous Falls; The Love Song (of Today); When the Organ Plays/W: Zelda Sears, M: Harold A. Levey. *Naughty Riquette* (Cosmopolitan, "Riquette Duval," Sept. 13, 1926): Alcazar; Make Believe You're Mine; Somehow I'd Rather Be Good; Two Are Company/W: Harry B. Smith, M: Oscar Straus — I May; Naughty Riquette/W: Harry B. Smith, M: Maurie Rubens, Kendall Burgess. *The Madcap* (Royale, "Chibi," Jan. 31, 1928): Birdies; I Want to Tell You a Story; Odle-De-O Do, I Do; Step to Paris Blues/W: Clifford Grey, M: Maurie Rubens — Stop! Go!/W: Clifford Grey, M: Maurie Rubens, J. Fred Coots. *Sari* (Liberty, revival, "Sari Racz," Jan. 29, 1930): same as above.

3945. Alan Hale (Feb. 10, 1892–Jan. 22, 1950) B: Washington, D.C. His career included newspaper work, singing with the Metropolitan Opera, directing movies and inventing the sliding theater seat. From 1911, he appeared in more than 100 films. *Rock-a-Bye Baby* (Astor, "Monte," May 22, 1918): The Big Spring Drive; I Believed All They Said; I Can Trust Myself with a Lot of Girls; One, Two, Three; Stitching, Stitching/W: Herbert Reynolds, M: Jerome Kern. *A Lonely Romeo* (Shubert > Casino, "Gilbert Grant," June 10, 1919): Any Old Place with You [Aug. 26, 1919]/W: Lorenz Hart, M: Richard Rodgers — Don't Do Anything Till You Hear from Me/W: Robert B. Smith, M: Malvin F. Franklin — Jolly Me; You Never Can Tell/W: Robert B. Smith, M: Robert Hood Bowers.

3946. Chester Hale (Jan. 15, 1899–) B: New York, NY. *Peg o' My Dreams* (Al Jolson, "Alexis," May 5, 1924): All Alone/W: Anne Caldwell, M: Hugo Felix.

3947. Elizabeth Hale (Jan. 15, 1947–) B: Brooklyn, NY. *Fiddler on the Roof* (Winter Garden, revival, "Tzeitel," Dec. 28, 1976): Matchmaker, Matchmaker/W: Sheldon Harnick, M: Jerry Bock.

3948. Frank Hale *Pom-Pom* (Cohan, "Gigolo," Feb. 28, 1916): Mister Love/W: Anne Caldwell, M: Hugo Felix.

3949. Georgie Hale *The Midnight Rounders*

of 1920 (Century roof, CR, revue, Oct. 4, 1920): Three Little Marys/W: Alfred Bryan, M: Jean Schwartz. *The Rise of Rosie O'Reilly* (Liberty, "Pete," Dec. 25, 1923): My Gang/WM: George M. Cohan. *The Greenwich Village Follies of 1924* (Shubert > Winter Garden, revue, Sept. 16, 1924): Brittany; The Follies Girls and Their Collies [Oct. 27, 1924]; Syncopated Pipes of Pan; Two Little Babes in the Wood/WM: Cole Porter — Happy Melody/W: Irving Caesar, John Murray Anderson, M: Phil Charig. *Puzzles of 1925* (Fulton, revue, Feb. 2, 1925): The Doo Dab/W: Bert Kalmar, M: Harry Ruby. *The Cocoanuts* (Lyric, "Eddie," Dec. 8, 1925): The Bellhops; They're Blaming the Charleston; We Should Care/WM: Irving Berlin. *Bye, Bye, Bonnie* (Ritz, "Charles Phillips," Jan. 13, 1927): Have You Used Soft Soap?; Lovin's Off My Mind; Promise Not to Stand Me Up Again/W: Neville Fleeson, M: Albert Von Tilzer. *Peggy-Ann* (Vanderbilt, CR, "Freddie Shawn," Sept. 1927): Chuck It!; Havana (Havana Opening); Hello!/W: Lorenz Hart, M: Richard Rodgers.

3950. Helen Hale M: WILLIAM T. HODGE. *Peggy from Paris* (Wallack's, "Lily Ann Lynch," Sept. 10, 1903): We Are the Principals/W: George Ade, M: William Lorraine. *Woodland* (New York > Herald Square, "Miss Jenny Wren," Nov. 21, 1904): Bye-Bye Baby; If You Love Me, Lindy, Tell Me So/W: Frank Pixley, M: Gustav Luders. *The Man from Now* (New Amsterdam, "Gasolina" and "Samsonia," Sept. 3, 1906): Girls Just Girls/W: Isabel deWitt Kaplan, M: ?— I Want to Go Home Now; Liquid Air; My Gasoline Maid/W: John Kendrick Bangs, M: Manuel Klein — What's the Matter with Our Team?/W: ?, M: Harry Von Tilzer. *The Yankee Tourist* (Astor, "Blanche Bailey," Aug. 12, 1907): Come and Have a Smile with Me; Wouldn't You Like to Have Me for a Sweetheart?/W: Wallace Irwin, M: Alfred G. Robyn — The Teddy Girl/W: William Jerome, M: Jean Schwartz.

3951. John Hale *Earl Carroll's Vanities of 1930* (New Amsterdam, revue, July 1, 1930): Going Up; I Came to Life; Love Boats/W: E.Y. Harburg, M: Jay Gorney — The March of Time; One Love/W: Ted Koehler, M: Harold Arlen. *Earl Carroll's Vanities of 1932* (Broadway, revue, Sept. 27, 1932): Love You Are My Inspiration/W: Ted Koehler, M: Andre Renaud — My Darling/W: Edward Heyman, M: Richard Myers. *Earl Carroll's Sketch Book of 1935* (Majestic, revue, CR, Sept. 9, 1935): At Last!/W: Charles Tobias, Sam M. Lewis, M: Henry Tobias — Silhouettes Under the Stars; Through These Portals Pass the Most Beautiful Girls in the World/ W: Charles Newman, Charles Tobias, M: Murray Mencher — There's Music in a Kiss/WM: Abner Silver, Al Lewis, Al Sherman.

3952. Ruth Hale (c 1886–Sept. 18, 1934) B: Rogersville, TN. M: HEYWOOD BROUN. *Poor Little Ritz Girl* (Central, "Marguerite," July 28, 1920): The Bombay Bombashay/W: Alex Gerber, M: Sigmund Romberg, Ray Perkins.

3953. Sonnie Hale (May 1, 1902–June 9, 1959) B: London, England. British star of stage and screen. M: EVELYN LAYE, 1926–1931; JESSIE MATTHEWS, 1931–1944. *Wake Up and Dream* (Selwyn, revue, Dec. 30, 1929): Looking at You/WM: Cole Porter.

3954. Royal Halee *The Greenwich Village Follies of 1925* (46th Street, revue, Dec. 24, 1925): White Cargo/WM: ?.

3955. Bernice Haley *His Little Widows* (Astor, "Dahlia," Apr. 30, 1917): When the Animals Are Gone/W: Thomas Gray, M: Malvin F. Franklin.

3956. Grace Haley *His Little Widows* (Astor, "Lily," Apr. 30, 1917): same as BERNICE HALEY.

3957. Jack Haley (Aug. 10, 1899–June 6, 1979) B: Boston, MA. Best remembered for his screen role as the Tin Woodman in *The Wizard of Oz* (1939). *Round the Town* (Century roof, revue, May 21, 1924): Liza Jane/W: Ned Wever, M: Alfred Nathan. *Gay Paree* (Shubert, revue, Aug. 18, 1925): Baby's Baby Grand/W: Clifford Grey, M: J. Fred Coots — (My) Sugar Plum/W: B.G. DeSylva, M: Joseph Meyer, J. Fred Coots — Wonderful Girl/W: Clifford Grey, M: Alfred Goodman, J. Fred Coots. *Gay Paree* (Winter Garden, revue, Nov. 9, 1926): There Never Was a Town Like Paris/W: Mann Holiner, M: Alberta Nichols. *Follow Thru* (46th Street, "Jack Martin," Jan. 9, 1929): Button Up Your Overcoat; I Could Give Up Anything but You/W: B.G. DeSylva, Lew Brown, M: Ray Henderson. *Free for All* (Manhattan, "Stephen Potter, Jr.," Sept. 8, 1931): The Girl Next Door; Not That I Care/W: Oscar Hammerstein II, M: Richard A. Whiting. *Take a Chance* (Apollo, "Duke Stanley," Nov. 26, 1932): She's Nuts About Me; Turn Out the Lights; You're an Old Smoothie/W: B.G. DeSylva, M: Richard A. Whiting, Nacio Herb Brown. *Higher and Higher* (Shubert, "Zachary Ash," Apr. 4, 1940): A Barking Baby Never Bites; Disgustingly Rich; From Another World; How's Your Health?; I'm Afraid/W: Lorenz Hart, M: Richard Rodgers. *Inside U.S.A.* (New Century, revue, Apr. 30, 1948): Rhode Island Is Famous for You; We

Won't Take It Back/W: Howard Dietz, M: Arthur Schwartz.

3958. Lucile Haley M: JACK NORTON. *His Little Widows* (Astor, "Tulip," Apr. 30, 1917): same as BERNICE HALEY.

3959. Mabel Haley *His Little Widows* (Astor, "Rose," Apr. 30, 1917): same as BERNICE HALEY.

3960. Adelaide Hall (Oct. 20, 1895–Nov. 7, 1993) B: Brooklyn, NY. One of the greatest jazz singers of all time. Her father taught music at Pratt Institute, where she studied. After moving to London in the 1930s and performing there and in Paris, she became an international cabaret star. *Runnin' Wild* (Colonial, revue, "Adelade," Oct. 29, 1923): Ginger Brown; Love Bug [Apr. 7, 1924]; Old Fashioned Love; Set 'Em Sadie/W: Cecil Mack, M: James P. Johnson. *My Magnolia* (Mansfield, revue, "Jenny," July 8, 1926): Gee Chee Charleston; Jazz Land Ball; Spend It/W: Alex Rogers, M: C. Luckeyth Roberts. *Blackbirds of 1928* (Liberty > Eltinge, revue, May 9, 1928): Bandanna Babies; Diga Diga Doo; Here Comes My Blackbird; I Must Have That Man/W: Dorothy Fields, M: Jimmy McHugh. *Brown Buddies* (Liberty, "Betty Lou Johnson," Oct. 7, 1930): Happy/W: Bob Joffe, M: Nat Reed. *Jamaica* (Imperial, "Grandma Obeah," Oct. 31, 1957): Cocoanut Sweet; For Every Fish There's a Little Bigger Fish; Savannah's Wedding Day/W: E.Y. Harburg, M: Harold Arlen.

3961. Albert Hall (Nov. 10, 1937–) B: Boothton, AL. *Ain't Supposed to Die a Natural Death* (Ethel Barrymore, Oct. 20, 1971): Three Boxes of Longs Please/WM: Melvin Van Peebles.

3962. Berniece Hall *Trumpets of the Lord* (Brooks Atkinson, "Female Voice," Apr. 29, 1969): Didn't It Rain; In His Care; Soon One Morning/WM: based on gospel hymns.

3963. Bettina Hall (1906–Aug. 6, 1997) B: North Easton, MA. Sister of NATALIE HALL. *The Little Show* (Music Box, revue, Apr. 30, 1929): A Little Hut in Hoboken/WM: Herman Hupfeld — Little Old New York/W: Howard Dietz, M: Arthur Schwartz — Or What Have You?/W: Grace Henry, M: Morris Hamilton — Six Little Sinners/W: Earle Crooker, M: Frank Grey. *Three Little Girls* (Shubert, "Marie" and "Mme. Morrossoni," Apr. 14, 1930): Dream On; I'll Tell You; A Lesson in Letter Writing/W: Harry B. Smith, M: Walter Kollo — Love Comes Only Once in a Lifetime/W: Stella Unger, M: Harold Stern, Harry Perella. *Meet My Sister* (Shubert > Imperial, "Dolly Molinar," Dec. 30, 1930): Always in My Heart; Birds in the Spring;

Friendship; It's Money — It's Fame — It's Love; Look and Love Is Here; Love Is Faded Away; Radziwill; She Is My Ideal; Tell Me What Can This Be/WM: Ralph Benatzky. *The Cat and the Fiddle* (Globe, "Shirley Sheridan," Oct. 15, 1931): Ha! Cha! Cha!; One Moment Alone; She Didn't Say Yes; Try to Forget/W: Otto Harbach, M: Jerome Kern. *The Only Girl* (44th Street, revival, "Ruth Wilson," May 21, 1934): The Compact; When You're Away; You're the Only One for Me/W: Henry Blossom, M: Victor Herbert. *Anything Goes* (Alvin > 46th Street, "Hope Harcourt," Nov. 21, 1934): All Through the Night; The Gypsy in Me/WM: Cole Porter.

3964. Cardell Hall *Your Arms Too Short to Box with God* (Lyceum, revue, Dec. 22, 1976): Your Arms Too Short to Box with God/WM: Alex Bradford.

3965. Carl Hall *Inner City* (Ethel Barrymore, revue, Dec. 19, 1971): Ding Dong Bell; The Great If; Jack Be Nimble; Now I Lay Me; One, Two; The Pickpocket; Street Sermon; Taffy/W: Eve Merriam, M: Helen Miller. *The Wiz* (Lunt-Fontanne, revival, "The Wiz," May 24, 1984): If You Believe (Believe in Yourself); So You Wanted to Meet the Wizard; Y'all Got It!/WM: Charlie Smalls.

3966. Carol Hall *The Best Little Whorehouse in Texas* (46th Street, CR, "Doatsey Mae," Jan. 1, 1979): Doatsey Mae; Texas Has a Whorehouse in It/WM: Carol Hall.

3967. Cliff (Sharlie) Hall (c 1894–Oct. 6, 1972) Straight man to comedian JACK PEARL as Baron Munchhausen on radio's *The Jack Pearl Show* (1932), from which came the phrase "Vas you dere, Sharlie?." *Here's Love* (Shubert, "Judge Martin Group," Oct. 3, 1963): My State, My Kansas, My Home/WM: Meredith Willson. *Sherry!* (Alvin, "Dr. Bradley," Mar. 27, 1967): With This Ring/W: James Lipton, M: Laurence Rosenthal.

3968. Delores Hall *Inner City* (Ethel Barrymore, revue, Dec. 19, 1971): Half Alive; If Wishes Were Horses; Law and Order; Now I Lay Me; Starlight Starbright; Summer Nights/W: Eve Merriam, M: Helen Miller. *Dude* (Broadway, "Bread," Oct. 9, 1972): Baby Breath; I Love My Boo Boo; A Song to Sing; Undo/W: Gerome Ragni, M: Galt MacDermot. *The Night That Made America Famous* (Ethel Barrymore, revue, Feb. 26, 1975): Too Much World; Welfare Rag; When I Look Up; When Maudey Wants a Man/WM: Harry Chapin. *Your Arms Too Short to Box with God* (Lyceum, revue, Dec. 22, 1976): The Band; I Love You So Much Jesus; Your Arms Too Short to Box with God/WM:

Alex Bradford. *The Best Little Whorehouse in Texas* (46th Street, "Jewel," June 19, 1978/Jan. 18, 1982): Girl, You're a Woman; No Lies; Twenty-Four Hours of Lovin'/WM: Carol Hall.

3969. Donald Hall (Aug. 14, 1867–July 25, 1948) B: Morree, Northwest Province, East India. *The Shop Girl* (Palmer's, CR, "Charles Appleby," early 1896): And Her Golden Hair Was Hanging Down Her Back/W: Monroe H. Rosenfeld, M: Felix McGlennon.

3970. Fred Hall *Bombo* (Al Jolson > Winter Garden, "Count Garibaldi" and "Prince Don," Oct. 6, 1921): In the Way Off There!/W: Harold Atteridge, M: Sigmund Romberg.

3971. George Hall (Nov. 19, 1916–) B: Toronto, Canada. *Call Me Mister* (National > Plymouth, revue, Apr. 18, 1946): The Senators' Song/WM: Harold Rome. *Lend an Ear* (National > Broadhurst, revue, Dec. 16, 1948): Power of the Press/WM: Joseph Stein, Will Glickman.

3972. Glenn Hall *The Madcap Duchess* (Globe, "Renaud, Prince of St. Pol in Artois," Nov. 11, 1913): Aurora Blushing Rosily; The Deuce, Young Man!; Do You Know?; Goddess of Mine; The Pledge; Star of Love/W: David Stevens, M: Victor Herbert. *Kitty Darlin'* (Casino, "Lieut. Lord Verney," Nov. 7, 1917): Just We Two; The Sword of My Father/W: P.G. Wodehouse, M: Rudolf Friml — Kitty Darlin'/W: Otto Harbach, M: Rudolf Friml —'Twas Pretense/WM: ?.

3973. Grayson Hall (Sept. 18, 1923–Aug. 7, 1985) B: Philadelphia, PA. *Happy End* (Martin Beck, revival, "The Fly," May 7, 1977): Ballad of the Lily of Hell/W: Bertolt Brecht, M: Kurt Weill.

3974. Isobel Hall *Winsome Winnie* (Casino, "Marjorie," Dec. 1, 1903): Jenny/WM: Henry Paulton, Edward Jakobowski. *The Prince of Pilsen* (Daly's, revival, "Edith Adams," Apr. 4, 1904): The Field and Forest; The Message of the Violet; We Know It's Wrong to Flirt/W: Frank Pixley, M: Gustav Luders.

3975. Jane Hall (Feb. 15, 1880–Oct. 13, 1975) B: Winona, MN. *The Soul Kiss* (New York, "Angela," Jan. 28, 1908): The Soul Kiss (Just for You from Above)/W: Lewis Gates, M: Maurice Levi.

3976. Josephine Hall (?–Dec. 5, 1920) B: East Greenwich, RI. *The Girl from Paris* (Herald Square, "Ruth," Dec. 8, 1896): Sister Mary Jane's Top Note/W: F. Bowyer, M: Ivan Caryll — Tootle, Tootle; Upon the Stage Let's Have a Fling/W: George Dance, M: Ivan Caryll. *The Military Maid* (Savoy, "Fleurette D'Norville," Oct. 8, 1900): Sister Mary Has the Measles/W: George V. Hobart, M: Alfred E. Aarons. *The Knickerbocker Girl* (Herald Square, "Mehitable Merton," June 15, 1903): Brother Bill; Country Life; Dolly Daily; Espanola Viva; A Little Bird Is Looking All the Time; She's All Right/W: George Totten Smith, M: Alfred E. Aarons.

3977. Josephine Hall *Rang-Tang* (Royale, revue, July 12, 1927): Come to Africa; Some Day; Summer Nights; Sweet Evening Breeze/W: Jo Trent, M: Ford Dabney. *Keep Shufflin'* (Daly's > Eltinge, revue, "Ruth," Feb. 27, 1928): Dusky Love/W: Henry Creamer, M: Will Vodery — Pining/WM: Con Conrad, Henry Creamer, Clarence Todd.

3978. Juanita Hall (Nov. 6, 1901–Feb. 28, 1968) B: Keysport, NJ. She was a regular on a live TV variety show called *Captain Billy's Mississippi Music Hall* (1948). *Sing Out Sweet Land* (International, revue "Watermelon Woman," Dec. 27, 1944): Watermelon Cry/WM: trad. *St. Louis Woman* (Martin Beck, "Leah," Mar. 30, 1946): Racin' Form/W: Johnny Mercer, M: Harold Arlen. *South Pacific* (Majestic, "Bloody Mary," Apr. 7, 1949): Bali Ha'i; Happy Talk/W: Oscar Hammerstein II, M: Richard Rodgers. *House of Flowers* (Alvin, "Madame Tango," Dec. 30, 1954): Madame Tango's Tango; Slide, Boy, Slide; Smellin' of Vanilla (Bamboo Cage)/WM: Truman Capote, Harold Arlen. *Flower Drum Song* (St. James, "Madam Liang," Dec. 1, 1958): Chop Suey; A Hundred Million Miracles; The Other Generation; You Are Beautiful/W: Oscar Hammerstein II, M: Richard Rodgers.

3979. Katherine Hall *Walk a Little Faster* (St. James, revue, Dec. 7, 1932): Mayfair/W: Roland Leigh, M: William Walter — Off Again, On Again/W: E.Y. Harburg, M: Vernon Duke.

3980. Natalie Hall (Sept. 23, 1904–Mar. 4, 1994) B: Providence, RI. Sister of BETTINA HALL. *Three Little Girls* (Shubert, "Beate-Marie" and "Beate," Apr. 14, 1930): Dream On; A Lesson in Letter Writing; Letter Song; Love's Happy Dream/W: Harry B. Smith, M: Walter Kollo — Love Comes Only Once in a Lifetime/W: Stella Unger, M: Harold Stern, Harry Perella. *Through the Years* (Manhattan, "Moonyeen," and "Kathleen," Jan. 28, 1932): I'll Come Back to You; Kathleen, Mine; Through the Years; You're Everywhere/W: Edward Heyman, M: Vincent Youmans. *Music in the Air* (Alvin > 44th Street, "Frieda Hatzfeld," Nov. 8, 1932): I Am So Eager; I'm Alone; Night Flies By; The Song Is You/W: Oscar Hammerstein II, M: Jerome Kern. *Music Hath Charms* (Majestic,

"Maria Sovrani" and "Marchese Maria," Dec. 29, 1934): Exquisite Moment; Frutti Di Mare; It's You I Want to Love Tonight; Let Me Be Free; Love Is Only What You Make It; Midnight Flirtation; My Heart Is Yours; My Palace of Dreams; Romance/W: Rowland Leigh, John Shubert, M: Rudolf Friml.

3981. Pamela Hall (Oct. 16, 1946–) B: Champaign, IL. *Dear World* (Mark Hellinger, "Nina," Feb. 6, 1969): I've Never Said I Love You/WM: Jerry Herman. *1776* (46th Street, CR, "Martha Jefferson," Apr. 13, 1971): He Plays the Violin/WM: Sherman Edwards. *A Funny Thing Happened on the Way to the Forum* (Lunt-Fontanne, revival, "Philia," Mar. 30, 1972): Echo Song; Lovely/WM: Stephen Sondheim. *Sondheim: A Musical Tribute* (Shubert, revue, Mar. 11, 1973): Your Eyes Are Blue/WM: Stephen Sondheim.

3982. Patricia Hall *Annie Get Your Gun* (Music Theater of Lincoln Center > Broadway, revival > return engagement, "Mrs. Schuyler Adams," May 31, 1966): There's No Business Like Show Business/WM: Irving Berlin.

3983. Pauline Hall (Feb. 26, 1860–Dec. 29, 1919) B: Cincinnati, OH. *Hiawatha* (Standard, "Honey Dew," Feb. 21, 1880): Pretty Little Boys/W: Nathaniel Childs, M: Edward E. Rice. *Erminie* (Casino, "Erminie de Pontvert," May 10, 1886): At Midnight on My Pillow Lying; Dear Mother, In Dreams I See Her; Lullaby/W: Claxson Bellamy, Harry Paulton, M: Edward Jakobowski. *Erminie* (Casino, revival, "Erminie de Pontvert," Nov. 20, 1889/May 23, 1898): same as above.

3984. Richard Hall *Love o' Mike* (Maxine Elliott, CR, "Jack Vaughn," Mar. 19, 1917): Don't Tempt Me; Lulu/W: Harry B. Smith, M: Jerome Kern.

3985. Steve Hall (June 4, 1958–) B: Washington, DC. *Marlowe* (Rialto, "Capt. Townsend," Oct. 12, 1981): The Funeral Dirge; Rocking the Boat/WM: Leo Rost, Jimmy Horowitz.

3986. Thurston Hall (May 10, 1882–Feb. 20, 1958) B: Boston, MA. In 1917 he debuted in films as Marc Antony in *Cleopatra* with Theda Bara, and went on to make 100 or more costume vehicles and comedies. *The Only Girl* (39th Street > Lyric, "Alan Kimbrough [Kim]," Nov. 2, 1914): Be Happy, Boys, Tonight; The Compact; Here's to the Land We Love, Boys!; You're the Only One for Me/W: Henry Blossom, M: Victor Herbert. *Have a Heart* (Liberty, "Ruddy Schoonmaker," Jan. 11, 1917): And I Am All Alone; Have a Heart; My Wife — My Man; The

Road That Lies Before/W: P.G. Wodehouse, M: Jerome Kern.

3987. William Hall see WILLIAM LANGAN.

3988. Jack Hallett (Nov. 7, 1948–) B: Philadelphia, PA. *The First* (Martin Beck, "Huey," Nov. 17, 1981): Is This Year Next Year?/W: Martin Charnin, M: Bob Brush.

3989. Beryl Halley *Half a Widow* (Waldorf, "June Love," Sept. 12, 1927): Step, Step, Step/WM: Jack Murray, Joe Brandfon. *Rio Rita* (Lyric, CR, "Montezuma's Daughter," Jan. 30, 1928): Montezuma's Daughter/W: Joseph McCarthy, M: Harry Tierney.

3990. Bud Halliday *Strut Miss Lizzie* (Times Square, revue, June 19, 1922): Breakin' the Leg; I Love Sweet Angeline; Mandy/WM: Henry Creamer, Turner Layton.

3991. Buzz Halliday *The Girls Against the Boys* (Alvin, revue, Nov. 2, 1959): The Girls Against the Boys/W: Arnold B. Horwitt, M: Richard Lewine.

3992. Frances Halliday *Blossom Time* (Ambassador, "Kitzi," Sept. 29, 1921): Lonely Heart; Love Is a Riddle; Three Little Maids/W: Dorothy Donnelly, M: Sigmund Romberg. *Half a Widow* (Waldorf, "Edith Proctor," Sept. 12, 1927): Under the Midsummer Moon/W: Harry B. Smith, M: Shep Camp — You're a Wonderful Girl/W: Frank Dupree, Harry B. Smith, M: Shep Camp.

3993. Gordon Halliday (Apr. 2, 1952–) B: Providence, RI. *Shenandoah* (Alvin, "Sam," Jan. 7, 1975): Violets and Silverbells/W: Peter Udell, M: Gary Geld.

3994. Heller Halliday Daughter of MARY MARTIN. *Peter Pan* (Winter Garden, "Liza," Oct. 20, 1954): I've Gotta Crow/W: Carolyn Leigh, M: Moose Charlap.

3995. Hildegarde Halliday (Sept. 12, 1907– Oct. 10, 1977) B: Nutley, NJ. *The Garrick Gaieties of 1930* (Guild, revue, June 4, 1930): Do Tell/W: Henry Myers, M: Charles M. Schwab. *New Faces of 1934* (Fulton, revue, Mar. 15, 1934): Something You Lack/W: June Sillman, Nancy Hamilton, M: Warburton Guilbert — You're My Relaxation/W: Robert Sour, M: Charles M. Schwab.

3996. Robert Halliday (Apr. 11, 1893–) B: Loch Lomond, Scotland. M: EVELYN HERBERT. The baritone studied engineering at Glasgow University and came to the U.S. in 1913. *Dew Drop Inn* (Astor, "Bobby Smith," May 17, 1923): Goodbye Forever; We Two/W: Cyrus D. Wood, M: Alfred Goodman, Rudolf Friml — The Primrose Path/W: Cyrus D. Wood, M: Alfred Goodman. *Paradise Alley* (Casino, CR,

"Jack Harriman," May 19, 1924): Friendship Leads Us to Love/W: Howard Johnson, M: A. Dorian Otvos — Put on the Ritz/W: Howard Johnson, M: Irving Bibo — Tell Me Truly/W: Howard Johnson, M: Carle Carleton — Those Beautiful Chimes; Your Way or My Way/W: Howard Johnson, M: Harry Archer — What You Could Be If You Had Me (If I Had You and You Had Me); Where Have the Old Timers Gone/W: Howard Johnson, M: Harry Archer, Carle Carleton. *Topsy and Eva* (Harris, CR, "George Shelby," Dec. 29, 1924): Give Me Your Heart and Give Me Your Hand; Kiss Me; Rememb'ring/WM: Vivian Duncan, Rosetta Duncan. *Holka-Polka* (Lyric, "Karel Boleslav," Oct. 14, 1925): Holka-Polka; This Is My Dance/W: Gus Kahn, Raymond B. Egan, M: Will Ortman — In a Little While/W: Raymond B. Egan, M: Will Ortman. *Tip-Toes* (Liberty, "Rollo Metcalf," Dec. 28, 1925): Nice Baby!/W: Ira Gershwin, M: George Gershwin. *The Desert Song* (Casino, "Red Shadow" and "Pierre Birabeau," Nov. 30, 1926): The Desert Song; Farewell; I Want a Kiss; One Alone; The Riff Song; Then You Will Know/W: Otto Harbach, Oscar Hammerstein II, M: Sigmund Romberg. *The New Moon* (Imperial > Casino, "Robert Mission," Sept. 19, 1928): An Interrupted Love Song; Lover, Come Back to Me; Marianne; Stouthearted Men; Wanting You/W: Oscar Hammerstein II, M: Sigmund Romberg. *Princess Charming* (Imperial, "Capt. Torelli of the Cruiser Elyria," Oct. 13, 1930): Here Is a Sword; I'll Never Leave You; Trailing a Shooting Star; You/W: Arthur Swanstrom, M: Arthur Schwartz, Albert Sirmay. *The Only Girl* (44th Street, revival, "Alan Kimbrough [Kim]," May 21, 1934): Be Happy, Boys, Tonight; The Compact; Here's to the Land We Love, Boys!; You're the Only One for Me/W: Henry Blossom, M: Victor Herbert. *Music Hath Charms* (Majestic, "Duke of Orsano" and "Charles Parker," Dec. 29, 1934): Exquisite Moment; Ladies, Beware; Love Is Only What You Make It; Maria; Midnight Flirtation; My Heart Is Yours/W: Rowland Leigh, John Shubert, M: Rudolf Friml. *White Horse Inn* (Center, "Donald Hutton," Oct. 1, 1936): Blue Eyes/W: Irving Caesar, M: Robert Stolz — The Waltz of Love/W: Irving Caesar, M: Richard Fall — The White Horse Inn/W: Irving Caesar, M: Ralph Benatzky — White Sails/W: Irving Caesar, M: Vivian Ellis. *Three Wishes for Jamie* (Mark Hellinger, "Tim Shanahan," Mar. 21, 1952): I'll Sing You a Song/WM: Ralph Blane — Love Has Nothing to Do with Looks/W: Charles Lederer, M: Ralph Blane.

3997. Edith Hallor (Mar. 26, 1896–May 21, 1971) B: Washington, DC. *Ziegfeld Follies of 1917* (New Amsterdam, revue, June 12, 1917): Hello, My Dearie!; Same Old Moon/W: Gene Buck, M: Dave Stamper — In the Beautiful Garden of Girls/W: Gene Buck, M: Raymond Hubbell. *Leave It to Jane* (Longacre, "Jane Witherspoon," Aug. 28, 1917): The Crickets Are Calling; Leave It to Jane; The Siren's Song; There It Is Again; Wait Till Tomorrow; What I'm Longing to Say/W: P.G. Wodehouse, M: Jerome Kern. *Broadway Brevities of 1920* (Winter Garden, revue, Sept. 29, 1920): Beautiful Faces (Need Beautiful Clothes) [Nov. 1, 1920]/WM: Irving Berlin — Love Me While the Snow Flakes Fall (Snow Flakes); Lu Lu/W: Arthur Jackson, M: George Gershwin.

3998. Edith Kingdon Hallor (1862–Nov. 13, 1921) B: England. *The Peasant Girl* (44th Street, "Countess Napolska," Mar. 2, 1915): Advice to the Young/W: ?, M: Oscar Nedbal.

3999. Violet Halls *The Mocking Bird* (Bijou, "Manon de Lange," Nov. 10, 1902): A Stale World and a Pale World/W: Sydney Rosenfeld, M: A. Baldwin Sloane.

4000. Nan Halperin (c 1898–May 30, 1963) B: Odessa, Russia. She grew up in Minneapolis, MN. A singing comedienne, known in vaudeville as America's Famous Satirist. M: composer William B. Friedlander. *Make It Snappy* (Winter Garden, revue, Apr. 13, 1922): Cheeky Kiki; He Was the Only Man I Ever Loved; A Modern Lullaby/WM: William B. Friedlander — The Flapper/W: Harold Atteridge, M: Jean Schwartz. *Little Jessie James* (Longacre, "Jessie Jamieson," Aug. 15, 1923): From Broadway to Main Street; Little Jack Horner; Little Jessie James; My Home Town in Kansas/W: Harlan Thompson, M: Harry Archer.

4001. Morty Halpern *Sing Out Sweet Land* (International, revue, "Old Timer," Dec. 27, 1944): Casey Jones/W: T. Lawrence Seibert, M: Eddie Newton.

4002. Helen Halpin *Catch a Star!* (Plymouth, revue, Sept. 6, 1955): The Story of Alice/W: Larry Holofcener, M: Jerry Bock.

4003. General MacArthur Hambrick *Cats* (Winter Garden, CR, "Alonzo"): Macavity/W: T.S. Eliot, M: Andrew Lloyd Webber.

4004. Janet Hamer *Song of Norway* (Imperial, "Sigrid," Aug. 21, 1944): Freddy and His Fiddle/WM: Robert Wright, George Forrest, based on Edvard Grieg.

4005. Nigel Hamer *Shenandoah* (Virginia, revival, "Nathan," Aug. 8, 1989): Next to Lovin' (I Like Fightin')/W: Peter Udell, M: Gary Geld.

4006. Mark Hamill (Sept. 25, 1951–) B: Oakland, CA. Leading man of TV and movies from 1975. He was Luke Skywalker in the movie *Star Wars* and its sequels (1977); and the voice of The Joker in TV's *Batman* cartoon series (1992). *Harrigan 'n Hart* (Longacre, "Tony Hart," Jan. 31, 1985): If I Could Trust Me; I've Come Home to Stay; Something New, Something Different; That's My Partner; We'll Be There/W: Peter Walker, M: Max Showalter — The Mulligan Guard; Such an Education Has My Mary Ann/W: Edward Harrigan, M: Dave Braham — Put Me in My Little Bed; She's Our Gretel; Wonderful Me/WM: ?.

4007. Bruce Hamilton *Oklahoma!* (St. James, CR, "Jud Fry," May 1946/Sept. 1946): Lonely Room; Pore Jud/W: Oscar Hammerstein II, M: Richard Rodgers.

4008. Caroline Hamilton *Robin Hood* (Standard, "Maid Marian," Sept. 28, 1891): All Nature Is at Peace and Rest (The Forest Song); Churning, Churning; Come Dream So Bright; I Come as a Cavalier; Though It Was Within This Hour We Met/W: Harry B. Smith, M: Reginald De Koven.

4009. Eric Hamilton (Dec. 27, 1954–) B: Bridgeport, CT. *The King and I* (New York City Center, revival, "Louis Leonowens," May 23, 1968): I Whistle a Happy Tune/W: Oscar Hammerstein II, M: Richard Rodgers.

4010. Ethel Hamilton *The Baron Trenck* (Casino, "Ella," Mar. 11, 1912): Cupid Is a Cruel Master/W: Henry Blossom, M: Alfred G. Robyn.

4011. Gloria Hamilton B: St. Louis, MO. *The Chocolate Soldier* (Century, revival, "Mascha," Mar. 12, 1947): After Today; Seek the Spy; The Tale of a Coat; Thank the Lord the War Is Over; That Would Be Lovely; We Too, Are Lonely/W: Stanislaus Stange, M: Oscar Straus. *Oklahoma!* (St. James, CR, "Laurey Williams," Aug. 1947): Many a New Day; Oh, What a Beautiful Mornin'; Oklahoma!; Out of My Dreams; People Will Say We're in Love; The Surrey with the Fringe on Top/W: Oscar Hammerstein II, M: Richard Rodgers. *Lend an Ear* (National > Broadhurst, revue, Dec. 16, 1948): Friday Dancing Class; The Gladiola Girl; I'll Be True to You; I'm on the Lookout; In Our Teeny Little Weeny Nest; Molly O'Reilly; When Someone You Love Loves You/WM: Charles Gaynor. *Courtin' Time* (National, "Cathy Rilling," June 13, 1951): Choose Your Partner; Goodbye, Dear Friend, Goodbye; Johnny Ride the Sky; An Old Fashioned Glimmer in Your Eye; The Wishbone Song/W: Jack Lawrence, M: Don Walker.

4012. Grace Hamilton *Springtime of Youth* (Broadhurst, "Mistress Prudence Stokes," Oct. 26, 1922): Love While You May; Our Busy Needles Fly/W: Cyrus D. Wood, M: Sigmund Romberg.

4013. James Hamilton *The Matinee Girl* (Forrest, "Jack Sterling," Feb. 1, 1926): At the Matinee; Waiting All the Time for You; When My Little Ship Comes In/W: McElbert Moore, Bide Dudley, M: Frank Grey — Mash Notes; Only One/W: McElbert Moore, M: Frank Grey.

4014. Laura Hamilton *The Whirl of Society* (Winter Garden, revue, Mar. 5, 1912): Hypnotizing Man/W: Harold Atteridge, M: Louis A. Hirsch. *The Man with Three Wives* (Weber and Fields, CR, "Olivia," Mar. 3, 1913): All in a Little Dance; Love's Flower Is Always Blooming; We Are Free/W: Paul M. Potter, Harold Atteridge, M: Franz Lehar. *The Passing Show of 1913* (Winter Garden, revue, July 24, 1913): Foolish Cinderella Girl/W: Harold Atteridge, M: Al W. Brown. *The Dancing Duchess* (Casino, "Celestine," Aug. 20, 1914): Celestine; On with the Dance; The Ragtime Whirl/W: R.H. Burnside, M: Milton Lusk. *Odds and Ends of 1917* (Bijou, revue, Nov. 19, 1917): My Lady's Clothes/W: Bide Dudley, Jack Norworth, M: James Byrnes. *The Rainbow Girl* (New Amsterdam, "Daisy Meade," Apr. 1, 1918): Mister Drummer Man; Won't Some Nice Boy Marry Me?/W: Rennold Wolf, M: Louis A. Hirsch. *Judy* (Royale, "Babette," Feb. 7, 1927): Hard to Get Along With; One Baby; When Gentlemen Grew Whiskers and Ladies Grew Old/W: Leo Robin, M: Charles Rosoff.

4015. Lawrence Hamilton (Sept. 14, 1954–) B: Ashdown, AR. *Uptown...It's Hot!* (Lunt-Fontanne, revue, Jan. 29, 1986): Ain't Too Proud to Beg/WM: Eddie Holland, Norman Whitfield — Dinah/W: Sam M. Lewis, Joe Young, M: Harry Akst — His Eye Is on the Sparrow/WM: trad. — Johnny B. Goode/WM: Chuck Berry — Old Landmark/WM: M.A. Brunner — Why Do Fools Fall in Love?/WM: Frank Lymon, Morris Levy.

4016. Margaret Hamilton (Dec. 9, 1902– May 16, 1985) B: Cleveland, OH. The former kindergarten teacher is best remembered as the Wicked Witch of the West in the classic movie *The Wizard of Oz* (1939). *Goldilocks* (Lunt-Fontanne, "Bessie," Oct. 11, 1958): Bad Companions; Two Years in the Making/W: Joan Ford, Walter Kerr, Jean Kerr, M: Leroy Anderson. *Show Boat* (New York State, revival, "Parthy Ann Hawks," July 19, 1966): Why Do I Love You?/W: Oscar Hammerstein II, M: Jerome Kern. *Come Summer* (Lunt-Fontanne, "Dorinda Pratt," Mar. 18, 1969): Moonglade/W: Will Holt, M: David

Baker. *Oklahoma!* (Music Theater of Lincoln Center, revival, "Aunt Eller Murphy," June 23, 1969): The Farmer and the Cowman; Kansas City; Oklahoma!; The Surrey with the Fringe on Top/W: Oscar Hammerstein II, M: Richard Rodgers.

4017. Marion Hamilton *Lady Butterfly* (Globe > Astor, "Ruth," Dec. 22, 1923): Waltz Time/W: Clifford Grey, M: Werner Janssen.

4018. Mitzi Hamilton *A Chorus Line* (Shubert, CR, "Val," Mar. 1, 1977/Mar. 1978/Jan. 1980/May 1980/Oct. 1980/July 1981/c 1985): And...; Dance: Ten, Looks: Three/W: Edward Kleban, M: Marvin Hamlisch.

4019. Nancy Hamilton (July 27, 1908–1985) B: Sewickley, PA. She began her acting career in 1933 as an understudy to KATHARINE HEPBURN. *New Faces of 1934* (Fulton, revue, Mar. 15, 1934): On the Other Hand/W: Nancy Hamilton, M: Martha Caples. *One for the Money* (Booth, revue, Feb. 4, 1939): The Yoo Hoo Blues/W: Nancy Hamilton, M: Morgan Lewis.

4020. Patrick Hamilton *The Best Little Whorehouse in Texas* (46th Street > Eugene O'Neill, CR, "Governor" and "Traveling Salesman" and "Scruggs," May 1980): The Sidestep; Texas Has a Whorehouse in It; 20 Fans/WM: Carol Hall.

4021. Patricia Hammerlee (Nov. 9, 1929–) B: Wilmington, NC. *New Faces of 1952* (Royale, revue, May 16, 1952): Lizzie Borden/WM: Michael Brown. *Seventh Heaven* (ANTA, "Collette," May 26, 1955): Camille, Collette, Fifi; Love, Love, Love; Love Sneaks Up on You/W: Stella Unger, M: Victor Young. *The Vamp* (Winter Garden, "Elsie Chelsea," Nov. 10, 1955): Four Little Misfits; You're Colossal/W: John Latouche, M: James Mundy.

4022. Elaine Hammerstein (1897– Aug. 13, 1948) B: Philadelphia, PA. The daughter of producer Arthur Hammerstein, she starred in a number of silent movies. She died in a car accident in Mexico. *High Jinks* (Lyric > Casino, "Florence," Dec. 10, 1913): High Jinks; Something Seems Tingle-ingleing; When Sammy Sang the Marseillaise/W: Otto Harbach, M: Rudolf Friml.

4023. John Hammil (May 9, 1948–) B: New York, NY. *Woman of the Year* (Palace, CR, "Chip Salisbury," Feb. 1983): It Isn't Working/ W: Fred Ebb, M: John Kander.

4024. Earl Hammond (?–2002) He played Sgt. Lane on the TV police drama *Rocky King, Inside Detective* (1950). *Juno* (Winter Garden, "Charlie Bentham," Mar. 9, 1959): My True Heart/WM: Marc Blitzstein.

4025. Burford Hampden *Sally, Irene and Mary* (Casino, "Percy Fitzgerald," Sept. 4, 1922): Something in Here; Stage Door Johnnies; Wedding Time/W: Raymond Klages, M: J. Fred Coots. *Sally, Irene and Mary* (44th Street, revival, "Percy Fitzgerald," Mar. 23, 1925): same as above.

4026. Ethel Hampton *On Your Toes* (Imperial > Majestic, "Lil Dolan," Apr. 11, 1936): Two-a-Day for Keith/W: Lorenz Hart, M: Richard Rodgers.

4027. Hope Hampton (Feb. 19, 1897–Jan. 23, 1982) B: Philadelphia, PA. The socialite actress was a leading lady in silent movies from 1921. *My Princess* (Shubert, "Minnie Johnson [Mimosa]," Oct. 6, 1927): Follow the Sun to the South; I Wonder Why; Our Bridal Night/W: Dorothy Donnelly, M: Sigmund Romberg.

4028. Stephen Hanan (Jan. 7, 1947–) B: Washington, DC. *Cats* (Winter Garden, "Bustopher Jones" and "Asparagus" and "Growltiger," Oct. 7, 1982): Bustopher Jones; Growltiger's Last Stand; Gus: The Theater Cat/W: T.S. Eliot, M: Andrew Lloyd Webber. *Peter Pan* (Lunt-Fontanne, revival, "Captain Hook," Dec. 13, 1990): Another Princely Scheme (Tarantella); Pirate Song; A Princely Scheme (Hook's Tango)/W: Carolyn Leigh, M: Moose Charlap — Captain Hook's Waltz; Mysterious Lady/W: Betty Comden, Adolph Green, M: Jule Styne.

4029. Allen Handley *New Faces of 1934* (Fulton, revue, Mar. 15, 1934): You're My Relaxation/W: Robert Sour, M: Charles M. Schwab.

4030. Roshi Handwerger *Mame* (Gershwin, revival, "Patrick Dennis, age 10," July 24, 1983): The Fox Hunt; Mame; My Best Girl; St. Bridget; We Need a Little Christmas/WM: Jerry Herman.

4031. Clarence Handyside (c 1854–Dec. 20, 1931) B: Montreal, Quebec, Canada. *The Vanderbilt Cup* (Broadway, CR, "Curt Willets," Jan. 16, 1906): If You Were I and I Were You/W: Henry Blossom, M: Victor Herbert.

4032. Jean Handzlik *Music in My Heart* (Adelphi, "Gypsy," Oct. 2, 1947): The Balalaika Serenade/W: Forman Brown, M: Franz Steininger, based on Peter I. Tchaikovsky. *The Liar* (Broadhurst, "Innkeeper's Wife," May 18, 1950): The Ladies' Opinion/W: Edward Eager, M: John Mundy — Women's Work/W: Edward Eager, M: A. Lehman Engel.

4033. Abigale Haness *The Rocky Horror Show* (Belasco, "Janet," Mar. 10, 1975): Over at the Frankenstein Place; Wedding Song/WM: Richard O'Brien.

4034. Carol Haney (Dec. 24, 1924–May 10, 1964) B: New Bedford, MA. M: LARRY BLYDEN. *The Pajama Game* (St. James, "Gladys," May 13, 1954): Her Is; Hernando's Hideaway; Steam Heat/WM: Richard Adler, Jerry Ross.

4035. Felix Haney *Fad and Folly [orig. Tommy Rot]* (Mrs. Osborn's Playhouse, "Sammy," Nov. 27, 1902): Run, Boy, Run/W: Paul West, M: Henry Waller. *A Yankee Circus on Mars* (Hippodrome, "King Borealis," Apr. 12, 1905): The Bogie Man; Get a Horse; Hold Your Horses/W: Harry Williams, M: Jean Schwartz. *A Society Circus* (Hippodrome, "The Major Domo," Dec. 13, 1905): But It Ain't; The Conspiracy/WM: Sydney Rosenfeld, Manuel Klein. *The Free Lance* (New Amsterdam, "Emperor of Braggadocia," Apr. 16, 1906): Come Ye Heroes All (The Emperor's War Song); Friendship's Sacred Touch; I Do It All by Proxy/W: Harry B. Smith, M: John Philip Sousa. *Around the World* (Hippodrome, revue, "McShane," Sept. 2, 1911): Blarney of Killarney/WM: Manuel Klein. *Miss Princess* (Park, "Sgt. Tim McGrew," Dec. 23, 1912): Ay-Oomps; Behind the Scenes/W: Will Johnstone, M: Alexander Johnstone — A Little Red Book and a Five Cent Bag/W: Hiram E. Russell, M: Alexander Johnstone.

4036. Eddie Hanley (May 17, 1904–Mar. 29, 1997) *Top Banana* (Winter Garden, "Danny," Nov. 1, 1951): O.K. for TV; Slogan Song (You Gotta Have a Slogan)/WM: Johnny Mercer.

4037. Ellen Hanley (May 15, 1926–) B: Lorain, OH. *Barefoot Boy with Cheek* (Martin Beck, "Clothilde Pfefferkorn," Apr. 3, 1947): Everything Leads Right Back to Love; I Knew I'd Know; When You're Eighteen/W: Sylvia Dee, M: Sidney Lippman. *Two's Company* (revue, Alvin, Dec. 15, 1952): Haunted Hot Spot; Roundabout/W: Ogden Nash, M: Vernon Duke. *First Impressions* (Alvin, "Charlotte Lucas," Mar. 19, 1959): Wasn't It a Simply Lovely Wedding?/WM: Robert Goldman, Glenn Paxton, George Weiss. *First Impressions* (Alvin, CR, "Elizabeth Bennet," May 1959): Fragrant Flower; The Heart Has Won the Game; I Suddenly Find You Agreeable; I'm Me; Let's Fetch the Carriage; Love Will Find Out the Way; A Perfect Evening; This Really Isn't Me; Wasn't It a Simply Lovely Wedding?/WM: Robert Goldman, Glenn Paxton, George Weiss. *Fiorello!* (Broadhurst, "Thea LaGuardia," Nov. 23, 1959): 'Til Tomorrow; When Did I Fall in Love?/W: Sheldon Harnick, M: Jerry Bock. *1776* (46th Street, CR, "Abigail Adams," Dec. 1969): Till Then; Yours, Yours, Yours/WM: Sherman Edwards.

4038. Katie Hanley (Jan. 17, 1949–) B: Evanston, IL. *Grease* (Eden > Broadhurst,

"Marty," June 7, 1972): Freddy, My Love/WM: Jim Jacobs, Warren Casey.

4039. Matthew Hanley *Natja* (Knicker-bocker, "Baron Wronsky," Feb. 16, 1925): You'll Have to Guess/W: Harry B. Smith, M: Karl Hajos, based on Peter I. Tchaikovsky.

4040. George Hanlon (c 1839–Nov. 5, 1926) B: England. *The Passing Show of 1913* (Winter Garden, revue, July 24, 1913): Reflections/W: Harold Atteridge, M: Jean Schwartz.

4041. Toma Hanlon Male impersonator in vaudeville. *Paris by Night* (Madison Square roof garden, "Magnolia Goldstein," July 2, 1904): The Convivial Girl [July 11, 1904]/W: Henry I. Marshall, M: Robert W. Edwards — The Girl with the Changeable Eyes/W: Estella Acres, M: Alfred Solman — The U.S. Volunteers/WM: Julius Adler.

4042. Daniel P. Hannafin (Feb. 8, 1933–) B: New York, NY. *Wonderful Town* (New York City Center, revival, "Drunk" and "Policeman," Mar. 5, 1958): My Darlin' Eileen/W: Betty Comden, Adolph Green, M: Leonard Bernstein. *South Pacific* (New York City Center, revival, "Sgt. Kenneth Johnson," Apr. 13, 1961): There Is Nothin' Like a Dame/W: Oscar Hammerstein II, M: Richard Rodgers. *Oklahoma!* (New York City Center, revival, "Jud Fry," Feb. 27, 1963/May 15, 1963/Dec. 15, 1965): Lonely Room; Pore Jud/W: Oscar Hammerstein II, M: Richard Rodgers.

4043. Cook Hanneford *Earl Carroll's Vanities of 1928* (Earl Carroll, revue, Aug. 6, 1928): The Dryad; Tell Me Truly [Dec. 10, 1928]/WM: George Bagby; G. Romilli.

4044. Edwin (Poodles) Hanneford (June 14, 1891–Dec. 9, 1967) B: Barnsley, England. Famous clown and bareback rider, for many years a member of the Ringling Brothers and Barnum and Bailey Circus. *The Circus Princess* (Winter Garden, "1st Waiter," Apr. 25, 1927): Waiters/W: Harry B. Smith, M: Emmerich Kalman.

4045. Kimberly Hannon *The Who's Tommy* (St. James, CR, "Tommy, age 4," c 1994): Listening to You/WM: Pete Townshend. *Les Misérables* (Broadway, CR, "Young Cosette," June 1996): Castle on a Cloud/W: Herbert Kretzmer, M: Claude-Michel Schonberg.

4046. Elizabeth Hansen *Do Black Patent Leather Shoes Really Reflect Up?* (Alvin, "Sister Helen," May 27, 1982): The Greatest Gift/WM: James Quinn, Alaric Jans.

4047. John Hansen *A Funny Thing Happened on the Way to the Forum* (Lunt-Fontanne, revival, "Hero," Mar. 30, 1972): Echo Song;

Free; Impossible; Love, I Hear; Lovely/WM: Stephen Sondheim.

4048. Tripp Hanson *Crazy for You* (Sam S. Shubert, "Mingo," Feb. 19, 1992): Bidin' My Time; The Real American Folk Song (Is a Rag)/W: Ira Gershwin, M: George Gershwin.

4049. Ernest Harada (Oct. 20, 1946–) B: Honolulu, HI. *Pacific Overtures* (Winter Garden, "Physician" and "Madam," Jan. 11, 1976): Chrysanthemum Tea; Welcome to Kanagawa/WM: Stephen Sondheim.

4050. Buddy Harak *Hold Everything!* (Broadhurst, "Marty," Oct. 10, 1928): Don't Hold Everything; Genealogy; We're Calling on Mr. Brooks/W: B.G. DeSylva, Lew Brown, M: Ray Henderson.

4051. Marian Haraldson (Sept. 5, 1933–) B: Northwood, ND. *The Girl Who Came to Supper* (Broadway, "Jessie Maynard," Dec. 8, 1963): Swing Song/WM: Noel Coward. *The Merry Widow* (New York State Theater, revival, "Olga, Mme. Novikovich," Aug. 17, 1964): When in France/W: Forman Brown, M: Franz Lehar. *Woman of the Year* (Palace, "Cleaning Woman," Mar. 29, 1981): I Wrote the Book/W: Fred Ebb, M: John Kander.

4052. Don Harden *The Illustrators' Show* (48th Street, revue, Jan. 22, 1936): I Love a Polka So/W: Carl Randall, M: Berenice Kazounoff— I Want to Play with the Girls/W: Milton Pascal, M: Edgar Fairchild — I'm You/W: Frank Loesser, M: Irving Actman — Let's Talk About the Weather/WM: Charlotte Kent.

4053. Marcella Hardie *I'll Say She Is* (Casino, "Marcella," May 19, 1924): Break Into Your Heart; Wall Street Blues/W: Will B. Johnstone, M: Tom Johnstone.

4054. Phyllis Harding *This Year of Grace* (Selwyn, revue, Nov. 7, 1928): Mother's Complaint/WM: Noel Coward.

4055. Mark Hardwick (Apr. 18, 1954–) *Pump Boys and Dinettes* (Princess, "L.M.," Feb. 4, 1982): Farmer Tan; Serve Yourself; T.N.D.P.W.A.M./WM: Jim Wann.

4056. CJay Hardy *Big* (Sam S. Shubert, "Deathstarette," Apr. 28, 1996): Dr. Deathstar/W: Richard Maltby, Jr., M: David Shire.

4057. Michele Hardy *Half a Sixpence* (Broadhurst, "Flo," Apr. 25, 1965): All in the Cause of Economy/WM: David Heneker.

4058. Samuel B. Hardy (Mar. 21, 1883–Oct. 16, 1935) B: New Haven, CT. *The Princess Pat* (Cort, "Bob Darrow," Sept. 29, 1915): Little World of Two/W: Henry Blossom, M: Victor Herbert. *Ziegfeld Follies of 1916)* (New Amsterdam, revue, June 12, 1916): Ain't It Funny What a Difference Just a Few Drinks Make?/W: Gene Buck, M: Jerome Kern — Six Little Wives of the King/W: Gene Buck, M: Louis A. Hirsch. *The Riviera Girl* (New Amsterdam, "Sam Springer," Sept. 24, 1917): Bungalow in Quogue/W: P.G. Wodehouse, M: Jerome Kern — Sometimes I Feel Just Like Grandpa; Why Don't You Hand It to Me?/W: P.G. Wodehouse, M: Emmerich Kalman. *The Canary* (Globe, "Ned Randolph," Nov. 4, 1918): Only in Dreams/W: Harry B. Smith, M: Ivan Caryll — This Is the Time/WM: Clifton Crawford.

4059. William Hardy, Jr. *Your Arms Too Short to Box with God* (Lyceum, revue, Dec. 22, 1976): The Band; Didn't I Tell You; There's a Stranger in Town; We Are the Priests and Elders; When the Power Comes/WM: Alex Bradford.

4060. Ernest Hare *Havana* (Casino, CR, "Diego de la Concha," Sept. 6, 1909): The Sun Is Down and Over the Town; Zara/W: Adrian Ross, M: Leslie Stuart. *Up and Down Broadway* (Casino, revue, July 18, 1910): Chinatown, My Chinatown/W: William Jerome, M: Jean Schwartz. *Vera Violetta* (Winter Garden, CR, "Claude," Feb. 24, 1912): Rum Tum Tiddle/W: Edward Madden, M: Jean Schwartz — That Haunting Melody/WM: George M. Cohan. *The Whirl of Society* (Winter Garden, CR, revue, June 24, 1912): My Sumurun Girl/W: Al Jolson, M: Louis A. Hirsch. *The Passing Show of 1912* (Winter Garden, revue, July 22, 1912): The Metropolitan Squawk-tette; A Policeman's Lot Is a Happy One/W: Harold Atteridge, M: Louis A. Hirsch — When Was There Ever a Night Like This?/WM: Louis A. Hirsch. *The Peasant Girl* (44th Street, "Von Mirski," Mar. 2, 1915): Advice to the Young/W: ?, M: Oscar Nedbal — Love's Awakening/W: ?, M: Rudolf Friml, Oscar Nedbal. *The Passing Show of 1915* (Winter Garden, revue, May 29, 1915): My Hula Maid/W: Harold Atteridge, M: Leo Edwards.

4061. Burt Harger *Merry-Go-Round* (Klaw, revue, CR, July 18, 1927): In the Park/WM: ?. *Early to Bed* (Broadhurst, "Burt," June 17, 1943): Early to Bed; Slightly Less Than Wonderful; There's Yes in the Air (Martinique)/W: George Marion, Jr., M: Fats Waller.

4062. Gary Harger (Aug. 19, 1951–) B: New Haven, CT. *Shenandoah* (Alvin, "Corporal," Jan. 7, 1975): The Only Home I Know/W: Peter Udell, M: Gary Geld.

4063. William Hargrave *Tattle Tales* (Broadhurst, revue, June 1, 1933): The First Spring Day/W: Edward Eliscu, M: Howard Jackson — Hasta Manana (So This Is Havana)/WM: Howard Jackson. *Saluta* (Imperial, "Priest," Aug.

28, 1934): Help the Seamen/W: Will Morrissey, M: Frank D'Armond.

4064. Norma Hark *Fifty-Fifty, Ltd.* (Comedy, "Marian Carter," Oct. 27, 1919): Nanette/WM: Leon DeCosta.

4065. Sam Harkness *Reggae* (Biltmore, "Binghi Maytal," Mar. 27, 1980): Reggae Music Got Soul/WM: Jackie Mittoo — Talkin' 'Bout Reggae/WM: Kendrew Lascelles, Jackie Mittoo, Michael Kamen, Stafford Harrison.

4066. Otis Harlan (Dec. 29, 1865–Jan. 20, 1940) B: Zanesville, OH. *Broadway to Tokio* (New York, "Calcium Lightwayte," Jan. 23, 1900): Story of the Dance; When I'm Traveling on the Road/W: Louis Harrison, M: A. Baldwin Sloane. *The Vanderbilt Cup* (Broadway, "Theodore Banting," Jan. 16, 1906): Wine, Women and Song/W: Raymond W. Peck, M: Robert Hood Bowers. *A Parisian Model* (Broadway, CR, "Silas Goldfinch," Dec. 10, 1906): The Gibson Girl/W: Harry B. Smith, M: Max Hoffmann — In Washington/W: Vincent Bryan, M: Gertrude Hoffmann — Kiss, Kiss, Kiss (If You Want to Learn to Kiss Me)/W: Harry B. Smith, M: Gertrude Hoffmann. *Dream City* (Weber's, "J. Bilkington Holmes," Dec. 25, 1906): Improvements; In Vaudeville/W: Edgar Smith, M: Victor Herbert. *A Broken Idol* (Herald Square, "Doc Whatt," Aug. 16, 1909): Cured; What Makes the World Go Round/W: Harry Williams, M: Egbert Van Alstyne. *Little Boy Blue* (Lyric, "Dupont," Nov. 27, 1911): Detective; You're Very Like Your Sister, Dear/W: Edward A. Paulton, M: Henry Bereny — Two Cockatoos/WM: Edward A. Paulton. *The Dancing Duchess* (Casino, "Richter," Aug. 20, 1914): I've Been Looking for You; Looking for a Girl Like Venus /W: R.H. Burnside, M: Milton Lusk.

4067. Beatrice Harlowe *Bringing Up Father* (Lyric, "Maggie," Apr. 6, 1925): Wedding Chimes/W: R.F. Carroll, M: Seymour Furth, Leo Edwards.

4068. Paul Harman (July 29, 1952–) B: Mineola, NY. *Chess* (Imperial, "Arbiter," Apr. 28, 1988): Arbiter's Song; Chess Hymn; A Model of Decorum & Tranquility/W: Tim Rice, M: Benny Anderson, Bjorn Ulvaeus. *Cats* (Winter Garden, CR, "Bustopher Jones" and "Asparagus," and "Growltiger," c 1988): Bustopher Jones; Growltiger's Last Stand; Gus: The Theater Cat/W: T.S. Eliot, M: Andrew Lloyd Webber.

4069. Lucille Harmon *Sunkist* (Globe, revue, "Gladys Sullivan," May 23, 1921): They Call Me Pollyanna/WM: Fanchon Wolff, Marco Wolff.

4070. Mary Harmon *By the Beautiful Sea* (Majestic, "Cora Belmont," Apr. 8, 1954): Good Time Charlie; Throw the Anchor Away/W: Dorothy Fields, M: Arthur Schwartz.

4071. Peggy Harmon *Big River: The Adventures of Huckleberry Finn* (Eugene O'Neill, "Susan Wilkes," Apr. 25, 1985): You Oughta Be Here with Me/WM: Roger Miller.

4072. Ben Harney (Aug. 29, 1952–) B: Brooklyn, NY. *Treemonisha* (Palace, "Zodzetrick," Oct. 21, 1975): The Bag of Luck; Treemonisha in Peril/WM: Scott Joplin. *Pippin* (Imperial, CR, "Leading Player," Jan. 12, 1976): Glory; On the Right Track; Simple Joys/WM: Stephen Schwartz. *Dreamgirls* (Imperial, "Curtis Taylor, Jr.," Dec. 20, 1981/Aug. 1984): Cadillac Car; Family; Heavy; Only the Beginning; The Rap; Steppin' to the Bad Side; When I First Saw You/W: Tom Eyen, M: Henry Krieger.

4073. Andrew Harper *The Passing Show of 1916* (Winter Garden, revue, June 22, 1916): Roosevelt, Wilson and Hughes/WM: ?.

4074. Belle Harper *The Geisha* (Daly's, revival, "Nami," Mar. 21, 1898): The Dear Little Jappy-jap-jappy/W: Henry Greenbank, M: Sidney Jones.

4075. Dolores Harper *House of Flowers* (Alvin, "Tulip," Dec. 30, 1954): Has I Let You Down?; Husband Cage; A Sleepin' Bee; Smellin' of Vanilla (Bamboo Cage); Waitin'/WM: Truman Capote, Harold Arlen.

4076. Fred Harper *Cherry Blossoms* (44th Street > Cosmopolitan, "Kamura," Mar. 28, 1927): If You Know What I Think/W: Harry B. Smith, M: Sigmund Romberg.

4077. J.W. (James) Harper (Oct. 8, 1948–) B: Bell, CA. *The Robber Bridegroom* (Harkness, "Little Harp," Oct. 7, 1975): Poor Tied Up Darlin'/W: Alfred Uhry, M: Robert Waldman.

4078. Mary Harper *The Sweetheart Shop* (Knickerbocker, "Mildred Blount," Aug. 31, 1920): The Sweetheart Shop/W: Anne Caldwell, M: Hugo Felix.

4079. Mary Louise Harper *Earl Carroll's Sketch Book of 1935* (Majestic, revue, CR, Oct. 14, 1935): At Last/W: Charles Tobias, Sam M. Lewis, M: Henry Tobias.

4080. Marcy Harriell *Rent* (Nederlander, CR, "Mimi Marquez," Apr. 5, 1997): Another Day; Goodbye, Love; Happy New Year; Light My Candle; Out Tonight; Voice Mail #3; Without You/WM: Jonathan Larson.

4081. Maida Harries *Elsie* (Vanderbilt, "Bunny," Apr. 2, 1923): Pretty Little Firefly/WM: Monte Carlo, Alma Sanders.

4082. Edward Harrigan (Oct. 26, 1844–June 6, 1911) B: New York, NY. Father of WILLIAM HARRIGAN. Comedy partner of TONY HART in the team of Harrigan and Hart. Harrigan wrote and produced all the material for their act. *The Mulligan Guards' Ball* (Comique, "Dan Mulligan," Jan. 13, 1879): The Mulligan Guard/W: Edward Harrigan, M: Dave Braham. *The Mulligan Guards' Christmas* (Comique, "Dan Mulligan," Nov. 17, 1879): The Pitcher of Beer; Tu-ri-ad-i-lum, or Santa Claus Has Come/W: Edward Harrigan, M: Dave Braham. *The Mulligan Guards' Surprise* (Comique, "Dan Mulligan," Feb. 16, 1880): Dat Citron Wedding Cake; The Full Moon Union; Never Take the Horse Shoe from the Door; Whist! The Bogie Man/W: Edward Harrigan, M: Dave Braham. *The Mulligans' Silver Wedding* (Comique, "Dan Mulligan," Feb. 21, 1881): Wheel the Baby Out/W: Edward Harrigan, M: Dave Braham.

4083. William Harrigan (Mar. 27, 1893–Feb. 1, 1966) B: New York, NY. M: LOUISE GROODY. Son of EDWARD HARRIGAN. In movies from 1917. *The Three Romeos* (Globe, CR, "Dick Dawson," Dec. 11, 1911): Along Broadway; In the Spring It's Nice to Have Someone to Love You/W: R.H. Burnside, M: Raymond Hubbell.

4084. C.J. Harrington *Little Johnny Jones* (Liberty > New York, "Capt. Squirvy" and "Jenkins," Nov. 7, 1904): Captain of a Ten-Day Boat; The Cecil in London Town/WM: George M. Cohan.

4085. Hamtree Harrington *Strut Miss Lizzie* (Times Square, revue, June 19, 1922): I'm Nobody's Gal/WM: Henry Creamer, Turner Layton. *Dixie to Broadway* (Broadhurst, revue, Oct. 29, 1924): Hanging Around/W: Grant Clarke, Roy Turk, M: George W. Meyer, Arthur Johnston. *Change Your Luck* (George M. Cohan, "Ebenezer Smart," June 6, 1930): Change Your Luck/WM: James C. Johnson.

4086. Pat Harrington (1900–Sept. 2, 1965) B: Montreal, Quebec, Canada. *Panama Hattie* (46th Street, "Skat Briggs," Oct. 30, 1940): Fresh as a Daisy; God Bless the Women; Join It Right Away; You Said It/WM: Cole Porter. *Star and Garter* (Music Box, revue, June 24, 1942): For a Quarter/W: Jerry Seelen, M: Lester Lee. *Call Me Madam* (Imperial, "Congressman Wilkins," Oct. 12, 1950): They Like Ike/WM: Irving Berlin.

4087. Robert Harrington *A Stubborn Cinderella* (Broadway, "Skeeter," Jan. 25, 1909): If They'd Only Left Poor Adam's Rib Alone; I'm in Love with All the Girls I Know/W: Will M. Hough, Frank R. Adams, M: Joseph E. Howard.

4088. Robert Harrington *Peter Pan* (Winter Garden, "John," Oct. 20, 1954): I'm Flying; Tender Shepherd/W: Carolyn Leigh, M: Moose Charlap.

4089. Alice Harris *The Cohan Revue of 1916* (Astor, revue, "Sadie Love," Feb. 9, 1916): Busy, Busy, Busy; That Frisco Melody/WM: George M. Cohan.

4090. Barbara Harris (July 25, 1935–) B: Evanston, IL. *On a Clear Day You Can See Forever* (Mark Hellinger, "Daisy Gamble," Oct. 17, 1965): Hurry! It's Lovely Up Here; On the S.S. Bernard Cohn; Tosy and Cosh; Wait 'Til We're Sixty-Five; What Did I Have That I Don't Have?/W: Alan Jay Lerner, M: Burton Lane. *The Apple Tree* (Shubert, "Eve" and "Princess Barbara" and "Ella" and "Passionella," Oct. 18, 1966/July 31, 1967): Feelings; Forbidden Love (in Gaul); Friends; Lullaby (Go to Sleep, Whatever You Are); Gorgeous; Here in Eden; I've Got What You Want; Oh to Be a Movie Star; Tiger, Tiger; Wealth; What Makes Me Love Him?; Which Door?/W: Sheldon Harnick, M: Jerry Bock.

4091. Brenda Harris *Greenwillow* (Alvin, "Sheby Briggs," Mar. 8, 1960): Clang Dang the Bell/WM: Frank Loesser.

4092. Charlene Harris (Mar. 16, 1925–) B: Chicago, IL. *Bless You All* (Mark Hellinger, revue, Dec. 14, 1950): Don't Wanna Write About the South/WM: Harold Rome. *But Never Jam Today* (Longacre, "White Queen," July 31, 1979): But Never Jam Today/WM: Bob Larimer, Bert Keyes.

4093. Cynthia Harris (Aug. 9–) B: New York, NY. *Company* (Alvin, CR, "Sarah," July 12, 1971): Poor Baby/WM: Stephen Sondheim.

4094. Daniel Harris *Forbidden Melody* (New Amsterdam, "Kazdu," Nov. 2, 1936): Bucharest; Just Hello; Lady in the Window/W: Otto Harbach, M: Sigmund Romberg.

4095. Hazel Harris *Lovely Lady* (Sam H. Harris, "Lisette," Dec. 29, 1927): Make Believe You're Happy/W: Cyrus D. Wood, M: Dave Stamper, Harold A. Levey. *Artists and Models of 1930 [Paris-Riviera Edition]* (Majestic, revue, "Nanette," June 10, 1930): Parisian Tango/WM: Harold Stern, Ernie Golden.

4096. Holly Harris *Bloomer Girl* (New York City Center, revival, "Octavia," Jan. 6, 1947): Welcome Hinges; When the Boys Come Home/W: E.Y. Harburg, M: Harold Arlen. *Kiss Me, Kate* (New Century, CR, "Lilli Vanessi" and "Katherine," July 1951): I Am Ashamed That Women Are So Simple; I Hate Men; Kiss Me, Kate; So in Love; We Open in Venice; Wunderbar/WM: Cole Porter. *Kiss Me, Kate* (Broadway,

revival, "Lilli Vanessi" and "Katherine," Jan. 8, 1952): same as above.

4097. Jeff Harris *South Pacific* (New York City Center, revival, "Stewpot," Apr. 13, 1961): There Is Nothin' Like a Dame/W: Oscar Hammerstein II, M: Richard Rodgers.

4098. Jonathan Harris (Nov. 6, 1914–) B: New York, NY. He played Dr. Zachary Smith on the TV sci-fi series *Lost in Space* (1965). *Hazel Flagg* (Mark Hellinger, "Oleander," May 16, 1953): Make the People Cry/W: Bob Hilliard, M: Jule Styne.

4099. Julie Harris (Dec. 2, 1925–) B: Grosse Pointe, MI. Actress of stage, TV and films, especially admired for her work on Broadway in *The Lark* and *Member of the Wedding*. *Skyscraper* (Lunt-Fontanne, "Georgina," Nov. 13, 1965): Don't Worry, Don't Worry (I Don't Worry); Everybody Has a Right to Be Wrong; An Occasional Flight of Fancy; Opposites; Spare That Building; Wrong!/W: Sammy Cahn, M: James Van Heusen.

4100. Lloyd Harris *70, Girls, 70* (Broadhurst, Apr. 15, 1971): Broadway, My Street; You and I, Love/W: Fred Ebb, M: John Kander.

4101. Lowell Harris M: INGE SWENSON. *Blood Red Roses* (John Golden, "Cornet Edwin May," Mar. 22, 1970): The Fourth Light Dragoons/W: John Lewin, M: Michael Valenti.

4102. Marion Harris (1905–Apr. 23, 1944) B: Henderson, KY. Singer in vaudeville and nightclubs. In the 1930s she moved to London where she became quite popular. She died in a hotel fire in New York. *Yours Truly* (Shubert, "Mary Stillwell," Jan. 25, 1927): Look at the World and Smile; Lotus Flower; Somebody Else; Yours Truly/W: Anne Caldwell, M: Raymond Hubbell. *The Second Little Show* (Shubert, revue, CR, Oct. 20, 1930): I Started on a Shoestring/W: Edward Heyman, M: Johnny Green.

4103. Nat Harris (c 1873–Apr. 29, 1913) *The International Cup* (Hippodrome, "George Gulliver," Sept. 3, 1910): Take a Trip to the Seaside/WM: Manuel Klein.

4104. Niki Harris (July 20, 1948–) B: Pittsburgh, PA. *A Day in Hollywood/A Night in the Ukraine* (John Golden > Royale, "Masha," May 1, 1980): A Night in the Ukraine/W: Dick Vosburgh, M: Frank Lazarus.

4105. Richard Harris (Oct. 1, 1930–Oct. 25, 2002) B: Limerick, Ireland. In movies from 1958. *Camelot* (Winter Garden, revival, "King Arthur," Nov. 15, 1981): Camelot; How to Handle a Woman; I Wonder What the King Is Doing Tonight; The Jousts; What Do the Simple Folk Do?/W: Alan Jay Lerner, M: Frederick Loewe.

4106. Robert H. Harris (July 15, 1909–Nov. 30, 1981) B: New York, NY. He played Jake Goldberg on the TV sitcom *The Goldbergs* (1953). *Foxy* (Ziegfeld, "Bedrock," Feb. 16, 1964): Money Isn't Everything/W: Johnny Mercer, M: Robert Emmett Dolan.

4107. Rosalind Harris (Dec. 22–) B: White Plains, NY. *Fiddler on the Roof* (Imperial, CR, "Tzeitel," Feb. 1970): Matchmaker, Matchmaker/W: Sheldon Harnick, M: Jerry Bock.

4108. Sadie Harris (Dec. 7, 1888–May 15, 1933) B: New York, NY. M: ARTHUR AYLESWORTH. *Moonshine* (Liberty, "Sadie Short," Oct. 30, 1905): How Happy Would This Chappie Be/W: George V. Hobart, M: Silvio Hein — A Hundred Years from Now/W: George V. Hobart, Edwin Milton Royle, M: Silvio Hein.

4109. Sam Harris (June 4, 1961–) B: Cushing, OK. *Grease* (Eugene O'Neill, revival, "Doody," May 11, 1994): Rock 'n' Roll Party Queen; Those Magic Changes/WM: Jim Jacobs, Warren Casey.

4110. Tom Harris (Feb. 17, 1949–) B: Kingston, PA. *Grease* (Broadhurst, "Eugene Florczyk," Feb. 14, 1972): Alma Mater/WM: Jim Jacobs, Warren Casey.

4111. Juan Harrison *Dixie to Broadway* (Broadhurst, revue, Oct. 29, 1924): If My Dreams Came True/WM: ?.

4112. Lee Harrison (1866–Oct. 29, 1916) B: Newark, IL. *Rogers Brothers in London* (Knickerbocker, "Will Conn," Sept. 7, 1903): In Gay New York/W: Ed Gardenier, M: Max Hoffmann.

4113. Louis Harrison (1859–Oct. 23, 1936) B: Philadelphia, PA. Performer, director and lyricist. *Hiawatha* (Standard, "Remus Brown," Feb. 21, 1880): Conspirators Three; Yah! Yoh! Yum!/W: Nathaniel Childs, M: Edward E. Rice. *The Jersey Lily* (Victoria, "Don Pedro de la Platza," Sept. 14, 1903): Aurora/W: George V. Hobart, M: Reginald De Koven — Lobster and the Lady/WM: Ernest Hanegan. *Babette* (Broadway, "Van Tympel," Nov. 16, 1903): Clock Maker's Song; It's a Way We Have in Spain; On the Stage; There Once Was an Owl; To the Sound of the Pipe and the Roll of the Drum/W: Harry B. Smith, M: Victor Herbert. *Lifting the Lid* (New Amsterdam roof, "I. Just Doothem," June 5, 1905): Albany; Line It Out, Mr. Maginnity; There's Nothing Doing in the Old, Old Town/W: William Jerome, M: Jean Schwartz. *Fascinating Flora* (Casino, "Alphonse Allegretti," May 20, 1907): I'm a Marvelous Musician; Nice Little Girls and Boys; What Will Happen Then?/W: R.H. Burnside, M: Gustave Kerker —

Romance and Reality/W: Louis Harrison, M: A. Baldwin Sloane — The Subway Express/W: James O'Dea, M: Jerome Kern. *The Golden Butterfly* (Broadway, "Baron Von Affenkoff," Oct. 12, 1908): Great Musicians; Singing Lesson/W: J. Hayden-Clarendon, M: Reginald De Koven. *He Came from Milwaukee* (Casino, "Napoleon Ravachal," Sept. 21, 1910): Tie a Red Ribbon on Me/W: Edward Madden, M: Ben M. Jerome, Louis A. Hirsch.

4114. Rex Harrison (Mar. 5, 1908–June 2, 1990) B: Huyton, Lancaster, England. The ultimate Henry Higgins, on stage and screen. *My Fair Lady* (Mark Hellinger, "Henry Higgins," Mar. 15, 1956): A Hymn to Him; I'm an Ordinary Man; I've Grown Accustomed to Her Face; The Rain in Spain; Why Can't the English?; You Did It/ W: Alan Jay Lerner, M: Frederick Loewe. *My Fair Lady* (Uris, revival, "Henry Higgins," Aug. 18, 1981): same as above.

4115. Stanley Harrison (?–Feb. 16, 1950) B: Glasgow, Scotland. *Music Hath Charms* (Majestic, "Sen. Nocio," Dec. 29, 1934): Scandal Number/W: Rowland Leigh, John Shubert, M: Rudolf Friml.

4116. James Harrod *The Lilac Domino* (44th Street, "Elledon," Oct. 28, 1914): Ladies Day; The Lilac Domino; True Love Will Find a Way/W: Robert B. Smith, M: Charles Cuvillier.

4117. Jack Harrold (?–July 22, 1994) B: Atlantic City, NJ. Son of ORVILLE HARROLD. Brother of PATTI HARROLD. A tenor, he sang with the New York City Opera for nearly 50 seasons. *The Cradle Will Rock* (New York City Center, revival, "Editor Daily," Feb. 11, 1960): Freedom of the Press; Honolulu/WM: Marc Blitzstein. *The Unsinkable Molly Brown* (Winter Garden, "Monsignor Ryan," Nov. 3, 1960): Are You Sure?/WM: Meredith Willson.

4118. Lizzie Harrold *Evangeline, or The Belle of Arcadia* (Daly's, revival, "Evangeline," June 4, 1877): Come Back to the Heart That Is Thine; Fie Upon You, Fie; Go Not Happy Day; My Best Beloved; Thinking, Love, of Thee; Where Art Thou Now, My Beloved?/W: J. Cheever Goodwin, M: Edward E. Rice.

4119. Orville Harrold (c 1878–1933) Father of JACK HARROLD and PATTI HARROLD. The tenor sang at the Metropolitan Opera from 1919 to 1924. *Naughty Marietta* (New York, "Capt. Richard Warrington," Nov. 7, 1910): Ah! Sweet Mystery of Life; I'm Falling in Love with Someone; It Never Never Can Be Love; Live for Today; Tramp! Tramp! Tramp!/W: Rida Johnson Young, M: Victor Herbert. *Hip-Hip Hooray* (Hippodrome, revue, "The Hero," Sept. 30,

1915): Chin Chin (Open Your Heart and Let Me In)/WM: A. Seymour Brown — My Land, My Flag/W: Marc Connelly, M: Zoel Parenteau. *Holka-Polka* (Lyric, "Peter Novak [Nobody]," Oct. 14, 1925): Home of My Heart; Spring in Autumn; When Love Is Near/W: Gus Kahn, Raymond B. Egan, M: Will Ortman.

4120. Patti Harrold Daughter of ORVILLE HARROLD. Sister of JACK HARROLD. *Irene* (Vanderbilt, CR, "Alice Blue Gown"): Alice Blue Gown; Irene; Sky Rocket; To Be Worthy (Worthy of You)/W: Joseph McCarthy, M: Harry Tierney. *Glory* (Vanderbilt, "Glory Moore," Dec. 25, 1922): Glory/W: James Dyrenforth, M: Maurice DePackh — A Little White House with Green Blinds; Mother's Wedding Dress; Popularity; Post Office; The Same Old Story/W: Joseph McCarthy, M: Harry Tierney. *Big Boy* (Winter Garden > 44th Street, "Annabelle Bedford," Jan. 7, 1925): Born and Bred in Old Kentucky; The Dance from Down Yonder; Tap the Toe; True Love/W: B.G. DeSylva, M: Joseph Meyer, James F. Hanley. *Holka-Polka* (Lyric, "Peterle Novak," Oct. 14, 1925): Fairy Tale; Holka-Polka; I Want to Be a Bad Little Boy; Spring in Autumn; This Is My Dance; When Love Is Near/W: Gus Kahn, Raymond B. Egan, M: Will Ortman — In a Little While/W: Raymond B. Egan, M: Will Ortman.

4121. Jackee Harry (Aug. 14, 1956–) B: Winston-Salem, NC. *A Broadway Musical* (Lunt-Fontanne, "Melinda Bernard," Dec. 21, 1978): A Broadway Musical/W: Lee Adams, M: Charles Strouse.

4122. Albert Hart (c 1875–1940) *The Casino Girl* (Casino, "Fromage," Mar. 19, 1900): It's the Chink, Chink, Chink/W: Harry B. Smith, M: Harry T. MacConnell. *Florodora* (Winter Garden, CR, "Cyrus W. Gilfain," Jan. 27, 1902): I Want to Marry a Man, I Do/W: Paul Rubens, M: Leslie Stuart — Phrenology; When You're a Millionaire/W: Ernest Boyd-Jones, M: Leslie Stuart. *The Free Lance* (New Amsterdam, "Duke of Graftiana," Apr. 16, 1906): Friendship's Sacred Touch/W: Harry B. Smith, M: John Philip Sousa. *The Dollar Princess* (Knickerbocker, "Tom Cowder," Sept. 6, 1909): A Boat Sails on Wednesday/W: Adrian Ross, George Grossmith, M: Jerome Kern — Hip, Hip, Hurrah!; Souvenir/W: George Grossmith, M: Leo Fall. *Gypsy Love* (Globe, "Moschu," Oct. 17, 1911): Matrimony/W: Harry B. Smith, Robert B. Smith, M: Franz Lehar. *Hop o' My Thumb* (Manhattan Opera House, "Ogre," Nov. 26, 1913): The Date Tree; Fee, Fi, Fo, Fum; Run Along, Mr. Ogre Man/W: Sydney Rosenfeld, M: Manuel Klein.

4123. Bernice Hart Sister of IRENE HART. *Silks and Satins* (George M. Cohan, revue, July 15, 1920): I Want to Be Somebody's Baby/W: Ed Smalle, M: Jesse Greer — Sunday's Child/W: Louis Weslyn, M: Leon Rosebrook. *Bombo* (Al Jolson > Winter Garden, "Twilight" and "Estelle," Oct. 6, 1921): Bylo Bay; Sleepy Village/W: Harold Atteridge, M: Sigmund Romberg.

4124. Charles H. Hart *The Spring Maid* (New Amsterdam, revival, "Baron Rudi," Jan. 27, 1913): The Fountain Fay Protective Institution, Limited/W: Robert B. Smith, M: Heinrich Reinhardt — Take Me Dear/W: Robert B. Smith, M: Robert Hood Bowers.

4125. Emily Hart (May 1986–) B: Smithtown, NY. *The Who's Tommy* (St. James, CR, "Tommy, age 4," c 1994): Listening to You/WM: Pete Townshend.

4126. Augusta (Gussie) Hart (c 1860–Feb. 19, 1906) B: New York, NY. *Marty Malone* (Bijou, Aug. 31, 1896): Savannah Sue/W: Edward Harrigan, M: Dave Braham.

4127. Harry Hart *Sing for Your Supper* (Adelphi, revue, Apr. 24, 1939): At Long Last; Bonnie Banks/W: Robert Sour, M: Lee Wainer.

4128. Irene Hart (1903–Aug. 6, 1922) B: Salem Center, IN. Sister of BERNICE HART. *Silks and Satins* (George M. Cohan, revue, July 15, 1920): I Want to Be Somebody's Baby/W: Ed Smalle, M: Jesse Greer — Sunday's Child/W: Louis Weslyn, M: Leon Rosebrook. *Bombo* (Al Jolson > Winter Garden, "Twinkle" and "Adele," Oct. 6, 1921): Bylo Bay; Sleepy Village/W: Harold Atteridge, M: Sigmund Romberg.

4129. J. Richard Hart *A Chorus Line* (Shubert, CR, "Mike," Aug. 1984): I Can Do That/W: Edward Kleban, M: Marvin Hamlisch.

4130. Joseph Hart (June 8, 1858–Oct. 3, 1921) B: Boston, MA. M: CARRIE DE MAR. *Foxy Grandpa* (14th Street, "Goodelby Goodman," Feb. 17, 1902): The First Submarine Boat; The Story of Two Bad Boys/WM: Joseph Hart, R. Melville Baker — The Funny Family; The Tight Rope Walker/WM: ?.

4131. Kathryn Hart *Shubert Gaieties of 1919* (44th Street, revue, July 14, 1919): Rainbow Ball/W: Alfred Bryan, M: Jean Schwartz — Vamp a Little Lady (The Vamp)/WM: Byron Gay.

4132. Linda Hart (Aug. 1, 1950–) B: Dallas, TX. *Anything Goes* (Vivian Beaumont, revival, "Erma," Oct. 19, 1987/July 1989): Buddy, Beware/WM: Cole Porter. *Anything Goes* (Vivian Beaumont, revival, CR, "Reno Sweeney," June 28, 1988): Anything Goes; Blow, Gabriel, Blow; Friendship; I Get a Kick Out of You; You're the Top/WM: Cole Porter.

4133. Mark Hart *Fritz in Tammany Hall* (Herald Square, "Pat McCann," Oct. 16, 1905): In Tammany Hall; Yankee Doodle Boodle/W: William Jerome, M: Jean Schwartz.

4134. Melissa Hart *Cabaret* (Broadway, CR, "Sally Bowles," July 28, 1969): Cabaret; Don't Tell Mama; Perfectly Marvelous; Why Should I Wake Up?/W: Fred Ebb, M: John Kander. *Georgy* (Winter Garden, "Meredith," Feb. 26, 1970): A Baby; Gettin' Back to Me; Howdjadoo; Just for the Ride/W: Carole Bayer Sager, M: George Fischoff.

4135. Teddy Hart (Sept. 25, 1897–Feb. 17, 1971) B: New York, NY. Younger brother of lyricist Lorenz Hart. *The Boys from Syracuse* (Alvin, "Dromio of Ephesus," Nov. 23, 1938): Big Brother; What Can You Do with a Man?/W: Lorenz Hart, M: Richard Rodgers. *One Touch of Venus* (Imperial, "Taxi Black," Oct. 7, 1943): The Trouble with Women/W: Ogden Nash, M: Kurt Weill.

4136. Toni Hart B: New York, NY. *Bloomer Girl* (Shubert, "Julia," Oct. 4, 1944): Welcome Hinges; When the Boys Come Home/W: E.Y. Harburg, M: Harold Arlen.

4137. Tony Hart (July 25, 1855–Nov. 4, 1891) B: Worcester, MA. Legendary comedic partner of EDWARD HARRIGAN from 1872 to 1885. Nat C. Goodwin said of him: "He sang like a nightingale, danced like a fairy, and acted like a master comedian." He died in an insane asylum. *The Mulligan Guards' Ball* (Comique, "Rebecca Allup," Jan. 13, 1879): The Mulligan Guard/W: Edward Harrigan, M: Dave Braham. *The Mulligan Guards' Christmas* (Comique, "Rebecca Allup," Nov. 17, 1879): The Sweet Kentucky Rose/W: Edward Harrigan, M: Dave Braham. *The Mulligan Guards' Surprise* (Comique, Feb. 16, 1880): Dat Citron Wedding Cake; The Full Moon Union; Never Take the Horse Shoe from the Door; Whist! The Bogie Man/W: Edward Harrigan, M: Dave Braham. *The Mulligans' Silver Wedding* (Comique, "Dennis Mulligan," Feb. 21, 1881): South Fifth Avenue/W: Edward Harrigan, M: Dave Braham.

4138. Tony Hart (c 1871–Jan. 13, 1912) B: Worcester, MA. *By the Sad Sea Waves* (Grand Opera House, revival, "Theodore Thomas Liszt," Mar. 5, 1900): The Under-Takers' Frolic/W: Harry Bulger, J. Sherrie Mathews, M: Gustav Luders.

4139. Vivian Hart (Sept. 25, 1896–Nov. 8, 1970) B: Texas. *Countess Maritza* (Shubert, "Lisa," Sept. 18, 1926): Golden Dreams/W: Harry B. Smith, M: Harry K. Morton — I'll Keep on Dreaming/W: Harry B. Smith, M:

Emmerich Kalman. *Good Boy* (Hammerstein's, CR, "Betty Summers," Nov. 1928): Manhattan Walk; Nina; Some Sweet Someone/W: Bert Kalmar, M: Harry Ruby, Herbert Stothart. *The Silver Swan* (Martin Beck, "Gabrielle," Nov. 27, 1929): I Love You, I Adore You; Trial Song/W: William Brady, M: H. Maurice Jacquet — Till I Met You/W: William Brady, Alonzo Price, M: H. Maurice Jacquet. *The Prince of Pilsen* (Jolson, revival, "Nellie Wagner," Jan. 13, 1930): Pictures in the Smoke; Song of the Nightingale; The Tale of the Sea Shell/W: Frank Pixley, M: Gustav Luders. *The Chocolate Soldier* (Jolson, revival, CR, "Mascha," 1930): Falling in Love; The Tale of a Coat/W: Stanislaus Stange, M: Oscar Straus. *The Chocolate Soldier* (Erlanger's, revival, "Mascha," Sept. 21, 1931): Falling in Love/W: Stanislaus Stange, M: Oscar Straus. *Robin Hood* (Erlanger's, revival, "Annabel," Feb. 8, 1932): Milkmaid's Song; When a Maiden Weds/W: Harry B. Smith, M: Reginald De Koven.

4140. Marion Harte *The Office Boy* (Victoria, "Jeanette," Nov. 2, 1903): After Business Hours/W: Harry B. Smith, M: Ludwig Englander.

4141. Arthur Hartley *Linger Longer Letty* (Fulton, "Walter," Nov. 20, 1919): Did You, My Boy, Did You?/W: Bernard Grossman, M: Alfred Goodman — Slow Town Is Jazz Town Now/W: Bernard Grossman, George Yoerger, M: Alfred Goodman. *Here's Howe!* (Broadhurst, "Edwin Treadwell," May 1, 1928): Beauty in the Movies/W: Irving Caesar, M: Joseph Meyer, Roger Wolfe Kahn. *Who Cares?* (46th Street, revue, July 8, 1930): Believe It or Not; Sun Up/W: Harry Clark, M: Percy Wenrich.

4142. Jack Hartley *My Girl* (Vanderbilt, "Harold Gray," Nov. 24, 1924): Before the Dawn; Desert Isle; They Say/W: Harlan Thompson, M: Harry Archer.

4143. David Hartman (May 19, 1935–) B: Pawtucket, RI. At one time an anchorman for TV's *Good Morning America*. He played David Sutton on the TV Western *The Virginian* (1968). *Hello, Dolly!* (St. James, "Rudolph," Jan. 16, 1964): Hello, Dolly!/WM: Jerry Herman. *The Yearling* (Alvin, "Oliver," Dec. 10, 1965): Everything in the World I Love; I'm All Smiles/W: Herbert Martin, M: Michael Leonard.

4144. Ferris Hartman (c 1861–Aug. 31, 1931) Father of PAUL HARTMAN. He managed musical comedies on the West Coast, in which his son sometimes danced. *The Man in the Moon* (New York, "Sherlock Holmes," Apr. 24, 1899): In Spite of Puck and Judge/W: Louis Harrison,

Stanislaus Stange, M: Ludwig Englander. *Treasure Girl* (Alvin, "Mortimer Grimes," Nov. 8, 1928): According to Mr. Grimes/W: Ira Gershwin, M: George Gershwin.

4145. Grace Hartman (Jan. 7, 1907–Aug. 8, 1955) B: San Francisco, CA. Her father was a ship's captain. She began dancing at the age of 5. M: PAUL HARTMAN, when she was 15 and he was 1917; they divorced in 1951. The couple became well known as comedic-satiric ballroom dancers in clubs and on Broadway and TV. *All for Love* (Mark Hellinger, revue, Jan. 22, 1949): It's a Living/WM: Allan Roberts, Lester Lee — We Can't Dance [added]/W: Milton Pascal, M: Clay Warnick. *Tickets, Please!* (Coronet, revue, Apr. 27, 1950): You Can't Take It with You/WM: Lyn Duddy, Joan Edwards.

4146. Paul Hartman (Oct. 25, 1904–Oct. 2, 1973) B: San Francisco, CA. Son of FERRIS HARTMAN. M: GRACE HARTMAN. He appeared on TV sitcoms such as *Petticoat Junction* (1968) and *Mayberry RFD* (1968). *All for Love* (Mark Hellinger, revue, Jan. 22, 1949): It's a Living/WM: Allan Roberts, Lester Lee — We Can't Dance [added]/W: Milton Pascal, M: Clay Warnick. *Tickets, Please!* (Coronet, revue, Apr. 27, 1950): Back at the Palace/W: Mel Tolkin, Lucille Kallen, Jack Fox, M: Clay Warnick. *Of Thee I Sing* (Ziegfeld, revival, "Alexander Throttlebottom," May 5, 1952): Who Is the Lucky Girl to Be?/W: Ira Gershwin, M: George Gershwin. *The Pajama Game* (New York City Center, revival, "Hines," May 15, 1957): I'll Never Be Jealous Again; The Pajama Game; Think of the Time I Save/WM: Richard Adler, Jerry Ross.

4147. Patricia Harty (Nov. 5, 1941–) B: Washington, DC. *Sail Away* (Broadhurst, "Nancy Foyle," Oct. 3, 1961): Beatnik Love Affair; When You Want Me; Where Shall I Find Him?/WM: Noel Coward.

4148. Thomas (Tom) Harty *Everybody's Welcome* (Shubert, "A Drunk," Oct. 13, 1931): You've Got a Lease on My Heart/W: Irving Kahal, M: Sammy Fain. *Ballyhoo of 1932* (44th Street, revue, Sept. 6, 1932): Falling Off the Wagon; Man About Yonkers [Oct. 31, 1932]/W: E.Y. Harburg, M: Lewis E. Gensler.

4149. Eivind Harum (May 24, 1944–) B: Stavanger, Norway. *West Side Story* (New York State, revival, "Riff," June 24, 1968): Cool/W: Stephen Sondheim, M: Leonard Bernstein. *Woman of the Year* (Palace, "Alexi Petrikov," Mar. 29, 1981): Happy in the Morning/W: Fred Ebb, M: John Kander.

4150. Clarence Harvey (c 1865–May 3, 1945) *His Honor the Mayor* (New York > Wallack's, "Hon. Teddy Todd," May 28, 1906): I'll Travel the Links with You/W: Charles J. Campbell, Ralph M. Skinner, M: Alfred E. Aarons — The Mayor of Kankakee; Military Willie/W: Charles J. Campbell, Ralph M. Skinner, M: Julian Edwards. *Tillie's Nightmare* (Herald Square, "Harvey Tinker," May 5, 1910): There Goes Another One/W: Edgar Smith, M: A. Baldwin Sloane. *The Passing Show of 1912* (Winter Garden, revue, July 22, 1912): Handy Andy/W: Harold Atteridge, M: Louis A. Hirsch. *The Girl from Brazil* (44th Street > Shubert, "Col. Zamzelius," Aug. 30, 1916): Oh You Lovely Ladies/W: Matthew Woodward, M: Sigmund Romberg. *La, La, Lucille* (Henry Miller, "Johnathon Jaynes," May 26, 1919): Too-Oodle-Um-Bum-Bo; When You Live in a Furnished Flat/W: Arthur Jackson, B.G. DeSylva, M: George Gershwin. *The Mimic World* (Century roof, revue, Aug. 17, 1921): Gay Brazilian/WM:?.

4151. Georgette Harvey (c 1882–Feb. 17, 1952) B: St. Louis, MO. *Strut Miss Lizzie* (Times Square, revue, June 19, 1922): Dear Old Southland/WM: Henry Creamer, Turner Layton. *Runnin' Wild* (Colonial, "Angelina Brown," revue, Oct. 29, 1923): Log Cabin Days/W: Cecil Mack, M: James P. Johnson.

4152. James Harvey *The King and I* (New York State Theater, revival, "Louis Leonowens," July 6, 1964): I Whistle a Happy Tune/W: Oscar Hammerstein II, M: Richard Rodgers.

4153. Jane Harvey *Bless You All* (Mark Hellinger, revue, Dec. 14, 1950): I Can Hear It Now; A Rose Is a Rose; Take Off the Coat/WM: Harold Rome.

4154. Kenneth Harvey (Dec. 25, 1918–1980) B: Montreal, Canada. *Pipe Dream* (Shubert, "Joe," Nov. 30, 1955): Bums' Opera/W: Oscar Hammerstein II, M: Richard Rodgers.

4155. Morris Harvey (Sept. 25, 1877–Aug. 24, 1944) B: London, England. *Hammerstein's Nine O'Clock Revue* (Century roof, revue, Oct. 4, 1923): Lucky Bargee/WM: ?.

4156. Robert Harvey B: Lynchburg, VA. *John Henry* (44th Street, "Hell Buster," Jan. 10, 1940): I Want Jesus to Walk with Me; I'm Gonna Git Down on My Knees/W: Roark Bradford, M: Jacques Wolfe.

4157. Roslyn Harvey *Sing for Your Supper* (Adelphi, revue, Apr. 24, 1939): At Long Last/W: Robert Sour, M: Lee Wainer.

4158. James Harwood *Razzle Dazzle* (Arena, revue, Feb. 19, 1951): Frivolity Frolics/W: Michael Stewart, M: Leo Schumer.

4159. John Harwood (Feb. 29, 1876–Dec. 26, 1944) B: London, England. Actor, producer, director. *The Star Gazer* (Plymouth, "Peckham," Nov. 26, 1917): A Bachelor's Button; If a Bachelor in Love Should Fall/W: Matthew Woodward, M: Franz Lehar.

4160. Lon Hascall (?–Dec. 13, 1932) B: Grand Rapids, MI. *Toot Sweet* (Princess > Nora Bayes, revue, May 7, 1919): Toot Sweet/W: Raymond B. Egan, M: Richard A. Whiting. *The Passing Show of 1919* (Winter Garden, revue, Oct. 23, 1919): Seven Ages of Women/W: Harold Atteridge, M: Sigmund Romberg, Jean Schwartz. *Hold Everything!* (Broadhurst, CR, "Nosey Bartlett," Aug. 12, 1929): Genealogy/W: B.G. DeSylva, Lew Brown, M: Ray Henderson.

4161. Jack Haskell (Apr. 30, 1919–Sept. 26, 1998) B: Akron, OH. An early member of Dave Garroway's TV show, *Garroway at Large* (1949), he also appeared regularly on the Jack Paar and Johnny Carson shows. *Mr. President* (St. James, "Pat Gregory," Oct. 20, 1962): Empty Pockets Filled with Love; I've Got to Be Around; Meat and Potatoes; Pigtails and Freckles/WM: Irving Berlin.

4162. James Haskins *Marilyn* (Minskoff, "Photographer," Nov. 20, 1983): Swing Shift (Miss Parachute)/WM: Beth Lawrence, Norman Thalheimer.

4163. Bert Haslem (?–Nov. 11, 1903) B: Colesburg, Cape, South Africa. Actor and dancer. *A Gaiety Girl* (Daly's, revival, "Rev. Montague Brierly," May 7, 1895): Jimmy on the Chute/WM: Harry Greenbank.

4164. George Hassell (May 4, 1881–Feb. 17, 1937) B: Birmingham, Warwick, England. *The Girl from Brazil* (44th Street > Shubert, "Herr Torkel," Aug. 30, 1916): Ivy and Oak/W: Matthew Woodward, M: Sigmund Romberg. *Good Morning Judge* (Shubert, "Horatio Meebles," Feb. 6, 1919): I Want to Go Bye-Bye; Oh That We Two Were Maying; Sporty Boys/W: Percy Greenbank, M: Lionel Monckton — Young Folks and Old Folks/WM: ?. *Florodora* (Century, revival, "Anthony Tweedlepunch," Apr. 5, 1920): I Want to Marry a Man, I Do/W: Paul Rubens, M: Leslie Stuart. *The Circus Princess* (Winter Garden, "Grand Duke Sergius," Apr. 25, 1927): The Hussars' Song/W: Harry B. Smith, M: Emmerich Kalman. *Artists and Models of 1930* (Majestic, revue, "Maurice," June 10, 1930): I Want You to Love Me/WM: Harold Stern, Ernie Golden.

4165. Thomas Hasson *West Side Story* (Winter Garden, revival, "Riff," Apr. 27, 1960): Cool/W: Stephen Sondheim, M: Leonard Bernstein.

4166. Bill Hastings (July 30, 1952–) B:

Vinita, OK. *Sweet Charity* (Minskoff, revival, CR, "Dark Glasses," Mar. 1987): You Should See Yourself/W: Dorothy Fields, M: Cy Coleman.

4167. Alonzo Hatch *The Royal Middy* (Daly's, "Don Lamberto," Jan. 28, 1880): Again Enfolded Within Thine Arms; All We Seem to Agree; Have You Forgot; Of All the Fine Fellows That Sail on the Sea; Sword in Hand, Man to Man; To Our Flag; To Thee My Queen/W: F. Zell, M: Richard Genee.

4168. William Riley Hatch (Sept. 2, 1862–Sept. 6, 1925) *The Burgomaster* (Manhattan, "Col. Krall" and "The Harlem Spider," Dec. 31, 1900): Good-Bye New Amsterdam; The Modern Gladiator/W: Frank Pixley, M: Gustav Luders. *Comin' Thro' the Rye* (Herald Square, "William Cactus Claude," Jan. 9, 1906): Whoa, Bill/W: George V. Hobart, M: A. Baldwin Sloane.

4169. Mary Hatcher B: Haines City, FL. *Oklahoma!* (St. James, CR, "Laurey Williams," Dec. 1946): Many a New Day; Oh, What a Beautiful Mornin'; Oklahoma!; Out of My Dreams; People Will Say We're in Love; The Surrey with the Fringe on Top/W: Oscar Hammerstein II, M: Richard Rodgers. *Texas, Li'l Darlin'* (Mark Hellinger, "Dallas Smith," Nov. 25, 1949): Affable, Balding Me; A Month of Sundays; Ride 'Em, Cowboy; They Talk a Different Language (The Yodel Blues); Whichaway'd They Go/W: Johnny Mercer, M: Robert Emmett Dolan.

4170. Linzi Hateley (Oct. 23, 1970–) B: Marsden Green, Birmingham, England. *Carrie* (Virginia, "Carrie White," May 12, 1988): And Eve Was Weak; Carrie; The Destruction; Dream On; Evening Prayers; Heaven; I'm Not Alone; Open Your Heart; Unsuspecting Hearts/W: Dean Pitchford, M: Michael Gore.

4171. Lansing Hatfield B: Virginia. He joined the Metropolitan Opera in 1941. *Virginia* (Center, "Capt. Boyd," Sept. 2, 1937): Virginia/W: Al Stillman, M: Arthur Schwartz. *Sadie Thompson* (Alvin, "Rev. Alfred Davidson," Nov. 16, 1944): (You'll Be) Born All Over Again; Garden in the Sky/W: Howard Dietz, M: Vernon Duke.

4172. Dorothy Hathaway *The Greenwich Village Follies of 1925* (Shubert, revue, CR, Mar. 15, 1926): How Do You Do?/W: Owen Murphy, M: Harold A. Levey — Wouldn't You?/WM: Owen Murphy.

4173. Tom Hatten (1927–) B: Jamestown, ND. *Annie* (Alvin, CR, "FDR," Aug. 18, 1982): A New Deal for Christmas; Tomorrow/W: Martin Charnin, M: Charles Strouse.

4174. Brad Hatton *Top Banana* (Winter

Garden, "Mr. Parker," Nov. 1, 1951): Slogan Song (You Gotta Have a Slogan)/WM: Johnny Mercer.

4175. Elaine Hausman (June 8, 1949–) B: Sacramento, CA. *Brigadoon* (Majestic, revival, "Meg Brockie," Oct. 16, 1980): Down on Mac-Connachy Square; The Love of My Life/W: Alan Jay Lerner, M: Frederick Loewe.

4176. Arthur Havel (c 1897–Mar. 29, 1965) B: Brooklyn, NY. He and his brother, MORTON HAVEL, began on the stage as children. *Just a Minute* (Ambassador > Century, "Joe Winston," Oct. 8, 1928): Anything Your Heart Desires; We'll Just Be Two Commuters/W: Walter O'Keefe, M: Harry Archer. *A Night in Venice* (Shubert, "Bud O'Neill," May 21, 1929): Sliding Down a Silver Cloud/W: J. Keirn Brennan, M: Lee David — The Stork Don't Come Around Anymore/WM: Betty Morse Laidlaw.

4177. Morton Havel B: Brooklyn, NY. Brother of ARTHUR HAVEL. *Just a Minute* (Ambassador > Century, "Charlie Winston," Oct. 8, 1928): same as above. *A Night in Venice* (Shubert, "Jack Graham," May 21, 1929): same as above.

4178. June Havoc (Nov. 8, 1916–) B: Seattle, WA. Sister of GYPSY ROSE LEE. Starting at age 2 in a Hal Roach comedy, Havoc was billed as Baby June, the Darling of Vaudeville. She became a popular film star. *Forbidden Melody* (New Amsterdam, "Rozsa," Nov. 2, 1936): How Could a Fellow Want More?/W: Otto Harbach, M: Sigmund Romberg. *Pal Joey* (Ethel Barrymore, "Gladys Bumps," Dec. 25, 1940): The Flower Garden of My Heart; Plant You Now, Dig You Later; That Terrific Rainbow; You Mustn't Kick It Around/W: Lorenz Hart, M: Richard Rodgers. *Mexican Hayride* (Winter Garden, "Montana," Jan. 28, 1944): Abracadabra; Count Your Blessings; There Must Be Someone for Me/WM: Cole Porter. *Sadie Thompson* (Alvin, "Sadie Thompson," Nov. 16, 1944): Fisherman's Wharf; If You Can't Get the Love You Want [Dec. 10, 1944]; Life's a Funny Present from Someone; The Love I Long For; Poor as a Church Mouse; Sailing at Midnight/W: Howard Dietz, M: Vernon Duke. *Annie* (Alvin, CR, "Miss Hannigan," Oct. 6, 1982): Easy Street; Little Girls/W: Martin Charnin, M: Charles Strouse.

4179. Harris Hawkins *Oklahoma!* (New York City Center, revival, "Will Parker," Aug. 31, 1953): All er Nothin'; The Farmer and the Cowman; Kansas City/W: Oscar Hammerstein II, M: Richard Rodgers.

4180. Ira Hawkins *Timbuktu!* (Mark Hel-

linger, "Hadji," Mar. 1, 1978): And This Is My Beloved; Fate; Gesticulate; Night of My Nights; Rhymes Have I; Sands of Time/WM: Robert Wright, George Forrest, M: based on Alexander Borodin. *The Tap Dance Kid* (Broadhurst, CR, "William Sheridan," Feb. 5, 1985): William's Song/W: Robert Lorick, M: Henry Krieger. *Honky Tonk Nights* (Biltmore, "Billy Sampson," Aug. 7, 1986): Honky Tonk Nights; Lily of the Alley/W: Ralph Allen, David Campbell, M: Michael Valenti.

4181. Iris Hawkins *Hop o' My Thumb* (Manhattan Opera House, "Hop o' My Thumb," Nov. 26, 1913): Hop, Hop, Hop/W: Sydney Rosenfeld, M: Manuel Klein.

4182. June Hawkins B: Minneapolis, MN. *Carmen Jones* (Broadway, "Frankie," Dec. 2, 1943): De Cards Don't Lie; Poncho de Panther from Brazil; Whizzin' Away Along de Track/W: Oscar Hammerstein II, M: Georges Bizet. *Carmen Jones* (Broadway, CR, "Myrt," Jan. 14, 1945): Beat Out Dat Rhythm on a Drum; De Cards Don't Lie; Poncho de Panther from Brazil; Whizzin' Away Along de Track/W: Oscar Hammerstein II, M: Georges Bizet. *St. Louis Woman* (Martin Beck, "Lila," Mar. 30, 1946): I Had Myself a True Love; Sleep Peaceful, Mr. Used-to-Be/W: Johnny Mercer, M: Harold Arlen.

4183. Sidney (Sid) Hawkins *Sunny Days* (Imperial, "Robert," Feb. 8, 1928): A Belle, a Beau and a Boutonniere/W: Clifford Grey, William Cary Duncan, M: Jean Schwartz. *Keep It Clean* (Selwyn, revue, June 24, 1929): I See You but What Do You See in Me?/WM: Lester Lee — Just a Little Blue for You/WM: James F. Hanley.

4184. Stanley Hawkins *The Show Girl or The Cap of Fortune* (Wallack's, "Capt. E. Ross Armor," May 5, 1902): As the Prince Waked the Princess/WM: ? — Lover's Lane; Waltz Song/WM: H.L. Heartz — One That He Loves Best; Psyche; A Rose and a Lily/WM: Edward W. Corliss — Sometime, Perhaps/W: D.K. Stevens, M: L.S. Thompson. *The Silver Slipper* (Broadway, CR, "Donald Gregor," Mar. 9, 1903): Tessie, You Are the Only, Only, Only/WM: Will R. Anderson — Two Eyes of Blue/W: Charles H. Taylor, M: Leslie Stuart. *The Red Feather* (Lyric, "H.R.H. Crown Prince of Romancia," Nov. 9, 1903): A Lesson in Verse; A Prince of Good Fellows/W: Charles Emerson Cook, M: Reginald De Koven. *Lady Teazle* (Casino, "Joseph Surface," Dec. 24, 1904): Dear Old London Town; The Hypocrite; The Pretty Little Milliner; Were I Happily Married/W: John Kendrick Bangs, M: A. Baldwin Sloane. *The Duke of Duluth* (Majestic, "Dennis O'Hara," Sept. 11, 1905): Give Me Death or Victory; Sweetheart of My Childhood/W: George Broadhurst, M: Max S. Witt.

4185. Charles R. Hawley *The Serenade* (Knickerbocker, CR, "Carlos Alvarado," Apr. 13, 1897): Don Jose of Sevilla; I Love Thee, I Adore Thee; The Serenade; With Cracking of Whip and Rattle of Spur/W: Harry B. Smith, M: Victor Herbert.

4186. Ida Hawley (?–Dec. 9, 1908) B: Belleville, Ontario, Canada. *A Million Dollars* (New York, "Phyllis Vandergold," Sept. 27, 1900): Believe Me/W: Louis Harrison, George V. Hobart, M: A. Baldwin Sloane. *The Prince of Pilsen* (Broadway, CR, "Edith Adams," June 20, 1903): The Field and Forest; The Message of the Violet; We Know It's Wrong to Flirt/W: Frank Pixley, M: Gustav Luders. *Babette* (Broadway, "Vinette," Nov. 16, 1903): My Lady of the Manor; On the Other Side of the Wall/W: Harry B. Smith, M: Victor Herbert. *The Pearl and the Pumpkin* (Broadway, "Polly Premier," Aug. 21, 1905): Come My True Love; Honeymoon Hall; Lily White/W: Paul West, M: John W. Bratton. *The Lady from Lane's* (Lyric > Casino, "Florence Gilbert," Aug. 19, 1907): Four Little Pigs [Sept. 16, 1907]; Take a Maid; You, Just You/W: George Broadhurst, M: Gustave Kerker — Rosita [Sept. 16, 1907]/W: George Broadhurst, M: Max S. Witt.

4187. Jennie Hawley *Hodge, Podge & Co.* (Madison Square, "Carmenita Hodge," Oct. 23, 1900): Dream Days of Seville/W: Walter Ford, M: John W. Bratton — What a Funny Story/W: Walter Ford, M: Herman Perlet. *The Toreador* (Knickerbocker, "Donna Teresa," Jan. 6, 1902): My Toreador/WM: Paul Rubens.

4188. Jill Haworth (Aug. 15, 1945–) B: Sussex, England. At 12 she became a member of the Sadler's Wells Ballet. She appeared in several films in the U.S., working for Otto Preminger, and in France. *Cabaret* (Broadhurst, "Sally Bowles," Nov. 20, 1966): Cabaret; Don't Tell Mama; Perfectly Marvelous; Why Should I Wake Up?/W: Fred Ebb, M: John Kander.

4189. Jim Hawthorne *South Pacific* (Majestic > Broadway, "Marine Cpl. Hamilton Steeves," Apr. 7, 1949): There Is Nothin' Like a Dame/W: Oscar Hammerstein II, M: Richard Rodgers. *The Merry Widow* (New York City Center, revival, "Camille De Jolidon," Apr. 10, 1957): A Dutiful Wife/W: Adrian Ross, M: Franz Lehar.

4190. Nellie Hawthorne *By the Sad Sea Waves* (Herald Square, "Charity Grace," Feb. 21, 1899): Honolulu Lady; Military Model/WM: J. Sherrie Mathews, Harry Bulger — The Willow Pattern Plate/W: Nellie Hawthorne, M: Leslie Stuart.

4191. Edgar Lee Hay *The Lady of the Slipper* (Globe, "Atzel," Oct. 28, 1912): Fond of the Ladies/W: James O'Dea, M: Victor Herbert.

4192. Mary Hay (Aug. 22, 1901–June 4, 1957) B: Fort Bliss, TX. She and CLIFTON WEBB were a popular dancing couple in vaudeville, though he was 6 ft. 2 to her 4 ft. 10. *Sally* (New Amsterdam, "Rosalind Rafferty," Dec. 21, 1920): The Church 'Round the Corner; Way Down East/W: Clifford Grey, P.G. Wodehouse, M: Jerome Kern — The Lorelei/W: Anne Caldwell, M: Jerome Kern — On with the Dance/W: Clifford Grey, M: Jerome Kern. *Marjolaine* (Broadhurst, "Barbara Sternroyd," Jan. 24, 1922): Cuddle Up Together (My Old Brown Coat); Don't!/W: Brian Hooker, M: Hugo Felix — I Want You/W: Anne Caldwell, M: Hugo Felix. *Mary Jane McKane* (Imperial, "Mary Jane McKane," Dec. 25, 1923): Just Look Around [Feb. 1924]; Laugh It Off; Mary Jane McKane/W: William Cary Duncan, Oscar Hammerstein II, M: Vincent Youmans, Herbert Stothart — Stick to Your Knitting/W: William Cary Duncan, Oscar Hammerstein II, M: Herbert Stothart — Toodle-oo/W: William Cary Duncan, Oscar Hammerstein II, M: Vincent Youmans. *Sunny* (New Amsterdam, "Weenie Winters," Sept. 22, 1925): Let's Say Goodnight Till It's Morning; Strolling, or What Have You?; Two Little Bluebirds/W: Otto Harbach, Oscar Hammerstein II, M: Jerome Kern. *Treasure Girl* (Alvin, "Polly Tees," Nov. 8, 1928): I've Got a Crush on You; K-ra-zy for You; What Causes That?/W: Ira Gershwin, M: George Gershwin.

4193. Gloria Hayden *Along Fifth Avenue* (Broadhurst, revue, Jan. 13, 1949): Vacation in the Store/W: Tom Adair, M: Gordon Jenkins.

4194. Michael Hayden (July 28, 1963–) B: St. Paul, MN. *Carousel* (Lincoln Center, revival, "Billy Bigelow," Mar. 24, 1994): If I Loved You; Soliloquy/W: Oscar Hammerstein II, M: Richard Rodgers.

4195. Sophie Hayden (Feb. 23–) B: Miami, FL. *The Most Happy Fella* (Booth, revival, "Rosabella," Feb. 13, 1992): Don't Cry; Happy to Make Your Acquaintance; How Beautiful the Days; My Heart Is So Full of You; Please Let Me Tell You; Somebody Somewhere; Warm All Over/WM: Frank Loesser.

4196. Tamra Hayden (Aug. 18, 1962–) B: Littleton, CO. *Les Miserables* (Broadway, CR, "Cosette," c 1994): A Heart Full of Love; In My Life/W: Herbert Kretzmer, M: Claude-Michel Schonberg.

4197. Carl Haydn *Happyland or The King of Elysia* (Lyric > Casino > Majestic, "Adonis," Oct. 2, 1905): Happy Is the Summer's Day/W: Frederic Ranken, M: Reginald De Koven. *Gypsy Love* (Globe, "Fedor," Oct. 17, 1911): Love Is Like the Rose/W: Harry B. Smith, Robert B. Smith, M: Franz Lehar.

4198. Martin Haydon *The Little Cherub* (Criterion, "Alderman Briggs," Aug. 6, 1906): My Wife Will Be My Lady [Oct. 22, 1906]/W: Owen Hall, M: Ivan Caryll. *The Princess Pat* (Cort, "Thomas," Sept. 29, 1915): Allies/W: Henry Blossom, M: Victor Herbert.

4199. Bill Hayes (June 5, 1925–) B: Harvey, IL. *Me and Juliet* (Majestic, "Larry," May 28, 1953): The Big Black Giant; I'm Your Girl; No Other Way; That's the Way It Happens/W: Oscar Hammerstein II, M: Richard Rodgers. *Brigadoon* (New York City Center, revival, "Tommy Albright," Dec. 13, 1967): Almost Like Being in Love; From This Day On; The Heather on the Hill; There but for You Go I/W: Alan Jay Lerner, M: Frederick Loewe.

4200. Frank Hayes *The Student King* (Garden, "Grumblekoff," Dec. 25, 1906): In Bohemia; Opposites Are We/W: Stanislaus Stange, M: Reginald De Koven.

4201. Georgie Hayes *Hello, Paris* (Shubert, "Fleurie Capel," Nov. 15, 1930): Paris/WM: ?.

4202. Grace Hayes (Aug. 23, 1895–Feb. 1, 1989) B: San Francisco, CA. Mother of PETER LIND HAYES. A stage and film actress, singer of comic material in vaudeville and nightclubs. *The Bunch and Judy* (Globe, "Grace Hayes," Nov. 28, 1922): Have You Forgotten Me Blues/W: Anne Caldwell, M: Jerome Kern. *The Merry World* (Imperial, revue, June 8, 1926): White Rose, Red Rose/WM: R. Moreiti. *A Night in Spain* (44th Street, revue, May 3, 1927): International Vamp; A Spanish Shawl/W: Alfred Bryan, M: Jean Schwartz. *Ballyhoo* (Hammerstein's, "Flora Fay," Dec. 22, 1930): Blow Hot — Blow Cold; Good Girls Love Bad Men/W: Harry Ruskin, Leighton K. Brill, M: Louis Alter — No Wonder I'm Blue/W: Oscar Hammerstein II, M: Louis Alter. *A Little Racketeer* (44th Street, "Ethel Pierson," Jan. 18, 1932): Blow, Gabriel/W: Edward Eliscu, M: Henry Sullivan — Mr. Moon/W: Lupin Fein, Moe Jaffe, M: Lee Wainer.

4203. Helen Hayes (Oct. 10, 1900–Mar. 17, 1993) B: Washington, DC. Known as The First Lady of the American Theater. *The Never Homes* (Broadway, "Fannie Hicks," Oct. 5, 1911): There's a Girl in Havana/WM: E. Ray Goetz, Irving Berlin, Ted Snyder.

4204. Peter Lind Hayes (June 25, 1915–Apr. 21, 1998) B: San Francisco, CA. Son of GRACE HAYES; they toured together in vaudeville. M: MARY HEALY; they worked together on live TV in the 1950s. *Heaven on Earth* (New Century, "James Aloysius McCarthy," Sept. 16, 1948): Don't Forget to Dream; In the Back of a Hack; The Letter; Wedding in the Park; What's the Matter with Our City?/W: Barry Trivers, M: Jay Gorney.

4205. Richard Hayes *The Beast in Me* (Plymouth, revue, May 16, 1963): Eat Your Nice Lily, Unicorn; So Beautiful; What Do You Say?/W: James Costigan, M: Don Elliott.

4206. Jimmy Hayeson (June 27, 1924–) B: Carthage, NC. *Ain't Supposed to Die a Natural Death* (Ethel Barrymore, Oct. 20, 1971): The Dozens; You Ain't No Astronaut/WM: Melvin Van Peebles.

4207. Coreania Hayman *Carmen Jones* (New York City Center, revival, "Cindy Lou," Apr. 7, 1946): My Joe; You Talk Jus' Like My Maw/W: Oscar Hammerstein II, M: Georges Bizet.

4208. Lillian Hayman (July 17, 1922–1994) *Kwamina* (54th Street, "Mammy Trader," Oct. 23, 1961): One Wife/WM: Richard Adler. *Hallelujah, Baby!* (Martin Beck, "Momma," Apr. 26, 1967): Back in the Kitchen; I Don't Know Where She Got It; Smile, Smile/W: Betty Comden, Adolph Green, M: Jule Styne. *70, Girls, 70* (Broadhurst, Apr. 15, 1971): Believe; Boom Ditty Boom; Broadway My Street; Coffee (in a Cardboard Cup); The Elephant Song; Home/W: Fred Ebb, M: John Kander. *No, No, Nanette* (46th Street, revival, CR, "Pauline," Oct. 30, 1972): Take a Little One-Step/W: Zelda Sears, M: Vincent Youmans. *Doctor Jazz* (Winter Garden, "Georgia Sheridan," Mar. 19, 1975): Georgia Shows 'Em How; We've Got Connections/WM: Buster Davis — Good-Time Flat Blues/WM: A.J. Piron.

4209. Daniel L. Haynes (c 1894–July 28, 1954) B: Atlanta, GA. *Rang-Tang* (Royale, revue, July 12, 1927): Jungle Rose/W: Jo Trent, M: Ford Dabney.

4210. Lawrence Haynes *Ziegfeld Midnight Frolic [4th Edition]* (New Amsterdam roof, revue, Oct. 3, 1916): Mavis; The Melting Pot; When He Comes Back to Me/W: Gene Buck, M: Dave Stamper.

4211. Tiger Haynes (Dec. 13, 1907–Feb. 15, 1994) B: St. Croix, Virgin Islands. He went to New York as a boy. During the Great Depression of the 1930s, he traveled the U.S., working as a lumberjack and a prizefighter, and changing his name from George to Tiger. Playing the guitar and singing, with Roy Testamark on piano and Bill Pollard on bass, he was part of the popular trio called The Three Flames. Their big hit was the song "Open the Door Richard" (1947). *Finian's Rainbow* (New York City Center, revival, "3rd Passion Pilgrim Gospeler," Apr. 27, 1960): The Begat/W: E.Y. Harburg, M: Burton Lane. *Fade Out—Fade In* (Mark Hellinger, "Lou Williams," May 26, 1964/Feb. 15, 1965): You Mustn't Be Discouraged/W: Betty Comden, Adolph Green, M: Jule Styne. *Kiss Me, Kate* (New York City Center, revival, "Paul," May 12, 1965): Too Darn Hot/WM: Cole Porter. *Finian's Rainbow* (New York City Center, revival, "2nd Passion Pilgrim Gospeler," Apr. 5, 1967): The Begat/W: E.Y. Harburg, M: Burton Lane. *The Wiz* (Majestic, "Tinman," Jan. 5, 1975): Slide Some Oil to Me; What Would I Do If I Could Feel/WM: Charlie Smalls. *A Broadway Musical* (Lunt-Fontanne, "Sylvester Lee," Dec. 21, 1978): The 1934 Hot Chocolate Jazz Babies Revue/W: Lee Adams, M: Charles Strouse. *Comin' Uptown* (Winter Garden, "Marley," Dec. 20, 1979): Get Your Act Together/W: Peter Udell, M: Garry Sherman. *My One and Only* (St. James, CR, "Rt. Rev. J.D. Montgomery," Nov. 1, 1984): Just Another Rhumba/W: Ira Gershwin, M: George Gershwin—Kickin' the Clouds Away/W: B.G. DeSylva, Ira Gershwin, M: George Gershwin.

4212. Rex Hays (June 17, 1946–) B: Hollywood, CA. *Angel* (Minskoff, "Joe Tarkington," May 10, 1978): Fingers and Toes/W: Peter Udell, M: Gary Geld. *Onward Victoria* (Martin Beck, "William Evarts," Dec. 14, 1980): Curiosity/W: Charlotte Anker, Irene Rosenberg, M: Keith Herrmann.

4213. Ina Hayward *The Passing Show of 1921* (Winter Garden, revue, Dec. 29, 1920): Hello Miss Knickerbocker; Silks and Satins; Tip Top Toreador/WM: ?—My Lady of the Lamp/W: Harold Atteridge, M: Lew Pollack. *Fashions of 1924* (Lyceum, revue, July 18, 1923): One Last Waltz (One More Waltz); A Violet in Broadway's Garden/W: Harry B. Smith, M: Ted Snyder. *The Merry Malones* (Erlanger's, "Mrs. Van Buren," Sept. 26, 1927): Behind the Mask/WM: George M. Cohan. *Billie* (Erlanger's, "Mrs. Ambrose Gerard," Oct. 1, 1928): Bluff; Come to St. Thomas's/WM: George M. Cohan.

4214. Billie Haywood *New Faces of 1934* (Fulton, revue, Mar. 15, 1934): The Coal Bin/WM: George Hickman—He Loves Me/W: Nancy Hamilton, M: Cliff Allen—My Last Affair/WM: Haven Johnson. *Fools Rush In* (The

Playhouse, revue, Dec. 25, 1934): Rhythm in My Hair; Shoes/W: Norman Zeno, M: Will Irwin—Sixty Second Romance/W: Lawrence Harris, M: Bud Harris. *New Faces of 1936* (Vanderbilt, revue, May 19, 1936): I Was a Gyp in Egypt; Sixty Second Romance [May 25, 1936]/W: Lawrence Harris, M: Bud Harris—It Must Be Religion/WM: Forman Brown.

4215. Nancy Haywood *The Beast in Me* (Plymouth, revue, May 16, 1963): What Do You Say?/W: James Costigan, M: Don Elliott.

4216. Yochai Hazani *To Live Another Summer, To Pass Another Winter* (Helen Hayes, revue, Oct. 21, 1971): The Sacrifice/W: David Paulsen, M: Dov Seltzer.

4217. Rupert Hazell *Pins and Needles* (Shubert, revue, CR, Feb. 6, 1922): Slow Movies/WM: ?—South Sea Sweetheart/W: Irving Caesar, M: Maurice Yvain.

4218. John E. Hazzard (Feb. 22, 1881–Dec. 2, 1935) B: New York, NY. M: ALICE DOVEY. *The Hurdy Gurdy Girl* (Wallack's, "Judge Terence Fitzgerald," Sept. 23, 1907): Stories/W: Richard Carle, M: H.L. Heartz. *The Red Rose* (Globe, "Ludwig Spiegle," June 22, 1911): A Brass Band's Good Enough for Me/W: James Harvey, M: Robert Hood Bowers—I'd Like to Go on a Honeymoon with You; The Old Ballet Days/W: Harry B. Smith, Robert B. Smith, M: Robert Hood Bowers. *The Lilac Domino* (44th Street, "Prosper," Oct. 28, 1914): Ladies Day; Still We Smile/W: Robert B. Smith, M: Charles Cuvillier. *Very Good Eddie* (Princess > Casino > 39th Street > Princess, "Al Cleveland," Dec. 23, 1915): I'd Like to Have a Million in the Bank/W: Herbert Reynolds, M: Jerome Kern. *Miss Springtime* (New Amsterdam, "Michael Robin," Sept. 25, 1916): All Full of Talk/W: P.G. Wodehouse, M: Jerome Kern—Life Is a Game of Bluff/W: Herbert Reynolds, M: Emmerich Kalman—This Is the Existence/WM: ?—Throw Me a Rose/W: P.G. Wodehouse, Herbert Reynolds, M: Emmerich Kalman. *The Girl Behind the Gun* (New Amsterdam, "Pierre Breval," Sept. 16, 1918): Back to the Dear Old Trenches; I Like It; Women Haven't Any Mercy on a Man/W: P.G. Wodehouse, M: Ivan Caryll. *La, La, Lucille* (Henry Miller, "John Smith," May 26, 1919): The Best of Everything; From Now On; It's Hard to Tell [Sept. 8, 1919]; The Ten Commandments of Love (There's Magic in the Air)/W: Arthur Jackson, B.G. DeSylva, M: George Gershwin. *The Night Boat* (Liberty, "Bob White," Feb. 2, 1920): Good Night Boat/W: Anne Caldwell, Frank Craven, M: Jerome Kern. *Tangerine* (Casino, "King Home-Brew," Aug. 9,

1921): Civilization/W: Howard Johnson, M: Monte Carlo, Alma Sanders — She Was Very Dear to Me/WM: Benjamin Hapgood Burt. *For Goodness Sake* (Lyric, "Perry Reynolds," Feb. 20, 1922): Hubby [Mar. 31, 1922]; In the Days of Wild Romance/W: Arthur Jackson, M: Paul Lannin, William Daly — Tra-La-La/W: Ira Gershwin, M: George Gershwin. *The Greenwich Village Follies of 1922* (Shubert, revue, Sept. 12, 1922): Goodbye to Dear Old Alaska/W: Irving Caesar, John Murray Anderson, M: Louis A. Hirsch. *One Kiss* (Fulton, "Gen. Pas-De-Vis," Nov. 27, 1923): In My Day; A Little Bit of Lace/W: Clare Kummer, M: Maurice Yvain. *Bye, Bye, Barbara* (National, "The Great Karloff," Aug. 25, 1924): As Kipling Says; I Learned About Women from Her/WM: Benjamin Hapgood Burt — Why Don't They Leave the Sheik Alone?/WM: Monte Carlo, Alma Sanders. *The Houseboat on the Styx* (Liberty, "Capt. William Kidd," Dec. 25, 1928): An Irate Pirate Am I/W: Monte Carlo, M: Alma Sanders. *Shoot the Works!* (George M. Cohan, revue, July 21, 1931): Back in Circulation Again/W: Max Lief, Nathaniel Lief, M: Michael Cleary.

4219. George L. Headley *The Girl from Nantucket* (Adelphi, "Tom Andrews," Nov. 8, 1945): Sons of the Sea/W: Kay Twomey, M: Jacques Belasco.

4220. Anthony Heald (Aug. 25, 1944–) B: New Rochelle, NY. *Anything Goes* (Vivian Beaumont, revival, "Lord Evelyn Oakleigh," Oct. 19, 1987): The Gypsy in Me/WM: Cole Porter.

4221. Eunice Healey *Girl Crazy* (Alvin, "Flora James," Oct. 14, 1930): Barbary Coast/W: Ira Gershwin, M: George Gershwin. *The Laugh Parade* (Imperial, revue, Nov. 2, 1931): Excuse for Song and Dance; Punch and Judy Man/W: Mort Dixon, Joe Young, M: Harry Warren. *Thumbs Up!* (St. James, revue, Dec. 27, 1934): Zing! Went the Strings of My Heart!/WM: James F. Hanley. *Hold On to Your Hats* (Shubert, "Shirley," Sept. 11, 1940): Don't Let It Get You Down; The World Is in My Arms/W: E.Y. Harburg, M: Burton Lane. *Two for the Show* (Booth, revue, Feb. 8, 1940): That Terrible Tune/W: Nancy Hamilton, M: Morgan Lewis. *Beat the Band* (46th Street, "Princess," Oct. 14, 1942): America Loves a Band; Free, Cute and Size Fourteen; The Steam Is on the Beam/W: George Marion, Jr., M: Johnny Green.

4222. Dan (Daniel) Healy (Nov. 3, 1888– Sept. 1, 1969) B: Rochester, NY. M: HELEN KANE. The song and dance man of the 1920s was known as Broadway's Boy and the Night Mayor of Broadway. *A World of Pleasure* (Win-

ter Garden, revue, CR, Jan. 3, 1916): Fifth Avenue/W: Harold Atteridge, M: Sigmund Romberg. *Yip, Yip, Yaphank* (Century > Lexington, revue, Aug. 19, 1918): Mandy/WM: Irving Berlin. *The Sweetheart Shop* (Knickerbocker, "Freddie," Aug. 31, 1920): The Dresden China Belle; Oh, Mr. Postman; Ring Those June Bells/W: Anne Caldwell, M: Hugo Felix. *Adrienne* (George M. Cohan, "Bob Gordon," May 28, 1923): Cheer Up; Dance with Me; The Hindoo Hop/W: A. Seymour Brown, M: Albert Von Tilzer. *Plain Jane* (New Amsterdam, "Happy Williams," May 12, 1924): Come On Feet, Let's Go; Puttin' on the Ritz/W: Phil Cook, M: Tom Johnstone. *Betsy* (New Amsterdam, "Moe," Dec. 28, 1926): The Kitzel Engagement/W: Lorenz Hart, M: Richard Rodgers. *Good Boy* (Hammerstein's, "Bobby Darnell," Sept. 5, 1928): I Wanna Be Loved by You; Manhattan Walk; Oh, What a Man/W: Bert Kalmar, M: Harry Ruby, Herbert Stothart.

4223. Mary Healy (Apr. 14, 1918–) B: New Orleans, LA. M: PETER LIND HAYES. Teamed with her husband on 1950s radio and TV shows. *Count Me In* (Ethel Barrymore, "Sherry," Oct. 8, 1942): We're Still on the Map; The Woman of the Year; You've Got It All/WM: Ann Ronell. *Around the World in Eighty Days* (Adelphi, "Mrs. Aouda," May 31, 1946): The Marine's Hymn/W: Henry C. Davis, M: based on Jacques Offenbach — Should I Tell You I Love You/WM: Cole Porter.

4224. Ted Healy (Oct. 1, 1896–Dec. 19, 1937) B: Houston, TX. Vaudeville comedian who originated the idea of the Three Stooges in slapstick comedy sketches. Moe and Shemp Howard, his childhood friends, and Larry Fine, were the first Stooges. In 1930, Healy was paid $6,000 a week to headline at the New York Palace, but he died penniless. *The Gang's All Here* (Imperial, "Dr. Indian Ike Kelly," Feb. 18, 1931): Adorable Julie/W: Owen Murphy, Robert A. Simon, M: Lewis E. Gensler. *Crazy Quilt* (44th Street, revue, May 19, 1931): I Found a Million Dollar Baby (in a Five and Ten Cent Store)/W: Mort Dixon, Billy Rose, M: Harry Warren — I Want to Do a Number with the Boys/W: Ned Wever, M: Rowland Wilson — It's in the Air/W: E.Y. Harburg, Billy Rose, M: Louis Alter.

4225. George Hearn (June 18, 1934–) B: St. Louis, MO. *1776* (46th Street, CR, "John Dickinson," Aug. 30, 1971): Cool, Cool, Considerate Men/WM: Sherman Edwards. *I Remember Mama* (Majestic, "Papa," May 31, 1979): A Little Bit More/W: Raymond Jessel, M: Richard Rodgers — You Could Not Please Me

More/W: Martin Charnin, M: Richard Rodgers. *Sweeney Todd, the Demon Barber of Fleet Street* (Uris, CR, "Sweeney Todd, "Mar. 4, 1980): The Barber and His Wife; Epiphany; Final Sequence; God, That's Good!; Johanna; A Little Priest; My Friends; No Place Like London; Pirelli's Miracle Elixir; Pretty Women/WM: Stephen Sondheim. *A Doll's Life* (Mark Hellinger, "Johan," Sept. 23, 1982): At Last; New Year's Eve; There She Is; You Interest Me/W: Betty Comden, Adolph Green, M: Larry Grossman. *La Cage aux Folles* (Palace, "Albin," Aug. 21, 1983/Oct. 22, 1984): The Best of Times; I Am What I Am; La Cage aux Folles; A Little More Mascara; Masculinity; Song on the Sand; With You on My Arm/WM: Jerry Herman. *Meet Me in St. Louis* (Gershwin, "Alonzo Smith," Nov. 2, 1989): A Day in New York; Paging Mr. Sousa; Wasn't It Fun?/WM: Hugh Martin, Ralph Blane. *Sunset Boulevard* (Minskoff, "Max von Mayerling," Nov. 17, 1994): The Greatest Star of All; New Ways to Dream/W: Don Black, Christopher Hampton, M: Andrew Lloyd Webber.

4226. Lew Hearn (Feb. 15, 1882–Feb. 1965) B: Poland. Great comic straight man of vaudeville. *Suzi* (Casino > Shubert, "Herr Horn," Nov. 3, 1914): Heaven Measured You for Me; The Match Makers; Secrets/W: Otto Harbach, M: Aladar Renyi — Teenie-Eenie-Weenie/W: Otto Harbach, M: Paul Lincke. *Make It Snappy* (Winter Garden, revue, Apr. 13, 1922): Good-Bye Main Street; (Tell Me What's the Matter) Loveable Eyes/W: Harold Atteridge, M: Jean Schwartz. *Innocent Eyes* (Winter Garden, revue, May 20, 1924): Damn Clever, These Chinese/WM: ?—Innocent Eyes/W: McElbert Moore, M: J. Fred Coots, Jean Schwartz. *Lady Do* (Liberty, "Pat Perkins," Apr. 18, 1927): Little Miss Small Town/W: Sam M. Lewis, Joe Young, M: Abel Baer.

4227. Roma Hearn *Anne of Green Gables* (City Center 55th Street, "Mrs. Blewett" and "Miss Stacy," Dec. 21, 1971): The Facts /WM: Donald Harron, Norman Campbell.

4228. Sam Hearn (c 1889–1964) *Spice of 1922* (Winter Garden, revue, July 6, 1922): Two Little Wooden Shoes/W: Jack Stanley, M: James F. Hanley. *Mercenary Mary* (Longacre, "Grandpa Skinner," Apr. 13, 1925): They Still Look Good to Me/WM: William B. Friedlander, Con Conrad. *The Greenwich Village Follies of 1925* (46th Street, revue, Dec. 24, 1925): The Window Cleaners/W: Bert Kalmar, M: Harry Ruby — Wouldn't You? [Mar. 15, 1926]/WM: Owen Murphy. *Good Boy* (Hammerstein's, "Pa Meakin," Sept. 5, 1928): Down in Arkansas; I

Have My Moments; I Wanna Be Loved by You/W: Bert Kalmar, M: Harry Ruby, Herbert Stothart.

4229. Nan C. Hearne *This Year of Grace* (Selwyn, revue, Nov. 7, 1928): Mother's Complaint/WM: Noel Coward.

4230. D. Michael Heath (Sept. 22, 1953–) B: Cincinnati, OH. *Starlight Express* (Gershwin, "Hashamoto," Mar. 15, 1987): First Final; Race Two/W: Richard Stilgoe, M: Andrew Lloyd Webber.

4231. Dody Heath (Aug. 3, 1928–) B: Seattle, WA. *A Tree Grows in Brooklyn* (Alvin, "Hildy," Apr. 19, 1951): Love Is the Reason; Mine Till Monday/W: Dorothy Fields, M: Arthur Schwartz.

4232. Frankie Heath *The Passing Show of 1919* (Winter Garden, revue, Oct. 23, 1919): So Long, Sing Song Girl/W: Harold Atteridge, M: Sigmund Romberg — Tumble Inn/W: Harold Atteridge, M: Jean Schwartz. *The Greenwich Village Follies of 1922* (Shubert, revue, Sept. 12, 1922): A Chauve-Souris of Our Own/WM: Irving Caesar — Manhattan Nights/W: Irving Caesar, John Murray Anderson, M: Louis A. Hirsch.

4233. Ray Heatherton (c 1909–Aug. 15, 1997) B: New Jersey. Father of singer dancer Joey Heatherton. He was a big band singer in the 1930s and 40s and *The Merry Mailman* on TV in the 1950s. *The Garrick Gaieties of 1930* (Guild, revue, June 4, 1930): Johnny Wanamaker/W: Paul James, M: Kay Swift. *Babes in Arms* (Shubert > Majestic, "Val Lamar," Apr. 14, 1937): All at Once; Babes in Arms; Where or When/W: Lorenz Hart, M: Richard Rodgers.

4234. Peggy Heavens *Parisiana* (Edyth Totten, revue, Feb. 9, 1928): Who Wouldn't?/WM: Vincent Valentini.

4235. Rich Hebert (Dec. 14, 1956–) B: Quincy, MA. *Rock 'n Roll! The First 5,000 Years* (St. James, revue, Oct. 24, 1982): American Pie/WM: Don McLean — Good Vibrations/WM: Mike Love, Brian Wilson — Stayin' Alive/WM: Barry Gibb, Maurice Gibb, Robin Gibb.

4236. Paul Hecht (Aug. 16, 1941–) B: London, England. *1776* (46th Street, "John Dickinson," Mar. 16, 1969): Cool, Cool, Considerate Men/WM: Sherman Edwards. *The Rothschilds* (Lunt-Fontanne, "Nathan Rothschild," Oct. 19, 1970): Bonds; Everything; I'm in Love! I'm in Love!; Rothschild & Sons; This Amazing London Town/W: Sheldon Harnick, M: Jerry Bock.

4237. F. Stanton Heck *A Parisian Model* (Broadway, CR, "Hercule," Dec. 10, 1906): The Gibson Girl/W: Harry B. Smith, M: Max Hoffmann. *The Little Cafe* (New Amsterdam, "Col.

Klink," Nov. 10, 1913): The Beauty Contest/W: C.M.S. McLellan, M: Ivan Caryll. *Katinka* (Lyric, CR, "Arif Bey," Aug. 16, 1916): Skidiski-schatch/W: Otto Harbach, M: Rudolf Friml.

4238. Eileen Heckart (Mar. 29, 1919–Jan. 31, 2001) B: Columbus OH. Solid character actress with a longtime career on stage, screen and TV. *Pal Joey* (New York City Center, revival, "Melba Snyder," May 31, 1961): Zip/W: Lorenz Hart, M: Richard Rodgers. *A Family Affair* (Billy Rose, "Tilly Siegal," Jan. 27, 1962): Beautiful; Harmony; I'm Worse Than Anybody; Kalua Bay; My Son, the Lawyer; Summer Is Over/W: James Goldman, William Goldman, M: John Kander.

4239. Florence Hedges *Up in the Clouds* (Lyric, "Louise," Jan. 2, 1922): Passing of Six Months/W: Will B. Johnstone, M: Tom Johnstone. *I'll Say She Is* (Casino, "Social Secretary," May 19, 1924): Give Me a Thrill; Glimpses of the Moon; Pretty Girl; San Toy; The Wonderful Nile/W: Will B. Johnstone, M: Tom Johnstone.

4240. Charles Hedley *Three Little Girls* (Shubert, "Hendrik Norgard" and "Karl Norgard," Apr. 14, 1930): A Lesson in Letter Writing; Love's Happy Dream/W: Harry B. Smith, M: Walter Kollo.

4241. John Heffernan (May 30, 1934–) B: New York, NY. *Purlie* (Broadway, "Ol' Cap'n," Mar. 15, 1970): Big Fish, Little Fish/W: Peter Udell, M: Gary Geld.

4242. Marta Heflin (May 29, 1945–) B: Washington, D.C. *Hair* (Biltmore, CR, "Sheila," Mar. 1971): Easy to Be Hard; Good Morning, Starshine; I Believe in Love; Let the Sunshine In (The Flesh Failures)/W: Gerome Ragni, James Rado, M: Galt MacDermot. *Jesus Christ Superstar* (Mark Hellinger, CR, "Mary Magdalene," Apr. 17, 1972): Could We Start Again, Please; Everything's Alright; I Don't Know How to Love Him; Peter's Denial; What's the Buzz/W: Tim Rice, M: Andrew Lloyd Webber.

4243. Alice Hegeman *The Pink Lady* (New Amsterdam, "Mme. Dondidier," Mar. 13, 1911): Donny Didn't, Donny Did/W: C.M.S. McLellan, M: Ivan Caryll. *Miss Daisy* (Shubert > Lyric, "Anastasia," Sept. 9, 1914): Interruptions; You Can't Stop Me from Thinking/W: Philip Bartholomae, M: Silvio Hein.

4244. Loulou Hegoburu *A Night in Paris* (Casino de Paris, Century roof, revue, Jan. 5, 1926): Powder Puff/W: Clifford Grey, McElbert Moore, M: J. Fred Coots, Maurie Rubens.

4245. Althea Heinly *Three Cheers* (Globe, CR, "Floria Vance," Mar. 4, 1929): The Amer-icans Are Here/W: B.G. DeSylva, M: Ray Henderson — Because You're Beautiful/W: B.G. DeSylva, Lew Brown, M: Ray Henderson — My Silver Tree/W: Anne Caldwell, M: Raymond Hubbell. *Ripples* (New Amsterdam, "Mrs. John Pillsbury," Feb. 11, 1930): Gentlemen of the Press/W: Irving Caesar, Graham John, M: Oscar Levant, Albert Sirmay.

4246. Ann Heinricher *A Chorus Line* (Shubert, CR, "Maggie," Aug. 1984): At the Ballet/W: Edward Kleban, M: Marvin Hamlisch.

4247. Helen Heins *Hip! Hip! Hooray!* (Music Hall, revue, CR, "Tootsie Tripper,"1907): The Frolics of Pierrot; Let's Wander Off Nowhere; Little Tootsie Tripper/W: Edgar Smith, M: Gus Edwards.

4248. Elisa Heinsohn (Oct. 11, 1962–) B: Butler, PA. *The Phantom of the Opera* (Majestic, "Meg Giry," Jan. 26, 1988): Angel of Music; Magical Lasso; Notes; Prima Donna/W: Charles Hart, Richard Stilgoe, M: Andrew Lloyd Webber.

4249. Anna Held (Mar. 18, 1865–Aug. 13, 1918) B: Warsaw, Poland. She grew up in Paris. M: producer Florenz Ziegfeld, 1897-1913. One of the most popular and highly paid stars of her time; at her death, thousands crowded into services at St. Patrick's Cathedral in New York. *The Little Duchess* (Casino, "The Little Duchess" and "Claire de Brion," Oct. 14, 1901): Chloe, I'm Waiting; A Dip in the Ocean; Make Allowances for Love/W: Harry B. Smith, M: Reginald De Koven — The Maiden with the Dreamy Eyes/W: James Weldon Johnson, M: Bob Cole — Pretty Mollie Shannon (She's the Real, Real Thing)/W: George H. Ryan, M: Walter Wolfe — Sadie/W: J.P. Barrington, M: Leo LeBrunn — Those Great Big Eyes/W: Harry B. Smith, M: Leo LeBrunn. *Mam'selle Napoleon* (Knickerbocker, "Mlle. Mars," Dec. 8, 1903): The A La Mode Girl; The Art of Stimulation; The Cockatoo and the Chimpanzee; Flowers, Feathers, Ribbons and Laces; I'll Love You Then as Now; The Language of Love; The Lion and the Mouse; Queen of the Comedie Francaise; The Two Dolls and the Glory of France/W: Joseph W. Herbert, M: Gustav Luders. *Higgledy-Piggledy* (Weber Music Hall, "Mimi de Chartreuse," Oct. 20, 1904): A Game of Love; Nancy Clancy/W: Edgar Smith, M: Maurice Levi. *A Parisian Model* (Broadway, "Anna," Nov. 27, 1906): Be My Little Teddy Bear/W: Vincent Bryan, M: Max Hoffman — A Gown for Each Hour of the Day/W: Harry B. Smith, M: Max Hoffmann — I Just Can't Make My Eyes Behave/W: Will D. Cobb, M: Gus Edwards — It's Delightful to Be Married/W:

Anna Held, M: Vincent Scotto — Kiss, Kiss, Kiss (If You Want to Learn to Kiss Me)/W: Harry B. Smith, M: Gertrude Hoffmann. *Miss Innocence* (New York, "Anna," Nov. 30, 1908): I Have Lost My Little Brown Bear (I Have Lost My Teddy Bear)/WM: Bob Cole, J. Rosamond Johnson — I Wonder What's the Matter with My Eyes; We Two in an Aeroplane/W: Harry Williams, M: Egbert Van Alstyne — I'm Learning Something Every Day/WM: Nora Bayes, Jack Norworth — Please Tell Me What They Mean/W: Harry B. Smith, M: Ludwig Englander. *Follow Me* (Casino, "Claire La Tour," Nov. 29, 1916): Adam Was the Only Lover; Stop Tickling Me/W: Robert B. Smith, M: Sigmund Romberg — Follow Me/WM: Helen Trix — I Want to Be Good but My Eyes Won't Let Me/W: Alfred Bryan, Anna Held, M: Harry Tierney — My Bohemian Fashion Girl/W: Alfred Bryan, M: Harry Tierney.

4250. Lillian Held *Yours Is My Heart* (Shubert, "Princess Mi," Sept. 5, 1946): Chingo-Pingo; Ma Petite Cherie (The Land of Smiles); Men of China/W: Karl Farkas, Ira Cobb, Harry Graham, M: Franz Lehar.

4251. Vera Hellaire *Letty Pepper* (Vanderbilt, "Corolie Van Ness," Apr. 10, 1922): Dope Song/W: Leo Wood, Irving Bibo, M: Werner Janssen.

4252. George Heller *The Grand Street Follies of 1928* (Booth, revue, May 28, 1928): Briny Blues/W: Agnes Morgan, M: Serge Walter. *The Grand Street Follies of 1929* (Booth, revue, May 1, 1929): Rome Is Burning/W: Agnes Morgan, M: Arthur Schwartz. *The Threepenny Opera* (Empire, "Legend Singer," Apr. 13, 1933): Legend of Mackie Messer/W: Bertolt Brecht, M: Kurt Weill.

4253. Jackie Heller *Yokel Boy* (Majestic, "Spud," July 6, 1939): A Boy Named Lem (and a Girl Named Sue); Hollywood and Vine; I Can't Afford to Dream; It's Me Again/W: Lew Brown, Charles Tobias, M: Sam H. Stept.

4254. Marc Heller *The Sound of Music* (New York State, revival, "Rolf Gruber," Mar. 8, 1990): Sixteen, Going on Seventeen/W: Oscar Hammerstein II, M: Richard Rodgers.

4255. Randee Heller *Hurry, Harry* (Ritz, "Helena" and "Native No. 4," Oct. 12, 1972): Africa Speaks; When a Man Cries/W: David Finkle, M: Bill Weeden. *Grease* (Broadhurst, CR, "Betty Rizzo," May 1974): Freddy, My Love; Look at Me, I'm Sandra Dee; There Are Worse Things I Could Do/WM: Jim Jacobs, Warren Casey.

4256. Bonnie Hellman (Jan. 10, 1950–) B: San Francisco, CA. *The Utter Glory of Morrissey*

Hall (Mark Hellinger, "Angela," May 13, 1979): Oh, Sun; You Will Know When the Time Has Arrived/WM: Clark Gesner.

4257. June Helmers (Oct. 21, 1941–) B: Middletown, OH. *Hello, Dolly!* (St. James, CR, "Irene Molloy," Apr. 1967/Dec. 26, 1969): Dancing; It Only Takes a Moment; Ribbons Down My Back/WM: Jerry Herman — Elegance; Motherhood/WM: Bob Merrill, Jerry Herman. *Johnny Johnson* (Edison, revival, "French Nurse," Apr. 11, 1971): Mon Ami, My Friend/W: Paul Green, M: Kurt Weill. *Tricks* (Alvin, "Zerbinetta," Jan. 8, 1973): Gypsy Girl; How Sweetly Simple/W: Lonnie Burstein/M: Jerry Blatt.

4258. Tom Helmore (Jan. 4, 1912–1995) B: London, England. *The Day Before Spring* (National, "Gerald Barker," Nov. 22, 1945): Friends to the End/W: Alan Jay Lerner, M: Frederick Loewe. *My Fair Lady* (Mark Hellinger, CR, "Henry Higgins," Aug. 17, 1956): A Hymn to Him; I'm an Ordinary Man; I've Grown Accustomed to Her Face; The Rain in Spain; Why Can't the English?; You Did It/W: Alan Jay Lerner, M: Frederick Loewe.

4259. Victor R. Helou *Something More!* (Eugene O'Neill, "Tony Santini" and "Luigi," Nov. 10, 1964): Bravo, Bravo, Novelisto; Don't Make a Move/W: Marilyn Bergman, Alan Bergman, M: Sammy Fain. *Kiss Me, Kate* (New York City Center, revival, "Second Man," May 12, 1965): Brush Up Your Shakespeare/WM: Cole Porter.

4260. Percy Helton (Jan. 31, 1894–Sept. 11, 1971) B: New York, NY. In Hollywood from 1937, he appeared in more than 200 movies. On the TV sitcom *The Beverly Hillbillies* (1968) he played Homer Crachit. *Happy* (Earl Carroll > Daly's, "Siggy Sigler," Dec. 5, 1927): If You'll Put Up with Me; Sunny Side of You; The Younger Generation/W: Earle Crooker, McElbert Moore, M: Frank Grey.

4261. Carl Hemmer *The O'Brien Girl* (Liberty, "Gerald Morgan," Oc.t 3, 1921): Learn to Smile; That O'Brien Girl/W: Otto Harbach, M: Louis A. Hirsch.

4262. Aida Hemmi *The Knickerbocker Girl* (Herald Square, "Roxie," June 15, 1903): Devotion; I Wouldn't, Would You?; Pretty Polly Primrose/W: George Totten Smith, M: Alfred E. Aarons. *The Jersey Lily* (Victoria, "Sara de Vries," Sept. 14, 1903): Dreaming, Dreaming (The Moon Song); Sweetheart Mine/W: George V. Hobart, M: Reginald De Koven.

4263. Sherman Hemsley (Feb. 1, 1938–) B: Philadelphia, PA. He played George Jefferson in the TV sitcom *All in the Family* (1973) and on *The Jeffersons* (1975). *Purlie* (Broadway, "Gitlow," Mar. 15, 1970): The Harder They Fall; Skinnin' a Cat/W: Peter Udell, M: Gary Geld. *Purlie* (Billy Rose, revival, "Gitlow," Dec. 27, 1972): same as above.

4264. Winston DeWitt Hemsley (May 21, 1947–May 9, 1989) B: Brooklyn, NY. The actor, dancer, choreographer was found beaten to death in his Las Vegas home. *Hello, Dolly!* (St. James, CR, "Barnaby Tucker," Nov. 12, 1967): Dancing; Put on Your Sunday Clothes/WM: Jerry Herman — Elegance; Motherhood/WM: Bob Merrill, Jerry Herman. *Rockabye Hamlet* (Minskoff, "Guildenstern," Feb. 17, 1976): Have I Got a Girl for You; Hey…!/WM: Cliff Jones. *A Chorus Line* (Shubert, CR, "Richie," Apr. 26, 1976): And…/W: Edward Kleban, M: Marvin Hamlisch. *Eubie!* (Ambassador, revue, CR, July 1979): Dixie Moon; If You've Never Been Vamped by a Brownskin, You've Never Been Vamped at All; I'm Just Wild About Harry; There's a Million Little Cupids in the Sky/W: Noble Sissle, M: Eubie Blake — You've Got to Git the Gittin While the Gittin's Good/W: Flournoy E. Miller, M: Eubie Blake.

4265. Percy Hemus (?–Dec. 22, 1943) *The Love Song* (Century, CR, "Col. Bugeaud," Feb. 16, 1925): Follow the Flag We Love; Soldiers When Your Country Needs You/W: Harry B. Smith, M: Edward Kunneke, Jacques Offenbach.

4266. Robert Hendersen *Candide* (Broadway, revival, "Servant" and "Agent of Inquisition" and "Spanish Don" and "Cartagenian Sailor," Mar. 10, 1974): I Am Easily Assimilated; O Miserere/W: Richard Wilbur, M: Leonard Bernstein.

4267. Florence Henderson (Feb. 14, 1934–) B: Dale, IN. Appealing singer and actress. She played Carol Brady on the TV sitcom *The Brady Bunch* (1967). *Oklahoma!* (New York City Center, revival, "Laurey Williams," Aug. 31, 1953): Many a New Day; Oh, What a Beautiful Mornin'; Oklahoma!; Out of My Dreams; People Will Say We're in Love; The Surrey with the Fringe on Top/W: Oscar Hammerstein II, M: Richard Rodgers. *Fanny* (Majestic, "Fanny," Nov. 4, 1954): Be Kind to Your Parents; Fanny; Happy Birthday Song (Nursery Round); I Have to Tell You; The Thought of You/WM: Harold Rome. *The Girl Who Came to Supper* (Broadway, "Mary Morgan," Dec. 8, 1963): The Coconut Girl; Coronation Chorale (Westminster Abbey); Here and Now; I've Been Invited to a Party; Paddy MacNeil and His Automobile; Six Lillies of the Valley; Soliloquies; Swing Song;

This Time It's True Love; The Walla Walla Boola; Welcome to Pootzie Van Doyle/WM: Noel Coward. *South Pacific* (Music Theater of Lincoln Center, revival, "Ensign Nellie Forbush," June 12, 1967): A Cockeyed Optimist; Honey Bun; I'm Gonna Wash That Man Right Outa My Hair; Some Enchanted Evening; Twin Soliloquies (Wonder How I'd Feel); A Wonderful Guy/W: Oscar Hammerstein II, M: Richard Rodgers.

4268. Isabel Henderson *Gypsy Blonde* (Lyric, "Arline," June 25, 1934): Come with the Gypsy Bride; I Dreamt I Dwelt in Marble Halls; I'm a Gypsy Blonde; In the Gypsy's Life; Ombo/W: Frank Gabrielson, M: Michael Balfe.

4269. Jack Henderson (c 1878–Jan. 1, 1957) B: Syracuse, NY. *Fad and Folly [orig. Tommy Rot]* (Mrs. Osborn's Playhouse, "Eric Leicester," Nov. 27, 1902): My Kimona Queen/WM: Henry Blossom, Jr., William F. Peters. *The Girl Question* (Wallack's, "Harold Sears," Aug. 3, 1908): College Days; When Eyes Like Yours Looked Into Eyes Like Mine/W: Frank R. Adams, Will H. Hough, M: Joseph E. Howard. *Three Twins* (Herald Square > Majestic, CR, "Ned Moreland," Nov. 30, 1908): Little Miss Up-to-Date/W: Otto Harbach, M: Karl Hoschna. *The Summer Widowers* (Broadway, "Hunter Lamb," June 4, 1910): Flying High; There's No Place Like Home Boys When Your Wife Has Gone Away/W: Glen MacDonough, M: A. Baldwin Sloane. *The Happiest Night of His Life* (Criterion, "Tom Dawson," Feb. 20, 1911): The Fiddler Must Be Paid; The Happiest Night of His Life; Jane; A Joy Ride; Nectar for the Gods; Oh, What a Beautiful Morning/W: Junie McCree, M: Albert Von Tilzer. *The Pink Lady* (New Amsterdam, "Lucien Garidel," Mar. 13, 1911): Donny Didn't, Donny Did; The Duel; I'm Single for Six Weeks More (I'm Going to Be Married in June); The Intriguers/W: C.M.S. McLellan, M: Ivan Caryll. *Papa's Darling* (New Amsterdam, "Marcel du Parvis," Nov. 2, 1914): The Land of the Midnight Sun; Where Shall We Go for Our Honeymoon?; Who Cares?/W: Harry B. Smith, M: Ivan Caryll.

4270. Joe Henderson *Strut Miss Lizzie* (Times Square, revue, June 19, 1922): Breakin' the Leg; I Love Sweet Angeline; Mandy/WM: Henry Creamer, Turner Layton.

4271. Marcia Henderson (July 22, 1929–) B: Andover, MA. *Peter Pan* (Imperial, "Wendy," Apr. 24, 1950): My House; Peter, Peter; Who Am I?/WM: Leonard Bernstein.

4272. Melanie Henderson (Sept. 20, 1957–) B: New York, NY. *The Me Nobody Knows* (Helen

Hayes, "Rhoda," Dec. 18, 1970): Black; Robert, Alvin, Wendell and Jo Jo; Something Beautiful/W: Will Holt, M: Gary William Friedman.

4273. Rose Henderson *Yeah Man* (Park Lane, revue, May 26, 1932): The Spell of Those Harlem Nights/WM: Al Wilson, Charles Weinberg, Ken Macomber.

4274. A.H. Hendricks *Little Nemo* (New Amsterdam, "An Officer of the Continentals," Oct. 20, 1908): Remember the Old Continentals/W: Harry B. Smith, M: Victor Herbert.

4275. Ben Hendricks (July 5, 1868–Apr. 30, 1930) B: Buffalo, NY. Actor and playwright. *The Spring Maid* (Liberty, CR, "Prince Nepomuk," May 1, 1911): Interrupted Allegory; The Next May Be the Right/W: Robert B. Smith, M: Heinrich Reinhardt. *Miss Princess* (Park, "Baron Gustav von Vetter," Dec. 23, 1912): Behind the Scenes/W: Will Johnstone, M: Alexander Johnstone. *Little Simplicity* (Astor > 44th Street, "Sheik of Kudah," Nov. 4, 1918): Women/W: Rida Johnson Young, M: Augustus Barratt.

4276. John Hendricks (c 1872–Feb. 26, 1949) *The Isle of Spice* (Majestic, "Kashon," Aug. 23, 1904): Star of Fate/W: George E. Stoddard, M: Paul Schindler. *My Best Girl* (Park, "Col. Wellington Bollivar," Sept. 12, 1912): Howdy-Do/W: Clifton Crawford, M: A. Baldwin Sloane — Love and the Automobile/W: Rennold Wolf, M: Augustus Barratt. *Hello, Broadway!* (Astor, revue, "Mr. Wu," Dec. 25, 1914): Look Out for Mr. Wu/WM: George M. Cohan. *Cheer Up* (Hippodrome, revue, Aug. 23, 1917): Cheer Up, Liza!; Melody Land/W: John L. Golden, M: Raymond Hubbell. *The Girl from Home* (Globe, "Jose Dravo," May 3, 1920): Our Presidents/W: Frank Craven, M: Silvio Hein. *The Girl in the Spotlight* (Knickerbocker, "John Rawlins," July 12, 1920): A Savage I Remain/W: Robert B. Smith, M: Victor Herbert. *Sue, Dear* (Times Square, "Le Comte Emile Pouchez," July 10, 1922): Foolishment; That Samson and Delilah Melody/W: Bide Dudley, M: Frank Grey. *Gypsy Blonde* (Lyric, "Phillip Arnheim," June 25, 1934): The Heart Bow'd Down/W: Frank Gabrielson, M: Michael Balfe.

4277. Flora Hengler (July 29–Sept. 7, 1968) B: New York, NY. Sister of MAY HENGLER. *The Sleeping Beauty and the Beast* (Broadway, "Lord Jocelyn," Nov. 4, 1901): Let Them Go/W: J. Cheever Goodwin, M: Frederic Solomon, J.M. Glover. *The Runaways* (Casino, CR, "Amelie Heaves," Aug. 17, 1903): Pretty Maid Adelaide; Way Down South/W: Addison Burkhardt, M: Raymond Hubbell.

4278. May Hengler (May 2, 1884–Mar. 15, 1952) B: New York, NY. *The Sleeping Beauty and the Beast* (Broadway, "Flossie," Nov. 4, 1901): same as FLORA HENGLER. *The Runaways* (Casino, CR, "Mary McShane," Aug. 17, 1903): same as FLORA HENGLER.

4279. Andi Henig (May 6–) B: Washington, DC. *Big River: The Adventures of Huckleberry Finn* (Eugene O'Neill, "Joanna Wilkes," Apr. 25, 1985): You Oughta Be Here with Me/WM: Roger Miller.

4280. Marilu Henner (Apr. 6, 1952–) B: Chicago, IL. She played Elaine Nardo in the TV sitcom *Taxi* (1980) and Ava Evans Newton in *Evening Shade* (1990). *Grease* (Broadhurst, CR, "Marty"): Freddy, My Love/WM: Jim Jacobs, Warren Casey.

4281. Nina Hennessey (July 1, 1957–) B: Deven, CO. *Cats* (Winter Garden, CR, "Jellyorum" and "Griddlebone," June 22, 1992): Bustopher Jones; Growltiger's Last Stand; Gus: The Theater Cat; The Old Gumbie Cat/W: T.S. Eliot, M: Andrew Lloyd Webber.

4282. Amy N. Henning *Cats* (Winter Garden, CR, "Cassandra," c 1993): The Old Gumbie Cat/W: T.S. Eliot, M: Andrew Lloyd Webber.

4283. Doug Henning (May 3, 1947–Feb. 7, 2000) B: Winnipeg, Canada. *Merlin* (Mark Hellinger, "Merlin," Feb. 13, 1983): The Elements; He Who Knows the Way; It's About Magic; Put a Little Magic in Your Life; Something More/W: Don Black, M: Elmer Bernstein.

4284. Leo Henning *Snapshots of 1921* (Selwyn, revue, June 2, 1921): Deburau/W: Alex Gerber, M: Malvin F. Franklin — Futuristic Melody/W: E. Ray Goetz, M: George Gershwin — Sky High Bungalow/W: E. Ray Goetz, M: George Meyer. *Bringing Up Father* (Lyric, "Patsy Moore," Apr. 6, 1925): Wedding Chimes; When Dad Was Twenty-One; When It Gets Dark/W: R.F. Carroll, M: Seymour Furth, Leo Edwards. *Belmont Varieties* (Belmont, revue, Sept. 26, 1932): Hitting the New High; I Paused, I Looked, I Fell/W: Sam Bernard, Jr., Bobby Burk, M: Henry Lloyd — Something New and It's You/W: Mildred Kaufman, M: Alvin Kaufman.

4285. Henrietta *Murray Anderson's Almanac* (Erlanger's, revue, Aug. 14, 1929): The Almanac Covers/W: Edward Eliscu, M: Henry Sullivan — Educate Your Feet/W: Jack Yellen, M: Milton Ager — Tiller, Foster, Hoffman, Hale and Albertina Rasch/W: Henry Myers, M: Henry Sullivan.

4286. Bette (Betty) Henritze (May 23–) B: Betsy Lane, KY. *Here's Where I Belong* (Billy

Rose, "Mrs. Bacon," Mar. 3, 1968): Pulverize the Kaiser/W: Alfred Uhry, M: Robert Waldman.

4287. Deborah Henry (c 1952–Feb. 6, 1996) *A Chorus Line* (Shubert, CR, "Val," Oct. 1979/Feb. 1980/May1980): And...; Dance: Ten, Looks: Three/W: Edward Kleban, M: Marvin Hamlisch. *A Chorus Line* (Shubert, CR, "Cassie," Oct. 1980): The Music and the Mirror/W: Edward Kleban, M: Marvin Hamlisch.

4288. Eleanor Henry *Sweethearts* (Liberty, CR, "Liane," Dec. 1, 1913): Jeannette and Her Little Wooden Shoes; Smiles/W: Robert B. Smith, M: Victor Herbert. *The Girl from Utah* (Knickerbocker, "Dora Manners," Aug. 24, 1914): Dance with Me; Una; When We Meet the Mormon [Sept. 30, 1914]/W: Percy Greenbank, M: Paul Rubens — Only to You/WM: Paul Rubens. *90 in the Shade* (Knickerbocker, "Madge," Jan. 25, 1915): Courtship de Dance; I've Been About a Bit/WM: ? — Wonderful Days/WM: Clare Kummer. *A Lonely Romeo* (Shubert > Casino, "Kitty Blythe," June 10, 1919): Don't Do Anything Till You Hear from Me/W: Robert B. Smith, M: Malvin F. Franklin — Jolly Me; Leave It to Your Milliner/W: Robert B. Smith, M: Robert Hood Bowers. *Linger Longer Letty* (Fulton, "Nancy," Nov. 20, 1919): Did You, My Boy, Did You?/W: Bernard Grossman, M: Alfred Goodman.

4289. Hank Henry (July 6, 1906–Mar. 31, 1981) B: New York, NY. At the time he appeared in *This Is the Army*, he was serving as a Private in the U.S. Army. *This Is the Army* (Broadway, revue, July 4, 1942): This Is the Army, Mr. Jones/WM: Irving Berlin. *Kiss Me, Kate* (Broadway, revival, "First Man," Jan. 8, 1952): Brush Up Your Shakespeare/WM: Cole Porter.

4290. Jack F. Henry *Marriage a la Carte* (Casino, "Eustace Haws," Jan. 2, 1911): Toddle Go the Girls; When Zim, Zim Go the Cymbals/W: C.M.S. McLellan, M: Ivan Caryll.

4291. Sara Henry *Cats* (Winter Garden, CR, "Cassandra," c 1993): The Old Gumbie Cat/W: T.S. Eliot, M: Andrew Lloyd Webber.

4292. John E. Henshaw *The Man in the Moon* (New York, "Willie Bullion," Apr. 24, 1899): Liberty Hall; The Man in the Moon/W: Louis Harrison, Stanislaus Stange, M: Ludwig Englander. *The Sho-Gun* (Wallack's, CR, "William Henry Spangle," Feb. 2, 1905): The Games We Used to Play; The Irrepressible Yank; Love, You Must Be Blind; Schemes/W: George Ade, M: Gustav Luders. *Old Dutch* (Herald Square, "Leopold Mueller," Nov. 22, 1909): Pretending/W: George V. Hobart, M: Victor Herbert. *Some Party* (Al Jolson, revue, Apr. 15, 1922):

Minstrel Days/W: R.H. Burnside, M: Percy Wenrich.

4293. Dale Hensley (Apr. 9, 1954–) B: Nevada, MO. *Anything Goes* (Vivian Beaumont, revival, "Sailor"): There's No Cure Like Travel/WM: Cole Porter. *Guys and Dolls* (Martin Beck, revival, "Rusty Charlie," c 1993): Fugue for Tinhorns/WM: Frank Loesser. *Cats* (Winter Garden, CR, "Bustopher Jones" and "Asparagus" and "Growltiger"): Bustopher Jones; Growltiger's Last Stand; Gus: The Theater Cat/W: T.S. Eliot, M: Andrew Lloyd Webber. *Sunset Boulevard* (Minskoff, CR, "Manfred," Sept. 1995): The Lady's Paying/W: Don Black, Christopher Hampton, M: Andrew Lloyd Webber.

4294. Gladys Henson (Sept. 27, 1897–Jan. 1983) B: Dublin, Ireland. In movies from 1945, often playing motherly or grandmotherly characters. *Set to Music* (Music Box, revue, Jan. 18, 1939): Mad About the Boy/WM: Noel Coward.

4295. John Henson *The Most Happy Fella* (Imperial > Broadway, "Ciccio" and "Jake," May 3, 1956): Abbondanza; Benvenuta; Sposalizio; Standing on the Corner/WM: Frank Loesser.

4296. Katharine Hepburn (Nov. 9, 1907–) B: Hartford, CT. A megastar of the silver screen. *Coco* (Mark Hellinger, "Coco Chanel," Dec. 18, 1969): Always Mademoiselle; Coco; Mademoiselle Cliche de Paris; The Money Rings Out Like Freedom; On the Corner of the Rue Cambon; Ohrbach's, Bloomingdale's, Best and Saks; The Preparation; The World Belongs to the Young/W: Alan Jay Lerner, M: Andre Previn.

4297. Evelyn Herbert (1898–) B: Philadelphia, PA. M: ROBERT HALLIDAY. She sang opera in Chicago and New York before arriving on Broadway. *Stepping Stones* (Globe, "Lupina," Nov. 6, 1923): Babbling Babette; Because You Love the Singer; Once in a Blue Moon; Our Lovely Rose/W: Anne Caldwell, M: Jerome Kern. *The Love Song* (Century, "Herminie," Jan. 13, 1925): He Writes a Song/W: Harry B. Smith, M: Jacques Offenbach — In Gardens Where Roses Bloom; Not for a Year, Not for a Day; Tell Me Not That You Are Forgetting/W: Harry B. Smith, M: Edward Kunneke, Jacques Offenbach — Love Will Find You Some Day [Feb. 16, 1925]/W: Harry B. Smith, M: Edward Kunneke. *Princess Flavia* (Century, "Princess Flavia," Nov. 2, 1925): Convent Bells Are Ringing; I Dare Not Love You; Twilight Voices/W: Harry B. Smith, M: Sigmund Romberg. *The Merry World* (Imperial, revue, June 8, 1926): Beauty Adorned/W: Clifford Grey, M: J. Fred Coots, Maurie Rubens — Girofle-Girofla/W: Harry B. Smith, M: Charles Lecocq — Heroes of Yesterday/WM: ?—

Whispering Trees/W: Herbert Reynolds, M: J. Fred Coots — You and I (in Old Versailles)/W: B.G. DeSylva, M: George Gershwin, Jack Green. *My Maryland* (Al Jolson, "Barbara Frietchie," Sept. 12, 1927): Mother; Mr. Cupid; Old John Barleycorn; The Same Silver Moon; Something Old, Something New; Won't You Marry Me?; Your Land and My Land/W: Dorothy Donnelly, M: Sigmund Romberg. *The New Moon* (Imperial > Casino, "Marianne Beaunoir," Sept. 19, 1928): The Girl on the Prow; An Interrupted Love Song; Lover, Come Back to Me; Never for You; One Kiss Is Waiting for One Man; Wanting You/W: Oscar Hammerstein II, M: Sigmund Romberg. *Princess Charming* (Imperial, "Princess Elaine of Novia," Oct. 13, 1930): I'll Never Leave You; Palace of Dreams; Trailing a Shooting Star; You/W: Arthur Swanstrom, M: Arthur Schwartz, Albert Sirmay. *Melody* (Casino, "Paula de Laurier" and "Andree de Namours," Feb. 14, 1933): Give Me a Roll on the Drum; Good Friends Surround Me; I Am the Singer, You Are the Song; In My Garden; Melody; Tonight May Never Come Again/W: Irving Caesar, M: Sigmund Romberg. *Bitter Sweet* (44th Street, revival, "Marchioness of Shayne" and "Madame Sari Linden" and "Sarah Millick," May 7, 1934): The Call of Life; Dear Little Cafe; I'll See You Again; Peace Enfold You (Evermore and a Day); What Is Love?; Zigeuner/WM: Noel Coward.

4298. Joseph W. Herbert (Nov. 27, 1863–Feb. 18, 1923) B: Liverpool, England. Actor, playwright, author of librettos. *Aladdin, Jr.* (Broadway, "Ki Yi," Apr. 8, 1895): Beauteous Widow Bohea; An Emperor's Lot; The Stars Alone Can Tell; The Way He Arranges His Face; Women, Wine and Song/W: J. Cheever Goodwin, M: W. H. Batchelor. — Love Among the Freaks/W: Joseph W. Herbert, M: Gustave Kerker. *The Girl from Paris* (Herald Square, "Auguste Pompier," Dec. 8, 1896): Cock-a-doodle; I'm All the Way from Gay Paree; Tootle, Tootle/W: George Dance, M: Ivan Caryll. *The Little Duchess* (Casino, "Maurice de Champignon," Oct. 14, 1901): The Man with the Tamborine/W: Harry B. Smith, M: Reginald De Koven. *Mam'selle Napoleon* (Knickerbocker, "Miche," Dec. 8, 1903): Life's No Blooming Airy Bubble; My Heart Will Be True to You (Too-Whoo); Out with the Boys!/W: Joseph W. Herbert, M: Gustav Luders. *It Happened in Nordland* (Lew Fields, "Duke of Toxen," Dec. 5, 1904): Tell It All/W: Glen MacDonough, M: Victor Herbert. *Mexicana* (Lyric, "Capt. Carmona," Jan. 29, 1906): How Do You Account

for That?/W: Robert B. Smith, M: Raymond Hubbell. *A Waltz Dream* (Broadway, "Prince Lothar," Jan. 27, 1908): Two Is Plenty/W: Joseph W. Herbert, M: Oscar Straus. *The Baron Trenck* (Casino, "Marquis D'Aucuneterre," Mar. 11, 1912): When I Get Married/W: Henry Blossom, M: Alfred G. Robyn. *Oh, I Say!* (Casino, "Buzot," Oct. 30, 1913): A Woman's Heart/W: Harry B. Smith, M: Jerome Kern. *The Beauty Shop* (Astor, "Phil Farraday," Apr. 13, 1914): Come Along, Little Girl, Come Along; Give Us Your Kind Applause; The Sunshine Maxixe/W: Rennold Wolf, M: Charles J. Gebest — Love's Hesitation/W: Maurice E. Marks, M: Charles J. Gebest. *Odds and Ends of 1917* (Bijou > Norworth, revue, Nov. 19, 1917): Sister Susie Glide/W: Bide Dudley, Jack Norworth, M: James Byrnes — There's a Lovely Crop of Girls This Year/W: R.P. Weston, M: Jack Norworth.

4299. Joseph Herbert, Jr. *Tangerine* (Casino, "Fred Allen," Aug. 9, 1921): It's Great to Be Married (and Lead a Single Life)/W: Howard Johnson, M: Monte Carlo, Alma Sanders, Carle Carlton — Love Is a Business; South Sea Island Blues/W: Howard Johnson, M: Monte Carlo, Alma Sanders — Man Is the Lord of It All/W: Carle Carlton, M: Jean Schwartz.

4300. Tim Herbert (June 22, 1914–June 20, 1986) Son of HERMAN TIMBERG. *Follow the Girls* (New Century > 44th Street, "Spud Doolittle, Apr. 8, 1944): Thanks for a Lousy Evening; A Tree That Grows in Brooklyn/W: Dan Shapiro, Milton Pascal, M: Phil Charig.

4301. Victoria Herbert *George White's Scandals of 1921* (Liberty, revue, July 11, 1921): Drifting Along with the Tide; Where East Meets West/W: Arthur Jackson, M: George Gershwin.

4302. David Herblin *Yours Truly* (Shubert, "Phil," Jan. 25, 1927): Follow the Guide/W: Anne Caldwell, M: Raymond Hubbell.

4303. Jeff Herbst (Jan. 8, 1963–) B: Sioux Falls, SD. *A Change in the Heir* (Edison, "Princess Agnes," Apr. 29, 1990): Duet; A Fairy Tale; Happily Ever After, After All; I Tried and I Tried and I Tried; Look at Me; Take a Look at That/W: George H. Gorham, M: Dan Sticco.

4304. Wilson Jermaine Heredia (Dec. 2, 1971–) B: Brooklyn, NY. *Rent* (Nederlander, "Angel Schunard," Apr. 29, 1996): Happy New Year; I'll Cover You; Today 4 U; Voice Mail #3; You Okay Honey?; You'll See/WM: Jonathan Larson.

4305. Kathryn Hereford *Three Cheers* (Globe, "Wellington Westland," Oct. 15, 1928): Because You're Beautiful/W: B.G. DeSylva, Lew Brown, M: Ray Henderson. *Show Girl* (Ziegfeld,

"Bobby," July 2, 1929): So Are You!/W: Ira Gershwin, Gus Kahn, M: George Gershwin. *Ripples* (New Amsterdam, "Jane Martin," Feb. 11, 1930): I'm a Little Bit Fonder of You/WM: Irving Caesar. *Smiles* (Ziegfeld, "Pat," Nov. 18, 1930): Clever, These Chinese/W: Harold Adamson, Clifford Grey, M: Vincent Youmans.

4306. Frederic Heringes B: Santa Maria, CA. *The Phantom of the Opera* (Majestic, CR, "Ubaldo Piangi," c 1993): Notes; Prima Donna; Twisted Every Way/W: Charles Hart, Richard Stilgoe, M: Andrew Lloyd Webber.

4307. Lillian Herlein (Mar. 11, 1895–Apr. 13, 1971) *The Rose of Algeria* (Herald Square, "Zoradie," Sept. 20, 1909): The Lady Sleeps; Rose of the World (My Life I Love Thee); Twilight in Barakeesh/W: Glen MacDonough, M: Victor Herbert. *The Never Homes* (Broadway, "Mrs. Talkington Louder," Oct. 5, 1911): First Love Days/W: E. Ray Goetz, M: A. Baldwin Sloane — In the Shadows/W: E. Ray Goetz, M: Herman Finck.

4308. Eileen Herlie (Mar. 8, 1919–) B: Glasgow, Scotland. Mainly a stage actress, her first major screen success was as Gertrude opposite Laurence Olivier in *Hamlet* (1948). *Take Me Along* (Shubert, "Lily," Oct. 22, 1959): But Yours; I Get Embarrassed; Oh, Please; Promise Me a Rose; Take Me Along; We're Home/WM: Bob Merrill. *All American* (Winter Garden, "Elizabeth Hawkes-Bullock," Mar. 19, 1962): If I Were You; Once Upon a Time; Our Children; The Real Me/W: Lee Adams, M: Charles Strouse.

4309. Joy Hermalyn *Cyrano: The Musical* (Neil Simon, "Chaperone," Nov. 21, 1993): A Message from Roxane/W: Peter Reeves, Koen Van Dijk, add. W: Sheldon Harnick, M: Ad Van Dijk. *A Christmas Carol* (Paramount Madison Square Garden, "Mrs. Cratchit," Dec. 1, 1994): Christmas Together/W: Lynn Ahrens, M: Alan Menken. *A Christmas Carol* (Paramount Madison Square Garden, return engagement, "Mrs. Fezziwig," Nov. 20, 1995): Mr. Fezziwig's Annual Christmas Ball/W: Lynn Ahrens, M: Alan Menken. *A Christmas Carol* (Madison Square Garden, return engagement, "Mrs. Fezziwig," Nov. 22, 1996): same as above.

4310. Cynthia Herman (July 23, 1947–) B: Peoria, IL. *The Beggar's Opera* (Billy Rose, revival, "Polly Peachum," Dec. 22, 1973): Come Sweet Lass; Is Then His Fate Decreed, Sir?; No Power on Earth Can E'er Divide; O, What Pain It Is to Part; Our Polly Is a Sad Slut; The Turtle Thus with Plaintive Crying; Virgins Are Like the Fair Flower; Were I Laid on Greenland

Coast; Why How Now Madam Flirt; Would I Might Be Hanged/WM: John Gay.

4311. Danny Herman (Nov. 2, 1960–) B: Pittsburgh, PA. *A Chorus Line* (Shubert, CR, "Mike," Apr. 1983/c 1985/c 1988): I Can Do That/W: Edward Kleban, M: Marvin Hamlisch.

4312. George Herman *Criss Cross* (Globe, "The Curé," Oct. 12, 1926): The Ali Baba Babies/W: Anne Caldwell, Otto Harbach, M: Jerome Kern.

4313. Helene Herman *The Matinee Girl* (Forrest, "Lucy Peters," Feb. 1, 1926): The Biggest Thing in My Life/W: McElbert Moore, Bide Dudley, M: Frank Grey — Do I, Dear? I Do/WM: McElbert Moore.

4314. Garda Hermany *The Music Man* (New York City Center, revival, "Amaryllis," June 16, 1965): Piano Lesson/WM: Meredith Willson.

4315. Richard Hermany *The Golden Apple* (Alvin, CR, "Patroclus," Aug. 2, 1954): Come Along, Boys; Helen Is Always Willing; It Was a Glad Adventure/W: John Latouche, M: Jerome Moross.

4316. Harry Hermsen *The Lilac Domino* (44th Street, "Istvan," Oct. 28, 1914): Cupid Keeps the Love Light Burning/W: Robert B. Smith, M: Charles Cuvillier. *Enchanted Isle* (Lyric, "Enoch," Sept. 19, 1927): Jazz/WM: Ida Hoyt Chamberlain.

4317. Philip Hernandez (Dec. 12, 1959–) B: Queens, NY. *Les Miserables* (Broadway, CR, "Jean Valjean," c 1995): Bring Him Home; Come to Me; In My Life; Soliloquy; Thenardier Waltz; Who Am I?/W: Herbert Kretzmer, M: Claude-Michel Schonberg.

4318. Vivian Hernandez *South Pacific* (New York City Center, revival, "Ngana," Apr. 26, 1961): Dites-Moi/W: Oscar Hammerstein II, M: Richard Rodgers.

4319. Dorie Herndon *Starlight Express* (Gershwin, CR, "Volta," c 1987): AC/DC; First Final; Pumping Iron; Race Two; Wide Smile, High Style, That's Me/W: Richard Stilgoe, M: Andrew Lloyd Webber.

4320. Jan Leigh Herndon (Apr. 9, 1955–) B: Raleigh, NC. *A Chorus Line* (Shubert, CR, "Sheila," Sept. 1982): At the Ballet/W: Edward Kleban, M: Marvin Hamlisch.

4321. Edward Heron *The Pied Piper* (Majestic, "Sammy Struggles," Dec. 3, 1908): It All Depends/W: R.H. Burnside, M: Manuel Klein.

4322. John Herrera (Sept. 21, 1955–) B: Havana, Cuba. *The Mystery of Edwin Drood* (Imperial, "Neville Landless," Dec. 2, 1985): Ceylon; No Good Can Come from Bad/WM: Rupert Holmes. *Shogun: The Musical* (Marquis,

"Father Alvito," Nov. 20, 1990): Absolution; Assassination; How Nice to See You/W: John Driver, M: Paul Chihara.

4323. Ralph Herz (Mar. 25, 1878–July 12, 1921) B: Paris, France. M: LULU GLASER. *Miss Dolly Dollars* (Knickerbocker > New Amsterdam, "Finney Doolittle," Sept. 4, 1905): An Educated Fool; It Keeps Me Guessing All the Time/W: Harry B. Smith, M: Victor Herbert. *The White Hen* (Casino, "Erich Weiss," Feb. 16, 1907): Follow, Follow, Follow; Very Well Then/W: Paul West, M: Gustave Kerker. *Lola from Berlin* (Liberty, "Richard Winchester Chorttle," Sept. 16, 1907): I'd Sooner Be a Has-Been Than a Never Was at All; Signs/W: William Jerome, M: Jean Schwartz. *The Soul Kiss* (New York, "J. Lucifer Mephisto," Jan. 28, 1908): I Wonder Where They'll Go; There Were Actors Then; Very Well Then [Apr. 13, 1908]/W: Harry B. Smith, M: Maurice Levi — The Soul Kiss (Just for You from Above)/W: Lewis Gates, M: Maurice Levi — That Wasn't All/W: Addison Burkhardt, M: Louis A. Hirsch. *Madame Sherry* (New Amsterdam, "Theophilus Sherry," Aug. 30, 1910): The Smile She Means for You; We Are Only Poor Weak Mortals, After All/W: Otto Harbach, M: Karl Hoschna — You Can't Argue/WM: ?. *Dr. Deluxe* (Knickerbocker, "John Truesdale," Apr. 17, 1911): It's a Lie; No One But You!/W: Otto Harbach, M: Karl Hoschna — What We Want and What We Get/WM: Edward Laska. *The Whirl of the World* (Winter Garden, revue, "Marquis Tullyrand," Jan. 10, 1914): The Noble Cause of Art; The Whirl of the World/W: Harold Atteridge, M: Sigmund Romberg. *Hands Up* (44th Street, "Fake Kennedy," July 22, 1915): It's a Clue/W: E. Ray Goetz, M: Sigmund Romberg. *Good Night, Paul* (Hudson, "Paul Forster," Sept. 3, 1917): Nothing Seems Right, Oh! The World Is All Wrong/W: Roland Oliver, Charles Dickson, M: Harry B. Olsen. *Always You* (Central, "Montmorency Jones," Jan. 5, 1920): My Pousse-Cafe; Woman/W: Oscar Hammerstein II, M: Herbert Stothart.

4324. Kimberly Hester *The Will Rogers Follies* (Palace, CR, "Ziegfeld's Favorite," May 4, 1993): Will-a-Mania/W: Betty Comden, Adolph Green, M: Cy Coleman.

4325. Barbara Heuman (Feb. 24, 1944–) B: Montrose, PA. *No, No, Nanette* (46th Street, revival, CR, "Nanette," Dec. 1972): I Want to Be Happy; Tea for Two/W: Irving Caesar, M: Vincent Youmans — I've Confessed to the Breeze; No, No, Nanette; Peach on the Beach; Waiting for You/W: Otto Harbach, M: Vincent Youmans.

4326. John Hewer (Jan. 13, 1922–) B: London, England. *The Boy Friend* (Royale, "Tony," Sept. 30, 1954): I Could Be Happy with You; A Room in Bloomsbury/WM: Sandy Wilson.

4327. Christopher Hewett (Apr. 5, 1922–Aug. 3, 2001) B: Worthing, Sussex, England. He played Lawrence on the TV drama *Fantasy Island* (1983), and starred in the sitcom *Mr. Belvedere* (1985). *First Impressions* (Alvin, "Collins," Mar. 19, 1959): Fragrant Flower; Wasn't It a Simply Lovely Wedding?/WM: Robert Goldman, Glenn Paxton, George Weiss. *Kean* (Broadway, "Barnaby," Nov. 2, 1961): Chime In!; The Fog and the Grog; Fracas at Old Drury; King of London; Queue at Drury Lane/WM: Robert Wright, George Forrest. *The Sound of Music* (New York City Center, revival, "Max Detweiler," Apr. 26, 1967): How Can Love Survive?; No Way to Stop It/W: Oscar Hammerstein II, M: Richard Rodgers. *Music Is* (St. James, "Malvolio," Dec. 20, 1976): I Am It/W: Will Holt, M: Richard Adler. *Peter Pan, or The Boy Who Wouldn't Grow Up* (Lunt-Fontanne, revival, CR, "Captain Hook," Oct. 17, 1979): Another Princely Scheme (Tarantella); Pirate Song; A Princely Scheme (Hook's Tango)/W: Carolyn Leigh, M: Moose Charlap — Captain Hook's Waltz; Mysterious Lady/W: Betty Comden, Adolph Green, M: Jule Styne.

4328. Peggy Hewett (c 1946–Mar. 1, 2002) *A Day in Hollywood/A Night in the Ukraine* (John Golden > Royale, "Mrs. Pavlenko," May 1, 1980): Doin' the Production Code; A Night in the Ukraine/W: Dick Vosburgh, M: Frank Lazarus — Double Trouble/W: Leo Robin, M: Ralph Rainger, Richard A. Whiting — Just Go to the Movies; Nelson/WM: Jerry Herman — On the Good Ship Lollipop/W: Sidney Clare, M: Richard A. Whiting.

4329. Edmund Hewitt *The Cradle Will Rock* (Mansfield > Broadway, revival, "Prof. Mamie," Dec. 26, 1947): Triple Flank Maneuver/WM: Marc Blitzstein.

4330. Georgiana Hewitt (?–Feb. 20, 1923) *Frank Fay's Fables* (Park, revue, Feb. 6, 1922): Fables (Don't Believe Their Fables); That Swanee River Melody; Two Are One (You Need Two Souls but One Thought)/WM: Frank Fay, Clarence Gaskill.

4331. David Hibbard (June 21, 1965–) *Cats* (Winter Garden, CR, "Rum Tum Tugger," Sept. 20, 1993): Mr. Mistoffolees; Old Deuteronomy; Rum Tum Tugger/W: T.S. Eliot, M: Andrew Lloyd Webber. *Once Upon a Mattress* (Broadhurst, revival, "Jester," Dec. 19, 1996): The Minstrel, the Jester and I; Normandy; Very

Soft Shoes/W: Marshall Barer, M: Mary Rodgers.

4332. Edna Hibbard (1895–Dec. 26, 1942) B: California. *Rock-a-Bye Baby* (Astor, "Zoie Hardy," May 22, 1918): According to Dr. Holt; The Big Spring Drive; I Never Thought; My Own Light Infantry (Nursery Fanfare); Stitching, Stitching; There's No Better Use for Time Than Kissing/W: Herbert Reynolds, M: Jerome Kern. *Tumble Inn* (Selwyn, "Kitty McNair," Mar. 24, 1919): I've Told My Love; The Laugh; Serve It Only for Two; The Thoughts That I Wrote on the Leaves of My Heart; The Wedding Blues/W: Otto Harbach, M: Rudolf Friml. *Queen o' Hearts* (George M. Cohan, "Myra," Oct. 10, 1922): Dear Little Girlie/W: Nora Bayes, M: Dudley Wilkinson — A Long Time Ago/W: Morrie Ryskind, M: Lewis E. Gensler, Dudley Wilkinson — Marriage C.O.D./W: Oscar Hammerstein II, M: Lewis E. Gensler, Dudley Wilkinson — That's That/W: Nora Bayes, Harry Richman, M: Dudley Wilkinson.

4333. Edward Hibbert (Sept. 9, 1955–) B: New York, NY. *Me and My Girl* (Marquis, revival, CR, "Hon. Gerald Bolingbroke," Oct. 1987): The Sun Has Got His Hat On/W: Ralph Butler, M: Noel Gay — Thinking of No One but Me/W: Douglas Furber, M: Noel Gay.

4334. Geoffrey Hibbert (June 2, 1920–Feb. 3, 1969) B: Hull, Yorkshire, England. *The Boy Friend* (Royale, "Lord Brockhurst," Sept. 30, 1954): It's Never Too Late to Fall in Love/WM: Sandy Wilson.

4335. Eddie Hickey *The Mimic World* (Century roof, revue, Aug. 17, 1921): Any Night on Old Broadway/W: Harold Atteridge, M: Jean Schwartz.

4336. Louise Hickey *Mail* (Music Box, "Power Lady," Apr. 14, 1988): We're Gonna Turn Off Your Juice/W: Jerry Colker, M: Michael Rupert.

4337. William Hickey (Sept. 19, 1928–June 29, 1997) B: Brooklyn, NY. He taught acting for over 40 years. *The Body Beautiful* (Broadway, "Albert," Jan. 23, 1958): The Art of Conversation; Pffft!/W: Sheldon Harnick, M: Jerry Bock.

4338. Alfred Hickman (Feb. 25, 1872–Apr. 9, 1931): B: England. *Nancy Brown* (Bijou, "Vanderhyphen Jenks," Feb. 16, 1903): Cupid's Ramble /W: Bob Cole, James Weldon Johnson, M: J. Rosamond Johnson — A Little Birdie Told Me/W: Frederick Ranken, M: Henry Hadley. *The Orchid* (Herald Square, "Hon. Guy Scrymageour," Apr. 8, 1907): I Must Propose to You/WM: Paul Rubens — Oh, Mr. Registrar!/W: Percy Greenbank, M: Lionel Monckton.

4339. Darryl Hickman (July 28, 1930–) B: Hollywood, CA. A star at age 7, he appeared in more than 200 movies as a child. He later wrote for TV and became a programmer at CBS. *How to Succeed in Business Without Really Trying* (46th Street, CR, "J. Pierpont Finch," Oct. 7, 1963): Been a Long Day; Brotherhood of Man; The Company Way; Grand Old Ivy; How To; I Believe in You; Rosemary/WM: Frank Loesser. *Where's Charley?* (New York City Center, revival, "Charley Wykeham," May 25, 1966): Better Get Out of Here; Make a Miracle; The New Ashmoleon Marching Society and Students Conservatory Band; Once in Love with Amy; Pernambuco/WM: Frank Loesser.

4340. James Hickman (Feb. 12, 1932–) B: Beaver, UT. *I Can Get It for You Wholesale* (Shubert, "Tootsie Maltz," Mar. 22, 1962): What Are They Doing to Us Now?/WM: Harold Rome.

4341. D'Atra Hicks *Smokey Joe's Cafe* (Virginia, revue, CR, c 1996): Dance with Me; Fools Fall in Love; Hound Dog; I'm a Woman; Kansas City; Neighborhood; Saved; Some Cats Know/WM: Jerry Leiber, Mike Stoller.

4342. Kenneth Hicks *Treemonisha* (Palace, "Andy," Oct. 21, 1975): Abuse; Conjurer's Forgiven; Treemonisha's Return; We Will Trust You As Our Leader/WM: Scott Joplin.

4343. Leonard Hicks (Feb. 24, 1918–Aug. 8, 1971) He appeared with the NY Shakespeare Festival. *Naughty-Naught ['00]* (Old Knickerbocker Music Hall, revival, "Frank Plover," Oct. 19, 1946): Love Makes the World Go Round/W: Ted Fetter, M: Richard Lewine.

4344. Malcolm Hicks *Marjolaine* (Broadhurst, CR, "Punch and Judy Man," Feb. 6, 1922): Punch and Judy/W: Brian Hooker, M: Hugo Felix.

4345. Rodney Hicks (Mar. 28, 1974–) B: Philadelphia, PA. *Rent* (Nederlander, "Paul," Apr. 29, 1996): Life Support/WM: Jonathan Larson.

4346. Seymour Hicks (Jan. 30, 1871–Apr. 6, 1949) B: St. Helier's, Isle of Jersey. Actor, manager, playwright. *The Shop Girl* (Palmer's, "Charles Appleby," Oct. 28, 1895): And Her Golden Hair Was Hanging Down Her Back/W: Monroe H. Rosenfeld, M: Felix McGlennon.

4347. Shauna Hicks (Jan. 15, 1962–) B: Neenah, WI. *Blood Brothers* (Music Box, CR, "Linda," c 1993): Kids Game/WM: Willy Russell.

4348. Sue Hicks *Walk a Little Faster* (St. James, revue, Dec. 7, 1932): Where Have We Met Before?/W: E.Y. Harburg, M: Vernon Duke.

4349. Daniel Higgins *Merry-Go-Round* (Klaw, revue, May 31, 1927): If Love Should Come to Me; Sentimental Silly; Something Tells Me; Tampa/W: Howard Dietz, Morrie Ryskind, M: Henry Souvaine, Jay Gorney.

4350. Joel Higgins (Sept. 28, 1943–) B: Bloomington, IL. *Shenandoah* (Alvin, "James," Jan. 7, 1975): Next to Lovin' (I Like Fightin'); Violets and Silverbells/W: Peter Udell, M: Gary Geld. *Music Is* (St. James, "Sebastian," Dec. 20, 1976): Hate to Say Goodbye to You; Please Be Human/W: Will Holt, M: Richard Adler. *Angel* (Minskoff, "Ben Gant," May 10, 1978): A Dime Ain't Worth a Nickel; Fatty; Like the Eagles Fly; Make a Little Sunshine; A Medley/W: Peter Udell, M: Gary Geld. *Oklahoma!* (Palace, revival, CR, "Curly McLain," May 12, 1980): The Farmer and the Cowman; Oh, What a Beautiful Mornin'; Oklahoma!; People Will Say We're in Love; Pore Jud; The Surrey with the Fringe on Top/W: Oscar Hammerstein II, M: Richard Rodgers. *City of Angels* (Virginia, CR, "Stone," Aug. 27, 1991): Double Talk; Ev'rybody's Gotta Be Somewhere; The Tennis Song; With Every Breath I Take; You're Nothing Without Me/W: David Zippel, M: Cy Coleman.

4351. Minnie Higgins (?–Mar. 27, 1914) *The Newlyweds and Their Baby* (Majestic, "Dora," Mar. 22, 1909): Ev'ry Baby Is a Sweet Bouquet/W: A. Seymour Brown, M: Nat D. Ayer — Supper Out of Doors/WM: ?.

4352. Peter Higgins *Free for All* (Manhattan, "Michael Byrne," Sept. 8, 1931): Free for All; Slumber Song (Goodnight); Tonight/W: Oscar Hammerstein II, M: Richard A. Whiting. *Earl Carroll's Sketch Book of 1935* (Winter Garden, revue, June 4, 1935): At Last/W: Charles Tobias, Sam M. Lewis, M: Henry Tobias — Silhouettes Under the Stars; Through These Portals Pass the Most Beautiful Girls in the World/W: Charles Newman, Charles Tobias, M: Murray Mencher — There's Music in a Kiss/WM: Abner Silver, Al Lewis, Al Sherman.

4353. Robert Higgins *Glory* (Vanderbilt, "Ansel Tollet," Dec. 25, 1922): The Goodly Little Things We Do; When the Tenor Married the Soprano (and the Alto Married the Bass)/W: James Dyrenforth, M: Maurice DePackh.

4354. Andrew Higginson *The Amber Express* (Globe, "Harry Austin," Sept. 19, 1916): You're a Hero/W: Marc Connelly, M: Zoel Parenteau, Robert Planquette.

4355. Pearl Hight *Oh, Please!* (Fulton, "Miss Fall River," Dec. 17, 1926): Homely but Clean/W: Anne Caldwell, M: Vincent Youmans.

4356. Susan Hight *Two's Company* (Alvin, revue, Dec. 15, 1952): Out of the Clear Blue Sky/W: Ogden Nash, M: Vernon Duke. *Guys and Dolls* (46th Street, CR, "Sarah Brown," Mar. 1953): Follow the Fold; If I Were a Bell; I'll Know; I've Never Been in Love Before; Marry the Man Today/WM: Frank Loesser.

4357. Gerald Hiken (May 23, 1927–) B: Milwaukee, WI. *Foxy* (Ziegfeld, "Shortcut," Feb. 16, 1964): Money Isn't Everything; This Is My Night to Howl/W: Johnny Mercer, M: Robert Emmett Dolan.

4358. Katherine Hilgenberg *Carousel* (New York State, revival, "Nettie Fowler," Aug. 10, 1965): June Is Bustin' Out All Over; A Real Nice Clambake; You'll Never Walk Alone/W: Oscar Hammerstein II, M: Richard Rodgers.

4359. Annabelle Hill *Kiss Me, Kate* (New Century, "Hattie," Dec. 30, 1948): Another Op'nin', Another Show/WM: Cole Porter.

4360. Arthur Hill (c 1875–Apr. 9, 1932) *The Top o' th' World* (Majestic > Casino, "Friendly Bear," Oct. 19, 1907): My Shaggy Old Polar Bear/W: James O'Dea, M: Anne Caldwell.

4361. Arthur Hill (Aug. 1, 1922–) B: Melfort, Saskatchewan, Canada. He starred in the TV legal drama *Owen Marshall, Counselor at Law* (1971). *Something More!* (Eugene O'Neill, "Bill Deems," Nov. 10, 1964): Bravo, Bravo, Novelisto; Ode to a Key; Something More/W: Marilyn Bergman, Alan Bergman, M: Sammy Fain — The Straw That Broke the Camel's Back/W: Marilyn Bergman, Alan Bergman, M: Jule Styne.

4362. Barre Hill *George White's Music Hall Varieties* (Casino, revue, Nov. 22, 1932): Hold Me Closer/WM: Jack Scholl, Max Rich, Frank Littau — The Waltz That Brought You Back to Me/W: Irving Caesar, M: Carmen Lombardo.

4363. Bobby Hill *Don't Bother Me, I Can't Cope* (Playhouse, revue, Apr. 19, 1972): Fighting for Pharoah; I Gotta Keep Movin'; Lookin' Over from Your Side; Love Power; So Long Sammy; Thank Heaven for You/WM: Micki Grant. *Your Arms Too Short to Box with God* (Lyceum, revue, Dec. 22, 1976): We Are the Priests and Elders/WM: Alex Bradford.

4364. Frank Hill *Dew Drop Inn* (Astor, "Reggie Murray," May 17, 1923): The Primrose Path/W: Cyrus D. Wood, M: Alfred Goodman.

4365. J. Leubrie Hill *Mr. Lode of Koal* (Majestic, "Buttram," Nov. 1, 1909): Can Song/W: J.A. Shipp, Alex Rogers, M: J. Rosamond Johnson, Bert Williams.

4366. Katheryn Hill *Dancing Around* (Winter Garden, CR, "Patricia," Dec. 7, 1914): An Afternoon Tea/WM: ?.

4367. Ruby Hill (1922–) B: Danville, VA. *St. Louis Woman* (Martin Beck, "Della Green," Mar. 30, 1946): Any Place I Hang My Hat Is Home; Come Rain or Come Shine; I Wonder What Became of Me; Lullaby/W: Johnny Mercer, M: Harold Arlen.

4368. Stephanie Hill *Flora, the Red Menace* (Alvin, "Elsa," May 11, 1965): All I Need (Is One Good Break); You Are You/W: Fred Ebb, M: John Kander.

4369. Fred Hillebrand (Dec. 25, 1893–Sept. 15, 1963) B: Brooklyn, NY. Actor and composer of stage scores and songs. M: VERA MICHELENA. *The Rose Girl* (Ambassador, "Filipe Telicot," Feb. 11, 1921): Flirtation Quartette; Quarrel Number; The Rose Girl Blues; When Our Sundays Are Blue/W: William Cary Duncan, M: Anselm Goetzl — My Old New Jersey Home/W: Ballard Macdonald, M: Nat Vincent. *Pleasure Bound* (Majestic, revue, "Bob Stewart," Feb, 18, 1929): Park Avenue Strut/W: Moe Jaffe, Harold Atteridge, M: Phil Baker, Maurie Rubens — We'll Get Along/W: Max Lief, Nathaniel Lief, M: Muriel Pollock.

4370. Jack Hilliard *Ziegfeld Follies of 1943* (Winter Garden, revue, CR, Oct. 17, 1943): Come Up and Have a Cup of Coffee; This Is It/W: Jack Yellen, M: Ray Henderson.

4371. Walter Hilliard *Americana of 1926* (Belmont, revue, "4th barber in Pan American Quartette," July 26, 1926): Swanee River Melody [added]/W: Al Wilson, M: Charles Weinberg — Thanks Awful/W: Sam M. Lewis, Joe Young, M: Con Conrad — That Lost Barber Shop Chord/W: Ira Gershwin, M: George Gershwin — The Volga Boatman/W: Dailey Paskman, M: Alexei Archangelsky.

4372. Bert Hillner *Gypsy Lady* (Century, "M. Guilbert Armand," Sept. 17, 1946): Young Lady a la Mode/W: Robert Wright, George Forrest, M: Victor Herbert.

4373. John Hillner (Nov. 5, 1952–) B: Evanston, IL. *Crazy for You* (Sam S. Shubert, "Lank Hawkins," Feb. 19, 1992): Naughty Baby/W: Ira Gershwin, Desmond Carter, M: George Gershwin.

4374. Alice Hills *The Golden Butterfly* (Broadway, "Wanda," Oct. 12, 1908): The Elf King/W: J. Hayden-Clarendon, M: Reginald De Koven. *The Girl of My Dreams* (Criterion, "Daphne Daffington," Aug. 7, 1911): What's Sauce for the Gander Is Sauce for the Goose/W: Otto Harbach, M: Karl Hoschna. *Take It from Me* (44th Street, "Ella Abbott," Mar. 31, 1919): It's Different Now [Apr. 7, 1919]; The Kiss/W: Will B. Johnstone, M: Will R. Anderson.

4375. Ferdinand Hilt *Magdalena* (Ziegfeld, "Major Blanco," Sept. 20, 1948): Come to Colombia; My Bus and I; Travel, Travel, Travel/W: Robert Wright, George Forrest, M: Heitor Villa-Lobos. *Can-Can* (New York City Center, revival, "Hilaire Jussac," May 16, 1962): Come Along with Me/WM: Cole Porter. *Where's Charley?* (New York City Center, revival, "Sir Francis Chesney," May 25, 1966): The New Ashmoleon Marching Society and Students Conservatory Band/WM: Frank Loesser.

4376. Dora Hilton *Tick-Tack-Toe* (Princess, revue, Feb. 13, 1920): Chinese-American Rag/WM: Herman Timberg.

4377. Lola Hilton *Odds and Ends of 1917* (Norworth, revue, CR, Feb. 4, 1918): Where Did You Get Those Irish Eyes?/W: Bide Dudley, Jack Norworth, M: James Byrnes.

4378. Marie Hilton *The Ballet Girl* (Manhattan, "Bedalia," Dec. 21, 1897): In the Ballet/WM: E.E. Rice. *The Show Girl or The Cap of Fortune* (Wallack's, "Vivien Epps," May 5, 1902): Adeline/W: D.K. Stevens, M: Edward W. Corliss — Invocation to Pie/W: D.K. Stevens, M: M.W. Daniels.

4379. Ross Himes *Topsy and Eva* (Harris, "Rastus," Dec. 23, 1924): Kiss Me/WM: Vivian Duncan, Rosetta Duncan. *Here's Howe!* (Broadhurst, "Mr. Petrie," May 1, 1928): I'd Rather Dance Here Than Hereafter/W: Irving Caesar, M: Joseph Meyer, Roger Wolfe Kahn.

4380. James Hindman (Mar. 25, 1960–) B: Detroit, MI. *City of Angels* (Virginia, "Mahoney," Dec. 11, 1989): All Ya Have to Do Is Wait/W: David Zippel, M: Cy Coleman.

4381. Esther Hinds *Porgy and Bess* (Uris, revival, "Bess," Sept. 25, 1976): Bess, You Is My Woman Now; I Loves You, Porgy/W: Ira Gershwin, DuBose Heyward, M: George Gershwin — Leavin' fo' de Promis' Land; What You Want wid Bess?/W: DuBose Heyward, M: George Gershwin — There's a Boat Dat's Leavin' Soon for New York/W: Ira Gershwin, M: George Gershwin.

4382. Babe Hines *Dance Me a Song* (Royale, revue, Jan. 20, 1950): Love/WM: James Shelton. *Almost Crazy* (Longacre, revue, June 20, 1955): Don't Bait for Fish You Can't Fry/WM: Portia Nelson — Love in the Barnyard/WM: Ray Taylor — Easy/WM: James Shelton.

4383. Elizabeth Hines (Jan. 8, 1894–Feb. 19, 1971) B: New York, NY or Albany, NY. *See-Saw* (Cohan, "Helen," Sept. 23, 1919): Peep-Peep; Senorita-Senorita; A World Full of Girls/W: Earl Derr Biggers, M: Louis A. Hirsch. *Love Birds* (Apollo, "Allene Charteris," Mar. 15,

1921): Is It Hard to Guess?; A Little Dream That Lost Its Way; The Trousseau Incomplete/W: Ballard Macdonald, M: Sigmund Romberg. *The O'Brien Girl* (Liberty, "Alice O'Brien," Oct. 3, 1921): I Wonder How I Ever Passed You By; I'm So Excited; Learn to Smile; That O'Brien Girl/W: Otto Harbach, M: Louis A. Hirsch. *Little Nellie Kelly* (Liberty, "Nellie Kelly," Nov. 13, 1922): All in the Wearing; (They're) All My Boys; The Voice in My Heart; When You Do the Hinky Dee; You Remind Me of My Mother/WM: George M. Cohan. *Marjorie* (Shubert > 44th Street, "Marjorie Daw," Aug. 11, 1924): Happy Ending; What Do You Say?/W: Clifford Grey, M: Herbert Stothart — Leading Man/W: Harold Atteridge, M: Stephen Jones — My Twilight Rose/W: Clifford Grey, M: Sigmund Romberg — Song of Love/W: Harold Atteridge, M: Sigmund Romberg.

4384. Gregory Hines (Feb. 14, 1946–) B: New York, NY. Actor, dancer brother of MAURICE HINES, performing together in theaters and nightclubs all over the country. *The Girl in Pink Tights* (Mark Hellinger, "Shoe Shine Boy," Mar. 5, 1954): Up in the Elevated Railway/W: Leo Robin, M: Sigmund Romberg. *Eubie!* (Ambassador, revue, Sept. 20, 1978): Baltimore Buzz; Dixie Moon; Hot Feet; If You've Never Been Vamped by a Brownskin (You've Never Been Vamped at All); Low Down Blues; There's a Million Little Cupids in the Sky/W: Noble Sissle, M: Eubie Blake. *Comin' Uptown* (Winter Garden, "Scrooge," Dec. 20, 1979): Born Again; Christmas Is Comin' Uptown; Have I Finally Found My Heart?; Now I Lay Me Down to Sleep; What Better Time for Love/W: Peter Udell, M: Garry Sherman. *Sophisticated Ladies* (Lunt-Fontanne, revue, Mar. 1, 1981): Do Nothin' Till You Hear from Me; Don't Get Around Much Anymore/W: Bob Russell, M: Duke Ellington — Drop Me Off in Harlem/W: Nick Kenny, M: Duke Ellington — Duke's Place/W: Bill Katz, R. Thiele, M: Duke Ellington — I'm Beginning to See the Light/WM: Duke Ellington, Don George, Johnny Hodges, Harry James — I'm Just a Lucky So and So/W: Mack David, M: Duke Ellington — Ko-Ko/WM: Duke Ellington — Something to Live For/WM: Duke Ellington, Billy Strayhorn — Sophisticated Lady/W: Mitchell Parish, Irving Mills, M: Duke Ellington. *Jelly's Last Jam* (Virginia, "Jelly Roll Morton," Apr. 26, 1992): The Chicago Stomp; Good Ole New York; In My Day; Somethin' More; That's the Way We Do Things in New Yawk; The Whole World's Waitin' to Sing Your Song/W: Susan Birkenhead,

M: Jelly Roll Morton — Dr. Jazz/W: Susan Birkenhead, M: Walter Melrose, King Oliver — Get Away, Boy; Street Scene; Too Late, Daddy/W: Susan Birkenhead, M: Luther Henderson — The Last Chance Blues; Lonely Boy Blues; That's How You Jazz/WM: trad. — The Last Rites/W: Susan Birkenhead, M: Luther Henderson, Jelly Roll Morton.

4385. Harry Hines (Apr. 28, 1889–May 3, 1967) *Silks and Satins* (George M. Cohan, revue, July 15, 1920): He Went In Like a Lion and Came Out Like a Lamb/W: Andrew B. Sterling, M: Harry Von Tilzer.

4386. Jackson Hines *Kitty Darlin'* (Casino, "Sir Jasper Standish," Nov. 7, 1917): Am I to Blame?/W: P.G. Wodehouse, M: Rudolf Friml — I Want a Man Who's Gentle/WM: ?. *The Maid of the Mountains* (Casino, "Carlo," Sept. 11, 1918): Dividing the Spoils/W: Clifford Harris, M: Harold Fraser-Simpson.

4387. Johnny Hines (July 25, 1895–1970) B: Golden, CO. Star of comic silent films. *Just a Minute* (Cort, CR, "Will U. Tell," Nov. 10, 1919): I'm Going to Be Lonesome; Just Imagine; Over and Over Again; Wonderful Day/WM: Harry L. Cort, George E. Stoddard, Harold Orlob.

4388. Laurence Hines *Blackbirds of 1939* (Hudson, revue, Feb. 11, 1939): Dixie Isn't Dixie Anymore; Jojo the Cannibal Kid/W: Johnny Mercer, M: Rube Bloom.

4389. Maurice Hines (1944–) B: New York, NY. Brother of GREGORY HINES. *The Girl in Pink Tights* (Mark Hellinger, "Newspaper Boy," Mar. 5, 1954): Up in the Elevated Railway/W: Leo Robin, M: Sigmund Romberg. *Eubie!* (Ambassador, revue, Sept. 20, 1978): Dixie Moon; If You've Never Been Vamped by a Brownskin (You've Never Been Vamped at All); I'm Just Wild About Harry; There's a Million Little Cupids in the Sky/W: Noble Sissle, M: Eubie Blake — You Got to Git the Gittin While the Gittin's Good/W: Flourney E. Miller, M: Eubie Blake. *Bring Back Birdie* (Martin Beck, "Mtobe," Mar. 5, 1981): Bring Back Birdie; There's a Brand New Beat in Heaven/W: Lee Adams, M: Charles Strouse. *Sophisticated Ladies* (Lunt-Fontanne, revue, CR, Jan. 5, 1982): Do Nothin' Till You Hear from Me; Don't Get Around Much Anymore/W: Bob Russell, M: Duke Ellington — Drop Me Off in Harlem/W: Nick Kenny, M: Duke Ellington — Duke's Place/W: Bill Katz, R. Thiele, M: Duke Ellington — I'm Beginning to See the Light/WM: Duke Ellington, Don George, Johnny Hodges, Harry James — I'm Just a Lucky So and So/W: Mack

David, M: Duke Ellington — Kinda Dukish; Ko-Ko/WM: Duke Ellington — Music Is a Woman/W: John Guare, M: Duke Ellington — Something to Live For/WM: Duke Ellington, Billy Strayhorn — Sophisticated Lady/W: Mitchell Parish, Irving Mills, M: Duke Ellington. *Uptown...It's Hot!* (Lunt-Fontanne, revue, Jan. 29, 1986): Body and Soul/W: Edward Heyman, Robert Sour, Frank Eyton, M: Johnny Green — Ill Wind; Stormy Weather/W: Ted Koehler, M: Harold Arlen — When Your Lover Has Gone/WM: E.A. Swan.

4390. Mimi Hines (July 17, 1933–) B: Vancouver, Canada. M: PHIL FORD. *Funny Girl* (Winter Garden, CR, "Fanny Brice," Dec. 27, 1965): Cornet Man; His Love Makes Me Beautiful; I Want to Be Seen with You Tonight; I'm the Greatest Star; The Music That Makes Me Dance; People; Rat-Tat-Tat-Tat; Sadie, Sadie; Who Are You Now?; You Are Woman/W: Bob Merrill, M: Jule Styne. *Grease* (Eugene O'Neill, revival, CR, "Miss Lynch," c 1994): Alma Mater; Born to Hand-Jive/WM: Jim Jacobs, Warren Casey.

4391. Bill Hinnant (Aug. 28, 1935–Feb. 17, 1978) B: Chincoteague Island, VA. *Frank Merriwell, or Honor Challenged* (Longacre, "Manuel," Apr. 24, 1971): Manuel Your Friend/WM: Larry Frank, Skip Redwine.

4392. Bernice Hirsch *Linger Longer Letty* (Fulton, "Ethelmay," Nov. 20, 1919): Ssh! Ssh! Ssh!/W: Bernard Grossman, M: Alfred Goodman — A Twentieth Century Lullaby/W: Bernard Grossman, George Yoerger, M: Alfred Goodman, W. Frisch.

4393. Fluffer Hirsch *Inner City* (Ethel Barrymore, revue, Dec. 19, 1971): Christmas Is Coming; I Had a Little Teevee; Jack Be Nimble; Lucy Locket; Taffy/W: Eve Merriam, M: Helen Miller.

4394. Raymond Hitchcock (Oct. 22, 1865–Nov. 24, 1929) B: Auburn, NY. M: FLORA ZABELLE. Known as Hitchy, the comic star of vaudeville and the musical stage appeared in 3 Mack Sennett silent films in 1915. *King Dodo* (Daly's, "King Dodo," May 12, 1902): A Jolly Old Potentate; The Tale of a Bumble Bee/W: Frank Pixley, M: Gustav Luders — They Gave Me a Medal for That/W: Glen MacDonough, M: Raymond Hitchcock. *The Yankee Consul* (Broadway > Wallack's, "Abijah Booze," Feb. 22, 1904): Ain't It Funny What a Difference Just a Few Hours Make?; In Old New York; In the Days of Old/W: Henry Blossom, M: Alfred G. Robyn. *The Yankee Tourist* (Astor, "Copeland Schuyler," Aug. 12, 1907): Come and Have a

Smile with Me; The Yankee Millionaire/W: Wallace Irwin, M: Alfred G. Robyn — So What's the Use?/WM: Edward Montagu. *The Red Widow* (Astor, "Cicero Hannibal Butts," Nov. 6, 1911): I Shall Never Look at a Pretty Girl Again/W: Rennold Wolf, Channing Pollock, M: Charles J. Gebest — I'm a Wonderful Man in Yonkers/W: William Jerome, M: Charles J. Gebest. *The Beauty Shop* (Astor, "Dr. Arbutus Budd," Apr. 13, 1914): Give Us Your Kind Applause; Saturday Afternoon on Broadway; When the Creditor Comes to Call/W: Rennold Wolf, M: Charles J. Gebest — I Love You Just the Same/W: Gene Buck, M: Dave Stamper — When You're All Dressed Up and No Place to Go/W: Benjamin Hapgood Burt, M: Silvio Hein. *Betty* (Globe, "Lord D'Arcy Playne," Oct. 3, 1916): Here Comes the Groom/WM: Benjamin Hapgood Burt — I Feel So Happy/WM: Paul Rubens, Adrian Ross — Sometime/W: William Jerome, M: Harry Tierney. *Hitchy-Koo of 1917)* (Cohan and Harris > Liberty > 44th Street, revue, June 7, 1917): The Girls of Home Sweet Home; When You've Picked Your Basket of Peaches/WM: E. Ray Goetz. *Hitchy-Koo of 1918* (Globe, revue, June 6, 1918): It'll All End Up with the Right End Up/WM: Henry I. Marshall. *Hitchy-Koo of 1919* (Liberty, revue, Oct. 6, 1919): I Introduced; My Cozy Little Corner in the Ritz; Peter Piper/WM: Cole Porter. *Hitchy-Koo of 1920* (New Amsterdam, revue, Oct. 19, 1920): Buggy Riding/W: Anne Caldwell, M: Jerome Kern — Old New York; The Star of Hitchy-Koo/W: Glen MacDonough, Anne Caldwell, M: Jerome Kern. *Ziegfeld Follies of 1921* (Globe, revue, June 21, 1921): If Plymouth Rock Had Landed on the Pilgrims (Plymouth Rock)/W: Channing Pollock, M: Dave Stamper. *Just Fancy* (Casino, "Charlie Van Bibber," Oct. 11, 1927): Naughty Boy/W: Leo Robin, M: Joseph Meyer, Phil Charig.

4395. Mabel Hite (May 30, 1885–Oct. 22, 1912) B: Ashland, KY. M: MICHAEL (MIKE) J. DONLIN. *A Certain Party* (Wallack's, "Norah," Apr. 24, 1911): Emerald Isle; I Want Another Situation Just Like That; The Walking Delegate/W: Edgar Smith, M: Robert Hood Bowers — Get the Hook; Turkey Trot/W: Edgar Smith, M: Tom Kelly — You're Going to Lose Your Husband If You Do/WM: Mabel Hite.

4396. Elsie Hitz *Miss Daisy* (Shubert > Lyric, "Fern Randolph," Sept. 9, 1914): Kissing; My Little Queen Bee; Pierrot's Ball; Tea Leaves; Won't You Dance?; Youth/W: Philip Bartholomae, M: Silvio Hein.

4397. Hal Hixon *The Midnight Rounders of*

1920 (Century roof, revue, July 12, 1920): Who Cares/W: Howard E. Rogers, M: Leo Edwards.

4398. Lindiwe Hlengwa *Sarafina!* (Cort, "Lindiwe," Jan. 28, 1988): Talking About Love/ WM: Hugh Masekela, Mbongeni Ngema.

4399. Bruce Hlibok (July 31, 1960–June 23, 1995) B: New York, NY. The deaf actor wrote several plays that were produced Off Broadway, and a book called *Silent Dancer*, about how his deaf sister learned to dance at the Joffrey Ballet School. *Runaways* (Plymouth, "Hubbell," May 13, 1978): Lullaby from Baby to Baby/WM: Elizabeth Swados.

4400. Bess Hoban *Sinbad* (Casino, CR, Oct. 18, 1918): On Cupid's Green/W: Harold Atteridge, M: Sigmund Romberg.

4401. Stella Hoban (c 1890–Jan. 24, 1962) *The Man from Cook's* (New Amsterdam, "Marjorie Benton," Mar. 25, 1912): All for You; You and I/W: Henry Blossom, M: Raymond Hubbell — A Little World for Two/W: Glen MacDonough, M: Raymond Hubbell. *Oh! Oh! Delphine* (Knickerbocker > New Amsterdam, "Simone," Sept. 30, 1912): The Maxim Girl; The Quarrel/W: C.M.S. McLellan, M: Ivan Caryll. *The Passing Show of 1916* (Winter Garden, revue, June 22, 1916): Romeo and Juliet/W: Harold Atteridge, M: Sigmund Romberg, Otto Motzan. *The Night Boat* (Liberty, "Mrs. Hazel White," Feb. 2, 1920): Good Night Boat/W: Anne Caldwell, Frank Craven, M: Jerome Kern — Left All Alone Again Blues/W: Anne Caldwell, M: Jerome Kern. *Helen of Troy, New York* (Selwyn > Times Square, "Grace Yarrow," June 19, 1923): I Like a Big Town, I Like a Small Town; We Must Be Up on Our Toes/W: Bert Kalmar, M: Harry Ruby.

4402. Robert Hobbs *Charlot Revue of 1924* (Times Square > Selwyn, revue, Jan. 9, 1924): Limehouse Blues/W: Douglas Furber, M: Philip Braham — You Were Meant for Me [Apr. 21, 1924]/WM: Noble Sissle, Eubie Blake. *The Nightingale* (Jolson, "Capt. Joe Archer," Jan. 3, 1927): Two Little Ships/W: P.G. Wodehouse, M: Armand Vecsey. *Lew Leslie's International Revue* (Majestic, revue, Feb. 25, 1930): Keys to Your Heart/W: Dorothy Fields, M: Jimmy McHugh.

4403. I.M. Hobson *Dance a Little Closer* (Minskoff, "Rev. Oliver Boyle," May 11, 1983): I Don't Know/W: Alan Jay Lerner, M: Charles Strouse.

4404. James Hobson *The Most Happy Fella* (New York City Center, revival, "Clem," May 11, 1966): Standing on the Corner/WM: Frank Loesser.

4405. Maude Hobson (?–Jan. 6, 1913) B: Australia. *A Gaiety Girl* (Daly's, "Lady Virginia Forrest," Sept. 17, 1894): High Class Chaperone/WM: ?.

4406. May Hobson *The Belle of Mayfair* (Daly's, "Lady Jay," Dec. 3, 1906): Eight Little Debutantes Are We/W: William Caine, M: Leslie Stuart.

4407. Leah Hocking *Grease* (Eugene O'Neill, revival, CR, "Marty," c 1994): Freddy, My Love/WM: Jim Jacobs, Warren Casey.

4408. Ann Hodapp (May 6, 1946–) B: Louisville, KY. *Fearless Frank* (Princess, "Nursemaid" and "Actress" and "Bootblack" and "Topsy" and "Newsboy" and "Enid," June 15, 1980): Free Speech, Free Thought, Free Love; Oh, Catch Me, Mr. Harris, Cause I'm Falling for You!/W: Andrew Davies, M: Dave Brown.

4409. Gloria Hodes (Aug. 20–) B: Norwich, CT. *Gantry* (George Abbott, "Adelberta Shoup," Feb. 14, 1970): He's Never Too Busy; We Can All Give Love/W: Fred Tobias, M: Stanley Lebowsky.

4410. William (Will) T. Hodge (Nov. 1, 1874–Jan. 30, 1932) B: Albion, NY. M: HELEN HALE. *The White Cat* (New Amsterdam, "Jonah the Thirteenth," Nov. 2, 1905): Antonio; Get the Money/W: William Jerome, M: Jean Schwartz — Graft/W: Harry B. Smith, M: Ludwig Englander. *Dream City* (Weber's, "Seth Hubbs," Dec. 25, 1906): Bound for the Opera; The Volunteer Fireman/W: Edgar Smith, M: Victor Herbert.

4411. Ann Hodges B: Elizabethtown, KY. *No Strings* (54th Street, "Gabrielle Bertin," Mar. 15, 1962): Be My Host/WM: Richard Rodgers. *Heathen!* (Billy Rose, "Hepsibah Burnham," May 21, 1972): The Word of the Lord/WM: Eaton Magoon, Jr.

4412. Eddie Hodges *The Music Man* (Majestic, "Winthrop Paroo," Dec. 19, 1957): Gary, Indiana; Wells Fargo Wagon/WM: Meredith Willson.

4413. Joy Hodges (Jan. 29, 1915–Jan. 19, 2003) B: Des Moines, IA. Singer and dancer, she appeared in a dozen movies, usually as a showgirl or singer. She helped Ronald Reagan begin his acting career, and stayed in touch with him for 60 years. *I'd Rather Be Right* (Alvin > Music Box, "Peggy Jones," Nov. 2, 1937): Have You Met Miss Jones?; I'd Rather Be Right; Sweet Sixty-Five/W: Lorenz Hart, M: Richard Rodgers. *Dream with Music* (Majestic, "Marian" and "Jasmin," May 18, 1944): Be Glad You're Alive; Love at Second Sight; Relax and Enjoy It/W: Edward Eager, M: Clay Warnick. *Nellie Bly* (Adelphi, "Nellie Bly," Jan. 21, 1946): All Around the World; Just My Luck; Sky High; You May

Not Love Me [Jan. 28, 1946]/W: Johnny Burke, M: James Van Heusen. *No, No, Nanette* (46th Street, revival, CR, "Sue Smith," Nov. 13, 1972): I Want to Be Happy/W: Irving Caesar, M: Vincent Youmans — Take a Little One-Step/W: Zelda Sears, M: Vincent Youmans.

4414. Claire Hodgson *The Magic Melody* (Shubert, "Mlle. Fleurie," Nov. 11, 1919): We Are the Fixers/W: Frederic Arnold Kummer, M: Sigmund Romberg.

4415. Dennis Hoey (Mar. 30, 1893–July 25, 1960) B: London, England. Character actor in movies; he played Lestrade to Basil Rathbone's Sherlock Holmes. *Katja* (44th Street, "Ivo," Oct. 18, 1926): Dance with You/W: Harry Graham, M: Jean Gilbert.

4416. Evelyn Hoey (c 1910–Sept. 11, 1935) *Fifty Million Frenchmen* (Lyric, "May de Vere," Nov. 27, 1929): The Boy Friend Back Home [Dec. 16, 1929]; Find Me a Primitive Man; I'm Unlucky at Gambling; Let's Step Out [Mar. 24, 1930]/WM: Cole Porter. *The Vanderbilt Revue* (Vanderbilt, revue, Nov. 5, 1930): Blue Again; Button Up Your Heart/W: Dorothy Fields, M: Jimmy McHugh — I Give Myself Away/W: Edward Eliscu, M: Jacques Fray — What's My Man Gonna Be Like?/WM: Cole Porter. *Walk a Little Faster* (St. James, revue, Dec. 7, 1932): April in Paris; Unaccustomed as I Am [Jan. 2, 1933]/W: E.Y. Harburg, M: Vernon Duke — Mayfair/W: Roland Leigh, M: William Waliter — So Nonchalant/W: E.Y. Harburg, Charles Tobias, M: Vernon Duke.

4417. Herbert Hoey *Ziegfeld Midnight Frolic [11th Edition]* (New Amsterdam roof, revue, Feb. 9, 1921): The Compere; Pretty Faces; Summertime/W: Gene Buck, M: Dave Stamper. *Ziegfeld Follies of 1921* (Globe, revue, June 21, 1921): Now I Know/W: Grant Clarke, M: James V. Monaco. *Sally, Irene and Mary* (44th Street, revival, "Clarence Edwards," Mar. 23, 1925): Opportunity; Stage Door Johnnies; Wedding Time/W: Raymond Klages, M: J. Fred Coots.

4418. Iris Hoey (July 17, 1885–May 13, 1979) B: London, England. *Tonight's the Night* (Shubert, "Beatrice Carraway," Dec. 24, 1914): Boots and Shoes; Too Particular/WM: Paul Rubens, Percy Greenbank.

4419. William F. Hoey (Jan. 1, 1854–June 29, 1897) B: New York, NY. Actor and manager. His nickname was Old Hoss. *The Flams* (Bijou, "Marmaduke Flam," Nov. 26, 1894): Dandy Colored Coon/W: Richard Norton, M: George LeBrunn — The Man Who Broke the Bank at Monte Carlo/WM: Fred Gilbert — Ours Is a Happy Little Home/WM: J.W. Sewell — Private

Tommy Atkins/W: Henry Hamilton, M: S. Potter.

4420. Edwin W. Hoff *Robin Hood* (Standard, "Robin Hood," Sept. 28, 1891): Come Dream So Bright; O, See the Lambkins Play!; An Outlaw's Life's the Life for Me; Then Hey for the Merry Greenwood; Though It Was Within This Hour We Met; A Troubador Sang to His Love/W: Harry B. Smith, M: Reginald De Koven. *The Knickerbockers* (Garden, "Hendrick," May 29, 1893): Sing Your Merriest Lays/W: Harry B. Smith, M: Reginald De Koven.

4421. Louise Hoff (c 1923–June 1, 1992) *From A to Z* (Plymouth, revue, Apr. 20, 1960): I Said to Love/W: Fred Ebb, M: Paul Klein.

4422. Vanda Hoff *Two Little Girls in Blue* (George M. Cohan, "Cecile," May 3, 1921): Just Like You/W: Ira Gershwin, M: Paul Lannin.

4423. Llora Hoffman *Shubert Gaieties of 1919* (44th Street, revue, July 14, 1919): Lamp of Love/W: Alfred Bryan, M: Jean Schwartz. *Cinderella on Broadway* (Winter Garden, revue, June 24, 1920): The Last Waltz I Had with You; Wheel of Fate/W: Harold Atteridge, M: Bert Grant. *The Dancing Girl* (Winter Garden, "Singer" and "Mrs. Sheldon" and "Dellisho," Jan. 24, 1923): Hail U.S.A.; That Romance of Mine; Venetian Carnival/W: Harold Atteridge, M: Sigmund Romberg — You and I (in Old Versailles)/W: B.G. DeSylva, M: George Gershwin, Jack Green. *Topics of 1923* (Broadhurst, revue, Nov. 20, 1923): Queens of Long Ago/W: Harold Atteridge, M: Jean Schwartz, Alfred Goodman. *Artists and Models of 1925* (Winter Garden, revue, June 24, 1925): Follow Your Star/W: Clifford Grey, M: J. Fred Coots — Mothers of the World/W: Clifford Grey, M: Sigmund Romberg.

4424. Matthew Hoffman *A Christmas Carol* (Madison Square Garden, return engagement, "Scrooge at 12," Nov. 22, 1996): A Place Called Home/W: Lynn Ahrens, M: Alan Menken.

4425. Otto Hoffman (May 2, 1879–June 23, 1944) B: New York, NY. *A Broken Idol* (Herald Square, "J. Ely Muddleford, D.Z.," Aug. 16, 1909): Poor Old Dad in New York for the Summer/W: Harry Williams, M: Egbert Van Alstyne.

4426. Philip Hoffman (May 12, 1954–) B: Chicago, IL. Character actor in movies from 1991. *Is There Life After High School?* (Ethel Barrymore, revue, May 7, 1982): For Them; I'm Glad You Didn't Know Me/WM: Craig Carnelia. *Baby* (Ethel Barrymore, "Mr. Weiss," Dec. 4, 1983): Fatherhood Blues/W: Richard Maltby, M: David Shire.

4427. Gertrude Hoffmann (1886–Oct. 21, 1966) B: San Francisco, CA. Mother of MAX HOFFMAN, JR. An interpretive dancer in vaudeville, she had her own troupe and introduced the provocative Salome dance to American audiences in 1908. *The Honeymooners* (New Amsterdam roof, "Madeline Tiger," June 3, 1907): The Musical Comedy Maid/WM: George M. Cohan.

4428. Max Hoffmann, Jr. (Dec. 13, 1902–Mar. 31, 1945) B: Norfolk, VA. M: NORMA TERRIS; HELEN KANE. His mother was GERTRUDE HOFFMANN. *Queen o' Hearts* (George M. Cohan, "Tom," Oct. 10, 1922): A Long Time Ago/W: Morrie Ryskind, M: Lewis E. Gensler, Dudley Wilkinson — Sizing Up the Girls/W: Oscar Hammerstein II, M: Lewis E. Gensler, Dudley Wilkinson. *Captain Jinks* (Martin Beck, "Lieut. Charles Martin," Sept. 8, 1925): Fond of You; Wanna Lotta Love/W: B.G. DeSylva, M: Lewis E. Gensler — Pals; Strictly Business/W: B.G. DeSylva, M: ?. *Gay Paree* (Winter Garden, revue, Nov. 9, 1926): There Never Was a Town Like Paris/W: Mann Holiner, M: Alberta Nichols. *Sweet Adeline* (Hammerstein's, "Tom Martin," Sept. 3, 1929): First Mate Martin; Out of the Blue; Some Girl Is on Your Mind/W: Oscar Hammerstein II, M: Jerome Kern. *America's Sweetheart* (Broadhurst, CR, "Michael Perry," June 1931): How About It?; I've Got Five Dollars; We'll Be the Same/W: Lorenz Hart, M: Richard Rodgers. *Shady Lady* (Shubert, "Geoffrey Benson," July 5, 1933): Any Way the Wind Blows; Live, Laugh and Love; Swingy Little Thingy/W: Bud Green, M: Sam H. Stept — Isn't It Remarkable; You're Not the One/W: Stanley Adams, M: Jesse Greer.

4429. Celeste Hogan *Jesus Christ Superstar* (Longacre, revival, "Maid by the Fire," Oct. 12, 1971): Peter's Denial/W: Tim Rice, M: Andrew Lloyd Webber.

4430. Edward Hogan *The Garrick Gaieties of 1925* (Garrick, revue, May 17, 1925): The Guild Gilded/W: Lorenz Hart, M: Richard Rodgers — Stage Managers' Chorus (Walk Upon Your Toes)/W: Dudley Digges, Lorenz Hart, M: Richard Rodgers. *The Garrick Gaieties of 1926* (Garrick, revue, "Sir Lancelot," May 10, 1926): Idles of the King/W: Lorenz Hart, M: Richard Rodgers.

4431. Ernest Hogan (c 1859–May 20, 1909) B: Bowling Green, KY. Black performer who appeared in nonblack as well as black productions. *Rufus Rastus* (American, "Rufus Rastus," Jan. 29, 1906): Oh, Say, Wouldn't It Be a Dream?/W: Earl C. Jones, M: Joe Jordan.

4432. Marie Hogan *The Maids of Athens* (New Amsterdam, "Mrs. Rosamond Barley," Mar. 18, 1914): One or Another/W: Carolyn Wells, M: Oscar Haase — Rosie/WM: Frederic Norton.

4433. Roland Hogue (c 1882–Oct. 7, 1958) *Little Boy Blue* (Lyric, CR, "Capt. Graham," Feb. 26, 1912): Aeroplane Duet/W: Grant Stewart, M: Henry Bereny. *Sky High* (Shubert > Winter Garden > Casino, "Montague Lush," Mar. 2, 1925): Find a Good Time/W: Clifford Grey, M: Carleton Kelsey, Maurie Rubens.

4434. William Hogue *Happy as Larry* (Coronet, "6th Tailor," Jan. 6, 1950): And So He Died; The Dirty Dog; Give the Doctor the Best in the House; He's a Bold Rogue; Mrs. Larry, Tell Me This; Oh, Mrs. Larry; Without a Stitch/W: Donagh MacDonagh, M: Mischa Portnoff, Wesley Portnoff.

4435. Dick Hoh *The Student Gypsy or The Prince of Liederkranz* (54th Street, "Colonel Helmet Blunderbuss," Sept. 30, 1963): The Drinking Song; The Grenadiers' Marching Song; Ting-a-Ling Dearie; A Woman Is a Woman Is a Woman/WM: Rick Besoyan.

4436. Michael Hoit B: Highland Park, IL. *Hair* (Biltmore, revival, "Berger," Oct. 5, 1977): Donna; Don't Put It Down; Going Down; Hair/W: Gerome Ragni, James Rado, M: Galt MacDermot.

4437. Florence Holbrook M: CECIL LEAN. *The Soul Kiss* (New York, "Suzette," Jan. 28, 1908): Any Old Place in the World with You; Let's Pretend/W: Harry B. Smith, M: Maurice Levi. *Bright Eyes* (New York, "Dorothy Mayland," Feb. 28, 1910): Cheer Up My Honey; For You Bright Eyes; The Mood You Are In/W: Otto Harbach, M: Karl Hoschna — Mrs. Casey/W: Collin Davis, Cecil Lean, M: Florence Holbrook.

4438. Hal Holbrook (Feb. 17, 1916–) B: Cleveland, OH. M: DIXIE CARTER, 1984. Best known for his portrayal of Mark Twain in his one-man show *Mark Twain Tonight!* (1966). *The Apple Tree* (Shubert, CR, "Adam" and "Captain Sanjar" and "Flip, the Prince Charming," Apr. 6, 1967): Beautiful, Beautiful World; Eve; Forbidden Love (in Gaul); George L.; It's a Fish; Which Door?; You Are Not Real/W: Sheldon Harnick, M: Jerry Bock. *Man of La Mancha* (Martin Beck, CR, "Don Quixote," July 1, 1968): The Combat; Dulcinea; Golden Helmet; The Impossible Dream (The Quest); Man of La Mancha (I, Don Quixote)/W: Joe Darion, M: Mitch Leigh.

4439. Harry Holbrook *Holka-Polka* (Lyric,

"Max Munz," Oct. 14, 1925): Goodfellow Days; Spring in Autumn/W: Gus Kahn, Raymond B. Egan, M: Will Ortman.

4440. William Holbrook (c 1895–Aug. 6, 1971) B: New York, NY. A dancer who sometimes sang. *Puzzles of 1925* (Fulton, revue, Feb. 2, 1925): The Doo Dab/W: Bert Kalmar, M: Harry Ruby. *A la Carte* (Martin Beck, revue, Aug. 17, 1927): Give Trouble the Air/W: Leo Robin, M: Louis Alter — Sunny Spain/WM: Norma Gregg. *Ned Wayburn's Gambols* (Knickerbocker, revue, Jan. 15, 1929): In the Days Gone By/W: Morrie Ryskind, M: Walter G. Samuels — Sweetest Little Fellow/WM: ?. *The Garrick Gaieties of 1930* (Guild, revue, return engagement, Oct. 16, 1930): Rose of Arizona/W: Lorenz Hart, M: Richard Rodgers.

4441. Geoffrey Holder (Aug. 1, 1930–) B: Trinidad. He won Tony awards as director and costume designer for *The Wiz* (1975). *House of Flowers* (Alvin, "The Champion," Dec. 30, 1954): Smellin' of Vanilla (Bamboo Cage)/WM: Truman Capote, Harold Arlen.

4442. Ronald Holgate (May 26, 1937–) B: Aberdeen, SD. M: DOROTHY COLLINS. *A Funny Thing Happened on the Way to the Forum* (Alvin, "Miles Gloriosus," May 8, 1962): Bring Me My Bride/WM: Stephen Sondheim. *1776* (46th Street, "Richard Henry Lee," Mar. 16, 1969/May 11, 1971): The Lees of Old Virginia/WM: Sherman Edwards. *Sondheim: A Musical Tribute* (Shubert, revue, Mar. 11, 1973): Beautiful Girls/WM: Stephen Sondheim. *The Grand Tour* (Palace, "Col. Tadeusz Boleslav Stjerbinsky," Jan. 11, 1979): For Poland; I Think, I Think; Marianne; More and More, Less and Less; One Extraordinary Thing; We're Almost There; You I Like/WM: Jerry Herman. *Musical Chairs* (Rialto, "Joel Preston," May 14, 1980): My Time; There You Are/WM: Tom Savage.

4443. Bob Holiday *Fiorello!* (Broadhurst, "Neil," Nov. 23, 1959): On the Side of the Angels/W: Sheldon Harnick, M: Jerry Bock. *It's a Bird It's a Plane It's Superman* (Alvin, "Superman" and "Clark Kent," Mar. 29, 1966): Doing Good; Pow! Bam! Zonk!; The Strongest Man in the World; We Need Him/W: Lee Adams, M: Charles Strouse.

4444. Loretta Holkmann *Porgy and Bess* (Radio City Music Hall, revival, "Maria," Apr. 7, 1983): I Hate Your Struttin' Style/W: DuBose Heyward, M: George Gershwin — Oh, Bess, Oh Where's My Bess?/W: Ira Gershwin, M: George Gershwin — Oh, Doctor Jesus/W: DuBose Heyward, Ira Gershwin, M: George Gershwin.

4445. Betty Lou Holland (Dec. 25. 1926–)

B: New York, NY. *Call Me Mister* (National > Plymouth, revue, Apr. 18, 1946): A Home of Our Own; Yuletide, Park Avenue/WM: Harold Rome.

4446. C. Maurice Holland (Sept. 11, 1896–Nov. 14, 1974) He began in vaudeville and appeared in silent films. For more than 10 years, in the so-called Golden Age of Television, he produced and directed the *Kraft Television Theatre*, a program of live dramas. *Love Dreams* (Times Square > Apollo, "Billy Parks," Oct. 10, 1921): Entre Nous; The Toddle Top Whirl; Two's Company, Three's a Crowd/W: Oliver Morosco, M: Werner Janssen. *Marjolaine* (Broadhurst, "Basil Pringle," Jan. 24, 1922): Cuddle Up Together (My Old Brown Coat)/W: Brian Hooker, M: Hugo Felix — I Want You/W: Anne Caldwell, M: Hugo Felix. *Sue, Dear* (Times Square, "Dave Craig," July 10, 1922): Foolishment; Key to My Heart; Love's Corporation/W: Bide Dudley, M: Frank Grey. *Lady Butterfly* (Astor, CR, "Billy Browning," Mar. 26, 1923): Doll's House; Girls I've Never Met; Good Evening, Good Night; Sway with Me; Waltz Time; When the Wedding Bells Ring Out/W: Clifford Grey, M: Werner Janssen. *Sunny Days* (Imperial, "Victor Duval," Feb. 8, 1928): One Sunny Day; Orange Blossoms/W: Clifford Grey, William Cary Duncan, M: Jean Schwartz. *White Lilacs* (Shubert, "Gaston De Flavigny," Sept. 10, 1928): Adorable You/W: David Goldberg, M: Maurice Rubens — Our Little Castle of Love/W: J. Keirn Brennan, M: Sam Timberg.

4447. Dorothy Holland (Feb. 11, 1945–) B: Indianapolis, IN. *Onward Victoria* (Martin Beck, "Susan B. Anthony," Dec. 14, 1980): The Age of Brass; Victoria's Banner/W: Charlotte Anker, Irene Rosenberg, M: Keith Herrmann.

4448. David Holliday (Aug. 4, 1937–) B: Illinois. *Man of La Mancha* (ANTA Washington Square, CR, "Don Quixote," Oct. 12, 1968 mats.): The Combat; Dulcinea; Golden Helmet; The Impossible Dream (The Quest); Man of La Mancha (I, Don Quixote)/W: Joe Darion, M: Mitch Leigh. *Man of La Mancha* (ANTA Washington Square, CR, "Dr. Carrasco,"1969): I'm Only Thinking of Him/W: Joe Darion, M: Mitch Leigh. *Coco* (Mark Hellinger, "Georges," Dec. 18, 1969): Let's Go Home; A Woman Is How She Loves/W: Alan Jay Lerner, M: Andre Previn. *Music Is* (St. James, "Duke Orsino," Dec. 20, 1976): The Tennis Song; When First I Saw My Lady's Face/W: Will Holt, M: Richard Adler. *Man of La Mancha* (Marquis, revival, "The Innkeeper," Apr. 24, 1992): Knight of the Woeful Countenance (The Dubbing)/W: Joe Darion, M: Mitch Leigh.

4449. Jennifer Holliday (Oct. 19, 1960–) B: Houston, TX. *Dreamgirls* (Imperial, "Effie Melody White," Dec. 20, 1981): And I Am Telling You I'm Not Going; Faith in Myself; I Am Changing; I Miss You Old Friend; One Night Only; Only the Beginning/W: Tom Eyen, M: Henry Krieger. *Grease* (Eugene O'Neill, revival, CR, "Teen Angel," c 1994): Beauty School Dropout/WM: Jim Jacobs, Warren Casey.

4450. Judy Holliday (June 21, 1921–June 7, 1965) B: Bronx, NY. Gifted comedic actresss known for her stage work, particularly in the play *Born Yesterday,* whose role of Billie Dawn she recreated on screen, and such other films as *Adam's Rib* (1949) and *The Solid Gold Cadillac* (1956). *Bells Are Ringing* (Shubert, "Ella Peterson," Nov. 29, 1956): Better Than a Dream [Apr. 14, 1958]; Drop That Name; Hello, Hello There!; I'm Goin' Back; Is It a Crime?; It's a Perfect Relationship; Just in Time; Long Before I Knew You; Mu-Cha-Cha; The Party's Over/W: Betty Comden, Adolph Green, M: Jule Styne. *Hot Spot* (Majestic, "Sally Hopwinder," Apr. 19, 1963): Gabie; Hey Love (See What You Can Do for Me); I Had Two Dregs; A Little Trouble (Goes a Long, Long Way); A Matter of Time; Smiles; That's Good, That's Bad/W: Martin Charnin, M: Mary Rodgers — Don't Laugh/ WM: Martin Charnin, Stephen Sondheim, Mary Rodgers.

4451. Hilda Hollins *Piff! Paff!! Pouf!!!* (Casino, "Encora Melon," Apr. 2, 1904): We Really Ought to Be Married/W: William Jerome, M: Jean Schwartz.

4452. Mabel Hollins (Dec. 25, 1887–Apr. 8, 1955) B: London, England. *Piff! Paff!! Pouf!!!* (Casino, "Nora Melon," Apr. 2, 1904): Under the Goo-Goo Tree/W: Stanislaus Stange, M: Jean Schwartz — We Really Ought to Be Married/W: William Jerome, M: Jean Schwartz. *His Honor the Mayor* (New York, "Daisy," May 28, 1906): The Dainty Milliners; A Little Girl Like Me/W: Charles J. Campbell, Ralph Skinner, M: Alfred E. Aarons — The Little Girl from Illinois/W: Charles J. Campbell, Ralph Skinner, M: Julian Edwards. *The Little Cherub* (Criterion, "Lady Dorothy Congress," Aug. 6, 1906): Cupid's Rifle Range [Oct. 22, 1906]/W: Adrian Ross, M: Frank Tours — Dear Little Girls; Olympian Octet/W: Owen Hall, M: Ivan Caryll — I Should So Love to Be a Boy/W: C.H. Bovill, M: Frank Tours. *The Girls of Gottenburg* (Knickerbocker, "Minna," Sept. 2, 1908): The Girls of Gottenburg/W: Adrian Ross, M: Ivan Caryll.

4453. Joan Holloway (Dec. 22, 1929–) B: Providence, RI. *Can-Can* (Shubert, CR, "Claudine," 1955): Can-Can; If You Loved Me Truly/WM: Cole Porter. *Shangri-La* (Winter Garden, "Rita Henderson," June 13, 1956): Every Time You Danced with Me; Second Time in Love; Talkin' with Your Feet/W: Jerome Lawrence, Robert E. Lee, M: Harry Warren.

4454. Julian Holloway (June 24, 1944–) B: Watlington, England. *My Fair Lady* (Virginia, revival, "Alfred P. Doolittle," Dec. 9, 1993): Get Me to the Church on Time; With a Little Bit of Luck/W: Alan Jay Lerner, M: Frederick Loewe.

4455. Stanley Holloway (Oct. 1, 1890–Jan. 30, 1982) B: London, England. Originally a seaside concert artist, he started on the stage in 1919. In movies from 1921; during the next 50 years he appeared in more than 100, many of them classics. *My Fair Lady* (Mark Hellinger, "Alfred P. Doolittle," Mar. 15, 1956): Get Me to the Church on Time; With a Little Bit of Luck/W: Alan Jay Lerner, M: Frederick Loewe. *Laughs and Other Events* (Ethel Barrymore, one-person revue, Oct. 10, 1960): And Yet I Don't Know; Any Old Iron; Brahn Boots; The Christening; A Cup o' Tea; The Gay Young Farmer; Gunner Joe; I Knew a Private; I Love Mary; I Must Go Home Tonight; I'm 'Enery the VIII; It'll Be All the Same; Je Sais Que Vous Etes Jolie; The Lion and Albert; A Little Bit of Cucumber; The Little Shirt My Mother Made for Me; My Word, You Do Look Queer; Old Sam; The 'Ole in the Ark; On Strike; Poppies; Return of Albert; Sentry Song; Signalman Dan; Three Ha' Pence a Foot; Two Lovely Black Eyes; Wotcher; You Gotta Get Aut/WM: Stanley Holloway — Champagne Charley Was His Name/W: H.J. Whymark, M: Alfred Lee — Going to the Derby; Green Peas; So We Will Sing/WM: old tavern songs.

4456. Sterling Holloway (Jan. 14, 1905– Nov. 22, 1992) B: Cedartown, GA. In movies he often played country bumpkins. He was the voice of several animated Disney characters, such as Dumbo and Bambi. He was Waldo Binney on the TV sitcom *The Life of Riley* (1953). *The Garrick Gaieties of 1925* (Garrick, revue, May 17, 1925): Manhattan; Sentimental Me; Soliciting Subscriptions; The Three Musketeers/W: Lorenz Hart, M: Richard Rodgers — Stage Managers' Chorus (Walk Upon Your Toes)/W: Dudley Digges, Lorenz Hart, M: Richard Rodgers. *The Garrick Gaieties of 1926* (Garrick, revue, May 10, 1926): Allez-Up [added]; Mountain Greenery; Sleepyhead; What's the Use of Talking?/W: Lorenz Hart, M: Richard Rodgers. *The*

Garrick Gaieties of 1930 (Guild, revue, June 4, 1930): Four Infant Prodigies; Love Is Like That/W: Allen Boretz, M: Ned Lehac — I Am Only Human After All/W: E.Y. Harburg, Ira Gershwin, M: Vernon Duke — Out of Breath/ W: Johnny Mercer, M: Everett Miller — Scheherezade/WM: Harold Goldman. The Garrick Gaieties of 1930 (Guild, revue, return engagement, Oct. 16, 1930): The Butcher, the Baker, the Candle-Stick Maker/W: Benjamin M. Kaye, M: Mana-Zucca — Four Infant Prodigies/W: Allen Boretz, M: Ned Lehac — I Am Only Human After All/W: E.Y. Harburg, Ira Gershwin, M: Vernon Duke — Out of Breath/W: Johnny Mercer, M: Everett Miller — Rose of Arizona; The Three Musketeers/W: Lorenz Hart, M: Richard Rodgers — Shavian Shivers; Unaccustomed As I Am/W: E.Y. Harburg, M: Vernon Duke.

4457. Celeste Holm (Apr. 29, 1919–) B: New York, NY. Skillful and versatile actress, memorable in such films as Gentleman's Agreement (1947) and All About Eve (1950). On TV she played Anna Rossini in the drama Falcon's Crest (1985). Oklahoma! (St. James, "Ado Annie Carnes," Mar. 31, 1943/Dec. 1947): All er Nothin'; The Farmer and the Cowman; I Cain't Say No/W: Oscar Hammerstein II, M: Richard Rodgers. Bloomer Girl (Shubert, "Evelina Applegate," Oct. 5, 1944): Evelina; It Was Good Enough for Grandma; Lullaby (Satin Gown and Silver Shoe); The Rakish Young Man with the Whiskers; Right as the Rain; Welcome Hinges/ W: E.Y. Harburg, M: Harold Arlen. The King and I (St. James, CR, "Anna Leonowens," July 30, 1952): Getting to Know You; Hello, Young Lovers; I Whistle a Happy Tune; The Royal Bangkok Academy; Shall I Tell You What I Think of You?; Shall We Dance?/W: Oscar Hammerstein II, M: Richard Rodgers. Mame (Winter Garden, CR, "Mame Dennis," Aug. 15, 1967): Bosom Buddies; If He Walked into My Life; It's Today; The Man in the Moon; My Best Girl; Open a New Window; That's How Young I Feel; We Need a Little Christmas/WM: Jerry Herman. The Utter Glory of Morrissey Hall (Mark Hellinger, "Julia Faysle, Headmistress," May 13, 1979): Give Me That Key; Proud, Erstwhile, Upright, Fair; Reflection; See the Blue; Way Back When/WM: Clark Gesner.

4458. Libby Holman (May 23, 1906–June 18, 1971) B: Cincinnati, OH. The torch singer's short marriage to young tobacco heir Zachary Smith Reynolds created a scandal by ending with his suicide. As her own life apparently did, too. The Garrick Gaieties of 1925 (Garrick, revue, May 17, 1925): Black and White; Ladies of the Boxoffice/W: Lorenz Hart, M: Richard Rodgers. Merry-Go-Round (Klaw, revue, May 31, 1927): Hogan's Alley; New York Town (Is Wearing Its Bandannas on Broadway); (He Said:) What D'Ya Say?/W: Howard Dietz, Morrie Ryskind, M: Henry Souvaine, Jay Gorney — Topics of the Day [July 18, 1927]/WM: Harry Richman, Cliff Friend. Rainbow (Gallo, "Lotta," Nov. 21, 1928): I Like You as You Are; I Want a Man; Let Me Give All My Love to Thee/W: Oscar Hammerstein II, M: Vincent Youmans. Ned Wayburn's Gambols (Knickerbocker, revue, Jan. 15, 1929): Mothers o' Men/W: Morrie Ryskind, M: Walter G. Samuels. The Little Show (Music Box, revue, Apr. 30, 1929): Can't We Be Friends?/W: Paul James, M: Kay Swift — Moanin' Low/W: Howard Dietz, M: Ralph Rainger — Six Little Sinners/W: Earle Crooker, M: Frank Grey. Three's a Crowd (Selwyn, revue, Oct. 15, 1930): Body and Soul/W: Edward Heyman, Robert Sour, Frank Eyton, M: Johnny Green — Right at the Start of It; Something to Remember You By/W: Howard Dietz, M: Arthur Schwartz — Yaller/W: Henry Myers, M: Charles M. Schwab. Revenge with Music (New Amsterdam, "Maria," Nov. 28, 1934): Maria; Wand'ring Heart; When You Love Only One; You and the Night and the Music/W: Howard Dietz, M: Arthur Schwartz. You Never Know (Winter Garden, "Mme. Baltin [Jeanne Montaigne]," Sept. 21, 1938): No, You Can't Have My Heart/WM: Dana Suesse — What Is That Tune?; You Never Know/WM: Cole Porter.

4459. Ben Holmes (Nov. 6, 1890–Dec. 2, 1943) B: Richmond, VA. Gay Paree (Winter Garden, revue, Nov. 9, 1926): There Never Was a Town Like Paris/W: Mann Holiner, M: Alberta Nichols.

4460. Jered Holmes That's Entertainment (Edison, revue, "Richard," Apr. 14, 1972): Absent Minded; Everything; I'm Glad I'm Single; Miserable with You; Triplets; You're Not the Type/W: Howard Dietz, M: Arthur Schwartz.

4461. Maynard Holmes The Cradle Will Rock (Windsor > Mercury, "Junior Mister" and "Rev. Salvation," Jan. 3, 1938): Croon-Spoon; Honolulu; Let's Do Something/WM: Marc Blitzstein.

4462. Millie Holmes Change Your Luck (George M. Cohan, "Passionate Sadie," June 6, 1930): Open That Door/WM: James C. Johnson.

4463. Prudence Wright Holmes B: Boston, MA. Happy End (Martin Beck, revival, "Sister Mary," May 7, 1977): Brother, Give Yourself a

Shove; Don't Be Afraid; In Our Childhood's Bright Endeavor; Lieutenants of the Lord; The Liquor Dealer's Dream; March Ahead/W: Bertolt Brecht, M: Kurt Weill.

4464. Rayley Holmes *Miss Millions* (Punch and Judy, "Horace Honeydew," Dec. 9, 1919): Dreams [Dec. 15, 1919]; My Advice/W: R.H. Burnside, M: Raymond Hubbell.

4465. Scott Holmes (May 30, 1952–) B: West Grove, PA. *Evita* (Broadway, CR, "Che," Apr. 5, 1983): The Actress Hasn't Learned (The Lines You'd Like to Hear); And the Money Kept Rolling In (And Out); Goodnight and Thank You; High Flying Adored; Lament; A New Argentina; Oh What a Circus; Peron's Latest Flame; Rainbow Tour; Waltz for Eva and Che/W: Tim Rice, M: Andrew Lloyd Webber. *The Rink* (Martin Beck, "Dino," Feb. 9, 1984): Blue Crystal; Not Enough Magic/W: Fred Ebb, M: John Kander. *Jerome Kern Goes to Hollywood* (Ritz, revue, Jan. 23, 1986): All the Things You Are; Can I Forget You?; The Folks Who Live on the Hill; I Have the Room Above Her; I Still Suits Me; I've Told Ev'ry Little Star; The Last Time I Saw Paris; Ol' Man River; The Song Is You/W: Oscar Hammerstein II, M: Jerome Kern — Bojangles of Harlem; A Fine Romance; I Dream Too Much; Remind Me; The Way You Look Tonight/W: Dorothy Fields, M: Jerome Kern — Californ-i-ay/W: E.Y. Harburg, M: Jerome Kern — Day Dreaming/W: Gus Kahn, M: Jerome Kern — Don't Ask Me Not to Sing; Yesterdays/W: Otto Harbach, M: Jerome Kern — Here Comes the Show Boat/W: Billy Rose, M: Maceo Pinkard — Long Ago and Far Away; The Show Must Go On/W: Ira Gershwin, M: Jerome Kern — Look for the Silver Lining/W: B.G. DeSylva, M: Jerome Kern — Make Way for Tomorrow/W: E.Y. Harburg, Ira Gershwin, M: Jerome Kern — They Didn't Believe Me/W: Herbert Reynolds, M: Jerome Kern — Till the Clouds Roll By/WM: P.G. Wodehouse, Guy Bolton, Jerome Kern — Who?/W: Oscar Hammerstein II, Otto Harbach, M: Jerome Kern. *The Best Little Whorehouse Goes Public* (Lunt-Fontanne, "Sam Dallas," May 10, 1994): Brand New Start; Change in Me; It's Been a While; Piece of the Pie/WM: Carol Hall.

4466. Taylor Holmes (May 16, 1872–Sept. 30, 1959) B: Newark, NJ. A matinee idol of the stage and silent screen; in later films he often played crooked politicians. *The Midnight Sons* (Broadway, CR, "Tom," Nov. 8, 1909): Yankee Honeymoon/W: Glen MacDonough, M: Raymond Hubbell. *Somewhere Else* (Broadway, "Billy Gettaway," Jan. 20, 1913): Can You Do

This?; Dingle-Dangle; How Do You Do/W: Avery Hopwood, M: Gustav Luders. *The Hotel Mouse* (Shubert, "Wally Gordon," Mar. 13, 1922): I'll Dream of You; One Touch of Loving; Rhyming/W: Clifford Grey, M: Armand Vecsey — Little Mother; Romance/W: Clifford Grey, M: Armand Vecsey, Ivan Caryll. *Happy Go Lucky* (Liberty, "Chester Chapin," Sept. 30, 1926): Happy Go Lucky/W: Helena Evans, M: Lucien Denni — Sing a Little Song/W: Gwynne Denni, M: Lucien Denni. *I'd Rather Be Right* (Alvin > Music Box, "The Secretary of the Treasury," Nov. 2, 1937): A Baby Bond for Baby/W: Lorenz Hart, M: Richard Rodgers.

4467. Tony Holmes *Shenandoah* (Alvin, CR, "Gabriel," Oct. 5, 1976): Freedom; Why Am I Me?/W: Peter Udell, M: Gary Geld.

4468. Lawrence Holofcener (Feb. 23, 1926–) B: Baltimore, MD. *Hello, Dolly!* (St. James, CR, "Cornelius Hackl"): Dancing; It Only Takes a Moment; Put on Your Sunday Clothes/WM: Jerry Herman — Elegance; Motherhood/WM: Bob Merrill, Jerry Herman.

4469. Calvin Holt *Catch a Star!* (Plymouth, revue, Sept. 6, 1955): The Story of Alice/W: Larry Holofcener, M: Jerry Bock.

4470. Henry Holt *The Girl and the Wizard* (Casino, CR, "Carl Behrend," Nov. 1, 1909): When I Sang Toreador/WM: Melville Gideon.

4471. Vivian Holt *Hello, Alexander* (44th Street, "Aunt Jemima," Oct. 7, 1919): Hawaiian Moonlight/W: Alfred Bryan, M: Jean Schwartz — Ma Curly Headed Babby/WM: George H. Clutsam — Roses of Picardy/W: Frederick Edward Weatherly, M: Haydn Wood. *Red Pepper* (Shubert, "Nokomis," May 29, 1922): Hiawatha's Melody of Love; Mississippi Cradle/WM: Howard E. Rogers, Albert Gumble, Owen Murphy.

4472. Lou Holtz (Apr. 11, 1898–Sept. 22, 1980) B: San Francisco, CA. The popular dialect comedian, who often worked in blackface, was discovered by ELSIE JANIS when he was 15, performing in a San Francisco road house. He often appeared on Jack Paar's late night TV show. *A World of Pleasure* (Winter Garden, revue, Oct. 14, 1915): I'll Make You Like the Town/W: Harold Atteridge, M: Sigmund Romberg — Syncopation [Jan. 3, 1916]/WM: J. Leubrie Hill. *Tell Me More!* (Gaiety, "Monty Sipkin," Apr. 13, 1925): In Sardinia (Where the Delicatessen Flows); Kickin' the Clouds Away; Mr. and Mrs. Sipkin (Monty! Their Only Child); Why Do I Love You/W: Ira Gershwin, B.G. DeSylva, M: George Gershwin — O Sola Mi, Whose Soul Are You?/W: Sam M. Lewis, Joe Young, M: Abel Baer. *Manhattan Mary* (Apollo,

"Sam Katz," Sept. 26, 1927): Broadway (The Heart of the World)/W: B.G. DeSylva, Lew Brown, M: Ray Henderson. *You Said It* (46th Street, "Pinkie Pinkus," Jan. 19, 1931): It's Different with Me/W: Jack Yellen, M: Harold Arlen.

4473. Terri Homberg (Jan. 5, 1959–) B: Jacksonville, FL. *Jerry's Girls* (St. James, revue, Dec. 18, 1985): Have a Nice Day; It Takes a Woman; It's Today; Just Go to the Movies; La Cage aux Folles; Mame; Milk and Honey; Song on the Sand; Take It All Off/WM: Jerry Herman.

4474. Arabella Hong *Flower Drum Song* (St. James, "Helen Chao," Dec. 1, 1958): Love, Look Away/W: Oscar Hammerstein II, M: Richard Rodgers.

4475. Keith Hong *Miss Saigon* (Broadway, CR, "Tam," c 1993): Little God of My Heart/W: Richard Maltby, Jr., Alain Boublil, M: Claude-Michel Schonberg.

4476. Howard Honig *The Rothschilds* (Lunt-Fontanne, CR, "Mayer Rothschild," Aug. 17, 1971): He Tossed a Coin; In My Own Lifetime; One Room; Rothschild & Sons; Sons/W: Sheldon Harnick, M: Jerry Bock.

4477. Walter Hook *Anya* (Ziegfeld, "Yegor," Nov. 29, 1965): That Prelude!/WM: Robert Wright, George Forrest.

4478. Robert Hooks (Apr. 18, 1937–) B: Washington, DC. A leading man, with many TV credits. Founder of the Negro Ensemble Co. *Hallelujah, Baby!* (Martin Beck, "Clem," Apr. 26, 1967): Another Day; I Don't Know Where She Got It; The Slice; Smile, Smile; Talking to Yourself; Watch My Dust/W: Betty Comden, Adolph Green, M: Jule Styne.

4479. Lee Hooper *West Side Story* (New York State, revival, "Consuelo," June 24, 1968): Somewhere/W: Stephen Sondheim, M: Leonard Bernstein. *Lost in the Stars* (Imperial, revival, "Answerer," Apr. 18, 1972): The Hills of Ixopo/W: Maxwell Anderson, M: Kurt Weill.

4480. Isabella Hoopes (Apr. 21, 1893–Aug. 7, 1987) *Show Boat* (New York City Center, revival, "Parthy Ann Hawks," Apr. 12, 1961): Why Do I Love You?/W: Oscar Hammerstein II, M: Jerome Kern.

4481. Legotie Hoover *The Magic Melody* (Shubert, "Mlle. Cherie," Nov. 11, 1919): We Are the Fixers/W: Frederic Arnold Kummer, M: Sigmund Romberg.

4482. Peggy Hoover *Hello Yourself!!!!* (Casino, "Isabel Manning," Oct. 30, 1928): Bobby's Nightmare; You've Got a Way with You/W: Leo Robin, M: Richard Myers.

4483. Bob Hope (May 26, 1903–July 27,

2003) B: Eltham, England. Megastar comedian, actor and singer, with a long career in vaudeville, standup comedy, movies, radio and TV. *Ballyhoo of 1932* (44th Street, revue, Sept. 6, 1932): Old Fashioned Wedding/W: E.Y. Harburg, M: Lewis E. Gensler. *Roberta* (New Amsterdam, "Huckleberry Haines," Nov. 18, 1933): Alpha Beta Pi; Don't Ask Me Not to Sing; Let's Begin; Something Had to Happen; You're Devastating/W: Otto Harbach, M: Jerome Kern. *Say When* (Imperial, "Jimmy Blake," Nov. 8, 1934): Don't Tell Me It's Bad/W: Ted Koehler, M: Ray Henderson. *Ziegfeld Follies of 1936* (Winter Garden, revue, Jan. 30, 1936): Fancy, Fancy; I Can't Get Started/W: Ira Gershwin, M: Vernon Duke — The Gazooka/WM: Ira Gershwin, David Freedman. *Red, Hot and Blue!* (Alvin, "Bob Hale," Oct. 29, 1936): It's De-Lovely; You've Got Something/WM: Cole Porter.

4484. Flossie Hope *Buster Brown* (Majestic, CR, "Susie Sweet," Feb. 27, 1905): Bo-Peep/WM: ? — Sue, Sue I Love You/WM: Billee Taylor. *The Rich Mr. Hoggenheimer* (Wallack's, "Tom Brown," Oct. 22, 1906): Poker Love (Card Duet)/WM: Paul West, Jerome Kern. *The Dairymaids* (Criterion, "Eliza," Aug. 26, 1907): Mary McGee/W: M.E. Rourke, M: Jerome Kern. *The Sunshine Girl* (Knickerbocker, "Marie Silvaine," Feb. 3, 1913): The Butler; Get a Move On!; Two Nuts/WM: Paul Rubens, Arthur Wimperis — You Can't Play Every Instrument in the Band/W: Joseph Cawthorn, M: John L. Golden.

4485. Peggy Hope *The Greenwich Village Follies of 1921* (Shubert, revue, Aug. 31, 1921): I Want a Picture of You/WM: Percy Wenrich.

4486. Angus Hopkins *Meet the People* (Mansfield, revue, Dec. 25, 1940): American Plan; Let's Steal a Tune (from Offenbach); Senate in Session/W: Henry Myers, M: Jay Gorney.

4487. Ethel Hopkins *Cheer Up* (Hippodrome, revue, Aug. 23, 1917): Beautiful Queen of the Nile; Gee! What a Wonderful Mate You'll Be/W: John L. Golden, M: Raymond Hubbell.

4488. Linda Hopkins (1925–) B: New Orleans, LA. *Inner City* (Ethel Barrymore, revue, Dec. 19, 1971): Deep in the Night; Fee Fi Fo Fum; It's My Belief; One Man; Urban Renewal; Winter Nights; You'll Find Mice/W: Eve Merriam, M: Helen Miller. *Me and Bessie* (Ambassador > Edison, revue, Oct. 22, 1975): After You've Gone/W: Henry Creamer, M: Turner Layton — Do Your Duty; Gimme a Pigfoot/WM: Wesley Wilson — Empty Bed Blues/WM: James C. Johnson — Fare Thee Well; God Shall Wipe All the Tears Away; I Feel Good; Jazzbo

Brown; Mama Don't 'Low; The Man's Alright; Moan You Mourners; Preach Them Blues; Put It Right Here; Trombone Cholly; Trouble/WM: ?—A Good Man Is Hard to Find/WM: Eddie Green — Hot Time in the Old Town Tonight/W: Joe Hayden, M: Theodore H. Metz — Kitchen Man/W: Andy Razaf, M: Alex Belledna — New Orleans Hop Scop Blues/WM: George W. Thomas — Nobody Knows You When You're Down and Out/WM: Jimmy Cox — Romance in the Dark/WM: Lil Green — 'Taint Nobody's Biz-ness If I Do/WM: Clarence Williams, Porter Grainger, Graham Prince — You've Been a Good Ole Wagon but You've Done Broke Down/WM: Ben Harney. *Black and Blue* (Minskoff, revue, Jan. 26, 1989): After You've Gone/W: Henry Creamer, M: Turner Layton — Come Sunday/ WM: Duke Ellington — I'm a Woman/WM: Elias McDaniel, Cora Taylor — I'm Gettin' 'Long Alright/WM: Bobby Sharp, Charles Singleton — 'Taint Nobody's Biz-ness If I Do/WM: Clarence Williams, Porter Grainger, Graham Prince.

4489. May Hopkins *The Grass Widow* (Liberty > Princess, "Angie," Dec. 3, 1917): All the Girls Have Got a Friend in Me; C.D.Q./W: Channing Pollock, Rennold Wolf, M: Louis A. Hirsch.

4490. Miriam Hopkins (Oct. 18, 1902–Oct. 9, 1972) B: Bainbridge, GA. Sophisticated blonde and versatile leading lady on Broadway and in movies from 1930. *Little Jessie James* (Longacre, "Juliet," Aug. 15, 1923): Quiet Afternoon/W: Harlan Thompson, M: Harry Archer.

4491. Peggy Hopkins see PEGGY HOPKINS JOYCE

4492. Ryan Hopkins *The King and I* (Neil Simon, revival, "Louis Leonowens," Apr. 11, 1996): I Whistle a Happy Tune/W: Oscar Hammerstein II, M: Richard Rodgers.

4493. De Wolf Hopper (Mar. 30, 1858–Sept. 23, 1935) B: New York, NY. M: Hedda Hopper, Hollywood gossip writer; EDNA WALLACE HOPPER; DELLA FOX; NELLA BERGEN. Important comedy, acting and singing star of the theater and early movies. In 1888, he gave his first performance on stage of the popular poem "Casey at the Bat" by Ernest Lawrence Thayer; during his lifetime he went on to repeat it 10,000 times. *The Black Hussar* (Wallack's, "Theophil Hackenback," May 4, 1885): Read the Answer in the Stars/W: Sydney Rosenfeld, M: Carl Millocker. *Wang* (Broadway, "Wang," May 4, 1891): Ask the Man in the Moon; The Man with an Elephant on His Hands/W: J. Cheever Goodwin, M: Woolson Morse. *El Capitan* (Broadway, "Don Errico Medigua, El Cap-

itan," Apr. 20, 1896): A Typical Tune of Zanzibar/W: Thomas Frost, M: John Philip Sousa. *Fiddle-Dee-Dee* (Weber and Fields Music Hall, "Hoffman Barr," Sept. 16, 1900): The Comic Opera; That's About the Size of It [Feb. 18, 1901]/W: Edgar Smith, M: John Stromberg. *Hoity-Toity* (Weber and Fields Music Hall, "General Steele," Sept. 5, 1901): The American Billionaire; Love a la Mode/W: Edgar Smith, M: John Stromberg. *Mr. Pickwick* (Herald Square, "Mr. Pickwick," Jan. 19, 1903): Boys Will Be Boys; The Forest Air; The Lay of the Merry Ha! Ha!; The Pickwick Club/W: Grant Stewart, M: Manuel Klein. *Wang* (Lyric, revival, "Wang," Apr. 18, 1904): same as above. *Happyland or The King of Elysia* (Lyric > Casino > Majestic, "Ecstaticus, King of Elysia," Oct. 2, 1905): Girls, Girls, Girls; How I Love Flowers; Mimette, the Human Mermaid; Oh, Joy! Oh, Bliss!/W: Frederick Ranken, M: Reginald De Koven. *The Pied Piper* (Majestic, "The Pied Piper," Dec. 3, 1908): I Should Like to Know the Reason; It's the Little Things That Count in Life; Nursery Rhymes; Woman's a Wonderful Thing/W: R.H. Burnside, M: Manuel Klein. *A Matinee Idol* (Daly's > Lyric, "Medford Griffin," Apr. 28, 1910): If You Could Only See Yourself as Other People Do/WM: ?— Nonsense/W: A. Seymour Brown, M: Silvio Hein — Won't You Write Your Autograph in My Album/W: E. Ray Goetz, M: Silvio Hein. *Lieber Augustin* (Casino, "Bogumid," Sept. 3, 1913): I'm the Patsy Bolivar of All the World/WM: Dick Temple — The Truth Must Come Out Some Day/WM: ?. *Hop o' My Thumb* (Manhattan Opera House, "King of Mnemonica," Nov. 26, 1913): No Damaged Goods; Those Seven League Boots/W: Sydney Rosenfeld, M: Manuel Klein. *The Passing Show of 1917* (Winter Garden, revue, Apr. 26, 1917): The Ready Made Sandwich/WM: ? *Everything* (Hippodrome, revue, Aug. 22, 1918): A Rainbow from the U.S.A./W: William Jerome, Jack F. Mahoney, M: Percy Wenrich. *Erminie* (Park, revival, "Ravennes," Jan. 3, 1921): Downy Jailbirds of a Feather/W: Claxson Bellamy, Harry Paulton, M: Edward Jakobowski. *White Lilacs* (Shubert, "Dubusson," Sept. 10, 1928): Words, Music, Cash/W: J. Keirn Brennan, M: Karl Hajos, based on Frederic Chopin.

4494. Edna Wallace Hopper (Jan. 17, 1864–Dec. 14, 1959) M: DE WOLF HOPPER. The comedian and actress was known as The Eternal Flapper. *Florodora* (Casino > New York, "Lady Holyrood," Nov. 10, 1900): I Want to Marry a Man, I Do; Tact; When I Leave Town/W: Paul Rubens, M: Leslie Stuart — I've an Inkling/WM:

Paul Rubens. *The Silver Slipper* (Broadway, "Wrenne," Oct. 27, 1902): The Baby with the Dimple and the Smile; Four and Twenty Little Men; If I Were a Girl Instead/WM: Leslie Stuart—The Girl You Love [Mar. 9, 1903]/WM: Paul Rubens—Ping Pong Duet/W: Percy Greenbank, M: Ivan Caryll. *About Town* (Herald Square, "Fannie Frivol" and "Duchess of Ehwattington," Oct. 29, 1906): I'm a Fickle Maid; In Amsterdam/W: Addison Burkhardt, M: Melville Ellis—When Tommy Atkins Marries Dolly Gray/W: Will D. Cobb, M: Gus Edwards. *Fifty Miles from Boston* (Garrick, "Sadie Woodis," Feb. 3, 1908): Jack and Jill; Waltz with Me/WM: George M. Cohan. *Girl o' Mine* (Bijou, "Lulu," Jan. 28, 1918): Rug Snug; Shrug Your Shoulders/W: Philip Bartholomae, M: Frank Tours.

4495. Irene Hopping *The Girl Who Smiles* (Lyric > Longacre, "Madeline," Aug. 9, 1915): A Breath from Bohemia/WM: Edward A. Paulton, Adolf Philipp, Jean Briquet.

4496. Bill Horan *Texas, Li'l Darlin'* (Mark Hellinger, "Muleshoes," Nov. 25, 1949): They Talk a Different Language (The Yodel Blues); Whoopin' and a-Hollerin'/W: Johnny Mercer, M: Robert Emmett Dolan.

4497. Mary Horan *Sons o' Guns* (Imperial, "Bernice Pearce," Nov. 26, 1929): Let's Merge; Red Hot and Blue Rhythm; There's a Rainbow on the Way/W: Arthur Swanstrom, Benny Davis, M: J. Fred Coots.

4498. Marie Horgan *The Road to Mandalay* (Park, "Mrs. Everleigh Fitzhugh," Mar. 1, 1916): Bright Day Dawning; Till You Try/W: William J. McKenna, M: Oreste Vessella.

4499. Patrick Horgan (May 26, 1929–) B: Nottingham, England. *Baker Street* (Broadway > Martin Beck, "Capt. Gregg," Feb. 16, 1965): It's So Simple/WM: Marian Grudeff, Raymond Jessel.

4500. Gen Horiuchi *Cats* (Winter Garden, CR, "Mistoffolees," Mar. 18, 1995): The Invitation to the Jellicle Ball; Mr. Mistoffolees; Mungojerrie and Rumpleteazer/W: T.S. Eliot, M: Andrew Lloyd Webber.

4501. Frank Horn *Nina Rosa* (Majestic, "Tom," Sept. 20, 1930): Nina Rosa/W: Irving Caesar, M: Sigmund Romberg.

4502. Roderick Horn *Oliver!* (Mark Hellinger, revival, "Mr. Sowerberry," Apr. 29, 1984): That's Your Funeral/WM: Lionel Bart.

4503. Frank Hornaday *Night of Love* (Hudson, "Rubero," Jan.7, 1941): Chiquitin Trio; I'm Thinking of Love; My Loved One/W: Rowland Leigh, M: Robert Stolz. *The Student Prince* (Broadway, revival, "Prince Karl Franz," June 8, 1943): Deep in My Heart, Dear; Golden Days; Nevermore; Serenade; Student Life/W: Dorothy Donnelly, M: Sigmund Romberg.

4504. C. Morton Horne *Marriage a la Carte* (Casino, "Hon. Richard Mirables," Jan. 2, 1911): Of All Her Sex a Paragon; Silly Cock-a-doodle-doo; Such a Bore!; Walking on a Wire; You, You/W: C.M.S. McLellan, M: Ivan Caryll. *Little Boy Blue* (Lyric, "Capt. Graham," Nov. 27, 1911): Aeroplane Duet/W: Grant Stewart, M: Henry Bereny. *Mlle. Modiste* (Globe, revival, "Capt. Etienne de Bouvray," May 26, 1913): The Time and the Place and the Girl/W: Henry Blossom, M: Victor Herbert.

4505. Lena Horne (June 30, 1917–) B: Brooklyn, NY. Star singer and actress, memorable in movies such as *Stormy Weather* (1943) and *Cabin in the Sky* (1945). *Blackbirds of 1939* (Hudson, revue, Feb. 11, 1939): Name It and It's Yours/WM: Mitchell Parish, Abner Silver, Sammy Fain—Shake Your Bluesies with Dancing Shoesies; Thursday/W: Dorothy Sachs, M: Louis Haber—Swing Struck/W: Irving Taylor, M: Vic Mizzy—You're So Indiff'rent/W: Mitchell Parish, M: Sammy Fain. *Jamaica* (Imperial, "Savannah," Oct. 31, 1957): Ain't It de Truth?; Cocoanut Sweet; I Don't Think I'll End It All Today; Napoleon; Pity de Sunset; Pretty to Walk With (That's How a Man Gets Got); Push de Button; Savannah; Take It Slow, Joe/W: E.Y. Harburg, M: Harold Arlen. *Lena Horne: The Lady and Her Music* (Nederlander, revue, May 12, 1981): As Long as I Live; Raisin' the Rent; Stormy Weather/W: Ted Koehler, M: Harold Arlen—Better Than Anything/WM: William Loughborough, D. Wheat—Bewitched, Bothered and Bewildered; The Lady Is a Tramp; A Lady Must Live; Where or When/W: Lorenz Hart, M: Richard Rodgers—Can't Help Lovin' Dat Man/W: Oscar Hammerstein II, M: Jerome Kern—Copper-Colored Gal/WM: Benny Davis, J. Fred Coots—'Deed I Do/W: Walter Hirsch, M: Fred Rose—Fly/WM: Martin Charnin—From This Moment On; Just One of Those Things/WM: Cole Porter—I Got a Name/W: Norman Gimbel, M: Charles Fox—I Want to Be Happy/W: Irving Caesar, M: Vincent Youmans—If You Believe (Believe in Yourself); That's What Miracles Are All About/WM: Charlie Smalls—I'm Glad There Is You/W: Paul Madeira, M: Jimmy Dorsey—I'm Gonna Sit Right Down and Write Myself a Letter/W: Joe Young, M: Fred E. Ahlert—Lady with the Fan/WM: Cab Calloway, Jeanne Burns, Al Brackman—Push de Button/W: E.Y. Harburg, M: Harold Arlen — Life Goes On/WM: Craig Doerge, Paul Williams — Love/WM: Ralph Blane, Hugh Martin — The Surrey with the Fringe on Top/W: Oscar Hammerstein II, M: Richard Rodgers — Watch What Happens/ W: Norman Gimbel, M: Charles Fox.

4506. William Horne In 1942, he was a Private in the U.S. Army. *This Is the Army* (Broadway, revue, July 4, 1942): I'm Getting Tired So I Can Sleep/WM: Irving Berlin. *Helen Goes to Troy* (Alvin, "Paris," Apr. 24, 1944): Come with Me; Is It a Dream?; The Judgment of Paris; The Shepherd Song; Sweet Helen/W: Herbert Baker, M: Jacques Offenbach, adapted by Eric Wolfgang Korngold.

4507. Cara Horner *A Christmas Carol* (Paramount Madison Square Garden, return engagements, "Grace Smythe," Nov. 20, 1995 > Nov. 22, 1996): Street Song/W: Lynn Ahrens, M: Alan Menken.

4508. Lacey Hornkohl *The Who's Tommy* (St. James, CR, "Sally Simpson," c 1994): Sally Simpson/WM: Pete Townshend. *Grease* (Eugene O'Neill, revival, CR, "Sandy Dumbrowski"): It's Raining on Prom Night; Look at Me, I'm Sandra Dee; Rydell Fight Song; Since I Don't Have You; Summer Nights/WM: Jim Jacobs, Warren Casey.

4509. Jannet Horsley *A Chorus Line* (Shubert, CR, "Judy," Sept. 1980): And.../W: Edward Kleban, M: Marvin Hamlisch.

4510. Del Horstmann *Oklahoma!* (Music Theater of Lincoln Center, revival, "Slim," June 23, 1969): The Farmer and the Cowman/W: Oscar Hammerstein II, M: Richard Rodgers.

4511. Robert Horton (July 29, 1924–) B: Los Angeles, CA. He played Flint McCullough on the long-running TV Western *Wagon Train* (1957). *110 in the Shade* (Broadhurst, "Bill Starbuck," Oct. 24, 1963): Is It Really Me?; Melisande; The Rain Song; Wonderful Music; You're Not Foolin' Me/W: Tom Jones, M: Harvey Schmidt.

4512. David Horwitz *Candide* (Broadway, revival, "Huntsman" and "1st Recruiting Officer" and "Agent" and "Spanish Don" and "Cartagenian" and "Priest" and "Sailor" and "Eunuch," Mar. 10, 1974): I Am Easily Assimilated/W: Richard Wilbur, M: Leonard Bernstein.

4513. John Hoshko (July 28, 1959–) B: Bethesda, MD. *Prince of Central Park* (Belasco, "Young Richard," Nov. 9, 1989): We Were Dancing/W: Gloria Nissenson, M: Don Sebesky.

4514. Robert Hoshour *Romance Romance* (Helen Hayes, "Lenny," May 1, 1988): My Love

for You; Plans A & B; Small Craft Warnings; Think of the Odds/W: Barry Harman, M: Keith Herrmann.

4515. Beverly Hosier *Billion Dollar Baby* (Alvin, "Neighbor," Dec. 21, 1945): Who's Gonna Be the Winner?/W: Betty Comden, Adolph Green, M: Morton Gould. *Lend an Ear* (National > Broadhurst, revue, Dec. 16, 1948): Friday Dancing Class; Molly O'Reilly/WM: Charles Gaynor.

4516. Alice Hosmer (c 1860–Jan. 12, 1911) B: Washington, D.C. *The Love Cure* (New Amsterdam, "Mrs. Julia Silliman," Sept. 1, 1909): Peek-a-boo!/W: Oliver Herford, M: Edmund Eysler.

4517. Dee Hoty (Aug. 16, 1952–) B: Lakewood, OH. *The Five O'Clock Girl* (Helen Hayes, revival, "Cora Wainwright," Jan. 28, 1981): Manhattan Walk/W: Bert Kalmer, M: Harry Ruby, Herbert Stothart. *Me and My Girl* (Marquis, revival, CR, "Lady Jacqueline Carstone," Feb. 23, 1988): The Sun Has Got His Hat On/W: Ralph Butler, M: Noel Gay — Thinking of No One but Me; You Would If You Could/W: Douglas Furber, M: Noel Gay. *City of Angels* (Virginia, "Alaura Kingsley," Dec. 11, 1989): Double Talk; The Tennis Song/W: David Zippel, M: Cy Coleman. *The Will Rogers Follies* (Palace, "Betty Blake," May 1, 1991): The Big Time; My Big Mistake; My Unknown Someone; No Man Left for Me; Without You/W: Betty Comden, Adolph Green, M: Cy Coleman. *The Best Little Whorehouse Goes Public* (Lunt-Fontanne, "Mona Stangley," May 10, 1994): Brand New Start; Call Me; I'm Leavin' Texas; It's Been a While; Nothin' Like a Picture Show; Piece of the Pie/WM: Carol Hall.

4518. Billy House (May 7, 1890–Sept. 23, 1961) B: Mankato, MN. A character actor who started out as a trumpet player. *Luckee Girl* (Casino, "Hercules," Sept. 15, 1928): Come On and Let's Make Whoopee/W: Mann Holiner, M: Werner Janssen — A Good Old Egg/WM: ? — I'll Take You to the Country/W: Max Lief, Nathaniel Lief, M: Maurice Yvain. *Murder at the Vanities* (New Amsterdam > Majestic, "Walter Buck," Sept. 12, 1933): Weep No More, My Baby/W: Edward Heyman, M: Johnny Green. *All the King's Horses* (Imperial, CR, "Con Conley," Apr. 1934): I've Gone Nuts Over You; Ouch; Tamboree/W: Frederick Herendeen, M: Edward A. Horan. *Show Boat* (New York City Center, revival, "Cap'n Andy Hawks," Sept. 7, 1948): Why Do I Love You?/W: Oscar Hammerstein II, M: Jerome Kern.

4519. Elizabeth Houston *The Illustrators' Show* (48th Street, revue, Jan. 22, 1936): I Love a Polka So/W: Carl Randall, M: Berenice Kazounoff— I'm You/W: Frank Loesser, M: Irving Actman — Let's Talk About the Weather/ WM: Charlotte Kent.

4520. Ethel Dufre Houston *The Baron Trenck* (Casino, "Frau Cornelia Stecher," Mar. 11, 1912): In Merry, Merry May/W: Frederick F. Schrader, M: Felix Albini. *The Peasant Girl* (44th Street, "Jadwiga Pawlowa," Mar. 2, 1915): Advice to the Young/W: ?, M: Oscar Nedbal — Love's Awakening/W: ?, M: Rudolf Friml, Oscar Nedbal. *Come Along* (Nora Bayes > 39th Street, "Mrs. Crosby," Apr. 8, 1919): Doughnuts for Doughboys/W: Bide Dudley, M: John L. Nelson.

4521. George Houston (Jan. 11, 1896–Nov. 12, 1944) B: Hampton, NJ. He sang with the American Opera Company; he also starred as The Lone Rider in a series of low budget Western movies (1940). *Chee-Chee* (Mansfield, "The Tartar Chief," Sept. 25, 1928): Singing a Love Song; The Tartar Song/W: Lorenz Hart, M: Richard Rodgers. *Fioretta* (Earl Carroll, "Orsino D'Andrea," Feb. 5, 1929): Blade of Mine/W: Grace Henry, M: George Bagby — Carissimi/W: Grace Henry, M: G. Romilli — Dream Boat/W: Grace Henry, Jo Trent, M: George Bagby. *The New Moon* (Casino, CR, "Robert Mission," Aug. 1929): An Interrupted Love Song; Lover, Come Back to Me; Marianne; Stouthearted Men; Wanting You/W: Oscar Hammerstein II, M: Sigmund Romberg. *Melody* (Casino, "Pierre," Feb. 14, 1933): Good Friends Surround Me/W: Irving Caesar, M: Sigmund Romberg. *Cavier* (Forrest, "Dimitri," June 7, 1934): Night Wind; Silver Sails/W: Edward Heyman, M: Harden Church. *Thumbs Up!* (St. James, revue, CR, Jan. 1935): Autumn in New York/WM: Vernon Duke.

4522. Peggy Hovenden *New Faces of 1934* (Fulton, revue, Mar. 15, 1934): Music in My Heart/ M: June Sillman, M: Warburton Guilbert. *Fools Rush In* (The Playhouse, revue, Dec. 25, 1934): Wicked, Unwholesome, Expensive/ WM: John Rox.

4523. Benjamin Howard *The Girl from Paris* (Herald Square, CR, "Tom Everleigh," Aug. 28, 1897): The Festive Continong; Somebody/W: George Dance, M: Ivan Caryll.

4524. Bob Howard (June 20, 1906–) B: Newton, MA. Swing pianist and vocalist in the tradition of FATS WALLER. *Early to Bed* (Broadhurst, "Pooch," June 17, 1943): Hi De Hi Ho in Harlem; Slightly Less Than Wonderful; Supple Couple; When the Nylons Bloom Again/ W: George Marion, Jr., M: Fats Waller.

4525. Charles (Charlie) Howard *Innocent Eyes* (Winter Garden, revue, May 20, 1924): Damn Clever, These Chinese/WM: ?. *Fioretta* (Earl Carroll, "Marquis Filippo Di Livio," Feb. 5, 1929): Wicked Old Willage of Wenice/WM: G. Romilli. *Something for the Boys* (Alvin, CR, "Mr. Tobias Twitch," Sept. 5, 1943): There's a Happy Land in the Sky/WM: Cole Porter.

4526. Cheryl Howard *Dance a Little Closer* (Minskoff, "Bebe," May 11, 1983): Happy, Happy New Year; Homesick; I Don't Know; I Got a New Girl; It Never Would Have Worked; Mad/W: Alan Jay Lerner, M: Charles Strouse.

4527. Don Howard *Earl Carroll's Sketch Book of 1929* (Earl Carroll > 44th Street > 46th Street, revue, July 1, 1929): Don't Hang Your Dreams on a Rainbow/W: Irving Kahal, M: Arnold Johnson — Like Me Less, Love Me More/ W: E.Y. Harburg, M: Jay Gorney — Song of Symbols/WM: ?— Song of the Moonbeams/W: Charles Tobias, Harry Tobias, M: Vincent Rose.

4528. Esther Howard (Apr. 4, 1892–Mar. 8, 1965) B: Montana. In movies from 1931. *The Sweetheart Shop* (Knickerbocker, "Minerva Butts," Aug. 31, 1920): I Want to Be a Bride; My Caravan; She's Artistic/W: Anne Caldwell, M: Hugo Felix. *Wildflower* (Casino, "Lucrezia La Roche," Feb. 7, 1923): I'll Collaborate with You; The World's Worst Woman/W: Otto Harbach, Oscar Hammerstein II, M: Herbert Stothart. *Tell Me More!* (Gaiety, "Jane Wallace," Apr. 13, 1925): Kickin' the Clouds Away; My Fair Lady (Lady Fair); When the Debbies Go By; Why Do I Love You?/W: Ira Gershwin, B.B. DeSylva, M: George Gershwin. *Allez-Oop* (Earl Carroll, revue, Aug. 2, 1927): What Did William Tell?/ W: Leo Robin, M: Phil Charig, Richard Myers. *The New Moon* (Imperial > Casino, "Clotilde Lombaste," Sept. 19, 1928): Funny Little Sailor Men; Love Is Quite a Simple Thing; The Trial/ W: Oscar Hammerstein II, M: Sigmund Romberg.

4529. Eugene Howard (July 7, 1880–Aug. 1, 1965) B: Neustadt, Germany. Older brother, partner and manager of WILLIE HOWARD. *The Passing Show of 1912* (Winter Garden, revue, July 22, 1912): Cohen's Yiddisha Band/WM: Ballard Macdonald, M: Al Piantadosi — The Metropolitan Squawk-tette/W: Harold Atteridge, M: Louis A. Hirsch. *The Whirl of the World* (Winter Garden, revue, "Steward of the Amber Club," Jan. 10, 1914): Ragtime Arabian Nights/W: Harold Atteridge, M: Sigmund Romberg. *The Passing Show of 1915* (Winter Garden, revue, May 29, 1915): Billy Shakespeare (The Shakespearian Rag/W: Harold Atteridge,

M: Leo Edwards — Isle d'Amour/W: Earl Carroll, M: Leo Edwards — My Trilby Maid/WM: Will Morrissey, Bobby Jones. *The Show of Wonders* (Winter Garden, revue, Oct. 26, 1916): Aladdin/W: Harold Atteridge, M: Sigmund Romberg — Mendelssohn and Liszt/W: Harold Atteridge, M: ?. *The Passing Show of 1921* (Winter Garden, revue, Dec. 29, 1920): My Wife/WM: ?. *The Passing Show of 1922* (Winter Garden, revue, Sept. 20, 1922): Carolina in the Morning/W: Gus Kahn, M: Walter Donaldson — Do You, Don't You, Will You, Won't You/WM: George A. Little, Larry Schaetzlein, Willie Howard, Eugene Howard — In Italy; My Coal Black Mammy/W: Harold Atteridge, M: Alfred Goodman. *George White's Scandals of 1926* (Apollo, revue, June 14, 1926): Walking Dogs Around/W: B.G. DeSylva, Lew Brown, M: Ray Henderson. *George White's Scandals of 1928)* (Apollo, revue, July 2, 1928): Bums; Second Childhood/W: B.G. DeSylva, Lew Brown, M: Ray Henderson. *Ziegfeld Follies of 1934* (Winter Garden, revue, Jan. 4, 1934): The Last Round-up/WM: Billy Hill. *The Show Is On* (Winter Garden, revue, CR, Sept. 18, 1937): Parade Night/W: Norman Zeno, M: Will Irwin.

4530. Garland Howard *Change Your Luck* (George M. Cohan, "Hot Stuff Jackson," June 6, 1930): Mr. Mammy Man; Sweet Little Baby o' Mine/WM: James C. Johnson.

4531. George Howard *Hiawatha* (Standard, "Mr. Lo," Feb. 21, 1880): A Marriageable Daughter/W: Nathaniel Childs, M: Edward E. Rice. *Adonis* (Bijou, "Bunion Turke," Sept. 4, 1884): Go Basest Lord/W: William F. Gill, Henry E. Dixey, M: Edward E. Rice. *Adonis* (Star, revival, "Bunion Turke," Nov. 22, 1888): same as above. *The Girl from Kay's* (Herald Square, "Harry Gordon," Nov. 2, 1903): I Don't Care/WM Paul Rubens — Make It Up/W: Claude Aveling, M: Ivan Caryll — Matilda and the Builder/W: J. Hickory Wood, M: Ernest Bucalossi — Semi-Detached/W: Adrian Ross, M: Ivan Caryll.

4532. H.C. Howard *The Student Prince* (Majestic, revival, "Lucas," Jan. 29, 1931): Serenade; Student Life; To the Inn We're Marching/W: Dorothy Donnelly, M: Sigmund Romberg.

4533. Joanna Howard *A Christmas Carol* (Paramount Madison Square Garden, return engagement, "Grace Smythe," Nov. 20, 1995): Nothing to Do with Me/W: Lynn Ahrens, M: Alan Menken.

4534. John Howard *Hazel Flagg* (Mark Hellinger, "Wallace Cook," Feb. 11, 1953): How Do You Speak to an Angel?; A Little More Heart; The World Is Beautiful Today/W: Bob Hilliard, M: Jule Styne.

4535. Joseph E. Howard (Feb. 12, 1867– May 19, 1961) B: New York, NY. M: MABEL BARRISON, one of nine wives. A musical comedy and vaudeville star, he also composed more than 200 songs, many among them standards. The movie *I Wonder Who's Kissing Her Now* (1947) portrays a version of his life. *The District Leader* (Wallack's, "Jack Dunning," Apr. 30, 1906): The Big Banshee/WM: Joseph E. Howard. *The Land of Nod* (New York, "The Man in the Moon," Apr. 1, 1907): Cross Your Heart; The Same Old Moon/W: Will M. Hough, Frank R. Adams, M: Joseph E. Howard.

4536. Ken Howard (Mar. 28, 1944–) B: El Centro, CA. He played Garrett Boydston on the TV drama *Dynasty* (1985). *1776* (46th Street, "Thomas Jefferson," Mar. 16, 1969): But, Mr. Adams; The Egg/WM: Sherman Edwards. *Seesaw* (Uris, "Jerry Ryan," Mar. 18, 1973): Chapter 54, Number 1909; In Tune; My City; Spanglish; We've Got It; You're a Lovable Lunatic/W: Dorothy Fields, M: Cy Coleman. *1600 Pennsylvania Avenue* (Mark Hellinger, "The President," May 4, 1976): I Love This Land; The Little White Lie; On Ten Square Miles by the Potomac River; President Jefferson Sunday Luncheon Party March; Rehearse!; Take Care of This House; We Must Have a Ball/W: Alan Jay Lerner, M: Leonard Bernstein.

4537. Larry Howard (?–1993) A major researcher into the John F. Kennedy assassination. He died in Dallas, TX. *By the Beautiful Sea* (Majestic, "Lenny," Apr. 8, 1954): Good Time Charlie/W: Dorothy Fields, M: Arthur Schwartz.

4538. Marcella Howard *I Married an Angel* (Shubert, "2nd Vendeuse" and "Philomena," May 11, 1938): Angel Without Wings; The Modiste/W: Lorenz Hart, M: Richard Rodgers.

4539. Tom Howard (June 16, 1885–Feb. 27, 1955) B: Co. Tyrone, Ireland. The burlesque and vaudeville comedian was host of the very funny radio quiz show takeoff *It Pays to Be Ignorant* (1942). *The Greenwich Village Follies of 1925* (46th Street, revue, Dec. 24, 1925): Go Ahead, Sing/WM: ?.

4540. William Howard *Keep Kool* (Morosco > Globe > Earl Carroll, revue, May 22, 1924): In They Go, Out They Come/W: Paul Gerard Smith, M: Jack Frost.

4541. Willie Howard (Apr. 13, 1883–Jan. 12, 1949) B: Neustadt, Germany. M: EMILY MILES. The legendary comic star was younger brother and partner of EUGENE HOWARD.

Brought to New York at the age of one year; in 1897 he debuted as a boy soprano at Proctor's 125th Street, a vaudeville theater. *The Passing Show of 1912* (Winter Garden, revue, July 22, 1912): The Bacchanal Rag; The Metropolitan Squawk-tette/W: Harold Atteridge, M: Louis A. Hirsch — Cohen's Yiddisha Band/W: Ballard Macdonald, M: Al Piantadosi — The Ragtime Jockey Man/WM: Irving Berlin. *The Whirl of the World* (Winter Garden, revue, "Sammy Meyers," Jan. 10, 1914): Nobody Was in Love with Me/W: Harold Atteridge, M: Sigmund Romberg — Ragtime Pinafore/WM: Henry Lehman. *The Passing Show of 1915* (Winter Garden, revue, May 29, 1915): Billy Shakespeare (The Shakespearian Rag)/W: Harold Atteridge, M: Leo Edwards — Broadway Sam/W: Blanche Merrill, M: Leo Edwards — Isle d'Amour/W: Earl Carroll, M: Leo Edwards. *The Show of Wonders* (Winter Garden, revue, Oct. 26, 1916): Mendelssohn and Liszt/W: Harold Atteridge, M: ? — Yaaka Hula Hickey Dula (Hawaiian Love Song)/WM: E. Ray Goetz, Joe Young, Pete Wendling. *The Passing Show of 1921* (Winter Garden, revue, Dec. 29, 1920): Becky from Babylon/W: Alex Gerber, M: Abner Silver — My Wife/WM: ?. *The Passing Show of 1922* (Winter Garden, revue, Sept. 20, 1922): Carolina in the Morning/W: Gus Kahn, M: Walter Donaldson — Do You, Don't You, Will You, Won't You/WM: George A. Little, Larry Schaetzlein, Willie Howard, Eugene Howard — In Italy; My Coal Black Mammy/W: Harold Atteridge, M: Alfred Goodman. *Sky High* (Shubert > Winter Garden > Casino, "Sammy Myers," Mar. 2, 1925): The Barbering Wop of Seville; The Best Song of All; Why Are They Following Me?/W: Clifford Grey, M: Carleton Kelsey, Maurie Rubens — Let It Rain/WM: Hal Dyson, James Kendis. *George White's Scandals of 1926* (Apollo, revue, June 14, 1926): Walking Dogs Around/W: B.G. DeSylva, Lew Brown, M: Ray Henderson. *George White's Scandals of 1928* (Apollo, revue, July 2, 1928): Bums; Second Childhood/W: B.G. DeSylva, Lew Brown, M: Ray Henderson. *George White's Scandals of 1929* (Apollo, revue, Sept. 23, 1929): Sittin' in the Sun (Just Wearing a Smile)/WM: George White, Cliff Friend. *Girl Crazy* (Alvin, "Geiber Goldfarb," Oct. 14, 1930): But Not for Me; Goldfarb! That's I'm!/W: Ira Gershwin, M: George Gershwin. *George White's Scandals of 1931* (Apollo, revue, Sept. 14, 1931): Those Were the Good Old Days/W: Lew Brown, M: Ray Henderson. *Ballyhoo of 1932* (44th Street, revue, Sept. 6, 1932): Ballyhujah; Man About Yonkers; What Have You Got to Have? [added]/W: E.Y.

Harburg, M: Lewis E. Gensler. *George White's Scandals of 1936* (New Amsterdam, revue, Dec. 25, 1935): I'm the Fellow Who Loves You/W: Jack Yellen, M: Ray Henderson. *The Show Is On* (Winter Garden, revue, CR, Sept. 18, 1937): Song of the Woodman/W: E.Y. Harburg, M: Harold Arlen. *My Dear Public* (46th Street, revue, "Barney Short," Sept. 9, 1943): If You Want to Make a Deal with Russia/WM: ?. *Sally* (Martin Beck, revival, "The Grand Duke Constantine," May 6, 1948): Look for the Silver Lining/W: B.G. DeSylva, M: Jerome Kern — Tulip Time in Sing Sing/W: P.G. Wodehouse, M: Jerome Kern.

4542. Elizabeth Howell (Dec. 24, 1914–July 14, 1999) B: Provo, Utah. *The Sound of Music* (Lunt-Fontanne, "Sister Berthe," Nov. 16, 1959): Maria/W: Oscar Hammerstein II, M: Richard Rodgers. *The Sound of Music* (Lunt-Fontanne, CR, "The Mother Abbess," Oct. 1961): Climb Ev'ry Mountain; Maria; My Favorite Things/W: Oscar Hammerstein II, M: Richard Rodgers.

4543. Helen Howell M: movie director, Frank Capra. She was a dancer. *Merry-Go-Round* (Klaw, revue, CR, July 18, 1927): In the Park/WM: ?.

4544. Lottice Howell (Nov. 14, 1897–Oct. 24, 1982) B: Bowling Green, KY. *Bye, Bye, Bonnie* (Ritz > Cosmopolitan, "Virginia Shrivell," Jan. 13, 1927): In My Arms Again; Love Is Like a Blushing Rose; Starlight/W: Neville Fleeson, M: Albert Von Tilzer.

4545. Sally Ann Howes (July 20, 1930–) B: London, England. M: songwriter Richard Adler. A child actress in films from 1943, she was the daughter of British actor Bobby Howes. *My Fair Lady* (Mark Hellinger, CR, "Eliza Doolittle," Feb. 3, 1958): I Could Have Danced All Night; Just You Wait; The Rain in Spain; Show Me; Without You; Wouldn't It Be Loverly?/W: Alan Jay Lerner, M: Frederick Loewe. *Kwamina* (54th Street, "Eve," Oct. 23, 1961): Another Time, Another Place; Did You Hear That?; One Wife; Ordinary People; What Happened to Me Tonight?; What's Wrong with Me?; You're As English As/WM: Richard Adler. *Brigadoon* (New York City Center, revival, "Fiona MacLaren," May 30, 1962): Almost Like Being in Love; From This Day On; The Heather on the Hill; Waitin' for My Dearie/W: Alan Jay Lerner, M: Frederick Loewe. *Brigadoon* (New York City Center, revival, "Fiona MacLaren," Jan. 30, 1963): same as above. *What Makes Sammy Run?* (54th Street, "Kit Sargent," Feb. 27, 1964): Kiss Me No Kisses; Lites — Camera — Platitude; Maybe Some Other Time; A Room Without

Windows; Something to Live For; A Tender Spot/WM: Ervin Drake.

4546. James Howkins *White Lights* (Ritz, "George," Oct. 11, 1927): An Eyeful of You/W: Al Dubin, M: J. Fred Coots.

4547. Beth Howland (May 28, 1941–) B: Boston, MA. She played Vera Louise Gorman on the TV sitcom *Alice* (1976). *High Spirits* (Alvin, "Beth," Apr. 7, 1964): The Sandwich Man/WM: Hugh Martin, Timothy Gray. *Darling of the Day* (George Abbott, "Rosalind," Jan. 27, 1968): What Makes a Marriage Merry/W: E.Y. Harburg, M: Jule Styne. *Company* (Alvin, "Amy," Apr. 26, 1970/Oct. 25, 1971): Getting Married Today; Poor Baby/WM: Stephen Sondheim. *Sondheim: A Musical Tribute* (Shubert, revue, Mar. 11, 1973): Getting Married Today/WM: Stephen Sondheim.

4548. Jobyna Howland (Mar. 31, 1880–June 7, 1936) B: Indianapolis, IN. Comic actress and model for the artist Charles Dana Gibson. *Kid Boots* (Earl Carroll > Selwyn, "Dr. Josephine Fitch," Dec. 31, 1923): Down 'Round the 19th Hole/W: Joseph McCarthy, M: Harry Tierney.

4549. Olin Howland (Feb. 10, 1896–Sept. 20, 1957) B: Denver, CO. Also known as Olin Howlin. He played small character roles in Hollywood movies for more than 40 years. *Leave It to Jane* (Longacre, "Bub Hicks," Aug. 28, 1917): I'm Going to Find the Girl; Sir Galahad/W: P.G. Wodehouse, M: Jerome Kern. *She's a Good Fellow* (Globe, "Chester Pollard," May 5, 1919): The Bumble Bee; I've Been Waiting for You All the Time; Oh, You Beautiful Person!/W: Anne Caldwell, M: Jerome Kern. *Linger Longer Letty* (Fulton, "Jim," Nov. 20, 1919): It's Just the Movement; Let's Pretend/W: Bernard Grossman, M: Alfred Goodman — Linger Longer Letty/W: Oliver Morosco, M: Alfred Goodman. *Two Little Girls in Blue* (George M. Cohan, "Morgan Atwell," May 3, 1921): I'm Tickled Silly (Slapstick); Wonderful U.S.A. (Your Wonderful U.S.A.)/W: Ira Gershwin, M: Paul Lannin — There's Something About Me They Like/W: Ira Gershwin, Fred Jackson, M: Vincent Youmans. *Just Because* (Earl Carroll, "Foster Phillips," Mar. 22, 1922): Associated Press; Eloping; Oh, Those Jazzing Toes/W: Helen S. Woodruff, M: Madelyn Sheppard. *Our Nell* (Nora Bayes, "Chris Deming," Dec. 4, 1922): The Cooney County Fair; Walking Home with Angeline/W: Brian Hooker, M: George Gershwin — Names I Love to Hear/W: Brian Hooker, M: George Gershwin, William Daly. *Wildflower* (Casino, "Gabrielle," Feb. 7, 1923): Course I Will; I Love You, I Love You, I Love You/W: Otto Harbach, Oscar

Hammerstein II, M: Vincent Youmans — I'll Collaborate with You; The World's Worst Woman/W: Otto Harbach, Oscar Hammerstein II, M: Herbert Stothart. *Golden Dawn* (Hammerstein's, "Sir Alfred Hammersley," Nov. 30, 1927): We Two/W: Oscar Hammerstein II, Otto Harbach, M: Emmerich Kalman, Herbert Stothart.

4550. Anna Hoy Sister of MARIETTA HOY and MARY HOY, known as the Hoy Sisters. *Jack O'Lantern* (Globe, "Princess Nougat," Oct. 16, 1917): Oh, Papa/W: Anne Caldwell, R.H. Burnside, M: Ivan Caryll.

4551. Marietta Hoy *Jack O'Lantern* (Globe, "Countess Caramel," Oct. 16, 1917): same as ANNA HOY.

4552. Mary Hoy *Jack O'Lantern* (Globe, "Duchess of Marshmallow," Oct. 16, 1917): same as ANNA HOY.

4553. Roy Hoyer *Tip Top* (Globe, revue, Oct. 5, 1920): The Girl Who Keeps Me Guessing; Life Is Like a Punch and Judy Show/W: Anne Caldwell, M: Ivan Caryll. *Stepping Stones* (Globe, "Prince Silvio," Nov. 6, 1923): In Love with Love; Once in a Blue Moon/W: Anne Caldwell, M: Jerome Kern. *Stepping Stones* (Globe, revival, "Prince Silvio," Sept. 1, 1924): same as above. *Criss Cross* (Globe, "Capt. Carleton," Oct. 12, 1926): The Portrait Parade; You Will, Won't You?/W: Anne Caldwell, Otto Harbach, M: Jerome Kern. *Angela* (Ambassador, "Count Bernadine," Dec. 3, 1928): The Baron, the Duchess and the Count; I Can't Believe It's True; You've Got Me Up a Tree [added]/W: Mann Holiner, M: Alberta Nichols. *Pleasure Bound* (Majestic, revue, "Tom Westover," Feb. 18, 1929): Just Suppose/W: Sid Silvers, Moe Jaffe, M: Phil Baker, Maurie Rubens — Park Avenue Strut/W: Harold Atteridge, Moe Jaffe, M: Phil Baker, Maurie Rubens.

4554. John Hoysradt (Oct. 5, 1904–Sept. 15, 1991) B: Bronxville, NY. Later known as John Hoyt. He played Grandpa Stanley Kanisky on the TV sitcom *Gimme a Break* (1982). *Allah Be Praised!* (Adelphi, "Emir," Apr. 20, 1944): Katinka to Eva to Francis/W: George Marion, Jr., M: Don Walker. *Maggie* (National, "Venables," Feb. 18, 1953): It's Only Thirty Years/WM: William Roy.

4555. Lon Hoyt (Apr. 6, 1958–) B: Roslyn, NY. *Rock 'n Roll! The First 5,000 Years* (St. James, revue, Oct. 24, 1982): Bennie and the Jets/WM: Elton John, Bernie Taupin — Message in a Bottle/WM: Gordon Sumner — Stayin' Alive/WM: Barry Gibb, Maurice Gibb, Robin Gibb.

4556. Vonnie Hoyt *Dream City* (Weber's,

"Maude," Dec. 25, 1906): Down a Shady Lane/ W: Edgar Smith, M: Victor Herbert.

4557. Alma Hubbard *Porgy and Bess* (44th Street > New York City Center, revival, "Serena," Sept. 13, 1943): My Man's Gone Now/W: DuBose Heyward, M: George Gershwin — Oh, Bess, Oh Where's My Bess?/W: Ira Gershwin, M: George Gershwin.

4558. Bruce A. Hubbard *Porgy and Bess* (Uris, revival, "Jake," Sept. 25, 1976): It Takes a Long Pull to Get There; A Woman Is a Sometime Thing/W: DuBose Heyward, M: George Gershwin. *Timbuktu!* (Mark Hellinger, "Chief Policeman," Mar. 1, 1978): Golden Land, Golden Life/WM: Robert Wright, George Forrest. *Show Boat* (Uris, revival, "Joe," Apr. 24, 1983): Can't Help Lovin' Dat Man; Ol' Man River/W: Oscar Hammerstein II, M: Jerome Kern.

4559. Elizabeth Hubbard (Dec. 22–) B: New York, NY. *A Time for Singing* (Broadway, "Bronwen Jenkins," May 21, 1966): Three Ships/ WM: Gerald Freedman, John Morris. *I Remember Mama* (Majestic, "Aunt Trina," May 31, 1979): Uncle Chris/W: Raymond Jessel, M: Richard Rodgers. *Dance a Little Closer* (Minskoff, "Contessa Carla Pirianno," May 11, 1983): I Don't Know/W: Alan Jay Lerner, M: Charles Strouse.

4560. Karen Hubbard *Hello, Dolly!* (Minskoff, revival, "Ermengarde," Nov. 6, 1975): Put on Your Sunday Clothes/WM: Jerry Herman.

4561. Margie Hubbard *Blackbirds of 1928* (Liberty > Eltinge, revue, May 9, 1928): Shuffle Your Feet (and Just Roll Along)/W: Dorothy Fields, M: Jimmy McHugh.

4562. Janet L. Hubert *The First* (Martin Beck, "Opal," Nov. 17, 1981): You Do-Do-Do-It Good!/W: Martin Charnin, M: Bob Brush. *Cats* (Winter Garden, "Tantomile," Oct. 7, 1982): The Moments of Happiness/W: T.S. Eliot, M: Andrew Lloyd Webber.

4563. David Huddleston (Sept. 17, 1930–) B: Vinton, VA. Actor and producer, often in Westerns. *The First* (Martin Beck, "Branch Rickey," Nov. 17, 1981): The Brooklyn Dodger Strike; Is This Year Next Year?; It's a Beginning; Jack Roosevelt Robinson; The Opera Ain't Over/W: Martin Charnin, M: Bob Brush.

4564. Johnny Hudgins *Lucky Sambo* (Colonial, "Sho Nuff," June 6, 1925): Porterology/ WM: Porter Grainger, Freddie Johnson.

4565. Wayne Hudgins (June 19, 1950–) B: Amarillo, TX. *Shenandoah* (Alvin, CR, "James," Feb. 17, 1976): Next to Lovin' (I Like Fightin'); Violets and Silverbells/W: Peter Udell, M: Gary Geld.

4566. Helen Hudson *George White's Scandals of 1923* (Globe, revue, June 18, 1923): Look in the Looking Glass; There Is Nothing Too Good for You/W: B.G. DeSylva, E. Ray Goetz, M: George Gershwin. *George White's Scandals of 1924* (Apollo, revue, June 30, 1924): I Need a Garden; Year After Year (We're Together)/W: B.G. DeSylva, M: George Gershwin. *George White's Scandals of 1925* (Apollo, revue, June 22, 1925): Beware of a Girl with a Fan/W: B.G. DeSylva, Lew Brown, M: Ray Henderson — Fly, Butterfly; Say It with a Sable/W: B.G. DeSylva, M: Ray Henderson.

4567. Muriel Hudson *Flora Bella* (Casino > 44th Street, "Countess Ola Drubetzkoy," Sept. 11, 1916): Cat, You Can't Leave Mice Alone; On to Petrograd/W: Percy Waxman, M: Charles Cuvillier — Creep, Creep, the World's Asleep/W: Victor Schertzinger, M: Milton Schwarzwald — Good Day, Good Night/W: Percy Waxman, M: Milton Schwarzwald.

4568. Teddy Hudson *Papa's Darling* (New Amsterdam, "Florine," Nov. 2, 1914): The Land of the Midnight Sun; The Popular Pop/W: Harry B. Smith, M: Ivan Caryll. *The Velvet Lady* (New Amsterdam, "Teddy," Feb. 3, 1919): I've Danced to Beat the Band/W: Henry Blossom, M: Victor Herbert. *Be Yourself!* (Sam H. Harris, "Betty," Sept. 3, 1924): Bongo Boo [Sept. 29, 1924]/W: Owen Murphy, M: Jay Gorney, Milton Schwarzwald — The Wrong Thing at the Right Time [Sept. 29, 1924]/W: Ira Gershwin, George S. Kaufman, Marc Connelly, M: Milton Schwarzwald.

4569. Travis Hudson (Feb. 2–Jan. 21, 1994) B: Amarillo, TX. *New Faces of 1962* (Alvin, revue, Feb. 1, 1962): Moral Rearmament/WM: Jack Holmes. *Pousse-Cafe* (46th Street, "Havana," Mar. 18, 1966): Goodbye Charlie/W: Marshall Barer, Fred Tobias, M: Duke Ellington — The Spider and the Fly/W: Herbert Martin, M: Michael Leonard. *Very Good Eddie* (Booth, revival, "Mme. Matroppo," Dec. 21, 1975): Katy-did/W: Harry B. Smith, M: Jerome Kern — Moon of Love/W: Anne Caldwell, M: Jerome Kern. *The Grand Tour* (Palace, "Mme. Marville" and "Mother Madeleine," Jan. 11, 1979): For Poland; We're Almost There/WM: Jerry Herman.

4570. Richard Huey *Bloomer Girl* (Shubert, "Alexander," Oct. 5, 1944): I Got a Song/W: E.Y. Harburg, M: Harold Arlen.

4571. Forrest Huff (Aug. 22, 1876–Aug. 21, 1947) B: Cleveland, OH. M: FRITZI VON BUSING. *The Ham Tree* (New York, "Ernest Everhart," Aug. 28, 1905): On an Automobile

Honeymoon/W: William Jerome, M: Jean Schwartz. *A Broken Idol* (Herald Square, "Jack Mason," Aug. 16, 1909): That's the Sign of a Honeymoon; What Makes the World Go Round/W: Harry Williams, M: Egbert Van Alstyne. *The Chocolate Soldier* (Casino, CR, "Lieut. Bumerli," Apr. 18, 1910): The Chocolate Soldier; The Letter Song; Seek the Spy; Sympathy; The Tale of a Coat; That Would Be Lovely/W: Stanislaus Stange, M: Oscar Straus. *The Belle of Bond Street* (Shubert, "Harry Gordon," Mar. 30, 1914): A Honeymoon Trip All Alone; Too Many Cooks/WM: ?. *Lady Luxury* (Casino > Comedy, "Sam Warren," Dec. 25, 1914): Dream On, My Princess; Hi There, Buddy; Life Is Just a Joke [Jan. 4, 1915]; Longing Just for You; When I Sing in Grand Opera/W: Rida Johnson Young, M: William Schroeder. *Sinbad* (Winter Garden > Century > Casino, "Van Rennsellar Sinbad," Feb. 14, 1918): I'll Tell the World/WM: Harold Atteridge, B.G. DeSylva — A Thousand and One Arabian Nights/W: Harold Atteridge, M: Sigmund Romberg. *Bombo* (Al Jolson > Winter Garden, "Jack Christopher" and "Christopho Columbo," Oct. 6, 1921): In the Way Off There; Through the Mist/W: Harold Atteridge, M: Sigmund Romberg. *The Serenade* (Jolson's, revival, "Duke of Santa Cruz," Mar. 4, 1930): Dreaming, Dreaming; The Funny Side of That; Woman, Lovely Woman/W: Harry B. Smith, M: Victor Herbert.

4572. Cady Huffman (Feb. 2, 1965–) B: Santa Barbara, CA. *The Will Rogers Follies* (Palace, "Ziegfeld's Favorite," May 1, 1991/Jan. 27, 1992): Will-a-Mania/W: Betty Comden, Adolph Green, M: Cy Coleman.

4573. Rosanna Huffman *Half a Sixpence* (Broadhurst, CR, "Ann Pornick"): Flash! Bang! Wallop!; Half a Sixpence; I Know What I Am; Long Ago/WM: David Heneker.

4574. Susan Hufford *Fiddler on the Roof* (Imperial, CR, "Hodel," Nov. 2, 1970): Far from the Home I Love; Matchmaker, Matchmaker; Now I Have Everything/W: Sheldon Harnick, M: Jerry Bock.

4575. Barnard Hughes (July 16, 1915–) B: Bedford Hills, NY. *How Now, Dow Jones* (Lunt-Fontanne, "Senator McFetridge," Dec. 7, 1967): A Little Investigation/W: Carolyn Leigh, M: Elmer Bernstein.

4576. J.J. Hughes He and his partner Adelaide were a popular dance team in vaudeville, specializing in a Pierrot and Pierette ballet. *The Passing Show of 1912* (Winter Garden, revue, July 22, 1912): My Reuben Girlie/W: Harold Atteridge, M: Louis A. Hirsch.

4577. Leila Hughes M: producer and composer, Alfred E. Aarons. *Two Little Brides* (Casino > Lyric, "Tatjana," Apr. 23, 1912): Are We Widows, Wives or What?; I Like All Girls; Kiss Me Again, Bebe; Meet Me at Eight in the Hall (The Letter Song); Snow Drops in the Spring; You Remind Me of Someone I Used to Know/W: Arthur Anderson, M: Gustave Kerker — Love Is Knocking at the Door/WM: ? — Somehow, Sometime, Somewhere/WM: Louis A. Hirsch. *The Maids of Athens* (New Amsterdam, "Mary Louise," Mar. 18, 1914): The Girl He Couldn't Kiss; When the Heart Is Young/W: Carolyn Wells, M: Franz Lehar.

4578. Mildred Hughes *Tickets, Please!* (Coronet, revue, Apr. 27, 1950): The Moment I Looked in Your Eyes/WM: Lyn Duddy, Joan Edwards. *Almost Crazy* (Longacre, revue, June 20, 1955): Mother's Day/W: Joyce Geary, M: Portia Nelson.

4579. Renee Hughes *Broadway Brevities of 1920* (Winter Garden, revue, Sept. 29, 1920): We've Got the Stage Door Blues/W: Bert Kalmer, M: Harry Ruby.

4580. Revella Hughes (1895–Oct. 24, 1987) B: Huntington, WV. *Runnin' Wild* (Colonial, revue, "Ethel Hill," Oct. 29, 1923): Open Your Heart; Swannee River/W: Cecil Mack, M: James P. Johnson. *Hot Rhythm* (Times Square > Waldorf, revue, Aug. 21, 1930): Loving You the Way I Do/W: Jack Scholl, Will Morrissey, M: Eubie Blake — Tropical Moon/W: Donald Heywood, M: Porter Grainger.

4581. Rhetta Hughes *Don't Play Us Cheap!* (Ethel Barrymore, "Earnestine," May 16, 1972): Ain't Love Grand/WM: Melvin Van Peebles. *Got Tu Go Disco* (Minskoff, "Snap-Flash," June 25, 1979): Chic to Cheap/WM: Kenny Lehman, John Davis, Ray Chew, Nat Adderley, Jr., Thomas Jones, Wayne Morrison, Steve Boston, Eugene Narmore, Betty Rowland, Jerry Powell. *Amen Corner* (Nederlander, "Margaret Alexander," Nov. 10, 1983): Amen Corner; Everytime We Call It Quits; Love Dies Hard; Rise Up and Stand Again; You Ain't Gonna Pick Up Where You Left Off/W: Peter Udell, M: Garry Sherman.

4582. Robert Hughes *The Red Mill* (Ziegfeld, revival, "Capt. Hendrick Van Damn," Oct. 16, 1945): I Want You to Marry Me; In the Isle of Our Dreams; Moonbeams; Wedding Bells (Wedding Chorus)/W: Henry Blossom, Forman Brown, M: Victor Herbert.

4583. Jack Hulbert (Apr. 24, 1892–Mar. 25, 1978) B: Ely, England. M: CICELY COURTNEIDGE. Actor, singer, dancer, director;

comedic star of British stage and screen. *Hassard Short's Ritz Revue* (Ritz > Winter Garden, revue, Sept. 17, 1924): Uking the Uke/WM: W. Franke Harling. *By the Way* (Gaiety > Central, revue, Dec. 28, 1925): All Day Long [Apr. 19, 1926]/W: Bert Lee, M: R.P. Weston — I Know Someone Loves Me/W: Graham John, M: Vivian Ellis — I Was Meant for Someone [Apr. 19, 1926]/W: Ballard Macdonald, M: James F. Hanley — I've Found the Bluebird [Apr. 19, 1926]; Looking Around [Apr. 19, 1926]/W: Leo Robin, M: Richard Myers — No One's Ever Kissed Me/W: Ronald Jeans, M: Philip Braham.

4584. Otto Hulett (Feb. 27, 1898–Sept. 1983) *The Grand Street Follies of 1928* (Booth, revue, May 28, 1928): Briny Blues/W: Agnes Morgan, M: Serge Walter. *The Garrick Gaieties of 1930* (Guild, revue, CR, Oct. 6, 1930): I Am Only Human After All/W: E.Y. Harburg, Ira Gershwin, M: Vernon Duke — I'm Grover/W: Newman Levy, M: Vernon Duke. *The Garrick Gaieties of 1930* (Guild, revue, return engagement, Oct. 16, 1930): Four Infant Prodigies/W: Allen Boretz, M: Ned Lehac — I Am Only Human After All/same as above — Rose of Arizona/W: Lorenz Hart, M: Richard Rodgers.

4585. Arthur Stuart Hull (May 8, 1878–Feb. 28, 1951) B: Pennsylvania. *Going Up* (Liberty, "James Brooks," Dec. 25, 1917): Down! Up! Left! Right!/W: Otto Harbach, M: Louis A. Hirsch.

4586. Esther Hull *Florodora* (New York, CR, "Valleda," during run, 1901): We Got Up at 8/WM: Leslie Stuart.

4587. Warren Hull (Jan. 17, 1903–Sept. 14, 1974) B: Gasport, NY. Emcee of the popular TV game show *Strike It Rich* (1951). *My Maryland* (Al Jolson, "Jack Negly," Sept. 12, 1927): Won't You Marry Me?/W: Dorothy Donnelly, M: Sigmund Romberg. *Rain or Shine* (George M. Cohan, "Jack Wayne," Feb. 9, 1928): Forever and Ever; Glad Tidings; Rain or Shine/W: Jack Yellen, M: Milton Ager — Roustabout Song (We Follow the Trail)/W: Jack Yellen, M: Milton Ager, Owen Murphy.

4588. Nancy Hume *Teddy & Alice* (Minskoff, "Alice Roosevelt," Nov. 12, 1987): But Not Right Now; The Fourth of July; Leg o' Mutton; Nothing to Lose; Perfect for Each Other/W: Hal Hackady, M: John Philip Sousa, Richard Kapp.

4589. Dorothy Humphreys *The Houseboat on the Styx* (Liberty, "Capt. of Police," Dec. 25, 1928): Hell's Finest/W: Monte Carlo, M: Alma Sanders. *The Little Show* (Music Box, revue, Apr. 30, 1929): Get Up on a New Routine; The Theme Song/W: Howard Dietz, M: Arthur Schwartz.

4590. Barry Humphries (Feb. 17, 1934–) B: Melbourne, Australia. *Oliver!* (Imperial, "Mr. Sowerberry," Jan. 6, 1963): That's Your Funeral/WM: Lionel Bart.

4591. Julie Humphries *Allegro* (Majestic, "Millie," Oct. 10, 1947): Money Isn't Ev'rything/W: Oscar Hammerstein II, M: Richard Rodgers.

4592. John Hundley (1900–Apr. 17, 1990) B: Hightstown, NJ. *Merry, Merry* (Vanderbilt, "Stephen Brewster," Sept. 24, 1925): My Own; Step, Step Sisters/W: Harlan Thompson, M: Harry Archer. *The Girl Friend* (Vanderbilt, "Thomas Larson," Mar. 17, 1926): Creole Crooning Song; Good Fellow Mine/W: Lorenz Hart, M: Richard Rodgers. *Just Fancy* (Casino, "Jack Warren," Oct. 11, 1927): Coo-Coo; Humpty-Dumpty/W: Leo Robin, M: Joseph Meyer, Phil Charig. *Just a Minute* (Ambassador > Century, "Jerry Conklin," Oct. 8, 1928): Anything Your Heart Desires; Pretty, Petite and Sweet/W: Walter O'Keefe, M: Harry Archer. *Polly* (Lyric, "Rex Van Zile," Jan. 8, 1929): Sing a Song in the Rain/W: Douglas Furber, Irving Caesar, M: Harry Rosenthal — Sweet Liar/W: Irving Caesar, M: Herbert Stothart. *Spring Is Here* (Alvin, "Stacy Haydon," Mar. 11, 1929): With a Song in My Heart/W: Lorenz Hart, M: Richard Rodgers. *Walk a Little Faster* (St. James, revue, Dec. 7, 1932): Mayfair/W: Roland Leigh, M: William Waliter — Time and Tide; Where Have We Met Before?/W: E.Y. Harburg, M: Vernon Duke.

4593. Cynthia Hunt *Evita* (Broadway, CR, "Peron's Mistress," c 1980): Another Suitcase in Another Hall/W: Tim Rice, M: Andrew Lloyd Webber.

4594. Ida Brooks Hunt *Woodland* (New York > Herald Square, "Miss Nightingale," Nov. 21, 1904): The Message of Spring; Time Is Flying/W: Frank Pixley, M: Gustav Luders. *Algeria* (Broadway, "Zoradie," Aug. 31, 1908): Rose of the World; Twilight in Barakeesh/W: Glen MacDonough, M: Victor Herbert. *The Chocolate Soldier* (Lyric > Herald Square > Lyric > Casino, "Nadina Popoff," Sept. 13, 1909): After Today; The Chocolate Soldier; The Letter Song; My Hero; Never Was There Such a Lover; Seek the Spy; Sympathy; The Tale of a Coat; That Would Be Lovely; We Too, Are Lonely/W: Stanislas Stange, M: Oscar Straus.

4595. Lois Hunt (Nov. 26, 1925–) B: York, PA. *Buttrio Square* (New Century, "Marisa D'Alessandro," Oct. 14, 1952): I'll Tell the World; Let's Make It Forever; More and More; One Is a Lonely Number/W: Gen Genovese, M: Fred Stamer. *The Sound of Music* (Lunt-Fontanne,

CR, "Elsa Schraeder," Oct. 1961): How Can Love Survive?; No Way to Stop It/W: Oscar Hammerstein II, M: Richard Rodgers.

4596. Alberta Hunter (Apr. 1, 1895–Oct. 17, 1984) B: Memphis, TN. International blues singer and recording artist. Coming out of retirement in 1977, she began appearing to great acclaim at The Cookery in New York City's Greenwich Village. *Change Your Luck* (George M. Cohan, "Mary Jane," June 6, 1930): Change Your Luck; Travellin'; Waisting Away/WM: James C. Johnson.

4597. Anne Hunter *The Girl from Wyoming* (American Music Hall, "Chiquori," Oct. 29, 1938): Manuelo/W: Ted Fetter, M: Richard Lewine.

4598. Eddie Hunter *My Magnolia* (Mansfield, revue, "Sherman," July 8, 1926): Baby Wants; Gallopin' Dominoes; Hard Times/W: Alex Rogers, M: C. Luckeyth Roberts.

4599. Edna Hunter (c 1877–Feb. 5, 1920) *The Liberty Belles* (Madison Square, "Daisy Field," Sept. 30, 1901): Lesson Book Song/W: ?, M: Aimee Lachaume — Shopping Chorus; A Spring Hat/W: Harry B. Smith, M: A. Baldwin Sloane. *Over the River* (Globe, "Sarah Parke," Jan. 8, 1912): I Want Him Saved/WM: John L. Golden.

4600. Glenn Hunter (1893–Dec. 30, 1945) B: Highland Mills, NY. *Spring Is Here* (Alvin, "Terry Clayton," Mar. 11, 1929): What a Girl; Yours Sincerely/W: Lorenz Hart, M: Richard Rodgers.

4601. JoAnn M. Hunter *Shogun: The Musical* (Marquis, "Kiku," Nov. 20, 1990): Pillowing/W: John Driver, M: Paul Chihara.

4602. Leslye Hunter *Christine* (46th Street, "Jaya," Apr. 28, 1960): I'm Just a Little Sparrow/W: Paul Francis Webster, M: Sammy Fain.

4603. Louise Hunter *Golden Dawn* (Hammerstein's, "Dawn," Nov. 30, 1927): Dawn/W: Oscar Hammerstein II, Otto Harbach, M: Robert Stolz, Herbert Stothart — Here in the Dark; My Bwana/W: Oscar Hammerstein II, Otto Harbach, M: Robert Stolz, Herbert Stothart.

4604. Nina Hunter *How Come?* (Apollo, "Dolores Love," Apr. 16, 1923): Charleston Cutout; Pretty Malinda; Syncopated Strain/WM: Ben Harris, Henry Creamer, Will Vodery.

4605. Walt Hunter *The Lieutenant* (Lyceum, "Captain," Mar. 9, 1975): At 0700 Tomorrow; Massacre; Something's Gone Wrong; Twenty-Eight/WM: Gene Curty, Nitra Scharfman, Chuck Strand.

4606. William Gregg Hunter *Rock 'n Roll! The First 5,000 Years* (St. James, revue, Oct. 24, 1982): Blueberry Hill/WM: Al Lewis, Larry Stock, Vincent Rose — Everybody Is a Star/WM: Sylvester Stewart — Land of 1000 Dances/WM: Chris Kenner, Fats Domino — Nothing from Nothing/WM: Billy Preston, Bruce Fisher — Why Do Fools Fall in Love?/WM: Frank Lymon, Morris Levy.

4607. Dorothy Hunting *Rogers Brothers in Paris* (New Amsterdam, "Emilie Lamson," Sept. 5, 1904): By the Old Oak Tree; Soldier Boy/W: George V. Hobart, M: Max Hoffmann.

4608. Tony Hunting *The Passing Show of 1913* (Winter Garden, revue, July 24, 1913): That Good Old Fashioned Cake Walk/W: Harold Atteridge, M: Jean Schwartz.

4609. Grace Huntington *Gentleman Joe, the Hansom Cabby* (Bijou, "Mrs. Ralli Carr," Jan. 30, 1896): Put It Down; Trovatore/W: Basil Hood, M: Walter Slaughter.

4610. G.P. Huntley (July 13, 1868–Sept. 21, 1927) B: Fermoy, Co. Cork, Ireland. *Three Little Maids* (Daly's > Garden, "Lord Cheyne," Sept. 1, 1903): Algy's Simply Awfully Good at Algebra/WM: Paul Rubens. *Hitchy-Koo of 1920* (New Amsterdam, revue, Oct. 19, 1920): The Star of Hitchy-Koo/W: Glen MacDonough, Anne Caldwell, M: Jerome Kern. *Peg o' My Dreams* (Al Jolson, "Alaric," May 5, 1924): Door Mats; Haven't We Met Before?/W: Anne Caldwell, M: Hugo Felix. *Be Yourself!* (Sam H. Harris, "Joseph Peabody Prescott," Sept. 3, 1924): Life in Town/WM: ?.

4611. G.P. Huntley, Jr. (Feb. 26, 1904–June 26, 1971) B: Boston, MA. Son of G.P. HUNTLEY. *This Year of Grace* (Selwyn, revue, Nov. 7, 1928): Chauve-Souris/WM: Noel Coward. *Gay Divorce* (Ethel Barrymore > Shubert, "Teddy," Nov. 29, 1932): Salt Air/WM: Cole Porter.

4612. Laurel Hurley (Feb. 14, 1927–) B: Allentown, PA. *Show Boat* (New York City Center, revival, "Magnolia Hawks Ravenal" and "Kim," Apr. 8, 1954): After the Ball/WM: Charles K. Harris — Can't Help Lovin' Dat Man; Make Believe; Why Do I Love You?; You Are Love/W: Oscar Hammerstein II, M: Jerome Kern.

4613. Dorothy Hurst *By the Way* (Gaiety > Central, revue, Dec. 28, 1925): In the Same Way I Love You/W: Eric Little, M: H.M. Tennant — My Castle in Spain/WM: Isham Jones.

4614. Frank Hurst *The Mimic World* (Century roof, revue, Aug. 17, 1921): Fine Feathers/W: Harold Atteridge, M: Sigmund Romberg — My Screen Maid; Old Fashioned Sweetheart/WM: ? — Star of Love/W: William Le Baron, M: Fritz Kreisler.

4615. James Hurst *Sail Away* (Broadhurst, "John Van Mier," Oct. 3, 1961): Don't Turn Away from Love; Go Slow, Johnny; Later Than Spring; Sail Away/WM: Noel Coward.

4616. Vera Hurst *Cape Cod Follies* (Bijou, revue, Sept. 18, 1929): The Lure of the Cape/W: Stewart Baird, M: Alex Fogarty.

4617. Woody Hurst *The Unsinkable Molly Brown* (Winter Garden, "Charlie," Nov. 3, 1960): I've A'ready Started In/WM: Meredith Willson.

4618. Jo Hurt *The Cradle Will Rock* (Mansfield > Broadway, revival, "Sister Mister," Dec. 26, 1947): Croon Spoon; Honolulu; Let's Do Something/WM: Marc Blitzstein.

4619. Ron Husmann (June 30, 1937–) B: Rockford, IL. *Tenderloin* (46th Street, "Tommy," Oct. 17, 1960): Artificial Flowers; My Miss Mary; The Picture of Happiness; What's in It for You?/W: Sheldon Harnick, M: Jerry Bock. *All American* (Winter Garden, "Edwin Bricker," Mar. 19, 1962): I Couldn't Have Done It Alone; I've Just Seen Her; We Speak the Same Language/W: Lee Adams, M: Charles Strouse. *Lovely Ladies, Kind Gentlemen* (Majestic, "Capt. Fisby," Dec. 28, 1970): Call Me Back; If It's Good Enough for Lady Astor; Right Hand Man; This Time/WM: Franklin Underwood, Stan Freeman. *On the Town* (Imperial, revival, "Gabey," Oct. 31, 1971): Lonely Town; Lucky to Be Me; New York, New York/W: Betty Comden, Adolph Green, M: Leonard Bernstein. *Irene* (Minskoff, revival, CR, "Donald Marshall," June 4, 1973): The Great Lover Tango/W: Otis Clements, M: Charles Gaynor — You Made Me Love You (I Didn't Want to Do It)/W: Joseph McCarthy, M: James V. Monaco. *Can-Can* (Minskoff, revival, "Judge Aristide Forestier," Apr. 30, 1981): C'est Magnifique; I Am in Love; It's All Right with Me; Never, Never Be an Artist/WM: Cole Porter.

4620. Jimmy Hussey *Puzzles of 1925* (Fulton, revue, Feb. 2, 1925): The Undecided Blues/WM: Elsie Janis — We're Jumping Into Something/WM: Blanche Merrill. *Betsy* (New Amsterdam, "Louie," Dec. 28, 1926): The Kitzel Engagement/W: Lorenz Hart, M: Richard Rodgers — Leave It to Levy/WM: Irving Caesar — The Tales of Hoffman/WM: Irving Caesar, A. Segal.

4621. Josephine Huston *Earl Carroll's Vanities of 1932* (Broadway, revue, Sept. 27, 1932): Along Came Love/W: Haven Gillespie, Charles Tobias, M: Henry Tobias — Forsaken Again; My Darling/W: Edward Heyman, M: Richard Myers — Take Me Away/W: Sidney Clare, Charles Tobias, M: Peter Tinturin. *Pardon My English* (Majestic, "Ilse Bauer," Jan. 20, 1933): Isn't It a Pity?; So What?; Tonight/W: Ira Gershwin, M: George Gershwin. *The Threepenny Opera* (Empire, "Lucy Brown," Apr. 13, 1933): Jealousy Duet; Lucy's Song/W: Bertolt Brecht, M: Kurt Weill. *Ziegfeld Follies of 1934* (Winter Garden, revue, CR, May 28, 1934): Green Eyes/W: E.Y. Harburg, M: Robert Emmett Dolan — The House Is Haunted (By the Echo of Your Last Goodbye)/W: Billy Rose, M: Basil G. Adlam — Suddenly/W: E.Y. Harburg, Billy Rose, M: Vernon Duke — What Is There to Say?/W: E.Y. Harburg, M: Vernon Duke. *Life Begins at 8:40* (Winter Garden, revue, Aug. 27, 1934): What Can You Say in a Love Song? (That Hasn't Been Said Before?)/W: Ira Gershwin, E.Y. Harburg, M: Harold Arlen.

4622. Philip Huston (Mar. 14, 1910–July 25, 1980) B: Goshen, VA. He worked mainly in the legitimate theater, in classical plays. *The Girl from Wyoming* (American Music Hall, "Ben Longwood," Oct. 29, 1938): Boston in the Spring; Our Home; Stay East, Young Man/W: Ted Fetter, M: Richard Lewine.

4623. Walter Huston (Apr. 6, 1884–Apr. 7, 1950) B: Toronto, Canada. The famous stage and film actor began in vaudeville with comedy sketches and song and dance. *Knickerbocker Holiday* (Ethel Barrymore, "Pieter Stuyvesant," Oct. 19, 1938): The One Indispensable Man; One Touch of Alchemy; The Scars; September Song; To War!/W: Maxwell Anderson, M: Kurt Weill.

4624. LeVern Hutcherson *Carmen Jones* (New York City Center, revival, "Joe," Apr. 7, 1946): Dere's a Cafe on de Corner; Dis Flower; If You Would Only Come Away; You Talk Jus' Like My Maw/W: Oscar Hammerstein II, M: Georges Bizet. *Porgy and Bess* (Ziegfeld, revival, "Porgy," Mar. 10, 1953): Bess, You Is My Woman Now; I Got Plenty o' Nuttin'; I Loves You, Porgy/W: Ira Gershwin, DuBose Heyward, M: George Gershwin — Oh, Bess, Oh Where's My Bess?/W: Ira Gershwin, M: George Gershwin — They Pass By Singing/W: DuBose Heyward, M: George Gershwin.

4625. David Hutcheson (June 14, 1905–Feb. 18, 1976) B: Craigmore, Bute, Scotland. *Sons o' Guns* (Imperial, "Maj. Archibald Ponsonby-Falcke, of the British R.F.A.," Nov. 26, 1929/Mar. 3, 1930): Let's Merge/W: Arthur Swanstrom, Benny Davis, M: J. Fred Coots. *Meet My Sister* (Shubert, CR, "Marquis de Chatelard," Jan. 19, 1931): I Like You/W: Mack Gordon, M: Harry Revel. *Free for All* (Manhattan, "Joe Butler," Sept. 8, 1931): I Love Him, the Rat; Living in Sin; Nevada Moonlight/W: Oscar Hammerstein II, M: Richard A. Whiting.

4626. Brice Hutchins see ROBERT (BOB) CUMMINGS.

4627. Harriet Hutchins *Keep Moving* (Forrest, revue, Aug. 23, 1934): A Bit of Optimism; The Torch Singer/W: Jack Scholl, M: Max Rich.

4628. Catherine Hutchinson *The Girl from Kay's* (Herald Square, "Norah Chalmers," Nov. 2, 1903): Bride's Song/WM: Bernard Rolt — Semi Detached/W: Adrian Ross, M: Ivan Caryll.

4629. Kathryn Hutchinson *The Show Girl or The Cap of Fortune* (Wallack's, "Cecelia Gay," May 5, 1902): As the Prince Waked the Princess/W: D.K. Stevens, M: H.L. Heartz — Invocation to Pie/W: D.K. Stevens, M: M.W. Daniels — A Rose and a Lily; Where Jasmine Flowers Are Twining/W: D.K. Stevens, M: Edward W. Corliss. *The Pearl and the Pumpkin* (Broadway, "Mother Carey," Aug. 21, 1905): The Submarine Fire Brigade (Fighters of Flame Are We)/W: Paul West, M: John W. Bratton. *The Rich Mr. Hoggenheimer* (Wallack's, "Lady Mildred Vane," Oct. 22, 1906): Au Revoir My Little Hyacinth [Oct. 29, 1906]/W: A.E. Sidney Davis, M: Herman Darewski — Cupid's Auctioneer/W: Harry B. Smith, M: Ludwig Englander.

4630. Mark Michael Hutchinson *Blood Brothers* (Music Box, "Eddie," Apr. 25, 1993): I'm Not Saying a Word; Long Sunday Afternoon; My Friend; That Guy/WM: Willy Russell.

4631. Chad M. Hutchison (Apr. 28, 1980–) B: Indianapolis, IN. *Peter Pan* (Lunt-Fontanne, revival, "Michael Darling," Dec. 13, 1990): I'm Flying; Tender Shepherd/W: Carolyn Leigh, M: Moose Charlap.

4632. Jim Hutchison *The Pajama Game* (St. James, CR, "2nd Helper," Nov. 29, 1954): Steam Heat/WM: Richard Adler, Jerry Ross.

4633. Betty Hutton (Feb. 26, 1921–) B: Battle Creek, MI. Blonde, vivacious singer and dancer of many 1940s Hollywood musicals. *Two for the Show* (Booth, revue, Feb. 8, 1940): Calypso Joe/W: Nancy Hamilton, M: Morgan Lewis. *Panama Hattie* (46th Street, "Florrie," Oct. 30, 1940): All I've Got to Get Now Is My Man; Fresh as a Daisy; They Ain't Done Right By Our Nell/WM: Cole Porter. *Annie* (Alvin, CR, "Miss Hannigan," Sept. 17, 1980): Easy Street; Little Girls/W: Martin Charnin, M: Charles Strouse.

4634. Bill Hutton (Aug. 5, 1950–) B: Evansville, IN. *Joseph and the Amazing Technicolor Dreamcoat* (Royale, revival, "Joseph," Jan. 27, 1982): Any Dream Will Do; The Brothers Came to Egypt; Close Ev'ry Door to Me; A Coat of Many Colors; Go, Go, Go, Joseph; Grovel, Grovel; Jacob and Sons; Joseph All the Time; Joseph's Dreams; Pharaoh's Dream Explained; Potiphar; Stone the Crows; Who's the Thief?/W: Tim Rice, M: Andrew Lloyd Webber.

4635. John Hyams (July 6, 1869–Dec. 9, 1940) B: Syracuse, NY. M: LEILA MCINTYRE. *The Belle of Bohemia* (Casino, "Chick Riley," Sept. 24, 1900): Strolling By the River/W: Harry B. Smith, M: Ludwig Englander. *The Sleeping Beauty and the Beast* (Broadway, "Doctor Squills," Nov. 4, 1901): When the Cure You Try/W: J. Cheever Goodwin, M: Frederic Solomon. *Piff! Paff!! Pouf!!!* (Casino, "Macaroni Paffle," Apr. 2, 1904): Lutie; M.A.C.A.R.O.N.I./ W: William Jerome, M: Jean Schwartz. *The Dancing Duchess* (Casino, "Count Gabor Von Bereny," Aug. 20, 1914): The Bumble Bee and the Butterfly; Fol-De-Rol-Lol; It's the Girls; Never Worry; That's the Kind of Man You Ought to Marry; That's the Way to Win a Girl/W: R.H. Burnside; M: Milton Lusk.

4636. F. Stuart Hyatt *The Red Feather* (Lyric, "Bagstock Bowler," Nov. 9, 1903): And Dost Observe How Well I Dust; Our Cabinet/W: Charles Emerson Cook, M: Reginald De Koven.

4637. Bruce Hyde (Sept. 14, 1941–) B: Dallas, TX. *Canterbury Tales* (Eugene O'Neill, "Absalon" and "John" and "Young Knight," Feb. 3, 1969): Beer Is Best (Beer, Beer, Beer); Darling, Let Me Teach You How to Kiss; What Do Women Want/W: Nevil Coghill, M: Richard Hill, John Hawkins.

4638. Frances Hyde *The Garrick Gaieties of 1925* (Garrick, revue, May 17, 1925): Stage Managers' Chorus (Walk Upon Your Toes)/W: Dudley Digges, Lorenz Hart, M: Richard Rodgers.

4639. Walter Hyde *Robin Hood* (New Amsterdam, revival, "Robin Hood," May 6, 1912): Roundelay/W: Harry B. Smith, M: Reginald De Koven.

4640. Constance Hyem *The School Girl* (Daly's > Herald Square, "Cicely Marchmont," Sept. 1, 1904): A Honeymoon Girl/WM: Leslie Stuart — If Ma Says No/WM: ?.

4641. Frank Hyers *Panama Hattie* (46th Street, "Windy Deegan," Oct. 30, 1940): Fresh as a Daisy; God Bless the Women; Join It Right Away; You Said It/WM: Cole Porter. *Something for the Boys* (Alvin, CR, "Harry Hart," Sept. 5, 1943): There's a Happy Land in the Sky; When We're Home on the Range/WM: Cole Porter.

4642. Evelyn Hylton With KATE HYLTON and MARGO HYLTON, they were known as the Hylton Sisters. *The Streets of Paris*

(Broadhurst, revue, June 19, 1939): Reading, Writing and Rhythm; South American Way; Thanks for the Francs; Three Little Maids/W: Al Dubin, M: Jimmy McHugh.

4643. Kate Hylton same as EVELYN HYLTON.

4644. Margo Hylton same as EVELYN HYLTON.

4645. Phyllis Hyman (July 6, 1941–July 1, 1995): B: Philadelphia, PA. *Sophisticated Ladies* (Lunt-Fontanne, revue, Mar. 1, 1981): I Got It Bad (and That Ain't Good)/W: Paul Francis Webster, M: Duke Ellington — I'm Checking Out, Go'om Bye/WM: Billy Strayhorn, M: Duke Ellington — In a Sentimental Mood/W: Manny Kurtz, Irving Mills, M: Duke Ellington — It Don't Mean a Thing/W: Irving Mills, M: Duke Ellington — Mood Indigo/WM: Albany Bigard, Irving Mills, Duke Ellington — Take the A Train/WM: Billy Strayhorn.

4646. Robert Hyman (Nov. 10, 1956–) B: Boston, MA. *Joseph and the Amazing Technicolor Dreamcoat* (Royale, revival, "Reuben," Jan. 27, 1982): Those Canaan Days/W: Tim Rice, M: Andrew Lloyd Webber.

4647. Jeff Hyslop *Anne of Green Gables* (City Center 55th Street, "Gilbert Blythe," Dec. 21, 1971): I'll Show Him; Where Did the Summer Go To?; Wondrin'/WM: Donald Harron, Norman Campbell. *A Chorus Line* (Shubert, CR, "Mike," Jan. 1979): I Can Do That/W: Edward Kleban, M: Marvin Hamlisch. *Kiss of the Spider Woman* (Broadhurst, CR, "Molina"): Anything for Him; Bluebloods; Dear One; Dressing Them Up; Gimme Love; Good Times; Her Name Is Aurora; I Draw the Line; Mama, It's Me; Only in the Movies; Over the Wall II; Russian Movie; She's a Woman; A Visit/W: Fred Ebb, M: John Kander.

4648. Carl Hyson M: DOROTHY DICKSON. They were a famous ballroom dance team, until their divorce. *Girl o' Mine* (Bijou, "Toby," Jan. 28, 1918): The Winning Race/W: Philip Bartholomae, M: Frank Tours. *Rock-a-Bye Baby* (Astor, "Archie," May 22, 1918): The Big Spring Drive; I Believed All They Said; I Can Trust Myself with a Lot of Girls; Motoring Along the Old Post Road; One, Two, Three; There's No Better Use for Time than Kissing/W: Herbert Reynolds, M: Jerome Kern. *Lassie* (Nora Bayes, "Philip Grayson," Apr. 6, 1920): Boo-Hoo; Flirting; Lady Bird; Skeletons; A Teacup and a Spoon/W: Catherine Chisholm Cushing, M: Hugo Felix. *Kissing Time* (Lyric, CR, "Paul Pommery," Oct. 25, 1920): Keep a Fox Trot for Me/W:?, M: Ivan Caryll — Mimi Jazz/WM: ?.

4649. Somegoro Ichikawa *Man of La Mancha* (ANTA Washington Square, CR, "Don Quixote," Mar. 2, 1970): The Combat; Dulcinea; Golden Helmet; The Impossible Dream (The Quest); Man of La Mancha (I, Don Quixote)/W: Joe Darion, M: Mitch Leigh.

4650. Loida Iglesias see LOIDA (IGLESIAS) SANTOS

4651. Thomas Ikeda *My Favorite Year* (Vivian Beaumont, "Rookie Carroca," Dec. 10, 1992): Welcome to Brooklyn/W: Lynn Ahrens, M: Stephen Flaherty.

4652. Margaret Illmann B: Adelaide, Australia. Before Broadway, she was principal dancer with the National Ballet of Canada. *The Red Shoes* (Gershwin, "Victoria Page," Dec. 16, 1993): Alone in the Light; Am I To Wish Her Love; The Audition; Top of the Sky; When You Dance for a King/W: Bob Merrill, M: Jule Styne.

4653. Angelique Ilo (Aug. 23, 1957–) B: Japan. *A Chorus Line* (Shubert, CR, "Judy," Aug. 1979/Apr. 24, 1989): And…/W: Edward Kleban, M: Marvin Hamlisch. *A Chorus Line* (Shubert, CR, "Cassie," Oct. 1984/July 1986): The Music and the Mirror/W: Edward Kleban, M: Marvin Hamlisch.

4654. Roger Imhof (Apr. 15, 1875–Apr. 15, 1958) B: Rock Island, IL. A vaudeville actor for over 20 years on the Orpheum and Keith circuits. *Jack and Jill* (Globe, "Daniel Malone," Mar. 22, 1923): Girls Grow More Wonderful Day by Day/W: Otto Harbach, M: Augustus Barratt.

4655. Carlo Imperato (Aug. 8, 1963–) B: Bronx, NY. *Runaways* (Plymouth, "A.J.," May 13, 1978): Every Now and Then/WM: Elizabeth Swados.

4656. H. Inez *Music Box Revue of 1921* (Music Box, revue, CR, Sept. 18, 1922): Dancing the Seasons Away/WM: Irving Berlin.

4657. Alvin Ing (May 26, 1938–) B: Honolulu, HI. *Pacific Overtures* (Winter Garden, "Shogun's Mother" and "American Admiral," Jan. 11, 1976): Chrysanthemum Tea; Please Hello/WM: Stephen Sondheim.

4658. Barrie Ingham (Feb. 10, 1934–) B: Halifax, Yorkshire, England. *Copperfield* (ANTA, "Uriah Heep," Apr. 13, 1981): 'Umble; Up the Ladder; Villainy Is the Matter/WM: Al Kasha, Joel Hirschhorn. *Aspects of Love* (Broadhurst, CR, "George Dillingham," Jan. 7, 1991): Falling; The First Man You Remember; A Memory of a Happy Moment; Other Pleasures; She'd Be Far Better Off with You; Stop. Wait. Please./W: Don Black, Charles Hart, M: Andrew Lloyd Webber.

4659. Rose Inghram B: Pelmyra, MO. *By Jupiter* (Shubert, "2nd Sentry," June 3, 1942): Jupiter Forbid/W: Lorenz Hart, M: Richard Rodgers. *Helen Goes to Troy* (Alvin, "Discordia," Apr. 24, 1944): The Judgment of Paris/W: Herbert Baker, M: Jacques Offenbach, adapted by Eric Wolfgang Korngold. *Polonaise* (Alvin, "Countess Ludwika Zaleski," Oct. 6, 1945): Au Revoir, Soldier; The Next Time I Care/W: John Latouche, M: Bronislau Kaper. *Three to Make Ready* (Adelphi, revue, Mar. 7, 1946): If It's Love; Tell Me the Story/W: Nancy Hamilton, M: Morgan Lewis. *Where's Charley?* (Broadway, CR, "Donna Lucia D'Alvadorez," Jan. 29, 1951): Lovelier Than Ever/WM: Frank Loesser.

4660. Violet Inglefield *Buzzin' Around* (Casino, "La Belle Violet," July 6, 1920): Pip Pip?/WM: Will Morrissey, Edward Madden.

4661. Georgia Ingram *Oh! Oh! Oh! Nurse* (Cosmopolitan, "Peggy," Dec. 7, 1925): Pierre/ W: Monte Carlo, M: Alma Sanders.

4662. Michael Ingram *Sarava* (Mark Hellinger, "Teo," Jan. 11, 1979): Muito Bom; Nothing's Missing; A Simple Man/W: N. Richard Nash, M: Mitch Leigh. *Sweet Charity* (Minskoff, revival, CR, "Herman," Mar. 1987): I Love to Cry at Weddings/W: Dorothy Fields, M: Cy Coleman.

4663. Rex Ingram (Oct. 20, 1894–Sept. 19, 1969) B: Cairo, IL. After graduating from medical school, the black actor was discovered by a casting director in Los Angeles. His career on stage, in TV and movies lasted 50 years. *Sing Out the News* (Music Box, revue, Sept. 24, 1938): F.D.R. Jones/WM: Harold Rome. *Cabin in the Sky* (Martin Beck, "Lucifer, Jr.," Oct. 25, 1940): Do What You Wanna Do/W: John Latouche, M: Vernon Duke.

4664. Tad Ingram (Sept. 11, 1948–) B: Pittsburgh, PA. *The Red Shoes* (Gershwin, "Sergei Ratov," Dec. 16, 1993): Do Svedanya/W: Bob Merrill, Marsha Norman, M: Jule Styne — It's a Fairy Tale/W: Bob Merrill, M: Jule Styne.

4665. Tonia Ingre *The Vanderbilt Revue* (Vanderbilt, revue, Nov. 5, 1930): I'm from Granada/W: David Sidney, M: Mario Braggiotti — Lady of the Fan/WM: ?.

4666. Frederick C. Inkley *Les Miserables* (Broadway, CR, "Jean Valjean," c 1995): Bring Him Home; Come to Me; In My Life; Soliloquy; Thenardier Waltz; Who Am I?/W: Herbert Kretzmer, M: Claude-Michel Schonberg.

4667. Page Inness *Nikki* (Longacre, "Page Innes," Sept. 29, 1931): Now I Know/W: James Dyrenforth, M: Phil Charig.

4668. Christopher Innvar *Les Miserables* (Broadway, CR, "Javert," Oct. 15, 1996): Soliloquy; Stars/W: Herbert Kretzmer, M: Claude-Michel Schonberg.

4669. Ethel Intropidi (c 1896–Dec. 18, 1946) B: New York, NY. Daughter of JOSIE INTROPIDI. *Rogers Brothers in Ireland* (Liberty > New York, "Mary O'Gaffeny," Sept. 4, 1905): When I Rode on the Choo Choo Cars/W: George V. Hobart, M: Max Hoffmann. *The Madcap* (Royale, "Claire Valmont," Jan. 31, 1928): Honeymooning Blues/W: Clifford Grey, M: Maurie Rubens.

4670. Josie Intropidi (c 1866–Sept. 19, 1941) B: New York, NY. Mother of ETHEL INTROPIDI. Especially well known for roles in Gilbert and Sullivan operas. *When Sweet Sixteen* (Daly's, "Mrs. Hammond," Sept. 14, 1911): It's Always Going to Be That Way/W: George V. Hobart, M: Victor Herbert. *The Laughing Husband* (Knickerbocker, "Lucinda," Feb. 2, 1914): In Beautiful Italiano/W: Arthur Wimperis, M: Edmund Eysler. *Her Regiment* (Broadhurst, "Lisette Berlier," Nov. 12, 1917): You Never Can Tell How a Marriage Will Take/W: William Le Baron, M: Victor Herbert. *Fiddlers Three* (Cort, "Suzanne Foppitt," Sept. 3, 1918): All on Account of Nipper!/W: William Cary Duncan, M: Alexander Johnstone.

4671. Daisie Irving *The Show of Wonders* (Winter Garden, revue, Oct. 26, 1916): Back to Nature; Wedding by the Sea/WM: ?.

4672. Dorothy Irving *Puzzles of 1925* (Fulton, revue, Feb. 2, 1925): Titina/W: Bertal Maubon, E. Ronn, M: Leo Daniderff— You've Got to Dance/WM: Elsie Janis.

4673. George S. Irving (Nov. 1, 1922–) B: Springfield, MA. M: MARIA KARNILOVA. *Call Me Mister* (National > Plymouth, revue, Apr. 18, 1946): Yuletide, Park Avenue/WM: Harold Rome. *Gentlemen Prefer Blondes* (Ziegfeld, "Josephus Gage," Dec. 8, 1949): Homesick Blues; I'm a'Tingle, I'm a'Glow/W: Leo Robin, M: Jule Styne. *Can-Can* (Shubert, CR, "Boris Adzinidzinadze," July 1954): Come Along with Me; If You Loved Me Truly; Never, Never Be an Artist/WM: Cole Porter. *The Beggar's Opera* (New York City Center, revival, "Mr. Peachum," Mar. 13, 1957): Hanging Is My Only Sport; In the Days of My Youth; Is Then His Fate Decreed, Sir?; Our Polly Is a Sad Slut; Through All the Employments of Life/WM: John Gay. *Irma La Douce* (Plymouth, "Police Inspector," Sept. 29, 1960): But; She's Got the Lot; Sons of France/W: Julian More, David Heneker, Monty Norman, M: Marguerite Monnot. *Bravo Giovanni* (Broadhurst, "Signor Bellardi," May 19,

1962): The Argument; Bravo, Giovanni; Uriti; Virtue Arrivederci/W: Ronny Graham, M: Milton Schafer. *Tovarich* (Broadway, "Charles Davis," Mar. 18, 1963): Say You'll Stay/W: Anne Crosswell, M: Lee Pockriss. *Anya* (Ziegfeld, "Chernov," Nov. 29, 1965): Here Tonight, Tomorrow Where?; On That Day; Six Palaces; So Proud; That Prelude!/WM: Robert Wright, George Forrest. *Irene* (Minskoff, revival, "Madame Lucy," Mar. 13, 1973): They Go Wild, Simply Wild, Over Me/W: Joseph McCarthy, M: Fred Fisher — We're Getting Away with It/W: Joseph McCarthy, M: Harry Tierney — You Made Me Love You (I Didn't Want to Do It)/W: Joseph McCarthy, M: James V. Monaco. *So Long, 174th Street* (Harkness, "Marlowe" and "Butler" and "Judge," Apr. 27, 1976): The Butler's Song; If You Want to Break Your Father's Heart/WM: Stan Daniels. *I Remember Mama* (Majestic, "Uncle Chris," May 31, 1979): Easy Come, Easy Go/W: Raymond Jessel, M: Richard Rodgers — It's Going to Be Good to Be Gone/W: Martin Charnin, M: Richard Rodgers. *Copperfield* (ANTA, "Mr. Micawber," Apr. 13, 1981): Something Will Turn Up; Up the Ladder; Villainy Is the Matter/WM: Al Kasha, Joel Hirschhorn. *On Your Toes* (Virginia, revival, "Sergei Alexandrovitch," Mar. 6, 1983/Sept. 6, 1983): Quiet Night; Too Good for the Average Man/W: Lorenz Hart, M: Richard Rodgers. *Me and My Girl* (Marquis, revival, "Sir John Tremayne," Aug. 10, 1986): Love Makes the World Go Round/WM: Noel Gay.

4674. Irma Irving *Puzzles of 1925* (Fulton, revue, Feb. 2, 1925): same as DOROTHY IRVING. *Oh, Please!* (Fulton, "Jane Jones," Dec. 17, 1926): I'd Steal a Star/W: Anne Caldwell, M: Vincent Youmans.

4675. Margaret Irving *Ziegfeld Midnight Frolic of 1919 [9th Edition]* (New Amsterdam roof, revue, Oct. 3, 1919): Surprise Package/W: Gene Buck, M: Dave Stamper. *Mercenary Mary* (Longacre, "June Somers," Apr. 13, 1925): Charleston Mad; Everything's Going to Be All Right/WM: William B. Friedlander, Con Conrad. *The Desert Song* (Casino, "Clementina," Nov. 30, 1926): My Little Castagnette; One Good Man Gone Wrong; Song of the Brass Key/W: Otto Harbach, Oscar Hammerstein II, M: Sigmund Romberg. *Hold On to Your Hats* (Shubert, "Sierra," Sept. 11, 1940): Don't Let It Get You Down/W: E.Y. Harburg, M: Burton Lane.

4676. Paul Irving *Afgar* (Central, "Houssain," Nov. 8, 1920): Ceremony of Veils/W: Douglas Furber, M: Charles Cuvillier.

4677. Charles Irwin (Jan. 31, 1887–Nov. 2, 1969) B: Curragh, County Kildare, Ireland. *A la Carte* (Martin Beck, revue, Aug. 17, 1927): Palm Beach Baby/WM: Herman Hupfeld. *Up in Central Park* (Century, "Timothy Moore," Jan. 27, 1945): The Birds and the Bees; Boss Tweed; Up from the Gutter; When the Party Gives a Party/W: Dorothy Fields, M: Sigmund Romberg.

4678. Flo Irwin (c 1859–Dec. 20, 1930) B: Whitby, Ontario, Canada. Sister of MAY IRWIN. *Gentleman Joe, the Hansom Cabby* (Bijou, "Lalage Potts," Jan. 30, 1896): Dat Nigger wid a White Spot on His Face/WM: ? — Does You Love Your Man/W: Walter Ford, M: John W. Bratton — In Gay Paree; Lalage Potts, That's Me/W: Basil Hood, M: Walter Slaughter. *Glory* (Vanderbilt, "Sarah King," Dec. 25, 1922): The Goodly Little Things We Do; When the Tenor Married the Soprano (and the Alto Married the Bass)/W: James Dyrenforth, M: Maurice DePackh.

4679. Helen Irwin *The Knickerbocker Girl* (Herald Square, "Miss Madison," June 15, 1903): Just a Smile/W: George Totten Smith, M: Alfred E. Aarons.

4680. Holly Irwin *Peter Pan* (Lunt-Fontanne, revival, "Tiger Lily," Dec. 13, 1990): Indians!/W: Carolyn Leigh, M: Moose Charlap — Ugg-a-Wugg/W: Betty Comden, Adolph Green, M: Jule Styne.

4681. May Irwin (June 27, 1862–Oct. 26, 1938) B: Whitby, Ontario, Canada. Sister of FLO IRWIN. Known as the Dean of Comediennes. May was 12 when she and her sister began singing and dancing in vaudeville. They split up in 1883. In 1896 she appeared in a short silent film, The Kiss. *A Country Sport* (Bijou, "Elizabeth Alwright, B.A., P.O.P.C.," Dec. 25, 1893): Mamie, Come Kiss Your Honey/WM: May Irwin — Molly O'Moore/WM: ?. *Courted into Court* (Bijou, "Dottie Dimple," Dec. 26, 1896): All Coons Look Alike to Me/WM: Ernest Hogan — Crappy Dan; Ma Lulu/WM: ? — Hot Time in the Old Town Tonight/W: Joe Hayden, M: Theodore H. Metz — Mamie, Come Kiss Your Honey [Apr. 5, 1897]/WM: May Irwin — Mister Johnson, Turn Me Loose/WM: Ben Harney. *The Belle of Bridgeport* (Bijou, "Ariel Smith," Oct. 29, 1900): Angeline; Bullfrog Ben/WM: Cissie Loftus — I Ain't Gwinter Work No More; I've Got Troubles of My Own; Magdalene, My Southern Queen; Why Don't the Band Play?/W: Bob Cole, James Weldon Johnson, M: J. Rosamond Johnson. *Mrs. Black Is Back* (Bijou, "Mrs. Black," Nov. 7, 1904): Bible Stories/W: John Lee Clarke, M: Al Johns — Dat Ain't Nothin' but

Talk/WM: Harry Brown, Chris Smith — Guess, Guess, Guess (Can't You Guess)/W: Paul West, M: John W. Bratton — I Love to Two Step with My Man/WM: Hughie Cannon — I'm Worried to Death About That/WM: May Irwin — In the Shadow of the Pyramid/W: Cecil Mack, M: Ernest R. Ball — Tennessee, That's the Place for Me/W: Harry Williams, M: Jean Schwartz.

4682. Nadine Isenegger *Cats* (Winter Garden, CR, "Victoria," July 25, 1994): The Invitation to the Jellicle Ball/W: T.S. Eliot, M: Andrew Lloyd Webber — Memory/W: Trevor Nunn, based on T.S. Eliot, M: Andrew Lloyd Webber.

4683. Burl Ives (June 14, 1909–Apr. 14, 1995) B: Hunt City Township, IL. Balladeer who crossed the country in the 1930s, earning a living by playing his banjo and singing the songs he learned from those he met along the way. In the 1940s, he sang these songs on the radio and recorded them, calling himself The Wayfaring Stranger. *Sing Out Sweet Land* (International, revue, "Fiddler" and "Bonaforte" and "First Soldier" and "Jolly Tramp" and "Petty Officer, Dec. 27, 1944): Big Rock Candy Mountain; The Foggy Foggy Dew; Frankie and Johnny; Marching Along Down This Road; Sea Chanty/WM: trad. — Blue-Tail Fly/WM: Daniel Decatur Emmett. *Paint Your Wagon* (Shubert, CR, "Ben Rumson"): I Still See Elisa; Wand'rin Star; Whoop-ti-ay!/W: Alan Jay Lerner, M: Frederick Loewe. *Show Boat* (New York City Center, revival, "Cap'n Andy Hawks," May 5, 1954): Why Do I Love You?/W: Oscar Hammerstein II, M: Jerome Kern.

4684. George Ives (Jan. 19, 1922–) B: New York, NY. *Happy Town* (54th Street, "Sib Richards," Oct. 7, 1959): It Isn't Easy/WM: Paul Nassau, Harry M. Haldane, Gordon Duffy.

4685. Dana Ivey (Aug. 12, 1941–) B: Atlanta, GA. *Sunday in the Park with George* (Booth, "Yvonne," May 2, 1984): The Day Off; Gossip; No Life/WM: Stephen Sondheim.

4686. Delores Ivory-Davis *Porgy and Bess* (Uris, revival, "Serena," Sept. 25, 1976): My Man's Gone Now; Time and Time Again/W: DuBose Heyward, M: George Gershwin.

4687. Karen Jablons (July 19, 1951–) B: Trenton, NJ. *Where's Charley?* (Circle in the Square, revival, "Young Lady," Dec. 20, 1974): The Gossips; Lovelier Than Ever/WM: Frank Loesser. *A Chorus Line* (Shubert, CR, "Val," Oct. 1976/Dec. 1977): And...; Dance: Ten, Looks: Three/W: Edward Kleban, M: Marvin Hamlisch.

4688. Hope Jackman *Oliver!* (Imperial,

"Mrs. Corney," Jan. 6, 1963): I Shall Scream; Oliver!/WM: Lionel Bart.

4689. Anna Jackson *Set to Music* (Music Box, revue, Jan. 18, 1939): Debutantes/WM: Noel Coward.

4690. Crawford Jackson *Blackbirds of 1928* (Liberty > Eltinge, revue, May 9, 1928): Bandanna Babies/W: Dorothy Fields, M: Jimmy McHugh. *Blackbirds of 1930* (Royale, revue, Oct. 22, 1930): Blackbirds on Parade/W: Andy Razaf, M: Eubie Blake.

4691. David Jackson (Dec. 4, 1948–) B: Philadelphia, PA. *Eubie!* (Ambassador, revue, CR, Sept. 1979): Baltimore Buzz; If You've Never Been Vamped by a Brownskin (You've Never Been Vamped at All); In Honeysuckle Time; There's a Million Little Cupids in the Sky/W: Noble Sissle, M: Eubie Blake — Goodnight Angeline/W: Noble Sissle, James Reese Europe, M: Eubie Blake. *Grand Hotel* (Martin Beck, "Jimmy," Nov. 12, 1989): Maybe My Baby Loves Me/WM: Robert Wright, George Forrest.

4692. Eddie Jackson (Feb. 19, 1896–July 16, 1980) B: Brooklyn, NY. With LOU CLAYTON and JIMMY DURANTE, part of the vaudeville team of Clayton, Jackson and Durante. On TV he was a regular on the live comedy variety Jimmy Durante Show (1954). *Show Girl* (Ziegfeld, "Deacon," July 2, 1929): Can Broadway Do Without Me?/WM: Jimmy Durante — Follow the Minstrel Band/W: Ira Gershwin, Gus Kahn, M: George Gershwin — Spain/W: Gus Kahn, M: Isham Jones. *The New Yorkers* (Broadway, "Grover Monahan," Dec. 8, 1930): Data; The Hot Patata; Money; Sheikin Fool; Wood/WM: Jimmy Durante — Venice/WM: Cole Porter.

4693. Edward Jackson Part of the singing quintette known as the Charioteers. *Hellzapoppin* (46th Street > Winter Garden, revue, Sept. 22, 1938): Abe Lincoln/W: Alfred Hayes, M: Earl Robinson — We Won't Let It Happen Here/WM: Don George, Teddy Hall.

4694. Ernestine Jackson (Sept. 18–) B: Corpus Christi, TX. *Hello, Dolly!* (St. James, CR, "Irene Molloy," Dec. 6, 1969): Dancing; It Only Takes a Moment; Ribbons Down My Back/WM: Jerry Herman — Elegance; Motherhood/WM: Bob Merrill, Jerry Herman. *Tricks* (Alvin, "Ernestina," Jan. 8, 1973): Believe Me; Enter Hyacinthe; Gypsy Girl; Love or Money; A Man of Spirit; Somebody's Doin' Somebody All the Time; A Sporting Man; Who Was I?/W: Lonnie Burstein, M: Jerry Blatt. *Raisin* (46th Street, "Ruth Younger," Oct. 18, 1973): He Come Down This Morning; It's a Deal; Not Anymore; Sweet Time; Whose Little Angry

Man/W: Robert Brittan, M: Judd Woldin. *Guys and Dolls* (Broadway, revival, "Sister Sarah Brown," July 21, 1976): Follow the Fold; If I Were a Bell; I'll Know; I've Never Been in Love Before; Marry the Man Today/WM: Frank Loesser.

4695. Ethel Jackson (Nov. 1, 1877–Nov. 23, 1957) B: New York, NY. She studied in Paris, Dresden and Vienna, and began her career at the Savoy in London with the D'Oyly Carte Opera. She returned to the U.S. in 1898. *A Runaway Girl* (Daly's > Fifth Avenue, CR, "Winifred Grey," 1899): The Boy Guessed Right/WM: Lionel Monckton — The Cigarette Song/W: Aubrey Hopwood, M: Lionel Monckton — No One in the World Like You/W: Aubrey Hopwood, M: Alfred D. Cammeyer — The Singing Girl/WM: ?. *The Blue Moon* (Casino, "Chandra Nil," Nov. 3, 1906): Little Blue Moon/W: Percy Greenbank, M: Howard Talbot. *The Merry Widow* (New Amsterdam, "Sonia, the Widow," Oct. 21, 1907): I Love You So (The Merry Widow Waltz); In Marsovia; The Silly Cavalier; Vilia/W: Adrian Ross, M: Franz Lehar.

4696. Harriett Jackson *Porgy and Bess* (Majestic, revival, "Clara," Jan. 22, 1942): Summertime/W: DuBose Heyward, M: George Gershwin. *Porgy and Bess* (44th Street > New York City Center, revival, "Clara," Sept. 13, 1943): same as above. *Carib Song* (Adelphi, "The Singer," Sept. 27, 1945): Oh, Lonely One; Sleep, Baby, Don't Cry/W: William Archibald, M: Baldwin Bergersen.

4697. Lorna Doone Jackson *Robin Hood* (Jolson, revival, "Allan-a-Dale," Nov. 18, 1929): The Bells of St. Swithins; Come the Bowmen in Lincoln Green; Milkmaid's Song/W: Harry B. Smith, M: Reginald De Koven — Oh, Promise Me/W: Clement Scott, M: Reginald De Koven. *The Serenade* (Jolson, revival, "Dolores," Mar. 4, 1930): The Angelus; Don Jose of Sevilla; I Love Thee, I Adore Thee/W: Harry B. Smith, M: Victor Herbert.

4698. Robert Jackson *Raisin* (46th Street, "Joseph Asagai," Oct. 18, 1973): Alaiyo/W: Robert Brittan, M: Judd Woldin. *Comin' Uptown* (Winter Garden, "Christmas Future," Dec. 20, 1979): Goin', Gone; Nobody Really Do/W: Peter Udell, M: Garry Sherman.

4699. Stewart Jackson (c 1890–July 13, 1919) *The Passing Show of 1916* (Winter Garden, revue, June 22, 1916): Broadway School Days/WM: ?. *The Girl from Brazil* (44th Street > Shubert, "Lieut. Olaf Nansen," Aug. 30, 1916): A Bachelor Girl and Boy; Oh You Lovely Ladies/W: Matthew Woodward, M: Sigmund Romberg —

Darling, I Love You So!/W: Matthew Woodward, M: Robert Winterberg.

4700. Zaidee Jackson *Rang-Tang* (Royale, revue, July 12, 1927): Brown/W: Jo Trent, M: Ford Dabney.

4701. Lou Jacobi (Dec. 28, 1913–) B: Toronto, Canada. Character actor in movies from 1960. *Fade Out— Fade In* (Mark Hellinger, "Lionel Z. Governor," May 26, 1964/Feb. 15, 1965): Close Harmony; The Dangerous Age/W: Betty Comden, Adolph Green, M: Jule Styne.

4702. Jacob Jacobs *The President's Daughter* (Billy Rose, "Nathan," Nov. 3, 1970): I Have What You Want; An Old Man Shouldn't Be Born; Welcome, Mr. Golden!; What Would You Do?/W: Jacob Jacobs, M: Murray Rumshinsky.

4703. Will Jacobs (July 14, 1945–) B: Center, TX. *Mother Earth* (Belasco, revue, Oct. 19, 1972): Rent a Robot/W: Ron Thronson, M: Toni Shearer.

4704. Danny Jacobson B: New York, NY. TV producer and writer; co-creator of the sitcom *Mad About You* (1992). *Grease* (Broadhurst, CR, "Kenickie," Apr. 1980): Greased Lightnin'/WM: Jim Jacobs, Warren Casey.

4705. Henrietta Jacobson (c 1906–Oct. 9, 1988) B: Chicago, IL. *70, Girls, 70* (Broadhurst, Apr. 15, 1971): Broadway, My Street; Go Visit Your Grandmother/W: Fred Ebb, M: John Kander.

4706. Irving Jacobson *Man of La Mancha* (ANTA Washington Square, "Sancho Panza," Nov. 22, 1965/July 19, 1966): The Combat; Golden Helmet; I Really Like Him; Knight of the Woeful Countenance (The Dubbing); A Little Gossip; Man of La Mancha (I, Don Quixote)/W: Joe Darion, M: Mitch Leigh. *Man of La Mancha* (Vivian Beaumont, revival, "Sancho Panza," June 24, 1972): same as above.

4707. Vernon Jacobson (c 1899–Dec. 13, 1955) M: SARAH EDWARDS. *Rain or Shine* (George M. Cohan, "Grocko, the Clown," Feb. 9, 1928): Hey, Rube/W: Jack Yellen, M: Milton Ager — Laugh, Clown, Laugh/WM: ?.

4708. Mark Jacoby (May 21, 1947–) B: Johnson City, TN. *Sweet Charity* (Minskoff, revival, "Vittorio Vidal," Apr. 27, 1986): Too Many Tomorrows/W: Dorothy Fields, M: Cy Coleman. *The Phantom of the Opera* (Majestic, CR, "The Phantom of the Opera," Feb. 21, 1991): All I Ask of You; Bravo, Bravo; I Remember; Little Lotte; The Mirror; The Music of the Night; Notes; The Point of No Return; Prima Donna; Stranger Than You Dreamt It; Twisted Every Way; Wandering Child/W: Charles Hart, Richard Stilgoe, M: Andrew Lloyd Webber —

The Phantom of the Opera/W: Mike Batt, Richard Stilgoe, M: Andrew Lloyd Webber. *Show Boat* (Gershwin, revival, "Gaylord Ravenal," Oct. 2, 1994): I Have the Room Above Her; Make Believe; Till Good Luck Comes My Way; Where's the Mate for Me?; You Are Love/W: Oscar Hammerstein II, M: Jerome Kern.

4709. Scott Jacoby (Nov. 19, 1956–) B: Chicago, IL. *Golden Rainbow* (Shubert, "Ally," Feb. 4, 1968): Taking Care of You; We Got Us/WM: Walter Marks. *Cry for Us All* (Broadhurst, "Miggsy," Apr. 8, 1970): The Broken Heart, or The Wages of Sin; The Cruelty Man; Home Free All; I Lost It; See No Evil/W: William Alfred, Phyllis Robinson, M: Mitch Leigh.

4710. Ray Jacquemot B: New Brunswick, NJ. *Louisiana Lady* (New Century, "El Gato," June 4, 1947): Gold, Women and Laughter; Just a Bit Naive; Louisiana's Holiday; The Night Was All to Blame; No, No, Mam'selle; When You Are Close to Me/W: Monte Carlo, M: Alma Sanders.

4711. Laura Jaffray *A Country Girl* (Herald Square, revival, "Madame Sophie," May 29, 1911): I'm a Naughty Girl/W: Adrian Ross, M: Sidney Jones — Two Little Chicks/W: Percy Greenbank, M: Paul Rubens.

4712. Sati Jamal *Ain't Supposed to Die a Natural Death* (Ethel Barrymore, Oct. 20, 1971): Come On Feet Do Your Thing/WM: Melvin Van Peebles.

4713. Alfred P. James *Sally* (New Amsterdam, "Pops," Dec. 21, 1920): This Little Girl/W: Clifford Grey, P.G. Wodehouse, M: Jerome Kern.

4714. Dorothea James *Harry Delmar's Revels* (Shubert, revue, Nov. 28, 1927): If You Have Troubles Laugh Them Away (Laff 'Em Away)/WM: Lester Lee. *Princess Charming* (Imperial, "Lulu," Oct. 13, 1930): The Panic's On; A Wonderful Thing for the King/W: Arthur Swanstrom, M: Arthur Schwartz, Albert Sirmay.

4715. Eddie James *Kismet* (New York State, revival, "Assiz," June 22, 1965): He's in Love!; Not Since Ninevah/WM: Robert Wright, George Forrest.

4716. Frankie James (? –Feb. 13, 1974) The musical comedy actress retired in 1942 and married the president of UI Studios. *Big Boy* (Winter Garden > 44th Street, "Dolly Graham," Jan. 7, 1925): Lackawanna/W: B.G. DeSylva, M: Joseph Meyer, James F. Hanley.

4717. Gladys James *The Mimic World* (Century roof, revue, Aug. 17, 1921): Broadway Pirates; Midnight Rounders/WM: ?.

4718. Ida James *Laffing Room Only* (Winter Garden, revue, Dec. 23, 1944): Got That Good Time Feelin'/WM: Burton Lane. *Memphis Bound!* (Broadway > Belasco, "Penny Paradise," May 24, 1945): Love or Reason; Sorry Her Lot/WM: Clay Warnick, Don Walker, based on William S. Gilbert and Arthur Sullivan.

4719. Jessica James (Oct. 31, 1933–May 7, 1990) B: Los Angeles, CA. *Little Me* (Eugene O'Neill, revival, "Belle [today]," Jan. 21, 1982): Don't Ask a Lady; Here's to Us; Little Me/W: Carolyn Leigh, M: Cy Coleman. *42nd Street* (Winter Garden, CR, "Maggie Jones," Oct. 4, 1982): Getting Out of Town/W: Mort Dixon, M: Harry Warren — Go Into Your Dance; Shadow Waltz; Shuffle Off to Buffalo/W: Al Dubin, M: Harry Warren.

4720. Joseph James *Love Life* (46th Street, Oct. 7, 1948): Economics/W: Alan Jay Lerner, M: Kurt Weill. *Lost in the Stars* (Music Box, "Answerer," Oct. 30, 1949): The Hills of Ixopo/W: Maxwell Anderson, M: Kurt Weill. *Porgy and Bess* (Ziegfeld, revival, "Jake," Mar. 10, 1953): It Takes a Long Pull to Get There; A Woman Is a Sometime Thing/W: DuBose Heyward, M: George Gershwin. *Carmen Jones* (New York City Center, revival, "Rum," May 31, 1956): Poncho de Panther from Brazil; Whizzin' Away Along de Track/W: Oscar Hammerstein II, M: Georges Bizet.

4721. Julia James (Dec. 28, 1890–July 1964) B: London, England. *Our Miss Gibbs* (Knickerbocker, "Lady Elizabeth Thanet," Aug. 29, 1910): Bedtime at the Zoo/W: Percy Greenbank, Leslie Mayne, M: Lionel Monckton.

4722. Kelli James (Mar. 18, 1959–) B: Council Bluffs, IA. *Les Miserables* (Broadway, CR, "Eponine," Sept. 15, 1987): A Heart Full of Love; In My Life; A Little Fall of Rain; On My Own/W: Herbert Kretzmer, M: Claude-Michel Schonberg.

4723. Marcia James *Sweethearts* (Shubert, revival, "Doreen," Jan. 21, 1947): Every Lover Must Meet His Fate; Game of Love; Sweethearts/W: Robert B. Smith, M: Victor Herbert.

4724. Olga James She played Cosby's sister-in-law, Verna Kincaid, on the TV sitcom The Bill Cosby Show (1969). *Mr. Wonderful* (Broadway, "Ethel Pearson," Mar. 22, 1956): Ethel Baby; I've Been Too Busy; Mr. Wonderful; Talk to Him/W: Larry Holofcener, George David Weiss, M: Jerry Bock.

4725. Polly James (July 8, 1941–) B: Lancashire, England. *Half a Sixpence* (Broadhurst, "Ann Pornick," Apr. 25, 1965): Flash! Bang! Wallop!; Half a Sixpence; I Know What I Am; Long Ago/WM: David Heneker.

4726. Stephen James (Feb. 2, 1952–) B: Mt. Vernon, OH. *A Day in Hollywood/A Night in the Ukraine* (John Golden > Royale, "Constantine," May 1, 1980): Again; Doin' the Production Code; Just Like That; A Night in the Ukraine/W: Dick Vosburgh, M: Frank Lazarus — Japanese Sandman/W: Raymond B. Egan, M: Richard A. Whiting — Sleepy Time Gal/W: Joseph R. Alden, Raymond B. Egan, M: Ange Lorenzo, Richard A. Whiting — Just Go to the Movies/WM: Jerry Herman.

4727. William James (Apr. 29, 1938–) B: Jersey City, NJ. *Maggie Flynn* (ANTA, "Timmy," Oct. 23, 1968): Never Gonna Make Me Fight/WM: Hugo Peretti, Luigi Creatore, George David Weiss.

4728. Joyce Jameson (Nov. 26, 1932–Jan. 16, 1987) B: Chicago, IL. *The Billy Barnes People* (Royale, revue, June 13, 1961): Second Best; There's Nothing Wrong with Our Values; Where Is the Clown?/WM: Billy Barnes.

4729. D. Jamin-Bartlett (May 21, 1948–) B: New York, NY. *A Little Night Music* (Shubert, "Petra," Feb. 25, 1973): The Miller's Son/WM: Stephen Sondheim.

4730. Judith Jamison (May 1, 1934–) B: Philadelphia, PA. Lead dancer in Alvin Ailey's Dance Theater, 1967 to1980, later its director. *Sophisticated Ladies* (Lunt-Fontanne, revue, Mar. 1, 1981): I Let a Song Go Out of My Heart/W: Henry Nemo, John Redmond, Irving Mills, M: Duke Ellington — I Love You Madly/WM: Duke Ellington — I'm Beginning to See the Light/WM: Duke Ellington, Don George, Johnny Hodges, Harry James — Music Is a Woman/W: John Guare, M: Duke Ellington — Old Man Blues/W: Irving Mills, M: Duke Ellington — Perdido/W: Hans Lengsfelder, Ervin Drake, M: Juan Tizol — Solitude/W: Eddie DeLange, Irving Mills, M: Duke Ellington — Sophisticated Lady/W: Mitchell Parish, Irving Mills, M: Duke Ellington.

4731. Dorothy Janice *Sitting Pretty* (Fulton, "Empress Eugenie," Apr. 8, 1924): Days Gone By/W: P.G. Wodehouse, M: Jerome Kern.

4732. Beverly Janis *Street Scene* (Adelphi, "Jennie Hildebrand," Jan. 9, 1947): Wrapped in a Ribbon (and Tied in a Bow)/W: Langston Hughes, M: Kurt Weill.

4733. Elsie Janis (Mar. 16, 1889–Feb. 26, 1956) B: Delaware, OH. Urged on by her mother, the talented songwriter and performer made her New York debut in 1900 at the Casino roof garden, doing impersonations. She was billed as America's Wonder Child and The Cleverest Girl in the World, and later when she

sang for American servicemen in WWI, The Sweetheart of the Armed Forces. Her close childhood friend, film star Mary Pickford, was with her when she died. *The Vanderbilt Cup* (Broadway > New York, "Dorothy Willetts," Jan. 16, 1906): If You Were I And I Were You; Let Me Be Your House Boat Beau; So I've Been Told/W: Raymond W. Peck, M: Robert Hood Bowers. *The Lady of the Slipper* (Globe, "Cinderella," Oct. 28, 1912): All Hallowe'en; Cinderella's Dream; I Like a Real, Real Man; Meow! Meow! Meow!; Princess of Far-Away/W: James O'Dea, M: Victor Herbert. *Miss Information* (George M. Cohan, "Dot from Nowhere," Oct. 5, 1915): Some Sort of Somebody (All of the Time)/W: Elsie Janis, M: Jerome Kern. *The Century Girl* (Century, revue, "Peggy O'Brien," Nov. 6, 1916): The Chicken Walk; They've Got Me Doin' It Now/WM: Irving Berlin — It Takes an Irishman to Make Love/WM: Elsie Janis, Irving Berlin. *Elsie Janis and Her Gang* (Gaiety, revue, Jan. 16, 1922): All the World Is Wonderful/W: Elsie Janis, M: Seymour Simons — I've Waited All My Life; Memories/WM: Elsie Janis — Mon Homme/W: Albert Willemetz, M: Maurice Yvain — Nuthin'/WM: Seymour Simons. *Puzzles of 1925* (Fulton, revue, Feb. 2, 1925): Je Vous Aime/WM: Arthur L. Beiner — Tra-la-la-la/WM: Elsie Janis, Vincent Scotto — The Undecided Blues/WM: Elsie Janis.

4734. Vivian Janis *Ziegfeld Follies of 1934* (Winter Garden, revue, CR, Feb. 5, 1934): I Like the Likes of You/W: E.Y. Harburg, M: Vernon Duke — This Is Not a Song/W: E.Y. Harburg, E. Hartman, M: Vernon Duke.

4735. Leon Janney (Apr. 1, 1917–Oct. 28, 1980) B: Ogden, UT. A child star in movies, he was one of the original Our Gang performers. *Kelly* (Broadhurst, "Augie Masters," Feb. 6, 1965): Six Blocks from the Bridge/W: Eddie Lawrence, M: Moose Charlap.

4736. Robert Janowski (Mar. 22, 1961–) *Metro* (Minskoff, "Jan," Apr. 16, 1992): Benjamin Franklin, in God We Trust; Bluezwis; But Not Me; Love Duet; Love Duet II; Metro; Uciekali/W: Mary Bracken Phillips, M: Janusz Stoklosa.

4737. Harry Jans (June 6, 1898–Feb. 4, 1962) B: Connecticut. *The Greenwich Village Follies of 1928* (Winter Garden, revue, Apr. 9, 1928): What's the Reason?/W: Harold Atteridge, M: Maurie Rubens. *Luana* (Hammerstein's, "Sure-Fire Thompson," Sept. 17, 1930): Shore Leave; Wanapoo Bay; Yankyula/W: J. Keirn Brennan, M: Rudolf Friml.

4738. Jim Jansen (July 27, 1945–) B: Salt

Lake City, UT. *Onward Victoria* (Martin Beck, "Anthony Comstock," Dec. 14, 1980): The Age of Brass; Everyday I Do a Little Something for the Lord; Read It in the Weekly/W: Charlotte Anker, Irene Rosenberg, M: Keith Herrmann.

4739. Lois January (Oct. 5, 1913–) B: Fort Worth, TX. *Yokel Boy* (Majestic, "Mary Hawkins," July 6, 1939): Let's Make Memories Tonight; The Ship Has Sailed/W: Lew Brown, Charles Tobias, M: Sam H. Stept. *High Kickers* (Broadhurst, "Kitty McKay," Oct. 31, 1941): A Panic in Panama; The Time to Sing; Waltzing in the Moonlight; You're on My Mind/W: Bert Kalmar, M: Harry Ruby.

4740. Emma Janvier (May 1–Aug. 31, 1924) B: New York, NY. *The Mayor of Tokio* (New York, "Mme. Stitch," Dec. 4, 1905): Cheer Up Everybody; Is Marriage a Failure?/W: Richard Carle, M: William F. Peters. *The Spring Chicken* (Daly's > New Amsterdam > Daly's, "Mrs. Girdle," Oct. 8, 1906): I Don't Know but I Guess/W: Adrian Ross, M: Lionel Monckton. *Fifty Miles from Boston* (Garrick, "Mrs. Tilford," Feb. 3, 1908): Ain't It Awful/WM: George M. Cohan. *Miss Innocence* (New York, "Miss Sniffins," Nov. 30, 1908): Perfectly Terrible, Dear/W: Harry Williams, M: Egbert Van Alstyne. *The Silver Star* (New Amsterdam, "Mrs. Vera Willing," Nov. 1, 1909): It May Be So but I Doubt It/W: Harry B. Smith, M: Robert Hood Bowers— They're Not Doing That This Season/W: Harry B. Smith, M: Albert Gumble. *The Amber Express* (Globe, "Mrs. Harriet Scott," Sept. 19, 1916): Gossip/WM: ?. *Go To It* (Princess, "Mrs. Piggot Luce," Oct. 24, 1916): Extra!/WM: ?. *Two Little Girls in Blue* (George M. Cohan, "Hariette Neville," May 3, 1921): The Silly Season/W: Ira Gershwin, M: Vincent Youmans. *Molly Darling* (Liberty, "Mrs. Redwing," Sept. 1, 1922): Mellow Moon/W: Phil Cook, M: Tom Johnstone.

4741. Frank Jaquet (Mar. 16, 1885–May 11, 1958) B: Wisconsin. *The Red Mill* (Ziegfeld, revival, "Burgomaster," Oct. 16, 1945): Moonbeams; Wedding Bells (Wedding Chorus)/W: Henry Blossom, Forman Brown, M: Victor Herbert.

4742. Dorothy Jardon (June 1, 1889– ?) B: New York, NY. M: lyricist Edward Madden. *The Yankee Girl* (Herald Square, "Loleta," Feb. 10, 1910): Maid of Sevilla/W: George V. Hobart, M: Silvio Hein. *Madame Sherry* (New Amsterdam, "Pepita," Aug. 30, 1910): The Kiss You Gave; The Mad Madrid and the Dance of Danger/W: Otto Harbach, M: Karl Hoschna. *La Belle Paree* (Winter Garden, "La Duchesse," Mar. 20, 1911): Sing Trovatore/W: Edward Madden, M: Jerome

Kern. *The Revue of Revues* (Winter Garden, revue, Sept. 27, 1911): The Carmen Girl; Oriental Eyes/WM: ?— I Sang Tra-la/W: Harold Atteridge, M: Louis A. Hirsch. *The Wedding Trip* (Broadway, "Aza," Dec. 25, 1911): Gypsy Kiss; Le Beau Sabreur; The Sea Shell Telephone; Soldier's Song/W: Harry B. Smith, M: Reginald De Koven. *A Winsome Widow* (Moulin Rouge, CR, "Mrs. Guyer," July 1, 1912): Call Me Flo/WM: John L. Golden, Jerome Kern— A Girl Like Me/W: Robert B. Smith, M: Raymond Hubbell— Songs of Yesterday; They Mean More/W: Harry B. Smith, M: Raymond Hubbell— A Winsome Widow Am I/W: Edward Madden, M: Gus Edwards. *The Pleasure Seekers* (Winter Garden, revue, "Mlle. Marcelle," Nov. 3, 1913): Faust Up to Date; Love Me to a Viennese Melody/WM: E. Ray Goetz— Follow the Midnight Girl/WM: E. Ray Goetz, Bert Grant. *The Dancing Duchess* (Casino, "Countess Pauline Von Bereny," Aug. 20, 1914): I Like You; Nay, Nay Pauline; The Song of Songs; The Tango Breakfast; That's the Kind of Man You Ought to Marry/W: R.H. Burnside, M: Milton Lusk. *Papa's Darling* (New Amsterdam, "Zozo," Nov. 2, 1914): A Certain Little Way of My Own/WM: ?— Dolores; Oh, This Love; Sparkling Moselle/ W: Harry B. Smith, M: Ivan Caryll.

4743. Jill Jaress *No, No, Nanette* (46th Street, revival, CR, "Betty Brown"): Telephone Girlie/W: Otto Harbach, M: Vincent Youmans.

4744. M. De Jari *Fashions of 1924* (Lyceum, revue, July 18, 1923): Love Through the Ages; Passing Fancies/W: Harry B. Smith, M: Ted Snyder.

4745. Sunshine (Jarmann) Jarmon *Artists and Models of 1925* (Winter Garden, revue, June 24, 1925): The Rotisserie/W: Clifford Grey, M: Alfred Goodman, Maurie Rubens, J. Fred Coots. *Americana of 1926* (Belmont, revue, CR, Aug. 30, 1926): Blowin' the Blues Away/W: Ira Gershwin, M: Phil Charig— Why Do Ya Roll Those Eyes?/W: Morrie Ryskind, M: Phil Charig.

4746. Dorothy Jarnac B: Sacramento, CA. *Heaven on Earth* (New Century, "Friday," Sept. 16, 1948): Apple Jack; The Letter/W: Barry Trivers, M: Jay Gorney.

4747. Lori Ada Jaroslow *Fiddler on the Roof* (New York State, revival, "Tzeitel," July 9, 1981): Matchmaker, Matchmaker/W: Sheldon Harnick, M: Jerry Bock.

4748. Ruth Jaroslow (May 22–) B: Brooklyn, NY. *Fiddler on the Roof* (Imperial, CR, "Yente," Aug. 19, 1971): Anatevka; I Just Heard/ W: Sheldon Harnick, M: Jerry Bock. *Fiddler on the Roof* (Winter Garden, revival, "Yente," Dec.

28, 1976): same as above. *Fiddler on the Roof* (New York State, revival, "Yente," July 9, 1981): same as above. *Fiddler on the Roof* (Gershwin, revival, "Yente," Nov. 18, 1990): The Rumor/W: Sheldon Harnick, M: Jerry Bock.

4749. Howard Jarratt *My Darlin' Aida* (Winter Garden, "Raymond Demarest," Oct. 27, 1952): Away; I Don't Want You; Knights of the White Cross; Land of Mine; Love Is Trouble; Master and Slave; Me and Lee; My Darlin' Aida; There'll Have to Be Changes Made; Why Ain't We Free?; You Are My Darlin' Bride/W: Charles Friedman, M: Hans Spialek, based on Giuseppe Verdi.

4750. Al Jarreau (Mar. 12, 1940–) B: Milwaukee, WI. Grammy winning vocalist of the 1970s and 80s. He co-wrote and sang the theme for the Cybill Shepherd-Bruce Willis TV comedy-drama Moonlighting (1985). *Grease* (Eugene O'Neill, revival, CR, "Teen Angel"): Beauty School Dropout/WM: Jim Jacobs, Warren Casey.

4751. Art Jarrett (Feb. 5, 1884–June 12, 1960) B: Marysville, CA. *Hot-cha!* (Ziegfeld, CR, "Jack Whitney," May 1932): Say (What I Wanna Hear You Say); You Can Make My Life a Bed of Roses/W: Lew Brown, M: Ray Henderson. *Walk with Music* (Ethel Barrymore, "Steve Harrington," June 4, 1940): Friend of the Family; Smile for the Press; Today I Am a Glamour Girl; Wait Till You See Me in the Morning; What'll They Think of Next/W: Johnny Mercer, M: Hoagy Carmichael.

4752. Dorothy Jarrett *Lovely Lady* (Sam H. Harris, "Yvonne," Dec. 29, 1927): At the Barbecue/W: Harry A. Steinberg, Edward Ward, M: Dave Stamper, Harold A. Levey — Lingerie; Make Believe You're Happy/W: Cyrus D. Wood, M: Dave Stamper, Harold A. Levey.

4753. Jerry Jarrett (Sept. 9, 1918–May 16, 2001) B: Brooklyn, NY. *Fiddler on the Roof* (Imperial, CR, "Avram"): Anatevka/W: Sheldon Harnick, M: Jerry Bock. *Fiddler on the Roof* (Imperial, CR, "Tevye," May 12, 1969/Jan. 1, 1970/Oct. 12, 1970/Oct. 11, 1971): Anatevka; Do You Love Me?; If I Were a Rich Man; Sabbath Prayer; Sunrise, Sunset; The Tailor, Motel Kamzoil; To Life; Tradition/W: Sheldon Harnick, M: Jerry Bock.

4754. Jack Jarrott *The Sun Dodgers* (Broadway, "Y. De Wake Taylor," Nov. 30, 1912): Down in the Old Rathskellar; Rag Me Around/W: E. Ray Goetz, M: A. Baldwin Sloane.

4755. Bobby (Robert C.) Jarvis (c 1892–Nov. 13, 1971) For many years he directed the Lambertville Music Circus in New Jersey. *The*

Desert Song (Casino, CR, "Bennie Kidd," June 1927): It; One Good Man Gone Wrong/W: Otto Harbach, Oscar Hammerstein II, M: Sigmund Romberg. *America's Sweetheart* (Broadhurst, CR, "Larry Pitman," Apr. 1931): How About It?; My Sweet; There's So Much More; We'll Be the Same; You Ain't Got No Savoir Faire/W: Lorenz Hart, M: Richard Rodgers. *The Cat and the Fiddle* (Globe, CR, "Alexander Sheridan," July 1932): Try to Forget/W: Otto Harbach, M: Jerome Kern.

4756. Scott Jarvis (c 1942–Feb. 26, 1990) *1776* (46th Street, "Courier," Mar. 16, 1969): Momma Look Sharp/WM: Sherman Edwards.

4757. Sydney (Sidney) Jarvis (Jan. 11, 1878–June 6, 1939) B: Toronto, Ontario, Canada. *The Little Millionaire* (George M. Cohan, "Roscoe Handover," Sept. 25, 1911): Oh, You Wonderful Girl; We Do the Dirty Work/WM: George M. Cohan. *A Winsome Widow* (Moulin Rouge, "Bryton Early," Apr. 11, 1912): Oh, You Fascinating Girl/W: Frank Tinney, Sidney Jones, M: Fred Strasser — Pousse Cafe; Songs of Yesterday/W: Harry B. Smith, M: Raymond Hubbell. *Hello, Broadway!* (Astor, revue, "Kick In McCluskey," Dec. 25, 1914): Broadway Tipperary; It Pays to Advertise/WM: George M. Cohan. *Her Regiment* (Broadhurst, "Eugene de Merriame," Nov. 12, 1917): The Art Song/W: William Le Baron, M: Victor Herbert. *Monte Cristo, Jr.* (Winter Garden, "Harry Sterling," Feb. 12, 1919): Carnival Time; Just My Type (They're All My Type); Sentimental Knights/W: Harold Atteridge, M: Sigmund Romberg, Jean Schwartz.

4758. Michael Jason *Jesus Christ Superstar* (Mark Hellinger, "Peter," Oct. 12, 1971): The Arrest; Could We Start Again, Please; Peter's Denial/W: Tim Rice, M: Andrew Lloyd Webber.

4759. Mitchell Jason *Fade Out— Fade In* (Mark Hellinger, "Ralph Governor," May 26, 1964/Feb. 15, 1965): Fear/W: Betty Comden, Adolph Green, M: Jule Styne. *Darling of the Day* (George Abbott, "Duncan," Jan. 27, 1968): A Gentleman's Gentleman/W: E.Y. Harburg, M: Jule Styne. *Fiddler on the Roof* (Imperial, CR, "Avram"): Anatevka/W: Sheldon Harnick, M: Jerry Bock. *Tricks* (Alvin, "Argante," Jan. 8, 1973): Where Is Respect/W: Lonnie Burstein, M: Jerry Blatt.

4760. Sylvia Jason *The Debutante* (Knickerbocker, "Hon. Spencer Mainwaring Cavendish," Dec. 7, 1914): The Baker's Boy and the Chimney Sweep; On a Sunny Afternoon/W: Robert B. Smith, M: Victor Herbert. *Follow Me* (Casino, "Miss Watchcharm," Nov. 29, 1916): The Girls

Are Getting Wiser Every Day/W: Alfred Bryan, Anna Held, M: Harry Tierney — Happyland; It's the Little Things That Count Most Ev'ry Way/W: Alfred Bryan, M: Harry Tierney. *Doing Our Bit* (Winter Garden, "Sylvia Farnsbee," Oct. 18, 1917): I May Be Small but I Have Big Ideas; A Loving Daddy/W: Harold Atteridge, M: Sigmund Romberg, Herman Timberg. *Little Simplicity* (Astor > 44th Street, CR, "Maude Mc-Call," Dec. 2, 1918): A Military Fox Trot Tune/W: Rida Johnson Young, M: Augustus Barratt.

4761. Martin Jaycox *The Gospel at Colonus* (Lunt-Fontanne, "Choragos," Mar. 24, 1988): No Never; Who Is This Man?/W: Lee Breuer, M: Bob Telson.

4762. Estelle Jayne *All the King's Horses* (Imperial, CR, "Sherry Shannon," May 1934): Tamboree/W: Frederick Herendeen, M: Edward A. Horan.

4763. Zizi Jeanmaire (Apr. 29, 1924–) B: Paris, France. Before going to Broadway she danced with the Monte Carlo Ballet and Ballet Russe. *The Girl in Pink Tights* (Mark Hellinger, "Lisette Gervais," Mar. 5, 1954): In Paris and in Love; My Heart Won't Say Goodbye; Up in the Elevated Railway; When I Am Free to Love/W: Leo Robin, M: Sigmund Romberg. *Can-Can* (Minskoff, revival, "La Mome Pistache," Apr. 30, 1981): Allez-Vous-En (Go Away); Can-Can; C'est Magnifique; I Love Paris; Live and Let Live; Never Give Anything Away/WM: Cole Porter.

4764. Mary Jeffery *China Rose* (Martin Beck, CR, "Sis Ta," Mar. 16, 1925): I'm No Butterfly/W: Harry L. Cort, George E. Stoddard, M: A. Baldwin Sloane.

4765. Dawn Jeffory *The Utter Glory of Morrissey Hall* (Mark Hellinger, "Frances," May 13, 1979): Oh, Sun; You Will Know When the Time Has Arrived/WM: Clark Gesner.

4766. Anne Jeffreys (Jan. 26, 1923–) B: Goldsboro, NC. M: movie actor Robert Sterling, 1951. They starred together on the TV sitcom Topper (1953). *Street Scene* (Adelphi, "Rose Maurrant," Jan. 9, 1947): Don't Forget the Lilac Bush; I Loved Her, Too; There'll Be Trouble/W: Langston Hughes, Elmer Rice, M: Kurt Weill — Remember That I Care; We'll Go Away Together; What Good Would the Moon Be?/W: Langston Hughes, M: Kurt Weill. *My Romance* (Shubert > Adelphi, "Mme. Marguerita Cavallini," Oct. 19, 1948): Aria; Bella Donna; From Now Onward; If Only; In Love with Romance; Love and Laughter; Paradise Stolen; Written in Your Hand/W: Rowland Leigh, M: Sigmund Romberg. *Kiss Me, Kate* (New Century, CR, "Lilli Vanessi" and "Katherine," June 1950): I

Am Ashamed That Women Are So Simple; I Hate Men; Kiss Me, Kate; So in Love; We Open in Venice; Wunderbar/WM: Cole Porter. *Three Wishes for Jamie* (Mark Hellinger, "Maeve Harrigan," Mar. 21, 1952): April Face; Goin' on a Hayride; It Must Be Spring; It's a Wishing World; My Home's a Highway (Sunday Night Supper); What Do I Know?/WM: Ralph Blane. *Kismet* (New York State, revival, "Lalume," June 22, 1965): Not Since Ninevah; Rahadlakum/WM: Robert Wright, George Forrest.

4767. John Jellison *Crazy for You* (Sam S. Shubert, CR, "Bela Zangler"): What Causes That?/W: Ira Gershwin, M: George Gershwin.

4768. Allen Jenkins (Apr. 9, 1900–July 20, 1974) B: New York, NY. Comic actor who appeared in more than 175 movies, often as a tough guy. On TV he played the cabdriver on the sitcom Hey Jeannie (1956). *Something for the Boys* (Alvin, "Harry Hart," Jan. 7, 1943): There's a Happy Land in the Sky; When We're Home on the Range/WM: Cole Porter.

4769. Daniel H. Jenkins (Jan. 17, 1963–) B: New York, NY. *Big River: The Adventures of Huckleberry Finn* (Eugene O'Neill, "Huckleberry Finn," Apr. 25, 1985): I, Huckleberry, Me; Leavin's Not the Only Way to Go; Muddy Water; River in the Rain; Waitin' for the Light to Shine; When the Sun Goes Down in the South; Worlds Apart/WM: Roger Miller. *Big* (Sam S. Shubert, "Josh Baskin," Apr. 28, 1996): Coffee, Black; Cross the Line; Fun; I Want to Go Home; Stars, Stars, Stars; This Isn't Me; When You're Big/W: Richard Maltby, Jr., M: David Shire.

4770. Ken Jenkins (1940–) B: Kentucky. *Big River: The Adventures of Huckleberry Finn* (Eugene O'Neill, CR, "The Duke," Jan. 7, 1986): The Royal Nonesuch; When the Sun Goes Down in the South/WM: Roger Miller.

4771. Wesley Jenkins *The Shoo Fly Regiment* (Bijou, "Bro. Doolittle," Aug. 6, 1907): De Bode o' Edicashun/W: James Weldon Johnson, M: J. Rosamond Johnson. *The Red Moon* (Majestic, "Bill Armour," May 3, 1909): Keep on Smilin'/W: Bob Cole, M: J. Rosamond Johnson.

4772. Myvanwy Jenn B: Wales. *Oh What a Lovely War* (Broadhurst, revue, Sept. 30, 1964): Keep the Home Fires Burning/W: Lena Guilbert-Ford, M: Ivor Novello. *I Remember Mama* (Majestic, "Dame Sybil Fitzgibbons," May 31, 1979): Fair Trade/W: Martin Charnin, M: Richard Rodgers.

4773. Trixie Jennery *The Little Cherub* (Criterion, "Eliza," Aug. 6, 1906): Won't You Waltz?/W: Owen Hall, M: Ivan Caryll.

4774. Ken Jennings (Oct. 10, 1947–) B: Jersey City, NJ. *Sweeney Todd, the Demon Barber of Fleet Street* (Uris, "Tobias Ragg," Mar. 1, 1979): God, That's Good!; Not While I'm Around; Pirelli's Miracle Elixir/WM: Stephen Sondheim. *A Christmas Carol* (Paramount Madison Square Garden, "Lamplighter" and "Ghost of Christmas Past," Dec. 1, 1994): The Lights of Long Ago; Nothing to Do with Me/W: Lynn Ahrens, M: Alan Menken. *A Christmas Carol* (Paramount Madison Square Garden > Madison Square Garden, return engagements, "Lamplighter" and "Ghost of Christmas Past," Nov. 20, 1995 > Nov. 22, 1996): same as above.

4775. O'Malley Jennings *Around the Map* (New Amsterdam, revue, "Toto de Beers," Nov. 1, 1915): Here Comes Tootsi/W: C.M.S. McLellan, M: Herman Finck.

4776. Robert Jennings *By the Beautiful Sea* (Majestic, "Half-Note," Apr. 8, 1954): Coney Island Boat/W: Dorothy Fields, M: Arthur Schwartz.

4777. Adele Jerome *Of V We Sing* (Concert, revue, Feb. 11, 1942): Sisters Under the Skin/W: Sylvia Marks, M: Baldwin Bergersen — You've Got to Appease with a Strip Tease/W: Lewis Allan, M: Toby Sacher.

4778. Clara Belle Jerome *An English Daisy* (Casino, "Henriette," Jan. 18, 1904): Big Indian Chief/W: Bob Cole, M: J. Rosamond Johnson — I Adore a Certain Party/W: Edgar Smith, M: A.M. Norden.

4779. Timothy Jerome (Dec. 29, 1943–) B: Los Angeles, CA. *The Rothschilds* (Lunt-Fontanne, "Amshel Rothschild," Oct. 19, 1970): Bonds; Everything; Rothschild & Sons/W: Sheldon Harnick, M: Jerry Bock. *The Rothschilds* (Lunt-Fontanne, CR, "Nathan Rothschild," June 7, 1971): Bonds; Everything; I'm in Love! I'm in Love!; Rothschild & Sons; This Amazing London Town/W: Sheldon Harnick, M: Jerry Bock. *The Magic Show* (Cort, CR, "Feldman," July 25, 1975): Before Your Very Eyes; A Bit of Villainy; The Goldfarb Variations; Style/WM: Stephen Schwartz. *The Moony Shapiro Songbook* (Morosco, revue, May 3, 1981): Climbin'; Don't Play That Lovesong Any More; Golden Oldie; Meg; Nazi Party Pooper; When a Brother Is a Mother to His Sister/W: Julian More, M: Monty Norman. *Me and My Girl* (Marquis, revival, "Herbert Parchester," Aug. 10, 1986): The Family Solicitor/W: L. Arthur Rose, Douglas Furber, M: Noel Gay. *Grand Hotel* (Martin Beck, "Gen. Dr. Preysing," Nov. 12, 1989): The Boston Merger; The Crooked Path/WM: Robert Wright, George Forrest, Maury Yeston — Everybody's Doing

It/WM: Maury Yeston. *Cats* (Winter Garden, CR, "Bustopher Jones" and "Asparagus" and "Growltiger"): Bustopher Jones; Growltiger's Last Stand; Gus: The Theater Cat/W: T.S. Eliot, M: Andrew Lloyd Webber. *Beauty and the Beast* (Palace, CR, "Maurice," c 1996): No Matter What/W: Tim Rice, M: Alan Menken.

4780. George Jessel (April 3, 1898–May 24, 1981) B: Bronx, NY. Actor, producer, screenwriter. M: FLORENCE COURTNEY; LOIS ANDREWS; silent film star Norma Talmadge. The comedian, who called himself The Toastmaster General of the United States, was best known for his phone calls to his mother. *Sweet and Low* (46th Street > 44th Street, revue, Nov. 17, 1930): Dancing with Tears in Their Eyes/W: Mort Dixon, Billy Rose, M: Will Irwin — Mr. Jessel/WM: Charlotte Kent — When a Pansy Was a Flower/W: Malcolm McComb, Billy Rose, M: Will Irwin. *High Kickers* (Broadhurst, "George M. Krause," Oct. 31, 1941): Memories/W: Bert Kalmar, M: Harry Ruby.

4781. Stanley Jessup (c 1877–Oct. 26, 1945) B: Chester, NY. *The Arcadians* (Liberty > Knickerbocker, "Astrophel," Jan. 17, 1910): The Joy of Life/W: Arthur Wimperis, M: Howard Talbot. *Two Little Girls in Blue* (George M. Cohan, "Capt. Morrow," May 3, 1921): We're Off on a Wonderful Trip/W: Ira Gershwin, M: Vincent Youmans.

4782. Michael Jeter (Aug. 26, 1952–) B: Lawrenceburg, TN. He played the wimpy math teacher Herman Stiles on the TV sitcom Evening Shade (1990). *Grand Hotel* (Martin Beck, "Otto Kringelein," Nov. 12, 1989): At the Grand Hotel/WM: Maury Yeston — Table with a View; We'll Take a Glass Together/WM: Robert Wright, George Forrest, Maury Yeston — Who Couldn't Dance with You?/WM: Robert Wright, George Forrest.

4783. Phil Jethro (Sept. 10, 1947–) B: Minneapolis, MN. *Jesus Christ Superstar* (Mark Hellinger, "Annas," Oct. 12, 1971): The Arrest; Damned for All Time; Judas' Dream; This Jesus Must Die/W: Tim Rice, M: Andrew Lloyd Webber.

4784. James Jewell (Oct. 20, 1925–) B: Gainesville, GA. *Razzle Dazzle* (Arena, revue, Feb. 19, 1951): Then I'm Yours/W: Michael Stewart, M: Leo Schumer. *John Murray Anderson's Almanac* (Imperial, revue, Dec. 10, 1953): Nightingale, Bring Me a Rose/W: Irving Caesar, John Murray Anderson, M: Louis A. Hirsch.

4785. Ann Jillian (Jan. 29, 1951–) B: Cambridge, MA. At age 12 she was in the movie version of Gypsy. *Sugar Babies* (Mark Hellinger,

"Jillian," Oct. 8, 1979): Exactly Like You/W: Dorothy Fields, M: Jimmy McHugh — I Want a Girl (Just Like the Girl That Married Dear Old Dad) [added]/W: William Dillon, M: Harry Von Tilzer — I'm Keeping Myself Available for You/W: Arthur Malvin, M: Jimmy McHugh — The Sugar Baby Bounce/WM: Jay Livingston, Ray Evans — Warm and Willing/W: Jay Livingston, Ray Evans, M: Jimmy McHugh.

4786. Joyce Jillson (Dec. 26, 1946–) B: Cranston, RI. *La Grosse Valise* (54th Street, "Baby," Dec. 14, 1965): For You; Hawaii; La Java/W: Harold Rome, M: Gerard Calvi.

4787. Marion Jim (Oct. 22, 1927–Dec. 10, 1978) B: Hawaii. *Ride the Winds* (Bijou, "Toki," May 16, 1974): Breathing the Air; Every Days/WM: John Driver.

4788. Jodi Jinks *Blood Brothers* (Music Box, CR, "Miss Jones," c 1993): Take a Letter, Miss Jones/WM: Willy Russell.

4789. Patti Jo *Purlie* (Broadway, CR, "Lutiebelle," Mar. 30, 1971): The Harder They Fall; He Can Do It; I Got Love; Purlie/W: Peter Udell, M: Gary Geld. *Purlie* (Billy Rose, revival, "Lutiebelle," Dec. 27, 1972): same as above.

4790. Joanne *Orchids Preferred* (Imperial, "June," May 11, 1937): The Echo of a Song (Echoes of Love); Sub-Debs' First Fling/W: Frederick Herendeen, M: Dave Stamper.

4791. Andy Jobe *A Christmas Carol* (Paramount Madison Square Garden, "Jack Smythe," Dec. 1, 1994): Dancing on Your Grave; Nothing to Do with Me/W: Lynn Ahrens, M: Alan Menken.

4792. Gwennllyan Jocelyn *Miss Daisy* (Shubert > Lyric, "Maisie Dearborn," Sept. 9, 1914): Tea Leaves; Won't You Dance?; Youth/W: Philip Bartholomae, M: Silvio Hein.

4793. Cameron Johann (c 1972–) B: *Nine* (46th Street, "Guido [young]," May 9, 1982): Getting Tall/WM: Maury Yeston.

4794. John Johann (Dec. 23, 1942–) B: Madison, WI. *Follies* (Winter Garden, CR, "Young Ben," Aug. 23, 1971): Waiting for the Girls Upstairs/WM: Stephen Sondheim.

4795. Don Johanson (Oct. 19, 1952–) B: Rock Hill, SC. *Cats* (Winter Garden, CR, "Mistoffolees," c 1986): The Invitation to the Jellicle Ball; Mr. Mistoffolees; Mungojerrie and Rumpleteazer/W: T.S. Eliot, M: Andrew Lloyd Webber.

4796. Michael John *Rex* (Lunt-Fontanne, "Prince Edward," Apr. 25, 1976): Christmas at Hampton Court; In Time; The Masque; The Wee Golden Warrior/W: Sheldon Harnick, M: Richard Rodgers.

4797. Brooke Johns (Dec. 24, 1893–Dec. 3, 1987) B: Washington, DC. *Tangerine* (Casino, CR, "Jack Floyd," Apr. 10, 1922): Isle of Tangerine; Love Is a Business; South Sea Island Blues/W: Howard Johnson, M: Monte Carlo, Alma Sanders — It's Great to Be Married (and Lead a Single Life)/W: Howard Johnson, M: Monte Carlo, Alma Sanders, Carle Carlton — Man Is the Lord of It All/W: Carle Carlton, M: Jean Schwartz. *Ziegfeld Follies of 1922* (New Amsterdam, revue, June 5, 1922): Some Sweet Day/W: Gene Buck, M: Louis A. Hirsch, Dave Stamper. *Ziegfeld Follies of 1922 [Summer Edition]* (New Amsterdam, revue, June 25, 1922): Pep It Up/W: Gene Buck, M: Dave Stamper — Some Sweet Day/W: Gene Buck, M: Louis A. Hirsch, Dave Stamper. *Jack and Jill* (Globe, "Donald Lee," Mar. 22, 1923): Married Life Blues/W: Otto Harbach, M: Augustus Barratt — My Cherokee Rose/WM: John Murray Anderson, Augustus Barratt — Pretty City Girl/W: Otto Harbach, M: William Daly — Voodoo Man/W: Otto Harbach, M: Alfred Newman. *Ziegfeld Follies of 1923* (New Amsterdam, revue, Oct. 20, 1923): Broadway Indians; Shake Your Feet; Swanee River Blues/W: Gene Buck, M: Dave Stamper — Take Oh Take Those Lips Away/W: Joseph McCarthy, M: Harry Tierney. *Piggy* (Royale, "Bobby Hunter," Jan. 11, 1927): I Need a Little Bit, You Need a Little Bit (A Little Bit of Love)/W: Lew Brown, M: Cliff Friend.

4798. Florence Johns *Toot-Toot!* (George M. Cohan, "Pandora," Mar. 11, 1918): It's Greek to Me/W: Berton Braley, M: Jerome Kern.

4799. Glynis Johns (Oct. 5, 1923–) B: Pretoria, South Africa. She performed on the London stage from 1935, and starred in the TV sitcom Glynis (1963). She was Mrs. Banks, the mother, in the movie Mary Poppins (1964). *A Little Night Music* (Shubert, "Desiree Armfeldt," Feb. 25, 1973): The Glamorous Life; Send in the Clowns; You Must Meet My Wife/WM: Stephen Sondheim.

4800. Kurt Johns (Feb. 28, 1954–) B: Cincinnati, OH. *Aspects of Love* (Broadhurst, "2nd Barker," Apr. 8, 1990): Everybody Loves a Hero/W: Don Black, Charles Hart, M: Andrew Lloyd Webber.

4801. Alma Johnson *Porgy and Bess* (Uris, revival, "Clara," Sept. 25, 1976): Summertime/W: DuBose Heyward, M: George Gershwin.

4802. Audrey Johnson *Company* (Alvin, CR, "Sarah," July 1, 1971): Poor Baby/WM: Stephen Sondheim.

4803. Betty Johnson *Take Me Along* (Martin Beck, revival, "Essie Miller," Apr. 14, 1985):

Knights on White Horses; Oh, Please/WM: Bob Merrill.

4804. Bill (William) Johnson (Mar. 22, 1918–Mar. 6, 1957) B: Baltimore, MD. M: SHIRL CONWAY. Known as Bill Johnson until 1955. *Two for the Show* (Booth, CR, revue, May 13, 1940): At Last It's Love; A House with a Little Red Barn; That Terrible Tune/W: Nancy Hamilton, M: Morgan Lewis. *All in Fun* (Majestic, revue, Dec. 27, 1940): How Did It Get So Late So Early?/W: June Sillman, M: Will Irwin — It's All in Fun/W: Bob Russell, M: Baldwin Bergersen — My Memories Started with You/W: June Sillman, M: Baldwin Bergersen — Where Can I Go from You?/W: Virginia Faulkner, M: Baldwin Bergersen. *Banjo Eyes* (Hollywood, "Charlie," Dec. 25, 1941): A Nickel to My Name; Not a Care in the World/W: John Latouche, M: Vernon Duke. *Something for the Boys* (Alvin, "Staff Sgt. Rocky Fulton," Jan. 7, 1943): Could It Be You?; Hey, Good Lookin'; There's a Happy Land in the Sky; When My Baby Goes to Town/WM: Cole Porter. *The Day Before Spring* (National, "Alex Maitland," Nov. 22, 1945): The Day Before Spring; God's Green World; I Love You This Morning; You Haven't Changed at All/W: Alan Jay Lerner, M: Frederick Loewe. *Pipe Dream* (Shubert, "Doc," Nov. 30, 1955): All at Once You Love Her; All Kinds of People; How Long?; The Man I Used to Be; The Next Time It Happens; The Tide Pool; Will You Marry Me?/W: Oscar Hammerstein II, M: Richard Rodgers.

4805. Bobby Johnson *Kiss Me, Kate* (Broadway, revival, "Paul," Jan. 8, 1952): Too Darn Hot/WM: Cole Porter.

4806. Chic Johnson (Mar. 5, 1891–Feb. 26, 1962) B: Chicago, IL. With comedy partner OLE OLSEN, they were known as Olsen and Johnson. *Take a Chance* (Apollo, CR, "Louie Webb," June 1933): Turn Out the Light/W: B.G. DeSylva, M: Richard A. Whiting, Nacio Herb Brown.

4807. Christine Johnson *Great Lady* (Majestic, "Housekeeper," Dec. 1, 1938): Madame Is at Home/W: Earle Crooker, M: Frederick Loewe. *Carousel* (Majestic, "Nettie Fowler," Apr. 19, 1945): June Is Bustin' Out All Over; A Real Nice Clambake; You'll Never Walk Alone/W: Oscar Hammerstein II, M: Richard Rodgers. *Carousel* (New York City Center > Majestic, revival, "Nettie Fowler," Jan. 25, 1949): same as above.

4808. Cora Johnson *Treemonisha* (Palace, "Lucy," Oct. 21, 1975): Confusion; We Will Trust You As Our Leader; We're Goin' Around; The Wreath/WM: Scott Joplin.

4809. David Lawrence Johnson *The Human Comedy* (Royale, "Trainman," Apr. 5, 1984): Hi Ya, Kid/W: William Dumaresq, M: Galt MacDermot.

4810. Eddie Johnson *Meet the People* (Mansfield, revue, Dec. 25, 1940): It's the Same Old South/W: Edward Eliscu, M: Jay Gorney — Let's Steal a Tune (from Offenbach)/W: Henry Myers, M: Jay Gorney — Union Label/W: Henry Myers, Edward Eliscu, M: Jay Gorney.

4811. Edward Johnson (Aug. 22, 1878–Apr. 20, 1959) B: Guelph, Ontario, Canada. The tenor lived for a time in Italy under the name Eduardo di Giovanni. He sang with the Metropolitan Opera from 1922 until 1935, when he became its manager. *A Waltz Dream* (Broadway, "Lieut. Niki," Jan. 27, 1908): The Family's Ancient Tree; Love Cannot Be Bought; Love's Roundelay; Sweetest Maid of All; Two Is Plenty/W: Joseph W. Herbert, M: Oscar Straus — I Love and the World Is Mine/W: Florence Earle Coates, M: Charles Gilbert Spross.

4812. Eric Johnson *Aspects of Love* (Broadhurst, "1st Barker," Apr. 8, 1990): Everybody Loves a Hero/W: Don Black, Charles Hart, M: Andrew Lloyd Webber.

4813. Ethel Johnson (c 1888–May 23, 1964) M: producer, songwriter E. Ray Goetz. *The Tenderfoot* (New York, "Patsy," Feb. 22, 1904): Dancing/W: Richard Carle, M: H.L. Heartz. *The Pearl and the Pumpkin* (Broadway, "Sally Simkins," Aug. 21, 1905): My Combination Girl; When the Moon Is in the Sky (Shadow Song)/W: Paul West, M: John W. Bratton. *The Red Mill* (Knickerbocker, "Tina," Sept. 24, 1906): Go While the Goin' Is Good; I Want You to Marry Me; Mignonette; Whistle It/W: Henry Blossom, M: Victor Herbert. *Judy Forgot* (Broadway, "Rosa," Oct. 6, 1910): My Soldier Boy/W: Avery Hopwood, M: Silvio Hein. *The Hen-Pecks* (Broadway, "Henolia Peck," Feb. 4, 1911): It's the Skirt; Just Tell Me with Your Eyes; Try This on Your Pianna, Anna/W: E. Ray Goetz, M: A. Baldwin Sloane.

4814. Frank Johnson *Better Times* (Hippodrome, revue, Sept. 2, 1922): Just a Fan/W: R.H. Burnside, M: Raymond Hubbell.

4815. Freddie Johnson *Lucky Sambo* (Colonial, "Jack Stafford," June 6, 1925): Coal Oil; June/WM: Porter Grainger, Freddie Johnson.

4816. Howard Johnson *Angel Face* (Knickerbocker, "Rockwell Gibbs," Dec. 29, 1919): How Do You Get That Way?; My Idea of Something to Go Home To; Sow Your Wild Oats Early/W: Robert B. Smith, M: Victor Herbert.

4817. J. Rosamond Johnson (Aug. 11,

1873–Nov. 11, 1954) B: Jacksonville, FL. Actor and composer. One of his songwriting partners was his brother, James Weldon Johnson. *The Shoo Fly Regiment* (Bijou, Aug. 6, 1907): If Adam Hadn't Seen the Apple Tree; There's Always Something Wrong/W: Bob Cole, M: J. Rosamond Johnson — Won't You Be My Little Brown Bear?/W: James Weldon Johnson, M: J. Rosamond Johnson. *The Red Moon* (Majestic, "Plunk Green," May 3, 1909): Big Red Shawl/W: Bob Cole, M: J. Rosamond Johnson — Don't Tell Tales Out of School; I Love but You/WM: ?. *Porgy and Bess* (Alvin, "Frazier," Oct. 10, 1935): Woman to Lady/W: DuBose Heyward, M: George Gershwin. *Porgy and Bess* (Majestic, revival, "Frazier," Jan. 22, 1942): same as above.

4818. Judy Johnson *Guys and Dolls* (New York City Center, revival, CR, "Miss Adelaide," May 31, 1955): Adelaide's Lament; A Bushel and a Peck; Marry the Man Today; Sue Me; Take Back Your Mink/WM: Frank Loesser.

4819. Julie Johnson (1903–Sept. 28, 1973) M: GEORGE MURPHY. *Shoot the Works!* (George M. Cohan, revue, July 21, 1931): Begging for Love/WM: Irving Berlin — Do What You Like/W: Leo Robin, M: Phil Charig — I Want to Chisel In on Your Heart/W: Max Lief, Nathaniel Lief, M: Michael Cleary.

4820. Marilyn J. Johnson *The Best Little Whorehouse in Texas* (46th Street, CR, "Jewel," Dec. 21, 1981): Girl, You're a Woman; No Lies; Twenty-Four Hours of Lovin'/WM: Carol Hall.

4821. Mel Johnson, Jr. (Apr. 16, 1949–) B: New York, NY. *Eubie* (Ambassador, revue, Sept. 20, 1978): Baltimore Buzz; Dixie Moon; If You've Never Been Vamped by a Brownskin (You've Never Been Vamped at All); There's a Million Little Cupids in the Sky/W: Noble Sissle, M: Eubie Blake — Goodnight Angeline/W: Noble Sissle, James Reese Europe, M: Eubie Blake — My Handyman Ain't Handy No More/W: Andy Razaf, M: Eubie Blake. *The Rink* (Martin Beck, "Hiram" and "Mrs. Jackson," Feb. 9, 1984): Not Enough Magic; What Happened to the Old Days?/W: Fred Ebb, M: John Kander. *Big Deal* (Broadway, "Sunnyboy," Apr. 10, 1986): Ain't She Sweet?; Happy Days Are Here Again/W: Jack Yellen, M: Milton Ager — Pick Yourself Up/W: Dorothy Fields, M: Jerome Kern.

4822. Myra Johnson B: Orangeburg, SC. *John Henry* (44th Street, "Poor Selma," Jan. 10, 1940): Stingaree Song/W: Roark Bradford, M: Jacques Wolfe.

4823. Naomi Johnson *Earl Carroll's Vanities of 1928* (Earl Carroll, revue, Aug. 6, 1928): My

Arms Are Open/W: Ned Washington, M: Michael H. Cleary — Wheels/W: Grace Henry, M: Morris Hamilton.

4824. Orrin Johnson (Dec. 1, 1865–Nov. 24, 1943) B: Louisville, KY. *Love Dreams* (Times Square > Apollo, "Dr. Duncan Pell," Oct. 10, 1921): My Dream of Love Is You/W: Oliver Morosco, M: Werner Janssen.

4825. Reginald Vel Johnson *But Never Jam Today* (Longacre, "Duchess" and "Humpty-Dumpty," July 31, 1979): A Real Life Lullabye; Riding for a Fall/WM: Bob Larimer, Bert Keyes.

4826. Ruth Johnson M: GROUCHO MARX. She was his first wife; they divorced after 21 years of marriage. *Blackbirds of 1928* (Liberty > Eltinge, revue, May 9, 1928): Bandanna Babies; Shuffle Your Feet (and Just Roll Along)/W: Dorothy Fields, M: Jimmy McHugh.

4827. Susan Johnson (July 6, 1927–Feb. 24, 2003) B: Columbus, OH. *Buttrio Square* (New Century, "Terry Patterson," Oct. 14, 1952): Get Me Out; You're Mine, All Mine/W: Gen Genovese, M: Fred Stamer — I Keep Telling Myself/W: Gen Genovese, M: Arthur Jones. *The Most Happy Fella* (Imperial > Broadway, "Cleo," May 3, 1956): Big D; Happy to Make Your Acquaintance; I Like Ev'rybody; Ooh! My Feet!/WM: Frank Loesser. *Oh Captain!* (Alvin, "Mae," Feb. 4, 1958): Give It All You Got; Love Is Hell; The Morning Music of Montmartre/WM: Jay Livingston, Ray Evans. *Whoop-Up* (Shubert, "Glenda Swenson," Dec. 22, 1958): Flattery; Glenda's Place; Men; Montana; Quarrel-tet; When the Tall Man Talks/W: Norman Gimbel, M: Moose Charlap. *Donnybrook!* (46th Street, "Kathy Carey," May 18, 1961): Dee-lightful Is the Word; I Wouldn't Bet One Penny; Mr. Flynn; Sad Was the Day/WM: Johnny Burke.

4828. Tina Johnson (Oct. 27, 1951–) B: Wharton, TX. *The Best Little Whorehouse in Texas* (46th Street, CR, "Angel," c 1980): Hard-Candy Christmas/WM: Carol Hall. *State Fair* (Music Box, "Vivian," Mar. 27, 1996): The Man I Used to Be/W: Oscar Hammerstein II, M: Richard Rodgers.

4829. Tommi Johnson B: Austin, TX. *Uptown...It's Hot!* (Lunt-Fontanne, revue, Jan. 29, 1986): Just a Closer Walk with Thee/WM: Red Foley — Old Landmark/WM: M.A. Brunner — Why Do Fools Fall in Love?/WM: Frank Lymon, Morris Levy — You Send Me/WM: L.C. Cooke.

4830. Van Johnson (Aug. 25, 1916–) B: Newport, RI. Likeable star of light romantic movies of the 1940s and 50s, often playing the boy next door. *Pal Joey* (Ethel Barrymore > Shubert > St. James, "Victor," Dec. 25, 1940): That

Terrific Rainbow/W: Lorenz Hart, M: Richard
Rodgers. *Too Many Girls* (Imperial, CR, "Clint
Kelley," Apr. 1960): I Didn't Know What Time
It Was; I Like to Recognize the Tune; Love
Never Went to College; Spic and Spanish;
Tempt Me Not/W: Lorenz Hart, M: Richard
Rodgers. *La Cage aux Folles* (Palace, CR,
"Georges," Jan. 7, 1985): Cocktail Counterpoint;
Look Over There; Masculinity; Song on the
Sand; With You on My Arm/WM: Jerry Her-
man.

4831. Winni Johnson *Early to Bed* (Broadhurst, "Euphenia," Oct. 3, 1943): A Girl Should
Never Ripple When She Bends/W: George Marion, Jr., M: Fats Waller.

4832. Carolyn Johnson-White *The Gospel
at Colonus* (Lunt-Fontanne, "Choir Soloist,"
Mar. 24, 1988): Lift Him Up/W: Lee Breuer,
M: Bob Telson.

4833. Fannie Johnston *Florodora* (Casino >
New York, "Dolores," Nov. 10, 1900): The
Queen of the Philippine Islands/WM: Paul
Rubens — Somebody; When We're on the Stage/
WM: ?.

4834. Grace Johnston *Free for All* (Manhattan, "Silver Dollar Kate," Sept. 8, 1931): When
Your Boy Becomes a Man/W: Oscar Hammerstein II, M: Richard A. Whiting.

4835. Jane A. Johnston (Aug. 4, 1934–) B:
Akron, OH. *The Cradle Will Rock* (New York
City Center, revival, "Ella Hammer," Feb. 11,
1960): Joe Worker/WM: Marc Blitzstein. *Company* (Alvin, CR, "Jenny," May 13, 1971): Getting
Married Today; Poor Baby/WM: Stephen Sondheim.

4836. Johnny Johnston (Dec. 1, 1915–Jan. 6,
1996) B: St. Louis, MO. M: KATHRYN GRAY-
SON, 1947 to 1951. The popular baritone, who
began his career as a band singer in the 1930s,
sang in several 1940s movies. *A Tree Grows in
Brooklyn* (Alvin, "Johnny Nolan," Apr. 19, 1951):
Don't Be Afraid; Growing Pains; I'll Buy You a
Star; I'm Like a New Broom; Look Who's Dancing; Make the Man Love Me; Mine Till Mon-
day/W: Dorothy Fields, M: Arthur Schwartz.

4837. Justine Johnston (June 13–) B:
Evanston, IL. *How to Succeed in Business With-
out Really Trying* (New York City Center, revival,
"Miss Jones," Apr. 20, 1966): Brotherhood of
Man; Paris Original/WM: Frank Loesser. *Follies*
(Winter Garden, "Heidi Schiller," Apr. 4, 1971):
One More Kiss/WM: Stephen Sondheim. *Sond-
heim: A Musical Tribute* (Shubert, revue, Mar. 11,
1973): One More Kiss/WM: Stephen Sondheim.

4838. Norman Johnston *Blossom Time*
(Jolson, revival, "Kupelweiser," Mar. 8, 1926):

Keep It Dark; My Springtime Thou Art; Sere-
nade/W: Dorothy Donnelly, M: Sigmund
Romberg.

4839. Justine Johnstone (Jan. 31, 1895–
Sept. 3, 1982) B: Englewood, NJ. M: movie pro-
ducer, Walter Wanger. *Betty* (Globe, "Chi-
quette," Oct. 3, 1916): I Love the Girls/WM:
Paul Rubens, Adrian Ross. *Oh, Boy!* (Princess >
Casino, "Polly Andrus," Feb. 20, 1917): A Pack-
age of Seeds/W: Herbert Reynolds, P.G. Wode-
house, M: Jerome Kern. *Over the Top* (44th
Street roof, revue, Nov. 28, 1917): My Rainbow
Girl; Posterland/W: Philip Bartholomae, M:
Sigmund Romberg, Herman Timberg.

4840. Russ Jolly (Sept. 23. 1961–) B: Bossier
City, LA. *Big River: The Adventures of Huckle-
berry Finn* (Eugene O'Neill, CR, "Young Fool"):
Arkansas/WM: Roger Miller.

4841. Al Jolson (Mar. 26, 1886–Oct. 23,
1950) B: Seredzius, Lithuania. M: RUBY
KEELER. Singing megastar of the stage, radio
and talking pictures. Eddie Cantor said of him:
"He was the King — and the King could do no
wrong." *La Belle Paree* (Winter Garden, "Evas-
tus Sparkler," Mar. 20, 1911): Paris Is a Paradise
for Coons/W: Edward Madden, M: Jerome
Kern. *Vera Violetta* (Winter Garden, "Claude,"
Nov. 20, 1911): Rum Tum Tiddle/W: Edward
Madden, M: Jean Schwartz — That Haunting
Melody/WM: George M. Cohan. *The Whirl of
Society* (Winter Garden, revue, Mar. 5, 1912):
My Sumurun Girl/W: Al Jolson, M: Louis A.
Hirsch — Row, Row, Row/W: William Jerome,
M: James V. Monaco — Snap Your Fingers; The
Villain Still Pursued Her/W: William Jerome,
M: Harry Von Tilzer — Waiting for the Robert
E. Lee/W: L. Wolfe Gilbert, M: Lewis F. Muir.
The Honeymoon Express (Winter Garden, "Gus,"
Feb. 6, 1913): Down Where the Tennessee Flows
[Apr. 28, 1913]/W: Ray Sherwood, M: Bert
Rule — Goodbye, Boys (I'm Going to Be Mar-
ried Tomorrow) [Apr. 28, 1913]/W: Andrew B.
Sterling, M: Harry Von Tilzer — I Love Her
(Oh! Oh! Oh!) [Apr. 28, 1913]/W: Joseph Mc-
Carthy, Edward P. Moran, M: James V. Mon-
aco — My Yellow Jacket Girl; That Gal of Mine/
W: Harold Atteridge, M: Jean Schwartz — Upon
the Hudson Shore (Give Me the Hudson Shore)/
W: ?, M: Al Jolson — Who Paid the Rent for
Mrs. Rip Van Winkle When Rip Van Winkle
Went Away? [added]/W: Alfred Bryan, M: Fred
Fisher — You Made Me Love You (I Didn't Want
to Do It) [Apr. 28, 1913]/W: Joseph McCarthy,
M: James V. Monaco. *Dancing Around* (Winter
Garden, "Gus," Oct. 10, 1914): Bring Along Your
Dancing Shoes/W: Gus Kahn, M: Grace Le

Boy — Dancing the Blues Away/WM: Joseph McCarthy, Howard Johnson, Fred Fisher — I Want to Be in Norfolk; The Shuffling Shiveree/W: Harold Atteridge, M: Harry Carroll — I'm Seeking for Siegfried; Venetia/WM: ? — Sister Susie's Sewing Shirts for Soldiers/W: R.P. Weston, M: Herman E. Darewski — Tennessee, I Hear You Calling/W: Jeff Godfrey, M: Harry Robe — When Grown Up Ladies Act Like Babies/W: Joe Young, Edgar Leslie, M: Maurice Abrahams. *Robinson Crusoe, Jr.* (Winter Garden, "Gus Jackson," Feb. 17, 1916): Down Where the Swanee River Flows/W: Charles McCarron, Charles S. Alberte, M: Albert Von Tilzer — Now He's Got a Beautiful Girl/W: Edgar Leslie, Ted Snyder, M: Grant Clarke — Tillie Titwillow/W: Harold Atteridge, M: Phil Schwartz — Where Did Robinson Crusoe Go with Friday on Saturday Night?/W: Sam M. Lewis, Joe Young, M: George W. Meyer — Where the Black-eyed Susans Grow/W: Dave Radford, M: Richard A. Whiting — Yaaka Hula Hickey Dula (Hawaiian Love Song)/WM: E. Ray Goetz, Joe Young, Pete Wendling. *Sinbad* (Winter Garden > Century > Casino, "Gus," Feb. 14, 1918): Cleopatra/W: Alfred Bryan, M: Harry Tierney — I Wonder Why She Kept on Saying Si-Si-Si-Si Senor!/W: Sam M. Lewis, Joe Young, M: Ted Snyder — I'll Say She Does; 'N' Everything/WM: Al Jolson, B.G. DeSylva, Gus Kahn — On the Road to Calais/W: Alfred Bryan, M: Al Jolson — Rock-a-Bye Your Baby with a Dixie Melody; Why Do They All Take the Night Boat to Albany?/W: Sam M. Lewis, Joe Young, M: Jean Schwartz. *Bombo* (Al Jolson > Winter Garden, "Gus" and "Bombo," Oct. 6, 1921): April Showers/W: B.G. DeSylva, M: Louis Silvers — Down South; Give Me My Mammy/W: B.G. De Sylva, M: Walter Donaldson — That Barber in Seville/W: ?, M: Con Conrad — Toot, Toot, Tootsie, Goodbye/WM: Ted Fiorito, Robert A. King, Gus Kahn, Ernie Erdman — Who Cares?/W: Jack Yellen, M: Milton Ager — Yoo-Hoo/W: B.G. DeSylva, M: Al Jolson. *Big Boy* (Winter Garden > 44th Street, "Gus," Jan. 7, 1925): As Long as I've Got My Mammy/W: B.G. DeSylva, M: Joseph Meyer, James F. Hanley — Hello, 'Tucky; If You Knew Susie (Like I Know Susie)/W: B.G. DeSylva, M: Joseph Meyer; Keep Smiling at Trouble/W: Al Jolson, B.G. DeSylva, M: Lewis E. Gensler — (Lead 'Em On) Miami; Nobody but Fanny/W: Al Jolson, B.G. DeSylva, M: Con Conrad — Who Was Chasing Paul Revere?/W: B.G. DeSylva, M: Joseph Meyer, Lewis E. Gensler. *The Wonder Bar* (Nora Bayes, "Mon. Al," Mar. 17, 1931): Good Evening, Friends; I'm Falling in

Love/W: Irving Caesar, M: Robert Katscher — Lenox Avenue/WM: Irving Caesar, Al Jolson, Joseph Meyer — Ma Mere/WM: Irving Caesar, Al Jolson, Harry Warren — Oh, Donna Clara/W: Irving Caesar, M: J. Petersburski. *Hold On to Your Hats* (Shubert, "Lone Rider," Sept. 11, 1940): Don't Let It Get You Down; Down on the Dude Ranch; Old Timer; She Came, She Saw, She Can-Canned; There's a Great Day Coming, Manana; Walkin' Along Mindin' My Business; Would You Be So Kindly?/W: E.Y. Harburg, M: Burton Lane.

4842. Joanne Jonas *Candide* (Broadway, revival, CR, "Old Lady," Sept. 1975): The Best of All Possible Worlds/W: Stephen Sondheim, M: Leonard Bernstein — I Am Easily Assimilated/W: Richard Wilbur, M: Leonard Bernstein.

4843. Roberta Jonay (Oct. 15, 1921–Apr. 19, 1976) B: Philadelphia, PA. *Allegro* (Majestic, "Jennie Brinker," Oct. 10, 1947): Money Isn't Ev'rything/W: Oscar Hammerstein II, M: Richard Rodgers.

4844. Allan Jones (Oct. 14, 1907–June 27, 1992) B: Old Forge, PA. Singing star of movies from 1935, especially Marx Brothers comedies such as A Night at the Opera (1935) and A Day at the Races (1937). *Bitter Sweet* (44th Street, revival, "Carl Linden," May 7, 1934): Dear Little Cafe; If You Could Only Come with Me; I'll See You Again; Tokay/WM: Noel Coward. *Jackpot* (Alvin, "Hank Trimble," Jan. 13, 1944): I Kissed My Girl Goodbye; It Was Nice Knowing You; I've Got a One-Track Mind; A Piece of a Girl; What Happened?/W: Howard Dietz, M: Vernon Duke.

4845. Anne Jones *Once Upon a Mattress* (Alvin, "Lady Larken," Nov. 25, 1959): In a Little While; Normandy; An Opening for a Princess; Yesterday I Loved You/W: Marshall Barer, M: Mary Rodgers.

4846. Benny Jones *The Red Moon* (Majestic, "Bill Simmons," May 3, 1909): I Ain't Had No Lovin' in a Long Time (an' Lovin' Is a Thing I Need)/W: Bob Cole, M: James Reese Europe — Keep on Smilin'/W: Bob Cole, M: J. Rosamond Johnson.

4847. Broadway Jones *Blackbirds of 1930* (Royale, revue, Oct. 22, 1930): Roll Jordan/W: Andy Razaf, M: Eubie Blake. *Sugar Hill* (Forrest, "Gyp Penrose," Dec. 25, 1931): Hanging Around Yo' Door; Hot Harlem/W: Jo Trent, M: James P. Johnson.

4848. Byron Jones *Dixie to Broadway* (Broadhurst, revue, Oct. 29, 1924): Prisoner's Up to Date/W: Grant Clarke, Roy Turk, M: George W. Meyer, Arthur Johnston. *Keep*

Shufflin' (Daly's > Eltinge, revue, Feb. 27, 1928): Choc'late Bar/W: Andy Razaf, M: Fats Waller.

4849. Carleton T. Jones *A Chorus Line* (Shubert, CR, "Richie," Mar. 1980): And.../W: Edward Kleban, M: Marvin Hamlisch.

4850. Charlotte Jones (Jan. 1, c 1916–Nov. 6, 1992) B: Chicago, IL. *Mame* (Winter Garden, "Mother Burnside," May 24, 1966): The Fox Hunt/WM: Jerry Herman. *How Now, Dow Jones* (Lunt-Fontanne, "Mrs. Millhauser," Dec. 7, 1967): Step to the Rear/W: Carolyn Leigh, M: Elmer Bernstein. *Johnny Johnson* (Edison, revival, "Aggie Tompkins," Apr. 11, 1971): Aggie's Sewing Machine Song/W: Paul Green, M: Kurt Weill.

4851. Chester Jones (Jan. 22, 1899–June 27, 1975) B: Kentucky. *Blackbirds of 1928* (Liberty, revue, CR, June 18, 1928): I Can't Give You Anything but Love/W: Dorothy Fields, M: Jimmy McHugh.

4852. Dale Jones *Just a Minute* (Ambassador > Century, "Tom," Oct. 8, 1928): Doggone/W: Walter O'Keefe, M: Harry Archer. *The Music Man* (New York City Center, revival, "Olin Britt," June 16, 1965): It's You; Lida Rose; Sincere/WM: Meredith Willson.

4853. Dave Jones *On Your Toes* (Imperial > Majestic, "Phil Dolan II," Apr. 11, 1936): Two-a-Day for Keith/W: Lorenz Hart, M: Richard Rodgers.

4854. Davey Jones *The Second Little Show* (Royale > Shubert, revue, Sept. 2, 1930): Foolish Face; What a Case I've Got on You!/W: Howard Dietz, M: Arthur Schwartz.

4855. David Jones (Dec. 30, 1946–) B: Manchester, England. On TV he was the guitar playing Davy in the sitcom The Monkees (1966). *Oliver!* (Imperial, "The Artful Dodger," Jan. 6, 1963): Be Back Soon; Consider Yourself; I'd Do Anything/WM: Lionel Bart.

4856. Dean Jones (Jan. 25, 1930–) B: Decatur, AL. Leading man in movies from 1956, especially The Love Bug (1969) and other Disney features. *Company* (Alvin, "Robert," Apr. 26, 1970): Barcelona; Being Alive; Company; Side by Side by Side; Someone Is Waiting; What Would We Do Without You?/WM: Stephen Sondheim. *Into the Light* (Neil Simon, "James Prescott," Oct. 22, 1986): Be There; The Data; It Can All Be Explained; Let There Be Light; Neat/Not Neat; Rainbow Logic; A Talk About Time; The Testing; The Three of Us; To Measure the Darkness/W: John Forster, M: Lee Holdridge.

4857. Eleanor Jones *If the Shoe Fits* (Century, "Lady Guinevere," Dec. 5, 1946): Night After Night/W: June Carroll, M: David Raksin.

4858. Floyd Jones *Hassard Short's Ritz Revue* (Winter Garden, revue, CR, Feb. 2, 1925): Monsieur Beaucaire; Our Crystal Wedding Day/W: Anne Caldwell, M: Frank Tours.

4859. Gattison Jones *Spice of 1922* (Winter Garden, revue, July 6, 1922): Burglar Inn/W: Edward P. Moran, M: Seymour Furth — Egyptian Melange/WM: James F. Hanley, Jack Stanley. *Angela* (Ambassador, "Duke of Berascon," Dec. 3, 1928): Bundle of Love; Don't Forget Your Etiquette; Oui, Oui!!; The Regal Romp; Tally-Ho/W: Mann Holiner, M: Alberta Nichols.

4860. James Earl Jones (Jan. 17, 1931–) B: Arkabutla, MS. Distinguished actor of the stage, films and TV. Son of ROBERT EARL JONES. *A Hand Is on the Gate* (Longacre, program of poetry and song, Sept. 21, 1966): Harlem Sweeties/WM: Langston Hughes.

4861. Jen Jones (Mar. 23, 1927–) B: Salt Lake City, UT. *The Music Man* (City Center 55th Street, revival, "Eulalie Mackecknie Shinn," June 5, 1980): It's You; Pick-a-Little, Talk-a-Little/WM: Meredith Willson.

4862. John Christopher Jones *The Goodbye Girl* (Marquis, "Mark," Mar. 4, 1993): Richard Interred/W: David Zippel, M: Marvin Hamlisch.

4863. John Price Jones (c 1891–Apr. 7, 1961) B: Nashville, TN. *Ziegfeld Midnight Frolic of 1919 [9th Edition]* (New Amsterdam roof, revue, CR, Jan. 26, 1920): Dearest/W: Gene Buck, M: Dave Stamper. *Pitter Patter* (Longacre, "Bob Livingston," Sept. 28, 1920): Any Afternoon; I'm a Bachelor/W: ?, M: William B. Friedlander — Baghdad on the Subway; Since You Came Into My Life; The Wedding Blues; You Can Never Tell/WM: William B. Friedlander — Send for Me/WM: Will M. Hough, William B. Friedlander. *Good Morning, Dearie* (Globe, "George Mason," Nov. 1, 1921): Every Girl/W: Anne Caldwell, M: Jerome Kern. *One Kiss* (Fulton, "Jean," Nov. 27, 1923): Don't Ever Be a Poor Relation/W: Clare Kummer, M: Maurice Yvain. *Oh! Oh! Oh! Nurse* (Cosmopolitan, "Dr. Sidney Killmore," Dec. 7, 1925): Good Night My Lady Love; I'll Give the World to You; The Newlywed Express/W: Monte Carlo, M: Alma Sanders. *Rufus Le Maire's Affairs* (Majestic, revue, Mar. 28, 1927): Bring Back Those Minstrel Days; Dancing by Moonlight; Down Where the Morning Glories Twine; Mexico/W: Ballard Macdonald, M: Martin Broones — I Can't Get Over a Girl Like You (Loving a Boy Like

Me)/W: Harry Ruskin, M: Martin Broones. *Good News!* (46th Street, "Tom Marlowe," Sept. 6, 1927): The Best Things in Life Are Free; Happy Days; On the Campus/W: B.G. DeSylva, Lew Brown, M: Ray Henderson. *Lady Fingers* (Vanderbilt > Liberty, "Dick Tain," Jan. 31, 1929): I Love You More Than Yesterday/W: Lorenz Hart, M: Richard Rodgers — My Wedding; You're Perfect/W: Edward Eliscu, M: Joseph Meyer.

4864. Kid Jones *Cohan and Harris Minstrels* (New York, revue, Aug. 16, 1909): Oh! You Coon/WM: George M. Cohan.

4865. Lauren Jones (Sept. 7–) B: Boston, MA. *Ain't Supposed to Die a Natural Death* (Ethel Barrymore, Oct. 20, 1971): Sera Sera Jim/WM: Melvin Van Peebles.

4866. Leilani Jones (May 14, 1957–) B: Honolulu, HI. *Grind* (Mark Hellinger, "Satin," Apr. 16, 1985): All Things to One Man; A Century of Progress; A Sweet Thing Like Me; Who Is He?; Why, Mama, Why/W: Ellen Fitzhugh, M: Larry Grossman.

4867. Neal Jones (Jan. 2, 1960–) B: Wichita, KS. *Big River: The Adventures of Huckleberry Finn* (Eugene O'Neill, CR, "Young Fool"): Arkansas/WM: Roger Miller.

4868. Patricia Jones *Angel in the Wings* (Coronet, revue, Dec. 11, 1947): Breezy/WM: Bob Hilliard, Carl Sigman.

4869. Paulette Ellen Jones *Inner City* (Ethel Barrymore, revue, Dec. 19, 1971): Hushabye Baby; Man in the Doorway; My Mother Said; Summer Nights; Wino Will/W: Eve Merriam, M: Helen Miller.

4870. Reed Jones (June 30, 1953–June 19, 1989) B: Portland, OR. Actor and choreographer. *Cats* (Winter Garden, "Skimbleshanks," Oct. 7, 1982/c 1988): Skimbleshanks/W: T.S. Eliot, M: Andrew Lloyd Webber.

4871. Robert Earl Jones (Feb. 3, 1900 or 1911–) B: Coldwater, MS. Father of JAMES EARL JONES. He was a prizefighter before becoming an actor. *The Gospel at Colonus* (Lunt-Fontanne, "Creon," Mar. 24, 1988): All My Heart's Desire/W: Lee Breuer, M: Bob Telson.

4872. Roy L. Jones *Dreamgirls* (Ambassador, revival, "Marty," June 28, 1987): Cadillac Car; I Miss You Old Friend; The Rap/W: Tom Eyen, M: Henry Krieger.

4873. Shirley Jones (Mar. 31, 1934–) B: Smithton, PA. M: JACK CASSIDY. Mother of SHAUN and PATRICK CASSIDY; stepmother of DAVID CASSIDY. A leading lady with a lovely singing voice, she was in movies from 1955. On TV she played the mother in the sit-com The Partridge Family (1970). *The Beggar's Opera* (New York City Center, revival, "Polly Peachum," Mar. 13, 1957): Come Sweet Lass; Is Then His Fate Decreed, Sir?; No Power on Earth Can E'er Divide; O, What Pain It Is to Part; Our Polly Is a Sad Slut; The Turtle Thus with Plaintive Crying; Virgins Are Like the Fair Flower; Were I Laid on Greenland Coast; Why How Now Madam Flirt; Would I Might Be Hanged/WM: John Gay. *Maggie Flynn* (ANTA, "Maggie Flynn," Oct. 23, 1968): Don't You Think It's Very Nice?; How About a Ball?; I Won't Let It Happen Again; I Wouldn't Have You Any Other Way; Maggie Flynn; Mr. Clown; Pitter Patter; The Thank You Song/WM: Hugo Peretti, Luigi Creatore, George David Weiss.

4874. Starr Jones *The Garrick Gaieties of 1925* (Garrick, revue, May 17, 1925): Stage Managers' Chorus (Walk Upon Your Toes)/W: Dudley Digges, Lorenz Hart, M: Richard Rodgers.

4875. Todd Jones *Cry for Us All* (Broadhurst, "Cabbage," Apr. 8, 1970): The Broken Heart, or The Wages of Sin; The Cruelty Man; Home Free All; I Lost It; See No Evil/W: William Alfred, Phyllis Robinson, M: Mitch Leigh.

4876. Walter Jones (1872–May 25, 1922) B: Springfield, OH. M: BLANCHE DEYO. *Excelsior, Jr.* (Olympia > Broadway, "William Tell," Nov. 29, 1895): Grandpa's Hat/W: R.A. Barnet, M: A. Baldwin Sloane. *The Man in the Moon* (New York, "Continuous Proctor," Apr. 24, 1899): Billy, You're Off Again/W: Louis Harrison, Stanislaus Stange, M: Gustave Kerker. *The Chaperons* (New York > New York roof, "Algernon O'Shaunessy," June 5, 1902): Somehow It Made Me Think of Home/W: Frederick Ranken, M: Isidore Witmark — Talk, Talk, Talk/WM: George V. Hobart. *Oh, I Say!* (Casino, "Portal," Oct. 30, 1913): Each Pearl a Thought; I Know and She Knows; A Woman's Heart/W: Harry B. Smith, M: Jerome Kern. *Rock-a-Bye Baby* (Astor, "Jimmy Jinks," May 22, 1918): According to Dr. Holt/W: Herbert Reynolds, M: Jerome Kern.

4877. George Jongeyans see GEORGE GAYNES.

4878. Claudia Jordan *Bloomer Girl* (Shubert, "Lydia," Oct. 4, 1944): Welcome Hinges; When the Boys Come Home/W: E.Y. Harburg, M: Harold Arlen.

4879. Dorothy Jordan (Aug. 9, 1906–Dec. 7, 1988) B: Clarkesville, TN. Her first movie was an early talkie version of Shakespeare's The Taming of the Shrew (1929), starring Douglas Fairbanks and Mary Pickford. *The Garrick Gaieties of 1926* (Garrick, revue, May 10, 1926): Mountain Greenery/W: Lorenz Hart, M: Richard Rodgers. *Treasure Girl* (Alvin, Nov. 8, 1928): Got a Rainbow/W: Ira Gershwin, M: George Gershwin.

4880. Jack Jordan, Jr. *Best Foot Forward* (Ethel Barrymore, "Dutch Miller," Oct. 1, 1941): The Guy Who Brought Me/WM: Hugh Martin, Richard Rodgers — Three Men on a Date/WM: Hugh Martin, Ralph Blane.

4881. Marc Jordan *The Apple Tree* (Shubert, "King Arik," Oct. 18, 1966): Make Way; Which Door?/W: Sheldon Harnick, M: Jerry Bock. *Darling of the Day* (George Abbott, "Bert," Jan. 27, 1968): A Gentleman's Gentleman; It's Enough to Make a Lady Fall in Love; Money, Money, Money; Not on Your Nellie; What Makes a Marriage Merry/W: E.Y. Harburg, M: Jule Styne. *The Pajama Game* (Lunt-Fontanne, revival, "Prez," Dec. 9, 1973): Her Is; 7½ Cents/WM: Richard Adler, Jerry Ross. *Music Is* (St. James, "Antonio," Dec. 20, 1976): Hate to Say Goodbye to You/W: Will Holt, M: Richard Adler.

4882. Edouard Jose (1880–Dec. 18, 1930) B: Antwerp, Belgium. *The Ballet Girl* (Manhattan, "Eugene Taradelle," Dec. 21, 1897): A Boom; Clear! Clear!; Dancing/W: Adrian Ross, M: Carl Kiefert.

4883. Hermosa Jose *Shubert Gaieties of 1919* (44th Street, revue, July 14, 1919): Rainbow Ball/W: Alfred Bryan, M: Jean Schwartz.

4884. David Josefsberg *Grease* (New York City Center, return engagement, "Roger," Nov. 29, 1996): Mooning/WM: Jim Jacobs, Warren Casey.

4885. Jackie Joseph (Nov. 7, 1936–) B: Los Angeles, CA. *The Billy Barnes People* (Royale, revue, June 13, 1961): Don't Bother/WM: Billy Barnes.

4886. Lois Josephine *The Wall Street Girl* (Cohan, "Sunshine Reilly," Apr. 15, 1912): You're Some Girl/W: A. Seymour Brown, M: Nat D. Ayer. *The Passing Show of 1913* (Winter Garden, revue, July 24, 1913): The Golden Stairs of Love; It Won't Be the Same Old Broadway/W: Harold Atteridge, M: Jean Schwartz. *Oh, I Say!* (Casino, "Julie," Oct. 30, 1913): Katy-Did/W: Harry B. Smith, M: Jerome Kern. *Ned Wayburn's Town Topics* (Century, revue, "Dorothy Doolittle," Sept. 23, 1915): The Old Fashioned Groom and the Up-to-Date Bride; Take It from Me/W: Robert B. Smith, M: Harold Orlob. *Go To It* (Princess, "Lucy," Oct. 24, 1916): Love Me Just a Little Bit/WM: Schuyler Greene, Worton David, William Hargreaves — When You're in Love You'll Know/WM: John L. Golden, Jerome

Kern — You're the Girl (That Sets Me Stuttering)/W: Schuyler Greene, M: Charles N. Grant.

4887. Betsy Joslyn (Apr. 19, 1954–) B: Staten Island, NY. *Sweeney Todd, the Demon Barber of Fleet Street* (Uris, CR, "Johanna," Jan. 22, 1980): City on Fire!; Green Finch and Linnet Bird; Kiss Me/WM: Stephen Sondheim. *A Doll's Life* (Mark Hellinger, "Nora," Sept. 23, 1982): Jailer, Jailer; Learn to Be Lonely; Letter to the Children; No More Mornings; Power; Rare Wines; Stay with Me, Nora; A Woman Alone/W: Betty Comden, Adolph Green, M: Larry Grossman. *Sunday in the Park with George* (Booth, CR, "Dot" and "Marie," Feb. 26, 1985): Children and Art; Color and Light; Everybody Loves Louis; Move On; Sunday in the Park with George; We Do Not Belong Together/WM: Stephen Sondheim. *Into the Woods* (Martin Beck, CR, "Witch," Mar. 29, 1988/ July 5, 1988): Children Will Listen; Lament (Children Won't Listen); Last Midnight; Stay with Me; Your Fault/WM: Stephen Sondheim.

4888. Carol Joyce *Bunk of 1926* (Heckscher, revue, Feb. 16, 1926): Cuddle Up/W: Gene Lockhart, M: Robert Armbruster — A Geisha Legend; How Very Long Ago It Seems; The Milky Way/W: Percy Waxman, M: Gene Lockhart.

4889. Elaine Joyce (Dec. 19, 1945–) B: Cleveland, OH. M: BOBBY VAN. *Sugar* (Majestic, "Sugar Kane," Apr. 9, 1972): Hey, Why Not!; We Could Be Close; What Do You Give to a Man Who's Had Everything?; When You Meet a Man in Chicago/W: Bob Merrill, M: Jule Styne.

4890. Laura Joyce (May 6, 1858–May 29, 1904) B: Newbury, Berkshire, England. M: DIGBY BELL, 1883. A singer of comic opera, she came to the U.S. in the 1870s. *Cinderella at School* (Daly's, "Merope Mallow," Mar. 5, 1881): I'm Sure to Astonish You All; I've Got a Letter from My Jack; 'Tis Not Becoming in a Maiden; What a Shocking Sight/WM: Woolson Morse.

4891. Peggy Hopkins Joyce (May 23 or 26, 1893–June 12, 1957) B: Norfolk, VA. Internationally celebrated showgirl, known for her jewels and 6 marriages. *Miss 1917* (Century, revue, Nov. 5, 1917): Sammy/W: James O'Dea, M: Edward Hutchinson — Who's Zoo in Girl Land/W: P.G. Wodehouse, M: Jerome Kern. *Earl Carroll's Vanities of 1923* (Earl Carroll, revue, July 5, 1923): Pretty Peggy; Queen of All [Dec. 17, 1923]/WM: Earl Carroll.

4892. Juanita Juarez *Beat the Band* (46th Street, "Mamita," Oct. 14, 1942): America Loves a Band; The Four Freedoms/W: George Marion, Jr., M: Johnny Green.

4893. Carl Judd *Pom-Pom* (Cohan, "Flic," Feb. 28, 1916): Mister Love/W: Anne Caldwell, M: Hugo Felix.

4894. Patrick Jude (Feb. 25, 1951–) B: Jersey City, NJ. *Jesus Christ Superstar* (Mark Hellinger, CR, "Judas Iscariot," July 5, 1972): Damned for All Time; Everything's Alright; Heaven on Their Minds; Judas' Dream; The Last Supper; Strange Thing Mystifying; Superstar/W: Tim Rice, M: Andrew Lloyd Webber. *Jesus Christ Superstar* (Longacre, revival, "Judas Iscariot," Nov. 23, 1977): same as above. *Got Tu Go Disco* (Minskoff, "Billy," June 25, 1979): Cassie; Disco Shuffle; Takin' the Light/WM: Kenny Lehman, John Davis, Ray Chew, Nat Adderley, Jr., Thomas Jones, Wayne Morrison, Steve Boston, Eugene Narmore, Betty Rowland, Jerry Powell. *Charlie and Algernon* (Helen Hayes, "Frank," Sept. 14, 1980): Jelly Donuts and Chocolate Cake; Midnight Riding/W: David Rogers, M: Charles Strouse. *Marlowe* (Rialto, "Christoper Marlowe," Oct. 12, 1981): Can't Leave Now; Emelia; Higher Than High; I'm Coming 'Round to Your Point of View; Live for the Moment; The Madrigal Blues/WM: Leo Rost, Jimmy Horowitz. *The News* (Helen Hayes, "Reporter," Nov. 7, 1985): Beautiful People; Classifieds; The Contest; Editorial; Front Page Expose; Horoscope; Hot Flashes I; Hot Flashes II; Hot Flashes III; Personals; Pyramid Lead; Super Singo; Violent Crime; What in the World; What's the Angle/WM: Paul Schierhorn.

4895. Charles Judels (Aug. 17, 1881–1969) B: Amsterdam, Holland. *The Knickerbocker Girl* (Herald Square, "Capt. Nunez," June 15, 1903): Contrary Mary/WM: M.E. Rourke, Ellis R. Ephram. *Old Dutch* (Herald Square, "Joseph Cusinier," Nov. 22, 1909): I Love Ze Parisienne/W: George V. Hobart, M: Victor Herbert. *Ziegfeld Follies of 1912* (Moulin Rouge, revue, Oct. 21, 1912): The Broadway Glide/W: A. Seymour Brown, M: Bert Grant — Follow the Circus Band; You Might as Well Stay on Broadway/W: Harry B. Smith, M: Raymond Hubbell. *Nobody Home* (Princess > Maxine Elliott, "Rolando D'Amorini," Apr. 20, 1915): You Don't Take a Sandwich to a Banquet/WM: Worton David, J.P. Long. *Go To It* (Princess, "The Colonel," Oct. 24, 1916): Girls, If You Ever Get Married/W: Schuyler Greene, M: Charles N. Grant — Go To It/W: John L. Golden, M: Raymond Hubbell, Max Darewski. *My Lady's Glove* (Lyric, "Col. Bombarde," June 18, 1917): Amorous Rose/W: Edward A. Paulton, M: Oscar

Straus. *Doing Our Bit* (Winter Garden, "John Lee," Oct. 18, 1917): The Fashion Show/W: Harold Atteridge, M: Sigmund Romberg, Herman Timberg. *Head Over Heels* (George M. Cohan, "Bambinetti," Aug. 29, 1918): Me/W: Edgar Allan Woolf, M: Jerome Kern. *Mary* (Knickerbocker, "Gaston Marceau," Oct. 18, 1920): Every Time I Meet a Lady; The Love Nest; Money, Money, Money/W: Otto Harbach, M: Louis A. Hirsch. *The Love Letter* (Globe, CR, "Eugene Bernard," Oct. 24, 1921): Scandal Town/W: William Le Baron, M: Victor Jacobi — Twiddle Your Thumbs/WM: ?. *For Goodness Sake* (Lyric, "Count Spinagio," Feb. 20, 1922): The French Pastry Walk/W: Arthur Jackson, Ira Gershwin, M: William Daly — Greatest Team of All; When You're in Rome/W: Arthur Jackson, M: Paul Lannin, William Daly. *Wildflower* (Casino, "Gaston La Roche," Feb. 7, 1923): Some Like to Hunt/W: Otto Harbach, Oscar Hammerstein II, M: Herbert Stothart.

4896. Nicholas Judels *He Came from Milwaukee* (Casino, CR, "Napoleon Ravachal," Aug. 28, 1911): Tie a Red Ribbon on Me/W: Edward Madden, M: Ben M. Jerome, Louis A. Hirsch.

4897. Alice Judson *Broadway to Tokio* (New York, "Patti Cadenza," Jan. 23, 1900): The Lovelorn Lily/W: Louis Harrison, George V. Hobart, M: A. Baldwin Sloane.

4898. Charles Judson *Hello, Alexander* (44th Street, "Muggs Casey," Oct. 7, 1919): Pantomime Baseball/W: Alfred Bryan, M: Jean Schwartz.

4899. James Judson *Up in Central Park* (New York City Center, revival, "Andrew Monroe," May 19, 1947): Boss Tweed; When the Party Gives a Party/W: Dorothy Fields, M: Sigmund Romberg.

4900. Bernard Jukes *Sari* (Liberty, revival, "Cadeaux," Jan. 29, 1930): Paris? (Oh My! Yes, Dear)/W: C.C.S. Cushing, E.P. Heath, M: Emmerich Kalman.

4901. Raul Julia (Mar. 9, 1940–Oct. 24, 1994) B: San Juan, Puerto Rico. *Two Gentlemen of Verona* (St. James, "Proteus," Dec. 1, 1971): Calla Lily Lady; Dragon Fight; Follow the Rainbow; I Love My Father; I'd Like to Be a Rose; Love's Revenge; Symphony; That's a Very Interesting Question; Thou, Julia, Thou Hast Metamorphosed Me; What Does a Lover Pack?; What's a Nice Girl Like Her/W: John Guare, M: Galt MacDermot — Who Is Silvia?/W: William Shakespeare, M: Galt MacDermot. *Via Galactica* (Uris, "Gabriel Finn," Nov. 28, 1972): Children of the Sun; Four Hundred Girls Ago; The Gospel of Gabriel Finn; Helen of Troy;

Hush; Shall We Friend?/W: Christopher Gore, M: Galt MacDermot. *Where's Charley?* (Circle in the Square, revival, "Charley Wykeham," Dec. 20, 1974): Better Get Out of Here; Make a Miracle; The New Ashmoleon Marching Society and Students Conservatory Band; Once in Love with Amy; Pernambuco/WM: Frank Loesser. *Threepenny Opera* (Vivian Beaumont, revival in new translation, "Mack the Knife," May 1, 1976): Ballad in Which Macheath Begs All Men for Forgiveness; Ballad of Gracious Living; Ballad of Immoral Earnings; Call from the Grave; The Cannon Song; Liebeslied; What Keeps Mankind Alive?/W: Bertolt Brecht, M: Kurt Weill. *Nine* (46th Street, "Guido Contini," May 9, 1982/Jan. 24, 1983): The Bells of St. Sebastian; The Grand Canal; Guido's Song; I Can't Make This Movie; Long Ago; A Man Like You; Nine; Only with You; Unusual Way/WM: Maury Yeston. *Man of La Mancha* (Marquis, revival, "Don Quixote," Apr. 24, 1992): The Combat; Dulcinea; Golden Helmet; The Impossible Dream (The Quest); Man of La Mancha (I, Don Quixote)/W: Joe Darion, M: Mitch Leigh.

4902. Miss Juliet (Feb. 23, 1889–Mar. 24, 1962) B: New York, NY. Her real name was Juliet Delf. *The Cohan Revue of 1916* (Astor, revue, "Emma McChesney" and "Gaby de Lys," Astor, Feb. 9, 1916): Busy, Busy, Busy; Gaby/WM: George M. Cohan.

4903. June (June 11, 1901–Jan. 14, 1985) B: Blackpool, Lancaster, England. Her name at birth was June Howard Tripp. She began her career as a ballet dancer. *Polly* (Lyric, "Polly Shannon," Jan. 8, 1929): Comme Ci, Comme Ca; Little Bo-Peep; Polly/W: Irving Caesar, M: Phil Charig — Sing a Song in the Rain/W: Douglas Furber, Irving Caesar, M: Harry Rosenthal — Sweet Liar/W: Irving Caesar, M: Herbert Stothart.

4904. Roma June *See America First* (Maxine Elliott, "Ethel," Mar. 28, 1916): Beautiful, Primitive Indian Girls; Indian Girls' Chant/WM: T. Lawrason Riggs, Cole Porter. *Some Night* (Harris, "Dorothy Wayne," Sept. 23, 1918): Alone in a Great Big World; Once Upon a Time; Painting My Picture of You/WM: Harry Delf.

4905. Jimmy Justice (Dec. 31, 1941–) B: Erie, PA. *Hello, Dolly!* (St. James, CR, "Rudolph," c 1968): Hello, Dolly!/WM: Jerry Herman.

4906. Roger Kachel *Starlight Express* (Gershwin, CR, "Krupp," c 1987): AC/DC; Wide Smile, High Style, That's Me/W: Richard Stilgoe, M: Andrew Lloyd Webber. *Cats* (Winter Garden, CR, "Mungojerrie," May 11, 1992): Mungojerrie and Rumpleteazer/W: T.S. Eliot, M: Andrew Lloyd Webber.

4907. Judy Kahan (May 24, 1948–) B: New York, NY. Her TV credits include a stint on the soap opera spoof *Mary Hartman, Mary Hartman* (1977). *A Little Night Music* (Shubert, "Fredrika Armfeldt," Feb. 25, 1973): The Glamorous Life/WM: Stephen Sondheim.

4908. Howard Kahl (Sept. 17, 1930–) B: New Albany, IN. *Hot Spot* (Majestic, "A Minister of State," Apr. 19, 1963): Smiles/W: Martin Charnin, M: Mary Rodgers.

4909. Madeline Kahn (Sept. 29, 1942–Dec. 3, 1999) B: Boston, MA. Comic actress, especially remembered for the movies she made with Mel Brooks. *New Faces of 1968* (Booth, revue, May 2, 1968): Das Chicago Song/W: Tony Geiss, M: Michael Cohen — Luncheon Ballad/W: Michael McWhinney, M: Jerry Powell — Toyland/WM: Gene P. Bissell. *Two by Two* (Imperial, "Goldie," Nov. 10, 1970): The Golden Ram/W: Martin Charnin, M: Richard Rodgers. *On the Twentieth Century* (St. James, "Mildred Plotka" and "Lily Garland," Feb. 19, 1978): Babette; Indian Maiden's Lament; I've Got It All; Lily, Oscar; Never; Our Private World; Sign, Lily, Sign (Sextet); Veronique/W: Betty Comden, Adolph Green, M: Cy Coleman.

4910. Ursuline Kairson B: Chicago, IL. *Bubbling Brown Sugar* (ANTA, CR, "Marsha" and "Young Irene," Feb. 15, 1977): God Bless the Child/WM: Arthur Herzog, Jr., Billie Holiday — Solitude/W: Eddie DeLange, Irving Mills, M: Duke Ellington — Sweet Georgia Brown/WM: Ben Bernie, Maceo Pinkard, Ken Casey.

4911. Keith Kaldenberg *The Most Happy Fella* (Imperial > Broadway, "Doc," May 3, 1956): Song of a Summer Night/WM: Frank Loesser. *The Most Happy Fella* (New York City Center, revival, "Doc," Feb. 10, 1959): same as above. *The Cradle Will Rock* (New York City Center, revival, "Junior Mister," Feb. 11, 1960): Croon-Spoon; Honolulu; Let's Do Something/WM: Marc Biltzstein. *Street Scene* (New York City Center, revival, "Daniel Buchanan," Feb. 13, 1960): When a Woman Has a Baby/W: Langston Hughes, Elmer Rice, M: Kurt Weill.

4912. Bob Kaliban (Nov. 6, 1933–) *Ben Franklin in Paris* (Lunt-Fontanne, "Pierre Caron de Beaumarchais," Oct. 27, 1964): God Bless the Human Elbow; Half the Battle; I Love the Ladies/W: Sidney Michaels, M: Mark Sandrich, Jr.

4913. Alexandre Kalioujny (1923–198?) B: Czechoslovakia. *The Girl in Pink Tights* (Mark Hellinger, "Volodya Kuzentsov," Mar. 5, 1954):

Up in the Elevated Railway/W: Leo Robin, M: Sigmund Romberg.

4914. Armand Kaliz (Oct. 23, 1887–Feb. 1, 1941) B: Paris, France. *The Kiss Burglar* (Cohan, "Bert Duvivier," May 9, 1918): Because You Do Not Know; The Girl I Can't Forget; Since I Met Wonderful You; Your Kiss Is Champagne/W: Glen MacDonough, M: Raymond Hubbell. *Spice of 1922* (Winter Garden, revue, July 6, 1922): I'm in Love with You/W: Armand Kaliz, M: Kenneth Keith.

4915. Dick Kallman (July 7, 1933–Feb. 22, 1980) B: Brooklyn, NY. *Seventeen* (Broadhurst, "Joe Bullitt," June 21, 1951): After All, It's Spring; If We Only Could Stop the Old Town Clock; Summertime Is Summertime; Things Are Gonna Hum This Summer; Weatherbee's Drug Store/W: Kim Gannon, M: Walter Kent. *Half a Sixpence* (Broadhurst, CR, "Arthur Kipps," July 4, 1966): All in the Cause of Economy; Flash! Bang! Wallop!; Half a Sixpence; If the Rain's Got to Fall; Long Ago; Money to Burn; The Party's on the House; A Proper Gentleman; She's Too Far Above Me/WM: David Heneker.

4916. Paul Kandel (Feb. 15, 1951–) B: Queens, NY. *The Who's Tommy* (St. James, "Uncle Ernie," Apr. 22, 1993): Fiddle About/ WM: John Entwistle — Tommy's Holiday Camp/ WM: Keith Moon. *A Christmas Carol* (Paramount Madison Square Garden, return engagement, "Ghost of Jacob Marley," Nov. 20, 1995/ Nov. 22, 1996): Link by Link/W: Lynn Ahrens, M: Alan Menken.

4917. Brad (Bradley) Kane (Sept. 29, 1973–) B: New Rochelle, NY. *She Loves Me* (Roundabout, revival, "Arpad Laszlo," June 10, 1993): Good Morning, Good Day; Ilona; Try Me/W: Sheldon Harnick, M: Jerry Bock.

4918. Donna Kane (Aug. 12, 1962–) B: Beacon, NY. *Meet Me in St. Louis* (Gershwin, "Esther Smith," Nov. 2, 1989): The Boy Next Door; Diamonds in the Starlight; Have Yourself a Merry Little Christmas; A Touch of the Irish; The Trolley Song; You Are for Loving/WM: Hugh Martin, Ralph Blane — Skip to My Lou/ WM: Hugh Martin, Ralph Blane, trad.— Under the Bamboo Tree (If You Lak-a Me Lak I Lak-a You)/W: Bob Cole, M: J. Rosamond Johnson. *Les Miserables* (Broadway, CR, "Fantine," c1992): Come to Me; I Dreamed a Dream/W: Herbert Kretzmer, M: Claude-Michel Schonberg.

4919. Dorothy Kane *Babes in Toyland* (Imperial, revival, "Contrary Mary," Dec. 22, 1930): Barney O'Flynn; Beatrice Barefacts; Before and After/W: Glen MacDonough, M: Victor Herbert.

4920. Edward Kane *Stars in Your Eyes* (Majestic, "3rd Assistant Director" and "Photographer," Feb. 9, 1939): This Is It/W: Dorothy Fields, M: Arthur Schwartz.

4921. Helen Kane (Aug. 4, 1903–Sept. 26, 1966) B: Bronx, NY. M: DAN HEALY; MAX HOFFMAN, JR. Known as the "boop boop a doop girl," she appeared in several early talking pictures and was immortalized by the animated cartoon character, Betty Boop. Portrayed by DEBBIE REYNOLDS in the movie *Three Little Words (1950). A Night in Spain* (44th Street, revue, May 3, 1927): Bambazoola [Nov. 7, 1927]; The Curfew Walk; De Dum Dum; Hot Hot Honey/W: Alfred Bryan, M: Jean Schwartz. *Good Boy* (Hammerstein's, "Patsy McManus," Sept. 5, 1928): I Wanna Be Loved by You; The Three Bears/W: Bert Kalmar, M: Harry Ruby, Herbert Stothart. *Shady Lady* (Shubert, "Millie Mack," July 5, 1933): Everything but My Man/ W: Charles Kenny, M: Serge Walter — I'll Betcha That I'll Getcha; Where, Oh Where Can I Find Love?/W: Stanley Adams, M: Jesse Greer.

4922. Irene Kane *Tenderloin* (46th Street, "Jessica," Oct. 17, 1960): Dear Friend/W: Sheldon Harnick, M: Jerry Bock.

4923. John Kane *Happy Go Lucky* (Liberty, "Robert Chapin," Sept. 30, 1926): You're the Fellow the Fortune Teller Told Me All About/W: Helena Evans, M: Lucien Denni. *Happy* (Earl Carroll > Daly's, "Bill Wentworth," Dec. 5, 1927): Black Sheep; Mad About You; Sunny Side of You; The Younger Generation/W: Earle Crooker, McElbert Moore, M: Frank Grey.

4924. Karol Kane *Keep It Clean* (Selwyn, revue, June 24, 1929): I See You but What Do You See in Me?/WM: Lester Lee — Just a Little Blue for You/WM: James F. Hanley.

4925. Lida Kane (c 1885–Oct. 7, 1955) *Judy* (Royale, "Mrs. Maguire," Feb. 7, 1927): What a Whale of a Difference a Woman Can Make/W: Leo Robin, M: Charles Rosoff.

4926. Jeri Kansas (Mar. 10, 1955–) B: Jersey City, NJ. *42nd Street* (Winter Garden, "Phyllis," Aug. 25, 1980): Go Into Your Dance; We're in the Money/W: Al Dubin, M: Harry Warren.

4927. Kenneth Kantor (Apr. 6, 1949–) B: Bronx, NY. *Mame* (Gershwin, revival, "Uncle Jeff," July 24, 1983): The Fox Hunt/WM: Jerry Herman.

4928. Jonathan Kaplan (July 5, 1980–) B: Detroit, MI. *Falsettos* (John Golden, revival, "Jason," Apr. 29, 1992): Another Miracle of Judaism; Cancelling the Bar Mitzvah; Everyone Hates His Parents; Everyone Tells Jason to See a Psychiatrist; Father to Son; The Fight; Four

Jews in a Room Bitching; The Games I Play; I Never Wanted to Love You; Jason's Therapy; Love Is Blind; Making a Home; March of the Falsettos; A Marriage Proposal; Marvin at the Psychiatrist; Marvin Hits Trina; My Father's a Homo; Please Come to My House; This Had Better Come to a Stop/WM: William Finn.

4929. Alfred Kappeler (c 1876–Oct. 29, 1945) B: Zurich, Switzerland. *The Arcadians* (Liberty > Knickerbocker, "Bobby," Jan. 17, 1910): Back Your Fancy; Truth Is So Beautiful [Feb. 2, 1910]/W: Arthur Wimperis, M: Lionel Monckton—The Ladies [Feb. 2, 1910]/W: Adrian Ross, M: Lionel Monckton. *A Certain Party* (Wallack's, "George Caldwell," Apr. 24, 1911): I Want a Boy/W: Edgar Smith, M: Tom Kelly—Love's Wireless Telephone/W: Raymond W. Peck, M: Robert Hood Bowers. *The Three Romeos* (Globe, "Dick Dawson," Nov. 13, 1911): Along Broadway; It's Nice to Have Someone to Love You/W: R.H. Burnside, M: Raymond Hubbell. *Oh, Look!* (Vanderbilt, "Sam Welch," Mar. 7, 1918): Wherever There's Music and Beautiful Girls/W: Joseph McCarthy, M: Harry Carroll. *China Rose* (Martin Beck, "Bang Bang," Jan. 19, 1925): Maiden Fair; Who Am I Thinking Of?/W: Harry L. Cort, George E. Stoddard, M: A. Baldwin Sloane.

4930. Tommy Karaty (Mar. 25, 1940–) Paterson, NJ. *Pousse-Café* (46th Street, "Harry," Mar. 18, 1966): The Eleventh Commandment/W: Herbert Martin, M: Michael Leonard—Rules and Regulations/W: Marshall Barer, M: Duke Ellington.

4931. Simeon Karavaeff *A la Carte* (Martin Beck, revue, Aug. 17, 1927): The Calinda/WM: Herman Hupfeld.

4932. Ras Karbi *Reggae* (Biltmore, "Natty," Mar. 27, 1980): Promised Land; Rise Tafari/WM: Ras Karbi—Star of Zion/WM: Michael Kamen.

4933. Tom Karl (Jan. 19, 1846–Mar. 19, 1916) B: Dublin, Ireland. Principal tenor of the comic opera touring company called The Bostonians. *Robin Hood* (Standard, "Robin Hood," Sept. 28, 1891): Come Dream So Bright; O, See the Lambkins Play!; An Outlaw's Life's the Life for Me; Then Hey for the Merry Greenwood; Though It Was Within This Hour We Met; A Troubador Sang to His Love/W: Harry B. Smith, M: Reginald De Koven.

4934. Gregory V. Karliss *Hair* (Biltmore, CR, "Berger"): Donna; Don't Put It Down; Going Down; Hair/W: Gerome Ragni, James Rado, M: Galt MacDermot.

4935. Boris Karloff (Nov. 23, 1887–Feb. 2, 1969) B: Dulwich, England. Best remembered for the Frankenstein films. *Peter Pan* (Imperial, "Captain Hook," Apr. 24, 1950): The Pirate Song; The Plank/WM: Leonard Bernstein.

4936. Sylvia Karlton *Allegro* (Majestic, "Dot," Oct. 10, 1947): Money Isn't Ev'rything/W: Oscar Hammerstein II, M: Richard Rodgers.

4937. Michael (Mickey) Karm (Oct. 24, 1941–) B: Chicago, IL. *South Pacific* (Music Theater of Lincoln Center, revival, "Professor," June 12, 1967): There Is Nothin' Like a Dame/W: Oscar Hammerstein II, M: Richard Rodgers. *Two by Two* (Imperial, "Ham," Nov. 10, 1970): Put Him Away; You Have Got to Have a Rudder on the Ark/W: Martin Charnin, M: Richard Rodgers.

4938. Christine Karner *Sing Out Sweet Land* (International, revue, "Nellie Bly," Dec. 27, 1944): Frankie and Johnny/WM: trad.

4939. Maria Karnilova (Aug. 3, 1920–Apr. 20, 2001) B: Hartford, CT. M: GEORGE S. IRVING. On stage as a child with the Metropolitan Opera Children's Ballet. *Gypsy* (Broadway, "Tessie Tura," May 21, 1959): You Gotta Have a Gimmick/W: Stephen Sondheim, M: Jule Styne. *Bravo Giovanni* (Broadhurst, "Signora Pandolfi," May 19, 1962): Breachy's Law; Jump In! (Connubiality); The Kangaroo; Signora Pandolfi/W: Ronny Graham, M: Milton Schafer. *Fiddler on the Roof* (Imperial, "Golde," Sept. 22, 1964): Anatevka; Do You Love Me?; Sabbath Prayer; Sunrise, Sunset; The Tailor, Motel Kamzoil/W: Sheldon Harnick, M: Jerry Bock. *Zorba* (Imperial, "Hortense," Nov. 17, 1968): Goodbye, Canavaro; Happy Birthday; No Boom Boom; Only Love; Y'assou/W: Fred Ebb, M: John Kander. *Gigi* (Uris, "Inez Alvarez [Mamita]," Nov. 13, 1973): The Contract; I Remember It Well; The Night They Invented Champagne/W: Alan Jay Lerner, M: Frederick Loewe. *Fiddler on the Roof* (New York State, revival, "Golde," July 9, 1981): Anatevka; Do You Love Me?; Sabbath Prayer; Sunrise, Sunset; The Tailor, Motel Kamzoil/W: Sheldon Harnick, M: Jerry Bock.

4940. Joan Karr *Allez-Oop* (Earl Carroll, revue, Aug. 2, 1927): In the Heart of Spain; Pull Yourself Together; Where Have You Been All My Life?/W: Leo Robin, M: Phil Charig, Richard Myers.

4941. Patti Karr (July 10, 192?–) B: St. Paul, MN. *New Faces of 1962* (Alvin, revue, Feb. 1, 1962): A Moment of Truth/WM: Jack Holmes. *Different Times* (ANTA, "Kimberly Langley," May 1, 1972): Here's Momma; I Dreamed About Roses; The Life of a Woman;

One More Time; The Words I Never Said/WM: Michael Brown. *Irene* (Minskoff, revival, CR, "Helen McFudd"): The Great Lover Tango/W: Otis Clements, M: Charles Gaynor — We're Getting Away with It/W: Joseph McCarthy, M: Harry Tierney. *Seesaw* (Uris, CR, "Gittel Mosca," Oct. 1, 1973/Oct. 29, 1973): Chapter 54, Number 1909; He's Good for Me; I'm Way Ahead; In Tune; Nobody Does It Like Me; Poor Everybody Else; Seesaw; Spanglish; Welcome to Holiday Inn!/W: Dorothy Fields, M: Cy Coleman. *Pippin* (Imperial, CR, "Fastrada," Aug. 5, 1974): Spread a Little Sunshine/WM: Stephen Schwartz. *A Broadway Musical* (Lunt-Fontanne, "Maggie Simpson," Dec. 21, 1978): A Broadway Musical; It's Time for a Cheer-Up Song; You Gotta Have Dancing/W: Lee Adams, M: Charles Strouse. *Got Tu Go Disco* (Minskoff, "Antwerp," June 25, 1979): Gettin' to the Top/WM: Kenny Lehman, John Davis, Ray Chew, Nat Adderly, Jr., Thomas Jones, Wayne Morrison, Steve Boston, Eugene Narmore, Betty Rowland, Jerry Powell. *Musical Chairs* (Rialto, "Lillian," May 14, 1980): Hit the Ladies/WM: Tom Savage.

4942. David Kashner *The Vamp* (Winter Garden, "Whip Man," Nov. 10, 1955): Samson and Delilah/W: John Latouche, M: James Mundy.

4943. Peter Kastner (1944–) B: Canada. *Rainbow Jones* (The Music Box, "Joey Miller," Feb. 13, 1974): I'd Like to Know You Better; It's So Nice; A Little Bit of Me in You; One Big Happy Family; We All Need Love; Who Needs the Love of a Woman/WM: Jill Williams.

4944. Kurt Kasznar (Aug. 12, 1913–Aug. 6, 1979) B: Vienna, Austria. *Seventh Heaven* (ANTA, "Boule," May 26, 1955): C'est la Vie/W: Stella Unger, M: Victor Young. *The Sound of Music* (Lunt-Fontanne, "Max Detweiler," Nov. 16, 1959): How Can Love Survive?; No Way to Stop It/W: Oscar Hammerstein II, M: Richard Rodgers.

4945. Christian Kauffmann *Legs Diamond* (Mark Hellinger, "Bones," Dec. 26, 1988): Charge It to A.R./WM: Peter Allen.

4946. Caroline Kava B: Chicago, IL. *Threepenny Opera* (Vivian Beaumont, revival in new translation, "Polly Peachum," May 1, 1976): Barbara Song; Concerning the Insecurity of the Human State; For That's My Way; Jealousy Duet; Liebeslied; Polly's Lied/W: Bertolt Brecht, M: Kurt Weill.

4947. Lila Kavanagh *Adonis* (Star, revival, "Artea," Nov. 22, 1888): Golden Chains/W: J. Cheever Goodwin, M: Edward E. Rice.

4948. Albia Kaven *The Straw Hat Revue* (Ambassador, revue, Sept. 29, 1939): Four Young People/WM: James Shelton.

4949. Diana Kavilis *A Chorus Line* (Shubert, CR, "Val," Feb. 20, 1989): And...; Dance: Ten, Looks: Three/W: Edward Kleban, M: Marvin Hamlisch.

4950. Beatrice Kay (Apr. 21, 1907–Nov. 8, 1986) B: New York, NY. She became popular singing songs of vaudeville days at Billy Rose's Diamond Horseshoe Restaurant in New York City. *Rose-Marie* (Imperial, CR, "Lady Jane," Dec. 1925): One Man Woman; Only a Kiss; Why Shouldn't We?/W: Otto Harbach, Oscar Hammerstein II, M: Herbert Stothart.

4951. Alma Kaye (Apr. 21, 1925–) B: Stratford, CT. Her career began as a model for Harry Conover. *Sing Out Sweet Land* (International, revue, "Mohee" and "Frankie" and "Daisy," Dec. 27, 1944): A Bicycle Built for Two/WM: Harry Dacre — Frankie and Johnny; Little Mohee; The Roving Gambler/WM: trad.— Heaven Will Protect the Working Girl/W: Edgar Smith, M: A. Baldwin Sloane.

4952. Anne Kaye (Sept. 6, 1942–) B: New Haven, CT. *The Utter Glory of Morrissey Hall* (Mark Hellinger, "Marjorie," May 13, 1979): Oh, Sun; You Will Know When the Time Has Arrived/WM: Clark Gesner.

4953. A.P. Kaye (c 1878–Sept. 7, 1946) *Rosalie* (New Amsterdam, "Prince Rabisco," Jan. 10, 1928): At the Ex-King's Club/W: Ira Gershwin, M: George Gershwin.

4954. Danny Kaye (Jan. 18, 1913–Mar. 3, 1987) B: Brooklyn, NY. M: lyricist and composer Sylvia Fine. Comic actor of the stage, movies and TV. Best remembered for movies such as *The Secret Life of Walter Mitty* (1947) and *Hans Christian Anderson* (1952), and for comic patter songs, most written by his wife. *The Straw Hat Revue* (Ambassador, revue, Sept. 29, 1939): Anatole of Paris; The Swingaroo Trio/WM: Sylvia Fine. *Lady in the Dark* (Alvin, "Russell Paxton," Jan. 23, 1941): The Best Years of His Life; The Greatest Show on Earth; One Life to Live; Tschaikowsky/W: Ira Gershwin, M: Kurt Weill. *Let's Face It!* (Imperial, "Jerry Walker," Oct. 29, 1941): Baby Games; Ev'rything I Love; Farming; I Hate You, Darling; Let's Not Talk About Love/WM: Cole Porter — A Fairy Tale; Melody in 4-F/WM: Sylvia Fine. *Two by Two* (Imperial, "Noah," Nov. 10, 1970/Feb. 8, 1971): The Covenant; Hey, Girlie; Ninety Again!; Poppa Knows Best; Something, Somewhere; Two by Two; When It Dries; Why Me?; You; You Have Got to Have a Rudder on the Ark/W: Martin Charnin, M: Richard Rodgers.

4955. Estaire Kaye *Caroline* (Ambassador, CR, "Helen," June 1923): The Piper You Must Pay (Pay the Piper); Shoulder Arms; Telling Fortunes (Your Fortune); Will o' the Wisp/W: Harry B. Smith, M: Edward Kunneke — Way Down South/W: Harry B. Smith, M: Alfred Goodman.

4956. Judy Kaye (Oct. 11, 1948–) B: Phoenix, AZ. *Grease* (Broadhurst, CR, "Betty Rizzo," May 10, 1977): Freddy, My Love; Look at Me, I'm Sandra Dee; There Are Worse Things I Could Do/WM: Jim Jacobs, Warren Casey. *On the Twentieth Century* (St. James, CR, "Mildred Plotka" and "Lily Garland," Apr. 24, 1978): Babbette; Indian Maiden's Lament; I've Got It All; Lily, Oscar; Never; Our Private World; Sign, Lily, Sign (Sextet); Veronique/W: Betty Comden, Adolph Green, M: Cy Coleman. *The Moony Shapiro Songbook* (Morosco, revue, May 3, 1981): Climbin'; Don't Play That Lovesong Any More; The Girl in the Window; Happy Hickory; I Accuse; I Found Love; I'm Gonna Take Her Home to Momma; Mister Destiny; Pretty Face; A Storm in My Heart; Talking Picture Show; Your Time Is Different to Mine/W: Julian More, M: Monty Norman. *Oh, Brother!* (ANTA, "Saroyana," Nov. 10, 1981): How Do You Want Me?; What Do I Tell People This Time?/W: Donald Driver, M: Michael Valenti. *The Phantom of the Opera* (Majestic, "Carlotta Guidicelli," Jan. 26, 1988): Notes; Poor Fool, He Makes Me Laugh; Prima Donna; Think of Me; Twisted Every Way/W: Charles Hart, Richard Stilgoe, M: Andrew Lloyd Webber.

4957. Robert Kaye *Wonderful Town* (New York City Center, revival, "Robert Baker," Feb. 13, 1963): Conversation Piece (Nice Talk, Nice People); It's Love; A Quiet Girl; What a Waste/W: Betty Comden, Adolph Green, M: Leonard Bernstein. *Flora, the Red Menace* (Alvin, "Mr. Stanley," May 11, 1965): You Are You/W: Fred Ebb, M: John Kander. *Mame* (Winter Garden, CR, "Beauregard Jackson Pickett Burnside"): Mame; We Need a Little Christmas/WM: Jerry Herman. *Maggie Flynn* (ANTA, "Col. John Farraday," Oct. 23, 1968): Look Around Your Little World/WM: Hugo Peretti, Luigi Creatore, George David Weiss.

4958. Sparky Kaye (c 1906–Aug. 23, 1971) B: New York, NY. *Kiss Me, Kate* (Broadway, revival, "Second Man," Jan. 8, 1952): Brush Up Your Shakespeare/WM: Cole Porter.

4959. Stubby Kaye (Nov. 11, 1918–Dec. 14, 1997) B: Bronx, NY. The comic actor's long career included vaudeville, TV and movies. It began when he won the Major Bowes Amateur Hour radio contest in 1939. Best remembered as Nicely-Nicely. *Guys and Dolls* (46th Street, "Nicely-Nicely Johnson," Nov. 24, 1950): Fugue for Tinhorns; Guys and Dolls; The Oldest Established; Sit Down, You're Rockin' the Boat/WM: Frank Loesser. *Li'l Abner* (St. James, "Marryin' Sam," Nov. 15, 1956): The Country's in the Very Best of Hands; I'm Past My Prime; Jubilation T. Cornpone; The Matrimonial Stomp/W: Johnny Mercer, M: Gene de Paul. *Good News* (St. James, revival, "Pooch Kearney," Dec. 23, 1974): Keep Your Sunny Side Up; The Professor and the Students; Tait Song/W: B.G. DeSylva, Lew Brown, M: Ray Henderson. *Grind* (Mark Hellinger, "Gus," Apr. 16, 1985): Cadava; The Grind; I Get Myself Out; Never Put It in Writing/W: Ellen Fitzhugh, M: Larry Grossman.

4960. Lainie Kazan (May 15, 1940–) B: Brooklyn, NY. *My Favorite Year* (Vivian Beaumont, "Belle Steinberg Carroca," Dec. 10, 1992): Rookie in the Ring; Welcome to Brooklyn/W: Lynn Ahrens, M: Stephen Flaherty.

4961. Grace Keagy (Dec. 16–) B: Youngstown, OH. *Goodtime Charley* (Palace, "Isabella of Bavaria," Mar. 3, 1975): History/W: Hal Hackady, M: Larry Grossman. *The Grand Tour* (Palace, "Mme. Bouffier," Jan. 11, 1979): For Poland/WM: Jerry Herman. *Carmelina* (St. James, "Rosa," Apr. 8, 1979): Signora Campbell/W: Alan Jay Lerner, M: Burton Lane. *Musical Chairs* (Rialto, "Roberta," May 14, 1980): Better Than Broadway/WM: Tom Savage. *Woman of the Year* (Palace, "Helga," Mar. 29, 1981): I Told You So; It Isn't Working/W: Fred Ebb, M: John Kander.

4962. Kenny Kealey *The Conquering Hero* (ANTA, "Gene," Jan. 16, 1961): Rough Times; Wonderful, Marvelous You/W: Norman Gimbel, M: Moose Charlap. *Something More!* (Eugene O'Neill, "Freddy Deems," Nov. 10, 1964): Come Sta?; I've Got Nothin' to Do; Who Fills the Bill/W: Marilyn Bergman, Alan Bergman, M: Sammy Fain.

4963. Betty Kean (Dec. 15, 1915–Sept. 29, 1986) B: Hartford, CT. M: LEW PARKER. Sister of JANE KEAN. *Crazy with the Heat* (44th Street, revue, Jan. 14, 1941): Time of Your Life/W: Peter K. Smith, M: William Provost. *Ankles Away* (Mark Hellinger, "Elsey," Apr. 18, 1955): Eleven O'Clock Song; Here's to Dear Old Us; Honeymoon; Old-Fashioned Mothers; Skip the Build-Up; Walk Like a Sailor/W: Dan Shapiro, M: Sammy Fain.

4964. Jane Kean (Apr. 10, 1924–) B: Hartford, CT. Sister of BETTY KEAN. *Early to Bed* (Broadhurst, "Eileen," June 17, 1943): Get Away,

Young Man; The Ladies Who Sing with a Band; There's Yes in the Air (Martinique)/W: George Marion, Jr., M: Fats Waller. *The Girl from Nantucket* (Adelphi, "Dodey Ellis," Nov. 8, 1945): I Love That Boy; What's He Like?/W: Kay Twomey, M: Jacques Belasco — Let's Do and Say We Didn't/WM: Hughie Prince, Dick Rogers — When a Hick Chick Meets a City Slicker/W: Burt Milton, M: Jacques Belasco. *Call Me Mister* (National > Plymouth, revue, CR, Jan. 6, 1947): Military Life (The Jerk Song); South America, Take It Away; Surplus Blues (Little Surplus Me); Yuletide, Park Avenue/WM: Harold Rome. *Ankles Away* (Mark Hellinger, "Wynne," Apr. 18, 1955): Eleven O'Clock Song; His and Hers; Kiss Me and Kill Me with Love; Nothing at All; Nothing Can Replace a Man; Old-Fashioned Mothers; Walk Like a Sailor/W: Dan Shapiro, M: Sammy Fain. *The Pajama Game* (New York City Center, revival, "Babe Williams," May 15, 1957): I'm Not at All in Love; Once a Year Day; 7½ Cents; Sleep-Tite; Small Talk; There Once Was a Man/WM: Richard Adler, Jerry Ross. *Show Boat* (New York City Center, revival, "Ellie May Chipley," Apr. 12, 1961): Goodbye My Lady Love/WM: Joseph E. Howard — Life Upon the Wicked Stage/W: Oscar Hammerstein II, M: Jerome Kern. *Carnival!* (Imperial, CR, "The Incomparable Rosie," July 23, 1962): Direct from Vienna; Humming; It Was Always You; Magic, Magic/WM: Bob Merrill.

4965. George Keane (Apr. 26, 1917–) B: Springfield, MA. *Park Avenue* (Shubert, CR, "Mr. Meacham," Dec. 2, 1946): Sweet Nevada/ W: Ira Gershwin, M: Arthur Schwartz.

4966. Lew Keane (Lew Keen; Louis Keene) *Plantation Revue* (48th Street, revue, July 17, 1922): Robert E. Lee; A Southern Hobby/W: Roy Turk, M: J. Russel Robinson. *Dixie to Broadway* (Broadhurst, revue, Oct. 29, 1924): Prisoner's Up to Date/W: Grant Clarke, Roy Turk, M: George W. Meyer, Arthur Johnston. *Lucky Sambo* (Colonial, June 6, 1925): Logomania/WM: Porter Grainger, Freddie Johnson.

4967. Robert Emmett Keane (Mar. 4, 1883–July 2, 1981) B: New York, NY. *The Passing Show of 1914* (Winter Garden > Lyric, revue, June 10, 1914): The American Englishman [Oct. 5, 1914]; On a Modern Wedding Day/WM: ? *His Little Widows* (Astor, "Jack Grayson," Apr. 30, 1917): That Creepy Weepy Feeling/W: Rida Johnson Young, M: William Schroeder — A Wife for Each Day in the Week/W: William Cary Duncan, M: William Schroeder. *The Grass Widow* (Liberty > Princess, "Larry Doyle," Dec.

3, 1917): All the Girls Have Got a Friend in Me; C.D.Q/W: Channing Pollock, Rennold Wolf, M: Louis A. Hirsch. *Head Over Heels* (George M. Cohan, "Squibbs," Aug. 29, 1918): Funny Little Something; Ladies, Have a Care!; Vorderveele/W: Edgar Allan Woolf, M: Jerome Kern. *Face the Music* (44th Street, return engagement, "Hal Reisman," Jan. 31, 1933): City Hall/WM: Irving Berlin. *The Only Girl* (44th Street, revival, "Andrew McMurray [Bunkie]," May 21, 1934): Be Happy, Boys, Tonight; Connubial Bliss/W: Henry Blossom, M: Victor Herbert — When You're Wearing the Ball and the Chain/W: Harry B. Smith, M: Victor Herbert.

4968. Teri Keane (Oct. 24–) *The Vagabond King* (Shubert, revival, "Lady Mary," June 29, 1943): Serenade/W: Brian Hooker, M: Rudolf Friml.

4969. Jack Kearney *Be Yourself!* (Sam H. Harris, "Eustace Brennan," Sept. 3, 1924): Bongo Boo [Sept. 29, 1924]/W: Owen Murphy, M: Jay Gorney, Milton Schwarzwald — A Good Hand Organ and a Sidewalk's All We Need/ WM: ?

4970. John L. Kearney (c 1871–Aug. 3, 1945) B: New York, NY. *Modest Suzanne* (Liberty, "Mon. Pomeral," Jan. 1, 1912): A Model Married Pair [Jan. 8, 1912]/W: Robert B. Smith, M: Jean Gilbert.

4971. Lynn Kearney (Apr. 9, 1951–) B: Chicago, IL. *Annie* (Alvin, CR, "Grace Farrell," Jan. 22, 1979): Annie; I Think I'm Gonna Like It Here; A New Deal for Christmas; N.Y.C.; You Won't Be an Orphan for Long/W: Martin Charnin, M: Charles Strouse.

4972. Tyrone Kearney *On Your Toes* (Imperial > Majestic, "Phil Dolan III," Apr. 11, 1936): Two-a-Day for Keith/W: Lorenz Hart, M: Richard Rodgers. *Sleepy Hollow* (St. James, "Conscience," June 3, 1948): Ichabod/W: Miriam Battista, Russell Maloney, M: George Lessner.

4973. Allen Kearns (Aug. 14, 1894–Apr. 20, 1956) B: Brockville, Ontario, Canada. *The Red Petticoat* (Daly's > Broadway, "Slim," Nov. 13, 1912): Dance, Dance, Dance/W: Paul West, M: Jerome Kern. *Miss Daisy* (Shubert > Lyric, "Frederic," Sept. 9, 1914): Cheer Up; I Adore the American Girl; Kissing; Pierrot's Ball; The Race of Life; Won't You Dance?; Youth/W: Philip Bartholomae, M: Silvio Hein. *Good Morning Judge* (Shubert, CR, "Hughie Cavanagh," 1919): Dinky Doodle Dicky/W: Percy Greenbank, M: Howard Talbot — I Was So Young (You Were So Beautiful)/W: Irving Caesar, Alfred Bryan, M: George Gershwin — It's Nothing to Do with You; Sporty Boys/W: Percy Greenbank, M:

Lionel Monckton — I've Got a Pair of Swinging Doors (That Lead Right Into My Heart)/W: Sam M. Lewis, Joe Young, M: Bert Grant — Young Folks and Old Folks/WM: ?. *Come Along* (Nora Bayes > 39th Street, "Pvt. Peanuts Barker," Apr. 8, 1919): But You Can't Believe Them/WM: Blanche Merrill — Gas Mask/W: Bide Dudley, M: John L. Nelson — K.P.; Yankee Land/WM: John L. Nelson. *What's in a Name* (Maxine Elliott, revue, Mar. 19, 1920): Strike!; Without Kissing, Love Isn't Love [Mar. 22, 1920]/W: John Murray Anderson, Jack Yellen, M: Milton Ager. *Tickle Me* (Selwyn, "Jack Barton," Aug. 17, 1920): I Don't Laugh at Love Any More; If a Wish Could Make It So; Little Hindoo Man; A Perfect Lover; Temptation; Then Love Again; Until You Say Goodbye/W: Otto Harbach, Oscar Hammerstein II, M: Herbert Stothart. *Tangerine* (Casino, "Lee Loring," Aug. 9, 1921): (You and I) Atta Baby [Apr. 10, 1922]/W: Howard Johnson, M: Carle Carlton — It's Great to Be Married (and Lead a Single Life)/W: Howard Johnson, M: Monte Carlo, Alma Sanders, Carle Carlton — Love Is a Business; South Sea Island Blues; There's a Sunbeam for Every Drop of Rain; We'll Never Grow Old/W: Howard Johnson, M: Monte Carlo, Alma Sanders — Man Is the Lord of It All/W: Carle Carlton, M: Jean Schwartz. *Little Jessie James* (Longacre, "Tommy Tinker," Aug. 15, 1923): Come On, Let's Step, Step Around; The Knocking Bookworms; Little Jessie James; Quiet Afternoon; Such Is Life (in a Love Song)/W: Harlan Thompson, M: Harry Archer. *Lady Butterfly* (Globe, "Billy Browning," Dec. 22, 1923): Doll's House; Girls I've Never Met; Good Evening, Good Night; Sway with Me; Waltz Time; When the Wedding Bells Ring Out [Feb. 26, 1923]/W: Clifford Grey, M: Werner Janssen. *Mercenary Mary* (Longacre, "Jerry," Apr. 13, 1925): Beautiful Baby; Honey, I'm in Love with You; I've Got to Be a Chaste Woman; Over a Garden Wall/WM: William B. Friedlander, Con Conrad. *Tip-Toes* (Liberty, "Steve Burton," Dec. 28, 1925): It's a Great Little World!; Nightie-Night; That Certain Feeling; When Do We Dance?/W: Ira Gershwin, M: George Gershwin. *Betsy* (New Amsterdam, "Archie," Dec. 28, 1926): Birds on High (Birds Up High); If I Were You; In Our Parlor on the Third Floor Back; Sing/W: Lorenz Hart, M: Richard Rodgers. *Funny Face* (Alvin, "Peter Thurston," Nov. 22, 1927): He Loves and She Loves; 'S Wonderful/W: Ira Gershwin, M: George Gershwin. *Here's Howe!* (Broadhurst, "Billy Howe," May 1, 1928): Boston Post Road; Here's Howe; Imagination;

Life as a Twosome/W: Irving Caesar, M: Joseph Meyer, Roger Wolfe Kahn. *Hello, Daddy* (Mansfield, "Lawrence Tucker," Dec. 26, 1928): As Long as We're in Love; I Want Plenty of You; Let's Sit and Talk About You; Maybe Means Yes; Your Disposition Is Mine/W: Dorothy Fields, M: Jimmy McHugh. *Girl Crazy* (Alvin, "Danny Churchill," Oct. 14, 1930): Could You Use Me?; Embraceable You/W: Ira Gershwin, M: George Gershwin.

4974. Thomas F. Kearns *Monte Carlo* (Herald Square, "Sir Benjamin Currie," Mar. 21, 1898): The Dancing Dean/W: Henry Greenbank, M: Howard Talbot.

4975. Billy Keating *The Little Show* (Music Box, revue, CR, June 24, 1929): The Theme Song/W: Howard Dietz, M: Arthur Schwartz.

4976. Diane Keaton (Jan. 5, 1946–) B: Santa Ana, CA. In movies from 1970. Memorable in *Annie Hall* (1977). *Hair* (Biltmore, CR, "Sheila," July 1968): Easy to Be Hard; Good Morning, Starshine; I Believe in Love; Let the Sunshine In (The Flesh Failures)/W: Gerome Ragni, James Rado, M: Galt MacDermot.

4977. Mildred Keats *Pitter Patter* (Longacre, "Violet Mason," Sept. 28, 1920): Any Afternoon; I'm a Bachelor/W: ?, M: William B. Friedlander — Send for Me/WM: Will M. Hough, M: William B. Friedlander — You Can Never Tell/WM: William B. Friedlander. *Bombo* (Al Jolson > Winter Garden, "Hazel Downing" and "Hazella," Oct. 6, 1921): The Daffodil; The Globe Trot; Jazzadadadoo/W: Harold Atteridge, M: Sigmund Romberg. *Battling Buttler* (Selwyn, "Marigold," Oct. 8, 1923): As We Leave the Years Behind; Will You Marry Me?/W: Ballard Macdonald, M: Joseph Meyer — Dancing Honeymoon/W: Douglas Furber, Ballard Macdonald, M: Philip Braham. *Bye, Bye Barbara* (National, "Majorie Palmer," Aug. 25, 1924): Curiosity; Gee, You Must Be in Love; Kiss Invention; Pas Seul; Sittin' in Clover/WM: Monte Carlo, Alma Sanders. *Kitty's Kisses* (Playhouse, "Miss Wendel," May 6, 1926): Bounce Me; I Love to Dance; Mr. and Mrs.; Promise Your Kisses/W: Gus Kahn, M: Con Conrad.

4978. Gladys Keck *Take the Air* (Waldorf, CR, "Marguerite," May 7, 1928): All Aboard for Times Square/W: Gene Buck, M: Dave Stamper.

4979. Lila Kedrova (Oct. 9, 1918–Feb. 16, 2000) B: Leningrad, Russia. She grew up in Paris. She received an Oscar for the film version of *Zorba the Greek* (1964). *Zorba* (Broadway, revival, "Madame Hortense," Oct. 16, 1983/Jan. 31, 1984): Goodbye Canavaro; Happy Birthday;

No Boom Boom; Only Love/W: Fred Ebb, M: John Kander.

4980. Jonathan Keefe *Miss Jack* (Herald Square, "Silas Bean," Sept. 4, 1911): Old Deacon Pettigue; There Really Isn't Any More to Tell/W: Mark Swan, M: William F. Peters.

4981. Matt Keefe *The Big Show* (Hippodrome, revue, Aug. 31, 1916): On the Mountain/W: John L. Golden, M: Raymond Hubbell.

4982. Howard (Harold) Keel (Apr. 13, 1917–) B: Gillespie, IL. For 10 years the tall, handsome baritone played Clayton Farlow on TV's long-running drama *Dallas* (1981) *Carousel* (Majestic, CR, "Billy Bigelow," Aug. 1945/June 1946): Blow High, Blow Low; The Highest Judge of All; If I Loved You; Soliloquy/W: Oscar Hammerstein II, M: Richard Rodgers. *Oklahoma!* (St. James, CR, "Curly McLain," Sept. 1945/Sept. 1946): The Farmer and the Cowman; Oh, What a Beautiful Mornin'; Oklahoma; People Will Say We're in Love; Pore Jud; The Surrey with the Fringe on Top/W: Oscar Hammerstein II, M: Richard Rodgers. *Carousel* (New York City Center, revival, "Billy Bigelow," Sept. 11, 1957): same as above. *Saratoga* (Winter Garden, "Clint Maroon," Dec. 7, 1959): Countin' Our Chickens; Dog Eat Dog; A Game of Poker; The Man in My Life; Saratoga; You or No One/W: Johnny Mercer, M: Harold Arlen — Why Fight This?/WM: Johnny Mercer. *No Strings* (54th Street, CR, "David Jordan," June 1963): Be My Host; How Sad; Look No Further; Maine; No Strings; Nobody Told Me; The Sweetest Sounds/WM: Richard Rodgers. *Ambassador* (Lunt-Fontanne, "Lewis Lambert Strether," Nov. 19, 1972): All of My Life; Happy Man; Lambert's Quandary; Lilas, What Happened to Paris; Something More; Surprise; Thank You, No; That's What I Need Tonight; Too Much to Forgive/W: Hal Hackady, M: Don Gohman.

4983. Ruby Keeler (Aug. 25, 1909–Feb. 28, 1993) B: Halifax, Nova Scotia. M: AL JOLSON, 1928–1940. She met Jolson when she was 18 and had been dancing in nightclubs for several years. *Lucky* (New Amsterdam, "Mazie," Mar. 22, 1927): If the Man in the Moon Were a Coon/WM: Fred Fisher — Pearl of Broadway/W: Bert Kalmar, Otto Harbach, M: Harry Ruby — Without Thinking of You/WM: ?. *Sidewalks of New York* (Knickerbocker, "Mamie," Oct. 3, 1927): Way Down Town/W: Eddie Dowling, M: James F. Hanley. *Show Girl* (Ziegfeld, "Dixie Dugan," July 2, 1929): Do What You Do!; Harlem Serenade; I Must Be Home by Twelve O'Clock/W: Ira Gershwin, Gus Kahn, M:

George Gershwin. *No, No, Nanette* (46th Street, revival, "Sue Smith," Jan. 19, 1971/Aug. 31, 1971/Apr. 4, 1972/Aug. 14, 1972): I Want to Be Happy/W: Irving Caesar, M: Vincent Youmans — Take a Little One-Step/W: Zelda Sears, M: Vincent Youmans.

4984. Elizabeth Keene With MARGARET KEENE, they were known as the Keene Twins. *Mary Jane McKane* (Imperial, "Carrie," Dec. 25, 1923): Speed; Time-Clock Slaves/W: William Cary Duncan, Oscar Hammerstein II, M: Vincent Youmans, Herbert Stothart — Toodle-oo/W: William Cary Duncan, Oscar Hammerstein II, M: Vincent Youmans. *The Greenwich Village Follies of 1924* (Shubert > Winter Garden, revue, CR, Dec. 1, 1924): Do a Little This, Do a Little That/W: Benton Levy, M: Lee David — I'm in Love Again; Syncopated Pipes of Pan/WM: Cole Porter.

4985. Lew Keene see LEW KEANE.

4986. Louis Keene see LEW KEANE.

4987. Margaret Keene *Mary Jane McKane* (Imperial, "Cash," Dec. 25, 1923): same as ELIZABETH KEENE. *The Greenwich Village Follies of 1924* (Shubert > Winter Garden, revue, CR, Dec. 1, 1924): same as ELIZABETH KEENE.

4988. Mattie Keene (c 1862–Sept. 2, 1944) M: JOSEPH PHILLIPS. *Caroline* (Ambassador, "Amanda," Jan. 31, 1923): The Old Virginia Reel/W: Harry B. Smith, M: Edward Delaney Dunn, Edward Kunneke — Telling Fortunes (Your Fortune)/W: Harry B. Smith, M: Edward Kunneke.

4989. Richard (Dick) Keene (Sept. 16, 1899–Mar. 11, 1971) B: Philadelphia, PA. *Music Box Revue of 1921* (Music Box, revue, Sept. 22, 1921): Dancing the Seasons Away/WM: Irving Berlin. *Keep Kool* (Morosco > Globe > Earl Carroll, revue, May 22, 1924): In They Go, Out They Come; Shall I Sing It Now/W: Paul Gerard Smith, M: Jack Frost. *Marjorie* (44th Street, CR, "Eph Daw," Nov. 10, 1924): Good Things and Bad Things; Super-Sheik/W: Harold Atteridge, M: Sigmund Romberg — Nature/W: Harold Atteridge, M: Herbert Stothart — Popularity/W: Harold Atteridge, M: Stephen Jones — Shuffle Your Troubles Away/W: Henry Creamer, M: James F. Hanley. *Hello, Lola* (Eltinge, "Willie Baxter," Jan. 12, 1926): In the Dark; Little Boy Blue; My Baby Talk Lady; My Brother Willie; Swinging on the Gate/W: Dorothy Donnelly, M: William B. Kernell. *Sidewalks of New York* (Knickerbocker, "Mickey O'Brien," Oct. 3, 1927): Playground in the Sky; Wherever You Are/W: Eddie Dowling, M: James

F. Hanley. *Spring Is Here* (Alvin, "Steve Alden," Mar. 11, 1929): Rich Man! Poor Man!; Spring Is Here (in Person)/W: Lorenz Hart, M: Richard Rodgers. *The Only Girl* (44th Street, revival, "John Ayre [Fresh]," May 21, 1934): Be Happy, Boys, Tonight; Connubial Bliss/W: Henry Blossom, M: Victor Herbert — When You're Wearing the Ball and the Chain/W: Harry B. Smith, M: Victor Herbert.

4990. Suzanne Keener *Peg o' My Dreams* (Al Jolson, "Peg," May 5, 1924): The Gap in the Hedge; Love Is Like a Firefly; Love's Young Dream; Shy Little Irish Smile/W: Anne Caldwell, M: Hugo Felix.

4991. Grace Keeshon *Doing Our Bit* (Winter Garden, "Miss U.S.A.," Oct. 18, 1917): Doing My Bit/W: Harold Atteridge, M: Sigmund Romberg, Herman Timberg.

4992. Don (Donnie) Kehr (Sept. 18, 1963–) B: Washington, DC. M: LISA MORDENTE. *The Human Comedy* (Royale, "Marcus Macauley," Apr. 5, 1984): Dear Brother; Don't Tell Me; I'll Tell You About My Family; My Sister Bess/W: William Dumaresq, M: Galt MacDermot.

4993. Betty Lou Keim (Sept. 27, 1938–) B: Malden, MA. *Texas, Li'l Darlin'* (Mark Hellinger, "Dogie Smith," Nov. 25, 1949): Hootin' Owl Trail; Whichaway'd They Go; Whoopin' and a-Hollerin'/W: Johnny Mercer, M: Robert Emmett Dolan.

4994. Thomas F. Keirnes *The Girl from Paris* (Wallack's, revival, "Auguste Pompier," Jan. 17, 1898): I'm All the Way from Gay Paree/W: George Dance, M: Ivan Caryll.

4995. Gordon Keith *The Merry World* (Imperial, revue, CR, July 12, 1926): Deauville/WM: Herman Hupfeld — Tallahassee/WM: B.G. DeSylva, C. Luckyeth Roberts.

4996. Paul Keith (June 1, 1944–) B: Chicago, IL. *Show Boat* (Uris, revival, "Frank," Apr. 24, 1983): Goodbye, My Lady Love/WM: Joseph E. Howard.

4997. Roydon Keith *Iole* (Longacre, "Lethbridge," Dec. 29, 1913): If Dreams Come True/WM: ?— None but the Brave Deserve the Fair/W: Will M. Hough, Frank R. Adams, Joseph E, Howard. *Flora Bella* (44th Street, CR, "Baron Tigo Oblonsky," Dec. 4, 1916): Adam; The Hypnotizing Duet; On to Petrograd/W: Percy Waxman, M: Charles Cuvillier — Creep, Creep, the World's Asleep; Good Day, Good Night/W: Percy Waxman, M: Milton Schwarzwald.

4998. Julia Kelety (c 1887–Jan. 1, 1972) B: Budapest, Hungary. *Always You* (Central, "Julie Fontaine," Jan. 5, 1920): My Pousse-Cafe; A Wonderful War/W: Oscar Hammerstein II, M: Herbert Stothart. *Two Little Girls in Blue* (George M. Cohan, "Ninon La Fleur," May 3, 1921): The Gypsy Trail/W: Irving Caesar, M: Paul Lannin — Honeymoon (When Will You Shine for Me?)/W: Ira Gershwin, M: Paul Lannin. *Half a Widow* (Waldorf, "Nita," Sept. 12, 1927): Spanish Love; A Thousand Times/W: Frank Dupree, Harry B. Smith, M: Shep Camp.

4999. Jackie Kelk (Aug. 6, 1923–Sept. 5, 2002) B: Brooklyn, NY. *Me and Juliet* (Majestic, "Herbie," May 28, 1953): Intermission Talk/W: Oscar Hammerstein II, M: Richard Rodgers.

5000. Jack (Keller) Kellar *A Lonely Romeo* (Shubert > Casino, "Tom Thomas," June 10, 1919): I Want a Lonely Romeo; Underneath a Big Umbrella/W: Robert B. Smith, M: Malvin F. Franklin. *The Midnight Rounders of 1920* (Century roof, revue, CR, Oct. 4, 1920): La Veda; The Swing/W: Alfred Bryan, M: Jean Schwartz.

5001. Cecil Kellaway (Aug. 22, 1891–Feb. 28, 1973) B: Cape Town, South Africa. Actor, director, producer, screenwriter. In Hollywood from 1939, he appeared in more than 75 films, usually as loveable old gentlemen. *Greenwillow* (Alvin, "Reverend Birdsong," Mar. 8, 1960): The Sermon; What a Blessing (To Know There's a Devil)/WM: Frank Loesser.

5002. Alma Keller *Blossom Time* (Jolson, revival, "Fritzi," May 19, 1924): Lonely Heart; Love Is a Riddle; Three Little Maids/W: Dorothy Donnelly, M: Sigmund Romberg.

5003. Dorothy Keller *Follow the Girls* (New Century > 44th Street, "Peggy Baker," Apr. 8, 1944): Thanks for a Lousy Evening; You Don't Dance/W: Dan Shapiro, Milton Pascal, M: Phil Charig. *Heaven on Earth* (New Century, "Officer Jonesy," Sept. 16, 1948): Apple Jack; Bench in the Park; You're the First Cup of Coffee/W: Barry Trivers, M: Jay Gorney.

5004. Jeff Keller (Sept. 8, 1947–) B: Brooklyn, NY. *Fiddler on the Roof* (Winter Garden, revival, "Perchik," Dec. 28, 1976): Now I Have Everything/W: Sheldon Harnick, M: Jerry Bock. *Dance a Little Closer* (Minskoff, "Edward Dunlop," May 11, 1983): I Don't Know; Why Can't the World Go and Leave Us Alone?/W: Alan Jay Lerner, M: Charles Strouse. *The Phantom of the Opera* (Majestic, CR, "Monsieur Andre"): Notes; Prima Donna; Twisted Every Way/W: Charles Hart, Richard Stilgoe, M: Andrew Lloyd Webber. *The Phantom of the Opera* (Majestic, CR, "The Phantom of the Opera," c 1993): All I Ask of You; Bravo, Bravo; I Remember; Little Lotte; The Mirror; The Music of the Night; Notes; The Point of No Return; Prima Donna; Stranger Than You Dreamt It; Twisted Every Way; Wandering Child/W: Charles Hart, Richard Stilgoe, M: Andrew Lloyd Webber — The Phantom of the Opera/W: Mike Batt, Richard Stilgoe, M: Andrew Lloyd Webber. *A Christmas Carol* (Paramount Madison Square Garden, "Ghost of Jacob Marley," Dec. 1, 1994): Link by Link/W: Lynn Ahrens, M: Alan Menken.

5005. Marie Keller *The Man from Now* (New Amsterdam, "Electra," Sept. 3, 1906): The Wireless Telephone/W: ?, M: Harry Von Tilzer.

5006. Barry Kelley (Aug. 19, 1908–June 5, 1991) B: Chicago, IL. He often played gangsters in movies. On TV he was newspaper editor Charlie Anderson on the long-running drama *Big Town* (1954). *Oklahoma!* (St. James, "Ike Skidmore," Mar. 31, 1943): Oklahoma/W: Oscar Hammerstein II, M: Richard Rodgers.

5007. Louise Kelley *The Pink Lady* (New Amsterdam, "La Comtesse de Montanvert," Mar. 13, 1911): Donny Didn't, Donny Did/W: C.M.S. McLellan, M: Ivan Caryll. *The Only Girl* (39th Street > Lyric, "Birdie Martin," Nov. 2, 1914): Connubial Bliss; Equal Rights/W: Henry Blossom, M: Victor Herbert. *Good Night, Paul* (Hudson, "Madam Louise," Sept. 3, 1917): Gowns; I Like You/W: Roland Oliver, Charles Dickson, M: Harry B. Olsen. *Look Who's Here* (44th Street, "Caroline Holmes," Mar. 2, 1920): I Cannot Understand; If I Had Only Met You Dear; Love, Love, Love/W: Edward A. Paulton, M: Silvio Hein.

5008. Peter Kelley (Dec. 17, 1925–) B: Indianapolis, IN. *Two's Company* (Alvin, revue, Dec. 15, 1952): It Just Occurred to Me/W: Sammy Cahn, M: Vernon Duke — Out of the Clear Blue Sky/W: Ogden Nash, M: Vernon Duke.

5009. Mike Kellin (Apr. 26, 1922–Aug. 26, 1983) B: Hartford, CT. *Pipe Dream* (Shubert, "Hazel," Nov. 30, 1955): All Kinds of People; A Lopsided Bus; Thinkin'; The Tide Pool/W: Oscar Hammerstein II, M: Richard Rodgers.

5010. Lynn Kellogg (Apr. 2, 1944–) B: Appleton, WI. *Hair* (Biltmore, "Sheila," Apr. 29, 1968): Easy to Be Hard; Good Morning, Starshine; I Believe in Love; Let the Sunshine In (The Flesh Failures)/W: Gerome Ragni, James Rado, M: Galt MacDermot.

5011. Shirley Kellogg (1888– ?) *Miss Innocence* (New York, "Ella Lee," Nov. 30, 1908): Oh! That Yankiana Rag/W: E. Ray Goetz, M: Melville Gideon. *Ziegfeld Follies of 1910* (Jardin de Paris [New York roof], revue, June 20, 1910): My Yiddish Colleen/W: Edward Madden, M: Leo

Edwards — Oh! That Yankiana Rag/W: E. Ray Goetz, M: Melville Gideon — The Pensacola Mooch/W: Will Marion Cook, M: Ford Dabney. *The Three Romeos* (Globe, "Daisy Dean," Nov. 13, 1911): Moonlight; Oh, Romeo/W: R.H. Burnside, M: Raymond Hubbell. *The Passing Show of 1912* (Winter Garden, revue, July 22, 1912): In 2010/WM: ?— There You Have Old New York Town; The Wedding Glide/WM: Louis A. Hirsch.

5012. Viola Kellogg *Havana* (Casino, "Senora Donna Junenez," Feb. 11, 1909): How Did the Bird Know That?/W: George Arthurs, M: Leslie Stuart — The Yacht/WM: ?.

5013. Daren Kelly (Mar. 9–) B: California. *Woman of the Year* (Palace, "Chip Salisbury," Mar. 29, 1981): It Isn't Working/W: Fred Ebb, M: John Kander. *Crazy for You* (Sam S. Shubert, CR, "Lank Hawkins," Aug. 1995): Naughty Baby/W: Ira Gershwin, Desmond Carter, M: George Gershwin.

5014. David Patrick Kelly (Jan. 19, 1952–) B: Detroit, MI. On the TV soap *Twin Peaks* (1990), he played Jerry Hornel. *Working* (46th Street, "Copy Boy" and "Box Boy," May 14, 1978): Brother Trucker/WM: James Taylor — The Mason/WM: Craig Carnelia. *Is There Life After High School?* (Ethel Barrymore, revue, May 7, 1982): Beer; High School All Over Again; Second Thoughts/WM: Craig Carnelia.

5015. Dennis Kelly *Damn Yankees* (Marquis, revival, "Joe Boyd," Mar. 3, 1994): Goodbye, Old Girl; A Man Doesn't Know; Near to You; Six Months Out of Every Year/WM: Richard Adler, Jerry Ross.

5016. Edith Kelly (c 1888–Dec. 11, 1960) *The Girls of Gottenburg* (Knickerbocker, "Lucille," Sept. 2, 1908): Always Come Back to You/WM: ?. *Havana* (Casino, "Glady," Feb. 11, 1909): Way Down in Pensacola/WM: Leslie Stuart. *Pins and Needles* (Shubert, revue, Feb. 1, 1922): Jungle Bungalow (I'll Build a Home in the Jungle); The Syncopated Minuet/W: Ballard Macdonald, M: James F. Hanley — The Little Tin Soldier and the Little Rag Doll/W: Darl MacBoyle, M: James F. Hanley — Piccadilly Walk/W: Ira Gershwin, Arthur Riscoe, M: Edward A. Horan.

5017. Emmett Kelly (Dec. 9, 1895–Mar. 28, 1979) B: Sedan, KS. Remembered as the tramp, Weary Willie, the most famous clown of the Ringling Brothers Barnum and Bailey Circus. He began his career as a cartoonist. *Keep Off the Grass* (Broadhurst, revue, May 23, 1940): The Cabby's Serenade/W: Al Dubin, M: Jimmy McHugh — On the Old Park Bench/W: Howard Dietz, M: Jimmy McHugh.

5018. Ethel Amorita Kelly *A Winsome Widow* (Moulin Rouge, "Flirt," Apr. 11, 1912): Teach Me Everything You Know/W: ?, M: Raymond Hubbell. *Ziegfeld Follies of 1913* (New Amsterdam, revue, June 16, 1913): You Must Have Experience/W: George V. Hobart, M: Raymond Hubbell. *The Passing Show of 1914* (Winter Garden, revue, June 10, 1914): The Eagle Rock; Good Old Levee Days; The Moving Picture Glide/W: Harold Atteridge, M: Harry Carroll — The Sloping Path/WM: ?.

5019. Gene Kelly (Aug. 23, 1912–Feb. 2, 1996) B: Pittsburgh, PA. Dancer, singer, director, actor, choreographer. An all-time major talent of musical theater and movies. *One for the Money* (Booth, revue, Feb. 4, 1939): Teeter Totter Tessie/W: Nancy Hamilton, M: Morgan Lewis. *Pal Joey* (Ethel Barrymore > Shubert > St. James, "Joey Evans," Dec. 25, 1940): Chicago (A Great Big Town); Den of Iniquity; Happy Hunting Horn; I Could Write a Book; Pal Joey (What Do I Care for a Dame?); You Mustn't Kick It Around/W: Lorenz Hart, M: Richard Rodgers.

5020. Georgie Kelly *Dr. Deluxe* (Knickerbocker, "Mrs. Clara Houston," Apr. 17, 1911): That Will Keep Him True to You/W: Otto Harbach, M: Karl Hoschna.

5021. Harry Kelly (c 1873–Mar. 19, 1936) B: New York, NY. *A Female Drummer* (Star > Manhattan, "Uptown Downs," Dec. 26, 1898): Maggie O'Connor/W: Charles E. Blaney, M: Frank David. *The Messenger Boy* (Daly's, "Capt. Pott," Sept. 16, 1901): Captain Pott (They're All After Pott); Off to Cairo/W: Adrian Ross, M: Lionel Monckton. *The Knickerbocker Girl* (Herald Square, "Abner Merton," June 15, 1903): Country Life; Lalla; A Little Bird Is Looking All the Time/W: George Totten Smith, M: Alfred E. Aarons. *It Happened in Nordland* (Lew Fields, CR, "Prince George of Nebula," Nov. 13, 1905): Absinthe Frappe; My Catamaran/W: Glen MacDonough, M: Victor Herbert. *Little Nemo* (New Amsterdam, "Dancing Missionary," Oct. 20, 1908): Is My Face on Straight?; Newspaper Song (Read the Papers Every Day); There's Nothing the Matter with Me/W: Harry B. Smith, M: Victor Herbert. *Miss 1917* (Century, revue, Nov. 5, 1917): The Honor System; We're Crooks/W: P.G. Wodehouse, M: Jerome Kern — Sammy/W: James O'Dea, M: Edward Hutchinson. *Oh, Look!* (Vanderbilt, "Capt. West," Mar. 7, 1918): I'm Just a Good Man/W: Joseph McCarthy, M: Harry Carroll. *Springtime of Youth* (Broadhurst, "Deacon Stokes," Oct. 26, 1922): Won't You Take Me to Paris/W: Cyrus D. Wood, M: Sigmund

Romberg. *Sweetheart Time* (Imperial, "Detective James," Jan. 19, 1926): One Way Street/W: Ballard Macdonald, M: Walter Donaldson.

5022. John T. Kelly (Aug. 26, 1852–Jan. 5, 1922) B: Boston, MA. *Hurly-Burly* (Weber and Fields Music Hall, "Michael McCann," Sept. 8, 1898): Little Old New York Is Good Enough for Me/W: Harry B. Smith, Edgar Smith, M: John Stromberg. *Fiddle-Dee-Dee* (Weber and Fields Music Hall, "Ignatius McSorley," Sept. 16, 1900): The Tips of Gay Paree/W: Edgar Smith, M: John Stromberg. *Hoity-Toity* (Weber and Fields Music Hall, revue, "King Kazoo," Sept. 5, 1901): The Bloke That Monte Carlo Broke [Mar. 31, 1902]; King Kazoo of Kakaroo/W: Edgar Smith, M: John Stromberg. *Twirly-Whirly* (Weber and Fields Music Hall, "Roger McCracken," Sept. 11, 1902): Strike Out, McCracken/W: Edgar Smith, M: William T. Francis. *A Certain Party* (Wallack's, "Jerry Fogarty," Apr. 24, 1911): Fogarty/W: Edgar Smith, M: Robert Hood Bowers. *Hokey-Pokey; and Bunty, Bulls and Strings* (Broadway, "Jeremiah McCann," Feb. 8, 1912): If It Wasn't for the Irish and the Jews/W: William Jerome, M: Jean Schwartz.

5023. Kate Kelly *The Utter Glory of Morrissey Hall* (Mark Hellinger, "Dickerson," May 13, 1979): Lost; You Will Know When the Time Has Arrived/WM: Clark Gesner.

5024. Kitty Kelly (Apr. 27, 1902–June 24, 1968) B: New York, NY. *The Whirl of New York* (Winter Garden, "Kissie Fitzgarter," June 13, 1921): Dancing Fool/W: Harry B. Smith, Francis Wheeler, M: Ted Snyder. *Mary Jane McKane* (Imperial, "Maggie Murphy," Dec. 25, 1923): Down Where the Mortgages Grow/W: William Cary Duncan, M: Anselm Goetzl — Laugh It Off/W: William Cary Duncan, Oscar Hammerstein II, M: Vincent Youmans, Herbert Stothart — The Flannel Petticoat Gal/W: William Cary Duncan, Oscar Hammerstein II, M: Vincent Youmans. *Mystery Moon* (Royale, "Mildred Middleton," June 23, 1930): If You and I Incorporate; Mechanical Man; What Could I Do, but Fall in Love with You/W: Monte Carlo, M: Alma Sanders.

5025. Kristen Lee Kelly (1968–) *Rent* (Nederlander, "Mark's Mom," Apr. 29, 1996): Happy New Year; Tune Up; Voice Mail #1; Voice Mail #3; Voice Mail #5/WM: Jonathan Larson.

5026. Margot Kelly (c 1894–Mar. 10, 1976) *Florodora* (Century, revival, "Angela Gilfain," Apr. 5, 1920): Come to St. Georges/WM: Leslie Stuart — The Fellow Who Might/W: Ernest Boyd-Jones, M: Leslie Stuart — Hello People/W: George Arthurs, M: Leslie Stuart.

5027. Marie Kelly *George White's Scandals of 1939-40* (Alvin, revue, CR, Oct. 16, 1939): Smart Little Girls/W: Jack Yellen, M: Sammy Fain.

5028. Maud Alice Kelly *The Mocking Bird* (Bijou, "Countess Bellaire," Nov. 10, 1902): A Stale World and a Pale World/W: Sydney Rosenfeld, M: A. Baldwin Sloane.

5029. Maurice Kelly (c 1915–Aug. 28, 1974) B: ? In 1942, he was a Private in the U.S. Army. *This Is the Army* (Broadway, revue, July 4, 1942): I'm Getting Tired So I Can Sleep/WM: Irving Berlin.

5030. Nell Kelly *Ups-A-Daisy!* (Shubert, "Lurline," Oct. 8, 1928): A Great Little Guy; Hot!; Tell Me Who You Are/W: Robert A. Simon, M: Lewis E. Gensler. *Boom-Boom* (Casino, "Tilly McGuire," Jan. 28, 1929): Be That Way; He's Just My Ideal; We're Going to Make Boom-Boom; What a Girl/W: Mann Holiner, J. Keirn Brennan, M: Werner Janssen. *The Street Singer* (Shubert, "Annette," Sept. 17, 1929): I Am; Statues/WM: ?.

5031. Patricia Kelly *Here's Where I Belong* (Billy Rose, "Mrs. Heink," Mar. 3, 1968): Pulverize the Kaiser/W: Alfred Uhry, M: Robert Waldman.

5032. Patrick J. Kelly (July 18, 1891–Mar. 19, 1938) B: Philadelphia, PA. *Blossom Time* (Jolson, revival, "Baron Franz Schober," Mar. 8, 1926): Let Me Awake; Love Is a Riddle; Only One Love Ever Fills the Heart; Serenade/W: Dorothy Donnelly, M: Sigmund Romberg.

5033. Patsy Kelly (Jan. 12, 1910–Sept. 24, 1981) B: Brooklyn, NY. Comic actress and tap-dancer, in vaudeville from childhood, in movies from 1933. *Harry Delmar's Revels* (Shubert, revue, Nov. 28, 1927): The Jigaboo Jig/W: Billy Rose, Ballard Macdonald, M: Lester Lee. *Three Cheers* (Globe, "Bobbie Bird," Oct. 15, 1928): The Americans Are Here; Look Pleasant/W: B.G. DeSylva, M: Ray Henderson — Because You're Beautiful/W: B.G. DeSylva, Lew Brown, M: Ray Henderson. *Earl Carroll's Sketch Book of 1929* (Earl Carroll > 44th Street > 46th Street, revue, July 1, 1929): Fascinating You/WM: Vincent Rose, Charles Tobias, Henry Tobias, Benee Russell. *The Wonder Bar* (Nora Bayes, "Elektra Pivonka," Mar. 17, 1931): Elizabeth/W: Irving Caesar, M: Robert Katscher. *Flying Colors* (Imperial, revue, Sept. 15, 1932): All's Well; Fatal Fascination [added]; On the American Plan/W: Howard Dietz, M: Arthur Schwartz. *No, No, Nanette* (46th Street, revival, "Pauline," Jan. 19, 1971): Take a Little One-Step/W: Zelda Sears, M: Vincent Youmans. *Irene* (Minskoff, revival,

"Mrs. O'Dare," Mar. 13, 1973/Aug. 20, 1973): Mother Angel Darling/WM: Charles Gaynor — You Made Me Love You (I Didn't Want to Do It)/W: Joseph McCarthy, M: James V. Monoco.

5034. Paula Kelly (Oct. 21, 1943–) B: Jacksonville, FL. *Something More!* (Eugene O'Neill, "Mrs. Veloz," Nov. 10, 1964): Grazie Per Niente/W: Marilyn Bergman, Alan Bergman, M: Sammy Fain.

5035. Rachael Kelly *Runaways* (Plymouth, "Jackie," May 13, 1978): Appendectomy; Song of a Child Prostitute/WM: Elizabeth Swados.

5036. Renee Kelly (June 4, 1888–Aug. 28, 1965) B: London, England. *Peggy* (Casino, "Peggy Barrison," Dec. 7. 1911): Any Old Time at All/W: C.H. Bovill, M: Leslie Stuart.

5037. Walter C. Kelly (Oct. 29, 1873–Jan. 6, 1939) B: Mineville, NY. He was an uncle of actress Grace Kelly. Billed as The Virginia Judge, first presented by MARIE DRESSLER in her vaudeville act, he was famous for his monologues, often racist in tone, which he performed all over the world. *Great Day!* (Cosmopolitan, "Judge Totheridge," Oct. 17, 1929): The Wedding Bells Ring On/W: Billy Rose, Edward Eliscu, M: Vincent Youmans.

5038. James Kelso *Keep Kool* (Morosco > Globe > Earl Carroll, revue, May 22, 1924): In They Go, Out They Come/W: Paul Gerard Smith, M: Jack Frost.

5039. Mayme (May, Maym) Kelso (Feb. 28, 1867–June 5, 1946) B: Columbus, OH. *A Waltz Dream* (Broadway, "Friedericke," Jan. 27, 1908): The Family's Ancient Tree; A Husband's Love/W: Joseph W. Herbert, M: Oscar Straus — A Lesson in Love; A Soldier Stole Her Heart/WM: ?.

5040. Vernon Kelso (c 1908–Dec. 27, 1993) *My Princess* (Shubert, "Lord Barchester," Oct. 6, 1927): Dear Girls, Goodbye; My Passion Flower/W: Dorothy Donnelly, M: Sigmund Romberg.

5041. Pert Kelton (Oct. 14, 1907–Oct. 30, 1968) B: Great Falls, MT, on a cattle ranch. At age 4, she toured in vaudeville with her parents, later as a sister act with her mother. In 1929 she debuted in the movies as Rosie the maid, in the film version of the Broadway musical *Sally*. On radio and TV she worked opposite MILTON BERLE and JACKIE GLEASON, playing the original Alice Kramden in a 1951 variety sketch before *The Honeymooners* became a series. In the 1950s she was blacklisted as a Communist. *Sunny* (New Amsterdam, "Magnolia," Sept. 22, 1925): Magnolia in the Woods/WM: Pert Kelton. *The 5 O'Clock Girl* (44th Street, "Susan Snow," Oct. 10, 1927): Any Little Thing; Society Ladder; We

Want You/W: Bert Kalmar, M: Harry Ruby. *The DuBarry* (George M. Cohan, "Margot," Nov. 22, 1932): Ga-Ga; Gustave; In the Bois; On the Stage/W: Rowland Leigh, M: Carl Millocker. *The Music Man* (Majestic, "Mrs. Paroo," Dec. 19, 1957): Piano Lesson/WM: Meredith Willson. *Greenwillow* (Alvin, "Gramma Briggs," Mar. 8, 1960): Clang Dang the Bell; Could've Been a Ring/WM: Frank Loesser.

5042. Walter Kelvin *Two on the Aisle* (Mark Hellinger, revue, July 19, 1951): Show Train/W: Betty Comden, Adolph Green, M: Jule Styne.

5043. Colin Kemball *Oh What a Lovely War* (Broadhurst, revue, "Moltke" and "Belgium," Sept. 30, 1964): Far, Far from Wipers/WM: Bingham, Greene — Silent Night (Heilige Nacht)/W: Joseph Mohr, M: Franz Gruber — When This Lousy War Is Over (parody of When This Cruel War Is Over/W: Charles Carroll Sawyer, M: Henry Tucker.

5044. Anthony Kemble-Cooper (Feb. 6, 1904–Jan. 9, 2000) B: London, England. *Sweethearts* (Shubert, revival, "Hon. Butterfield Slingsby," Jan. 21, 1947): Jeannette and Her Little Wooden Shoes; Pilgrims of Love/W: Robert B. Smith, M: Victor Herbert.

5045. Charles Kemper (Sept. 6, 1900–May 12, 1950) B: Oklahoma. *You Never Know* (Winter Garden, "Henri Baltin," Sept. 21, 1938): For No Rhyme or Reason/WM: Cole Porter.

5046. Kuy Kendall *Shubert Gaieties of 1919* (44th Street, revue, July 14, 1919): Cosy Corner; Rainbow Ball/W: Alfred Bryan, M: Jean Schwartz.

5047. Terry Kendall *Sweet and Low* (44th Street, revue, CR, Jan. 19, 1931): Would You Like to Take a Walk? (Sump'n Good'll Come from That)/W: Mort Dixon, Billy Rose, M: Harry Warren.

5048. Pat Kendell *The Great Temptations* (Winter Garden, revue, May 18, 1926): The Sesquicentennial Baby/W: Clifford Grey, M: Maurie Rubens.

5049. Rexford Kendrick *Iole* (Longacre, "Harrow," Dec. 29, 1913): If Dreams Come True; None but the Brave Deserve the Fair/W: Will M. Hough, Frank R. Adams, M: Joseph E. Howard.

5050. Bob Kennedy *Oklahoma!* (St. James, CR, "Curly McLain," June 1945): The Farmer and the Cowman; Oh, What a Beautiful Mornin'; Oklahoma; People Will Say We're in Love; Pore Jud; The Surrey with the Fringe on Top/W: Oscar Hammerstein II, M: Richard Rodgers. *The Girl from Nantucket* (Adelphi, "Michael Nicholson," Nov. 8, 1945): From Morning Till Night; Hammock in the Blue; I

Want to See More of You; Your Fatal Fascination/W: Kay Twomey, M: Jacques Belasco.

5051. Don Kennedy *Great to Be Alive* (Winter Garden, "O'Brien," Mar. 23, 1950): Who Done It?/W: Walter Bullock, M: Abraham Ellstein.

5052. Ewing Kennedy *Good News!* (46th Street, CR, "Windy," Nov. 14, 1927): Flaming Youth; On the Campus; The Varsity Drag/W: B.G. DeSylva, Lew Brown, M: Ray Henderson.

5053. Frances Kennedy *Three Twins* (Herald Square > Majestic, "Mrs. Dick Winters," June 15, 1908): Boo-Hoo, Tee-Hee, Ta-Ha/W: Otto Harbach, M: Karl Hoschna. *The Belle of Brittany* (Daly's, "Madame Poquelin," Nov. 8, 1909): In the Chest; The Old Chateau/W: Percy Greenbank, M: Howard Talbot — The Trysting Tree/W: Percy Greenbank, M: Marie Horne. *The Red Petticoat* (Daly's > Broadway, "Sage Brush Kate," Nov. 13, 1912): Sing, Sing, You Tetrazinni/W: Paul West, M: Jerome Kern.

5054. Jack Kennedy (c 1888–1964) *Good News!* (46th Street, "Slats," Sept. 6, 1927): Flaming Youth/W: B.G. DeSylva, Lew Brown, M: Ray Henderson.

5055. John P. Kennedy *The Messenger Boy* (Daly's, "Capt. Naylor," Sept. 16, 1901): Off to Cairo/W: Adrian Ross, M: Ivan Caryll.

5056. Madge Kennedy (Apr. 19, 1890–June 9, 1987) B: Chicago, IL. Ladylike star of silent pictures, 1917–1926. *Poppy* (Apollo, "Poppy McGargle," Sept. 3, 1923): Choose a Partner Please [Oct. 8, 1923]/WM: ?— Fortune Telling [Oct. 8, 1923]; Poppy Dear; Two Make a Home/W: Dorothy Donnelly, M: Stephen Jones, Arthur Samuels — Hang Your Sorrows in the Sun/W: Dorothy Donnelly, M: John C. Egan.

5057. Memay Kennedy *The Sultan of Sulu* (Wallack's, "Miss Newton," Dec. 29, 1902): The Peachy Teacher; Ten Little Gentlemen of Spooney Town/W: George Ade, M: Alfred G. Wathall.

5058. Sandy Kennedy *The King and I* (St. James, "Louis Leonowens," Mar. 29, 1951): I Whistle a Happy Tune/W: Oscar Hammerstein II, M: Richard Rodgers.

5059. William Kennedy *Brigadoon* (New York City Center, revival, "Sandy Dean," Jan. 30, 1963): Down on MacConnachy Square/W: Alan Jay Lerner, M: Frederick Loewe.

5060. Zetti Kennedy *When Johnny Comes Marching Home* (New York, "Kate Pemberton," Dec. 16, 1902): The Drums; Fairyland; Love's Night [Feb. 2, 1903]; Spring, Sweet Spring; The Suwanee River; Who Knows?/W: Stanislaus Stange, M: Julian Edwards.

5061. Dorothy Kennedy-Fox *Fools Rush In* (The Playhouse, revue, Dec. 25, 1934): Rhythm in My Hair/W: Norman Zeno, M: Will Irwin.

5062. BK (Brian) Kennelly M: KRISTI LYNES. *Cats* (Winter Garden, CR, "Rum Tum Tugger," c 1992): Mr. Mistoffolees; Old Deuteronomy; The Rum Tum Tugger/W: T.S. Eliot, M: Andrew Lloyd Webber.

5063. Ed Kenney (Aug. 8, 1933–) B: Honolulu, HI. *Flower Drum Song* (St. James, "Wang Ta," Dec. 1, 1958): Like a God; You Are Beautiful/W: Oscar Hammerstein II, M: Richard Rodgers. *13 Daughters* (54th Street, "Mana, Prince of Hawaii," Mar. 2, 1961): Let-a-Go Your Heart; My Hawaii; When You Hear the Wind/ WM: Eaton Magoon, Jr.

5064. Charles Kenny (June 23, 1898–) B: Astoria, NY. Songwriter. *Belmont Varieties* (Belmont, revue, Sept. 26, 1932): Park Avenue/W: Charles Kenny, M: Serge Walter.

5065. Jack Kenny (Mar. 9, 1958–) B: Chicago, IL. *Fiddler on the Roof* (Gershwin, revival, "Motel," Nov. 18, 1990): Miracle of Miracles/W: Sheldon Harnick, M: Jerry Bock.

5066. Joseph (Joe) Keno M: ROSIE GREEN. Father of MITZI GREEN. *The Hen-Pecks* (Broadway, "Hiram," Feb. 4, 1911): Don't Forget the Beau You Left Behind/W: E. Ray Goetz, M: A. Baldwin Sloane. *Honey Girl* (Cohan and Harris, CR, "Timothy Smiley [Tip]," Aug. 23, 1920): I'm the Fellow; It's a Very Simple Matter; You're Just the Boy for Me/W: Neville Fleeson, M: Albert Von Tilzer. *The Whirl of New York* (Winter Garden, "Blinky Bill," June 13, 1921): The Belle of New York/W: Hugh Morton, M: Gustav Kerker — Dancing Fool/W: Harry B. Smith, Francis Wheeler, M: Ted Snyder.

5067. Craufurd Kent (Oct. 12, 1881–May 14, 1953) B: London, England. *Our Miss Gibbs* (Knickerbocker, "Lord Eynsford," Aug. 29, 1910): An English Gentleman/W: Percy Greenbank, M: Lionel Monckton. *The Pink Lady* (New Amsterdam, "Maurice D'Ulzac," Mar. 13, 1911): The Duel; When Love Goes A-Straying/ W: C.M.S. McLellan, M: Ivan Caryll. *Adele* (Longacre > Harris, "Robert Friebur," Aug. 28, 1913): The Clock Is Striking Ten; Matter of Opinion; A Waste of Time to Plan; When the Little Birds Are Sleeping; Yours for Me and Mine for You/WM: Edward A. Paulton, Adolf Philipp, Jean Briquet. *Yvette* (39th Street, "Robert De Villoc," Aug. 10, 1916): Love Letters; Love's Serenade; Since I Met You; Someone Just Like You/WM: Frederick Herendeen.

5068. Eleanor Kent (Dec. 6, 1880–Sept. 15, 1957) B: Illinois. *The Silver Slipper* (Broadway, CR, "Queen of Venus," Mar. 9, 1903): Invocation of Venus/WM: Leslie Stuart. *A Parisian Model* (Broadway, CR, "Violette," Jan. 28, 1907): On San Francisco Bay/W: Vincent Bryan, M: Gertrude Hoffmann.

5069. Mildred Kent *Flossie* (Lyric, "Nellie," June 3, 1924): Flossie; I Want to Be a Santa Claus/W: Ralph Murphy, M: Armand Robi.

5070. William (Billy) Kent (Apr. 29, 1886–Oct. 4, 1945) B: St. Paul, MN. *Toot-Toot!* (George M. Cohan, "Hyperion Buncombe," Mar. 11, 1918): If (There's Anything You Want); It's Greek to Me/W: Berton Braley, M: Jerome Kern. *Somebody's Sweetheart* (Central > Casino, "Sam Benton," Dec. 23, 1918): Is It Your Smile?; Somebody's Sweetheart; Then I'll Marry You; Twinkle/W: Alonzo Price, M: Antonio Bafunno. *Shubert Gaieties of 1919* (44th Street, revue, July 14, 1919): Please Don't Take Away the Girls/W: Alfred Bryan, M: Jean Schwartz. *Pitter Patter* (Longacre, "Dick Crawford," Sept. 28, 1920): Meet Your True Love Half Way/WM: William B. Friedlander. *Good Morning, Dearie* (Globe, "Steve Simmons," Nov. 1, 1921): Easy Pickin's; 'Melican Papa (Chink Song); Sing Song Girl/W: Anne Caldwell, M: Jerome Kern. *Battling Butler* (Selwyn, "Ernest Hozier," Oct. 8, 1923): In the Spring/W: Ballard Macdonald, M: Adorjan Otvos — Two Little Pals/W: Ballard Macdonald, M: Walter L. Rosemont. *Rose-Marie* (Imperial, "Hard-Boiled Herman," Sept. 2, 1924): Hard-Boiled Herman; The Minuet of the Minute; One Man Woman; Only a Kiss; Why Shouldn't We?/W: Otto Harbach, Oscar Hammerstein II, M: Herbert Stothart. *Funny Face* (Alvin, "Dugsie Gibbs," Nov. 22, 1927): Birthday Party; Once/ W: Ira Gershwin, M: George Gershwin. *Ups-A-Daisy!* (Shubert, "Montmorency Billings," Oct. 8, 1928): A Great Little Guy/W: Robert A. Simon, M: Lewis E. Gensler — Oh, How Happy We'll Be/W: Robert A. Simon, Clifford Grey, M: Lewis E. Gensler. *Girl Crazy* (Alvin, "Slick Fothergill," Oct. 14, 1930): Goldfarb! That's I'm!; Treat Me Rough/W: Ira Gershwin, M: George Gershwin. *A Little Racketeer* (44th Street, "Jay Slump," Jan. 18, 1932): Spring Tra La/W: Lupin Fein, Moe Jaffe, M: Lee Wainer — Throwing a Party/W: Edward Eliscu, M: Henry Sullivan. *Show Boat* (Casino, return engagement, CR, "Cap'n Andy Hawks," Oct. 1932): Why Do I Love You?/W: Oscar Hammerstein II, M: Jerome Kern. *Revenge with Music* (New Amsterdam, CR, "Don Emilio," Apr. 22, 1935): Think It Over/W: Howard Dietz, M: Arthur Schwartz.

5071. Albert Kenway *The Better 'Ole*

(Greenwich Village > Cort > Booth, "A Tommy," Oct. 19, 1918): Tommy/W: James Heard, M: Herman Darewski.

5072. Laura Kenyon (Nov. 23, 1947–) B: Chicago, IL. *On the Town* (Imperial, revival, "Senorita Dolores," Oct. 31, 1971): Nightclub Song (Spanish)/W: Betty Comden, Adolph Green, M: Leonard Bernstein.

5073. Leslie Kenyon (c 1871–Jan. 3, 1914) B: England. *The Man from Cook's* (New Amsterdam, "Lord Fitz-Bertie Baffingfone," Mar. 25, 1912): A Little Pot of Tea/W: Henry Blossom, M: Raymond Hubbell. *The Man with Three Wives* (Weber and Fields, "Baron Pickford," Jan. 23, 1913): Man Is Faithful Till He's Caught; Vengeance; We Are Free/W: Paul M. Potter, Harold Atteridge, M: Franz Lehar.

5074. Nancy Kenyon *Show Boat* (Ziegfeld, revival, CR, "Magnolia Hawks Ravenal" and "Kim," Apr. 1946): After the Ball/WM: Charles K. Harris — Can't Help Lovin' Dat Man; Make Believe; Nobody Else but Me; Why Do I Love You?; You Are Love/W: Oscar Hammerstein II, M: Jerome Kern.

5075. William Keough *The Governor's Son* (Savoy, "Hon. Theodore Wheelock," Feb. 25, 1901): Behold the Governor; Never Breathe a Word of This to Mother/WM: George M. Cohan. *Running for Office* (14th Street, "Sam Gayland," Apr. 27, 1903): Sweet Popularity/ WM: George M. Cohan. *The Honeymooners* (New Amsterdam roof, "Sam Gayland," June 3, 1907): I'm a Popular Man/WM: George M. Cohan.

5076. Paul Ker (c 1875–Mar. 31, 1929) B: Berlin, Germany. *The Midnight Girl* (44th Street, "Guiseppe," Feb. 23, 1914): Come Back to the Old Cabaret/WM: Adolf Philipp, Edward A. Paulton, Jean Briquet. *Blossom Time* (Ambassador, "Kupelweiser," Sept. 29, 1921): Keep It Dark; My Springtime Thou Art; Serenade/W: Dorothy Donnelly, M: Sigmund Romberg.

5077. Ken Kercheval (July 15, 1935–) B: Wolcottville, TN. He played Cliff Barnes in the TV drama *Dallas* (1978). *The Apple Tree* (Shubert, CR, "Adam" and "Captain Sanjar" and "Flip, the Prince Charming," Mar. 27, 1967): Beautiful, Beautiful World; Eve; Forbidden Love (in Gaul); George L.; It's a Fish; Which Door?; You Are Not Real/W: Sheldon Harnick, M: Jerry Bock. *Here's Where I Belong* (Billy Rose, "Aron Trask," Mar. 3, 1968): No Time; Soft Is the Sparrow; We Are What We Are; We're a Home/ W: Alfred Uhry, M: Robert Waldman. *Cabaret* (Broadhurst, CR, "Clifford Bradshaw," Aug. 26, 1968): Perfectly Marvelous; Why Should I Wake Up?/W: Fred Ebb, M: John Kander.

5078. Kalem Kermoyan *The Girl in Pink Tights* (Mark Hellinger, "Mike," Mar. 5, 1954): You've Got to Be a Little Crazy/W: Leo Robin, M: Sigmund Romberg.

5079. Michael Kermoyan (Nov. 29, 1921– Sept. 21, 1994) B: Fresno, CA. *Whoop-Up* (Shubert, "Jiggs Rock Medicine," Dec. 22, 1958): I Wash My Hands/W: Norman Gimbel, M: Moose Charlap. *Happy Town* (54th Street, "Glenn Richards," Oct. 7, 1959): It Isn't Easy/ WM: Harry M. Haldane, Gordon Duffy, Paul Nassau. *The Happiest Girl in the World* (Martin Beck, "Jupiter," Apr. 3, 1961): Eureka/W: E.Y. Harburg, M: Jacques Offenbach. *Tovarich* (Broadway, "Admiral Boris Soukhomine," Mar. 18, 1963): It Used to Be; Make a Friend; Nitchevo/W: Anne Crosswell, M: Lee Pockriss. *Something More!* (Eugene O'Neill, "Lepescu," Nov. 10, 1964): The Master of the Greatest Art of All/W: Marilyn Bergman, Alan Bergman, M: Sammy Fain. *Anya* (Ziegfeld, "Bounine," Nov. 29, 1965): Anya; If This Is Goodbye; Six Palaces; So Proud; That Prelude!; This Is My Kind of Love/WM: Robert Wright, George Forrest. *Carousel* (New York City Center, revival, "Jigger Craigin," Dec. 15, 1966): Blow High, Blow Low; There's Nothin' So Bad for a Woman/W: Oscar Hammerstein II, M: Richard Rodgers. *The King and I* (New York City Center, revival, "The King," May 23, 1968): A Puzzlement; Shall We Dance?; Song of the King/W: Oscar Hammerstein II, M: Richard Rodgers. *The Desert Song* (Uris, revival, "Ali Ben Ali," Sept. 5, 1973): Let Love Go; One Alone/W: Otto Harbach, Oscar Hammerstein II, M: Sigmund Romberg. *The King and I* (Uris, revival, CR, "The King," Apr. 11, 1978): same as above.

5080. David Kernan (June 23, 1939–) B: London, England. *Side by Side by Sondheim* (Music Box, revue, Apr. 18, 1977): Anyone Can Whistle; Barcelona; Beautiful Girls; Buddy's Blues (The God-Why-Don't-You-Love-Me Blues); Comedy Tonight; Company; Could I Leave You?; Everybody Says Don't; Getting Married Today; I Remember; The Little Things You Do Together; Love Is in the Air; Pretty Lady; Side by Side by Side; You Could Drive a Person Crazy; You Must Meet My Wife/WM: Stephen Sondheim — We're Gonna Be All Right/W: Stephen Sondheim, M: Richard Rodgers.

5081. Harry Kernell (July 18, 1888–) B: New York, NY. *Girlies* (New Amsterdam, "Burglar," June 13, 1910): Going Up (in My Aeroplane)/W: Harry Williams, M: Egbert Van Alstyne.

5082. Florence Kerns *Broadway Brevities of*

1920 (Winter Garden, revue, Sept. 29, 1920): We've Got the Stage Door Blues/W: Bert Kalmar, M: Harry Ruby.

5083. Rhoda Kerns *Catch a Star!* (Plymouth, revue, Sept. 6, 1955): One Hour Ahead of the Posse/W: Ray Golden, Dave Ormont, M: Phil Charig.

5084. Robert Kerns (June 8, 1933–Feb. 15, 1989) B: Detroit, MI. *The Cradle Will Rock* (New York City Center, revival, "Gus Polock," Feb. 11, 1960): Gus and Sadie Love Song/WM: Marc Blitzstein.

5085. Donald Kerr (Aug. 5, 1891–Jan. 25, 1977) B: Eagle Grove, IA. Partner of EFFIE WESTON. *The Passing Show of 1917* (Winter Garden, revue, Apr. 26, 1917): Same Old Song/W: Harold Atteridge, M: Sigmund Romberg, Otto Motzan. *Poor Little Ritz Girl* (Central, "Teddie Burns," July 28, 1920): The Bombay Bombashay/W: Alex Gerber, M: Sigmund Romberg, Ray Perkins. *Sunkist* (Globe, revue, "Assistant Director," May 23, 1921): The I Dun-No-Wat/WM: Fanchon Wolff, Marco Wolff. *The Greenwich Village Follies of 1921* (Shubert, revue, Aug. 31, 1921): Easin' Along/W: Irving Bibo, M: Thomas Morris — I Want a Picture of You/WM: Percy Wenrich.

5086. Nancy Kerr *Anne of Green Gables* (City Center 55th Street, "Mrs. Barry," Dec. 21, 1971): Did You Hear?/WM: Donald Harron, Norman Campbell.

5087. Anne Kerry B: Texas. *Annie* (Alvin, CR, "Grace Farrell," Apr. 29, 1981): Annie; I Think I'm Gonna Like It Here; A New Deal for Christmas; N.Y.C.; You Won't Be an Orphan for Long/W: Martin Charnin, M: Charles Strouse.

5088. Robin Kersey *Jerry's Girls* (St. James, revue, Dec. 18, 1985): Have a Nice Day; It Takes a Woman; It's Today; La Cage Aux Folles; Mame; Milk and Honey; Song on the Sand; Take It All Off/WM: Jerry Herman. *Honky Tonk Nights* (Biltmore, "Kitty Stark," Aug. 7, 1986): Roll with the Punches; The Sampson Beauties/W: Ralph Allen, David Campbell, M: Michael Valenti.

5089. Larry Kert (Dec. 5, 1930–June 5, 1991) B: Los Angeles, CA. Brother of ANITA ELLIS. *West Side Story* (Winter Garden, "Tony," Sept. 26, 1957): Maria; One Hand, One Heart; Something's Coming; Tonight/W: Stephen Sondheim, M: Leonard Bernstein. *West Side Story* (Winter Garden, revival, "Tony," Apr. 27, 1960): same as above. *A Family Affair* (Billy Rose, "Gerry Siegal," Jan. 27, 1962): Anything for You; There's a Room in My House; What I

Say Goes; Wonderful Party/W: James Goldman, William Goldman, M: John Kander. *I Can Get It for You Wholesale* (Shubert, CR, "Harry Bogen," June 1962): Ballad of the Garment Trade; Eat a Little Something; The Family Way; A Funny Thing Happened (On My Way to Love); A Gift Today (The Bar Mitzvah Song); Momma, Momma; The Sound of Money; The Way Things Are; When Gemini Meets Capricorn/WM: Harold Rome. *Cabaret* (Broadway, CR, "Clifford Bradshaw," Dec. 9, 1968): Perfectly Marvelous; Why Should I Wake Up?/W: Fred Ebb, M: John Kander. *La Strada* (Lunt-Fontanne, "Mario, the Fool," Dec. 14, 1969): Sooner or Later; You're Musical/W: Martin Charnin, M: Elliot Lawrence — There's a Circus in Town/WM: Lionel Bart. *Company* (Alvin, CR, "Robert," May 29, 1970/Aug. 23, 1971): Barcelona; Being Alive; Company; Side by Side by Side; Someone Is Waiting; What Would We Do Without You?/WM: Stephen Sondheim. *Sondheim: A Musical Tribute* (Shubert, revue, Mar. 11, 1973): Being Alive; Happily Ever After/WM: Stephen Sondheim. *A Musical Jubilee* (St. James, revue, Nov. 13, 1975): Ain't Misbehavin'/W: Andy Razaf, M: Fats Waller, Harry Brooks — The Best Things in Life Are Free/W: B.G. DeSylva, Lew Brown, M: Ray Henderson — The Bonnie Blue Flag/W: Annie Chambers-Ketchum, M: Harry MacCarthy — Fascinating Rhythm/W: Ira Gershwin, M: George Gershwin — How Jazz Was Born/W: Andy Razaf, Henry Creamer, M: Fats Waller — Oh, the Women/W: ?, M: Franz Lehar — Serenade/W: Dorothy Donnelly, M: Sigmund Romberg — Skip to My Lou; Whoa-Haw/WM: trad. — Sophisticated Lady/W: Mitchell Parish, Irving Mills, M: Duke Ellington — We're Blase/W: Bruce Sievier, M: Ord Hamilton. *Rags* (Mark Hellinger, "Nathan Hershkowitz," Aug. 21, 1986): Big Tim; Bread and Freedom (Sisters We Stand); Dancing with the Fools; In America; Uptown; Yankee Boy/W: Stephen Schwartz, M: Charles Strouse.

5090. Lenora Kerwin *Three Twins* (Herald Square > Majestic, "Isabel Howard," June 15, 1908): Little Miss Up-to-Date/W: Otto Harbach, M: Karl Hoschna.

5091. Zale Kessler *Dear World* (Hellinger, CR, "The Sewerman," Apr. 16, 1969): Garbage/WM: Jerry Herman. *Gantry* (George Abbott, "Prout," Feb. 14, 1970): Foresight/W: Fred Tobias, M: Stanley Lebowsky.

5092. Dave Ketchum (1925– ?) B: Quincy, IL. *The Billy Barnes People* (Royale, revue, June 13, 1961): Before and After; Dolls; The End?;

There's Nothing Wrong with Our Values/WM: Billy Barnes.

5093. J. Ward Kett *Moonshine* (Liberty, "Earl of Broadlawns," Oct. 30, 1905): A Hundred Years from Now/W: George V. Hobart, Edwin Milton Royle, M: Silvio Hein.

5094. Ilsa Kevin B: Rochester, NY. *New Faces of 1943* (Ritz, revue, Dec. 22, 1942): Animals Are Nice/W: J.B. Rosenberg, M: Lee Wainer — New Shoes/W: June Carroll, M: Will Irwin — Richard Crudnut's Charm School/W: June Carroll, John Lund, M: Lee Wainer.

5095. Peter Kevoian (Oct. 9, 1952–) *Zorba* (Broadway, revival, "Monk," Oct. 16, 1983): The Crow/W: Fred Ebb, M: John Kander.

5096. Daniel Keyes (Mar. 6, 1914–Oct. 11, 1995) B: Concord, MA. *Baker Street* (Broadway > Martin Beck, "Inspector Lestrade," Feb. 16, 1965): It's So Simple/WM: Marian Grudeff, Raymond Jessel. *Rainbow Jones* (The Music Box, "Uncle Ithaca," Feb. 13, 1974): It's So Nice/WM: Jill Williams.

5097. Evelyn Keyes (Nov. 20, 1919–) B: Port Arthur, TX. A dancer in nightclubs, she became a star of 1940s movies. Best known as Scarlet O'Hara's sister Suellen in the film *Gone with the Wind* (1939). M: director Charles Vidor; producer-director John Huston; bandleader Artie Shaw. *Keep Shufflin'* (Daly's > Eltinge, revue, "Evelyn," Feb. 27, 1928): Choc'-late Bar/W: Andy Razaf, M: Fats Waller.

5098. Joe Keyes, Jr. *Don't Play Us Cheap!* (Ethel Barrymore, "Trinity," May 16, 1972): Break That Party; I'm a Bad Character/WM: Melvin Van Peebles.

5099. Ramzi Khalaf (Jan. 17, 1982–) B: Lebanon. *A Christmas Carol* (Paramount Madison Square Garden, "Scrooge at 12," Dec. 1, 1994): A Place Called Home/W: Lynn Ahrens, M: Alan Menken.

5100. Leleti Khumalo (1970–) B: Durban, South Africa. *Sarafina!* (Cort, "Sarafina," Jan. 28, 1988): Bring Back Nelson Mandela/WM: Hugh Masekela.

5101. Mhlathi Khuzwayo (1959–) B: South Africa. *Sarafina!* (Cort, "S'Ginci" and "Police Sergeant," Jan. 28, 1988): Sarafina/WM: Hugh Masekela.

5102. Kathleen Kidd (1899–Feb. 23, 1961) B: England. *The Grand Street Follies of 1929* (Booth, revue, "Pierrette," May 1, 1929): I Need You So/W: David Goldberg, Howard Dietz, M: Arthur Schwartz.

5103. Jan Kiepura (May 16, 1902–Aug. 15, 1966) B: Sosnowiec, Poland. M: MARTA EGGERT. At age 21 he was Poland's most out-standing operatic tenor. Along with his wife, he went on to become a star of movies in Europe. They came to the U.S. in the late 1930s. *The Merry Widow* (Majestic, revival, "Prince Danilo," Aug. 4, 1943): I Love You So (The Merry Widow Waltz); Maxim's/W: Adrian Ross, M: Franz Lehar — Kuiawiak/W: Jan Kiepura, M: Henri Wieniawski. *The Merry Widow* (New York City Center, revival, "Prince Danilo," Oct. 8, 1944): same as above. *Polonaise* (Alvin, "Gen. Thaddeus Kosciusko," Oct. 6, 1945): Just for Tonight; Mazurka; Meadowlark; Now I Know Your Face by Heart; O Heart of My Country; Wait for Tomorrow/W: John Latouche, M: Bronislau Kaper, based on Frederic Chopin. *The Merry Widow* (New York City Center, revival, "Prince Danilo," Apr. 10, 1957): same as above.

5104. James A. Kiernan *Florodora* (Casino > New York, CR, "Anthony Tweedlepunch," Dec. 9, 1901): I Want to Marry a Man, I Do/W: Paul Rubens, M: Leslie Stuart — When We're on the Stage/WM: ?.

5105. Thomas A. Kiernan (? –Nov. 3, 1915) *By the Sad Sea Waves* (Grand Opera House, revival, "Manley Strong," Mar. 5, 1900): The Under-Takers' Frolic/W: Harry Bulger, J. Sherrie Mathews, M: Gustav Luders.

5106. Patricia Kies (Sept. 1, 1952–) B: Camp Atterbury, IN. *Camelot* (Gershwin, revival, "Queen Guenevere," June 21, 1993): Before I Gaze at You Again; Camelot; I Loved You Once in Silence; The Jousts; The Lusty Month of May; The Simple Joys of Maidenhood; What Do the Simple Folk Do?/W: Alan Jay Lerner, M: Federick Loewe.

5107. Shirley Kilduff *George White's Scandals of 1939-40* (Alvin, revue, CR, Oct. 16, 1939): Our First Kiss; Smart Little Girls/W: Jack Yellen, M: Sammy Fain.

5108. Richard Kiley (Mar. 31, 1922–Mar. 5, 1999) B: Chicago, IL. *Kismet* (Ziegfeld, "The Caliph," Dec. 3, 1953): And This Is My Beloved; He's in Love!; Night of My Nights; Stranger in Paradise/WM: Robert Wright, George Forrest. *Redhead* (46th Street, "Tom Baxter," Feb. 5, 1959): Behave Yourself; I'll Try; I'm Back in Circulation; Just for Once; Look Who's in Love; My Girl Is Just Enough Woman for Me; She's Not Enough Woman for Me/W: Dorothy Fields, M: Albert Hague. *No Strings* (54th Street, "David Jordan," Mar. 15, 1962): Be My Host; How Sad; Look No Further; Maine; No Strings; Nobody Told Me; The Sweetest Sounds/WM: Richard Rodgers. *Here's Love* (Shubert, CR, "Fred Gaily," May 1964): Here's Love; Look, Little Girl; My Wish; She Hadda Go Back/WM:

Meredith Willson. *I Had a Ball* (Martin Beck, "Stan the Shpieler," Dec. 15, 1964): The Affluent Society; Can It Be Possible?; Faith; Fickle Finger of Fate; The Other Half of Me/WM: Jack Lawrence, Stan Freeman. *Man of La Mancha* (ANTA Washington Square > Martin Beck, "Don Quixote," Nov. 22, 1965): The Combat; Dulcinea; Golden Helmet; The Impossible Dream (The Quest); Man of La Mancha (I, Don Quixote)/W: Joe Darion, M: Mitch Leigh. *Her First Roman* (Lunt-Fontanne, "Caesar," Oct. 20, 1968): Caesar Is Wrong; In Vino Veritas/W: Sheldon Harnick, M: Jerry Bock — Hail Sphinx; Kind Old Gentleman; Rome; Save Me from Caesar; The Things We Think We Are/WM: Ervin Drake. *Man of La Mancha* (Vivian Beaumont, revival, "Don Quixote," June 22, 1972): same as above. *Man of La Mancha* (Palace, revival, "Don Quixote," Sept. 15, 1977): same as above.

5109. Madelyn Killeen *Talk About Girls* (Waldorf, "Abigail," June 14, 1927): Oo, How I Love You; That's My Man/W: Irving Caesar, M: Harold Orlob.

5110. Nancy Killmer (Dec. 16, 1936–) B: Homewood, IL. *Goodtime Charley* (Palace, "Marie," Mar. 3, 1975): History/W: Hal Hackady, M: Larry Grossman.

5111. Jack Kilty *It Happens on Ice* (Center, revue, Oct. 10, 1940): What's on the Penny/W: Al Stillman, M: Fred E. Ahlert. *Stars on Ice* (Center, revue, July 2, 1942): Big Broad Smile; Gin Rummy, I Love You; Stars on Ice; You're Awfully Smart/W: Al Stillman, M: Paul McGrane — Like a Leaf Falling in the Breeze/W: Al Stillman, M: James Littlefield. *Oklahoma!* (St. James, CR, "Curly McLain," June 1946/Apr. 1947): The Farmer and the Cowman; Oh, What a Beautiful Mornin'; People Will Say We're in Love; Pore Jud; The Surrey with the Fringe on Top/W: Oscar Hammerstein II, M: Richard Rodgers. *Make Mine Manhattan* (Broadhurst, revue, Jan. 15, 1948): I Fell in Love with You; Phil the Fiddler; Saturday Night in Central Park/W: Arnold B. Horwitt, M: Richard Lewine.

5112. Mara Kim B: Los Angeles, CA. *Happy as Larry* (Coronet, "Clotho," Jan. 6, 1950): Three Old Ladies from Hades/W: Donagh MacDonagh, M: Mischa Portnoff, Wesley Portnoff.

5113. Taewon Kim (July 8, 1966–) B: Seoul, Korea. *The King and I* (Neil Simon, revival, "Lady Thiang," Apr. 11, 1996): Something Wonderful/W: Oscar Hammerstein II, M: Richard Rodgers.

5114. Christina Kumi Kimball *A Broadway Musical* (Lunt-Fontanne, "Kumi-Kumi" Dec. 21, 1978): Smoke and Fire/W: Lee Adams, M: Charles Strouse. *Cats* (Winter Garden, CR, "Cassandra"): The Old Gumbie Cat/W: T.S. Eliot, M: Andrew Lloyd Weber.

5115. Grace Kimball (Feb. 18, 1870–) B: Detroit, MI. *The Wizard of Oz* (Majestic, "Tryxie Trifle," Jan. 20, 1903): Sammy/W: James O'Dea, M: Edward Hutchison — When the Circus Comes to Town/W: James O'Dea, M: Bob Adams.

5116. Kathryn (Kay) Kimber *Two for the Show* (Booth, revue, Feb. 8, 1940): At Last It's Love; Fool for Luck; A House with a Little Red Barn/W: Nancy Hamilton, M: Morgan Lewis. *By Jupiter* (Shubert, "3rd Sentry," June 3, 1942): Jupiter Forbid/W: Lorenz Hart, M: Richard Rodgers.

5117. Charles Kimbrough (May 23, 1936–) B: St. Paul, MN. He played anchorman Jim Dial on the TV sitcom *Murphy Brown* (1988). *Company* (Alvin, "Harry," Apr. 26, 1970): Have I Got a Girl for You; Sorry-Grateful/WM: Stephen Sondheim. *Candide* (Broadway, revival, CR, "Dr. Voltaire" and "Dr. Pangloss" and "Governor" and "Host" and "Sage," Jan. 20, 1975): The Best of All Possible Worlds/W: Stephen Sondheim, M: Leonard Bernstein — Bon Voyage/W: Richard Wilbur, M: Leonard Bernstein — My Love/W: Richard Wilbur, John Latouche, M: Leonard Bernstein. *Sunday in the Park with George* (Booth, "Jules," May 2, 1984): The Day Off; Gossip; No Life/WM: Stephen Sondheim.

5118. Kenneth Kimmins (Sept. 4, 1941–) B: Brooklyn, NY. On TV he was Howard Burleigh on the sitcom *Coach* (1989) and Thornton McLeish on *Dallas* (1982). *The Fig Leaves Are Falling* (Broadhurst, "Charley Montgomery," Jan. 2, 1969): Old Fashioned Song/W: Allan Sherman, M: Albert Hague. *Company* (Alvin, CR, "Harry," May 13, 1971): Have I Got a Girl for You; Sorry-Grateful/WM: Stephen Sondheim. *The Magic Show* (Cort, CR, "Feldman," Dec. 29, 1974/Oct. 27, 1976): Before Your Very Eyes; A Bit of Villainy; The Goldfarb Variations; Style/WM: Stephen Schwartz.

5119. Eric Scott Kincaid *Cats* (Winter Garden, CR, "Skimbleshanks," June 3, 1994): Skimbleshanks/W: T.S. Eliot, M: Andrew Lloyd Webber.

5120. Alan King (Dec. 26, 1927–) B: Brooklyn, NY. Durable actor and comedian of night spots, TV and movies. *Guys and Dolls* (New York City Center, revival, "Nathan Detroit," Apr. 28, 1965): The Oldest Established; Sue Me/WM: Frank Loesser.

5121. Allyn King (c 1901–Mar. 30, 1930) *Ziegfeld Follies of 1917* (New Amsterdam, revue, June 12, 1917): Chu, Chin, Chow/W: Gene Buck, M: Dave Stamper — My Arabian Maid/ W: Gene Buck, M: Raymond Hubbell. *Ziegfeld Midnight Frolic of 1919* (New Amsterdam roof, revue, Oct. 3, 1919): Shanghai; Sweet Olden Days/W: Gene Buck, M: Dave Stamper. *Ziegfeld Follies of 1922* (New Amsterdam, revue, CR, Oct. 2, 1922): Songs I Can't Forget; Sunny South/W: Gene Buck, M: Louis A. Hirsch — Weaving My Dreams/W: Gene Buck, M: Victor Herbert. *Sun Showers* (Astor, "Alice Worthy," Feb. 5, 1923): Everyone Is Beautiful in Someone's Eyes; He Loves Me; The Joy of Living; Sun Showers; Worth Waiting For; Yours Truly/WM: Harry Delf. *Moonlight* (Longacre, "Louise Endicott," Jan. 30, 1924): Dancing; Say It Again/W: William B. Friedlander, M: Con Conrad.

5122. Carole King (Feb. 9, 1940–) B: Brooklyn, NY. Best selling, Grammy winning folk rock songwriter and singer. *Blood Brothers* (Music Box, CR, "Mrs. Johnstone," c 1993): Bright New Day; Easy Terms; Light Romance; Marilyn Monroe; My Child; Tell Me It's Not True/WM: Willy Russell.

5123. Charles E. King (Oct. 31, 1889–Jan. 11, 1944) B: New York, NY. M: LILA RHODES. The popular song and dance man started as a blackface comedian in vaudeville and burlesque. Best remembered for the still watched 1929 movie musical, *Broadway Melody*. *The Mimic World* (Casino, revue, "Artie," July 9, 1908): Ragtime Minstrel Man/W: E. Ray Goetz, M: Louis A. Hirsch — When Two Hearts Beat as One/W: Edward Laska, M: Samuel Lehman. *The Hen-Pecks* (Broadway, CR, "Ayer Castle," Aug. 14, 1911): It's the Skirt; Just Tell Me with Your Eyes; White Light Alley/W: E. Ray Goetz, M: A. Baldwin Sloane. *A Winsome Widow* (Moulin Rouge, "Wilder Daly," Apr. 11, 1912): Be My Little Baby Bumble Bee [May 6, 1912]/W: Stanley Murphy, M: Henry I. Marshall — String a Ring of Roses 'Round Your Rosie/W: William Jerome, M: Jean Schwartz — You're a Regular Girl/W: A. Seymour Brown, M: Nat D. Ayer. *The Honeymoon Express* (Winter Garden, CR, "Baudry," Feb. 6, 1913): You'll Call the Next Love the First/W: Harold Atteridge, M: Jean Schwartz. *The Geisha* (44th Street, revival, "Dick Cunningham," Mar. 27, 1913): The Dear Little Jappy-jap-jappy/W: Henry Greenbank, M: Sidney Jones. *The Passing Show of 1913* (Winter Garden, revue, July 24, 1913): When I Want to Settle Down/W: Harold Atteridge, M: Jean Schwartz — Won't You Come Into My Play-

house?/WM: ?. *Watch Your Step* (New Amsterdam, revue, "Algy Cuffs," Dec. 8, 1914): Play a Simple Melody; Settle Down in a One-Horse Town; They Always Follow Me Around/WM: Irving Berlin — When I Discovered You/WM: E. Ray Goetz, Irving Berlin. *Miss 1917* (Century, revue, Nov. 5, 1917): The Bumble Bee/W: Anne Caldwell, M: Jerome Kern — The Land Where the Good Songs Go; The Picture I Want to See/W: P.G. Wodehouse, M: Jerome Kern. *Good Morning Judge* (Shubert, "Hughie Cavanagh," Feb. 6, 1919): Dinky Doodle Dicky/W: Percy Greenbank, M: Howard Talbot — I Was So Young (You Were So Beautiful)/W: Irving Caesar, Alfred Bryan, M: George Gershwin — It's Nothing to Do with You; Sporty Boys/W: Percy Greenbank, M: Lionel Monckton — I've Got a Pair of Swinging Doors (That Lead Right Into My Heart)/W: Sam M. Lewis, Joe Young, M: Bert Grant — Young Folks and Old Folks/WM: ?. *George White's Scandals of 1921* (Liberty, revue, July 11, 1921): South Sea Isles (Sunny South Sea Islands); Where East Meets West /W: Arthur Jackson, M: George Gershwin. *Little Nellie Kelly* (Liberty, "Jerry Conroy," Nov. 13, 1922): Nellie Kelly, I Love You; When You Do the Hinky Dee; You Remind Me of My Mother/WM: George M. Cohan. *Keep Kool* (Morosco > Globe > Earl Carroll, revue, May 22, 1924): Dandelion Time; How You Gonna Keep Kool?/W: Paul Gerard Smith, M: Jack Frost — Nellie Kelly, I Love You/WM: George M. Cohan — Out Where the Pavement Ends/WM: Jack Frost. *Ziegfeld's American Revue of 1926 aka No Foolin'* (Globe, revue, June 24, 1926): Don't Do the Charleston/W: Irving Caesar, M: James F. Hanley — Honey, Be Mine/W: Gene Buck, M: James F. Hanley — Poor Little Marie/W: Gene Buck, M: James F. Hanley, Billy Rose — Wasn't It Nice?/W: Irving Caesar, M: Rudolf Friml. *Hit the Deck* (Belasco, "Bilge Smith," Apr. 25, 1927): Harbor of My Heart/W: Clifford Grey, Leo Robin, M: Vincent Youmans — Sometimes I'm Happy/W: Irving Caesar, M: Vincent Youmans. *Present Arms* (Mansfield, "Chick Evans," Apr. 26, 1928): Blue Ocean Blues; Do I Hear You Saying I Love You?; Down by the Sea (Whoopie); A Kiss for Cinderella; Tell It to the Marines (A Bunch o' Nuts)/W: Lorenz Hart, M: Richard Rodgers. *The New Yorkers* (Broadway, "Al Spanish," Dec. 8, 1930): Let's Fly Away; Sing Sing for Sing Sing; Where Have You Been?/WM: Cole Porter. *Sea Legs* (Mansfield, "Capt. Nordstrom," May 18, 1937): Catalina; Off on a Weekend Cruise; The Opposite Sex/W: Arthur Swanstrom, M: Michael H. Cleary.

5124. Dennis King, Sr. (Nov. 2, 1897–May 21, 1971) B: Coventry, England. Father of JOHN MICHAEL KING and DENNIS KING, JR. The handsome baritone settled in the U.S. in 1921 and became a star of musical comedy and movies. He co-starred with Jeanette MacDonald in the film version of *The Vagabond King* (1930). *Rose-Marie* (Imperial, "Jim Kenyon," Sept. 2, 1924): I Love Him; Indian Love Call; Rose-Marie/W: Otto Harbach, Oscar Hammerstein II, M: Rudolf Friml. *The Vagabond King* (Casino, "Francois Villon," Sept. 21, 1925): Love Me Tonight; Only a Rose; Song of the Vagabonds; Tomorrow/W: Brian Hooker, M: Rudolf Friml. *The Three Musketeers* (Lyric, "D'Artagnan," Mar. 13, 1928): Gascony Bred; Heart of Mine; A Kiss Before I Go (One Kiss); March of the Musketeers; My Sword and I/W: Clifford Grey, M: Rudolf Friml — Your Eyes/W: P.G. Wodehouse, M: Rudolf Friml. *Show Boat* (Casino, return engagement, "Gaylord Ravenal," May 19, 1932): Make Believe; Till Good Luck Comes My Way; Where's the Mate for Me?; Why Do I Love You?/W: Oscar Hammerstein II, M: Jerome Kern. *Frederika* (Imperial, "Goethe," Feb. 4, 1937): One; Rising Star; Rose in the Heather; A Word to Remind You/W: Edward Eliscu, M: Franz Lehar. *I Married an Angel* (Shubert, "Count Willy Palaffi," May 11, 1938): Did You Ever Get Stung?; I Married an Angel; The Modiste; Spring Is Here/W: Lorenz Hart, M: Richard Rodgers. *Music in the Air* (Ziegfeld, revival, "Bruno Mahler," Oct. 8, 1951): I Am So Eager; I'm Coming Home (Letter Song); One More Dance; The Song Is You/W: Oscar Hammerstein II, M: Jerome Kern. *Shangri-La* (Winter Garden, "Hugh Conway," June 13, 1956): Shangri-La/W: Jerome Lawrence, Robert E. Lee, M: Harry Warren.

5125. Dennis King, Jr. (July 6, 1921–Aug. 24, 1986) B: Birmingham, England. Son of DENNIS KING, SR. Singer and actor of stage, screen and TV. *The Cradle Will Rock* (Mansfield > Broadway, revival, "Junior Mister," Dec. 26, 1947): Croon Spoon; Honolulu; Let's Do Something/WM: Marc Blitzstein.

5126. Donna King B: Kansas City, MO. *The Best Little Whorehouse in Texas* (46th Street, "Linda Lou," June 19, 1978): Hard-Candy Christmas/WM: Carol Hall. *Can-Can* (Minskoff, revival, "Mimi," Apr. 30, 1981): It's All Right with Me/WM: Cole Porter. *Cats* (Winter Garden, "Bombalurina," Oct. 7, 1982): Bustopher Jones; Grizabella, the Glamour Cat; Macavity; The Old Gumbie Cat/W: T.S. Eliot, M: Andrew Lloyd Webber.

5127. Edith King (Apr. 12, 1898–Sept. 26, 1963) B: Dalton, GA. *Saratoga* (Winter Garden, "Mrs. Sophie Bellop," Dec. 7, 1959): Have You Heard? (Gossip Song)/W: Johnny Mercer, M: Harold Arlen. *Wildcat* (Alvin, "Countess Emily O'Brien," Dec. 16, 1960): Dancing on My Tippy Tippy Toes/W: Carolyn Leigh, M: Cy Coleman.

5128. Ginny King (May 12, 1957–) B: Atlanta, GA. *42nd Street* (Winter Garden, "Lorraine," Aug. 25, 1980): Go Into Your Dance; We're in the Money/W: Al Dubin, M: Harry Warren.

5129. Grace King *The Sho-Gun* (Wallack's, "Moo-Zoo May," Oct. 10, 1904): The Games We Used to Play; Little Moo-Zoo May/W: George Ade, M: Gustav Luders. *A Skylark* (New York, "Elberta Parling," Apr. 4, 1910): Broadway Lament; I Just Can't Wait; I'm Looking for a Little Girl Who's Looking for a Man; Style, Style, Style/W: William B. Harris, Jr., M: Frank Dossert.

5130. Jane King With her sister MARY KING, they were known as the King Sisters. *Jim Jam Jems* (Cort, "Jane King," Oct. 4, 1920): Jim Jam Jems; Just a Little Bit Behind the Times; Raggedy Ann/W: Harry L. Cort, George E. Stoddard, M: James F. Hanley. *Letty Pepper* (Vanderbilt, "Hattie," Apr. 10, 1922): Coo-ee-doo/W: Leo Wood, M: Werner Janssen, James F. Hanley — Every Little Miss; I Love to Dance/W: Leo Wood, Irving Bibo, M: Werner Janssen.

5131. John King *Cohan and Harris Minstrels* (New York, revue, Aug. 3, 1908): Good Bye, Mr. Ragtime/W: William Jerome, M: Jean Schwartz — I'll Be True to My Honey Boy/WM: George Evans. *Cohan and Harris Minstrels* (New York, revue, Aug. 16, 1909): Down Where the Watermelons Grow/W: Ren Shields, M: George Evans.

5132. John L. King *The Love Call* (Majestic, "Tim," Oct. 24, 1927): When I Take You All to London/W: Harry B. Smith, M: Sigmund Romberg.

5133. John Michael King (May 13, 1926–) B: New York, NY. Son of DENNIS KING; brother of DENNIS KING, JR. *My Fair Lady* (Mark Hellinger, "Freddy Eynsford-Hill," Mar. 15, 1956): On the Street Where You Live/W: Alan Jay Lerner, M: Frederick Loewe. *Anya* (Ziegfeld, "Prince Paul," Nov. 29, 1965): Hand in Hand; On That Day/WM: Robert Wright, George Forrest.

5134. Larry L. King (Jan. 1, 1929–) B: Putnam, TX. *The Best Little Whorehouse in Texas* (46th Street, CR, "Sheriff Ed Earl Dodd," Jan. 15, 1979): Good Old Girl/WM: Carol Hall.

5135. Mabel King (Dec. 25, 1932–Nov. 9, 1999) B: Charleston, SC. *Don't Play Us Cheap!* (Ethel Barrymore, "Mrs. Bowser," May 16, 1972): Feast on Me/WM: Melvin Van Peebles. *The Wiz* (Majestic, "Evillene," Jan. 5, 1975): No Bad News/WM: Charlie Smalls. *It's So Nice to Be Civilized* (Martin Beck, "Grandma," June 3, 1980): I've Still Got My Bite; Who's Going to Teach the Children?/WM: Micki Grant.

5136. Mary King *Jim Jam Jems* (Cort, "Mary King," Oct. 4, 1920): same as JANE KING. *Letty Pepper* (Vanderbilt, "Imogene," Apr. 10, 1922): same as JANE KING.

5137. Michael E. King *Snow White and the Seven Dwarfs* (Radio City Music Hall, "Dopey," Oct. 18, 1979): Bluddle-uddle-um-dum (The Washing Song); The Dwarf's Yodel Song (The Silly Song); Heigh-Ho/W: Larry Morey, M: Frank Churchill.

5138. Mollie King (Apr. 16, 1895–Dec. 28, 1981) B: New York, NY. *The Passing Show of 1913* (Winter Garden, revue, July 24, 1913): My Irish Romeo/W: Harold Atteridge, M: Al W. Brown. *Good Morning Judge* (Shubert, "Joy Chatterton," Feb. 6, 1919): Dinky Doodle Dicky/W: Percy Greenbank, M: Howard Talbot — A Game That Ends with a Kiss/W: Adrian Ross, Percy Greenbank, M: Lionel Monckton, Howard Talbot — I Was So Young (You Were So Beautiful)/W: Irving Caesar, Alfred Bryan, M: George Gershwin — It's Nothing to Do with You/W: Percy Greenbank, M: Lionel Monckton — There's More to the Kiss Than the Sound/W: Irving Caesar, M: George Gershwin. *Blue Eyes* (Casino, "Dorothy Manners," Feb. 21, 1921): Blue Eyes [Feb. 28, 1921]/W: George V. Hobart, Edward A. Paulton, M: Silvio Hein — When Gramercy Square Was Up Town; Without a Girl Like You/W: Zeke Meyers, M: I.B. Kornblum.

5139. Nellie King *The Mimic World* (Casino, revue, "Marey Carey," July 9, 1908): When Two Hearts Beat as One/W: Edward Laska, M: Samuel Lehman.

5140. Patsi King *Sophie* (Winter Garden, "Sylvain Krouse," Apr. 15, 1963): Queen of the Burlesque Wheel; Who Are We Kidding?/WM: Steve Allen.

5141. Ray King *Broadway Nights* (44th Street, revue, CR, "Stage Manager," July 22, 1929): Stranded in a One-Horse Town/WM: ?.

5142. Rose King *A la Carte* (Martin Beck, revue, Aug. 17, 1927): Sunny Spain/WM: Norma Gregg. *Take the Air* (Waldorf, "Goldie," Nov. 22, 1927): Carmen Has Nothing on Me/W: Gene Buck, M: Dave Stamper — On a Pony for Two/W: Gene Buck, M: James F. Hanley.

Thumbs Up! (St. James, revue, Dec. 27, 1934): A Taste of the Sea/W: Earle Crooker, M: Henry Sullivan. *The Show Is On* (Winter Garden, revue, CR, Sept. 18, 1937): Buy Yourself a Balloon/WM: Herman Hupfeld — Rhythm/W: Lorenz Hart, M: Richard Rodgers.

5143. Walter Woolf King (Nov. 2, 1899–Oct. 24, 1984) B: San Francisco, CA. Known as WALTER WOOLF before 1933. *The Passing Show of 1919* (Winter Garden, revue, Oct. 23, 1919): In Salem/W: Harold Atteridge, M: Sigmund Romberg, Jean Schwartz — So Long, Sing Song Girl/W: Harold Atteridge, M: Sigmund Romberg — Tumble Inn/W: Harold Atteridge, M: Jean Schwartz. *Florodora* (Century, revival, "Frank Abercoed," Apr. 5, 1920): The Shade of the Palm/W: Owen Hall, M: Leslie Stuart — Somebody/WM: ?. *The Midnight Rounders of 1920* (Century roof, revue, July 12, 1920): Beauty Is Like a Rose; My Lady of the Cameo; O You Heavenly Body/W: Alfred Bryan, M: Jean Schwartz. *The Last Waltz* (Century, "Lieut. Jack Merrington, U.S.N.," May 10, 1921): The Last Waltz; Now Fades My Golden Love Dream/W: Edward Delaney Dunn, M: Oscar Straus — Live for Today/W: Harold Atteridge, M: Alfred Goodman, A. Werau — Reminiscence/W: ?, M: Oscar Straus. *The Lady in Ermine* (Ambassador, "Col. Belovar," Oct. 2, 1922): Dear Old Land o' Mine/W: Cyrus D. Wood, M: Alfred Goodman — How Fiercely You Dance/W: Harry Graham, Cyrus D. Wood, M: Alfred Goodman, Jean Gilbert — Mariana/W: Harry Graham, M: Jean Gilbert. *The Dream Girl* (Ambassador, "Jack Warren," Aug. 20, 1924): All Year 'Round; Broad Highway/W: Harold Atteridge, M: Sigmund Romberg — My Dream Girl; My Hero/W: Rida Johnson Young, M: Victor Herbert. *Artists and Models of 1925* (Winter Garden, revue, June 24, 1925): Cellini's Dream; The Magic Garden of Love/WM: ? — Oriental Memories/W: Clifford Grey, M: Alfred Goodman, Maurie Rubens, J. Fred Coots. *Countess Maritza* (Shubert, "Count Tassilo Endrody," Sept. 18, 1926): (Come at the) Call of Love/W: Harry B. Smith, M: Alfred Goodman — Dear Home of Mine, Goodbye; Don't Tempt Me; In the Days Gone By; Play Gypsies, Dance Gypsies; Why Is the World So Changed Today?/W: Harry B. Smith, M: Emmerich Kalman — Golden Dreams/W: Harry B. Smith, M: Harry K. Morton. *The Red Robe* (Shubert, "Gil de Berault," Dec. 25, 1928): Cavalier/WM: Harden Church — Joy or Strife; Only a Smile; Where Love Grows/W: Harry B. Smith, M: Jean Gilbert — King of the Sword/W: J. Keirn Brennan, M: Robert Stolz, Maurie

Rubens—The One Girl [May 6, 1929]/W: Oscar Hammerstein II, M: Vincent Youmans. *Melody* (Casino, "George Richards," Feb. 14, 1933): Tonight May Never Come Again; The Whole World Loves/W: Irving Caesar, M: Sigmund Romberg. *May Wine* (St. James, "Baron Kuno Adelhorst," Dec. 5, 1935): Always Be a Gentleman; I Built a Dream One Day; Interlude in a Barbershop; Just Once Around the Clock; You Wait and Wait and Wait/W: Oscar Hammerstein II, M: Sigmund Romberg.

5144. Walter Kingsford (Sept. 20, 1881–Feb. 7, 1958) B: Red Hill, Nottinghamshire, England. In movies from the 1930s. *Song of Norway* (Imperial, "Father Grieg," Aug. 21, 1944): At Christmastime/WM: Robert Wright, George Forrest, M: based on Edvard Grieg.

5145. Gretchen Kingsley-Weihe (Oct. 6, 1961–) B: Washington, DC. *Sweeney Todd* (Circle in the Square, revival, "Johanna," Sept. 14, 1989): Ah, Miss; Green Finch and Linnet Bird; Kiss Me/WM: Stephen Sondheim.

5146. Patrick Kinser-Lau *Pacific Overtures* (Winter Garden, "Shogun's Companion," Jan. 11, 1976): Chrysanthemum Tea/WM: Stephen Sondheim.

5147. Richard Kinsey (Mar. 22, 1954–) *Les Miserables* (Broadway, CR, "Javert," Nov. 19, 1992): Soliloquy; Stars/W: Herbert Kretzmer, M: Claude-Michel Schonberg.

5148. Sadie Kirby *Monte Carlo* (Herald Square, "Gertie Galatine," Mar. 21, 1898): The Sisters Galatine/W: Harry Greenbank, M: Howard Talbot.

5149. Alyson Kirk (Jan. 14, 1970–) B: Waldwick, NJ. *Annie* (Alvin, CR, "Annie," Sept. 8, 1982): I Don't Need Anything But You; I Think I'm Gonna Like It Here; It's the Hard-Knock Life; Maybe; N.Y.C.; A New Deal for Christmas; Tomorrow/W: Martin Charnin, M: Charles Strouse. *Take Me Along* (Martin Beck, revival, "Mildred Miller," Apr. 14, 1985): Oh, Please/WM: Bob Merrill.

5150. Beverly Kirk *Great Lady* (Majestic, "Second Assistant Dressmaker," Dec. 1, 1938): Madame Is at Home/W: Earle Crooker, M: Frederick Loewe.

5151. George Kirk *Nina Rosa* (Majestic, "Dick," Sept. 20, 1930): Nina Rosa/W: Irving Caesar, M: Sigmund Romberg. *Flying Colors* (Imperial, revue, Sept. 15, 1932): Just Around the Corner/W: Howard Dietz, M: Arthur Schwartz. *Let 'Em Eat Cake* (Imperial, "Lieutenant," Oct. 21, 1933): The General's Gone to a Party; My Fellow Soldiers/W: Ira Gershwin, M: George Gershwin. *Revenge with Music* (New Amsterdam, "Eduardo," Nov. 28, 1934): My Father Said/W: Howard Dietz, M: Arthur Schwartz.

5152. Keith Byron Kirk (Aug. 11, 1968–) B: Oakland, CA. *Miss Saigon* (Broadway, CR, "John," c 1993): Bui-doi; The Confrontation; The Guilt Inside Your Head; Please; The Telephone/W: Richard Maltby, Jr., Alain Boublil, M: Claude-Michel Schonberg.

5153. Lisa Kirk (Sept. 18, 1925–Nov. 11, 1990) B: Roscoe, PA. *Allegro* (Majestic, "Emily West," Oct. 10, 1947): Allegro; The Gentleman Is a Dope/W: Oscar Hammerstein II, M: Richard Rodgers. *Kiss Me, Kate* (New Century, "Lois Lane" and "Bianca," Dec. 30, 1948): Always True to You in My Fashion; Tom, Dick or Harry; We Open in Venice; Why Can't You Behave?/WM: Cole Porter. *Here's Love* (Shubert, CR, "Doris Walker," 1964): Arm in Arm; Look, Little Girl; Nothing in Common; Pine Cones and Holly Berries; You Don't Know/WM: Meredith Willson. *Mack & Mabel* (Majestic, "Lottie Ames," Oct. 6, 1974): Big Time; Tap Your Troubles Away/WM: Jerry Herman.

5154. Van Kirk *'Tis of Thee* (Maxine Elliott, revue, Oct. 26, 1940): Noises in the Street/W: David Greggory, Peter Barry, M: Richard Lewine.

5155. Bradford Kirkbride *Princess Virtue* (Central, "Bruce Crawford," May 4, 1921): Dear Sweet Eyes; Smoke Rings/WM: Gitz Rice, B.C. Hilliam. *Sue, Dear* (Times Square, "Phillip West," July 10, 1922): Foolishment; Lover's Lane with You; My Little Full-Blown Rose/W: Bide Dudley, M: Frank Grey. *Helen of Troy, New York* (Selwyn, CR, "David Williams," July 23, 1923): It Was Meant to Be; Look for the Happy Ending; We'll Have a Model Factory/W: Bert Kalmar, M: Harry Ruby.

5156. Charles Kirke (c 1854–Apr. 30, 1903) *Broadway to Tokio* (New York, "Lee High Hung," Jan. 23, 1900): Story of the Dance/W: Louis Harrison, M: A. Baldwin Sloane.

5157. Hazel Kirke *Roly Poly* (Broadway, "Katrina," Nov. 21, 1912): Steinland; When I'm Waltzing/W: E. Ray Goetz, M: A. Baldwin Sloane. *Sweethearts* (New Amsterdam > Liberty, "Liane," Sept. 8, 1913): Jeannette and Her Little Wooden Shoes; Smiles/W: Robert B. Smith, M: Victor Herbert. *Iole* (Longacre, "Vanessa," Dec. 29, 1913): Back to Nature; Comes an Exquisite Situation; I Wonder Why; Oh Precious Thoughts; To Rent, to Let/W: Robert W. Chambers, M: William F. Peters—If Dreams Come True; Nude Descending a Staircase/WM: ?—None but the Brave Deserve the Fair/W: Will

M. Hough, Frank R. Adams, M: Joseph E. Howard. *The Road to Mandalay* (Park, "Rose Montgomery," Mar. 1, 1916): Bright Day Dawning/W: William J. McKenna, M: Oreste Vessella — The Road to Mandalay/W: Jack Appleton, M: Oreste Vessella. *Fiddlers Three* (Cort, "Bernice Brockway," Sept. 3, 1918): It Was All on Account of Nipper!/W: William Cary Duncan, M: Alexander Johnstone. *Oh, What a Girl!* (Shubert, "Margot Merrivale," July 28, 1919): The Breeze Through the Trees/W: Edgar Smith, M: Charles Jules, Jacques Presburg — Get Him Up/W: Edward Clark, M: Charles Jules, Jacques Presburg.

5158. Sam Kirkham (Apr. 28, 1923–) B: Gainesville, TX. *Oklahoma!* (Music Theater of Lincoln Center, revival, "Ike Skidmore," June 23, 1969): The Farmer and the Cowman; Oklahoma/W: Oscar Hammerstein II, M: Richard Rodgers.

5159. Jim (James) Kirkwood (Aug. 22, 1924–Apr. 21, 1989) B: Los Angeles, CA. Best-selling novelist and co-author of Pulitzer prizewinning musical *A Chorus Line*. *Small Wonder* (Coronet, revue, CR, Nov. 29, 1948): Ballad for Billionaires; William McKinley High/W: Burt Shevelove, M: Albert Selden.

5160. Josephine Kirkwood *The Governor's Son* (Savoy, "Mrs. Franklin-Jones Berrymore," Feb. 25, 1901): A Widow's Wile; Wine Divine/WM: George M. Cohan.

5161. Dale Kirstein see DALE KRISTIEN.

5162. Dorothy Kirsten (July 6, 1910–Nov. 18, 1992) B: Montclair, NJ. The singer and actress, a protege of GRACE MOORE, was one of the most successful crossover opera stars and recording artists. *Great Lady* (Majestic, "Maid," Dec. 1, 1938): Madame Is at Home/W: Earle Crooker, M: Frederick Loewe.

5163. Louise Kirtland (Aug. 4, 1919–) B: Lynn, MA. *Tell Her the Truth* (Cort, "Ethel," Oct. 28, 1932): Won't You Tell Me Why?/W: R.P. Weston, Bert Lee, M: Joseph Tunbridge, Jack Waller. *Shady Lady* (Shubert, "Peggy Stetson," July 5, 1933): Isn't It Swell to Dream/W: Bud Green, Stanley Adams, M: Sam H. Stept, Jesse Greer. *Murder at the Vanities* (Majestic, CR, "Sonya Sonya," Jan. 29, 1934): You Love Me/WM: Herman Hupfeld. *The Only Girl* (44th Street, revival, "Jane McMurray," May 21, 1934): Connubial Bliss; Tell It All Over Again/W: Henry Blossom, M: Victor Herbert. *Tovarich* (Broadway, "Grace Davis," Mar. 18, 1963): Say You'll Stay; A Small Cartel/W: Anne Crosswell, M: Lee Pockriss.

5164. Leonard Kirtley *Under Many Flags*

(Hippodrome, "Capt. Alan Strong," Aug. 31, 1912): Home Is Where the Heart Is; Temple Bells/WM: Manuel Klein.

5165. Franklin Kiser *Ben Franklin in Paris* (Lunt-Fontanne, "Temple Franklin," Oct. 27, 1964): Half the Battle; I Love the Ladies; Whatever Became of Old Temple; You're in Paris/W: Sidney Michaels, M: Mark Sandrich, Jr.

5166. Terry Kiser (Aug. 1, 1939–) B: Omaha, NE. *Shelter* (John Golden, "Michael," Feb. 6, 1973): Don't Tell Me It's Forever; It's Hard to Care; She's My Girl; Welcome to a New World/W: Gretchen Cryer, M: Nancy Ford.

5167. Mary Cory Kitchen *Plain Jane* (New Amsterdam, "Little Miss Ritz," May 12, 1924): I Love a Fight; Puttin' on the Ritz/W: Phil Cook, M: Tom Johnstone — If Flowers Could Speak/WM: Phil Cook, Tom Johnstone.

5168. Eartha Kitt (Jan. 17, 1927–) B: Columbia, SC. Best known as a cabaret singer, she started as a dancer with a scholarship from the KATHERINE DUNHAM dance troupe. *New Faces of 1952* (Royale, revue, May 16, 1952): Bal Petit Bal/WM: Francis Lemarque — Love Is a Simple Thing; Monotonous/W: June Carroll, M: Arthur Siegel — Waltzing in Venice with You/WM: Ronny Graham. *Mrs. Patterson* (National, "Teddy Hicks," Dec. 1, 1954): Be Good, Be Good, Be Good; If I Was a Boy; Mrs. Patterson; My Daddy Is a Dandy; Tea in Chicago/WM: James Shelton. *Timbuktu!* (Mark Hellinger, "Sahleem-la-Lume," Mar. 1, 1978): In the Beginning, Woman; Rahadlakum; Sands of Time/WM: Robert Wright, George Forrest, based on Alexander Borodin.

5169. Terri Klausner *Evita* (Broadway, "Eva," Sept. 25, 1979 matinees): The Actress Hasn't Learned (The Lines You'd Like to Hear); The Art of the Possible; Buenos Aires; Dice Are Rolling; Don't Cry for Me Argentina; Eva Beware of the City; Eva's Final Broadcast; Goodnight and Thank You; High Flying Adored; I'd Be Surprisingly Good for You; Lament; A New Argentina; Peron's Latest Flame; Rainbow High; Rainbow Tour; Waltz for Eva and Che/W: Tim Rice, M: Andrew Lloyd Webber. *Sophisticated Ladies* (Lunt-Fontanne, revue, Mar. 1, 1981): Bliblip/WM: Duke Ellington, Sid Kuller — Hit Me with a Hot Note and Watch Me Bounce/W: Don George, M: Duke Ellington — Imagine My Frustration/WM: Duke Ellington, Billy Strayhorn, Gerald Wilson — Just Squeeze Me/W: Lee Gaines, M: Duke Ellington — Mood Indigo/WM: Duke Ellington, Albany Bigard, Irving Mills.

5170. Paul Kleeman *Peg o' My Dreams* (Al

Jolson, "Arkady," May 5, 1924): Moscow Belles; Rose in the Snow/W: Anne Caldwell, M: Hugo Felix. *The Student Prince [in Heidelberg]* (Al Jolson, "Von Asterberg," Dec. 2, 1924): Come Boys, Let's All Be Gay, Boys (Students' March Song): Serenade; Student Life; To the Inn We're Marching/W: Dorothy Donnelly, M: Sigmund Romberg.

5171. Alisa Klein (June 10, 1971–) B: Cleveland, OH. *Grease* (New York City Center, return engagement, "Frenchy," Nov. 29, 1996): Beauty School Dropout/WM: Jim Jacobs, Warren Casey.

5172. Arthur Klein *Somebody's Sweetheart* (Central > Casino, "Roderic," Dec. 23, 1918): Spain/W: Arthur Hammerstein, M: Herbert Stothart.

5173. Reid Klein *The Sound of Music* (New York City Center, revival, "Rolf Gruber," Apr. 26, 1967): Sixteen, Going on Seventeen/W: Oscar Hammerstein II, M: Richard Rodgers. *Darling of the Day* (George Abbott, "Sydney," Jan. 27, 1968): Money, Money, Money/W: E.Y. Harburg, M: Jule Styne.

5174. Robert Klein (Feb. 8, 1942–) B: New York, NY. *New Faces of 1968* (Booth, revue, May 2, 1968): Love in a New Tempo/WM: Ronny Graham.

5175. Sally Klein (Jan. 21–) B: Toledo, OH. *Merrily We Roll Along* (Alvin, "Beth," Nov. 16, 1981): Bobby and Jackie and Jack; Opening Doors/WM: Stephen Sondheim.

5176. Stephen Klein *Jesus Christ Superstar* (Mark Hellinger, CR, "Caiaphas," 1972): The Arrest; Damned for All Time; Hosanna; Judas' Death; This Jesus Must Die; Trial Before Pilate/W: Tim Rice, M: Andrew Lloyd Webber.

5177. Werner Klemperer (Mar. 20, 1920– Dec. 6, 2000) B: Cologne, Germany. He played Col. Wilhelm Klink on the TV sitcom *Hogan's Heroes* (1965). *Cabaret* (Imperial, revival, "Herr Schultz," Oct. 22, 1987): It Couldn't Please Me More; Married; Meeskite/W: Fred Ebb, M: John Kander. *The Sound of Music* (New York State, revival, "Max Detweiler," Mar. 8, 1990): How Can Love Survive?; No Way to Stop It/W: Oscar Hammerstein II, M: Richard Rodgers.

5178. John Klendon *Poppy* (Apollo, CR, "Mortimer Pottle," May 19, 1924): A Picnic Party with You/W: Dorothy Donnelly, M: John C. Egan — What Do You Do Sunday, Mary?/W: Irving Caesar, M: Stephen Jones — When Men Are Alone/W: Dorothy Donnelly, M: Stephen Jones, Arthur Samuels.

5179. Dorothy Klewer *Miss 1917* (Century, revue, Nov. 5, 1917): Sammy/W: James O'Dea,

M: Edward Hutchinson — Who's Zoo in Girl Land/W: P.G. Wodehouse, M: Jerome Kern.

5180. Kevin Kline (Oct. 24, 1947–) B: St. Louis, MO. M: actress Phoebe Cates. Versatile, extremely popular actor of the stage and movies. *The Beggar's Opera* (Billy Rose, revival, "Macheath," Dec. 22, 1973): At the Tree I Shall Suffer with Pleasure; The Charge Was Prepar'd; Let Us Take the Road; My Heart Was So Free; O, What Pain It Is to Part; The Ways of the World; Were I Laid on Greenland Coast; Why How Now Madam Flirt; Would I Might Be Hanged/WM: John Gay. *The Robber Bridegroom* (Harkness, "Jamie Lockhart," Oct. 7, 1975): Love Stolen; The Real Mike Fink; Riches; Steal with Style/W: Alfred Uhry, M: Robert Waldman. *On the Twentieth Century* (St. James, "Bruce Granit," Feb. 19, 1978): Mine; Sign, Lily, Sign (Sextet)/W: Betty Comden, Adolph Green, M: Cy Coleman.

5181. Richard Kline (Apr. 29, 1944–) B: New York, NY. He played Larry Dallas in the TV sitcom *Three's Company* (1978). *City of Angels* (Virginia, CR, "Buddy Fidler," Apr. 23, 1991): The Buddy System; Double Talk/W: David Zippel, M: Cy Coleman.

5182. Helen Kling *Mary* (Knickerbocker, "Toddling Tessie," Oct. 18, 1920): Tom, Tom, Toddle/W: Otto Harbach, M: Louis A. Hirsch.

5183. Cindi Klinger *A Chorus Line* (Shubert, CR, "Judy," Nov. 23, 1987/c 1988): And.../W: Edward Kleban, M: Marvin Hamlisch.

5184. Pam Klinger *A Chorus Line* (Shubert, CR, "Maggie," Sept. 1981/c 1985/c 1987): At the Ballet/W: Edward Kleban, M: Marvin Hamlisch. *The Who's Tommy* (St. James, "Mrs. Simpson," Apr. 22, 1993): Sally Simpson/WM: Pete Townshend.

5185. Jack Klugman (Apr. 27, 1922–) B: Philadelphia, PA. Serious comic and dramatic actor from the theater to TV where he became Oscar Madison on the classic sitcom *The Odd Couple* (1970). *Gypsy* (Broadway, "Herbie," May 21, 1959): Small World; Together Wherever We Go; You'll Never Get Away from Me/W: Stephen Sondheim, M: Jule Styne.

5186. Judith (Judy) Knaiz (Nov. 7, 1940–) B: Pittsburgh, PA. *That's Entertainment* (Edison, revue, "Carol," Apr. 14, 1972): Confession; High and Low; How Low Can a Little Worm Go?; Miserable with You; Something to Remember You By; You're Not the Type/W: Howard Dietz, M: Arthur Schwartz. *No, No, Nanette* (46th Street, revival, CR, "Winnie Winslow," May 1, 1972): Telephone Girlie/W: Otto Harbach, M: Vincent Youmans.

5187. Dorothy Knapp (c 1900–) B: Dallas,

TX. Sometime girlfriend of Earl Carroll. As the star of *Fioretta*, she earned $1,000 a week until she was fired for lack of talent. The voluptuous Knapp sued and lost. *Earl Carroll's Vanities of 1923* (Earl Carroll, revue, July 5, 1923): The Band Plays Home Sweet Home [Dec. 17, 1923]; Get in a Bathing Suit/WM: Earl Carroll. *Ziegfeld Follies of 1924-1925* (New Amsterdam, revue, June 24, 1924): Home Again [Aug. 17, 1925]/W: Gene Buck, M: Raymond Hubbell — Someone, Someday, Somewhere [Mar. 10, 1925]/ W: Gene Buck, M: Rudolf Friml. *Fioretta* (Earl Carroll, "Fioretta Pepoli," Feb. 5, 1929): Dream Boat/W: Grace Henry, Jo Trent, M: George Bagby.

5188. Eleanore Knapp B: Passaic, NJ. *Man of La Mancha* (ANTA Washington Square, "The Housekeeper," Nov. 22, 1965): I'm Only Thinking of Him/W: Joe Darion, M: Mitch Leigh. *Man of La Mancha* (Vivian Beaumont, revival, "The Housekeeper," June 22, 1972): same as above.

5189. Marjorie Knapp B: Shreveport, LA. *Boys and Girls Together* (Broadhurst, revue, Oct. 1, 1940): Liable to Catch On/W: ?, M: Sammy Fain — Times Square Dance/W: Jack Yellen, M: Sammy Fain. *Star and Garter* (Music Box, revue, June 24, 1942): Brazilian Nuts [Jan. 31, 1943]/ W: Al Stillman, M: Dorival Caymmi — Bunny, Bunny, Bunny; Money [Jan. 31, 1943]/WM: Harold Rome — I Don't Get It/W: Sis Willner, M: Doris Tauber.

5190. Bernie Knee *Ballroom* (Majestic, "Nathan Bricker," Dec. 14, 1978): I've Been Waiting All My Life; More of the Same; One by One; A Song for Dancing/W: Alan Bergman, Marilyn Bergman, M: Billy Goldenberg.

5191. Tom Kneebone (1932–Nov. 15, 2003) B: Aukland, New Zealand. *Noel Coward's Sweet Potato* (Ethel Barrymore, revue, Sept. 29, 1968): Alice Is at It Again; I Wonder What Happened to Him?; Mad Dogs and Englishmen; Men About Town; Three White Feathers/WM: Noel Coward.

5192. Hildegarde Knef see HILDEGARDE NEFF.

5193. George S. Knight (Nov. 6, 1850–Jan. 14, 1892) B: Parkesburg, PA. *Evangeline, or The Belle of Arcadia* (Daly's, revival, "Capt. Dietrich," June 4, 1877): I'm in Lofe/W: J. Cheever Goodwin, M: Edward E. Rice.

5194. Hilda Knight *George White's Scandals of 1931* (Apollo, revue, Sept. 14, 1931): Back from Hollywood/W: Lew Brown, M: Ray Henderson. *Orchids Preferred* (Imperial, "Gertrude Devereaux," May 11, 1937): A Girl for the Man About Town/W: Frederick Herendeen, M: Dave Stamper.

5195. Jack Knight *Wonderful Town* (New York City Center, revival, "Wreck," May 17, 1967): Pass the Football/W: Betty Comden, Adolph Green, M: Leonard Bernstein.

5196. June Knight (Jan. 22, 1911–June 16, 1987) B: Los Angeles, CA.
Hot-cha! (Ziegfeld, "Dorothy Maxwell," Mar. 8, 1932): It's Great to Be Alive; There I Go Dreaming Again; You Can Make My Life a Bed of Roses/W: Lew Brown, M: Ray Henderson. *Take a Chance* (Apollo, "Toni Ray," Nov. 26, 1932): Oh, How I Long to Belong to You; Should I Be Sweet?; So Do I/W: B.G. DeSylva, M: Vincent Youmans — Turn Out the Light/W: B.G. DeSylva, M: Richard A. Whiting, Nacio Herb Brown. *Jubilee* (Imperial, "Karen O'Kane," Oct. 12, 1935): Begin the Beguine; Just One of Those Things; Mr. and Mrs. Smith; A Picture of Me Without You/WM: Cole Porter. *Sweethearts* (Shubert, revival, "Liane," Jan. 21, 1947): I Might Be Your Once-in-a-While; Jeannette and Her Little Wooden Shoes/W: Robert B. Smith, M: Victor Herbert.

5197. Patricia Knight (Apr. 28, 1918–) B: Boston, MA. M: film star Cornel Wilde, 1939-1951. *Sea Legs* (Mansfield, "Pat," May 18, 1937): Catalina; The Opposite Sex/W: Arthur Swanstrom, M: Michael H. Cleary.

5198. Percival Knight (c 1875–Nov. 27, 1923) B: Scotland. *Kitty Grey* (New Amsterdam, "Joseph," Jan. 25, 1909): A Gentleman's Gentleman/WM: Harold Lawson, Harold Samuels. *The Arcadians* (Liberty > Knickerbocker, "Peter Doody," Jan. 17, 1910): My Motter/W: Arthur Wimperis, M: Howard Talbot. *The Quaker Girl* (Park, "Jeremiah," Oct. 23, 1911): Just as Father Used to Do/W: Percy Greenbank, M: Lionel Monckton. *The Marriage Market* (Knickerbocker, "Lord Hurlingham," Sept. 22, 1913): Hand in Hand/W: Arthur Anderson, M: Victor Jacobi — I Always Come Back to You/W: Harry B. Smith, M: Leo Fall. *Go To It* (Princess, "The Private," Oct. 24, 1916): Extra!/WM: ?— Girls, If You Ever Get Married/W: Schuyler Greene, M: Charles N. Grant — Little by Little and Bit by Bit/W: Schuyler Greene, M: Worton David — There's Something About You Dear That Appeals to Me/W: Frank Craven, M: John L. Golden, Silvio Hein. *Apple Blossoms* (Globe, "Richard Stewart [Dickie]," Oct. 7, 1919): On the Banks of the Bronx/W: William Le Baron, M: Victor Jacobi — The Second Violin/W: William Le Baron, M: Fritz Kreisler.

5199. Bradley Knoche *Elsie Janis and Her*

Gang (Gaiety, revue, Jan. 16, 1922): Broadway/WM: Elsie Janis.

5200. Charles Knowlden *Tumble Inn* (Selwyn, CR, "Tom Harbison," June 2, 1919): Serve It Only for Two; The Thoughts That I Wrote on the Leaves of My Heart/W: Otto Harbach, M: Rudolf Friml.

5201. Alice Knowlton *The Belle of Mayfair* (Daly's, Dec. 3, 1906): My Lady Fair/W: ?, M: Leslie Stuart.

5202. Lola Knox *Starlight Express* (Gershwin, CR, "Buffy," c 1987): Engine of Love/W: Peter Reeves, Richard Stilgoe, M: Andrew Lloyd Webber — Lotta Locomotion; Pumping Iron; Race Two; Rolling Stock; U.N.C.O.U.P.L.E.D./ W: Richard Stilgoe, M: Andrew Lloyd Webber.

5203. Lucretia Knox *Runnin' Wild* (Colonial, revue, CR, "Mandy Little," Apr. 7, 1924): Old Fashioned Love/W: Cecil Mack, M: James P. Johnson.

5204. Teddy Knox (July 12, 1894–Dec. 1, 1974) B: Gateshead, England. Comedy partner of JIMMY NERVO. *Pins and Needles* (Shubert, revue, Feb. 1, 1922): Piccadilly Walk/W: Ira Gershwin, Arthur Riscoe, M: Edward A. Horan — Slow Movies/WM: ?.

5205. Kurt Knudson (Sept. 7, 1936–) B: Fargo, ND. *Take Me Along* (Martin Beck, revival, "Sid Davis," Apr. 14, 1985): But Yours; I Get Embarrassed; In the Company of Men; Little Green Snake; Sid Ole Kid; Take Me Along/WM: Bob Merrill. *Beauty and the Beast* (Palace, CR, "Maurice," c 1994): No Matter What/W: Tim Rice, M: Alan Menken.

5206. Ruth Kobart (Apr. 24, 1924–Dec. 14. 2002) B: Des Moines, IA. *Pipe Dream* (Shubert, CR, "Fauna," 20x during run): All at Once You Love Her; Bums' Opera; The Happiest House on the Block; How Long?; Suzy Is a Good Thing; Sweet Thursday; We Are a Gang of Witches; Will You Marry Me?/W: Oscar Hammerstein II, M: Richard Rodgers. *The Cradle Will Rock* (New York City Center, revival, "Mrs. Mister," Feb. 11, 1960): Ah, There You Are; Art for Art's Sake; Hard Times; War! War!/WM: Marc Blitzstein. *Street Scene* (New York City Center, revival, "Emma Jones," Feb. 13, 1960): Ain't It Awful, the Heat?; Get a Load of That; Ice Cream; When a Woman Has a Baby/W: Langston Hughes, Elmer Rice, M: Kurt Weill. *How to Succeed in Business Without Really Trying* (46th Street, "Miss Jones," Oct. 14, 1961): Brotherhood of Man; Paris Original/WM: Frank Loesser. *A Funny Thing Happened on the Way to the Forum* (Alvin, "Domina," May 8, 1962): That Dirty Old Man/WM: Stephen Sondheim.

Oklahoma! (New York City Center, revival, "Aunt Eller Murphy," Dec. 15, 1965): The Farmer and the Cowman; Kansas City; Oklahoma; The Surrey with the Fringe on Top/W: Oscar Hammerstein II, M: Richard Rodgers. *Annie* (Alvin, CR, "Miss Hannigan," Feb. 24, 1982): Easy Street; Little Girls/W: Martin Charnin, M: Charles Strouse.

5207. Michael Koetting *Cats* (Winter Garden, CR, "Alonzo"): Macavity/W: T.S. Eliot, M: Andrew Lloyd Webber.

5208. Florence Kolb *The Paradise of Mahomet* (Herald Square, "Babouch," Jan. 17, 1911): Gypsy Song/W: Harry B. Smith, M: Robert Planquette.

5209. Robert Kole *Wonderful Town* (Winter Garden, "Policeman," Feb. 25, 1953): My Darlin' Eileen/W: Betty Comden, Adolph Green, M: Leonard Bernstein.

5210. Joseph Kolinski (June 26, 1953–) B: Detroit, MI. *Dance a Little Closer* (Minskoff, "Heinrich Walter," May 11, 1983): What Are You Going to Do About It?/W: Alan Jay Lerner, M: Charles Strouse. *The Human Comedy* (Royale, "Tobey," Apr. 5, 1984): Everlasting; I'm Home; I've Known a Lot of Guys; Marcus, My Friend; An Orphan Am I/W: William Dumaresq, M: Galt MacDermot. *The Three Musketeers* (Broadway, revival, "Duke of Buckingham," Nov. 11, 1984): L'Amour, Toujours, L'Amour/W: Catherine Chisholm Cushing, M: Rudolf Friml — My Dreams/W: Clifford Grey, M: Rudolf Friml. *Les Misérables* (Broadway, CR, "Enjolras"): Do You Hear the People Sing?; Red and Black/W: Herbert Kretzmer, M: Claude-Michel Schonberg.

5211. Richard Kollmar (Dec. 31, 1910–Jan. 7, 1971) B: Ridgewood, NJ. M: journalist Dorothy Kilgalen, with whom he broadcast a popular breakfast hour radio program called *Dorothy and Dick* (1954). *Knickerbocker Holiday* (Ethel Barrymore, "Brom Broeck," Oct. 19, 1938): How Can You Tell an American?; It Never Was You; There's Nowhere to Go but Up; We Are Cut in Twain; Will You Remember Me?; Young People Think About Love/W: Maxwell Anderson, M: Kurt Weill. *Too Many Girls* (Imperial, "Clint Kelley," Oct. 18, 1939): I Didn't Know What Time It Was; I Like to Recognize the Tune; Love Never Went to College; Spic and Spanish; Tempt Me Not/W: Lorenz Hart, M: Richard Rodgers. *Crazy with the Heat* (44th Street, revue, Jan. 14, 1941): It Should Happen to Me/W: Richard Kollmar, M: Elsie Thompson — Some Day/W: Kurt Kasznar, Carl Kent, M: Rudi Revil. *Early to Bed* (Broadhurst, "El Magnifico," June 17, 1943): Long Time No Song; Me and

My Old World Charm; Supple Couple; There's Yes in the Air (Martinique); This Is So Nice/W: George Marion, Jr., M: Fats Waller.

5212. Bonnie Koloc (Feb. 6, 1946–) B: Waterloo, IA. *The Human Comedy* (Royale, "Mrs. Kate Macauley," Apr. 5, 1984): Daddy Will Not Come Walking Through the Door; Everything Is Changed; Long Past Sunset; Parting; Remember Always to Give; We're a Little Family; The World Is Full of Loneliness/W: William Dumaresq, M: Galt MacDermot.

5213. James (Jimmie) Komack (Aug. 3, 1924–Dec. 24, 1997) B: New York, NY. Writer, producer and actor, mostly for TV. *Damn Yankees* (46th Street, "Rocky," May 5, 1955): The Game; Heart/WM: Richard Adler, Jerry Ross.

5214. Philip Lyle Kong (Sept. 23, 1986–) B: Lattingtown, NY. *Miss Saigon* (Broadway, "Tam," Apr. 11, 1991, Mon., Wed., Fri., Sat. evenings): Little God of My Heart/W: Richard Maltby, Jr., Alain Boublil, M: Claude-Michel Schonberg.

5215. Norma Kopp M: WILLIAM DANFORTH. *The Idol's Eye* (Broadway, "Damayanti," Oct. 25, 1897): The Lady and the Kick/W: Harry B. Smith, M: Victor Herbert.

5216. Eddie Korbich (Nov. 6, 1960–) B: Washington, DC. *Sweeney Todd* (Circle in the Square, revival, "Tobias Ragg," Sept. 14, 1989): God, That's Good; Not While I'm Around; Parlor Songs; Pirelli's Miracle Elixir/WM: Stephen Sondheim. *Carousel* (Lincoln Center, revival, "Enoch Snow," Mar. 24, 1994): Geraniums in the Winder; Mister Snow; Stonecutters Cut It on the Stone; When the Children Are Asleep/W: Oscar Hammerstein II, M: Richard Rodgers.

5217. Alix (Alexandra) Korey (May 14–) B: Brooklyn, NY. *Hello, Dolly!* (Lunt-Fontanne, revival, "Minnie Fay," Mar. 5, 1978): Dancing/WM: Jerry Herman — Elegance; Motherhood/WM: Bob Merrill, Jerry Herman. *Ain't Broadway Grand* (Lunt-Fontanne, "Harriet Popkin," Apr. 18, 1993): Ain't Broadway Grand; They'll Never Take Us Alive/W: Lee Adams, M: Mitch Leigh.

5218. Richard Korthaze (Feb. 11–) B: Chicago, IL. *Chicago* (46th Street, "Sgt. Fogarty," June 3, 1975): Funny Honey/W: Fred Ebb, M: John Kander. *Chicago* (46th Street, CR, "Amos Hart," Aug. 1977): Mr. Cellophane/W: Fred Ebb, M: John Kander.

5219. Marie Kosco *The Greenwich Village Follies of 1928* (Winter Garden, revue, Apr. 9, 1928): Down at the Village/W: Max Lief, Nathaniel Lief, M: Maurie Rubens.

5220. Alexis Kosloff *The Show of Wonders* (Winter Garden, revue, Oct. 26, 1916): Diabolo/W: Harold Atteridge, M: Herman Timberg.

5221. Tessa Kosta (1893–Aug. 23, 1981) B: Chicago, IL. *The Beauty Shop* (Astor, "Anna Budd," Apr. 13, 1914): Come Along, Little Girl, Come Along; Give Us Your Kind Applause; The Tale of a Mermaid/W: Rennold Wolf, M: Charles J. Gebest — Love's Hesitation/W: Maurice E. Marks, M: Charles J. Gebest. *Chu Chin Chow* (Manhattan Opera House > Century, "Marjanah," Oct. 22, 1917): I Love You So/W: Hartley Carrick, M: Frederic Norton. *The Royal Vagabond* (Cohan and Harris, "Anitza Chefcheck," Feb. 17, 1919): Goodbye, Bargravia/WM: George M. Cohan — Love of Mine/W: William Cary Duncan, M: Anselm Goetzl — When the Cherry Blossoms Fall (Love Is Love)/W: Stephen Ivor Szinnyey, William Cary Duncan, M: Anselm Goetzl. *Lassie* (Nora Bayes, "Kitty McKay," Apr. 6, 1920): Echo; Fairy Whispers; Lovely Corals; A Teacup and a Spoon/W: Catherine Chisholm Cushing, M: Hugo Felix. *Princess Virtue* (Central, "Liane Demarest [Princess Virtue]," May 4, 1921): Princess Virtue; Smoke Rings; When I Meet Love/WM: Gitz Rice, B.C. Hilliam. *The Chocolate Soldier* (Century, revival, "Nadina," Dec. 12, 1921): The Chocolate Soldier; The Letter Song; My Hero; Never Was There Such a Lover; Seek the Spy; Sympathy; The Tale of a Coat; That Would Be Lovely/W: Stanislaus Stange, M: Oscar Straus. *The Rose of Stamboul* (Century, "Kondja Gul," Mar. 7, 1922): My Heart Is Calling; Waltz Duet; With Papers Duly Signed/W: Harold Atteridge, M: Sigmund Romberg. *Caroline* (Ambassador, "Caroline Lee," Jan. 31, 1923): Land of Enchantment (Land of Romance)/W: Harry B. Smith, M: Edward Kunneke, Alfred Goodman — The Man in the Moon; Sweetheart; Will o' the Wisp/W: Harry B. Smith, M: Edward Kunneke — Who Cares for a Name/W: Harry B. Smith, M: Edward Delaney Dunn, Edward Kunneke. *Princess April* (Ambassador, "April Daley," Dec. 1, 1924): Champagne; The Love Clock (Tick-Tock-Tick-Tock); Sweetheart of Mine; Tantalizing April/WM: Monte Carlo, Alma Sanders. *Song of the Flame* (44th Street, "Aniuta," Dec. 30, 1925): The Cossack Love Song (Don't Forget Me); Song of the Flame/W: Otto Harbach, Oscar Hammerstein II, M: George Gershwin, Herbert Stothart — Midnight Bells; The Signal/W: Otto Harbach, Oscar Hammerstein II, M: George Gershwin — Wander Away/W: Otto Harbach, Oscar Hammerstein II, M: Herbert Stothart. *The Fortune Teller* (Al Jolson, revival,

"Irma" and "Musette," Nov. 4, 1929): Always Do As People Say You Should; Gypsy Love Song (Slumber On, My Little Gypsy Sweetheart); The Lily and the Nightingale; Romany Life (Czardas)/W: Harry B. Smith, M: Victor Herbert.

5222. Dorothy Koster *George White's Scandals of 1939-40* (Alvin, revue, Aug. 28, 1939): Smart Little Girls/W: Jack Yellen, M: Sammy Fain.

5223. Nellie Kouns *Frivolities of 1920* (44th Street, revue, Jan. 8, 1920): Echo Song; A Spanish Aria/WM: William B. Friedlander.

5224. Sara Kouns *Frivolities of 1920* (44th Street, revue, Jan. 8, 1920): Echo Song; In Peacock Alley/WM: William B. Friedlander.

5225. Nikos Kourkoulos (Dec. 5, 1934–) B: Athens, Greece. *Illya Darling* (Mark Hellinger, "Tonio," Apr. 11, 1967): After Love; Birthday Song; Medea Tango; Po, Po, Po/W: Joe Darion, M: Manos Hadjidakis.

5226. Hizi Koyke *The Geisha* (Erlanger's, revival, "O Mimosa San," Oct. 5, 1931): The Amorous Goldfish; A Geisha's Life; The Kissing Duet/W: Harry Greenbank, M: Sidney Jones — The Jewel of Asia/W: Harry Greenbank, M: James Philp.

5227. Valentina Kozlova *A Christmas Carol* (Madison Square Garden, return engagement, "Ghost of Christmas Future," Nov. 22, 1996): Dancing on Your Grave/W: Lynn Ahrens, M: Alan Menken.

5228. Tony Kraber (c 1905–Sept. 9, 1986) Actor, director, singer, playwright. *Johnny Johnson* (44th Street, "Private Harwood," Nov. 19, 1936): Oh, the Rio Grande (Cowboy Song)/W: Paul Green, M: Kurt Weill. *The Girl from Wyoming* (American Music Hall, "Sleepy," Oct. 29, 1938): The Dying Cowboy; Lullaby of the Plain/W: Ted Fetter, M: Richard Lewine.

5229. William Krach *Gentlemen Prefer Blondes* (Ziegfeld, "Tenor," Dec. 8, 1949): Coquette/W: Leo Robin, M: Jule Styne.

5230. Jean Kraemer *Can-Can* (Shubert, "Celestine," May 7, 1953): If You Loved Me Truly/WM: Cole Porter.

5231. Beatrice Kraft B: Englewood, NJ. *Sadie Thompson* (Alvin, "Honeypie," Nov. 16, 1944): Barrel of Beads; Siren of the Tropics/W: Howard Dietz, M: Vernon Duke. *Kismet* (Ziegfeld, "Princess Samaris of Bangalore," Dec. 3, 1953): Rahadlakum/WM: Robert Wright, George Forrest, M: based on Alexander Borodin. *Kismet* (New York State, revival, "Princess Samaris of Bangalore," June 22, 1965): same as above.

5232. Charles Kraft *Early to Bed* (Broad-hurst, "Charles," June 17, 1943): Get Away, Young Man/W: George Marion, Jr., M: Fats Waller.

5233. Jack Kraft *Buzzin' Around* (Casino, "Little Jack," July 6, 1920): O-I-L Spells Oil; Voulez-Vous/WM: Will Morrissey, Edward Madden.

5234. Jane Krakowski (Oct. 11, 1968–) B: Parsippany, NJ. *Starlight Express* (Gershwin, "Dinah," Mar. 15, 1987): Engine of Love; Final Selection; First Final; A Lotta Locomotion; Pumping Iron; Race One; Rolling Stock; There's Me; U.N.C.O.U.P.L.E.D./W: Richard Stilgoe, M: Andrew Lloyd Webber. *Grand Hotel* (Martin Beck, "Flaemmchen," Nov. 12, 1989): I Want to Go to Hollywood/WM: Maury Yeston. *Once Upon a Mattress* (Broadhurst, revival, "Lady Larken," Dec. 19, 1997): In a Little While; Normandy; An Opening for a Princess; Yesterday I Loved You/W: Marshall Barer, M: Mary Rodgers.

5235. Heidi Krall *Dance Me a Song* (Royale, revue, Jan. 20, 1950): One Is a Lonely Number/W: Maurice Valency, M: Albert Hague.

5236. Marsha Kramer (June 19, 1945–) B: Chicago, IL. *Peter Pan, or The Boy Who Wouldn't Grow Up* (Lunt-Fontanne, revival, "Wendy," Sept. 6, 1979): Distant Melody/W: Betty Comden, Adolph Green, M: Jule Styne — I'm Flying; Tender Shepherd/W: Carolyn Leigh, M: Moose Charlap.

5237. Charlotte Krauss *Reunion in New York* (Little, revue, Feb. 21, 1940): Stars in Your Eyes/WM: Fritz Kreisler.

5238. Harold Kravitt *Cherry Blossoms* (44th Street > Cosmopolitan, "The Bonze," Mar. 28, 1927): Feast of the Lanterns [May 1927]; Japanese Serenade/W: Harry B. Smith, M: Sigmund Romberg.

5239. Gary Krawford (Mar. 23, 1941–) B: Kitchener, Ontario, Canada. *Pousse-Cafe* (46th Street, "John Harmon," Mar. 18, 1966): Rules and Regulations/W: Marshall Barer, M: Duke Ellington. *The Education of H*Y*M*A*N K*A*P*L*A*N* (Alvin, "Mr. Parkhill," Apr. 4, 1968): A Dedicated Teacher; OOOO-EEEE; Strange New World/WM: Paul Nassau, Oscar Brand. *Company* (Alvin, CR, "Robert," Dec. 27, 1971): Barcelona; Being Alive; Company; Side by Side by Side; Someone Is Waiting; What Would We Do Without You?/WM: Stephen Sondheim.

5240. Beatrice Krebs *Street Scene* (New York City Center, revival, "Olga Olsen," Feb. 13, 1960): Ain't It Awful, the Heat?; Get a Load of That; Ice Cream/W: Langston Hughes, Elmer Rice, M: Kurt Weill.

5241. Hans Kriefall *Cats* (Winter Garden, CR, "Alonzo," Apr. 24, 1995): Macavity/W: T.S. Eliot, M: Andrew Lloyd Webber.

5242. Ilene Kristen (July 30, 1952–) B: Brooklyn, NY. *Grease* (Broadhurst, "Patty Simcox," June 7, 1972): Alma Mater/WM: Jim Jacobs, Warren Casey.

5243. Robert Kristen *Bajour* (Shubert, "3rd Patrolman," Nov. 23, 1964): Living Simply/ WM: Walter Marks.

5244. Dale Kristien (May 18–) B: Washington, DC. *The Phantom of the Opera* (Majestic, CR, "Christine Daae," July 1988, Mon. and Wed. evenings): All I Ask of You; Angel of Music; Bravo, Bravo; I Remember; Little Lotte; The Mirror; The Phantom of the Opera; The Point of No Return; Raoul, I've Been There; Stranger Than You Dreamt It; Think of Me; Wandering Child; Why Have You Brought Me Here; Wishing You Were Somehow Here Again/W: Charles Hart, Richard Stilgoe, M: Andrew Lloyd Webber.

5245. Carol Kristy *Mother Earth* (Belasco, revue, Oct. 19, 1972): Corn on the Macabre/ WM: Ron Thronson, Roger Ailes, Ray Golden — Pills/WM: Ray Golden — Plow It All Under/W: Ron Thronson, M: Toni Shearer.

5246. Ronnie Kroll *Oliver!* (Imperial, CR, "Oliver Twist," Nov. 18, 1963): Be Back Soon; Consider Yourself; I'd Do Anything; Oliver!; Where Is Love?; Who Will Buy?; You've Got to Pick a Pocket or Two/WM: Lionel Bart.

5247. Jacques Kruger *The Hurdy Gurdy Girl* (Wallack's, "Old Bunn," Sept. 23, 1907): Stories/W: Richard Carle, M: H.L. Heartz.

5248. Ottillie Kruger (Nov. 20, 1926–) B: New York, NY. *Naughty-Naught ['00]* (Old Knickerbocker Music Hall, revival, "Claire Granville," Oct. 19, 1946): Love Makes the World Go Round/W: Ted Fetter, M: Richard Lewine.

5249. Dania Krupska M: TED THURSTON. *The Girl in Pink Tights* (Mark Hellinger, "Hattie Hopkins," Mar. 5, 1954): Up in the Elevated Railway/W: Leo Robin, M: Sigmund Romberg.

5250. Jack Kruschen (Mar. 20, 1922–Apr. 2, 2002) B: Winnipeg, Canada. *I Can Get It for You Wholesale* (Shubert, "Maurice Pulvermacher," Mar. 22, 1962): I'm Not a Well Man/ WM: Harold Rome.

5251. Michael Kubala (Feb. 4, 1958–) B: Reading, PA. *Dancin'* (Broadhurst, revue, CR, May 8, 1979): Easy; If It Feels Good, Let It Ride/WM: Carol Bayer Sager, Melissa Manchester — Was Dog a Doughnut/WM: Cat Stevens.

Jerome Robbins' Broadway (Imperial, revue, Feb. 26, 1989): Comedy Tonight/WM: Stephen Sondheim — New York, New York; Ya Got Me/ W: Betty Comden, Adolph Green, M: Leonard Bernstein.

5252. Marc Kudisch (Sept. 22, 1966–) B: Hackensack, NJ. *Joseph and the Amazing Technicolor Dreamcoat* (Minskoff, revival, "Reuben," Nov. 10, 1993): One More Angel in Heaven/ WM: Tim Rice, Andrew Lloyd Webber. *Beauty and the Beast* (Palace, CR, "Gaston," c 1994): Belle; Gaston; The Mob Song/W: Howard Ashman, M: Alan Menken — Maison des Lunes; Me/W: Tim Rice, M: Alan Menken.

5253. Judy Kuhn (May 20, 1958–) B: New York, NY. *The Mystery of Edwin Drood* (Imperial, "Alice," Dec. 2, 1985): Moonfall/WM: Rupert Holmes. *Rags* (Mark Hellinger, "Bella Cohen," Aug. 21, 1986): For My Mary; Rags/W: Stephen Schwartz, M: Charles Strouse. *Les Miserables* (Broadway, "Cosette," Mar. 12, 1987): A Heart Full of Love; In My Life/W: Herbert Kretzmer, M: Claude-Michel Schonberg. *Chess* (Imperial, "Florence," Apr. 28, 1988): Anthem; Heaven Help My Heart; How Many Women; I Know Him So Well; Lullaby (Apukad Eros Kesen); A Model of Decorum & Tranquility; Nobody's on Nobody's Side; Press Conference; So You Got What You Want; Someone Else's Story; Terrace Duet; You and I; You Want to Lose Your Only Friend?/W: Tim Rice, M: Benny Anderson, Bjorn Ulvaeus. *She Loves Me* (Roundabout, revival, "Amalia Balash," June 10, 1993): Dear Friend; I Don't Know His Name; Ice Cream; No More Candy; Three Letters; Where's My Shoe?; Will He Like Me?/W: Sheldon Harnick, M: Jerry Bock.

5254. Eric Kunze *Miss Saigon* (Broadway, CR, "Chris"): The Ceremony; The Confrontation; The Guilt Inside Your Head; The Last Night of the World; Sun and Moon; The Telephone; Why God Why?/W: Richard Maltby, Jr., Alain Boublil, M: Claude-Michel Schonberg. *Damn Yankees* (Marquis, revival, CR, "Joe Hardy," c 1994): Goodbye, Old Girl; A Man Doesn't Know; Near to You; Shoeless Joe from Hannibal, Mo./WM: Richard Adler, Jerry Ross. *Les Miserables* (Broadway, CR, "Marius"): Empty Chairs at Empty Tables; A Heart Full of Love; In My Life; A Little Fall of Rain; Red and Black/W: Herbert Kretzmer, M: Claude-Michel Schonberg.

5255. Alvin Kupperman (Oct. 14, 1945–) B: Brooklyn, NY. *Minnie's Boys* (Imperial, "Herbie Marx [Zeppo]," Mar. 26, 1970): The Act; Be Happy; Four Nightingales; If You Wind Me

Up; More Precious Far; The Smell of Christmas; Where Was I When They Passed Out Luck?; You Don't Have to Do It for Me/W: Hal Hackady, M: Larry Grossman.

5256. Vilma Kurer (Oct. 6, 1914–) B: Melk, Austria. *Reunion in New York* (Little, revue, Feb. 21, 1940): A Character in Search of a Character/W: David Greggory, M: Berenece Kazounoff — I'm Going Crazy with Strauss/WM: Werner Michel, Peter Barry — Where Is My Homeland/W: Werner Michel, August Spectorsky, M: Nelly Franck.

5257. Julie Kurnitz (Sept. 8, 1942–) B: Mt. Vernon, NY. *Minnie's Boys* (Imperial, "Mrs. McNish," Mar. 26, 1970): You Remind Me of You/W: Hal Hackady, M: Larry Grossman.

5258. Ron Kurowski (Mar. 14, 1953–) B: Philadelphia, PA. *A Chorus Line* (Shubert, CR, "Bobby," Jan. 1978/Aug. 1984): And.../W: Edward Kleban, M: Marvin Hamlisch.

5259. John Henry Kurtz *Marlowe* (Rialto, "Richard Burbage," Oct. 12, 1981): Because I'm a Woman; The Funeral Dirge; Higher Than High; So Do I (Ode to Virginity)/WM: Leo Rost, Jimmy Horowitz.

5260. Swoosie Kurtz (Sept. 6, 1944–) B: Omaha, NE. *A History of the American Film* (ANTA, revue, "Bette," Mar. 30, 1978): Apple Blossom Victory; Ostende Nobis Tosca; Pretty Pin-Up; They Can't Prohibit Love/W: Christopher Durang, M: Mel Marvin.

5261. Bill Kux (June 26, 1953–) B: Detroit, MI. *Ain't Broadway Grand* (Lunt-Fontanne, "Waldo Klein," Apr. 18, 1993): Ain't Broadway Grand; The Theater, The Theater/W: Lee Adams, M: Mitch Leigh.

5262. Kyme *Honky Tonk Nights* (Biltmore, "Ivy Vine," Aug. 7, 1986): Roll with the Punches; The Sampson Beauties; Tapaholics/W: Ralph Allen, David Campbell, M: Michael Valenti. *Oh, Kay!* (Richard Rodgers, revival, "Dolly Greene," Nov. 1, 1990): Show Me the Town; Slap That Bass; Sleepless Nights; You've Got What Gets Me/W: Ira Gershwin, M: George Gershwin.

5263. Jane LaBanz B: Cincinnati, OH. *Anything Goes* (Vivian Beaumont, revival, CR, "Young Girl"): There's No Cure Like Travel/WM: Cole Porter.

5264. Arthur Laceby *Our Miss Gibbs* (Knickerbocker, "Mr. Toplady," Aug. 29, 1910): An English Gentleman/W: Percy Greenbank, M: Lionel Monckton. *The Rose Maid* (Globe, "Chumley," Apr. 22, 1912): Money Talks; Telephone Song/W: Robert B. Smith, M: Bruno Granichstaedten.

5265. Florence Lacey *Hello, Dolly!* (Lunt-Fontanne, revival, "Irene Molloy," Mar. 5, 1978): Dancing; It Only Takes a Moment; Ribbons Down My Back/WM: Jerry Herman — Elegance; Motherhood/WM: Bob Merrill, Jerry Herman. *The Grand Tour* (Palace, "Marianne," Jan. 11, 1979): For Poland; I Belong Here; More and More/Less and Less; One Extraordinary Thing; We're Almost There/WM: Jerry Herman. *Evita* (Broadway, CR, "Eva," May 30, 1983): The Actress Hasn't Learned (The Lines You'd Like to Hear); The Art of the Possible; Dice Are Rolling; Don't Cry for Me Argentina; Eva Beware of the City; Eva's Final Broadcast; Goodnight and Thank You; High Flying Adored; I'd Be Surprisingly Good for You; Lament; A New Argentina; Peron's Latest Flame; Rainbow High; Rainbow Tour; Waltz for Eva and Che/W: Tim Rice, M: Andrew Lloyd Webber. *Hello, Dolly!* (Lunt-Fontanne, revival, "Irene Molloy," Oct. 19, 1995): same as above. *Les Miserables* (Broadway, CR, "Fantine," Sept. 10, 1996): Come to Me; I Dreamed a Dream/W: Herbert Kretzmer, M: Claude-Michel Schonberg.

5266. LaChanze (Dec. 16, 1961–) B: St. Augustine, FL. *Once on This Island* (Booth, "Ti Moune," Oct. 18, 1990): The Ball; Forever Yours; Pray; Ti Moune; Waiting for Life/W: Lynn Ahrens, M: Stephen Flaherty.

5267. Herndon Lackey *Les Miserables* (Broadway, CR, "Javert," Jan. 17, 1989): Soliloquy; Stars/W: Herbert Kretzmer, M: Claude-Michel Schonberg. *Kiss of the Spider Woman* (Broadhurst, "Warden," May 3, 1993): Over the Wall IV — Lucky Molina/W: Fred Ebb, M: John Kander.

5268. Harry Lacy *Cinderella at School* (Daly's, "Arthur Bicycle," Mar. 5, 1881): Maiden Fair Awake to Me; Pretty Little Shoe; 'Tis Not Becoming in a Maiden/WM: Woolson Morse.

5269. Hank Ladd (Dec. 12, 1908–June 9, 1982) B: Chicago, IL. M: FRANCETTA MALLOY. *Angel in the Wings* (Coronet, revue, Dec. 11, 1947): Long Green Blues; The Thousand Islands Song/WM: Bob Hilliard, Carl Sigman. *Along Fifth Avenue* (Broadhurst, revue, Jan. 13, 1949): Call It Applefritters/W: Milton Pascal, M: Richard Stutz.

5270. William Ladd *Peg o' My Dreams* (Al Jolson, "Chris," May 5, 1924): All Alone; Right-O/W: Anne Caldwell, M: Hugo Felix. *Hassard Short's Ritz Revue* (Ritz > Winter Garden, revue, Sept. 17, 1924): Beedle-Um-Bee/W: Eric Valentine, William Gaston, M: Martin Broones — The Little Black Cat/W: Anne Caldwell, M: Raymond Hubbell — Uking the Uke/WM: W.

Franke Harling — When You and I Were Dancing/W: Graham John, M: H.M. Tennant. *The Greenwich Village Follies of 1925* (46th Street, revue, Dec. 24, 1925): The Dancing Doctor; You Have Me — I Have You/W: Owen Murphy, M: Harold A. Levey.

5271. Robert La Fosse B: Beaumont, TX. *Jerome Robbins' Broadway* (Imperial, revue, Feb. 26, 1989): New York, New York/W: Betty Comden, Adolph Green, M: Leonard Bernstein.

5272. Irma-Estel LaGuerre *The King and I* (Broadway, revival, "Lady Thiang," Jan. 7, 1985): Something Wonderful; Western People Funny/W: Oscar Hammerstein II, M: Richard Rodgers.

5273. Rose La Harte (c 1891–Jan. 20, 1958) B: Cincinnati, OH. *The Fisher Maiden* (Victoria, "Georgiana," Oct. 5, 1903): Roses for the Girl I Love/W: Arthur J. Lamb, M: Harry Von Tilzer. *A Society Circus* (Hippodrome, "The Lady Volumnia," Dec. 13, 1905): The Laughing School; Tainted Gold/WM: Sydney Rosenfeld, Manuel Klein. *The Auto Race* (Hippodrome, revue, "Mrs. Gay Spanker," Nov. 25, 1907): Riding in a Motor Car/WM: Manuel Klein. *Around the World* (Hippodrome, revue, "Mrs. Grantwood Leigh," Sept. 2, 1911): Sweet Senorita/WM: Manuel Klein. *The Matinee Girl* (Forrest, "Maria Mendez," Feb. 1, 1926): His Spanish Guitar/W: McElbert Moore, Bide Dudley, M: Frank Grey. *Yvette* (39th Street, "Countess Rochebaron," Aug. 10, 1916): American Beauties/WM: Frederick Herendeen.

5274. Bert Lahr (Aug. 13, 1895–Dec. 4, 1967) B: New York, NY. Star actor and comedian of the stage and nightclubs for almost 40 years. Especially loved as the Cowardly Lion in the classic movie *The Wizard of Oz* (1939). *Hold Everything!* (Broadhurst, "Gink Schiner," Oct. 10, 1928): Oh, Gosh; When I Love, I Love/W: B.G. DeSylva, Lew Brown, M: Ray Henderson. *Flying High* (Apollo, "Rusty Krause," Mar. 3, 1930): Mrs. Krause's Blue-Eyed Baby Boy; This Will Be the First Time for Me/W: B.G. DeSylva, Lew Brown, M: Ray Henderson. *Hot-cha!* (Ziegfeld, "Alky Schmidt," Mar. 8, 1932): I Make Up for That in Other Ways; I Want Another Portion of That/W: Lew Brown, M: Ray Henderson. *George White's Music Hall Varieties* (Casino, revue, Nov. 22, 1932): A Bottle and a Bird/WM: Irving Caesar — Cabin in the Cotton/W: Irving Caesar, George White, M: Harold Arlen — Let's Put Out the Lights and Go to Sleep/WM: Herman Hupfeld — Two Feet in Two-Four Time/W: Irving Caesar, M: Harold Arlen. *Life Begins at 8:40* (Winter Garden, revue, Aug. 27, 1934): Life

Begins at City Hall (Beautifying the City); Quartet Erotica; Things!/W: Ira Gershwin, E.Y. Harburg, M: Harold Arlen. *George White's Scandals of 1936* (New Amsterdam, revue, Dec. 25, 1935): The Buxom Mrs. Bascom; I'm the Fellow Who Loves You/W: Jack Yellen, M: Ray Henderson. *The Show Is On* (Winter Garden, revue, Dec. 25, 1936): Song of the Woodman/W: E.Y. Harburg, M: Harold Arlen — Woof/W: Norman Zeno, M: Will Irwin. *Du Barry Was a Lady* (46th Street > Royale, "Louis Blore" and "Louis XV," Dec. 6, 1939): But in the Morning, No!; Friendship; It Ain't Etiquette/WM: Cole Porter. *Seven Lively Arts* (Ziegfeld, revue, Dec. 7, 1944): Drink, Drink, Drink/WM: Cole Porter. *Two on the Aisle* (Mark Hellinger, revue, July 19, 1951): Catch Our Act at the Met; The Clown/W: Betty Comden, Adolph Green, M: Jule Styne. *The Girls Against the Boys* (Alvin, revue, Nov. 2, 1959): Too Young to Live/W: Arnold B. Horwitt, M: Richard Lewine — Nobody Else but You/W: Arnold B. Horwitt, M: Albert Hague. *Foxy* (Ziegfeld, "Foxy," Feb. 16, 1964): Bon Vivant; Many Ways to Skin a Cat; Money Isn't Everything/W: Johnny Mercer, M: Robert Emmett Dolan.

5275. Barbara Lail (Apr. 6, 1950–) *Good News* (St. James, revival, "Babe O'Day," Dec. 23, 1974): Button Up Your Overcoat; Varsity Drag/W: B.G. DeSylva, Lew Brown, M: Ray Henderson.

5276. Cleo Laine (Oct. 28, 1927–) B: Southall, England. Jazz singer of international fame. *The Mystery of Edwin Drood* (Imperial, "Princess Puffer," Dec. 2, 1985): Don't Quit While You're Ahead; The Garden Path to Hell; Settling Up the Score; The Wages of Sin/WM: Rupert Holmes.

5277. George Laird *Parisiana* (Edyth Totten, revue, Feb. 9, 1928): Golliwog; Keep It Under Your Hat/WM: Vincent Valentini.

5278. Gladys Laird *The Garrick Gaieties of 1926* (Garrick, revue, May 10, 1926): Mountain Greenery/W: Lorenz Hart, M: Richard Rodgers.

5279. Harriette Lake (Jan. 22, 1909–Mar. 15, 2001) B: Valley City, ND. Known in her Hollywood years as ANN SOTHERN. She played Susie McNamara in the TV sitcom *Private Secretary* (1953). *America's Sweetheart* (Broadhurst, "Geraldine Marsh," Feb. 10, 1931): I've Got Five Dollars; We'll Be the Same/W: Lorenz Hart, M: Richard Rodgers. *Everybody's Welcome* (Shubert, "Ann Cathway," Oct. 13, 1931): (I'm) All Wrapped Up in You/W: Mack Gordon, Harold Adamson, M: Harry Revel — Even as You and I; You've Got a Lease on My

Heart/W: Irving Kahal, M: Sammy Fain — Ta Ta, Ol' Bean/W: Edward Eliscu, M: Manning Sherwin. *Of Thee I Sing* (Imperial, return engagement, CR, "Mary Turner," May 15, 1933): I'm About to Be a Mother (Who Could Ask for Anything More?); Of Thee I Sing; Who Cares?/W: Ira Gershwin, M: George Gershwin.

5280. Frank Lalor (Aug. 20, 1869–Oct. 15, 1932) B: Washington, DC. *The Show Girl or The Cap of Fortune* (Wallack's, "Dionysius Lye," May 5, 1902): The Family Ghost; I'm a Simple Author-Manager; Reggie's Family Tree/W: D.K. Stevens, M: H.L. Heartz — In Gay Japan; Invocation to Pie/W: D.K. Stevens, M: M.W. Daniels. *Mr. Wix of Wickham* (Bijou, "Shamus O'Scoot," Sept. 19, 1904): Googy-oo/WM: John Wagner, Edward E. Rice — Saturday 'Till Monday/WM: John Wagner, Jerome Kern. *The Bachelor Belles* (Globe, "Tim Jones," Nov. 7, 1910): Everybody Brushes By/W: Harry B. Smith, M: Raymond Hubbell — Those Good Old Days Can Never Come Again (They Were the Happy Days/W: Harry B. Smith, M: Karl Hoschna — What Has Become of the Girls I Used to Know?/W: Harry B. Smith, M: Gus Edwards. *The Pink Lady* (New Amsterdam, "Philippe Dondidier," Mar. 13, 1911): Donny Didn't, Donny Did; Hide and Seek; I Like It!; The Intriguers/W: C.M.S. McLellan, M: Ivan Caryll. *Iole* (Longacre, "Clarence Guilford," Dec. 29, 1913): Nude Descending a Staircase; Oh What's the Use?; Take It from Me; To Rent, to Let/WM: ? — Oh Precious Thoughts/W: Robert W. Chambers, M: William F. Peters. *Papa's Darling* (New Amsterdam, "Achille Petipas," Nov. 2, 1914): The Popular Pop; A Touch of Spring/W: Harry B. Smith, M: Ivan Caryll. *Stop! Look! Listen!* (Globe, revue, "Gideon Gay," Dec. 25, 1915): Stop! Look! Listen!/WM: Irving Berlin. *The Amber Express* (Globe, "Percival Hopkins," Sept. 19, 1916): There's Nothing So Uncertain As a Dead Sure Thing; They Can't Run Off the Reels Too Fast for Me; You're a Hero/W: Marc Connelly, M: Zoel Parenteau, Robert Planquette. *His Little Widows* (Astor, "Abijah Smith," Apr. 30, 1917): Saints of the Latter Day; A Wife for Each Day in the Week/W: William Cary Duncan, M: William Schroeder — Salt Lake City/W: Benjamin Hapgood Burt, M: Silvio Hein — This Is the Best We Ever Struck/WM: ?. *Good Night, Paul* (Hudson, "Frank Forster," Sept. 3, 1917): I Like You/W: Roland Oliver, Charles Dickson, M: Harry B. Olsen. *Suzette* (Princess, "Tony," Nov. 24, 1921): Bagdad; A Modern Diplomat; Oh, Waiter; Saturday Evening Post/W: Roy Dixon, M: Arthur

Gutman. *Luckee Girl* (Casino, "Pontaves," Sept. 15, 1928): When I'm in Paree/WM: ?. *The Street Singer* (Shubert, "Prefect of Police," Sept. 17, 1929): Oh, Theobold, Oh, Elmer/WM: ?. *Robin Hood* (Erlanger's, revival, "Friar Tuck," Feb. 8, 1932): O, See the Lambkins Play!/W: Harry B. Smith, M: Reginald De Koven.

5281. Eleanor La Mance *Robin Hood* (Erlanger's, revival, "Allan-a-Dale," Feb. 8, 1932): The Bells of St. Swithins; Come the Bowmen in Lincoln Green; In Sherwood Forest; Milkmaid's Song/W: Harry B. Smith, M: Reginald De Koven — Oh, Promise Me/W: Clement Scott, M: Reginald De Koven.

5282. Al Lamar *Buster Brown* (Majestic, CR, "Jack Wynn," Feb. 27, 1905): I'll Be Your Honey/WM: ? — Sue, Sue I Love You/WM: Billie Taylor.

5283. Fernando Lamas (Jan. 9, 1915–Oct. 8, 1982) B: Buenos Aires, Argentina. M: ARLENE DAHL, 1954 to 1960; Esther Williams, movie star swimmer, 1967. The handsome baritone made a dozen Spanish- speaking movies in Buenos Aires before going to Hollywood in the early 1950s. *Happy Hunting* (Majestic, "The Duke of Granada," Dec. 6, 1956): Happy Hunting; It's Like a Beautiful Woman; Mutual Admiration Society; This Much I Know/W: Matt Dubey, M: Harold Karr.

5284. Gil Lamb (June 14, 1906–Nov. 2, 1995) B: Minneapolis, MN. Comic actor who appeared in 1940s Hollywood movie musicals. *Hold On to Your Hats* (Shubert, "Slim," Sept. 11, 1940): Don't Let It Get You Down/W: E.Y. Harburg, M: Burton Lane. *Sleepy Hollow* (St. James, "Ichabod Crane," June 3, 1948): If; A Musical Lesson/W: Miriam Battista, Russell Maloney, M: George Lessner — There's History to Be Made/W: Ruth Hughes Aarons, Miriam Battista, Russell Maloney, M: George Lessner. *70, Girls, 70* (Broadhurst, Apr. 15, 1971): Believe; Boom Ditty Boom; Do We?; Home/W: Fred Ebb, M: John Kander.

5285. Mary Ann Lamb (July 4, 1959–) B: Seattle, WA. *Starlight Express* (Gershwin, "Volta," Mar. 15, 1987): AC/DC; First Final; Pumping Iron; Race Two; Wide Smile, High Style, That's Me/W: Richard Stilgoe, M: Andrew Lloyd Webber.

5286. Ernest Lambart (c 1874–June 27, 1945) B: Ireland. Popular comedian for over 30 years. *The Girl from Kay's* (Herald Square, "Hon. Percy Fitzthistle," Nov. 2, 1903): Glass Glass/W: Aubrey Fitzgerald, M: Paul Rubens — My Birthday Party/W: Percy Greenbank, M: Paul Rubens. *Twiddle-Twaddle* (Weber's Music Hall,

"Hon. Algernon Fitz-Haggis," Jan. 1, 1906): Hats; 'Tis Dreadful! 'Tis Astounding/W: Edgar Smith, M: Maurice Levi. *Algeria* (Broadway, "Van Cortlandt Parke," Aug. 31, 1908): Little Bird of Paradise/W: Glen MacDonough, M: Victor Herbert. *Havana* (Casino, "Don Adolfo," Feb. 11, 1909): Cupid's Telephone; Hello People/W: George Arthurs, M: Leslie Stuart — Would You Like to Motor with Mater?/W: Adrian Ross, M: Leslie Stuart. *Our Miss Gibbs* (Knickerbocker, "Hon. Hughie Pierrepoint," Aug. 29, 1910): Bertie the Bounder/W: George Grossmith, M: Clarke — Eight Little Girls/W: M.E. Rourke, M: Jerome Kern — An English Gentleman/W: Percy Greenbank, M: Lionel Monckton — I Don't Want You to Be a Sister to Me/W: Frederick Day, M: Jerome Kern — Not That Sort of Person/WM: George Grossmith, Lionel Monckton. *The Red Rose* (Globe, "Hon. Lionel Talboys," June 22, 1911): Hammock Song (Then You Swing, Swing, Swing); If You Can't Sing, Dance/W: Robert B. Smith, M: Robert Hood Bowers.

5287. Beverly Lambert (May 20, 1956–) B: Stamford, CT. *Brigadoon* (New York State, revival, "Fiona MacLaren," Feb. 28, 1986): Almost Like Being in Love; Come to Me, Bend to Me; From This Day On; The Heather on the Hill; Waitin' for My Dearie/W: Alan Jay Lerner, M: Frederick Loewe.

5288. Edward Lambert *Mr. Strauss Goes to Boston* (New Century, "Elmo Tilt," Sept. 6, 1945): Down with Sin; Mr. Strauss Goes to Boston/W: Robert Sour, M: Robert Stolz. *If the Shoe Fits* (Century, "King Kindly," Dec. 5, 1946): I'm Not Myself Tonight; What's the Younger Generation Coming To?/W: June Carroll, M: David Raksin.

5289. Gloria Lambert A regular on the TV musical variety show *Sing Along with Mitch* (1961). *West Side Story* (Winter Garden, revival, "Rosalia," Apr. 27, 1960): I Feel Pretty/W: Stephen Sondheim, M: Leonard Bernstein.

5290. Happy (Jack) Lambert (Dec. 29, 1899–Mar. 1976) B: Ardrossan, Ayrshire, Scotland. *Everything* (Hippodrome, revue, Aug. 22, 1918): The Circus Is Coming to Town/WM: Irving Berlin — Everything Is Hunky Dory Down in Honky Tonk Town/W: Joseph McCarthy, M: Harry Tierney. *Happy Days* (Hippodrome, revue, Aug. 23, 1919): Be a Party at the Party Tonight; Happy Days/W: R.H. Burnside, M: Raymond Hubbell. *Good Times* (Hippodrome, revue, Aug. 9, 1920): Hands Up; Hello Imagination/W: R.H. Burnside, M: Raymond Hubbell. *Better Times* (Hippodrome, revue, Sept. 2,

1922): Gloom and Joy; I Dreamt That I Went to the Grand Opera Ball/W: R.H. Burnside, M: Raymond Hubbell.

5291. Harry Lambert (July 9, 1876–June 11, 1949) B: Dublin, Ireland. *Some Night* (Harris, "Bobby," Sept. 23, 1918): Everything Is Going Higher; I'll Be Waiting for You; When We Are Married/WM: Harry Delf.

5292. John Lambert *Stepping Stones* (Globe, "Remus," Nov. 6, 1923): Because You Love the Singer; Once In a Blue Moon; Pie; Raggedy Ann/W: Anne Caldwell, M: Jerome Kern. *Stepping Stones* (Globe, revival, "Remus," Sept. 1, 1924): same as above. *Criss Cross* (Globe, "Prof. Mazeroux," Oct. 12, 1926): Rose of Delight/W: Anne Caldwell, Otto Harbach, M: Jerome Kern. *Three Cheers* (Globe, "Malotte," Oct. 15, 1928): Bride Bells/W: B.G. DeSylva, M: Ray Henderson.

5293. Juliet Lambert (Jan. 15, 1964–) B: Massachusetts. *Meet Me in St. Louis* (Gershwin, "Rose Smith," Nov. 2, 1989): Ice/WM: Hugh Martin — A Raving Beauty; A Touch of the Irish/WM: Hugh Martin, Ralph Blane — Skip to My Lou/WM: Hugh Martin, Ralph Blane, trad. *Les Miserables* (Broadway, CR, "Fantine," Mar. 12, 1997): Come to Me; I Dreamed a Dream/W: Herbert Kretzmer, M: Claude-Michel Schonberg.

5294. Marie Lambert *Bunk of 1926* (Broadhurst, revue, CR, Apr. 26, 1926): Chatter/WM: Gene Lockhart — Cuddle Up/W: Gene Lockhart, M: Robert Armbruster — Do You Do the Charleston?; How Very Long Ago It Seems; The Milky Way/W: Percy Waxman, M: Gene Lockhart.

5295. Mark Lambert M: VICTORIA MALLORY. *A Little Night Music* (Shubert, "Henrik Egerman," Feb. 25, 1973): Later; Soon/WM: Stephen Sondheim. *Sondheim: A Musical Tribute* (Shubert, revue, Mar. 11, 1973): Two Fairy Tales/WM: Stephen Sondheim.

5296. Maude Lambert *When Johnny Comes Marching Home* (New York, "Cordelia Allen," Dec. 16, 1902): But They Didn't; The Drums; I Could Waltz On Forever; 'Twas Down in the Garden of Eden; While You're Thinking/W: Stanislaus Stange, M: Julian Edwards. *Florodora* (Broadway, revival, "Dolores," Mar. 27, 1905): The Queen of the Philippine Islands/WM: Paul Rubens — Somebody; When We're on the Stage/WM: ?. *The White Cat* (New Amsterdam, "Prince Peerless," Nov. 2, 1905): Goodbye, Maggie Doyle; Highland Mary/W: William Jerome, M: Jean Schwartz. *The Babes and the Baron* (Lyric, "Robin Hood," Dec. 25, 1905): By the

Light of the Honeymoon, or Kiss Me and Say You'll Be Mine/W: James O'Dea, M: Anne Caldwell — How D'Ye Do?/WM: F.R. Babcock — If I But Dared/WM: Nat D. Mann — An Outlaw Bold/WM: Arthur Weld. *The Midnight Sons* (Broadway, CR, "Mrs. Carrie Margin," Nov. 8, 1909): The Billiken Man; Eily Riley; Yankee Honeymoon/W: Glen MacDonough, M: Raymond Hubbell — My Sist' Tetrazin'/W: Edward Madden, M: Anatole Friedland. *The Summer Widowers* (Broadway, "Fritzi Fluff," June 4, 1910): Oh You Summertime Romeo!/W: Glen MacDonough, M: A. Baldwin Sloane. *Over the River* (Globe, "Mrs. Madison Parke," Jan. 8, 1912): For de Lawd's Sake, Play a Waltz/WM: Elsie Janis — My Irish Senorita/WM: John L. Golden, Edward Griffin, Henry Murtagh. *Maid in America* (Winter Garden, revue, "Anna Gray," Feb. 18, 1915): I'm Looking for Someone's Heart/W: Harold Atteridge, M: Sigmund Romberg.

5297. Robert Lambert (July 28, 1960–) B: Ypsilanti, MI. *Gypsy* (St. James, revival, "Tulsa," Nov. 16, 1989): All I Need Is the Girl/W: Stephen Sondheim, M: Jule Styne. *Gypsy* (Marquis, return engagement of revival, "Tulsa," Apr. 28, 1991): same as above.

5298. Heath Lamberts *Beauty and the Beast* (Palace, "Cogsworth," Apr. 18, 1994): Be Our Guest; Something There/W: Howard Ashman, M: Alan Menken. *Once Upon a Mattress* (Broadhurst, revival, "King Sextimus," Dec. 19, 1996): Man to Man Talk; The Minstrel, the Jester and I; Normandy/W: Marshall Barer, M: Mary Rodgers.

5299. Margaret LaMee *Pump Boys and Dinettes* (Princess, CR, "Rhetta Cupp," Feb. 9, 1983): Be Good or Be Gone/WM: Jim Wann.

5300. Robin Lamont (June 2, 1950–) B: Boston, MA. *Grease* (Broadhurst, CR, "Sandy Dumbrowski"): All Choked Up; It's Raining on Prom Night; Look at Me, I'm Sandra Dee; Summer Nights/WM: Jim Jacobs, Warren Casey.

5301. Mark Lamos (Mar. 10, 1946–) B: Chicago, IL. *Cyrano* (Palace, "Christian de Neuvillette," May 13, 1973): From Now Till Forever; It's She and It's Me; Roxana/W: Anthony Burgess, M: Michael J. Lewis.

5302. Peggy Hagen Lamprey *Rainbow Jones* (The Music Box, "Leona," Feb. 13, 1974): Bad Breath; Do Unto Others; Her Name Is Leona; I'd Like to Know You Better; A Little Bit of Me in You; One Big Happy Family; Wait a Little While; We All Need Love/WM: Jill Williams.

5303. Albert Lamson *Dr. Deluxe* (Knickerbocker, "Toodlums," Apr. 17, 1911): For Every

Boy That's Lonely There's a Girl That's Lonely Too/W: Otto Harbach, M: Karl Hoschna.

5304. Lucie Lancaster (Oct. 15, 1907–) B: Chicago, IL. *70, Girls, 70* (Broadhurst, Apr. 15, 1971): Believe; Boom Ditty Boom; Do We?; Hit It, Lorraine; Home/W: Fred Ebb, M: John Kander. *Pippin* (Imperial, CR, "Berthe," Apr. 1973/ July 1974/Sept. 1, 1975): No Time at All/WM: Stephen Schwartz.

5305. Bella Land (?–Mar. 24, 1882) B: London, England. *The White Fawn* (Niblo's Garden, CR, "Prince Leander," June 1, 1868): Prince Leander Is My Name; Waking at Early Dawn/W: James Mortimer, M: Edward Mollenhauer.

5306. Matt Landers (Oct. 21, 1952–) B: Mohawk Valley, NY. *Grease* (Broadhurst, CR, "Kenickie"): Greased Lightnin'/WM: Jim Jacobs, Warren Casey. *Working* (46th Street, "Fireman" and "Tie Salesman," May 14, 1978): Brother Trucker/WM: James Taylor — Un Mejor Dia Vendra/W: Graciela Daniele, Matt Landers, M: James Taylor.

5307. Gloria Wills Landes see GLORIA WILLS.

5308. Marla Landi (c 1937–) *New Girl in Town* (46th Street, "Pearl," May 14, 1957): Flings/WM: Bob Merrill.

5309. Nils Landin *The Merry Widow* (New York City Center, revival, "Camille De Jolidon," Oct. 8, 1944): A Dutiful Wife; Women/W: Adrian Ross, M: Franz Lehar.

5310. Carole Landis (Jan. 1, 1919–July 5, 1948) B: Fairchild, WI. Married and divorced 4 times from the age of 15, the blonde actress appeared in about 2 dozen movies. She committed suicide allegedly over a romance with REX HARRISON. *A Lady Says Yes* (Broadhurst, "Ghisella," Jan. 10, 1945): Don't Wake Them Up Too Soon; I'm Setting My Cap for a Throne; Without a Caress; You're More Than a Name and Address/W: Stanley Adams, M: Fred Spielman, Arthur Gershwin.

5311. Neville Landor *Blossom Time* (46th Street, revival, "Kupelweiser," Dec. 26, 1938): My Springtime Thou Art; Serenade/W: Dorothy Donnelly, M: Sigmund Romberg.

5312. Jack Landron (June 2, 1938–) B: San Juan, PR. *Hurry, Harry* (Ritz, "Marco" and "Native No. 5" and "Chorus Boy," Oct. 12, 1972): Africa Speaks; Hurry, Harry; When a Man Cries/W: David Finkle, M: Bill Weeden.

5313. Glenda Landry *Anne of Green Gables* (City Center 55th Street, "Diana Barry," Dec. 21, 1971): Ice Cream; Kindred Spirits/WM: Donald Harron, Norman Campbell.

5314. Abbe Lane (Dec. 14, 1932–) B: Brooklyn, NY. M: Latin bandleader Xavier Cugat, 1956-1963. He led his band and played the violin while she sang and danced. *Oh Captain!* (Alvin, "Bobo," Feb. 4, 1958): Double Standard; Femininity; Keep It Simple; You Don't Know Him; You're So Right for Me/WM: Jay Livingston, Ray Evans.

5315. Betty Lane B: Detroit, MI. *Porgy and Bess* (Uris, revival, "Clara," Sept. 25, 1976): Summertime/W: DuBose Heyward, M: George Gershwin.

5316. Bradley F. Lane *The Love Call* (Majestic, "Mike," Oct. 24, 1927): When I Take You All to London/W: Harry B. Smith, M: Sigmund Romberg.

5317. Clara Lane (c 1865–Mar. 15, 1952) B: Ellsworth, ME. *An Arabian Girl and the Forty Thieves* (Herald Square, "Morgiana," Apr. 29, 1899): Dashing Militaire/WM: John Gilbert — I'm a Little Lady; To the Cave Away!/W: J. Cheever Goodwin, M: ?.

5318. Edith Lane *My Romance* (Adelphi, CR, "Veronica De Witt," Jan. 3, 1949): Debutante/W: Rowland Leigh, M: Sigmund Romberg.

5319. Elmira Lane *The Lady in Ermine* (Century, CR, "Rosina," Feb. 19, 1923): Follow You All Over the World (I'll Follow You to Zanzibar); The Lady in Ermine/W: Cyrus D. Wood, M: Alfred Goodman — My Silhouette (Silhouette Duet)/W: Harry Graham, Cyrus D. Wood, M: Alfred Goodman, Jean Gilbert — Play with Fire/W: Cyrus D. Wood, M: Sigmund Romberg, Alfred Goodman.

5320. George Lane *Up in Central Park* (Century, "Richard Connolly, Comptroller of the City of New York," Jan. 27, 1945): Boss Tweed/W: Dorothy Fields, M: Sigmund Romberg. *Up in Central Park* (New York City Center, revival, "Richard Connolly, Comptroller of the City of New York, May 19, 1947): same as above.

5321. Harry Lane *The Yankee Tourist* (Astor, "Capt. O'Malley," Aug. 12, 1907): Irish Memories/W: Wallace Irwin, M: Alfred G. Robyn.

5322. James C. Lane *Little Miss Fix-It* (Globe, "Harold Watson," Apr. 3, 1911): No More Staying Out Late/WM: Nora Bayes, Jack Norworth, Bert Lee — There Is a Happy Land (Tale of Woe) [May 8, 1911]/W: Jack Norworth, M: Jerome Kern.

5323. Julia Lane *Peg o' My Dreams* (Al Jolson, "Diane," May 5, 1924): Right O; Shy Little Irish Smile/W: Anne Caldwell, M: Hugo Felix.

5324. Kenneth Lane *The Most Happy Fella* (New York City Center, revival, "Giuseppe,"

Feb. 10, 1959): Abbondanza; Benvenuta; Sposalizio/WM: Frank Loesser.

5325. Leota (Leotabel) Lane (c 1913–July 25, 1963) The sister of Lola, Rosemary and Priscilla who did not go on to Hollywood. *The Greenwich Village Follies of 1925* (Shubert, revue, CR, Mar. 15, 1926): The Curse of Cinderella; Lady of the Snow/W: Owen Murphy, M: Harold A. Levey — Whistle Away Your Blues/W: Leo Robin, M: Richard Myers. *Babes in Toyland* (Jolson, revival, "Contrary Mary," Dec. 23, 1929): Barney O'Flynn; Beatrice Barefacts; Before and After/W: Glen MacDonough, M: Victor Herbert.

5326. Lola Lane (May 21, 1906–June 22, 1981) B: Macy, IN. With ROSEMARY LANE and Priscilla Lane, one of the 3 singing Lane Sisters in Warner Bros. movies. *The Greenwich Village Follies of 1925* (Shubert, revue, CR, Mar. 15, 1926): Whistle Away Your Blues/W: Leo Robin, M: Richard Myers.

5327. Lupino Lane (June 16, 1892–Nov. 10, 1959) B: London, England. The singer, actor, dancer and comedian was an uncle of screen star Ida Lupino. *Afgar* (Central, "Coucourli," Nov. 8, 1920): I Hate the Lovely Women/W: Joseph McCarthy, M: Harry Tierney — Man from Mexico; We're the Gentlemen of the Harem/W: Douglas Furber, M: Charles Cuvillier. *Ziegfeld Follies of 1924-1925* (New Amsterdam, revue, June 24, 1924): All Pepped Up; I'd Like to Put You in a Cage and Look at You All Day; The Old Town Band/W: Joseph McCarthy, M: Harry Tierney — March of the Toys/W: Glen MacDonough, M: Victor Herbert — A Night in June/W: Gene Buck, M: Raymond Hubbell.

5328. Marjorie Lane M: BRIAN DONLEVY. *The Rise of Rosie O'Reilly* (Liberty, "Lillian Smith," Dec. 25, 1923): The Arrival of the Plot; Let's You and I Just Say Goodbye; Stage Society/WM: George M. Cohan. *The Merry Malones* (Erlanger's, "Annabelle," Sept. 26, 1927): Like the Wandering Minstrel; Roses Understand/WM: George M. Cohan. *Billie* (Erlanger's, "Winnie Sheldon," Oct. 1, 1928): Bluff; Come to St. Thomas'; I'm a One Girl Man; They Fall in Love; The Two of Us/WM: George M. Cohan.

5329. Mary Lane *What's in a Name* (Maxine Elliott, revue, Mar. 19, 1920): The Jewels of Pandora; The Theatrical Blues; What's in a Name? (Love Is Always Love)/W: John Murray Anderson, Jack Yellen, M: Milton Ager.

5330. Midgie Lane *Fast and Furious* (New Yorker, revue, Sept. 15, 1931): Boomerang/WM: J. Rosamond Johnson, Joe Jordan.

5331. Nancy Lane (June 16, 1951–) B: Passaic, NJ. *A Chorus Line* (Shubert, "Bebe," July 25, 1975): At the Ballet/W: Edward Kleban, M: Marvin Hamlisch.

5332. Nathan Lane (Feb. 3, 1956–) B: Jersey City, NJ. *Merlin* (Mark Hellinger, "Prince Fergus," Feb. 13, 1983): Fergus's Dilemma; We Haven't Fought a Battle in Years/W: Don Black, M: Elmer Bernstein. *Wind in the Willows* (Nederlander, "Toad," Dec. 19, 1985): Brief Encounter; The Gasoline Can-Can; S-S-Something Comes Over Me; That's What Friends Are For; Where Am I Now?; You'll Love It in Jail/WM: Roger McGough, William Perry. *Guys and Dolls* (Martin Beck, revival, "Nathan Detroit," Apr. 14, 1992): The Oldest Established; Sue Me/WM: Frank Loesser. *A Funny Thing Happened on the Way to the Forum* (St. James, revival, "Prologus" and "Pseudolus," Apr. 18, 1996): Bring Me My Bride; Comedy Tonight; Everybody Ought to Have a Maid; Free; The House of Marcus Lycus; Lovely/WM: Stephen Sondheim.

5333. Rosemary Lane (Apr. 14, 1914–Nov. 25, 1974) B: Indianola, IA. With LOLA LANE and Priscilla Lane, one of the 3 singing Lane Sisters in Warners movies. *Best Foot Forward* (Ethel Barrymore, "Gale Joy," Oct. 1, 1941): Ev'ry Time; I'd Gladly Trade; That's How I Love the Blues/WM: Hugh Martin, Ralph Blane — The Guy Who Brought Me/WM: Richard Rodgers, Hugh Martin.

5334. Augusta Lang *The Red Widow* (Astor, "Princess Sophya," Nov. 6, 1911): In Society It's Always Dress Parade/W: Rennold Wolf, Channing Pollock, M: Charles J. Gebest.

5335. Barbara Lang *A Little Night Music* (Shubert, "Mrs. Anderssen," Feb. 25, 1973): Perpetual Anticipation/WM: Stephen Sondheim. *So Long, 174th Street* (Harkness, "Angela," Apr. 27, 1976): Say the Words/WM: Stan Daniels. *The Robber Bridegroom* (Biltmore, return engagement, "Salome," Oct. 9, 1976): The Pricklepear Bloom; Riches/W: Alfred Uhry, M: Robert Waldman. *A Doll's Life* (Mark Hellinger, "Astrid," Sept. 23, 1982): Arrival; Departure; Letter from Klemnacht/W: Betty Comden, Adolph Green, M: Larry Grossman.

5336. Eric Lang *Man on the Moon* (Little, "Ernie Hardy," Jan. 29, 1975): Boys from the South; Convent; Love Is Coming Back; Midnight Deadline Blastoff; Mission Control; Place in Space; Speed of Light; Star Stepping Stranger/WM: John Phillips.

5337. Gertrude Lang (c 1899–Oct. 2, 1941) *The Passing Show of 1922* (Winter Garden, revue,

Sept. 20, 1922): I Came, I Saw, I Fell/W: Harold Atteridge, M: Alfred Goodman — Radiance/W: Jack Stanley, M: Alfred Goodman. *Half a Widow* (Waldorf, "Babette," Sept. 12, 1927): It's Great to Be a Doughboy; Longing for You; Tell Me Again/W: Frank Dupree, M: Shep Camp — Soldier Boy/WM: ?. *Music in May* (Casino, "Vita," Apr. 1, 1929): I Found a Friend; Open Your Window/W: J. Keirn Brennan, M: Maurie Rubens — I'm in Love/W: J. Keirn Brennan, M: Maurie Rubens, Emile Berte — Unto My Heart/W: J. Keirn Brennan, M: Emile Berte.

5338. Harold Lang (Dec. 21, 1920–July 26, 1985) B: Daly City, CA. *Look Ma, I'm Dancin'* (Adelphi, "Eddie Winkler," Jan. 29, 1948): Gotta Dance; The Two of Us/WM: Hugh Martin. *Kiss Me, Kate* (New Century, "Bill Calhoun" and "Lucentio," Dec. 30, 1948): Bianca; I Sing of Love; Tom, Dick or Harry; We Open in Venice/WM: Cole Porter. *Make a Wish* (Winter Garden, "Ricky," Apr. 18, 1951): I'll Never Make a Frenchman Out of You; Take Me Back to Texas with You/W: Timothy Gray, M: Hugh Martin — Suits Me Fine; That Face!; Who Gives a Sou?/WM: Hugh Martin. *Pal Joey* (Broadhurst, revival, "Joey Evans," Jan. 3, 1952): Chicago (A Great Big Town); Den of Iniquity; Do It the Hard Way; Happy Hunting Horn; I Could Write a Book; Pal Joey (What Do I Care for a Dame?); You Mustn't Kick It Around/W: Lorenz Hart, M: Richard Rodgers. *Shangri-La* (Winter Garden, "Robert Henderson," June 13, 1956): Every Time You Danced with Me; Second Time in Love; Talkin' with Your Feet/W: Jerome Lawrence, Robert E. Lee, M: Harry Warren. *Ziegfeld Follies of 1957* (Winter Garden, revue, Mar. 1, 1957): (That) Element of Doubt/W: Howard Dietz, M: Sammy Fain — If You Got Music/W: David Rogers, M: Colin Romoff — Two a Day on the Milky Way/W: Marshall Barer, M: Dean Fuller. *I Can Get It for You Wholesale* (Shubert, "Teddy Asch," Mar. 22, 1962): Ballad of the Garment Trade; The Family Way; What's In It for Me?/WM: Harold Rome.

5339. Jeanie Lang *Ballyhoo* (Hammerstein's, "Ruth," Dec. 22, 1930): How I Could Go for You; If I Were You; Throw It Out the Window/W: Harry Ruskin, Leighton K. Brill, M: Louis Alter — No Wonder I'm Blue/W: Oscar Hammerstein II, M: Louis Alter.

5340. Lise Lang *Marilyn* (Minskoff, "Babs," Nov. 20, 1983): Jimmy Jimmy/WM: Jeanne Napoli, Doug Frank.

5341. Peter Lang (May 29, 1859–Aug. 20, 1932) *Robin Hood* (Standard, "Sir Guy of Gisborne," Sept. 28, 1891): Churning, Churning;

O, See the Lambkins Play!/W: Harry B. Smith, M: Reginald De Koven. *Honey Girl* (Cohan and Harris, "Judge Martin," May 3, 1920): Shopping/W: Neville Fleeson, M: Albert Von Tilzer.

5342. William Langan (Mar. 4, 1903–Sept. 1986) B: Brooklyn, NY. *Take the Air* (Waldorf, CR, "Capt. Halliday," May 7, 1928): Wings/W: Gene Buck, M: Dave Stamper.

5343. Sue Ane Langdon (Mar. 8, 1936–) B: Paterson, NJ. *The Apple Tree* (Shubert, CR, "Eve" and "Princess Barbara" and "Ella" and "Passionella," Nov. 1, 1967, evenings): Feelings; Forbidden Love (in Gaul); Friends; Lullaby (Go to Sleep, Whatever You Are); Gorgeous; Here in Eden; I've Got What You Want; Oh to Be a Movie Star; Tiger, Tiger; Wealth; What Makes Me Love Him?; Which Door?/W: Sheldon Harnick, M: Jerry Bock.

5344. Juliette Lange *Betsy* (Herald Square, "Abaloni," Dec. 11, 1911): Only a Voice; There Came a Vision/W: Will B. Johnstone, M: Alexander Johnstone.

5345. Bonnie Langford (July 22, 1964–) *Gypsy* (Winter Garden, revival, "Baby June," Sept. 23, 1974): May We Entertain You/W: Stephen Sondheim, M: Jule Styne.

5346. Frances Langford (Apr. 4, 1913–) B: Lakeland, FL. Her singing career was launched on Rudy Vallee's radio program from Tampa, Florida in 1931. In movie musicals 1935 to 1954. *Here Goes the Bride* (46th Street, "Rose," Nov. 3, 1931): Hello, My Lover, Goodbye/W: Edward Heyman, M: Johnny Green — Music in My Fingers/W: Edward Heyman, M: Richard Myers.

5347. Leland H. Langley *A Gaiety Girl* (Daly's, revival, "Charles Goldfield," May 7, 1895): Beneath the Skies; Sunshine Above/W: Harry Greenbank, M: Sidney Jones — Private Tommy Atkins/W: Henry Hamilton, M: S. Potter.

5348. Pvt. Stuart Langley (?–Apr. 2, 1970) *Best Foot Forward* (Ethel Barrymore, "Old Grad," Oct. 1, 1941): Buckle Down Winsocki/WM: Hugh Martin, Ralph Blane.

5349. Sylvain Langlois (c 1861–June 1921) B: Windsor, Ontario, Canada. *Sergeant Kitty* (Daly's, "Gen. Dubois," Jan. 18, 1904): War/W: R.H. Burnside, M: A. Baldwin Sloane. *The Mayor of Tokio* (New York, "Gen. Satake," Dec. 4, 1905): Conspirators Are We/W: Richard Carle, M: William F. Peters. *The Spring Chicken* (Daly's > New Amsterdam > Daly's, "Baron Papouche," Oct. 8, 1906): Baron Papouche/W: Adrian Ross, M: Ivan Caryll. *The Hurdy Gurdy Girl* (Wallack's, "Milo," Sept. 23, 1907): Hope On/W: Richard Carle, M: H.L. Heartz.

5350. Christine Langner *Cats* (Winter Garden, "Rumpleteazer," Oct. 7, 1982): Mungojerrie and Rumpleteazer/W: T.S. Eliot, M: Andrew Lloyd Webber.

5351. Shawni Lani *Belmont Varieties* (Belmont, revue, Sept. 26, 1932): Goona-Goona/W: Charles Kenny, M: Serge Walter.

5352. John Lankston *Pal Joey* (New York City Center, revival, "Louis," May 31, 1961): The Flower Garden of My Heart/W: Lorenz Hart, M: Richard Rodgers. *Pal Joey* (New York City Center, revival, "Louis," May 29, 1963): same as above. *Funny Girl* (Winter Garden, "Ziegfeld Tenor," Mar. 26, 1964): His Love Makes Me Beautiful/W: Bob Merrill, M: Jule Styne. *The Most Happy Fella* (New York State, revival, "Ciccio," Sept. 4, 1991): Abbondanza; Benvenuta/WM: Frank Loesser.

5353. Don Lanning *Who Cares?* (46th Street, revue, July 8, 1930): Make My Bed Down in Dixieland; Who Cares?/W: Harry Clark, M: Percy Wenrich.

5354. Jerry Lanning (May 17, 1943–) B: Miami, FL. *Mame* (Winter Garden, "Patrick Dennis, aged 19-29," May 24, 1966): My Best Girl/WM: Jerry Herman. *Sextet* (Bijou, "Leonard," Mar. 3, 1974): I Love You All the Time; Women and Men/W: Lee Goldsmith, M: Lawrence Hurwit. *Where's Charley?* (Circle in the Square, revival, "Jack Chesney," Dec. 20, 1974): At the Red Rose Cotillion; Better Get Out of Here; My Darling, My Darling; The New Ashmoleon Marching Society and Students Conservatory Band/WM: Frank Loesser. *My Fair Lady* (St. James, revival, "Freddy Eynsford-Hill," Mar. 25, 1976): On the Street Where You Live/W: Alan Jay Lerner, M: Frederick Loewe. *Anna Karenina* (Circle in the Square, "Prince Stephen Oblonsky," Aug. 26, 1992): Mazurka; There's More to Life Than Love/W: Peter Kellogg, M: Daniel Levine.

5355. Angela Lansbury (Oct. 16, 1925–) B: London, England. Longtime star of stage, screen and TV. She came to New York with her family in 1940. Her first film role as the cockney maid, Nancy Oliver, in *Gaslight* (1944) won her an Oscar. Best known to a worldwide audience as amateur sleuth Jessica Fletcher in the TV series *Murder, She Wrote* (1984). *Anyone Can Whistle* (Majestic, "Cora Hoover Hooper," Apr. 4, 1964): I've Got You to Lean On; Me and My Town; Miracle Song; A Parade in Town/WM: Stephen Sondheim. *Mame* (Winter Garden, "Mame Dennis," May 24, 1966/Feb. 27, 1967/ Aug. 29, 1967): Bosom Buddies; If He Walked into My Life; It's Today; The Man in the Moon;

My Best Girl; Open a New Window; That's How Young I Feel; We Need a Little Christmas/WM: Jerry Herman. *Dear World* (Hellinger, "Countess Aurelia, The Madwoman of Chaillot," Feb. 6, 1969): And I Was Beautiful; Dear World; Each Tomorrow Morning; Garbage; I Don't Want to Know; Kiss Her Now; One Person; Pearls; Thoughts/WM: Jerry Herman. *Sondheim: A Musical Tribute* (Shubert, revue, Mar. 11, 1973): Me and My Town; A Parade in Town/WM: Stephen Sondheim. *Gypsy* (Winter Garden, revival, "Rose," Sept. 23, 1974): Everything's Coming Up Roses; Mr. Goldstone, I Love You; Rose's Turn; Small World; Some People; Together Wherever We Go; You'll Never Get Away from Me/W: Stephen Sondheim, M: Jule Styne. *The King and I* (Uris, revival, CR, "Anna Leonowens," Apr. 11, 1978): Getting to Know You; Hello, Young Lovers; I Whistle a Happy Tune; The Royal Bangkok Academy; Shall I Tell You What I Think of You?; Shall We Dance?/W: Oscar Hammerstein II, M: Richard Rodgers. *Sweeney Todd, the Demon Barber of Fleet Street* (Uris, "Mrs. Lovett," Mar. 1, 1979/Sept. 12, 1979): By the Sea; God, That's Good!; A Little Priest; My Friends; Not While I'm Around; Parlor Songs; Pirelli's Miracle Elixir; Poor Thing; Wait; The Worst Pies in London/WM: Stephen Sondheim. *Mame* (Gershwin, revival, "Mame Dennis," July 24, 1983): same as above.

5356. Charlotte Lansing *The Desert Song* (Casino, CR, "Margot Bonvalet," June 1927): All Hail to the General; The Desert Song; French Military Marching Song; I Want a Kiss; Romance; The Sabre Song; Then You Will Know/W: Otto Harbach, Oscar Hammerstein II, M: Sigmund Romberg. *The New Moon* (Casino, CR, "Marianne Beaunoir," June 1929): The Girl on the Prow; An Interrupted Love Song; Lover, Come Back to Me; Never for You; One Kiss; Wanting You/W: Oscar Hammerstein II, M: Sigmund Romberg. *East Wind* (Manhattan, "Claudette Fortier," Oct. 27, 1931): Are You Love?; I Saw Your Eyes; I'd Be a Fool; It's a Wonderful World/W: Oscar Hammerstein II, M: Sigmund Romberg. *Robin Hood* (Erlanger's, revival, "Lady Marian Fitzwalter [Maid Marian])," Feb. 8, 1932): All Nature Is at Peace and Rest (Forest Song); Churning, Churning; Come Dream So Bright; I Come as a Cavalier/W: Harry B. Smith, M: Reginald De Koven. *Blossom Time* (46th Street, revival, "Bellabruna," Dec. 26, 1938): Keep It Dark; Let Me Awake; Melody Triste/W: Dorothy Donnelly, M: Sigmund Romberg.

5357. John Lansing (Oct. 16, 1949–) B: Baldwin, NY. *Grease* (Broadhurst, CR, "Danny Zuko," Nov. 1974): All Choked Up; Alone at a Drive-In Movie; Summer Nights/WM: Jim Jacobs, Warren Casey.

5358. Al Lanti *Wildcat* (Alvin, "Cisco," Dec. 16, 1960): El Sombrero/W: Carolyn Leigh, M: Cy Coleman.

5359. Maurice Lapue *Earl Carroll's Vanities of 1928* (Earl Carroll, revue, Aug. 6, 1928): Painting a Vanities Girl/WM: Ernie Golden. *The New Yorkers* (Broadway, "Alfredo Gomez," Dec. 8, 1930): I'm Getting Myself Ready for You/WM: Cole Porter.

5360. Cora La Redd *Say When* (Morosco, "Cora," June 26, 1928): One Step to Heaven/W: Raymond Klages, M: Jesse Greer. *Messin' Around* (Hudson, revue, Apr. 22, 1929): Skiddle-de-Skow/W: Perry Bradford, M: James P. Johnson. *Change Your Luck* (George M. Cohan, "Bandana Babe Peppers," June 6, 1930): Can't Be Bothered Now; My Regular Man; Percolatin'/WM: James C. Johnson.

5361. Norman A. Large *A Doll's Life* (Mark Hellinger, "Conductor" and "Mr. Gustafson," Sept. 23, 1982): New Year's Eve; A Woman Alone/W: Betty Comden, Adolph Green, M: Larry Grossman. *Les Miserables* (Broadway, CR, "Javert," Jan. 18, 1988/July 19, 1988): Soliloquy; Stars/W: Herbert Kretzmer, M: Claude-Michel Schonberg.

5362. Lucien la Riviere *Belmont Varieties* (Belmont, revue, Sept. 26, 1932): Back Seat of a Taxi/W: Charles Kenny, M: Serge Walter — Etiquette; You Took My Breath Away/W: Sam Bernard, Jr., Bobby Burk, M: Henry Lloyd — Yes and No/W: Lucien la Riviere, M: Von Egen.

5363. Anna Larkin *Hold Everything!* (Broadhurst, CR, "Gladys Martin," June 24, 1929): Don't Hold Everything/W: B.G. DeSylva, Lew Brown, M: Ray Henderson.

5364. Elizabeth Larner *Oliver!* (Mark Hellinger, revival, "Mrs. Bedwin" and "Mrs. Bumble," Apr. 29, 1984): Oliver!; Where Is Love?/WM: Lionel Bart.

5365. Mary La Roche *Laffing Room Only* (Winter Garden, revue, CR, Feb. 4, 1945): Got That Good Time Feelin'/WM: Burton Lane.

5366. Francine Larrimore (Aug. 22, 1898–Mar. 7, 1975) B: Verdun, France. Cousin of LUTHER ADLER. *Sometime* (Shubert, "Enid Vaughn," Oct. 4, 1918): Baby Doll; Sometime/W: Rida Johnson Young, M: Rudolf Friml.

5367. Martha Larrimore B: Chattanooga, TN. *The Golden Apple* (Alvin, CR, "Mother Hare," Aug. 2, 1954): Circe, Circe/W: John Latouche, M: Jerome Moross.

5368. Liz Larsen (Jan. 16, 1959–) B: Philadelphia, PA. *Fiddler on the Roof* (New York State, revival, "Chava," July 9, 1981): Matchmaker, Matchmaker/W: Sheldon Harnick, M: Jerry Bock. *The Most Happy Fella* (Booth, revival, "Cleo," Feb. 13, 1992): Big D; Happy to Make Your Acquaintance; I Like Ev'rybody; Ooh! My Feet!/WM: Frank Loesser. *Damn Yankees* (Marquis, revival, CR, "Gloria Thorpe," Mar. 12, 1995): Shoeless Joe from Hannibal, Mo.; Six Months Out of Every Year/WM: Richard Adler, Jerry Ross.

5369. William Larsen (Nov. 20, 1927–Jan. 21, 1996) B: Lake Charles, LA. *Half a Sixpence* (Broadhurst, CR, "Chitterlow"): Flash! Bang! Wallop!/WM: David Heneker. *Dear World* (Hellinger, "The Chairman of the Board," Feb. 6, 1969): The Spring of Next Year/WM: Jerry Herman.

5370. Lisby Larson (Oct. 23, 1951–) B: Washington, DC. *The Five O'Clock Girl* (Helen Hayes, revival, "Patricia Brown," Jan. 28, 1981): Thinking of You; Up in the Clouds; Who Did? You Did!/W: Bert Kalmar, M: Harry Ruby.

5371. Tom Larson *The Unsinkable Molly Brown* (Winter Garden, "Burt," Nov. 3, 1960): I've A'ready Started In/WM: Meredith Willson.

5372. Grace La Rue (Apr. 23, 1880–Mar. 13, 1956) B: Kansas City, MO. She began singing and acting at age 12, and appeared in vaudeville with Charles Burke, whom she later married, as Burke and La Rue. *The Tourists* (Majestic, "Julia Jellicoe," Aug. 25, 1906): Different Girls; The Tale of Mary's Lamb/W: Edward P. Moran, Will Heelan, M: Seymour Furth. *The Blue Moon* (Casino, "Evelyn Ormsby," Nov. 3, 1906): Don't You Think It's Time to Marry?/W: Addison Burkhardt, M: Gus Edwards — The Loveland Volunteers/WM: Percy Greenbank, Paul Rubens, Howard Talbot. *Ziegfeld Follies of 1907* (Jardin de Paris — New York roof > Liberty, revue, July 8, 1907): Pocahontas/WM: Edgar Selden, Seymour Furth. *Ziegfeld Follies of 1908* (Jardin de Paris — New York roof > New York, revue, June 15, 1908): Duchess of Table d'Hote/ W: Harry B. Smith, M: Maurice Levi — Goodbye, Mr. Ragtime/W: William Jerome, M: Jean Schwartz. *Madame Troubadour* (Lyric > 39th Street, "Henriette," Oct. 10, 1910): Oh, How That Taxi Got on My Nerves; Trou-Trou-Ba-Ba-Troubadour; Yesterday and Today/W: Joseph W. Herbert, M: Felix Albini — Please, Please/W: M.E. Rourke, M: Walter Kollo. *Betsy* (Herald Square, "Elizabeth Killigrew," Dec. 11, 1911): Aristocracy; Dream Love; First Gray Hair; Laughter and Love; Love's Conquests; There

Came a Vision/W: Will B. Johnstone, M: Alexander Johnstone. *The Honeymoon Express* (Winter Garden, CR, "Yvonne," Apr. 28, 1913): Bring Back Your Love; When the Honeymoon Stops Shining; You'll Call the Next Love the First/W: Harold Atteridge, M: Jean Schwartz. *Hitchy-Koo of 1917* (Cohan and Harris > Liberty > 44th Street, revue, June 7, 1917): The Girls of Home Sweet Home; When You've Picked Your Basket of Peaches/WM: E. Ray Goetz — I May Be Gone for a Long, Long Time/W: Lew Brown, M: Albert Von Tilzer — M-I-S-S-I-S-S-I-P-P-I/ W: Bert Hanlon, Ben Ryan, M: Harry Tierney. *Music Box Revue of 1922* (Music Box, revue, Oct. 23, 1922): Crinoline Days/WM: Irving Berlin.

5373. Gay La Salle *The New Yorkers* (Edyth Totten, revue, Mar. 10, 1927): Here Comes the Prince of Wales; A Song About Love/W: Henry Myers, M: Arthur Schwartz.

5374. Kendrew Lascelles Writer, musician, choreographer. *Wait a Minim!* (John Golden, revue, Mar. 7, 1966): Eine Kleine Bombardonmusik; Last Summer; The Love Life of a Gondolier; Tuba Man/WM: ?.

5375. Henry Lascoe (May 30, 1912–Sept. 1, 1964) B: New York, NY. *Silk Stockings* (Imperial, "Ivanov," Feb. 24, 1955): Hail, Bibinski; Siberia; Too Bad/WM: Cole Porter. *Carnival!* (Imperial, "Mr. Schlegel," Apr. 13, 1961): Direct from Vienna; Humming/WM: Bob Merrill.

5376. Charles Laskey *Marinka* (Ethel Barrymore, CR, "Lieut. Palafy," Nov. or Dec. 1945): Treat a Woman Like a Drum; Young Man Danube/W: George Marion, Jr., M: Emmerich Kalman.

5377. David Lasley (Aug. 20, 1947–) B: Sault-St.-Marie, MI. *Dude* (Broadway, "Sissy," Oct. 9, 1972): The Handsomest Man; A Song to Sing/W: Gerome Ragni, M: Galt MacDermot.

5378. Louise Lasser (Apr. 11, 1935–) B: New York, NY. M: Filmmaker Woody Allen, 1966 to 1971. Heroine of the TV soap spoof *Mary Hartman, Mary Hartman* (1976). *Henry, Sweet Henry* (Palace, "Stella," Oct. 23, 1967): Pillar to Post/WM: Bob Merrill.

5379. Franc Lassiter *Murray Anderson's Almanac* (Erlanger's, revue, Aug. 14, 1929): Schrafft's University/W: Edward Eliscu, M: Henry Sullivan.

5380. Warren Lassiter same as FRANC LASSITER.

5381. Blanche Latell *Oh, Please!* (Fulton, "Miss South Bend," Dec. 17, 1926): Homely but Clean/W: Anne Caldwell, M: Vincent Youmans.

5382. Dick Latessa *The Education of H*Y*M*A*N K*A*P*L*A*N* (Alvin, "Giovanni

Pastora," Apr. 4, 1968): Spring in the City/WM: Paul Nassau, Oscar Brand. *Rags* (Mark Hellinger, "Avram Cohen," Aug. 21, 1986): Children of the Wind; Kaddish; Rags; Three Sunny Rooms/W: Stephen Schwartz, M: Charles Strouse. *The Will Rogers Follies* (Palace, "Clem Rogers," May 1, 1991): It's a Boy!; Will-a-Mania/ W: Betty Comden, Adolph Green, M: Cy Coleman. *Damn Yankees* (Marquis, revival, "Van Buren," Mar. 3, 1994): Heart/WM: Richard Adler, Jerry Ross.

5383. Cynthia Latham (Apr. 21, 1897–) B: London, England. *Redhead* (46th Street, "Maude Simpson," Feb. 5, 1959): Behave Yourself/W: Dorothy Fields, M: Albert Hague.

5384. Bobbi Jo Lathan (Oct 5, 1951–) B: Dallas, TX. *The Best Little Whorehouse in Texas* (46th Street, CR, "Mona Stangley," Aug. 6, 1979): Bus from Amarillo; Girl, You're a Woman; A Li'l Ole Bitty Pissant Country Place; No Lies; 20 Fans/WM: Carol Hall. *The Best Little Whorehouse in Texas* (46th Street, CR, "Doatsey Mae," c 1980): Doatsey Mae; Texas Has a Whorehouse in It/WM: Carol Hall.

5385. Alton Lathrop *Bubbling Brown Sugar* (ANTA, "Gene" and "Gospel Lady's Son," Mar. 2, 1976): I'm Gonna Tell God All My Troubles/WM: ?— Rosetta/WM: Earl Hines, Henri Woode — Solitude/W: Eddie DeLange, Irving Mills, M: Duke Ellington.

5386. Anna Laughlin (Oct. 11, 1885–Mar. 6, 1937) B: Sacramento, CA. Mother of LUCY MONROE. *The Belle of Bohemia* (Casino, "La Sahara," Sept. 24, 1900): Strolling by the River/ W: Harry B. Smith, M: Ludwig Englander. *The Wizard of Oz* (Majestic, "Dorothy Gale," Jan. 20, 1903): Carrie Barry/W: Glen MacDonough, M: A. Baldwin Sloane — Honey, My Sweet/W: George Spink, M: Henry Blossom — Rosalie/W: Will D. Cobb, M: Gus Edwards — When You Love, Love, Love!/W: L. Frank Baum, M: Paul Tietjens. *The Top o' th' World* (Majestic > Casino, "Kokomo," Oct. 19, 1907): Busy Mr. Bee; Little Brown Hen; Why Don't You?/W: James O'Dea, M: Anne Caldwell — Side by Side [Nov. 4, 1907]/W: James O'Dea, M: Manuel Klein. *When Claudia Smiles* (39th Street > Lyric, "Kate Walker," Feb. 2, 1914): Boys, Boys, Boys/WM: ?— Dear Old Dinah/WM: Stanley Murphy, Henry I. Marshall — He's a Dear Old Pet/W: William Jerome, M: Jean Schwartz — I've Got Everything I Want but You; You're My Boy/W: Marion Sunshine, M: Henry I. Marshall.

5387. Jane Laughlin *Walking Happy* (Lunt-Fontanne, "Ada Figgins," Nov. 26, 1966): A Joyful Thing/W: Sammy Cahn, M: James Van Heusen.

5388. Larry Laurence (Mar. 3, 1920–) B: Milan, Italy. He later was known as ENZO STUARTI. *Around the World in Eighty Days* (Adelphi, "Pat Passepartout," May 31, 1946): Look What I Found; Pipe Dreaming; There He Goes, Mr. Phileas Fogg/WM: Cole Porter. *By the Beautiful Sea* (Majestic, "Burt Mayer," Apr. 8, 1954): Throw the Anchor Away/W: Dorothy Fields, M: Arthur Schwartz.

5389. Paula Laurence (Jan. 25, 1916–) B: Brooklyn, NY. Popular in nightclubs and cabarets. *Sing for Your Supper* (Adelphi, revue, Apr. 24, 1939): At Long Last; How Can We Sing It?; Young Man with a Horn/W: Robert Sour, M: Lee Wainer. *Something for the Boys* (Alvin, "Chiquita Hart," Jan. 7, 1943): By the Mississinewah; There's a Happy Land in the Sky; When We're Home on the Range/WM: Cole Porter. *One Touch of Venus* (Imperial, "Molly Grant," Oct. 7, 1943): Catch Hatch; One Touch of Venus; Very, Very, Very/W: Ogden Nash, M: Kurt Weill. *The Duchess Misbehaves* (Adelphi, "Queen of Spain" and "Mrs. Kiester," Feb. 13, 1946): The Honeymoon Is Over; Men/W: Gladys Shelley, M: Frank Black. *The Liar* (Broadhurst, "Colombina," May 18, 1950): A Jewel of a Duel; Spring; Truth/W: Edward Eager, M: John Mundy — Women's Work/W: Edward Eager, M: Lehman Engel. *The Beggar's Opera* (New York City Center, revival, "Mrs. Coaxer," Mar. 13, 1957): If the Heart of a Man; In the Days of My Youth/WM: John Gay. *Funny Girl* (Winter Garden, CR, "Mrs. Strakosh," June 1964): Find Yourself a Man; If a Girl Isn't Pretty/W: Bob Merrill, M: Jule Styne.

5390. Joe Laurie, Jr. (1892–Apr. 29, 1954) B: New York, NY. Comedian especially remembered as a panelist on the early TV series *Can You Top This?* (1950). *Plain Jane* (New Amsterdam, "Kid McGuire," May 12, 1924): Follow Your Footsteps [May 19, 1924]; I Love a Fight/ W: Phil Cook, M: Tom Johnstone.

5391. Joseph Lautner (Sept. 29, 1924–) B: Cambridge, MA. *New Faces of 1952* (Royale, revue, May 16, 1952): Lizzie Borden/WM: Michael Brown — Waltzing in Venice with You/ WM: Ronny Graham. *Me and Juliet* (Majestic, "Ruby," May 28, 1953): The Big Black Giant/W: Oscar Hammerstein II, M: Richard Rodgers.

5392. Madelon La Varre *The Midnight Rounders of 1920* (Century roof, revue, July 12, 1920): Chanson/W: Howard E. Rogers, M: Leo Edwards — Je Ne Comprends Pas; Josephine/W: Alfred Bryan, M: Jean Schwartz. *The Century Revue* (Century, revue, July 12, 1920): Marcelle/W: Alfred Bryan, M: Jean Schwartz.

5393. Marie Lavarre *Ned Wayburn's Town Topics* (Century, revue, Sept. 23, 1915): Wake Up! It's Cake Walk Day/W: Thomas Gray, M: Harold Orlob. *The Show of Wonders* (Winter Garden, revue, Oct. 26, 1926): Louisiana/WM: Harry Tierney — When Pavlova Starts Buck and Winging/W: Harold Atteridge, M: Sigmund Romberg — The Zoo Step/W: Homer Tutt, M: Clarence Wilson.

5394. Gertrude Lavella *Bringing Up Father* (Lyric, "Kitty," Apr. 6, 1925): Poppy the Dream Girl; Wedding Chimes; When It Gets Dark/W: R.F. Carroll, M: Seymour Furth, Leo Edwards.

5395. Mary Gail Laverenz (Dec. 28, 1948–) B: Moline, IL. *The Happy Time* (Broadway, "Dorine," Jan. 18, 1968): Catch My Garter; The Life of the Party; Tomorrow Morning/W: Fred Ebb, M: John Kander.

5396. Aric Lavie B: Germany. *Irma La Douce* (Plymouth, "Roberto-Les-Diams," Sept. 29, 1960): The Freedom of the Seas; From a Prison Cell; Le Grisbi Is le Root of le Evil in Man; Sons of France; That's a Crime; There Is Only One Paris for That/W: Julian More, David Heneker, Monty Norman, M: Marguerite Monnot. *To Live Another Summer, To Pass Another Winter* (Helen Hayes, revue, Oct. 21, 1971): The Boy with the Fiddle/WM: Alexander Argov — Don't Destroy the World; The Sacrifice; To Live Another Summer, To Pass Another Winter/W: David Paulsen, M: Dov Seltzer — Give me a Star/W: David Paulsen, M: David Krivoshei — Son of Man/WM: David Axelrod.

5397. Linda Lavin (Oct. 15, 1937–) B: Portland, ME. On TV she starred in the sitcom *Alice* (1976). *A Family Affair* (Billy Rose, "Fifi of Paris," Jan. 27, 1962): Harmony/W: James Goldman, William Goldman, M: John Kander. *It's a Bird It's a Plane It's Superman* (Alvin, "Sydney," Mar. 29, 1966): Ooh, Do You Love You!; You've Got Possibilities/W: Lee Adams, M: Charles Strouse. *Gypsy* (St. James, revival, CR, "Rose," July 30, 1990): Everything's Coming Up Roses; Mr. Goldstone, I Love You; Rose's Turn; Small World; Some People; Together Wherever We Go; You'll Never Get Away from Me/W: Stephen Sondheim, M: Jule Styne.

5398. Audrey Lavine B: Greensboro, NC. *Rags* (Mark Hellinger, "Rosa," Aug. 21, 1986): Bread and Freedom (Sisters We Stand)/W: Stephen Schwartz, M: Charles Strouse.

5399. Helen La Vonne *George White's Scandals of 1922* (Globe, revue, CR, Sept. 18, 1922): I Found a Four-Leaf Clover; Lady Fan [Oct. 16, 1922]/W: B.G. DeSylva, M: George Gershwin — I'll Build a Stairway to Paradise/W: B.G.

DeSylva, Arthur Francis, M: George Gershwin.

5400. Vera Lavrova *Innocent Eyes* (Winter Garden, revue, May 20, 1924): Day Dreams/W: Harold Atteridge, Tot Seymour, M: Sigmund Romberg — Inspiration/W: Clare Kummer, M: Leo Fall.

5401. Evelyn Law *Two Little Girls in Blue* (George M. Cohan, "Margie," May 3, 1921): The Silly Season/W: Ira Gershwin, M: Vincent Youmans — There's Something About Me They Like/W: Ira Gershwin, Fred Jackson, M: Vincent Youmans. *Betsy* (New Amsterdam, "Flora," Dec. 28, 1926): Cradle of the Deep; The Kitzel Engagement; My Missus; One of Us Should Be Two/W: Lorenz Hart, M: Richard Rodgers.

5402. Mildred Law *Artists and Models of 1943* (Broadway, revue, Nov. 5, 1943): Blowing My Top/W: Milton Pascal, Dan Shapiro, M: Phil Charig.

5403. Betty Lawford (1910–Nov. 20, 1960) B: London, England. Daughter of ERNEST E. LAWFORD. *Walk with Music* (Ethel Barrymore, "Carrie Gibson," June 4, 1940): Today I Am a Glamour Girl/W: Johnny Mercer, M: Hoagy Carmichael.

5404. Ernest E. Lawford (1870–Dec. 27, 1940) B: England. Father of BETTY LAWFORD. *White Lilacs* (Shubert, "Heinrich Heine," Sept. 10, 1928): Words, Music, Cash/W: J. Keirn Brennan, M: Karl Hajos, based on Frederic Chopin.

5405. Mark Lawhead *Man on the Moon* (Little, "Leroy [Little Red Box]," Jan. 29, 1975): Mission Control; Speed of Light; Truth Cannot Be Treason/WM: John Phillips.

5406. Marvin Lawler *Ziegfeld Follies of 1936-1937* (Winter Garden, revue, Sept. 14, 1936): Sentimental Weather/W: Ira Gershwin, M: Vernon Duke.

5407. William (Cooper) Lawley *The Love Song* (Century, "Pierre," Jan. 13, 1925): Not for a Year, Not for a Day; Tell Me Not That You Are Forgetting; When Your Life Seems a Rainy Day/W: Harry B. Smith, M: Edward Kunneke, Jacques Offenbach.

5408. Andrew Lawlor, Jr. *Three Showers* (Harris > Plymouth, "Willie Mobberly," Apr. 5, 1920): B Is the Note/W: Henry Creamer, M: Turner Layton.

5409. Mary Lawlor (1911–) B: Utica, NY. *The Rise of Rosie O'Reilly* (Liberty, "Polly," Dec. 25, 1923): Born and Bred in Brooklyn (Over the Bridge); Love Dreams/WM: George M. Cohan. *Annie Dear* (Times Square, "Gwen Morley," Nov. 4, 1924): Help, Help, Help/WM: Clare

Kummer — Louwanna/W: Clifford Grey, M: Sigmund Romberg, Jean Schwartz. *No, No, Nanette* (Globe, "Winnie," Sept. 16, 1925): Fight Over Me; Telephone Girlie/W: Otto Harbach, M: Vincent Youmans — I Want to Be Happy/W: Irving Caesar, M: Vincent Youmans. *Queen High* (Ambassador, "Polly Nettleton," Sept. 7, 1926): Cross Your Heart; Everything Will Happen for the Best; The Weaker Sex/W: B.G. DeSylva, M: Lewis E. Gensler — Don't Forget (Your Auntie)/W: B.G. DeSylva, M: James F. Hanley. *Good News!* (46th Street, "Connie Lane," Sept. 6, 1927): The Best Things in Life Are Free; Just Imagine; Lucky in Love/W: B.G. DeSylva, Lew Brown, M: Ray Henderson. *Cross My Heart* (Knickerbocker, "Sally Blake," Sept. 17, 1928): Come Along Sunshine; Dream Sweetheart; Lady Whippoorwill; Right Out of Heaven Into My Arms/W: Joseph McCarthy, M: Harry Tierney. *Hello, Daddy* (Mansfield, "Connie Block," Dec. 26, 1928): As Long as We're in Love; I Want Plenty of You; Let's Sit and Talk About You; Maybe Means Yes; Your Disposition Is Mine/W: Dorothy Fields, M: Jimmy McHugh. *You Said It* (46th Street, "Helen Holloway," Jan. 19, 1931): If He Really Loves Me; You Said It/W: Jack Yellen, M: Harold Arlen.

5410. Terry Lawlor *The Show Is On* (Winter Garden, revue, CR, Sept. 18, 1937): By Strauss/W: Ira Gershwin, M: George Gershwin — Casanova; Now/W: Ted Fetter, M: Vernon Duke — Long as You've Got Your Health/W: E.Y. Harburg, Norman Zeno, M: Will Irwin — The Show Is On/W: Ted Fetter, M: Hoagy Carmichael.

5411. Bob Lawrence *Jumbo* (Hippodrome, "Mr. Ball," Nov. 16, 1935): The Circus on Parade; Diavalo; Over and Over Again/W: Lorenz Hart, M: Richard Rodgers. *The Boys from Syracuse* (Alvin, "Singing Policeman," Nov. 23, 1938): Come with Me/W: Lorenz Hart, M: Richard Rodgers. *The Boys from Syracuse* (Alvin, CR, "Antipholus of Ephesus," May 1939): Come with Me; The Shortest Day of the Year/W: Lorenz Hart, M: Richard Rodgers. *Sunny River* (St. James, "Jean Gervais," Dec. 4, 1941): Along the Winding Road; Let Me Live Today; My Girl and I; Time Is Standing Still/W: Oscar Hammerstein II, M: Sigmund Romberg.

5412. Burke Lawrence (Apr. 7, 1959–) B: Montreal, Canada. *Shenandoah* (Virginia, revival, "Jacob," Aug. 8, 1989): Next to Lovin' (I Like Fightin')/W: Peter Udell, M: Gary Geld.

5413. Carol Lawrence (Sept. 5, 1932–) B: Melrose Park, IL. *New Faces of 1952* (Royale, revue, May 16, 1952): Waltzing in Venice with You/WM: Ronny Graham. *Ziegfeld Follies of 1957* (Winter Garden, revue, Mar. 1, 1957): Honorable Mambo/W: Marshall Barer, M: Dean Fuller — Salesmanship/W: Carolyn Leigh, M: Philip Springer. *West Side Story* (Winter Garden, "Maria," Sept. 26, 1957): A Boy Like That; I Feel Pretty; I Have a Love; One Hand, One Heart; Tonight/W: Stephen Sondheim, M: Leonard Bernstein. *Saratoga* (Winter Garden, "Clio Dulaine," Dec. 7, 1959): Countin' Our Chickens; A Game of Poker; I'll Be Respectable; Love Held Lightly; The Man in My Life; One Step — Two Step; Petticoat High; Saratoga/W: Johnny Mercer, M: Harold Arlen — Why Fight This?/WM: Johnny Mercer. *West Side Story* (Winter Garden, revival, "Maria," Apr. 27, 1960): same as above. *Subways Are for Sleeping* (St. James, "Angela McKay," Dec. 27, 1961): Be a Santa; Comes Once in a Lifetime; Girls Like Me; I Said It and I'm Glad; Ride Through the Night; Subway Directions; What Is This Feeling in the Air?; Who Knows What Might Have Been/W: Betty Comden, Adolph Green, M: Jule Styne. *I Do! I Do!* (46th Street, CR, "She [Agnes]," Oct. 18, 1967 matinees only/Dec. 4, 1967): All the Dearly Beloved; Flaming Agnes; Good Night; The Honeymoon Is Over; I Do! I Do!; Love Isn't Everything; My Cup Runneth Over; Nobody's Perfect; Roll Up the Ribbons; Someone Needs Me; Something Has Happened; This House; Together Forever; What Is a Woman?; When the Kids Get Married; Where Are the Snows/W: Tom Jones, M: Harvey Schmidt.

5414. Charles (Charlie) Lawrence (Apr. 21, 1896–Sept. 1984) B: Worcester, MA. *Elsie Janis and Her Gang* (Gaiety, revue, Jan. 16, 1922): Too Young to Love/WM: Elsie Janis. *Helen of Troy, New York* (Selwyn > Times Square, "Theodore Mince," June 19, 1923): I Like a Big Town, I Like a Small Town; If I Never See You Again; We'll Have a Model Factory; What Makes a Business Man Tired?/W: Bert Kalmar, M: Harry Ruby. *Kiss Me* (Lyric, "Eugene Moreaux," July 18, 1927): Always Another Girl; Dodo; I Have Something Nice for You; Two Is Company/W: Derick Wulff, M: Winthrop Cortelyou. *The Love Call* (Majestic, "Dr. Fenlon," Oct. 24, 1927): You Appeal to Me/W: Harry B. Smith, M: Sigmund Romberg. *Music in May* (Casino, "Popkin," Apr. 1, 1929): For the Papa/W: J. Keirn Brennan, M: Maurie Rubens — It's the Cooks, Not the Looks/WM: ?. *Mystery Moon* (Royale, "Sam Martin," June 23, 1930): Mechanical Man; What Could I Do, but Fall in Love with You; Why Couldn't We Incorporate?/W: Monte Carlo, M: Alma Sanders.

5415. David Lawrence *Parade* (Guild, revue, May 20, 1935): Bon Voyage/W: Kyle Crichton, M: Jerome Moross—Life Could Be So Beautiful/W: Paul Peters, George Sklar, M: Jerome Moross.

5416. Eddie Lawrence (Mar. 2, 1919–) B: Brooklyn, NY. He started in vaudeville, playing at the Brighton Beach Baths in Brooklyn. *Bells Are Ringing* (Shubert, "Sandor," Nov. 29, 1956): It's a Simple Little System; Salzburg/W: Betty Comden, Adolph Green, M: Jule Styne. *Sherry!* (Alvin, "Banjo," Mar. 27, 1967): The Fred Astaire Affair; Harriet Sedley; Marry the Girl Myself; Putty in Your Hands/W: James Lipton, M: Laurence Rosenthal.

5417. Georgie Lawrence (c 1877–Jan. 12, 1923) B: New York, NY. *The Good Mister Best* (Garrick, "Nanette," Aug. 30, 1897): Puff, Puff/W: John J. McNally, M: ?. *Hodge, Podge & Co.* (Madison Square, "Minnie Rausmittem," Oct. 23, 1900): The Town Folks Will Be Pleased/WM: ?—*It Happened in Nordland* (Lew Fields, CR, "Parthenia Schmitt," Nov. 13, 1905): Jack O'Lantern Girl/W: Glen MacDonough, M: Victor Herbert—The Man Meant Well/WM: ? *The Lady from Lane's* (Lyric > Casino, "Mamie Morris," Aug. 19, 1907): The Correspondence School; That Really Was a Lovely Place for Me/W: George Broadhurst, M: Gustave Kerker—Four Little Pigs [Sept. 16, 1907]/WM: ? When the Troupe Comes Back to Town [Sept. 16, 1907]/W: George Totten Smith, M: Harry Von Tilzer.

5418. Gertrude Lawrence (July 4, 1898–Sept. 6, 1952) B: London, England. One of the brightest stars of her time. In 1910 she made her first stage appearance, in Brixton, dancing in a pantomime, *The Babes in the Wood*. The glamorous and sophisticated actress was a close friend of Noel Coward; he wrote plays and songs for her to perform. *Charlot Revue of 1924* (Times Square > Selwyn, revue, Jan. 9, 1924): I Don't Know; I Might/W: Ronald Jeans, M: Philip Braham—Limehouse Blues/W: Douglas Furber, M: Philip Braham—Parisian Pierrot/WM: Noel Coward—You Were Meant for Me/WM: Eubie Blake, Noble Sissle. *Charlot Revue of 1926* (Selwyn, revue, Nov. 10, 1925): A Cup of Coffee, a Sandwich and You/W: Billy Rose, Al Dubin, M: Joseph Meyer—I Don't Know/W: Ronald Jeans, M: Philip Braham—Let's All Go Raving Mad/W: Hugh E. Wright, M: Philip Braham—Poor Little Rich Girl; Russian Blues/WM: Noel Coward. *Oh, Kay* (Imperial, "Kay Denham," Nov. 8, 1926): Dear Little Girl (I Hope You've Missed Me); Do Do Do; Maybe; Someone to Watch Over Me/W: Ira Gershwin, M: George Gershwin—Oh, Kay!/W: Ira Gershwin, Howard Dietz, M: George Gershwin. *Treasure Girl* (Alvin, "Ann Wainwright," Nov. 8, 1928): Feeling I'm Falling; I Don't Think I'll Fall in Love Today; What Are We Here For?; Where's the Boy? Here's the Girl!/W: Ira Gershwin, M: George Gershwin. *Lew Leslie's International Revue* (Majestic, revue, Feb. 25, 1930): Cinderella Brown; Exactly Like You; International Rhythm/W: Dorothy Fields, M: Jimmy McHugh. *Tonight at 8:30* (National, "Lily Pepper" and "Jane" and "Victoria Gayforth" and "Louise Charteris," Nov. 24, 1936): Drinking Song; Has Anybody Seen Our Ship?; Hearts and Flowers; Men About Town; Music Box; Play, Orchestra, Play!; Then; We Were Dancing; You Were There/WM: Noel Coward. *Lady in the Dark* (Alvin, "Liza Elliott," Jan. 23, 1941): The Best Years of His Life; Huxley; My Ship; One Life to Live; The Princess of Pure Delight; The Saga of Jenny; This Is New; The World's Inamorata/W: Ira Gershwin, M: Kurt Weill. *Tonight at 8:30* (National, revival, "Lily Pepper" and "Jane" and "Victoria Gayforth," Feb. 20, 1948): Drinking Song; Has Anybody Seen Our Ship?; Hearts and Flowers; Men About Town; Music Box; Play, Orchestra, Play!; Then; You Were There/WM: Noel Coward. *The King and I* (St. James, "Anna Leonowens," Mar. 29, 1951): Getting to Know You; Hello, Young Lovers; I Whistle a Happy Tune; The Royal Bangkok Academy; Shall I Tell You What I Think of You?; Shall We Dance?/W: Oscar Hammerstein II, M: Richard Rodgers.

5419. Henry Lawrence *Brigadoon* (New York City Center, revival, "Sandy Dean," Dec. 13, 1967): Down on MacConnachy Square/W: Alan Jay Lerner, M: Frederick Loewe. *Jimmy* (Winter Garden, "Stanislaus Kazimir Wojciezkowski," Oct. 23, 1969): It's a Nice Place to Visit; They Never Proved a Thing/WM: Bill Jacob, Patti Jacob.

5420. Jane Lawrence B: Bozeman, MT. *Where's Charley?* (St. James, "Donna Lucia D'Alvadorez," Oct. 11, 1948): Lovelier Than Ever/WM: Frank Loesser.

5421. Larry Lawrence *Two on the Aisle* (Mark Hellinger, revue, July 19, 1951): Show Train/W: Betty Comden, Adolph Green, M: Jule Styne.

5422. Madge Lawrence *Paris by Night* (Madison Square roof garden, "Mme. Bon Bon," July 2, 1904): I Loves You Lady Deed I Do/WM: Joseph Nathan—Maudie; Sweet Rose of Mexico [July 11, 1904]; That Horrid Mosquito/WM: ?. *Jim Jam Jems* (Cort, "Miss Sextette," Oct. 4,

1920): Poor Old Florodora Girl/W: Ballard Macdonald, M: James F. Hanley.

5423. Norman Lawrence *Earl Carroll's Vanities of 1940* (St. James, revue, Jan. 13, 1940): Charming/W: Dorcas Cochran, M: Charles Rosoff— The Starlit Hour/W: Mitchell Parish, M: Peter De Rose. *Sadie Thompson* (Alvin, "Private Griggs," Nov. 16, 1944): Barrel of Beads; Siren of the Tropics/W: Howard Dietz, M: Vernon Duke. *Follow the Girls* (44th Street > Broadhurst, CR, "Bob Monroe," Feb. 11, 1945): John Paul Jones; Today Will Be Yesterday Tomorrow; Where You Are/W: Dan Shapiro, Milton Pascal, M: Phil Charig.

5424. Sharon Lawrence (June 29, 1961–) B: Charlotte, NC. She played Asst. DA Sylvia Costas on the TV police drama *N.Y.P.D. Blue* (1994). *Fiddler on the Roof* (Gershwin, revival, "Tzeitel," Nov. 18, 1990): Matchmaker, Matchmaker/W: Sheldon Harnick, M: Jerry Bock.

5425. Stephanie Lawrence (Dec. 16, 1956–Nov. 4, 2000) B: Newcastle upon Tyne, England. *Blood Brothers* (Music Box, "Mrs. Johnstone," Apr. 25, 1993): Bright New Day; Easy Terms; Light Romance; Marilyn Monroe; My Child; Tell Me It's Not True/WM: Willy Russell.

5426. Steve Lawrence (July 8, 1935–) B: Brooklyn, NY. M: singer EYDIE GORME, 1957. The star pop singer began his career in 1953 on Steve Allen's late night TV show. *What Makes Sammy Run?* (54th Street, "Sammy Glick," Feb. 27, 1964/July 20, 1964): I Feel Humble; I See Something; Kiss Me No Kisses; Lites — Camera — Platitude; My Hometown; A New Pair of Shoes; A Room Without Windows; Some Days Everything Goes Wrong; You Can Trust Me; You Help Me; You're No Good/WM: Ervin Drake. *Golden Rainbow* (Shubert, "Larry Davis," Feb. 4, 1968): All in Fun; Desert Moon; For Once in Your Life; I've Got to Be Me; Kid; We Got Us/WM: Walter Marks.

5427. Walter Lawrence *The Man from Now* (New Amsterdam, "Jack Raleigh," Sept. 3, 1906): Coaxing/W: ?, M: Bernard Rolt — I Will Love You Forever, My Dear/WM: Manuel Klein. *The Hurdy Gurdy Girl* (Wallack's, "Tom Otis," Sept. 23, 1907): Come Little Dearie; The Hurdy Gurdy Girl/W: Richard Carle, M: H.L. Heartz — In Bohemia/WM: Richard Carle. *The Soul Kiss* (New York, CR, "Ketcham Short," Mar. 2, 1908): Any Old Place in the World with You; I'm the Human Night Key of New York; Let's Pretend/W: Harry B. Smith, M: Maurice Levi — Rah! Rah! Rah! (Those College Yells)/W: Cecil Lean, M: C.M. Chapel. *The Mimic World*

(Casino, revue, "Prince Danillo," July 9, 1908): I'm No Stingy Romeo/W: Edgar Smith, M: Carl Rehman — My Lady Wine/W: Addison Burkhardt, M: Carl Rehman — Mary Carey/W: Addison Burkhardt, M: Max Hoffmann. *Two Little Brides* (Casino > Lyric, "Count Boris Rimanow," Apr. 23, 1912): Buzz On, Little Busy Bees!; Kiss Me Again, Bebe; You Remind Me of Someone I Used to Know/W: Arthur Anderson, M: Gustave Kerker — Love Is Knocking at the Door/ WM: ? — Somehow, Sometime, Somewhere/ WM: Louis A. Hirsch. *The Woman Haters* (Astor, "Maj. John Von Essenburg," Oct. 7, 1912): Comes a Feeling [Oct. 14, 1912]; It Was Marie; The Letters That Never Were Written/ W: George V. Hobart, M: Edmund Eysler. *Eva* (New Amsterdam, "Dagobert Millefleurs," Dec. 30, 1912): Joy and Glass; On the Day I Marry; The Quarrel; Starlight Guards; The Up-to-Date Troubador/W: Glen MacDonough, M: Franz Lehar.

5428. Ted Lawrie (May 22, 1923–) B: New York, NY. *Follies* (Winter Garden, CR, "Theodore Whitman," May 1972): Rain on the Roof/ WM: Stephen Sondheim.

5429. Jerry Laws (Mar. 25, 1912–Sept. 7, 1976) B: New Haven, CT. Actor, singer, stage manager. *Finian's Rainbow* (46th Street, "1st Passion Pilgrim Gospeler," Jan. 10, 1947): The Begat/W: E.Y. Harburg, M: Burton Lane. *Finian's Rainbow* (New York City Center, revivals, "1st Passion Pilgrim Gospeler," Apr. 27, 1960/ Apr. 5, 1967): same as above.

5430. Arthur Lawson *Bloomer Girl* (New York City Center, revival, "Augustus," Jan. 6, 1947): I Got a Song/W: E.Y. Harburg, M: Harold Arlen.

5431. Kate Drain Lawson (July 27, 1894–Nov. 14, 1977) B: Washington. *The Garrick Gaieties of 1930* (Guild, revue, June 4, 1930): Do Tell/W: Henry Myers, M: Charles M. Schwab — Scheherezade/WM: Harold Goldman.

5432. Roger Lawson (Oct. 11, 1942–) B: Tarrytown, NY. *Hello, Dolly!* (St. James, CR, "Ambrose Kemper," Nov. 12, 1967): Come and Be My Butterfly; Put on Your Sunday Clothes/ WM: Jerry Herman.

5433. Lillian Lawton (?–May 29, 1940) *The Earl and the Girl* (Casino, CR, "Daisy Fallowfield"): The Poor Little Marionette [Jan. 15, 1906]/WM: R.A. Browne, William H. Penn — Shopping; Sporting Song/W: Percy Greenbank, M: Ivan Caryll.

5434. Miriam Lax *Princess Flavia* (Century, "Marta," Nov. 2, 1925): Yes or No?/W: Harry B. Smith, M: Sigmund Romberg.

5435. Dilys Lay (Mar. 11, 1934–) B: London, England. *The Boy Friend* (Royale, "Dulcie," Sept. 30, 1954): The Boy Friend; It's Never Too Late to Fall in Love; Perfect Young Ladies; Riviera; Sur La Plage; The You Don't Want to Play with Me Blues/WM: Sandy Wilson.

5436. Evelyn Laye (July 10, 1900–Feb. 17, 1996) B: London, England. M: SONNIE HALE. Major star of operetta and musical comedy in Britain. *Bitter Sweet* (Ziegfeld, "Marchioness of Shayne" and "Madame Sari Linden" and "Sarah Millick," Nov. 5, 1929): The Call of Life; Dear Little Cafe; I'll See You Again; Peace Enfold You (Evermore and a Day); What Is Love?; Zigeuner/WM: Noel Coward. *Between the Devil* (Imperial, "Natalie Rives," Dec. 22, 1937): Bye-Bye Butterfly Lover; Celina Couldn't Say No; I See Your Face Before Me; Why Did You Do It?/W: Howard Dietz, M: Arthur Schwartz.

5437. Si Layman *Mary* (Knickerbocker, "Whirlwind Willie," Oct. 18, 1920): Tom, Tom Toddle/W: Otto Harbach, M: Louis A. Hirsch.

5438. Turner Layton (1894–Feb. 6, 1978) B: Washington, DC. Composer, pianist, singer, performer. *Spice of 1922* (Winter Garden, revue, July 6, 1922): Way Down Yonder in New Orleans/W: Henry Creamer, M: Turner Layton.

5439. Jerry LaZarre *Pipe Dream* (Shubert, "Esteban," Nov. 30, 1955): All at Once You Love Her/W: Oscar Hammerstein II, M: Richard Rodgers.

5440. Frank Lazarus (May 4, 1939–) B: Cape Town, South Africa. *A Day in Hollywood/A Night in the Ukraine* (John Golden, "Carlo," May 1, 1980): Doin' the Production Code; It All Comes Out of the Piano; A Night in the Ukraine/W: Dick Vosburgh, M: Frank Lazarus — I Love a Film Cliche/W: Dick Vosburgh, M: Trevor Lyttleton — Just Go to the Movies/WM: Jerry Herman.

5441. Roy Lazarus *The Most Happy Fella* (Imperial > Broadway, "Al," May 3, 1956): Standing on the Corner/WM: Frank Loesser. *The Most Happy Fella* (New York City Center, revival, "Al," Feb. 10, 1959): same as above.

5442. Kay Lazell *The Little Show* (Music Box, revue, CR, July 15, 1929): Get Up on a New Routine/W: Howard Dietz, M: Arthur Schwartz.

5443. Emilie Lea *High Jinks* (Lyric > Casino, "Chi-Chi," Dec. 10, 1913): The Bubble; Chi-Chi/W: Otto Harbach, M: Rudolf Friml. *Lady Luxury* (Casino > Comedy, "Madame Mischkowa," Dec. 25, 1914): That Rag-Tag Dance/W: Rida Johnson Young, M: William Schroeder. *The Love Mill* (48th Street, "Lucille," Feb. 7,

1918): Follow Mama's Advice; Watch the Things You Eat/W: Earl Carroll, M: Alfred Francis. *Glorianna* (Liberty, "Jessica," Oct. 26, 1918): Chianti; Toodle-oo/W: Catherine Chisholm Cushing, M: Rudolf Friml. *Angel Face* (Knickerbocker, "Tessie Blythe," Dec. 29, 1919): I Don't Want to Go Home; I Might Be Your Once-in-a-While; Say When; Tip Your Hat to Hattie/W: Robert B. Smith, M: Victor Herbert.

5444. Flora Lea *Ziegfeld Midnight Frolic [7th Edition]* (New Amsterdam roof, revue, CR, Aug. 19, 1918): Here Come the Yanks; Try a Ring, Dear!; We Are the Bright Lights of Broadway/W: Gene Buck, M: Dave Stamper. *Topics of 1923* (Broadhurst, revue, Nov. 20, 1923): Rin Tin Tin/W: Harold Atteridge, M: Jean Schwartz, Alfred Goodman. *Artists and Models of 1924* (Astor > Casino, revue, Oct. 15, 1924): Dancing Colors; Off to Greenwich Village/WM: ?.

5445. Archie Leach (Jan. 18, 1904–Nov. 29, 1986) B: Bristol, England. In Hollywood, he changed his name to CARY GRANT. *Boom-Boom* (Casino, "Reggie Phipps," Jan. 28, 1929): Nina/W: Mann Holiner, J. Keirn Brennan, M: Werner Janssen. *Nikki* (Longacre, "Cary Lockwood," Sept. 29, 1931): On Account of I Love You; Taking Off/W: James Dyrenforth, M: Phil Charig.

5446. Clare Leach *42nd Street* (Winter Garden, CR, "Peggy Sawyer," Sept. 17, 1985/Sept. 16, 1986): About a Quarter to Nine; 42nd Street; Go Into Your Dance; We're in the Money; Young and Healthy; You're Getting to Be a Habit with Me/W: Al Dubin, M: Harry Warren.

5447. Marjory (Marjorie) Leach *Innocent Eyes* (Winter Garden, revue, "Esther," May 20, 1924): Damn Clever, These Chinese/WM: ?— Let's Have a Rattling Good Time/W: Alfred Bryan, M: Jean Schwartz. *Music in May* (Casino, "Zenzi," Apr. 1, 1929): For the Papa/W: J. Keirn Brennan, M: Maurie Rubens — It's the Cooks, Not the Looks/WM: ?.

5448. Cloris Leachman (Apr. 30, 1925–) B: Des Moines, IA. Sister of CLAIBORN CARY. Talented actress whose performances in film and TV include the role of Phyllis Lindstrom on *The Mary Tyler Moore Show* (1970). She won an Oscar for *The Last Picture Show* (1971). *South Pacific* (Majestic, CR, "Ensign Nellie Forbush," Oct. 1952): A Cockeyed Optimist; Dites-Moi; Honey Bun; I'm Gonna Wash That Man Right Outa My Hair; Some Enchanted Evening; Twin Soliloquies (Wonder How I'd Feel); A Wonderful Guy/W: Oscar Hammerstein II, M: Richard Rodgers.

5449. Sundy Leigh Leake *Cats* (Winter Garden, CR, "Tantomile"): The Moments of Happiness/W: T.S. Eliot, M: Andrew Lloyd Webber.

5450. Cecil Lean (July 8, 1878–July 18, 1935) B: London, Ontario, Canada. M: CLEO MAYFIELD. *The Soul Kiss* (New York, "Ketcham Short," Jan. 28, 1908): Any Old Place in the World with You; I'm the Human Night Key of New York; Let's Pretend/W: Harry B. Smith, M: Maurice Levi — Rah! Rah! Rah! (Those College Yells)/W: Cecil Lean, M: C.M. Chapel. *Bright Eyes* (New York, "Tom Genowin," Feb. 28, 1910): Cheer Up My Honey; The Lines in Molly's Hand; The Mood You Are In/W: Otto Harbach, M: Karl Hoschna — He's a Fan, Fan, Fan/W: Cecil Lean, M: Florence Holbrook. *The Man with Three Wives* (Weber and Fields, "Hans Ziffer," Jan. 23, 1913): The Temporary Widow; Woman of Temperament/WM: ? — The Vale of Dreaming/W: Paul M. Potter, Harold Atteridge, M: Franz Lehar — When You're Traveling/W: Cecil Lean, M: Al W. Brown. *The Blue Paradise* (Casino > 44th Street, "Rudolph Stoeger," Aug. 5, 1915): Auf Wiedersehn/W: Herbert Reynolds, M: Sigmund Romberg — Here's to You, My Sparkling Wine/W: Blanche Merrill, M: Leo Edwards — The Tune They Croon in the U.S.A./WM: Cecil Lean — Vienna, How D'Ye Do?; Vienna, Vienna/W: Herbert Reynolds, M: Edmund Eysler. *Miss 1917* (Century, revue, Nov. 5, 1917): Dinah/WM: ? — Goodbye Broadway, Hello France/W: C. Francis Reisner, Benny Davis, M: Billy Baskette — The Palm Beach Girl; We're Crooks/W: P.G. Wodehouse, M: Jerome Kern. *Look Who's Here* (44th Street, "Robert W. Holmes," Mar. 2, 1920): (I'll Make) Bubbles; Look Who's Here/W: Edward A. Paulton, M: Silvio Hein — I Know and You Know; Love Never Changes; The Turk Has the Right Idea/W: Edward A. Paulton, Cecil Lean, M: Silvio Hein — Since My Wife Got Fat/W: Cecil Lean, M: Silvio Lean. *The Blushing Bride* (Astor, "Coley Collins," Feb. 6, 1922): Bad Little Boy and Good Little Girl; Cazazza; Different Days; Goodbye; I'll Bet on Anything but Girls; Mister and Missus; Springtime Is the Time for Loving/W: Cyrus D. Wood, M: Sigmund Romberg. *Innocent Eyes* (Winter Garden, revue, "Prof. Honore Longuebois," May 20, 1924): Croony Spoony Tune/W: Tot Seymour, M: Jean Schwartz — Dear Old Moulin Rouge; Our Emblem Is the Lily/WM: ? — Innocent Eyes/W: McElbert Moore, M: J. Fred Coots, Jean Schwartz. *Allez-Oop* (Earl Carroll, revue, CR, Nov. 7, 1927): What Did William Tell?/W: Leo Robin, M: Phil Charig, Richard Myers.

5451. Tommy Leap *The Sound of Music*

(Lunt-Fontanne, CR, "Kurt," Aug. 1962): Do Re Mi; Edelweiss; The Lonely Goatherd; So Long, Farewell; The Sound of Music/W: Oscar Hammerstein II, M: Richard Rodgers. *The King and I* (New York City Center, revival, "Louis Leonowens," June 12, 1963): I Whistle a Happy Tune/W: Oscar Hammerstein II, M: Richard Rodgers.

5452. Ford Leary (Sept. 5, 1908–June 4, 1949) B: Lockport, NY. In the 1930s and 1940s he was a trombonist and vocalist with big bands such as Bunny Berigan and Larry Clinton. *Follow the Girls* (44th Street > Broadhurst, CR, "Goofy Gale," June 3, 1945): A Tree That Grows in Brooklyn; You're Perf/W: Dan Shapiro, Milton Pascal, M: Phil Charig.

5453. Lois Leary *How to Succeed in Business Without Really Trying* (46th Street, CR, "Rosemary," Aug. 1962): Been a Long Day; Cinderella Darling; Happy to Keep His Dinner Warm; I Believe in You; Paris Original; Rosemary/WM: Frank Loesser.

5454. Thomas Leary (c 1868–June 13, 1923) *The Sho-Gun* (Wallack's, "Hanki-Pank," Oct. 10, 1904): Flutter Little Bird; Teach the Young Idea How to Shoot/W: George Ade, M: Gustav Luders. *The Student King* (Garden, "Merrilaff," Dec. 25, 1906): In Bohemia; Opposites Are We/W: Frederick Ranken, Stanislaus Stange, M: Reginald De Koven. *Mecca* (Century, "Wei San Wei," Oct. 4, 1920): Me Welly Poor Old Chinaman/W: Oscar Asche, M: Percy E. Fletcher.

5455. Beth Leavel (Nov. 1, 1955–) B: Raleigh, NC. *Crazy for You* (Sam S. Shubert, "Tess," Feb. 19, 1992): Slap That Bass/W: Ira Gershwin, M: George Gershwin. *Show Boat* (Gershwin, revival, CR, "Ellie," Nov. 1995): Goodbye, My Lady Love/WM: Joseph E. Howard — Life Upon the Wicked Stage/W: Oscar Hammerstein II, M: Jerome Kern.

5456. Douglas Leavitt (c 1883–Mar. 3, 1960) *Take It from Me* (44th Street, "Dick Roller," Mar. 31, 1919): I Like to Linger in the Lingerie/W: Will B. Johnstone, M: Will R. Anderson. *Innocent Eyes* (Winter Garden, revue, CR, "Prof. Honore Longuebois," July 7, 1924): Croony Spoony Tune/W: Tot Seymour, M: Jean Schwartz — Dear Old Moulin Rouge; Our Emblem Is the Lily/WM: ? — Innocent Eyes/W: McElbert Moore, M: J. Fred Coots, Jean Schwartz. *Gay Paree* (Winter Garden, revue, Nov. 9, 1926): There Never Was a Town Like Paris/W: Mann Holiner, M: Alberta Nichols.

5457. Flora Le Breton (1898–) B: Croydon, Surrey, England. *The Optimists* (Casino de Paris, revue, Jan. 30, 1928): Dreamy Days/WM: ?. *Pre-*

sent Arms (Mansfield, "Lady Delphine Wither-spoon," Apr. 26, 1928): Do I Hear You Saying I Love You?; Is It the Uniform?/W: Lorenz Hart, M: Richard Rodgers. *The Cat and the Fiddle* (Globe, "Maizie Gripps," Oct. 15, 1931): I Watch the Love Parade/W: Otto Harbach, M: Jerome Kern.

5458. Henry Le Clair (July 27–) B: Cranston, RI. *1776* (46th Street, "Robert Livingston," Mar. 16, 1969): But, Mr. Adams/WM: Sherman Edwards.

5459. Charles Le Clercq (c 1841–Sept. 20, 1895) B: England. *The Royal Middy* (Daly's, "Don Domingos Domingos De Barros," Jan. 28, 1880): Of All the Fine Fellows That Sail on the Sea; Sword in Hand, Man to Man; To Our Flag/W: F. Zell, M: Richard Genee. *Cinderella at School* (Daly's, "Lord Lawntennys," Mar. 5, 1881): My Dear Young Ladies/WM: Woolson Morse.

5460. William Ledbetter *Brigadoon* (New York State, revival, "Archie Beaton," Feb. 28, 1986): Down on MacConnachy Square/W: Alan Jay Lerner, M: Frederick Loewe. *Wonderful Town* (New York State, revival, "Guide," Nov. 8, 1994): Christopher Street/W: Betty Comden, Adolph Green, M: Leonard Bernstein.

5461. Baayork Lee *Flower Drum Song* (St. James, CR, "Night Club Singer," Feb. 1960): Fan Tan Fannie/W: Oscar Hammerstein II, M: Richard Rodgers. *Promises, Promises* (Shubert, "Miss Wong," Dec. 1, 1968): Turkey Lurkey Time/W: Hal David, M: Burt Bacharach.

5462. Beatrice Lee *No, No, Nanette* (Globe, "Betty," Sept. 16, 1925): Fight Over Me; Telephone Girlie/W: Otto Harbach, M: Vincent Youmans — I Want to Be Happy/W: Irving Caesar, M: Vincent Youmans.

5463. Bernice Lee *Walk a Little Faster* (St. James, revue, Dec. 7, 1932): Off Again, On Again; A Penny for Your Thoughts [Jan. 2, 1933]; Unaccustomed as I Am/W: E.Y. Harburg, M: Vernon Duke.

5464. Dorothy Lee (May 23, 1911–June 24, 1999) B: Los Angeles, CA. She appeared in comedy films with BERT WHEELER and ROBERT WOOLSEY. *Hello Yourself!!!!* (Casino, "Sue Swift," Oct. 30, 1928): Bobby's Nightmare; I Want the World to Know; We Might Play Tiddle De Winks/W: Leo Robin, M: Richard Myers.

5465. Emilie Lee *Hands Up* (44th Street, "Mlle. Marcelle," July 22, 1915): On the Levee Along Broadway; Orange Girl/W: E. Ray Goetz, M: Sigmund Romberg. *Love Birds* (Apollo, "Mme. Delaunois" and "Velouka," Mar. 15,

1921): Carnival Night/W: Ballard Macdonald, M: Sigmund Romberg — Persian Fantasy (Persiana)/W: Jack Stern, Clarence Marks, M: Sigmund Romberg.

5466. Eullah Lee *The Mocking Bird* (Bijou, return engagement, CR, "Manon de Lange," May 25, 1903): A Stale World and a Pale World/W: Sydney Rosenfeld, M: A. Baldwin Sloane.

5467. Graham Lee *Alive and Kicking* (Winter Garden, revue, Jan. 17, 1950): One! Two! Three!/W: Ray Golden, Paul Francis Webster, M: Sonny Burke.

5468. Gypsy Rose Lee (Feb. 9, 1913–Apr. 26, 1970) B: Seattle, WA. Sister of JUNE HAVOC. Actress and dancer, and the world's best known and classiest stripper. The hit musical *Gypsy* was based on their lives. *Ziegfeld Follies of 1936-1937* (Winter Garden, revue, Sept. 14, 1936): The Economic Situation; I Can't Get Started/W: Ira Gershwin, M: Vernon Duke — The Gazooka/WM: Ira Gershwin, David Freedman. *Du Barry Was a Lady* (Royale, CR, "May Daley" and "Du Barry," Oct. 1940): But in the Morning, No!; Come On In; Do I Love You?; Du Barry Was a Lady; Friendship; Give Him the Oo-La-La; Katie Went to Haiti; When Love Beckoned/WM: Cole Porter. *Star and Garter* (Music Box, revue, June 24, 1942): Star and Garter/W: Jerry Seelen, M: Lester Lee.

5469. Harriette Lee *Sun Showers* (Astor, "Minnie Silver," Feb. 5, 1923): I'm a Greenwich Village Chambermaid; Speak Without Compunction/WM: Harry Delf.

5470. Helen Lee *Miss Daisy* (Shubert > Lyric, "Elvira Walsh," Sept. 9, 1914): Kissing; My Little Queen Bee; Pierrot's Ball; Tea Leaves/W: Philip Bartholomae, M: Silvio Hein. *Girl o' Mine* (Bijou, "Mildred," Jan. 28, 1918): Girl o' Mine; Love Is Just a Fairy Tale/W: Philip Bartholomae, M: Frank Tours.

5471. Henrietta Lee *Mary's Lamb* (New York, "Sylvia Montrose," May 25, 1908): Jamais d'la Vie; The Modest Little Model/WM: Richard Carle. *The Girl of My Dreams* (Criterion, "Helen Bombastino," Aug. 7, 1911): What's Sauce for the Gander Is Sauce for the Goose/W: Otto Harbach, M: Karl Hoschna.

5472. Irving Allen Lee (Nov. 21, 1948–Sept. 5, 1992) B: New York, NY. *Ride the Winds* (Bijou, "Musashi," May 16, 1974): The Emperor Me; Loving You; Someday I'll Walk; Those Who Speak; You're Loving Me/WM: John Driver. *Pippin* (Imperial, CR, "Leading Player," June 1975): Glory; On the Right Track; Simple Joys/WM: Stephen Schwartz. *Rockabye Hamlet*

(Minskoff, "Player," Feb. 17, 1976): Something's Rotten in Denmark; The Wart Song/WM: Cliff Jones. *A Broadway Musical* (Lunt-Fontanne, "James Lincoln," Dec. 21, 1978): Broadway, Broadway; A Broadway Musical; It's Time for a Cheer-Up Song; The 1934 Hot Chocolate Jazz Babies Revue; Smoke and Fire; Together; You Gotta Have Dancing/W: Lee Adams, M: Charles Strouse. *Sweet Charity* (Minskoff, revival, "Daddy Johann Sebastian Brubeck," Apr. 27, 1986): The Rhythm of Life/W: Dorothy Fields, M: Cy Coleman.

5473. Jae Woo Lee *Pacific Overtures* (Winter Garden, "Fisherman," Jan. 11, 1976): Four Black Dragons/WM: Stephen Sondheim.

5474. James Lee *The Girl from Paris* (Wallack's, revival, "Cecil Smyth," Jan. 17, 1898): The Festive Continong/W: George Dance, M: Ivan Caryll.

5475. Joan Lee *A Night in Paris* (Casino de Paris [Century roof], revue, CR, Jan. 11, 1926): Louisiana/W: McElbert Moore, M: J. Fred Coots, Maurie Rubens.

5476. Kathryn Lee (Sept. 1, 1926–) B: Denison, TX. *Allegro* (Majestic, "Hazel Skinner," Oct. 10, 1947): Money Isn't Ev'rything/W: Oscar Hammerstein II, M: Richard Rodgers.

5477. Laura Lee (1910–) M: DWIGHT FRYE. *The Greenwich Village Follies of 1928* (Winter Garden, revue, Apr. 9, 1928): Dirty Dig/W: Max Lief, Nathaniel Lief, M: Maurie Rubens — Get Your Man/W: Max Lief, Nathaniel Lief, M: Ray Perkins — Padlock Your Blues/WM: ?— What's the Reason?/W: Harold Atteridge, M: Maurie Rubens. *Broadway Nights* (44th Street, revue, "Flo DeForrest," July 15, 1929): Bracelets/W: J. Keirn Brennan, M: Maurie Rubens — Come Hit Your Baby; White Lights Were Coming; Why Don't We?/W: Moe Jaffe, M: Sam Timberg, Maurie Rubens — The Lobster Crawl/W: Benny Davis, M: Ted Lewis — Stranded in a One-Horse Town/WM: ?— Your Broadway and Mine/W: Moe Jaffe, M: Maurie Rubens.

5478. Lillian Lee *Dream City* (Weber's, "Maria Dinglebender," Dec. 25, 1906): Bound for the Opera/W: Edgar Smith, M: Victor Herbert.

5479. Lois Lee M: HARVEY STONE. *High Button Shoes* (New Century, "Fran," Oct. 9, 1947): Can't You Just See Yourself?; Next to Texas, I Love You; You're My Girl/W: Sammy Cahn, M: Jule Styne.

5480. Lovey Lee *Peg o' My Dreams* (Al Jolson, "Blanche," May 5, 1924): All Alone; Lily Bell Polka; Right-O/W: Anne Caldwell, M: Hugo Felix. *The Magnolia Lady* (Shubert, "Stella Hallett," Nov. 25, 1924): A la Gastronome/W: Anne Caldwell, M: Harold A. Levey. *Tip-Toes* (Liberty, "Denise Marshall," Dec. 28, 1925): It's a Great Little World; Sweet and Low-Down; When Do We Dance?/W: Ira Gershwin, M: George Gershwin.

5481. Mable Lee *Shuffle Along of 1952* (Broadway, revue, "Mable," May 8, 1952): Bongo-Boola/W: Noble Sissle, M: Eubie Blake — Here 'Tis/W: Floyd Huddleston, M: Joseph Meyer.

5482. Margaret Lee *Follow Thru* (46th Street, "Babs Bascomb," Jan. 9, 1929): It's a Great Sport; Married Men and Single Men; Then I'll Have Time for You/W: B.G. DeSylva, Lew Brown, M: Ray Henderson. *Three's a Crowd* (Selwyn, revue, Oct. 15, 1930): All the King's Horses/WM: Howard Dietz, Edward Brandt, Alec Wilder — Forget All Your Books/W: Howard Dietz, Samuel Lerner, M: Burton Lane — Je T'Aime/W: Howard Dietz, M: Arthur Schwartz — Out in the Open Air/W: Howard Dietz, Ted Pola, M: Burton Lane — Practising Up on You/W: Howard Dietz, M: Phil Charig. *Face the Music* (New Amsterdam, "Pickles," Feb. 17, 1932): I Don't Want to Be Married; You Must Be Born with It/WM: Irving Berlin. *Face the Music* (44th Street, return engagement, "Pickles," Jan. 31, 1933): same as above. *Revenge with Music* (New Amsterdam, "Margarita," Nov. 28, 1934): My Father Said; Never Marry a Dancer; Once-in-a-While/W: Howard Dietz, M: Arthur Schwartz.

5483. Michele Lee (June 24, 1942–) B: Los Angeles, CA. She played Karen Fairgate MacKenzie on the TV drama *Knots Landing* (1979). *Vintage '60* (Brooks Atkinson, revue, Sept. 12, 1960): Five Piece Band/WM: Jack Wilson, Alan Jeffreys, Maxwell Grant. *Bravo Giovanni* (Broadhurst, "Miranda," May 19, 1962): Breachy's Law; I'm All I've Got; One Little World Apart; Steady, Steady/W: Ronny Graham, M: Milton Schafer. *How to Succeed in Business Without Really Trying* (46th Street, CR, "Rosemary," Oct. 8, 1962): Been a Long Day; Cinderella Darling; Happy to Keep His Dinner Warm; I Believe in You; Paris Original; Rosemary/WM: Frank Loesser. *Seesaw* (Uris, "Gittel Mosca," Mar. 18, 1973/Oct. 15, 1973): Chapter 54, Number 1909; He's Good for Me; I'm Way Ahead; In Tune; Nobody Does It Like Me; Poor Everybody Else; Seesaw; Spanglish; Welcome to Holiday Inn!/W: Dorothy Fields, M: Cy Coleman.

5484. Myra Lee *Blossom Time* (Jolson, revival, "Greta," Mar. 8, 1926): Lonely Heart/W: Dorothy Donnelly, M: Sigmund Romberg.

5485. Peggy Lee (May 26, 1920–Jan. 21, 2002) B: Jamestown, ND. Pop singer, songwriter, recording artist. One of the best. She began her career as a vocalist in a Fargo North Dakota nightclub, and sang over radio station WDAY. *Peg* (Lunt-Fontanne, one-woman revue, Dec. 14, 1983): Angels on Your Pillow; Daddy Was a Railroad Man; Flowers and Flowers; He'll Make Me Believe That He's Mine; Mama; No More Rainbows; The Other Part of Me; Sometimes You're Up; Soul; That Old Piano; That's How I Learned to Sing the Blues; There Is More; What Did Dey Do to My Goil?/W: Peggy Lee, M: Paul Horner — Big Spender/W: Dorothy Fields, M: Cy Coleman — Fever/WM: John Davenport, Eddie Cooley, Peggy Lee — Goody Goody/W: Johnny Mercer, M: Matt Malneck — I Don't Know Enough About You; It's a Good Day; Manana/WM: Peggy Lee, Dave Barbour — I Love Being Here with You; One Beating a Day/WM: Peggy Lee — I'm a Woman; Is That All There Is?/WM: Jerry Leiber, Mike Stoller — Lover/W: Lorenz Hart, M: Richard Rodgers — Stay Away from Louisville Lou/W: Jack Yellen, M: Milton Ager — Why Don't You Do Right?/WM: Joe McCoy.

5486. Phoebe Lee *Ziegfeld Follies of 1920* (New Amsterdam, revue, June 22, 1920): Tell Me, Little Gypsy/WM: Irving Berlin.

5487. Richard L. Lee (June 1, 1872–July 24, 1931) B: New York, NY. *Miss Hook of Holland* (Criterion, "Ludwig Schnapps," Dec. 31, 1907): A Little Bit of Cheese/WM: Paul Rubens.

5488. Ruth Lee (c 1896–1975) *The Yankee Princess* (Knickerbocker, "Fifi," Oct. 2, 1922): Lotus Flower/W: B.G. DeSylva, M: Emmerich Kalman.

5489. Sam Lee *The 5 O'Clock Girl* (44th Street, "Oswald," Oct. 10, 1927): Following in Father's Footsteps; Society Ladder; We Want You/W: Bert Kalmar, M: Harry Ruby. *Pleasure Bound* (Majestic, revue, "Packy," Feb. 18, 1929): Cross Word Puzzles/WM: ?.

5490. Sammy Lee (May 26, 1890–Mar. 30, 1968) B: New York, NY. Producer, choreographer, director. *The Firefly* (Lyric > Casino, "Pietro," Dec. 2, 1912): De Trop; The Latest Thing from Paris; A Trip to Bermuda/W: Otto Harbach, M: Rudolf Friml.

5491. Sondra Lee (Sept. 30, 1930–) B: Newark, NJ. *Peter Pan* (Winter Garden, "Tiger Lily," Oct. 20, 1954): Indians!/W: Carolyn Leigh, M: Moose Charlap — Ugg-a-Wugg/W: Betty Comden, Adolph Green, M: Jule Styne. *Street Scene* (New York City Center, revival, "Mae Jones," Feb. 13, 1960): Moon-Faced, Starry-Eyed/W: Langston Hughes, M: Kurt Weill. *Hello, Dolly!* (St. James, "Minnie Fay," Jan. 16, 1964): Dancing/WM: Jerry Herman — Elegance; Motherhood/WM: Bob Merrill, Jerry Herman.

5492. Sylvan Lee *Naughty Riquette* (Cosmopolitan, "Jean," Sept. 13, 1926): He May Say Yes Today/W: Harry B. Smith, M: Oscar Straus — Someone/W: Harry B. Smith, M: Alfred Goodman, Maurie Rubens. *Lady Do* (Liberty, "Jack," Apr. 18, 1927): Snap Into It; You Can't Eye a Shy Baby/W: Sam M. Lewis, Joe Young, M: Abel Baer.

5493. Thelma Lee *Fiddler on the Roof* (Winter Garden, revival, "Golde," Dec. 28, 1976): Anatevka; Do You Love Me?; Sabbath Prayer; Sunrise, Sunset; The Tailor, Motel Kamzoil/W: Sheldon Harnick, M: Jerry Bock.

5494. Valerie Lee B: New York, NY. *Here's Love* (Shubert, "Susan Walker," Oct. 3, 1963): Arm in Arm; My Wish; Pine Cones and Holly Berries/WM: Meredith Willson.

5495. Al Leech *The Jolly Bachelors* (Broadway, "Chase Payne," Jan. 6, 1910): Walk This Way/W: Glen MacDonough, M: Raymond Hubbell. *The Never Homes* (Broadway, "Daly Bunn," Oct. 5, 1911): I'm All for You/W: E. Ray Goetz, M: Raymond Hubbell — That Spooky Tune/W: E. Ray Goetz, M: A. Baldwin Sloane.

5496. Beverly Leech *City of Angels* (Virginia, CR, "Alaura Kingsley," Mar. 1991): Double Talk; The Tennis Song/W: David Zippel, M: Cy Coleman.

5497. Edna Leedom *Ziegfeld Follies of 1923* (New Amsterdam, revue, Oct. 20, 1923): I'm a Manicurist/WM: Blanche Merrill — Little Old New York/W: Gene Buck, M: Victor Herbert — What Thrills Can There Be?/W: Harry Ruskin, M: Dave Stamper. *Ziegfeld Follies of 1924-1925* (New Amsterdam, revue, June 24, 1924): The Great Wide Open Spaces/W: Gene Buck, M: Dave Stamper — The Old Town Band/W: Joseph McCarthy, M: Harry Tierney. *Lovely Lady* (Sam H. Harris, "Folly Watteau," Dec. 29, 1927): Boy Friends; Breakfast in Bed; Lovely Lady/W: Cyrus D. Wood, M: Dave Stamper, Harold A. Levey.

5498. Harry Leeds Partner of TRIXIE LE MAR. They were billed as Leeds and Le Mar. *The Revue of Revues* (Winter Garden, revue, Sept. 27, 1911): College Boys; On the Congo/ WM: ?.

5499. Jordan Leeds (Nov. 29, 1961–) B: Queens, NY. *Sunset Boulevard* (Minskoff, CR, "Artie Green," Sept. 1995): Every Movie's a Circus; This Time Next Year/W: Don Black, Christopher Hampton, M: Andrew Lloyd Webber.

5500. Lyda Sue Leeds *The Show Is On* (Winter Garden, revue, CR, Sept. 18, 1937): Little Old Lady/W: Stanley Adams, M: Hoagy Carmichael — What Has He Got?/W: Ted Fetter, M: Vernon Duke.

5501. Michael Leeds (Nov. 14, 1951–) B: New York, NY. *Pal Joey* (Circle in the Square, revival, "Victor," June 27, 1976): That Terrific Rainbow/W: Lorenz Hart, M: Richard Rodgers.

5502. Peter Leeds (May 30, 1917–Nov. 12, 1996) B: Bayonne, NJ. The comedy actor was in movies from 1941 and on TV for over 5,000 appearances. *Sugar Babies* (Mark Hellinger, revue, "Peter," Oct. 8, 1979): I Want a Girl (Just Like the Girl That Married Dear Old Dad)/W: William Dillon, M: Harry Von Tilzer — Let Me Be Your Sugar Baby/WM: Arthur Malvin.

5503. Phil Leeds (c 1916–Aug. 16, 1998) B: New York, NY. *Of V We Sing* (Concert, revue, Feb. 11, 1942): Brooklyn Cantata/W: Mike Stratton, M: George Kleinsinger — Juke Box/W: Alfred Hayes, M: Alex North — You've Got to Appease with a Strip Tease/W: Lewis Allan, M: Toby Sacher. *Let Freedom Sing* (Longacre, revue, Oct. 5, 1942): Flowers in Bloom/W: David Gregory, M: Jack Gerald — Johnny Is a Hoarder/WM: Harold Rome. *Can-Can* (Shubert, "Theophile," May 7, 1953): If You Loved Me Truly; Never, Never Be an Artist/WM: Cole Porter. *Christine* (46th Street, "Uncle," Apr. 28, 1960): Freedom Can Be a Most Uncomfortable Thing; How to Pick a Man a Wife; Welcome Song/W: Paul Francis Webster, M: Sammy Fain. *Nowhere to Go but Up* (Winter Garden, "Hop Wong" and "Hymie," Nov. 10, 1962): Follow the Leader Septet; The We Makin' Cash with Sour Mash: No Rickie-Tickie No Licq-ie Rag/W: James Lipton, M: Sol Berkowitz. *Sophie* (Winter Garden, "William Morris," Apr. 15, 1963): Hold On to Your Hats/WM: Steve Allen. *Hurry, Harry* (Ritz, "Town Drunk" and "Dr. Krauss" and "Chorus Boy," Oct. 12, 1972): Hurry, Harry; When a Man Cries; You Won't Be Happy/W: David Finkle, M: Bill Weeden.

5504. Jeni Le Gon *Black Rhythm* (Comedy, "Jenny," Dec. 19, 1936): Here 'Tis/WM: Donald Heywood. *Early to Bed* (Broadhurst, "Lily-Ann," June 17, 1943): Hi De Hi Ho in Harlem; Slightly Less Than Wonderful; Supple Couple; When the Nylons Bloom Again/W: George Marion, Jr., M: Fats Waller.

5505. Phyllis Le Grand *Orange Blossoms* (Fulton, "Helene de Vasquez," Sept. 19, 1922): Because I Love You So; I Can't Argue with You; Then Comes the Dawning/W: B.G. DeSylva, M: Victor Herbert.

5506. David Le Grant *Oklahoma!* (New York City Center, revival, "Ali Hakim," Aug. 31, 1953): It's a Scandal! It's a Outrage!/W: Oscar Hammerstein II, M: Richard Rodgers.

5507. Stephen Lehew *Brigadoon* (Majestic, revival, "Charlie Dalrymple," Oct. 16, 1980): Come to Me, Bend to Me; I'll Go Home with Bonnie Jean/W: Alan Jay Lerner, M: Frederick Loewe.

5508. Philip Lehl (Apr. 29, 1964–) B: Terra Haute, IN. *Blood Brothers* (Music Box, CR, "Mickey," c 1993): Kids Game; Long Sunday Afternoon; My Friend; That Guy/WM: Willy Russell.

5509. Russell Leib *Big River: The Adventures of Huckleberry Finn* (Eugene O'Neill, CR, "The Duke," Sept. 2, 1985): The Royal Nonesuch; When the Sun Goes Down in the South/WM: Roger Miller.

5510. Marie Leidal *The Cradle Will Rock* (Mansfield > Broadway, revival, "Sadie Polock," Dec. 28, 1947): Gus and Sadie Love Song/WM: Marc Blitzstein.

5511. Harriet Leidy *The Yankee Girl* (Herald Square, CR, "Rosie," Feb. 21, 1910): I'll Make a Ring Around Rosie/W: George V. Hobart, M: Silvio Hein.

5512. Grace (Gracie) Leigh (c 1875–June 24, 1950) M: LIONEL MACKINDER. *Ziegfeld Follies of 1908* (Jardin de Paris — New York roof > New York, revue, June 15, 1908): Mosquito Song/W: Harry B. Smith, M: Maurice Levi — Take Me 'Round in a Taxicab/W: Edgar Selden, M: Melville Gideon. *The Little Cafe* (New Amsterdam, "Katziolinka," Nov. 10, 1913): I'm a-Hunting Jaguar; Just Because It's You/W: C.M.S. McLellan, M: Ivan Caryll. *The Girl Who Smiles* (Lyric > Longacre, "Alphonse Duttier," Aug. 9, 1915): My Pauline; You Are My Little Cupid/WM: Edward A. Paulton, Adolf Philipp, Jean Briquet. *Roly-Boly Eyes* (Knickerbocker, CR, "Mrs. Penelope Giddings," Oct. 13, 1919): A Matron's Good Night's Sleep/W: Edgar Allen Woolf, M: Eddy Brown, Louis Gruenberg.

5513. Leslie Leigh *The Isle of Spice* (Majestic, "Trinket," Aug. 23, 1904): Peggy Brady/W: Allen Lowe, M: Paul Schindler, Ben M. Jerome — Star of Fate/W: George E. Stoddard, M: Paul Schindler. *Sporting Days and Battle in the Skies* (Hippodrome, CR, "Kitty Vanderveer," Jan. 4, 1909): When the Circus Comes to Town/WM: Manuel Klein.

5514. Lois Leigh (c 1902–Sept. 2, 1921) *The Magic Melody* (Shubert, "Melody of Dance," Nov. 11, 1919): Melody of Dance/W: Alex Gerber, M: Sigmund Romberg. *The Night Boat*

(Liberty, "Susan," Feb. 2, 1920): Girls Are Like a Rainbow; I Love the Lassies (I Love Them All/W: Anne Caldwell, M: Jerome Kern.

5515. Vivien Leigh (Nov. 5, 1913–July 8, 1967) B: Darjeeling, India. M: Laurence Olivier. A great beauty, best remembered as Scarlet O'Hara in the classic film *Gone with the Wind* (1939). *Tovarich* (Broadway, "Tatiana," Mar. 18, 1963): All for You; I Know the Feeling; Make a Friend; The Only One; Wilkes-Barre, PA.; You Love Me/W: Anne Crosswell, M: Lee Pockriss — You'll Make an Elegant Butler (I'll Make an Elegant Maid)/WM: Joan Javits, Philip Springer.

5516. Trixie Le Mar Partner of HARRY LEEDS. They were billed as Leeds and Le Mar. *The Revue of Revues* (Winter Garden, revue, Sept. 27, 1911): College Boys; On the Congo/WM: ?.

5517. William LeMassena (May 23, 1916–Jan. 19, 1993) B: Glen Ridge, NJ. *Come Summer* (Lunt-Fontanne, "Francis Faucett," Mar. 18, 1969): Moonglade/W: Will Holt, M: David Baker.

5518. Harvey Lembeck (Apr. 15, 1923–Jan. 5, 1982) B: Brooklyn, NY. *Oklahoma!* (New York City Center, revival, "Ali Hakim," Mar. 19, 1958): It's a Scandal! It's a Outrage!/W: Oscar Hammerstein II, M: Richard Rodgers.

5519. Marguerite Lemon *The Geisha* (Daly's, revival, "O Mimosa San," Mar. 21, 1898): The Amorous Goldfish; A Geisha's Life; The Kissing Duet/W: Harry Greenbank, M: Sidney Jones — The Jewel of Asia/W: Harry Greenbank, M: James Philp.

5520. Robert Lenn (June 13, 1914–Jan. 15, 1980) B: Courtland, NY. *Whoop-Up* (Shubert, "Hotel Proprietor," Dec. 22, 1958): Quarrel-tet/W: Norman Gimbel, M: Moose Charlap. *High Spirits* (Alvin, "Bob," Apr. 7, 1964): The Sandwich Man/WM: Hugh Martin, Timothy Gray.

5521. Robert Emmett Lennon *The Ham Tree* (New York, CR, "Ike Mainstem," Sept. 25, 1905): Goodbye Sweet Old Manhattan Isle/W: William Jerome, M: Jean Schwartz. *The Yankee Prince* (Knickerbocker, "Duke of Dollsford," Apr. 20, 1908): A Song of the King/WM: George M. Cohan.

5522. Fred Lennox *The Girl from Paris* (Wallack's, revival, "Ebenezer Honeycomb," Jan. 17, 1898): So Take You a Warning/W: George Dance, M: Ivan Caryll. *An English Daisy* (Casino, "Hiram Smart," Jan. 18, 1904): Big Indian Chief/W: Bob Cole, M: J. Rosamond Johnson. *The Three Romeos* (Globe, "Timothy Stubbs," Nov. 13, 1911): Along Broadway; He's Crazy; She

Didn't Seem to Care/W: R.H. Burnside, M: Raymond Hubbell.

5523. Jane Lennox *By the Sad Sea Waves* (Grand Opera House, revival, "Lily Flower," Mar. 5, 1900): Japanese Baby; Soldiers in Love's War; This Dear Little Fellow Was Cupid/W: Harry Bulger, J. Sherrie Mathews, M: Gustav Luders.

5524. William Lennox *Fifty-Fifty, Ltd.* (Comedy, "Monty," Oct. 27, 1919): Along the Hudson/WM: Arthur Swanstrom, Carey Morgan.

5525. Rosetta LeNoire (Aug. 8, 1911–Mar. 17, 2002) B: New York, NY. Actress of the stage, movies and TV; founder of Amas Repertory Theatre. She played Grandma Winslow on the TV sitcom *Family Matters* (1989). *The Hot Mikado* (Broadhurst, "Peep-Bo," Mar. 23, 1939): So Pardon Us; Three Little Maids/W: William S. Gilbert, M: Arthur Sullivan. *South Pacific* (New York City Center, revival, "Bloody Mary," Apr. 13, 1961): Bali Ha'i; Happy Talk/W: Oscar Hammerstein II, M: Richard Rodgers. *Sophie* (Winter Garden, "Mollie," Apr. 15, 1963): Hold On to Your Hats; Patsy; When I'm in Love; You've Got to Be a Lady/WM: Steve Allen. *I Had a Ball* (Martin Beck, "Ma Maloney," Dec. 15, 1964): Coney Island, U.S.A.; The Neighborhood Song; Think Beautiful/WM: Jack Lawrence, Stan Freeman. *Show Boat* (New York State, revival, "Queenie," July 19, 1966): Can't Help Lovin' Dat Man; Queenie's Bally-hoo/W: Oscar Hammerstein II, M: Richard Rodgers.

5526. Adriane Lenox (Sept. 11, 1956–) B: Memphis, TN. *Ain't Misbehavin'* (Longacre, revue, CR, Sept. 24, 1979): How Ya Baby/W: James C. Johnson, M: Fats Waller — I Can't Give You Anything but Love/W: Dorothy Fields, M: Jimmy McHugh — I've Got My Fingers Crossed/W: Ted Koehler, M: Jimmy McHugh — Keepin' Out of Mischief Now/W: Andy Razaf, M: Fats Waller — Lounging at the Waldorf/W: Richard Maltby, Jr., M: Fats Waller — When the Nylons Bloom Again/W: George Marion, Jr., M: Fats Waller — Yacht Club Swing/W: James C. Johnson, M: Fats Waller, Herman Autry.

5527. Lotte Lenya (Oct. 18, 1898–Nov. 27, 1981) B: Vienna, Austria. M: composer Kurt Weill, whose songs she sang. They settled in New York in 1937. *The Firebrand of Florence* (Alvin, "Duchess," Mar. 22, 1945): The Little Naked Boy; Sing Me Not a Ballad/W: Ira Gershwin, M: Kurt Weill. *Cabaret* (Broadhurst, "Fraulein Schneider," Nov. 20, 1966/Feb. 26, 1968/Oct. 7, 1968): It Couldn't Please Me More;

Married; So What?; What Would You Do/W: Fred Ebb, M: John Kander.

5528. Daisy Leon *The Pearl Maiden* (New York, "Talulu," Jan. 22, 1912): A Coral Isle; That Typical, Topical, Tropical Tune/W: Arthur F. Kales, Earle C. Anthony, M: Harry Auracher.

5529. Dorothy Leon *Grease* (Broadhurst, "Miss Lynch," June 7, 1972): Alma Mater/WM: Jim Jacobs, Warren Casey.

5530. Joseph Leon (June 8, 1923–Mar. 25, 2001) B: New York, NY. *The Merry Widow* (New York State, revival, "General Novikovich," Aug. 17, 1964): Women/W: Forman Brown, M: Franz Lehar.

5531. Billie Leonard *You Said It* (46th Street, "Grace Carroll," Jan. 19, 1931): Wha'd' We Come to College For?/W: Jack Yellen, M: Harold Arlen. *You Said It* (46th Street, CR, "Hattie Hudson," May 18, 1931): They Learn About Women from Me; You'll Do/W: Jack Yellen, M: Harold Arlen. *Caviar* (Forrest, "Helen," June 7, 1934): Haywire/WM: Edward Heyman — My Heart's an Open Book; One in a Million/W: Edward Heyman, M: Harden Church.

5532. Eddie Leonard (Oct. 18, 1875–July 29, 1941) B: Richmond, VA. A blackface minstrel, comedian, vaudeville headliner and songwriter for 45 years. *Lifting the Lid* (New Amsterdam roof, "Willie Steele [Texas Dan]," June 5, 1905): Coonland/WM: Kenneth Clark — Texas Dan/W: William Jerome, M: Jean Schwartz. *Cohan and Harris Minstrels* (New York, revue, Aug. 3, 1908): Big Brown Boo Loo Eyes/WM: Eddie Leonard. *Roly-Boly Eyes* (Knickerbocker, "Billy Emerson," Sept. 25, 1919): Ida, Sweet as Apple Cider/WM: Eddie Leonard, Eddie Munson — Just a Girl, Just a Boy; Minstrel Serenade; That Minstrel Man; Your Voice I Hear/W: Edgar Allen Woolf, M: Eddy Brown, Louis Gruenberg.

5533. Freda Leonard *Shubert Gaieties of 1919* (44th Street, revue, July 14, 1919): Vamp a Little Lady (The Vamp)/WM: Byron Gay.

5534. Leon Leonard *Flo Flo* (Cort, "Billy Cope," Dec. 20, 1917): Business Is Business; I Don't Know What You See in Me; There's Only One Little Girl; Would You Say No?/W: Edward A. Paulton, M: Silvio Hein — When a Small Town Girl Meets a Small Town Boy/W: George Edwards, M: Silvio Hein.

5535. Lu Leonard (1932–) B: Long Beach, NY. She played Gertrude the secretary on the TV legal drama *Jake and the Fatman* (1987). *The Happiest Girl in the World* (Martin Beck, "Myrrhina," Apr. 3, 1961): Love-Sick Serenade/W:

E.Y. Harburg, M: Jacques Offenbach. *The Gay Life* (Shubert, "Frau Brandel," Nov. 18, 1961): You Will Never Be Lonely/W: Howard Dietz, M: Arthur Schwartz. *Drat! The Cat!* (Martin Beck, "Kate Purefoy," Oct. 10, 1965): She's Roses/W: Ira Levin, M: Milton Schafer.

5536. Queenie Leonard (Apr. 7, 1905–Jan. 17, 2002) B: Manchester, England. The actress and singer appeared in more than 30 movies in Hollywood, as well as in cabaret in the U.S. and Britain. *This Year of Grace* (Selwyn, revue, Nov. 7, 1928): Little Women; Lorelei; Try to Learn to Love/WM: Noel Coward.

5537. Robert Z. Leonard (Feb. 22, c 1889– Jan. 5, 1948) B: Poland. M: MAE MURRAY. *Kosher Kitty Kelly* (Times Square > Daly's 63rd St., "Moses Ginsburg," June 15, 1925): What's in Store for You/WM: Leon DeCosta.

5538. Urylee Leonardos (May 14–Apr. 25, 1986) B: Charleston, SC. *Carmen Jones* (New York City Center, revival, "Carmen Jones," Apr. 7, 1946): Dat Ol' Boy; Dat's Love; Dere's a Cafe on de Corner; If You Would Only Come Away; Whizzin' Away Along de Track/W: Oscar Hammerstein II, M: Georges Bizet. *Porgy and Bess* (Ziegfeld, revival, "Bess," Mar. 10, 1953): Bess, You Is My Woman Now; I Loves You, Porgy/W: Ira Gershwin, DuBose Heyward, M: George Gershwin — Leavin' fo' de Promis' Lan'; What You Want wid Bess?/W: DuBose Heyward, M: George Gershwin — There's a Boat Dat's Leavin' Soon for New York/W: Ira Gershwin, M: George Gershwin. *1600 Pennsylvania Avenue* (Mark Hellinger, "Rachel," May 4, 1976): Welcome Home Miz Adams/W: Alan Jay Lerner, M: Leonard Bernstein.

5539. Henry Leone (Mar. 30, 1857–June 9, 1922) B: Constantinople, Turkey. Also known as HENRI LEONI. *An English Daisy* (Casino, "Compte Dubois," Jan. 18, 1904): Spin Again/ W: Percy Greenbank, M: Alfred Muller-Norden. *A Parisian Model* (Broadway, "Julien de Marsay," Nov. 27, 1906): An American Girl in Paris/W: Harry B. Smith, Vincent Bryan, M: Max Hoffmann — I Want Yer Ma Honey/WM: Fay Templeton — I Love You, Ma Cherie/WM: Paul Rubens — Lots of Good Fish in the Sea [Dec. 10, 1906]/WM: ?. *Miss Princess* (Park, "Prince Alexis," Dec. 23, 1912): Behind the Scenes; I Never Had a Kiss; Queen Thou Art; The Wireless Way/W: Will Johnstone, M: Alexander Johnstone. *Mlle. Modiste* (Globe, revival, "Henri de Bouvray, Compte de St. Mar," May 26, 1913): I Want What I Want When I Want It/W: Henry Blossom, M: Victor Herbert. *Sari* (New Amsterdam, CR, "Pali Racz," May 11,

1914): Long Live the King (Vive le Roi); Marry Me; My Faithful Stradavari; Stop It, Stop It; Time, Oh Time, You Tyrant King; Triumphant Youth/W: C.C.S. Cushing, E.P. Heath, M: Emmerich Kalman. *Fiddlers Three* (Cort, "Carlo Andreani," Sept. 3, 1918): When the Fiddle Bows Begin to Fly/W: William Cary Duncan, M: Alexander Johnstone.

5540. John Leone (Apr. 7, 1964–) B: Weymouth, MA. *Les Miserables* (Broadway, CR, "Marius"): Empty Chairs at Empty Tables; A Heart Full of Love; In My Life; A Little Fall of Rain; Red and Black/W: Herbert Kretzmer, M: Claude-Michel Schonberg.

5541. Maud Leone (c 1885–Mar. 13, 1930) *Roly-Boly Eyes* (Knickerbocker, "Mrs. Penelope Giddings," Sept. 25, 1919): A Matron's Good Night's Sleep/W: Edgar Allen Woolf, M: Eddy Brown, Louis Gruenberg.

5542. Ray Leone *Earl Carroll's Vanities of 1928* (Earl Carroll, revue, Aug. 6, 1928): Forever Mine/WM: George Bagby, G. Romilli.

5543. Adrienne Leonetti *The Most Happy Fella* (Majestic, revival, "Marie," Oct. 11, 1979): How Beautiful the Days; Young People/WM: Frank Loesser.

5544. Henri Leoni see HENRY LEONE.

5545. Sharon Lerit *Bye Bye Birdie* (Martin Beck, "Sad Girl" and "Alice," Apr. 14, 1960): One Boy; Put on a Happy Face/W: Lee Adams, M: Charles Strouse.

5546. Hal LeRoy (Dec. 10, 1913–May 2, 1985) B: Cincinnati, OH. *Thumbs Up!* (St. James, revue, Dec. 27, 1934): Lily Belle May June/W: Earle Crooker, M: Henry Sullivan — Zing! Went the Strings of My Heart!/WM: James F. Hanley. *Too Many Girls* (Imperial, "Al Terwilliger," Oct. 18, 1939): I Like to Recognize the Tune; Spic and Spanish/W: Lorenz Hart, M: Richard Rodgers. *Count Me In* (Ethel Barrymore, "Alvin," Oct. 8, 1942): Someone in the Know/WM: Ann Ronell.

5547. Ken LeRoy (Aug. 17, 1927–) B: Detroit, MI. *I Can Get It for You Wholesale* (Shubert, "Meyer Bushkin," Mar. 22, 1962): Ballad of the Garment Trade; The Family Way; A Gift Today (The Bar Mitzvah Song); Have I Told You Lately?/WM: Harold Rome. *Fiddler on the Roof* (New York State, revival, "Mendel," July 9, 1981): Anatevka/W: Sheldon Harnick, M: Jerry Bock.

5548. Victor Le Roy *Oh, My Dear!* (Princess > 39th Street, "Willie Love," Nov. 27, 1918): Ask Dad; If They Ever Parted Me from You/W: P.G. Wodehouse, M: Louis A. Hirsch — A Moment of Peace [Apr. 21, 1919]/WM: ?.

5549. Walter (William) Le Roy *The American Idea* (New York, "Daniel Sullivan," Oct. 5, 1908): F-A-M-E; Sullivan/WM: George M. Cohan.

5550. Joseph Lertora *Miss Daisy* (Shubert > Lyric, "Duke of Tormina," Sept. 9, 1914): I Adore the American Girl; I Love You, Dear, I Love but You; Interruptions; Little Girl, What Have You Done to Me?; Shadows; Weave from Your Looms; You Were Made for Love; Youth/W: Philip Bartholomae, M: Silvio Hein. *The Princess Pat* (Cort, Prince Antonio di Montaldo [Toto]," Sept. 29, 1915): All for You!; Neapolitan Love Song (Sweet One How My Heart Is Yearning)/W: Henry Blossom, M: Victor Herbert. *Going Up* (Liberty, "Jules Gaillard," Dec. 25, 1917): Kiss Me; There's a Brand New Hero/W: Otto Harbach, M: Louis A. Hirsch. *Glorianna* (Liberty, "Lieut. Dick Pennington," Oct. 28, 1918): Love! Love! Love! [Nov. 11, 1918]; When a Girl/W: Catherine Chisholm Cushing, M: Rudolf Friml. *The Sweetheart Shop* (Knickerbocker, "Julian Lorimer," Aug. 31, 1920): Didn't You?; Life Is a Carousel; My Caravan/W: Anne Caldwell, M: Hugo Felix — Waiting for the Sun to Come Out/W: Arthur Francis, M: George Gershwin. *Helen of Troy, New York* (Selwyn > Times Square, "Baron De Cartier," June 19, 1923): Advertising; Nijigo Novgo Glide; What Makes a Business Man Tired?/W: Bert Kalmar, M: Harry Ruby. *The Chiffon Girl* (Lyric, "Mario Navarro," Feb. 19, 1924): The Cafe Boheme; Did You Come Back?; My Tonita; Till the End of Time; We're Sweethearts/WM: Monte Carlo, Alma Sanders. *June the 14th* (Cosmopolitan, "Capt. Gallifet," Mar. 3, 1925): Follow the Rajah/W: Arthur Wimperis, M: Sigmund Romberg. *Twinkle Twinkle* (Liberty, "Jack Wyndham," Nov. 16, 1926): Get a Load of This; I Hate to Talk About Myself; You Know, I Know/W: Harlan Thompson, M: Harry Archer. *Lady Do* (Liberty, "Duke De Corsona," Apr. 18, 1927): In My Castle in Sorrento; Live Today; O Sole Mi — Whose Soul Are You?/W: Sam M. Lewis, Joe Young, M: Abel Baer. *Say When* (Morosco, "Count Scippio Varelli," June 26, 1928): Cheerio/W: James J. Walker, M: Jesse Greer. *Music in May* (Casino, "Baron Metternich," Apr. 1, 1929): Lips That Laugh at Love/W: J. Keirn Brennan, M: Maurie Rubens. *There You Are* (George M. Cohan, "Don Jose Gomez," May 16, 1932): Haunting Refrain/WM: William Heagney, Tom Connell.

5551. Elene Leska *Somewhere Else* (Broadway, "Chloe," Jan. 20, 1913): As Birds Greet Morning Skies; Can You Do This?; For You Dear

Heart; If I Kissed You/W: Avery Hopwood, M: Gustav Luders.

5552. Charlotte Leslay *Alma, Where Do You Live?* (Weber's, "Louise," Sept. 26, 1910): Boo Hoo Hoo/W: George V. Hobart, M: Jean Briquet.

5553. Bert Leslie *Fluffy Ruffles* (Criterion, "Noggie Noggles," Sept. 7, 1908): I Wonder Why Jane Is a Suffragette/W: Wallace Irwin, M: William T. Francis. *Our Miss Gibbs* (Knickerbocker, "Slithers," Aug. 29, 1910): An English Gentleman/W: Percy Greenbank, M: Lionel Monckton — A Little Change/W: Basil Hood, M: Walter Slaughter — Will You Sing This Glee with Me?/W: George Arthurs, M: Harold Lonsdale. *The Hen-Pecks* (Broadway, "Dr. I. Stall," Feb. 4, 1911): He's the Wonder of Them All/ WM: ?.

5554. Doree Leslie *Simple Simon* (Ziegfeld, "Elaine King" and "Cinderella," Feb. 18, 1930): I Can Do Wonders with You; Send for Me/W: Lorenz Hart, M: Richard Rodgers.

5555. Earl Leslie *Innocent Eyes* (Winter Garden, revue, "Harry," May 20, 1924): Let's Have a Rattling Good Time/W: Alfred Bryan, M: Jean Schwartz — Organdie Days/W: Tot Seymour, M: Jean Schwartz — Surrounded by the Girls/ WM: ?.

5556. Ellen Leslie *Bloomer Girl* (New York City Center, revival, "Lydia," Jan. 6, 1947): Welcome Hinges; When the Boys Come Home/W: E.Y. Harburg, M: Harold Arlen.

5557. Eva Leslie *By the Sad Sea Waves* (Herald Square, "Babette," Feb. 21, 1899): Calisthenic Song/W: ?, M: Barney Fagan.

5558. Fred Leslie (May 19, 1881–Aug. 1, 1945) B: London, England. *Charlot Revue of 1924* (Times Square > Selwyn, revue, Jan. 9, 1924): Limehouse Blues/W: Douglas Furber, M: Philip Braham. *Sweetheart Time* (Imperial, "Lord Hector Raybrook," Jan. 19, 1926): Cocktail Melody/W: Ballard Macdonald, M: Walter Donaldson — Step on It/W: Irving Caesar, M: Joseph Meyer.

5559. George W. Leslie (c 1863–Aug. 15, 1911) B: Philadelphia, PA. M: LOUISE WILLIS-HEPNER. *Alma, Where Do You Live?* (Weber's, "Gaston," Sept. 26, 1910): Boogie Boo; Never More/W: George V. Hobart, M: Jean Briquet.

5560. May (Mae) Leslie (?–July 21, 1965) *About Town* (Herald Square, CR, "Mattahnac," Nov. 15, 1906): The Legend of the Mojaves/W: Joseph W. Herbert, M: Gustave Kerker. *Miss 1917* (Century, revue, Nov. 5, 1917): We Want to Laugh; Who's Zoo in Girl Land/W: P.G. Wodehouse, M: Jerome Kern. *Morris Gest Midnight*

Whirl (Century Grove, revue, Dec. 27, 1919): Limehouse Nights/W: B.G. DeSylva, John Henry Mears, M: George Gershwin.

5561. Sylvia Leslie *Bitter Sweet* (Ziegfeld, "Gussie," Nov. 5, 1929): Ladies of the Town/ WM: Noel Coward. *Conversation Piece* (44th Street, "Sophie Otford," Oct. 23, 1934): Charming, Charming; Dear Little Soldiers; There's Always Something Fishy About the French/ WM: Noel Coward.

5562. Amy Lesser *Hodge, Podge & Co.* (Madison Square, "Evangeline Hodge," Oct. 23, 1900): A Billet Doux/W: Walter Ford, M: George V. Hobart — What a Funny Story/W: Walter Ford, M: Herman Perlet.

5563. Florence Lessing (c 1916–Sept. 6, 2002) *Kismet* (Ziegfeld, "Princess Zubbediya of Damascus" and "Street Dancer," Dec. 3, 1953): Bazaar of the Caravans; Rahadlakum/WM: Robert Wright, George Forrest.

5564. Madge Lessing (1866–1932) *Wang* (Lyric, revival, CR, "Mataya," May 16, 1904): Ask the Man in the Moon; Baby, Baby, Dance My Darling Baby; No Matter What Others May Say; A Pretty Girl, a Summer Night; Where Are You Going, My Pretty Maid?/W: J. Cheever Goodwin, M: Woolson Morse — Tizan, My Maid of Hindoostan/W: George Lieb, M: Leo Friedman.

5565. Dorothy Lester *The Liberty Belles* (Madison Square, "Ruth Leslie," Sept. 30, 1901): Lesson Book Song/W: ?, M: Aimee Lachaume.

5566. Florence Lester *Lola from Berlin* (Liberty, "Edith Westervelt," Sept. 16, 1907): Beneath the Moon; I Think of You the Whole Year Round/W: William Jerome, M: Jean Schwartz.

5567. Jerry Lester (Feb. 16, 1910–Mar. 23, 1995) B: Chicago, IL. The boisterous comedian hosted *Broadway Open House* (1950), the first successful late-night network TV talk and variety show. *Beat the Band* (46th Street, "Hugo Dillingham," Oct. 14, 1942): America Loves a Band; The Four Freedoms; Free, Cute and Size Fourteen; I'm Physical, You're Cultured/W: George Marion, Jr., M: Johnny Green. *Jackpot* (Alvin, "Jerry Finch," Jan. 13, 1944): (I'm in Love with) My Top Sergeant; A Piece of a Girl; Sugarfoot; What's Mine Is Yours/W: Howard Dietz, M: Vernon Duke. *A Funny Thing Happened on the Say to the Forum* (Alvin, CR, "Prologus" and "Pseudolus," Dec. 17, 1962/Oct. 21, 1963): Bring Me My Bride; Comedy Tonight; Free; Lovely; Pretty Little Picture/WM: Stephen Sondheim.

5568. Todd Lester *Starlight Express* (Gershwin, "Flat-Top," Mar. 15, 1987): Belle/W: Richard Stilgoe, M: Andrew Lloyd Webber. *Cats*

(Winter Garden, CR, "Mistoffolees"): The Invitation to the Jellicle Ball; Mr. Mistoffolees; Mungojerrie and Rumpleteazer/W: T.S. Eliot, M: Andrew Lloyd Webber. *Cats* (Winter Garden, CR, "Mungojerrie"): Mungojerrie and Rumpleteazer/W: T.S. Eliot, M: Andrew Lloyd Webber.

5569. Val Lester *Just Fancy* (Casino, CR, "Jill" and "Kay," Nov. 14, 1927): Ain't Love Grand; Dressed Up for Your Sunday Beau; Shake, Brother!; You Came Along/W: Leo Robin, M: Joseph Meyer, Phil Charig.

5570. Robert Lett *King Dodo* (Daly's, CR, "Dr. Fizz," May 26, 1902): The Eminent Doctor Fizz; In Lands Unknown/W: Frank Pixley, M: Gustav Luders. *The Fisher Maiden* (Victoria, "Sir George Gilding," Oct. 5, 1903): Coo-ee, Coo-ee; He Dandled Me on His Knee; Let the Band Play a Pleasing Tune/W: Arthur J. Lamb, M: Harry Von Tilzer.

5571. Larry Leung *Flower Drum Song* (St. James, CR, "Frankie Wing," Dec. 1959): Gliding Through My Memoree/W: Oscar Hammerstein II, M: Richard Rodgers.

5572. Estelle Levelle *Artists and Models of 1923* (Shubert > Winter Garden, revue, Aug. 20, 1923): Say It with a Ukelele/WM: Art Conrad — Take Me Back to Samoa Some More/W: Cyrus D. Wood, M: Jean Schwartz.

5573. Sam Levene (Aug. 28, 1905–Dec. 28, 1980) B: New York, NY. *Guys and Dolls* (46th Street, "Nathan Detroit," Nov. 24, 1950): The Oldest Established; Sue Me/WM: Frank Loesser. *Let It Ride!* (Eugene O'Neill, "Patsy," Oct. 12, 1961): If Flutterby Wins; I'll Learn Ya; Let It Ride/WM: Jay Livingston, Ray Evans. *Cafe Crown* (Martin Beck, "Hymie, the Busboy," Apr. 17, 1964): Magical Things in Life; So Long as It Isn't Shakespeare; That's the Life for Me; What's the Matter with Buffalo?/W: Marty Brill, M: Albert Hague.

5574. Emma Levey *The Good Mister Best* (Garrick, "Lizette," Aug. 30, 1897): Puff, Puff/W: John J. McNally, M: ?.

5575. Ethel Levey (Nov. 22, 1880–Feb. 27, 1955) B: San Francisco, CA. M: GEORGE M. COHAN, c 1900–1907. The hugely popular singer and dancer also starred for nearly ten years in British stage revues and music halls. *The Governor's Son* (Savoy, "Emerald Green," Feb. 25, 1901): And the Manager Said...; Lucy; The Quakertown Cadets/WM: George M. Cohan. *Running for Office* (14th Street, "Gertie Gayland," Apr. 27, 1903): I'll Be There in the Public Square; Kid Days; The Reubens on Parade/WM: George M. Cohan. *Little Johnny Jones*

(Liberty > New York, "Goldie Gates," Nov. 7, 1904): A Girl I Know; Goodbye Flo; Mam'selle Fauchette/WM: George M. Cohan. *George Washington, Jr.* (Herald Square > New York, "Dolly Johnson," Feb. 12, 1906): Ethel Levey's Virginia Song (I Was Born in Virginia); Wedding of the Blue and the Gray/WM: George M. Cohan. *Nearly a Hero* (Casino, "Angeline De Vere," Feb. 24, 1908): I'm So Particular; The Queen of Belle Paree/WM: ?— My Sahara Belle/W: Harry B. Smith, M: Edward B. Claypoole. *Go Easy, Mabel* (Longacre, "Mabel Montmorency," May 8, 1922): Ethel Levey's Smile Song; Go Easy, Mabel; I Want a Regular Man; Oh, Papa; When You Dance with the Girl You Love/WM: Charles George. *Sunny River* (St. James, "Lolita," Dec. 4, 1941): The Butterflies and the Bees; Sunny River/W: Oscar Hammerstein II, M: Sigmund Romberg.

5576. Charles Levin *City of Angels* (Virginia, CR, "Buddy Fidler," Mar. 1991): The Buddy System; Double Talk/W: David Zippel, M: Cy Coleman.

5577. Patrick Levis (Jan. 23, 1982–) B: Silver Springs, MD. *Big* (Sam S. Shubert, "Young Josh," Apr. 28, 1996): Can't Wait; I Want to Know; Talk to Her/W: Richard Maltby, Jr., M: David Shire.

5578. Helen Le Von *Broadway Brevities of 1920* (Winter Garden, revue, Sept. 29, 1920): We've Got the Stage Door Blues/W: Bert Kalmar, M: Harry Ruby.

5579. Jaime Lewin *The President's Daughter* (Billy Rose, "Reb Yosel," Nov. 3, 1970): Love at Golden Years; Welcome, Mr. Golden!/W: Jacob Jacobs, M: Murray Rumshinsky.

5580. Abby Lewis (Jan. 14, 1910–Nov. 22, 1997) B: Mesilla Park, NM. M: JOHN D. SEYMOUR, 1951. She worked in early TV until her death. *70, Girls, 70* (Broadhurst, Apr. 15, 1971): You and I, Love/W: Fred Ebb, M: John Kander.

5581. Ada Lewis (Mar. 17, 1872–Sept. 24, 1925) B: New York, NY. M: JOHN W. PARR. The original "tough girl" of Harrigan and Hart vaudeville shows. *Courted into Court* (Bijou, "Mlle. Nocodi," Dec. 26, 1896): The Oompah/W: Fred Bowyer, M: John Baker. *Fritz in Tammany Hall* (Herald Square, "Lil McGrain," Oct. 16, 1905): East Side Lil/W: William Jerome, M: Jean Schwartz. *Old Dutch* (Herald Square, "Alma Villianyi," Nov. 22, 1909): Pretending/W: George V. Hobart, M: Victor Herbert. *The Dancing Duchess* (Casino, "Tilly," Aug. 20, 1914): I've Been Looking for You/W: R.H. Burnside, M: Milton Lusk. *The Night Boat* (Liberty, "Mrs. Maxim," Feb. 2, 1920): Good Night

Boat/W: Anne Caldwell, Frank Craven, M: Jerome Kern.

5582. Alde Lewis, Jr. *Big Deal* (Broadway, "Otis," Apr. 10, 1986): Hold Tight, Hold Tight/WM: Leonard Kent, Edward Robinson, Leonard Ware, Jerry Brandow, Willie Spotswood — Pick Yourself Up/W: Dorothy Fields, M: Jerome Kern.

5583. Bob Lewis (Mar. 16, 1909–Nov. 23, 1997) B: Brooklyn, NY. *Johnny Johnson* (44th Street, "Mayor," Nov. 19, 1936): Over in Europe/W: Paul Green, M: Kurt Weill.

5584. Bobo Lewis (May 14, 1926–Nov. 6, 1998) B: Miami, FL. *Working* (46th Street, "Rose Hoffman," May 14, 1978): Nobody Tells Me How/W: Susan Birkenhead, M: Mary Rodgers. *42nd Street* (Winter Garden, CR, "Maggie Jones," July 21, 1987): Getting Out of Town/W: Mort Dixon, M: Harry Warren — Go Into Your Dance; Shadow Waltz; Shuffle Off to Buffalo/W: Al Dubin, M: Harry Warren.

5585. Boncellia Lewis *The First* (Martin Beck, "Ruby," Nov. 17, 1981): You Do-Do-Do-It Good!/W: Martin Charnin, M: Bob Brush.

5586. Brenda Lewis (Mar. 2, 1921–) B: Harrisburg, PA. *Regina* (46th Street, "Birdie Hubbard," Oct. 31, 1949): Lionnet/WM: Marc Blitzstein. *The Girl in Pink Tights* (Mark Hellinger, "Lotta Leslie," Mar. 5, 1954): The Cardinal's Guard Are We; Love Is the Funniest Thing; You've Got to Be a Little Crazy/W: Leo Robin, M: Sigmund Romberg. *Cafe Crown* (Martin Beck, "Mme. Cole," Apr. 17, 1964): Au Revoir Poland; A Lifetime Love; Make the Most of Spring; A Mother's Heart; On This Wedding Day; That's the Life for Me/W: Marty Brill, M: Albert Hague.

5587. Carol Jean Lewis *Purlie* (Broadway, CR, "Missy," Mar. 30, 1971): Down Home; The Harder They Fall; He Can Do It/W: Peter Udell, M: Gary Geld. *Sarava* (Mark Hellinger, "Dionisia," Jan. 11, 1979): I'm Looking for a Man; You Do/W: N. Richard Nash, M: Mitch Leigh.

5588. Catherine Lewis (May 6, 1853–Feb. 15, 1942) B: Swansea, Wales. *The Royal Middy* (Daly's, "Fanchette," Jan. 28, 1880): All We Seem to Agree; Have You Forgot; I Am So Sick; In Woman's Heart Alone; My Name Is Fanchette; Sword in Hand, Man to Man; Through the Night; To Our Flag; Who Is the Woman/W: F. Zell, M: Richard Genee.

5589. Dave Lewis (1870–Nov. 18, 1924) B: U.S.A. *The District Leader* (Wallack's, "Tom Cole," Apr. 30, 1906): A Heart to Let/WM: Joseph E. Howard. *Ziegfeld Follies of 1907* (Jardin de Paris — New York roof > Liberty, revue,

July 8, 1907): Reincarnation/W: Vincent Bryan, M: E. Ray Goetz.

5590. E.W. Lewis *The Burgomaster* (Manhattan, "Foreman," Dec. 31, 1900): We Always Work the Public/W: Frank Pixley, M: Gustav Luders.

5591. Flo Lewis *Tick-Tack-Toe* (Princess, revue, Feb. 13, 1920): I'd Like to Know Why I Fell in Love with You; My Manicure Maids; Shimmy All the Blues Away; Take Me Back to Philadelphia, Pa.; Where's My Sweet and Pretty Man?/WM: Herman Timberg. *Big Boy* (Winter Garden > 44th Street, "Tessie Forbes," Jan. 7, 1925): The Dance from Down Yonder; Lead 'Em On; Something for Nothing/W: B.G. DeSylva, M: Joseph Meyer, James F. Hanley. *Twinkle Twinkle* (Liberty, "Bessie Smith," Nov. 16, 1926): Day Dreams [Apr. 4, 1927]/W: Bert Kalmar, M: Harry Ruby — Reuben; When We're Bride and Groom/W: Harlan Thompson, M: Harry Archer.

5592. Frank Lewis *Fluffy Ruffles* (Criterion, "Tom Jones," Sept. 7, 1908): Won't You Let Me Carry Your Parcel?/W: C.H. Bovill, M: Jerome Kern.

5593. Fred Irving Lewis *Let's Face It!* (Imperial, "Judge Henry Clay Pigeon," Oct. 29, 1941): I've Got Some Unfinished Business with You/WM: Cole Porter.

5594. Hazel Lewis *Ziegfeld Follies of 1912* (Moulin Rouge, revue, Oct. 21, 1912): Beautiful Girl/W: John E. Hazzard, M: Raymond Hubbell.

5595. Henry Lewis (1891–Feb. 1922) *Follow Me* (Casino, "Adolph Knutt," Nov. 29, 1916): Oh Johnny, Oh Johnny, Oh!/W: Ed Rose, M: Abe Olman — There's Just a Little Bit of Monkey Still Left in You and Me/W: Grant Clarke, M: James V. Monaco — What Do You Want to Make Those Eyes at Me For (When They Don't Mean What They Say!)/WM: Howard Johnson, Joseph McCarthy, James V. Monaco. *Frivolities of 1920* (44th Street, revue, Jan. 8, 1920): Squidgulums/WM: William B. Friedlander.

5596. James Lewis (Oct. 5, 1837–Sept. 10, 1896) B: Troy, NY. Leading comedian with Augustin Daly's company from 1869 until his death. *Cinderella at School* (Daly's, "Syntax," Mar. 5, 1881): A Cotton Cloth Ghost; Courting in the Moonlight; You Are an Orphan/WM: Woolson Morse.

5597. Jennifer Lewis (Jan. 25, 1957–) B: St. Louis, MO. *Eubie!* (Ambassador, revue, CR, Sept. 1979): If You've Never Been Vamped by a Brownskin (You've Never Been Vamped at All); I'm Craving for That Kind of Love; I'm Just

Wild About Harry/WM: Noble Sissle, Eubie Blake. *Rock 'n Roll! The First 5,000 Years* (St. James, revue, Oct. 24, 1982): Love to Love You, Baby/WM: Pete Bellotte, Giorgio Moroder, Donna Summer — You Keep Me Hangin' On/ WM: Eddie Holland, Lamont Dozier, Brian Holland.

5598. Jerry Lewis (Mar. 16, 1926–) B: Newark, NJ. Popular slapstick comedian, in movies from 1949. He and singer Dean Martin were partners until 1956. *Damn Yankees* (Marquis, revival, CR, "Applegate," Mar. 12, 1995): Those Were the Good Old Days; Two Lost Souls/WM: Richard Adler, Jerry Ross.

5599. Jessie Lewis (July 8, 1890–Apr. 6, 1971) B: New York, NY. *The Girl in the Spotlight* (Knickerbocker, "Clare," July 12, 1920): Come Across; In My Looking Glass/W: Robert B. Smith, M: Victor Herbert.

5600. Marcia Lewis (Aug. 18, 1938–) B: Melrose, MA. *Annie* (Alvin, CR, "Miss Hannigan," Apr. 29, 1981/Mar. 10, 1982): Easy Street; Little Girls/W: Martin Charnin, M: Charles Strouse. *Rags* (Mark Hellinger, "Rachel Halpern," Aug. 21, 1986): Penny a Tune; Three Sunny Rooms/W: Stephen Schwartz, M: Charles Strouse. *Roza* (Royale, "Mme. Katz," Oct. 1, 1987): Different/W: Julian More, M: Gilbert Becaud. *Fiddler on the Roof* (Gershwin, revival, "Golde," Nov. 18, 1990): Do You Love Me?; The Dream; Sabbath Prayer; Sunrise, Sunset/W: Sheldon Harnick, M: Jerry Bock. *Grease* (Eugene O'Neill, revival, "Miss Lynch," May 11, 1994): Alma Mater; Born to Hand-Jive/WM: Jim Jacobs, Warren Casey. *Chicago* (Richard Rodgers, revival, "Matron Morton [Mama]," Nov. 14, 1996): Class; When You're Good to Mama/W: Fred Ebb, M: John Kander.

5601. Mary Lewis *The Greenwich Village Follies of 1920* (Shubert, revue, Jan. 3, 1921): I'll Be Your Valentine; Parfum d'Amour/W: Arthur Swanstrom, John Murray Anderson, M: A. Baldwin Sloane — Just Snap Your Fingers at Care/W: B.G. DeSylva, M: Louis Silvers. *Ziegfeld Follies of 1922* (New Amsterdam, revue, June 5, 1922): Dreams for Sale/W: Herbert Reynolds, M: James F. Hanley — List'ning on Some Radio/W: Gene Buck, M: Louis A. Hirsch, Dave Stamper — Songs I Can't Forget; Sunny South/W: Gene Buck, M: Louis A. Hirsch — Weaving My Dreams/W: Gene Buck, M: Victor Herbert. *Rufus Le Maire's Affairs* (Majestic, revue, Mar. 28, 1927): Travel On/W: Ballard Macdonald, M: Martin Broones.

5602. Maxine Lewis Film actress of the 1930s and 40s. *A la Carte* (Martin Beck, revue,

Aug. 17, 1927): The Calinda; Palm Beach Baby/WM: Herman Hupfeld — Give Trouble the Air/W: Leo Robin, M: Louis Alter.

5603. Nadine Lewis B: Chicago, IL. *The Sound of Music* (Lunt-Fontanne, CR, "Sister Margaretta," Aug. 20, 1962): Maria/W: Oscar Hammerstein II, M: Richard Rodgers — *The Sound of Music* (New York City Center, revival, "Sister Margaretta," Apr. 26, 1967): same as above. *Johnny Johnson* (Edison, revival, "Goddess of Liberty," Apr. 11, 1971): Song of the Goddess/W: Paul Green, M: Kurt Weill.

5604. Norm Lewis *The Who's Tommy* (St. James, "Specialist," Apr. 22, 1993): Go to the Mirror/WM: Pete Townshend.

5605. Ralph Lewis B: New York, NY. *New Faces of 1943* (Ritz, revue, Dec. 22, 1942): Love, Are You Raising Your Head Again?; Radio City, I Love You/W: June Carroll, M: Lee Wainer — Richard Crudnut's Charm School/W: June Carroll, John Lund, M: Lee Wainer — Yes, Sir, I've Made a Date/W: J.B. Rosenberg, M: Lee Wainer.

5606. Ruby Lewis *Hip! Hip! Hooray!* (Music Hall, revue, "Alvie Holbrook," Oct. 10, 1907): Let's Wander Off Nowhere/W: Edgar Smith, M: Gus Edwards. *The Girl in the Spotlight* (Knickerbocker, "Margot," July 12, 1920): Catch 'Em Young, Treat 'Em Rough, Tell 'Em Nothing/W: Robert B. Smith, M: Victor Herbert.

5607. Ted Lewis (June 6, 1890–Aug. 25, 1971) B: Circleville, OH. His greeting to audiences, "Is ev'rybody happy?" became his trademark. For 56 years the famous showman, bandleader, singer and composer remained married to Adah Becker, a burlesque performer who became his business partner and secretary. *The Greenwich Village Follies of 1919* (Nora Bayes, revue, c Sept. 15, 1919): When My Baby Smiles at Me/W: Andrew B. Sterling, Ted Lewis, M: Bill Munro. *The Greenwich Village Follies of 1921* (Shubert, revue, Aug. 31, 1921): Bang! Bang! Bang!/W: John Murray Anderson, Arthur Swanstrom, M: Carey Morgan. *The Greenwich Village Follies of 1922* (Shubert, revue, Sept. 12, 1922): Georgette/W: Lew Brown, M: Ray Henderson. *Rufus Le Maire's Affairs* (Majestic, revue, Mar. 28, 1927): Land of Broken Dreams; Mexico/W: Ballard Macdonald, M: Martin Broones. *Artists and Models of 1927* (Winter Garden, revue, Nov. 15, 1927): Is Everybody Happy Now?/W: Jack Osterman, Ted Lewis, M: Maurie Rubens — Start the Band/WM: ?.

5608. Tom Lewis (May 17, 1867–Oct. 19, 1927) B: New Brunswick, NJ. *Hip! Hip! Hooray!* (Music Hall, revue, "Washington Deecy," Oct. 10, 1907): Coon College/W: Edgar Smith, M:

Gus Edwards. *The Yankee Prince* (Knickerbocker, "Steve Daly," Apr. 20, 1908): M-O-N-E-Y/WM: George M. Cohan. *The Sunshine Girl* (Knickerbocker, "Steve Daly," Feb. 3, 1913): The Butler; The Kitchen Range; Who's the Boss?/WM: Paul Rubens, Arthur Wimperis. *High Jinks* (Lyric > Casino, "Mr. J.J. Jeffreys," Dec. 10, 1913): Come Hither Eyes/WM: ?. *Molly O'* (Cort, "Dan O'Malley," May 17, 1916): Little Women/W: Robert B. Smith, M: Carl Woess. *The Blushing Bride* (Astor, "Christoper Pottinger," Feb. 6, 1922): Different Days/W: Cyrus D. Wood, M: Sigmund Romberg. *Helen of Troy, New York* (Selwyn > Times Square, "Elias Yarrow," June 19, 1923): What Makes a Business Man Tired?/W: Bert Kalmar, M: Harry Ruby.

5609. Vicki Lewis (Mar. 17, 1960–) B: Cincinnati, OH. *Do Black Patent Leather Shoes Really Reflect Up?* (Alvin, "Virginia Lear," May 27, 1982): Mad Bombers and Prom Queens/WM: James Quinn, Alaric Jans. *Wind in the Willows* (Nederlander, "Mole," Dec. 19, 1985): The Day You Came Into My Life; Follow Your Instinct; I'd Be Attracted; Messing About in Boats; That's What Friends Are For; The World Is Waiting for Me/WM: Roger McGough, William Perry. *Damn Yankees* (Marquis, revival, "Gloria Thorpe," Mar. 3, 1994): Shoeless Joe from Hannibal, Mo.; Six Months Out of Every Year/WM: Richard Adler, Jerry Ross.

5610. Kecia Lewis-Evans *Once on This Island* (Booth, "Asaka," Oct. 18, 1990): And the Gods Heard Her Prayer; Mama Will Provide/W: Lynn Ahrens, M: Stephen Flaherty.

5611. Drue Leyton (June 12, 1906–Feb. 8, 1997) B: Somers, WI. *A Hero Is Born* (Adelphi, "Lady Rosalind," Oct. 1, 1937): The Last Word; We Believe/W: Agnes Morgan, M: A. Lehman Engel.

5612. Sonya Leyton *Blossom Time* (Century, CR, "Kitzi," Nov. 20, 1922): Lonely Heart; Love Is a Riddle; Three Little Maids/W: Dorothy Donnelly, M: Sigmund Romberg.

5613. Don Liberto (June 10, 1915–) B: Pittsburgh, PA. *Look Ma, I'm Dancin'* (Adelphi, "Wotan," Jan. 29, 1948): Jazz; Shauny O'Shay/WM: Hugh Martin.

5614. Anna Lichter *The Prince of Pilsen* (Broadway, "Edith Adams," Mar. 17, 1903): The Field and Forest; The Message of the Violet; We Know It's Wrong to Flirt/W: Frank Pixley, M: Gustav Luders.

5615. James Liddy (c 1894–Feb. 18, 1936) *Artists and Models of 1923* (Shubert > Winter Garden, revue, Aug. 20, 1923): Flower of the Woodland/W: Cyrus D. Wood, Harold Atteridge, M: Jean Schwartz — Somehow/W: Cyrus D. Wood, M: Jean Schwartz. *Sky High* (Winter Garden, CR, "Horace Deveridge," Mar. 23, 1925): Give Your Heart in June-Time/W: Clifford Grey, Harold Atteridge, M: Victor Herbert — Intermezzo; The Letter Song/W: Harold Atteridge, M: Robert Stolz. *The Vagbond King* (Casino, CR, "Francois Villon," Nov. 1926): Love Me Tonight; Only a Rose; Song of the Vagabonds; Tomorrow/W: Brian Hooker, M: Rudolf Friml. *Castles in the Air* (Selwyn, CR, "John Brown," Dec. 13, 1926): If You Are in Love with a Girl; Latvia; Love Rules the World; My Lips, My Love, My Soul!; The Rainbow of Your Smile/W: Raymond W. Peck, M: Percy Wenrich.

5616. Lora Lieb *His Honor the Mayor* (New York > Wallack's, "Marjorie Vayne," May 28, 1906): Flower Song/WM: ?.

5617. Evanna Lien *The Sound of Music* (Lunt-Fontanne, "Gretl," Nov. 16, 1959): Do Re Mi; Edelweiss; The Lonely Goatherd; So Long, Farewell; The Sound of Music/W: Oscar Hammerstein II, M: Richard Rodgers — *The Sound of Music* (Lunt-Fontanne, CR, "Marta," Aug. 1962): same as above.

5618. Jennifer Light *Nine* (46th Street, CR, "Saraghina"): Be Italian; Ti Voglio Bene/WM: Maury Yeston.

5619. J.E. Lightfoot *Mr. Lode of Koal* (Majestic, "Sarg," Nov. 1, 1909): Bygone Days in Dixie/W: Alex Rogers, M: Bert Williams.

5620. Winnie Lightner (Sept. 17, 1899–Mar. 5, 1971) B: Greenport, NY. M: movie director Roy del Ruth. She was known in vaudeville as The Song a Minute Girl. She also appeared in several early talking pictures, including *Gold Diggers of Broadway* (1929). *George White's Scandals of 1922* (Globe, revue, Aug. 28, 1922): I'll Build a Stairway to Paradise/W: B.G. DeSylva, Arthur Francis, M: George Gershwin — Where Is the Man of My Dreams?/W: B.G. DeSylva, E. Ray Goetz, M: George Gershwin. *George White's Scandals of 1923* (Globe, revue, June 18, 1923): Last Night on the Back Porch (I Loved Her Best of All)/W: Lew Brown, M: Carl Schraubstader — Throw 'Er in High! [June 25, 1923] W: B.G. DeSylva, E. Ray Goetz, M: George Gershwin. *George White's Scandals of 1924* (Apollo, revue, June 30, 1924): Somebody Loves Me/W: B.G. DeSylva, Ballard Macdonald, M: George Gershwin — Tune in (to Station J.O.Y.)/W: B.G. DeSylva, M: George Gershwin. *Gay Paree* (Shubert, revue, Aug. 18, 1925): Give Me the Rain/WM: Lester Allen, Henry Creamer, Maurie Rubens — I Can't Believe That

You're in Love with Me/W: Clarence Gaskill, M: Jimmy McHugh — Oh! Boy, What a Girl/W: Bud Green, M: Frank Wright Bessinger — (My) Sugar Plum/W: B.G. DeSylva, M: Joseph Meyer, J. Fred Coots — Wide Pants Willie/W: Harold Atteridge, Henry Creamer, M: James F. Hanley — Toddle Trot/WM: ?. *Gay Paree* (Winter Garden, revue, Nov. 9, 1926): College Days/WM: ?— Paris Is a Paradise for Coons/W: Edward Madden, M: Jerome Kern. *Harry Delmar's Revels* (Shubert, revue, Nov. 28, 1927): I Love a Man in a Uniform/W: Billy Rose, Ballard Macdonald, M: James V. Monaco — Naga Saki/W: Billy Rose, Ballard Macdonald, M: Jesse Greer.

5621. George Liker *West Side Story* (Winter Garden, revival, "Action," Apr. 27, 1960): Gee, Officer Krupke!/W: Stephen Sondheim, M: Leonard Bernstein.

5622. Carolyn Lilja *Woodland* (New York > Herald Square, CR, "Miss Turtle Dove," Dec. 5, 1904): Dainty Little Ingenue; The Tale of a Turtle Dove/W: Frank Pixley, M: Gustav Luders.

5623. James A. Lillard *The Hot Mikado* (Broadhurst, "Pish-Tush," Mar. 23, 1939): Our Great Mikado; So Pardon Us; Young Men Despair/W: William S. Gilbert, M: Arthur Sullivan.

5624. Harry Lillford (?–Jan. 9, 1931) *Sitting Pretty* (Fulton, "Roper," Apr. 8, 1924): There Isn't One Girl/W: P.G. Wodehouse, M: Jerome Kern.

5625. Beatrice Lillie (May 29, 1894–Jan. 20, 1989) B: Toronto, Canada. The comic actress moved to England in her teens and appeared on the music hall stage from age 16. *Charlot Revue of 1924* (Times Square > Selwyn, revue, Jan. 9, 1924): March with Me!/W: Douglas Furber, M: Ivor Novello — There Are Times/W: Ronald Jeans, M: Ivor Novello — There's Life in the Old Girl Yet/WM: Noel Coward. *Charlot Revue of 1926* (Selwyn, revue, Nov. 10, 1925): March with Me!/W: Douglas Furber, M: Ivor Novello — Mouse! Mouse!/W: Hilda Brighten, M: Muriel Lillie — Susannah's Squeaking Shoes/W: Arthur Weigall, M: Muriel Lillie. *Oh, Please!* (Fulton, "Lily Valli," Dec. 17, 1926): The Girls of the Old Brigade/WM: ?— I Know That You Know; Like He Loves Me; Love and Kisses 'n' Everything; Nicodemus/W: Anne Caldwell, M: Vincent Youmans — Love Me/W: Reginald Arkell, M: Philip Braham. *She's My Baby* (Globe, "Tilly," Jan. 3, 1928): A Baby's Best Friend; Camera Shoot; The Swallows; When I Go on the Stage; Whoopsie/W: Lorenz Hart, M: Richard Rodgers — March with Me! [Feb. 1928]/W: Douglas Furber, M: Ivor Novello. *This Year of Grace* (Selwyn, revue, Nov. 7, 1928): Britannia Rules the Waves; Chauve-Souris; I Can't Think; Lilac Time; World Weary/WM: Noel Coward. *The Third Little Show* (Music Box, revue, June 1, 1931): Cinema Lorelei; Sevilla/W: Edward Eliscu, M: Ned Lehac — Mad Dogs and Englishmen/WM: Noel Coward — There Are Fairies at the Bottom of My Garden/W: Rose Fyleman, M: Liza Lehmann. *Walk a Little Faster* (St. James, revue, Dec. 7, 1932): End of a Perfect Night/W: E.Y. Harburg, M: Vernon Duke — Frisco Fanny/W: Earle Crooker, M: Henry Sullivan — Mayfair/W: Roland Leigh, M: William Waliter. *At Home Abroad* (Winter Garden > Majestic, revue, Sept. 19, 1935): Get Yourself a Geisha; O Leo!; Paree /W: Howard Dietz, M: Arthur Schwartz. *The Show Is On* (Winter Garden, revue, Dec. 25, 1936): Buy Yourself a Balloon/WM: Herman Hupfeld — Josephine Waters/W: E.Y. Harburg, M: Harold Arlen — Rhythm/W: Lorenz Hart, M: Richard Rodgers. *Set to Music* (Music Box, revue, Jan. 18, 1939): I Went to a Marvelous Party; I'm So Weary of It All; Mad About the Boy/WM: Noel Coward. *Seven Lively Arts* (Ziegfeld, revue, Dec. 7, 1944): Dancin' to a Jungle Drum; When I Was a Little Cuckoo/WM: Cole Porter. *Inside U.S.A.* (New Century, revue, Apr. 30, 1948): At the Mardi Gras; We Won't Take It Back/W: Howard Dietz, M: Arthur Schwartz. *Ziegfeld Follies of 1957* (Winter Garden, revue, Mar. 1, 1957): Intoxication/W: Marshall Barer, M: Dean Fuller — Miss (All You Don't Catch) Follies of 192-/WM: Herman Hupfeld. *High Spirits* (Alvin, "Madame Arcati," Apr. 7, 1964): The Bicycle Song; Go Into Your Trance; Talking to You/WM: Hugh Martin, Timothy Gray.

5626. William Lilling *Blossom Time* (Jolson, revival, "Von Schwind," May 19, 1924): Keep It Dark; My Springtime Thou Art; Serenade/W: Dorothy Donnelly, M: Sigmund Romberg.

5627. Lilo (Mar. 2, 1925–) B: France. *Can-Can* (Shubert, "La Mome Pistache," May 7, 1953): Allez Vous En (Go Away); Can-Can; C'est Magnifique; Every Man Is a Stupid Man; I Love Paris; Live and Let Live; Never Give Anything Away/WM: Cole Porter. *Pousse-Cafe* (46th Street, "Solange," Mar. 18, 1966): C'est Comme Ca; Easy to Take; Follow Me Up the Stairs; The Good Old Days; Let's; Thank You, Ma'am/W: Marshall Barer, M: Duke Ellington.

5628. Christina Lind *Sing Out the News* (Music Box, revue, Sept. 24, 1938): How Long Can Love Keep Laughing?/WM: Harold Rome.

5629. Della Lind *The Streets of Paris* (Broadhurst, revue, June 19, 1939): Danger in the Dark; Is It Possible?; South American Way/W: Al Dubin, M: Jimmy McHugh. *Music in My Heart* (Adelphi, "Princess Katherine Dolgorvki," Oct. 2, 1947): Stolen Kisses; Three's a Crowd/W: Forman Brown, M: Franz Steininger, based on Peter I. Tchaikovsky.

5630. Gloria Lind *Sweethearts* (Shubert, revival, "Nadine," Jan. 21, 1947): Every Lover Must Meet His Fate; Game of Love; Sweethearts/W: Robert B. Smith, M: Victor Herbert.

5631. Homer Lind *When Johnny Comes Marching Home* (New York, "Gen. William Allen," Dec. 16, 1902): The Drums; The Suwanee River; When Our Lips in Kisses Met/W: Stanislaus Stange, M: Julian Edwards. *The Gingerbread Man* (Liberty > New York, "Machevalius Fudge," Dec. 25, 1905): The Evil Eye; Incantation; That Awful Bogie Man/W: Frederick Ranken, M: A. Baldwin Sloane.

5632. Linda *Sidewalks of New York* (Knickerbocker, "Dorothy Brewster," Oct. 3, 1927): Just a Little Smile from You; Wherever You Are/W: Eddie Dowling, M: James F. Hanley.

5633. Stanley Lindahl *The Garrick Gaieties of 1925* (Garrick, revue, May 17, 1925): Stage Managers' Chorus (Walk Upon Your Toes)/W: Dudley Digges, Lorenz Hart, M: Richard Rodgers.

5634. Hal Linden (Mar. 20, 1931–) B: Bronx, NY. He began his career playing saxophone and singing with bands such as Sammy Kaye and Bobby Sherwood. On TV he starred as *Barney Miller* (1975). *Bells Are Ringing* (Shubert, CR, "Jeff Moss," July 1958): Hello, Hello There!; I Met a Girl; Independent (On My Own); It's Better Than a Dream; Just in Time; Long Before I Knew You; You've Got to Do It/W: Betty Comden, Adolph Green, M: Jule Styne. *Something More!* (Eugene O'Neill, "Dick," Nov. 10, 1964): Who Fills the Bill/W: Marilyn Bergman, Alan Bergman, M: Sammy Fain. *The Education of H*Y*M*A*N* K*A*P*-L*A*N* (Alvin, "Yissel Fishbein," Apr. 4, 1968): Old Fashioned Husband/WM: Paul Nassau, Oscar Brand. *The Rothschilds* (Lunt-Fontanne, "Mayer Rothschild," Oct. 19, 1970/Aug. 31, 1971): He Tossed a Coin; In My Own Lifetime; One Room; Rothschild & Sons; Sons/W: Sheldon Harnick, M: Jerry Bock. *The Pajama Game* (Lunt-Fontanne, revival, "Sid Sorokin," Dec. 9, 1973): Hernando's Hideaway; Hey, There; A New Town Is a Blue Town; Once a Year Day; Small Talk; There Once Was a Man/M: Richard Adler, Jerry Ross.

5635. Margaret Linden *Head Over Heels* (George M. Cohan, "Mrs. Montague," Aug. 29, 1918): At the Thé Dansant; The Moments of the Dance/W: Edgar Allan Woolf, M: Jerome Kern.

5636. May Florine Linden *The Merry Whirl* (New York, "Mrs. Morgan Rogers" and "Baronne De Cammembert," May 30, 1910): Love's Rainbow; Tulips; When I Waltz with You/W: Ed Ray, M: Leo Edwards.

5637. Paul Lindenberg *From Vienna* (Music Box, revue, June 20, 1939): Journey to Paradise/W: Jura Soyfer, John Latouche, M: Otto Andreas — Musical Day/W: Hans Weigel, Werner Michel, M: Walter Drix. *Reunion in New York* (Little, revue, Feb. 21, 1940): I'm Going Crazy with Strauss/WM: Werner Michel, Peter Barry.

5638. Viveca Lindfors (Dec. 29, 1920–Oct. 25, 1995) B: Uppsala, Sweden. In films from 1947. *Pal Joey* (New York City Center, revival, "Vera Simpson," May 29, 1963): Bewitched, Bothered and Bewildered; Den of Iniquity; Take Him; What Is a Man?/W: Lorenz Hart, M: Richard Rodgers.

5639. Karen Lindgren *The Liar* (Broadhurst, "Beatrice Balanzoni," May 18, 1950): A Jewel of a Duel; Truth/W: Edward Eager, M: John Mundy.

5640. Abraham Lind-Oquendo B: New York, NY. *Porgy and Bess* (Uris, revival, "Porgy," Sept. 25, 1976): Bess, You Is My Woman Now; I Got Plenty o' Nuttin'; I Loves You, Porgy/W: Ira Gershwin, DuBose Heyward, M: George Gershwin — Oh, Bess, Oh Where's My Bess?/W: Ira Gershwin, M: George Gershwin — They Pass By Singing/W: DuBose Heyward, M: George Gershwin.

5641. John V. Lindsay (Nov. 24. 1921–Dec. 19, 2000) B: New York, NY. For 7 minutes on this date, the Mayor of the City of New York stole the show from KEN HOWARD. *Seesaw* (Uris, CR, "Jerry Ryan," Mar. 23, 1973): My City/W: Dorothy Fields, M: Cy Coleman.

5642. Kevin (Kevin-John) Lindsay (Sept. 7, 1957–) B: New York, NY. *The Me Nobody Knows* (Helen Hayes > Longacre, "William," Dec. 18, 1970): Black; Light Sings; Robert, Alvin, Wendell and Jo Jo/W: Will Holt, M: Gary William Friedman.

5643. Robert Lindsay (Dec. 13, 1949–) B: Ilkeston, Derbyshire, England. *Me and My Girl* (Marquis, revival, "Bill Snibson," Aug. 10, 1986/Dec. 23, 1986): Hold My Hand/W: Harry Graham, M: Maurice Elwin, Noel Gay — The Lambeth Walk; Me and My Girl; You Would If You Could/W: L. Arthur Rose, Douglas Furber, M: Noel Gay — Leaning on a Lamppost; Love

Makes the World Go Round; Song of Hare-ford/WM: Noel Gay.

5644. Carl Lindstrom (Dec. 9, 1938–) B: Portland, OR. *A Funny Thing Happened on the Way to the Forum* (Lunt-Fontanne, revival, "Miles Gloriosus," Mar. 30, 1972): Bring Me My Bride/WM: Stephen Sondheim.

5645. Richie Ling (c 1867–Mar. 5, 1937) B: London, England. M: LOTTA FAUST; ROSE WINTER. *The Defender* (Herald Square, "Charles Dare," July 3, 1902): Anglo-Saxons of Today; The Lighthouse and the Boat/W: Allen Lowe, M: Charles Denee. *The Jewel of Asia* (Criterion > Daly's, "Yussuf Potiphar," Feb. 16, 1903): Love Is a Game [Mar. 16, 1903]/W: Harry B. Smith, M: Ludwig Englander — Oh! Thou Art Fair My Love/W: Frederick Ranken, M: Ludwig Englander. *A Princess of Kensington* (Broadway, "Lieut. Brook Green," Aug. 31, 1903): Love in a Cottage; Now, Here's to the 'Prentices; Seven O'Clock in the Morning; Who That Knows How I Love You, Love/W: Basil Hood, M: Edward German. *Babette* (Broadway, "Marcel," Nov. 16, 1903): I'll Bribe the Stars; My Lady of the Manor; There Once Was an Owl/W: Harry B. Smith, M: Victor Herbert. *Chu Chin Chow* (Manhattan Opera House > Century, CR, "Ali Baba"): Any Time's Kissing Time/WM: Frederic Norton — When a Pullet Is Plump It's Tender/W: Oscar Asche, M: Frederic Norton.

5646. Peter Link (June 19, 1944–) B: St. Louis, MO. *Hair* (Biltmore, CR, "Berger"): Donna; Don't Put It Down; Going Down; Hair/W: Gerome Ragni, James Rado, M: Galt Mac-Dermot.

5647. Bambi Linn (Apr. 26, 1926–) B: Brooklyn, NY. She studied dance with choreographer Agnes de Mille. With dancer Rod Alexander, she was a regular on the TV comedy/variety program *Your Show of Shows* (1952). *Sally* (Martin Beck, revival, "Sally Green," May 6, 1948): Look for the Silver Lining/W: B.G. DeSylva, M: Jerome Kern — Sally (Dear Little Girl); Wild Rose/W: Clifford Grey, M: Jerome Kern — The Siren's Song/W: P.G. Wodehouse, M: Jerome Kern. *Great to Be Alive* (Winter Garden, "Bonnie," Mar. 23, 1950): Headin' for a Weddin'; When the Sheets Come Back from the Laundry/W: Walter Bullock, M: Abraham Ellstein. *I Can Get It for You Wholesale* (Shubert, "Blanche Bushkin," Mar. 22, 1962): Ballad of the Garment Trade; The Family Way; A Gift Today (The Bar Mitzvah Song); Have I Told You Lately?/WM: Harold Rome.

5648. Ben Linn *So Long Letty* (Shubert, "Billy Monday," Oct. 23, 1916): Blame It on the Girls; Mr. Patrick Henry Must Have Been a Married Man/WM: Earl Carroll. *Caroline* (Ambassador, "Hannibal," Jan. 31, 1923): The Old Virginia Reel/W: Harry B. Smith, M: Edward Delaney Dunn, Edward Kunneke — Telling Fortunes (Your Fortune)/W: Harry B. Smith, M: Edward Kunneke.

5649. Betty Linn *The Greenwich Village Follies of 1921* (Shubert, revue, CR, Nov. 14, 1921): That Reminiscent Melody/W: John Murray Anderson, Jack Yellen, M: Milton Ager.

5650. Ralph Linn *Two's Company* (Alvin, revue, Dec. 15, 1952): Roll Along, Sadie/W: Ogden Nash, M: Vernon Duke. *Li'l Abner* (St. James, "Dr. Krogmeyer," Nov. 15, 1956): Oh Happy Day/W: Johnny Mercer, M: Gene de Paul.

5651. Mark Linn-Baker (June 17, 1954–) B: St. Louis, MO. *Doonesbury* (Biltmore, "Mark," Nov. 21, 1983): Another Memorable Meal; Baby Boom Boogie Boy; Graduation; Muffy & the Topsiders/W: Garry Trudeau, M: Elizabeth Swados. *A Funny Thing Happened on the Way to the Forum* (St. James, revival, "Hysterium," Apr. 18, 1996): Everybody Ought to Have a Maid; I'm Calm; Lovely/WM: Stephen Sondheim.

5652. Lotta Linthicum (?–Mar. 19, 1952) *The Little Whopper* (Casino, "Mrs. MacGregor," Oct. 13, 1919): The Kiss/W: Otto Harbach, Bide Dudley, M: Rudolf Friml.

5653. Betty Hyatt Linton (June 12, 1930–) B: Jacksonville, FL. *How to Succeed in Business Without Really Trying* (New York City Center, revival, "Hedy La Rue," Apr. 20, 1966): Been a Long Day; Love from a Heart of Gold/WM: Frank Loesser.

5654. Albert Linville (June 19, 1918–Mar. 1, 1985) *A Tree Grows in Brooklyn* (Alvin, "Swanswine," Apr. 19, 1951): Is That My Prince?/W: Dorothy Fields, M: Arthur Schwartz. *Wonderful Town* (Winter Garden, "Associate Editor" and "Policeman," Feb. 25, 1953): My Darlin' Eileen; What a Waste/W: Betty Comden, Adolph Green, M: Leonard Bernstein. *Damn Yankees* (46th Street, "Vernon," May 5, 1955): Heart/WM: Richard Adler, Jerry Ross. *Let It Ride!* (Eugene O'Neill, "Charlie," Oct. 12, 1961): Broads Ain't People; He Needs You; If Flutterby Wins/WM: Jay Livingston, Ray Evans.

5655. Freda Linyard *The Soul Kiss* (New York, "Satanella," Jan. 28, 1908): The Dollar Sign/W: Jessie Villars, M: Fleta Jan Brown.

5656. Beth Lipari *Grease* (Eugene O'Neill, revival, CR, "Frenchy," c 1996): Beauty School Dropout/WM: Jim Jacobs, Warren Casey.

5657. Lydia Lipkowska She sang at the

Imperial Opera in Petrograd (now St. Petersburg) Russia before coming to the U.S. *The Merry Widow* (Knickerbocker, revival, "Sonia, the Widow," Sept. 5, 1921): I Love You So (The Merry Widow Waltz); In Marsovia; Vilia/W: Adrian Ross, M: Franz Lehar.

5658. Clara Lipman (Dec. 6, 1869–June 22, 1952) B: Chicago IL. M: LOUIS MANN. Actress, playwright. *The Girl from Paris* (Herald Square, "Mlle. Julie Bon-Bon," Dec. 8, 1896): Cock-a-doodle; I'm All the Way from Gay Paree; It's a Good Thing to Have; The Proper Air [June 28, 1897]; Reste La [June 28, 1897]; Tweedledum and Tweedledee/W: George Dance, M: Ivan Caryll.

5659. David Lipman (May 12, 1938–) B: Brooklyn, NY. *My Favorite Year* (Vivian Beaumont, "Uncle Monty," Dec. 10, 1992): Welcome to Brooklyn/W: Lynn Ahrens, M: Stephen Flaherty. *Ain't Broadway Grand* (Lunt-Fontanne, "Reuben Pelish," Apr. 18, 1993): Ain't Broadway Grand/W: Lee Adams, M: Mitch Leigh.

5660. Juliette Lippe *The Whirl of the World* (Winter Garden, revue, "Nanette," Jan. 10, 1914): How Do You Do, Goodbye; Life's a Dress Parade/W: Harold Atteridge, M: Sigmund Romberg. *The Passing Show of 1915* (Winter Garden, revue, May 29, 1915): The Primrose Way/W: Harold Atteridge, M: Leo Edwards. *Flora Bella* (Casino > 44th Street, "Mme. Vera Ludoffska," Sept. 11, 1916): Creep, Creep, the World's Asleep/W: Percy Waxman, M: Milton Schwarzwald — We'll Dance Till Dawn of Day/WM: ?.

5661. Arthur Lipson *Madame Sherry* (New Amsterdam, CR, "Phillippe," Sept. 26, 1910): The Other Fellow/WM: ?. *When Sweet Sixteen* (Daly's, "Mon. Beaucaire," Sept. 14, 1911): It's Always Going to Be That Way; Little Fifi; My Toast to You; There's a Raft of Money in Graft! Graft! Graft!/W: George V. Hobart, M: Victor Herbert. *Rock-a-Bye Baby* (Astor, "Pasquale," May 22, 1918): Bella Mia/W: Herbert Reynolds, M: Jerome Kern. *Oh! Oh! Oh! Nurse* (Cosmopolitan, "Mon. Louis d'Brac," Dec. 7, 1925): Pierre; Who Bites the Holes in Schweitzer Cheese?/W: Monte Carlo, M: Alma Sanders.

5662. Paul Lipson (Dec. 23, 1913–Jan. 3, 1996) B: Brooklyn, NY. He played the role of Tevya more than 2,000 times. *Carnival in Flanders* (New Century, "Butcher," Sept. 8, 1953): Ring the Bell; You're Dead!/W: Johnny Burke, M: James Van Heusen. *The Vamp* (Winter Garden, "Barney Ostertag," Nov. 10, 1955): I'm Everybody's Baby/W: John Latouche, M: James Mundy. *Fiorello!* (New York City Center, revival, "Morris Cohen," June 13, 1962): Marie's Law;

On the Side of the Angels/W: Sheldon Harnick, M: Jerry Bock. *The Sound of Music* (Lunt-Fontanne, CR, "Max Detweiler," July 1962): How Can Love Survive?; No Way to Stop It/W: Oscar Hammerstein II, M: Richard Rodgers. *Fiddler on the Roof* (Imperial, "Avram," Sept. 22, 1964): Anatevka/W: Sheldon Harnick, M: Jerry Bock. *Fiddler on the Roof* (Imperial, CR, "Lazar Wolf," Aug. 1965): Anatevka; To Life/W: Sheldon Harnick, M: Jerry Bock. *Fiddler on the Roof* (Imperial, CR, "Tevye," Jan. 19, 1970/Oct. 19, 1970/Oct. 18, 1971/May 2, 1972): Anatevka; Do You Love Me?; If I Were a Rich Man; Sabbath Prayer; Sunrise, Sunset; The Tailor, Motel Kamzoil; To Life; Tradition/W: Sheldon Harnick, M: Jerry Bock. *Fiddler on the Roof* (Winter Garden, revival, "Lazar Wolf," Dec. 28, 1976): same as above. *Fiddler on the Roof* (New York State, revival, "Lazar Wolf," July 9, 1981): same as above.

5663. Blanche Lipton *High Jinks* (Casino, CR, "Sylvia Dale," June 8, 1914): The Bubble; Is This Love at Last?; Love's Own Kiss/W: Otto Harbach, M: Rudolf Friml.

5664. Celia Lipton (Dec. 25, 1923–) B: Edinburgh, Scotland. *Maggie* (National, "Sybil Tenterdon," Feb. 18, 1953): People in Love/WM: William Roy. *John Murray Anderson's Almanac* (Imperial, revue, Dec. 10, 1953): If Every Month Were June/W: John Murray Anderson, M: Henry Sullivan.

5665. Luba Lisa (c 1941– Dec. 15, 1972) B: Brooklyn, NY. The actress was killed in a plane crash in Vermont. *I Can Get It for You Wholesale* (Shubert, "Manette," Mar. 22, 1962): What Are They Doing to Us Now?/WM: Harold Rome. *West Side Story* (New York City Center, revival, "Anita," Apr. 8, 1964): America; A Boy Like That; I Have a Love/W: Stephen Sondheim, M: Leonard Bernstein. *I Had a Ball* (Martin Beck, "Addie," Dec. 15, 1964): Addie's At It Again; Boys, Boys, Boys; Can It Be Possible?; You Deserve Me/WM: Jack Lawrence, Stan Freeman.

5666. Margaret Liste *Lovely Lady* (Sam H. Harris, "Yvette," Dec. 29, 1927): At the Barbecue/W: Harry A. Steinberg, Edward Ward, M: Dave Stamper, Harold A. Levey — Lingerie; Make Believe You're Happy/W: Cyrus D. Wood, M: Dave Stamper, Harold A. Levey.

5667. Leslie Litomy *The Cradle Will Rock* (Mansfield, revival, "Prof. Trixie," Dec. 26, 1947): Listen, Fellas!/WM: Marc Blitzstein.

5668. Jim Litten *The Lieutenant* ("Clergyman" and "1st Reporter," Mar. 9, 1975): He Wants to Put the Army in Jail; The Star of This War/WM: Gene Curty, Nitra Scharfman,

Chuck Strand. *A Chorus Line* (Shubert, CR, "Mike," June 1977): I Can Do That/W: Edward Kleban, M: Marvin Hamlisch.

5669. Brad Little *The Phantom of the Opera* (Majestic, CR, "Raoul, Vicomte de Chagny," c 1994): All I Ask of You; Bravo, Bravo; Little Lotte; The Mirror; Notes; Prima Donna; Raoul, I've Been There; Think of Me; Twisted Every Way; Wandering Child; Why Have You Brought Me Here/W: Charles Hart, Richard Stilgoe, M: Andrew Lloyd Webber.

5670. Cleavon Little (June 1, 1939–Oct. 22, 1992) B: Chickasha, OK. The actor and comedian won a Tony for his role in *Purlie*. Best remembered as the black sheriff in the Mel Brooks movie *Blazing Saddles* (1974). *Purlie* (Broadway, Mar. 15, 1970): Down Home; The Harder They Fall; New-Fangled Preacher Man/ W: Peter Udell, M: Gary Geld.

5671. Nick Littlefield *Kismet* (New York State, revival, "Wazir's Guard," June 22, 1965): Was I Wazir?/WM: Robert Wright, George Forrest.

5672. Sarah E. Litzsinger (Oct. 22, 1971–) B: Indianapolis, IN. *Oliver!* (Mark Hellinger, revival, "Bet," Apr. 29, 1984): I'd Do Anything; It's a Fine Life/WM: Lionel Bart.

5673. Delyse Lively-Mekka *A Chorus Line* (Shubert, CR, "Val," c 1986/c 1987): And...; Dance: Ten, Looks: Three/W: Edward Kleban, M: Marvin Hamlisch.

5674. Eleanor Livingston *Head Over Heels* (George M. Cohan, "Miss Hammond," Aug. 29, 1918): With Type a-Ticking/W: Edgar Allan Woolf, M: Jerome Kern.

5675. Jose Llana B: Philippines. *The King and I* (Neil Simon, revival, "Lun Tha," Apr. 11, 1996): I Have Dreamed; We Kiss in a Shadow/ W: Oscar Hammerstein II, M: Richard Rodgers.

5676. Dorothy Llewellyn *Cape Cod Follies* (Bijou, revue, Sept. 18, 1929): Clutching at Shadows/W: Seymour Morris, M: Alex Fogarty — In a Cape Cod Garden/W: Stewart Baird, M: Alex Fogarty — That's Why We Misbehave/ W: Edith Lois, Urana Clarke, M: Alex Fogarty.

5677. Harry Llewellyn *Marjolaine* (Broadhurst, CR, "Admiral Sir Peter Antrobus," Apr. 3, 1922): Punch and Judy/W: Brian Hooker, M: Hugo Felix.

5678. Alice Lloyd (Oct. 20, 1873–Nov. 16, 1949) B: London, England. M: TOM MC-NAUGHTON. Her birth name was ALICE WOOD. *Animal Crackers* (44th Street, "Arabella Rittenhouse," Oct. 23, 1928): When Things Are Bright and Rosy/WM: Bert Kalmar, Harry Ruby.

5679. Christopher Lloyd (Oct. 22, 1928–) B: Stamford, CT. He was Reverend Jim Ignatowski on the TV sitcom *Taxi* (1979). *Happy End* (Martin Beck, revival, "Bill Cracker," May 7, 1977): The Bilbao Song; Song of the Big Shot/ W: Bertolt Brecht, M: Kurt Weill.

5680. Doris Lloyd (July 3, 1896–May 21, 1968) B: Liverpool, England. She began as a child star on the British stage, then went to Hollywood in the 1920s and played ingenues. *The Show of Wonders* (Winter Garden, revue, Oct. 26, 1916): Angels/W: Harold Atteridge, M:?.

5681. George Lloyd *'Tis of Thee* (Maxine Elliott, revue, Oct. 26, 1940): What's Mine Is Thine/W: Alfred Hayes, M: Al Moss.

5682. Violet Lloyd (Nov. 25, 1879–Oct. 20, 1924) B: London, England. *The Geisha* (Daly's, "Molly Seamore," Sept. 9, 1896): Chon Kina; The Interfering Parrot; The Toy Duet/W: Harry Greenbank, M: Sidney Jones.

5683. Virginia Lloyd *Mayflowers* (Forrest, "Mary," Nov. 24, 1925): Oh! Sam/W: Clifford Grey, M: J. Fred Coots, Maurie Rubens — Put Your Troubles in a Candy Box/W: Clifford Grey, M: J. Fred Coots — Whoa, Emma!/W: Clifford Grey, M: Edward Kunneke.

5684. Randon Lo (June 12, 1949–) B: Oakland, CA. *Joseph and the Amazing Technicolor Dreamcoat* (Royale, revival, "Mrs. Potiphar," Jan. 27, 1982): Potiphar/WM: Tim Rice, Andrew Lloyd Webber.

5685. Mary Loane *Sherry!* (Alvin, "Daisy Stanley," Mar. 27, 1967): Turn on Your Radio/ W: James Lipton, M: Laurence Rosenthal.

5686. Lee Lobenhofer (June 25, 1955–) B: Chicago, IL. *Shogun: The Musical* (Marquis, "Capt. Gen. Ferriera," Nov. 20, 1990): Assassination/W: John Driver, M: Paul Chihara.

5687. David Lober *Touch and Go* (Broadhurst > Broadway, revue, Oct. 13, 1949): Easy Does It/W: Walter Kerr, Jean Kerr, M: Jay Gorney.

5688. Joe Locarro (Feb. 26, 1959–) B: East Rutherford, NJ. *Les Miserables* (Broadway, CR, "Enjolras," Jan. 15, 1990): Do You Hear the People Sing?; Red and Black/W: Herbert Kretzmer, M: Claude-Michel Schonberg.

5689. Anna Locke *Hold Everything!* (Broadhurst, "Gladys Martin," Oct. 10, 1928): Don't Hold Everything/W: B.G. DeSylva, Lew Brown, M: Ray Henderson.

5690. Harry Locke *Hold Everything!* (Broadhurst, "Mack," Oct. 10, 1928): Don't Hold Everything; Genealogy; We're Calling on Mr. Brooks/W: B.G. DeSylva, Lew Brown, M: Ray Henderson.

5691. Mary Susan Locke *The Sound of Music* (Lunt-Fontanne, "Marta," Nov. 16, 1959): Do Re Mi; Edelweiss; The Lonely Goatherd; So Long, Farewell; The Sound of Music/W: Oscar Hammerstein II, M: Richard Rodgers. *The Sound of Music* (Lunt-Fontanne, CR, "Brigitta," Aug. 1962): same as above.

5692. Ralph Locke *Plain Jane* (New Amsterdam, "Julian Kingsley," May 12, 1924): Winning the Prize/W: Phil Cook, M: Tom Johnstone.

5693. Calvin Lockhart (1934–) B: Nassau, West Indies. *Reggae* (Biltmore, "Ras Joseph," Mar. 27, 1980): No Sinners in Jah Yard/WM: Max Romeo, Ras Karbi — Rasta Roll Call; Rise Up Jah-Jah Children/WM: Ras Karbi — Roots of the Tree/WM: Kendrew Lascelles, Ras Karbi.

5694. Gene Lockhart (July 18, 1891–Mar. 31, 1957) B: London, Ontario, Canada. Father of actress June Lockhart. Actor, singer, director, producer, screenwriter, songwriter. He appeared in dozens of movies from 1922 until his death. *Bunk of 1926* (Heckscher > Broadhurst, revue, Feb. 16, 1926): Bunk/WM: Gene Lockhart — Pan/W: Percy Waxman, M: Gene Lockhart.

5695. Helen Lockhart *Just a Minute* (Ambassador > Century, "May," Oct. 8, 1928): Coming Out of the Garden; Doggone/W: Walter O'Keefe, M: Harry Archer.

5696. Danny Lockin (July 13, 1943–Aug. 21, 1977) B: Hawaii. A talented dancer and singer, he played Barnaby in the movie version of *Hello, Dolly!* (1969) before appearing opposite ETHEL MERMAN in the role on Broadway. He was found murdered. *Hello, Dolly!* (St. James, CR, "Barnaby Tucker," Dec. 26, 1969): Dancing; Put on Your Sunday Clothes/WM: Jerry Herman — Elegance; Motherhood/WM: Bob Merrill, Jerry Herman.

5697. Peter Lockyer *Les Miserables* (Broadway, CR, "Marius," Mar. 12, 1997): Empty Chairs at Empty Tables; A Heart Full of Love; In My Life; A Little Fall of Rain; Red and Black/W: Herbert Kretzmer, M: Claude-Michel Schonberg.

5698. Philip Loeb (1892–Sept. 1, 1955) B: Philadelphia, PA. The actor ended his life with sleeping pills. *The Garrick Gaieties of 1926* (Garrick, revue, "Suzanne Lenglen" and "Sir Galahad," May 10, 1926): Idles of the King; Tennis Champs (Helen! Suzanne! and Bill!)/W: Lorenz Hart, M: Richard Rodgers. *Merry-Go-Round* (Klaw, revue, May 31, 1927): In the Bathroom Tra La (Bathroom Tenor)/W: Howard Dietz, M: Jay Gorney. *The Garrick Gaieties of 1930* (Guild, revue, June 4, 1930): Four Infant Prodigies/W: Allen Boretz, M: Ned Lehac — I Am Only Human After All/W: E.Y. Harburg, Ira Gershwin, M: Vernon Duke — I'm Grover/W: Newman Levy, M: Vernon Duke — Scheherezade/WM: Harold Goldman. *The Garrick Gaieties of 1930* (Guild, return engagement, Oct. 16, 1930): In the Bathroom Tra La (Bathroom Tenor)/W: Howard Dietz, M: Jay Gorney — Rose of Arizona; The Three Musketeers/W: Lorenz Hart, M: Richard Rodgers — Unaccustomed as I Am/W: E.Y. Harburg, M: Vernon Duke. *The Band Wagon* (New Amsterdam, revue, June 3, 1931): Nanette/W: Howard Dietz, M: Arthur Schwartz. *Flying Colors* (Imperial, revue, Sept. 15, 1932): Just Around the Corner/W: Howard Dietz, M: Arthur Schwartz. *Let 'Em Eat Cake* (Imperial, "Kruger," Oct. 21, 1933): Down with Ev'rything That's Up; A Hell of a Hole; Let 'Em Eat Caviar; That's What He Did; Throttle Throttlebottom/W: Ira Gershwin, M: George Gershwin. *Sing Out the News* (Music Box, revue, Sept. 24, 1938): We've Got the Song; Yip-Ahoy (Adrift on the Lo-one Prairie)/WM: Harold Rome.

5699. Emily Loesser (June 2, 1965–) B: New York, NY. M: WILLIAM STEPHENSON. Her father was composer and lyricist Frank Loesser. *The Sound of Music* (New York State, revival, "Liesel," Mar. 8, 1990): Sixteen, Going on Seventeen/W: Oscar Hammerstein II, M: Richard Rodgers.

5700. Robert Loftin *Mail* (Music Box, "LIFE Exec" and "Con Ed Man," Apr. 14, 1988): It's Your Life; It's Your Life II; We're Gonna Turn Off Your Juice/W: Jerry Colker, M: Michael Rupert.

5701. Linda Loftis *Oh What a Lovely War* (Broadhurst, revue, Sept. 30, 1964): Roses of Picardy/W: Frederick Edward Weatherley, M: Haydn Wood.

5702. Cissie (Cecilia) Loftus (Oct. 22, 1876–July 12, 1943) B: Glasgow, Scotland. Famous in vaudeville as the Queen of Mimics for her impressions of celebrities of the day. *Dream City* (Weber's, "Nancy," Dec. 25, 1906): In Vaudeville; A Shy Suburban Maid/W: Edgar Smith, M: Victor Herbert.

5703. Ella Logan (Mar. 6, 1913–May 1, 1969) B: Glasgow, Scotland. She moved to the U.S. in 1932, appearing on radio and in films during the 1930s. *Calling All Stars* (Hollywood, revue, Dec. 13, 1934): If It's Love/W: Lew Brown, M: Harry Akst. *George White's Scandals of 1939-40* (Alvin, revue, Aug. 28, 1939): Are You Havin' Any Fun?; In Waikiki; The Song's for Free/W: Jack Yellen, M: Sammy Fain — The Mexiconga; Something I Dreamed Last Night [added]/W: Herb Magidson, Jack Yellen, M: Sammy Fain. *Sons o' Fun* (Winter Garden, revue, Dec. 1, 1941): Happy in Love; It's a Mighty Fine Country We Have Here; It's a New Kind of Thing; Oh, Auntie!; Thank You, South America/W: Jack Yellen, M: Sammy Fain. *Finian's Rainbow* (46th Street, "Sharon McLonergan," Jan. 10, 1947): How Are Things in Glocca Morra?; If This Isn't Love; Look to the Rainbow; Old Devil Moon; Something Sort of Grandish; That Great Come-and-Get-It Day; When the Idle Poor Become the Idle Rich/W: E.Y. Harburg, M: Burton Lane.

5704. Michael Logan *Pickwick* (46th Street, "Mr. Wardle," Oct. 4, 1965): Very/W: Leslie Bricusse, M: Cyril Ornadel.

5705. Stacey Logan *Crazy for You* (Sam S. Shubert, "Patsy," Feb. 19, 1992): Slap That Bass/W: Ira Gershwin, M: George Gershwin. *Beauty and the Beast* (Palace, "Babette," Apr. 18, 1994): Be Our Guest; Human Again/W: Howard Ashman, M: Alan Menken.

5706. Ben Lokey *A Chorus Line* (Shubert, CR, "Al," Apr. 1977): Sing!/W: Edward Kleban, M: Marvin Hamlisch.

5707. Hal Loman (July 16, 1929–) B: Brooklyn, NY. *Mr. Wonderful* (Broadway, "Hal," Mar. 22, 1956): 1617 Broadway/W: Larry Holofcener, George David Weiss, M: Jerry Bock.

5708. Peter Lombard (Oct. 12, 1935–) B: Spokane, WA. *The Conquering Hero* (ANTA, "Pfc. Pasco," Jan. 16, 1961): Five Shots of Whiskey; One Mother Each/W: Norman Gimbel, M: Moose Charlap. *1776* (46th Street, CR, "Thomas Jefferson," Nov. 24, 1969): But, Mr. Adams; The Egg/WM: Sherman Edwards.

5709. Joan Lombardo *Oliver!* (Imperial, CR, "Bet"): I'd Do Anything; It's a Fine Life/WM: Lionel Bart.

5710. Bobby London *Jesus Christ Superstar* (Longacre, revival, "Simon Zealotes," Nov. 23, 1977): Simon Zealotes/W: Tim Rice, M: Andrew Lloyd Webber.

5711. David London *The Merry Malones* (Erlanger's, "Carlysle," Sept. 26, 1927): Like the Wandering Minstrel; Roses Understand/WM: George M. Cohan. *Billie* (Erlanger's, "Harry Thompson," Oct. 1, 1928): Bluff; The Cause of the Situation; I'm a One Girl Man; They Fall in Love; The Two of Us/WM: George M. Cohan. *Cape Cod Follies* (Bijou, revue, Sept. 18, 1929): Clutching at Shadows; That's the Time When I Miss You/W: Seymour Morris, M: Alex Fogarty — Wondering Who/W: George Fitch, M: Alex Fogarty.

5712. Zach London *A Christmas Carol* (Paramount Madison Square Garden, return engagement, "Tiny Tim," Nov. 20, 1995): Christmas Together/W: Lynn Ahrens, M: Alan Menken.

5713. Lenore Lonergan (June 2, 1928–1989) B: Toledo, OH. She played Fuffy Adams in the long running Broadway play, *Junior Miss* (1941). *Alive and Kicking* (Winter Garden, revue, Jan. 17, 1950): Cry, Baby, Cry; French with Tears; Love, It Hurts So Good/WM: Harold Rome. *Of Thee I Sing* (Ziegfeld, revival, "Diana Devereaux," May 5, 1952): Because, Because; I Was the Most Beautiful Blossom; Jilted! Jilted!/W: Ira Gershwin, M: George Gershwin.

5714. Avon Long (June 18, 1910–Feb. 15, 1984) B: Baltimore, MD. *Black Rhythm* (Comedy, "Rhythm," Dec. 19, 1936): Black Rhythm/WM: Donald Heywood. *Porgy and Bess* (Majestic, revival, "Sportin' Life," Jan. 22, 1942): It Ain't Necessarily So; There's a Boat Dat's Leavin' Soon for New York/W: Ira Gershwin, M: George Gershwin. *Porgy and Bess* (44th Street > New York City Center, revival, "Sportin' Life," Sept. 13, 1943): same as above. *Memphis Bound!* (Broadway > Belasco, "Winfield Carter [Windy]," May 24, 1945): Fair Moon; I Am the Captain of the Pinafore; Old Love and Brand New Love; Stand Around the Band; Things Are Seldom What They Seem; Trial by Jury/WM: Clay Warnick, Don Walker, based on William S. Gilbert and Arthur Sullivan. *Carib Song* (Adelphi, "The Fisherman," Sept. 27, 1945): Woman Is a Rascal/W: William Archibald, M: Baldwin Bergersen. *Shuffle Along of 1952* (Broadway, revue, "Lieut. Jim Crocker," May 8, 1952): Bitten by Love; My Day/W: Floyd Huddleston, M: Joseph Meyer — Love Will Find a Way/W: Noble Sissle, M: Eubie Blake. *Don't Play Us Cheap!* (Ethel Barrymore, "David," May 16, 1972): Break That Party; The Phoney Game/WM: Melvin Van Peebles. *Bubbling Brown Sugar* (ANTA, "John Sage" and "Rusty," Mar. 2, 1976/July 4, 1977): Brown Gal/WM: Avon Long, Lil Armstrong — In Honeysuckle Time/WM: Noble Sissle, Eubie Blake — Honeysuckle Rose/W: Andy Razaf, M: Fats Waller — Nobody/W: Alex Rogers, M: Bert Williams.

5715. Brenda Long *Saratoga* (Winter Garden, "Maudey," Dec. 7, 1959): One Step, Two Step/W: Johnny Mercer, M: Harold Arlen.

5716. J.N. Long *A Pullman Palace Car* (Haverley's Lyceum, "Sir Henry Cashmere" and "Louis" and "Mr. St. Clair," Nov. 3, 1879): 'Tis Time to Say Good Night/W: ?, M: Alfred Cellier.

5717. Nick Long *The Girl from Paris* (Herald Square, CR, "Auguste Pompier," Aug. 28,

1897): Cock-a-doodle; I'm All the Way from Gay Paree; Tootle, Tootle/W: George Dance, M: Ivan Caryll.

5718. Nick Long, Jr. (c 1906–Aug. 31, 1949) B: New York, NY. He died in an auto accident. *Lollipop* (Knickerbocker, "Omar K. Garrity," Jan. 21, 1924): When We Are Married/W: Zelda Sears, M: Vincent Youmans. *Kitty's Kisses* (Playhouse, "Philip Dennison," May 6, 1926): Bounce Me; I Love to Dance; Mr. and Mrs./W: Gus Kahn, M: Con Conrad — Steppin' on the Blues/ W: Otto Harbach, M: Con Conrad, Walter Donaldson. *Oh, Please!* (Fulton, "Jack Gates," Dec. 17, 1926): I'd Steal a Star; I'm Waiting for a Wonderful Girl/W: Anne Caldwell, M: Vincent Youmans. *She's My Baby* (Globe, "Dance Director," Jan. 3, 1928): I Need Some Cooling Off; This Goes Up; Wasn't It Great? (It's All Over Now)/W: Lorenz Hart, M: Richard Rodgers. *The Street Singer* (Shubert, "Ronnie," Sept. 17, 1929): Somebody Quite Like You; Statues; You Never Can Tell/WM: ?. *Through the Years* (Manhattan, "Willie Ainley," Jan. 28, 1932): An Invitation; Kinda Like You; The Road to Home; The Trumpeter and the Lover/W: Edward Heyman, M: Vincent Youmans. *Say When* (Imperial, "Reginald Pratt," Nov. 8, 1934): It Must Have Been the Night; Let's Take Advantage of Now/W: Ted Koehler, M: Ray Henderson. *Louisiana Purchase* (Imperial, "Lee Davis," May 28, 1940): Louisiana Purchase; You Can't Brush Me Off/WM: Irving Berlin. *Artists and Models of 1943* (Broadway, revue, Nov. 5, 1943): Blowing the Top/W: Milton Pascal, Dan Shapiro, M: Phil Charig.

5719. Ray Long *Ziegfeld Follies of 1943* (Winter Garden, revue, Apr. 1, 1943): Swing Your Lady, Mister Hemingway/W: Jack Yellen, M: Ray Henderson.

5720. Shorty Long (Oct. 31, 1923–) B: Reading, PA. *The Most Happy Fella* (Imperial > Broadway, "Herman," May 3, 1956): Big D; I Like Ev'rybody; Standing on the Corner/WM: Frank Loesser.

5721. Tamara Long (Nov. 7, 1941–June 8, 2002) B: Oklahoma City, OK. *Lorelei or Gentlemen Still Prefer Blondes* (Palace, "Dorothy Shaw," Jan. 27, 1974): Coquette; I Love What I'm Doing; It's High Time; Keeping Cool with Coolidge/W: Leo Robin, M: Jule Styne — I Won't Let You Get Away; Miss Lorelei Lee/W: Betty Comden, Adolph Green, M: Jule Styne.

5722. Walter H. Long *Toplitzky of Notre Dame* (Century, "Roger," Dec. 26, 1946): Baby Let's Face It; A Slight Case of Ecstasy/W: George Marion, Jr., M: Sammy Fain.

5723. Amelia Loomis *Lucky Sambo* (Colonial, "Nimble Foote," June 6, 1925): Stop; Strolling/WM: Porter Grainger, Freddie Johnson.

5724. Joe E. Loomis *Americana of 1926* (Belmont, revue, "2nd barber in Pan American Quartette," July 26, 1926): Swanee River Melody [added]/W: Al Wilson, M: Charles Weinberg — Thanks Awful/W: Sam M. Lewis, Joe Young, M: Con Conrad — That Lost Barber Shop Chord/W: Ira Gershwin, M: George Gershwin — The Volga Boatman/W: Dailey Paskman, M: Alexei Archangelsky. *Swing It* (Adelphi, "Bud," July 22, 1937): I Praise Sue/W: Cecil Mack, Milton Reddie, M: Eubie Blake.

5725. Rod Loomis (Apr. 21, 1942–) B: St. Albans, VT. *Sunset Boulevard* (Minskoff, CR, "Cecil B. DeMille," Jan. 1997): Surrender/W: Don Black, Christopher Hampton, M: Andrew Lloyd Webber.

5726. Lita Lope *Belmont Varieties* (Belmont, revue, Sept. 26, 1932): Bonbonera/W: Charles Kenny, M: Serge Walter.

5727. Carmen Lopez *The Land of Joy* (Park > Knickerbocker, "Torerito" and "Jerezanos," Oct. 31, 1917): Jerezanos; Torerito, Torerazo/W: Ruth Boyd Ober, M: Joaquin Valverde.

5728. Priscilla Lopez (Feb. 26, 1948–) B: Bronx, NY. *Company* (Alvin, CR, "Kathy," Oct. 25, 1971): You Could Drive a Person Crazy/WM: Stephen Sondheim. *Pippin* (Imperial, CR, "Fastrada," Jan. 6, 1974): Spread a Little Sunshine/ WM: Stephen Schwartz. *A Chorus Line* (Shubert, "Diana," July 25, 1975): Nothing; What I Did for Love/W: Edward Kleban, M: Marvin Hamlisch. *A Day in Hollywood/A Night in the Ukraine* (John Golden > Royale, "Gino," May 1, 1980): The Best in the World; Just Go to the Movies/WM: Jerry Herman — Doin' the Production Code; Famous Feet; A Night in the Ukraine/W: Dick Vosburgh, M: Frank Lazarus — Japanese Sandman/W: Raymond B. Egan, M: Richard A. Whiting. *Nine* (46th Street, CR, "Liliane La Fleur," Nov. 8, 1982): Folies Bergeres/WM: Maury Yeston.

5729. Denise Lor (May 3, 1929–) B: Los Angeles, CA. *42nd Street* (Winter Garden, CR, "Maggie Jones," c 1986): Getting Out of Town/ W: Mort Dixon, M: Harry Warren — Go Into Your Dance; Shadow Waltz; Shuffle Off to Buffalo/W: Al Dubin, M: Harry Warren.

5730. Milton Lorance *The New Yorkers* (Edyth Totten, revue, Mar. 10, 1927): Here Comes the Prince of Wales; 99% Pure/W: Henry Myers, M: Arthur Schwartz — Triangle/W: Henry Myers, M: Charles M. Schwab.

5731. **Martha Lorber** (June 11, 1900–July 3, 1983) B: Brooklyn, NY. *Tangerine* (Casino, "Kate Allen," Aug. 9, 1921): Man Is the Lord of It All/W: Carle Carlton, M: Jean Schwartz. *Ziegfeld Follies of 1924-1925* (New Amsterdam, revue, June 24, 1924): Montmartre/W: Gene Buck, M: Raymond Hubbell. *Three Little Girls* (Shubert, "Annette," Apr. 14, 1930): Annette; A Cottage in the Country; A Lesson in Letter Writing; Waltz with Me/W: Harry B. Smith, M: Walter Kollo.

5732. **Helen Lord** (1878–Jan. 2, 1911) B: Hornell, NY. M: composer Raymond Hubbell. *Miss Simplicity* (Casino, "Mlle. Clair de Loinville," Feb. 10, 1902): Charity; Some Do! Some Don't!; Sweet Ecstasy; When Will My Dreams Come True, Love?/W: R.A. Barnet, M: H.L. Heartz. *The Runaways* (Casino, "Dorothy Maynard," May 11, 1903): Love Is an Ailment; Strolling/W: Addison Burkhardt, M: Raymond Hubbell.

5733. **Sylvia Lord** *New Faces of 1962* (Alvin, revue, Feb. 1, 1962): In the Morning/WM: Ronny Graham — Love Is Good for You/W: June Carroll, M: Arthur Siegel — Over the River and Into the Woods/WM: Jack Holmes.

5734. **Fred Lorenz** (Jan. 1, 1907–July 25, 1984) B: Vienna, Austria. *From Vienna* (Music Box, revue, June 20, 1939): Salzburg Puppet-Show/W: Lothar Metzl, Werner Michel, Eva Franklin, M: Otto Andreas.

5735. **John A. Lorenz** (Dec. 6, 1886–Apr. 30, 1972) B: Buffalo, NY. *Hello, Paris and A La Broadway* (Folies Bergere, revue, "Nick O'Teene," Sept. 22, 1911): Antics of the Comics/W: William Le Baron, Mabel H. Hollins, M: Harold Orlob.

5736. **Dee Loretta** *Glorianna* (Liberty, CR, "Therese," Jan. 6, 1919): Frocks and Frills/W: Catherine Chisholm Cushing, M: Rudolf Friml.

5737. **Estelle Loring** (Feb. 13, 1925–) B: New York, NY. She appeared on the early TV quiz show *Stop the Music* (1949). *The Cradle Will Rock* (Mansfield > Broadway, revival, "Moll," Dec. 26, 1947): I'm Checkin' Home Now; Nickel Under the Foot; Polyphonic; So That's the Way/WM: Marc Blitzstein. *Inside U.S.A.* (New Century, revue, Apr. 30, 1948): Haunted Heart; Rhode Island Is Famous for You/W: Howard Dietz, M: Arthur Schwartz.

5738. **Michael Loring** *Who's Who* (Hudson, revue, Mar. 1, 1938): Croupier; Train Time/W: June Sillman, M: Baldwin Bergersen — Glee Club/WM: James Shelton — It's You I Want/W: Al Stillman, M: Paul McGrane. *Sing Out the News* (Music Box, revue, Sept. 24, 1938): How Long Can Love Keep Laughing?; My Heart Is Unemployed/WM: Harold Rome.

5739. **Andree Lorraine** *The Girl from Paris* (Wallack's, revival, "Norah," Jan. 17, 1898): Somebody/W: George Dance, M: Ivan Caryll.

5740. **Lillian Lorraine** (Jan. 1, 1892–Apr. 17, 1955) B: San Francisco, CA. Once billed as the Highest Salaried Show Girl in the World, Miss Lorraine had a long affair with Flo Ziegfeld and was named the other woman in his divorce from ANNA HELD. *Miss Innocence* (New York, "Angele," Nov. 30, 1908): My Post Card Girl/W: Addison Burkhardt, M: Louis A. Hirsch — Shine On, Harvest Moon/WM: Nora Bayes, Jack Norworth. *Ziegfeld Follies of 1909* (Jardin de Paris — New York roof, revue, June 14, 1909): By the Light of the Silvery Moon; Up! Up! Up! in My Aeroplane/W: Edward Madden, M: Gus Edwards — It's Nothing but a Bubble/W: Harry B. Smith, M: Maurice Levi. *Ziegfeld Follies of 1910* (Jardin de Paris — New York roof, revue, June 20, 1910): I'll Get You Yet/W: Addison Burkhardt, M: Albert Von Tilzer — I'm in Love with You/W: Harry B. Smith, M: Gus Edwards — Sweet Kitty Bellaires [Aug. 22, 1910]/W: Robert B. Smith, M: Gus Edwards — Kidland; Rosalie/W: Will D. Cobb, M: Gus Edwards — Swing Me High, Swing Me Low/W: Ballard Macdonald, M: Victor Hollander. *Over the River* (Globe, "Myrtle Mirabeau," Jan. 8, 1912): Chop Stick Rag/W: Edward Clark, M: Jean Schwartz — The Raggety Man/W: Harry Williams, M: Egbert Van Alstyne — Ring-a-Ting-a-Ling/W: William Jerome, M: Jean Schwartz — When There's No Light at All/WM: John L. Golden. *Ziegfeld Follies of 1912* (Moulin Rouge, revue, Oct. 21, 1912): Daddy Has a Sweetheart and Mother Is Her Name/W: Dave Stamper, M: Gene Buck — Row, Row, Row/W: William Jerome, M: James V. Monaco — There's One in a Million Like You/W: Grant Clarke, M: Jean Schwartz. *The Whirl of the World* (Winter Garden, revue, "Fifi," Jan. 10, 1914): Hello, Little Miss U.S.A./WM: Harry Gifford, Fred Godfrey — My Cleopatra Girl; This Is the Life for Me/W: Harold Atteridge, M: Sigmund Romberg. *Odds and Ends of 1917* (Bijou > Norworth, revue, Nov. 19, 1917): Dear Old Bronx; Hector; Sister Susie Glide/W: Bide Dudley, Jack Norworth, M: James Byrnes. *Ziegfeld Midnight Frolic [7th Edition]* (New Amsterdam roof, revue, Apr. 24, 1918): The Big Spring Drive/W: Herbert Reynolds, M: Jerome Kern — The Broadway Blues [added]/W: Arthur Swanstrom, M: Carey Morgan — Swinging Along; Victory/W: Gene Buck, M: Dave Stamper — Tackin' 'Em Down/

W: B.G. DeSylva, M: Albert Gumble. *Ziegfeld Follies of 1918* (New Amsterdam > Globe, revue, June 18, 1918): Any Old Time at All/W: Gene Buck, M: Louis A. Hirsch — The Blue Devils of France/WM: Irving Berlin — Garden of My Dreams/W: Gene Buck, M: Louis A. Hirsch, Dave Stamper — Starlight; When I'm Looking at You/W: Gene Buck, M: Dave Stamper. *Ziegfeld Nine O'Clock Revue and Midnight Frolic* (New Amsterdam roof, revue, Dec. 9, 1918): Tipperary Mary/W: Gene Buck, M: Dave Stamper. *The Little Blue Devil* (Central, "Paulette Divine [The Little Blue Devil]," Nov. 3 1919): Dancing Shoes; Hello, Everybody; I'm So Sympathetic; Just a Kiss; The Little Blue Devil; Shimmy-Shaking Love/W: Harold Atteridge, M: Harry Carroll. *The Blue Kitten* (Selwyn, "Totoche," Jan. 13, 1922): Cutie; When I Waltz with You/W: Otto Harbach, M: Rudolf Friml.

5741. Ted Lorraine *The Blue Paradise* (Casino > 44th Street, "Rudolph Oberdorher," Aug. 5, 1915): I Had a Dog/W: Herbert Reynolds, M: Leo Edwards. *Over the Top* (44th Street roof, revue, Nov. 28, 1917): The Girl for Me; Greenwich Village Belle; Over the Top; That Airship of Mine/W: Philip Bartholomae, M: Sigmund Romberg, Herman Timberg — The Justine Johnstone Rag/W: Charles Manning, M: Frank Carter, Sigmund Romberg. *The Melting of Molly* (Broadhurst, "Tom Morgan," Dec. 30, 1918): Bridesmaids; Dancing School; Floating Down a Moonlight Stream; I Want My Husband When I Wed; Jazz, How I Love to Hear It/W: Cyrus D. Wood, M: Sigmund Romberg — Jazz All Your Troubles Away/W: Augustus Barratt, M: Sigmund Romberg. *Shubert Gaieties of 1919* (44th Street, revue, July 14, 1919): Lamp of Love/W: Alfred Bryan, M: Jean Schwartz. *The Midnight Rounders of 1920* (Century roof, revue, July 12, 1920): Chanson/W: Howard E. Rogers, M: Leo Edwards — The Mansion of Roses; Three Little Marys/W: Alfred Bryan, M: Jean Schwartz. *The Last Waltz* (Century, "Lieut. Mat Lain," May 10, 1921): Ladies' Choice/WM: ? — The Next Dance with You/W: Harold Atteridge, M: Louis Friedman, Alfred Goodman.

5742. Remo Lota *Street Scene* (Adelphi, "Daniel Buchanan," Jan. 9, 1947): When a Woman Has a Baby/W: Langston Hughes, Elmer Rice, M: Kurt Weill.

5743. Mark Lotito *The Most Happy Fella* (Booth, revival, "Pasquale," Feb. 13, 1992): Abbondanza; Benvenuta/WM: Frank Loesser.

5744. Harry Lott *Dolly Varden* (Herald Square, "Lieut. Marlow," Jan. 27, 1902): Brides and Grooms; Loveable Love/W: Stanislaus Stange, M: Julian Edwards.

5745. David Loud *Merrily We Roll Along* (Alvin, "Ted," Nov. 16, 1981): Bobby and Jackie and Jack/WM: Stephen Sondheim.

5746. Dorothy Loudon (Sept. 17, 1933– Nov. 15, 2003) B: Boston, MA. Actress, comedian, cabaret artist. She won a Tony for her role as Miss Hannigan. *Nowhere to Go but Up* (Winter Garden, "Wilma Risque," Nov. 10, 1962): Baby, Baby; Follow the Leader Septet; I Love You for That; Live a Little; Nowhere to Go but Up; The Odds and Ends of Love/W: James Lipton, M: Sol Berkowitz. *Noel Coward's Sweet Potato* (Ethel Barrymore, revue, Sept. 29, 1968): If Love Were All; Mad About the Boy; Mad Dogs and Englishmen; Men About Town; A Room with a View; Teach Me to Dance Like Grandma; Three White Feathers; Useless Useful Phrases/WM: Noel Coward. *The Fig Leaves Are Falling* (Broadhurst, "Lillian Stone," Jan. 2, 1969): All of My Laughter; For the Rest of My Life; Lillian, Lillian, Lillian; We/W: Allan Sherman, M: Albert Hague. *Annie* (Alvin, "Miss Hannigan," Apr. 21, 1977): Easy Street; Little Girls/W: Martin Charnin, M: Charles Strouse. *Ballroom* (Majestic, "Bea Asher," Dec. 14, 1978): Fifty Percent; I Love to Dance; I Wish You a Waltz; Somebody Did Alright for Herself; A Terrific Band and a Real Nice Crowd/W: Alan Bergman, Marilyn Bergman, M: Billy Goldenberg. *Sweeney Todd, the Demon Barber of Fleet Street* (Uris, CR, "Mrs. Lovett," Mar. 4, 1980): By the Sea; God, That's Good!; A Little Priest; My Friends; Not While I'm Around; Parlor Songs; Pirelli's Miracle; Poor Thing; Wait; The Worst Pies in London/WM: Stephen Sondheim. *Jerry's Girls* (St. James, revue, Dec. 18, 1985): The Best of Times; Dickie; Have a Nice Day; Hello, Dolly!; Just Leave Everything to Me; Mame; The Man in the Moon; My Type; Nelson; Put on Your Sunday Clothes; Song on the Sand; Take It All Off; Tap Your Troubles Away; Time Heals Everything; Two-a-Day/WM: Jerry Herman.

5747. Basil Loughrane *Kosher Kitty Kelly* (Times Square > Daly's 63rd Street, "Morris Rosen," June 15, 1925): Dancing Toes; I'll Cuddle Up to You; What's in Store for You/WM: Leon DeCosta.

5748. Mary Louise (July 10–) B: Baltimore, MD. *Hello, Dolly!* (Minskoff, revival, "Irene Molloy," Nov. 6, 1975): Dancing; It Only Takes a Moment; Ribbons Down My Back/WM: Jerry Herman — Elegance; Motherhood/WM: Bob Merrill, Jerry Herman.

5749. Merle Louise *Company* (Alvin, "Susan," Apr. 26, 1970): Poor Baby/WM: Stephen Sondheim. *Sweeney Todd, the Demon Barber of Fleet Street* (Uris, "Beggar Woman," Mar. 1, 1979): Ah, Miss; God, That's Good!; No Place Like London/WM: Stephen Sondheim. *La Cage aux Folles* (Palace, "Mme. Dindon," Aug. 21, 1983): Cocktail Counterpoint/WM: Jerry Herman. *Kiss of the Spider Woman* (Broadhurst, "Molina's Mother," May 3, 1993): Dear One; You Could Never Shame Me/W: Fred Ebb, M: John Kander.

5750. Tina Louise (Feb. 11, 1934–) B: New York, NY. On TV she played Ginger Grant in *Gilligan's Island* (1964) and Julie Grey in *Dallas* (1978). *Fade Out—Fade In* (Mark Hellinger, "Gloria Currie," May 26, 1964): Close Harmony/W: Betty Comden, Adolph Green, M: Jule Styne.

5751. James Lounsbery *Girl o' Mine* (Bijou, "Duc de Bouvais," Jan. 28, 1918): Rug, Snug; The Winning Race/W: Philip Bartholomae, M: Frank Tours.

5752. Allan Louw *The Yearling* (Alvin, "Buck Forrester," Dec. 10, 1965): What a Happy Day/W: Herbert Martin, M: Michael Leonard.

5753. Darlene Love (July 26, 1938–) B: Los Angeles, CA. In the 1960s she was lead singer with Phil Spector on hit singles such as "He's a Rebel." In movies she played Danny Glover's wife in the *Lethal Weapon* series (1988). *Leader of the Pack* (Ambassador, revue, Apr. 8, 1985): Christmas—Baby Please Come Home; Not Too Young (to Get Married); River Deep—Mountain High; Wait 'Til My Bobby Gets Home/WM: Jeff Barry, Ellie Greenwich, Phil Spector—Maybe I Know/WM: Jeff Barry, Ellie Greenwich—Today I Met the Boy I'm Gonna Marry; Why Do Lovers Break Each Others' Hearts/WM: Ellie Greenwich, Tony Powers, Phil Spector—We're Gonna Make It (After All)/WM: Ellie Greenwich. *Carrie* (Virginia, "Miss Gardner," May 12, 1988): Alma Mater; Heaven; In; Unsuspecting Hearts/W: Dean Pitchford, M: Michael Gore. *Grease* (Eugene O'Neill, revival, CR, "Teen Angel"): Beauty School Dropout/WM: Jim Jacobs, Warren Casey.

5754. Edward Love (June 29, 1952–Dec. 27, 1991) B: Toledo, OH. *A Chorus Line* (Shubert, CR, "Richie," June 1977): And.../W: Edward Kleban, M: Marvin Hamlisch. *Dancin'* (Broadhurst, revue, Mar. 27, 1978): Dixie/WM: Daniel Decatur Emmett—Easy; If It Feels Good, Let It Ride/WM: Melissa Manchester, Carol Bayer Sager—I've Got Them Feelin' Too Good Today Blues/WM: Jerry Leiber, Mike Stoller.

5755. Ellen Love B: Boston, MA. *Cape Cod Follies* (Bijou, revue, Sept. 18, 1929): In the Swim (The Jolly Bather)/W: Stewart Baird, M: Alexander Fogarty—Looking at Life Through a Rainbow/WM: Walter Craig, Kenneth Burton—That's the Time When I Miss You/W: Seymour Morris, M: Alex Fogarty. *Sing Out Sweet Land* (International, revue, "Frankie's Mother," Dec. 27, 1944): The Roving Gambler/WM: trad.

5756. Alex (Alec) Lovejoy *How Come?* (Apollo, "Brother Ham," Apr. 16, 1923): Count Your Money/WM: Ben Harris, Henry Creamer, Will Vodery. *Change Your Luck* (George M. Cohan, "Big Bill," June 6, 1930): Ain't Puttin' Out Nothin'/WM: James C. Johnson.

5757. Jane Lovell *The Ham Tree* (New York, "Daisy of Savannah," Aug. 28, 1905): On an Automobile Honeymoon/W: William Jerome, M: Jean Schwartz.

5758. Louise Lovelle *Hummin' Sam* (New Yorker, "Louise Lovelle," Apr. 8, 1933): Answer My Heart; How the First Song Was Born/WM: Alexander Hill.

5759. Helen Lovett *Morris Gest Midnight Whirl* (Century Grove, revue, Dec. 27, 1919): Limehouse Nights/W: B.G. DeSylva, John Henry Mears, M: George Gershwin.

5760. Marcus Lovett (1965–) B: Glen-Ellen, IL. *The Phantom of the Opera* (Majestic, CR, "The Phantom of the Opera," c 1992/May 1994): All I Ask of You; Bravo, Bravo; I Remember; Little Lotte; The Mirror; The Music of the Night; Notes; The Point of No Return; Prima Donna; Stranger Than You Dreamt It; Twisted Every Way; Wandering Child/W: Charles Hart, Richard Stilgoe, M: Andrew Lloyd Webber—The Phantom of the Opera/W: Mike Batt, Richard Stilgoe, M: Andrew Lloyd Webber.

5761. Max Loving *Roza* (Royale, "Young Momo," Oct. 1, 1987): Get the Lady Dressed; Is Me; Moon Like a Silver Window/W: Julian More, M: Gilbert Becaud.

5762. Betty Low *Great to Be Alive* (Winter Garden, "Prudence," Mar. 23, 1950): Headin' for a Weddin'; When the Sheets Come Back from the Laundry/W: Walter Bullock, M: Abraham Ellstein.

5763. Isabelle Lowe *The Melting of Molly* (Broadhurst, "Molly Carter," Dec. 30, 1918): Darling; Dear Old Gown; Lodger; Reminiscence; Rolling Exercise; You Remember Me/W: Cyrus D. Wood, M: Sigmund Romberg—Jazz All Your Troubles Away/W: Augustus Barratt, M: Sigmund Romberg.

5764. Jackie Lowe *The Tap Dance Kid* (Broadhurst, "Carole," Dec. 21, 1983): Dance If

It Makes You Happy; Fabulous Feet; I Could Get Used to Him/W: Robert Lorick, M: Henry Krieger. *Wind in the Willows* (Nederlander, "Wayfarer Rat," Dec. 19, 1985): Mediterranean/ WM: Roger McGough, William Perry. *Ain't Misbehavin'* (Ambassador, revue, revival, CR, Dec. 20, 1988): How Ya Baby/W: James C. Johnson, M: Fats Waller — I Can't Give You Anything but Love/W: Dorothy Fields, M: Jimmy McHugh — I've Got My Fingers Crossed/ W: Ted Koehler, M: Jimmy McHugh — Keepin' Out of Mischief Now/W: Andy Razaf, M: Fats Waller — Lounging at the Waldorf/W: Richard Maltby, Jr., M: Fats Waller — When the Nylons Bloom Again/W: George Marion, Jr., M: Fats Waller — Yacht Club Swing/W: James C. Johnson, M: Fats Waller, Herman Autry.

5765. John V. Lowe *La, La, Lucille* (Henry Miller, "Allan Brady," May 26, 1919): It's Great to Be in Love/W: Arthur Jackson, B.G. DeSylva, M: George Gershwin. *The Midnight Rounders of 1920* (Century roof, revue, July 12, 1920): The Swing/W: Alfred Bryan, M: Jean Schwartz. *The Last Waltz* (Century, "Capt. Kaminski," May 10, 1921): Ladies' Choice/WM: ? — The Next Dance with You/W: Harold Atteridge, M: Louis Friedman, Alfred Goodman. *Fashions of 1924* (Lyceum, revue, July 18, 1923): Bring on the Girls/ W: Harry B. Smith, M: Ted Snyder. *Vogues of 1924* (Shubert, revue, Mar. 27, 1924): Medicos/ W: Clifford Grey, M: Herbert Stothart.

5766. Helen Lowell (June 2, 1866–June 28, 1937) B: New York, NY. *The Red Petticoat* (Daly's > Broadway, "Sophie Brush," Nov. 13, 1912): The Correspondence School; A Prisoner of Love; Since the Days of Grandmamma; Where Did the Bird Hear That?/W: Paul West, M: Jerome Kern. *The Grass Widow* (Liberty > Princess, "Annette," Dec. 3, 1917): Soup/WM: ?.

5767. Cary Scott Lowenstein (May 24, 1962–Nov. 29, 1992) *A Chorus Line* (Shubert, CR, "Mike," July 1981): I Can Do That/W: Edward Kleban, M: Marvin Hamlisch.

5768. David Lowenstein *Jerome Robbins' Broadway* (Imperial, revue, Feb. 26, 1989): New York, New York/W: Betty Comden, Adolph Green, M: Leonard Bernstein.

5769. Mae Lowery *The Burgomaster* (Manhattan, CR, "Daisy," Jan. 14, 1901): The Bathing Girls; The Little Soubrette; Reaching for the Cake/W: Frank Pixley, M: Gustav Luders.

5770. Jeannette Lowrie (1862–Feb. 22, 1937) B: Cardiff, Wales. M: THOMAS Q. SEABROOKE. *Florodora* (New York, CR, "Angela Gilfain," Dec. 9, 1901): The Fellow Who Might/ W: Hickory Wood, M: Leslie Stuart — Gallop-

ing/W: Ernest Boyd-Jones, M: Leslie Stuart. *The Wizard of Oz* (Majestic, CR, "Cynthia Cynch," June 1, 1903): Things That We Don't Learn at School/W: Ed Gardenier, M: Edwin S. Brill. *The Medal and the Maid* (Broadway, "Miss Ventnor," Jan. 11, 1904): Frills Upon Their Petticoats; In My Curriculum; Publicity/W: Charles H. Taylor, M: Sidney Jones. *The Free Lance* (New Amsterdam, "Griselda," Apr. 16, 1906): Come, My Dear; The Goose Girl; The Mystery of History/W: Harry B. Smith, M: John Philip Sousa. *The Love Mill* (48th Street, "Mrs. Thompson," Feb. 7, 1918): Follow Mama's Advice/W: Earl Carroll, M: Alfred Francis.

5771. Master Lowrie *Betty* (Globe, "David Playne," Oct. 3, 1916): On a Saturday Afternoon/WM: Paul Rubens, Adrian Ross.

5772. Ed Lowry *Broadway Sho-Window* (Broadway, revue, Apr. 12, 1936): Hitch Your Wagon to a Star/W: Ted Fetter, M: Richard Lewine — Poverty Row or Luxury Lane/W: Howard Johnson, M: Gus Edwards.

5773. Lily Lubell *The Grand Street Follies of 1928* (Booth, revue, May 28, 1928): Just a Little Love Song/WM: Max Ewing.

5774. Edna Luby (Oct. 12, 1884–Oct. 1, 1928) B: New York, NY. *Babette* (Broadway, "Greta," Nov. 16, 1903): There Once Was an Owl/W: Harry B. Smith, M: Victor Herbert. *Fascinating Flora* (Casino, CR, "Rose Gayboy," June 10, 1907): What Will Happen Then?/W: R.H. Burnside, M: Gustave Kerker. *Fascinating Flora* (Casino, CR, "Dolly Wagner," July 15, 1907): In Paris/W: R.H. Burnside, M: Gustave Kerker.

5775. Craig Lucas (Apr. 30, 1951–) B: Atlanta, GA. *Shenandoah* (Alvin, CR, "Nathan," Sept. 26, 1976): Next to Lovin' (I Like Fightin')/ W: Peter Udell, M: Gary Geld.

5776. Helene Lucas *The Liberty Belles* (Madison Square, "Juana Gomez," Sept. 30, 1901): Lesson Book Song/W: ?, M: Aimee Lachaume.

5777. J. Frank Lucas B: Houston, TX. *The Best Little Whorehouse in Texas* (46th Street, "Mayor Rufus Poindexter" and "Senator Wingwoah," June 19, 1978): The Sidestep; Texas Has a Whorehouse in It/WM: Carol Hall.

5778. Jonathan Lucas (Aug. 14, 1922–) B: Sherman, TX. *Small Wonder* (Coronet, revue, Sept. 15, 1948): No Time; Nobody Told Me/W: Phyllis McGinley, M: Baldwin Bergersen — William McKinley High/W: Burt Shevelove, M: Albert Selden. *Touch and Go* (Broadhurst > Broadway, revue, Oct. 13, 1949): Highbrow, Lowbrow; Mister Brown, Miss Dupree/W: Walter Kerr, Jean Kerr, M: Jay Gorney. *Of Thee I*

Sing (Ziegfeld, revival, "Sam Jenkins," May 5, 1952): Hello, Good Morning/W: Ira Gershwin, M: George Gershwin. *The Golden Apple* (Alvin, "Paris," Apr. 20, 1954): Introducin' Mr. Paris; Lazy Afternoon; My Picture in the Papers/W: John Latouche, M: Jerome Moross.

5779. Mary Lucas *Judy* (Royale, "Dorothy," Feb. 7, 1927): Looking for a Thrill/W: Leo Robin, M: Charles Rosoff.

5780. Nick Lucas (Aug. 22, 1897–July 28, 1982) B: Newark, NJ. Billed in vaudeville as The Singing Troubadour, his tenor voice and easygoing style while accompanying himself on the guitar appealed to large audiences in the 1920s. He made hundreds of recordings but was most identifed with the song, "Tip Toe Through the Tulips," which he introduced in the movie musical, *Gold Diggers of Broadway* (1929). *Show Girl* (Ziegfeld, "Nick Lucas," July 2, 1929): Liza (All the Clouds'll Roll Away)/W: Ira Gershwin, Gus Kahn, M: George Gershwin.

5781. Roxie Lucas (Aug. 25, 1951–) B: Memphis, TN. *The Best Little Whorehouse in Texas* (Eugene O'Neill, CR, "Ginger," May 1982): Hard-Candy Christms/WM: Carol Hall. *Harrigan 'n Hart* (Longacre, "Ada Lewis," Jan. 31, 1985): Maggie Murphy's Home/W: Edward Harrigan, M: David Braham — Sweetest Love/ W: Peter Walker, M: Max Showalter.

5782. Sam Lucas (1840–Jan. 10, 1916) B: Washington, OH. One of the greatest black minstrels and actors of his time. *The Shoo Fly Regiment* (Bijou, "Bro. Doless," Aug. 6, 1907): De Bode o' Edicashun/W: James Weldon Johnson, M: J. Rosamond Johnson. *The Red Moon* (Majestic, "Bill Webster," May 3, 1909): Keep on Smilin'/W: Bob Cole, M: J. Rosamond Johnson.

5783. Claire (Clair) Luce (Oct. 15, 1901–Aug. 31, 1989) B: Syracuse, NY. *Gay Divorce* (Ethel Barrymore > Shubert, "Mimi Pratt," Nov. 29, 1932): I've Got You on My Mind; Night and Day; You're in Love/WM: Cole Porter.

5784. Leola Lucey *The Road to Mandalay* (Park, "Lily Montgomery," Mar. 1, 1916): Bright Day Dawning; Firefly; Heart of My Heart; Ocean of Dreams/W: William J. McKenna, M: Oreste Vessella.

5785. Leo Lucker (c 1913–Feb. 1, 1977) B: Chicago, IL. *Annie Get Your Gun* (New York City Center, revival, "Foster Wilson," Feb. 19, 1958): Doin' What Comes Natur'lly/WM: Irving Berlin.

5786. Susan Luckey *Take Me Along* (Shubert, "Muriel Macomber," Oct. 22, 1959): I Would Die/WM: Bob Merrill.

5787. Lorna Luft (Nov. 21, 1952–) B: Hollywood, CA. Daughter of JUDY GARLAND. Half sister of LIZA MINNELLI. *Promises, Promises* (Shubert, CR, "Fran Kubelik," Oct. 1971): I'll Never Fall in Love Again; Knowing When to Leave; Whoever You Are, I Love You; You'll Think of Someone/W: Hal David, M: Burt Bacharach.

5788. Carol Jo Lugenbeal (July 14, 1952–) B: Detroit, MI. *Where's Charley?* (Circle in the Square, revival, "Kitty Verdun," Dec. 20, 1974): At the Red Rose Cotillion; Better Get Out of Here; My Darling, My Darling; The New Ashmoleon Marching Society and Students Conservatory Band/WM: Frank Loesser.

5789. James Luisi (Nov. 11, 1928–June 7, 2002) B: New York, NY. *Sweet Charity* (Palace, "Vittorio Vidal," Jan. 29, 1966): Too Many Tomorrows/W: Dorothy Fields, M: Cy Coleman.

5790. Paul Lukas (May 26, 1887–Aug. 15, 1971) B: Budapest, Hungary. Leading man in Hollywood from the late 1920s, often playing villains. *Call Me Madam* (Imperial, "Cosmo Constantine," Oct. 12, 1950): The Best Thing for You; Lichtenburg; Marrying for Love/WM: Irving Berlin.

5791. Keye Luke (June 18, 1904–Jan. 12, 1991) B: Canton, China. He appeared in 150 movies, including 13 as Charlie Chan's Number One Son. *Flower Drum Song* (St. James, "Wang Chi Yang," Dec. 1, 1958): A Hundred Million Miracles; The Other Generation/W: Oscar Hammerstein II, M: Richard Rodgers.

5792. Rebecca Luker (Apr. 17, 1961–) B: Helena, AL. Talented actress with a crystal soprano voice. *The Phantom of the Opera* (Majestic, CR, "Christine Daae," Mar. 1989, Monday and Wednesday evenings/June 5, 1989): All I Ask of You; Angel of Music; Bravo, Bravo; I Remember; Little Lotte; The Mirror; Notes; The Point of No Return; Raoul, I've Been There; Stranger Than You Dreamt It; Think of Me; Twisted Every Way; Wandering Child; Why Have You Brought Me Here; Wishing You Were Somehow Here Again/W: Charles Hart, Richard Stilgoe, M: Andrew Lloyd Webber — The Phantom of the Opera/W: Mike Batt, Richard Stilgoe, M: Andrew Lloyd Webber. *The Secret Garden* (St. James, "Lily," Apr. 25, 1991): A Bit of Earth; Come Spirit, Come Charm; Come to My Garden; A Girl in the Valley; How Could I Ever Know; I Heard Someone Crying; Opening Dream; Quartet/W: Marsha Norman, M: Lucy Simon. *Show Boat* (Gershwin, revival, "Magnolia," Oct. 2, 1994): After the Ball/WM: Charles

K. Harris — Can't Help Lovin' Dat Man; Dance Away the Night; I Have the Room Above Her; Make Believe; You Are Love/W: Oscar Hammerstein II, M: Jerome Kern.

5793. Alvin Lum (May 28, 1931–) B: Honolulu, HI. *Two Gentlemen of Verona* (St. James, "Eglamour," Dec. 1, 1971): Dragon Fight; Eglamour/W: John Guare, M: Galt MacDermot. *City of Angels* (Virginia, "Yamato," Dec. 11, 1989): All Ya Have to Do Is Wait/W: David Zippel, M: Cy Coleman.

5794. Barbara Luna (Mar. 2, 1937–) B: New York, NY. In movies from 1960, often playing the beautiful foreigner. *South Pacific* (Majestic > Broadway, "Ngana," Apr. 7, 1949): Dites-Moi/W: Oscar Hammerstein II, M: Richard Rodgers. *West Side Story* (New York State, revival, "Anita," June 24, 1968): America; A Boy Like That; I Have a Love/W: Stephen Sondheim, M: Leonard Bernstein. *A Chorus Line* (Shubert, CR, "Diana," Apr. 26, 1976): Nothing; What I Did for Love/W: Edward Kleban, M: Marvin Hamlisch.

5795. Cornilla Luna *The King and I* (Neil Simon, revival, CR, "Tuptim," 1996): I Have Dreamed; My Lord and Master; We Kiss in a Shadow/W: Oscar Hammerstein II, M: Richard Rodgers.

5796. Art Lund (Apr. 1, 1920–May 31, 1990) B: Salt Lake City, UT. The baritone, first known as Art London, sang for many years with Benny Goodman's orchestra, *The Most Happy Fella* (Imperial > Broadway, "Joe," May 3, 1956): Cold and Dead; Don't Cry; Fresno Beauties; How Beautiful the Days; Joey, Joey, Joey/WM: Frank Loesser. *The Most Happy Fella* (New York City Center, revival, "Joe," Feb. 10, 1959): same as above. *Donnybrook!* (46th Street, "John Enright," May 18, 1961): The Day the Snow Is Meltin'; Ellen Roe; For My Own; I Have My Own Way; The Loveable Irish; A Quiet Life/WM: Johnny Burke. *Fiorello!* (New York City Center, revival, "Ben Marino," June 13, 1962): The Bum Won; Little Tin Box; Politics and Poker/W: Sheldon Harnick, M: Jerry Bock. *Sophie* (Winter Garden, "Frank Westphal," Apr. 15, 1963): Fast Cars and Fightin' Women; Hold On to Your Hats; I Love You Today; I'd Know It; They've Got a Lot to Learn; Waltz; When I'm in Love; When You Carry Your Own Suitcase/WM: Steve Allen. *The Most Happy Fella* (New York City Center, revival, "Joe," May 11, 1966): same as above.

5797. John Lund (Feb. 6, 1911–May 10, 1992) B: Rochester, NY. M: MARIE LUND. He began his stage career in the Railroad on Parade

Pageant of the 1939 World's Fair. *New Faces of 1943* (Ritz, revue, Dec. 22, 1942): Land of Rockefellera/W: John Lund, M: Lee Wainer — Radio City, I Love You/W: June Carroll, M: Lee Wainer — Yes, Sir, I've Made a Date/W: J.B. Rosenberg, M: Lee Wainer.

5798. Marie Lund M: JOHN LUND. She was a Conover model. *New Faces of 1943* (Ritz, revue, Dec. 22, 1942): Land of Rockefellera/W: John Lund, M: Lee Wainer — Richard Crudnut's Charm School/W: June Carroll, John Lund, M: Lee Wainer — Yes, Sir, I've Made a Date/W: J.B. Rosenberg, M: Lee Wainer.

5799. Gene Luneska *The Golden Butterfly* (Broadway, "Tina Korbay," Oct. 12, 1908): Off to Russia; The Queen of the Ring/W: J. Hayden-Clarendon, M: Reginald De Koven.

5800. Barry Lupino (Jan. 7, 1884–Sept. 26, 1962) B: London, England. Comedian and pantomimist. Older brother of STANLEY LUPINO. *Robinson Crusoe, Jr.* (Winter Garden, Feb. 17, 1916): (Go Ahead and) Dance a Little More/W: Harold Atteridge, M: James F. Hanley — When You're Starring in the Movies/W: Harold Atteridge, M: Sigmund Romberg. *The Love Call* (Majestic, "Reginald Pargester," Oct. 24, 1927): If That's What You Want; Spanish Love; When I Take You All to London; You Appeal to Me/W: Harry B. Smith, M: Sigmund Romberg. *The Red Robe* (Shubert, "Hercule," Dec. 25, 1928): I've Got It/W: Mann Holiner, M: Alberta Nichols — Oh, How the Girls Adore Me!; The Thrill of a Kiss/W: Harry B. Smith, M: Jean Gilbert.

5801. Stanley Lupino (May 15, 1893–June 10, 1942) B: London, England. Younger brother of BARRY LUPINO. Father of screen actress Ida Lupino. He began his career as an acrobat, and appeared on the musical comedy stage in London from 1900. *Naughty Riquette* (Cosmopolitan, "Theophile Michu," Sept. 13, 1926): In Armenia; Me; Somehow I'd Rather Be Good/W: Harry B. Smith, M: Oscar Straus — What Great Men Cannot Do/W: Bert Lee, M: R.P. Weston. *The Nightingale* (Jolson, "Mr. Carp," Jan. 3, 1927): Breakfast in Bed; He Doesn't Know; Santa Claus/W: P.G. Wodehouse, M: Armand Vecsey — Josephine/W: Clifford Grey, M: Armand Vecsey.

5802. Patti LuPone (Apr. 21, 1949–) B: Northport, NY. *The Beggar's Opera* (Billy Rose, revival, "Lucy Lockit," Dec. 22, 1973): Come Sweet Lass; I'm Like a Skiff on the Ocean Toss'd; Is Then His Fate Decreed, Sir?; Why How Now Madam Flirt; Would I Might Be Hanged/WM: John Gay. *The Robber Bridegroom* (Harkness,

"Rosamund," Oct. 7, 1975): Nothin' Up; Riches; Sleepy Man/W: Alfred Uhry, M: Robert Waldman. *Evita* (Broadway, "Eva," Sept. 25, 1979): The Actress Hasn't Learned (The Lines You'd Like to Hear); The Art of the Possible; Buenos Aires; Dice Are Rolling; Don't Cry for Me Argentina; Eva Beware of the City; Eva's Final Broadcast; Goodnight and Thank You; High Flying Adored; I'd Be Surprisingly Good for You; Lament; A New Argentina; Peron's Latest Flame; Rainbow High; Rainbow Tour; Waltz for Eva and Che/W: Tim Rice, M: Andrew Lloyd Webber. *Oliver!* (Mark Hellinger, revival, "Nancy," Apr. 29, 1984): As Long as He Needs Me; I'd Do Anything; It's a Fine Life; Oom-Pah-Pah/WM: Lionel Bart. *Anything Goes* (Vivian Beaumont, revival, "Reno Sweeney," Oct. 19, 1987/July 5, 1988): Anything Goes; Blow, Gabriel, Blow; Friendship; I Get a Kick Out of You; You're the Top/WM: Cole Porter. *Patti LuPone on Broadway* (Walter Kerr, one person revue, Oct. 12, 1995): Ain't Nobody Here but Us Chickens/WM: Alex Kramer, Joan Whitney — Always; Lonely Heart/WM: Irving Berlin — Anything Goes; I Get a Kick Out of You/WM: Cole Porter — As If We Never Said Goodbye/W: Don Black, Christopher Hampton, M: Andrew Lloyd Webber — As Long as He Needs Me/WM: Lionel Bart — Being Alive/WM: Stephen Sondheim — Bewitched, Bothered and Bewildered/W: Lorenz Hart, M: Richard Rodgers — Don't Cry for Me Argentina/W: Tim Rice, M: Andrew Lloyd Webber — I Dreamed a Dream/W: Alain Boublil, Herb Kretzmer, M: Claude-Michel Schonberg — It Never Was You/W: Maxwell Anderson, M: Kurt Weill — Meadowlark/WM: Stephen Schwartz — My Ship/W: Ira Gershwin, M: Kurt Weill — Sleepy Man/W: Alfred Uhry, M: Robert Waldman.

5803. Robert Lupone (July 29, 1956–) B: Brooklyn, NY. *The Magic Show* (Cort, "Manny," May 28, 1974): The Goldfarb Variations; Sweet, Sweet, Sweet/WM: Stephen Schwartz. *Late Nite Comic* (Ritz, "David Ackerman," Oct. 15, 1987): The Best in the Business; Dance; Gabrielle; Having Someone; It Had to Happen Sometime; It's Such a Different World; Late Nite Comic; Relax with Me, Baby; Stand-Up; Think Big; This Lady Isn't Right for Me/WM: Brian Gari.

5804. Carol Lurie *Mame* (Gershwin, revival, "Cousin Fan," July 24, 1983): The Fox Hunt/WM: Jerry Herman.

5805. Marlena Lustik (Aug. 22, 1944–) B: Milwaukee, WI. *Pousse Café* (46th Street, "Louise," Mar. 18, 1966): Let's/W: Marshall Barer, M: Duke Ellington.

5806. Franc (Frank) Luz (Dec. 22–) B: Cambridge, MA. *Whoopee!* (ANTA, revival, "Wanenis," Feb. 14, 1979): I'm Bringing a Red, Red Rose; Out of the Dawn/W: Gus Kahn, M: Walter Donaldson. *City of Angels* (Virginia, CR, "Stone"): Double Talk; Ev'rybody's Gotta Be Somewhere; The Tennis Song; With Every Breath I Take; You're Nothing Without Me/W: David Zippel, M: Cy Coleman.

5807. Madelaine Luzon *Artists and Models of 1927* (Winter Garden, revue, CR, Feb. 20, 1928): Bangaway Isle/WM: ?.

5808. George Lydecker *The Girl from Montmartre* (Criterion, "Lieut. Corignon," Aug. 5, 1912): Bohemia/W: Robert B. Smith, M: Jerome Kern — Love Will Win/W: Arthur Wimperis, M: Lionel Monckton. *Nobody Home* (Princess > Maxine Elliott, "Jack Kenyon," Apr. 20, 1915): In Arcady/W: Herbert Reynolds, M: Jerome Kern.

5809. Robert (Bob) Lydiard (Apr. 28, 1944–) B: Glen Ridge, NJ. *Hello, Dolly!* (Lunt-Fontanne, revival, "Barnaby Tucker," Mar. 5, 1978): Dancing; Put on Your Sunday Clothes/WM: Jerry Herman — Elegance; Motherhood/WM: Bob Merrill, Jerry Herman.

5810. Maude Lydiati *The Gingham Girl* (Earl Carroll, CR, "Ann," Mar. 5, 1923): The 42nd Street and Broadway Strut; Sweet Cookie/W: Neville Fleeson, M: Albert Von Tilzer.

5811. Beth Lydy *Step This Way* (Shubert > Astor, May 29, 1916): All for You/W: E. Ray Goetz, M: Bert Grant. *The Girl from Brazil* (44th Street > Shubert, "Hilma," Aug. 30, 1916): Childhood Days; Come Back Sweet Dream; My Senorita; Stolen Kisses/W: Matthew Woodward, M: Sigmund Romberg. *Her Soldier Boy* (Astor > Lyric > Shubert, "Marlene Delaunay," Dec. 6, 1916): Fairy Song; He's Coming Home; The Kiss Waltz; The Lonely Princess (The Sleeping Princess)/W: Rida Johnson Young, M: Sigmund Romberg — Golden Sunshine/W: Rida Johnson Young, M: Emmerich Kalman. *The Rainbow Girl* (New Amsterdam, "Mollie Murdock," Apr. 1, 1918): Just You Alone; Love's Ever New; My Rainbow Girl; We Fear You Will Not Do, Lady Wetherell/W: Rennold Wolf, M: Louis A. Hirsch.

5812. Aubrey (A.L.) Lyles (c 1884–July 28, 1932) B: Jackson, TN. Vaudeville and musical comedy partner of FLOURNOY E. MILLER. He died of tuberculosis. *Shuffle Along of 1921* (63rd Street Music Hall, revue, "Sam Peck," May 23, 1921): If You've Never Been Vamped by a Brown Skin (You've Never Been Vamped at All)/W: Noble Sissle, M: Eubie Blake. *Rang-*

Tang (Royale, revue, July 12, 1927): Monkey Land/W: Jo Trent, M: Ford Dabney. *Keep Shufflin'* (Daly's > Eltinge, revue, "Sam Peck," Feb. 27, 1928): Give Me the Sunshine/WM: Con Conrad, Henry Creamer, James P. Johnson.

5813. Michael (Sutherland) Lynch (Nov. 14, 1964–) B: El Paso, TX. *Jerome Robbins' Broadway* (Imperial, revue, Feb. 26, 1989): Gotta Dance/WM: Hugh Martin. *Les Miserables* (Broadway, CR, "Marius," c 1992): Empty Chairs at Empty Tables; A Heart Full of Love; In My Life; A Little Fall of Rain; Red and Black/W: Herbert Kretzmer, M: Claude-Michel Schonberg.

5814. Nellie Lynch *Aladdin, Jr.* (Broadway, "Poo See Wee Lo," Apr. 8, 1895): Dorothy Flop/W: J. Cheever Goodwin, M: W.H. Batchelor. *The Gingerbread Man* (Liberty > New York, "Margery Daw," Dec. 25, 1905): Evil Eye/W: Frederick Ranken, M: A. Baldwin Sloane.

5815. Teddy Lynch *New Faces of 1934* (Fulton, revue, Mar. 15, 1934): The Coal Bin/WM: George Hickman — Gloomy Heaven/W: Harold Goldman, W: Walter Feldkamp — So Low/W: June Sillman, Nancy Hamilton, M: Donald Honrath — Visitors Ashore/W: Everett Marcy, Nancy Hamilton, M: Warburton Guilbert — Wedding Song [May 21, 1934]/WM: James Shelton. *Fools Rush In* (Playhouse, revue, Dec. 25, 1934): Building Up to a Let-Down/W: Lee Brody, Norman Zeno, M: Will Irwin — I'm So in Love; Rhythm in My Hair; Two Get Together/W: Norman Zeno, M: Will Irwin.

5816. Betty Lynd B: Los Angeles, CA. *A Chorus Line* (Shubert, CR, "Maggie," June 5, 1979): At the Ballet/W: Edward Kleban, M: Marvin Hamlisch.

5817. Helen Lynd (Jan. 18, 1902–Apr. 1, 1992) B: Jersey City, NJ. As a child she appeared with Gus Edwards in his vaudeville act. *Yes, Yes, Yvette* (Harris, "Mabel Terry," Oct. 3, 1927): Maybe I Will/W: Irving Caesar, M: Harold Orlob — Pack Up Your Blues and Smile/W: Jo Trent, M: Peter DeRose, Albert Von Tilzer — You're So Nice to Me/W: Irving Caesar, M: Phil Charig, Ben M. Jerome. *Rain or Shine* (George M. Cohan, "Frankie Schultz," Feb. 9, 1928): Add a Little Wiggle; Feelin' Good/W: Jack Yellen, M: Owen Murphy. *Rainbow* (Gallo, "Penny," Nov. 21, 1928): The Bride Was Dressed in White; Diamond in the Rough; My Mother Told Me Not to Trust a Soldier/W: Oscar Hammerstein II, M: Vincent Youmans. *The Little Show* (Music Box, revue, Apr. 30, 1929): I've Made a Habit of You/W: Howard Dietz, M: Arthur Schwartz — Six Little Sinners/W: Earle

Crooker, M: Frank Grey — Stick to Your Dancing, Mabel/WM: Charlotte Kent — What Every Little Girl Should Know/W: Henry Myers, M: Arthur Schwartz. *Earl Carroll's Vanities of 1931* (Earl Carroll > 44th Street, revue, Aug. 27, 1931): It's Great to Be in Love/WM: Cliff Friend. *The Illustrators' Show* (48th Street, revue, Jan. 22, 1936): I Like to Go to Strange Places/W: Frank Loesser, M: Irving Actman — Wherefore Art Thou, Juliet/WM: Charlotte Kent.

5818. Percy Lyndal *Bright Eyes* (New York, "Mr. Hunter-Chase," Feb. 28, 1910): The Mood You Are In/W: Otto Harbach, M: Karl Hoschna.

5819. Janice Lynde (Mar. 28, 1947–) B: Houston, TX. *The Me Nobody Knows* (Longacre, CR, "Catherine," Nov. 1971): Fugue for Four Girls; How I Feel; Sounds/W: Will Holt, M: Gary William Friedman. *Applause* (Palace, CR, "Eve Harrington," Nov. 22, 1971): The Best Night of My Life; One Halloween/W: Lee Adams, M: Charles Strouse.

5820. Paul Lynde (June 13, 1926–Jan. 11, 1982) B: Mt. Vernon, OH. *New Faces of 1952* (Royale, revue, May 16, 1952): Lizzie Borden/WM: Michael Brown. *Bye Bye Birdie* (Martin Beck, "Mr. MacAfee," Apr. 14, 1960): Hymn for a Sunday Evening; Kids!/W: Lee Adams, M: Charles Strouse.

5821. Edmund Lyndeck (Oct. 4, 1925–) B: Baton Rouge, LA. *Sweeney Todd, the Demon Barber of Fleet Street* (Uris, "Judge Turpin," Mar. 1, 1979): Pretty Women; Quartet/WM: Stephen Sondheim. *A Doll's Life* (Mark Hellinger, "Eric," Sept. 23, 1982): New Year's Eve; Rare Wines; There She Is/W: Betty Comden, Adolph Green, M: Larry Grossman. *Merlin* (Mark Hellinger, "Wizard," Feb. 13, 1983): The Elements; He Who Knows the Way; Nobody Will Remember Him/W: Don Black, M: Elmer Bernstein. *Into the Woods* (Martin Beck, CR, "Mysterious Man," July 19, 1988): No More/WM: Stephen Sondheim.

5822. John Lynds *Where's Charley?* (St. James > Broadway, "Brassett," Oct. 11, 1948): The New Ashmoleon Marching Society and Students Conservatory Band; Where's Charley?/WM: Frank Loesser.

5823. Kristi Lynes M: BK (BRIAN) KENNELLY. *Cats* (Winter Garden, CR, "Rumpleteazer," c 1988): Mungojerrie and Rumpleteazer/W: T.S. Eliot, M: Andrew Lloyd Webber. *How to Succeed in Business Without Really Trying* (Richard Rodgers, revival, "Miss Krumholtz," Mar. 23, 1995): How To; Paris Original/WM: Frank Loesser.

5824. Nora Mae Lyng (Jan. 27, 1951–) B:

Jersey City, NJ. *Wind in the Willows* (Nederlander, "Jailer's Daughter," Dec. 19, 1985): Brief Encounter/WM: Roger McGough, William Perry. *Cabaret* (Imperial, revival, "Fraulein Kost," Oct. 22, 1987): Tomorrow Belongs to Me/W: Fred Ebb, M: John Kander.

5825. Bebe Lynn *Messin' Around* (Hudson, revue, Apr. 22, 1929): I Don't Love Nobody but You; Roust-Abouts/W: Perry Bradford, M: James P. Johnson.

5826. Billy Lynn *The Star Gazer* (Plymouth, "Horace Bowyer, Esq.," Nov. 26, 1917): My Heart Is Like a Bird in May/W: Matthew Woodward, M: Franz Lehar. *The Girl from Nantucket* (Adelphi, "Capt. Matthew Ellis," Nov. 8, 1945): Boukra Fill Mish Mish; What's a Sailor Got?/W: Kay Twomey, M: Jacques Belasco.

5827. Elaine Lynn *Plain and Fancy* (Mark Hellinger, "Another Young Miller," Jan. 27, 1955): Plenty of Pennsylvania/W: Arnold B. Horwitt, M: Albert Hague.

5828. Eve Lynn Along with ALAN HALE, she introduced the first Rodgers and Hart song ever to appear in a Broadway show. The show had opened in June; the song was added to the score in August. *A Lonely Romeo* (Casino, CR, Aug. 26, 1919): Any Old Place with You/W: Lorenz Hart, M: Richard Rodgers.

5829. Joe Lynn (July 4, 1947–Dec. 2, 1987) B: Ohio. *Dreamgirls* (Imperial, "Tiny Joe Dixon," Dec. 20, 1981): Takin' the Long Way Home/W: Tom Eyen, M: Henry Krieger.

5830. Judy Lynn *Top Banana* (Winter Garden, "Sally Peters," Nov. 1, 1951): O.K. for TV; Only If You're in Love; Slogan Song (You Gotta Have a Slogan); That's for Sure/WM: Johnny Mercer.

5831. Leni Lynn (May 3, 1925–) B: Waterbury, CT. She starred in several unexceptional British musicals. *All for Love* (Mark Hellinger, revue, Jan. 22, 1949): My Heart's in the Middle of July; Run to Me, My Love/WM: Allan Roberts, Lester Lee.

5832. Lorna Lynn *Panama Hattie* (46th Street, CR, "Geraldine Bullett," Aug. 4, 1941): Let's Be Buddies/WM: Cole Porter.

5833. Mara Lynn (July 17, 1927–Apr. 6, 1988) B: Chicago, IL. *The Body Beautiful* (Broadway, "Gloria," Jan. 23, 1958): Gloria; The Honeymoon Is Over/W: Sheldon Harnick, M: Jerry Bock. *Can-Can* (New York City Center, revival, "Claudine," May 16, 1962): Can-Can; Come Along with Me; If You Loved Me Truly/WM: Cole Porter.

5834. William Lynn (c 1889–Jan. 5, 1952) B: Providence, RI. *Something for the Boys* (Alvin, "Mr. Tobias Twitch," Jan. 7, 1943): There's a Happy Land in the Sky/WM: Cole Porter.

5835. Ada Lynne (Sept. 7, 1928–) B: Chicago, IL. *Hold It!* (National, "Millie Henderson," May 5, 1948): Friendly Enemy; Fundamental Character; Hold It!; It Was So Nice Having You; Roll 'Em/W: Sam Lerner, M: Gerald Marks.

5836. Phyllis Lynne *Toplitzky of Notre Dame* (Century, "Patti," Dec. 26, 1946): All American Man; A Slight Case of Ecstasy; Wolf Time/W: George Marion, Jr., M: Sammy Fain.

5837. Damon Lyon (c 1865–July 5, 1918) B: Syracuse, NY. *San Toy* (Daly's, revival, "Sing-Hi," Apr. 7, 1902): We're the Cream of Courtly Creatures/W: Harry Greenbank, Adrian Ross, M: Sidney Jones.

5838. Fred Lyon *George White's Scandals of 1929* (Apollo, revue, CR, Jan. 6, 1929): You Are My Day Dream/W: Irving Caesar, M: Cliff Friend.

5839. Robert Lyon *Bloomer Girl* (Shubert, "Joshua Dingle," Oct. 5, 1944): The Farmer's Daughter; Welcome Hinges/W: E.Y. Harburg, M: Harold Arlen.

5840. Wanda Lyon *Robinson Crusoe, Jr.* (Winter Garden, Feb. 17, 1916): Spinning a Yarn/WM: John L. Golden. *The Passing Show of 1917* (Winter Garden, revue, Apr. 26, 1917): (I'll Be a) College Boy's Dear; Won't You Write to Me? (Won't You Send a Letter to Me?)/W: Harold Atteridge, M: Sigmund Romberg. *The Star Gazer* (Plymouth, "Martha Hornblower," Nov. 26, 1917): As a Butterfly Sips the Roses; My Heart Is Like a Bird in May; Rhyming for a Dance; Twinkle, Twinkle; Won't You Come Up to the Table?/W: Matthew Woodward, M: Franz Lehar. *Flo Flo* (Cort, "Angelina Stokes," Dec. 20, 1917): Good-Bye Happy Days/W: Edward A. Paulton, M: Silvio Hein — When a Small Town Girl Meets a Small Town Boy/W: George Edwards, M: Silvio Hein. *Madame Pompadour* (Martin Beck, "Belotte," Nov. 11, 1924): Magic Moments; One, Two and One, Two, Three; Tell Me What Your Eyes Were Made For/W: Clare Kummer, M: Leo Fall — When the Cherry Blossoms Fall (Love Is Love)/W: William Cary Duncan, M: Anselm Goetzl. *Piggy* (Royale, "Suzanne Fair," Jan. 11, 1927): The Music of a Little Rippling Stream/W: Lew Brown, M: Cliff Friend.

5841. Collette Lyons (Oct. 3, 1908–Oct. 5, 1986) B: Massachusetts. *Artists and Models of 1943* (Broadway, revue, Nov. 5, 1943): How'ja Like to Take Me Home; Sears Roebuck/W: Milton Pascal, Dan Shapiro, M: Phil Charig. *Show Boat* (Ziegfeld, revival, "Ellie May Chipley," Jan. 5, 1946): Goodbye, My Lady Love/WM: Joseph

E. Howard — Life Upon the Wicked Stage/W: Oscar Hammerstein II, M: Jerome Kern.

5842. Helen Lyons *The Rose Girl* (Ambassador, "Felice," Feb. 11, 1921): The Proteges/W: William Cary Duncan, M: Anselm Goetzl. *Music Box Revue of 1923* (Music Box, revue, CR): Maid of Mesh/WM: Irving Berlin.

5843. John Lyons *The Magic Ring* (Liberty, "Policeman," Oct. 1, 1923): Deep in Someone's Heart; Education/W: Zelda Sears, M: Harold A. Levey.

5844. Pat Lysinger *No, No, Nanette* (46th Street, revival, "Winnie Winslow," Jan. 19, 1971): Telephone Girlie/W: Otto Harbach, M: Vincent Youmans. *Going Up* (John Golden, revival, "Miss Zonne," Sept. 19, 1976): Hello Frisco! (I Called You Up to Say Hello!)/W: Gene Buck, M: Louis A. Hirsch — My Sumurun Girl/W: Al Jolson, M: Louis A. Hirsch — Paging Mr. Street/ W: Otto Harbach, M: Louis A. Hirsch.

5845. David H. Lythgoe *The Ballet Girl* (Manhattan, "Reuben Van Eyt," Dec. 21, 1897): A Boom; My Home; Romance; She's the Girl I Love; A Stitch in Time; Vanity of Human Wishes; Wedding Bells/W: Adrian Ross, M: Carl Kiefert. *Miss Simplicity* (Casino, "Philip Montford," Feb. 10, 1902): Rosalie/W: R.A. Barnet, M: Edward W. Corliss — Some Do! Some Don't!; When Will My Dreams Come True, Love?/W: R.A. Barnet, M: H.L. Heartz. *Mr. Wix of Wickham* (Bijou, "Tom," Sept. 19, 1904): Cupid's Garden/WM: Max C. Eugene — Military Maids; Susan/WM: Jerome Kern.